Psychology and Life

Diamond Printing
Ninth Edition

S0-BHY-196

Philip G. Zimbardo
Stanford University

in consultation with
Floyd L. Ruch
University of Southern California

Contributors/**RESEARCH FRONTIERS**
Elliot Aronson • University of California, Santa Cruz
Albert Bandura • Stanford University
Sandra Lipsitz Bem • Stanford University
John D. Bonvillian • Vassar College
Robert Buckhout • Brooklyn College, C.U.N.Y.
Ruth S. Day • Yale University
Jane Elliott • Riceville, Iowa, Public Schools
Christina Maslach • University of California, Berkeley
Richard E. Nisbett • University of Michigan
Erik Peper • San Francisco State University
David L. Rosenhan • Stanford University
Martin E. P. Seligman • University of Pennsylvania
Philip Teitelbaum • University of Illinois

Scott, Foresman and Company
Glenview, Illinois
Dallas, Tex.
Oakland, N.J.
Palo Alto, Cal.
Tucker, Ga.
Abingdon, England

Fitz Memorial Library
Endicott College
Beverly, Massachusetts 01915

Preface

I am pleased that the Ninth Edition of *Psychology and Life* has proven to be at least as popular with a wide range of student readers as the long line of successful previous editions written by Floyd L. Ruch has been since 1937.[1]

Traditionally, a major revision, and hence a new edition, is undertaken once every four years. But we have decided to try something different this time around.

The text has been updated and modified on the basis of new information not available a few years ago when the Ninth Edition was being written. It has also been improved in a number of places through incorporating the constructive feedback students and faculty users have passed along to me. But the major innovation you will find here consists of a group of original essays by exciting researchers whose work and thinking are at the frontiers of psychological knowledge. Thus you have thirteen essays, a baker's dozen, written especially for our book that were not part of the 1975 edition. Because these changes go well beyond those in the usual reprinting, but are not so thorough as I shall make in the Tenth Edition, the current text is identified as a Diamond Printing.

A word about the Research Frontier articles. Following each chapter summary is a brief essay, four or six pages in length, on a subject related to the basic content of that chapter. Some of these essays present new theoretical ideas, while others offer refined methodology and systematic programs of investigation to discover psychological truths. There is a balance of hard, rigorous research with selections of a more speculative, reflective, analytical nature. There are detailed observations on a single case as well as experiments with thousands of subjects. Some essays focus on basic research, others on the practical application of such research. Some of the authors are the most eminent scholars in their fields, others are the rising young thinkers whose ideas are just beginning to have an impact on their fields.

[1]Both the title and the approach of this book are represented by the symbol at the top of this page, a combination of the ancient Egyptian ankh, symbolic of *life*, with the Greek letter psi, ψ, which has come to stand for *psychology*.

44202

1BF
121
R 8R 79
1977

Library of Congress Cataloging in Publication Data
Zimbardo, Philip G
  Psychology and life.

1st-8th editions by Floyd L. Ruch.
  Bibliography: p.
  Includes indexes.
  1. Psychology. I. Ruch, Floyd Leon, 1903–
joint author. II. Title.
BF121.R77 1977   150   76-21847
ISBN 0-673-15011-9

Copyright © 1977, 1975, 1971, 1967 Scott, Foresman and Company.
All Rights Reserved.
Printed in the United States of America.

1 2 3 4 5 6 7 8 -RRC- 82 81 80 79 78 77 76

These people have tried to communicate to you in a direct way what they are studying, why they have chosen to study it, and what they are discovering. It is not easy to distill a lifetime's work or even one major research project into a brief essay suitable for newcomers to the complex realm of psychology. So for your part you will have to give something too: you will have to read with more attention than is perhaps customary. These authors have tried to explain their work as clearly as possible, but not condescendingly. They are talking to you at a personal level, but they never talk *down* to you. I'd like to know which essays you find most valuable, along with your positive and negative reactions to the rest of the text. The feedback page at the end of the book will make it easy for you to respond.

It is the goal of this newest edition of *Psychology and Life* to retain those basic features which have always set it apart from its competitors, while adding new dimensions, style, and emphasis. We believe this edition to be more rigorous, relevant, and readable than ever before. We have broadened the scientific research foundation of the evidence on which conclusions are drawn, while at the same time we have focused greater attention on humanistic, personal concerns about which psychology has something relevant to offer. We have tried to speak directly to our student reader at a level appropriate for any intelligent, interested nonprofessional person. Much effort has gone into the attempt to demonstrate the contemporary significance of psychological analysis to understanding problems of personal, social, and political interest to today's students. In addition, many of today's "hottest" topics of theoretical and empirical interest to psychology as a discipline are presented. The emphasis in the Ninth Edition is squarely on understanding the dynamics of human behavior and consciousness. In the course of describing how psychologists go about this task, we have tried to engage our reader in a lively scenario. It is a book about life as much as it is about psychology. We hope it will be both an enjoyable and profitable experience for you.

Using This Book

There is a lot of reading ahead of you in this course; *Psychology and Life* is a big book with much to say. We believe you will find it worthwhile. In order to aid in your fuller appreciation of the materials we have prepared and also to help enhance your mastery of them, we have utilized a number of special features to which we want to call your attention. Our recommendation for reading each assigned chapter is to first look over the table of contents, then turn to the end of the chapter and carefully read the Chapter Summary to get an overview of what will be covered and in what order. Then read once through the entire chapter lightly to familiarize yourself with the basic orientation, concepts, and conclusions.

Now go back and read closely, *actively* reviewing each major section of the chapter. Active participation that involves underlining, making notations in the margin, and, ideally, taking notes on what you have read is superior to passive reading for later test-taking. It takes time now, but your grades will reflect that extra effort later.

The material in each chapter is subdivided so as to facilitate comprehension and study. Major topics come under *first-level headings* (brown type), which always appear at the top of a column. Be sure you note the styles of type used in the various levels of headings because they indicate the structure of the chapter and the relationships of the ideas. These headings organize the content for you and help you plan your reading for each period of study. Important terms and concepts are *italicized* to highlight them. Reports of interesting or critical research are printed in italicized sections. When a figure or illustration is mentioned in the text, it is followed by one of these symbols: ● ▲ ■ ◆. The same symbol appears with the caption of the appropriate chart or photo. A special feature of our book is the use of *P&L Close-ups* in which some item of special interest is set apart from the body of the text for detailed presentation. Each one appears on or close to the page in the text where it is cited, and should be read at that time even though you may have to pass over some material in order to get to it.

References to research, scholarly sources, and mass-media sources appear throughout the text. The authors' names and date of publication will be listed in parentheses (e.g., Zimbardo & Ruch, 1975); complete citations are listed in the References at the end of the book in alphabetical order. These references establish the basis of our conclusions and also direct you to more complete information if you are especially interested in any given idea. We should also alert you to other pedagogically valuable aids at the end of the book: an Appendix containing basic information on measurement and statistics; a full glossary of psychological terms and concepts used in *Psychology and Life* (indicating the pages on which they are discussed); a subject index of important concepts; and a name index of the individuals whose ideas we cite.

It will become obvious to you that this is not only a basic text introducing you to the field of psychology, but a valuable reference book that will be useful in later psychology courses or for term papers for other courses. For example, most psychology majors prepare for Graduate Record Examinations by reviewing their introductory psychology text. In short, you should think of this book as part of your personal library of resource materials.

Finally, we would like to know what *you* think of this book, what you like and want us to do more of in our next edition; as well as what you dislike, are bored with, or find trivial or wrong. We read every student feedback evaluation sent to us and personally respond to as many as we can. Much of what is good in the Ninth Edition of *Psychology and Life* is due to the advice we received from students who took the time to tell us how they felt about the last edition. Won't you help shape the Tenth Edition by sharing your evaluation with us? (Forms are provided at the end of the book after the Index—no postage required.)

Special Acknowledgments

Any book of this scope and complexity requires the cooperation of many people for its realization in the final form you see here. We called upon researchers, teachers, and students to evaluate the strengths and weaknesses of the previous edition of our text, to assist us in the initial preparation of some new materials, to track down references, and to judge the educational and scientific adequacy of each section of the new manuscript. We are very grateful for this invaluable aid to: Karl Minke, University of Hawaii; Leonore Tiefer, Colorado State University; Scott Fraser, University of Southern California; Richard Nisbett, University of Michigan; and Arthur Hastings, Hastings Associates. At Stanford University, we relied upon the expertise of Jeff Wine, Karl Pribram, Edward Smith, Barbara Sackitt, Ervin Staub, and Lee Ross of the faculty, while from graduate and undergraduate students considerable creative and critical help were contributed by Trudy Solomon, Eileen Sobeck, Eugene Eberts, James Newton, Paul Pilkonis, Michael Jennings, Thomas Devine, Paige Jenson, Gary Marshall, and Dean Funabiki.

We were especially fortunate to have the statistics appendix prepared by William W. Ruch of Psychological Services Inc. and the glossary prepared by Eileen Sobeck. Rosanne Saussotte not only typed the entire manuscript from often illegible handwriting, but efficiently organized and coordinated the various parts and stages in the processing of this text. At Scott, Foresman and Company we were blessed with editors who were not only knowledgeable about psychology and expert in editorial matters, but who remained primarily concerned for the prospective student reader of this text: Louise Howe, Marguerite Clark, and Joanne Tinsley. Finally, Christina Maslach, of the University of California at Berkeley, helped, aided, and abetted every stage in this transformation of idea to printed word, as informed, critical colleague; as supportive, encouraging friend; and as loving wife.

Phil Zimbardo

Overview

Contents

Psychology and Life

Diamond Printing
Ninth Edition

Learning is acquired by reading books; but the much
more necessary learning, the knowledge of the world,
is only to be acquired by reading men [and women],
and studying all the various editions of them.

Lord Chesterfield, *Letters to His Son,* March 16, 1752.

PART 1
Foundations

1

Unraveling the Mystery of Human Behavior

All persons are puzzles until at last we find in some word or act the key to the man, to the woman: straightway all their past words and actions lie in light before us.

Ralph Waldo Emerson, *Journals*, 1842

Psychology is the scientific study of the behavior of organisms. It is learning what makes people tick and finding out how the mind works. Psychology is a way of thinking about how living creatures cope with their environment and interact with each other; as such it is at the intersection of philosophy, biology, sociology, physiology, and anthropology. Psychology is what distinguishes humans from machines. Perhaps most importantly, psychology is a kind of knowledge and approach that can be used to improve the quality of human life.

It is virtually impossible today to read a newspaper or magazine or watch television without having some supposed psychological truth thrust upon you. The seventies have become the era of psychology—a time when everybody is a psychologist of sorts. So by now, in your own personal attempt to make the most out of life, you have already become something of a psychologist. You have undoubtedly wondered about your own behavior and the things that sometimes cause others to act so differently from the way you do under the same circumstances. If you are a perceptive, sensitive individual, it is probable that you often try to understand the behavior patterns you observe and how they are related to personality characteristics. Most likely, you have come to be pretty good at anticipating the consequences of your own actions and also at predicting how you will act under various conditions. But it is not enough to be able to predict your behavior. There are probably many times when you wish you had better control over what you do and over what other people do that affects you.

Common-sense psychology may be adequate for many tasks, but it can also at times lead you to false conclusions and ineffective actions. This may be because of faulty assumptions about human nature, cultural and personal biases and prejudices, poorly controlled observations, or an uncritical acceptance of information provided by your senses, by so-called authorities, or by the mass media. To be a good psychologist, you need to learn how to check your assumptions, observe accurately, weigh evidence objectively, and draw valid conclusions.

We believe that a careful reading of *Psychology and Life* can help pave your way toward becoming an effective psychologist. To complete the journey, of course, will require not only additional reading and course work, but a continued openness to new experiences, ideas, and people, as well as curiosity to discover all you can about the psychology of *you*. It can be an exciting, unique adventure — one that will enable you to understand better the secrets of why people think and feel and act as they do. (See *P&L* Close-up, p. 7.)

Psychology in Action: Research on Two Basic Questions About Mind and Behavior

Let us begin your introduction to psychology by posing two questions of considerable importance and examining the processes by which psychologists have set about answering them. In doing so, we will prepare the stage for discussing the major issues psychology deals with, the assumptions it is based on, its goals, and the methods it employs to achieve those goals and resolve the issues. Subsequent chapters will then both expand on and analyze in depth these issues, assumptions, goals, and methods.

Could Lack of Love and Affection Turn a Child into a Dwarf?

Are love and affection necessary for physical well-being and normal growth, or would good food and other good physical conditions be enough? This question is important not only in and of itself but also because it is part of a much broader question: how are mental and physical processes related to each other? Does either one control the other? Is one more "real" than the other? Much psychological research takes a position on these questions or casts light on the likely answers.

Long before the science of psychology was born, Frederick II, a thirteenth-century ruler of Sicily and a master of languages, believed that every person was born with innate, already existing, knowledge of an ancient language. According to him, a child would begin to use this built-in language without any training or experience as soon as he or she was old enough. Learning was necessary, then, only to perfect a person's innate language or to add additional languages to one's repertoire.

To test his hypothesis, Frederick conducted an experiment. A group of foster mothers were put in charge of a number of newborn infants. They were to care for the babies in silence, never to speak to them or allow them to hear human sounds. When at last they spoke, it would reveal, according to Frederick, the true natural language they had inherited, since nothing could be attributed to their upbringing.

Chronicles of history give us the unexpected results of this experiment: "But he labored in vain, because the children all died. For they could not live without the petting and the joyful faces and loving words of their foster mothers."

A fable? Folklore? Do you believe that emotional deprivation could have such a profound effect? Writing in 1760, a Spanish churchman noted, "In the foundling home the child becomes sad, and many of them die of sorrow." In 1915, a doctor at Johns Hopkins Hospital reported that despite adequate physical care, 90 percent of the infants admitted to orphanages in Baltimore died within the first year. In 1942, a researcher at New York University began to record the effects on children of being removed from their home environment for prolonged hospital treatment. Besides becoming apathetic and depressed, they soon were observed to develop respiratory infections and fevers of unknown origin and to fail to gain weight at the normally expected rate. All this occurred even though their nutritional intake was carefully regulated. But when the hospitalized children were returned home, these symptoms disappeared.

Subsequent studies of hospitalized infants over a period of nine years (1935–43) by Margaret Ribble revealed signs of physiological de-

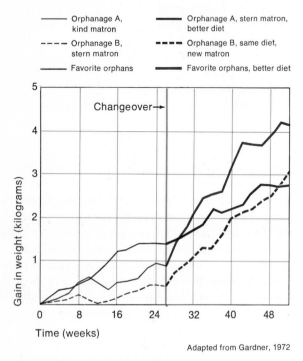

Adapted from Gardner, 1972

■ AN EXPERIMENT OF NATURE ON QUALITY OF HUMAN KINDNESS

The importance of quality of care is illustrated by these curves showing the weight gain of children in two German orphanages after World War II. For the first 26 weeks, both groups of children received the same basic rations, yet those in orphanage A, with a kind and loving matron, showed greater weight gain than those in orphanage B, where the matron was harsh and stern. The stern matron was then transferred to orphanage A, where a better diet was begun at the same time. At orphanage B the diet remained the same as before, but the weight gain increased sharply. The colored line shows the increasing weight gain of a group of the stern matron's favorites, whom she took with her when she moved.

terioration (diarrhea, decrease in muscle tone, and eating difficulties) that were alarming enough for her to conclude that absence of normal mother-child interaction was "an actual privation which may result in biological, as well as psychological, damage to the infant." A study of children in postwar German orphanages traced the relationship of weight changes to quality of care. ■

A little later, investigators Rene Spitz and Katherine Wolf (1946) carefully took histories of ninety-one infants in foundling homes in the United States and Canada. They found reliable evidence of anxiety, sadness, physical retardation, insomnia, stupor, and abnormal weight loss among the children. "In spite of good food and meticulous medical care," thirty-four of these ninety-one infants died—most during the period from the seventh to the twelfth month of life.

Recently, Lytt Gardner (1972) of Syracuse's Upstate Medical Center reported an intensive study of six "thin dwarfs"—children who were underweight and short and had retarded skeletal development, with a "bone age" much less than their chronological age. All had come from family environments marked by emotional detachment and lack of normal affectional bonds between parents and children. This condition has been called *deprivation dwarfism*. Gardner showed that it was indeed the physical consequence of emotional deprivation. He found that such children gain weight and begin to grow when they are removed from the hostile environment, and their growth again becomes stunted if they are returned to it. An extended exposure to such deprivation in early life, however, leaves a permanent mark on the child's body size, intellect, and personality.

Not only has a relationship between emotional deprivation and defective physical growth been demonstrated, but a physiological link between them has been found. Two structures in the brain are involved in this link: with emotional starvation, a region called the *hypothalamus* (which plays a central role in frequent emotional arousal) fails to have its usual stimulating effect on the *pituitary gland* (whose function it is to secrete growth hormones). It is through such a mechanism that lack of love and human attention at critical, sensitive periods in the development of the infant can affect the body—producing deprivation dwarfism in those babies who manage to live at all. Gardner concluded: "Deprivation dwarfism is a concrete example—an 'experiment of nature,' so to speak—that demonstrates the delicacy, complexity and crucial importance of infant-parent interactions" (1972, p. 82).

More recent research leads to the conclusion that retarded growth due to adverse social environments is more widespread than we suspect. The best indicator of this stress-produced short stature is the marked reversal when the youngsters are put in foster or convalescent homes. They grow nearly 8 inches in a year, whereas 2.4 inches is normal. The exact process by which deprivation dwarfism works is not yet known. However, it seems to be related to the impact of emotional strain on the production of pituitary and growth hormones. Most growth hormone is secreted during sleep, and these children may not sleep properly in their stress-filled homes.

Would You Electrocute a Stranger, If I Asked You?

Our other sample question is quite different but also is representative of a recurring issue in psychology: to what extent is behavior caused by characteristics inside the person, and to what extent is it caused by conditions in the environment?

What made Eichmann and the other Nazis do what they did to the Jews? How was it possible for them systematically to destroy millions of people in the gas chambers of the concentration camps? How can civilized people—American college students of the 1970s—understand the basis for such mass violence? Was it a character defect of the Germans that they blindly obeyed authority, willingly carrying out orders from Adolf Hitler, even if the orders violated their own values and beliefs?

What other explanation might there be? Is it conceivable that the behavior in question was not peculiar to the people who engaged in it in Nazi Germany but rather was the result of environmental conditions that those people happened to face? Might you have acted in the same way?

Not a very pleasant thought, to be sure, but one that would suggest a very different approach to preventing such behavior in the future. If there are situations that increase the probability that you or I will act the way Eichmann did in Germany or Lieutenant Calley did at My Lai, then we want to identify those conditions so we can avoid them or work to change them so they will not affect others. Solutions then would be phrased not in terms of what should be done with "problem people" but of how we should change problem situations that might give rise to such psychological and social consequences in any of us.

Close-up
The Domain of Psychology

"In regard to human knowledge there are two questions that may be asked: first, what do we know? and second, how do we know it? The first of these questions is answered by science, which tries to be as impersonal and as dehumanized as possible. In the resulting survey of the universe it is natural to start with astronomy and physics, which deal with what is large and what is universal; life and mind, which are rare and have, apparently, little influence on the course of events, must occupy a minor position in this impartial survey. But in relation to our second question—namely, how do we come by our knowledge—psychology is the most important of the sciences. Not only is it necessary to study psychologically the processes by which we draw inferences, but it turns out that all the data upon which our inferences should be based are psychological in character; that is to say, they are experiences of single individuals. The apparent publicity of our world is in part delusive and in part inferential; all the raw material of our knowledge consists of mental events in the lives of separate people. In this region, therefore, psychology is supreme."

Sir Bertrand Russell, *Human Knowledge, Its Scope and Limits*, 1948, pp. 52–53

How might these competing alternative explanations be separated and their influence investigated? Often inner and outer forces are hopelessly entangled.

Stanley Milgram (1965, 1974), of the City University of New York, set out to investigate this question. To do so, he devised a measure of obedience to authority and a procedure by which he could vary factors in a given situation and measure personality traits. His subjects were all volunteer adult males who were paid $4.50 for taking part in the experiment. He began using Yale students as subjects but eventually expanded the sample to represent a wide cross section of the population varying in age from twenty to fifty years, in occupation from unskilled workers to white-collar workers and professionals, and in education from elementary-school dropouts to doctoral graduates.

The subjects were led to believe that the purpose of the study was to investigate the effect of punishment on memory. Every subject was told that he was to be a "teacher" and that his task was to administer punishment (an electric shock) to a "learner" whenever the latter made a mistake on a learning test. The learner, "Mr. Wallace," was a pleasant, mild-mannered man, about fifty years old, who was an accountant. It was made to look as though assignment to the two roles had been by a chance drawing of lots.

After the subject-teacher himself received a sample shock of 45 volts and saw the learner strapped into an "electric chair" in an adjacent room, the experiment began. The subject was directed to choose from among thirty clearly marked positions ranging from "Slight Shock" (15 volts) to "Danger: Severe Shock" (450 volts) and then was commanded to increase the shock to the next level each time the learner

■ In the photo above, the experimenter instructs the subject in the use of the shock generator. The other photo shows the "victim" being strapped into the shock apparatus. Suppose for a moment that you were the subject-teacher. How far would you go in administering the shocks? Which of the thirty levels of shock would be the absolute limit beyond which you would refuse to continue? How far do you think the average subject in Milgram's experiment actually went? Indicate your estimates below.

1. I would refuse to shock the other person beyond voltage level (circle one number):

0	15	30	45	60	75	90	120	135	150
165	180	195	210	225	240	255	270	285	300
315	330	345	360	375	390	405	420	435	450

2. The average subject probably stopped at: _____ volts.

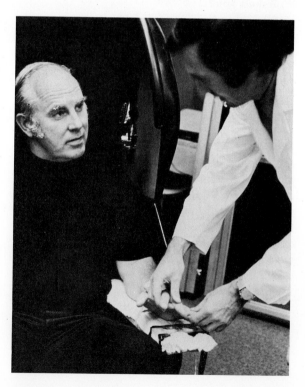

made an error or failed to respond. Since the learner made many errors, the level of punishment escalated rapidly.

The protests of the victim, heard over an intercom, rose with the shock level being administered. At 75 volts he began to moan and grunt; at 150 volts he demanded to be released from the experiment; at 180 volts he cried out that he could not stand the pain any longer. At 300 volts he insisted that he would no longer take part in the experiment and must be freed. He yelled out about his heart condition, screamed, and then failed to respond at all over the last series of trials.

If the subject hesitated or protested against delivering the next shock, the experimenter told him, "Teacher, you have no other choice; you must go on!" "Your job is to punish the learner's mistakes." The experimenter insisted that absence of a response must also be punished, because the rule stated that this was to be considered an error. ■

When forty psychiatrists were asked to predict the performance of subjects in this experiment, they estimated that most subjects would not go beyond 150 volts, that at 300 volts fewer than 4 percent of the subjects would still be obedient, and that only about 0.1 percent would go all the way up to 450 volts—obviously, only those few individuals who were abnormal in some way. How close are your predictions to theirs?

As you might imagine, the situation was not an enjoyable one for the subjects. In fact, it produced considerable anguish in many. To shock an innocent stranger at such high voltage levels obviously was an act of extreme violence against another human being. Most subjects complained and protested. As they became alarmed that they might even kill the learner if one of their shocks caused him to have a heart attack, they insisted they could not go on with their job. That the experimental situation produced considerable conflict is readily apparent from a sample of the transcript given here:

"*180 volts delivered: 'He can't stand it! I'm not going to kill that man in there! You hear him hollering? He's hollering. He can't stand it. What if something happens to him? . . . I mean who is going to take the responsibility if anything happens to that gentleman?' (The experimenter accepts responsibility.) 'All right.'*

"*195 volts delivered: 'You see he's hollering. Hear that. Gee, I don't know.' (The experimenter says: 'The experiment requires that you go on.')—'I know it does, sir, but I mean—huh—he don't know what he's in for. He's up to 195 volts.' . . .*

"*240 volts delivered: 'Aw, no. You mean I've got to keep going up with that scale? No sir, I'm not going to kill that man! I'm not going to give him 450 volts!'*" *(1965, p. 67)*

After the ominous silence from the learner's room, trial after trial, some subjects would even call out to him to respond, urging him to get the answer right so they would not have to continue shocking him, all the while protesting loudly to the experimenter.

There is no such thing in man's nature as a settled and free resolve either for good or evil, except at the very moment of execution.
Nathaniel Hawthorne, *Twice-Told Tales*, 1837

The majority of the subjects—students just like you, older people just like us—dissented, *but they did not disobey*. Nearly two thirds of the subjects (62 percent) kept pressing the levers all the way to the very last switch that delivered 450 volts, the maximum punishment possible!

Even including the minority who refused to obey the authority's request, the mean maximum level of shock administered was nearly 370 volts. None of the subjects who got within five switches of the end ever refused to go all the way. By then, their resistance was broken; they had resolved their own conflict. And later, when this study was repeated in a social setting that increased the prestige and power of the experimenter by using high-school students tested at Princeton University, an amazing 85 percent went to the very end (Rosenhan, 1969).

In all these studies, the "victim" was in reality a confederate of the experimenter and his protests were standardized, tape-recorded responses to the various shock levels—none of which he actually received. But the subjects believed the shocks were real.

Personality tests administered to the subjects did *not* reveal any traits that differentiated those who obeyed from those who refused. Nor did the tests show any psychological disturbance or abnormality in the obedient "executioners."

Thus, we are forced to conclude from this research and variations on the basic design conducted by Milgram and others (discussed further in Chapter 14) that forces in the situation may override our attitudes and values and lead us to do things that we could not imagine ourselves doing when we are not actually enmeshed in the situation.

In these studies those situational forces are identified as: the presence of a "legitimate" authority who assumes responsibility for the consequences of one's actions; a victim who is physically remote; acceptance of a subordinate role with functions governed by rules; and finally, allowing oneself to become part of a social system where public etiquette and protocol are more important to maintain than one's personal values and private beliefs.

An experiment such as this one is valuable not only because it provides answers, but also because it raises new questions and compels us to rethink some of our assumptions about human nature. It shatters the myth that evil is alien to Everyman and Everywoman and lurks only in particular other people who are different from us. It is a convincing demonstration that the "Eichmann phenomenon" could be reproduced in the majority of ordinary American citizens under specifiable social conditions.

It also should make you wonder why you (probably) underestimated the percentage of people who would blindly obey. And what about your illusion of invulnerability that leads you to believe that *you* would have been able to resist the social forces even though the majority of your peers could not? What experiences in

our homes and schools prepare us to be "good little conformists" so readily manipulated by authority and rules? Under what conditions might the majority of subjects refuse to shock at all, or break off long before dealing the ultimate blow to the victim?

The methodology used in this study is *not typical* of the average experiment you may participate in as a research subject. Most psychological research does not involve deception or such a complicated scenario. And if you are disturbed by the ethics of such a study, you will be interested to know that many psychologists are too. In fact, a special group in the American Psychological Association (the leading professional organization of psychologists) is now trying to work out specific guidelines regarding this and other aspects of treatment of subjects in psychological experiments. It is a tricky problem. Subjects must be safeguarded but without unduly hindering the search for knowledge. We will have more to say elsewhere, particularly in the Epilogue, about the ethical and moral issues involved in experimentation, therapy, and other forms of intervention in our lives.

These two questions—Could lack of affection stunt physical growth? and What conditions could produce an Eichmann?—exemplify the wide range of questions that psychologists are investigating. Is there a common denominator in their searching?

Assumptions and Basic Issues

Psychologists begin by making certain assumptions about nature, people, behavior, mind, and appropriate methods for studying them. On some of these assumptions there is general agreement; others represent continuing unresolved issues in psychology.

The assumptions of natural order, determinism, and empiricism. The starting point of scientific inquiry is neatly captured in these two statements:

The chess-board is the world, the pieces are the phenomena of the universe, the rules of the game are what we call laws of Nature.

Thomas H. Huxley, *A Liberal Education*, 1868

Nature goes her own way, and all that to us seems an exception is really according to order.

Johann W. Goethe, *Conversations with Goethe*, 1824

The scientist assumes an underlying order in nature, a system of events, processes, and phenomena that are predictable because they occur repeatedly with some sort of regularity. The goal of research, then, is to uncover this lawfulness, and the patterns of systematic relationship that underlie apparently unique, unrelated events. The quest is to peer beneath the surface of differences and particulars to the foundation of similarities and generalities.

This approach is in sharp contrast with that of many poets and artists who make the assumption that nature is inherently mysterious, changing, chaotic, in constant flux. For them, the task of art is to impose an artificial structure and permanence on this transience. ●

Associated with the scientist's assumption of an ordered universe are the assumptions of determinism and causality. It is assumed that all events have causes—conditions that preceded them and determined that they would happen. These antecedent conditions and their relationships to consequent events are assumed to be invariant and thus in theory knowable and predictable. Given knowledge of all the relevant *variables* (conditions), it should be possible to make a deterministic prediction of when and how a given event or phenomenon will occur. At the present, such absolute knowledge is lacking in the field of psychology, however, and psychologists must talk in probabilistic terms: "the probability is X percent that cause A will result in effect B under Y conditions."

Can we ever really know all the relevant variables that "determine" a given behavior? What you do in a particular situation—for example, when someone threatens you—is determined by the history of your species, your culture, your heredity, your psychological and physical make-up, your upbringing and other past experience, the availability or unavailability of a weapon, the existing laws, your anticipation of the consequences of your actions, and a thousand other things. There are so many determinants operating that it seems impossible ever to know all of them. But this does *not* mean that they do not fully determine the behavior and that behavior is therefore a matter of "free will" or "free choice."

The philosophical debate between "determinism" and "free will" has been a lively one for centuries and is not resolvable by logical argument. It is important simply to realize that scientists and psychologists *must* accept the assumptions of determinism and causality if they are to proceed to study human nature by means of experimental research. Unless they assume regularity and predictability, there is no point in looking for "laws of behavior."

● The scientist sees nature as orderly and seeks to determine its underlying structure. The artist, on the other hand, sees nature as changing and changeable and may seek to impose a new order on it, as in this painting by Marc Chagall entitled *I and the Village*, 1911.

Oil on Canvas, 75⅝ × 59⅝". Collection, The Museum of Modern Art, New York. Mrs. Simon Guggenheim Fund.

They assume further that the only acceptable type of knowledge in science is *empirical* knowledge: information about the environment, events, and actions that is gained through sensory experience—seeing, hearing, touching, smelling, and tasting. This empirical information must also be such that it can be verified by one or more independent observers or appropriate instruments of detection. Metaphysical statements or questions—which involve concepts that go beyond the realm of the observable and empirically testable—are not scientifically acceptable. If *in principle* a phenomenon cannot be measured or demonstrated, it does not exist scientifically.

About theological or metaphysical "reality," science is simply *agnostic*. It does not know. It has nothing to say because the evidence cannot be checked out by the senses. It must be pointed out, however, that in their personal lives, many psychologists maintain a belief (have faith) in some divine purpose or force of creation beyond human nature. But such religious faith coexists with their assumptions of determinism, causality, and empiricism in their scientific endeavor.

Conflicting assumptions about "human nature."
Although research psychologists agree on the basic assumptions that must guide their scientific investigations, they differ considerably on a range of issues dealing with "human nature"— how best to conceptualize what human nature is, how we have become what we are, and how our behavior can be changed—if indeed it can be.[1]

Mind vs. body. The findings on deprivation dwarfism run counter to a commonly held assumption among psychologists that events in consciousness are simply *epiphenomena*, by-products of the real events—the neurological processes—with no part in the causal chain. In keeping with this assumption and the emphasis on sticking to overt, observable behavior, the

[1]See Wertheimer, 1972, and Hitt, 1969, for fuller discussions.

terms *mind* and *mental processes* early fell into disrepute, and psychology students were taught never to use them.

More recently, however, many strands of research are challenging this assumption. Research on the effects of life stresses on physical health, studies of perceptual, cognitive, and language development in terms of the processes involved rather than simply the products, studies of states of consciousness and the effects of mind-expanding drugs, and studies of the effects of things like feelings of helplessness, expectations, and aspirations—all these have stirred a new interest in such processes and a recognition that they must be included in an adequate account of behavior. Even though they cannot be observed directly, their effects can be seen and their operation inferred indirectly through many observable processes. Most psychologists are still more comfortable calling them "psychological processes" or "cognitive processes" rather than "mental processes," however, and many psychologists still see no need to study them at all.

Nature vs. nurture. To what extent are you a product of your heredity, and to what extent the result of your life's experiences? This basic issue, debated for centuries by philosophers, is still argued with much gusto. John Locke propounded the notion that at birth we are nothing but a blank tablet (*tabula rasa*) on which experience makes impressions. This *environmentalist* position—placing emphasis on nurture as the determining factor of our individuality—is at odds with that of the *nativists*, who hold that what we are is determined by our genes, nervous system, physical structure, and all that is present at birth. For them, nurture just develops the nature we are born with.

This basic issue has been argued in many forms. For example, there are arguments as to the relative contributions of *innate* versus *learned* factors in determining intelligence and personality, and arguments about the importance of unlearned, *maturational* processes versus specific training and *learning* experiences in the development of skills.

This issue is important because advocates of the extreme nativist position see more severe limits on the degree to which behavior, performance, and skills can be modified by learning, knowledge, practice, and education. A sociopolitical implication of this position is that if some people are born "stupid," there is no sense in wasting (taxpayers') money trying to educate them. The environmentalists, by contrast, see human nature as essentially pliable, modifiable, perfectable. Such a view has been the cornerstone of the approach taken by psychologists who have made *learning* the core of American psychology. It is a democratic belief, one that gives every child the same opportunity at birth—assuming, of course, that he or she can have access to the same enriched, rewarding environment. If this ideal is false, its danger lies less in wasted funds than in the frustrated expectations of a nation of children who believe they can become anything they want to because "practice makes perfect."

Our evil being vs. our inherent goodness. The religious themes of evil–good, sin–grace, and devil–god have carried over into alternative views of what we are and what motivates us to act the way we do. ◆

On the dark side of the ledger, human nature is seen as basically evil—*hedonistic* (pleasure seeking), self-centered, driven by irrational impulses, mechanistic, materialistic, and concerned with power, control of others, self-aggrandizement, and destruction. It is the task of the state and its social institutions, therefore, to constrain this animal-like nature in us, or else all hell will break loose.

We ride through life on the beast within us. Beat the animal, but you can't make it think.
    Luigi Pirandello, *The Pleasure of Honesty,* 1917

But what about the innocence of youth, the sacrifice of martyrs, the gift of altruistic concern for the well-being of others, the multitudes whose lives are guided by moral choices and ethical decisions? Is it not the exploits of the few who act in evil ways that give the name to the many who inconspicuously go about their lives in quiet goodness? Many psychologists reject the pessimistic view that we are essentially evil, dominated by fate and impulses, acting only to avoid pain and satisfy animal drives. For them, human nature is *potential*, good unless perverted. Living fully is becoming, creating, and actualizing one's potential for growth, beauty, and joy. Behavior can be the outcome of rational choice, mind can transcend the confines of biological matter, and life can be a process of discovering freedom where society often imposes coercive restrictions. In their view, the role of social institutions should be to enable, not to restrict.

Universal laws vs. individual uniqueness. Psychological laws are generalizations about causes and their consequences. Can they ever explain why, how, and when an individual does what he or she does? Psychologists working in counseling and therapy generally assume that to understand an individual case, they must explore that person's unique past experience, view of the world, and other special circumstances that make him or her unique. This is termed the *idiographic* approach. Many similarities and predictable sequences are found, of course, but each case is unique in some ways.

◆ How do you see human nature? Which stands out, the angelic or the demonic?

The Nyakyusa Rush in Where Psychiatrists Fear to Tread

In our society, a person experiencing emotional disturbance is frequently urged by family or friends to "Pull yourself together!" If, as often happens, the individual is unable to do so, he or she is likely to be abandoned by close associates at the first signs of "bizarre" behavior. This is reported to have been the case with the high-school friends of Lee Harvey Oswald (the assassin of President Kennedy) who inadvertently helped turn him into an alienated loner by avoiding him when he started acting in unusual ways. Thus, in addition to the stress that induces the emotional and behavioral problems, the suffering person also has to feel "abnormal," rejected, and guilty for having any problems at all. Often this leads to attempts to conceal such problems from others rather than to seek counsel. The society and the psychiatrist step in only *after* the problem has become severe.

A remarkable contrast is provided by the Nyakyusa, an African society of nearly a quarter of a million people. In this agricultural, cattle-raising culture, there is an ever present concern for *preventing* mental illness because of its disruptive effects on the entire community. Whenever a situation arises that has the potential for causing someone severe distress, members of the community intervene immediately with established rituals. These rituals are not only curative, but they place the responsibility for the problem on forces outside the individual.

Anthropologist Monica Wilson (1970) who has studied these rituals extensively over many years reports that they appear to work so well that there is virtually no incidence of behaviors that could be characterized as "crazy," "mad," or "psychotic." One wonders whether the growing frequency of mental illness in the United States is in part due to our feeling personally responsible for our failures, sorrows, frustration, and distress, coupled with the *asocial* response of our peers and loved ones at the time we need them most.

Other psychologists take a *nomothetic* approach, trying to establish general relationships between behavior and causal conditions that hold for all of us. Most psychological tests take the nomothetic approach in specifying a series of traits or dimensions on which we all can be placed, differing only in our position on each scale. A profile of a person's scores on these scales is assumed to be an adequate description of the person.

Psychologists who follow the idiographic approach study why people behave differently in the same situation, while those who take the nomothetic road investigate what makes such seemingly different people as we all are behave so similarly in many situations.

Causes in the person vs. causes in the environment. Where shall we look for the wellsprings of human action? Are the determinants of behavior to be found inside the person, in one's character, personality traits, and dispositions to act? Or are they outside, in the situation? Is our behavior caused by us or by our environment? Psychologists use the terms *dispositional* and *situational* attribution to indicate whether behavior is attributed to causes within the person or in his or her external situation.

The many psychologists who try to measure and diagnose human "types" and those in the helping professions whose goal it is to cure the individual of personal pathologies and socially deviant behavior assume causes to be dispositional, or in the person. Such a position in psychology has resulted in political legislation and social institutions designed to identify "problem people" whose freedom is a threat to the majority or who are seen as in need of treatment of some kind. Once the problem (of violence, crime, deviance, or any antisocial behavior) is judged to be inherent in, and limited to, certain kinds of people, then proposed solutions follow quite naturally: reeducate, reform, rehabilitate, treat, cure, hospitalize, segregate, imprison, punish, or, finally, execute.

A body of recent investigation, however, supports situational attribution of causes and claims that personality traits are poor predictors of behavior (Mischel, 1968). Moreover, many psychologists are demonstrating in their studies that acts can be induced, maintained, and altered by specified variables in the environment regardless of what dispositions may reside within the actor. Milgram's studies of obedience (see pp. 8–10) are an example. This controversy has important implications for programs of education, therapy, and social change as well as for an accurate intellectual understanding of the causes of human behavior.

Person vs. group as the unit of study. Given our economic doctrine of individual enterprise and capitalism, and our social history and folklore of rugged individualism, it is no wonder that psychology in America has been the psychology of the individual, of the ego. The study of individual uniqueness, of individual reactions, of personality has been a dominant theme in much of psychology from its start. Indeed, the very popularity of psychology as an area of study in the United States stems, in part, from its relevance for understanding "personal problems." In a society where "I've gotta be me," it is natural that people want a psychology of "me-ness."

Although social psychology is a partial corrective to this overconcern for the individual, through studying the behavior of individuals as influenced by others, it, too, has tended to ignore important variables that operate at a level beyond that of the individual organism. Ecological variables (space, time, and place) and system variables (power, authority, institutional rules, etc.) have until very recently been overlooked because the perspective was of the person rather than of people.

Where the important unit is not the individual, but the group, the society, the family, or the culture, then a very different psychology emerges. For example, in Japan, group action is considered preferable to individual initiative because it minimizes individual responsibility and failure while increasing the chances of shared success. There one finds less emphasis on the study of guilt (an individual phenomenon) than on shame (a more social relationship). Similarly, African psychology puts survival of the tribe at its core, rather than successful coping by the individual. (See *P&L* Close-up, p. 14.)

What to study and how. How one poses the questions determines the kinds of answers that are possible. Different questions lead to looking for quite different phenomena, which means developing different research tools and strategies, collecting different data, and ultimately developing radically different perspectives about the human condition. For example, how a research question is posed determines whether the researcher:

a) studies only *overt behavior,* observable to all, or *psychological processes* like thoughts and feelings;

b) accepts only *objective* behavioral data or includes also the subjects' *subjective* analysis of their own experience;

c) studies all living, behaving *organisms* or only *humans;*

d) emphasizes *precision and simplicity* or *complexity and richness* in description and explanation;

e) analyzes behavior into the smallest functional *parts* or deals with *whole,* integrated systems of behavior;

f) focuses on the *past* history of the individual or on *present* conditions;

g) collects *data* without bias of theory or starts with a *theory* to guide the data collection, gathering data to test or extend the theory;

h) conducts research for its own intellectual, *scientific value* or for its *application* to the solution of practical problems;

i) studies the *process* of psychological events (reasoning, problem solving) or the *product* (success, failure).

It is not an uncommon pattern to find psychologists whose work is characterized as the scientific study of the behavior of organisms and who seek data that are objective, overt, specific, localized responses to specific stimuli, precisely measured and simply interrelated. Such psychologists are called *behaviorists.* They believe that the basis of reality is to be found in the objective, material world of physical actions. They look for predictable relationships between specific responses and conditions in the environment and see no need to look for causes within the person.

When the unit studied is the stimulus-response connection, behaviorism is also known as *S – R psychology*. Behaviorists tend toward the "scientific" in their approach to psychology: they prefer "hard," numerical data to "soft," qualitative data and typically collect their data from controlled laboratory experiments with a large number of subjects, using electronic apparatus and computers to present stimuli and record responses. They insist on precise definitions, special vocabulary, and rigorous standards of evidence; often they use animal subjects because control can be much more complete than with human subjects and because the processes being studied occur in simpler form.

Early behaviorists such as Clark Hull, Kenneth Spence, and Edward Guthrie developed elaborate theories that generated much pure research — primarily on simple organisms such as the white rat, in artificial, simplified environments. More recently, the inability of these theories to account for the complex behavior of people in natural settings has led behaviorists to abandon these grand schemes in favor of "mini-theories." Such theories are used to account for a limited set of relationships, and to emphasize application of their principles of learning to changing specific behaviors of people in a variety of institutional settings — schools, mental hospitals, prisons, and the military. The well-known modern behaviorist B. F. Skinner, of Harvard University, sees no need for any theory at all but still bases his research on assumptions about where the causes of behavior lie (in the environment).

Phenomenologists are in many ways the opposite of the behaviorists. For these psychologists, the basis of reality is found in the subjective world of individual experience. Their primary emphasis is on understanding consciousness rather than controlling behavior. Mental processes and introspective reports of unobservable, unique experiences are their province.

The richness of human nature is studied not through analysis of its parts, but as a whole, interdependent system — a dynamic system of potentiality. (See *P&L* Close-up, p. 17.)

The English essayist William Hazlitt captured a basic tenet of this approach to psychology when he wrote:

We do not see nature with our eyes but with our understanding and our hearts.

"On Taste," 1839

There are other major approaches to studying psychological processes that also take stands on these perennial issues. The orthodox psychoanalytic approach of Freud, for example, focuses on early life experiences and traumatic historical events as influencing adult life. The psychoanalyst's data come from uncontrolled sources such as dreams, fantasies, interviews, case studies, and therapy with individual patients. This analytic approach attends to the *process* by which certain beliefs, values, and symptoms develop.

Using a similar analytic approach in a different area of psychology is the Swiss psychologist Jean Piaget. Piaget's intensive study of *how* a child develops modes of thinking, perceiving, and relating tells us something about the cognitive processes going on in the child's mind while solving a problem and not merely whether or not the child solves the problem.

These issues and differing approaches will recur in different guises throughout this text. We hope that the brief outline of them presented here will help illuminate for you some of the alternative ways of studying psychology. They should also provide groundwork for understanding and predicting your own behavior and thus for achieving greater control over your life.

The Goals of Psychology

What are psychologists basically trying to do? What are the goals that form the foundation of the whole psychological enterprise?

For the research psychologist, these goals are description, explanation, prediction, and control. For the applied psychologist, who conducts research on practical problems or puts into practice the findings derived from other research, there is a fifth goal, that of improving the quality of human life. As psychological control techniques become more powerful, there is an increasing feeling that the research psychologist, too, must be concerned about this fifth goal.

Description: Reporting What Really Happens

In a court of law it is imperative that the evidence presented by both prosecution and defense be as objective and specific as possible. Although the evidence introduced is intended to lead the judge and jury toward a given conclusion for one or the other side, any given piece of evidence must stand alone as a "fact"; it must not be someone's interpretation of the facts. *Res ipsa loquitur* — the fact speaks for itself. Either the evidence must be described in such a manner that different jurors can agree as to what it represents, or it must be available for their personal inspection. "What occurred" and "what is" are carefully distinguished from "what could have been" and "what seems to be." Inference is not acceptable in a statement of facts.

In science, too, the first task is to "get the facts." And there are a number of parallels between the standards of trial evidence and those of scientific evidence. In science, too, conclusions must be based on objective observation. And the observation must be reported in such a way that others' knowledge of what you are describing is as identical to yours as possible and would correspond to the observations they would make if they had access to the same events.

Data and facts. In science, the evidence is comprised of *data*. Data are reports or measurements of observed events. They are the building

Close-up
The Humanistic Revolution

Humanistic psychology has much in common with phenomenology, but it is less a research-oriented approach to studying psychology and more a program of ideals about what *should* be the proper study of psychology. It is a reaction against behaviorism as much as it is against Freudian psychoanalysis. The humanists contend that Freud's deterministic view of people results in the pessimism of control by irrational forces programmed into us at various stages of our (psychosexual) development. We are portrayed as "victim-spectators" of blind forces working from within to control our thinking and action. In behaviorism, too, there are controlling forces, but they work on us from without, from the environment.

The former president of the American Association for Humanistic Psychology, Floyd Matson, attacks a considerable number of working psychologists when he says:

"I know of no greater disrespect for the human subject than to treat him as an object — unless it is to demean that object further by fragmenting it into drives, traits, reflexes, and other mechanical hardware." (1971, p. 7)

In brief, what humanistic psychology stands for is: a commitment to human becoming, an emphasis on the wholeness and uniqueness of the individual, a concern for improving the human condition as well as for understanding the individual. Psychologists in this humanist tradition, such as Rollo May, Carl Rogers, and Abraham Maslow, believe that psychological inquiry should be directed toward concepts of self-identity, choice, freedom, certainty, hope, and self-fulfillment — and toward means of achieving or optimizing these processes in our selves.

blocks of psychology or any other science. Data distinguish scientific thought from logical, rational, philosophical, mathematical, and religious thought.

Every grain of sand on a beach, every smile of a stranger, every silence in a conversation is a potential source of data. One's dreams are not data because only the person dreaming has direct access to them. But *reports* of dreams can stand as data, as can changes in brain-wave patterns or eye movements during the periods in sleep when people say they have been dreaming. Such data, when collected, are available for scrutiny and evaluation by independent investigators.

The psychologist must be constantly on guard to separate *observations* ("The patient's hands trembled and he did not make eye contact with the therapist") from *inferences* that go beyond the observations ("The patient was anxious"). If a patient complains of a headache, all those present could hear the statement and agree that the patient had made it, but they might disagree about the presence of the headache.

To report any event as *it is* requires stripping away the observer's expectations and suppositions as well as minimizing the blinders imposed by personal history, culture, and values. It is a difficult, if not impossible requirement, despite our best intentions and efforts.

Hugo Münsterberg, one of the first research psychologists at Harvard University, provided us with this remarkable account of the different observations made by reporters who covered a speech on peace that he gave to a large audience in New York:

"The reporters sat immediately in front of the platform. One man wrote that the audience was so surprised by my speech that it received it in complete silence; another wrote that I was constantly interrupted by loud applause, and that at the end of my address the applause continued for minutes. The one wrote that during my opponent's speech I was constantly smiling; the other noticed that my face remained grave and without a smile. The one said that I grew purple-red from excitement; and the other found that I grew white like chalk. The one told us that my critic, while speaking, walked up and down the large stage; and the other, that he stood all the while at my side and patted me in a fatherly way on the shoulder." (1908, pp. 35–36)

Surely, someone was not telling it like it was.

Data become meaningful facts when they provide support for (or challenge the adequacy of) what we believe to be true. However objectively gathered, data are often—perhaps always—collected and presented to bolster someone's point of view. Thus what is gathered and reported may be only part of what was there to be seen.

Psychologists thoroughly appreciate the validity of the old adage, "What you look for, you will find." In designing their experiments, they try to safeguard against this tendency. For example, psychologists studying the effects of a certain drug or other treatment would conduct a *double-blind* test. That is, they would arrange that the individuals evaluating the behavior of the subjects would not know until they had completed this evaluation which subjects had received the treatment and which had not. Nor would the subjects themselves know which group they were in or even that there were two conditions being tested.

In new areas of research particularly, it is often difficult for investigators to maintain their objectivity. The closer they come to a discovery that might be a real breakthrough, the harder it becomes for them not to let what they wish to see stand in the way of unbiased observation or interpretation of their data—no matter how good their intentions. When we read of "astounding new discoveries" in psychology, or in any science, it is well to be cautious about accepting them until time has proved their worth.

Operationism. If internal events like dreams and "anxiety" or "frustration" cannot serve as data, how can they be studied? You report that you feel "shy"; one observer reports your behavior as "aloof," another as "introverted," a third as "alienated." Which is it?

An approach advocated by the physicist Percy Bridgeman (1927) to remove surplus meaning and ambiguity from terms and concepts is called *operationism*. In this approach, a concept is defined by the operations used in measuring it. For example, hunger is an internal event, not available for direct observation by an outsider. But if you define hunger operationally, as a certain number of hours without food, then anyone reading about your research will know exactly what you mean when you say your subjects were "hungry." Your experiment could be repeated by someone else with confidence that comparable conditions were being used. If there are no operations appropriate for describing a concept, then it cannot be used in scientific ways, although it still may be of value in philosophy or ordinary discourse.

For many concepts in psychology, different measuring procedures have been used in different studies. For example, in studies of "psychological stress" several different kinds of measurements have been used as definitions of "stress." In communicating the results of a study, it is important that researchers make known what operational procedures they used to define their concepts so that in comparing the results of different studies we can know whether they really are about the same concept. Otherwise two studies of "stress" could be about quite different processes. For example, if one researcher used "muscular tension" as the definition of stress and another used "headaches" or "days absent from work" as the definition, they would measure different things and might report quite different findings about "stress."

Sometimes where no one operational definition captures the whole concept, several can be used together to identify what we mean by the concept through a kind of triangulation process. Thus "emotional arousal" might be defined by a combination of self-reports, ratings by trained observers, physiological changes, and scores on selected performance tasks.

Explaining What Happens

What we want to know is not merely what happens, but how two or more events are related. The quest of science is a search for patterns of regularity, for consistent relationships. It is this search that uncovers and creates "facts" from prehistoric scribbles on a cave wall, balls rolling down inclined planes, molds on bread, dogs salivating to the sound of a bell, and changes in the electrical resistance of one's skin.

"What" and "how," not "why." Although the process of explanation begins with attempts to answer "why," scientific research is designed to answer questions of "what" and "how," to which descriptive answers can be given. The "why" question is not scientifically acceptable because it cannot be answered satisfactorily as long as another "why" is still possible. "Why" questions demand an infinite regression to ever more profound "whys" and eventually ultimate, absolute causes and metaphysical truths that are beyond the range of empirical demonstration, and thus beyond the province of science.

Types of explanation in psychology. Many different types of explanation are possible to help make sense of a given event, experience, or personal problem. One is to infer *mentalistic* or *psychic* causes, such as feelings or wishes. Consider the following "explanation" offered by a biochemist, Myron Tumbleson, for the drinking habits of pigs given a mixture of alcohol and orange juice. Prior to their introduction to alcohol, the pigs had established an order of dominance (comparable to a "pecking order" in chickens) that determined the order in which they lay down—the dominant pig consistently taking the most prized position in the corner, followed by the others in descending order, ending with the lowliest pig, who was continually forced to have his hindquarters in the breeze.

" 'The king pig drank so heavily that he lost his status within 24 hours,' reported Tumbleson. 'The No. 3 pig drank very little and became king pig.' However, the morning after was a salutary one for the original No. 1, and within

72 hours he was back on top of the pecking order. Said Tumbleson, 'He never became inebriated again.'

"After that experience, the pigs settled into drinking patterns that were apparently determined by their feelings about their social status. 'The heaviest drinker was the pig that ranked No. 6 in the seven-pig social order,' explained Tumbleson. 'Apparently he is frustrated about his position and has resorted to drink.' The experiment may also have provided good news for the perennial losers of the world: the low pig in the pen apparently felt no need to drown his sorrows. 'No. 7 knows he's last,' said the Missouri researcher, 'and has accepted that.'" (Newsweek, *July 30, 1973*)

Here we are asked to believe that some pigs were experiencing feelings of frustration, some pigs were experiencing an awareness of status variation, and some pigs were able to resign themselves to, and even accept, the knowledge that they were the lowliest of creatures. This is an extreme example of both explanation by mentalistic reasons and *anthropomorphism,* attributing human qualities to lower animals.

Mentalistic explanations ascribe inner reasons, desires, wishes, impulses, and purposes as the causes of behavior: he did what he did because he wanted to. But if his wants are unobservable, then to say, "He did what he did because he wanted to" adds no information to the report that he did it. As we have seen, however, there is a new interest in studying conscious phenomena scientifically by specifying operations or visible behaviors that can be used as objective indicators of the inferred inner events.

Another kind of explanation is in terms of *physiological* events in the brain, nerve cells, glands, and countless other areas of the body. Many introductory psychology students believe that physiology is the key to all behavior: that when we know enough about physiology and biochemical reactions, nothing more will remain to be explained. But while physiological explanations may account for a given behavior, questions often remain about how the physiological process operates and what sets it off.

There are also behavioral events that are too broad in scope to be explained meaningfully at the highly specific level of brain physiology. When what is sought is an explanation for why a vice-president of the U.S. allegedly took bribes, it does not satisfy the questioner to explain how the muscles of the hand contract to pick up money placed in it. The explanation must be appropriate to the level of the question that is asked.

Another form of explanation is through the use of *analogy.* A new occurrence is explained by its similarity to already known common events. This form of explanation loses much of its value when the common occurrence itself is not well understood or the similarity between the new and the familiar is limited or irrelevant. The use of analogy is quite typical in children's explanations, as we see in the answers to the question "What do you think a hangover is?" (See *P&L* Close-up, p. 21.)

These children's explanations of hangovers also reveal another form that many scientific explanations take: that of *enumerating the boundary conditions* under which the event occurs and is altered. Hangovers are thus described as events more typically found in adults, events taking place in the morning after some prior night's experience, and solitary experiences made worse by noise and better by taking the medicine "chasers." Such empirical statements may not be accurate, but at least they can be readily tested and verified.

A related though more sophisticated version of this approach is called the *functional* explanation. Behavior is explained by the stimulus conditions of which it is a function. Finding observable, measurable stimulus conditions that are consistently related to an observable, measurable response is regarded as adequate explanation of the response. For example, if the frequency of a behavior is consistently related to the pleasant or unpleasant consequences it has brought the organism in the past, then it is said to be explained by—to be a function of—those consequences. No other causes need be sought. This is the position of B. F. Skinner, who champions the functional explanation as the only acceptable form that explanations should take.

Such explanations do not tell us *how* the two things are related, only *that* they are, that one regularly follows the other.

Models and *simulations* are still other tools for explaining behavior. To reason by use of a model is to apply a conceptual or theoretical framework developed in one field to guide research and thinking in a less advanced field of knowledge. In explaining abnormal behavior, for example, Sigmund Freud called upon an energy model drawn from physics ("psychic energy") and a hydraulic model drawn from engineering to represent how the driving forces in the "id" supposedly direct much of our behavior—for example, how unacceptable impulses, pushed down out of consciousness, push up in such everyday psychopathologies as certain types of forgetting, slips of the tongue, accidents, and other forms. But such models do not really explain behavior; they only make it seem more familiar.

With the advent of computers, a new form of explanation has emerged, that of reasoning by *simulation* of a given behavioral process. In the mid-1950s, Newell, Shaw, and Simon at Carnegie Tech had the foresight to realize that because computers were symbol-manipulating machines, they might be used to demonstrate the processes by which humans manipulate symbols when they think or solve problems. Since then, many computer simulations have been carried out. A model of learning or memory, for example, is developed and programmed into the computer, which processes new information in the way the model specifies. The process and outcome are then compared with results from experiments on living subjects. Where there is a good "fit" between the two, the computer simulation model is thought to provide an adequate explanation of what is probably going on in the "black box" of the human brain.

In building psychological models, "what we are ultimately attempting to simulate . . . is not [merely] the observed behavior of an organism but rather the behavioral repertoire from which the observed behavior is drawn" (Fodor, 1968, p. 133). The explanatory power of such a technique increases as it describes the *potential* behavior of the organism in addition to its actual past performance.

The grandest attempt at explanation comes with *theoretical explanation*. To explain by means of a theory is to deduce a particular instance from more general principles, perhaps even before it has been observed—in the latter case confirming it subsequently by observation and experimentation.

In common-sense terms, we often use "theory" as interchangeable with "explanation," as when we ask "What is your theory as to why females have higher verbal scores on college entrance examinations than males?" In contrast, a *formal theory* in psychology consists of a systematic statement of the relationship of several assumptions, some principles of behavior, a va-

Close-up

What Do You Think a Hangover Is?

Anthony — Age 8

"You have to be grown up to get one. A hangover, it's, well, it's kind of like a quarrel. But you don't have to have two people to have a hangover. Just one person can get a hangover. I don't know how you get a hangover, but you have to be very quiet when you have one."

David — Age 10

"It's something that happens to people after they go to bed. After they've been having fun, about a couple of hours later it happens. They get a headache and feel terrible. There's a medicine they take for it. It's called Chasers. I've got a friend and his father's always taking Chasers. It's supposed to relieve you."

Jennifer — Age 7

"It's something like a problem. When you grow up it's a problem you get sometimes. It has something to do with their life. It happens to people in the morning. When you grow up and in the morning when you wake up if you have a problem, it's called a hangover. I think that's what it is, anyway. I don't know anyone that has ever had one." (O'Hara, 1972)

riety of deductions, and a body of observed pertinent facts. The value of a theory is assessed in terms of: (a) its ability to give meaning and order to known facts, (b) whether it reveals relationships among concepts and observations previously seen as unrelated, and (c) its usefulness in generating new ideas that can be tested in further research.

It is theory that determines which observations will become "data" and which data are entitled to become relevant facts. When new facts are shown to be inconsistent with the theory, either the theory is modified to accommodate them or (less scientifically but more typically) the facts are simply ignored. It is almost never the case that a theory is overthrown and discarded by facts to the contrary. Instead, worthless theories persist with a life of their own until replaced by others proven to be less objectionable. This reluctance to give up an old theory for a new one is evidenced in the persistence of Ptolemy's theory that the earth was the center of the universe long after Copernicus' heliocentric theory was empirically and logically proven to be a better model of planetary motion.

It is the nature of [a theory], when once a man has conceived it, that it assimilates everything to itself as proper nourishment, and, from the first moment of your begetting it, it generally grows the stronger by everything you see, hear, read, or understand.

Laurence Sterne, *Tristram Shandy*, 1759–67

The psychologist's second goal, then—of explaining behavior—involves finding order, simplicity, and regularity in the apparent confusion, complexity, and randomness of observed events.

Predicting What Will Happen

In addition to their desire to understand nature, human beings throughout history have sought to know the future—to predict and prepare for events in advance of their happening. In ancient times, oracles and soothsayers held positions of great honor, for they were credited with a supernatural ability to reveal the future by reading signs from the gods. Today we rely primarily on science for predictions of the future. Accurate prediction helps us guide our present behavior so as to avoid danger, pain, and disappointment

▲ Stonehenge, a massive structure on England's Salisbury Plain dating from neolithic times, bears silent testimony to the human passion for predicting the secrets of nature. At dawn on Midsummer Day (the summer solstice), the first rays of the rising sun strike through the arch in exact alignment with the giant "heel stone." On the basis of careful study, astronomer Gerald Hawkins (1965) has concluded that Stonehenge is actually an accurate, if primitive, computer capable not only of predicting the yearly solstices, but also of forecasting the most terrifying of celestial events, eclipses of the sun and moon.

Throughout this book we will be exploring various ways psychology touches each one of our lives. These twelve pages of photographs highlight some aspects of life in our contemporary society that the study of psychology can help illuminate. Among these are confrontations between differing generations, cultures, and life-styles (this page) and the search for a source of spiritual meaning and stability (opposite).

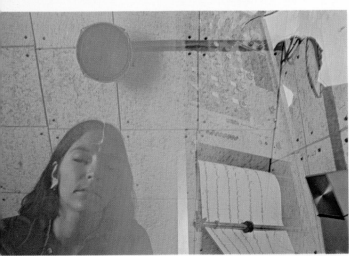

New ways of inner experiencing are being sought by many — through such diverse means as the centuries-old sacred mushroom cults of Mexico, biofeedback training, and techniques of transcendental meditation.

Loss of control over inner experiencing is evidenced in mental disturbance. The paintings of cats were made in the course of a sequence of schizophrenic episodes.

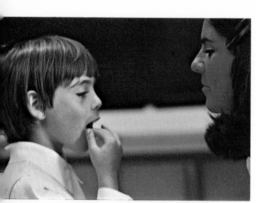
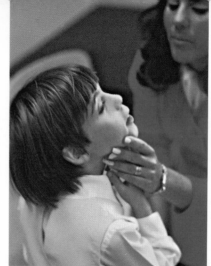

Therapy can take many forms—from one-to-one treatment of an autistic child to psychodrama sessions for groups of patients (opposite). But therapy may also be for healthy individuals who seek through various types of experiential groups to enhance their human potential for sensitivity, openness, and sharing.

Government Bureau, by George Tooker

Modern life can be dehumanizing and deindividuating (this page)—and such conditions may be part of the underlying causes of the violence that has become a way of life both in this country and in places like Northern Ireland (opposite).

Our "world is so full of a number of things"—so many cars, so many possessions, so much noise and visual stimulation—that it sometimes becomes difficult to figure out who we are and where we are going.

But many people have a dream for the future and are making positive choices—both for themselves and for their environment.

while gaining security, pleasure, and satisfaction. Successful prediction reduces uncertainty and confers a sense that we understand what is going on around and within us. ▲

While some psychologists are content with understanding and explaining as the goal of their inquiry, others insist that if you cannot predict the conditions under which a given behavior will appear or vary, then you simply have not understood it. For them, the operational test of explanation is predicting what will happen, or being able to make it happen, or both.

Actuarial prediction vs. prediction through understanding. Some predictions are averages made on the basis of relationships observed in the past. This is the type employed to tell us in advance of each Labor Day weekend how many motorists will die in auto accidents. Such predictions are called *actuarial* predictions. They are made for groups, not for individuals. The whole concept of life insurance is based on the ability to predict very accurately the life-span of different classes and types of people. Actuarial prediction does not depend on an understanding of the life-death cycles but merely on observed past relationships.

The goal of most scientific prediction, however, is to understand cause-and-effect relationships well enough to be able to describe the exact conditions under which an event will occur or even to predict an event that has not been previously observed.

Hypotheses about relationships. Every investigation into causes starts with a hypothesis. A *hypothesis* is a statement of possible ways two or more events or variables may be related. Some hypotheses are general, stating only that there is a relationship; others are more specific, stating how two things are related. For example, one hypothesis of the latter type might be that as anonymity increases, there will be more violence. Hypotheses must be made in such a way that they can be tested by observation, or by logical inference, or perhaps by both.

When does a relationship indicate causality? Just a few of the possible answers to this question are given in the *P&L* Close-up on this page.

Close-up
On Causation

The cause is hidden, the effect is known.

Ovid, *Metamorphoses*

Everything in nature is a cause from which there flows some effect.

Benedictus de Spinoza, *Ethica*, 1675

Chance is a word devoid of sense;
Nothing can exist without a cause.

Voltaire, *Philosophical Dictionary*, 1764

Nothing can happen without a sufficient reason.

Gottfried Wilhelm Leibniz, *Monadology*, 1714

[Cast an] eye on any two objects, which we call cause and effect, and turn them on all sides, in order to find that impression, which produces an idea of such prodigious consequence.

David Hume, *A Treatise of Human Nature*, 1739–40

The most important events are often determined by very trivial causes.

Marcus Tullius Cicero, *Orationes Philippicae*

Every effect becomes a cause.

Buddhist maxim

There are such things in nature as parallel cases; that what happens once, will, under a sufficient degree of similarity of circumstances, happen again.

John Stuart Mill, *A System of Logic*, 1843

EFFECT (noun): The second of two phenomena which always occur together in the same order. The first, called a Cause, is said to generate the other—which is no more sensible than it would be for one who has never seen a dog except in pursuit of a rabbit to declare the rabbit the cause of the dog.

Ambrose Bierce, *The Devil's Dictionary*, 1911

Discovering causality is one of the primary tasks of psychological research. It has also been an ageless problem for philosophical analysis to determine the conditions that satisfy the criteria of causality. For events to be considered causally related, they must occur together (be invariably contiguous: if A, then always B), and it is assumed that the "cause" must occur prior to or simultaneously with the "effect." But a relationship established by research states only *that* the events in question occurred together in the manner prescribed. Any explanation of *how* the two variables are related is a theoretical interpretation that must be assessed against other alternatives. There is almost always more than one possible explanation for *how* two related things are related. Causality itself is a concept; one does not see it but only infers it.

A critical task for the researcher or scholar is to try to specify all the alternative hypotheses that might explain a phenomenon. Each of these is tested against available information or current theories or in new experiments, and by a strategy of elimination all but one is rejected as unsatisfactory. As false hypotheses are eliminated, the investigator emerges with a single hypothesis that seems preferable to its rivals.

Confidence is never absolute, however. A hypothesis can be supported by evidence, but it can never be proved true. Even after hypotheses have been supported by the results of many studies and thus given the elevated status of "laws" of behavior, they are not considered to be proved in any absolute sense. They still are regarded as only provisional—the best available knowledge at this time. Thus psychological research transforms "uncertainty" to "tentativeness" while moving in the direction of, but never quite realizing, the impossible dream of "certainty."

Correlation and causation. Cause-and-effect predictions are only one form that predictions may take, and indeed are not the common "garden" variety with which you are probably most familiar. Your "success in college" was predicted from your College Entrance Board scores, but your scores are not causing your success. Much of the time you are making predictions of future behavior from your current behavior. You estimate how you will do on the final exam from how you are doing on the quizzes. On the basis of how much you enjoyed your partner on the first date, you predict what the next encounters will be like and pursue or abandon the relationship. Psychologists who are interested in studying individual differences between people—in intelligence, personality, achievement, abilities, or whatever—devise tests whose scores will predict certain behaviors they are interested in predicting.

All these are examples of predictions relating one behavior to another rather than relating behavior to environmental conditions. They are *correlations,* simply statements of relationship. While it is possible to make accurate predictions based on correlational data, one is *never* justified in assuming that such data describe direct causal relations. If events A and B are found to be highly correlated, any of the following causal connections may be responsible for that observed correlation: A may cause B. B may cause A. A may cause X, which then causes B, or the opposite. X may cause both A and B. X may cause A, Y may cause B, and X and Y may tend to occur together. And finally there is always the chance that A and B are occurring together only by coincidence. (See *P&L* Close-up, p. 25.)

There is a correlation between number of ice-cream cones eaten by students at the University of Delaware and deaths in Calcutta, India, but it is not a causal one. Each part of the relation is produced independently as a function of summer heat. The Surgeon General's Report (1964) claims that a "definite link" has been established between number of cigarettes smoked and probability of getting cancer and other fatal diseases.

Tranquil Texans and Testy Tyrants: Correlations and Causation

It has been "discovered" that in El Paso, Texas, the local water acts as a tranquilizer for residents, giving them a healthier outlook on life and fewer mental problems than residents of Dallas. The chemical lithium, widely used in treating extremely depressed, hospitalized mental patients, is found in high levels in El Paso's water because it comes from deep supply wells. In Dallas, however, the water supply comes from surface wells, and lithium levels are low.

A biochemist at the 1971 meeting of the American Medical Association reported the finding of a "mathematically proven" relationship between lithium levels and mental hospital admissions in cities throughout Texas. Dallas has more than ten times as many of its citizens admitted to state hospitals as does El Paso. In 1970 the figures were 2697 to 238; convincing data, but a causal connection?

The causal waters are muddied by the following additional bits of data: the nearest mental hospital is 350 miles from El Paso, while there is one only 35 miles from Dallas; there are many differences between the cities in socioeconomic level and population density, and though lithium calms manic-depressive patients it has not been shown to have a tranquilizing effect on "normal" people. So much for your causation! (Associated Press release, Sept. 2, 1971)

Researchers at the Yerkes Primate Center in Georgia have demonstrated a correlation between rank or status in social groups of monkeys and levels of testosterone, the male gonadal hormone. Although several factors influence testosterone levels in adult males, those males with high social rank tend to have higher hormone levels. This correlation leaves open the question of whether a leader becomes a leader because of his higher hormonal levels or whether his testosterone levels rise after he becomes a leader.

Attempts to answer this question included experimental removal of higher ranking males to allow subordinates to become leaders, and placement of former group leaders into new groups where they could only achieve subordinate positions. The results were consistent: variations in status caused variations in male hormone levels. The investigators, Irwin Bernstein, Tom Gordon, and Bob Rose agree: "If you depose a leader, his testosterone level falls; if you create a leader, it rises" (Bernstein, 1974).

The cigarette companies have rejected the idea that this correlation is a causal connection between the two events: maybe the people who smoke more are more nervous and irritable to begin with, and this nervous irritability predisposes them to disease and premature death, as well as to smoking.

Why such a big deal about the difference, you ask? It becomes important when you start making recommendations about how to control the behavior in question by varying the predictor. For example, if cigarette smoking causes cancer, stopping smoking will reduce the probability of the disease. If, on the other hand, nervous irritability causes both events, then stopping smoking might put people under more stress and increase the likelihood of the disease. It is only by eliminating the alternative explanations through amassing a network of correlational data that researchers from the American Cancer Society can predict that reduction of the incidence of respiratory and circulatory disease will follow cessation of smoking and can recommend that smoking be stopped. In general, causal connections are sought between behavior and stimulus conditions rather than between two behaviors.

Controlling What Happens

Psychologists are not content to try to understand and predict behavior, but strive to know how to control it as well. This has been the ultimate goal of much psychological effort for two reasons.

First, the ultimate test of the validity of any causal explanation of behavior lies in being able to demonstrate the conditions under which the behavior can be started, stopped, maintained, or altered. It is by such demonstrations that we are able to establish that we know the *necessary and sufficient conditions* for the behavior to occur. For example, there is a correlation between amount of sunlight a plant receives and its growth; but sunlight alone is not enough. It is a necessary, but not a sufficient condition for controlling the growth of plants—water and soil nutrients being other necessary conditions. Similarly, the *desire* to stop smoking, drinking, or shooting heroin may be a necessary condition to actually stop these addictive behaviors, but it must usually be supplemented by a variety of environmental changes before the behavior can be controlled. Knowledge of how to control an undesirable behavior usually depends on understanding not only how it started but how it is maintained—what keeps it going.

The second reason for an emphasis on control is less related to "pure knowledge" than to utility. Psychology is a practical, pragmatic discipline often concerned with "problem behaviors" or "problem situations" and how to change or improve them. Fear, anxiety, mental illness, suicide, retarded learning, worker alienation, battered children, sexism, racism, conformity—these are just a few of the topics and "problems" psychologists study, with an eye toward change.

In an interesting book, *The Human Use of Human Beings,* Norbert Weiner (1954) defined *control* as "nothing but the sending of messages" that effectively change the behavior of the recipient. He had in mind the way a thermostat controls a furnace through receiving information about room temperature and sending out messages that activate electrical relays, which in turn vary the activity of the furnace. It is known as *cybernetic* or *feedback* control. You use it every time you engage in social dancing and manage to keep from dancing on your partner's toes.

There are many other forms of behavior control, including changing the environment to induce the desired behavior, giving verbal instructions, establishing rules and laws, and administering tranquilizing or energizing drugs. We are all controlled by an infinite array of physiological, social, environmental, legal, religious, and political processes and forces. Indeed, we rarely realize the extent to which our behavior is under the control of subtle situational variables. During the rioting in Watts a few years ago, when people were defying usual restraints by breaking windows, setting fires, and battling with police, many of these same people were observed "stopping at traffic lights and driving with caution. Examples were given during the study interviews of looters apologizing when bumping into each other" (Bernstein, 1970, p. 199).

"Control" has become a term loaded with the negative connotations of robots guided by "Big Brother" via electrodes in our brains, subliminal commands relayed to us on TV, and mind-binding chemicals slipped into our coffee. But although we resent being controlled, we buy millions of Dale Carnegie's recipes for *How to Win Friends and Influence* [*control*] *People*. We are all persuaders. Some of us work for better schools, others for more humane prisons, still others for stiffer laws, less permissive judges, less violence on children's TV programs, and so on. All are instances of attempts at social control. (See *P&L* Close-up below.)

Close-up
A Lesson in Street-Corner Psychology of Control

Bill Wells might be described as a collector of rare coins—he is a professional beggar who uses "street psychology" quite effectively in his trade.

"'Sure I'm a panhandler,' he says defiantly. 'What's wrong with that?'

"Not a thing, you tell him, offering a few coins for the secret of his success.

"'Now you just stand over there in that doorway and watch my pitch.'

"Bill picks out a businessman in a three-button suit and goes into his routine, an expert combination of lies, wheedling and facial expressions designed to flatter, cajole and reprimand at the same time.

"'Could you help a poor fellow out? I haven't eaten today.' The hand goes out, palm up, after the last word, and he stoops a bit to look suitably small in the eyes of his prospective benefactor.

"He calls it his hungry routine. Bill actually looks hungry whether he's had breakfast or not, and he usually has.

"The three-button suit stares at Bill coldly and passes by. So do the next two prospects. But the third man quickly digs into his pocket and comes up with a quarter. Bill has scored.

"On the surface, his pitch appears to lack style and originality. The words are commonplace, and you assess his performance as short of any real talent.

"But it works to the tune of better than a dollar an hour, and you have to ask him why.

"'Well,' he says, 'if you'll buy me just one drink, I'll explain it to you.' And over a Tom Collins he does.

"'You see, it's psychologically sound. There has to be plenty of contrast in appearances. My clothes are old but clean; they're a size too large, and my shoes look like they're coming apart.

"'A well-dressed man is proud of his looks and he notices the contrast right away. And there's another thing:

"'I don't ask for a specific amount like a dime or a quarter. I leave size of the coin up to the prospect, and this gives him an opportunity to make a decision when he gets his hand in his pocket. Men like to make decisions.

"'Then, you notice that I inform him that I haven't eaten which is a rebuke because he's probably had breakfast and a coffee break, and he's already thinking about where he'll have lunch.

"'Also notice that I've told him I'm a 'poor fellow.' This is obvious, of course, but it makes him feel good because the prospect is elevated by my admitting I've been defeated in life.

"'Could you help a poor fellow out? I haven't eaten today. Think about the words. They say a lot.'" (Blake, 1972)

The tools of psychology, like any other tools, can be used for good or evil — to help achieve our goals, meet our needs, or to diminish us. Control of our movements by others in many everyday situations is essential, nonfrightening, and accepted by all, as, for example, the control exercised here by a French policeman, or similar control by a traffic signal. On the other hand, the idea of computerized electronic control by means of electrodes implanted in the brain seems a terrifying prospect. Yet such techniques make it possible for the monkey shown here to raise an otherwise paralyzed arm; thus they hold tremendous potential for enabling people with physical disabilities to regain control over their bodily functioning — for example, for the blind to "see" by electronic signals. Control also has its humorous aspects, as shown in the cartoon. Just as even the most powerful dictator is dependent on his people in that he can maintain his power only so long as he can get the response he needs from them, control in the laboratory is, in the last analysis, a reciprocal relationship in which the psychologist and the subject "control" each other.

"Boy, do we have this guy conditioned. Every time I press the bar down he drops a pellet in."

But how do you feel about the following kind of control? What would your recommendation be to this concerned father who wrote to a national magazine's advice column?

"I am very pro-American. I have a small son and have hopes that when he grows up he will join one of the armed forces. To ensure this, I have thought of talking to him while he is sleeping—no great speech, but a little patriotism and the suggestion that an army career would be good. Can this type of suggestion help, or will it cause him to rebel?" (McCall's, Nov. 1969, p. 65)

Do we not expect children to be controlled by their parents as well as by teachers, ministers, police, and physicians? When is control good, and when is it evil? Serious ethical issues are involved in any effort to control other people's behavior—whether it is in the psychological laboratory or in psychotherapy or in everyday settings in which others control us or we control them. (See *P&L* Close-up, p. 28.)

Robert Oppenheimer, the well-known physicist, said in a speech to the American Psychological Association:

". . . The psychologist can hardly do anything without realizing that for him the acquisition of knowledge opens up the most terrifying prospects of controlling what people do and how they think and how they behave and how they feel. This is true for all of you who are engaged in practice, and as the corpus of psychology gains in certitude and subtlety and skill, I can see that the physicist's pleas that what he discovers be used with humanity and be used wisely will seem rather trivial compared to those pleas which you will have to make and for which you will have to be responsible." (1956, p. 128)

Improving the Quality of Life by Changing What Happens

It is essential that detachment and objectivity be used in gathering and interpreting data. But following the rules of scientific method only tells you how to get evidence that you can trust. It does not tell you what evidence to look for or how to use the knowledge and tools you develop. So increasingly, as their knowledge grows and their tools become sharper, psychologists are accepting responsibility for seeing that their tools are used to enrich human life, not to diminish it.

Until comparatively recently, academic psychologists had been reluctant to be concerned with values, partly from a feeling that concern with values was not "objective" and "scientific" and partly from a sense of modesty about whether psychology was really ready to make a contribution to the public good. For though "psychology has a long past, it has a short history." The first formal experimental laboratory was founded less than a century ago—in 1879—by Wilhelm Wundt in Leipzig, Germany. Many of the most exciting and relevant areas of study in psychology have emerged only within the last decade or two. "Science proceeds cautiously" is a reminder of those who claim that psychologists need to know much more before being arrogant enough to try to formulate solutions to social problems.

"Ready or not, you better come out!" is the cry from other quarters. The pressing social and personal needs of today cannot wait until tomorrow. George Miller, in a presidential address to the American Psychological Association, argued that besides being good scientists, psychologists must also be advocates of ways to improve the quality of human life. In his "revolutionary" speech, Miller (1969) stated:

". . . Changing behavior is pointless in the absence of any coherent plan for how it should be changed. It is our plan for using control that the public wants to know about. Too often, I fear, psychologists have implied that acceptable uses for behavior control are either self-evident or can be safely left to the wisdom and benevolence of powerful men. Psychologists must not surrender the planning function so easily. . . . Psychology has at least as much, probably more, to contribute to the diagnosis of personal and social problems as it has to the control of behavior. . . .

". . . I want to try to make the case that understanding and prediction are better goals for psychology than is control—better both for psychology and for the promotion of human welfare—because they lead us to think, not in terms of coercion by a powerful elite, but in terms of the diagnosis of problems and the development of programs that can enrich the lives of every citizen. . . .

". . . So let us continue our struggle to advance psychology as a means of promoting human welfare, each in our own way. For myself, however, I can imagine nothing we could do that would be more relevant to human welfare, and nothing that could pose a greater challenge to the next generation of psychologists, than to discover how best to give psychology away." (pp. 1068–74)

Scientific Inquiry and Experimental Method

Stripped of all its glamour, scientific inquiry is nothing more than a way of limiting false conclusion-drawing about natural events. This superficially simple goal is exceedingly difficult to achieve. It requires a set of special attitudes on the part of the investigator as well as explicit procedures for stating, testing, and evaluating propositions that might become general conclusions. Taken together, these attitudes, orientations, and procedures are what is meant by the *scientific method*. (See *P&L* Close-up, p. 31.)

Scientific inquiry involves four major steps: getting a worthwhile idea, testing it, drawing conclusions, and reporting what has been found in such a way that another investigator could *replicate* (repeat) the study for verification or challenge. Each investigator can thus build on what others have contributed and make new findings available for later searchers to start with.

There are no guidelines on how to get good ideas—that is the creative part of science, the art in the process. It depends on the scientist's knowledge, creativity, ability to analyze and synthesize, and sometimes, as we shall see, pure chance. But even in the face of a "lucky" or chance discovery (such as Fleming's discovery of penicillin from moldy bread or Pavlov's discovery of the phenomenon of classical conditioning from dogs salivating at the sight of food), "chance favors only the prepared mind," as was pointed out by Louis Pasteur.

Ideas formulated as testable hypotheses come from many sources, among them: (a) derivations from theories, (b) conflicting observations or conclusions, (c) a puzzling phenomenon that questions or challenges traditional thinking, (d) the need to change some condition of life (infection, anxiety, pollution), (e) a chance event or observation, called *serendipity*, (f) an intensive analysis of one's own experiences and behavior. For the psychologist, there is no substitute for a sensitivity to the dynamics of human behavior, for "people watching," for rigorous self-appraisal, and for caring about improving the human condition.

While most laypersons now accept the role of sense experience as the legitimate grounds for arriving at knowledge of nature, such was not always the case. Truth as divinely revealed in the Scriptures has been the dogma of faith upon which many people have insisted on basing their view of the universe. The trial of Galileo is a reminder of the time when this philosophy was dominant. Galileo's data, secured through precise observation, had to be rejected because they supported Copernicus' theory of a heliocentric universe (in which the sun is the center). The Church of that period held that the universe was geocentric — with the central point being man and his earth. In 1615, Galileo was denounced by the Church for his heretical views, and when he did not cease and desist, he was tried in 1633. The wording of his sentencing and abjuration provide a valuable lesson for us which needs no further comment.

Sentence of the Tribunal of the Supreme Inquisition Against Galileo Galilei,
Given the 22nd Day of June of the Year 1633.

"It being the case that thou, Galileo, son of the late Vincenzio Galilei, a Florentine, now aged seventy, wast denounced in this Holy Office in 1615:

"That thou heldest as true the false doctrine taught by man, that the Sun was the centre of the universe and immovable, and that the Earth moved, and had also a diurnal motion: That on this same matter thou didst hold a correspondence with certain German mathematicians: That thou hadst caused to be printed certain letters entitled "on the Solar Spots," in which thou didst explain the said doctrine to be true. . . .

"This Holy Tribunal desiring to obviate the disorder and mischief which had resulted from this, and which was constantly increasing to the prejudice of the Holy Faith; by order of our Lord (Pope) and of the most Eminent Lords Cardinals of this supreme and universal Inquisition, the two propositions of the stability of the Sun and of the motion of the Earth were by the qualified theologians thus adjudged:

"That the Sun is the centre of the universe and doth not move from his place is a proposition absurd and false in philosophy, and formally heretical; being expressly contrary to Holy Writ: That the Earth is not the centre of the universe nor immovable, but that it moves, even with a diurnal motion, is likewise a proposition absurd and false in philosophy, and considered in theology ad minus erroneous in faith.

"We say, pronounce, sentence, and declare, that thou, the said Galileo, by the things deduced during this trial, and by thee confessed as above, hast rendered thyself vehemently suspected of heresy by this Holy Office, that is, of having believed and held a doctrine which is false, and contrary to the Holy Scriptures, to wit: that the Sun is the centre of the universe, and that it does not move from east to west, and that the Earth moves and is not the centre of the universe: and that an opinion may be held and defended as probable after having been declared and defined as contrary to Holy Scripture; and in consequence thou hast incurred all the censures and penalties of the Sacred Canons, and other Decrees both general and particular, against such offenders imposed and promulgated."

Galileo's Abjuration

"I, Galileo Galilei, . . . after having been admonished by this Holy Office entirely to abandon the false opinion that the Sun was the centre of the universe and immovable, and that the Earth was not the centre of the same and that it moved, and that I was neither to hold, defend, nor teach in any manner whatever, either orally or in writing, the said false doctrine; and after having received a notification that the said doctrine is contrary to Holy Writ, I did write and cause to be printed a book in which I treat of the said already condemned doctrine, and bring forward arguments of much efficacy in its favor. . . .

"I abjure with a sincere heart and unfeigned faith, I curse and detest the said errors and heresies, and generally all and every error and sect contrary to the Holy Catholic Church. And I swear that for the future I will neither say nor assert in speaking or writing such things as may bring upon me similar suspicion. . . ."

Horse Sense (or, How Clever Hans Tapped His Way to Stardom)

How is it possible that a horse, "Clever Hans," could deceive not only his trainer but also a reputable, scientifically oriented Investigating Commission in Berlin who came as skeptics of his cleverness and left convinced that he was a horse of another color? It appeared that Hans had a remarkable memory and could spell, read, comprehend complex questions, count, and perform mathematical operations. The investigators carefully observed the horse's feats but could find no deliberate trickery, since the horse performed as well for them as for his trainer. They concluded that he could reason and think at least as well as most humans. After reading about what Hans could do, can you detect how he did it and recommend to the Commission the necessary controls to correct their observation?

". . . The stately animal, a Russian trotting horse, stood like a docile pupil, managed not by means of the whip, but by gentle encouragement and frequent reward of bread or carrots. He would answer correctly nearly all of the questions which were put to him in German. If he understood a question, he immediately indicated this by a nod of the head; if he failed to grasp its import, he communicated the fact by a shake of the head. We were told that the questioner had to confine himself to a certain vocabulary, but this was comparatively rich and the horse widened its scope daily without special instruction, but by simple contact with his environment. . . .

"Our intelligent horse was unable to speak, to be sure. His chief mode of expression was tapping with his right forefoot. A good deal was also expressed by means of movements of the head. Thus 'yes' was expressed by a nod, 'no' by a deliberate movement from side to side; and 'upward,' 'upper,' 'downward,' 'right,' 'left,' were indicated by turning the head in these directions. . . ."

"Let us turn now to some of his specific accomplishments. He had, apparently, completely mastered the cardinal numbers from 1 to 100 and the ordinals to 10, at least. Upon request he would count objects of all sorts, the persons present, even to distinctions of sex. Then hats, umbrellas, and eyeglasses. . . . Small numbers were given with a slow tapping of the right foot. With larger numbers he would increase his speed, and would often tap very rapidly right from the start. . . . After the final tap he would return his right foot—which he used in his counting—to its original position. . . .

"But Hans could not only count, he could also solve problems in arithmetic. The four fundamental processes were entirely familiar to him. Common fractions he changed to decimals and vice versa. . . .

"Hans, furthermore, was able to read the German readily, whether written or printed. . . . If a series of placards with written words were placed before the horse, he could step up and point with his nose to any of the words required of him. He could even spell some of the words. This was done by the aid of a table devised by Mr. von Osten, in which every letter of the alphabet, as well as a number of diphthongs had an appropriate place which the horse could designate by means of a pair of numbers. . . ." (Pfungst, 1911, pp. 18–24)

It was some time before the Commission found that Hans could not solve any problems if he wore blinders, if the trainer stood behind him, or if the person who posed the question did not himself know the answer. These *controls* on the observation of Hans' behavior make it immediately obvious that Hans was merely responding to subtle, unintentional, visual cues given by the questioner as to when he should start tapping and when he should stop. Hans had learned to do what is done consciously by "mind-reading" entertainers.

Because of instances such as these, the scientist learns that the "raw appearance" of things is only one source of data about reality. It must be checked against a variety of other observations of the same phenomena. How do you convince a child that the earth is not flat or that the sun does not rise in the east, move across the sky, and set in the west?

Ground Rules for Collecting Data

Once you know what you want to study, you must decide how to define and measure the things whose relationships you want to investigate. For example, if you wanted to investigate the relationship between apple-polishing and school success, you would need measures of both. For "school success" you would probably use grades, though you might use other measures too. For "apple-polishing" you might use "number of minutes per day spent helping the teacher."

In looking for a relationship between these two things, you will be looking for two *signals* (apple-polishing and school success) against a background of the *"noise"* of all the other things that are happening at the same time. In your search there will be two sources of contamination that are especially troublesome—conditions or events that conceal the true signal by adding to the background noise, and conditions or events that make it appear as if there is a true signal when there is only noise. For example, if all the students were having many active, cooperative contacts with the teacher, it would be hard to distinguish the signal "apple-polishing" from the "noise" of all the other kinds of contact that were taking place. ● A good example of detection of a nonexistent signal was the famous case of Clever Hans. (See *P&L* Close-up, p. 32.)

Once you have defined the things whose relationship you plan to study, your next step would be to formulate a testable hypothesis—perhaps that students who spend more than X amount of time a day apple-polishing receive higher grades than those who don't. Actually, for convenience in later use of statistical checks, the hypothesis is usually stated negatively, as a *null hypothesis* —in this case that apple-polishing will *not* make a difference in grades. But the evidence you gather is the same.

● The relation of signal to noise is like the relation of a visual figure to the background. A clear figure against a gray background stands out clearly, whereas the more structured and heterogeneous the background becomes, the more difficult it is to identify the outlines of the figure and distinguish it clearly from the background.

The variables being investigated in psychological research are like the figures in pictures. Often, especially in "real life," they do not stand out clearly enough from the context in which we see them operating to let us identify and measure them. By studying them in the laboratory we get both the advantage of being rid of the "noise" of the background and the disadvantage of having to create the figure artificially, with the result that it may be a weak or incomplete representation of the variable that occurs naturally outside the laboratory.

When you are studying the influence of a stimulus condition (S) on a response (R), the first is called the *independent variable* and the second, the one influenced, is called the *dependent variable*. The independent variable is either manipulated (for example, you might systematically arrange for different students to spend different amounts of time apple-polishing), or it is measured as it occurs naturally and then is used as a predictor of the dependent variable. School success is the dependent variable in this example, the one whose variation you think will be *dependent on* (affected by) variations in apple-polishing.

If you are in the lucky position of being able to manipulate the independent variable, you are using the *experimental method,* which gives you much more opportunity to find causal relationships. By holding constant all other variables that might affect the behavior and then systematically varying the independent variable, you can find just which aspects of it are necessary and sufficient for a particular form of the dependent variable (the response) to occur under that particular set of conditions. ("Varying the independent variable" might mean either exposing one group of subjects to it but not another or comparing the effects of different strengths of the independent variable.)

The essentials of a typical psychological experiment involve randomly assigning subjects to different conditions, manipulating one or more independent variables, and carefully measuring the responses. To check your hypothesis about apple-polishing, you might randomly assign some students to an "experimental" group who would be instructed to do apple-polishing so many minutes a day, and other students to a "control group," who would be given no special instructions and probably would not even know they were in one of your groups.

You would need to assign students randomly to each group to be sure that the two groups were comparable at the start of the experiment. If you had more students who were articulate or bright or already in favor with the teacher in one of your groups, then you couldn't be sure that any later differences in grades that you found between the two groups were due to the apple-polishing variable itself.

If you were not able to intervene in the natural ongoing behavior to get one group to do apple-polishing, you would have to identify some natural apple-polishers, match them for similarity in as many other respects as you could with another group of students who were not apple-polishers, and then compare the scores of the two groups on your measures of school success.

You would also have to be as certain as possible that all the other things that might affect grades were held constant (operated in similar ways for the two groups) during the period of observation. Control of all conditions that might prevent a clear, unambiguous test of the hypothesis is the most crucial feature of an experiment.

These and other controls will be illustrated more concretely when we analyze specific experiments throughout the remainder of this book. Unfortunately, the variables affecting the behavior of organisms are not easily separable for analytical purposes. The major criticism leveled against most experiments is their failure to include some control group or procedure that is logically necessary in order to rule out an alternative hypothesis. (See *P&L* Close-up, p. 35.)

Drawing Conclusions

"There is nothing that spoils a good conclusion like disagreeable data," is a sentiment shared by many psychologists of the *"Bubba psychology"* school. *Bubba psychology* represents the grandmotherly wisdom of common sense, intuition, and making up your mind of what's right before you have all (or sometimes any) of the facts. Consider what kinds of data you would need to convince your *bubba* that a date she thought was not good enough for you, was, in fact, good enough.

Well, sometimes scientists have as much vested interest in proving they are right as do parents, lawyers, and politicians. But scientific researchers are a little more scrupulous in their effort to let the data decide, to have conclusions follow rather than anticipate the data. Without some formalized and standard procedure for drawing conclusions from a given set of observations, there could be no objective and impartial way of establishing when a result was "significant" or a difference really demonstrated.

Assume that data have been collected properly, and a behavioral difference between the experimental and control groups emerges. Can we conclude that the independent variable was responsible for this difference, and thus that the experimental hypothesis has been supported? After all this investment of time, energy, intellect, and money, our objective scientist might be inclined to see any difference, however accidental or trivial, as a "real" one. The safeguard against such a temptation comes from agreeing in advance to a convention shared by all psychological researchers on what will be regarded as a *significant difference.*

Remember, the experiment began with the statement of a *null hypothesis* — that there would be no difference between the two groups after the experimental treatment. If you do find a difference, you need to know whether it is big enough to be considered a real one or whether it could have occurred by chance. If chance could have accounted for it, you cannot draw any conclusions about a relationship between your variables. Only if the difference is big enough, can you reject the null hypothesis and conclude that the difference is real (that there probably is a relationship between apple-polishing and school success, in our earlier example).

The particular statistical tests used vary according to the nature of the data collected, but all yield the same final *probability statement,* an estimate of the probability that the difference is a chance occurrence. This probability statement is what makes it possible for psychologists to adopt a common rule for deciding when an experiment has "worked." A result is accepted as a *real* one and is labeled "statistically signifi-

Close-up
A Typical Experimental Design

Two groups are chosen randomly from the same population. Both are given the same pretest and posttest, during which all relevant variables (directions, room temperature, time allowed, and so on) are the same for both groups. So far as is known, the only systematic difference during the interval between pretest and posttest for the two groups is the difference in the experimental treatment. The change in learning performance for each group is determined by subtracting pretest from posttest scores. If the experimental group has changed more than the control group, the difference is attributed to the difference in the experimental treatment. Is it clear to you what the independent and dependent variables are here?

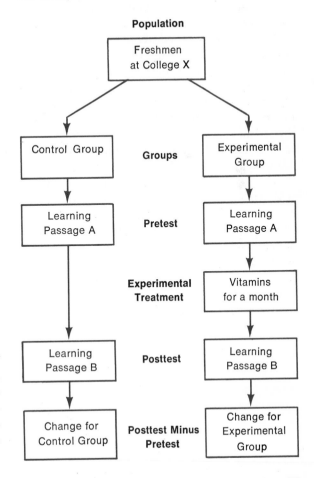

In our discussion of research findings we will occasionally mention the terms *mean, variability,* and *correlation.* Their meanings are briefly summarized here. For a fuller explanation of statistical terms and statistical inference, see the Appendix.

1. To describe a group's performance (and be able to compare it with that of another group), you need two things: a single number *typical* enough to represent the whole group of scores, and a number that tells how different the scores are: how widely they *vary.*

a) The most typical number is a *measure of central tendency,* or *average.* The three kinds of average most often used are the *mean* (sum of the scores divided by the number of scores and abbreviated M or $\bar{X}$), the *median* (the score in the middle when all the scores are lined up in order; 50% of the scores are above and 50% below the median), and the *mode* (the most frequently occurring single score).

b) Measures of variability tell whether the scores cluster closely or are spread out. The measures of variability most often used are the *range* of the scores (from lowest to highest) and the *standard deviation,* a measure of the average variation of the individual scores from the group mean. The bigger the standard deviation, the more the scores vary from the mean score.

2. To describe the relationships between two sets of scores for the same individuals (intelligence and grades, for example), you use a statistical formula to obtain a *coefficient of correlation* (r). This statistic tells you whether there is a positive or negative relationship and how strong or weak it is.

Coefficients of correlation range from *minus one* (-1.0), which would mean perfect *negative* correlation (as intelligence gets higher, grades get lower), through *zero* (0), which would mean no correlation at all, to *plus one* $(+1.0)$, which would mean perfect *positive* correlation (as intelligence goes up so do grades). Perfect correlations are rarely found. A "moderate" correlation might be between .25 and .60 (either + or −), a "high" correlation between .60 and .99.

cant" only when the probability (p) that the difference could have occurred by chance is less than five in one hundred. (The notation $p < .05$ is used to indicate "probability is less than 5 percent.") This is the most lenient level of significance permitted, and for some problems it is not acceptable. More stringent requirements are imposed on conclusion drawing as the consequences of reaching a false conclusion become more important. For example, in predicting suicides, the researcher might demand a probability level of .01, .001, or greater. This and other statistical techniques for deciding the degree of confidence you can have in measures you get are described in the Appendix. There also are techniques for finding out how far you can generalize your findings with a particular sample of subjects to apply to others in the same general category. You have to know how representative your sample is of a larger group before you can generalize your findings to the group as a whole. (See *P&L* Close-up at left.)

Two other cautions are in order in this quick and necessarily simplified account of using the experimental method and drawing valid conclusions from your findings. Suppose you have found a statistically significant difference and have rejected the null hypothesis, concluding that your manipulation of the independent variable has indeed changed a particular behavior. You still cannot legitimately say that the independent variable causes the behavior, but only that changes in the independent variable produce changes in the behavior. Nor can you say that the independent variable is the only influence on (or cause of) the behavior, but only that what you found was true when all the other relevant variables that might also have been affecting the behavior were held at some constant level. If they were at different levels, your changes in the independent variable might have different effects. And if your independent variable were held constant and one of the other variables manipulated, you might find just as big a relationship between this independent variable and your dependent variable.

For example, if you are teaching an animal to make some response, you may find that one pattern of food reward will be much more effective than another in getting the animal to perform the response, so long as you make sure that the animal's hunger level is comparable when you try the different patterns. But if you tried the same patterns with an animal that is not hungry at all, you might get quite different results. And if you used just one pattern of food reward and varied the degree of hunger, you would probably conclude that the degree of hunger was the important variable in how fast the animal learned the response.

This is another example of how the question you ask determines the kind of answer you will get. The psychologist studying learning and reward holds motivation constant and focuses attention on differences in reward patterns; conclusions about learning and reward are then all about the effect of reward. The psychologist studying motivation, however, would hold reward constant and vary motivation; in this case, conclusions would be about different motivational states and *their* influence on behavior. Likewise a psychologist studying personality would hold situational factors constant; a psychologist studying the effects of situational factors would hold personality characteristics constant. Their conclusions would vary accordingly.

This elaborate procedure of gathering data and drawing conclusions is what distinguishes scientific conclusions from those advanced by philosophers, theologians, and journalists as well as by the rest of us in our daily rounds of concluding what is and what is not and what we ought to believe in and support. Unfortunately, not all the conclusions that others want us to act on are so valid; in fact, many—including some that claim to be based on "scientific fact"—represent serious psychological traps.

Psychological Traps

If it sounds easy to "gather only objective information and draw conclusions according to rules agreed on in advance," consider the following examples of traps you are invited to fall into every day.

The Truth of the Ad Is in the Comparison

Advertising is aimed openly at manipulating not only behavior but ideas. Do ads fool you? For example, if you wanted a pill to relieve the pain from the ordinary headaches to which millions of Americans are heir, would you conclude that Bayer aspirin really is best because "Government tests have proven that no pain reliever is stronger or more effective than Bayer aspirin"?

What ads like this fail to mention is that those government tests, which were sponsored by the Federal Trade Commission and published in the *Journal of the American Medical Association*, actually found *no difference* at all among the five headache preparations tested, either in speed or in effectiveness of pain relief. True, none was more effective than Bayer aspirin, but neither was any *less* effective. Adding that second comparison puts the conclusion in quite a different light.

And what about your cavities? You should know by now that "it has been found that people who use Crest regularly had 38 percent fewer cavities." Makes sense then to take the recommended action and buy a tube, no? Maybe yes, maybe no. *"Fewer than what?"* Than *irregular* Crest users? Than children who *never* brushed their teeth? Than those who brushed but did not have regular dental checkups and oral hygiene treatments? Than *chimpanzees* who used Crest regularly?

We all know those TV ads touting the Ford LTD as "quieter than even the most expensive imports" (implying a comparison with the famed quiet of Rolls Royce). When the Federal Trade Commission ordered an independent substantiation of this and other claims made in auto advertisements, it was disclosed that comparison tests showed the new Ford was quieter than a 1963 Daimler with 37,225 miles clocked on it, and

Psychological Clues Detected in Elderly Year Before Death

CHICAGO, Nov. 11 (AP) — A researcher at the University of Chicago says that older persons show definite psychological changes about a year before death occurs.

Morton A. Lieberman, an associate professor of psychiatry at the university's medical school, wrote in the school's journal, Reports, that the changes included the intellectual and emotional areas.

Professor Lieberman tested 80 persons between the ages of 70 and 95. Forty have died since his study began. Of these, 34 showed a distinct awareness of signs of death more than a year before it occurred,

"There was no evidence in these psychological changes that these people had any increased concern or fear, only that they were monitoring signs within themselves that became symbolized as death," he said.

He emphasized that "these people were not obviously physically ill when they began to show these signs."

"The psychology of death may begin in middle age," Mr. Lieberman said. "People may begin coping with the problem in their late fifties. By the time they truly are old, most have come to terms with the situation.

The crisis of anticipation of a radical change, plus the move itself, are the most critical stages for the aged, Mr. Lieberman said.

The most noted radical change was being placed in an old age institution.

Mr. Lieberman cited figures showing that 24 per cent of ... persons placed in an old ... died within the ...

THEORIES ABOUND ON BIRTH INCREASE

Possible Link With Blackout Will Not Be Determined for Two More Weeks

HOSPITALS REPORT RISE

Many Parents Join Fertility Experts and Sociologists in Sifting Phenomenon

By MARTIN TOLCHIN

... crease in births in several hospitals continued ... day, nine months aft- ... power blackout, as ... mothers joined ... fertility ...

SMOKING LINKED TO POOR GRADES

Habit in Freshmen Is Also Tied to Campus Activity

By JANE E. BRODY

The freshman college student is more likely to smoke if he has poor grades and fails to participate in campus activities, a University of Illinois study has shown.

It was found that the more spending money the student had, the more likely he was to smoke. The results showed also that the smokers were more likely to have at least one parent who smoked.

Of the 3,567 freshman questioned at the university, 40 per cent were smokers. Nearly half of them said they wanted to stop smoking.

These findings, gleaned from an ongoing study of student smoking habits, are described in the current issue of the Journal of the American Medical Association published yesterday.

---

also quieter than a Jaguar—a 1964 oldie but goodie with over 20,000 miles (United Press, Oct. 7, 1972).

MORAL: The whole is more truthful than the part.

Did You Know That VISTA Volunteers Were "Radicalized by Their Experiences"?

"The exposure of thousands of young, middle-class Americans to the conditions of poverty through their enlistment in the VISTA program has sharply 'radicalized' about one third of them and moved most others toward a more left social and political posture, according to a government sponsored study" (The New York Times Service, *May 24, 1971*).

Before you conclude that VISTA is a communist indoctrination program subsidized by the taxpayers, ask about the comparison group. The change in VISTA volunteers was gauged against a group of VISTA volunteers who were "no shows"—who failed, for various reasons, to serve the one-year enlistment period. What the data actually show is that 6 percent of this control group described themselves as having changed from "conservative" or "moderate" to "liberal" or "radical left," while the comparison figure for the VISTA group was 17 percent—

only an 11 percent difference and hardly a "sharp radicalization of a third of the group."

MORAL: Compare before you conclude.

Smoke Gets in Their Eyes

How do you know when you can believe what you read in the papers? What would you conclude from the article on smoking and grades reprinted in part above? If freshmen hope to be academically successful, must they stop smoking?

Here we need question neither the data nor the correlation between the two sets of behaviors (the students' smoking and the teachers' assignment of grades to them). Rather, we must focus on the implied *causality*. What leads to what? Will grades go up if smoking goes down? This will occur only if the two events are directly linked in a causal fashion. However, we can readily posit several equally likely causal sequences that fit the observed relationship. First, perhaps smoking does cause poor grades. If so, the number of cigarettes smoked ought to correlate negatively with grade-point average, and grades should change as smoking patterns are varied. But suppose poor grades can cause smoking. In fact, the newspaper article notes "that students with poor grades had a 'certain psychological reaction' that often leads them to nervous habits such as smoking or nibbling." If so, changing the effect (smoking) would not change the cause (poor grades).

It could also be that both events are caused by a third factor, such as "nervous irritability." This factor would lead to smoking behavior and also to poor study habits, which result in poor grades. By this argument, reducing smoking might increase nervousness, which in turn would result in more distraction when studying and eventually in poorer grades. So we might conclude (if we were in the employ of a tobacco company) that smoking is a safety valve that helps some students get "A" averages.

So until more is known, several explanations are equally plausible. In the example above, we can add at least one more alternative (can you supply any others?). It might be that teachers dislike students who smoke in class (it looks as though they are not enraptured by the lecture, not studious, etc.) and therefore are predisposed to give poorer grades to smokers. In such a case, stopping smoking might lead to better grades, *not* by directly changing the students' study habits, attitudes, or psychic health, but by changing the teacher's perception of them.

MORAL: One correlation does not a causation make.

Sex Can Make You Crazy

Another newspaper article reported a university psychiatrist's findings that 86 percent of a group of women who were psychiatric patients had indulged in intercourse, as compared with only 22 percent of a group of women at the same university who were not psychiatric patients. The figures had been obtained through questionnaires, and the psychiatrist was quoted as concluding that his patients were "casualties of the sexual revolution." From the information given, would you agree with his conclusion?

Two claims are involved here: (a) that a much higher percentage of patients than comparable nonpatients had had intercourse, and (b) that the sexual activity of the patients was a causal factor in their emotional problems. Again the conclusion may be true, but before accepting it (or before you allow your parents to arm themselves with new "authoritative" arguments on how to preserve your mental health), you must raise several questions.

First, how large was the sample of psychiatric patients? The surprisingly high figure of "86 percent" could be the data for only six women out of a grand total of seven. The conclusion as stated goes far beyond the original *sample* of students questioned. It is generalized to the entire *population* of all college women, but we do not know how large the sample was or whether it was representative of college women in general.

It is also conceivable that the nonpatient coeds were giving a more "socially desirable" self-report in which they underestimated their actual promiscuity, while those under psychiatric care either were more truthful or were bragging. The psychiatrist's conclusion was not about the women's *self-reports* but about the *behavior* referred to in those reports; but we can never assume that *self-reports* and *actual behavior* are the same. Differences between groups on self-report measures may reflect differences *not* in the behavior under consideration but in what the two groups were trying to prove about themselves. In fact, the members of the patient group may even have regarded their sexual activity as one of the few healthy aspects of their lives and may have sought psychiatric help for other reasons entirely. So we end up knowing only that the patient group *reported* more intercourse than the nonpatient group.

MORAL: There's many a slip between observing the word and generalizing about the deed.

Blackout Baby Boom
(or, What to Do 'til the Lights Go On Again)

It is remarkable how many things are correlated in nature and how that number increases when human beings are involved. In August 1966, newspapers in New York heralded an above-average increase in births "in several leading hospitals," "nine months after the 1965 power blackout." This claim was generally accepted without question, and people proceeded to try to explain it.

Among the thirty million people affected by the November 9 blackout on the East Coast were those who later theorized "that natural disasters lead people to turn to each other. Excavations of Pompeii, for example, showed couples embracing during the volcanic eruption." Said a mother at Brookdale Hospital: "I wouldn't go to bed by myself." A new father attributed the birth increase to his belief that "New Yorkers are very romantic. It was the candlelight." A more somber appraisal was offered by an official of the Planned Parenthood Federation of America:

"Sexuality is a very powerful force, and people would normally indulge in sex if they didn't have anything else to do. All the substitutes for sex— meetings, lectures, card parties, theaters, saloons—were eliminated that night. What else could they do?" (The New York Times, *Aug. 11, 1966*)

Again we see a causal inference from a correlation of two events. The frequency with which this type of thinking occurs attests to our predilection to go beyond observations and seek the lawfulness that we believe must explain them. This is an admirable venture, but may be nothing more than an intellectual explanation in search of a nonfact. Two possibilities exist in this example, which we have not considered in the earlier ones: (a) the data cannot be trusted, or (b) the relationship is coincidental.

Although one New York hospital (St. Luke's) reported three times the average number of daily births for each of the seven key days, the numbers were small, only about 10 extra babies a day. And the sixteen other hospitals combined reported an increase of only 47 births—2.9 babies per hospital. This output seems even less significant when we remind ourselves that in New York City there were probably three million women with childbearing capabilities who were in the dark of that November night. And can we assume that all those women who gave birth in August had even been involved in the blackout nine months earlier?

In order to discover whether there is, in fact, a fact to be explained, a statistician (J. Richard Udrey of the School of Public Health, University of North Carolina) compared the "blackout birth rates" with those of earlier years. There was *no difference* between the proportion of the total year's births that fell approximately nine months after the November 9 conception date (from June 27 to August 14) and the proportion usually born during that time period in any of the five preceding years.

An epilogue to the New York story was provided by the experience of Chicago the following year. Based on the New York claim, Chicago hospitals braced themselves for a baby boom in the fall of 1967 as a memento of their 23-inch snowstorm in January of that year. But statistics for the three fall months, compared with those of the corresponding months the year before and the year after, showed only slight fluctuations, with slightly fewer births than the previous year and slightly more than the following year.

Such myths die slowly because they get into the common folklore and most people never see the evidence to the contrary. Seven years after the New York blackout, the claim surfaced again, in exaggerated form, in a United Press release. Los Angeles City Councilman Donald Lorenzen, worried about the possibility of no lights or TV because of the energy crisis, was reported as saying, "I know what happened in New York when they had the blackout. Everybody went to bed and population zero went to hell. There were more kids born after that period than at any other time." (United Press, Nov. 23, 1973)

MORAL: Elaborate explanations for nonfacts are the cotton candy of reality: a mouthful of fluff but an empty stomach.

Ah, to Be Black Now That the Police Are Beating Up Whites

"Poor whites are more affected than Negroes" by use of unnecessary police force, according to a July 1968 news story. "Race prejudice is not a major factor in any beatings of poor people by the police . . . whites are more likely to be handled roughly by the police than are Negroes." Thirty-six observers who worked with the police in Boston, Washington, and Chicago during the summer of 1966 reported that of 643 white suspects, 27 were hit unnecessarily (a rate of 41.9 per 1000). Of 751 black suspects, only 17 were hit unnecessarily (a rate of 22.9 per 1000). Thus, allegations by civil rights groups of police brutality toward blacks are not supported by this data. ■

Taken as they stand, however, these data have at least three possible interpretations: (a) they may be accurate, as is stated in the report; (b) they may be due to the uncertainty principle; (c) they may be due to observer bias or inaccuracy.

The physicist Heisenberg gave us the *principle of uncertainty*—that the act of measuring a process may change the process itself. Although he was referring to the speed and location of an electron in a cloud chamber, his statement is frequently true of psychological measurement. When the behavior being measured is influenced by people's awareness that they are being observed, the observer no longer gets an accurate picture. Rather, the measure may be distorted by attempts to deceive, to present a favorable image, to react against being a "guinea pig," or to "psych out" the observer—to be or do what you think is wanted. Thus, in this study of police brutality, the police might have changed their pattern of cracking heads because they knew they were being watched by observers riding around with them in their squad cars.

The conclusion may also be affected by the observers' definitions of "unnecessary force." Maybe they had different definitions for black and white suspects. It is possible that the police hit as many black suspects as white ones—maybe even more—but that more of the hitting of blacks was regarded as "necessary" by the observers.

MORAL: When we report on "the way things are," we really mean the "way they seem" given what we have been conditioned to notice, how we define and measure what we are looking for, and what others want us to see.

The Tyranny of Numbers: Can Statistics Lie?

Crime is one of the nation's number one concerns, according to most of the public opinion polls that are taken today. But just how bad is the picture? The answer depends on comparative crime statistics of criminal offenses over the past years. But it also depends on whether you want the statistics to prove that: (a) the situation is getting worse (that is, when there is a lobby for a bigger law enforcement budget or when there is an attack on the present administration) or (b) the situation is getting better (to justify the past expenditure of taxes for law enforcement or prove that the administration's policies of crime control have been effective).

■ "At least we can't be accused of racism—hitting whites was just as much fun as hitting blacks."

The crime rise reported by the FBI in the chart portrays a clear message: Help! ▲ But the Attorney General's office disputed this pessimistic view of things (*The New York Times*, Sept. 18, 1971) and supplied statistics to prove that the previously high crime rate (under Democratic administrations) was tapering off under Nixon's "Law and Order" programs.

Although FBI statistics revealed that major crimes had risen from 4.4 million in 1968 to 5.5 million in 1970—a 25 percent increase, the programs of the Justice Department are nevertheless succeeding. How, you ask? Well, according to the Attorney General's statistics, it is obvious that the "rate-of-increase" of crime is decreasing. In 1967 the crime rate rose by 16 percent over 1966, by 17 percent the next year, then by 12 percent in 1969, and by 11 percent in 1970. Thus, the increased crime rate we are experiencing represents an actual decreased rate of increase at this point in time. (Something to cheer about behind your triple-locked doors, no?)

MORAL: A statistic is a number, until you want it to prove your conclusion—then it is a weapon.

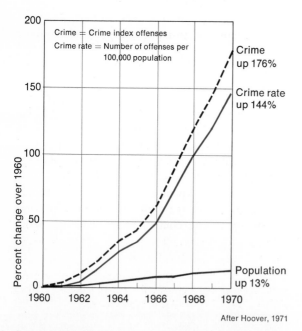

Crime = Crime index offenses
Crime rate = Number of offenses per 100,000 population

Crime up 176%

Crime rate up 144%

Population up 13%

Percent change over 1960

After Hoover, 1971

▲ **OUR DECREASINGLY INCREASING CRIME RATE**

A Case History in the Instant Creation of a Scientific Authority

As a final cautionary tale in our review of the hazards of accepting at face value pronouncements about what "science" has supposedly discovered, we offer the following personal case history.

"The use of obscene language among women, from the coeds of the New Left to the proper matrons at swank Manhattan cocktail parties, has risen sharply in the last few years, according to some leading psychologists."

Thus began an article in *The New York Times* (Leo, 1968) that, as you can imagine, provoked considerable national interest. What is most interesting for our purposes is that the reputed "leading authority" on this topic was one of the authors of *Psychology and Life*. The article commented further upon his observations:

"Philip Zimbardo, a Stanford University psychologist, said that in observing agitated patients at two East Coast mental hospitals over a long period of time, he noted that the language of the women was more obscene than that of the men."

This report was picked up by the news services, reprinted in various forms in papers throughout the country, given a splashy *Newsweek* treatment under the heading "Girl Talk: **%#!," commented upon by Dr. Joyce Brothers in her syndicated column, and finally boxed in the Forum Newsfront of *Playboy Magazine!* Offers for this authority to appear on radio and television "talk" programs, as well as a rash of requests for reprints of his writings on the topic (some from as far away as South America) followed *The New York Times* report. We are in the unique position of being able to trace this widely circulated and fully accepted conclusion from its uncertain, speculative origin to its final, convincing, authoritative status as "fact of human nature."

It appears that one of the editors of *The New York Times* was cursed out by a woman at a party, and he promptly assigned a reporter to find out whether this was a unique experience, or part of a regularly occurring social phenomenon, or something about him that the particular guest did not like.

The reporter telephoned several social scientists who might know something about the issue, one of whom (for some unknown reason) directed him to Zimbardo. Protests about not having any relevant evidence and the statement that no one was engaged in research on this particular problem were not accepted, since there was a deadline to be met the next morning. What was said, then, to the reporter was that "a number of years ago (ten to be exact), in two mental hospitals in Connecticut, in informal observations in the back wards (where chronic schizophrenics were kept), the women's wards seemed to be noisier and to have a greater amount of exhibitionism and obscenity than the men's wards."

Because the observer was not testing a hypothesis about obscenity, he did not record any data other than his general impressions. There was no independent verification by other observers of the same data, no explicit definition of obscenity, and no comparability of observation periods of men and women. It is possible that the observer was simply more aware of female obscenity because of its usual lesser frequency in everyday life: it may have occurred with the same frequency as among the male schizophrenics, or its frequency might even have been lower. Or perhaps there were simply a few very loudly obscene female patients in that ward. In any event, with no systematically collected and recorded data, we cannot separate distortions in Zimbardo's recall (ten years later) of what he witnessed from either his original observations or the actual behavior that was occurring.

In *The New York Times* report, the casual "observed a number of years ago" became "observed over a long period of time" and "chronic schizophrenics" became "agitated patients." In *Newsweek* the original casual observations that were "noted" in the *Times* report became a relationship that was "found"—"women patients in mental hospitals are much more likely to

swear than men" (notice the addition of "much"). In Dr. Brothers' column, the "back ward schizophrenics" became "female mental patients"—a term that could include relatively normal outpatients in therapy.

The modern authority on all matters sexual—*Playboy*—simplified matters for its readers with the broad overgeneralization that "a number of psychologists, *The New York Times* reports, have found that women of every social level have become increasingly uninhibited in their use of obscene language" (*Playboy*, 1969). The only psychologist mentioned is the now well-known authority, Philip Zimbardo, whose comprehensive research "confirms" the above principle of human behavior.

The latest addition to this media pollution is that the unconfirmed, biased (maybe sexist) observation has now passed into the lofty realm of scientific generalization—soon to become an honest-to-goodness truth. Would you believe the following "believe it or not" account from a syndicated column in the *San Francisco Chronicle?* (Nov. 13, 1971)

> ### ∼ Grab Bag ∼
>
> ## *Everyone Is Scared Of Something*
>
> #### L. M. Boyd
>
> OPEN QUESTION: It's a proven peculiarity that the woman patient in a mental hospital is far more likely to swear a blue streak than is the man patient. How do you account for that?

Unfortunately, contest rules prohibit any person of either sex who has read this text from submitting explanations for this "proven peculiarity."

MORAL: Authorities are only as reliable as their weakest evidence, their most questionable premises, and their doubting critics.

Levels of Psychological Analysis

In studying any given phenomenon or process, it is possible for a researcher to ask questions, use techniques, and collect data that are appropriate to quite different levels of analysis—all the way from the highly detailed, minute, and specific to the general, broad, and gross. We can distinguish three levels of analysis in psychological research: the microscopic level, the molecular level, and the molar level.

At the *microscopic* (or *micro*) level, interest is centered on the smallest possible parts, events, and subunits of the whole organism. Precision, specificity, rigorous methods of data collection, and quantitative analysis are the hallmarks of research at this level. A researcher who studied chemical transformations within cells of the eye during transmission of a nerve impulse would be operating at this micro level.

The *molecular* level is also geared to a concern for detail—for small, quantifiable units of measurement. However, the units studied are bigger than at the micro level, since larger processes are investigated, which themselves are composed of subunits. Psychologists who work in the areas of learning, perception, psycholinguistics, and information processing, for example, probably operate most frequently at the molecular level. They often attempt to develop causal laws relating internal processes (such as color vision or memory) to external, manipulated variables.

At the *molar* level, the object of study is either the whole functioning organism or systems of behavior that involve much of the total organism. The personality psychologist, the clinical psychologist (who does diagnosis and therapy of mental and emotional disorders), and the social psychologist typically are among those who utilize the molar level of analysis. At this level, the data are often more qualitative than quantitative, the research methodology is less rigorous and controlled, and the conclusions are much broader but less precise than at the micro or molecular levels. Psychologists who operate at this level are willing to make inferences about

unobservable events and processes (for example, values, the superego, cultural deprivation) and to attribute behavior to historical, mental, environmental, social, and even political causes.

Despite the general agreement on goals of psychology and on standards for dependable data collection and conclusion drawing, there is no agreement among psychologists on what level of analysis is best. Typically, a researcher chooses to function primarily at the level that suits his or her own interests, training, and abilities. And there is an interplay between one's assumptions about causes and consequences of human behavior and the level of analysis at which one studies the processes. If you assume that behavior is controlled largely by genetic influences, you do not study attitudes, childrearing patterns, and self-awareness. If you function at the "looser," "softer," less specific, molar level, you are less likely to be interested in physiological processes and more likely to assume that the important determiners of behavior are to be found in the individual's social environment.

Although the particular level at which any psychologist functions may be just a matter of personal preference, many come to feel that their level is the best or indeed the only right way to study psychology. The history of psychology is filled with the names of "schools" of psychology that have arisen to defend a particular set of assumptions about what should be the legitimate study of psychology and/or how that study should be conducted. Names such as "structuralism," "functionalism," "introspectionism," "behaviorism," and others describe alternative approaches to the study of psychology. They are defined in the glossary and discussed in the text where appropriate. Our own approach will be *eclectic*—that is, one that tries to present you with the widest variety of the best available research, theory, and speculation, regardless of the orientation or level of analysis of the researcher or the philosophical and political assumptions of the theorist.

A useful way to think about the issue of levels of analysis is in terms of the different kinds of *maps* you would need in order to go from your college campus to some desired other place. If you wanted to find the administration building or the gym, a campus map with each building identified would be the most appropriate one. If, however, you wanted to bike to a movie downtown, then you would be better off with a map showing streets of the town. To go on a vacation to a nearby city would require a map with state and county routes, while a cross-country jaunt on your freewheeling motorcycle would necessitate a national map of the United States with states, cities, interstate highways, and other features shown.

Although each map may be an accurate and valid representation of the information it provides, it may be totally inappropriate if you do not need that information for your particular trip. To be "relevant" the map you use must be at the level of detail or generality appropriate to the demands you impose on it. Therefore, to go from where you are at this moment to Istanbul requires a whole set of maps, perhaps starting and ending with local ones but employing global ones as well, in order to give you general direction and the overall picture.

Maps differ not only in their scale of detail but also in the kinds of features they show. A relief map may not show auto routes or cities. Such differences may correspond to the difference in psychology between studying physical events and studying conscious experience. Some psychologists would deny this, having faith that ultimately all psychological events will be describable in neurological or biochemical terms. This position is called *reductionism* (see p. 52).

In this text, you will be introduced to research growing out of all these approaches. You will have a chance yourself to wrestle with the question of what is the best level for understanding and explaining what we do and how we feel — or whether perhaps different levels must be used for different purposes.

The text is so organized that as you go from chapter to chapter you will move from micro to molecular to increasingly larger molar levels of analysis. Chapter 2, dealing with physiological psychology, is the most specific, while in the last two chapters, on social pathology and ecological psychology, we use the broadest levels of analysis in attempting to describe the human condition. In between these extremes, we will keep an eye on the ultimate goal of our journey, so as not to be confused by too many minor paths and diversions; but at the same time, we will try to be aware of and appreciate the local terrain that will make our trip together interesting and unusual.

Chapter Summary

Psychology is *the scientific study of the behavior of organisms*. Through the study of psychology we learn about how living creatures (including human beings) interact with their environment and with each other. Every one of us functions informally as a "psychologist" — assessing and predicting our own behavior and that of other people. In this text we shall be studying the ways in which psychologists have formalized the study of behavior: checking their assumptions, making accurate observations, weighing evidence objectively, and drawing valid conclusions.

All psychologists begin by making certain assumptions about the nature of the world. (a) Like other scientists, they assume that there is an underlying *order* in nature; that patterns of systematic relationship can be found. (b) They make an assumption of *determinism;* that is, they assume that all events have causes, and that an understanding of these causes makes it possible to predict the occurrence of future events. (c) They restrict themselves to *empirical* knowledge: information that can be objectively observed and independently verified.

Although psychologists agree on the basic assumptions underlying scientific research, they may operate on the basis of differing assumptions about human nature and human behavior. Psychologists differ as to the existence—and the importance—of *cognitive* or *mental* processes. They differ as to the importance of *nature* (the influence of heredity) as opposed to *nurture* (the influence of the environment). They differ as to whether "human nature" is inherently *good* or inherently *evil*. Some psychologists take a *nomothetic* approach, seeking universal laws that will explain the behavior of all people. Others prefer an *idiographic* approach, seeking to determine why people differ in their behavior. Some look for *dispositional* causes within persons. Others look for *situational* causes in the environment. Some concentrate on the study of *individuals;* others on the behavior of *groups.*

How the psychologist poses the questions will determine the kind of answers that are obtained. Psychologists who are interested in studying overt responses to specific stimuli are called *behaviorists*. Those who prefer to study subjective individual experience are called *phenomenologists.*

The research psychologist has four basic goals: *description, explanation, prediction,* and *control.* To these the applied psychologist adds a fifth: utilizing the findings of research to improve the quality of human life.

Description requires objective observations. This means gathering *data:* reports or measurements of observed events. In gathering data it is important to distinguish between what is actually *observed* and what is only *inferred.* To make sure that their data are not ambiguous, psychologists rely on *operationism.* They construct *operational definitions,* in which concepts are defined in terms of the specific operations used in measuring them.

Explanation in psychology is concerned with answering the questions of "what" and "how" rather than "why." Many types of explanation may be used, depending on the event to be explained. In general, psychologists tend to avoid *mentalistic* explanations that infer feelings or wishes. Many, however, use *physiological* explanations, based on nerve cell activity, etc., to explain specific units of behavior. Some use *analogy,* explaining an event in terms of its similarity to some better known process or occurrence. In *functional* explanation, behavior is explained in terms of the stimulus conditions of which it is a function. *Models* or theoretical frameworks from one field may be of help in attempts to explain behavior in another area but do not serve as complete explanations. Computer science has given rise to a new tool for explanation: *simulation* of behavioral processes. In working with symbol-manipulating computer programs, psychologists can learn much about human information processing. The most elaborate form of scientific explanation is *theoretical* explanation. A *theory* is a statement of the relationship between a set of assumptions, principles, deductions, and observations.

On the basis of their theories, psychologists attempt to predict the occurrence and/or the consequences of behavior. Such prediction begins with a *hypothesis:* a statement concerning a possible relationship between two or more *variables.* Hypotheses are tested by experimentation, and while they may be supported with a reasonable degree of certainty, they are never actually considered proved.

Correlations are a useful tool in psychological prediction. These are precise statistical statements of the relationship between two variables. It is important to note that a correlation between two variables does *not* necessarily mean one is *causing* the other, only that they co-vary.

Controlling the behavior of oneself or others is possible only when the conditions under which such behavior occurs are understandable and predictable. *Feedback* concerning the results of behavior is an important element in control. Psychologists are becoming increasingly concerned about using their ability to predict and control behavior in ways that will enrich rather than diminish the quality of human life.

The *experimental method* is the basis of scientific inquiry. This method involves four major steps: formulating a hypothesis, testing it, drawing conclusions, and reporting the results in such a manner that the experiment can be *replicated* by other scientists. The research psychologist begins by deciding how the variables to be studied are to be defined and measured and by formulating a hypothesis. The variable whose effects are being studied is called the *independent variable*. This is the one the experimenter changes, or *manipulates*. The *dependent variable* is the behavior that is expected to change when the independent variable is manipulated.

A typical experiment involves two groups of subjects: an *experimental group* and a *control group*. The independent variable is manipulated for the experimental group but held constant for the control group. (All other variables that might possibly influence the results are held constant for both groups.) If the dependent variable changes for the experimental group but not for the control group, the difference can be attributed to the changes in the independent variable. Actually, most behaviors have multiple causes and a network of interrelated effects. Where variables cannot be held constant, control is achieved by other means. The crucial element in experimentation is the *random* assignment of subjects to different experimental conditions.

It is important to know whether there is a *significant difference* between the groups, or whether the difference could have occurred by chance. This must be determined by statistical tests which result in a *probability statement*. This is an estimate of the probability that the difference occurred by chance. If this probability is small enough (say, less than 5 chances in 100), the hypothesis of a chance result is rejected and the difference is considered to be *statistically significant*—due not to chance but to the experimental manipulation of variables.

Conclusions drawn from scientific experiments are only as sound as the data they are based on and the objectivity with which they are interpreted. We are bombarded by the media every day with purported "scientific conclusions" whose worth we must be able to evaluate if we are to avoid falling into psychological "traps."

The psychological investigations we shall be studying throughout this text can be categorized according to the *level of analysis* at which they are carried out. Studies involving subunits of an organism, such as the behavior of individual cells, are generally at the *microscopic* level of analysis. Studies of larger units of behavior, such as those involved in perception or information processing, are at the *molecular* level. Broader investigations involving the behavior of an entire organism or groups of organisms are said to be at the *molar* level of analysis. The level of analysis at which a particular psychologist functions is determined by his or her theoretical assumptions and by the nature of the processes to be investigated. In this text we shall take an *eclectic* approach to the study of psychology, drawing on various theoretical assumptions and levels of analysis as the need arises.

2

The Physiological Bases of Behavior

What a piece of work is a man! how noble in reason! how infinite in faculty! in form and moving how express and admirable!
>   William Shakespeare, *Hamlet*, II:ii

We are in the operating room of the Montreal Neurological Institute observing brain surgery on Buddy, a young man with uncontrollable epileptic seizures. The surgeon wants to operate to remove a tumor, but first he must discover what the consequences will be of removing various portions of the brain tissue surrounding the tumor. In effect, he must draw a *map* of a portion of the patient's brain — a map relating particular sites in the brain to the psychological functions they affect or control. Therefore, Buddy is kept conscious under local anesthesia so he can report what he experiences as the surgeon probes his brain.

The thick, bony layer of skull that shields and protects the delicate biological organ housed within is removed. We can now see the outermost, deeply wrinkled surface of the brain, called the *cortex*. The point of a thin wire, held like a pencil in the surgeon's skilled hand, gently touches one area of the cortex, stimulating it with minute electrical current.

"Nil, nil, no reaction noted," states the nurse. The electrode is then carefully placed on another spot only millimeters away. "Fist clenching, hand raising, twitching reaction observed." Again the same area is stimulated, and the nurse reports a similar motor reaction. This procedure of stimulating one area of the surface of the brain after another while observing the changes in behavior produced is slowly putting together the map the surgeon must use to guide his operation through the innumerable hills and valleys of the patient's brain.

Suddenly, an unexpected response occurs.

"The patient is grinning; he is smiling; eyes opening when that area is stimulated."

"Buddy, what happened, what did you just experience?"

"Doc, I heard a song, or rather a part of a song, a melody."

"Buddy, have you ever heard it before?"

"Yes, I remember having heard it a long time ago, but I can't remember the name of the tune."

When another brain site is stimulated, the patient recalls in vivid detail a thrilling childhood experience.

In a similar operation, a woman patient "relived" the experience she had during delivery of her baby. As if by pushing an electronic memory button, the surgeon, Dr. Wilder Penfield, has touched memories stored silently for years in the recesses of his patients' brains (Penfield & Baldwin, 1952). ■

But where did the memories come from? How were they stored in the brain so they could be released so instantly? How does exactly the same kind of electrical stimulation produce a motor response in one part of the brain, a sensory response in another, a memory recall in a third, and so on? Is every one of the estimated million billion bits of information our senses pick up from the environment during our lifetime stored somewhere in our brains? Even more puzzling, how are we able to "read" and report on the contents of our own brain—to know, to be conscious of what is going on in there, behind our eyes, at this very moment?

These are but a few of the questions you might want to pose to a *physiological psychologist*—a psychologist whose primary concern is relating behavior and experience to the biological functioning of an organism. In this chapter we shall begin a systematic inquiry into the genetic and physiological bases of behavior. Throughout, our purpose will be to try to understand behavior and the "mental" processes. But to do so, we will have to remember that ultimately we are biological creatures, composed of a great many glands, muscles, and other structures, with a nervous system that coordinates the parts and makes the whole enterprise work pretty well. By understanding how these parts developed and how they function, we may ultimately be able to direct the future of the species onto more constructive and harmonious paths.

Physiology Opens the Black Box

For countless centuries, philosophers, theologians, and laity have been intrigued by the problem of how the external world is perceived and represented in human consciousness. Is there an "animal spirit" or "vital fluid" that enables the "mind" to make contact with properties of the physical world? Medieval investigators wrestled with the tricky question of how the soul guides human perception. They were inevitably unsuccessful in their venture—primarily because they began by asking the wrong questions and failed to distinguish between questions of physics, physiology, and psychology.

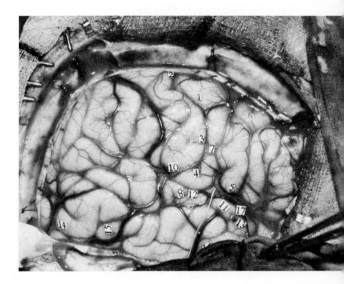

■ This is the right cerebral cortex of an epileptic patient. It has been exposed for surgery with the patient fully conscious. The numbers indicate spots at which electrical stimulation produced positive responses—simple sensory and motor responses at spots 2, 3, 7, 4, and 8 and flashback experiences at spots 11, 12, 15, and 14. For example, when spot 11 was stimulated, the patient reported hearing a neighborhood mother calling her little boy. She identified the experience as "something that happened years ago" (Penfield, 1958).

Descartes and Helmholtz

It was the French philosopher and mathematician René Descartes, often called the founder of physiological psychology, who began to ask the right questions in the early 1600s. He began with a view of the body as an "animal machine" that could be understood scientifically. He then raised purely physiological questions, questions of bodily mechanics of motion, that could be separated from psychological questions of how people sense, know, or experience the qualities of the world. Thus to understand the physiology of vision required a knowledge of the physical laws governing the transmission of light through lenses. Descartes' insistence upon reducing complex sensory processes to their underlying physical basis has been termed the *mechanistic* approach to the study of physiological processes.

A contemporary of Descartes was the astronomer Kepler, whose precise, mathematically based observations of the movements of celestial bodies was providing a firm support for Copernicus' revolutionary theory of a solar system in which the sun and not the earth was at the center. Kepler wrote of his work on the motion of planets, "My goal is to show that the heavenly machine is not a kind of divine living being but similar to a clockwork" (see Crombie, 1964).

Because Descartes was a devoutly religious man, however, he could not dispense with the soul in his theory of body functioning. Yet because of his belief in the appropriateness of a mechanistic view of perception and other sensory processes, he could not allow the soul to direct such processes. How, then, could he resolve this dilemma?

Descartes' intellectual feat was postulating a *dualism* to separate the action of the mechanistic body and brain from that of the spiritual soul and ephemeral mind, thereby rendering the body and its processes available for naturalistic study. Although the soul was assumed to be united to the entire body, it could not act upon all parts of the body or be acted upon by all parts. If it could, the body would not be a perfect machine but rather an "unaccountable mechanism."

According to Descartes, the soul and body interact at the only part of the brain that is not duplicated in the two halves, or cerebral hemispheres: the *pineal gland*. His view was that the soul acts upon the extended substance of the body only at this point, but is not confined to this space. (See *P&L* Close-up, p. 51.)

Not until the nineteenth century, however, with the discovery of a way to generate and store electricity (by Galvani and Volta), was it possible to demonstrate that the "will" to act and the "action" were distinguishable events. Using electricity to stimulate successive points along the nerve of a frog, a German physiologist, Helmholtz, measured the delay time for the corresponding muscle to twitch. He then stimulated a man on the toe and the thigh and observed the differences in time required to react to this stimulation. In both cases, he found that it took *time* for the stimulation to produce a reaction—and more time when the distance was greater. In fact, to everyone's surprise, it turned out that the transmission of the nerve impulse was relatively slow (less than 90 feet per second in the frog's motor nerve). Until then, many people had believed it to be instantaneous, faster even than the speed of light.

Of Helmholtz's demonstration, a modern experimentalist and historian of psychology, E. G. Boring, wrote: "To separate the movement in time from the event of will that caused it was in a sense to separate the body from the mind, and almost from the personality or self" (1950, p. 42). Helmholtz paved the way for research that used reaction time to measure how long thinking and other mental events took (see Chapter 5). And he raised deeper issues: it was obvious that response to stimulation was being delayed in the nervous system. But where and how? Answers to these questions are still being sought by modern researchers in physiological psychology.

Close-up
New Light on the Old Pineal Gland

As portrayed in this 1686 woodcut, Descartes believed that information about the outside world was received by the eyes and transmitted by "strings in the brain" to the pineal gland. This gland, he explained, was filled with "animal humors" that poured out whenever a light stimulus made contact with the pineal gland, causing it to tilt downward. The humors then flowed through "hollow tubes" (nerve fibers) until they reached muscles, causing them to expand or contract in response to the environmental input.

Since Descartes' time, most physiologists have tended to view the pineal gland as nothing more than a useless remnant of evolution—functional at some earlier time in the history of the species but no longer necessary. Recent research, however, indicates that despite his picturesque concepts of strings and tubes, Descartes may not have been far from the truth. Through an extensive series of rigorous experiments begun in the 1960s, the mysteries of this tiny neglected gland, tucked away in the middle of the brain, are slowly being unraveled in the laboratories of researchers Julius Axelrod and Richard Wurtman. Their basic findings support some of the "primitive" ideas of Descartes, but go even further to implicate the pineal gland in an amazing array of physiological functions.

The pineal gland apparently acts as a "biological synchronizer that keeps an animal in tune with [its] environment by altering brain chemistry according to day and night" (Luce, 1970). The size of the pineal gland and its enzyme activity were found to be affected by the amount of light in the animal's environment. But how could light reach this gland, deeply buried in the darkness of the brain? It was found that when light enters the eyes, the signal travels a roundabout route through a special optic nerve system (the inferior optic tract) and past intermediary stations in the neck and lower brain, eventually reaching the pineal gland and controlling its activity.

The pineal gland is unique in secreting the enzyme *melatonin*, which blanches the skin and influences sex hormones. In addition, this gland has been found to be rich in other significant enzymes and biochemicals, among them, *serotonin*—important in inducing nightly sleep—and *noradrenaline*—vital to the transmission of sensory information throughout the nervous system. It is conjectured that the pineal gland employs these as "transmitter substances" or messengers to inform the rest of the brain of changes in time. Thus this tiny biological time-clock may play a crucial role in affecting body chemistry, emotions, and behavior, all of which change as we pass from day to night and from season to season (Wurtman, Axelrod, & Kelly, 1968; Axelrod & Wurtman, 1970).

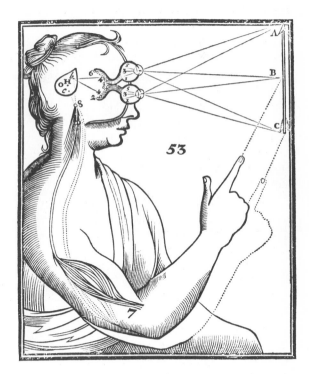

Reductionism—and Other Approaches

Before introducing you to some of the exciting research and ideas in this area, it may be appropriate to consider briefly some basic differences between the ways physiological psychologists and nonphysiological psychologists try to understand, predict, and control behavior.

The inclination of physiological psychologists is to try to understand the brain by taking it apart. Thus they dissect and analyze everything into smaller components—reflexes, nerve impulses, chemical reactions, and so on. Investigators who work in this area generally assume that this is the way the ultimate answers will be found.

This basic approach is called *reductionism*. In the reductionist approach, complex acts and processes are assumed to be understood best by study of simpler neurological or biochemical

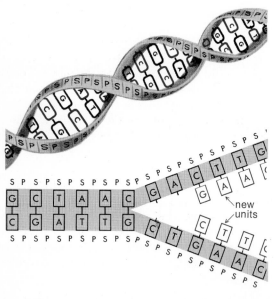

Adapted from Beadle, 1964

● THE STRUCTURE OF DNA

A DNA molecule replicates itself by unwinding, separating down the middle like a long zipper, and picking up the appropriate new units from the surrounding fluid. DNA is so tiny that all the DNA strands in the egg cells that have given rise to the approximately three billion people living today would fit into a ⅛-inch cube (Beadle, 1964).

units of analysis. Thus the study of human behavior becomes an analysis of the brain's many structures, which are made up of nerve cells, which, in turn, are made up of biochemical substances and events, and so on down to atoms and electrons.

There is a danger in the reductionist approach, however. Separating the parts from the whole produces new structures, different processes, and unique events; the parts removed from their usual context may no longer behave in the same ways. Thus some psychologists take a *holistic* approach, advocating that the proper study of behavior should be in terms of the whole organism, not of its functioning parts.

Another position contrary to physiological reductionism is that of many experimental psychologists, of whom Harvard's B. F. Skinner is an example. It is unnecessary, he argues, to look inside the "black box" (the organism, animal or human) to predict and control behavior. Do you have to look inside and "understand" the wiring of your radio or TV set in order to control its action to your satisfaction? Hardly! It is enough to know what switches to throw and what knobs to adjust. But if for some reason it does not work properly, *someone* will have to know how to get inside and repair it, so that *you* can afford to remain ignorant of how it works. The physiological psychologist is one of the many people in the health sciences whose primary interest is in getting inside the human black box to understand how it works, as well as what happens when something goes berserk.

Still another approach holds that psychological events should not be translated into physiological ones because conscious events can never be fully encompassed in neurological terms. Surely biochemical events and nerve impulses underlie experiences such as beauty or ecstasy or love, but are they identical? If not, something will be lost in the translation.

Environment As Taskmaster

Life is never a material, a substance to be molded. If you want to know, life is the principle of self-renewal, it is constantly renewing and remaking and changing and transfiguring itself.

Boris Pasternak, *Doctor Zhivago*, 1958

To understand the adaptive capacity of any species, we have to ask what it was developed to do, and this means asking what demands the environment was making on the organism when that capacity developed. Contemporary biology views the environment as an active force that constantly poses challenges to the organism, challenges that may change radically from time to time (Dobzhansky, 1957). Of the one hundred million species of animals and plants that have inhabited the surface of the earth since the first organisms appeared, barely 2 percent are still surviving. The rest did not succeed in meeting the challenges of the environment and have gone the way of the great dinosaurs into extinction.

When a species changes in a new environment, it is not because the environment has changed the genetic structure of the individuals, as was once believed. But if the needed genes are already present in some individuals, their descendants can pass this new environmental test of who is fit to survive, while other members of the species, or other species, perish.

This sequence was demonstrated recently in our use of DDT. Most insects died when exposed to the lethal environment it created, but a few of them had a "built-in" genetic resistance. These insects survived the DDT-ridden environment and mated, while others of the species died. The immunity-producing genes were in turn passed on to their offspring. In this way, a DDT-resistant strain of insects was "created."

Can the human race survive the environmental tests it is creating as it fills the atmosphere with nuclear radiation, industrial chemical wastes, smog, medical X rays? We do not know. Unfortunately, all of these can contribute not only to disease and death but also to genetic damage that is passed on to future generations.

Genes and Mutations

In the nucleus of every one of the billions of cells in the human organism are large molecules called *chromosomes*. More poetically, they have been called the *threads of life*, for they direct the activities of the cells and make possible the growth and development of the individual from conception to and through adulthood. It is their ability to make copies of themselves that makes possible the creation of new cells within the body as well as whole new individuals.

The chromosomes are large molecules consisting mainly of DNA (deoxyribonucleic acid) and proteins. The chemical structure of DNA is simple—long chains consisting of pairs of nucleotide bases, arranged like a twisted ladder or spiral staircase. Watson and Crick, who discovered the structure of DNA, called it a "double helix" (1968). ●

The *genes* are strings of these nucleotide bases that function as units in providing many kinds of "instructions" for the development and functioning of the body. Only four bases are present—*guanine* paired with *cytosine* and *adenine* with *thymine*—but a single gene may contain thousands of these bases in a long chain.

To form a new cell, the DNA in the existing cell uncoils and "unzips" down the middle of the "ladder." Each half then acts as a template and picks up the complementing bases in the proper sequence from unattached ones present in the surrounding cytoplasm. When this process is complete, the cell then divides into two cells, each of which has a complete set of DNA. The DNA also contains the instructions for making proteins, which are the building blocks of the body.

We can speculate about the development of life and evolution in the light of the following "bio-logic." At some point in time, strands of DNA must have formed that contained sequences of bases that could produce useful proteins. These proteins enabled the cell to break down nutrients into energy and to reproduce—thus to maintain itself and grow and, over the eons, to produce many kinds of alterations in the DNA.

Sickle-Cell Anemia in Two Environments

Sickle-cell anemia is a disease in which the red blood cells, carriers of oxygen through the bloodstream, become crescent shaped instead of rounded. Once sickled, the cells are unable to glide smoothly through the capillaries, causing blockage and ultimately starving the body's tissues of nourishment. Most of those afflicted with the disease die young, often before age twenty.

This potential killer is a hereditary disease that occurs almost entirely among blacks and is found only in individuals who receive sickle-cell genes from both their parents. Thus the genes are called "recessive" genes, since people who carry only one such gene never develop the disease. According to genetic theory, any gene that causes a lethal disease should become rare, but sickle-cell anemia is actually rather common. In some places in Africa as high as 35 percent of the people are carriers. About fifty thousand American blacks have two sickle genes and thus the disease, and almost 10 percent are thought to be carriers.

Genetic theory also has it that when a condition so lethal is also so common, it must offer some special advantage. On the basis of research over the last two decades, it is now widely accepted that possession of one sickle hemoglobin gene confers protection against malaria. Unfortunately, this trait, which is highly adaptive in Africa due to the high incidence of malaria, may be worse than useless for blacks in America.

Diagnostic tests for the presence of the sickle-cell gene can now provide information to help prospective parents decide whether they want to take the risk of having a child with the disease. There is controversy within the black community in America as to the intention behind the availability of such tests. Some say they prevent a tragic waste of human life; others say they are being promoted as a scientifically legitimized way of suppressing the black birthrate. Whatever the case, sickle-cell anemia is fast becoming a rather unique medical phenomenon: a political disease (Powledge, 1973).

Such alterations in the DNA are called *mutations*. A change in a single base in a DNA molecule will change the corresponding amino acid sequence in the proteins it forms. Some mutations occur spontaneously; others are caused by environmental pollutants. They may be beneficial, harmful, or lethal for the species or its offspring; most are harmful.

Most of the human cost of genetic misfiring occurs during the early stages of fertilization and pregnancy, accounting for considerable fetal wastage. Of babies that survive to be born, about 2 percent suffer from a recognizable, discrete genetic defect. This is just the tip of the iceberg; the heritability of many common diseases suggests that from one fourth to one half of *all* disease is of genetic origin, for there are important variations in people's susceptibility to even extreme environmental insults (Lederberg, 1971, p. 10).

Since every cell of the body is programmed by a copy of the individual's DNA, every cell is subject to mutation. If a mutation occurs in *body cells*, it will affect the person but will not have an effect on his or her children. Such mutations are suspected in leukemia and also in the process of aging; they may act by disorganization of an increasing proportion of body cells as new, crippled cells are formed. When a mutation occurs in the *germ cells*—either sperm or egg—it has no effect on the individual's body but may be passed on to the offspring through sexual reproduction. (See *P&L* Close-up at left.)

Sexual Reproduction and Adaptive Capacity

At the time of conception, two living *germ cells*—the *sperm* from the male and the *ovum*, or *egg*, from the female—unite to produce a new individual. The male and female germ cells are known technically as *gametes*, and the single cell they form at the moment of conception—which becomes the new organism—is called the *zygote*. The human zygote contains 46 chromosomes—23 from each parent. As it divides and redivides into more cells, the chromosomes are duplicated each time so that there still are 46 chromosomes in each new cell. The only exceptions to this rule will be the sex cells, which in their last division do not duplicate their chromosomes first but simply split, each new cell carrying half of the available chromosomes. The 23 chromosomes contained in each egg or sperm thus represent a variety of combinations from among the 46 possible ones. Different combinations, in different matings of the same two parents, account for the wide genetic differences among their children.

It is the sexual union of individuals who differ in some of their genes that gives rise to the tremendous variability present in a population. This *hybridization*—mating of dissimilar individuals—freely deals the existing genes and their mutations into new arrangements. Thus it is sex that puts enough variety in the shows it sends on the road to guarantee, in most cases, that at least some will survive the severest environmental critics. The infinite variety, originality, and uniqueness of the human form can be traced to sexual reproduction.

Each healthy creature is a living trophy of the successes its ancestors had in meeting their environmental challenges. Its own capacity to adapt to the demands of *its* environment is in part dependent on a complex set of interactions that took place in earlier generations of its species. The evolutionary nature of this adaptive capacity is illustrated in the recurring cyclical patterns outlined in the diagram. ◆

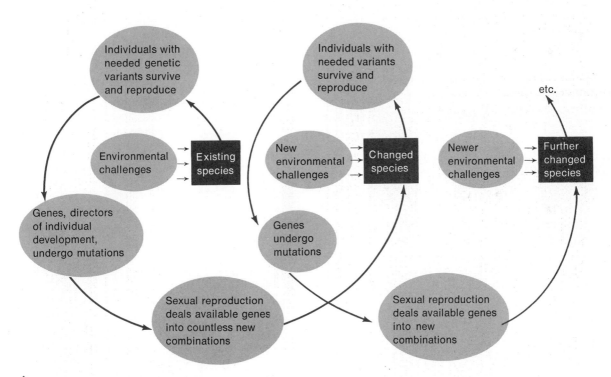

◆ **THE EVOLUTION OF ADAPTIVE CAPACITY**

The effects of heredity and environment are cumulative and interweaving. Environment keeps presenting challenges. Only members of the existing species that have the capacity to meet the challenges survive and reproduce; the others do not. As time goes on, new mutations keep occurring, some lethal, some harmful or adaptive, some with no immediate effects. As the gradually changing genes are dealt into ever new combinations through sexual reproduction, the species keeps changing. The environment keeps challenging it, often with new problems, and again only those who can survive and reproduce pass on their genetic inheritance.

The Evolution of You from It

As you look at a one-celled organism, such as a *paramecium*, swimming about on a microscopic stage, it seems inconceivable that the complexity that is *you*—with billions of cells (10^{12} brain cells alone)—has evolved from such apparent simplicity. Our forebears found it inconceivable too. A Dutch microscopist, Hartsoeker, used a crude viewing instrument in 1694 to look at a sperm cell and thought what he saw was a completely formed, miniature human figure, a *homunculus*. This creature needed only nourishment and time to develop into an adult. Moreover, each homunculus was thought to contain tiny sex cells with smaller homunculi; they in turn contained others, and so on, thereby explaining both individual development and the sequence of the generations. ■

The appealing simplicity of such ideas has been incorporated into theories in which all organisms are thought to have once upon a time been "infolded" in some primordial cell, to be "unfolded" at later times in the development of the species. Such theories view evolution as the progressive manifestation of latent forms of preexisting life, a process called *orthogenesis*.

Aristotle advanced an alternative view that is more in line with what has been discovered about embryonic development. He believed that organs were formed only gradually out of simple, unformed substances in the fertilized egg. He called this process *epigenesis*, a term still used by embryologists. ●

Before we examine the epigenetic interactions that result in the differentiation of a fertilized egg cell into the specialized tissues of the organism, we might ask why early organisms were not content to remain one-celled but evolved into protozoa, worms, fish, reptiles, mammals, and human beings. (See *P&L* Close-up, p. 57.)

■ This drawing of a sperm cell by Niklaas Hartsoeker depicts a completely formed miniature human being. The photo shows actual sperm cells highly magnified by modern photographic techniques.

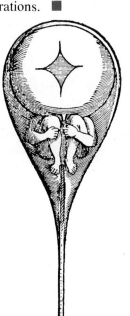

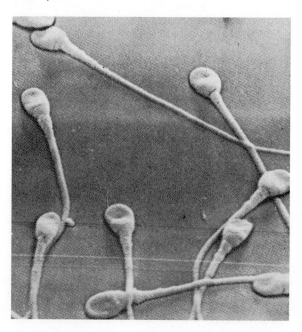

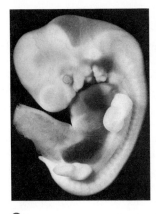 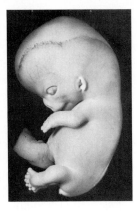

● The photos show the developing human embryo at 34 and 44 days after conception. At 34 days the facial features, hands, and feet are beginning to develop and the internal organs are forming. When the embryo is 44 days old, it possesses all the features and organs it will have as an adult, although it is still less than an inch long. The beginnings of fingers, toes, eyelids, teeth, and the tongue are visible. By the 150th day, the fetus will be completely formed. It will continue to grow and mature for another four months before birth.

Close-up

**Down from the Heavens . . .
or Up from the Muck?**

With the publication of his famous book, *The Origin of Species by Natural Selection,* in 1859, Charles Darwin dropped a bombshell upon accepted beliefs about the origins of life on this planet—and human life in particular. The theory of evolution he proposed was in direct opposition to the idea of divine creation as set forth in the Book of Genesis:

"In the beginning God created the heaven and the earth. . . . And God said, Let the earth bring forth the living creature after his kind, cattle, and creeping thing, and beast of the earth after his kind: and it was so. . . . And God said, Let us make man in our image, after our likeness: and let them have dominion over the fish of the sea, and over the fowl of the air, and over the cattle, and over all the earth. . . ." (Genesis I:1, 24, 26)

Those who interpret the Biblical account of creation as fact believe the earth is relatively young—instantaneously called into being only six thousand years ago with its full complement of plants and animals. Radioactive decay data indicating that the earth is closer to three billion years old are discounted by these creationists as the result of "special creative processes" that "only make it seem that way" (see Dolinar, 1973).

Evolutionists believe in a slow, gradual process of the development of complex organisms from simple predecessors on the basis of mutations that allowed adaptation to dramatic environmental changes (in the manner outlined earlier). Their theory places the start of life in the seas billions of years ago: ". . . under a deadly sun, in an ammoniated ocean topped by a poisonous atmosphere, in the midst of a soup of organic molecules, a nucleic acid molecule came accidentally into being that could somehow bring about the existence of another like itself" (Asimov, 1960).

Eventually these molecules formed simple organisms that evolved into fish. Some fish with lungs left the murky seas for land and evolved into reptiles, some of which evolved into birds, some of which evolved into mammals, some of which were apes, some of which evolved into human beings. Thus evolutionary theory not only suggests we are "descended from monkeys" but portrays us as having come up the hard way from the muck and mire. The fossil records used to bolster this theory are convincing evidence to its adherents, but are held by creationists to be full of gaps.

On the basis of available data, most scientists believe that the theory of evolution offers the more probable explanation of the beginnings of human life. And many individuals, scientists and nonscientists alike, feel that acceptance of the evolutionary process in no way rules out belief in the existence of a divine Creator—whether the process of creation was completed in seven days or has been going on for three billion years.

The Single Cell

A single-celled organism would seem to contain all the material necessary for survival: (a) *cytoplasm*, which is the substance in which most of the cell's biochemical reactions take place and in which the breakdown of nutrients into body energy (*metabolism*) occurs; (b) an *outer membrane*, which keeps the internal contents separate from the external environment and, through its contractions, provides one means of locomotion; (c) a *nucleus*, which directs the activities in the cytoplasm through the production of various nucleic acids. The cell can also divide to reproduce and perpetuate itself.

But a single cell is not designed to adapt to changes in the environment that interfere with its usual functioning. Thus a cell's mobility is too limited when rapid motion is required; it may have nutritional problems because it is not flexible enough to synthesize new substances when its regular food supply is unavailable. And the new, duplicate single cells that it produces will be no better suited to a changing, hostile environment than the parent cell.

The Multi-Celled Organism

For greater complexity and flexibility, a multi-celled organism with specialized cells is the only answer. Every cell in your body still has cytoplasm, a membrane, and a nucleus, which perform the general functions described above, but what the cells themselves do, and hence their makeup and ways of functioning, have become specialized.

Cell differentiation, specialization, and redundancy. The development of cellular differentiation is highly specific, such that one system of cells forms a given, distinct end-product (such as a kidney or liver), while another forms a different end-product (for example, nervous tissue). In addition, each system manages to give rise to its normal end-product, even when the conditions during its development are somewhat abnormal. (This control breaks down, of course, if the conditions are *too* abnormal.)

Within these systems, the various cells have developed widely differing capacities. Thus sensory receptors have specialized in detecting sights, sounds, and smells. Endocrine cells have specialized in developing an efficient way of synthesizing hormones through enzyme action. The neural membrane has specialized in being able to propagate information without itself physically moving. And so on.

These highly specialized functions of individual types of cells are duplicated innumerable times over in many cells as a kind of "margin of safety" to guarantee that the specific job will get done even if some cells are damaged. Thus physiological psychologists have discovered that not only are there more cell assemblies in the brain and body than are required to execute various functions, but there are a number of functions vital to survival that can continue even though massive sections of the brain are removed. This duplication or *redundancy* has thus increased the flexibility of the organism, while its cell specialization has increased the variety of situations to which it can respond or adapt.

But at what cost have these positive features been added to the once "simple-Simon" cell? In order to gain these advantages, what price was paid?

The demands upon the multi-celled organism. When you increase the number of cells and give them specialized jobs, new problems arise. The major problem is that the cells can no longer work independently, but must operate in a coordinated fashion. Consider the analogy to doing a writing project all by yourself versus doing it with a group of other students. In a group, some can do the library work, some the statistical or laboratory work. Some may know how to write well; others can type. When you do it alone, you have to do it all. But when a group does it, someone must coordinate the individual functions to have a polished, finished-on-time product.

Or imagine a more lowly example, a worm crawling along. Suddenly its head receptors detect hostile stimulation. Unless that information can be transmitted quickly to the tail, the tail will just keep moving on, pushing the head to its destruction.

Smooth workin', fast talkin' neurons. The problem of coordination and rapid intercommunication faced by complex, multi-celled organisms has been solved by the evolution of specialized cells called *nerve cells*, or *neurons*. *Neurons* have all the general characteristics of other cells and, in addition, are highly specialized to receive, carry, and transmit information in electrochemical form. These messages about the state of the external environment, or the organism's reaction to it, are called *nerve impulses*.

Neurons are unique in their ability to transmit information over long distances without any loss in the strength of the signal from the time it is picked up to when it finally reaches its destination. *Motor neurons* signal the muscles to relax or contract and the glands to secrete; *sensory neurons* carry information from the eye, ear, nose, skin, and so on to the brain about changes in the environment. In between, in the brain and spinal cord, are various types of connecting and coordinating neurons. Different types of neurons vary greatly in size and shape. The parts of a "typical" neuron are shown in the diagram. ▲

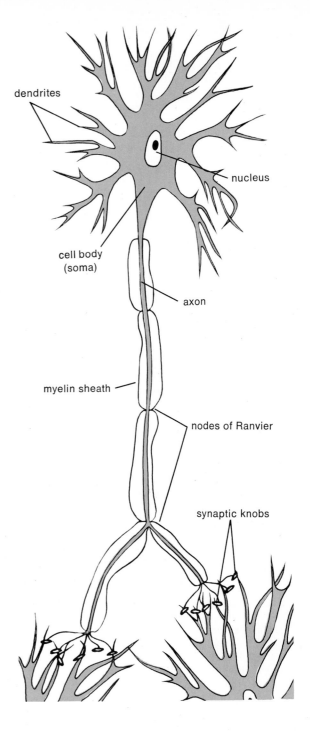

▲ ANATOMY OF A NEURON

The *cell body* of a neuron is somewhat spherical in shape and contains the *nucleus*. Projecting from the cell body are two types of fiberlike extensions: one *axon* and several *dendrites*. The axon is a long fiber, sometimes branched, that terminates in *end feet* (also called *synaptic knobs*). The length of axons varies considerably depending on the type of neuron; some are several meters long. The axon transmits nerve impulses from the cell body to the dendrites or to cell bodies of other neurons or to muscles. Large axons are often covered with a *myelin sheath* of fatty material that insulates the axon and speeds transmission of nerve impulses. This sheath is missing at points called the *nodes of Ranvier*. (The diameter of the axon and myelin sheath are greatly exaggerated relative to the axon length.)

The dendrites are typically short, multiple, and branched. They serve to receive nerve impulses and conduct them to the cell body. The neurons in a chain do not actually touch. There is a microscopic space, called a *synapse*, between the synaptic knobs of one neuron and the dendrite or cell body of the next, which the nerve impulse must "jump" across.

Going Through Channels

The nervous system can be viewed as an extremely complex communication network that developed to help meet the need for internal coordination when cells became specialized. Given the necessity of communication, the question then becomes, "Just *how* do the various parts of the nervous system 'talk' to each other?"

To understand better the system that has evolved, you might think about the necessary requirements for a reliable communication system. First of all, different parts of the system must be able to send and receive information over long distances rapidly and accurately, with-

out loss or distortion. This would presuppose one or more common languages of communication between the parts. Secondly, there must be a means by which many different bits of information can be processed and integrated.

Get the Message?

Although the details of how the nervous system processes information are very complex (and not completely understood yet), the mechanisms by which a nerve cell reacts to stimulation and spreads the word to other cells can be described rather simply.

Each sensory neuron is programmed to convey messages about a specific type of energy (pressure, temperature, light, sound) coming from the immediate environment. This energy is detected by the sensory neuron itself or by special receptor cells. It is then converted into the "common language" of the nervous system—the *nerve impulse*. Thus nerve impulses about pressure, temperature, light, and sound are all alike while they are traveling along the sensory neurons. It is their destination in the brain that determines whether we see, hear, or smell as a result of the stimulation we have received.

In addition to this information, there is also a lot of irrelevant, low-level energy called *noise* in the environment. Luckily for us, the energy reaching receptor cells has to exceed a particular level, or *stimulation threshold*, before the sensory neuron bothers to do anything about it. When it does, though, it really does!

Axonal conduction. In every nerve cell, solutions of two different chemicals, sodium and potassium, are found on both sides of the axon membrane. This membrane is selectively permeable, which means that ions of one element (in this case, the potassium) can move through it more readily than those of the other (sodium). As a result of this selective permeability, the concentration of sodium ions is much higher on the outer side, while the concentration of potassium ions is much higher inside the axon. For complicated reasons, this leads to a voltage difference between the external and internal solutions, with the inside of the axon most of the time being

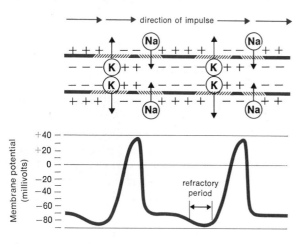

◆ AXONAL CONDUCTION OF IMPULSES
The movement of a nerve impulse down an axon is shown in the upper part of the diagram. The impulse travels along the axon as membrane "gates" are opened that allow sodium ions to move inside the membrane, depolarizing it. After the impulse has passed, the negative potential is restored.

The membrane potential (voltage) is shown in the lower part of the figure. The spike corresponds to the point at which the electrical potential becomes positive enough for the axon to "fire." Just after firing, at the point where potassium ions are flowing out, there is a brief refractory period in which the electrical potential becomes even more negative than usual. During this period it is difficult or impossible for the axon to fire.

Information is conveyed in the form of the number of impulses per second and the number of neurons activated. Once an impulse starts down an axon, it is virtually never diminished in strength.

electrically negative with respect to the outside. In this condition, the nerve cell is at rest and is said to be *polarized.*

When the energy of a stimulus exceeds the stimulation threshold, there is a change in the permeability of the membrane; sodium ions rush in, depolarizing the cell. The nerve impulse corresponds to this depolarization, which spreads from one area to the next along the axon like a lit fuse (except that the sudden change is in voltage rather than in heat).

For a few milliseconds after the axon has "fired," the membrane is temporarily unexcitable and the axon cannot be fired again, regardless of the strength of a stimulus. This interval is known as the *absolute refractory period.* There is a short period just before the membrane returns to normal during which a stronger-than-normal stimulus is required to fire another impulse; this is called the *relative refractory period.* ◆

The speed of axonal transmission is faster where the diameter of the axon is wider and where there is a coating around it known as a *myelin sheath.* In fact, to improve the reliability and velocity of signal transmission along axons, there is even a special "express" service by which impulses can jump from one point to another along the axon or even skip some stops in between. These are points where the myelin sheath is constricted; they are known as the *nodes of Ranvier* (Tasaki, 1953). This process activates several points along the axon almost simultaneously.

If the stimulus strength is anywhere above threshold—whether barely above or far above—the axon fires with the same full response. It fires either completely or not at all; this is known as the *all-or-none principle.* The size of the nerve impulse is always the same for any particular axon, regardless of the strength of the stimulus—as long as the stimulus is above the threshold. This feature ensures that the message will not fade away as it travels from one end of the nerve fiber to the other—you can depend on the service.

But if this is true, you are no doubt wondering how the neuron communicates information about stimuli of *different* intensities. A good

question. Only the axon's activities are "all-or-none." Graded incoming responses are coded into a series of impulses all of the same magnitude, but the interval between them varies: with a stronger stimulus there are more impulses per second. In addition, the stronger the stimulus, the more neurons it will excite. (See *P&L* Close-up below.)

Synaptic transmission. As remarkable as axonal conduction is for rapid, reliable delivery of coded information, the real key to the complexity and subtlety of the information carried by our nervous system lies in the activities that take place at the *synapses*—the tiny spaces between the end feet of one neuron and the dendrites or cell body of the next neuron (or neurons).

Close-up
Nerves and Puffer Fish

A *neurotoxin* is a poison that kills by disrupting the nervous system. The Japanese puffer fish contains in its liver and ovaries an extremely powerful neurotoxin called *tetrodotoxin* or TTX. TTX is a molecule that locks shut the tiny "gates" in the nerve cell axon that normally permit sodium to flow inside during an action potential, and hence blocks all nerve conduction. Since the motor nerves to the muscles necessary for breathing are included in this general block, only a small amount of TTX can cause death by asphyxiation.

Puffer fish are considered a delicacy in Japan. They are served in special restaurants, where all preparation is done by government-licensed chefs, who are experts at removing the poison gland. Nevertheless, several people die each year because of reactions to the tiny amounts of poison usually present. The true afficionado is said to delight in a slight numbness and tingling of the lips experienced during a meal of puffer fish, the numbness being produced by partial block of some sensory nerves. (If the numbness persists or spreads, see your doctor ASAP!!)

In our simplified diagrams and textbook descriptions, we portray a single neuron as sending a kind of dash-dash-dash Morse code message relaying that a stimulus is out there. But consider for a moment your different reactions to the stimulus of the same flashing police light, depending on whether you've been speeding or are in need of help. The stimulus energies are identical in the two cases; the messages circulated in your nervous system are certainly not. Or how do we ever go beyond "yes"/"no" detection of the presence of a stimulus and perceive the beauty of a summer sunset, a friend's face in a crowded lecture hall, the pattern of a tapestry, or the differences between the music of Mozart, Montovani, and the Rolling Stones?

Part of the answer to the richness of the quality of information transmitted and of our reactions to it lies in the astronomical network of billions upon billions of neurons, each one of which has hundreds of receiving points along its cell body and dendrites. At each of these, it is possible for the coded information coming down the preceding axon to be inhibited, to be passed along to the next neuron more or less rapidly, or to be added to or subtracted from related information reaching the synapse at the same time from other axons.

The synapse, this miniscule space of five millionths of an inch, may indeed be nature's most amazing invention. By not having a direct connection between any two neurons, but rather having each one indirectly linked to hundreds of others by synaptic connections, nature has made it possible for more complex messages to be simultaneously transmitted to many parts of the entire system, and for the system to work even if many neurons become damaged or defective. By analogy, the receiving sites are like great telephone switchboards into which a hundred calls can be received at once. Even if a number of the incoming cables are cut, broken,

■ The remarkable photo on the left was made possible by a new technique of scanning electron microscopy of specially prepared tissue. It shows the synaptic knobs of many axons synapsing on what appears to be a cell body.

On the right is a highly magnified view of one synapse, showing the synaptic knob of an axon, a dendrite of another neuron, and the tiny space between them. You can also see the cluster of vesicles in which the chemical transmitter is stored. In fact, clusters of vesicles like these enable researchers to tell which direction the impulse can flow across the synapse.

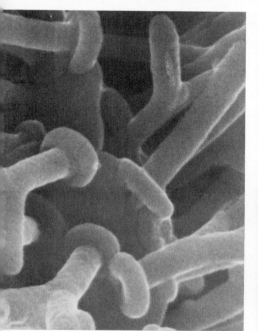

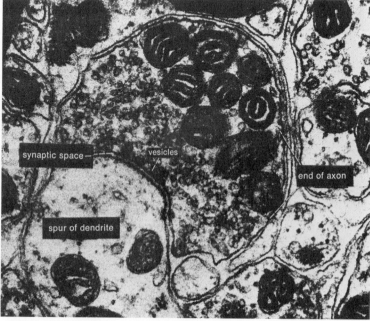

synaptic space

vesicles

end of axon

spur of dendrite

or out of order, the message can still get sent through.

When a nerve impulse reaches synaptic knobs on the end of an axon, it triggers an electrochemical disturbance that releases minute quantities of chemical messengers called *transmitter substances.* ■ These then diffuse across the synaptic gap and interact with specific receptor sites on the membranes of adjacent neurons. The effect may be either *excitatory* or *inhibitory* for the *postsynaptic membrane,* the membrane of the next neuron. The signal may be propagated along the new axon, or the depolarization of the membrane may be inhibited, thus preventing the signal from going on. But the "absence" of parts of a total incoming message still conveys information, just as black (the absence of light) does in an overall black/white pattern.

Although we have been talking of one neuron activating a second one, this is actually somewhat misleading. Generally the amount of chemical transmitter released by only a single nerve impulse is insufficient to fire a second impulse. Usually a second neuron can be activated only by more than one active nerve ending. The graded responses of several different axon inputs are summed to produce a large enough postsynaptic potential. In *spatial summation,* several inputs that arrive at the same time are added together. In *temporal summation,* several inputs that arrive in rapid succession are summed. Thus transmission across the synapse involves inputs of varying strength and is said to follow a *more-or-less principle.*

This necessity for summation in synaptic transmission means that information from many different neurons is being integrated and passed on in a new form. Obviously, a great amount of interaction is possible between excitatory and inhibitory inputs to a neuron, as outlined in the diagram. ●

After a transmitter substance does its job, it must be removed from the synapse or else it will continue to influence the membrane of the cell body. Removal is accomplished by the release of an enzyme that destroys the transmitter substance by breaking it down into its constituent parts. These parts are then recycled, resynthesized into the transmitter substance again, and the whole process is ready to be repeated—at least hundreds of times per second!

It is still not known exactly how many different transmitter substances may be used by the nervous system. There may be five or more, but the available evidence clearly substantiates the widespread presence of two—*norepinephrine* (also known as noradrenaline) and *acetylcholine.*

1. Input from one weak excitatory fiber

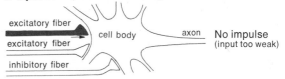

2. Input from two weak excitatory fibers

3. Input from two excitatory fibers and one inhibitory fiber

4. Input from inhibitory fiber only

● **EFFECTS OF EXCITATORY AND INHIBITORY INPUT**
Different amounts and combinations of input to a motor neuron produce different results. Four possibilities are shown here in simplified form.
The electrical events in the neural input are the same whether the impulses are carried by excitatory or inhibitory fibers. Their effects on the next neuron are different because different chemicals are released at the synapse.

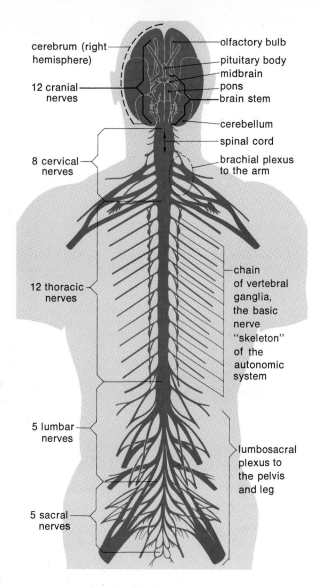

cerebrum (right hemisphere)

olfactory bulb

pituitary body

midbrain

pons

brain stem

12 cranial nerves

cerebellum

spinal cord

brachial plexus to the arm

8 cervical nerves

chain of vertebral ganglia, the basic nerve "skeleton" of the autonomic system

12 thoracic nerves

5 lumbar nerves

lumbosacral plexus to the pelvis and leg

5 sacral nerves

◆ THE NERVOUS SYSTEM

All the neurons (or parts of neurons) *within* the brain and spinal cord make up the central nervous system; all those *outside* make up the peripheral nervous system. Many individual neurons thus start in one system and end in the other.

Twelve important nerves in the peripheral system originate in the brain itself and are thus called *cranial* nerves (though one, the *vagus* nerve, wanders through the body and innervates most of the visceral organs along the way). The other main peripheral nerves connect with the spinal cord between the vertebrae all the way down and have more localized functions.

Variations in the concentration of these chemicals may influence whether the individual reacts to environmental tests swiftly and effectively or with a nonproductive overreaction. Abnormalities in these and related biochemicals may predispose people to severe mental and emotional disturbances.

One-way traffic control. Hundreds or thousands of neurons may be involved in the transmission of the same message, and the basic activity of the single nerve cell is continuously being repeated in all parts of the body in connection with many simultaneous messages. Because the many interconnections and interactions make the nervous system truly staggering in its complexity, there must be a mechanism to prevent these messages from going in all directions and turning into meaningless nonsense. There is; all neural activity follows the *law of forward conduction*. The coded information in the form of nerve impulses travels only in one direction: from the axon across the synapse to the dendrites and cell body of the next neuron. It cannot cross the synapse in the opposite direction from dendrites to axons because the transmitter substances necessary to bridge the gap are found only in the knobs of the axon.

The Input-Output Network: The Peripheral Nervous System

Another mechanism for avoiding the potential chaos of such a massive communication system is the organization of neurons within the nervous system. Essentially, the nervous system consists of two subsystems, the central and the peripheral. The *central nervous system* is made up of the brain and the spinal cord. Its function is to correlate and integrate—to make the various parts of the body work together. The *peripheral nervous system* consists of nerve fibers that connect the central nervous system to cells that are sensitive to stimulus energy (*receptors*) and to the muscles and glands (*effectors*), which perform the adjustive actions of the organism. ◆

Frequently a number of axons (or *nerve fibers*, as they are more generally called) are gathered into bundles that have a common place of origin and destination. Within the central nervous system, such bundles are known as *nerve tracts* or *pathways*. When these bundles connect the central nervous system with other parts of the body, they are called *nerve trunks*, or simply *nerves*, and contain both sensory and motor fibers. There also are certain areas in the brain called *nuclei*, where the cell bodies (and hence their nuclei) are concentrated. Finally, the entire complex of neurons is embedded in a network of *neuroglia*, or *glial cells*, which nourish and protect the delicate neurons. Some think these more recently discovered glial cells also play a critical role in nerve functioning, but this has not yet been proved.

The *peripheral nervous system* has both *somatic* components, which control the skeletal muscles, and *visceral* components, which control the glands and the special kinds of smooth muscle found in the heart, blood vessels, eyes, and internal organs. Neurons of the somatic system have all their synapses in the brain and spinal cord; neurons in the visceral portion always synapse *outside* the central nervous system. The centers controlling both systems are located in the brain, with the important difference that the visceral control centers are largely in the lower, evolutionarily older parts of the brain,

whereas the somatic control centers are in the higher centers (although the older structures contribute to final motor acts). Thus while control of the skeletal muscles can be either voluntary or reflexive, very little voluntary control of visceral functions is possible without special training. The nature of this special visceral training is described in the next chapter.

Somatic components. Although sensory and motor neurons send impulses in opposite directions—sensory neurons toward the spinal cord, motor neurons away from it—they travel in the same trunks over most of their length. Thus they enter or leave the spinal cord at the same level, and the motor fibers end in or near muscles close to the receptors that activate the sensory components.

Sensory neurons have their cell bodies near the spinal cord and send their axons into it. This means that for some sensory neurons, such as those coming from arms or legs, the dendrites will be very long. Most other neurons, as we have seen, have very short dendrites and longer axons. The motor neurons have their dendrites and cell bodies in the spinal cord; only their axons extend outside it. ▲

▲ KINDS OF NEURONS

Three kinds of neurons are represented here:
(a) a sensory (afferent) neuron, different from most neurons in having a long dendrite and relatively short axon; (b) an interneuron, with its many tiny branches, well designed for its job of providing multiple connections among many neurons; and (c) a motor

neuron, with its long axon traveling most of the distance in the same nerve trunk as the sensory neuron and ending at effectors near the origin of the sensory input. In a sensory input-motor output arc such as this, all synapses are in the spinal cord.

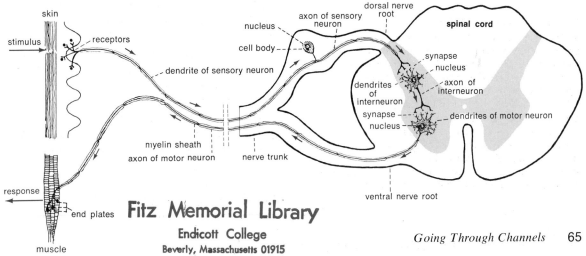

Fitz Memorial Library
Endicott College
Beverly, Massachusetts 01915

44202

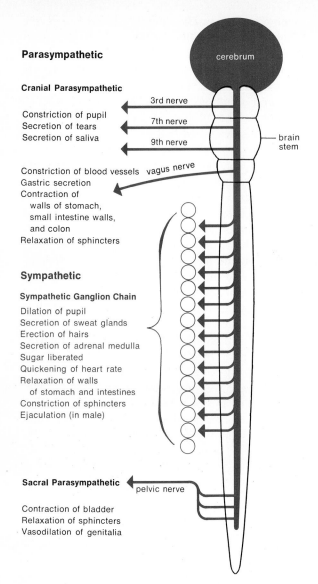

Parasympathetic

Cranial Parasympathetic

Constriction of pupil
Secretion of tears
Secretion of saliva

Constriction of blood vessels
Gastric secretion
Contraction of
   walls of stomach,
   small intestine walls,
   and colon
Relaxation of sphincters

Sympathetic

Sympathetic Ganglion Chain

Dilation of pupil
Secretion of sweat glands
Erection of hairs
Secretion of adrenal medulla
Sugar liberated
Quickening of heart rate
Relaxation of walls
   of stomach and intestines
Constriction of sphincters
Ejaculation (in male)

Sacral Parasympathetic

Contraction of bladder
Relaxation of sphincters
Vasodilation of genitalia

cerebrum

3rd nerve
7th nerve
9th nerve
brain stem
vagus nerve
pelvic nerve

● **THE AUTONOMIC NERVOUS SYSTEM**
This is a highly simplified and diagrammatic portrayal of
the parts of the autonomic nervous system—where they
originate and what their main functions are. For
simplicity, the system on only one side of the body is
shown. Parasympathetic parts and functions are labeled
in black and sympathetic ones in brown.

Visceral components. The visceral portion of the peripheral nervous system is called the *autonomic nervous system*. While some of the functions it controls, such as digestion, are truly autonomous and regulate themselves, other functions, especially those involved in the experience and expression of *emotion*, are not autonomous.

There are two divisions of the autonomic system—the *sympathetic* and the *parasympathetic*—that originate from different sections of the brain stem and spinal cord and that often oppose each other's functions. ●

The sympathetic division. In this part of the autonomic system, the nerve fibers originate only in the middle part of the spinal cord—in the segments between the neck and the lower spine. These nerves run only into a nearby, vertical chain of *ganglia* (collections of nerve cell bodies); one such chain lies on each side of the spinal cord. Fibers then run up and down this chain, synapsing with neurons that lead to the visceral organs.

The sympathetic division was so named because early anatomists believed that it was supposed to make the visceral organs work "in sympathy." It does in fact usually work as a coordinated whole, with all or most of its functions coming into play when it becomes active. The sympathetic division can be regarded as the trouble-shooter that takes charge in cases of emergency. It operates when life is threatened, when we are engaging in strenuous effort or exercise, and when we are experiencing such strong emotions as fear and rage. Essentially, the system prepares the body for action by speeding up the heart rate, causing the liver to release sugar to be used by the muscles, stimulating the flow of adrenaline, stopping the digestive processes so that the blood normally going to the stomach can be diverted to the muscles, and so on.

The parasympathetic division. The fibers in this division branch off from the central nervous system above and below the sympathetic nerve fibers, thus giving it the name *parasympathetic* (*para* means "next to"). The majority of the functions of this division are controlled by the fibers originating from above, in the brain stem.

Most of the vital functions of life are governed by the parasympathetic division. Basically, it carries out the body's housekeeping chores, such as digestion, elimination of wastes, protection of the visual system, and, generally, the conservation of bodily energy. In contrast to the sympathetic division, the parasympathetic system does not respond as a whole but activates only whatever functions are necessary at a particular time.

Coordination of the two divisions. Most organs of the chest and abdomen receive fibers from both systems; where this happens, the action of the two divisions is always antagonistic. If one system excites the organ to increased activity, the other inhibits or decreases its activity. For example, the sympathetic division inhibits digestive processes, while the parasympathetic system facilitates them. However, there are times when the two systems are both active and work together in sequence. Sexual response in the male is an example; it requires first erection (a parasympathetic function) and then ejaculation (a sympathetic function).

The Connection: The Central Nervous System

The billions of neurons, synapses, and transmitter substances organized in functional arrangements within the brain and the spinal cord constitute the *central nervous system* (CNS). This system provides the basis for connecting the vast network of sensory receptors and incoming *afferent* nerve fibers to the outgoing *efferent* nerve fibers to muscles and glands. Input sensory pathways and output motor pathways are interconnected within the CNS by a net of *associative* neurons (also called *interneurons* or *internuncial* neurons).

The CNS is much more than merely a connecting switchboard, however, for it also integrates and coordinates the stimulus input and response output. The higher the species, the more highly developed are the mechanisms for integration and coordination. In some species that have developed a highly specialized CNS, neural facilities are provided to store both sensory information and information concerning the

consequences of past actions. It then becomes possible to compare stored information with present input as well as to reorganize both input and output (creativity) and plan for future action (anticipation).

Parts of this system also have the capacity for spontaneous activity regardless of whether there is sensory input. How do "worrying," "dreaming," "self-satisfaction," "nostalgia," and other *internal*, nonstimulus-bound states come about in you? The answers to these apparently simple questions are quite complex and not yet fully understood.

The sensory-motor arc. Response to a stimulus follows a basic pattern. The stimulus is first detected by the appropriate receptors; for example, a light touch is detected by special cells in the skin. This information is then conducted along the *sensory nerve cells* to the spinal cord, where central processing begins. Usually the processed information is then relayed to the brain; here the information is further processed, and a particular response is "selected." This decision is then sent via the *motor nerve cells* to the appropriate effectors, which make the behavioral response (for example, the hand will move away from a painful stimulus). The basic pattern of *sensory input→central nervous system →behavioral output* is known as the *sensory-motor arc;* actually it is duplicated many times in any single stimulus-response act. ■ (p. 68)

The reflex action of the spinal cord. In the course of evolution, the development of the "thinking" brain came after the development of the more primitive spinal cord. The functions of protecting the organism from injury, keeping the internal machinery operating, and maintaining the animal's posture are basic to survival of the organism. Thus these functions could not await development of the brain, and were built into the spinal cord. It is therefore possible to understand why animals that have had their brains surgically separated from their spinal cords (*decortication*) can still react to stimuli and even show simple learning.

If a baby's finger is pinched, the whole arm is drawn away. The localized stimulus (of potential danger) results in the activation of muscles over a large area of the body as a result of the network of neurons in the spinal cord. This network does four things: (a) it enables impulses from a single receptor to reach many muscles (divergence); (b) it permits the same muscle to be used in reflexes by stimulation from many points on the skin (convergence); (c) it extends a response in time (due to feedback loops); and (d) it causes impulses to be long-circuited to the brain. ◆

What is the basis on which the nervous system decides which of many simultaneous messages will be transmitted most rapidly, and which will be delayed or inhibited? For example, it is possible to be hungry, tired, bored, have a toothache, and get stung by a bee all at the same time. Which message would get priority and how? A simple answer is that painful stimuli, strong stimuli, or stimuli of special significance to the organism have the right of way, whereas a continued stimulus ceases to arouse us and a repeated response may give way to a rival response. A fuller answer takes us into the mysteries of orienting and habituating.

To Orient or to Habituate? That Is the Question

In a world filled with an immense number and variety of sounds, lights, smells, and other stimuli constantly impinging on your sense receptors, you need an environmental detection system that will alert you to possible emergencies but tune out the noise and useless nonsense. Orienting and habituation are the mechanisms that serve these needs. Although present in some form in all species, orienting is more pronounced among the more highly developed animals than among the simpler ones. In addition, since they are equipped to extract more information per stimulus exposure, higher animals also show more rapid habituation.

■ **A SENSORY-MOTOR ARC**

Response to a stimulus requires all five of the steps shown in this diagram except in rare cases where there is no interneuron in the spinal cord. No response will be able to take place if the stimulation is too weak or of a kind to which the receptors are not sensitive, or if the neural impulse fails to cross any of the synapses in the chain, or if the impulse finally reaching the muscles or glands is too weak to activate them, or if the muscles are unable to respond (perhaps because of fatigue).

A single chain is drawn here with one interneuron. Actually, this simple arc is duplicated many times in a stimulus-response act, and typically interneurons bring

involvement of segments of the spinal cord above and below the one shown.

Not evident in this diagram is an essential feature of sequential behavior—and most of our behavior is actually continuing action, not just one stimulus-response circuit. As our action proceeds, we get *sensory feedback* indicating the consequences of our ongoing motor output or other changes in the environment. We keep monitoring this feedback and adjusting our output to meet the changing requirements.

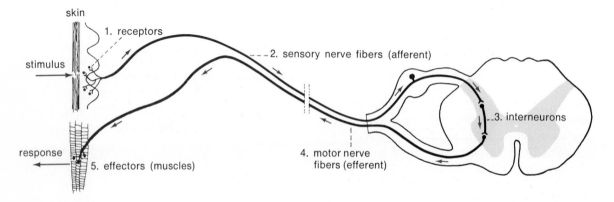

skin

1. receptors

stimulus

2. sensory nerve fibers (afferent)

3. interneurons

response

5. effectors (muscles)

4. motor nerve fibers (efferent)

Orienting: The "what-is-it?" reaction. The organism's mechanism for paying attention to a change in environmental stimulation is called the *orienting reaction.*

Components of the orienting reaction. Many internal changes accompany the apparently simple turning toward the source of the stimulus. They serve the dual role of maximizing sensitivity to informational input while simultaneously preparing the body for emergency action. Components of the orienting reaction include:

1. *Increased sensitivity.* Auditory and visual thresholds are lowered (resulting in response to less intense stimuli than usually needed); the pupil dilates to let in more light; and the ability to discriminate between similar stimuli is increased.

2. *Specific skeletal muscle changes.* Depending on the species, muscles that direct the sense organs operate to turn the head, focus the eyes, prick up the ears, and so on.

3. *General muscle changes.* Ongoing activities are suspended; general muscle tonus rises, and electrical activity in the muscles increases.

4. *Brain-wave changes.* The pattern of the brain waves is modified toward increased arousal, with fast, low-amplitude activity predominating.

5. *Visceral changes.* Blood vessels in the limbs constrict, while those in the head dilate. The galvanic skin response (GSR)—a change in the electrical resistance of the skin—occurs, breathing becomes deeper and slower, and (in humans and some other animals) heart rate decreases.

Conditions that elicit orienting. For simplicity, we may distinguish three classes of stimuli that evoke orienting reactions (based on a categorization developed by Dan Berlyne, 1960).

1. *Novel or complex stimuli.* Events that are different from those recently experienced, or arranged in a novel sequence, creating "surprise," elicit orienting. Monkeys trained to find a banana under a cup showed marked orienting reactions when instead they found lettuce there (Tinklepaugh, 1928).

In addition, stimuli of moderate to high intensity elicit orienting, as do varicolored stimuli and complex or incongruous figures.

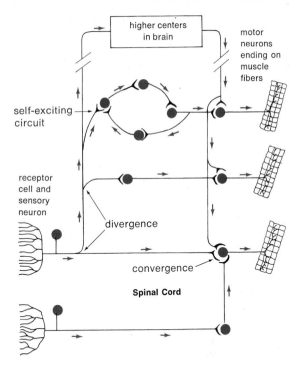

◆ COORDINATION IN THE SPINAL CORD

The spinal cord is a versatile distributing system whose first stage is provided by the sensory neuron. On entering the spinal cord, it divides into ascending and descending parts, giving off collaterals (branches) at each level of the spinal cord. Each of these collaterals, in turn, can connect with an *interneuron*, which also runs up and down the cord, at each level giving off collaterals to *motor neurons*. This type of distribution is called *divergence.*

A reverse consequence of this arrangement is called *convergence.* Impulses from many afferent neurons can ultimately reach the same motor neuron, the system acting much like a funnel. Convergence makes it possible for the same muscle fiber to take part in many different reflexes.

Some of the interneurons are arranged in *self-exciting circuits.* Through such reverberating circuits, or *feedback loops,* a momentary stimulus can cause a response that continues long after the stimulus has been withdrawn. The effect of such a feedback loop may be either excitatory or inhibitory.

In the intact animal, some interneurons and collaterals from incoming afferent neurons form long circuits that carry impulses to the brain. These keep "headquarters" informed, and the brain may then modify the activity of the simpler reflex arcs.

2. *Conflicting stimuli.* When an organism must make a difficult perceptual discrimination between similar stimulus events, one of which has been associated with positive consequences and the other with negative consequences, strong orienting reactions occur. A conflict between required motor or verbal responses can also result in orienting.

3. *Significant (signal) stimuli.* When a stimulus has acquired special significance for a subject, its presentation elicits orienting. Furthermore, it continues to elicit orienting even though it is repeated, is not novel, and produces no conflict. Your own name, "Watch out," and "Danger" (either seen or heard) are examples of a class of stimuli that continue to call forth the orienting reaction, whereas many nonsignificant stimuli that are presented equally often produce no reaction.

The importance of orienting to survival is indicated by the observation that for each species there are stimuli of special significance that consistently elicit orienting behavior. For example, rustling noises evoke a strong orienting reaction in hares that does not diminish over 240 repeated trials, while domesticated dogs show only very weak orienting to such stimuli. Similarly, owls continue to orient to the sight of cats, beavers to the sound of splintering wood, or fish to the sound of splashing waves (Klimova, 1958). It is not known whether such reactions are genetically built in or are the consequence of early learning.

Habituation: The "so-what's-new?" reaction. Most stimuli cease to evoke an orienting reaction merely by being repeated in identical form. With such repetition the organism *habituates* to the stimulus, both physiologically and psychologically, and stops responding to it. It is as if a stimulus ceases to exist once it stops carrying new or significant information of potential value to the organism.

Repeated stimulation, even by stimuli of moderate intensity, can produce drowsiness and eventually sleep (a fact you must have experienced while reading certain introductory textbooks or listening to canned lectures delivered in a droning monotone). It has been shown that many normal, well-rested adults fall asleep after being exposed to only eight minutes of repetitive stimulation (Gastaut & Bert, 1961).

Sometimes a decrease in responding to a continued stimulus is the result of adaptation in the receptors (called *sensory adaptation*) or fatigue of the muscles. *Habituation* is defined specifically as a decrease in response brought about by some kind of change in the central nervous system, rather than in the peripheral receptors or effectors. It may be measured by a decrease in force or amplitude of a body movement or by a change in brain waves or blood pressure. In the simplest physiological terms, habituation means that the transmission of sensory information through central pathways is decreased.

There are only two ways in which such a decrease in central transmission can occur: either there is some sort of *intrinsic fatigue* in the pathways themselves, or the transmission pathway is being *inhibited* by a blocking action initiated by some part of the brain. Most of the physiological evidence obtained so far favors the first explanation. The "fatigue" apparently occurs at synaptic junctions and is referred to as *synaptic depression.* The evidence supporting this mechanism of habituation comes from animals as diverse as crayfish and cats. Studies on several invertebrates indicate that a reduced amount of chemical transmitter substances is released during habituation. No transmitter, no message across the synapse.

The brain as monitor. Since habituation can occur in animals with only a spinal cord, the brain evidently is not *necessary* for habituation to occur. However, it is still possible that there is a kind of habituation in which cortical inhibitory control operates.

A research finding that cannot be explained in terms of the simple intrinsic fatigue conception of habituation is the *"missing-stimulus"* effect. A series of repetitive stimuli are presented to the subject, and somewhere along the line, one of them is omitted; then the series continues, as in reading aloud the number three, once per second:

$$-3-3-3-3-3-3-3-3-3-3- \ -3-3-3.$$

When the gap occurs, there is an increased response, a sudden loss of habituation. *Dishabituation* is said to occur. (See *P&L* Close-up below.)

Such demonstrations call for some mechanism that tunes out information that is *expected* to be identical to prior information—and thus of little significance—but catches a break in the pattern. An elegant model to account for how this may all be monitored in the brain has been proposed by a Russian psychologist, Sokolov (1960), and generally supported by neurophysiological evidence. The essential feature of this proposed explanation is a system for comparing incoming events with previously experienced

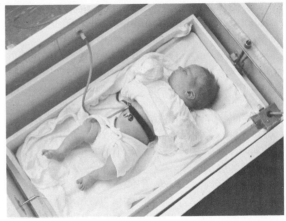

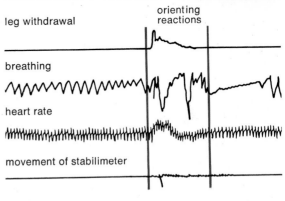

leg withdrawal

breathing

heart rate

movement of stabilimeter

orienting reactions

stimulus present

Close-up
Detective Work via Dishabituation

The phenomenon of dishabituation has made possible an ingenious technique developed by Lewis Lipsitt and his colleagues (1963, 1966) for studying infants' ability to discriminate between different odors. When babies only a few days old are presented with certain olfactory stimuli, they respond with bodily movements and changes in breathing and heart rate, as shown in the record at right. These responses indicate that the infants are sensitive to these stimuli. The apparatus used is shown in the photograph.

Such a stimulus is presented repeatedly until habituation occurs; then the experimenter presents another stimulus. If the infant can detect the difference, dishabituation occurs and there is a reappearance of the olfactory response. If the new stimulus is perceived as "not different," however, habituation should continue.

The graph shows an infant's habituation curve to a mixture of three chemicals. The strength of the response to this mixture decreases with each successive presentation over the course of five blocks of trials. But when one of the components of the mixture is presented alone, a strong response reappears, indicating dishabituation and, by inference, the ability to distinguish between the original mixture and the single element.

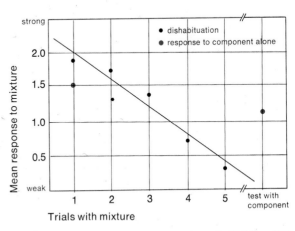

After Lipsitt, 1966 and Engen, Lipsitt, & Kaye, 1963

events. It accounts for habituation to stimulus sequences, as well as to individual stimuli, and thus predicts the missing-stimulus effect. ▲

Sokolov's model has an interesting historical predecessor worthy of mention. The late eighteenth-century French physiologist Xavier Bichat distinguished between the vegetative functions basic to primitive survival needs (such as metabolism, digestion, and excretion) and the animal functions essential for perception, response, movement, and emotions. In his classic work (modestly titled: *Physiological Investigations on Life and Death*), he too envisioned a cortical process matching new sensations with previously experienced ones.

"The action of the mind on each feeling of pain or pleasure, arising from a sensation, consists in a comparison between that sensation and those which have preceded it. The greater the difference between the actual and past impressions, the more ardent will be the feeling. That sensation would affect us most which we had never experienced before. . . .

"The nature of pleasure and of pain is thus to destroy themselves, to cease to exist, because they have existed. The art of prolonging the duration of our enjoyments consists in varying their causes." (Bichat, 1809)

An interesting study with monkeys showed that learning changed habituation — and by inference that the brain was involved in determining when and whether habituation would occur.

Microelectrodes were first placed in isolated cells of the auditory cortex of the brain in order to record evoked potentials in response to a variety of acoustic stimuli. Then one group was trained to depress a key whenever a light signal appeared and to release it at the onset of an auditory stimulus. A dollop of applesauce reinforced "good" performance and encouraged the monkeys to attend to the stimuli and respond rapidly. Another group was not trained in this task.

Responses of both groups to repetitive acoustic stimuli were then measured, and marked differences in habituation of cortical activity were found between the trained and untrained subjects. In the untrained animals, more than 85 percent of the individual cells that were measured showed the expected habituation, often after as few as four presentations. In contrast, monkeys trained to perform the auditory task showed no evidence of habituation to repetitive auditory stimuli — the individual cells of their auditory cortex continued to respond consistently.

Even when these trained animals were tested under conditions where no overt response was required, the cortical cells showed little sign of habituation to the repetitive sounds, although their rate of firing was somewhat reduced.

The investigators concluded that the cortical cell activity clearly depended not only on physiological conditions but also on both prior training and current behavioral state (J. M. Miller et al., 1972).

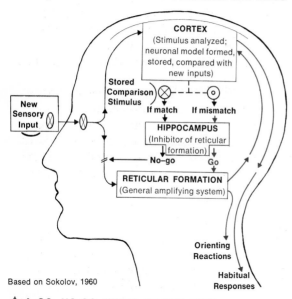

Based on Sokolov, 1960

▲ A GO, NO-GO MODEL OF THE MIND

This is a simplified diagram of Sokolov's model of what takes place in the brain during orientation and habituation.

1. Sensory input of stimulus patterns is analyzed in the cortex, and a neuronal model is formed.
2. New stimulus is matched against this model.
3. Where the new stimulus is different from the stored companion model, *mismatch* occurs; the hippocampus releases its inhibition over the reticular activating system, and orienting reactions are elicited.
4. Where the new input and model match, the hippocampus inhibits the reticular formation, blocking input from the afferent nerves, and habituation results.

The Quintessence of Essence: The Brain

Imagine a small, portable computer weighing only a few pounds, with the following features: immense memory capacity for possibly all important inputs it will receive during seventy years or more; discriminative capacities diverse enough to detect a vintage-year wine, the difference between two perfumes, and whether a sphere traveling at great velocity toward it will be a "strike" or "ball"; the ability to plan its own reproduction and know how to win friends and influence people. Finally, can you imagine a computer that could program its own destruction and that of its species? The human brain is a mass of tissue organized into just such a computer system—which also allows you to imagine its feats, and allows scientists to probe its as yet unattained potential.

Techniques of Probing Its Secrets

The secrets of the brain's functioning, like some great treasure hidden in a vault, have eluded discovery for centuries because of its protected location. The thick, bony skull cap shields it from exposure, and even when the skull is removed, only the surface *cortex* is revealed—the rest remains still concealed below. Anatomists have, of course, provided us with pictures of the brain, by cutting brains out of human and animal cadavers. But a physiological psychologist interested in the relationship between brain processes and behavior must study a behaving—*living*—organism.

The study of brain processes in living subjects has awaited technological discoveries. Most of these methodological breakthroughs have occurred only in the last few decades, but already they have generated an enormous yield of exciting information about how our brains work. The three most basic techniques employed by researchers to probe the neural activity of the brains of living humans and lower animals are: (a) lesions, (b) electrical recording of brain cell activity, and (c) direct electrical or chemical stimulation of brain sites.

Lesions. A *lesion* is a destroyed area of brain cells. Some lesions occur naturally through disease, tumors, accidents, or injuries sustained in war. Early work in physiology relied almost exclusively on correlating the deficits in behavior that occurred with the location of these lesions. But the obvious drawback in such research is that the general condition of the subject is often deteriorated by the time the behavioral analysis is done. There is no "before" record to compare it with, and the generalized effects of the lesion and the shock to the organism are unknown. And there is inefficiency in waiting for natural disasters to strike and having no choice about where the lesions are made.

Karl Lashley (1929) was one of the pioneers in the use of experimentally induced lesions to study brain-behavior relations. Using laboratory rats, he systematically destroyed different brain regions and different amounts of brain tissue and then gave the animal behavioral tests at different intervals afterward to see what defects in performance resulted from the loss of specific brain tissue.

Lashley found that although destruction of some areas resulted in permanent loss of a given function, damage to other areas was only temporarily incapacitating. In some cases, loss of function even seemed less dependent on the *location* of the brain tissue removed than on the total *amount* removed.

From the early days of raw empiricism, when the question posed was "I wonder what will happen if I cut out this part of the brain?" the lesioning approach has now been refined so that very specific structures can be lesioned and subtle changes in behavior measured. The questions being asked now (see M. Wilson, 1973; P. Meyer, 1973) focus on learning about the exact brain processes that normally underlie particular behavior. If a change is observed, is it limited to only one sense modality (vision or hearing, for example) or is it more general? Is it temporary or permanent? Can the lost behavior be recovered through drug therapy, retraining, or other treatment? Of course, the major drawback of lesioning as a research approach is that some of its effects are permanent, and the animal may be adversely affected for life.

Electrical recording of brain activity. Electrical recording of neural impulses has been developed into one of the most powerful tools for studying brain function. Because of their characteristic of producing repeated, all-or-none action potentials, activated neurons sound like machine guns if their electrical activity is amplified. Indeed, early researchers listened to these amplified nerve impulses on loud speakers. But modern electronic techniques allow the researcher to see the nerve impulse in action on a TV-like screen called an *oscilloscope*. (See *P&L Close-up*, p. 75.)

Electrical recording is combined with the "evoked-potential" method in the following way. A light or sound is presented that *evokes* neural impulses; these impulses then travel to the brain, where they are detected as localized changes in electrical *potential* by electrodes placed at different areas of the brain. Wherever a change in potential occurs, it is electronically amplified and its form is displayed visually on the oscilloscope. Earlier, only surface electrodes were used, but now it is possible to implant electrodes deep within the brain and to detect discharges even in single cells (See Thompson, Robertson, & Mayers, 1973).

Direct stimulation of the brain. Stimulation of the brain by minute amounts of electrical current passed through microelectrodes has become a very popular psychophysiological technique for mapping the functions of the brain. Different areas are stimulated under varying conditions and the resulting sensations or behavior noted. The modern era of brain stimulation began with W. R. Hess' precision instrumentation and detailed research on over 4500 stimulated points in nearly 500 cats. He was able to study fully awake, moving animals only minimally restrained by cables connecting electrodes permanently implanted in their brains to the stimulator source (see Gloor, 1954, for the English version of Hess' work).

Wilder Penfield's use of electrical stimulation to map the functions of brain areas of epileptic patients prior to brain surgery was reported in the introduction to this chapter. At Tulane University, Robert Heath and his colleagues have been studying the deep regions of the brains of schizophrenic patients in this way since 1951 (Heath & Mickle, 1960).

Perhaps the greatest impetus to the widespread use of brain stimulation research came from a discovery of James Olds, of the University of Michigan. He found that if electrodes are implanted in certain areas of a rat's brain, the rat will work hard or even suffer pain just to reach a lever that delivers electrical stimulation to one of these areas. In fact, rats will stimulate themselves as many as seven thousand times an hour, even passing up food and water though they are hungry and thirsty.

Olds called these areas "pleasure centers" (Olds & Milner, 1954; Olds, 1973). Other areas of rats' brains appear to be punishing sites, and still others are both pleasurable and painful. Similar areas have been found in other species, including humans.

Chemical stimulation of the brain is also used. Many advantages are claimed for it in studying the relationship of specific brain areas to memory, learning, eating, drinking, and other behavioral processes. Compared to electrical stimulation, the effects of injections of chemicals into the brain are longer lasting; unlike lesions, the effects are reversible. The effects of the chemicals on the regions directly altered can be monitored on an oscilloscope when recording electrodes are also utilized. But the main reason for studying the brain by means of chemical injections is that there are many areas where complex neural pathways overlap geographically and it is difficult or impossible to study these areas by lesions or electrical stimulation, both of which affect too many layers of cells.

A technique has been developed by Sebastian Grossman (1967) to stimulate or suppress the activity of neural pathways in the deep regions of the brain by microinjections of chemicals that

Close-up
Nerve Watching on the Oscilloscope

The major tool used by scientists who study the brain's activity is the oscilloscope. With it, nerve impulses can be observed visually on a fluorescent screen and their characteristics precisely measured. Photos or illustrations of a neuron firing or of a nerve impulse being transmitted (as on p. 60) are taken from the oscilloscope.

Think of aiming a thin flashlight beam so that it makes a dot on a screen, then rapidly move it across the screen, then up and down. What you would see would be a horizontal, then a vertical line. Similarly, in an oscilloscope there is a dot of light that is in reality a beam of electrons. This beam becomes illuminated and visible when it hits the phosphor-coated screen of the oscilloscope.

Electrons are *negatively* (−) charged particles that are attracted by positive (+) electrical charges and repelled by other negative charges. Thus in the series of figures, you can see the effects of putting either + or − charges on one or the other of the four plates that surround the beam (A). The beam moves rapidly to the left if a + voltage is applied there (B). It shifts to the right if the left side is made − and the right is made + (C). The speed with which it traverses the screen depends on the relative strengths of the charges on either side. Obviously the beam can move in the vertical dimension by electrically charging either the upper or the lower plate (D), or it can be made to bounce back and forth by alternating the charges on the plates (E).

In recording from neurons in the brain, the experimenter determines how fast the beam sweeps from left to right; the rate of this movement is the measurement of *time*. The vertical movement of the beam represents changes in voltage of the membrane of the neuronal cell being studied. When a neuron "fires," it produces a momentary change in voltage so rapid that the beam is deflected and returned to its original position within a millisecond — 1/1000th of a second. (The voltage change must be amplified thousands of times before it can influence the oscilloscope beam.) When the beam is moving slowly across the screen from left to right, the sudden voltage change of the firing neuron makes the deflection look like a "spike" or a sudden "impulse" on the record (F). The terms *nerve impulse, nerve spike,* and *nerve action potential* are used interchangeably.

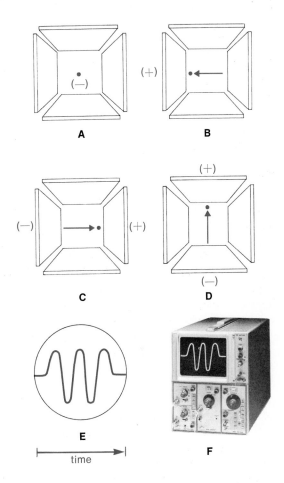

A   B

C   D

E
time

F

vary the concentration of synaptic chemical transmitter substances. Basically, the technique consists of permanently implanting a double tube (cannula) in the animal's skull. The inner cannula is removed, sterilized, filled with crystals of a given chemical, and reinserted through the outer tube into the brain area being investigated. With the same implanted tube, Grossman has been able to reliably elicit eating by injecting one chemical and drinking by injecting another. Since the brain consists largely of fluids and a variety of biochemical substances, the chemical stimulation technique is especially useful for temporarily altering brain processes in precise ways.

Where the Action Is

Back in the early 1800s, a movement called *phrenology* developed. Its basic principle was that the mind was not a unity, but rather was composed of various distinct powers. These powers, argued the originators of phrenology, Gall and Spurzheim, could be found in various "organs" of the brain. The places they identified as the seats of various functions can be seen in the phrenologist's chart. ● Their method of identification—their technique for probing the powers of the mind—consisted of locating bumps on people's heads. Each bump indicated the point where the organ for a particular power was located. Supposedly, each individual's personality could thus be determined from the shape of his or her head.

Modern neurophysiologists have come to the same general conclusion, not about the powers of the mind nor about the relation of bumps on the head to naive categories of behavior and personality postulated by the phrenologists, but about the fact of specialized functions. But matters are considerably more complex than the phrenologists thought, as we shall see. In this section we will start by outlining some general features of the brain's anatomy so you will know what is where. Then we will describe briefly which parts of the brain do what.

Although we will be talking about various parts of the brain as if they were separate structures, this is not really so. The main thing to remember about the brain is that it is made up of clusters of neurons that perform the same function. Often (not always) their nuclei are close together, but their axons may extend into distant areas. Therefore, the parts of the brain that *look* like separate structures when the brain is dissected are not as separate as they look because they may contain parts of many neurons whose nuclei are somewhere else. Exact boundaries between the actual functional groups of neurons could not possibly be drawn. Our labels of parts of the brain reflect the fact that the earliest study was of visually distinguishable parts. Later study has found that the parts most closely related to each other functionally may be quite different from these visual divisions. In addition, boundaries between parts in more simple brains have often become obliterated with the evolutionary development of more complex brains. ▲

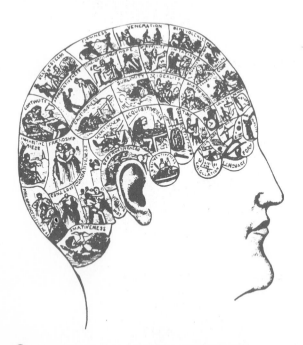

● This phrenological map shows the locations ascribed to the various presumed powers or faculties of the mind—largely social-moral personality traits.

The new brain: The neocortex. If you were looking in at the top of the brain of a surgical patient, you would see a mass of gray tissue separated into two halves, each covered with ridges and convolutions, much like an oversized walnut. The two halves are called *cerebral hemispheres;* their wrinkled outer surface is a layer less than a tenth of an inch thick called the *cortex*, meaning "bark." This tissue is made up largely of the dendrites and gray cell bodies of neurons that have axons extending into the interior part of the brain.

The cortex is also called the *neocortex* because in the course of evolution it is a relatively new development. Fish have no neocortex, while amphibians, reptiles, and birds, in that order, have increasingly more. In mammals the neocortex becomes much larger, until in humans it achieves its greatest size.

The two cerebral hemispheres are in fact not separated; communication between them occurs primarily through a bundle of nerve fibers, the *corpus callosum*. Each hemisphere can be divided functionally into four lobes by reference to two deep grooves (fissures). Each of these lobes identifies an area where certain functions predominate.

Beneath the cortical layer is the larger portion of the new brain, which is almost all white due to the presence of the white myelin sheaths covering countless axons. Some of these fibers are sensory fibers coming up to the cortex from the spinal cord by way of relay centers in the older parts of the brain; some are motor fibers going down from the cortex to the spinal cord; others connect one area of the cortex with an-

▲ THE HUMAN BRAIN

Shown here are three views of the intact human brain with the main parts labeled. The fourth view shows a cross section of the front part of the brain where the two hemispheres are not yet linked by the corpus callosum. It shows how much the cortex is increased by the formation of convolutions around the edge. In general, the higher the species, the more convolutions there are and the deeper they become—an ingenious way to get more surface area into the same small space.

These views show the cerebral hemispheres and the cerebellum. Structures in the subcortex are shown on page 78.

View from Above

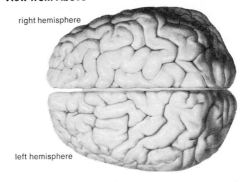

right hemisphere

left hemisphere

View from Underneath

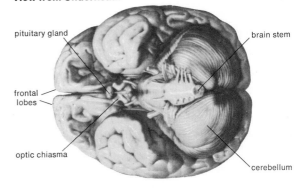

pituitary gland

brain stem

frontal lobes

optic chiasma

cerebellum

View from the Left

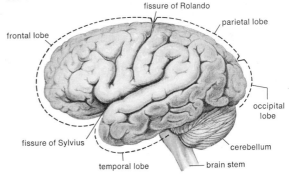

fissure of Rolando

parietal lobe

frontal lobe

occipital lobe

fissure of Sylvius

cerebellum

temporal lobe

brain stem

Cross Section Through Frontal Lobes

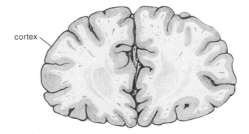

cortex

other area of the same hemisphere, with areas on the opposite side of the brain, or with a variety of separate subcortical structures. (See *P&L Close-up*, p. 79.)

The old brain: The subcortex. The prominent position of the cortex at the top of the nervous system and its greater development in higher species—as well as its accessibility to surgical and stimulation research—led investigators at first to the false conclusion that it alone was responsible for almost all complex adaptive behavior. Recently, however, it has become clear that humans, like other animals, still do much of their living in the old brain. Our appetites (hunger, thirst, sex), aversions (fears), consummatory behavior (eating, drinking, mating), sleep, arousal, and temperature control are all under the influence of parts of the subcortex. Finally, housed deep within these primitive structures are centers that play a vital role in emotional behavior. Paths to and from the cortex pass through the old brain, and there is ample two-way communication between it and the higher centers.

Recently, several investigators have proposed a model of brain organization and function in which the neocortex is seen as being the newer, efficient system for all discriminational functions, while the old brain is the more generalized system for receiving nonspecific, heterogeneous input. According to this model, some brain processes operate independently in parallel systems, while others are more closely interrelated (Semmes, 1969; Gross, 1973).

The subcortex has several parts. Most important for our purposes are the partly overlapping structures of the *brain stem* and the *limbic system*.

The brain stem. The brain stem is a general name for a collection of smaller structures that connect the new brain to the spinal cord; it was the earliest beginning of a "central headquarters" in the nervous system. The main parts of the brain stem are the *thalamus*, the *hypothalamus*, and the *reticular formation*. In the human brain, the *thalamus*, as you can see in the diagram, is in almost the center. ◆ It is an important relay station for incoming sensory messages from all parts of the body. Directly below

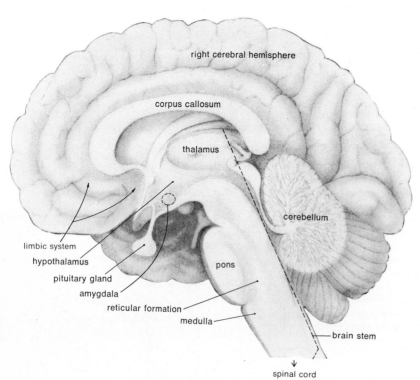

right cerebral hemisphere

corpus callosum

thalamus

cerebellum

limbic system
hypothalamus
pituitary gland
amygdala
reticular formation
medulla

pons

brain stem

↓
spinal cord

◆ **MIDLINE VIEW OF THE BRAIN**

In this view, the brain has been cut through the middle from front to back. The front and upper parts thus show surfaces of the right hemisphere, whereas the various structures below are all cut areas. The corpus callosum has been cut crosswise through the exact center. Below it are subcortical structures. The limbic system cannot be seen on the midline surface, being deeper within the hemisphere.

the thalamus and merging into it is the *hypothalamus* (*hypo* means "below"), in which important centers are located for the regulation of metabolism, body temperature, hunger, thirst, and emotional behavior. It has been shown that stimulation of the back of the hypothalamus will produce reactions of the sympathetic nervous system (increase in heart rate and blood pressure), while stimulation of the front part produces parasympathetic reactions (slowing of heart rate, dilation of blood vessels in the intestine and stomach). The hypothalamus is sensitive to changes in the external environment that demand either "fight or flight." It is also sensitive to internal requirements of the body and is important in maintaining the exchange of energy between the organism and its environment.

The *reticular formation* is a tangled mass of nuclei and fibers in the core of the brain stem just above the spinal cord. Fibers both *to* and *from* the cortex pass through it, and it has two important functions. By responding to fibers coming down to it from the various higher centers, it suppresses some incoming sensory messages and facilitates others. Through fibers going upward from it to all the higher centers, it acts as a general arousal system: stimulation in this area causes a sleeping animal to awaken and one already awake to become more alert. It is therefore called the *reticular activating system.*

The limbic system. The other important region of the old brain, the limbic system, forms a border around the upper end of the brain stem. Originally it was thought to be simply the "nose brain," serving as "odor decoder," because nerves from smell receptors project into a part of it called the *rhinencephalon.* Now we know that in addition it has parts that are active in functions as different as attention, emotion, and remembering. In fact, one researcher believes that the two basic life principles, preservation of self and preservation of the species, are localized within the limbic system (MacLean, 1958).

Close-up
Illuminating the Brain

In this highly magnified section of a cat's brain, some of the neurons have been stained with a special dye to make them more visible. No two-dimensional view can convey the full complexity of the three-dimensional neural network, however. In any slice of tissue, you see only a small portion of a neuron; most of its parts would be nearer or farther away. So you need to visualize a three-dimensional structure built up of the connections shown here—and many more connections.

Another even more spectacular technique for making neurons visible has been developed by researchers in Sweden. This technique involves inducing a chemical reaction between neurotransmitter molecules and formaldehyde vapors to yield a fluorescent compound so that the neurons glow brightly when irradiated with ultraviolet light. Since the reaction is specific to certain neurotransmitters that are located in discrete neuron pathways in the brain, the technique makes it possible to follow the course of these neurons through the brain.

When a slice of brain tissue illuminated in this way is viewed through a microscope, it resembles the view from an airplane at night. Brightly glowing axons crisscross the field of vision like highways, and clusters of cell bodies in nuclei are reminiscent of the lights of small towns. This technique is of vital importance, for it forges strong links between the disciplines of anatomy, cellular neurophysiology, and psychopharmacology; also, it allows a more accurate portrait of the nervous system to be painted.

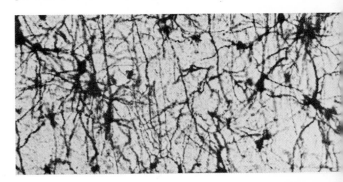

Stimulation of many of these structures produces an *attention response* in which the animal alertly searches its environment. Stimulation of a limbic structure called the *amygdala* brings responses of flight and defense. ● Lesions made in the amygdala or in another structure, the *cingulate gyrus*, can tame a wild animal, while lesioning the nearby *septal area* can induce vicious rage in a previously tame animal. Selective initiation or suppression of behavior in adapting to environmental demands has also been shown to involve the limbic system.

Still another part of the limbic system, the *hippocampus*, is involved in at least two very different behaviors, mating and remembering. Electrical stimulation of this region can produce an erection of the male sex organ. Patients with damage to the hippocampus have great difficulty remembering new events unless they keep their attention focused on them. Although they exhibit normal intelligence, reasoning, and vocabulary, they suffer from *retrograde amnesia*. This is a memory defect in which old habits and events are well remembered, but more recent ones are increasingly less well remembered.

A similar phenomenon seems to accompany senility: along with aging and hardening of the arteries (and less oxygen to the brain) comes a loss in memory, especially for more recently experienced information. Exploratory research appears to show that daily administration of doses of pure oxygen prevents this loss in memory efficiency of older people (Jacobs, Winter, Alvis, & Small, 1969). These changes in functioning remind us that memory is ultimately a physical process, related in some way to the neurophysiology of nerve impulses.

The cerebellum. The *cerebellum*, tucked in under the back of the cerebral hemispheres, is the least psychologically interesting portion of the brain because its vital functions appear to be primarily maintenance of balance, posture, breathing, and other basic regulatory mechanisms. Recent work, however, suggests that the cerebellum also plays a role in initiating voluntary movements and possibly even in motor learning and adaptation to distorted sensory input.

What Action!

When all is said and done about the anatomy of the brain and the neurophysiology of nerve

● José Delgado is a pioneer in the brain implantation of radio-activated electrodes. His ability to find an exact spot in an animal's brain is so precise that he can trust his life to it. Here, even after the bull has started to charge, Delgado can stop it by a radio message to electrodes planted in its brain. After repeated experiences such as this, the animal becomes permanently less aggressive.

transmission, the critical issue is what our brains enable us to do. For convenience, their functional activities can be grouped into three categories: sensory, motor, and association. We are especially interested here in what the new brain contributes to these functions.

Sensory functions. Though stimulation of different sensory nerves gives rise to different kinds of sensation, this is not because the impulses are different. As we already have seen, nerve impulses differ only in amplitude and rate of propagation. They yield different sensations because they end at different locations in the brain.

The most highly developed receiving areas, making possible the most precise discriminations, are in the cerebral cortex. All the senses are represented to a greater or lesser extent by lower receiving areas also, however. Thus if the higher centers are destroyed, lower ones can take over at least part of the same decoding of the incoming message.

Sensory messages from the various parts of the body surface cross over to the other side in the spinal cord or brain and are projected on the *somatosensory* areas. ◆ The primary somatosensory area runs along behind the fissure of Rolando, across it from the primary motor centers. The body is represented upside down,

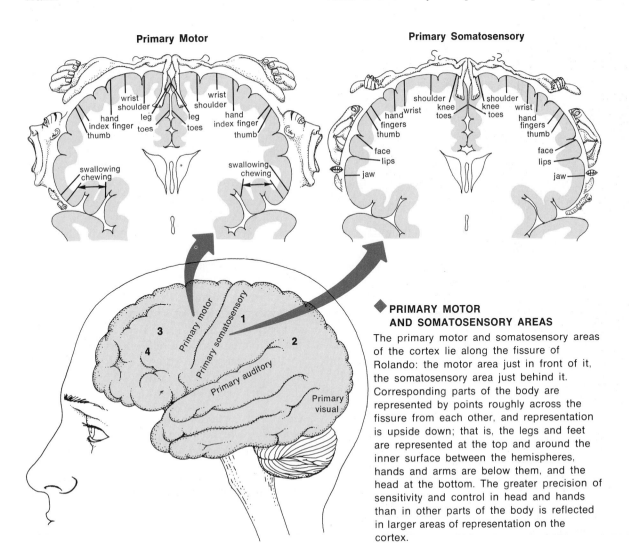

◆**PRIMARY MOTOR AND SOMATOSENSORY AREAS**

The primary motor and somatosensory areas of the cortex lie along the fissure of Rolando: the motor area just in front of it, the somatosensory area just behind it. Corresponding parts of the body are represented by points roughly across the fissure from each other, and representation is upside down; that is, the legs and feet are represented at the top and around the inner surface between the hemispheres, hands and arms are below them, and the head at the bottom. The greater precision of sensitivity and control in head and hands than in other parts of the body is reflected in larger areas of representation on the cortex.

with far more cortical area devoted to face and hands than to the rest of the body. Centers for taste are close to those for touch sensitivity for the tongue.

The highest visual centers lie in the occipital lobe at the back of the brain. Destruction of these areas in humans destroys vision, except perhaps for some primitive ability for gross discrimination of lightness and darkness. In lower animals, however, more ability for visual discrimination remains after cortical damage.

Auditory centers lie along the fissure of Sylvius in the upper part of the temporal lobe. They are close to, and to some extent intermingled with, some of the receiving areas for touch. As mentioned previously, smell is decoded in the *rhinencephalon*—located deep inside the hemispheres.

Besides the primary receiving areas shown in the diagram, various adjacent areas—or in some cases areas some distance away—are also involved in the analysis and organization of the sensory input and hence in complex perceptions. For example, although the primary auditory receiving area is along the lower surface of the fissure of Sylvius in the top of the temporal lobe, patients with injuries in many other parts of the brain may also have difficulty in recognizing sounds.

A major methodological problem in determining sensory functions lies in the type of *behavioral tests* used to measure the effects of lesions or stimulation. For example, to label a part of the brain simply as the "visual sensory" area is to fail to distinguish between visual pattern discrimination, visual intensity discrimination, visual memory, color discrimination, visual spatial discrimination, visual factual discrimination, and still others. Ultimately, assessment of what functions take place in an area of the brain must rely on behavioral tests of sufficient variety, precision, and subtlety to reveal the complexity of the cortical processes. (See *P&L* Close-up, p. 83.)

Motor functions. The primary motor area is concentrated immediately in front of the fissure of Rolando, across from the somatosensory area. Here, too, the feet are represented at the upper part, the trunk farther down, and the hands still farther down; nerve centers controlling motions of the face and tongue are localized at the bottom.

Long axons lead down from this area of the brain through the spinal cord directly or through interneurons to the motor neurons supplying the muscles of the body and the extremities on the other side of the body. Thus when a part of this brain area is stimulated, some voluntary muscle group on the other side of the body responds, and when areas in this region of the brain are destroyed, movement is impaired accordingly.

Because of the clear connection between this brain area and activity of the voluntary muscles, it was long believed that control of the muscles was centered in this strip of brain. But Luria (1970) has pointed out that to make such an assumption is like assuming that all merchandise exported from a particular port has been manufactured there. Actually, several parts of the brain play important roles in organizing voluntary motion. For example:

1. Feedback from the sensory area across the fissure is necessary for precise regulation of the movement. Without such feedback, pairs of opposing muscles would be innervated indiscriminately, and organized motion would be impossible.

2. Proper organization of an action in space requires the action of cells still farther back in the parietal-occipital area. With lesions here, the individual may confuse left and right or get lost in a familiar place. But are visual-motor responses controlled entirely even by *this* area of the brain? The following study suggests not.

Cats with extensive neocortical lesions were unable to put their forepaws down on a table properly, a task requiring visual-motor coordination. Thus it appeared that the lesions had destroyed the area necessary to perform this motor response. However, when the animals were given injections of a drug (dR-amphetamine), the lost responses appeared, only to dis-

appear again when the drug effect wore off. Apparently, the drug-activated subcortical pathways carried sufficient visual-motor information for the habit to be performed (Meyer, Horel, & Meyer, 1963).

3. For a coordinated sequence of actions, there must be termination of each link as it is completed so that the next one can occur. With a lesion in the area in front of the primary motor area, the individual may keep repeating the first part of an action.

4. Planning and carrying out a coordinated sequence requires the action of an area still farther forward in the frontal lobe. If this area is damaged, the individual repeats links already completed or responds impulsively to outside stimuli; purposive, goal-directed action cannot be carried through (Luria, 1970). These four areas are indicated by 1, 2, 3, and 4 on the diagram on page 81.

Besides all the cortical areas mentioned and perhaps others, subcortical areas of the brain also play a role in organizing voluntary motion—for example, in filtering or magnifying incoming messages, in inducing a particular level of energy mobilization, and in other ways just being discovered. There is considerable vertical interaction between cortical and subcortical levels in both the analysis of sensory input and the shaping of an adaptive motor output.

Association functions. If we make a drawing of the human cerebral cortex and mark off areas known to be involved in motor and sensory functions, we find that by far the larger portion is not touched by our pencil. These parts are the *association areas,* so named because it was originally assumed that it must be here that new "associations"—that is, learning—took place. Although much remains to be learned about these areas, it is now recognized that this picture is far too simple.

The association areas of each side of the cerebral cortex are connected with each other, with motor and sensory areas, with corresponding areas on the opposite side, and with inner parts of the brain. They are thought to correlate and integrate the simpler functions of the sensory

and motor areas. In fact, as we have seen, the sensory areas act essentially as gateways into the cortex, and the motor area as the exit. Thus injuries to the cortex outside but near the primary visual area do not cause blindness but destroy awareness of depth and recognition of visual objects.

Close-up

Are There "Grandmother Cells" in the Brain?

In the early 1960s, neuroscientists began to find neurons in the visual systems of animals that responded only to very specific stimuli. For example, a small erratically moving dark dot in the visual field of a frog would cause a certain cell to fire, but no other stimulus (such as turning the lights up and down, or jiggling a small spot of light) was effective. Jerome Lettvin, of the Massachusetts Institute of Technology, dubbed these cells "bug detectors" and suggested that cells with exceedingly complex stimulus requirements might be found in the brain. As an extreme example, he speculated half jokingly on the existence of a "grandmother cell," a neuron in the brain that would only respond to the features of one's grandmother.

Recently, however, investigators at Princeton discovered a cell in the brain of the monkey that responded best to a silhouette of the monkey's hand. The stimuli used in this study are shown below, arranged from left to right in the sequence of their increasing ability to trigger response (Gross et al., 1972). We will have more to say about such "prewired circuits" in Chapter 6.

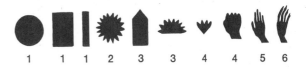

| 1 | 1 | 1 | 2 | 3 | 3 | 4 | 4 | 5 | 6 |

Areas of the cortex between the primary sensory areas that have not shown observable evoked potentials to peripheral stimulation used to be called the *silent cortex,* and a variety of functions were hypothesized for them. Richard Thompson of Harvard University has been able to make this silent cortex "talk" and tell us some surprising things.

Surmising that the barbiturate anesthetic formerly used in research on the cortex had itself depressed the evoked potentials, Thompson substituted a new anesthetic. Sure enough, with the new anesthetic he soon found regions that did respond to sensory stimulation in other parts of the body. He terms these regions *association response areas.*

His careful research revealed that when cats are stimulated by visual flashes, auditory clicks, and shocks to the paws, 82 percent of the cells in these association response areas respond to all three modalities. Some cells, however, are more likely to respond to one or the other. When different combinations and series of stimuli are used, many of the cells also show *response plasticity*—a variable reaction rather than a fixed one.

In addition, Thompson has found "novelty" cells—cells that respond only when there are intervals of thirty seconds or more between stimuli (compared with the usual response after intervals of a second or less)—and "number-coding" cells, each of which responds to a particular numbered stimulus in a series. For example, a given cell will fire only when the seventh stimulus in an array is presented, regardless of the stimulus modality or the interval between stimuli (Thompson, Robertson, & Mayers, 1973).

Disease in or injury to certain association areas brings about a condition in which the person is unable to recognize objects by their "feel." A familiar object like a door key or a pencil can be handled indefinitely and still not be recognized. Patients who show this type of disorder are still capable of experiencing normal elementary sensations; their difficulty is in organizing these elements into normal perceptions.

Similar disorders of perception are found in other sensory fields. These disorders are called *agnosias,* or "inabilities to know," and are classified on the basis of the nature of the function that is impaired. Related disorders affecting language are called *aphasias.* One example is inability to recognize spoken words, sometimes called "word deafness." Agnosias and aphasias are associated with lesions in the association regions that lie close to the various sensory areas of the cortex. (See *P&L* Close-up at left.)

In the brain areas identified with a particular function, there are aggregates of cells that perform that function. Such duplication (redundancy) of function means that important functions can continue reliably even if some of the cells in the area are destroyed, since others are still carrying the work.

However, it has become increasingly evident that though one area may normally play a primary role in a given function, there is much integration between regions, and given functions are represented at more than one place. Thus while it may be convenient to parcel the areas and functions of cerebral neocortex into "sensory," "motor," and "association," such distinctions actually are not valid in any absolute sense. After surveying over four hundred reports of investigations into the role of the cortex in behavior, a recent reviewer was forced to conclude: "Almost every report cited here either demonstrates, suggests, or refers to, non-sensory functions in sensory areas, nonmotor functions in motor areas, or nonassociative functions in association areas. . . . [Until an alternative of comparable generality is developed] it can only be hoped that these outmoded terms will not be taken seriously by those outside the field, nor especially by new generations of students" (Masterton & Berkley, 1974, pp. 294–95). (See *P & L* Close-up at right.)

Dominance and specialization in the cerebral hemispheres. As we have seen, the new brain is composed of two cerebral hemispheres, each of which receives sensory inputs from the opposite side of the body and also controls bodily responses on that opposite side. The left hemisphere has sensory and motor areas for the right visual field and the right side of the body, while the right hemisphere has similar areas for the left visual field and the left side of the body. The two hemispheres communicate through the corpus callosum, which makes possible an integration of the separate inputs and outputs into coordinated perception and behavior.

Competition between the two hemispheres is normally avoided by dominance of one hemisphere over the other. This asymmetry of brain function is much like the asymmetry of most people in writing with their left and right hands. In the space below, write your name, using your right hand; then do so with your left hand.

Right hand_____

Left hand_____

Any difference in the effort required to perform each task or in the appearance of the autographs? Does one look rather childish, as it does for most people? Just as one hand (the right one usually) dominates over the other, one hemisphere (usually the left) dominates in controlling speech, reading, writing, and mathematical calculations. The nondominant hemisphere is the silent, nonverbal partner. It is terrible in arithmetic but excels in perceptual tasks of spatial orientation, recognizes shapes and textures, and has a good musical memory (Sperry, Gazzaniga, & Bogen, 1969). Each hemisphere is thus specialized to do certain tasks that the other cannot do at all or does poorly.

To study the operation of each hemisphere in a normal individual with intact interconnections between the hemispheres, researchers have recently turned to measuring the electrical activity of the two hemispheres as the person performs a

Close-up
Holograms in the Head

A truly innovative conception of how the memory store is organized in the brain is Karl Pribram's model of the brain as a hologram. A *hologram* is a filter of sorts in which an image becomes diffused in such a way that each local area of the filter contains elements from every other area. One characteristic of such a filter is that the whole image can thus be reconstructed from any of its parts when the reverse of the diffusion process occurs.

There is evidence that might support the holographic brain. Even a patient who has had a stroke that has injured very large parts of the brain does not forget part of the family, or part of the language, and so on. The remaining brain functions in lieu of the whole. There is other, more direct, electrical evidence also that an input through each of the senses becomes represented and distributed over large areas of the brain.

How then does the brain work with these memory stores? Because of the distributed nature of brain storage, mechanisms must operate to "get it all together" when necessary. Such control programs have been shown to operate much as in a computer, where an input program calls up from various parts what is relevant to that program.

Some novel implications of the holographic model are: (a) that apparently unorganized (random appearing) physical systems may in fact be highly organized along holographic principles; (b) that such principles may apply not only to brain (a microcosm of the individual) but also to social organization: even when you "do your own thing," you reflect to some extent the total organization of which you are a part.

variety of tasks. The voltage shown in recordings of brain-wave activity of each hemisphere varies, depending on the nature of the task, and shows which side is dominant for that activity (Galin & Ornstein, 1972).

It appears that the dominant hemisphere, whichever it is, represents the intellectual, analytical, critical side, while the other hemisphere is more intuitive, artistic, and perhaps also sensual. The normal brain seems to function best when one side is temporarily idling while the other operates at full throttle. But there are probably people who have learned to rely too much on one-sided brain activity and cannot alternate effectively to use whichever mode of brain operation is most appropriate to each situation. (See *P&L* Close-up, p. 87.)

Research is presently in progress to determine if subjects can be trained to increase or suppress the activity of either hemisphere voluntarily. If they can, what will be the effects on their learning and creative abilities as well as on their sense of self-contentment and appreciation of their natural environment? The answers to such provocative questions await the next round of psychophysiological research.

Efferent control of afferent input. The input *to* the nervous system obviously influences and directs action, but does it ever work the other way? Can it be shown that the brain influences the physiological processing of afferent (input) activity, either at the receptors or elsewhere as a sensory message travels upward? To what extent is the nervous system a two-way thoroughfare rather than a network of independent one-way streets?

Karl Pribram, of Stanford University, has investigated this question with fascinating results. He has found convincing evidence that activity in the sensory and motor cortex and in an association area (the lower part of the temporal cortex) can influence the nerve impulse generated in the eye by a flash of light.

The technique involved measuring the refractory period between two successive flashes of light that produced evoked potential in the primary visual cortex. In one condition the association cortex was independently stimulated at the same time as the visual cortex. In a second condition, only the visual cortex was stimulated. The refractory period was longer when the association cortex was also being stimulated, thus indicating that activity in one part of the brain influenced processing in the other part of the brain. The efferent control of afferent input was further revealed since the effects of stimulation of these association areas were shown to influence incoming nerve impulses as far down as the optic nerve (the nerve that carries impulses from the retina to the brain).

Thus there remains little doubt that activity in the association cortex can influence the processing of incoming visual stimuli in the primary sensory system (Spinelli & Pribram, 1967).

Subsequent experiments showed that brain-wave activity initiated by a particular sensory input also changes with time as a result of the consequences of previous responses to that sensory message (Rothblat & Pribram, 1972).

Evoked responses to visual stimuli were recorded in the visual association cortex while monkeys were learning a discrimination. They had to learn to respond to either the color *or the* shape *of a colored pattern and to inhibit response to the other. One group was reinforced for responding positively to the color; another group, for responding positively to the shape.*

After the monkeys had learned the discrimination, their patterns of neural activity were different even though they were receiving the same retinal stimulation. Furthermore, the differential neural activity became evident about 5 milliseconds before *the overt response, whereas early in learning the brain-wave activity was identical before the two responses. Evidently the activity of the visual association cortex was being affected not only by the current retinal stimulation but also by the consequences of previous responses. Such feedback presumably had been stored in some way in the brain.*

The implications for psychology of this new view of how the brain works are considered by many researchers to be revolutionary. During the 1920s and 1930s and even into the 1950s, a strict stimulus → response, input → output, reflex-arc model of central nervous system functioning guided research and theory. The result was the classical behaviorism of that period, which conceived the behavior of organisms to be guided exclusively by the environmental input — stimulus conditions. With the revised view of the nervous system as a steering, cybernetic, feedback-influenced mechanism came the realization that sensory receptors were as much at the mercy of the brain as of the environment (Miller, Galanter, & Pribram, 1960; Pribram, 1971). Thus since the 1960s the processes of cognitive control of behavior have become a major focus of inquiry, vastly aided by the new resource of computer simulation.

Brain waves. From before birth until the moment of death, the brain never stops its constant activity, never "rests" even for a minute. Recordings of the electrical activity of the brain (*electroencephalograms*, EEGs) from elec-

Close-up
Brain Splitting: Two Minds in One Body

Occasionally, when epileptic seizures are very severe and cannot be controlled by medication, an operation is performed to sever the corpus callosum, the connection between the two cerebral hemispheres. Without such surgery, the seizures may become fatal; with it, the patient is freed from seizures and reports an improvement in well-being.

A by-product of this surgery is the natural experiment created by making two brains operate within a single body. Each half acts independently of the other, and each seems to have its own sensations, perceptions, and memories, as well as cognitive and emotional experiences.

Although the split-brain patients quickly learn ways to compensate for the loss of coordination, it has been shown experimentally by Roger Sperry that they are living with two separately functioning brains. As you can see in the diagram below, coordination between eye and hand is normal if the split-brain patients use their left hand to find and match an object that appears in the left visual field. However, when they are asked to recognize objects that they touch with their right hand, in order to match the pear seen in the left visual field, they cannot do so. Here the cup is misperceived as matching the pear. All messages from the patient's right hand are going to the left cerebral hemisphere, from which there is no longer a connection to the right visual cortex.

But there are some situations when two brains would be better than one, as when you have to respond to two sets of sensory inputs. It takes you less time to react to a single stimulus than to have to press one button with your right hand when a light on your left side flashes on and to press another with your left hand when a right-side light is presented. Not so for the split-brain patient: response to the double reaction-time situation is as fast as to the simple one. Each reaction is independent of the other; thus no time is lost thinking about or coordinating what is happening in each hemisphere of the brain. This is indeed a case where it is better that the right hand doesn't know what the left hand is doing (Gazzaniga, 1970).

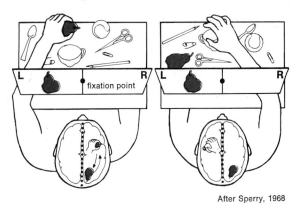

After Sperry, 1968

trodes attached to the scalp have established that even during sleep the brain maintains a constantly high level of electrical activity. These spontaneous EEGs, like the potentials evoked by stimulation, discussed earlier, are made visible by means of an oscilloscope. The difference is that in the case of EEGs it is patterns that are being sought, and the record represents a complex, continuing average of many signals rather than the discrete response to a particular stimulus.

What *are* brain waves, and what do they tell us about the physiological basis of experience and behavior, the problem of primary concern to us in this chapter? Brain waves probably reflect the alternating states of excitability and refractoriness of neurons. Many nerve fibers are activated along parallel pathways at each synaptic junction along the routes through the brain, forming a wave of varying electrical voltage. At each relay stage of the cortex, there may be as many as 100 neurons; accordingly, an advancing wave may, in a second, sweep over 100,000 neurons. This wave front may follow diverse pathways through a mosaic of neurons, and may even double back on itself, forming a reverberatory circuit.

These wave fronts may be both the carriers of the sensory nerve impulse frequency code and the means by which parts of the message are organized to form a meaningful sensory experience. As you have seen, the sensory information started at the receptors comes to the cortex as a specific signal that can be picked up even in single cells in the appropriate sensory projection area of the cortex. But since different cortical cells decode information about different characteristics of an object (size, shape, movement, color, texture, weight, odor, temperature, and so on), all this information must be integrated somehow. This integration may occur between the wave fronts generated by each of these receptor-organ impulses. Some researchers speculate that these constantly flowing wave fronts interlock and integrate every sense organ input and response output.

All this activity of the brain requires an enormous expenditure of energy in the form of cell metabolism. In fact, this metabolism utilizes 20 percent of the total oxygen consumption of the whole body at rest. As brain activity increases with the stress of anxiety or with concentration, the brain uses more oxygen. In contrast, when brain functioning starts to decline (as in elderly people with senile psychosis), or almost comes to a standstill (as in surgical anesthesia or alcoholic coma), the brain consumes much less oxygen—sometimes less than half the normal requirement. It is believed that processes that interfere with synaptic transmission decrease cerebral oxygen consumption (Kety, 1967b).

The practical applications of brain-wave research now in progress sound a bit like science fiction. Only a few examples can be mentioned here.

Research being conducted at the U.S. Naval Academy compared the EEG signals from the brains of twenty-five A students with those of an equal number of C students while the subjects performed a number of tasks. The A students had significantly different brain-wave production on different tasks or situations—resting, solving problems, or under stress; the C students did not show this appropriately differentiated EEG response. The top academic students also were able to produce greater amounts of a slow brain-wave pattern known as alpha *(described in Chapter 7).*

Could the less gifted students change their brain-wave patterns to make them resemble the patterns of their high-scoring peers? As this is written, a group of C students is being trained to control their alpha pattern and most have been successful. Whether their grades will be affected is yet to be established.

Analysis of EEG records has also been made as subjects shifted from concentration to aimless daydreaming (where are you *at this moment?). This work has led to the development of an "Attention-Level Analyzer" that monitors level of concentration and sounds a warning tone when the subject's mind is wandering. If daydreaming continues, a second alarm sounds, notifying another person.*

This device has worked with about three fourths of the subjects tested. The researcher suggests that it could be used to notify pilots or truck drivers when their vigilance was below what it should be; likewise it could enable air controllers, radar and sonar operators, and their supervisors to know when not enough attention was being paid to the task at hand (Montor, 1973).

Another exciting new area of practical research involves stimulation of "pleasure centers" (see page 74) to teach the brain to control its own activity. The discovery that there are "pleasure centers" in the brain that motivate a high level of purposeful responding has begun a new era in brain research and behavior control.

One set of experiments has studied the extent to which the brain can be trained to manipulate the firing of groups of neurons in the visual pathway. The evoked potential from a light flashed in the animal's eye is monitored by electrodes implanted in sensory neurons in the brain; they discharge with a characteristic amplitude and frequency. Whenever the evoked potential activity changes a slight amount in a preselected direction, the brain is rewarded with direct pleasurable stimulation. By this biofeedback procedure, the amplitude of these evoked potentials can be doubled or totally suppressed.

In this way, the brain can learn not only to fire single neurons in uncharacteristic ways, but also to change and modulate broad activity patterns. The sensory-motor rhythm, for example, is a particular EEG pattern (of 12–16 cycles per second) generated by the sensory-motor cortex. A cat's brain waves were passed through a special filtering device that electrically activated a food dispenser whenever the "right" waves appeared. The task was for a hungry cat's brain to produce more of these sensory-motor rhythms in order for the cat to get fed. Whether or not the hungry cat ate was left entirely up to whether the brain could alter its own waves.

After twenty training sessions, the right rhythms were being emitted more frequently than before. Then, when the cat was no longer rewarded for producing the rhythms, the brain reduced its output of them (reported by Chase, 1973).

There are probably few more capable and willing learners than the brain—as was shown in further studies where the sensory-motor rhythm was conditioned to occur in only one cerebral hemisphere. When these cats were asleep, only that side of the brain continued to be influenced by what it had trained itself to do while awake.

Most provocative of all is an experiment by M. B. Sterman (1971) in which reactions to a poisonous drug were compared in cats who had been trained to control their brain waves and cats who had been given no special training. Sterman says of the trained cats:

"It was interesting to watch these animals. Although they had been trained long before, they seemed to be controlling the seizures in their brains by adopting odd motionless postures, often staring off into space, or gazing at an inert, lifted paw. They had apparently learned how to inhibit motor activity, and thus delay and even prevent the motor symptoms, convulsions, of this extremely toxic drug." (p. 341)

The extent to which we might be able to program our own brains in life-sustaining and enhancing ways appears to be limitless.

Chapter Summary

The scientific study of the human brain began in the early sixteenth century. By assuming that the body and brain were mechanistic, as distinct from the soul, which was spiritual, René Descartes overcame religious objections to studying the workings of the mind.

The physiological psychologists who have succeeded Descartes tend to follow a *reductionist* approach, seeking to understand complex behavioral processes by studying simpler neurological or biochemical events. Many other psychologists prefer a *holistic* approach, studying the organism as whole rather than its functioning parts.

Demands imposed by the environment mold the characteristics of living species by ensuring the survival and reproduction of those individuals best suited to adapt. It is the *chromosomes* within living cells that transmit characteristics from generation to generation. Chromosomes are made up of *genes*—long twisted strings of deoxyribonucleic acid *(DNA)*. DNA controls the reproduction of body cells and the manufacture of proteins. *Mutations*, or changes in the structure of DNA, may result in favorable or unfavorable changes being passed on to future generations.

In sexual reproduction, two *germ cells* (male *sperm* and female *ovum*) come together to form the *zygote*—a single cell that will develop into a new individual. Since the sperm and ovum each contain only half the chromosomes necessary to new body cells, the genes present in a species are constantly being dealt into new combinations.

While single-celled organisms contain the essentials for survival, their adaptability is limited. Multi-celled organisms are much more flexible due to the *specialization* of cells for various types of functions. Specialized cells that make up the *nervous system* enable the organism to process and respond to information from the environment.

The basic units of the nervous system are the *nerve cells,* or *neurons,* which transmit information in the form of *nerve impulses*. Neurons differ in size and shape, but each consists of a *cell body, dendrites,* which receive nerve impulses, and an *axon,* which transmits impulses to other neurons. *Axonal conduction* carries information within a neuron; *synaptic transmission* carries it across a synapse to another neuron.

In the resting state, an axon is *polarized,* with the inside electrically negative relative to the outside. A nerve impulse occurs when stimulation is strong enough to *depolarize* the membrane; this change in *membrane potential* then travels down the nerve fiber. The axon transmits on an *all-or-none* basis; it transmits either a full impulse or nothing at all. Information about intensity of stimulation is conveyed by the number of neurons that fire and how often they fire.

In *synaptic transmission,* the message is carried across the synapse (the tiny space between one neuron and the next) by *chemical transmitter substances* that affect the polarization of the second neuron. If the polarization of the *postsynaptic* membrane is decreased, the second neuron fires. By means of *spatial* and *temporal summation,* the input from several neurons can be added together. Thus synaptic transmission is said to follow a *more-or-less* principle. Impulses travel in one direction only, following the law of *forward conduction:* from dendrite to axon across the synapse to the dendrites or cell body of the next neuron.

The nervous system consists of two main parts: the *central nervous system* (the brain and spinal cord) and the *peripheral nervous system,* which connects the CNS to receptors and effectors throughout the body. The *somatic* part of the peripheral nervous system controls the skeletal muscles. The *visceral* part (the *autonomic nervous system*) connects the central nervous system with the internal organs. The autonomic nervous system in turn has two divisions: the *sympathetic,* which regulates emergency functioning, and the *parasympathetic,* which governs continuing vital functions.

Interneurons or *associative neurons* within the central nervous system provide the interconnections between *afferent* impulses coming from sensory receptors and *efferent* impulses to the muscles and glands. The basic pattern of any stimulus-response act is the *sensory-motor arc,* consisting of stimulus input, CNS processing, and behavioral output. In *reflex action,* the simplest form of behavior, CNS processing may take place entirely in the spinal cord, without involving higher brain centers. The network of neurons in the spinal cord makes possible *divergence, convergence, feedback* loops, and the *long-circuiting* of information to the brain.

In the presence of novel, conflicting, or especially significant stimuli, the organism experiences an *orienting reaction,* which includes increased sensitivity, heightened muscle activity, general arousal, and visceral changes that prepare the body for action. When stimuli become familiar, *habituation* occurs, and responding decreases or ceases. After *habituation* has occurred, a change in the stimulus can bring about *dishabituation* and reinstate the orienting reaction.

Brain functions have been studied through *lesions* (the destruction of brain tissue), through electronic *recording* of brain activity, and through electrical or chemical *stimulation* of the brain. The brain consists of two *hemispheres,* connected by the *corpus callosum;* each hemisphere has four lobes: *frontal, temporal, parietal,* and *occipital.* The outer layer of these hemispheres is called the *cortex* or *neocortex.*

The evolutionarily older *subcortex* controls primitive functions such as appetites, pleasure, and pain. An important part of the subcortex is the *brain stem,* which contains the *thalamus,* an important relay station for sensory information, the *hypothalamus,* which controls many vital functions, and the *reticular formation,* a general arousal system. The *limbic system* is primitive cortical tissue involved in functions as diverse as attention, emotion, and memory. Within the limbic system are located the *rhinencephalon,* involved in odor detection, and the *hippocampus,* involved in both mating and memory.

Primary *sensory* reception areas are located in relatively specific parts of the cortex, with auditory functions in the *temporal* lobe and visual functions in the occipital lobe. Primary *motor* functions are localized in the cortical area just forward from the fissure of Rolando. The remaining areas of the cortex are *association* areas, where sensory and motor functions are integrated. Damage to these areas may impair understanding or use of language. There is a great deal of *redundancy* of function in the brain, so that if some areas are damaged, their functions may be taken over by other parts of the brain.

Each of the cerebral hemispheres receives input from and sends messages to the opposite side of the body. One hemisphere (usually the left) is *dominant* for most functions, but there is much specialization of function. There is some evidence for *efferent control of afferent input;* that is, messages from the brain can influence the transmission of incoming sensory impulses.

Brain waves, measured by electroencephalograms *(EEGs),* reflect the spontaneous activity of neurons in the brain. Brain activity accounts for about a fifth of the oxygen consumed by the body.

RESEARCH FRONTIER

The Physiological Analysis of Motivated Behavior
Philip Teitelbaum University of Illinois

To many students, physiological psychology appears to be largely concerned with the neural mechanisms underlying behavior rather than with behavior itself. Thus, using anatomical methods, physiological psychologists often try to localize the parts of the brain involved in psychologically interesting phenomena such as learning, perception, motivation, and cognition. They may study brain wave patterns or autonomic changes associated with such behavioral events. Their research can lead them deep into the structure and function of the nervous system, but often seems to have little relevance for the behavioral studies that characterize other areas of psychology.

However, physiological psychology can also be a very powerful direct approach to the analysis of behavior. When a part of the brain is damaged, the behavior controlled by it may disappear completely or decompose into only a very simple fragmentary form. Then, as recovery from such damage takes place, the behavior gradually re-integrates itself, giving us a view of the levels of organization involved. In brief, we can use brain damage to simplify behavior, and recovery to see how behavioral components can be put back together again to form an effectively functioning organism.

For example, brain systems running through the hypothalamus have long been known to play an important role in motivated behavior. Brief electrical stimulation in the lateral hypothalamus can elicit pleasure in people, and animals will press a lever thousands of times to stimulate themselves in that region, indicating that they too find it reinforcing. Sustained lateral hypothalamic stimulation can elicit eating or drinking in satiated animals, or even mating or attack.

If we damage the lateral hypothalamus on both sides then rats, cats, dogs, monkeys, and even people will stop eating and drinking. In animals, the refusal to eat (aphagia) and to drink (adipsia) may persist until the animal dies. However, laboratory studies have shown that if such animals are kept alive by force-feeding, they will eventually recover the ability to eat and drink (Teitelbaum & Epstein, 1962).

The behavioral pattern of recovery in adult lateral hypothalamic rats is summarized diagrammatically in Figure 1. A striking fact about this syndrome is that every lateral hypothalamic animal shows the same *sequence* of recovery, although the rate may vary. Since all behavior reflects the action of the brain, such reorganization of brain function should give us a clue as to how behavior is organized.

In some ways, the lateral hypothalamic rat during its recovery is like an infant rat. For instance, during the stage of aphagia, when it refuses dry food and water, it will suckle reflexively at the nipple of a bottle. Later in its recovery, although it eats dry food and drinks water, it still does not respond fully to dehydration. Normal weanling animals show similar deficits in drinking behavior. If a parallel exists between recovery and development, each stage in recovery from the lateral hypothalamic syndrome should also occur in proper sequence

	Stage I Adipsia, Aphagia	Stage II Adipsia, Anorexia	Stage III Adipsia, Dehydration-Aphagia	Stage IV Recovery
Eats wet palatable foods	No	Yes	Yes	Yes
Regulates food intake & body wt. on wet palatable foods	No	No	Yes	Yes
Eats dry foods (if hydrated)	No	No	Yes	Yes
Drinks water. survives on dry food and water.	No	No	No	Yes

Figure 1   States of recovery seen in the lateral hypothalamic syndrome (from Teitelbaum & Epstein, 1962).

during development in infancy. To study this, we slowed down the course of normal development by surgically removing the thyroid gland in newborn rats. We hoped to reveal the slow development of elements of regulation just as the slow course of recovery reveals the elements of regulation in the lateral hypothalamic syndrome (Teitelbaum, Cheng, & Rozin, 1969).

The effects of thyroidectomy in retarding both weight gain and growth were clearly evident. When tested at the normal weaning age of 21 days, the thyroidectomized rats displayed every stage of the lateral hypothalamic syndrome. Those most severely retarded in development were completely aphagic and adipsic when offered wet palatable foods or ordinary food and water. They nursed reflexively, but like adult aphagic lateral hypothalamic rats they did not voluntarily ingest food or water no matter how palatable. Others, more fully developed at weaning, accepted wet, palatable foods but did not eat enough to maintain their weight. If this stage lasted too long, they died. Other weanlings, even less retarded, gained weight and regulated their caloric intake of a liquid diet but were still adipsic and would have died (some did die) if later offered only dry food and water. Finally, the least retarded weanlings accepted dry food and water, but drank only when they ate and not in response to body dehydration. Thus, depending on the degree of retardation, every stage of the adult lateral hypothalamic syndrome as shown in Figure 1 was seen in these infant rats.

In a separate experiment, we severely starved infant rats throughout the suckling period by systematically limiting access to the mother from birth until weaning (Cheng, Rozin, & Teitelbaum, 1971). Control litters with unlimited access to their mother developed normally. The starvation-produced runts, when tested at weaning (21 days of age), showed every stage of the lateral hypothalamic syndrome. Like thyroidectomized infants, those that survived progressed through the various stages as they developed. Produced by either of these methods, then, retardation in development shows a remarkable parallel to the lateral hypothalamic syndrome.

Parallels in Another System

One could be more sure of the validity of such a parallel between adult recovery and infant development if it could be found in another brain system, unrelated to feeding and drinking. Such a parallel has in fact been demonstrated in studies of how people recover voluntary use of the hand following a stroke. Early studies had shown that even though a paralyzed limb could not be used for voluntary actions, several types of reflexive movements could be elicited. In the hand, for instance, three types of reflexive grasping have been identified: (1) the traction response, where a pull against the flexed arm causes closure of the fist; (2) the true grasp, where the touch of a finger or a rod moving across the palm will cause closure of the fingers; and (3) the instinctive grasp reaction, in which the hand orients to the stimulus and gropes after it if it moves away. Twitchell (1951) showed that these grasping reflexes recover one after the other in distinct stages of recovery of voluntary use of the hand. Later, Twitchell (1970) identified very similar stages in the normal development of voluntary control of grasping in newborn infants. Thus we may conclude that in human beings as well as in rats, adult recovery parallels infant development.

How nervous tissue recovers after damage is not yet understood. In the remaining fragment of a partially destroyed system, increased synthesis of neural transmitters, increased sensitivity to such transmitters, sprouting of neurons and synaptic formation may be involved. The parallel to development suggests that nervous connections which develop first are also the first to recover after damage.

From a behavioral point of view, there are important implications in the parallel between recovery and development. Motivated behavior must be organized, as is the nervous system whose action it reflects, in terms of levels of integration. That is what the stages of development and stages of recovery have in common. Consider once again the behavior involved in feeding. The earliest type of behavior to appear in the human fetus is the total withdrawal pattern response of head and body to tactile stimulation around the mouth. As development progresses, response to such stimulation changes: head movements toward the stimulation (rooting reflexes) are elicited and differentiated local reflexes of mouth opening and closing, swallowing, and sucking eventually appear. We know that such reflexes do not require the function of the hypothalamus or any part of the brain above the level of the midbrain, since they can be seen in infants born with part or all of their brain missing and in adult animals with their cerebrum removed. In such cases, however, these reflexes never become further elaborated into more complex feeding patterns. Incorporation and transformation of the simple reflex patterns into more complex feeding behavior does occur in the normal infant as development proceeds; therefore, the development of higher parts of the nervous system must be necessary for the transformation of simple reflexive feeding patterns into motivated regulatory behavior. Immediately after lesion, adult animals with extensive lateral hypothalamic damage show only reflexive sucking behavior; their recovery is similar to the slowed development of infants. Thus we may conclude that in development, behavior is *encephalized;* in recovery, it is *reencephalized.*

This view provides us with a powerful way of thinking and experimenting on both brain and behavior. With respect to the organization of the nervous system, it means that we need not think merely in terms of localized centers of function, but rather in terms of vertically organized brain systems, with new levels of complexity added by each way-station from spinal cord to cortex. Correspondingly, to understand any behavioral phenomenon, we must view it as we would a stage of development or recovery. These only make sense as a transformation from the stage of integration that preceded it (a lower level of encephalization) towards a higher level of integration. *Behavior, like the nervous system, is a hierarchically organized structure.*

Let us use this way of thinking to find new insights into the lateral hypothalamic syndrome. If the localized damage affects not merely the hypothalamus, but an entire vertically organized system running from spinal cord to cortex, then abnormalities produced by central nervous damage at any level might be similar to deficits produced in lateral hypothalamic animals. Alerted for such similarities,

we note that adult monkeys or humans suffering from parietal lobe damage display some symptoms that are reminiscent of lateral hypothalamic-damaged animals. For instance, they turn away from food, and may refuse to eat altogether. One aspect of a parietal patient's behavior is particularly striking. If damaged on one side, say the right parietal lobe, he does not pay attention to anything on his opposite side. He orients and attends quite well on the same side, but neglects the other. He may fail to dress his left side, comb his hair only from the midline to the right, or even fail to recognize his left hand as it moves into view.

Is there a similar deficit in attention in the first stage of lateral hypothalamic recovery, when animals do not voluntarily eat or drink at all? Marshall, Turner, and I (1971) damaged rats on one side of the lateral hypothalamus only. We then applied a series of simple neurological tests. A normal rat investigates a stimulus by orienting its head toward it. This natural response was used to determine the responsivity of rats before and after lateral hypothalamic damage. Damaging the lateral hypothalamus on one side profoundly impaired the rat's ability to orient to the stimuli on the side opposite the lesion. Such rats showed no orientation to visual, olfactory, or tactile stimulation on the opposite side, whereas they responded promptly to the same stimuli on the same side. Rats with lesions on both sides of the brain did not respond to sensory stimuli on either side of the body.

This orientation impairment does not seem to be a motor paralysis, since these animals remain able to perform normal grooming movements on both sides of the body. Nor is it an inability to sense the stimuli, since eye movement and respiratory changes often occur when the stimulus is presented. Rather, the deficit seems to be a kind of "neglect." The rat is unable to integrate the sensory information with the adaptive motor patterns involved in orienting toward a stimulus.

Such sensory neglect can drastically affect the instinctive behavior patterns involved in eating, drinking, and attack. For example, after unilateral damage, rats that normally killed mice ignored a mouse when it was on the opposite side of the visual field. However, as soon as the mouse moved into the other half of the field, the rats attacked normally.

There is another lesson to be learned from the reflexive behavior of brain-damaged animals. For example, we are accustomed to thinking both of lateral hypothalamic aphagia and *anorexia* (a disorder in which a person refuses to eat) in terms of *motivational* impairment — a lack of desire for food. This was particularly so, because palatable foods can transform such a starving animal into one that eats enough to maintain itself. The one-sided deficit forces us to change our concepts. We now think in terms of *sensory neglect* — a kind of loss of reflexive orientation — rather than a *loss of motivation*. The control of the behavior has shifted to the environment, rather than being focused in an independent central state of motivation. Many complex motivated voluntary acts may similarly be illuminated by an analysis of the underlying reflexive patterns.

Relevance for Human Functioning

One point of persistent misunderstanding about physiological psychology should be clarified. Because physiological psychologists often produce brain damage to study its effects on behavior, they must work on animals. Many students taking introductory psychology feel that work on animals has little to offer for an understanding of human behavior. Nothing could be further from the truth. The simplifications of behavior that result from brain damage in animals often reveal components of normal human behavior that we would not have suspected. Let me show you how this comes about.

A cat exhibits exquisitely precise complex sensorimotor behavior; therefore, when its brain is damaged, we may gain insights into the deficits that are not as readily apparent in the rat. Wolgin and I (1975) found that bilateral hypothalamic damage in cats produced the same disruptions of feeding and drinking behavior and the same stages of recovery seen in rats. They also show sensory neglect. During the early stage of complete aphagia, as shown in Figure 2 left, they typically become cataleptic, clinging reflexively with the forelimbs for long periods when placed on the back of a chair, supporting some of their weight also on the hind legs and keeping the head upright. Similar cataleptic clinging is produced by drugs that block the catecholamine systems in the brain. Seeking to test the

Figure 2   Bandage-backfall reaction in bilateral hypothalamic adult cat.

role of vision in allowing a cat to keep its head erect during this drug-induced clinging, Van Harreveld and Bogen (1961) covered the eyes by bandaging the entire head and neck. The animal's head then fell slowly backwards, the forelimbs extended, and the forepaws gradually released their grasp, causing the animal to fall backwards off the chair. Further research, however, showed that this "backfall reaction" is not due to lack of vision, since it does not occur when unbandaged animals are tested in total darkness. But if head and neck are bandaged without covering the eyes, the backfall reaction does occur. Thus it appears to be induced by pressure on certain facial and cervical nerves.

When undrugged lateral hypothalamic cataleptic cats (like drugged but intact cats) are wrapped with an elastic bandage, they also slowly fall backwards (Figure 2, right). But as these animals recover and begin to walk spontaneously, clinging and backfall no longer occur. Instead, like normal animals, they climb upwards over the back of the chair or turn to the side and jump down to the floor.

One of the brain areas affected in lateral hypothalamic damage is the nigrostriatal pathway, an area known to be involved in Parkinson's disease. Therefore, it seemed reasonable to look for the bandage-backfall reaction in severely debilitated Parkinson patients. Figure 3, top left, shows a patient suffering from Parkinsonism who was confined to a wheelchair because he could not walk by himself. He seemed to be aware of his environment, but could not speak more than a word at a time in response to direct questions. In the wheelchair, he sat slumped forward but was able to hold his head and neck erect. Allowing him to grasp a wooden rod, held horizontally, one of us raised it, lifting the patient's arms above his head. Then his wheelchair was tilted backwards to an angle of about 45 degrees. In this position, he maintained his head erect, even though this required active support by neck muscles. However, when the maneuver was repeated with his head and neck bandaged, his head sagged backwards (Figure 3, top right). Even when his arms were lowered and the wheelchair was returned to the upright position, his head remained back (Figure 3, bottom left). As soon as we unwrapped the bandage, he raised his head to an erect position (Figure 3, bottom right). As with the drugged or brain-damaged cat, *pressure,* not vision, seemed to be the effective variable. Three other Parkinson patients who were less severely affected than this man did not show the bandage-backfall. Because the bandage-backfall reaction appears after lateral hypothalamic damage in animals, and in severe human Parkinsonism, both of

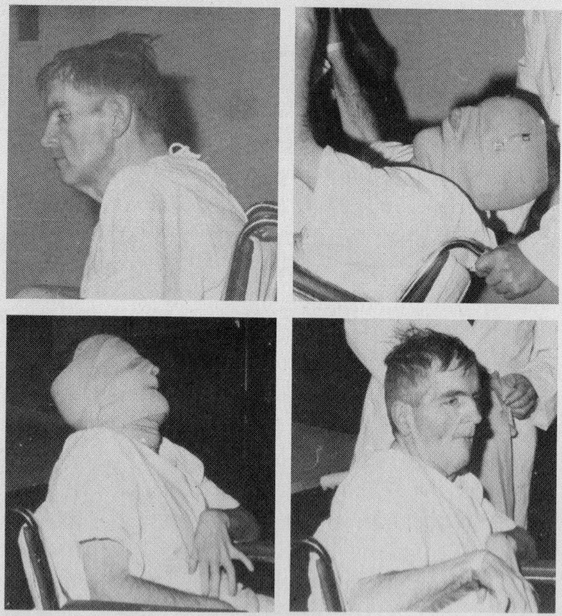

Figure 3 Bandage-backfall reaction in post-encephalic Parkinsonism patient.

which involve the region of the nigrostriatal pathway, further study should be of great value in neurological diagnosis of humans.

This reaction may also shed light on normal developmental processes. As we have seen, the stages of recovery of eating seen in the adult lateral hypothalamic rat closely parallel the development of feeding in infancy. The bandage-backfall in the lateral hypothalamic-damaged cat is present only during the initial, aphagic, stage of the syndrome. As recovery proceeds, it disappears. If the recovery-development parallel holds for catalepsy as it does for feeding, the bandage-backfall reaction should appear in very young normal infants. Then, as encephalization proceeds with age, it should disappear—and tests with kittens, puppies, and infant baboons show that it does!

We also tested nine human infants, ranging in age from 4 to 13½ weeks. With upper torso leaning 10–15 degrees back (Figure 4, bottom left), an 8-week-old baby held its head easily erect. However, when the head and neck were bandaged, the head fell sharply backward (Figure 4, bottom right). When the bandage was removed, the infant was again able to hold its head erect. In six of these infants (ranging from 4 weeks to 11 weeks) the bandage-backfall could be elicited. Three infants, 10 to 13½ weeks old, held their heads up quite well, whether bandaged or not. Thus, by about 3 months of age, in normal human infants, the bandage reaction seems no longer evident. (Since excess pressure on the neck could obstruct breathing and endanger a baby's life, we always worked with a physician present when bandaging young infants.)

Soon after an infant is able to hold up its head, the bandage-backfall reaction can be demonstrated. Later it disappears. A possible explanation is that the infantile inhibitory pathways (from bandaged receptors) are themselves inhibited by later developing catecholaminergic brain systems. In adults, lateral hypothalamic damage or drugs that antagonize catecholamines can produce catalepsy. In that state, the primitive inhibitory system is released, and, as in normal infancy, a bandage around the head and neck will once again cause the backfall reaction.

Figure 4 Bandage-backfall reaction in newborn kitten, 2-week-old infant baboon, and 8-week-old human infant.

In summary, we have seen that physiological psychology can be a very powerful direct approach to the analysis of animal and human behavior. Localized brain damage can simplify a behavioral system and the study of recovery can show us how it is put back together again. The abnormalities of brain damage may represent simpler levels of behavior, which are also present, though often unsuspected, in normal infant development.

References

Cheng, M. F., Rozin, P., & Teitelbaum, P. Semi-starvation retards development of food and water regulations. *Journal of Comparative and Physiological Psychology,* 1971, *76,* 206–218.

Marshall, J. F., Turner, B. H., & Teitelbaum, P. Sensory neglect produced by lateral hypothalamic damage. *Science,* 1971, *174,* 523–525.

Teitelbaum, P., Cheng, M. F., & Rozin, P. Development of feeding parallels its recovery after hypothalamic damage. *Journal of Comparative and Physiological Psychology,* 1969, *67,* 430–441.

Teitelbaum, P. & Epstein, A. N. The lateral hypothalamic syndrome: recovery of feeding and drinking after lateral hypothalamic lesions. *Psychological Review,* 1962, *69,* 74–90. Copyright © 1962, American Psychological Association. Figure 1 reprinted by permission.

Teitelbaum, P. & D. L. Wolgin. Neurotransmitters and the regulation of food intake. In W. H. Gispen et al., *Progress in Brain Research,* Vol. 42, pp. 235–249. Amsterdam: Elsevier Scientific Publishing Co., 1975.

Teitelbaum, P., Wolgin, D. L., De Ryck, M., & Marin, O. S. M. Bandage-backfall reaction: Occurs in infancy, brain damage and catalepsy. *Proceedings of the National Academy of Science,* 1976, in press.

Twitchell, T. E. The restoration of motor function following hemiplegia in man. *Brain,* 1951, *74,* 443–480.

Twitchell, T. E. Reflex mechanisms and the development of prehension. In Connally, K. J. (Ed.), *Mechanisms of Motor Skill Development.* New York, Academic Press, 1970, 25–45.

Van Harreveld, A. & Bogen, J. E. The clinging position of the bulbocapninized cat. *Experimental Neurology,* 1961, *4,* 241–261.

3

Adaptive Behavior: Conditioning and Learning

It is likely that snow was falling in St. Petersburg when Ivan Petrovich Pavlov prepared to board the train on his journey to Stockholm. It was 1904, and Pavlov was on his way to accept the highest tribute for a contribution to basic knowledge: the Nobel Prize. The Russian physiologist had devised a technique for studying the functioning of the digestive glands in intact animals. The role of salivary and other secretions involved in digestion could now be studied by extracting them from the body through tubes implanted in the glands and viscera of experimental dogs.

Surprisingly, Pavlov was more troubled than happy as he departed. It appeared that recent problems in his own laboratory were calling into question the usefulness of his approach to studying the physiology of digestion.

At an early stage in an experiment, his dogs would salivate shortly after food was placed in their mouths. This was as it should be, because food is the natural stimulus for a dog's salivation—saliva making it possible to digest the food. However, after this procedure was repeated a number of times, the animals began to salivate *before* they tasted the food. First, the sight of the food made them salivate; then, later on, the sight of the experimenter who brought the food, and finally even the experimenter's footsteps would suffice to elicit salivation. Pavlov's assistants were at a loss to understand how they could get rid of this undesirable effect, which was a source of error and was complicating the simple process they wished to study. How could it be that any stimulus that regularly preceded the food came to evoke the same reaction as did the food itself?

The interference of this "psychic process" on the basic physiological process under investigation intrigued Pavlov. The leading physiologist of the time, Sir Charles Sherrington, advised him not to get sidetracked by such psychical nonsense, but Pavlov's scientific curiosity was stimulated, and his receptive mind was able to appreciate that he had stumbled onto something of importance. He persisted and eventually was able to turn this chance observation into one of the major discoveries of our time—uncovering the basic laws of conditioning.

The implications of Pavlov's psychological contribution to our knowledge of how organisms learn to adjust to novel stimuli in their environment became immediately apparent. So much so, that when the historian H. G. Wells was asked to judge whether Pavlov or his literary contemporary, George Bernard Shaw, was more important to society, he answered by stating that if they were both drowning and he had but one life preserver, he would throw it to Pavlov.

What Organisms Must Learn

It is through the process of learning that human beings gain the fullest measure of autonomy and freedom from the restrictions set by their natural environment as well as from the constraints imposed by their physiological and anatomical inheritance and the history of their species or social community. Humans have learned to fly, to live in space stations orbiting in outer space, to extend the limits of their sensory capacities through electron microscopes and radio telescopes, to prolong life through adequate diet, medicine, and surgery, and to change the environment through irrigation, air conditioning, and nuclear heating plants.

These and other accomplishments of the human animal are, to a large extent, attributable to learning how to become accurate, consistent predictors. There are two basic kinds of predictions that we must learn to make reliably: first, which events follow which other events in us or in the environment, and secondly, which events follow our own actions or responses. With this knowledge, we may then move from prediction to control—intervening to change environmental events (or their impact on us), modifying the behavior of other people, and altering our own behavior to make it more appropriate and effective.

All living organisms possess the capacity to learn about these two basic kinds of relationships. Lower organisms possess it to a lesser degree: their responses tend to be more predetermined and stereotyped, and there is little variability from individual to individual. For them the history and biology of the entire species is evidenced in the reactions of any given member of the species to an environmental input.

Organisms higher up on the phylogenetic scale are capable of learning more complex and more subtle relationships than are lower ones. Also they are more able to alter their behavior so as to achieve the best "fit" to the particular environmental information they are receiving. When we reach humans, we see the extent to which individuals have gone beyond simply adapting to their environment to forcing the environment to adapt to them.

What Events Are Signals?

By learning about the regularity with which certain events occur together (co-vary), we identify environmental correlations. The complete set of these correlations becomes our representation of the environment and the basis on which we make predictions about the likelihood of future events from knowledge of present or past events. A stimulus becomes a signal to the extent that it provides information about the probability that another stimulus will occur.

By learning how to detect and decipher the signal value of stimuli, we are thereby better prepared for those events that they forecast. A given stimulus may be a signal for subsequent events that have very different meanings or significance: danger, safety, relief, hope, despair, or pleasure. (See *P&L* Close-up, p. 94.)

A clanging bell at a railroad crossing signals the danger of an oncoming train; its cessation or the raising of the striped crossbar (a second, back-up signal) is the "Go ahead" safety signal. During World War II, civil-defense sound signals warned the people of air raids; then a different pattern of sound was used as the all-clear signal. To the bored student, the lecturer's phrase, "and in conclusion . . ." signals relief on the way: the seemingly endless lecture will, in fact, soon terminate.

Temporal or spatial patterning can also be a signal. Thus the obstetrician uses the timing of the contractions of the uterus of a pregnant woman to predict how soon the baby will be delivered.

But there are an infinite variety of stimulus events in our environment, and only some of them are related to others in the informational way we have described here. How, then, do we learn to extract from these myriad possibilities those that are genuine signals? Aristotle in his classical work *De Anima* suggested that for ideas (or events) to be associated in our minds, they must occur in conjunction or *contiguity* with each other. The signal and the thing signaled must be experienced close enough together in space and time that we will see them as related; thereafter, the former will remind us to pay at-

Close-up
Seeing Red and Acting Green

A young psychologist presenting a research report at his first international conference was delighted to discover that his paper was one of those chosen for simultaneous translation from English into French and German. But after having presented the introduction and procedure section of his report, with apparent positive feedback from the audience, he noticed a small light on the lectern beginning to flash on and off. He assumed he was running out of time, and having forgotten his wristwatch, could not judge how long he had spoken or how much time he had left.

As he continued, the light flashed more rapidly, and in his gradually increasing anxiety over not finishing, the neophyte psychologist spoke faster and faster. Soon his rate of delivery matched that of the flashing light. As he neared the end of his speech, the light abruptly stopped flashing and the members of the audience in dismay removed their earphones. The translator had quit because his flashing red light—which was designed to signal the speaker to *slow down* his delivery—had been ignored; the speaker, for some apparently perverse reason, spoke faster rather than slower, eventually making translation impossible.

Would *you* have known intuitively the correct signal value of the flashing light? How would you design a signal system to avoid such a misreading even by an overanxious psychologist?

tention: the latter is coming soon. Psychologists today believe that contiguity is not *sufficient* to account for learning associations, but it seems to be *necessary* in most cases. A high frequency or repetitiveness of the events to be associated also enhances the learning of their relationship.

When the second stimulus in a pair is unpleasant, noxious, or potentially lethal, individuals are motivated to search for naturally occurring, neutral signals that anticipate the dangerous one and thus can enable them to avoid its serious consequences. In addition, in the examples of air-raid sirens or traffic lights, human beings go beyond merely using existing signals; they create new ones to help them predict other events—and then instruct members of their language community as to the significance of these signals.

Thus, in learning about relationships between stimulus events ($S-S$ relationships), we come to learn about *the nature of the environment* in which we behave. We also learn what responses are related to each other and then can make predictions accordingly. Often clusters of responses tend to occur together. For example, when a response toward some desired goal is blocked or frustrated, aggressive responses of some kind typically follow. As fear responses increase in potency, avoidance or escape reactions are likely. At a finer level of analysis, any integrated, coordinated behavior involving a sequence of responses, such as learning to count from one to ten, playing a violin, tying one's shoelaces, or learning to say "antidisestablishmentarianism," consists of components, each of which is both a response and a signal as to what response should follow.

Sometimes there is a lack of consistency between a person's responses so that one is *not* a predictable signal of another. When a person's words and actions are inconsistent on issues judged to be important by the society, that person is labeled a "hypocrite"—the expected correlation is nonexistent or even negative. In contrast, when the correlation is consistently positive, we judge the person to be dependable. Of such people, we say as a compliment, "Their word is their deed." From such response correlations ($R-R$ relationships), we come to learn about *the structure of behavior*—first our own, and then, by observation and inference, that of other people.

Another kind of relationship between events is *the impact that the environment has on us* ($S \rightarrow R$ relationships). Scalding water will burn your skin. A bright light shining in your eyes makes the pupils constrict, causes tearing, eventually will fatigue your eyes, and may lead to a headache. People with allergies must learn which foods, flowers, or other environmental conditions will induce allergic reactions in them if they are to avoid those unpleasant and occasionally fatal stimulus events. On a more positive note, we also come to predict fairly accurately which stimuli will make us feel happy, proud, satisfied, or sexually aroused—and then try to arrange our lives so that the environment has a good opportunity to do its good things to us.

What Actions and Consequences Are Related?

The second general type of correlation to be learned is that between a response we make and the consequences it has on the environment. Some things we do have an effect, while other things we do have none. Consider the behavioral act of crying, for example. You do not have to learn to cry; the response mechanisms involved in crying are physiologically wired in at birth. Crying is elicited in any infant by intense, disturbing stimuli, such as hunger pangs, cold, pain, and noise. Indeed, infant crying is a signal to adult caretakers that something is probably bothering the baby. But the child soon learns under which conditions crying is followed by the appearance of parents or grandparents, and often "uses" crying as a means to get their attention, to avoid being alone, to be picked up and cuddled, and so forth. So the child does not learn how to cry, but rather when crying is effective. Children raised in orphanages or children who are long-term hospital patients cry less often than children in their own homes, because the institutional staff members respond less often to their crying.

In many societies, male children learn that the consequences that follow their crying are nega-

tive—they will be teased or embarrassed and labeled "sissies" or "cry babies." For such males, the act of crying becomes inhibited when they learn to predict that it will have aversive consequences. By the time these males reach adulthood, stimulus events that would be expected to elicit crying, such as extreme pain or even the death of a loved one, no longer do so.

When your actions do affect the environment in predictable ways, you discover what features of the environment are susceptible to control and at the same time you learn something about yourself as an agent of control. When you raise your hand in class, does the teacher notice you? When you smile, do people smile back at you? When you hit someone bigger, do you get away with it? When you throw water on a gasoline fire, does it go out? When you cry "Wolf" or "Help" does anyone come to your aid? It is from the answers you discover to these and other pairs of responses and consequences ($R \rightarrow S$ relationships) that you learn to understand *the impact you have—and can have—on your social and physical environment.*

The poor plumbing found in many college dormitories and apartment houses offers us an excellent example for illustrating most of the basic points about both of these fundamental relationships (between events, and about consequences).

Imagine taking a warm, soothing shower after a hard day's work. As the water pours down against your back, you soon relax contentedly and become oblivious to everything but the comforting warmth. Suddenly, your relaxation is smashed by the awareness that the water has become scalding hot. Someone has flushed a toilet, and when that happens, there is no cold water to temper the shower. The heat burns your back, causing considerable pain. Just as quickly, the temperature of the water returns to its previous condition, and you continue your shower, although unable to regain your former state of contented oblivion. But soon you detect that the water pressure has abruptly and momentarily dropped. Bam! On comes the red-hot flow again, accompanied by curses from you—but that response does not make the water cooler.

You did not have to learn to experience pain

when skin tissue was damaged. Those connections are physiologically built in. But you did have to learn the connection between the event and its effect on you—namely, "very hot water burns my skin." You also had to discover that the drop in water pressure was a signal for the scalding water.

That one association between water-pressure reduction and heat increase may be sufficient to develop an "expectancy" in which the former forecasts the impending danger of the latter. Certainly, if the two stimulus changes occurred together repeatedly, you would learn to perceive the first event as a signal for the second.

So you have experienced an association between two stimuli: namely, there is a high degree of correlation between reduction in cold water pressure and subsequent rise in water temperature. One is a dependable *signal* for the other. Unless you can put such knowledge to work on your behalf, however, you will be smarter but not in less pain.

Originally, many behavioral reactions may accompany your pain response, such as screaming, crying, cursing, stomping, kicking the wall, tearing the shower curtain, and so on. What you

Close-up
"Solution for a Burning Issue"

"A soldier with an engineering degree has licked a barracks plumbing problem at Aberdeen Proving Ground that has burned up Army men for years.

"Specialist 4th David Ursin and his bunkmates are the only enlisted men at this weapons test center who no longer worry about sudden flashes of scalding water in the barracks shower each time someone flushes a toilet.

"'After repeatedly getting burned,' Ursin said, 'I had to do something.'

"So he invented the 'accumulator,' a quart-sized metal cylinder that fits behind the shower head and takes the peril out of barracks bathing.

"The accumulator holds enough water during latrine flushing to eliminate surges of hot water through the shower head."

Associated Press, Aug. 16, 1971

obviously must learn is which reaction from your total repertoire of responses will be adaptive—will terminate or better yet prevent the painful experience the next time you shower. In this case you would learn to get out of the path of the shower right after you noticed the water pressure drop and before the torrent of scalding water. This is the second kind of association you must learn—the association between your behavior and its consequences. Such actions on your part involve *operating* on the environment or your relation to it in order to change it in a desired way. (See *P&L* Close-up at left.)

This kind of environmental control is vastly extended in humans by the use of language. Thus not every resident or visitor in a dormitory with this plumbing problem has to go through the painful process of discovering it personally. It becomes part of the storehouse of knowledge that can be passed from one person to another through words. In the two chapters that follow, we will see further what a remarkable degree of control over our environment we gain by manipulation of words and other symbols.

The study of learning processes is fundamental to any understanding of human behavior. The characteristic that most distinguishes higher organisms from lower forms of animal life is the relative independence of their behavior from unchangeable, inherited physiological mechanisms and the greater modifiability of behavior through learned encounters with the environment. We learn how to become human beings, to live with others, to speak, to attend, to perceive, to reason—as well as to act. Our attitudes, tastes, idiosyncrasies, loves, hates, fears, prejudices, and even neurotic symptoms are all learned. It is not surprising, therefore, that basic to almost any analysis of human behavior will be a consideration of principles of learning.

The present chapter focuses primarily on the learning of the two basic patterns by which learning ties things together (signal learning and consequence learning). Subsequent chapters that focus on complex human learning and on other psychological phenomena, such as perception, social interaction, and therapy for mental illness, will often rely either implicitly or explicitly on this foundation of learning principles.

Pavlov's Respondent Conditioning

Basically, what Pavlov discovered from his extended series of experiments on conditioning in dogs were the conditions under which an irrelevant, often insignificant stimulus event could become relevant and powerful. His investigations centered on one class of behaviors—reflexes and responses under the control of the autonomic nervous system (ANS), and especially that division that operates in emotional reactions, the sympathetic nervous system. Each of these behaviors—such as salivation, pupil contraction, knee jerk, leg flexion, or eye blink—is *elicited* by a stimulus event of a particular kind. The connections between these specific stimuli and the responses they elicit are determined genetically in the species and fixed in the individual at or soon after birth. The behaviors are automatic and unlearned and temporarily change the organism in some way to promote its adaptation to the environment. In making these *involuntary responses* to an eliciting stimulus, the organism is responding to a stimulus by doing something to itself, not to its environment. Such behavior is termed *respondent* behavior.

The Basic Paradigm

A *paradigm* is a symbolic model or diagram that can help us understand the essential features of a process. The respondent conditioning paradigm begins with the relationship between a stimulus and a reflex that it reliably elicits. Pavlov called the normal eliciting stimulus the *unconditioned* or *unconditional stimulus* (UCS, or sometimes abbreviated US). He called the response that inevitably follows it the *unconditioned response* (UCR, or UR).

What Pavlov found was that when he presented meat powder and observed the automatic, unlearned response of salivation, it was not long before other stimuli occurring shortly before it (sight of food, sight or sound of experimenter) also became capable of eliciting salivation. When salivation was elicited by these other stimuli, it was called a *conditioned* or *conditional response* (CR). ∎

∎ Ivan Pavlov and his staff are shown here with the apparatus used in his conditioning experiments. The dog was harnessed to the wooden frame; a tube conducted its saliva to a measuring device that recorded quantity and rate of salivation to stimuli.

Close-up
Hi-Yo Silver!

The conditioning of words as symbols is effectively demonstrated in a humorous "experiment" conducted by two young pranksters. Their pompous old minister, who rode his horse to church each Sunday, insisted that they clean the horse and do other duties without payment or thanks. To get even, they conditioned the horse by riding him, calling out "Whoa" (CS), and thereupon sticking him in the behind with a pin (UCS). You can imagine the CR that happened the next Sunday when the horse trotted up to the church, and the minister, sitting proudly on its back, called out the familiar "Whoa."

When respondent conditioning takes place, the organism learns a new correlation between two previously unrelated stimulus events—the conditioned stimulus (CS) now signals the onset of the unconditioned stimulus (UCS). Once this S–S pairing has been learned, the organism responds to the signal just as if it were the original, powerful instigating stimulus (for example, food or electric shock).

UCS - - - - → **Elicits** - - - - → **UCR**
(food)   (salivation)

CS - - - - - - - - - - → **Elicits** - - - - → **CR**
(bell)   (salivation)

In this procedure neither stimulus is under the organism's control; both occur regardless of what it does. Either they are programmed by the natural (or designed) environment (as with the water-pressure change and hot water in our shower example), or they are contrived by a "trainer" who sets out to establish a conditioned response in a human or animal subject. (See *P&L* Close-up at left.)

In addition to studying the conditioned salivary response (called *appetitive conditioning*), Pavlov also investigated *aversive conditioning* in dogs by using electric shock to the paw as the UCS, leg withdrawal or flexion as the UCR, and a variety of sound and visual stimuli as the CS. Since the pain of the shocks was unavoidable because the animal was strapped into a harness, the animal reacted to the noxious stimulus not only with leg flexion but also with a generalized fear response. Any conditioned stimulus that preceded the unconditioned one regularly—a bell, a tone, or even the sight of a cat, a dark experimental chamber, a smiling experimenter—came to elicit fear.

Suppose you were an observer in such a laboratory and were unaware of this conditioning history. What would you think when you saw the animal cringe, whine, and run away from a small cat, a dark room, or even a smiling observer? That it was "crazy"? What about human beings who have fears that are apparently irrational—"don't make sense"—fears of harmless insects, small spaces, darkness, hair, and literally hundreds of other objects and situations?

In the movie *The Diary of Anne Frank*, the arrival of Nazi SS troops was always preceded by the wailing siren of a squad car and followed by the perpetration of some horrifying action against the Jews. By the end of the movie, the peculiar sound of the siren alone (conditioned stimulus, CS) elicited strong feelings of revulsion (conditioned response, CR) in many members of the audience, in anticipation of the horror about to come (unconditioned stimulus, UCS)—as it undoubtedly did in those victims who actually experienced this symbol of danger and the events with which it came to be associated.

Not only physical stimuli but also words and other symbols can become conditioned stimuli. Such conditioning vastly extends the range of stimuli that can elicit reflexes, signal danger, or "stand in" for absent unconditioned stimuli. Words and symbols associated with significant events come to be substitutes for events, producing the same reaction as the events themselves. ▲ It is remarkable that many people all over the world experience strong internal reactions when a piece of cloth is raised on a pole and a band makes some musical sounds—if the cloth is their nation's flag and the sounds are the music of their national anthem.

Any stimulus that the organism can perceive can be used to elicit a conditioned response in any muscle or gland by an appropriate pairing of this conditioned stimulus with a biologically significant unconditioned stimulus.

One of the major trends in the psychology of learning over the last decade has been an ever widening view of the kinds of environmental events that can become conditioned stimuli. In fact, it appears that the only restrictions are the perceptual limitations of the organism. Whatever it can perceive, it can learn to value—or to see as frightening or dangerous.

In addition, the Russian investigator, Bykov (1957), after reviewing a large body of respondent conditioning research on the extent to which internal organs can be conditioned, concluded (our rough translation): "If it wiggles or squirts

naturally, it can be conditioned." So virtually anything we can become aware of can come to have meaning for us, positive or negative, and virtually any response we can make can come to be affected by these learned signals.

The Anatomy of Pavlovian Conditioning

How are these connections built up, and how are they broken when the environment changes and the conditioned stimulus is no longer a meaningful or trustworthy signal? The following is a summary of the major processes underlying respondent conditioning.

1. Generalized excitability. Even after a single pairing of a neutral and an unconditioned stimulus, the animal will respond to the conditioning situation by being more excitable. This may be great enough to trigger spontaneous motor reactions as well as glandular secretions. If it is a food response that is being conditioned, there is a "general alimentary excitation, a general preparation for future alimentary activity, the expectation of feeding in general that is supposed to

▲ This photo illustrates the commercial use of a conditioned stimulus. For word-saturated Americans, "WOW" has come to signal the height of intense, positive experience. Thus it is a powerful conditioned stimulus for advertisers to attach to a product about which they would like the public to feel intensely and positively.

follow. Then the reaction is concretized, and the animal awaits the definite conditioned stimulus that is followed by feeding, and focuses its attention on this stimulus" (Kupalov, 1961, p. 1050).

2. Temporal patterning (CS-UCS interval). Increasing the number of pairings of the conditioned and unconditioned stimuli increases the strength of the conditioned responses (up to some maximal level), but only under certain temporal relations between the two events. The most favorable interval between stimuli is about half a second between onset of CS and onset of UCS. This time interval is sufficient for the first stimulus to signal the second and to prepare the organism physiologically. Shorter time intervals reduce the signaling utility of the CS; longer ones allow time for other stimuli to occur, other responses to be activated, and a loss of attention to the specific CS.

The time interval itself can become the conditioned stimulus. If the unconditioned stimulus is presented repeatedly with a consistent interval between presentations, the subject learns to respond to the *interval* by making a response just before the time the UCS is due to appear. This is called *temporal conditioning*.

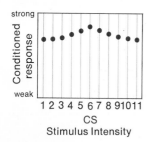 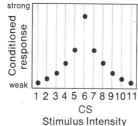

⬤ **STIMULUS GENERALIZATION GRADIENTS**

In the flat generalization gradient on the left, responses to stimuli of higher or lower intensity are similar to the response to the CS. In the steep gradient on the right, responses to stimuli of higher or lower intensity are sharply differentiated from response to the CS. Based on your own experience, if a conditioning procedure generates strong emotional responses, is the generalization gradient likely to be steep or flat?

3. Stimulus generalization. During the early stages of the development of a conditioned response, many signals similar to the primary one will evoke the response. This phenomenon is called *stimulus generalization*. The tendency to "confuse" stimuli early in conditioning occurs most readily between stimuli in the same sensory modality as the conditioned stimulus—tones of different pitch or lights of different brightness. For example, once you have learned about the discomfort that follows the sound of a dentist's drill, a similar sound that is higher or lower might set off the same response in you. But stimulus generalization can also occur between stimuli of different sensory modalities. The dog that is learning to salivate at the sound of a bell may also salivate if a bright light is flashed on.

If stimuli are arranged in a graduated series (e.g., from low to high) according to their relationship to the conditioned stimulus, the strength of response to each of the stimuli can be shown on a curve called a *stimulus generalization gradient*. When the organism responds similarly to many of the stimuli, its generalization gradient is said to be "flat"; when it discriminates among them and responds to each stimulus in proportion to its similarity to the original conditioned stimulus, the gradient is termed "steep." ⬤ As conditioning proceeds, the individual responds increasingly only to stimuli that are quite similar to the actual signal. As this happens, the gradient of generalization changes from a relatively flat curve to a steep one.

4. Discrimination and inhibition. While it may be initially useful for the organism to respond to all stimuli that might potentially have signal value, it must learn to differentiate or *discriminate* between relevant and irrelevant stimuli and to *inhibit* its response to all stimuli *not* associated with the unconditioned stimulus event. Conditioning can be thought of as a process in which differentiation wins over generalization.

The more distinguishable the *signal*, the more quickly it will be identified and attended to at the expense of the *noise* stimuli—irrelevant stimuli that are occurring at the same time. Thus a sharp discontinuity or difference in intensity between stimuli will speed up differentiation. In the shower example, the association between drop in water pressure and hotter water will be more quickly learned if the water-pressure change is marked and the rise in temperature is great than if the changes are small and gradual.

Even *not responding* can be a response. Although inhibition of a response is a passive act in a behavioral sense, it involves considerable activity at the neural level. All we see during conditioning is the overt activity, but many investigators believe that the most intriguing aspect of conditioning is the coordinating role of inhibitory processes in suppressing the inappropriate reactions to all the sensory inputs except the critical one.

After a response has been conditioned, of course, it may be temporarily disrupted by an unexpected noise or light or by stimulation from within the organism, such as fatigue, a full bladder, sexual arousal, or other motivational states.

5. Higher-order conditioning. One of Pavlov's colleagues, Krylov, found that after a morphine injection had elicited nausea and vomiting, the mere sight of the needle about to be injected could also produce vomiting—a typical conditioned response. But not only that: he found in addition that nausea came to be elicited by any stimulus regularly preceding the sight of a needle—alcohol on the skin, the box containing the needle, eventually even the laboratory room.

This process, by which a series of conditioned stimuli may, in turn, serve as a substitute for the original conditioned stimulus and themselves produce the response, is called *higher-order conditioning.* Once a conditioned stimulus has acquired the power to elicit a strong conditioned response, it can then be paired with any other stimulus that the organism can perceive and that second CS will come to elicit the conditioned response in the absence of both the original CS and the UCS. In this way, human behavior can come to be pervasively controlled by stimuli qualitatively very different from those originally present during conditioning. For example, gestures, words, or images can come to play this role.

6. Extinction. Since the actual connections between events in the environment change from time to time, it is vitally important that the connections established by conditioning not be permanent. Otherwise, we would not have the flexibility we need for responding appropriately to a changing environment. Once a conditioned stimulus no longer signals either danger or benefit, our continued response to it would be nonfunctional and perhaps harmful.

Fortunately for us, most such nonfunctional responding eventually stops when presentation of the conditioned stimulus is repeatedly *not* followed by the unconditioned stimulus: the conditioned response becomes weaker and eventually reaches zero intensity. The response is then said to be *extinguished,* and the trials that bring it about (CS + no UCS) are called *extinction trials.*

When a response is extinguished, does that mean it is gone forever? Not at all. Extinction is a special case of active inhibition, not loss of learning. This is demonstrated by the fact that after a rest period, the supposedly extinguished conditioned response comes to life again—though in somewhat weaker form—the first time the conditioned stimulus reoccurs. This phenomenon is called *spontaneous recovery.* If additional acquisition trials are given (CS + UCS), the response will return to its former vigor. If further extinction trials are given, it will become weaker and be permanently extinguished.

During extinction, a process takes place that is analogous to stimulus generalization during acquisition of a CR. Responses to stimuli not directly subjected to extinction training will also extinguish—in proportion to their similarity to

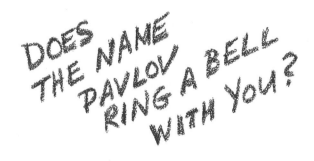

the conditioned stimulus. This spread of inhibition is known as *generalization decrement*.

Why do intense, irrational fear reactions, learned through respondent conditioning, sometimes persist and not extinguish even though no harm or danger ever follows? One answer is that people avoid situations where the thing they have learned to fear (snakes, small rooms, open spaces, heights) might appear, or they flee as soon as the feared object or situation is present or threatened. So there is never a chance to learn that it does not in fact signal danger or harm on the way. For the conditioned fear response to extinguish, conditions must be arranged so that the individual can experience the conditioned stimulus *not* being followed by danger or harm, or better yet being followed by a pleasant event, in which case new, *counterconditioning* can take place. These phenomena have been demonstrated in the laboratory.

When experimental dogs were trained to avoid a painful electric shock in the grill floor of one compartment of a shuttle-box by jumping quickly over a barrier into the "safe" side of the box, they learned to do so in only a few trials. After the tenth conditioning trial, shock was never presented in the formerly "danger" side of the box. Nevertheless, whenever the dogs were placed in that compartment they continued to jump into the other one—and did so without evidence of extinction for 500 trials! They never learned that the first side was now safe because they did not stay around long enough to learn that the correlation had been broken (Solomon, Kamin, & Wynne, 1953).

7. Strength of conditioning. We cannot measure the strength of conditioning directly but must infer it from some kind of observable, measurable behavior. Pavlov used *amplitude* of response—quantity of saliva secreted—as his measure of response strength. Other measures sometimes used are *latency* of response—how much time elapses between the onset of the conditioned stimulus and the response—and *frequency,* or rate of making a given response.

Strength of learning can also be measured by *resistance to extinction.* The more trials required to extinguish a conditioned response, the stronger it is assumed to have been.

Psychologists may use strength of conditioning to study not only learning ability but perceptual ability. We saw in Chapter 2 how Lipsitt and his colleagues tested whether infants could distinguish between two odors by determining whether the infants could learn to respond to one while inhibiting response to the other.

8. Pseudoconditioning. In some cases behavior similar to conditioned behavior occurs when in fact conditioning has not taken place. This phenomenon is generally due to a heightened state of excitability in the organism. In it, there is a change in the strength of responding as a result of experience but no actual learning of a specific stimulus-response association. (See *P&L* Close-up, p. 103.)

A Little Learning May Be a Dangerous Thing

If anything we perceive can come to be a signal for us and if any response we make naturally can come to be evoked by a learned signal, then we can expect that a vast amount of inappropriate conditioning will take place and for one reason or another continue to plague us instead of being extinguished. This is exactly what happens.

"Excess baggage" and schizokinesis. Some years ago, Liddell (1934), a psychologist at Cornell University, studied respondent conditioning using sheep as his subjects and electric shock as the unconditioned stimulus. The sheep soon learned to flex their about-to-be-shocked leg at the sound of a bell preceding the shock. But the leg flexion was also accompanied by marked changes in breathing, heart rate, and general activity. These responses, as well as the more specific one of leg withdrawal, were also undergoing conditioning: the CR had several components that the simple UCR did not.

More recently, Zeaman and Smith (1965) found that when light and shock are paired in conditioning the human cardiac response, a

The Worm That "Learns"
Turns on the Experimenter

What does a lowly flatworm have to tell us about the principles of conditioning? Planaria are the highest form of animal life capable of regeneration after being cut in half. They move by a process of muscular contraction and respond to aversive stimulation with such contractions. Early learning experiments (Thompson & McConnell, 1955) showed that these animals contract (UR) in response to an electric shock (US) and that this response can be conditioned to a light (CS). McConnell and his co-workers then sought to discover whether, if planaria so conditioned were cut in two and allowed to regenerate, the learning would be retained only by the animals with the conditioned heads, or by those grown from conditioned tails as well.

Half of a group of conditioned planaria were cut in two, while half remained intact. After the split halves had regenerated, all subjects were retested. Both groups of regenerated animals were found to have retained as much of the original learning as had the intact conditioned group (McConnell, Jacobson, & Kimble, 1959).

How far could such findings be extended? Does learning bring about a permanent change in body chemistry? Suppose the ground-up bodies of conditioned planaria were fed to unconditioned planaria — would the "cannibals" become superior learners? When McConnell tried this, the results appeared to support the hypothesis of a transfer of memory from a trained to an untrained generation of planaria (1962). You can imagine the excitement such a discovery created. Here at last was a use for old psychology professors: grind them up and feed them to the introductory psychology students!

But sadly, these provocative findings did not survive critical scrutiny by independent investigators. Hartry, Keith-Lee, and Morton (1964) employed rigorous controls in evaluating alternative explanations of the basis for superior learning in unconditioned planaria who had cannibalized their previously conditioned brethren. Seven different treatments were used in the experiment. One group of planaria was conditioned and then fed to other planaria; another was conditioned but remained intact. Other groups were not conditioned but were exposed to certain elements involved in the conditioning procedure (shock, light, or simply being handled by experimenters) and then fed to cannibals. Two groups received no stimulation of any kind; one of these groups became cannibal fodder; the other remained intact.

The five groups of cannibals and the two groups that had remained intact were then tested, using a double-blind technique, to see how many trials it took for them to reach the original criterion of learning. Experience made a difference. The unfed-inexperienced group performed worst. However, the actual process of conditioning the victims did not appear to be the critical factor in enhancing the conditionability of the cannibals. In fact, the cannibals that had eaten animals exposed to handling only and light only conditioned faster than those that had eaten "educated" animals. It appears that the faster learning, where it occurred, was not a function of an earlier conditioned memory trace, but simply of stimulation or nutrition. Other studies have had similar results (Jensen, 1965).

Thus the generalized enhancement of learning in cannibal planaria by means of prior "sensitization" of their victims appears to be nothing more than a form of *pseudoconditioning*. Our extended discussion of the controversy stirred up by the seemingly trivial question of what makes a worm turn shows the importance of several of the characteristics of psychological science we mentioned in Chapter 1:

1. There is many a slip between a psychological "discovery" and its "proof."

2. It is the most interesting ideas that have the greatest implications and become subjected to the most severe tests of disbelief.

3. The system of checks and balances inherent in the exercise of the scientific method must be policed by critical researchers who are willing to devote their efforts and talent to testing a conclusion independently before accepting it.

4. Even when the first explanation advanced for a "discovery" is proven untenable, further checking may yield other valuable explanations.

Pavlov's Respondent Conditioning   103

conditioning of respiratory responses also occurs. Similarly, Neal Miller (1969) reported a number of experiments in conditioning of autonomic responses in which responses other than those being conditioned were also affected. These other autonomic responses returned to their normal level of functioning only after continued training and differentiation of the selected conditioned response from the rest.

Because a conditioned muscular response may have autonomic and emotional components as well, extinction of a specific conditioned response does not guarantee that all the extra components of the response system will be extinguished too. Instead, they may linger on, resisting extinction indefinitely. As one psychologist has observed:

"The fact that conditional reflexes are so difficult to eradicate, once formed, makes the individual a museum of antiquities as he grows older. . . . He is encumbered with many reactions no longer useful or even . . . detrimental to life. This is especially true for the cardiovascular function, and it is these conditional reflexes that are most enduring. A person may be reacting to some old injury or situation which no longer exists, and he is usually unconscious of what it is that is causing an increase in heart rate or blood pressure. The result may be chronic hypertension. This may be the explanation of many cardiac deaths." (Gantt, 1966, p. 62)

Schizokinesis is the term coined by Gantt to refer to this dual reaction in which parts of a complex, conditioned response split and go their separate ways over the course of time. In many cases where individuals no longer show any overt behavioral response to the conditioned stimulus, it is still having an effect on them at a physiological level.

Such resistance to extinction of a once-significant signal stimulus long after it ceases to signal anything really coming is demonstrated in a study of reactions to "the call to battle stations" (Edwards & Acker, 1962).

Hospitalized Army and Navy veterans who had seen active service during World War II were exposed to a series of twenty sound stimuli, and their autonomic responses were measured by a recording of GSR changes. The biggest difference between men from the two services emerged when they heard a repetitive gong sounding at the rate of about 100 percussions a minute. This signal was used as a call to battle stations aboard U.S. Navy ships during the war, and it continued to elicit a strong autonomic response from the Navy veterans. Even though more than fifteen years had elapsed since this stimulus had signaled danger, the sailors showed a significantly more vigorous emotional response to it than did the soldiers. The probability of getting such a big difference by chance would have been less than one in a hundred.

Conditioned addictions. Of all addictions, the one that reduces life expectancy most is food addiction. Anyone can eat when hungry; the obese person learns to eat even when not hungry. Recent research (to be presented in Chapter 8) indicates that many extremely overweight people have a heightened sensitivity to cues associated with food and eating—the sight or smell of food, pictures of food, or seeing other people eating. Furthermore, environments in which overweight people normally eat when hungry become conditioned stimuli for eliciting eating even in the absence of hunger—while watching TV, movies, or sports events, listening to music, walking through the kitchen or dining room, and so on. One therapeutic procedure being tried out currently with some success involves decreasing these conditioned associations by restricting eating to just one place at predetermined times (Stunkard, 1972).

Experimental neurosis. Sometimes an extreme abnormal reaction pattern develops in subjects when the conditioning training places them under considerable stress. One of Pavlov's assistants first observed this reaction in a dog that had been conditioned to salivate in response to a circle projected on a screen. A discrimination was then established between the circle and an ellipse by a series of trials in which the circle was followed by food and the ellipse was not.

Next, the shape of the ellipse was changed by stages until it looked almost like a circle with one side slightly flattened. The dog continued to make appropriate discriminations, salivating only to the full circle, but when the point was reached where the two stimuli were almost the same, the discrimination broke down and got worse. Eventually, the animal could not even make the original simple discrimination. Even more dramatic were the accompanying behavioral changes. The formerly tranquil dog barked, squealed, tore at the apparatus, showed signs of fear of the room, and exhibited generalized inhibition leading to drowsiness and sleep. Similar reactions have been found in studies with rats, cats, and sheep.

This phenomenon has been called *experimental neurosis;* it is like neurosis in humans in that it:

a) results from prolonged stress, inescapable conflict, and inability to decide between competing alternatives;

b) involves behavior indicative of a generalized anxiety state;

c) is marked by "symptoms" — reactions that are unusual in the life of the organism and provide at best only a partial solution to the conflict; and

d) may persist without extinction for a lifetime, unless special counterconditioning therapy is provided.

Liddell (1956) reports symptoms enduring for thirteen or more years, as well as an increased incidence of premature deaths among sheep who were made experimentally neurotic. He relates one incident in which, when the experimenter returned after a year at another job, his 400-pound neurotic sow, Tiny, "by friendly overtures, lured him into a fence corner and attacked him so viciously that he required medical attention" (pp. 982–83).

The House That Pavlov Built

American behavioral scientists have surely added wings to the house that Pavlov built, but really only wings; the main house continues to overtower and to stand firm, little worn by wind and weather.

G. H. S. Razran, "Introductory Remarks" to *Pavlovian Conference,* 1961, p. 816

From Pavlov's serendipitous discovery of conditioned salivation in dogs while investigating the physiology of digestion has developed an approach to the study of behavior that to this day dominates many branches of Soviet psychology. In America, too, many psychologists who study the learning process consider themselves to be neo-Pavlovians, as do many neurophysiologists who are trying to identify what happens in the brain during the learning process.

In America, John B. Watson, the founder of the objective psychology *behaviorism,* went even further toward a psychology of stimulus-response connections and physiological events. He argued that behavior is composed *entirely* of glandular secretions and muscular movements and that these responses are determined by effective stimuli.

Thus for Watson the job of psychology was to identify and control the relationships between stimuli and these overt, observable responses. There was no point in studying conscious processes, mentalistic phenomena, or introspective accounts of the contents of the mind: behavior could be explained and predicted without them.

Watson's emphasis on observable, measurable responses as the basis for psychology ran counter to the prevailing trend of his time, which was to attribute all behavior to inherited tendencies and "instincts," ignoring the impact of environmental influences in shaping behavior. To those skeptical of the extent to which human behavior was modifiable through the process of conditioning, Watson pronounced:

"Give me a dozen healthy infants, well-formed, and my own specified world to bring them up in and I'll guarantee to take any one at random and train him to become any type of specialist

Close-up

The Sad Tale of Little Albert and the White Rat

Little Albert started out as a "normal," rather unemotional baby. He never reacted fearfully to any of the test situations devised by the experimenter. His reaction to the succession of objects suddenly thrust upon him was to reach and play. There were a white rat, a rabbit, a dog, a fur coat, a ball of cotton, and some masks. But he did startle and begin to cry at the unexpected loud noise of a steel bar being struck a sharp blow just behind him.

At the tender age of eleven months and three days, when the white rat was presented and he reached for it—*bong* went the steel bar. After two such experiences, the baby was whimpering. A week later when the rat again appeared on the scene, Albert had learned his lesson—he withdrew his hand before it touched his old playmate. Then systematic respondent conditioning was started in order to establish a strong negative emotional response to the white rat. For seven trials, rat and startling noise were paired. When next the rat was presented alone, Albert began to cry, turned, fell over, and crawled away with all his little might.

About a week later, the fear reaction had generalized from the white rat to the friendly rabbit. The dog frightened him, the fur coat made him cry, he pulled away from the cotton ball. Saddest of all, "he was again pronouncedly negative" when shown a Santa Claus mask. No such fear was shown to blocks or objects that did not share the apparently controlling stimulus dimension of "furriness."

Whether little Albert developed into a Scrooge who hated Christmas with its Santa Claus fear-reminders must remain a conjecture. The experimenters reported, "Unfortunately, Albert was taken from the hospital the day the above tests were made. Hence, the opportunity of building up an experimental technique by means of which we could remove the conditioned emotional responses was denied us" (Watson & Rayner, 1920).

I might select—doctor, lawyer, artist, merchant-chief, and, yes, even beggar-man and thief, regardless of his talents, penchants, tendencies, vocations, and race of his ancestors." (1926, p. 10)

Watson's work with one such healthy infant is described in the *P&L* Close-up at left.

The intervening years have brought convincing evidence that Watson's claim is far too extreme—that genetic structure as well as the social environment must be taken into account. As we shall see, too, evidence has accumulated that points to the need for studying cognitive factors in behavior. But even with these qualifications, the house that Pavlov built continues to be an impressive and much-lived-in edifice.

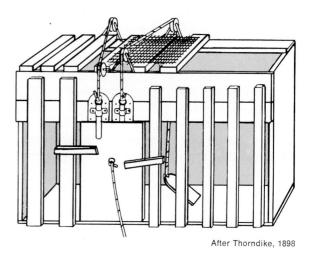

After Thorndike, 1898

◆ Thorndike's cats were confined in boxes like this one and food was placed outside of the box. To get out, the animal had to loosen a bolt, bar, or loop in order to release a weight that would pull the door open.

Conditioning Based on Consequences: Instrumental Conditioning

Learning what events in the environment are predictably related to each other is not enough for adaptation and survival. Any organism, as we have seen, must also learn what consistent relationships can be expected between its own actions and subsequent events in the environment—in particular, what changes it can achieve or prevent.

American psychology has from the first been centrally concerned with the study of learning and especially with the learning of this second kind of relationship—as befits a young, action-oriented, practical society, confident of its power to control its own destiny. Pioneering American psychologists developed their own techniques and concepts of what was happening, little influenced at first by the work going on elsewhere.

Thorndike's Cats in Puzzle Boxes

At about the same time that Russian dogs were salivating or flexing their muscles to assorted stimuli, American cats were learning to work their way out of strange boxes. In order to get out of their solitary confinement (and get food), hungry cats had to discover how to operate a latch on each of a series of seven different "puzzle boxes." American psychologist E. L. Thorndike, at Columbia University, reported the results of this pioneering study of the behavioral (as contrasted with Pavlov's more physiological) approach to learning back in 1898:

"When put into the box the cat would show evident signs of discomfort and of an impulse to escape from confinement. It tries to squeeze through any opening; it claws and bites at the bars or wire; it thrusts its paws out through any opening and claws at everything it reaches; . . . It does not pay very much attention to the food outside [the reward for the hungry cat], but seems simply to strive instinctively to escape from confinement. The vigor with which it struggles is extraordinary. For eight or ten minutes it will claw and bite and squeeze incessantly. With 13, an old cat, and 11, an uncommonly sluggish cat, the behavior was different. They did not struggle vigorously or continually. On some occasions they did not even struggle at all. It was therefore necessary to let them out of the box a few times, feeding them each time. After they thus associated climbing out of the box with getting food, they tried to get out whenever put in. . . . Whether the impulse to struggle be due to an instinctive reaction to confinement or to an association, it is likely to succeed in letting the cat out of the box. The cat that is clawing all over the box in her impulsive struggle will probably claw the string or loop or button so as to open the door. And gradually all the other nonsuccessful impulses will be stamped out and the particular impulse leading to the successful act will be stamped in by the resulting pleasure, until, after many trials, the cat will, when put in the box, immediately claw the button or loop in a definite way." (p. 13) ◆

From observations such as these on "trial-and-error learning," Thorndike began the study of what came to be known as *instrumental conditioning*. His methods and ideas became cornerstones in the American investigation of the learning process in humans and lower animals.

Let us briefly analyze what the cats did and how Thorndike explained what was happening in terms different from those used to explain respondent conditioning.

Mediating variables—drives, response hierarchies, and cues. To explain the cats' behavior, Thorndike inferred unseen, inner processes that *mediated*—intervened between—the observable events. For example, he believed that his cats in the puzzle boxes were motivated by *drive states*—strong internal stimuli that impelled them to action by energizing their behavior. Their behavior he thus saw as *emitted* behavior—behavior caused by internal conditions rather than *elicited* by an external, conditioned stimulus. ■

Thorndike viewed these inner drives as forcing a variety of responses from the individual—some innate and "wired in" according to the inherited nervous system of the species (meowing and hissing for cats, crying for human infants), others learned in previous experiences. All these responses, both innate and learned, made up the individual's response repertoire, some with a higher probability of being tried out than others.

When a cat was first put in a puzzle box, it tried many of these available responses, but in the course of several trials most of them dropped out. Although the responses were supposedly emitted in response to *internal* stimuli (hunger and fear being the likely candidates), the selection and narrowing down was guided by cues from *external* stimuli. Such external stimuli might help focus the subject's attention on the relevant parts of the environment (the latch or the food tray) or might serve as cues to indicate when a particular response was appropriate. For example, when a light was consistently on when food was available and off when

it was not, the animal's behavior would come to be guided by the presence or absence of the light. Although its "hunger" was constant, it would learn to work for food only when the light was on, since correct responding would be followed by food only then. In instrumental conditioning, the response to be learned is the one that is instrumental in obtaining the desired reward.

The law of effect. Like Thorndike's cats, you encounter many situations in which what you do makes a difference. If a coke machine regularly fails to deliver a coke after you deposit a coin, you learn that coin-dropping in that situation has no effect on that machine. Your behavior does not change the environment. But if you kick the machine and a cold coke appears and you quench your thirst, your behavior has had a consequence on the environment. Next time you are thirsty, you may go up to the coke machine and start kicking it (especially if no one is watching). Kicking the machine has thus become a dominant, highly probable response for you. If that fails to produce a coke, you may learn that the behavior that is followed by the coke is composed of two response units: first

Experimental Operations	Presumed Motivational State (Drive)	"Innate" Hierarchy of Overt Responses		Environmental Consequences (Stimulus Change)	What Is Learned
S_1 Confinement in a box ———→	Discomfort (fear) ———→	R_1 Meow ———→	None		Extinguished
		R_2 Hiss ———→	None		"
		R_3 Scratch ———→	None		"
		R_4 Freeze ———→	None		"
		⋮			
and		R_N Motion releasing ———→ latch	S_A	Escape confinement	S_1 ——→ R_N ——→ S_A
S_2 Deprived of ———→ food	Hunger ———→	R_1 Meow ———→	None		Extinguished
		R_2 Paw around ———→	None		"
		R_3 Sniff box ———→	None		"
		⋮			
		R_N Motion releasing ———→ latch	S_B	Obtain food reward	S_2 ——→ R_N ——→ S_B

■ **INSTRUMENTAL LEARNING: LETTING THE CAT OUT OF THE BOX**

In Thorndike's experimental situation two motives were assumed to be instigating action: fear and hunger. The same response leads to both escape and food. But Thorndike never knew whether both motivational states were necessary or whether the cats might have worked equally hard to get out if they had been well fed. Research today is more likely to study the result of one experimental operation at a time.

depositing the coin and then smartly kicking the recalcitrant machine. On subsequent occasions you will repeat the sequence, or else search for a coke machine that will deliver its contents for coin alone or for a more gentle kick.

In Thorndike's experiment, if the latch had been dropped by means of a sound-activated relay when the puzzled cats meowed or hissed, or if mama cat had come and opened the door then, the cats would have continued to meow or hiss on later trials. But meowing and hissing were not followed by freedom or food; in fact, they had no effect on the environment at all. So they were discontinued; in Thorndike's terminology, they moved down in the response hierarchy.

Thorndike thought that it was the *feeling of satisfaction* in accomplishment (another unobservable mediating variable) that made a successful response become more probable. He regarded these successful environmental consequences as goal events of "reinforcing states" and believed that connections between them and the responses that led to them were "stamped in" on successive training trials. According to his *law of effect,*

"Any act which in a given situation produces satisfaction becomes associated with that situation, so that when the situation recurs, the act is more likely than ever before to recur also. Conversely, any act which in a given situation produces discomfort becomes disassociated from that situation, so that when the situation recurs, the act is less likely than before to recur." (1905, p. 202)

Thorndike's law of effect was really little more than a modern restatement of the old doctrine of *hedonism* advanced by the philosopher Jeremy Bentham—that people will tend to behave in such a way as to gain pleasure and avoid pain. Nevertheless, for many years it served as the basic principle for that emerging American enterprise, "the psychology of learning."

Hull's Integrated Theory

Sometime later, Clark Hull (1943, 1952), at Yale University, attempted to formulate a comprehensive theory of learning that would not only integrate the findings of respondent and instrumental conditioning and make objective and precise the law of effect, but would be

applicable to social learning in humans as well as maze learning in lower animals. The major features of Hullian theory are:

a) What is learned is a connection between a stimulus and a response; the unit of learning is called *habit strength.*

b) *Reinforcement* is a necessary condition for learning. For a response to increase in habit strength, it must be followed immediately by a goal substance. Such substances, called *reinforcers,* gain their effectiveness by reducing the level of existing drive. The theory is therefore described as a *drive-reduction* theory of learning.

c) The learned connection between a stimulus and a response increases in magnitude gradually and continously with each reinforced practice trial; this learning represents a relatively permanent change in behavior.

Unfortunately, Hullian theory was left unfinished because of Hull's death in 1952. Its influence, however, has been a major one in American psychology, and other psychologists have refined and extended it (Spence, 1956).

▲ B. F. Skinner and friends.

Tolman's Purposive Behaviorism

On the west coast, E. C. Tolman (1932, 1950) at the University of California, Berkeley, rejected the view that learning involves the development of S–R bonds—"molecular" bits of behavior—in favor of a broader conception of learning. In Tolman's view, learning is represented by "molar" changes in cognitions as a result of interactions with one's environment. These "cognitions" are assumed to be built out of perceptions of and beliefs or knowledge about the experienced environment.

According to Tolman, organisms learn to expect an environment organized in meaningful patterns. They learn that some stimuli are signs that certain events will follow or are usually associated with other stimuli; thus stimuli not only function as response elicitors but also supply information, as cues or signs. These signs are part of a whole pattern that includes memories from past experience as well as data from current perceptions. Thus learned behavior is not merely the automatic, blind emission of responses that have been associated with particular stimuli and reward patterns in the past. Rather, learned behavior always involves implicit and explicit goals and also hypotheses and expectations about how to achieve them. Thus learning is purposive and rationally directed. Heresy for the traditional behaviorist—both in its attention to inner experience and in its assumptions of purposiveness and rationality!

Tolman's theory shares with Hull's an important role for needs and goals, but goes beyond what would be acceptable to a Hullian in the relationships postulated between them. According to Tolman's view, needs produce demands for goals, and rewards lead to *object-cathexis* (a term borrowed from Freud), which is the tendency to seek certain goals and avoid others.

Tolman's approach could also be described as one in which S–S connections, "cognitive maps," of the environment are learned. This cognitive approach maintains that the significant process in learning is the acquisition of *information* (including abstract concepts and generalizations) rather than of specific *responses.*

Conditioning Based on Consequences: Operant Conditioning

It is likely that along with Freud and Pavlov, B. F. Skinner was a familiar name to you even before you took a psychology course. Harvard's Professor Skinner is the author of a provocative novel, *Walden II* (1948)—which describes his behavioristically designed utopia—and more recently the chief prophet of "behavioral engineering" in his book *Beyond Freedom and Dignity* (1971). In between these literary efforts, Skinner has developed into a precise science what he calls the *experimental analysis of behavior* and has pioneered efforts to apply his techniques of learning in improving education and modifying the abnormal behavior of mental patients, delinquents, and other people with "behavior problems." ▲

From the outset, Skinner's approach has been characterized by its emphasis on observing the physical, measurable properties of responding and on developing a practical technology for controlling observable responses. There is no place in such an analysis of behavior for unobservable, inferred mental, motivational, or even physiological states or entities. For example, what did we really know about those cats of Thorndike's? What could we *see?* Meowing and scratching, yes; inner drives, no. Higher rate of occurrence of the successful response, yes; satisfaction, no. Cessation of the ineffective responses, yes; "stamping in" or "stamping out," no. In fact, if you conceptualize learning as a "stamping in" of connections, you may spend years looking for the wrong thing in the wrong place if what happens in learning is in fact quite different. Psychologists are much more aware today of the need to make their concepts precise and explicit and closely related to what *can* be observed.

Followers of Skinner hold that a learning situation can and should be described *entirely* in such terms that nothing need be said about what is happening within the organism. For example, they define "hunger" not by an inference about drives but by the experimental operation of with-holding food for a certain number of hours before the trial, or by a given percent of body weight loss after an organism has been on a deprivation schedule.

In this framework, instead of saying that hunger *motivated* the animal to work for food, they say that food deprivation made food a more effective reinforcer, as gauged by more rapid responding. Deprivation, amount and type of food, and rate of response are all overt, observable, measurable events.

Consequences, too, can be defined empirically. A *reinforcer* (or *reinforcing stimulus*) is defined as any stimulus that follows a response and increases the probability of its occurrence. If getting food as a result of opening a latch makes the latch-opening response more probable next time, then getting food is a reinforcer. In Skinner's words:

"A natural datum in a science of behavior is the probability that a given bit of behavior will occur at a given time. An experimental analysis deals with that probability in terms of frequency or rate of responding. . . . The task of an experimental analysis is to discover all the variables of which probability of response is a function." (1966, pp. 213, 214)

Operant Behavior

Like Thorndike, Skinnerian psychologists study behavior voluntarily emitted by the organism and then reinforced instead of involuntary behavior elicited automatically by a preceding stimulus. However, instead of using the term *instrumental*, which sounds uncomfortably purposive to psychologists who are trying to avoid mentalistic concepts, they use the term *operant*, indicating a response that operates on the environment (as distinguished from salivation and the other "respondents" studied by the Pavlovians). Actually, the terms *instrumental* and *operant* are used interchangeably by many psychologists, though *operant* remains Skinner's preferred term and that of his many students and disciples working in the field of behavior modification.

The "operant" responses studied by Skinner differ from the "instrumental" responses studied by Thorndike in one important way, however. Whereas Thorndike's cats had to learn new responses to escape from their puzzle boxes, Skinner's rats and pigeons are usually just learning to increase or decrease the rate of some response they are already making, such as pressing a lever or pecking a disk.

Operant level. The rate at which a freely available response occurs when its consequences are neither positive nor negative is called the *operant level* of that response. Each such response has an operant level for a given individual. The Skinnerian psychologist studies *change* in response rate as a result of various kinds, intensities, and timing of reinforcement. Stuttering, gesturing, swallowing while reading, and using plural nouns in speech are all examples of responses whose operant level might be studied or modified in human subjects.

What is a "reinforceable response"? Actually, what we arbitrarily designate as a "response" is only some segment of continuous behaving. Beyond the level of an efferent nerve impulse, there is no such thing as a single response. Even a muscle twitch is composed of many response components. The size of the unit we designate as a response can vary widely; if it is reinforced as a unit, the rate of the whole unit can be expected to increase. A hundred key presses, which as a unit produce reinforcement, could be an operant response, as could going to college for four years for one degree of reinforcement. So there is virtually no limit to how large or how small a "reinforceable response" can be.

Some units of behavior, such as muscle twitches, do not usually have a direct effect on the environment. But when an ingenious experimenter creates conditions in which they *do* have effects, their rate of occurrence changes accordingly. As we saw in the last chapter, even the rate of particular brain rhythms can be changed in

this way. Clearly, then, the claim of operant conditioning that *any response that can be reinforced quickly can be conditioned* rivals in significance that of respondent conditioning that *anything the organism can perceive can become a conditioned stimulus* and that anything that "wiggles or squirts naturally" can be conditioned.

The Basic Operant Conditioning Paradigm

Operant conditioning is the process by which behavior can be modified or, more specifically, by which the rate of emission of an operant response is controlled through environmental manipulations. The simple empirical statement for how this happens is:

If an operant response is emitted and followed by a reinforcing stimulus, the probability that it will occur again is increased

$$R \longrightarrow S^R$$

Those responses that have favorable environmental consequences are more likely to occur, and to do so at higher rates, than those that have no such effects. But the concept of reinforcement is not linked to any presumed drive states or "satisfactions." A *reinforcer* is simply defined empirically and pragmatically as any stimulus event that increases the probability of occurrence of any response. The relationship between the response and the reinforcer is arbitrary, and a stimulus is called a "reinforcer" only *after* it has been shown to influence the rate of responding.

The discriminative stimulus and stimulus control. Since the operant behavior is not the new thing to be learned (the organism already "knows" how to make sounds, move, touch, push, peck, etc.), what is learned is *when* to make the response that will be followed by reinforcing consequences. From all the available stimuli in their environment, animals and humans learn to identify—to *discriminate*—those particular ones that are signals for (correlated with) reinforcers that will come when they emit an operant response. These signals are called *discriminative stimuli* (symbolized by Skinner as S^D); they inform the organism of when a behavior will (or will not) be followed by a payoff. A discriminative stimulus "sets the stage" or "provides the occasion" for the organism to emit a voluntary operant response. It does not elicit the response in the sense that a bright light elicits an eye blink but simply signals, in effect, "If you do it now, you can get a reinforcer."

An extension of the basic operant conditioning paradigm that includes this discriminative stimulus is:

In the presence of a discriminative stimulus, an operant response is followed by a reinforcing stimulus.

$$S^D \qquad\qquad R \longrightarrow S^R$$

The dimming of lights in a public hall is the S^D for sitting in your seat, stopping talking, and attending to the (hopefully reinforcing) event about to unfold. Many professors who teach large lecture classes have difficulty getting their show going because they do not employ a salient, consistent discriminative stimulus that can be easily recognized—such as walking to the lectern and beginning to lecture immediately. One problem many students have on first dates is learning to "read" the discriminative stimuli projected by their date—they have to learn *when* it is OK to do what they already know how to do and receive the reinforcer they hope will be a consequence of doing it. Two practical applications of operant principles using discriminative stimuli are described in the *P&L* Close-up on p. 114.

Operant conditioners are concerned with bringing responding under the control of manipulable environmental stimuli. By controlling the reinforcing stimulus, they can control the rate or probability of a response. By controlling the appearance of the discriminative stimulus, they control when the response will be made. An organism is said to be "under stimulus control" when it responds consistently in the presence of a discriminative stimulus and not in its absence.

An organism's alertness to a discriminative stimulus can also be used to teach it to make discriminations between stimuli, even quite similar ones. The technique is to give reinforcement when responses are made in the presence of one stimuli but not when responses are made in the presence of the other. The first stimulus then becomes the *positive discriminative stimulus* (S^D), and the other becomes the negative discriminative stimulus (S$^\circ$ or S$^\blacktriangle$, pronounced "ess delta"). After repeated discrimination training, responding virtually always occurs in the presence of S^D only. (See *P&L* Close-up, below.) In fact, psychologists often use this technique to find out whether an organism can in fact distinguish between particular stimuli—between blue and green, for example, or between horizontal and vertical lines.

Close-up
To Err May Be Human, But . . .

Terrace (1963) has developed a technique for discrimination training in which subjects never make an error, even during the initial stages. What he did was to establish a red-green discrimination in pigeons (an easy discrimination for them to learn) and then superimpose horizontal lines on the red and vertical lines on the green (or the other way around). By fading the red and green gradually until only the horizontal and vertical lines were left, the subjects were able to learn the horizontal-vertical discrimination without making any mistakes.

Terrace's discovery is important for two reasons: (a) learning achieved in this way without errors is more stable later on, and, even more important, (b) it has provided a technique for teaching discriminations formerly thought to be impossible. For example, mental retardates have been taught perceptual discriminations that previously seemed to be beyond their capabilities (Sidman & Stoddard, 1969).

From Hunt and Peck to Search and Destroy

Operant conditioning of complex discriminations through appropriate reinforcement contingencies has many practical applications, some of which will be discussed in subsequent chapters. Two of the most fascinating applications of these principles have used pigeons: in one case, the pigeons substituted for workers on an assembly line in which defective drug capsules had to be found and sorted out; in the other, they were taught to guide missiles toward selected enemy targets during World War II.

Defective capsules, or "skags," made up about 10 percent of all capsules on the belt of an assembly line in a drug company. Employees had been performing the monotonous job of hunting for skags as the belt moved along endlessly. To emancipate them from this drudgery, Verhave (1966) trained pigeons to be quality-control inspectors. During training, capsules moved along on a belt at about two per second past a small window. Pecking a disk when a skag appeared delivered a reinforcement; pressing a different disk when the capsule was acceptable delivered no food but moved the next capsule into view. Wrong pecks brought no food and a thirty-second blackout. Within one week of daily discrimination training, the birds had become capable of taking over on the inspection line with 99 percent accuracy (and would have done so if the union had not intervened).

During World War II, B. F. Skinner reasoned that if pigeons could learn to vary their responses continuously according to the demands of a constantly changing stimulus situation, then they could be put in nose cones of missiles to guide them in searching out and destroying selected targets. The feasibility of such a scheme was demonstrated by Skinner as part of Project Orcon (ORganic CONtrol). During the discrimination training, reinforcement was made contingent on pecking only at the center of a target (in the form of an enemy ship) that appeared on a screen. When a gold electrode on the pigeon's beak touched the screen, an electronic circuit in the missile sensed the exact location of pecks on the screen. The missile was held on course when pecking was in the center of the screen, but changed its course depending on any other location of the pecks. Shown here are some frames of a patriotic bird's-eye view of a target about to be destroyed (Skinner, 1960).

Conditioned reinforcers. Any discriminative stimulus that predictably sets the occasion for reinforced responding can in time come to be itself reinforcing—to increase the rate of a response that it follows. When this happens, it is called a *conditioned reinforcer,* or *secondary reinforcer.* Thus if baby's approach in the presence of a smile is repeatedly followed by a tasty treat, the smile will become a conditioned reinforcer for approach even in the absence of the treat. In fact, in wealthy, technologically advanced countries, such conditioned reinforcements are far more important in controlling behavior than primary reinforcers that have biological consequences. Just consider, for example, the many responses you will emit to obtain a rectangular piece of green paper with the picture of a United States President on it.

Smiles, nods, pats on the back, and money all represent a class of *generalized conditioned reinforcers* that can be used to control a wide range of responding. Such reinforcers carry the burden of human social interaction and bridge the gap between behavior and its eventual primary reinforcement. In some cases, people treat the conditioned reinforcer as if it had biological significance and begin to value it for itself and hoard it. Know any such people?

Although conditioned reinforcers are more variable than primary reinforcers in their effect on learning, they are often more effective for a teacher or experimenter to use because: (a) they can be dispensed rapidly, (b) they are portable, (c) almost any available stimulus event can be used for a conditioned reinforcer, (d) they often do not lead to satiation, (e) their reinforcing effect may be more immediate since it depends only on perception and not on biological processing of primary reinforcers. We will see in Chapter 12 that the principle of reinforcing behavior with tokens exchangeable later for a variety of tangible rewards is now being used extensively in behavioral modification programs with humans.

Response-reinforcer contingencies. At the time you are making any response, many environmental events are occurring. Indeed, the environment is constantly changing even when you are *not* responding. How, then, do you know which events your behavior is affecting? It is generally agreed that you can say that an environmental event is *contingent* on your behavior—if it follows that behavior with some degree of regularity (a high probability but not necessarily 100 percent).

The idea of *behavioral contingency* is perhaps the most important concept in operant conditioning. By setting up different contingencies—different relationships between responses and reinforcers—those who use the operant conditioning approach can make a given response more or less probable over time. They do this through changing the timing and frequency of events known to be reinforcers, making them available after the desired response but not at other times. When a reinforcer is made contingent on (available only after) a desired response, that response becomes more probable.

Operant conditioners assume that any response that keeps occurring is being maintained by a payoff of some kind. Getting the payoff is contingent on making the response, so it continues—however undesirable or irrational or even bizarre it may appear to an observer and even though it brings other consequences that cause suffering for the individual. To understand it, one must discover what the payoff is. This is what operant conditioners mean by *experimental analysis of behavior.*

To change behavior, new payoff relationships must be arranged that make the payoff contingent on desired behavior instead and prevent payoff from being achieved by the undesirable behavior that is to be eliminated. For example, instead of paying attention to and giving in to a whining child (thus reinforcing and maintaining the whining), the parent is taught to reinforce desirable behavior and to do so only when the child is not whining.

Fuller discussion of the applications of these techniques will appear in later chapters. For now, it is important to note that in this approach, unlike many others in psychology, the cause of any conditioned behavior is assumed to be specifiable environmental contingencies and not mental events, personality characteristics, or other inner states.

Five kinds of contingencies are possible between responses and reinforcers—three that increase the rate of an operant response and two that decrease it. Response rate *increases* when responding is followed by (1) a positive reinforcing stimulus, (2) escape from an aversive stimulus, or (3) avoidance of an aversive stimulus. The rate *decreases* when responding is followed by (4) an aversive stimulus (*punishment*) or (5) the absence of any reinforcer (*extinction*). These five contingencies are diagrammed in the illustration. ◆

Superstitious relationships. Perhaps the most fascinating relationship between responses and stimuli that follow them occurs when, in fact, *no relationship* exists between them, but the individual believes that one does. One day a tennis player, in dressing for the game, puts on his left sock, right sock, right shoe, and left shoe in that order. He then wins the game. Next time, he puts his socks and shoes on in a different order, and he loses the game. With as little as one "learning" trial, some people (including at least one well-known former tennis star) have come to believe that the outcome of their game was contingent on the behavior of putting on their socks and shoes in one inviolable order.

Consider another example of this type of learning. A man who calls himself Orpheus tells you that he has the power to make the sun rise by singing to it. Being, by now, scientifically skeptical, you demand a demonstration of this environmental control. Orpheus begins to sing at about 5 A.M. and soon the sun rises. He can repeat this demonstration for you daily, showing that his response is always followed by this change in the environment. You now suggest another test; omit the singing and see if the sun still comes up. But Orpheus must reject such a test. The consequence of his not singing would surely be the sun's not rising, and for the sake of the world he dare not risk such a dire consequence.

This example can be seen as accidental operant strengthening of a *coincidental* relationship between behavior and reinforcers. The rituals gamblers use in trying to change their luck illustrate their learned belief that something they were doing caused the dice or cards to fall a certain way. Such accidentally conditioned responses are called *superstitions*.

When the environmental consequences are vital for an individual or a group, a superstitious response is extremely resistant to extinction. This is true for two reasons. First, as in the case of Orpheus, the risk involved in not making the response, *if* the connection *were* a causal one, would be greater than the gain in knowledge from finding out that one's behavior was not producing the effect. Second, if the individual believes in the validity of the superstition, refraining from the "necessary" act might produce other changes in his or her behavior that *would* directly affect the event in question. This is often seen among students who have a special pen or pair of jeans that they always use for taking final exams. If the pen is lost, or the filthy jeans are thrown out by an exasperated parent, they may indeed do poorly on the exam because of expectation of failure and distracting thoughts about "their luck running out."

The development of such superstitions can be easily demonstrated in the laboratory. A hungry pigeon is confined in a box with a feeding mechanism that automatically dispenses a pellet of food every fifteen seconds, regardless of what the pigeon does. Whatever response the pigeon happens to be making when the food is delivered then becomes a reinforced response, and the probability of its occurrence is increased. Different stereotyped behavior patterns are likely to emerge in different subjects—turning counterclockwise, turning in a circle several times before going to the food dispenser, jerking the head in one direction, as well as other "bizarre" movements.

1. Reward Conditioning   **increases operant rate**

S^D	R	is followed by	S^{R+}
Discriminative Stimulus	Operant Response		Positive Reinforcing Stimulus
[coke machine]	[put coin in slot]		[get refreshing drink]

2. Escape Conditioning   **increases operant rate**

S^D	R	is followed by	S^{R-}
Discriminative Stimulus	Operant Response		Negative Reinforcing Stimulus
[heat]	[fanning oneself]		[escape from heat]

An unpleasant situation (S^D) is escaped from by making a selected operant response. Escape is a reinforcing stimulus, and it is called a *negative* reinforcing stimulus because the event escaped is negative (undesirable).

3. Avoidance Conditioning   **increases operant rate**

S^D	R	is followed by	S^{R-}
Discriminative Stimulus	Operant Response		Negative Reinforcing Stimulus
[during WWII, in Britain, sound of rocket with time-delay explosives]	[run for shelter]		[avoid effects of explosion]

A stimulus signals the organism that an unpleasant event will occur soon; responding in the time interval between the discriminative stimulus and the signaled event avoids the feared event altogether. In animal learning research, the S^D is typically a light which signals electric shocks.

4. Punishment   **decreases operant rate**

S^D	R	is followed by	S^A
Discriminative Stimulus	Operant Rate		Aversive Stimulus
[attractive match box]	[playing with matches]		[getting burned]

When punishment contingencies are used, the individual cannot escape or avoid but experiences the aversive event each time the response is made.

5. Operant Extinction   **decreases operant rate**

R	is followed by	$\cancel{S^R}$
Conditioned Operant		No reinforcing stimulus

A conditioned respondent that is emitted and is *not* followed by a reinforcing stimulus decreases in rate and becomes more variable in its form (topography).

Punish the Response, Not the Person

It is written in the Bible: "He that spareth the rod hateth his own son" (Prov. 13:24). And a well-known Chinese proverb dispenses the wisdom, "Beat your child every day. If you don't know why, he does." Punishment is thus assumed by many to "build character," "teach right from wrong," and prevent children from becoming self-indulgent, strong-willed, spoiled tyrants. Indeed, the argument is that children must be punished for their own good.

Within psychology, too, there are advocates of punishment for directing behavior change: "There is no indication from any data that any one of these procedures [extinction, satiation, stimulus change, physical restraint, and response incompatibility] provides an effect which is as immediate, enduring, or generally effective as that produced by the proper use of punishment techniques" (Johnson, 1972, p. 1051).

But voices have been raised in opposition to the use of punishment in the management of human affairs. "All punishment is mischief. All punishment is itself evil," said English philosopher Jeremy Bentham. French essayist Montaigne wrote: "I have never observed other effects of whipping than to render boys more cowardly, or more wilfully obstinate." American writer Eric Hoffer pointed out the rewarding "side effects" of punishment to the punishing agent rather than to the one who is punished when he noted: "Our sense of power is more vivid when we break a man's spirit than when we win his heart." Black psychologists Grier and Cobbs maintain that "beating in childrearing actually has its psychological roots in slavery." Other psychologists report that it is a relatively inefficient means of exerting control, since it breeds rebellion and requires surveillance, and also that it is a statement of one's failure to use positive reinforcement contingencies effectively (Baer, 1970; Solomon, 1964).

Perhaps some of the heated controversy here may be resolved by reference to a semantic distinction that those in the field of behavior modification insist on:

Responses are reinforced,
people are rewarded.

Extending this distinction to the effective and humane use of punishment, we would add:

Undesirable *responses* may be punished;
people should not be.

And as a corollary, it is well for us, and punishing agents everywhere, to be reminded that:

Although *responses* may be undesirable, *people* should never be made to feel that *they* are undesirable.

Does punishment work? As we have seen, a stimulus is called a *positive reinforcer* if it is given as a consequence of a response and increases the probability of that response. It is called a *negative reinforcer* if avoidance or escape from it increases the probability of the response. A stimulus that is given as a consequence of an undesired response to achieve a *decreased* probability of that response is called *punishment*. In this perspective, the principles of punishment are comparable to those of positive reinforcement, except that punishment *decreases* anticipated probability of responding, whereas positive reinforcement *increases* it.

Stimuli that punish us are a regular part of our physical environment. When we bump into a chair in a dark room, we get hurt. But when should such stimuli be used in social situations—or should they at all?

The basic goals of even the most benevolent parents, teachers, and others involved in behavioral management are to *start* some behaviors, *maintain* some, and *stop* some others from occurring (especially at certain times and places). Positive reinforcement clearly is the most effective technique for the first two, starting and maintaining desired behavior—for getting something that is happening a little to happen more often or for getting a behavior you like to continue. But when you are trying to stop a persistent act that is for some reason undesirable, positive reinforcement alone may not be enough. In such cases, punishment that follows the principles outlined below may work, but if and only if

it is administered within an overall positive context. If not, you may win the battle but lose the war.

a) *Alternative responses.* There should always be available in the situation a response that the individual can make that will not receive the punishing stimulus, but will be positively reinforced.

b) *Response and situational specificity.* It should be made explicitly clear what specific response is being punished, why, and what alternatives are possible. In addition, the person whose responses are being punished should be made to realize that the aversive social interaction with the punisher is restricted to the situation in which the punished response occurs.

c) *Timing.* The punishment should follow the response immediately and on every occurrence of the response.

d) *Escape.* There should be no unauthorized means of escape, avoidance, or distraction.

e) *Intensity of punishing stimulus.* The punishing stimulus should be great and at the highest reasonable level.

f) *Duration.* Prolonged punishment is to be avoided.

g) *Conditioned punishing stimuli.* A neutral stimulus consistently paired with the noxious punishing stimulus may be used to reduce the frequency of responding without harming the individual.

h) *Displays of sympathy, affection, etc.* Punishers should *not* provide positive reinforcement in connection with punishment. If they do, it may be sufficient to sustain (become the reason for emitting) the to-be-punished response. Punishment should signal an extinction period for the punished response, a period when it wins no positive reinforcement.

i) *Time-outs.* Punishment effects are obtained with use of "time-out periods" in which desired positive reinforcement is withheld because of undesirable responses (no television viewing today because you didn't do your homework last night).

j) *Motivation.* Motivation for making the punished response should be reduced.

k) *Generalizations from acts to dispositions.* Under *no* circumstances should the punisher generalize from the specific response to character traits of the person ("You're no good," "stupid," "incorrigible," etc.) on the basis of the punished response. These inferences about personal traits remain in the person's consciousness long after the punished response has been extinguished and the punishment is forgotten. (List adapted from Parke & Walters, 1967; Azrin & Holz, 1966)

When is punishment counterproductive? Although there is substantial evidence for the effectiveness of the judicious, controlled use of punishment as one method in a program of behavior management that generally emphasizes positive reinforcement, punishment is usually counterproductive. This is because in its nonlaboratory use by teachers, parents, police, hospital aids, friends, spouses, bosses, and others it is rarely used in accordance with the principles listed above, which were derived from controlled research. Rather, it is used indiscriminately and typically because of the motives of the punisher, which are not pertinent to the task of reducing the probability of a specific punished response.

Let us review some of the reasons why the everyday use of punishment may elicit more undesirable responses than it reduces:

a) Punishment often arouses strong emotional responses in the punisher and the punished that generalize beyond the punishment situation (punisher may derive pleasure from it; punished may learn to fear, resent, hate punisher and/or have lower self-esteem).

b) It is often difficult to apply the punishing stimulus immediately and consistently.

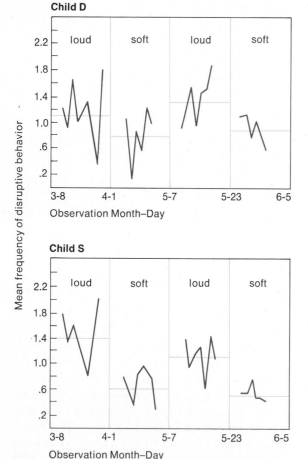

Child D

Mean frequency of disruptive behavior

Observation Month–Day

Child S

Observation Month–Day

After O'Leary et al., 1970

■ **DISRUPTIVE BEHAVIOR OF TWO CHILDREN WITH LOUD AND SOFT REPRIMANDS**

c) It is too easy for the punisher to underestimate the severity and intensity of the punishment and thus abuse it. (See *P&L* Close-up, p. 121.)

d) It becomes a general learning situation in which the meaning of "social power" is exemplified. The punisher, by virtue of age, sex, strength, or credentials, is seen as having the right to define what is "desirable" behavior and what is not, and to institute actions against the powerless person (which are condoned by society). Those who are punished learn to follow this model, also using punishing strategies for controlling the behavior of others.

e) As usually employed, punishment only suppresses and inhibits the response during surveillance. This leads to the twin beliefs that surveillance is necessary to assure good behavior and that the individuals being punished are unable to learn to manage their own behavior.

f) Punishment often occurs in social situations involving people other than the punisher and the person whose responses are being punished. The presence of these others may add to the humiliation felt by the individual; they may even add to the punishment. Or their presence may bias the behavior of the punisher. For example, the punisher may be concerned about his or her image and use punishment because any desired change that occurs will be "credited" to him or her rather than to the punished person. Or the punisher may overreact and use the occasion as a lesson for the group.

In a study of the spontaneous use of punishment by schoolteachers, two children from each of five classes were observed for a four-month period. These children had a high frequency of classroom behavior for which their teachers reprimanded them publicly. Almost all reprimands were loud, heard by most of the class. The reprimands were not particularly effective in reducing the frequency of the disruptive behavior.

During Phase 2 of the study, teachers were asked to use "soft" reprimands, audible only to the child being reprimanded. In almost all cases, disruptive behavior decreased when soft reprimands were used. In Phase 3, loud repri-

mands were reinstated with an accompanying increase in frequency of disruptive behavior. In Phase 4, to demonstrate convincingly the counterproductivity of loud, public reprimands and the effectiveness of soft, personal ones, soft personal ones were again used by the teachers. Again disruptive behavior declined in virtually all cases where the teacher made the punishing stimulus not a public announcement to the student's peers but a soft, personal reprimand intended only for the student (O'Leary et al., 1970). ■

A new area of research is emerging in which the focus is on the punisher rather than the punished. Efforts are being made to identify the particular social, cultural, and environmental variables that influence whether a person faced with the task of managing the behavior of other people will resort to punishment, to positive reinforcement, or to restructuring the environment (Banks, 1973; Banks, Zimbardo, & Phillips, 1974).

Close-up
**"There's Only One Way
to Teach the Little Brats . . ."**

Speak roughly to your little boy,
And beat him when he sneezes;
He only does it to annoy,
Because he knows it teases.

Lewis Carroll, *Alice's Adventures in Wonderland*, 1865

In many cases punishment of children is carried to extremes, such that children are seriously abused—physically and psychologically damaged. In fact, thousands are killed annually—at the hands of their parents.

The "battered-child syndrome" is analyzed in Chapter 14, but it is appropriate here to examine briefly the results of a series of interviews with the mothers of "abused" children and those in a comparison group whose children were not abused. *Abused* in this study was defined as "multiple bone fractures traceable to physical assault by parents" (Elmer, 1971).

In families where child abuse was present, discipline was achieved by a variety of physical means of control, including whipping, scolding, shaming, shaking, and deprivation. Reasoning or avoidance of conflicts were rare. "These parents tended to see even small infants as needing discipline and deliberately misbehaving" (p. 62). Many of these mothers believed that even very young, immature children of 6 to 9 months had "tempers," acted out of spite, knew right from wrong, and deliberately did the wrong thing. When asked how they would respond if their baby (of 6 months of age or older) struck or spat at them, the overwhelming majority replied that they would retaliate physically "to show him that he is *not* to do that kind of thing."

"The mothers involved in this study usually discriminated very little between discipline and teaching. When asked how they would attempt to teach the baby some new behavior representing a real learning effort for him, they most frequently responded in terms of scolding or spanking to get him to learn after first giving verbal instructions. The investigators feel that infants are punished physically more often than is realized. When it is common practice to strike babies, however lightly, with the goal of teaching them, the laws of probability indicate that some babies are going to be struck too hard and that some will be injured."(p. 78)

But many of the parents of nonabused children also punished their babies physically—the difference being in the severity and frequency of the punishment. Eighty-seven percent of *all* the mothers studied were slapping the hands or buttocks of their children by the time they were 24 months of age.

Interesting social class and sex differences were found. According to the mothers' reports, upper-class mothers tended to punish more for aggressive acts, middle-class mothers for excessive, irritating, or dangerous activities, and lower-class mothers for "misconduct," such as excessive demands, disobedience, or crying. Across all social classes more girls were punished at earlier ages: by 9 months, 31 percent of the girls but only 5 percent of the boys were being punished. At 18 months, 70 percent of the girls and 50 percent of the boys were being punished.

Skinner's Box and Cumulative Record

Special apparatus, electronic programming equipment, and a unique means of recording changes in the response rate have been designed for investigating the stimulus conditions that modify the rate of operant responding.

The apparatus (affectionately called a Skinner box) is a highly simplified, restricted environment in which the various discriminative stimuli to be studied can be presented clearly without interference from distracting, competing, or irrelevant stimuli that would occur in the organism's natural environment. Lights, colors, or shapes are typical S^D (used with pigeons, the typical subject in this research) and are presented on illuminated disks. The operant response of pecking a disk or pushing a lever is made more probable by having those items be the only aspects of the physical environment that the subject can easily manipulate, or operate upon. A food or water cup and a light to signal when a reinforcer is available in it, completes the Skinner box. ▲

Electronic programming equipment is necessary to control precisely the presentation of stimuli, monitor responses, and activate the reinforcing device. It also can arrange complex patterns of reinforcement.

Response rate is conveniently measured on a cumulative record. This record plots each response as it occurs, totaling them all up in cumulative fashion over each time interval. A pen is placed against a paper and either the pen or the paper (usually the latter) is moved along sideways at a constant speed, so many inches per period of time. As it moves, responses are recorded automatically: at each response, the pen moves upward a little. The more responses made in a given time period, the more accumulated upward steps of the recording pen there will be on the section of paper that has moved past the pen during that interval.

Time passing is thus shown by horizontal distance on the line; responses, by vertical distance. A high rate of responding gives a steep cumulative curve; a low rate of responding gives a less steep one.

It is also possible to look at the shape (*topography*) of a cumulative curve and see how the rate of responding has changed during the time interval recorded. Typically in a new situation, the curve goes up very slowly and irregularly at first, and there may be long pauses between responses; during these pauses, the recording pen simply moves horizontally along the paper. Then as learning proceeds, the cumulative curve shows less variability and becomes steeper. A skilled researcher can read a subject's response curve much like an X-ray plate, to see the changes over time and find out what the behavioral effects of different patterns of reinforcement were. ●

▲ The "Skinner box" designed for use with pigeons delivers a pellet of food (via the lower opening) when the bird pecks the key. The rat obtains food by pressing a bar. The floor grid of the rat's box can be electrified to deliver aversive stimulation.

Reinforcement Scheduling

Every reinforcement is part of some schedule, whether systematically arranged or haphazard. Modification of behavior requires discovering the schedule currently controlling an individual's pattern of responding, and then changing it.

Many years ago, when the then young B. F. Skinner was secluded in his laboratory over a long weekend, he stumbled by accident onto an important discovery: namely, that there are times when less of a good thing is better. Realizing that he had not stocked up enough food pellets for his hard-working animals, Skinner decided to make do by giving them a pellet only every other time they responded correctly.

Surprisingly, he found no difference in learning rate: *partial reinforcement* appeared to be as effective as *continuous reinforcement* (one response, one pellet). But the real discovery came when the subjects were put through *extinction* training. *Acquisition of responding under conditions of partial reinforcement made responding more resistant to extinction!* After being trained with only partial reinforcement, the subjects persevered longer when the reinforcer was no longer available. This "partial reinforcement effect" is a reliable one; it has been found repeatedly with many different animal species, including humans.

Thus, if you want someone to continue to emit a response when you are no longer around to reinforce it, it is better to have programmed your reinforcers initially so that they were part of a partial schedule of reinforcement even when you were there all the time.

Once we recognize the principle that reinforcers on other than a one-to-one relationship with responses can control responding in predictable ways, we can inquire into what ways different *schedules of intermittent reinforcement* affect behavior.

Ratio schedules. As we have seen, a "response" is sometimes considered to be made up of a class of response units, all of which must be run off before any reinforcement is presented. If the same number of units of work earns a rein-

forcement each time (like getting pay for piece work), the schedule is called a *fixed ratio (FR) schedule.* In the laboratory, a pigeon might have to peck a key anywhere from two to over a hundred times before getting a single pellet. "FR-25," for example, would be laboratory shorthand for "one reinforcement for each twenty-five responses." Winning the Perfect Attendance Award is on an FR schedule of the total number of days you must come to class before receiving the reinforcer. FR schedules produce very high rates of responding in the

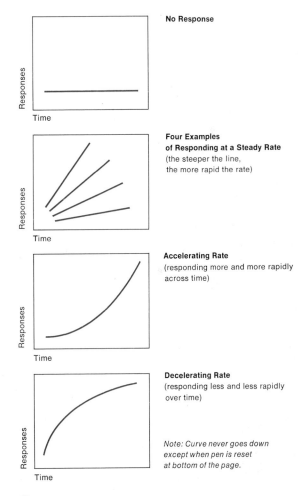

No Response

Four Examples of Responding at a Steady Rate
(the steeper the line, the more rapid the rate)

Accelerating Rate
(responding more and more rapidly across time)

Decelerating Rate
(responding less and less rapidly over time)

Note: Curve never goes down except when pen is reset at bottom of the page.

● **HOW TO READ A CUMULATIVE RECORD**

laboratory, as can be seen from the cumulative record shown in the diagram. Subjects learn to count on such schedules. ◆

But the world is not always arranged in so orderly a fashion as described by fixed ratios. Sometimes the world is a slot machine—you cannot tell whether one or a few or only a great many responses will eventually result in hitting the jackpot. As long as you occasionally get a payoff, this *variable ratio (VR) schedule* will keep you responding at a high rate for a long time. The possibility that the next response will get the big reward is what keeps gamblers gambling on VR schedules.

Interval schedules. It may be not *how much* work you do that brings the reinforcement but *when* you do it. Learning to look busy when the Man (employer, lab instructor, police officer, head resident) makes the rounds may be enough to assure getting your just rewards. When reinforcement is set on a temporal basis, it is theoretically being given at a single time for all the responses during the preceding interval. Actually, however, early responses bring no reinforcement and may not have any effect on whether it comes later. For a pigeon in a Skinner box, only the *last* response—the one that triggers the feeding mechanism—need be made.

If the interval is of a constant duration each time, say once every ten seconds, or even once every week (as with salaried workers), the schedule is called a *fixed interval (FI) schedule.* FI schedules reveal a typical, but peculiar,

curve with a "scalloped" typography. After each reinforced response, the subject ceases relevant responding for a time and performs "time-out" responses. As the time for the next payoff approaches, relevant responding switches on and increases sharply until the reinforcement occurs. This effect is called "scalloping." It looks as if the subjects are learning to tell time. Any work system employing long FI reinforcement schedules must use surveillance during the interval to keep the workers from dallying during the "time-out" period immediately following a reinforcement—the "Monday letdown" syndrome.

If reinforcement is given on a temporal basis but the interval varies from one time to the next, it is called a *variable interval (VI) schedule.* One time you might have to wait a long time before getting a single reward; then you might get a second or third reward or more after only a short wait. But when you think "you've got it!" the next reward may be a long time in coming. This appears to be the reinforcement history of many people in the entertainment field. Trout fishermen, who also live by VI schedules and don't quit, probably learn "patience" as a by-product of such a schedule.

Schedules of reinforcement may occur in mixed forms and may be quite complex; those described here are only the most basic varieties. Schedules can be designed to generate high levels of responding or to ensure continuous, steady responding over time. ■ Some schedules even suppress behavioral output, by reinforcing waiting and nonresponding. In fact, animals have even learned to run through a maze or down an alley at whatever speed yields a larger or more immediate reward (Logan, 1960, 1972). And there is evidence that humans not only learn to respond at particular speeds but even learn to *learn* at the particular speeds that are positively correlated with reward.

Delay of reinforcement: Late may not be better than never. Whatever the schedule of reinforcement, reinforcers, to be effective, must be "quick on the draw." The more prompt the better; in fact, if too much time elapses between the terminal response in a sequence of behavior

◆ "FR 25! PASS IT ON!"

and its reinforcement, the effect of reward is completely wasted.

One would think that educators would make use of this simple principle to be sure that good student performance was promptly reinforced, but alas, as your own reinforcement history most probably illustrates, this is not so. Too often, reinforcement in the classroom comes long after the effort expended, and when it comes, it is often a general evaluative grade rather than specific informational feedback for particular responses.

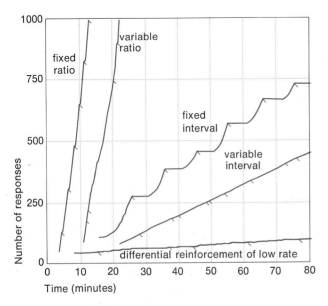

■ TYPICAL CURVES FOR DIFFERENT REINFORCEMENT SCHEDULES

These are typical "idealized" curves that have come to be identified with the main kinds of reinforcement schedules. These records are characteristic whether the subject is a rat or a pigeon or a child.

Both the ratio schedules typically maintain a high level of responding, as shown in the steepness of the curves. Interval schedules generally maintain a moderate rate of responding. The fixed interval schedule typically yields the "scalloped" curve shown here, reflecting the fact that the subject virtually stops responding after a reinforcement and waits until near the next scheduled reinforcement before responding actively again.

It is also possible, by reinforcing a low rate of responding, to get the almost flat curve of response shown here. (Figure redrawn from "Teaching Machines" by B. F. Skinner. Copyright © 1961 by Scientific American, Inc. All rights reserved.)

In teaching situations where the delay of reinforcement is unavoidable, a teacher may still improve pupil performance by:

1. Making sure that the correct completion of the response is so clear and unambiguous that both teacher and pupil will recognize it when it occurs.

2. Making explicit the reinforcement contingencies so that they never appear arbitrary or inconsistent but are seen as predictably dependent on particular behavior.

3. Using language and other reminders to establish the symbolic connection for the learner between a late-appearing reward and the long-gone response.

4. Employing conditioned reinforcers to "stand in" for the primary reinforcer along the way.

New Responses Through Operant Conditioning

Since only an act that has happened can be reinforced, you might think that an operant conditioner would have no way of using consequences to affect behavior that has not happened yet or in any case is not happening now. Not so, however. There are several ways in which the desired response can be induced, whether it be a response that is available but just not being made or a brand new response or sequence of behavior that the individual has never performed before.

Getting the first response. Let us assume that you are a benevolent parent, teacher, or animal trainer, and you have a pocketful of reinforcers you want to dispense—if only the individual will make the correct response. What procedures can you use to elicit the first correct response, so you can reinforce it and thus make it occur more frequently? This is a problem Pavlov never had because he was studying responses that could always be produced by careful presentation of the proper eliciting stimulus.

This is a crucial and basic problem in learning, to which all too little systematic attention has been given. All we will do here is outline and briefly comment on the possible effectiveness of several approaches. Some of the means of getting the individual to make that first correct response so you can reinforce it are: (a) increasing motivation; (b) lowering restraints; (c) structuring the environment; (d) forcing; (e) providing a model; (f) giving instructions; and (g) trial and error. Each of these techniques has certain advantages and disadvantages, depending on whether only immediate results or more permanent, long-term ones are desired. Because some of the consequences of applying these techniques are unintentionally negative, especially in the long run, we must be judicious in deciding which fits the particular learning situation best.

Increasing motivation. Prodding the organism into responding increases the probability that one of the responses will be the correct one. Electrifying a grid will get the rat moving about, and in the process it may discover an escape route. Here necessity is the mother of invention. Threats and promises of future reward (called "incentive motivation") as well as deprivation states or noxious stimulation all may be successfully used to motivate action.

There are, however, a number of potentially bad effects such motivators may have. Raising the level of motivation is not recommended if the individual does not have the response in his or her repertoire or does not have the ability to make it. For example, the mother who "won't love Johnny any more if Johnny soils his little diapers" will have no effect on changing the bowel movements if the child does not have sphincter muscle control yet. She may, however, produce both feelings of inferiority and a long-lasting resentment in her child. Such a procedure can also lead to conflict and stress if there is strong competing motivation. Finally, if the individual makes the response only because of the *extrinsic motivation* provided by avoidance of pain or anticipation of reward (perhaps a gold star or a dessert), he or she will be less likely to learn the intrinsic value of the task activity itself (studying or eating spinach).

Lowering restraints. If the organism has already learned the skills involved in making the correct response but does not emit it under mo-

tivating conditions, it may well be that the response is being inhibited or suppressed. Previously learned habits may be incompatible with emitting the desired response. The shy boy who knows the answer will not ever get reinforced for it unless he raises his hand and says it out loud, but this he cannot do because he has learned that it is very painful to him to talk in class. Many males cannot express "tender" responses such as love or grief because prior learning has defined them as "unmasculine" responses. To get soldiers to kill, or medical students to start to cut up a cadaver, techniques are used to lower learned restraints against such "antisocial" behavior. Discovering what are the competing motives and weakening them, or finding out what reinforcers are maintaining the inhibitions on behavior and removing them, may help to induce the "desired" response. On the negative side, whatever is inhibiting the behavior in question may also be holding in check other undesirable behaviors that you would *not* want to be released.

Structuring the environment. Suppose you want two competitive children to learn to cooperate with each other. One way to encourage this type of responding is to place them in an area containing toys that can be manipulated only by two or more children. If you want an animal to learn to press a bar, peck a key, open a latch, go through an escape hatch, or even consume an available reward, you can make the behavior more likely by removing distracting, irrelevant stimuli, simplifying the environment, making the *manipulandum* (bar, key, etc.) stand out more than other features of the environment. The change from Thorndike's relatively complicated puzzle box to the simplicity of the Skinner box (p. 122) is an illustration of making the desired response more likely by structuring the environment to remove most other possibilities. Of course, learning to survive in only a relatively simple environment may leave the organism overwhelmed by the stimulus variety if it encounters a complex environment (as when the country mouse goes to the city).

Forcing. Often the most efficient method of getting out that first correct response is to assist its execution physically. You take the child's hand with the spoonful of unfamiliar food and guide it mouthward. Then you reinforce putting-food-in-mouth (and hopefully swallowing it) with praise or whatever. To teach a dog to roll over, trainers first provide a verbal cue, then physically roll the dog over and praise or feed it each time until it "catches on."

This rapid response elicitation technique probably has the worst long-term consequences for human learners, especially if they are involuntary or unwilling participants or if the individual using the technique is inept. Guiding a learner in a dance step could be helpful, but imagine how our shy student would feel toward the teacher who forced the response of answering in class by picking up his hand. Regardless of the size of the subsequent reinforcement for the response, this crude type of forcing would likely develop negative emotional responses toward the coercive agent of reinforcement, deepen the sense of personal inadequacy, or lead the subject to make the correct response by rote without ever understanding the underlying principle involved.

Imitation of model. "*Répétez, s'il vous plaît*" says the French teacher, and the student attempts to imitate what the teacher has said—both the content and manner of delivery. Observational learning is also valuable where the details of a complex motor task cannot be easily communicated in words—as, for example, tying one's shoelaces, or hitting a baseball. This kind of learning is evidently important in the social learning of both animals and humans.

On the other hand, overdependence on models (who usually are "authority figures") may limit one's own initiative and teach one to be a conformist. It may also lead one to "pick up" a host of other responses made by the model. These may be responses correlated with the desired one, such as parents' speech habits, dialects, and so on, learned along with the language. Or they may be unrelated responses that just happen to be emitted with high frequency by the model, such as statements of prejudice against minority groups.

Verbal instruction. "Do what I say, not what I do," distinguishes this approach from the previous one. The ability to use language can clear-ly facilitate some kinds of learning and can greatly accelerate elicitation of the first correct response. In fact, verbal instructions can be used not only to outline how the response should be made, but also to provide a description of the happy consequences that such responding will bring. Complex sequences may be communicated, as well as abstract principles, information regarding delay of response, ways of using past learning, and instructions for the future.

Naturally, following verbal instructions presupposes understanding them, which is not always the case, as parents will testify who have tried in frustrating desperation to assemble a child's toy from the "easy-to-follow directions." Ambiguity in language usage, implied reliance on a set of concepts or skills, and the occasional difference between what is said and what is actually meant may all reduce the effectiveness of verbal instruction for many potential learners. On the other hand, overly explicit instructions can lead in the long run to a learned dependence on being told exactly what to do and how to do it—along with a loss of intellectual curiosity and a fear of taking risks.

Trial and error. This "sink or swim," survival-of-the-fittest method is peculiar in a number of ways. It is one of the least effective techniques for getting out that first correct response (in the absence of any other techniques), but it may have the most desirable long-term consequences when it works. It is a decidedly undemocratic, elitist approach, however, where many are called, but only a few are reinforced. For those who try and do succeed, the relative subjective reinforcement is greater when viewed in the perspective of all those who did not succeed. In addition, what is reinforced is not only the correct response, but the entire process of searching for a solution.

In contrast, for the many people whose trials end only in more errors, reinforcement for correct responding never comes. The effort and curiosity involved in the behavior are likely to undergo experimental extinction. This is especially true when grading is on a curve and half the members of a class are doomed to "below average" grades. On the other hand, a noncompetitive trial-and-error "inquiry" approach, with a watchful teacher to help structure the search so that students are constantly reaching beyond past achievements—but not too far beyond—can enable searchers to get enough reinforcement along the way to keep them going.

Shaping and chaining of behavior. Believe it or not, you can even use operant conditioning to do such unlikely things as getting a pigeon to play Ping-Pong, a rat to lift more than its body weight, or dolphins to jump through a hoop. The secret is that you start with something the animal already does and gradually change the exact response that you reinforce, "shaping" it closer and closer to the response you want.

For many behaviors that are complex and unlikely to occur in perfect form on the first trial, you would lower the criterion for reinforcement. At the beginning, you would decide that the "correct" response would be any overt response that was an approximation of (bore some resemblance to) even one step in the final sequence of action you wanted. Then, on successive trials, the response would have to be progressively closer to the desired act in order to earn reinforcement. Finally, several such shaped behaviors might be put together into a whole complex sequence. By the end of training, only the whole sequence would be followed by reinforcement. (See *P&L* Close-up, p. 129.)

You have undoubtedly seen trained animals on TV performing remarkable feats in which only the last response was followed by the carrot, sugar cube, or fish tidbit. An experimental demonstration of the procedure involved in producing such smart animals would show that the key ingredient is the patience and operant conditioning skill of the trainer.

Pierrel and Sherman (1963) were able to turn a rather commonplace little rat, "Barnabus,"

into an exotic performer, just as Professor Higgins did with his street waif in *My Fair Lady*. Barnabus learned to:

a) climb a spiral staircase,
b) cross a narrow drawbridge,
c) ascend a ladder,
d) pull a toy car over by a chain,
e) jump into the car,
f) pedal it to a second ladder,
g) climb this ladder,
h) crawl through a tube,
i) board an elevator,
j) pull a chain that raised a flag and that lowered him back to the starting platform, where he could
k) press a lever delivering a tiny food pellet and, after eating the food,
l) climb the spiral staircase . . .

To teach Barnabus to go through this remarkable sequence, the experimenters started not at the beginning of it but at the end. First Barnabus learned to press the lever to get food pellets. Next, they put him in the elevator, which, when lowered, gave him access to the food lever. Once he learned that elevator rides were followed by such happy results—and then how to achieve them by pulling a chain—it was no trick to get Barnabus to crawl through a tunnel to reach the elevator. And so on. Individual parts of the responses that were not originally in Barnabus' repertoire sometimes had to be induced by one or more special techniques developed by animal conditioners, such as showing him, putting him in the situation they wanted him to enter, making critical parts of the environment stand out more clearly, and so on. Approximations of the desired responses were then shaped toward the precise action desired. Eventually each link in the chain became a *discriminative stimulus* for the next step and a *conditioned reinforcer* for the preceding one.

We assume that some such pattern as this is involved when we learn a complex series of new responses like driving a car, playing the piano, or dancing. Component segments are emitted—sometimes first in rough form—and then are perfected by selective reinforcement and integrated into a sequence.

New Challenges
to the Traditional Paradigms

Introductory textbooks in all fields are in a sense like a house cleaned for unexpected company—the dirt is swept under the rugs, the rooms with unmade beds are closed off, and irrepressible little Willy is sent off to play at the neighbors. To "the company" there is a pleasant appearance of order and harmony. Authors of psychology textbooks would like to convey that same sense of simplicity, regularity, and everything in its proper place for their introductory students. For one thing, the material is easier to learn that way. But also it seems to put psychology in a better light by giving the impression that psychologists always know just what they are doing.

Because psychology is an evolving discipline, however—a science in progress—there is a great deal that cannot be neatly pigeonholed and tidily categorized. In fact, quite recently there has been some "disturbing" new research in the area of the psychology of learning that does not "make sense" in terms of the traditional textbook categories and differentiations. At the most, these findings challenge our basic conception; at the least, they force a recognition of the narrowness of the currently accepted view of what constitutes the psychology of learning.

Close-up
The Strength of Hercules

The photographs (right) illustrate how a meek laboratory rat, "Hercules," was transformed into a brute weightlifter capable of lifting as much as twice his own weight. First, any response of the hungry rat directed toward the food cup was followed by a loud click, a light on the food cup, and a pellet of food. Once he had become familiar with the feeding mechanism, he was rewarded only for movements of his body toward the bar, then only when he touched it, and then only when he pulled it down.

After this stage was completed, the effort required to depress the bar was gradually in-creased by the addition of small weights to the mechanism at the other end of it. By carefully spacing out the reinforcements and stepping up the weights systematically, the 250-gram rat became capable of lifting 515 grams of weight after only a few hours of weight lifting.

Note in the bottom photo how Hercules has also learned to adjust his posture in order to perform his feat. He must anchor the claws of his hind paws into the wire-mesh wall to keep from being pulled off his feet by the heavy bar as it springs up after he successfully pulls it down to make contact with the micro-switch that delivers a food pellet.

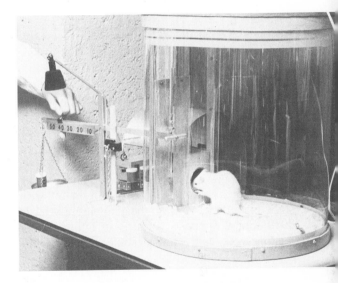

In this section, then, we think you might enjoy peeking into some of the "unmade" rooms of the house that Pavlov built and Skinner modified. After a brief respondent-operant comparison, we will consider research that demonstrates how a respondent reflex can be operantly conditioned; how an operant response can be respondently conditioned; and how genetic factors and even past experience can *prevent* learning from following the course that one would expect from our "laws of learning."

Respondent and Operant Conditioning Compared

It should be obvious to you that the unconditioned stimulus (UCS) in respondent conditioning is the same as the positive or negative reinforcer (S^R) in the operant case in providing reinforcement for the response. And the conditioned stimulus (CS), which stands in for the unconditioned stimulus in Pavlovian conditioning, comes to serve the same function as do the conditioned or secondary reinforcers in Skinnerian conditioning. What then are the major differences between the two types of learning? These differences are summarized in the chart. ◆

Now let's complicate the picture a bit with some exceptions to even these apparently basic distinctions. Suppose you are an infant. While feeding you, your mother smiles, then spoons out some of your favorite mush, and you salivate, eat the food, and smile back contentedly. It appears that you are being respondently conditioned: Momma's smile (CS) – Food (UCS) – Salivation (UCR). Eventually you will salivate (CR) to Momma's smile even before the food comes.

But what about from your perspective? Is it not possible that you will have learned to believe that your salivation, smiling, gurgling, and so on are instrumental in making the food appear? Once you are conditioned, the sequence is: Momma's smile – you respond – food appears. To you, it is an instrumental act – an operant conditioning paradigm – even if your mother views it as respondent conditioning. In fact, you are like Orpheus in our example of superstitious operant conditioning (see p. 116): you act *as if* the reinforcer were contingent on your response even though it is not, and you treat Momma's smile as a discriminative stimulus setting the stage for the $R \rightarrow S^R$ machinery to occur rather than as just the sweet, simple CS that it was intended to be. You would be convinced that you were wrong if you could be persuaded not to salivate or smile, and then see that the food would be administered anyway – but that's a tough job of persuasion to accomplish on a hungry, well-conditioned, smiling baby. So which is it: respondent conditioning or operant conditioning?

Let's turn to some additional, less prosaic complications.

◆ **RESPONDENT VS. OPERANT CONDITIONING**

	Respondent	Operant
Type of response	Involuntary, related to biological survival, produces change in organism, elicited by stimulus	Voluntary, operates on environment, emitted by organism
Contingencies	S–S, R–R, S → R	R → S
Preceding stimulus	Elicits response	Signals that reinforcement is available
Temporal relation of response to reinforcer (in acquisition)	Response follows	Response precedes
Functional relation of response to reinforcer	Presence of reinforcer independent of response	Presence of reinforcer contingent on response and changes probability of response
Timing between paired stimuli ($CS - UCS$; $S^D - S^R$)	Short, fixed	Variable, can be a long time

Operant Conditioning of Respondents

Respondents are acts closely related to the primitive biological survival of the organism. Digestion, salivation, dilation and contraction of blood vessels, perspiration, changes in heart rate, blood pressure, temperature, breathing, liver and kidney functions are some of the involuntary responses that keep us alive and usually occur without any effort on our part. We are rarely even aware of them until we have asthma, high blood pressure, colitis, ulcers, or any of a host of other disturbances of these normally unnoticed, efficient processes.

You may remember reading a few years ago about a seventeen-year-old girl who suddenly began to sneeze uncontrollably and could not stop. She sneezed more than once every waking minute, day after day, for months on end. No medicine, change of air, or folk remedy (scare her, put a paper bag over her head, etc.) had any effect on this unfortunate condition. If sneezing were an operant response, it would be possible to decrease its rate by what? Yes, by applying punishment contingencies.

Psychologist Malcolm Kusher decided to take a chance and apply operant procedures to cure this respondent behavior of uncontrollable sneezing. His approach was simple. The girl's sneezes were followed immediately by the inescapable, aversive consequences of electric shocks to her forearm. After about four hours of this pairing of sneeze and shock, the sneezing stopped and did not reoccur except as a normal, occasional, elicited response.

In another example the authors are personally familiar with, a young New York City boy developed acute asthmatic attacks every time his parents sent him to vacation with his country cousins in New Jersey. The condition was diagnosed as an allergic reaction to pollen, present in the country but not in the city. Curiously, however, he never had any respiratory problems when he camped out overnight in the New Jersey woods with his Boy Scout troop. "Being sent away to relatives" was for him an aversive consequence that perhaps he learned to escape by developing an asthmatic reaction — which forced his joyful return to his city friends and family.

If responses of the viscera, glands, and smooth internal muscles of the body can be shown to operate according to the same laws of learning as overt, voluntary, skeletal muscle responses, then the class of responses that can be changed through reinforcement becomes virtually unlimited. Moreover, if the smooth muscles and glands are responsive to environmental circumstances, we are in a position to discover how psychosomatic illness develops. We know that these physical ailments are somehow triggered by psychological stress, as in the case of the asthmatic city boy. Maybe they are under operant control. If they are, then, as with the chronically sneezing girl, they can be modified by operant procedures. Yet ordinarily, most responses of the autonomic nervous system have no effect on the environment. Thus they do not get reinforced by consequences and are not under environmental control.

To demonstrate that they could be *changed* through reinforcement and thus become controllable, Neal Miller and his colleagues at Rockefeller University (1969, 1970, 1973) developed an ingenious set of procedures in their attempt to demonstrate whether this "dumb" nervous system could learn to behave in a more "sophisticated," environment-sensitive way. In an extensive series of studies still under way, these researchers have been able to show that visceral operant learning is indeed possible, and moreover, that an exquisitely fine degree of behavior control can be achieved by such techniques.

Three procedures had to be devised by Miller and his associates in order to make it possible to reinforce responding of the autonomic nervous system:

1. They had to prevent skeletal responses such as breathing and moving, which might influence visceral responses. This was accomplished by administration of *curare*, which blocks all motor responses and reduces distractions by irrelevant stimuli, but does not eliminate consciousness. Breathing was maintained artificially, and nonhuman subjects were used.

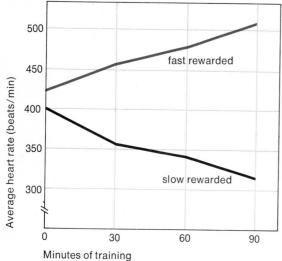

After Miller & DiCara, 1967

■ In this photo of Miller's apparatus, a rat, paralyzed by curare, is receiving artifical respiration through a nose cone. Through previously implanted electrodes, stimulation is delivered to the brain promptly after each autonomic change in the desired direction. The graph shows the curve over a ninety-minute period in rats rewarded for increasing their heart rate and a corresponding decreasing trend in rats rewarded for lowering it.

2. Small visceral responses had to be detected and amplified, and slight changes in amplitude or rate had to be reinforced immediately. This was accomplished with sophisticated physiological recording devices controlled by a small computer that could sense response change and initiate reinforcement.

3. The reinforcement had to be delivered immediately, have instant effectiveness, and not require the subject to make any motor responses (as eating would, if the reinforcer were food). This was accomplished by administering a small amount of electric current directly into specified regions of the brain stem already known to be "pleasure centers" (described in Chapter 2).

The precision of the control that is possible is hinted by the fact that even the time interval within a single heartbeat (from auricle to ventricle pumping) can be experimentally varied. Besides the heart-rate changes shown in the illustration, operant techniques have enabled researchers to control: salivation, blood pressure, intestinal contractions, rate of urine formation, and blood flow in the stomach wall, among other responses. ■

To demonstrate that operant reinforcement could have a highly specific effect on individual parts of the sympathetic nervous system—rather than a generalized, indiscriminate effect—rats were taught to "blush" in one ear but not the other. Photocells attached to the rats' ears indicated momentary changes in dilation of blood vessels. Whenever the vasodilation in one ear increased above some criterion, the rats received immediate reinforcement via brain stimulation. Of twelve rats, six were rewarded for producing more dilation (blushing) in the right ear, while six were rewarded only for left-ear blushing. All twelve subjects learned to blush only in the rewarded direction (Di Cara & Miller, 1968b).

Stimulated by the success of this research in animals, investigators at a number of university and medical laboratories are now at work extending the principles to the control of psychosomatic symptoms in humans. At present the results are promising but not as dramatic as in the better controlled animal experiments.

Part of the problem lies in the less immediate, potent reinforcer used with humans as compared to brain stimulation with animals. In human studies, for example, changes in the response are amplified, and when they exceed some criterion level, a light or a tone indicates "success" to the subject. This feedback is the reinforcer—that is, the sense of "competence" in being able to ring the bell or turn on the light. But even with the use of a less potent reinforcer with humans, it has proved possible to condition patients with a heart ailment to decrease their premature ventricular contractions, and half of a group of eight subjects have maintained this favorable state when retested nearly two years later (Weiss & Engel, 1971).

All of this proves that respondents can be operantly conditioned. Although it may initially muddy the once-clear distinction between the two types of learning, it may also eventually lead to clinical procedures for relieving serious illness by learning rather than medication.

Respondent Conditioning of Operants

Operant responses, we know, are strengthened by their consequences. The single operant response most often used in laboratory research is pecking by pigeons. Suppose it could be shown that pecking is elicited by a conditioned stimulus in a respondent conditioning paradigm where pecking does not affect the delivery of food.

Such a phenomenon has been found in experiments described as *autoshaping* (self-shaping), where an operant response is not shaped by the contingencies that follow it, but rather by self-generated reinforcers derived from the evolutionary history of the organism. Brown and Jenkins (1968) were the first to observe the following curious behavior.

Hungry pigeons placed in a Skinner box were presented with food shortly after a small disk was illuminated. The food was delivered on an irregular schedule regardless of what the pigeon was doing; the pairing of stimuli being clearly of the CS–UCS variety. Soon the pigeons began to peck the illuminated key even though pecking

was unrelated to food delivery. But they pecked the key only if it was a signal for food; if it was always illuminated, they ignored it.

Even more curious, in a related study, such autoshaped pecking persisted even when pecking the key actually prevented delivery of the food (Williams & Williams, 1969). Autoshaping has also been reported in quail, monkeys, fish, and rats.

This line of research suggests that although autoshaped animals are free to move about and the response conditioned is an operant one, the process involved is that of Pavlovian conditioning. Why should such an effect be possible? One reasonable answer is the natural adaptiveness of learning to approach environmental cues that signal food.

"The Pavlovian mechanism would be highly adaptive in most natural situations. It would cause the animal to return to places, or objects, or substances, or organisms in the presence of which it was likely to encounter the sorts of unconditioned stimuli which elicit approach reactions. . . . The striking simplicity of the Pavlovian process, and the economy with which it utilizes the instructive mechanisms already present in primitive organisms, would have given it an initial evolutionary advantage of considerable magnitude." (B. Moore, 1973, p. 183)

But do the animals really react to the conditioned stimulus as if it were the unconditioned stimulus, as happens in Pavlovian conditioning? Is the form of their response to it comparable to the form of their consummatory response when eating or drinking? The answer appears to be "yes." High-speed motion pictures of pigeons pecking a key associated with either food or water reveal that the autoshaped responses were different depending on the reinforcer and appropriate to it—for food, the beak was open and the pecks were sharp and vigorous; for water, the beak was closed, the pecks were slower and often accompanied by swallowing movements.

In a beautifully designed recent study, conditions were arranged such that for half the subjects (rats) one lever in a Skinner box was associated with the delivery of food (CS⁺), while a second lever was presented randomly (CS°). For a second group of subjects one lever was associated with reinforcing electrical stimulation of the brain (CS⁺), while again the appearance of a second lever had no relationship to the brain stimulation. The responses of the subjects had no contingent effect on the reinforcing stimulus. There were five sessions of forty trials of acquisition training, followed by extinction trials (no food or brain stimulation), reacquisition, and then reversal, in which the CS° lever was related to the reinforcer and the formerly CS⁺ lever had no functional significance.

As in previous autoshaping experiments, the subjects made considerable contact with the CS⁺ lever. These responses decreased rapidly during extinction, but were rapidly reacquired and easily shifted when the signal value of the two levers was reversed. ▲

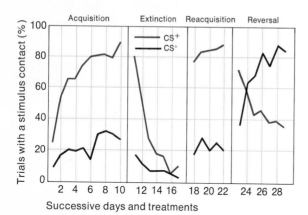

Adapted from Peterson et al., 1972

▲ The graph shows the percentage of trials on which subjects made contact with each lever during successive stages of the experiment. During the acquisition and reacquisition stages, CS⁺ signaled food, whereas CS° occurred randomly. During the extinction stage, no food was given. During the reversal stage, CS° signaled food and the former CS⁺ occurred randomly.

Of greater interest is the finding that the specific form of the contact made depended on the forthcoming unconditioned stimulus. When it was food, videotaped pictures revealed that the subjects made almost exclusively oral contacts with it, licking and gnawing. In contrast, the brain-stimulation subjects rarely licked the CS⁺ lever; instead they visually explored it, sniffed it, and touched it with their forepaws. The Pavlovian conditioned stimulus thus evoked specific skeletal responses similar to those elicited directly by the forthcoming unconditioned stimulus (Peterson, Ackil, Frommer, & Hearst, 1972).

Research of this kind makes us aware of the hitherto unappreciated role of Pavlovian conditioning in the appearance, maintenance, and modification of certain operant responses important for the organism's (and the species') survival.

Species-Specific Constraints on Conditioning

The laws of learning presented in this chapter are statements of functional relationships between certain classes of independent and dependent variables. The research foundation for such laws has been built on the assumption that the basic elements to be associated—stimuli, responses, and reinforcers—are arbitrary and can best be studied in highly simplified, artificial laboratory environments with tamed, laboratory-reared animals. Many psychologists within the animal-learning tradition have come to believe in the generality of their experimental operations—that their "laws of learning" are really principles of behavior for all organisms.

". . . we arbitrarily choose almost any act from the animal's repertoire and reinforce it with food, water, or whatever else the animal will work to obtain. Although typically we teach a rat to press a bar or a pigeon to peck a key to obtain a pellet of food, we can readily train either to dance around the cage if we so choose. We usually use a light to signal the delivery of a pellet, but we can use a tone or a buzzer or any other stimulus the animal can detect . . . . The same act can be used for any reinforcement . . . . In effect, in any operant situation, the *stimulus, the response, and the reinforcement are completely arbitrary and interchangeable. No one of them bears any biological built-in fixed connection to the others." (Teitelbaum, 1966, pp. 566–67)*

The appealing simplicity of such a view has come under attack recently by investigators who argue that an animal's capacity for learning is geared to the requirements for learning posed by conditions of its natural habitat and by *species-specific characteristics* — characteristics that are specific for a given species and different for other species (e.g., Shettlesworth, 1972; Rozin & Kalat, 1970). *Ethologists* (researchers who study animal behavior in its natural setting) have long emphasized that the behavior of any individual may be as characteristic of its species as is its physiology or anatomy. The laboratory study of animal learning violates the "ecological validity" of the species being studied — pigeons are not allowed to nest or fly, rats cannot gnaw or forage for food, monkeys are prevented from mating. There is little necessity for defensive, aggressive, exploratory, or vigilance reactions in the daily lives of laboratory animals. Subsystems of behavior that have evolved adaptively for each species over millions of years (such as avoidance of predators, migration, mating, feeding, care of young) probably follow laws of learning appropriate to them. There is increasing evidence of the need to modify current laws of learning to take into account such genetically based influences.

Instinctual drift.   Following long experience in trying to train animals such as pigs, hens, and raccoons for animal shows and displays, Breland and Breland (1966) reported a phenomenon that they called "instinctual drift." These nonlaboratory-bred animals often displayed responses that were counterproductive to the learning situation at hand, but resembled responses that they make "naturally" in their usual environment. For example, hungry pigs being trained to put a coin in a piggy bank (followed by a food reinforcer) would stop along the way to root it around and manipulate it instead. This type of reaction, reminiscent of that in autoshaping, was ob-

served to delay the food reinforcement in many other species too. They "did their own thing" instead of performing the response that the experimenter was patiently rewarding with food, a reinforcer generally assumed to control the behavior of a hungry organism.

Bait-shyness.   The avoidance of poison in foods is obviously a learned ability of considerable survival value for an animal like the rat. A number of recent experiments have shown that rats will learn to avoid a food they have eaten that was contaminated by irradiation or with substances that made them sick. Nothing very startling about that. What is news is twofold: (a) It is only the quality of the taste of the food that becomes a conditioned stimulus for avoidance. Rats do not later avoid foods that look similar to it, foods that have similar textures or temperatures, foods that were being eaten at the same time as the poisoned food, or even foods accompanied by electric shocks while they were eating the poisoned food. Thus there is no stimulus generalization such as usually occurs in conditioning. (b) Given only one learning trial, rats learn to associate the taste of the poisoned food (CS) with sickness (UCS), even though the sickness occurred some *hours* after eating. In the laboratory, many trials are usually necessary, and it is an axiom that the UCS must come very soon after the CS for conditioning to occur. In fact, according to the laws of learning, the ideal CS–UCS interval is less than a *second*, whereas here we have an instance of powerful, highly selective learning occurring despite an interval of hours between danger signal and dangerous event. This research by Garcia and his colleagues (1972) both questions the appropriateness of the basic laws of conditioning for explaining all learning and focuses our attention on the adaptive learning mechanisms that a given organism brings into any learning situation.

It is becoming increasingly clear that there are species differences in "predispositions" to learn certain things rather than others (pigeons learn color discriminations more readily than line-angle discriminations), the ease with which certain stimuli acquire discriminative control over behavior, the effectiveness of reinforcers (songs for birds, opportunity to display self for some fish), and the difficulty of conditioning or modifying some behavior subsystems compared to others. Acknowledging these constraints on learning will lead to a more comprehensive view of the learning process, although not necessarily as simple a view as has been traditionally advanced.

● Konrad Lorenz, the ethologist who pioneered in the study of imprinting, graphically demonstrates what can happen when young animals (in this case, goslings) become imprinted on someone other than their mother.

Imprinting (or, I'll follow you anywhere). In 1935, the famous ethologist Konrad Lorenz called attention to a phenomenon of significance both to the development of the individual and to the maintenance of the species—the imprinting of following and sexual responses. The term *imprinting* refers to an early experience in which a young animal follows an animal that is present during a critical time period in its development. Later, in adulthood, the individual selects an animal of that same species as a mate. The usual object of imprinting is, naturally enough, the infant's mother. ●

Illustrative of these phenomena, which have been studied primarily in mallard ducklings and chickens, are the two observations that a newly hatched duckling placed with a foster mother of another species: (a) will follow her rather than its biological mother, and (b) when it matures sexually, will select as a mate a member of the foster mother's species.

Hess (1959) has carried out controlled laboratory studies in which ducklings have been imprinted on a wooden duck decoy that is artificially made to move and render ducklike sounds. Using the apparatus shown in the drawing, he has verified the natural observations of ethologists that the critical period of positive following-imprinting (for mallard ducklings) is between five and twenty-four hours, with the peak at thirteen to sixteen hours. ■ After this time imprinting is rare, and strange objects are reacted to with shyness or fear. The corresponding period for dogs occurs at about the age of thirteen weeks, after which they cannot readily be made into pets. Similarly, kittens not handled during the first few weeks of life always show a fear of people.

Some of the remarkable features of imprinting that are relevant to the present discussion of constraints on the laws of learning are: (a) that the reaction can be "fixed" in a period as short as one minute's worth of following (Schutz, 1969); (b) that the reaction is stronger the *more effort* required to follow the model; and (c) that aversive stimulation, such as shocking the young followers, increases rather than decreases the effectiveness of the imprinting.

Under natural life conditions, the following reaction is important for the immediate survival of the helpless infant, which must attach itself to its mother for protection and nurturance. Imprinting to the mother also ensures later selection of a mate of the same species; normally this mechanism prevents crossbreeding.

The study of imprinting makes clear the interaction between inherited response mechanisms, maturational processes, and specific environmental experiences. While it might appear that humans are less subject to this process than lower animals, it is interesting to conjecture whether the permanent lack of sociability observed in some persons who spent their early childhood in institutions (Goldfarb, 1943) may be traced to a failure to experience normal contact with (and adequate "imprinting" on) people during a critical developmental period.

Past Learning As a Constraint on Conditioning

A few years ago, Martin Seligman and his associates, Maier and Overmier (1967), stumbled onto an interesting phenomenon while studying the carry-over effects of aversive Pavlovian conditioning on subsequent avoidance learning. Dogs restrained in the Pavlovian harness were conditioned to respond to a tone that signaled a painful shock. The next day they were put into an alley with the two compartments separated by a barrier, where they were to learn the simple instrumental response of jumping over the barrier to escape shock given in the first compartment.

Naive dogs, not previously shocked in the Pavlovian apparatus, when shocked for the first time in this "shuttlebox" run around wildly for about thirty seconds, howling, defecating, and urinating, then jump over the barrier and discover the safety of the other side. In a few more trials, these dogs learn to avoid the shock completely by jumping the barrier as soon as they are placed in the first compartment.

What about the dogs with prior shock experience? At first they reacted as did the naive ones, howling, running around, etc., but then they stopped responding, lay down, and whined quietly as they endured the traumatic electric

shock. They did not learn to jump the barrier to escape the shock but passively resigned themselves to taking it. Even when one of these dogs occasionally did jump over the barrier and the response enabled it to escape the shock, this reinforcement did not change its later behavior: on the next trial it simply stayed and took the full trauma of fifty seconds of pulsating shock.

This *learned helplessness* has some rather dramatic additional "side effects." Not only is such "adaptation" maladaptive in that needed responses are inhibited by the previous expe-

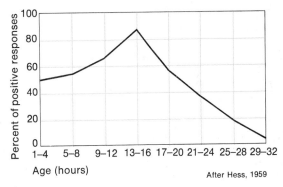

After Hess, 1959

■ IMPRINTABILITY AND CRITICAL AGE

The apparatus that Hess used to study imprinting (top) consisted of a decoy, suspended from a rotating arm, which the duckling followed around a circular runway. The controls and recording apparatus are shown in the foreground. The graph shows the percentage of positive responses made by groups of ducklings imprinted at different ages on test trials *after* imprinting sessions. Some imprinting occurred immediately after hatching and as late as thirty-two hours after hatching, but ducklings imprinted at an age of thirteen to sixteen hours consistently made the highest following scores.

rience of powerlessness, but physiological functioning suffers as well: there is loss of appetite and weight, and ulcers may develop.

Once the dogs had learned to be passive, Seligman found that it took many experiences (up to 200) of being forcibly dragged across from the shock compartment to the safe compartment for them to rediscover that responding could bring relief and thus to break out of the learned helplessness syndrome.

In Chapter 9 we will discuss learned helplessness in more detail, including learned helplessness in humans. We also will review Seligman's more recent work in "preventive therapy," in which an individual can be "inoculated" against learned helplessness by prior mastery training.

Chapter Summary

In order to survive, any organism must be capable of learning: (a) what things in the environment are related, and (b) how its own actions affect and are affected by environmental events. Such learning enables the organism to make predictions about future events and to use the environment to meet its needs.

A stimulus that elicits a response predictably prior to learning is called an *unconditioned stimulus* (US or UCS). A neutral stimulus that repeatedly occurs just before the onset of an unconditioned stimulus acquires the ability to elicit the response, thereby becoming a *conditioned stimulus* (CS). This process is called *respondent conditioning* or *classical conditioning*. In such learning, one stimulus comes to substitute for another as a signal that a *pleasant event* (perhaps food) or an *aversive event* (perhaps electric shock) is imminent. The originally automatic response is called an *unconditioned response* (UR, or UCR). The *conditioned response* (CR) elicited by the new signal may be very similar to the UCR or may have additional components. Not only physical stimuli but words and other symbols as well may become conditioned stimuli.

In a conditioning situation there is a generalized increase in *excitability*. The most favorable *interval* between onset of the CS and onset of the US is half a second. *Stimulus generalization* typically occurs, in which not only the precise conditioned stimulus but other stimuli somewhat similar to it also elicit the response. With continued trials in which reinforcement occurs only after the exact CS, the organism comes to respond only to the correct stimulus and to make only the precise response through *discrimination* and *inhibition of competing responses*. *Higher-order conditioning* may occur, in which the conditioned stimulus rather than the unconditioned stimulus serves as reinforcement in establishing second-order association. *Extinction*, due to active inhibition of the response, occurs after conditioning when the conditioned stimulus is regularly *not* followed by the unconditioned stimulus. *Spontaneous recovery* of the response can occur after a rest period following lengthy extinction training. The *strength of conditioning* can be measured by *resistance to extinction* as well as by *amplitude of response, frequency of response*, or *latency of response*. In *pseudoconditioning*, there is a change in the strength of responding, but no actual learning.

Past conditioning can leave unfortunate and often unrecognized residues. In *schizokinesis*, component parts of the conditioned response (changes in heart rate, for example) remain after the primary muscular or glandular response has been extinguished. Overeating may be the result of a *conditioned addiction* to food. When a conditioned animal is forced to make finer and finer discriminations, the original conditioned discrimination may be lost, and "neurotic" symptoms may appear, a phenomenon known as *experimental neurosis*.

Any stimulus the organism can perceive can be used to elicit a conditioned response in any muscle or gland by respondent conditioning procedures.

Conditioning based on the consequences of behavior was first studied by E. L. Thorndike with hungry cats confined to puzzle boxes. Here behavior is *instrumental in reaching a goal;* it is *emitted* by the organism rather than *elicited* by a stimulus, and reinforcement is given only if a particular response is made. To explain such instrumental conditioning, Thorndike postulated *mediating variables,* including *drive states, response hierarchies,* and *cues,* and a *law of effect:* that the feeling of satisfaction following a successful response made the response more likely next time.

Clark Hull sought to formulate a comprehensive *drive reduction* theory of learning based on simple stimulus-response associations. Tolman, however, developed a broader theory that viewed learning as *purposive,* involving changes in cognitions.

B. F. Skinner, a pioneer in the *experimental analysis of behavior,* and his followers hold that learning can and should be described entirely in terms of observable behavior. They study *operant conditioning,* also based on consequences, in which *rate of responding* rather than occurrence of new responses is measured. A *response* in this context may be a single behavioral act or a given number of behavioral acts reinforced as a group (such as 100 key presses). A *reinforcer* is defined operationally as any stimulus event following which a response becomes more probable.

A *discriminative stimulus* (S^D) is one that signals the availability of a reinforcer; rate of responding increases in its presence. A *negative discriminative stimulus* (S$^\triangle$) sets the occasion for a low rate of responding. A discriminative stimulus may itself become reinforcing; it is then said to be a *conditioned,* or *secondary, reinforcer.*

Five response-reinforcer contingencies are possible. Response rate *increases* when responding is followed by a *positive* reinforcing stimulus or by *escape* from or *avoidance* of an aversive stimulus; it decreases when followed by an aversive stimulus *(punishment)* or no reinforcer *(extinction). Superstitious* relationships occur when an individual assumes a stimulus-response relationship that does not in fact exist.

Punishment is the presentation of an aversive stimulus that *decreases* the probability of a response. While it can be effective under some circumstances, punishment must be used carefully if it is *not* to have undesired consequences. It should be made clear that the response, and not the person, is the object of punishment.

Response rate is recorded on a *cumulative recorder;* the more rapid the rate, the steeper the *cumulative response curve* will be. Once a response has been learned, it can be maintained by *intermittent reinforcement.* Four schedules of intermittent reinforcement are *fixed ratio, variable ratio, fixed interval,* and *variable interval* schedules; each induces a characteristic pattern of responding. The more prompt and specific the reinforcement, the more effective it will be in increasing rate of responding.

Since reinforcers can influence only responses that are already occurring, special means need to be devised for inducing the first response. Such means include increasing motivation, lowering restraints, structuring the environment, forcing, providing a model, giving instructions, inducing trial and error, and rewarding successive approximations *(shaping).* In *chaining,* a subject can be taught a sequence of responses in which the discriminative stimulus for one step becomes a *conditioned reinforcer* for the step preceding it.

To summarize, respondent conditioning involves involuntary biological responses which are *elicited* by presentation of a stimulus. It may involve S–S, R–R, or S→R contingencies. Operant conditioning, on the other hand, involves voluntary responses *emitted* by the organism and followed by a reinforcing stimulus; thus it involves R→S contingencies.

Many of the results of current research on conditioning cannot be neatly categorized; there are areas where operant conditioning of visceral activity (respondents), such as blushing, has been shown to occur. In *autoshaping,* on the other hand, respondent conditioning of operant behavior occurs. Species-specific characteristics may affect the learning process in an animal's natural setting. Examples include *instinctual drift, bait-shyness,* and *imprinting.* Past learning may also serve as a constraint on conditioning; for example, *learned helplessness* can lead to a passive lack of responding in stressful situations.

Self-reinforcement: The power of positive personal control

Albert Bandura Stanford University

How can we explain the variability, uniformities, and complexity of human functioning? Many different theories have been proposed over the years to account for why people behave as they do and to suggest how behavior may be changed. A particular theory usually focuses on one class of events while ignoring others. Furthermore, one's theoretical conceptions determine the ways in which one collects evidence, and this evidence in turn shapes one's particular theory.

For some time now, a number of theorists have held that the major causes of behavior are *motivational* forces within the individual. These inner determinants—needs, drives, and impulses—are not directly observable but have been inferred from the behaviors they supposedly cause. Eating was seen as evidence of a hunger drive, achievement-oriented behavior indicated the existence of an achievement drive, exploration of the environment was considered to be motivated by a curiosity drive, and so on. In psychodynamic theories of behavior, notably Freudian theory, these motivational forces were seen as operating beneath the level of consciousness, sometimes leading to behaviors which were the opposite of those that might be expected. Thus through the alleged mechanisms of "reaction formation" an intense aggressive drive could result in passive behavior rather than in aggressive conduct.

Such motivational conceptions have been criticized as being nonpredictive, descriptive rather than explanatory, incapable of experimental verification, and as disregarding the enormous complexity of human responsiveness. A major challenger has been *behavior theory,* which shifted the search for determinants of behavior from a study of vague internal states to a detailed examination of external influences on human behavior. Any given behavior can be analyzed into the external stimulus conditions that evoke it and the external reinforcing conditions that maintain it. There is much research to support the notion that human behavior is externally regulated. The empirical success of the operant conditioning approach has led many psychologists to abandon the view that human behavior is determined by factors within the individual. Instead, they emphasize the power of environmental forces over human behavior. However, radical behaviorism has been rejected by many people who refuse to see human beings as passive, controlled by an all-powerful environment. Other criticism is directed at the refusal of behavior theorists to recognize the significance of cognitive functioning in human behavior.

An alternative perspective, which we shall examine here, is provided by *social learning theory* (see Bandura, 1976a, b). In the social learning view, behavior, personal factors, and environmental factors all operate as interlocking determinants of each other. It is true that behavior is influenced by the environment, but the environment is partly of people's own making. Nor can "persons" be considered causes independent of their behavior. It is largely through their actions that people produce environmental conditions that affect their behavior in a reciprocal fashion. The experiences generated by behavior also partly determine what a person becomes and can do which, in turn, affects subsequent behavior. The relative influences exerted by these interdependent factors vary for different settings and for different behaviors. Sometimes environmental forces are the primary determinants of behavior regardless of the personality attitudes, values, or prior history of the individual. At other times, personal factors override the influences exerted by the environment.

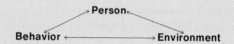

This conception of human functioning does not cast people into the role of being helplessly driven by inner forces nor that of being passively buffeted by environmental stimuli. People are seen as capable of exercising some degree of control over their own behavior. The impact of environmental stimuli is often mediated by cognitive processes through which people define, interpret, compare, contrast, give meaning to, and integrate stimulus events. People are able to remember the circumstances in which their behavior was followed by reinforcement and how often reinforcement occurred and thus, over time, to identify a pattern of contingent relationships. This integrating capacity depends on cognitive skills.

This cognitive orientation has guided social learning theorists to investigate neglected aspects of learning, such as observational learning, symbolic learning, and self-regulatory processes. Many behaviors vital for development and survival are acquired not by tedious trial and error but rather through the *observation* of models engaging in that behavior and of its consequences for the models. People often relate to each other and to their environment through the use of *symbols.* Verbal and imaginal symbols are representational forms that enable us to process, store in memory, and retrieve experiences that can serve as guides for future behavior. The cognitive power of symbolizing allows the learner to imagine alternative consequences of different actions, to test out problem-solving solutions mentally, and to give substance to abstract ideas such as "freedom," "dignity," "patriotism," and many others.

But one of the most distinguishing features of social learning theory is the importance it gives to *self-regulatory capacities.* People can create their own environmental inducements to action, generate cognitive support for choosing one course of action rather than another, and then supply their own reinforcers for such action.

Self-reinforcement occupies a prominent place among the various self-control processes we have investigated. Individuals regulate their behavior by rewarding themselves for meeting self-prescribed standards of performance. Results of research on self-regulatory processes are having a considerable impact in therapeutic programs designed to bring about personal change. Where the emphasis used to be on "managing" behavior by imposing stimulus contingencies, now it has shifted to developing personal skills in self-regulation. Control is vested in the individuals themselves, not in therapists, trainers, teachers, researchers, and other "agents of change." The individuals set their own goals, monitor their ongoing performance, evaluate it in terms of established criteria, and then decide to grant or deny reinforcers to themselves.

What constitutes a self-reinforcing event? A self-reinforcing event is one in which the individual exercises full control over a supply of freely available reinforcers, but does not administer them to himself or herself until a self-prescribed standard of performance has been attained. Performances that match or exceed these goals serve as discriminative cues for self-reward; all others signal an occasion of nonreinforcement. These performance standards usually involve comparison with (a) some *absolute level* of performance (such as 90 percent correct on a test, or bowling over 200); (b) one's own *previous personal standard* (such as reducing the number of cigarettes smoked in a day or increasing reading speed by a given amount); or (c) *social comparison* with the performance of others (such as doing as well as or better than your best friend on the test).

These features define the *operation* of self-reinforcement and should be distinguished from the *process* by which consequences affect behavior. The main differences between externally controlled reinforcements and those that are self-regulated arise *before* rewards are administered. Once the standard is met and the reward given, then the source of that reward does not matter—the process of reinforcement is the same.

Two separate lines of research have been designed to study when and how individuals choose to reward themselves, and whether these self-administered rewards can be shown to influence behavior. In the first line of research the *independent variables* are all those influences, such as the behavior of models, that are likely to affect the standards that are established for administering rewards. The *dependent variables* are the actual performance attainments which individuals do in fact self-reward or self-punish. The second line of research poses the question, do self-administered consequences in fact enhance performance? In this paradigm, the *independent variables* are the self-administered consequences and the *dependent variables* are the performance levels.

Let us consider briefly how performance standards are acquired and generalized to a variety of activities, and then turn to an analysis of conditions under which self-reinforcing contingencies are temporarily set aside.

Behavioral standards for determining when a self-reward is warranted are established by two processes, *modeling* and evaluative consequences. A considerable body of research demonstrates the influence of modeling in transmitting standards for self-reward. In a typical research design, children observe models performing a task in which the models adopt either high or low performance standards for self-reward. When that standard is reached or exceeded, the models reward and praise themselves; when they fall short of the standard, they withhold available rewards and criticize themselves. When children who have observed this situation are later allowed to perform and reward themselves, they tend to adopt the standards modeled, to judge their performance relative to those standards, and to reinforce themselves accordingly (Bandura & Kupers, 1964). Preferred reference models tend to be those whose ability is similar to one's own rather than models of considerably higher or lower ability. However, under special conditions observers may come to adopt the stringent standards of self-reward used by outstanding models even though they seldom attain these lofty standards. To create such "high ideals," the observer must be exposed to uniformly high standards, there must be a conducive relationship between models and observer, and public recognition must be bestowed on the model for upholding excellence (Bandura, Grusec & Menlove, 1967).

It should be mentioned in passing that acquisition of learning standards in everyday life is complicated because of inconsistencies in the standards of different models or of the same model in different circumstances, or because of contradictions between preached standards and practiced standards. The latter often turns up in the area of moral behavior and prejudice.

Transmitting performance standards by means of differential outcomes has only been studied in animal subjects (Bandura & Mahoney, 1974). After basic standards are established for instituting self-reward and negative consequences for insufficient performance, the response requirements are progressively raised. Animals come to adopt increasingly higher performance requirement standards for self-administered reward which then extend even to unfamiliar tasks.

The generalization of performance standards is a significant feature of self-reward. Indeed, the failure of many therapeutic and experimental training programs to break bad habits of food, drug, alcohol, and cigarette addiction can be attributed to failure of generalization of abstinence from the training situation to a variety of daily situations encountered by the person. I believe that the principal goal of social development is to transmit general standards of conduct that can serve as guides for self-regulation of behavior across a variety of activities. These generalized standards are best transmitted by varying the nature of the activities and the environmental setting while requiring a similar level of performance for self-reward.

After people learn to set standards for themselves and to react evaluatively to their own behavior, they can influence themselves by self-produced consequences. Results of numerous studies show that people can improve and maintain behavior on their own over long periods just as well as or better than when others apply incentives for change. The development of self-selective capabilities thus gives humans a capacity for self-direction.

Once internal control through self-produced consequences is established, it does not operate in an invariant and rigid way. Internal control may be temporarily suspended, making reprehensible conduct personally and socially acceptable by portraying it in the service of moral ends or by environmental arrangements that obscure or distort the relationship between one's actions and their effects (dropping a napalm bomb and not seeing the burning bodies).

People may engage in censurable conduct—immoral, illegal, evil behavior—without altering their moral standards and self-reinforcement systems because self-administered consequences can be discriminately disengaged in many ways, such as dehumanizing the people toward whom the actions are directed, misperceiving or misrepresenting the relationship between actions and consequences, or inventing moral justifications for the previously negative conduct. The violence of soldiers in military encounters against the "enemy," or "the gooks in My Lai" as contrasted with their peacetime, stateside conduct is a notable example of this process.

It is also important to recognize that many so-called external reward systems that promote prosocial responding are in fact human creations: grading systems, promotional schemes, reverence for slim bodies are not decrees of an autonomous impersonal environment. Thus there exists an interplay of self-generated and environmentally generated reward systems in which person and environment transform each other. In the search for prior causes, for every chicken discovered by a unidirectional environmentalist, a social learning theorist can identify an egg that came first.

Finally, the role of motivation in social learning theory must be acknowledged. Self-regulated reinforcement enhances performance mainly through its motivational function. By making self-reward conditional upon attaining a certain level of performance, individuals create self-inducements to persist in their efforts until their performances match their prescribed standards. External reinforcement also serves principally as a motivational operation rather than as a mechanical response strengthener. If valued rewards can be secured by performing certain activities, individuals are motivated by the incentives to engage in those activities. Therefore, from a social learning theory perspective it is more appropriate to speak of *regulation* of behavior by its consequences than of "reinforcement."

References

Bandura, A. *Social Learning Theory.* Englewood Cliffs, N.J.: Prentice-Hall, 1976a.

Bandura, A. Self-reinforcement: Theoretical and methodological considerations. *Behaviorism,* 1976b. In press.

Bandura, A., Grusec, J. E., & Menlove, F. L. Some social determinants of self-monitoring reinforcement systems. *Journal of Personality and Social Psychology,* 1967, *5,* 449–455.

Bandura, A., & Mahoney, M. J. Maintenance and transfer of self-reinforcement functions. *Behaviour Research and Therapy,* 1974, *12,* 89–97.

Bandura, A., & Kupers, C. J. Transmission of patterns of self-reinforcement through modeling. *Journal of Abnormal and Social Psychology,* 1964, *69,* 1–9.

PART 2
Human Information Processing

4

Language, Communication, and Memory

Consider the following transcript of an experimental session in a hypnosis research laboratory. What are some of the questions it raises in your mind about the function of language? the nature of memory? (Set aside for the moment your questions about hypnosis itself; we will consider this topic in depth in a later chapter.)

HYPNOTIST: "It's your birthday, Chuck. You are going back in time, getting younger and younger until once again you are only five years old. You can see the years on your personal calendar fade away as you slowly begin feeling younger than the eighteen years of age you are now. Becoming younger, sixteen . . . fourteen . . . twelve . . . ten years old . . . eight . . . seven . . . six . . . and now, you *are* a little boy of five years and it is your birthday party! Only five years old now and you are at your own birthday party."

CHUCK: "Oooo, ¡Mamí! ¡Qué linda! ¡Qué torta más grande y tantas velas! Hay uno, dos, tres, cuatro, cinco, y uno más para darme mi deseo especial. Quiero, quiero . . . una hermanita. Pero, ¿cómo voy a tener mi deseo si no puedo decirselo a nadie? ¿Puedo, puedo Mamí? ¿Puedo hacer lo que me prometiste? ¿Puedo meter un dedo en la torta para sacar la crema? Huiiii . . ."[1]

HYPNOTIST: "Now Chuck, once again you are going to become younger. You will be able to hear me and understand what I am saying, but soon you will feel and be only six months old. You will be six months old until I tap you on the shoulder, and then you will quickly return to the age you were when you came into the hypnosis research laboratory. You will once again be eighteen years old and a freshman at this college, able to remember and report all your experiences with age regression. The years are being removed from your calendar; five years old, four . . . three . . . becoming younger and younger, now two . . . then one, and soon you will be only a little baby lying in your

---

[1]"Oooh, Mommie, how beautiful, what a big cake and so many candles, there are one, two, three, four, five, and one more to give my special wish. I wish, I wish . . . a little sister. But how will I get my wish if I cannot tell anybody? Can I, can I Mommie? Can I do what you promised? Can I put my finger into the cake and scoop up the cream? . . . Wheeee . . ."

crib covered by a soft, warm blanket. A lovely, sweet baby of six months. Nice baby, Daddy loves his baby. Good baby."

OBSERVER'S NOTES: "Subject lying on floor of lab, begins curling up, thumb in mouth, saliva dripping from side of mouth, smiling . . . makes clenched fists, strained expression, on knees, violent rocking motion, head being repeatedly thrust forward toward and slightly above hands. Appears to be crying, without sound. Hypnotist tells subject he is being fed, Mother is feeding him warm milk. Rocking stops, lips pursed, lying down, sucking, hands raised near mouth, sucking stops, all motion stops, subject appears to be in deep sleep!"

Information gathered after the hypnotic session revealed that, although his family had spent several years in Mexico when he was a child, the student was unaware he knew any Spanish, and in fact could neither speak nor understand it when not under hypnosis. His mother recalled that for a period of time when he was a baby, Chuck would sometimes rock in his crib, smashing his head against the sides.

In this example, we can see that language apparently has the power to create images that can become interchangeable with the actual events they portray. The effects may be intensified under hypnosis, but the phenomenon occurs to some degree every time you get totally involved or "lost" in a good novel. Such images can serve not only as a link to re-creating the past, but also as a bridge to the future. Visions of what we will be, incentives and deterrents, goals and expectations guide our behavior along predictable channels. In some cultures, belief in the words of a curse pronounced by a powerful witch doctor can result in illness and eventually even death (see Chapter 9).

Although language serves both to structure reality and to stimulate fantasy, it can also become a barrier to the full experience of emotions by allowing us to substitute verbal descriptions of how we are (or ought to be) feeling in place of the feelings themselves. Language can thus be used to gain analytical distance from disturbing experiences by giving them a label, an explanation, and a time tag, which forces them into a specific historical niche.

A hypnotic subject who is undergoing age regression often begins by observing and silently commenting about past events that occur as if they were being shown on a private movie screen. It is only when the observer gives up this detached vantage point and becomes part of the action that the experience seemingly shifts from past to present tense, as in the case described above. In such instances aspects of memory that we ordinarily do not make much use of may come into play. Since human beings have become a language-dominated species, much of what we store in memory, and much of the process we use to retrieve this stored information, involves words. But there are other types of cues that can stimulate memories of long-past events, situations, and people. Emotional memories may be elicited by visual stimuli, odors, or other nonverbal cues associated with a particular experience. For example, strong feelings of guilt were unexpectedly aroused in a middle-aged man who had severely sprained his ankle and had to walk with a limp, supporting himself with a cane. He began to feel as if he *were* his younger brother who had had polio as a child. The man was reexperiencing the guilt he had felt watching his brother limp around with braces while he could run about freely—a memory triggered by postural cues and sensory feedback from his own limping.

It is through our mastery of language that human beings have been able to transmit the wisdom of one generation to the next, and through memory that we learn from our mistakes and profit from our successes. But where does our facility with language come from: is it learned, or is it the built-in product of endless years of evolution? And what has psychological investigation revealed about how we remember and how (all too often) we forget? These will be but a few of the questions we will examine as we consider those crowning achievements of our species—an incredible system of language and communication and a remarkable system of storing and retrieving what we have experienced and learned.

Learning and Using Language

It is a very inconvenient habit of kittens (Alice had once made the remark) that, whatever you say to them, they *always* purr. "If they would only purr for 'yes,' and mew for 'no,' or any rule of that sort," she had said, "so that one could keep up a conversation. But how *can* you talk with a person if they always say the same thing?"

Lewis Carroll, *Through the Looking Glass,* 1871

"We've got to communicate better." Phrases such as this have become very common in recent years, due in part to the growing influence of encounter and sensitivity-training groups, with their emphasis on learning how to relate to other people. But just what do we mean by "communicate"? In its broadest sense, communication is the process by which individuals give and receive information. The information to be communicated can be facts, ideas, or emotional feelings; it can be transmitted in a number of different ways, such as by speech, gestures, and pictorial or written symbols. When people use this process well, "communication" takes on the additional meaning of a more intimate sharing, and of a close relationship.

Although there are many means of communication, the most prominent one is that of verbal language. The development and use of a highly complex linguistic system is one of the most distinctive and curious accomplishments of human beings, and has become the focus of much research. Therefore we will begin this chapter with a discussion of spoken language, and then turn our attention to other forms (both verbal and nonverbal) of communication.

Possibly the greatest intellectual feat demonstrated by any human being is the learning of one's native language. This achievement takes place in the first few years of life, long before any formal schooling. Of course, it may not seem particularly impressive to you now, since you—and probably all the people you know—

have achieved this goal. But if you stop to think about the complexity of the way in which thousands of words are put together to produce meaningful utterances, you will undoubtedly agree on how astonishing it is that a small child can master such a system in so short a time. How is it done? Both psychologists and linguists have long sought the answers to this question, and their joint pursuit has brought into being the field of *psycholinguistics,* which involves the psychological study of language and speech. However, before we examine their theories about *how* language is learned, we must look at what language consists of and at the sequence of language development in children.

The Structure of Language

On the surface, human languages appear to be infinitely varied. To the student of psycholinguistics, however, it soon becomes apparent that they share certain universal properties. Thus while the specific sounds, words, and rules we shall consider in our discussion of language are those of English, the same broad principles are applicable to any language.

Levels of linguistic analysis. One of the properties common to all human languages is a basic linguistic structure—a hierarchical system building from simple sound units to structural units to complex idea units.

Phonological level. At the phonological level, we are concerned with the basic sound units that make up the stream of speech. A *phoneme* is a class of sounds that are recognized by speakers of a given language as having certain distinctive features that set them apart from other sounds and signal a difference in meaning. For example, while the sound of the letter *p* in *pan* is not entirely identical to that of the *p* in *plan*, any speaker of English would recognize them as instances of the same phoneme: /p/. Furthermore, an English-speaking person would make a clear distinction between this phoneme and the initial sound in the word *ban* (the phoneme /b/). Obviously, to understand any spoken language, a person must learn to make the necessary phonemic distinctions and identifications.

Grammatical level. The grammatical (or structural) level has two divisions: *morphology* and *syntax.* A *morpheme* is the smallest unit of speech that has a definable meaning; it may or may not be a word. Thus the word *tigers* is composed of two morphemes, the animal name and the *s* that indicates the plural. Words themselves can be thought of as speech units that communicate meaning and that are symbols for some class of objects, events, or activities.

Rules of *syntax,* or *grammar,* specify the permissible orders in which words and phrases may be arranged to form sentences. Chomsky (1957) postulated that the basic element of language at the syntactic level is a simple, active, declarative sentence, which he called a *kernel sentence.* This basic sentence can be given different meanings by applying certain *transformational rules.* For example, we can transform a kernel sentence such as "John hit the ball" to a passive sentence, "The ball was hit by John"; a negative sentence, "John did not hit the ball"; a question, "Did John hit the ball?"; or combinations of these such as "Wasn't the ball hit by John?" which is a passive, negative question. The specific rules vary from language to language, but certain aspects of these transformations are universal across languages of widely diverse cultures.

Semantic level. Some linguistic events have meaning, others are meaningless. The study of meaning is called *semantics.* Some words or word strings have arbitrarily agreed-upon meanings (such as the word *psychology*), or else acquire meaning through emotional or cognitive associations. The meaning of a word also depends on its immediate context and the inflection with which it is uttered relative to related words. For example, the simple word *run* has over twenty meanings. (How many of them can you list?) A "white house cat" becomes a very different thing depending on where the inflection falls: "a *white* house cat," "a *white house* cat," "a white *house* cat," and so on. The sentence, "The King is pregnant" is acceptable on the phonological and grammatical levels but not on the semantic level.

The psychological reality of linguistic analysis. Do these units, levels, and rules really possess psychological "reality" for the native speaker/listener? One research strategy employed by psycholinguists to answer this question involves changing a single linguistic element and then observing whether this has any effect on the subject's ability to perceive, learn, or remember a given utterance.

Studying phonemes. Investigators working at the phonological level have succeeded in determining the basic physical acoustic properties necessary to hear and identify a phoneme. Spoken sounds can be recorded and then converted to visual displays, called *spectrograms.* Plotted on these spectrograms are the frequency (cycles per second) of the sound and the amount of time needed to utter it. Researcher Ruth Day and her colleagues at the Haskins Laboratories in New Haven have developed a method for constructing simplified, idealized sound patterns from these actual spectrograms. ● With a special

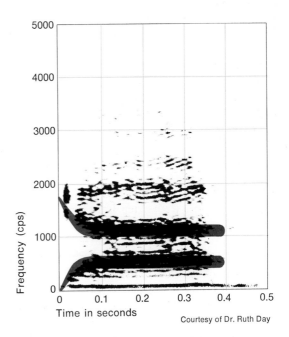

Courtesy of Dr. Ruth Day

● **ACTUAL AND IDEALIZED SPECTROGRAMS**
The actual spectrogram of the spoken syllable /ga/ is shown in black. Superimposed in color is the idealized spectrogram constructed by investigators at Haskins laboratory.

apparatus, these idealized patterns can be converted back to sound and played to listeners who are asked to report what they hear. The investigators have found that some very similar physical patterns are heard as different phonemes, as shown for /da/ and /ga/ in the top portion of the figure. ▲ Other very different physical patterns (as shown in the lower part of the figure) are often *not* distinguished by the listener as being different phonemes. The fact that no one pattern has been found that corresponds with a given phoneme (such as /d/) makes it all the more amazing that phonemes are so readily extracted from the stream of speech and recognized by listeners.

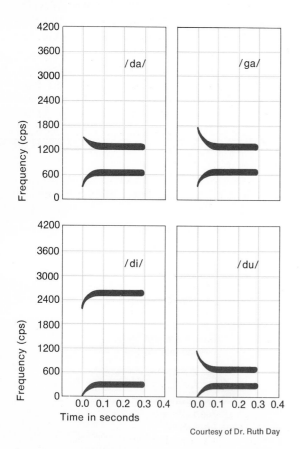

Courtesy of Dr. Ruth Day

▲ IDEALIZED SPECTROGRAMS OF FOUR SOUNDS

Studying morphemes. In English, the plural morpheme can take on any of three different sounds, depending on the last phoneme of the noun. Thus a voiceless *s* is added to a word like *trick*, a *z* sound is added to a word like *bird*, and an *ez* sound is added to a word like *glass*. Psycholinguists can specify the precise rules that determine when each form is used. But how can we tell whether children have actually learned these rules?

In an ingenious experiment, Joan Berko sought to determine whether preschool and first-grade children knew the rules for making plurals. For example, she showed each child a drawing of a birdlike creature and said, "This is a wug.*" Next, she pointed to a drawing with two of the same creatures and had the child complete the sentence, "There are two _____."* ■ *In this case, the correct plural form is* wugz. *Similarly, if the animal had been identified as a* niss, *then the child would be correct if he or she said that two of them were two* niss-ez.

The children were able to answer the questions consistently; the investigator concluded that "there can be no doubt that children in this age range operate with clearly defined morphological rules." Boys and girls performed equally well; first-graders performed significantly better than preschoolers on many of the items (Berko, 1958).

It is important to note that nonsense names were used in this study; had acceptable English

This is a wug.

Now there is another one.

There are two of them.
There are two_____.

After Berko, 1958

■ MATERIALS USED
IN STUDYING THE FORMATION OF PLURALS

names been used, such as *bird*, we would be unable to determine whether the children knew the rule, or whether they had heard both *bird* and *birds* before and had simply memorized both forms. What is meant by "knowing a linguistic rule" is not that the person can state the rule in all its technical glory, but that he or she can apply it correctly, especially in novel situations that arise.

Studying syntax and semantics. In a series of experiments, George Miller and his co-workers at Rockefeller University have studied the psychological effects of violating syntactic and semantic rules. Consider the five "normal sentences" in the table. ◆ Note that all follow the same syntactic sequence, namely (Subject) + (Verb) + (Direct Object) + (Preposition) + (the) + (Object of Preposition). From these, a new set of sentences was generated that violated semantic rules but preserved syntactic order. Each of these was prepared by selecting the first word of one normal sentence, the second word of the next normal sentence, the third word of the next normal sentence, and so on, yielding the string, "Gadgets kill passengers from the eyes." This procedure was continued until all words were used, yielding the second group of sentences in the table, which were grammatically correct but "semantically anomalous." A third set of sentences was generated by haphazardly rearranging the words of the normal sentences to destroy their normal syntactic structure, yielding the "ungrammatical strings" shown in the table. The sentences were tape-recorded, and the subjects were asked to "shadow" them by repeating them out loud as soon as they heard them. The subjects were able to correctly repeat 89 percent of the first group, 80 percent of the second group, and only 56 percent of the third, ungrammatical group. Similar results were found when subjects were asked to memorize these types of sentences. Thus both structure and meaning apparently affect our ability to hear accurately and to remember what we have heard (Miller & Isard, 1963; Marks & Miller, 1964).

Recent research on nonstandard English languages (dialects) spoken by various ethnic groups (particularly those in urban ghettos) has shown them to be well-developed linguistic systems with their own rules and contructions. Although these rules differ from those that guide speakers of standard English, the users of nonstandard English follow them with a consistency that allows them to be understood by others in their language community. (See *P&L* Close-up, pp. 148–49.)

The Development of Language

Up to this point, we have been speaking of language as though it were simply a way of expressing one's ideas. However, language is more than a medium of communication; it plays a basic role in ordering experience and in stabilizing the confusing world a young child faces. In fact, there are very few psychological processes that are not affected by the operation of language, verbal labels, and symbols. By "appropriately" using language, a child can have his or her biological needs better met, secure attention, and control the behavior of others.

Language also allows the child to represent things symbolically and thus operate intellec-

◆ **SENTENCES USED IN STUDYING CONSEQUENCES OF LINGUISTIC RULE VIOLATIONS**

Normal Sentences
1. Gadgets simplify work around the house.
2. Accidents kill motorists on the highways.
3. Trains carry passengers across the country.
4. Bears steal honey from the hive.
5. Hunters shoot elephants between the eyes.

Semantically Anomalous Sentences
1. Gadgets kill passengers from the eyes.
2. Accidents carry honey between the house.
3. Trains steal elephants around the highways.
4. Bears shoot work on the country.
5. Hunters simplify motorists across the hive.

Ungrammatical Strings
1. Around accidents country honey the shoot.
2. On trains hive elephants the simplify.
3. Across bears eyes work the kill.
4. From hunters house motorists the carry.
5. Between gadgets highways passengers the steal.

tually on an abstract level rather than the concrete level of immediate experience. Mastery of language is necessary if we are to recall, plan, reason, analyze, synthesize, explain inconsistencies, reduce uncertainty, and form a common bond of social reality with others in our shared language community.

The sequence of language development. Human language production can be roughly divided into four stages. These stages overlap and are not sharply differentiated, but they form a convenient chronology of early vocalization (Kaplan & Kaplan, 1970).

Stage 1. The study of language development in human children begins with the birth cry of the newborn. For the first three weeks, the infant's vocal repertoire is extremely limited. The basic cry may be modified somewhat to produce variations, from which the alert parent infers anger or physical pain. But cries, coughs, and gurgles make up the sum of the newborn's vocal production. (See *P&L* Close-up, p. 149.)

Stage 2. From about three weeks of age to four or five months, the infant introduces some pseudocries—cry vocalizations that are not simple cries. Variety in these sounds is produced by changes in duration, pitch, and articulation.

Stage 3. During the last half of the first year, the child's speech sounds become so varied and continuous that this period is known as the "babbling stage." In addition to producing both vowel-like and consonant-like sounds, the child begins to imitate adult intonation. Sounds that are easier to produce (such as the *e* in *bet*) appear earlier at this stage of vocalization than sounds (such as *oo* in *noon*) that are more difficult.

Stage 4. The beginnings of patterned, "true" speech occur some time near the end of the first year. The "prelinguistic" period of the previous stages gives way to the appearance of the child's

Close-up
"He Done Did Follow the Man's Rules": Nonstandard English

What is the difference between the following sentences: "He workin' when the boss come in" and "He be workin' when the boss come in"? According to the rules of standard English, both sentences are grammatically incorrect and imprecise. However, if the speaker is a black American, there is a significant difference in their meaning, one that is conveyed with considerable precision according to psycholinguists J. L. Dillard (1967, 1968, 1972) and William Labov (1969). The first statement means the worker performs his job *only* in the presence of his employer. The second indicates that the worker is conscientious about his work and works even in the absence of surveillance.

"I do," "I did," and "I have done" are the accepted forms of the verb "to do" in standard English, but the black child might say, "I do," "I done," and "I have did," or "I done did." Linguistic differences such as these have been assumed by many white educators to reflect "cultural deprivation" and cognitive inability to learn and process complex concepts.

At the heart of this controversy is whether nonstandard English is erratic and illogical or is a rule-governed language system. Resolution of the issue goes beyond satisfying academic curiosity because of its social, cultural, and political implications. Are black children and others who have learned to master their ethnic group's nonstandard English language system handicapped by having to unlearn it and acquire a "foreign" language that is the only accepted and correct form in school? Furthermore, since their language is not officially recognized as "legitimate"—as it would be if they spoke Russian, Arabic, or French—such children are often ridiculed for their "faulty" speech habits, thereby making school for them a place associated with feelings of inferiority. (Incidentally, there are, in fact, rules regarding verb forms in nonstandard English that are similar to those of Russian or Arabic and dissimilar to those of English.)

according to the rules of their dialect. Thus, when asked to repeat sentences containing the negative "nobody ever," black ghetto children consistently responded with "nobody never"—the correct form in black English (Labov et al., 1968).

The concern of linguists that black nonstandard English be recognized as a viable, legitimate language is eloquently stated by Labov:

"Teachers are now being told to ignore the language of Negro children as unworthy of attention and useless for learning. They are being taught to hear every natural utterance of the child as evidence of his mental inferiority. As linguists we are unanimous in condemning this view as bad observation, bad theory and bad practice. That educational psychology should be strongly influenced by a theory so false to the facts of language is unfortunate; but that children should be the victims of this ignorance is intolerable." (1969, p. 169)

Some instances of grammatical rules of black dialect are, for example: (a) when a word ends with two audible sounds the last is dropped—*fist* becomes *fis* and *desk* becomes *des*. Thus, with plurals *fis* transforms to *fisses* and *des* to *desses;* (b) whenever standard English can contract, black children use either the contracted verb form or the deleted form (called the *zero copula*)—"they mine," "you right"; (c) in long sentences additional predicate markers are used to remind the speaker and listener of the subject of the discussion, as in "You know that girl live on 151st street, dress real cool, work modeling downtown, got real deep eyes, *she* go to school with me."

Linguists have argued that aspects of nonstandard black English offer a better sense of the point in time, or the duration an action takes place. In addition, because this language is still closer to its oral, storytelling tradition than to written form, it employs grammatical devices, emphasis, and vocabulary to hold the listener's immediate attention. Even when listening to a sentence spoken in standard form and asked to repeat it, black research subjects "translate" it

Close-up
Crying Like a Baby

Infant cries show sufficiently regular patterning that analysis of distress cries can be used by investigators to detect certain brain disorders or genetic defects. When over 300 distress cries from thirteen infants were analyzed by means of sound spectrograms, there were distinct patterns and differences in pitch between those of "normal" infants and those diagnosed as "possibly abnormal" or "abnormal" (Ostwald & Peltzman, 1974). There were no differences in the duration of the cries, but there were distinct differences in their pitch patterns. The mean pitch values of the cries of abnormal infants were much higher than those of the normal babies and slightly higher than those from the possibly abnormal group.

first recognizable words. However, it is still not clear whether the prelinguistic stages are systematically related to the production of true speech. Some researchers maintain that in the babbling stage there is an ordered sequence of development: a preoccupation first with vowel sounds, then with consonant sounds, then with consonant-vowel combinations, and finally with consonant-vowel-consonant-vowel units that embody the rhythm and intonation of true language. This viewpoint is opposed by other theorists, who argue that the babbling sounds just "produce themselves" and have no systematic function. According to this position, the development of true language is completely discontinuous from prior linguistic behavior.

The average year-old child has an initial vocabulary of 2 to 3 words. This increases to about 50 words by twenty-four months and 1000 words by the age of three (Lenneberg, 1969). It is likely that the greater stimulation provided by daily exposure to television programming will be shown to accelerate vocabulary development, and if skillfully prepared (as on the program "Sesame Street") may have an impact on other areas of language development. ▲ One study (Irwin, 1960) demonstrated that when children of working-class parents were regularly read to for fifteen minutes a day from their thirteenth to their thirtieth month, their production of speech sounds was increasingly superior to that of matched controls from the age of seventeen months onward.

The pattern of language development. Once children are able to produce recognizable words, what do they say? The first meaningful utterances are single words, such as "mama," which often carry the force of a complete sentence. For example, "mama" could mean "That's Mama," "Mama, where are you?" "Mama, I'm hungry," or several other things, depending on the situation. Later on, the child begins to put words together to form two-word sentences. As we shall see, these word combinations are not random but show a definite, regular structure. While this structure changes with age, it does not always correspond to the structure of adult language.

▲ Snuffle-Upagus and Big Bird are among the residents of "Sesame Street" who devote their efforts to helping preschool children develop cognitive skills.

Putting words together. At about eighteen months of age, the child begins to use two-word, rather than one-word sentences. Investigators who have studied these sentences have identified two distinct *classes* of words (Braine, 1963; Miller & Ervin, 1964). One of these classes, which is relatively small, contains *pivot words*, while the second, larger class contains all other words in the child's vocabulary. A *pivot word* is one that can be attached to many other words to form a meaningful sentence. For example, the word "more" is a pivot word because the child can say many things ("More hot," "More milk," "More wet") by adding it to different words from the vocabulary class. The position of a particular pivot word in a two-word sentence is always fixed; it is either always in the first position ("Allgone milk," "Allgone Daddy") or always in the second position ("Mail come," "Mommy come"). ■

A second type of two-word sentence that the child begins to use at this time is one that combines two vocabulary words, rather than a pivot plus one vocabulary word. Such sentences seem to be expressing various types of relationships between things. For example, the sentence "Cup glass" could be signifying a *conjunction* ("I see a cup and a glass"). Similarly, *location* could be expressed by "hat chair" ("The hat is on the chair"), while "Party hat" might signify *attribution* ("This is a party hat"). A sentence such as "Mary ball" could indicate either *possession* ("Here is Mary's ball") or a *subject-object* relationship ("Mary throws the ball"). Obviously, two-word sentences such as these can only be understood in the context in which they are spoken.

The important thing to realize about the child's language at this stage is that it is *not* a direct copy of an adult's language. Although the words are the same, the child puts them together in a different way. The child's grammar has its own rules that do not correspond to those of the adult language that he or she hears every day and must eventually use in order to communicate effectively.

Organizing words and phrases. When children are about two years old, they begin to produce sentences that are longer than two words. Often, these longer sentences are expansions of shorter ones; the child first produces a short sentence and then apparently "plugs it in" to a more complex one. For example, a child will say, "Want that . . . Andrew want that" or "Stand up . . . Cat stand up . . . Cat stand up table." A careful examination of these longer sentences suggests that the child is actively analyzing each sentence into its structural subunits and is not just stringing words together.

As the child's language becomes more and more complex, he or she begins to put some order into it. The child begins applying patterns of regularity, or *rules*, and then uses them as often as possible. Sometimes the rule is applied too widely and results in incorrect linguistic forms. As an example, once the child learns that the general rule for making a plural (adding *"s"* to the noun), this rule will be extended to *all* plurals, producing such words as "foots" or "mouses." Similarly, when the child learns the past-tense rule for most verbs (adding *"ed"* to the verb), the *"ed"* will be added to *all* verbs, resulting in words such as "doed" and "breaked."

■ **A PORTION OF ONE CHILD'S PIVOT GRAMMAR**
With few exceptions, any of the pivot words followed by any of the vocabulary words can form a meaningful sentence in this child's language.

First Position Pivots	Vocabulary
allgone byebye big more pretty my see night-night hi	boy sock boat fan milk plane shoe vitamins hot Mommy Daddy . . .

After McNeill, 1966

This overgeneralization of a rule is especially interesting because it usually appears *after* the child has learned and used the correct forms of the verbs and nouns. That is, the child first uses the correct verb forms of "came" and "went," apparently because they were learned as separate vocabulary items. However, when the child later learns the general rule for past tenses, he or she immediately extends it to all verbs and starts to say "comed" and "goed," even though the child has never heard other people say such words. Sometimes these incorrect overgeneralizations last for several years, in spite of adult efforts to change them. It is from analysis of these mistakes that we can discover how language learning depends on acquisition of rules.

Up to this time, children's sentences have generally taken the form of simple statements, such as "More cookie" or "John want that." However, the child gradually begins to apply transformational rules and construct questions and negative statements. For example, the statement "He is doing it" can be turned into a question by making one transformation: "Is he doing it?" If you also add a "why" to the beginning of the sentence, so that the question becomes "Why is he doing it?" then you have made *two* transformations.

When children first learn how to do these transformations, they are unable to do more than one of them for a single sentence. For example, a child at this stage of development will add the "why" to the sentence but is not capable of also changing "he" and "is." The resulting question is "Why he is doing it?" At a later stage, the child will master the ability to do two transformations at once and will be able to phrase this question correctly. However, further linguistic development is required before the child is able to produce a sentence that requires *three* transformations, such as "Why is he *not* doing it?" (Bellugi-Klima, 1968)

Theories of Language Learning

Now that we have some idea of *what* children learn to say, we can begin to tackle the question of *how* they learn to say it. Where does this ability to produce a complex language come from? If you were to go out and ask people this question, they would probably say, "Oh, children just imitate what they hear, and if they make a mistake, their parents correct them." In fact, this imitation-and-correction model is one of the major theories of language acquisition and is generally known as the *learning theory approach*.

The learning theory approach. B. F. Skinner (1957), as a leading learning theorist, argues that children learn language in just the same way that they learn to perform all other behaviors, such as how to eat with a fork or chopsticks or how to hit a ball or herd sheep. They imitate the linguistic behavior of the adults around them and, if they do so correctly, the adults will reward them positively by praising them and telling them that what they have said is "right." However, if they make a mistake and say something ungrammatical, adults will withhold reinforcement, and sometimes provide punishment by saying "No, that's wrong" or "You can't talk like that." As a result of this selectively reinforced imitation of adult language, children gradually learn how to speak correctly.

There is evidence to support the view that vocalizations in three-month-old infants can be increased by providing social reinforcements when vocalizations occur (Rheingold, Gewirtz, & Ross, 1959). Other recent studies have shown that the incidence of a particular sound can be increased or decreased via reinforcement (see Routh, 1969).

Although this is a fairly simple, straightforward idea of how children learn a language, there are several major problems with it. First, the *variability* in environmental or reinforcing conditions from child to child should result in tremendous variability in language development and performance in different children. But this is not the case. Despite differences in the kind of opportunities for training and social reinforcement offered by the great variety of social environments in which language acquisition takes place, the development of language by children of various cultures and social classes seems to follow a relatively standardized, universal pattern. An unusual speech environment is provided by deaf parents, who would be unable to reinforce adult-like vocalizations selectively since they could not hear them. Eric Lenneberg (1969) reports a fascinating study in which he recorded the environmental sounds and the vocalizations of two groups of infants, six born of deaf parents and six of hearing parents. These observations were carried out twice a week for three months, starting before the babies were ten days old.

The children whose parents were both deaf experienced little in the way of normal speech sounds from them, and there was significantly less other sound (from TV, radio, and voices) in their homes than in the homes of the other children. However, these dramatic environmental differences made no difference between the babies in the two groups in their vocalizations (crying, cooing, and fussing). "Thus the earliest development of human sounds appears to be relatively independent of the amount, nature, or timing of the sounds made by parents." (p. 637)

Still another argument against the learning theory analysis of language is that children often say things that are clearly *not* imitations of adult speech. As we saw earlier, children will say "foots" and "goed," or will produce two-word sentences like "Allgone Daddy," none of which they have ever heard adults say. At certain stages of development, they are unable to make several grammatical transformations, even though they have always heard adults make them. Furthermore, parents actually do not correct the child's speech as often as the learning theorists contend they do. If we listen closely to the interaction between parent and child, we will see that the parent is more concerned with comprehending *what* the child is trying to say,

rather than with *how* it is being said. A true statement will often receive positive reinforcement from the parent, even if it is ungrammatical. For example, if a child says "Her curl my hair," the mother will probably answer "That's right" because she is, in fact, curling the child's hair. However, if a child makes the grammatically correct statement, "There's the animal farmhouse" but is pointing to a lighthouse, the parent will surely say "No, that's wrong" (Brown, Cazden, & Bellugi-Klima, 1969).

Most importantly, if children could say only sentences that they had successfully imitated and been reinforced for, then how could they ever produce new sentences that they had never heard before? Clearly, children and adults alike are continually producing sentences that are completely original; in fact, the total number of sentences that might be uttered by any human being is theoretically infinite. We must then look for a theory of language development that will take this into account.

The psycholinguistic approach. Skinner's learning theory analysis of language was strongly criticized by Noam Chomsky of M.I.T. (1968, 1969), who has become one of the leading proponents of the psycholinguistic theory of language acquisition. This approach argues that children learn a complex system of *rules*, rather than just many different strings of words, and that such a system allows them to generate an infinite number of new sentences. As we saw earlier, children's use of pivot grammar and their overgeneralization of the past tense form are clear evidence that they are using a system of rules. Not only do children acquire these rules without having someone formally teach them "as rules," but they do so at a very early age when they are not capable of other complex intellectual achievements. How do they manage to accomplish such an incredible feat?

Theorists such as Lenneberg (1969) stress the importance of biological aspects. All evidence indicates that the ability to develop a complex, abstract language system is *species specific;* that is, unique to human beings. Some animals, such as baboons, for example, have developed a reasonably complex signal system to communicate the presence of danger or food. However, such systems contain no means for novelty of expression or abstraction as in human language, and, as we shall see, the ability of such animals to learn human speech is limited.

Language capacity also seems to be *species uniform:* there is no known instance of a group of human beings without a language. Furthermore, there is little difference in the grammatical complexity of various human languages. Observations such as these have led a number of students of language processes to propose that many aspects of our linguistic ability are probably innate. That is, much of our ability to speak and understand a language is due to our genetic makeup rather than to the specific reinforcements to which we have been exposed. Lenneberg points out that "Children begin to speak no sooner and no later than when they reach a given stage of physical maturation" (1969, p. 635).

He has shown that language development correlates consistently with motor development and maturational indices of brain development. ●

If this theory of an innate ability is correct, then all intellectually competent children should be able to develop a rule system regardless of the language they speak—and, in fact, this seems to be true. A comparison of children all over the world shows that they learn their native language at approximately the same age and that they use similar rule systems (Slobin, 1971).

The psycholinguistic approach has focused particular attention on the *productive* aspects of language—that is, on how people are able to produce completely original sentences that they have not heard before. Presumably, this aspect of language is based on the ability to use various syntactic rules. According to Chomsky, these rules can be divided into two classes, depending on whether they determine the superficial or the underlying linguistic structure of language. The *surface structure* of a sentence refers to its component parts (such as noun, verb, object, etc.) and the relationship between them. This

● **CORRELATION OF MOTOR AND LANGUAGE DEVELOPMENT**

Age (years)	Motor Milestones	Language Milestones
0.5	Sits using hands for support; unilateral reaching	Cooing sounds change to babbling by introduction of consonantal sounds
1	Stands; walks when held by one hand	Syllabic reduplication; signs of understanding some words; applies some sounds regularly to signify persons or objects, that is, the first words
1.5	Prehension and release fully developed; gait propulsive; creeps downstairs backward	Repertoire of 3 to 50 words not joined in phrases; trains of sounds and intonation patterns resembling discourse; good progress in understanding
2	Runs (with falls); walks stairs with one foot forward only	More than 50 words; two-word phrases most common; more interest in verbal communication; no more babbling
2.5	Jumps with both feet; stands on one foot for 1 second; builds tower of six cubes	Every day new words; utterances of three and more words; seems to understand almost everything said to him; still many grammatical deviations
3	Tiptoes 3 yards (2.7 meters); walks stairs with alternating feet; jumps 0.9 meter	Vocabulary of some 1000 words; about 80 percent intelligibility; grammar of utterances close approximation to colloquial adult; syntactic mistakes fewer in variety, systematic, predictable
4.5	Jumps over rope; hops on one foot; walks on line	Language well established; grammatical anomalies restricted either to unusual constructions or to the more literate aspects of discourse

Lenneberg, 1969

structure of a sentence plays an important role in determining its meaning. Clearly, if we take the words in a sentence like "Lecturers like silent, happy audiences" and rearrange them in various combinations, the meaning they convey will be quite different. What a sentence means (its semantic interpretation) is determined by its underlying *deep structure*. Even if sentences have very different surface structure, they may be similar in their deep structure. For instance, the sentences "I asked Chris to come" and "What I asked of Chris was that she come" have the same deep structure and semantic interpretation, even though their surface structure differs.

It is this deep structure that is intuitively and unconsciously converted, by means of transformational rules, into the surface structure. Take, for example, the sentence "The man who is sitting at the head of the table is my father." We may consider this sentence to be composed of a transformed version of "The man is my father" and "The man is sitting at the head of the table." In this case the speaker has unconsciously transformed two separate "sentences" (at the conceptual level) into the single sentence that is spoken. Certain transformational rules have been used to *embed* one sentence in the other and make the morphological and syntactic changes necessary to produce a well-formed construction. The hearer of the sentence goes through the reverse procedure, transforming the surface structure into the deeper structures that reveal the underlying meaning.

The psycholinguistic approach is certainly a challenging alternative to learning theories, but it does not give the final answer to the problem of how a child learns his or her native language, and some of its basic assumptions have been questioned as well. We still do not know exactly what the "innate abilities" of the child's mind are, nor how they operate to produce various language skills. Much more research is needed before we really understand the development of language. Meanwhile, the debate between the followers of Chomsky and of Skinner on how much of language acquisition is innate and how much is learned will probably continue for some time.

Patterns of Communication

Imagine, if you will, that you and three other students are subjects in an experiment that involves a city-planning simulation. You are told that one of you will be chosen to be the designer and the others will serve as consultants working together to plan a model city. The person to be singled out for distinction is to be chosen on the basis of a series of tests and after a round-table discussion between all the participants. What would you do to communicate to the experimenter that you want the job of designer—without, of course, being so crude as to come right out and ask for it in so many words?

But wait! Are you sure you want to be singled out? In some situations the person in charge has to assume much responsibility, stress, and anxiety and receives little praise or reward. This was indeed true for half of the groups when this study was actually conducted; the designer was to be given electric shocks for every poor decision made—a hostile environment to work in. For the other half of the groups in the supportive environment condition, the designer was to receive a monetary reward for each good decision.

Now you are faced with deciding what to do, how to behave, in order to stand out from the crowd in the supportive, rewarding environment, while submerging yourself inconspicuously in the crowd when the environment is hostile and threatening.

In this experiment, conducted by Christina Maslach (1974) with Stanford University undergraduates, the subjects' verbal and nonverbal behaviors were videotaped and analyzed frame by frame to determine differences in communication patterns they used to get across the message that they wanted to be chosen, to be "outstanding," or wanted *not* to be noticed, to be "anonymous." Indeed, there were marked differences elicited by the two situations, and some features of these patterns of communication also differed depending on whether the subjects were female or male.

To stand out in a supportive environment, subjects gave unusual self-descriptions, accompanied by expressive arm gestures, lengthy comments, and unique, nonconforming test responses. Female subjects smiled more often than males, but made fewer bodily movements when someone else in the group was talking. Females who talked more about themselves made fewer total comments, although each of their comments was longer than the average.

The threatening environment elicited anxious, agitated responses in the subjects anticipating it. Surprisingly, they joked a lot, smiled, interrupted, and made many short comments. Although these "defensive" communications actually called attention to themselves, they consciously tried to meld into the group by giving highly conforming test responses and by avoiding statements that were personal or unusual.

On the basis of this research we can rephrase a familiar speech from Shakespeare's *As You Like It:* All the world's a stage on which people attempt to be either a part of the chorus in the background or the main actor; tragedies draw us back, while romances and comedies encourage us to step out into the spotlight.

We communicate to others our desire to be noticed or ignored not only by what we say but by how we say it, not only with the language of words but with the silent language of the body and our expressive style.

Communicating Without Words

Verbal language, with its intriguing complexity of structure and richness of vocabulary, is clearly the primary means by which people express their thoughts and feelings. However, to assume that verbal language is the *only* means of communication would be a major mistake. Facial expressions, body movements, gestures, and vocal characteristics (such as stammering) are all powerful modes of communication. The same words (such as "I love you") can be interpreted in many different ways, depending on whether they are said in a whisper, in a teasing tone of voice, with a sob, or with a hug. Our intuitive judgment that a person "doesn't sound sincere" is often based on the manner in which his or her words are expressed, rather than the content of the words themselves. A vivid example of nonlinguistic expressiveness is the reported behavior of prisoners of war, who would read aloud the statements that their captors demanded of them, but would vary their intonation so that their fellow prisoners and relatives would know that they didn't really believe what they were saying.

Although we are specifically trained in whatever language we speak, few of us, except drama students, are ever taught how to use these forms of nonlinguistic expressiveness. Some of them appear to be innate responses, such as crying and smiling. Others are learned informally, such as saying a positive phrase ("Oh, that's wonderful") in a negative tone of voice in order to express sarcasm. These nonverbal messages usually convey only a few basic dimensions of human feelings and attitudes (like–dislike, dominance or status, and responsiveness to others), rather than the more complex ones that can be expressed by a verbal language (Mehrabian, 1971b). The one important exception to this is the complex nonverbal sign language used by the deaf.

Nonverbal expressiveness. Broadly defined, *nonverbal expression* refers to any communication that does not rely solely on words or word symbols. Although such behaviors can be used in conjunction with verbal utterances (as when a person smiles or gestures while talking), they are not dependent on the production of words for their occurrence. The interest in nonverbal behaviors has centered on their use as a mode of communication—what expressions or movements do we use to convey our thoughts and feelings, and to infer those of other people?

Experimental research has focused on four general types of nonverbal expression. Many studies have been made of *facial display*, since the most important overt expression of emotion occurs in the face, at least for humans (see Chapter 9 for a discussion of this research).

Another area of study is *kinesics*, which is concerned with body positions, posture, gestures, and other body movements. *Proxemics* focuses on spatial distance between people interacting with each other, as well as their orientation toward each other (as reflected in touch and eye contact). A fourth area deals with *paralanguage*, which covers aspects of communication that are vocal but not verbal—voice qualities, such as pitch, intensity, and rate of speech; hesitations, errors, and other speech nonfluencies; and nonlanguage sounds, such as laughs and yawns.

An eye can threaten like a loaded and leveled gun, or can insult like hissing or kicking; or, in its altered mood, by beams of kindness, it can make the heart dance with joy.

Ralph Waldo Emerson, *Conduct of Life*, 1860

The eyes have it. The eyes have long been held to be one of the most expressive parts of the body. People "make eyes" at those to whom they're attracted, while antagonists have "eyeball-to-eyeball" confrontations. Untrustworthy characters "won't look you straight in the eye," while people who are embarrassed, shy, or respectful will "avert their gaze."

In general, it seems that eye contact helps establish the nature of the relationship between people—positive or negative, intimate or distant. People tend to engage in mutual glances, if they like the person they are with, but they will try to avoid looking at a companion they dislike (Exline & Winters, 1965). Extending this finding a bit, Rubin (1970) observed the eye-contact patterns of heterosexual couples who were waiting to participate in a psychology experiment together. Those couples who were in love were more likely to gaze into each other's eyes than those couples who were not. Although the implication of these two studies is that eye contact reflects a positive relationship, this is not always true. According to Ellsworth and Carlsmith (1968), eye contact serves to intensify the ongoing verbal content of a relationship, whether it be negative or positive. Thus if someone is paying me compliments, I will feel more positively about that person if he or she

looks at me rather than looks away. However, if someone is criticizing me, I will feel better about the relationship if the person avoids looking at me—the lack of eye contact makes the negative feedback seem less personal.

It has long been known that *staring* serves as a signal for threat in nonhuman primates and also that many cultures around the world have had a fear of the destructive magic of the "evil eye," which has resulted in taboos against staring. To find out how more "sophisticated" Americans would react to an intense stare from a stranger, Ellsworth and her associates conducted a very interesting field experiment simple enough to be replicated by any student who is interested in doing so.

The experimenter waited at the corner of a busy intersection until a car pulled up at the red light. As soon as the car stopped, the experimenter began to stare, calmly and continuously, at the driver. When the light changed to green, another experimenter started a concealed stopwatch and measured the time it took the driver to cross the intersection. For subjects in the control group, the experimenter simply stood on the corner—without looking directly at the drivers—and measured the time it took for their cars to cross.

The experiment was repeated several times, with a number of variations, and in each of the replications the results were the same: drivers who were stared at crossed the intersection significantly faster than those who were not stared at (Ellsworth, Henson, & Carlsmith, 1972).

In this case, eye contact was clearly a stimulus for avoidance behavior. In interpreting this finding, we do not need to conclude that the stare is an innate threat signal in humans or that modern-day Americans still harbor a secret belief in the evil eye. The experimenters suggest that in this situation staring had two major properties: (a) it created an incongruous situation in which the driver did not have any obvious, appropriate response, and (b) it was a strong enough stimulus that the driver felt he or she was involved and had to make a response.

Incongruity alone is not enough to account for the escape behavior. This was demonstrated by a control study in which the experimenter performed an incongruous act (pounding on the sidewalk with a hammer) that did not involve staring. On the average, drivers in this condition did not cross the intersection any faster than in the no-stare condition; they experienced incongruity but not involvement. Only when they were personally involved did the lack of an appropriate response apparently arouse tension and elicit escape at the earliest possible moment. When the starer provides additional "suggestive" cues, or stares in a situation where

approach responses are appropriate or might prove rewarding, then eye contact would be expected to be a "come-on" stimulus, rather than a "get-going" one.

Body and soul. Undoubtedly there have been times when you "knew" that someone else was interested in you, even though that person had not actually stated it in words. What nonverbal cues were you using to arrive at your judgment? As we have just seen, eye contact would be one clue to a person's interest. However, you would probably also recognize certain body movements and gestures as signs of involvement—for example, turning to face you, leaning toward you while you speak, reaching out as though to touch (as when someone raises a hand in greeting). All of these behaviors are signals that the individual's attention is being focused on you. The amount of information contained in attention movements such as these is well known to various "naive psychologists." (See *P&L* Close-up, p. 159.)

Body cues are also good (although subtle) indicators of people's status. When two people get together, the one who has the more relaxed posture is usually the one who has higher status. That is, the higher-status person is more likely to sit rather than stand, to recline or lean sideways rather than be erect, and to take a more asymmetrical stance (e.g., with legs crossed or arms akimbo). For the lower-status person to adopt a more relaxed posture is generally viewed as being disrespectful or defiant. Why should relaxation indicate high status? One explanation is that, historically, high status has been based on power. Powerful people are less fearful and less vigilant than weak ones, and thus can afford to relax or turn their back on others (Mehrabian, 1969b).

In addition to posture or stance, the way in which a person moves from one place to another is often expressive of self-confidence and status. Someone who walks stiffly or hesitantly will give a very different impression than someone who strides briskly and effortlessly. In some cases, the messages that are contained in the style of a person's walk are far more important than the fact that the person is heading for a particular destination. A particularly vivid example of this is the "black walk" that is fairly typical of young black males, particularly in ghetto areas. This walk is actually a stroll, with a casual and rhythmic gait. One arm swings at the side with the hand slightly cupped, while the other arm either hangs limply or has the fingers tucked in the pocket. Sometimes the head is slightly elevated and tipped to the side. Over and above this basic format, each man adds some original components to create a personal style. When they are "walking that walk," black men are communicating a number of messages, including self-esteem, masculinity, being "cool," and (when used in response to a reprimand) rejection of authority (Johnson, 1971).

Another expressive form of body movement is the use of gestures. Shaking or nodding one's head, shaking hands, folding one's arms, and pointing are all examples of this process. Like many other nonverbal behaviors, gestures can convey emotional feelings, status, and responsiveness or attention. (See *P&L* Close-up at right.)

Close-up
A Poker Body Is As Important As a Poker Face

Professional gamblers are well aware of how revealing their nonverbal behaviors can be. To prevent other players from guessing how good their hand is, they will always put on a "poker face" that is as devoid of any emotion or interest as possible. However, novice gamblers often do not realize that their body movements can be just as expressive as their faces. The strength of their hand can be assessed by a sharp-eyed opponent who notices whether they sit close to the table or lean back, place their bet quickly or slowly, put their chips in the center of the pot or closer to themselves, and so on. To protect themselves, good poker players maintain not only a constant facial expression but a constant, uniform *body* expression as well. Throughout the game, they keep the same posture, place their chips in the same spot, and make their bets with the same motion and the same speed.

Close-up
The Hands That Love to Teach

It has been suggested by some educators that teachers who gesture regularly get better results with their students.

If this observation proves to be true, how can we explain it? One answer is that frequent gesturing has been found to be part of a general affiliative style that conveys positive feelings (Mehrabian, 1971a). Such a style tends to elicit reciprocal liking and cooperation from

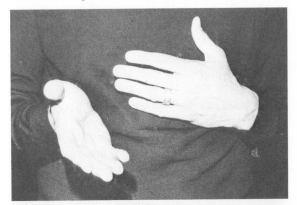

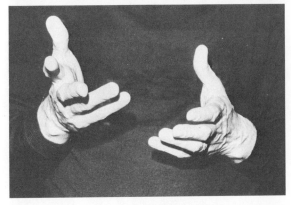

other people. Thus, a teacher who uses many gestures, like the one pictured here, is probably expressing a positive feeling for his students, leading to their greater involvement in the class. As for the teacher who is less loose and more controlled in gestures, the opposite results should occur. Since you have had a chance to observe a number of teachers in action, what is your conclusion? Or better, why not systematically collect data for a study of your own?

The importance of gestures (as well as other nonverbal behaviors) in the therapy situation has long been recognized by therapists but only recently has any systematic study been made of them. Ekman and Friesen (1968) have made some films of the clinical interviews of patients at the time of admission to a psychiatric hospital and shortly before discharge. By analyzing the gestures exhibited by the patients and the verbal content accompanying them, the researchers were able to identify individual patterns of verbal communication that reflected the patients' psychological functioning. For one patient, rubbing the arms of her chair seemed to indicate a state of agitated restlessness. For another, a characteristic tossing of the hands indicated frustrated anger.

Invisible walls. In response to our earlier question, How do you know when someone is interested in you? you may have thought (correctly) that the factor of *distance* would be important. In general, the more interest two people have in each other, the closer they get. However, studies in the area of proxemics have shown that there is a definite limit to how close people will allow each other to get, unless the relationship is an intimate one. For Americans, this invisible boundary or "bubble" of privacy is about eighteen to twenty-four inches around them. Anyone who violates this boundary by coming too close will usually elicit strong tension and discomfort in the individual, who will then try to reestablish the appropriate distance by backing off or moving away. Since different cultures have different ideas about what the "appropriate" distance is, misunderstandings can easily develop. For example, the invisible boundary for Latin Americans is smaller than that of North Americans. If a Latin American and a North American start talking to each other, the Latin American will tend to move closer, in order to establish the "appropriate" distance. In response, the North American will start to back away. Both people will probably end up with negative opinions of each other—the first will think the second is very cold and aloof, while the second will think the first is very pushy and aggressive (Hall, 1966).

But what if a person cannot back off from someone who has come too close—how is this enforced intimacy handled? A clear example of this problem is found in crowded elevators,

● Avoiding eye contact is one way in which a group of strangers in close proximity to one another tend to maintain their separateness.

where people are often very close to several strangers. For most individuals, the solution is to orient oneself away from the other people and to avoid eye contact. Thus, elevator occupants will usually stare in silence at either the door or the floor-indicator panel, in an attempt to establish a psychological distance where a physical one does not exist. ●

When the eyes say one thing, and the tongue another, a practised man relies on the language of the first.

Ralph Waldo Emerson, *Conduct of Life*, 1860

I can hear it on your lips but can't see it in your eyes. Although there are many different channels of expressive communication (verbal, vocal, facial, and motor), we usually assume that they all will say the same thing. That is, when people say "I'm happy," we expect that they will say so in a lighthearted, laughing way; that they will smile; and that they will be lively and carefree in their movements. But what if there is some discrepancy between the various channels? How do we then judge the reaction? Suppose, for example, that someone said "I'm happy" in a quavering voice, with trembling hands. Would you guess that he or she was actually feeling happy? Or would you be more inclined to label the response as one of nervousness or fear? If the latter, you would be relying more on the nonverbal cues than on the verbal ones.

This is the characteristic response to discrepant information, as researchers have begun to discover. On the basis of these findings, Mehrabian (1971a) has drawn up a tentative equation of the importance of each of the channels to the overall interpretation of the message: *Total feeling = 7 percent verbal feeling + 38 percent vocal feeling + 55 percent facial feeling.* Such an "equation" gives an estimate of the relative importance of these channels—it points out the fact that people tend to trust the face most and the words least. This may be because the verbal channel is the one most consciously controlled and monitored by the sender. Presumably the nonverbal channels are not so well controlled and thus more directly reflect the person's deep-down, true feelings and attitudes.

Sarcasm is a good example of the kind of inconsistent communication that we are talking about here. In a sarcastic statement, the person says a positive thing verbally (such as "That's great") but does so in a negative tone of voice and/or with a frown (which implies "That's terrible"). ◆ The opposite of sarcasm (for which there is no term in English) is also a typical type of inconsistent communication. A person says something negative (such as "You idiot") in such a positive nonverbal way that the overall message is interpreted as a loving, joking acceptance. These inconsistent communications often occur in situations where the speaker has mixed feelings about the person or event in question. For example, if a person says "You idiot" to a friend who has just made a silly mistake, the positive nonverbal components of the message indicate a continuing liking for the friend even though there is some momentary irritation or dismay over the error.

Sometimes the expression of these inconsistent messages can have a very negative and even damaging impact on people. Imagine a family situation in which the children are told verbally that they are loved, but consistently receive the nonverbal message that they are either insignificant or resented. What do you suppose the con-

◆ The various channels of communication may not always be expressing the same message.

**Birds of the Same "Dialect"
Flock Together**

You undoubtedly are able to identify the regional background of many of your classmates by certain characteristics of the way they use the English language—that is, the dialect they speak. But did you know that birds have "dialects," too? Investigators studying the white-crowned sparrow, a small North American songbird, have found that there are regional differences in their song, and that these differences have important behavioral correlates.

Analysis of sound spectrograms of the mating songs of 18 male white-crowned sparrows from three localities in the San Francisco Bay area revealed that song characteristics are consistent among birds in the same area, but are quite different from those of others of their species living as little as 60 miles away.

Studies by Peter Marler (1967) and his associates at Rockefeller University point out some interesting parallels to the development of speech in children and the concept of a "language community":

1. The white-crowned sparrow has a predisposition to learn some sound patterns rather than others, just as some aspects of human language appear to be innate.

2. The young bird must be able to hear its own voice; auditory feedback is needed if it is to translate the memory of the normal song of its parents into motor activity and produce a song of its own.

3. Song does not appear suddenly in young birds but develops over time with practice and is preceded by transitional stages termed *subsongs*.

4. Dialect patterns are transmitted by a learning process from one generation to the next.

5. The existence of dialects maintains the local populations as distinguishable units, since birds tend to mate with those who share the same dialect.

6. The behavior patterns that create this "common song community" are under environmental, rather than genetic, control.

sequences might be? This pattern of communication has been observed by therapists in families with a schizophrenic child, and has led to the proposal of a *"double-bind" theory of schizophrenia* (Bateson, Jackson, Haley, & Weakland, 1956). According to this theory, a "double-bind" communication is one that involves two or more inconsistent messages that require incompatible responses from the individual. As an example, Bateson and his colleagues cite the case of a young schizophrenic who was visited in the hospital by his mother. When he greeted her with a hug, she stiffened; when he then withdrew his arms from her, she said, "Don't you love me any more?" The young man was thus faced with an impossible dilemma: "If I am to keep my tie to Mother, I must not show her that I love her, but if I do not show her that I love her, then I will lose her." People who constantly receive such double-bind communications are thought to develop maladaptive patterns of interpersonal functioning, and often learn to respond with double-bind messages of their own. Thus, the son in the above example might tell his mother that he cannot hug her because his arm is injured or because "John" is holding him back (in both cases, the excuses are imaginary). With this double message, he expresses his wish to show affection to his mother but prevents himself from doing so.

Animal Communication

Is the gift of language unique to human beings? Or is it possible that other species have language systems of their own? While it is clear that animals do have signals for communicating with each other (such as courtship displays, warning cries, or fighting postures), there is really no solid evidence as yet that they possess a complex language system, complete with words and grammar, such as human beings have. To date, the only scientist who has been successful at discovering animal language is the fictional Dr. Doolittle, who not only understood animal tongues but could speak them as well. Nevertheless, much research continues to be done in this area, not only to understand just how animals communicate with each other, but to give us better insight into the unique aspects of human language. (See *P&L* Close-up, p. 162.)

Whistling dolphins. In recent years, much attention has been focused on the communication systems of dolphins, partially because the underwater sounds made by dolphins were thought to be a true language. One of these sounds is a series of "clicks." However, research has shown that these clicks serve only as an underwater sonar system for exploring the environment. By emitting a sound that is reflected back as an echo, the dolphin (much like the bat) can determine the position of objects.

Another sound made by dolphins is a "whistle." It is made by both sexes and by all age groups—even newborn infants. This unique sound is not at all typical of nonhuman mammals, and there has been much speculation about its possible function as a true language. The most recent investigations, however, seem to challenge this conclusion. It has been found that individual dolphin whistles are very stereotyped and very repetitive. Although there are differences among dolphins in the type of whistle they make, there are not sufficient variations in pattern within a particular whistle to justify thinking of it as a language. Rather, the whistle appears to serve four *social* functions: (1) the alerting of other dolphins to one dolphin's presence, (2) the identification of that particular dolphin, (3) the localization of that dolphin, and (4) a general indication of the emotional state of the animal doing the whistling (Caldwell & Caldwell, 1972).

Experimental evidence has been found to support these first three functions, and data is currently being collected on the fourth. The Caldwells have shown that dolphins can clearly distinguish between the whistles of other individual dolphins, of both their own and other species. Furthermore, dolphins can locate the position of another dolphin on the basis of its whistle. These researchers have also noted that dolphins whistle a great deal when they are in an excited emotional state, but stop immediately when they are afraid. ■ Apparently, dolphins have not learned the human trick of "whistling a happy tune" when afraid, in order to fool others into thinking that they are not!

It is sad, but true, that researchers who find evidence that destroys a popular myth often find themselves in an unpopular position and greeted with cries of "Say it isn't so!" As the Caldwells report:

"The surprise that we felt in finding that individual dolphin whistles are largely stereotyped has been nothing compared to the surprise felt at the unbridled anger that we evoke when forced to state this conclusion. It is an unpleasant experience, for we too want to be loved by our fellow man, to evoke social approval rather than anger. To have been cast into the role of destroyers of one of the few myths remaining to our own benighted species was forced upon us, not sought. We had rather hoped initially that dolphin whistles would at least prove to have songs like birds, but find no evidence of this. . . . On the basis of present evidence, and in conflict with some earlier writers, we do not believe that either whistles or burst-pulse sounds in dolphins are used for anything other than communication on a very general basis." (1972, pp. 25–26)

■ The streams of bubbles indicate that the dolphins are whistling. The sounds they make appear to serve as a means of identification rather than communication, however.

Studying monkey talk. Is the gift of language unique to human beings because of evolution and innately given mental structures or because of the ideal language learning environment to which other species do not have access?

In the last forty years, a number of experiments have been conducted to determine whether chimpanzees reared in home environments can develop communication skills comparable to those exhibited by children. The young chimp rapidly adapts to its physical and social environment, becomes strongly attached to its caretaker, imitates adult acts without any training, and develops its motor behavior more rapidly than a child of similar age. However, the results in terms of language development are dismal. None of the chimps studied ever copied or reproduced human word sounds spontaneously, nor was there any evidence of attempts to do so. There was not any period of babbling or random emission of sounds (other than the food-bark, the "oo oo" cry, and screeching).

One couple did manage to teach their chimp, Viki, to utter four words: "mama," "papa," "cup," and "up." Viki learned these words with great difficulty, only after considerable training, and even then could not really produce them easily and could not keep the sound patterns straight (Hayes & Hayes, 1952). On language comprehension, the chimps fared much better, with one showing fifty-eight specific correct response patterns to simple human commands over a nine-month period, compared with sixty-eight for her human companion, a little boy (Kellogg & Kellogg, 1933).

Washoe talks in American sign language . . . If chimps can comprehend, gesture, and imitate, then perhaps the key to language acquisition in this species is through voiceless communication by some type of signs. In June 1966, Allen and Beatrice Gardner, psychologists at the University of Nevada, began an intensive test of language acquisition in apes, with a female named Washoe. Using the American sign language (ASL), a code of arbitrary symbols devised for the deaf, and insisting that this be the only form of communication between human handlers and Washoe, the Gardners (1969) have reported remarkable progress and promise.

In the first seven months, Washoe acquired four signs that she used reliably: "come-gimme," "more," "up," and "sweet." Moreover, she understood more signs than she produced. In the next seven months, she added nine more signs and by the fall of 1970 had control over 160 signs. The stringent criterion of sign acquisition was one appropriate and nonimitated occurrence for each of fifteen consecutive days.

What has led psychologists like Roger Brown (1970) to sit up and take notice of what Washoe is saying is not the extent of her vocabulary, but rather that she spontaneously uses a great many (29) signs per day, has begun to string her sign words into simple phrases, and demonstrates both generalization and differentiation. For example, she uses the same sign, "more," for continued play and additional food; she uses "open" for opening a door, a soda bottle, or a stuck zipper. Her multi-sign sequences, such as "Gimme please food," "Please tickle more," "Hurry gimme toothbrush," "You me go there in," or "Roger Washoe tickle" are not just word strings but semantically valid constructions. They are not, however, syntactically acceptable, and they exhibit no rules for sign order. This is a major difference from language development in human children, and one that needs to be explored in future research.

Roger Fouts, a former graduate student of the Gardners, has moved with Washoe to the Institute for Primate Studies at Norman, Oklahoma, where research on use of ASL is being carried out with a growing number of chimps (Fleming, 1974).

. . . Sarah talks back . . . Using a slightly different approach, David Premack and his associates have had remarkable success in teaching their chimp, Sarah, to communicate by constructing sentences with colored chips of plastic on a magnetized board. Sarah first learned, through simple conditioning procedures, to associate a chip of a particular color and shape with a particular fruit—being allowed to eat the

correctly identified item as a reward. Other chips became the "names" of the experimenters or represented certain actions, and Sarah was soon comprehending and constructing sentences like "Mary give apple Sarah" and "Sarah insert banana pail."

The next step was to determine whether Sarah was capable of learning relational concepts such as "on" or "under." Working first with colored cards, then with plastic color names, she soon learned to follow instructions and place "red on green" or vice versa. Another type of relationship, still more abstract, can best be described as "name of." When presented with a symbol and a piece of fruit, Sarah readily learned to use symbols meaning "name of" or "not-name of" to construct such sentences as "(symbol) not-name of apple." Perhaps the high point of Sarah's "writing" career, however, was the day when, apparently bored with what was going on, she set up a string of incomplete sentences and gave her astonished trainer a multiple-choice sentence-completion test! (Premack, 1969, 1970)

. . . And Lana talks to a computer. At the Yerkes Primate Research Center in Georgia, a third method of studying language in chimps is being used. There, three-year-old Lana is learning to "read" symbols on a computer keyboard and type out her requests (for food, music, etc.). Only "grammatically correct sentences"—that is, correct sequences of signs—are rewarded by the computer, and Lana has learned not only to state her requests correctly but also to erase and correct "ungrammatical" sentences presented by the computer (Rumbaugh, Gill, & von Glasersfeld, 1973).

At latest count, Lana is effectively using over 74 word symbols. More impressively, she no longer waits passively for new instructions, but now asks her teachers to name objects that interest her. ●

● The chimps shown here are all very communicative, each in her own way. Washoe (top) asks for a drink in American Sign Language. Sarah (center) "writes" her request for chocolate on the magnetized board. Lana (bottom) types out sentences on an elaborate computer keyboard. All three of them are contributing to our understanding of communication processes.

And now, all join in . . .   Washoe and Sarah have learned their language systems from human beings, and Lana by interacting with a computer. So far, they have used them only to communicate with human beings. But suppose they were in the company of other chimps who also knew the same system. Would the chimps use this language to communicate with each other? The Oklahoma chimps, who have learned sign language from human trainers, often use the signs when communicating among themselves. For example, one chimp will usually respond to another's sign command to "Come, hug" or "Come, hurry." Sometimes the chimps use signs to play games, as when two chimps ask each other to "Come, tickle." One of the pair will run after the other, until the chase ends in a bout of mutual tickling.

Not only can the chimps use their sign language in dialogues with individuals other than their human trainers, but there is some evidence that they will invent signs of their own in order to communicate more clearly. In one instance, a chimp named Lucy approached the researchers and made a completely novel sign—bending her index finger into a hook shape and touching it to her neck. It did not take long for the psychologists to realize that the sign referred to Lucy's leash and that she was asking to be taken out for a walk.

A number of intriguing questions are raised by the findings of these studies. Does this language system allow the chimps to communicate more precisely? Could they now independently develop a language by creating many new signs of their own? Would it be possible for these chimps to teach other chimps to use their newly acquired language system? (Lucy once tried to teach it to a kitten, but gave up when her efforts bore no results.)

The accomplishments of Sarah, Lana, and the Oklahoma chimps clearly challenge previous conceptions of the linguistic limitations of subhuman species. The extent to which these chimps can communicate with human beings (as well as with each other) via a shared language system gives some hope that Dr. Doolittle's ability to "talk to the animals" may not be such a fantasy after all.

Memory

Think for a moment of all the complex information you have learned in school: grammar, foreign languages, chemical formulas, geometric proofs, syllogistic reasoning, and much more. Then consider how much more you have had to learn outside of class about your environment, especially about the people and institutions in it. Some of this learning has come easily and "naturally"; some of it you have had to work hard to learn.

Forgetting has not been the same for everything either. Have you had the experience of mastering material well enough to get an "A" only to find a few months later that you have forgotten most of what you knew? But can't you still remember all of the details associated with your first "real date"? College students frequently can remember the names of all their elementary school teachers, but forget the name of their psychology professor or their textbook the day after the final exam.

On the other hand, if you put on a pair of skates, began to skip rope, or tried a dance you had not done for years, you would probably find that in a short time you were almost as good as you ever were. Why do some things stay with you so much longer than others? Does the difference lie with the kind of material learned, or does something about the way you learn it determine how well you are able to remember it later? Or does it have something to do with the way your brain stores the information it has "learned"?

In our earlier discussions of conditioning and neural processes, we have spoken as if there is always a direct, one-to-one relationship between stimulus input and representation of this input by the nervous system. In many simple cases, we can assume that for all practical purposes the stimulus "out there" is the same as our perception of it and thus that the responses a given stimulus induces in our nervous system will generally be similar.

In most cases of human interaction with the environment, however, we are not so directly bound to the stimuli that impinge on us. We can process incoming information in various ways rather than reacting item for item or point for point. For human beings, far more than for other species, the processing of information includes not only receiving and literal coding of input but selectivity, reorganization, and transformation of the input that we receive. The major reason for this selective coding is simply that there is too much input for us to process each item separately. We can detect every stimulus within the range of each of our sensory systems and discrimination capacities, but to prevent our processing and storage capacities from becoming overloaded and thus inefficient, we have developed operations for selective organization and coding of all stimulus input. But does this rearranging of what comes in affect our access to it when we want to retrieve it later on? This is another question we will deal with in this chapter.

Most human learning is as much dependent on our special ability for processing information as on our ability to retain new knowledge or to change a way of responding. Thus processing and coding of information are important components of learning to perceive, learning skills, learning to speak, and acquisition and memory for verbal and conceptual material.

You may have noticed already that we have made a distinction between learning and memory. Psychologists usually make this distinction in their studies. A psychologist investigating learning looks at trial-to-trial changes in performance and how well a subject is ultimately able to perform on some task after different kinds of practice—a change in performance as a result of experience.

In studying memory, we are interested in whether material that has been learned at a given time in the past is available to the subject at a selected time in the present. Tests of memory, then, require that the past be brought back into the present. The psychological inquiry into memory processes is trying to develop an understanding of: (a) how knowledge is stored, (b) how well the stored knowledge is retained over time, and (c) how stored knowledge is retrieved for use. The stimuli most often used in these studies have been words (in some cases artificially constructed words), digits, and pictures. It is of historical interest that many of the psychologists who were studying animal learning and basic laws of conditioning and instrumental learning from the 1940s to the 1960s are now switching their focus of concern to "human information processing," "cognitive psychology," or "language and memory." The humans have won! Indeed, there is probably no area of psychology with a greater abundance of energetic innovative research under way than this one, nor any with greater potential for developing new conceptions of how the human mind works.

Now before reading what we know about human memory, stop and test your own memory power. (See *P&L* Close-up below.)

Close-up
Memory Test

Below is a series of twenty digits; either have a friend read them to you slowly or scan them yourself, looking at each only once for a few seconds. Then write down as many as you can remember, trying to reproduce them in the original sequence.

12, 3, 18, 27, 96, 41, 37, 82, 65, 54,
77, 8, 26, 75, 98, 6, 32, 56, 98, 40

It is likely that you were able to recall no more than about twelve of the numbers correctly, and only about seven in the proper sequence. What variables of training, practice, and testing do you think might improve your memory score? The techniques to be discussed at the end of this chapter should help you increase this ability considerably.

Classic Research on Memory and Forgetting

In laboratory studies memory is inferred by comparing how much is remembered after some period of time with how much was known immediately after learning. It is assumed that with perfect memory the two would be the same — there would be no loss. Actually, therefore, memory is usually assessed in terms of how much has been forgotten. This explains why much of what we say about "memory" in this section will be in terms of forgetting and, furthermore, why the most important theories about memory have been developed in terms of the process of forgetting.

General experimental procedure. The usual sequence by which memory is studied experimentally has already been implied. First, some task is presented to the experimental subject to be learned, and usually some measure is made of how much learning has taken place. Second, during some length of time the subject is asked to engage in specified types of activity (perhaps additional learning or perhaps some time-filling task, like doing arithmetic problems, that simply limits any thinking about the original task). Finally, the subject is tested on what he or she is able to remember from the original task, and this score is compared with the score that was obtained at the end of the learning session.

To measure the amount remembered, the investigator may use *recall, recognition,* or *relearning.*

1. *Recall.* Recall is reproduction of the learned material. If the exam question asks you to give the causes of the Civil War, you must dredge them up out of your memory and formulate a response that convinces your instructor you know them.

Two kinds of recall are distinguished by researchers. The first is *rote* or *verbatim recall.* Whenever we need to remember the exact form of things, especially arbitrary items like telephone numbers, we must store the entire information in order to reproduce it correctly. Most cases of recall that involve any complexity, however, require some *reconstruction.* In this case, we store and recall only part of the information but are able to reconstruct the rest of the event or fact from this partial information. For example, you could probably develop a theory of the causes of the Civil War on the basis of just a few remembered facts.

2. *Recognition.* Another technique of assessing remembering involves the ability to *recognize* something previously experienced. Think of the tremendous number of objects and people you can recognize. The streets and buildings of your neighborhood, the faces of numerous friends and acquaintances, words — the list is nearly endless. Furthermore, most of the things you can recognize you could not possibly reproduce from memory. On a multiple-choice test you often recognize many correct alternatives that you could not formulate on your own.

Recognition is usually tested by presenting a stimulus and asking the subject whether it is one of a set learned earlier or is a new one. Another method is to present several items and ask whether the subject recognizes any as previously experienced.

3. *Relearning.* A still more indirect measure of retention, *relearning,* incorporates the techniques of recall and recognition. A record is kept of the amount of time it takes to learn the material to some criterion, such as perfect recall twice in a row. Then, after some interval of time, the subject studies the material again until he or she can pass the same test equally well.

Psychologists use the term *savings* for the extent to which an experimental subject learns a task more quickly the second time than the first. This savings score is regarded as a measure of the extent to which the subject has retained the original learning.

The relearning technique is the most sensitive measure of all. Even when other tests do not reveal any evidence of remembering, relearning may be faster than original learning, indicating that the effects have not been entirely lost.

Depending on the interests of the experimenter and the hypotheses being tested, a particular study may involve manipulating conditions in the original learning, the intervening interval, or the final remembering phase. For example, the researcher may want to compare the effects of different original learning conditions on later retention. In this case, experimental and control subjects learn under different conditions, but their learning and later retention are measured in the same way, and conditions are the same for them during the intervening period between learning and remembering.

Perhaps the experimenter is interested in the effects of different activities during the time interval after original learning. In this case, conditions and degree of original learning must be the same for all subjects; otherwise, if they remembered different amounts later, one could not tell whether it was because of the different intervening activities or because of different original learning.

Reproductive memory. Within psychology, there have been two basic orientations to the study of memory. One of these views memory as a *reproductive* process that retrieves information that has been previously learned and "stored" in the brain. This approach stems from the classic experimental studies of Hermann Ebbinghaus in 1885. The second orientation, which views memory as *productive*, contends that we actively reconstruct what we remember, rather than simply pulling the memories out from storage. The earliest formulation of this approach appears in the work of Sir Frederick Bartlett, conducted in 1914–16.

Ebbinghaus and serial learning. The first significant study providing a truly quantitative measure of retention was performed by Ebbinghaus toward the end of the last century. Ebbinghaus invented the "nonsense syllable"—a meaningless three-letter unit consisting of a vowel between two consonants, such as *ceg*, *dax*, and so on. He used nonsense syllables because he wanted to obtain a "pure" measure of memory, uncontaminated by previous learning or associations that might otherwise have been brought to the task being studied. Using himself as his only subject, Ebbinghaus would study a list of such nonsense syllables until he could repeat the list perfectly, twice in a row. In addition, he would measure the amount of time it took him to learn the list. Then, after some fixed period of time—during which he would usually be learning other

lists—he would relearn the original list and again measure his learning time. The amount by which this second time was shorter—the *savings score*—was his measure of retention.

The type of result obtained by Ebbinghaus is shown in the figure, where percent of time saved in relearning is plotted as a function of the number of days since original learning. ▲ As you can see, there is a rapid initial loss, followed by a gradually slower decline. This curve is typical of results obtained in studies involving rote memorization.

The method of recall that Ebbinghaus developed for his research, known as *serial anticipation*, became one of the classic methods of studying verbal learning and memory. In this procedure, the subject looks at a list of words or nonsense syllables, and is then shown each of these items one at a time. As each item appears, the subject is asked to "anticipate" the item that follows it in the list and will appear next. In the laboratory, the typical procedure is to present each item for a fixed duration of time in the window of an apparatus called a *memory drum*. This continues for as many *trials* (presentations of the complete list) as are needed to meet whatever learning criterion the experimenter has established. In Ebbinghaus' case, as we have seen, the criterion was two trials without errors. Whatever the criterion de-

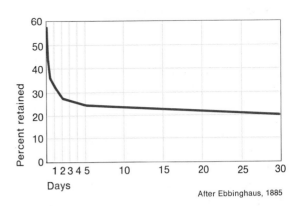

After Ebbinghaus, 1885

▲ **RETENTION OF NONSENSE SYLLABLES**

cided on, the same one is used again later, after relearning.

In any practical experience you have had in serial learning, you may have noticed a phenomenon that nearly always occurs. If you are learning a list of items—such as digits in a telephone number—the first and last numbers in the list seem easier to remember than those in the middle. This is called the *serial position effect*. ■ No one is completely certain why it occurs, but it has been observed consistently in experiments. So far, the accepted explanation is that the first and last items occupy unique positions in the list and thus are especially noticeable because they serve as markers for the beginning and the end of the list. For example, if there is no pause between the "last" and "first" item of the series—it is presented as a circular list—then the average serial position curve is markedly reduced. Sometimes the person apparently selects a subjective "starting point" for the series, and a serial position develops around that subjective anchor point.

Ebbinghaus' pioneering effort was important for several reasons. His approach marked a transition from philosophical speculation to scientific experimentation and thus set the stage for the appearance of modern learning theory. Ebbinghaus had been impressed by Fechner's rigorous analysis of sensation (see page 240) and was the first to try to apply the same rigor and precision to the study of higher mental processes. He did this in a systematic way, studying all the variables he could think of—number of syllables in a list, rehearsal time, trials, and so on—by varying them one at a time with other variables held constant. He used quantitative measures and special materials of comparable difficulty and for the first time measured learning and remembering separately and related retention to initial learning.

However, Ebbinghaus' reliance on meaningless nonsense syllables to study memory has been challenged by recent research. It has been found that subjects often figure out some way to transform each nonsense syllable into a meaningful word (such as *locomotive* for the nonsense syllable *loc*). They then remember the word plus the transformation (Prytulak, 1971). Although contemporary researchers share the same experimental goal as Ebbinghaus (namely, to understand memory), they believe that the way to reach this goal is to use *meaningful*, rather than meaningless, material. Memory for meaningless nonsense syllables may differ qualitatively from memory for meaningful material, rather than being the "pure" form of retention that Ebbinghaus assumed it was. Thus there is now a great deal of research on memory for sentences, or other meaningful material, and such research is a definite break from the Ebbinghaus tradition.

Paired-associate learning. Think of learning English equivalents of foreign vocabulary words, or of learning the capital cities of various states. In these cases, the information to be acquired is a set of pairs, such that one element of a pair goes with or is to be associated with the other element of the pair. These examples illustrate a second classic technique used to study memory, known as *paired-associate learning.* Typically the subject studies each pair for a short time until the entire list has been pre-

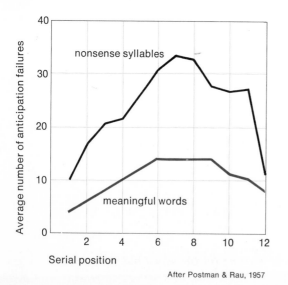

After Postman & Rau, 1957

■ SERIAL POSITION EFFECT

The items in the middle of the list are more difficult to remember than those at the beginning and end.

sented. Then the first item in each pair is presented alone and the subject is asked to recall the second item of the pair before it is exposed a few seconds later. This procedure is repeated until the subject can correctly anticipate the second item for each pair in the list before it is presented.

Free recall. Occasionally, instead of insisting that the recall be in the proper sequence or that the correct second member of each pair be given in response to the first member, the experimenter simply asks for *free recall* of all the items the subject can remember. Even here a serial position effect is typically found, with the beginning and end of the list learned earlier and the items just past the middle learned last.

Interference phenomena. Both serial-anticipation and paired-associate learning have been used extensively to investigate particular aspects of memory. One major line of investigation has been to study how the memory of one thing inhibits or interferes with remembering something else. In *proactive* (forward-working) *interference*, the memory for earlier material interferes with the memory for more recently acquired material. In *retroactive* (backward-working) *interference*, the process is just the reverse—the memory for material learned later interferes with the memory for material learned first.

One technique for studying interference processes has been to have subjects learn successive paired-associate lists in which the first items of the pairs never change but the items that they are paired with change from list to list. For example, if the pair of nonsense syllables *yuf-dax* is in the first list (X-A) then the second list (X-B) will contain a pair like *yuf-geb*. One way to test for *proactive* interference is to have subjects learn first the X-A list, and then the X-B list. Later, after some fixed period of time, they are tested for recall of the list learned second—the X-B pairs. The scores for these experimental subjects are then compared with the scores for control subjects, who have learned only the second list and spent the preceding interval in some nonlearning activity. Under such conditions, the control subjects will remember more of the X-B list than will the experimental

subjects, leading to the conclusion that the experimental group's memory of the first list must have interfered with their memory of the second list. ▲

To test *retroactive* interference, on the other hand, both groups learn the *first* list, with only the experimental group learning the second list while the control group does some irrelevant task. Both groups are then tested again on the first list as shown in the table. Again the control group usually does better, presumably because of less interference from the intervening activity.

Productive memory. We all know the way gossip changes the details of a story. One person hears a juicy morsel about somebody; by the time that person has a chance to tell someone else, his or her memory for the details seems to have changed the story slightly. After the story has passed among several people, the originator of the gossip may hear it and not even recognize it as the same story!

F. C. Bartlett, an Englishman, was not much concerned with gossip, but he was very sure that such systematic distortion is a real property of memory. His research was aimed at demonstrating and explaining this distortion. Thus it

▲ TYPICAL PARADIGMS FOR STUDYING INTERFERENCE IN VERBAL LEARNING

Proactive Inhibition

Group	Learn	Learn	⟶	Test on List B
Experimental	List A	List B ↑ (equally well) ↓	Passage of Time	poorer
Control	(none)	List B		better

Retroactive Inhibition

Group	Learn	Learn	⟶	Test on List A
Experimental	List A ↑ (equally well) ↓	List B	Passage of Time	poorer
Control	List A	(none)		better

represents a distinctly different type of investigation from that of the verbal learning tradition developed in America.

Successive reproduction. Bartlett developed a technique known as successive reproduction, in which some meaningful material was recalled several times by the subjects. Either the same subject was asked to reproduce the material at several different times after learning it, or a series of subjects transmitted what they remembered of the material to each other. For example, one person might be shown a picture and asked to remember it. After some time this person would be asked to draw the picture from memory. A second individual would be given the first person's drawing as the picture to be memorized and reproduced, and so on. The figure shows a typical result. ◆ In this figure the original picture of an owl was gradually transformed into one of a cat.

In other experiments, Bartlett read an American Indian folktale to his subjects. After fifteen minutes, they would be asked to reproduce the story, and again at later times. In general, subjects seemed to accurately remember the central meaningful "core" of the story, but they also added new material that had not been originally included. Often this new material involved alterations of the story to make it conform better with the subjects' cultural norms. Thus, the phrase "went down to the river to hunt seals" was remembered by one of the British subjects as "went fishing."

Bartlett's interpretation of these results was that memory is *productive* as well as *reproductive* and that this productivity induces certain predictable changes in what is stored. According to him:

"Remembering is not the re-excitation of innumerable fixed, lifeless and fragmentary traces. It is an imaginative reconstruction, or construction, built out of the relation of our attitude towards a whole active mass of organized past reactions or experience . . . . It is thus hardly ever really exact, even in the most rudimentary cases of rote recapitulation." (Bartlett, 1932, p. 213)

A recent version of Bartlett's original theory has been provided by Neisser (1967), who argues that good memory is more than just an efficient filing and storage system. Acts of memory are analogous to the work of a paleontologist, who starts with a few bone fragments and then reconstructs the form of a dinosaur or other creature. In a similar way, people reconstruct what they remember on the basis of a few recalled elements.

Memory for meaning. One of the differences between the approaches of Ebbinghaus and Bartlett is that the former used meaningless nonsense syllables, while the latter relied on meaningful material, such as stories. Because of the greater influence of Ebbinghaus on American research, most of the earlier experiments in this country used nonsense syllables. It is only recently that there has been a significant trend toward studying memory for meaningful material. One of the findings of this later research is that people do not have exact rote memory for the words they learn, but that they do remember

Original drawing   Reproduction 1   Reproduction 2

Reproduction 3   Reproduction 4   Reproduction 5   Reproduction 6

Reproduction 7   Reproduction 8   Reproduction 9   Reproduction 10

◆ The original figure is a stylized drawing of an owl. In successive reproductions it becomes increasingly ambiguous; by the tenth drawing it has definitely become a figure of a cat.

the general meaning of those words. Thus you will remember tomorrow some of what was said in this chapter, but you certainly will not remember the exact words that were used.

In one experiment, subjects were read a short story containing a particular sentence—such as, "He sent a letter about it to Galileo, the great Italian scientist." They were later given a recognition test for this sentence, which came after either 0, 80, or 160 additional syllables of story. On the test, a sentence was presented that was either identical to the original one, changed in form but not meaning ("A letter about it was sent to Galileo, the great Italian scientist"), or changed in meaning ("Galileo, the great Italian scientist, sent him a letter about it"). As can be seen in the figure, the subjects were very good at detecting changes in meaning but not so good either at recognizing verbatim wording as the same or at detecting changes in form when the meaning had been preserved (Sachs, 1967). ●

While studies such as these have focused on memory for individual sentences or words, other research has been concerned with memory for ideas. Such ideas are often based on many different sentences that express a common semantic content. The phenomenon of "idea acquisition and retention" has been demonstrated in a series of experiments by Bransford and Franks (1971). They found that subjects took the information expressed in a number of related sentences and spontaneously integrated them into a few complex ideas. Later on, these subjects were more likely to recognize, or "remember," sentences that communicated these complex ideas, rather than the simpler ones that they had originally heard. Findings such as these suggest that people often construct organizing schemes for the information they learn. As a result, they exhibit a constructive process in their memory of things, rather than a rote, verbatim recall. This work is clearly in line with Bartlett's original ideas about memory and has opened up a new and challenging area of psychological research (see Cofer, 1973).

Theories of Memory and Forgetting

Explanations of memory and forgetting focus on two related questions: What is happening when we forget? and How are memories stored in the brain and how are they retrieved?

Why do we forget? If there is one fact about learning that all of us know, it is that we do not remember everything. We forget people's names, we forget appointments, we forget the information that is crammed for an exam, we forget numbers just after dialing them on the telephone, and so on. Although forgetting is a very common experience for all of us, its explanation is not so easily found. Much research has been done on this topic, and several alternative theories have been proposed to explain how and why we seem to forget the material we have learned.

Decay theory. According to *decay theory,* learned material leaves a "trace" or impression

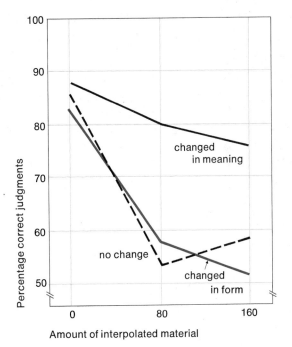

After Sachs, 1967

● MEMORY FOR MEANING VS. MEMORY FOR FORM

in the brain, and, if unused, this trace will disappear with time. In other words, the knowledge we have learned just fades away. Such decay can be prevented if we repeatedly use or practice the knowledge and thus maintain the trace. Although the decay theory is a very simple and straightforward explanation of forgetting, it has not been supported by recent research.

Interference theory. The basic notion in *interference theory* is that everything we learn will stay learned unless something new occurs to interfere with it. If there were nothing to interfere with our knowledge, we would never forget anything. However, interference is a daily occurrence in our lives, taking one of the two forms—proactive or retroactive—that were discussed earlier (p. 171).

As opposed to decay theory, which suggests that *time* itself is the critical factor in forgetting, interference theory argues that it is *what occurs* during that time period that is crucial. One of the earliest tests of these hypotheses was done by Jenkins and Dallenbach in 1924.

In this study, subjects learned lists of nonsense syllables and were later tested for recall of these lists at several different time intervals. The period between the subject's learning and recall was either spent in normal working activity or in sleep (during which, it is assumed, there is less interference). The results showed that less forgetting occurred after sleep than after waking activity. This supports the notion of interference theory that it is the nature of the intervening activity, and not time itself, that is critical to forgetting. ■

How does the interference process work? One hypothesis is that the interfering material "overpowers" the other learned material and becomes stronger and more dominant in our memory. An alternative idea (and one that has received more experimental support) is that the interfering material causes the other material to be *unlearned,* that is, we forget the prior material in order that we may learn the new material more readily.

Displacement theory. A hypothesis that is related to interference is that of *displacement theory* (Waugh & Norman, 1964). According to this principle, the memory store has a limited capacity, and thus, successive inputs to it will push out, or displace, items that are already there. If there is no new information over time, then no forgetting will occur. The difference between interference and displacement theories lies in their conceptualization of how new material causes other material to be forgotten; the former postulates a process of unlearning, while the latter argues that there is a limit to the storage capacity.

Forgetting as loss of access. A fourth hypothesis is that actually we never forget anything—that the things we seem to have forgotten have merely become temporarily inaccessible for one reason or another. In other words, all the information is there in the memory store but is inaccessible because of inadequate retrieval cues. If

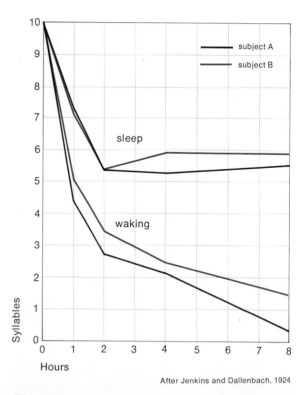

After Jenkins and Dallenbach, 1924

■ **FORGETTING AFTER SLEEPING VS. WAKING**
The graph shows the number of syllables recalled after various intervals of sleep or waking activity.

appropriate cues are available, then there is no forgetting. For example, if someone asked you if you remembered a man named John Doe, you might search your memory and say "no." However, if the person asked you if you remembered the John Doe who owned the corner ice-cream store, you might say "Oh, *that* John Doe—sure, I know him!" Clearly, you had not lost or "unlearned" this information; rather, the cue of the man's name was not adequate for retrieving the information from your memory store.

Psychologists have often demonstrated the role of different types of retrieval cues in forgetting and remembering. An elementary illustration is to read aloud some arbitrary set of twenty or thirty unrelated words and then request the listener to recall various parts of the list in response to different cues. Examples would be to recall all words that began with the letter *b*, all words denoting animals, all words that rhyme with *pear*, and so on. Any word, even one of singular meaning, is classifiable in multiple ways. Thus it has multiple possible access routes, and each of these can be tried to see whether it produces recall of the specific target word. The general outcome of such studies is the conclusion that a stimulus becomes a potent retrieval cue for an item only if the person thinks of the two as related at the time the item is studied. Thus, if the person thought of the word *Dizzy* solely as the name of a famous jazz musician, then "a word beginning with *d*" or "a bodily state" would be ineffectual retrieval cues.

One type of cue that has been studied recently is that of the environment or *context* in which material is learned and remembered. There is some evidence that information that is learned in one environmental context (such as a particular room) is easier to recall in that same context than in a different one. Similarly, it may be that the person's *internal* environmental context (such as mood, bodily state, etc.) can also influence memory and forgetting. Rand and Wapner (1967) tested this notion by varying the subjects' posture during a learning task. Subjects were either standing erect or lying down while they learned a word test and while they later tried to remember it. Those subjects who were in the same position for both learning and recall had a better memory for the test than those who changed their posture. Such material may also be recalled better when similar contextual sets are induced under hypnosis—remember Chuck and his birthday party?

Motivational theories. In all of the theories discussed so far, forgetting has been viewed as an automatic consequence of the memory system (displacement, interference) or as a system failure (decay, inadequate cues). A very different approach was taken by Sigmund Freud, who argued that forgetting may be *intentional*. His thesis was that the things we remember and the things we forget are related to their value and importance to us. Things that are very disturbing to us, for example, are likely to be made temporarily inaccessible by being driven out of our consciousness. Such *repression* is a device by which we unknowingly protect ourselves from unacceptable or painful information. As we shall see in Chapter 10, the "forgotten" material may persist at an unconscious level and produce emotional conflicts for years afterward.

At about the same time that Freud was talking about motives to repress negative information, Kurt Lewin and his students were looking at the effect of task motives on memory. Legend has it that they were puzzled by an occurrence in a Berlin beer garden. It seems there was a waiter with such a remarkable memory that he could retain long, detailed, complicated orders without writing them down. Once after the meal had been served and he had given the party their bill, however, someone asked him a simple question about the order. It turned out that he could remember very little of it once he had completed his task.

The result of this observation was a classic experiment that demonstrated greater recall of tasks before completion than of comparable tasks after completion. This effect of enhanced recall for uncompleted tasks was named the *Zeigarnik effect* after Bluma Zeigarnik, the young woman who carried out the study.

In this experiment the subjects performed simple tasks that they would be able to accomplish if given enough time, such as writing down a favorite quotation from memory, solving a riddle, and doing mental arithmetic problems. In some of the tasks, the subjects were interrupted before they had a chance to carry out the instructions in full. In others they were allowed to finish.

Despite the fact that the subjects spent more time on the completed tasks than on the interrupted ones, they tended to recall the unfinished tasks better than the finished ones when they were questioned a few hours later. This superiority of recall for the uncompleted tasks disappeared, however, within twenty-four hours. Apparently it was attributable to short-term motivational factors that affected the rehearsal process (Zeigarnik, 1927).

It may appear to you that the Zeigarnik effect is inconsistent with the notion of repression, since one might expect that people would repress their memory of things left unfinished, particularly if the lack of completion was viewed as a failure. Later research has suggested a resolution of this inconsistency by showing that the Zeigarnik effect only holds for tasks performed under nonstressful conditions. When noncompletion is ego-involving and threatens the individual's self-esteem, there is a tendency for the Zeigarnik effect to be reversed—that is, for completed tasks to be remembered better than uncompleted ones.

Further inhibiting effects of threatening experiences on memory have been demonstrated in a number of studies. In general, memory has been shown to be impaired when "anxiety" stimulus words are used, when there is a threat of failure associated with the material, or when frustration or other unpleasantness is experienced between learning and recall. Whether memory is facilitated or inhibited by motivation depends on the kind and intensity of emotion aroused as well as on the nature of the task, the kind of response called for, and the place in the sequence of learning and remembering at which the motivational conditions are introduced.

Current appraisal of theories of forgetting. Approximately twenty-three hundred years ago, Aristotle proposed a theory of memory and forgetting that emphasized the importance of such variables as contiguity, similarity, and contrast. Experimental research has substantiated some of Aristotle's thinking, but it has not really produced any dramatic new insights into the memory process. All of the different theories seem to "explain" some aspect of forgetting, but no one of them is sufficient to provide an overall answer to the question, Why do we forget? Hopefully, future research will either find ways of combining the current hypotheses into a more comprehensive theory or discover a completely new model for the workings of the human mind.

How do we remember? Although psychologists are still unsure about the explanations of memory and forgetting, they are fairly well agreed upon some of the characteristics of the memory process. Basically, there appear to be three different memory systems: sensory-information storage, short-term memory, and long-term memory.

Sensory-information storage. One of the memory systems preserves sensory information just long enough to be used in perceiving, remembering, judging, and so on, and is called *sensory-information storage.* It lasts only for a very brief time, usually less than half a second. (See *P&L* Close-up, p. 177.) From sensory-information storage, material may be passed on to short-term memory.

Short-term memory. The second memory system is *short-term memory,* in which limited amounts of information that the person has just learned remain in the memory for very short periods of time. The classic example of short-term memory is remembering an unfamiliar telephone number. After you look up the number in the directory, you can dial it immediately and perhaps even repeat it to someone else if necessary. Shortly after that, however, you probably cannot remember the number correctly.

Like sensory-information storage, short-term memory has a limited capacity and can only store a small amount of information. However, the information that is there is very accessible and can be recalled easily. To maintain information in short-term memory, it is necessary to rehearse it actively (as when we repeat a new telephone number over and over again). Nevertheless, most information in short-term memory is soon "lost" or forgotten. Research has shown that this type of forgetting is due to interference processes and not to simple decay, as was once hypothesized (Reitman, 1971).

The errors that occur in short-term memory are usually confusions of things that *sound* alike, even if they look different and have different meanings. For example, if people are trying to immediately recall lists of letters, they might remember *B* instead of *D*, or *S* instead of *X*. These short-term acoustic confusions occur even if people have seen the lists of letters, rather than heard them (Conrad, 1964). Such findings suggest that short-term memory involves some sort of "echo" process by which we remember the sound of things, rather than their meaning.

Long-term memory. Remembering the *meaning* of information appears to be characteristic of *long-term memory*. This third memory system is more permanent, with a theoretically unlimited capacity. However, unlike short-term memory, it is not always so easy to retrieve information from the long-term storage. Because the material is not immediately accessible, it takes more "searching" for appropriate cues to retrieve it.

In order for us to profit from our experience—not to make the same mistakes again—information must somehow get transferred to long-term memory. The first step in the process is that the new information passes immediately from the sensory-information storage into short-term memory. The period in short-term memory is a very fragile one, during which the information could easily be forgotten or lost from the system. Some recent experiments with animals as well as clinical observations of humans with brain injuries suggest that the memory for an event during this fragile period can be easily disrupted and "shaken out" of the system. In studies with animals, a standard technique for disrupting a recent memory is to give an electroconvulsive shock to the brain or induce unconsciousness and coma by a drug. It is found that

behavioral events occurring shortly before the convulsion or coma are almost totally erased from memory, so that little if any remnant of that information can be detected upon later testing. The longer the delay interval between the event and the trauma to the brain, the less the memory for an event is likely to be disrupted. This finding is in accord with the view that information transmitted to long-term memory increases with the time an item is able to remain in short-term memory without interference. However, it also raises the puzzling question of how the brain can discriminate and store *meanings*.

Patients who have had a part of their hippocampus (a structure in the subcortex) removed have no permanent memory for new information but can remember material learned prior to the operation (Milner & Penfield, 1955). Thus the hippocampus may be involved in the transfer of information from the short-term memory to long-term memory.

Several factors help to get the information transferred from the short-term system, where its rate of loss is great, to the long-term, where it is relatively more persistent. The likelihood of information getting into long-term storage is greater the smaller the amount of material pre-

Close-up
Fleeting Feelings

You can get some idea of what the sensory storage system is like if you try the following exercises:

"Tap four fingers against your arm. Feel the immediate sensations—note how they fade away so that first you still retain the actual feeling of the tapping, but later on only the recollection that you were tapped . . . . Wave a pencil (or even your finger) back and forth in front of your eyes while you stare straight ahead. See the shadowy image that trails behind the moving object." (Lindsay & Norman, 1972, pp. 287–88)

sented, the more novel it is, the more actively it is rehearsed, and the greater its meaning or significance for the individual's orienting to and coping with environmental demands. Unfortunately for those who hate commercials, much information that is of no value to us gets stored in long-term memory because it meets these criteria. Thus the messages of cigarette advertisements, which certainly have a negative value for human survival, seem to linger on and on. Consider:

"I'd walk a mile for a _____."
"_____ tastes good like a cigarette should."
"You can take _____ out of the country, but . . . ."

If you recognize these slogans, even though cigarette advertising has been banned from television for several years, you are cluttering up long-term memory storage with them and may remember them for the rest of your life.

Physiological bases of memory. Current hypotheses about how memories are stored are concerned with the possible neural mechanisms and with the question of whether one such mechanism can explain all the remembering we do. As we saw in the previous section, the loss of short-term memory as a result of brain injury or trauma suggests a relationship between memory and specific physiological processes in the brain. Unfortunately, however, we still know little about the neural basis of human memory despite considerable ongoing research and analysis. Almost fifty years ago, Karl Lashley set out to find just where memory traces, or *engrams,* might be stored in the brain. "In search of the engram," Lashley surgically removed various areas of the cortex in both primates and rats and observed the effects on their memory for learned tasks. His search ended in failure when he reported: "It is not possible to demonstrate the isolated localization of a memory trace anywhere within the nervous system" (1950, p. 501). From this he concluded that the engram probably consists of a "vast system of associations involving the interrelations of hundreds of thousands or millions of neurons" (p. 498).

Three hundred years earlier, Descartes had provided a clue to where a profitable search for memory might begin—namely with the differential transmission efficiency or receptivity at the synapses. It is revealing to review Descartes' early doctrine of the neural basis of memory and compare it with the current physiological approach to this problem. Descartes wrote:

"When the mind wills to recall something [directed attention], this volition causes the little [pineal] gland, by inclining successively to different sides, to impel the animal spirits [nerve impulses] toward different parts of the brain, until they come upon that part where the traces are left of the thing which it wishes to remember; for these traces are nothing else than the circumstance that the pores [synapses] of the brain through which the spirits have already taken their course on presentation of the object, have thereby acquired a greater facility than the rest to be opened again the same way by the spirits which come to them; so that these spirits coming upon the pores enter therein more readily than into the others." (quoted in Lashley, 1950, p. 478—his brackets)

Recent experiments with rats have used drugs to change synaptic transmission efficiency and have observed corresponding changes in memory efficiency. With drugs that block reception of the transmitter substance by the receiving neuron, memory is worse. With drugs that keep the transmitter substance from being destroyed, memory improves. Such evidence suggests that the physical change underlying learning is related to an increase in efficiency of the synapse to transmit impulses following use, whereas memory deficits may be due to reduction in efficiency of synaptic transmission for one reason or another (Deutsch & Deutsch, 1966).

Memory monitoring: Knowing what you know. You search through the stacks of a library for a specific book only if you have reasonable grounds for believing that it is there. It is of little use to search for esoteric, out-of-date government documents in a small bookmobile. Human memories seem to have a built-in monitor that tells you whether you are likely to know something—whether a more extensive search of your memories will prove fruitful in answering the question. For example, you know that you know your current address, and you know that you may possibly remember your previous addresses (or that they are on the "tip of your tongue"). However, you know surely that you do not know Mao Tse-tung's address in Peking. Experiments have shown that these feeling-of-knowing (or not-knowing) judgments can be quite accurate. (See *P&L* Close-up at right.)

In one experiment, college students were asked a number of general information questions (e.g., "Who invented the steam engine?"). If the students could not recall the answer to a particular question, they were asked to rate their "feeling of knowing" on a 5-point scale. Later they were given a multiple-choice test covering the same questions on which recall had been attempted. An analysis of only those items for which subjects could not recall the answer (which surely loaded the dice against them) revealed that their feeling-of-knowing judgments predicted whether or not they could recognize and select the correct answer on the multiple-choice test. The observed percentage of correct choices was about 63 percent for tests on items the subjects thought they knew versus 47 percent for tests on items they thought they did not know, as compared with the 25 percent correct that would have been expected by chance on the four alternate questions. In other words, the subjects could judge to some extent whether they knew information that they could not recall at the time (Hart, 1967).

This introspective monitoring, this knowledge of our own knowledge, is surely one of the more fascinating capabilities of the mind. It serves to inform us whether it is worthwhile to search our memory for some elusive item of information; by this means, time and effort are not wasted in hopeless and fruitless searches.

How Memory Can Be Improved

In this final section we shall review what research has to say about factors that can improve our ability to remember.

Close-up

Don't Tell Me—
It's on the Tip of My Tongue

What is the name of the waxy substance derived from sperm whales that is often used in perfumes? What is the name of the small boats used in the harbors and rivers of China and Japan? Do you know the name of the patronage bestowed in consideration of family relationship, not on the basis of merit? When these questions were asked of a large number of college students, there were three kinds of reactions: immediate recall of the correct word; failure to identify the word from the definition; and, most interestingly, awareness of knowing the right word, but not being able to recall it (Brown & McNeil, 1966). This last reaction is a common one we all experience when the name we are searching for is "on the tip of the tongue" (TOT).

If these TOT words are really known and stored in memory, but are not available in the person's active-recall vocabulary, then it should be possible to demonstrate that many characteristics of the word can be retrieved through questioning. When asked to write down all the words they were thinking of as possible answers, subjects gave words that are similar in *meaning* to the elusive TOT word, but more often they answered with words similar in *sound*. For the TOT word *sampan*, they tended to answer "Siam," "Cheyenne," "Sarong," or "Saipan" more frequently than "junk" or "barge." They were also able to recall other details of the target word, such as its number of syllables and first letter, even though the word itself was not recalled.

You might want to demonstrate this phenomenon for yourself using your roommate or relatives as subjects to see what they say while searching for *ambergris, sampan, nepotism,* and other words that might fall into the TOT category. From such research we learn that memory storage and retrieval is a complex, rather than an all-or-none process.

Practice strategies. Verbal learning research early identified three techniques for improving retention of learned material—overlearning, review, and recitation.

Overlearning. If your task is to learn a list, you might think that when you can recall the complete list without error, your learning is complete and there would be no point in studying it further. To the contrary: further practice, called *overlearning*, has a marked effect on how much of the material you will remember later.

In one study, subjects were asked to memorize several lists of words. As soon as they had done so, they were divided into three groups and given varying amounts of additional practice. One group practiced the words again for the same amount of time it had taken them to learn the words originally (100 percent), a second group practiced the words for half the time it took to learn them originally (50 percent), and a third group did not practice at all (0 percent). All three groups were tested for recall at intervals throughout the next month. As shown in the figure, the 100 percent group recalled about twice as many words as the 0 percent group on each of six tests, although by the twenty-eighth day, recall was very low for all groups. ▲

Review. If you read a book at the beginning of a term and expect to be tested on its contents some time later, you are likely to make a better showing if you review the material by periodically looking through it. It is thought that one reason such review is helpful is that it enables you to direct your attention to parts you did not learn thoroughly the first time. With periodic review, less and less review time is needed to maintain recall as time passes.

Active recitation. During original learning, writing and/or saying the material out loud (as well as reading it) leads to better retention of the material. Such *active recitation* ensures active attention rather than passive reception and also ensures that your learning has reached the degree necessary for recall rather than only recognition. It is even useful to test yourself on the material with the book closed—in other words, to recite the material without visually reviewing it. Psychologists have suggested that the effectiveness of such recitation, even in the absence of a check on accuracy, may lie in the opportunity it provides for practice in *retrieving* the information—perhaps devising the strategy that will be most effective later, when exam time comes.

"Chunking" and memory. Read the following sequence of letters once and then close your eyes and try to recite them from memory.

TH-EDO-GSA-WTH-ECA-T

Very probably a sequence of letters like this one is at or near the limit of your short-term memory capacity. The way the letters are organized into groups is probably meaningless; thus the letters must be remembered individually. However, if you had noticed that this sequence of letters, with different groupings, says "the dog saw the cat," then it would have been a simple matter to remember and recall the sequence.

Our ability to recall once-presented material depends on the number of organizational units, or *chunks*, we see in it. Many studies have shown that we can take in only somewhere between five and nine chunks in a brief time—as George Miller (1956) says, *seven plus or minus*

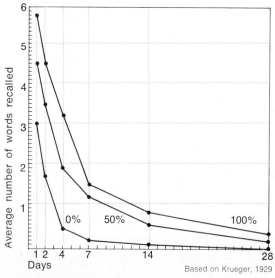

▲ **OVERLEARNING EFFECT**

Based on Krueger, 1929

two bits of information. This seems to be true whether the units are large or small, complex or simple. (Did you try to remember the sequence of letters as fifteen separate units?)

One psychologist taught himself to recode sequences of two digits in a random pattern—for example, 101100111010—by using a code that transformed every group of three digits into a single digit between 0 and 7. For example, the series above—grouped as 101,100,111,010—would be recoded as 5472.

He first determined how long a sequence of the original digits he could recall without recoding. Then he learned a recoded series. As expected, his recall increased just a bit less than threefold. Evidently what had been remembered as three chunks in the original sequence was being remembered as one chunk in the recoded series, with a corresponding increase in the amount that could be retained (S. Smith, cited in G. A. Miller, 1967).

Many studies have verified this tendency to recall a constant number of chunks, whatever their size or complexity. Thus when letters are grouped into words, there is about a sevenfold increase in the number of letters that can be retained, even though the words are more complex informational units. When the words are organized into sentences and the sentences into larger thought units, the amount of material we can take in increases accordingly.

This kind of evidence establishes quite well the notion of chunking and constant capacity for immediate memory in terms of chunks. It may be that our greater recall for meaningful than meaningless material (reported earlier in this chapter) results from the fact that meaningless items such as lists of nonsense syllables are composed of many small chunks that cannot be grouped into larger units and thus must each be processed separately. In any case, it is quite clear that we do indeed organize material to be learned into "meaning-encoded" units.

Mnemonic strategies. Until recently, those trying to apply psychological principles in the classroom have made little effort to deal directly with the organizational problems that confront the learner as the task of learning begins. With the discovery of chunking and the importance of hierarchical organization and meaningful encoding, however, psychologists have begun to investigate the mental processes by which material is encoded, and techniques for making this coding more efficient. Such techniques are called *mnemonic strategies.* The idea behind most mnemonic strategies is to use old knowledge as an anchor or context for new knowledge.

Using an existing framework. The subject may use the organization of some already well-known structure as an "outline" for new information. For example, the correct order of a group of items can be remembered more easily if they are assigned numbers in sequence. Many young musicians have learned to name the lines of the treble staff by reciting "Every Good Boy Does Fine." Or one can arrange the items in a list so that the initial letters spell a familiar word. For example, the names of the Great Lakes (Huron, Ontario, Michigan, Erie, Superior) spell *homes.*

Increasing meaningfulness. Since meaningful material is easier to learn and recall, another effective mnemonic strategy is to give meaning to relatively meaningless material.

One of the most effective mnemonic devices for increasing meaning in lists of words is to put them into a story or sentence. Bower and Clark (1969) demonstrated the effectiveness of this strategy for remembering a list of nouns.

Subjects were given a list of ten totally unrelated nouns that they had to learn in the order presented. The experimental subjects were told to construct a story in which these nouns appeared in the correct order. For example, a subject's story woven around the nouns (capitalized here) for one list was:

"A VEGETABLE *can be a useful* INSTRUMENT *for a* COLLEGE *student. A carrot can be a* NAIL *for your* FENCE *or* BASIN. *But a* MERCHANT *of the* QUEEN *would* SCALE *that fence and feed the carrot to a* GOAT."

Each subject learned twelve lists this way. For each narrative subject, a matched control sub-

ject was given the lists and given the same amount of time to study them that the narrative subject had used. The control subject was given no instructions about constructing stories.

Since there were only ten words in each list, both groups of subjects had almost perfect recall for each list immediately following the study period. After all the lists had been presented and learned, however, each subject was given the first word of each list and asked to recall the rest of each list in correct order. As you can see from the figure, the contrast was dramatic. ◆ Subjects who had made up stories were able to recall correctly 94 percent of the words from all the lists, as compared with only 14 percent for the control subjects. The mnemonic strategy had increased recall sevenfold.

Using visual imagery. Visual imagery is one more example of a mnemonic strategy. The technique is particularly effective when small groups of meaningful items such as words must be associated. In this technique, the objects to be associated are pictured as being in some vivid interacting scene. For example, if the pair *dog-bicycle* is part of a list for a paired-associate task, then the pair will likely be more rapidly

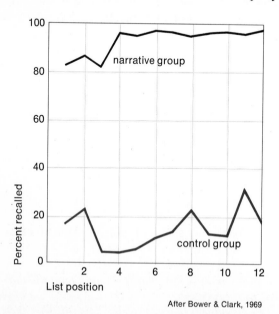

After Bower & Clark, 1969

◆ **INCREASING MEANING HELPS MEMORY**

learned and more accurately remembered if you picture a large, spotted dog pedaling a decorated child's bicycle. People's names, too, can often be remembered more easily by the use of such imagery. The more vivid and specific the imagery, the better.

The most appropriate mnemonic strategy to use depends somewhat on the type of material to be learned as well as the type of remembering that will be required. Such strategies have long been touted in the popular literature but have only recently begun to be studied seriously by psychologists such as Gordon Bower and by educators concerned with improving their students' memories for the vast amount of knowledge applicable to their lives.

Chapter Summary

Language plays an important role in human learning, communication, and memory. It serves both to structure reality and to stimulate fantasy, and provides the means whereby knowledge is transmitted from generation to generation.

Psycholinguistics, the study of the psychological aspects of language and language learning, begins with the study of the content and structure of language. Linguistic analysis takes place on three levels: (a) the *phonological level,* concerned with *phonemes,* the basic sound units of language; (b) the *grammatical level,* which includes *morphology,* the study of *morphemes* (words and meaningful word segments) and *syntax* (rules for combining words and phrases into sentences); and (c) the *semantic level,* concerned with meaning. *Sound spectrograms* have proved useful in studying the acoustical properties of phonemes. Both syntactical structure and meaning affect our ability to hear and remember accurately.

Language production during the first year of life is limited to various forms of crying and babbling. At the end of this year, recognizable words appear and true speech begins. From here, children go on to increase their vocabulary and develop their use of grammar. They begin by using single words and later progress to two-word sentences made up of a *pivot* and a *vocabu-*

lary word or two vocabulary words. By the age of two, they are capable of producing longer sentences, and soon begin to master the grammatical rules of adult speech.

Learning theorists hold that language, like any other behavior, is learned through *reinforcement* of correct responses that the infant produces spontaneously or through imitation of adults. Psycholinguists, on the other hand, argue that language production is an *innate* human ability, both *species specific* and *species uniform.* They believe it is based not on imitation, but rather on construction of a general theory of language based on *transformational rules* by which *deep structure*, or meaning, is converted into *surface structure.*

Communication does not always involve words, however. The study of *nonverbal communication* includes *facial display, kinesis* (body movements), *proxemics* (physical distance and orientation), and *paralanguage* (nonverbal aspects of vocal communication). Eye contact is an important factor in nonverbal expression. We tend to look directly at people we like and to avoid eye contact with those we dislike; inappropriate eye contact can be a source of discomfort. Body posture can give cues as to interest, status, or role, as can habitual gestures. The distance people keep from one another also signals the degree of intimacy desired. When vocal and other nonverbal cues transmit messages inconsistent with the spoken one, the nonverbal cues are likely to be more reliable.

Psychologists have long been intrigued by the question of whether the ability to use language is restricted to the human species. Studies of the whistling sounds made by dolphins have shown that they serve social rather than communication functions. Studies with chimpanzees have shifted from attempts at teaching the animals to speak words to studying their ability to use symbols. Several investigators are making considerable progress in this area.

The study of memory involves the questions of how knowledge is stored, retained, and retrieved. It is conducted by comparing the amount retained immediately after learning with the amount retained at some later time. Verbal learning studies use the methods of *recall* (eith-er verbatim or reconstructive), *recognition*, and *relearning* (in which the experimenter is interested in *savings* in learning time). The verbal learning tradition began with Ebbinghaus, who learned lists of nonsense syllables by the *method of serial anticipation.* Ebbinghaus found a typical rote retention curve with rapid forgetting at first, followed by a gradually slower decline, and also a *serial position effect* (a tendency for the first and last items in a series to be recalled most easily).

Also used in studying memory is the *paired-associate method*, in which the subject learns pairs of words and must recall one of the pair when given the other. *Free recall* is also studied. The paired-associate method has been used extensively in studying forward (*proactive*) and backward (*retroactive*) interference. Memory can also be *productive*, involving both reconstruction and distortion of details. Studies of this phenomenon employ the technique of *successive reproduction* of material.

Explanations of forgetting include the *decay theory*, the *interference theory*, the *displacement theory*, the *loss of access theory*, and *motivational theories* involving *repression*. Uncompleted tasks will be remembered better than completed ones (the *Zeigarnik effect*), except when anxiety is involved. The different theories account for different aspects of forgetting, but none of them provides an overall explanation.

There is general agreement that three different memory systems exist. *Sensory-information storage* preserves sensory information just long enough for immediate use in perception. In *short-term memory*, limited amounts of information are stored for brief periods of time. Content that is to be retained for longer periods must be transferred to *long-term memory.* Memory appears to be related to synaptic transmission processes rather than to the storage of specific memory traces, or *engrams.*

Principles gained from learning research that can be used to improve one's own learning and retention include *overlearning, review*, and *active recitation. Chunking* cuts down the number of units to be learned. Other *mnemonic strategies* include using an existing framework, increasing meaningfulness, and using visual imagery.

Breaking Through into the Silent World of an Autistic Child
John D. Bonvillian Vassar College

What is involved when a young child does not start to speak by the time he is three years old? In many cases, the child's language faculties prove to be intact, with the primary difference from normal development being a slower rate of language acquisition. Medical examinations reveal that many other cases are the result of hearing impairment. However, a small number of these mute children show no discernible hearing impairment or brain injury and yet they continue to fail to acquire speech. Ted was such a child. I would like to recount for you the story of a continuing venture to build an avenue of communication with this once isolated child.

From early infancy, Ted behaved very differently than had his older brothers and sister. Whereas they had frequently climbed into their parents' arms, Ted did not cuddle up to his parents. His siblings, like other normal children, had cried in response to pain; in contrast, Ted often appeared insensitive to pain. When he failed to speak by the time he was three years old, Ted's already worried parents sought the assistance of specialists in the areas of child language disorders and children's emotional problems. After several years of active participation in a number of therapeutic programs, Ted remained a mute and isolated child. However, agreement was reached as to the diagnosis of his rare constellation of behaviors: infantile autism.

Although the syndrome of early infantile autism has attracted considerable interest since it was first described over thirty years ago, only a very small number of children (about 4 per 10,000) are classified as infantile autistic. Historically, descriptions of autistic children have focused on several aspects of their behavior that clearly differentiate them from normal children. Autistic children are characterized as alone and detached from human relationships, as making bizarre, repetitive motor movements. In addition, they often show intense interest in mechanical objects and a desire for sameness, and they often fail to acquire communicative speech. The early analyses of autism also suggested that the child's abnormal development was a result of a marked lack of parental warmth and of interaction between parent and child. However, as more evidence has been collected, this view of the parents as causative agents has largely been rejected. Instead, more recent reviews have argued that disturbance in language function and symbolic processing are the primary handicaps of autism, from which subsequent severe social and behavioral abnormalities arise. Furthermore, it has been shown that the absence of functional speech by age five years in an autistic child is highly correlated with a poor prognosis for the child's later adjustment—it is unlikely that the child will ever make a "normal" adjustment to his or her environment.

Ted's and my paths first crossed several years ago. Several days before, I had lectured a small group of students at Stanford University on the structure and processing of the gestural or sign language of the deaf. In the class was an undergraduate whose fiancee's brother was a mute 15-year-old autistic boy. After some discussion, this young student and I decided that using some other avenue of communication than oral speech, namely sign language, might be worth a try. Dr. Gloria F. Leiderman, the director of the treatment center that the boy attended, suggested that we might try our idea first on 9-year-old Ted, who had failed to respond to all previous speech-oriented programs.

We reasoned that a predominantly visual-motor language might facilitate Ted's acquisition of communicative skills where speech had failed to develop. Previous research had indicated that the visual responses of autistic children were more similar to those of normal children than were their auditory and vocal skills. Thus, a visual-motor means of communication might take advantage of underlying skills that were relatively unimpaired in contrast to speech. In addition to this apparent advantage of utilizing Ted's vision-related skills, sign language, in comparison with speech, has the advantage of being easily "shaped"—teachers could readily mold Ted's hands into the appropriate gesture.

Signs in American Sign Language (ASL), the colloquial sign language of the deaf in the United States, are largely analogous to words in spoken languages. Like words, each sign represents an underlying concept or meaning. Similarly, a series of signs are combined to express a complete idea in much the same way words are grouped to form sentences. Recent analyses of ASL syntax and semantics indicate a high degree of structural consistency, suggesting a rule-based syntactic system. Each sign in ASL consists of a particular configuration of the hand or hands, movement, and a place

on or near the body where the sign begins or ends. Further evidence of similarity between sign language and speech is seen in studies comparing the acquisition of sign language in deaf children and of speech in normal hearing children. Many of the stages of sign language acquisition closely parallel the stages of language acquisition in hearing children. As the study progressed, we switched from ASL to SEE (Signing Exact English, a form of sign language that more closely approximates the grammar of English).

At the time we began teaching him sign language, Ted was nine years and one month old and had *never* produced communicative speech. However, he appeared receptive to sound, often turning and pointing when someone entered his therapy room. When he was much younger, an auditory examination had revealed his hearing to be within normal limits, as was an EEG recording. Beginning when he was three, Ted participated in a computer-aided language interaction program for eighteen months, and was the most unresponsive child in the program. In addition to the computer-aided language program, he was given individual language training and group play therapy; both were completely ineffective in stimulating speech or social responsiveness. His intelligence level was assessed at age five and was extremely low (an IQ of 46, when 100 would be considered "normal"). At age seven and a half Ted entered the day treatment and educational center he currently attends, Peninsula Children's Center in Palo Alto, California. Here he was introduced to a speech program based on operant conditioning procedures, but again he failed to generate any language, not even single words. It was apparent when the sign language training began, that if Ted were able to master sign language it would be his first use of productive language, and perhaps the first steps on his road to a more normal social life.

Ted received special training in sign language in a daily half-hour language session at his treatment center. In order to introduce him to a new sign, his teacher-therapist, Rachel Vasiliev, would usually show him a picture of the object or action for which he was to learn the sign, and then mold his hands

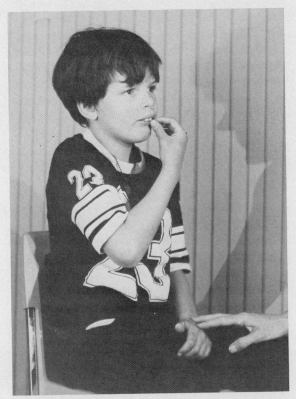

Ted is pictured here during one of his daily sessions with the teacher-therapist shortly after he began to acquire and use sign language.

into the appropriate gesture. As the next step, Rachel would model the correct sign for the picture and request that Ted imitate her. Finally, Ted learned to produce the correct sign in response to the picture alone. During the first months of acquiring a lexicon of signs, Ted was positively reinforced for successful performance. A token reward system was instituted whereupon he received a card after every time he successfully produced a sign. At the end of a language session, Ted was allowed to trade in his cards for a desired toy or the opportunity to play outside. In addition, Rachel verbally praised him after his correct sign productions and encouraged him throughout the language session. The daily language session was supplemented by informal training and interaction in sign language with his mother at home. Both Ted's mother and teacher-therapist received formal instruction and practice in sign language for at least one hour each week.

The table shows Ted's slow but consistent progress towards acquiring a vocabulary of signs across the first six months of the project. During this period, he acquired new signs at the average rate of slightly more than two new signs each week. Interestingly, if Ted used a sign correctly (without immediately preceding molding or modeling) once,

he was quite likely (in 96% of cases) to use it correctly on at least two other occasions. Over the two years, Ted's sign vocabulary continued to expand; current estimates of his total vocabulary indicate that he knows and uses nearly 400 individual signs.

Although the accurate use of individual signs was an important first step in Ted's learning of language, if he was to be effective in communicating with his family and the center staff it was necessary for him to learn to combine signs in order to express more complex meanings. Thus, you can imagine our delight when, after slightly more than three months of training on individual signs, we first observed Ted spontaneously combining signs to communicate his ideas. Comparisons of Ted's early sign combinations with the patterns of word combinations reported for children first learning to speak revealed a number of similarities. Analysis of the underlying semantic relations expressed in Ted's spontaneous two-sign combinations showed that they closely resembled normal children's two-word sentences in terms of structural meaning. Examples of Ted's two-sign combinations and their structural interpretations included: "boy drink" (agent & verb), "swim school" (verb & location), and "boy ball" (possession & object). Additional similarities included Ted's use of the sign "more"

TED'S ACQUISITION OF INDIVIDUAL SIGNS

TWICE-WEEKLY SESSIONS	1—10	11—20	21—30	31—40	41—51
Number of New Signs Introduced:	14	12	13	19	19
Number of New Signs Learned:	9	9	11	12	15
New Signs Learned:	yes	drink	boy	toilet	cry
	no	come	bicycle	baby	apple
	ball	good-by	school	on	break
	Ted	hello	shoe	me	month
	eat	haircut	telephone	off	Ruth
	Daddy	swim	work	bird	turkey
	book	town-dump	play	tomorrow	today
	sleep	car	cookie	tree	kitty
	Mother	go	more	golf	sick
			pants	coat	candy
			light	water	bath
				milk	chocolate
					love
					fix
					hat

to request or signal recurrence (e.g., "more milk," "more cookie") and his use of the sign for negation before another sign or sign combination (e.g., "no food," "no go") to indicate nonexistence or refusal. Also, his mother observed him occasionally signing to himself in a mirror—a behavior that resembles normal children's early word play.

Aside from the many parallels in the acquisition process, Ted's early sign combinations differed in at least two respects from a normal child's early utterances. First, after only two months of combining signs, Ted produced several coherent sign utterances of up to five signs in length (e.g., "no mother car play school"—Ted's mother was not coming to pick him up in the car because he was going to play at school) and second, he often used time referents correctly in his sentences (e.g., "Eat turkey tomorrow"). Such lengths of expression and accurate use of time referents are highly unusual for a child in the early stages of language acquisition.

In the last two years, the amount and complexity of Ted's signing have gradually increased, although his conversation is largely limited to his immediate experience. However, if the listener is familiar with Ted's view of the world, it is possible to engage Ted in a coherent conversation for up to several minutes. An example of his new level of language complexity and understanding occurred recently. When his teacher-therapist asked him what he planned to do when he grew up, Ted replied, "Ted big Daddy, have whiskers—street cleaner, doctor" ("When I get big like Daddy and have whiskers, I'm going to be a street cleaner or a doctor").

We have attempted over the past year to extend Ted's communication skills to include reading and spoken responses. His teacher-therapist began teaching Ted to read printed words by pairing them with their equivalent sign. After many months of training, Ted has begun to master the concept of correct word order and is now able to read and reproduce simple subject-verb-object sentences. Finally, Deborah Bresler, Ted's speech and language therapist, has been working with him on acquiring

spoken language. His gains in this area are very slow, as Ted lacks the ability to protrude his tongue or open his mouth on command. Training has focused on helping Ted gain control of purposeful oral movements. He practices tongue mobility by licking ice cream placed systematically on his lips. His first moderately intelligible word was "ice cream."

Accompanying Ted's developing facility in communication has been a marked improvement in his personal and social behavior. During the first six months of the project his incidence of soiling his pants decreased sharply from an average of over twice a day to about once a week. Now, for the first time, he appears to have complete control over both his bladder functions and bowel movements. The frequency of his temper tantrums both at home and school is now near zero, and his parents have removed from their home a specially constructed "time-out" room (a small, empty room where he had been previously placed to cool off after his tantrums or destructive episodes). Ted also appears to have improved in his ability to focus on and attend to different people and actions in his environment, and there has been a gradual reduction in his bizarre, stereotypic gestures or movements.

Overall, Ted has made great strides in learning to communicate over the two and a half years of participation in this personalized research-therapy project. He remains a markedly handicapped child who will probably need close supervision and support throughout his life. It is also evident from Ted's success with sign language that his cognitive and linguistic abilities had been relatively untapped by speech-oriented therapeutic settings. In addition, his success suggests that many other autistic and nonverbal children might have the cognitive capacity necessary to learn to communicate through sign language or another nonoral method. In fact, reports coming in from research and training centers throughout the country indicate that a number of autistic children are making progress in communication skills through the use of sign language.

5

Thinking, Reasoning, and Creativity

"What goes on four legs in the morning, on two legs at noon, and on three legs in the twilight?"

By answering "Man," Oedipus solved the riddle of the Sphinx and freed the people of Thebes from its tyranny. Our species is called *homo sapiens*—knowing man. By freely exercising our unique ability to think, reason, and solve problems, we free ourselves from the oppression of a life dominated by environmental forces and internal needs. To overcome the many obstacles in the path of our full human development, we have had to learn how to analyze what those problems were, and how to devise creative solutions to them, as well as how to carry them out.

Our ability to know includes the ability to think—to manipulate or organize elements in the environment by means of symbols instead of physical acts. Such symbols include words, numbers, gestures, pictures, diagrams, and visual images. Thinking can take many forms, ranging from reasoning out the solution of a practical problem to daydreaming and flights of fancy. But beyond our capacity to be riddle-solvers of everyday practical problems has been our emergence as *homo ludens*—playing man. We play with the environment, and with each other. We have learned how to take pleasure in reasoning for its own sake, to delight in games of skill, of chance, of daring. When uninhibited, highly imaginative thinking is used in the service of reality, we call it *creativity*.

This chapter will study these highly complex mental processes in the effort to understand how they work. As instances of *homo sapiens*, we are our own greatest challenges.

Indeed, in 1639 when Descartes uttered his famous words *Cogito, ergo sum*, "I think, therefore I am," he was telling us that human existence is predicated on an awareness of human thought. Would an organism that looked exactly like you physically but could not think still be a human being? How could *it* know whether or not it existed without the ability to think and without being able to monitor its own thought processes? The marvel of human thought is that not only do we think, but we are aware that we think and can even think about our thinking.

Thinking is the endeavor to capture reality by means of ideas.

José Ortega y Gasset, *The Dehumanization of Art*, 1925

Thinking is the most complex activity human beings ever perform. It involves the use of *symbols* to represent physical elements in the environment. It involves transformations of what is out there in empirical reality into: what it was (history and origins); what it might be related to (associations, categories, and identity); and what it could become (future, potentiality, and fantasy). Thinking thereby enables us to go beyond mere perception; with it we are able to form abstract concepts, such as "freedom," that may not even have a concrete referent. In this way, thought frees human action from the constraints imposed by the immediate material environment.

When our thoughts correspond closely to features and requirements of the objective, external situation, our thinking is said to be *realistic*. When realistic thinking is directed toward action, toward solving a problem, toward specifying the means necessary to achieve desired ends, it is called *reasoning*.

Autistic thinking is at the opposite end of the continuum that relates thought to the demands of reality. The stimulus for autistic thought is inner reality rather than external reality. It need not correspond to any elements in the "real" world, but may consist entirely of wishes, dreams, fantasies, responses to our own needs for self-gratification. However, a person whose thinking was primarily of this autistic type would have a hard time surviving in our physical and social environment. Such thinking would probably lead to inadequate coping with the demands, stresses, and threats posed by external reality, as well as a lack of the shared bond of consensual agreement with others. There could be no social community in a group of people whose thinking was autistic—they would only be isolated individuals thinking their own thing. We will see when we consider abnormal behavior in Chapter 11 that people diagnosed as schizophrenic are described as *losing* contact with reality, when it is more likely that they are using their autistically based inner reality as the foundation or validity check for external reality. When our ideas conflict with reality, we usually change them. But it is also possible to believe in the validity of one's ideas "no matter what" and try to change external reality, to restructure it, to minimize its importance, or in the extreme, to reject it entirely in favor of one's inner reality.

Creativity clearly involves going beyond what is apparent to everyone else and coming up with either new solutions or new ways of conceptualizing old problems. The creative act thus requires a high degree of autistic thinking that is not bound to the usual, the cliché, or the traditional mode of response. Creative problem solving that results in inventions combines autistic and realistic thinking. Creativity in artistic expression, of the kind revealed by Pablo Picasso, involves giving form to the autistic imaginings of the artist such that others may come to share and accept it. ● (p. 186) In science, creativity typically builds on a base of realistic thinking that incorporates the best available sources of evidence and then combines them in a new way, draws a novel conclusion from them, perceives a missing link, or discovers the fundamental unifying principle.

It is interesting to mention in passing that while recognition of creativity among Americans and Europeans tends to be for the original, the innovative, and the new form, the mark of creativity among Orientals is to reconceptualize the elements of an old form in a new way. For example, the creative Japanese poet is restricted to a rigid verse form in writing haiku—seventeen syllables in three unrhymed lines of five, seven, and five syllables respectively—usually about nature. But the variations on that theme within that prescribed formula are endless and allow considerable latitude for creative thought.

●A variety of creative approaches to the same subject, all by Pablo Picasso. (From top: *Visage*, Collection of The Detroit Institute of Arts, Gift of the Friends of Modern Art; *Woman Weeping*, The Roland Penrose Collection, London; *Girl Before Mirror*, March 14, 1932, Oil on Canvas, 64 × 51½″, Collection, The Museum of Modern Art, New York, Gift of Mrs. Simon Guggenheim.)

Cognitive Psychology

It is safe to say that the major area of interest in experimental psychology today is that of *cognitive processes*. Formerly, the emphasis was on "conditioning and learning," often in lower animals and typically of isolated, overt responses to physical stimuli. Textbooks and introductory psychology courses were, until recently, heavy on "rat psychology" and relatively sparse on the subject of human thought. Rats and pigeons were "in," people were out—except as caretakers of their valuable subjects.

The new approach that has emerged focuses on the ways in which human beings manipulate symbols in their heads. Cognition is the *process of knowing*, in the broadest sense, including perception, memory, judgment, language, and so on. But it is also the result or *product of the act of knowing*, as a thought, bit of information, memory element, and so forth. It is our unique cognitive capacity that enables us to go beyond concern for survival and preoccupation with adaptation to our own particular environment. When we make full use of our cognitive apparatus, we become active creators of new realities. We human beings transform external, empirical, nuts-and-bolts, bread-and-butter, here-and-now reality into something altogether different, by virtue of our symbolic representation of it.

"It isn't raining rain you know, it's raining violets."
"Every dark cloud has a silver lining."
"Wishing can make it so."

In technologically advanced societies we act less from the urgency of biological demands or from desperation in escaping predators and natural disasters, and more often from the myths we have created with our words, our daydreams, and ideas. We typically respond to our personal assessment or interpretation of a situation rather than to the "objective" situation itself. We deal in labels in place of the thing labeled, in concepts and generalizations in place of events, items, and specific physical stimuli.

Our life is what our thoughts make it.
　　　　　　　Marcus Aurelius, *Meditations*, 2nd Cent. A.D.

We have already discussed some aspects of cognitive psychology in the preceding chapter; in this chapter we will elaborate on other aspects of this general cognitive orientation. One perspective on what constitutes cognitive psychology is given by the British psychologist D. E. Broadbent (1971):

"The fashion of recent years has rather been to think of each sensory event as affecting a complex of interacting processes, many of which were already in progress before S [the stimulus] arrived. These processes may transform the information about S into another form, leave it temporarily aside and then take it up later, abstract certain features from it and neglect others, use it to modify an internal representation of the whole outside environment, manipulate this symbolic model of the world to represent events in space or time, start a movement or control it once initiated, and generally operate upon S rather than merely react to it by producing R [a response]." (p. 192)

We shall briefly summarize here the basic recurrent themes in research and theorizing on cognitive processes before turning to consider in detail what we know about how we know.

1. Intellectual development necessitates freeing conceptualization from its ties to the perceptual immediacy of external reality. By studying how children develop a logical understanding of their world, we may discover how facts of nature become principles of reasoning, how data become information, and how assumptions, rules, and categories come to replace experience. The symbols of the external world can be transformed by any one or a combination of processes that are generated by a whole family of internal cognitive operations.

2. There remains a lively debate as to the relative influence of nature and nurture on cognitive development. It is easy to conclude the existence of a strong innate basis because cognitive structure is so complex, children perform such high-level functions with so little training, and the stages of cognitive development appear in such an orderly sequence. However, individual cultural variations of sophistication in cognitive functions lead others to emphasize the pervasive, subtle effects of environmental factors such as learning, experience, and schooling.

3. Cognitive processes are continuous events, although for purposes of analysis they can be separated into successive phases that intervene between stimulus input and response output. These phases arbitrarily abstracted from the ongoing process by researchers include: detection of stimulus features; selection of features to attend to; recognition of the stimulus as novel or familiar; transformation or encoding of selected features; storage in memory; access to and retrieval of stored cognitions; verbal representation of ideas; specification of alternatives, consequences, and plans for action; and testing of actual outcomes against expectations.

4. To study cognitive processes is to examine patterns of behavior at different points along a time continuum. This includes studying developmental patterns that evolve over a period of years as well as emergent patterns of response that occur in minutes or even microseconds as a cognition is being sent through the human information-processing system.

5. Cognitive processes do not necessarily occur in an orderly, linear fashion, but may involve parallel, simultaneous processing of different types of information at different rates. For instance, you might be solving a math problem, planning your lunch, trying to recall a name that is "on the tip of your tongue," being distracted by the awareness of hunger pangs or sexual urges, noticing a hole in your sock, recalling a silly dream, and wondering what you're doing in college anyway, all within a few moments.

Ulric Neisser, one of the most influential thinkers in the field of cognitive psychology, provides us with a broad definition of what we shall mean when we refer to cognitive processes:

". . . Cognition refers to all the processes by which the sensory input is transformed, reduced, elaborated, stored, recovered, and used. It is concerned with those processes even when they operate in the absence of relevant [externally generated] stimulation, as in images and hallucinations." (1967, p. 4)

Approaches to Studying Cognitive Development

When Meno asked Socrates whether virtue can be taught by rational discussion, or requires practice, or is a natural inborn attitude or state, the basic question in child development was posed. Posed not necessarily with regard to the concept of "virtue," but more generally with regard to any aspect of human behavior. What would happen if nothing were done, if there were no teaching, no opportunity to observe other people, in short, no social environment? Would the child develop the same way?

Psychologists have long been concerned with questions of the processes underlying the cognitive development we observe as the mute, unintelligible infant becomes a perceptive, articulate child and eventually a philosopher/poet/scientist/adult. They have also argued over the *determinants* of that development, its *limits,* and whether its *sequence, rate,* and *qualitative* features are invariant or can be modified.

Piaget Sets the Stage

There is no one who has contributed more to our knowledge of how children think, reason, and solve problems than Swiss psychologist Jean Piaget. For nearly fifty years he has devoted his career to observing what children are able to do and how they explain what they can (and cannot) do at successive stages in their intellectual development. Piaget began by carefully observing the behavior of his own children as they were growing up. He would pose problems for them, alter the situation slightly, and then see how they would respond. His training as a zoologist probably provided the orientation that has characterized his research: intensive observations of the behavior and development of normal organisms in a natural environment. ■

Unlike many experimental psychologists who study cognitive information processing in laboratory settings by designing complex experiments that yield simple conclusions, Piaget has used simple experiments from which complex generalizations can be drawn.

From appearances to rules. Young children start their journey through life as *naive realists*—that is, they believe in what they see, trusting that appearance is the only reality. For many problems children face, this reliance on *perception* as the means of knowing the environment is adequate. But looks can be deceiving, as when we tell our children that "all that glitters is not gold."

Time strips our illusions of their hue
And one by one in turn, some grand mistake
Casts off its bright skin yearly like the snake.
Lord Byron, *Don Juan,* 1824

A central problem of cognitive development is how children manage to learn and use appropriately the *rules* that govern abstract relationships in their world. These rules embody the principles necessary to develop a logical understanding of the world. In Piaget's view (1970) this knowledge comes only when children free themselves from the dominant influence exerted by the perceptual immediacy of external reality. It is in the process of discovering, applying, and verifying the rules that underlie logical and mathematical relations that children learn what are the stable, invariant features of their world, and, in addition, learn about their relation to it and to the other people who also inhabit it.

■ Jean Piaget, the Swiss psychologist whose work is basic to our understanding of cognitive development in children.

The gospel according to Piaget. In summarizing the characteristic aspects of the Piagetian cognitive approach, the following ideas are the most significant.

1. The study of cognitive processes requires a *developmental* analysis of behavior over time; it necessitates intensive study of how the individual child thinks and reasons at successive stages of intellectual development.

2. There is a *discontinuity* between the cognitive processes of the child and the adult. It is assumed that children represent, understand, and react to the world in ways that are qualitatively different from those of adults. These processes must be studied in their own right and not as inferior versions of grown-up behavior.

3. This discontinuity between child and adult models of thought occurs because there are distinct stages of intellectual development over different periods of each individual's life. Although the boundaries between these stages cannot be precisely drawn, each stage represents abrupt, discontinuous changes rather than continuous or gradual changes. The top achievements realized at each stage are *qualitatively* different from each other and not merely of greater difficulty. But the structures and capacities developed at one stage are incorporated into the next one—which could not be attained without them.

4. There are four general stages of cognitive development (to be described later) that occur at different chronological ages in different children. However, the four stages occur in the same sequence in all children of all cultures. That is, Stage 3 appears only after Stages 1 and 2 have been reached and before Stage 4 becomes possible. The *rate* at which a child progresses through this fixed sequence, however, depends on individual biological and motivational factors as well as learning experiences.

5. A child's understanding, inferences, abstractions, logical rules, and problem-solving ability develop entirely from occasions of unsatisfactory *interaction* of the child with the environment *(states of tenuous equilibrium)*. Knowledge is structured, as is behavior, and these structures change only when there is a perceived *discrepancy* between them (or their level

of complexity) and the complexity of the environment. Out of these encounters between a child and the problems that are posed by the *physical* environment emerges the invariant sequence of cognitive developmental stages.

6. The overall process of development is (a) a function of the intellectual challenge that comes from confronting the child's existing cognitive structures with novel, challenging information from the environment, and (b) a continual process of internal, self-induced reorganizing and integrating of the contents and structures of human intellect.

7. The primary "shapers" of intellectual growth are certain *functional invariants* that enable the child to adapt successfully to its environment. Here Piaget suggests a similarity between intellectual functioning and biological functioning. The baby starts life with biologically inherited modes of interacting with the environment (called *functions*). These functions enable the child to perform acts that accomplish things necessary for survival, such as ingestion of food.

In the process of being carried out, these acts become organized into *structures* that are changed to adapt to varying environmental demands. The child thus develops cognitive structures that relate means (such as looking, reaching, manipulating) to ends (such as receiving particular kinds of stimulation). The two most important functional invariants are assimilation and accommodation. *Assimilation* is the process whereby new perceptual, cognitive elements are altered to make them more similar to familiar, already experienced ones. In this way, novelty is incorporated into existing cognitive structures. However, it is not always appropriate to transform the new into the old, since sometimes the new is more valuable and must change the old. *Accommodation* is the process whereby previously developed cognitive structures are modified on the basis of new experiences. The cognitive structures that are developed through accommodation are called *schemata* (the singular is *schema*). Schemata are characteristic patterns of particular means-ends relationships. Cognitive development, in Piaget's terms, consists of a succession of changes in these structures. It is these schemata that exert a guiding or controlling influence over what the child can understand and do at a given time.

The four stages of cognitive development. Based on his observations of young children, Piaget has delineated four successive stages of cognitive development: sensory-motor, preoperational thought, concrete operations, and formal operations.

Stage 1: Sensory-motor period (0–2 years). Simple, automatic reflexes and responses appear first. These are of limited duration and seem not to be affected by their consequences. As the infant matures, these reactions become organized and consolidated into patterns that more clearly influence the environment—they are repeated because they have consequences that are noticeable and presumably desirable. (This, as we have seen, is the basis of operant conditioning.) Thus Piaget reports that at three months of age his daughter Lucienne shook her crib repeatedly, apparently because this motion caused the dolls that hung from it to shake.

A third phase of development appears from twelve to eighteen months when mere repetition is transformed into *variation* of response patterns. The passive, self-centered infant becomes an active seeker of knowledge, an explorer. During this stage, then, many new schemata are produced, and they are intercoordinated across different senses and in response to different, new situations.

The most important and profound cognitive developments during this primary stage are those that combine to generate self-identification, efficacy, and causality.

The separation of the concept of self from external objects requires developing a concept of external reality as consisting of objects other than the self that exist in space. Initially, the child conceives of objects as permanent parts of the total perceptual field in which they were first experienced. The separation of figure from ground is an important cognitive structure basic to developing a sense of self as distinct from all that is nonself. Piaget's daughter Jacqueline, at the age of ten months, watched her father hide a toy parrot on her left twice and readily retrieved it. But after watching him hide it on her right, she attempted to retrieve it again by going back to the old hiding place on the left. She later learned to distinguish between such contextual variations.

Children come to learn about what they can do, how they can influence people and objects, how their intentions and needs become realized when their responses yield meaningful consequences. This vague sense of *efficacy* (personal competence, mastery, or self-worth) is perhaps the most important single kind of knowledge we ever develop. It is what enables us to experience many setbacks, frustrations, disappointments, extinctions, and still be able to function and "bounce back."

Of great significance during this primary cognitive stage is the beginning of causal thinking. It is essential for survival that we learn that events are related in ways that influence their occurrence and nonoccurrence. (See *P&L* Close-up, p. 191.) Children must learn to infer probable causes from observed effects and to predict effects from likely causes. This requires the assumption of *physical causality:* that antecedent events can be causes of other events only if there is some direct connection between them. This idea must replace the more "primitive" belief of *phenomenalism:* that sequential events can be causally related even if they occur in different places, without direct contact. Children must learn the psychological causality between their own intentions and actions—but must reject the belief that their desires necessarily cause external events to happen without intervening actions on their part.

Stage 2: Preoperational thought (2–7 years). The principal achievement during this second period is the development of the capacity to represent the external world *internally,* by means of symbols that come to stand for objects. This symbolic function enables the child to represent not only events taking place in the present environment but past and future events as well. The use of symbols helps the child escape from the rigid confines of the limited, concrete operations of the here-and-now, to plan and develop multiple alternative strategies to achieve the same end.

There are two limitations or constraints on the cognitive development of the child in this preoperational stage:

1. *Transductive reasoning:* In this type of reasoning, the child "reasons by simile," by comparison of particulars that are alike in some respect to the conclusion that they are alike in all respects. Thinking goes from *particular to particular* rather than *deductively* from general propositions to specific inescapable conclusions or *inductively* from observation of specific instances to generalizations.

2. *Egocentrism:* The failure to imagine the world from any perspective other than the child's own, and the inability to acknowledge that the child's own perspective is but one of many alternative ones is called *egocentrism.* This deficiency leads to much communication misunderstanding and limits the breadth of knowledge a child can acquire.

A recent study by John Flavell and his students at the University of Minnesota (1974) illustrates in a quite ingenious way how egocentrism affects the inferences a child makes about what other people are perceiving.

The task given the children used an eight-by-ten-inch opaque-white cardboard with a cutout of a dog on one side and a cat on the other. After the child had examined both sides, the cardboard was held up vertically between child and experimenter, and the child was asked two questions: "What do *you* see?" and "What do *I* see?" All the three-year-olds were able to take the other perspective, to infer what the other person was looking at that was different from their view. However, only about half of the two-year-olds were able to break through the egocentric orientation that results in the belief that others must be seeing what they see. It is as if the egocentric child modifies Descartes' assertion to "I see and think, therefore *you* see and exist."

Close-up
Train-in, Train-out

If a baby is watching a moving object that briefly disappears from sight, then reappears consistently at another place, will the baby visually track the extension of the observed trajectory of the object? Keith Nelson (1970) sought the answer to this question when he set up a research design that attempted to show how human infants supplement their inherited perceptual repertoire with acquired knowledge in order to make contact with, and understand, novel aspects of encountered phenomena.

Nelson began by recording the eye movements of eighty babies varying in age from 99 days to 264 days as they watched an electric train moving around a track. As soon as the babies spotted the train, all previous, random behavior stopped instantly. With feet or hands "frozen" in mid-air, they watched the moving train intently. On the first trial, seventy-three of the subjects tracked the train steadily, until it disappeared into a tunnel. They continued fixating on the entrance ("like cats at a mouse hole") and usually were unaware of its exit at the other end. However, on each of the next three successive runs, the babies looked progressively more toward the exit and spotted the reappearing train sooner and sooner, as is evident in the photo below of a seven-month-old baby intently waiting for the toy train to reappear from the tunnel. Visual tracking and anticipation in this complex, novel situation were learned in only a few trials, and more readily by seven-month-old babies than by those five months old.

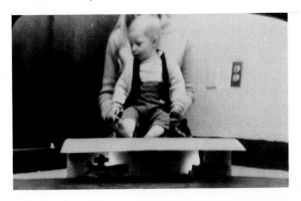

The developmental progression of the capacity to make nonegocentric inferences is clearly shown in another study (Strayer, Bigelow, & Ames, 1973) that used a similar picture task with young children of five age groups. The older children were able to make progressively more correct inferences on eight critical trials:

Age Group	Correct Inferences
19 months	0
22 months	0
25 months	1
28 months	2
31 months	6

These studies support Piaget's notion of egocentric perspective but indicate that the ability to make correct inferences about others' visual percepts develops earlier than Piaget postulated (Flavell, 1973).

Stage 3: Concrete operations (7–11 years). At this stage the child develops a cognitive system for organizing the events in the external world by means of logical-mathematical structures. The Stage 3 child masters operations of arithmetic, measurement, logical classes, class and set relationships, and conceptions of space. In addition, conservation is developed. *Conservation* refers to the knowledge that the amount of a substance is unchanged—conserved—even though its appearance is changed by transferring it to a different size or shape container or by combining its parts or separating the whole into its parts. To solve the conservation problems posed by Piaget (and by the natural environment), the child must learn to respond to two or more dimensions of the stimulus simultaneously.

Consider Piaget's lemonade study: an equal amount of lemonade is poured into two identical glasses. Who has more, the child or the experimenter? Swiss five-, six-, and seven-year-olds all report that they have the same amount. But now the lemonade from one glass is poured into a taller, thinner glass and given to the child. Who has more now? The five-year-olds are convinced they have more in their tall glasses; the six-year-olds are less certain, but say they too

have more; the seven-year-olds "know" there is no difference. When the lemonade is poured back into the identical glasses, the five-year-olds say there is more in the glass that came from the tall one, but the six-year-olds know there is again an equal distribution of lemonade. To a five-year-old, the salient cue of height usually is a reliable cue to the dimension of "more than." But when the dimension is volume, and height and width change simultaneously, then height cues are misleading. An "average" six-year-old realizes that something besides height is important, but can not yet integrate two dimensions at once conceptually. A seven-year-old has come to understand that the concept of amount depends on both height and width. If changes in one dimension are compensated for by equal changes in the other, then the underlying reality is *conserved* (that is, the reality remains unchanged even though the appearance varies). ▲

It is difficult for children to give up their trust in perceptual cues and learn to deal at a symbolic level with the operations made on those stimuli. In part, according to Harvard University's Jerome Bruner (1973) this is because the perceptual representation of stimuli are conceptually stored as *iconic* entities (*icon* means "image"). There is a conflict or interference between the symbolic operational processes and these symbolic representations of the physical stimuli. Bruner reasoned that more children would be able to solve the volume conservation problems if the water glasses were screened from view and only the pouring operations could be witnessed. When he did this, correct conservation responding among four-year-olds jumped from 0 to 50 percent; among five-year-olds, from 20 to 90 percent; and among six-year-olds, from 50 to 100 percent. When the children had made these judgments on the basis of the operations alone, the screen was removed and they were faced with the perceptual evidence. How do you think children reacted to this added source of information?

All the four-year-olds changed their minds. The perceptual display overwhelmed them and they decided that the wider glass had less water. But virtually all of the five-year-olds stuck to their judgment, often invoking the difference between appearance and reality — "It looks like more to drink, but it is only the same because it is the same water and it was only poured from there to there," to quote one typical five-year-old. All of the six- and seven-year-olds stuck to their judgment (Bruner, 1973, p. 336).

Stage 4: Formal operations (11 years and above). In the third stage, reasoning and inference are still dependent on visible evidence, concrete objects, and the immediate perceptual field. The fourth and final stage in cognitive development is one in which reasoning may proceed entirely from verbal descriptions, the form of an argument may be distinguished from its contents, and hypothetical or imagined consequences and means-ends relations are developed to coexist with those that are based on reality. The child's comprehension of the physical world and the logical realm now permits him or her to deal with concepts of negation, reciprocals, and other transformations.

American criticisms of this Swiss scenario. Until quite recently, Piaget's approach to cognitive development has not been well received by American psychologists, nor properly acknowledged for its influential contributions. There are a number of reasons (see Manis, 1971) for this critical view: (a) Piaget's structuralism rubs American functionalism the wrong way. (b) Behaviorists have had difficulty embracing a theory in which the response unit — schema — is so broad and vague, and where response and stimulus interact and are not isolatable. (c) The experimental testing situation used by Piaget was loose, unstructured, and poorly controlled, making it difficult to rule out the influence of Piaget the theoretician on Piaget the data gatherer. Piaget's observations were largely based on his own three children. How far can we generalize from this limited sample to a general theory of cognitive development, especially given the fact that these subjects were born of a remarkably brilliant father and reared in a rather unusual household? (d) Piaget overrelied on the child's overt descriptions of covert thought processes. The two are not perfectly related; a child may understand something without being able to explain it. Thus there is a need for test-

ing procedures that rely on nonverbal measures. (e) Piaget seems to believe that cognitions develop best in the absence of formal education and without incentives (see Kessen, 1965). In one of his rare public lectures on this continent, he startled educators by declaring: "Every time

▲ **PIAGET'S CONCEPTUAL CONSERVATIONS**
Illustrated here are some of the types of conservations studied by Piaget. The ages given are those at which the Swiss youngsters with whom he was working were able to master the various concepts. Note that there is a steady progression with age, and that conservation of volume is usually not grasped until youngsters are well into their teens.

Type of conservation	Dimension	Change in physical appearance
Number (Age 6-7)	Number of elements in a collection	Rearranging or displacing the elements
Substance (Age 7-8)	Amount of a deformable substance (e.g., clay)	Altering its shape
Length (Age 7-8)	Length of a line or object	Altering its shape or displacing it
Area (Age 8-9)	Amount of a surface covered by a set of plane figures	Rearranging the figures
Weight (Age 9-10)	Weight of an object	Altering its shape
Volume (Age 14-15)	Volume of an object (in terms of water displacement)	Altering its shape

you teach a child something you keep him from reinventing it."

The efforts of American educators to speed up the rate of cognitive development are a futile exercise in technology according to Piaget, who is content to allow "natural" development to occur at its own rate. However, he feels that programmed progressive discrepancies and environmental challenges at the limits of the child's current developmental stage should be part of the ideal learning situation.

Despite these and other criticisms, Piaget's work represents a landmark in psychology. He has helped inform us not only of how cognitive processes develop in infants and children, but more broadly of how we come to understand, relate to, and eventually master both the world around us and the reality within us.

The Influence of Culture on Cognitive Growth

In Piaget's studies of cognitive development, the age of the children is the only independent variable observed (that is, he studies how well a task is performed by children of different ages). This is understandable given his emphasis on biological maturation. However, with such an approach it is impossible to inquire what role, if any, environmental influences play in the development of thinking and reasoning, and therefore, in the emergence of intelligence.

To what extent is intelligence affected by the technology, value orientations, or language structure of a particular culture? This is the question posed by investigators who believe that "intelligence is to a great extent the internalization of tools provided by a given culture" (Greenfield & Bruner, 1973). (See *P&L* Close-up, p. 195.)

While American educators typically want to know whether Piaget's stages can be accelerated by special techniques, they may overlook

more fundamental questions of the way in which the structure and contents of cognitive growth are influenced by such variables as: schooling, the powerlessness of the social group, economic abundance or scarcity, and the extent to which members of a culture are encouraged to develop a self-conscious, individualistic orientation or only a collective identity where self is relatively unimportant (as in Russia and mainland China).

When children in Senegal, Africa (the Wolof society), were given Piaget's conservation tasks, their success as well as their explanations of what they observed differed not only as a function of their age, but also according to whether they had been educated and raised with urban influences. Rural unschooled children (from six to eleven years of age) were compared with other children from the bush who had had schooling and also with urban school children (Greenfield, 1966).

Those with schooling and urban experience not only were more successful, but showed greater understanding of the task itself. When the unschooled children were asked to give reasons for why the second glass held more, the same, or less liquid after the water had been poured, they were silent. They could not answer a question whose structure was, "Why do you say (or think) thus and such is true?" But they could when it was rephrased as, "Why is thus and such true?" For them, the external event could be explained, but not a *statement about* the external event. Further analysis of the way these children formed concepts and solved problems revealed that they do not distinguish between their own psychological reactions and external events; thus they have difficulty in categorizing the same stimuli according to several different criteria or alternative points of view.

What schooling does, and what is further emphasized in urban cultures and western societies, is provide *individualistic* orientation. Such an orientation recognizes and emphasizes individual initiative, intention, and desire as necessary to action and change. It also exaggerates an individual's sense of personal importance, responsibility, and self-consciousness. Cultures that promote individual self-consciousness will also promote the notion of individual mastery over the physical world and a separation of self from the external environment. In contrast, cultures where there is scarcity of resources, a subsistence economy, and a lack of technological control over nature, or where the important functional unit is not the individual but the group or tribe, will develop modes of thinking that can be called *collective*. In the collective

Close-up
The Importance of Cross-Cultural Psychological Research

Although psychology claims to be interested in understanding human behavior, it is remarkable how limited the range of behaviors and peoples studied has been. There exists a "lazy provincialism" that leads researchers to study what is at hand: people readily available in their own society. These populations are typically "captive" groups that have gathered in a given place for some purpose other than to be research subjects and that can be induced to become *subjects* — such as college and nursery school students, mental patients, military personnel, factory workers, prisoners, and so on. Limiting our investigations to such populations severely restricts the generality of the conclusions that may be drawn and limits the breadth of theories on which such studies may be based.

Cross-cultural research is necessary to guard against a biased, narrow definition of the determinants of human behavior. Such research investigates individual behavior as it occurs in cultures with different traditions, where individuals are confronted with environmental conditions divergent from our own. A good definition of *cross-cultural psychology* comes from Brislin, Lonner, and Thorndike's (1973) excellent summary of the methods and current state of this approach:

"Cross-cultural psychology is the empirical study of members of various culture groups who have had different experiences that lead to predictable and significant differences in behavior.

In the majority of such studies, the groups under study speak different languages and are governed by different political units." (p. 5)

Cross-cultural research is valuable in testing claims of the "universal" or innate nature of some trait, behavior, or psychological process; providing experimental variations unavailable in any one culture; highlighting patterns of behavior that do not exist in the researcher's own country; and studying how members of different cultural groups define their own subjective cultural experiences. The existence of cross-cultural area files at several major universities throughout the United States makes it possible for researchers to test hypotheses with large sets of data already gathered and catalogued by anthropologists, psychologists, and others who have filed reports on the cultures they have studied. An example of this methodology is presented in Chapter 14, where aggression in warfare is related to whether or not warriors in different cultures make themselves anonymous prior to battle (Watson, 1973).

A cogent example of the kind of psychological knowledge that can come from cross-cultural studies is Margaret Mead's classic study *Coming of Age in Samoa* (1938) where she showed that the physical and psychological turmoil commonly associated with puberty among adolescents in the United States does not occur among Samoan youth because of the less repressive cultural attitudes toward sex in Samoa.

In another study Mexican children from families of potters were compared on the Piaget conservation tasks with those from non-pottery-making families. The early experience of helping their parents roll and shape the clay led the children of potters to acquire conservation ability at a younger age than other Mexican children or those from industrialized cultures (Price-Williams, Gordon, & Ramirez, 1969). Thus cultural experience is shown to modify what is theorized to be a purely maturational process.

orientation, the individual's desires are subordinated to the needs and demands of the group. In this way individuals overcome feeling more powerless by collective action and adopt a world view in which attitudes, actions, and physical events are *not* categorized separately.

Eskimo children in Anchorage, Alaska, are trained to suppress attitudes of individualism, since survival of the society demands group action in its major activities of hunting, fishing, and sealing. These children do not go through the *egocentrism* stage that Piaget observed in European children because it is contrary to the dominant values of their culture (Reich, as reported in Bruner, Olver, Greenfield, et al., 1966).

Another consequence of schooling for cognitive development is that it creates cognitive structures that render "magical thinking" unlikely. Unschooled children were able to explain the discrepancy between the apparent amounts of water in the glasses of different sizes by attributing special magical powers to the adult experimenter: "They are now different because *you* poured the water." Magical thinking of this kind is nonexistent in other groups of Senegalese children who have had even half a year of schooling.

One way to break through the attribution of special magical powers to the adult experimenter is to have the children conduct the pouring operations themselves. When they do, conservation success goes up, magical explanations go down. When the child pours, the basis for the explanation is that "they were equal to start with and must still be so because *I* have done nothing to change them."

In the Tiv culture of Nigeria, children are encouraged to approach the physical world through active manipulation of it; thus when given the conservation task, they would *spontaneously* take over the pouring operations themselves and reverse the sequence of pouring, making it obvious that nothing had changed and thus achieving a high level of conservation (Price-Williams, 1961).

Basic Determinants of Cognitive Development

One way to recast much of our discussion about cognitive development is to ask, "How does a brain become a mind?" What is the process by which some protoplasm and the biochemical-electrical activity within cells become a system for perceiving, organizing, integrating, memorizing, planning, and directing action?

This "humanization of matter" has intrigued philosophers for centuries, but only recently has the basic philosophical question of "How do we know?" been modified to make it appropriate for psychological analysis. For psychologists the question has become, "What are the relative contributions of heredity and environment to the development of human intelligence?"

Philosophers such as Immanuel Kant maintained that there exist at birth in the organism many ideas and relationships that develop naturally as the child matures. The basis of human knowledge is to be found in innate ideas (*a priori* axioms) existing prior to any environmental experience. In twentieth-century terms, this position, which is called *nativism,* might describe the mind as a prewired kit that is inherited as part of one's native endowment and needs but to be tuned by experience.

The position of nativism was first opposed by Thomas Hobbes in the seventeenth century, who argued that sensations and experience are the source of all knowledge, and that memory and imagination are decaying sense impressions held together by association. Thus one should search for the origin of the mind in sensation and examine its development through association. This experiential basis of human knowledge is called *empiricism;* it found its champion in the renowned philosopher John Locke. He advanced the thesis that the infant's brain was like a blank tablet (a *tabula rasa,* in Latin), on which experience writes sense impressions by which the meaning of life is communicated.

In psychology, too, these extreme positions have found staunch supporters eager to do intellectual battle to defend either nature or nurture as the more important contributor to intelligence. Let us briefly examine some of the evidence used to support each side before considering what all the fuss is really about. Does it make any difference for your view of human potential if one side or the other is right?

Arguments for Nativism

Who says nature is the key to intelligence? What are the sources of evidence that have led social scientists to conclude that the limits of cognitive, intellectual development are set and determined by our genetic inheritance? In former times it was Galton, Dugdale, Goddard, and Terman; currently the standard-bearers for nativism are psychologist Arthur Jensen and physicist William Shockley. The evidence mustered to support their belief that the major portion of individual variation in intelligence is genetic has come from studies that compare the intelligence test scores of individuals who vary in their degree of genetic similarity.

The general conclusions of this research to be described are that: intelligence is largely an inheritable trait (that is, it "runs in families"); intelligence is positively related to socially desirable behaviors: higher intelligence is a "fair" predictor of attaining a higher quality of life, and lower intelligence is related to a variety of undesirable social qualities. In evaluating the validity of these conclusions, you are encouraged to recall our analysis of *psychological traps* in Chapter 1 to see if any of the "morals" cited there are appropriate in this context.

Galton's studies of eminent families. Sir Francis Galton, in 1869, published a monumental work entitled *Hereditary Genius: An Enquiry into Its Laws and Consequences.* In it he showed that eminence and genius run in families and concluded that they are therefore inherited. Galton's data, taken from the biographies of "great men," revealed that their children as well as their parents and forefathers were more likely than could be expected by chance to have achieved fame. Galton subsequently reported that he had replicated his findings: "During the fourteen years that have elapsed since the former book was published, numerous fresh in-

stances have arisen of distinction being attained by members of gifted families whom I quoted as instances of heredity, thus strengthening my arguments" (Galton, 1907, p. 57).

Galton, who was half cousin to Darwin, took the subtitle of Darwin's classic, *On the Origin of Species by Natural Selection, or the Preservation of Favored Races in the Struggle for Life,* quite literally and became the founder of the eugenics movement. (*Eugenics* is the science that deals with the improvement of species through the control of hereditary factors in mating.) A disciple of Galton's was the noted British statistician, Karl Pearson, who devised the formula for computing correlation (the Pearson product-moment coefficient of correlation). Pearson used his considerable mathematical skills to allegedly "demonstrate" the innate mental inferiority of certain ethnic groups—notably the Jews, who were at that time migrating into Great Britain.

Jukes and Kallikaks; the bad-seed theory. The case of inheritance was promoted by an ingenious tactic, attempting also to prove the reverse side of Galton's coin. While inheritance was being acclaimed in England as the causal agent in producing great men, it was "proven" in America to be the basis for the failings of two of the world's most infamous breeds, the Jukes and the Kallikaks.

Richard Dugdale's investigation of the inherited basis of "crime, pauperism, disease, and insanity," published in 1875, was accepted throughout the world as the best documented evidence of the bad-seed theory of evil. In his intensive analysis of the "Jukes" clan, Dugdale identified over 700 people "belonging to the Jukes blood," of whom more than 500 were social degenerates. There were those who were "immoral," "harlots," "lecherous," "paupers," "drunkards," "lazy," "fornicators," as well as murderers, rapists, and thieves. So evil and corrupt was this family line that during the seventy-three years of its studied existence, it cost the taxpayers of New York State over a million dollars.

In 1912 another researcher, Henry Goddard, found further support for the nativist position when he came upon a natural experiment in breeding. A Revolutionary War soldier, whom Goddard dubbed "Kallikak" (from the Greek *kalos*, "good" and *kakos*, "bad"), sired two families, one illegitimate and one legitimate. His first alliance was with a tavern maid who was reportedly mentally defective; he later married a young woman of "better stock." What were the consequences of these different unions? Only a few of the nearly 500 descendants from Martin Kallikak's legal marriage could be classified as "undesirable." In contrast, the son born of Martin's affair with the tavern maid produced a long line of defective descendants. Of 480 traced descendants, 143 were reported to be feeble-minded, 33 were sexually immoral, 24 were alcoholics, many died in infancy, and others were criminals, brothel keepers, and the like.

These studies led some criminologists to accept the theory that "social disease," as well as insanity and idiocy, could be inherited. The apparent inevitability that a tainted individual would pass the bad seed on to future generations was a powerful stimulus to the eugenics movement in America. Twenty-seven states proceeded to adopt compulsory sterilization laws to prevent the transmission of such "unalterable" defects.

Goddard's own eminence rose as a consequence of this famous study, and he was invited by the U.S. Public Health Service to test the intelligence of European immigrants arriving at New York's Ellis Island. Based on what he described in his 1913 report of the testing of the "great mass of average immigrants," Goddard claimed to have discovered the following percentages of *feeble-minded* individuals among them:

Russians	87%
Jews	83%
Hungarians	80%
Italians	79%

In 1917, Goddard was able to report a vast increase in deportation of immigrants whose feeble-mindedness was detected by the use of tests of mental ability.

Terman and the menace of the feeble-minded.
Lewis Terman is well known among psychologists for two contributions: his introduction into the United States in 1916 of a version of the IQ test developed by French psychologist Alfred Binet (to be discussed in Chapter 10) and his longitudinal study of the development of a group of children classified as geniuses on that "Stanford-Binet IQ test." (Terman was then a professor at Stanford University.) What is less well known is that Terman believed the feeble-mindedness uncovered by IQ tests represented a serious menace to society. He wrote in 1917 ". . . only recently have we begun to recognize how serious a menace it is to the social, economic and moral welfare of the state . . . . If we would preserve our state for a class of people worthy to possess it, we must prevent, as far as possible, the propagation of mental degenerates" (pp. 161, 165). Also after having found low IQ scores for a *pair* of Mexican and Indian children he tested, Terman generalized:

"Their dullness seems to be racial, or at least inherent in the family stocks from which they come. The fact that one meets this type with such extraordinary frequency among Indians, Mexicans and negroes suggests quite forcibly that the whole question of racial differences in mental traits will have to be taken up anew. . . . Children of this group should be segregated in special classes. . . . They cannot master abstractions, but they can often be made efficient workers. . . ." (1916, pp. 91–92)

Before we turn to the less dramatic but more quantitative support for the nativist position, consider briefly the sources of bias in this evidence. Of course, no one would dispute the fact that "eminence" as recognized social status runs in certain families — but is that support for inheritance or for the social, political, and economic *contacts* that eminent parents can provide for their offspring? Can we rule out the availability of advantageous social influences, supportive family environments, appropriate role models, and educational opportunities (limited in earlier times only to the rich)? And how was it possible to construct the genetic family trees of the Jukes and Kallikaks from a period of history when public record keeping of vital statistics was rare or incomplete—and *did not exist* for illegitimate births? How objective are the stigmatizing labels applied by the researchers to the bad-seed offspring: "immoral," "lazy," "perverted"? Is "fornication" an indicator of pathology? One must wonder at the "objective" criteria for assigning the categorical label "feeble-minded" in such a way as to include the vast majority of Eastern and Southern European immigrants. No less must the student of psychology speculate at the size of the inductive leap involved in generalizing from a tested sample of two children to many different ethnic and racial populations. Finally, after our lengthy consideration of the objectivity of the scientific method in Chapter 1, you may be puzzled by its apparent absence in this research. Perhaps this is one area of research where the personal values of researchers have interfered with proper utilization of the scientific method for collecting unbiased data and drawing valid conclusions from reliable evidence.

Modern studies of twins. If intelligence is an inherited attribute, one should be able to demonstrate that the similarity of the intelligence test scores of two persons is a function of their biological similarity—holding environment constant. The approach commonly used has been to compare the correlations between intelligence test scores of identical twins, ordinary siblings, parents and children, and unrelated individuals. This method is based on the premise that, to the extent that heredity influences intelligence, *monozygotic*, or identical, twins (from the same fertilized ovum and thus with identical genetic makeup) should vary less in intelligence than *dizygotic*, or fraternal, twins who develop from separate ova and whose genetic constitution is no more similar than that of any pair of siblings. Thus we should be more likely to find similar intelligence among identical twins, be it high or low, than among fraternal twins. This is indeed the case as the correlation coefficients shown in the table reveal. ◆

The higher IQ correlations for identical twins (.87) than for the other pairs is obvious, but the greater correlations for fraternal twins (.63) than

for siblings (.53) might be due to the fact that they experience greater similarity in environment than do siblings born several years apart. To separate these environmental factors from hereditary ones, evidence has been amassed from four studies in which identical twins were reared apart and unrelated children were reared together.

Separated identical twins. By studying IQ test scores of identical twins who were separated from each other shortly after birth and reared in different environments, it should be possible to show that their IQ correlations are still more similar than those of fraternal twins reared together in the same environment. The published data from four studies conducted in England, Denmark, and the United States on a total sample of 122 pairs of twins (all white) is the evidence currently being used by Jensen (1969, 1972) and Shockley (1972) to support their conclusion that genetic inheritance is the major contributor to intelligence, environment playing a relatively minor role.

The IQ correlations of the separated identical twins in these four studies are substantial: .62, .67, .77, .86. Those identical twins reared apart differ in mean IQ by about 5 IQ points, while those reared together differ by 2 or 3 points, and siblings as well as fraternal twins reared together differ by as much as 12 IQ points. Thus, Jensen concludes:

"The studies of identical twins show clearly that individuals who are genetically identical are almost as much alike in mental ability as they are in physical traits, and this is true even when they have grown up in different environments." (1972, p. 149)

◆ CORRELATIONS IN INTELLIGENCE

Types of Pairs	Number of Pairs	Correlation Coefficient (r)
Ordinary Siblings	384	.53
Fraternal Twins	482	.63
Identical Twins	687	.87

Based on McNemar, 1942; Nichols, 1965

Unrelated children reared together. When unrelated children are adopted at birth by foster parents and reared in the same environment, they still differ considerably in intelligence test scores—according to studies by Shields (1962) and Burt (1957, 1966). Such children differ by almost as many IQ points as do unrelated children from different homes in the same socio-economic class. Thus environmental rearing conditions are claimed to have little effect on influencing IQ correlations. This argument is strengthened further by the additional finding that the IQs of adopted children are unrelated to those of their foster parents but are almost as similar to those of their natural parents as are the IQ scores of children who have been reared by their natural parents.

Analysis of the existing data on these 122 twin pairs has led Shockley (1972) to conclude that the weight of genetic factors in intelligence, as measured by intelligence tests, is four times the environmental weight. In other words, he believes genetic inheritance accounts for 80 percent of the observed variability in intelligence while environment contributes only 20 percent. Earlier studies by Burks (1928) and Leahy (1935) support this same conclusion.

The Environmentalists' Rejoinder

The position advocated by most of those who might be called "environmentalists" is considerably less precise than that of the nativists in its assessment of the relative weights given to hereditary and environmental variables. They agree that since we are biological creatures whose evolution has been guided by genetic factors, intelligence must indeed be influenced to some degree by heredity. Their dispute is with any position that leaves little room for a variety of powerful environmental influences to have an impact on modifying any mental or physical variable. Their contention rests on two general lines of reasoning: (a) evidence of the kind presented throughout any basic psychology text of the importance of environmental forces and interventions on altering physiological functions, perceptual abilities, learning, and adaptive behavior in general, and (b) methodological criticism of the existing twin studies.

As we have seen, reflexes are least influenced by the environment, instincts a little more affected, and adaptive behavior most affected and most dependent on learning. Intelligent behavior is adaptive behavior, requiring flexibility, identification of the critical requirements of a problem, and selection of appropriate resources for solving it. Perceiving, integrating, memorizing, planning, and directing action are all parts of intelligent behavior, and environment plays an important role in their development. Thus environmentalists argue that potential for intelligent behavior does not simply unfold but requires particular kinds of experience.

Research carried out at the University of California at Berkeley by a team of physiologists and psychologists (Rosenzweig et al., 1969) indicates that rats randomly assigned to be raised in an "enriched environment," when compared to those assigned to be reared in an "impoverished" environment, not only were superior learners in adulthood, but had brains that were permanently altered. The animals with the favorable environmental history had larger brains with a thicker cortex, more of certain transmitter substances, and more of a particular enzyme in the cells that nourish nerve cells. These biochemical consequences of early environmental intervention were most noticeable in the occipital cortex, the center for many sensory inputs and sensory-motor integration. Other recent research in perception, to be discussed in the next chapter, indicates that the action of single sensory neurons can be greatly modified by the quality of early life experience (Hirsch, 1972; Barlow, 1972). Research on imprinting (Hess, 1972) clearly reveals that this important social reaction in infant birds depends on experiential conditions and maturational factors as well as species-specific variables. We shall also look later at classic research by Harlow that shows that healthy infant monkeys raised with inanimate terry-cloth "mothers" fail to ever develop normal social or heterosexual behavior and become seriously disturbed in many ways. The list of studies that demonstrates the importance of environmental variables in a wide range of behaviors, including cognitive development, is impressive. However, none of these studies attempts to isolate the relative contributions of environment as compared to heredity, and they have not been focused on human intelligence and its modifiability by environmental interventions.

Some critics of the genetic-nativist view of intellectual development (notably Jerry Hirsch, 1970; David McClelland, 1972; N. L. Gage, 1972; Leon Kamin, 1974) have marshaled impressive arguments in refutation of the conclusions based on the four major twin studies. In addition, criticism has been leveled against the political and social implications that have been drawn by some advocates of the nativist position. For a discussion of their views on some of the ways intelligence test scores have been and are being used, see the *P&L* Close-up, pp. 201–2.)

To establish fully the claim that intelligence is genetically determined, certain conditions would have to be met: (a) objective measurement of the intelligence of parents, twins, and siblings using the same standardized intelligence tests; (b) standardized conditions of testing; (c) random assignment of children to parents and environments; (d) assessment of the "intellectual quality" or "intelligence-encouraging status" of each of the environments into which the children are placed.

None of these conditions has been met by the research conducted to date. Instead, a careful analysis of each of the original studies reveals a number of questionable procedures that leave their results ambiguous. We saw in Chapter 1 that statistics can be used to "prove" any point—but they are only as good as the quality of the measurements that gave rise to them. Different types of intelligence tests were used in each of the reported twin studies: some group tests, some individual tests. Furthermore, some of the scores were adjusted according to "teacher's assessments." In some cases IQ scores for parents were not available, so educational level was substituted. Several of the tests had not been standardized for the population from which the research sample was drawn. There was no standardization of the test scores according to age and sex of the twins—and the correlation of IQ and age varies considerably between males and females.

Examination of the Shields study (1962) shows that when Shields tested the twins himself, their IQ difference score was only 8.5 points, but the co-twin difference among twin pairs *not* tested by him was a sizable 22.4 points—a statistically significant difference. It is possible that a researcher's bias might affect the IQ test scores of people known to be twins if the researcher is hoping to find that those people have the same scores. Therefore researchers should be "blind" to whether or not any given subject is an identical or fraternal twin or a twin at all (there is no evidence this was true in any of the studies conducted so far).

Close-up

The Tyranny of Intelligence Testing: A Personal Statement by Phil Zimbardo

When I was a student, the heredity-environment controversy was an abstract intellectual issue that did not seem to have "relevance" to real-life issues. "Tabula rasa," "heritability," "correlation coefficient," and the like were philosophical and psychological jargon that had no effect on more practical concerns; and in my early years of teaching I could not get my students seriously interested in the issue.

All that has changed. In the past few years it has been reported that compensatory education programs (Head Start and others) for "disadvantaged minorities" were of little value because genetically determined intelligence could not be significantly raised by education. This conclusion by Arthur Jensen in the *Harvard Educational Review* (1969) was based on his interpretation of the data from the four twin studies reported in the text. Jensen thus generalized from the data on IQ heritability among 122 pairs of white twins to account for the reported difference in IQ test scores (about 15 points) between white and black Americans.

It remained for William Shockley (Nobel Prize-winning co-inventor of the transistor) to carry the argument to one of its obvious conclusions. Shockley has advocated a national genetic control program to counteract what he terms "*dysgenics*—retrogressive evolution through the disproportionate reproduction of the genetically disadvantaged." His reading of the data (on the same 122 twin cases) "leads inescapably to the opinion that American Negro IQ and social deficits are primarily hereditary and racially genetic in origin" (1973, p. 3). Shockley recommends drastic social action: financial compensation for black people who undergo voluntary sterilization. Such an idea might have been dismissed out of hand were it not: (a) backed by the scientific and academic "credentials" that make such pronouncements newsworthy, (b) supported by the Jensen arguments, and (c) already endorsed by certain segments of the general population.

Let us briefly put the Jensen-Shockley position into its appropriate historical context before outlining its fallacies. This context includes the anti-immigrant hysteria that led Pearson and Moul to "prove" that Jews were "somewhat inferior physiologically and mentally to the native population" of Britain (1925, p. 126). In turn-of-the-century America the attempt to keep the American people "pure" also called on the mental test movement to provide the intellectual foundation for both eugenics programs and immigration quotas. Little distinction was made between various types of "degenerates"—the criminal, the insane, the poor, and the "feebleminded." They were housed in "charitable and correctional public institutions," many of which demanded their sterilization before release.

An influential book by Carl Bingham, *A Study of American Intelligence,* provided the necessary justification for Congress to pass in 1924 the first immigration law restricting immigration from various countries according to a "quota system." Bingham concluded, on the basis of a highly inappropriate set of correlations, that the Nordic and Alpine countries of Europe sent their better racial stock, while those who emigrated from Mediterranean countries were of biologically inferior racial stock. This generalization was based on the evidence that immigrants who had been in the U.S. more than 16

years scored higher on IQ tests than more recent immigrants. The more recent immigrants tended to be from southern Europe, while the established immigrants were from northern Europe. Thus time and place are confounded in this correlation. It is interesting to note that the highest intelligence test scores were found for white, Anglo-Saxon, male immigrants—the group that has traditionally held the positions of political, economic, and social power in the United States (and the general category into which most of the contemporary nativists fall).

Higher IQ *is* a predictor of a better quality of life *in an environment* that rewards verbal skills and intellectual performance with formal education, better jobs, and positions of eminence. Overall IQ predicts scholastic achievement well, but not many other skills important for coping and adapting to the nonscholastic environment that most people face every day. There is *no* available evidence for Shockley's "80 percent heredity" assertion in any group other than Caucasians. It is false logically and empirically to further assert that because of the heritability of IQ, environmental interventions—such as compensatory education—will have negligible effects on intelligence. Height, which is obviously an inherited characteristic, has been shown to be modifiable from one generation to the next by environmental changes (Cavalli-Sforza & Bodner, 1971). Heritability coefficients tell us nothing about the potential effectiveness of environmental changes. If Head Start programs are ineffective, it may not be because the *children* have failed, but because the *programs* were poorly designed. We will see throughout this text that whenever there are "social problems," the political reaction is to blame *people* rather than social situations. Nativist arguments have been quite influential in the search-and-destroy operations designed to eliminate "problem people."

I might well be stomping grapes in Sicily today instead of teaching at the university where Terman and Shockley did their work if all those "inferior" Mediterranean types had been restricted from entering this land of opportunity in my grandparents' day. I'm glad the nativists didn't win.

The alleged differences in environments for twins reared separately were never assessed in terms of psychological qualities of the environments—at most, socioeconomic variables and data on education of parents were noted. Since these studies are not "true experiments" (random assignment of children to environments would be unethical), there were selection factors operating that determined where the adoptive twins were placed. In many cases, as one might expect, twins put up for adoption were placed in homes of friends or relatives of the parents. When placed by agencies, the true mother's IQ or education is used to select a home of suitable quality for the adopted child, thereby building in a spurious correlation between the true mother's IQ and child's IQ through comparability of their environments—separate but similar. The foster parents in these studies have been shown to differ from the true parents on several dimensions that might affect environmental quality: they were older, wealthier, better educated, and had fewer children—thus, the "perfect matching" claimed by Jensen (1969) was not possible.

Rarely mentioned by nativists is the finding across three studies of similar IQ correlations of adoptive parents with their own children and with their adopted children. The IQ correlation of 48 adoptive parents and their true child was .35, while it was .26 between adoptive parents and a sample of 520 adopted children—a difference *not* statistically significant. (The studies compared are those of Leahy, 1935; Burks, 1928; and Freeman et al., 1928). Another point of contention is that, with few exceptions, most of the supporting evidence used by the nativists comes from research of an era (the 1920s and 1930s) when there was in general less methodological rigor and sophistication. The more recent classic study by Burt (1955) is, according to Kamin's (1974) review, replete with procedural problems that would require reanalysis of his original data. Unfortunately, Burt's data were lost after his death.

While in the past those overemphasizing the genetic aspect of cognitive development have adopted a fatalistic picture of human potential and have used their conclusions to justify simplistic solutions to social problems, those pushing the empiricist view have often erred in the opposite direction. The American behaviorist tradition has held that virtually all behavior is modifiable by experience and training. By disregarding genetic limitations, the environmentalists have sometimes raised unwarranted optimism about how much some upper individual limit might be modified.

Today the pendulum is starting on a less extreme swing as it becomes more and more evident that the two factors are in constant *interaction* from the moment an individual is conceived. Few would take either a pure nativist or a pure environmentalist position today. It is generally agreed that what we inherit from our parents—and through them from all of our ancestors—makes possible a range of behaviors and perhaps some maximum level of functioning within each of those behaviors. A group of fifty scientists and social scientists, concerned about the hue and cry over the influence of heredity on intelligence, recently drafted a resolution on the subject for publication in the major professional journal of the American Psychological Association. That resolution is reprinted in the *P&L* Close-up on p. 204.

It seems clear that genetic potentials can be realized only in a favorable environment, but that no environment can create potentials that do not exist. We cannot say at this time how much of a beneficial effect an ideal environment might have, because we do not know enough yet to design one.

Is Cognitive Development Stable and Predictable?

A great many studies have been carried out to determine whether intelligence test scores, used as indices of cognitive development, remain the same over a period of years. The universal conclusion is that they usually remain essentially constant when conditions remain the same—that is, when health, type of education, and

**A Resolution Concerning
the Study of Heredity**

. . . We the undersigned scientists from a variety of fields, declare the following beliefs and principles:

"1. We have investigated much evidence concerning the possible role of inheritance in human abilities and behaviors, and we believe such hereditary influences are very strong.

"2. We wish strongly to encourage research into the biological hereditary bases of behavior, as a major complement to the environmental efforts at explanation.

"3. We strongly defend the right, and emphasize the scholarly duty, of the teacher to discuss hereditary influences on behavior, in appropriate settings and with responsible scholarship.

"4. We deplore the evasion of hereditary reasoning in current textbooks, and the failure to give responsible weight to heredity in disciplines such as sociology, social psychology, social anthropology, educational psychology, psychological measurement, and many others.

"5. We call upon liberal academics—upon faculty senates, upon professional and learned societies, upon the American Association of University Professors, upon the American Civil Liberties Union, upon the University Centers for Rational Alternatives, upon presidents and boards of trustees, upon departments of science, and upon the editors of scholarly journals—to insist upon the openness of social science to the well-grounded claims of biobehavioral reasoning, and to protect vigilantly any qualified faculty members who responsibly teach, research, or publish concerning such reasoning.

"We so urge because as scientists we believe that human problems may best be remedied by increased human knowledge, and that such increases in knowledge lead much more probably to the enhancement of human happiness than to the opposite." (American Psychological Association, 1972, p. 660)

home situation do not change markedly. The single notable exception is in the case of very young children, whose potentialities may still be more variable, and with whom, in any case, there are special difficulties in designing and administering tests. For example, attention may be erratic, or poor motor coordination may prevent an accurate assessment. Another serious problem is that tests at different ages draw on different components of intelligence: those for young children test largely sensory and motor abilities, whereas those for older children are more dependent on verbal and conceptual abilities. This is undoubtedly one reason why scores obtained after age six usually correlate more highly with adult intelligence than do scores obtained during the preschool years. Scores obtained below the age of two are not very stable and in any case are more tests of general developmental level than specifically of mental ability.

Dramatic changes in the environment have been shown to bring about striking changes in intelligence test *scores*—a point in favor of the environmentalists. (See *P&L* Close-up, p. 205.) This is especially true when there has been severe deprivation in the past and when the child is quite young at the time of the change. It seems clear in such cases that the original intelligence test score was not a measure of the child's full potential. Unfortunately, we do not know to what extent this is true of test scores generally or how often — and at what ages — other children's scores would go up with a better programming of their environment.

Two longitudinal studies have helped us to pinpoint the factors responsible for constancy or change in particular cases. One study at the Fels Research Institute of Human Development in Ohio (Sontag, Baker, & Nelson, 1958) has complete records for twenty years on 200 noninstitutionalized subjects. The other study, directed by Nancy Bayley (1968) and Marjorie Honzik (1973) and their colleagues at the University of California at Berkeley, examined fifty-six "normal" people from birth to age thirty-six. The remarkable dedication of scientists engaged in long-term, complex studies like these has paid many dividends in new knowledge and in clues for further research. One of their most striking findings was how different the course of cognitive growth may be in different individuals. For example:

1. Both studies found that for many of the children they observed, there were changes in mental-ability scores not only during the preschool period but throughout childhood.

2. The *rates* of mental growth for individual children during the early years were unstable: growth seemed to show spurts and plateaus.

3. Different individuals showed different patterns of change in IQ: for some it did not change; for others, there was progressive increase or decrease; for still others the pattern was variable at different periods as they grew up.

4. The greatest gain observed was 73 points (from 107 at two-and-a-half years of age to 180 at ten years of age); the greatest loss seen was 40 points (from 142 at age three to 102 at age eight).

The Bayley study found many evidences of a different course of cognitive development for boys than for girls, as well as different relationships between cognitive development and various personality variables. Several consistent, stable correlations were found for the boys between behaviors during the first three years of life and verbal intelligence scores over the thirty-six-year span. For the girls, however, there were no striking consistencies between childhood behaviors and either concurrent or later intelligence. In fact, in some cases correlations found for the girls at age sixteen were reversed at age thirty-six. For the boys, too, there were some reversals: for example, boys who were highly active between ten and fifteen months tended to have low verbal scores later, whereas high activity in boys between eighteen and thirty-six months was predictive of high verbal scores later if the boys were also happy. At age one, shyness and unhappiness were predictive of later high verbal scores for girls, but for boys at the same age, happiness was a predictor of later high verbal scores. Shyness at age four was unrelated to later verbal scores for either boys or girls. Clearly, on this more analytical level,

Close-up

Enriched Environments Mend Malnourished Minds and Bodies

A recent study (Winick, Meyer, & Harris, 1975) indicates that enriching the environments of previously malnourished children also results in improved mental as well as physical development. Height, weight, IQ score, and achievement level scores of Korean orphans adopted before age 2 by American parents all showed marked effects of six years of rearing in middle-class homes. The sample of 141 children was divided into three subgroups according to the degree of malnourishment at the time of adoption—"malnourished," "moderately nourished," and "well nourished."

All three groups have passed the expected mean for Korean children in height and weight, but are below the 50th percentile of an American standard. Initial differences in physical size tended to persist, with those who were well nourished at 18 months being bigger at elementary-school age. Most striking, however, are their IQ scores. The malnourished children raised in the favorable environment provided by an American middle-class home have measured IQ's of about 40 points higher than those of similar children who were returned to their early (impoverished) home environments.

The stigma of early malnourishment does linger to some extent, since the mean IQ of the well-nourished Korean adoptees is some 10 points higher than their malnourished peers. The results for achievement scores are similar to those of IQ, increasing with initial degree of nourishment and all doing at least as well as the mean for U.S. school children. Indeed, the mean IQ of 112 for the well-nourished children is significantly greater than that of middle-class American children. The authors speculate that these children's "attainments may reflect the select character of adoptive parents and of the environment they provide to their adopted children."

many things are happening that are obscured by overall scores that represent averages from many individuals.

What effect does the quality of maternal behavior have on the development of intelligence and personality-related behaviors? Correlations of maternal behaviors with children's intelligence revealed a very interesting pattern. For boys, how their mothers responded to them during the first three years evidently had a permanent effect on their intelligence as measured at eighteen and even thirty-six years of age. Hostility in mothers was related to low adult intelligence in their offspring (correlations of around −.60), while maternal love and understanding were positively related to adult intelligence. The girls' intelligence scores, in contrast, were independent of the maternal *handling* they received, but were related to indices of parental *ability*. Bayley concludes:

"These sex differences in patterns of correlations led us to the suggestion that there are genetically determined sex differences in the extent to which the effects of early experiences (such as maternal love and hostility) persist. The girls appeared to be more resilient in returning to their own characteristic inherent response tendencies. Boys, on the other hand, were more permanently affected by the emotional climate in infancy whether it was one of warmth and understanding or of punitive rejection." (pp. 14–15)

More studies are needed that provide adequate data for understanding the specific ways in which heredity and environment interact to shape intelligence. The above findings would suggest that hereditary factors may be more potent contributors to intelligence for females than for males. Boys and men appear to be more susceptible to environmental influences than girls and women. This rather surprising finding

is supported consistently across a wide spectrum of behaviors. For example, males are more likely than females to die in infancy, to have reading problems, to develop childhood schizophrenia, to commit suicide, to commit acts of violence, to be hospitalized for physical and mental diseases. In fact, it has been reported that after the atomic bombing of Hiroshima, male fetuses were more likely to be born dead or defective than female fetuses (Maccoby, 1966).

The growth of cognitive ability cannot be separated from the basic growth of the individual since cognitive functioning determines what the individual can do in and to the environment. On the other hand, cognitive ability is but an extension of the individual's total personality. From our discussion so far, it can be seen that intelligence should not be viewed as a static, fixed entity—something people have inside of them. Measures of "intelligence" are always measures of an individual's *adaptive behavior* in meeting a particular set of environmental challenges. For complex adaptive behavior, the individual requires both the hereditary potential for dealing with complexity and the kinds of environmental encounters that permit the learning of the necessary component skills—perceptual, conceptual, motor, and perhaps also linguistic and social.

Researcher Honzik provides a concluding statement that is suitable for the entire issue of heredity versus environment and the long-term predictability of intelligence. She writes:

"Heredity sets the limits and is relevant to the child's intelligence as measured by his mental test performance but the correlations are low and suggest the effect that experiential factors may be having on the mental growth pattern. Environmental factors do not begin with the birth of the child but at conception or before. . . . As we provide more enriching programs for individuals from birth to senescence, we can measure the resulting patterns of abilities to see the extent of the plasticity of the human organism to develop its abilities." (1973, pp. 649, 653)

Thought Processes

It has been said that although the brain is in the head, we think with our whole body. More than just "ideas" and mental states seem to be involved in thinking; subvocal speech and bodily changes have also been implicated in the process. To some extent thinking is influenced by images we have of stimulus objects, by feedback we receive from hearing ourselves communicate thoughts, and by the kind of language we use to express what is "in our heads."

The Pictures in Our Heads

People sometimes think with *images,* which are mental pictures of actual sensory experiences. Most people seem to be strongest in visual imagery though some are strongest in auditory imagery, and a small minority report that images of touch, muscle movement, taste, or smell predominate for them.

Although some early psychologists believed that thought *required* the use of imagery, various studies through the years have indicated that thought can also proceed in the absence of images. For example, one pioneer study found that many scientists and mathematicians, though engaged in the highest and most complicated type of thinking, were actually quite deficient in visual imagery (Galton, 1883). Poincaré, the great French geometrician, described himself as lacking in the ability to visualize space. All this is not to deny that imagery is used in many kinds of thinking, but to point out that it is not always necessary.

Eidetic imagery. Before reading further, look at the photograph. ■ Some individuals possess imagery that is almost like actual perception in its clarity and accuracy. These strong images, usually visual, are called *eidetic images.* People with eidetic imagery can frequently tell the exact position of a formula or fact on the printed page of a textbook. They can even glance for a fraction of a second at an object, such as a comb, and then call up such a vivid image that they can give a complete description, including the number of teeth in the comb. In examinations, they may "copy" from their image of the printed page, performing with an accuracy as great as though the book were actually open before them (see Haber, 1968).

Striking examples of eidetic imagery have been documented in *The Mind of a Mnemonist,* a case study by the Russian psychologist Luria of a man with a "photographic" mind.

The subject had such powers of imagery that he was able to perform staggering feats of memo-

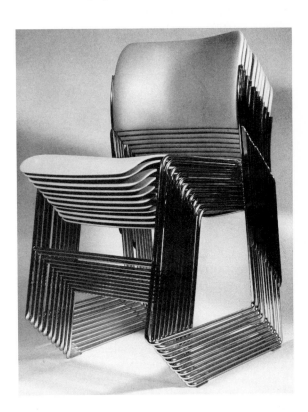

■ Look at this picture for about three seconds; then read the note at the bottom of page 208.

The kind of visualization that is useful in complex thought is not necessarily the same as visual imagery. This fact is brought out in an introspective account by a psychologist who is also a chess master capable of playing twelve boards of "blindfold" chess simultaneously. The player does not actually wear a blindfold, but sits facing away from the board or boards; a referee calls out the opponent's moves. Obviously, ability to visualize what is happening on the board is a primary factor in winning. However, such visualization is more a process of abstraction than a literal visualizing of all details. This psychologist-master summarizes it as follows:

1. As a result of long experience with the game, both the board and the pieces acquire many associations. It becomes impossible to think of the board and pieces separately.

2. It is also impossible to think of the moves separately from the special notation or symbolic language that chess players use to describe their plays. Simultaneous games are kept separate in the player's mind largely with the aid of such symbols. Games vary greatly in character according to the opening used, and as they progress and differences become greater, it is easier, rather than more difficult, to keep them separate.

3. A space-time Gestalt or pattern is formed of the entire board. That is, the position of the pieces changes in space and with time, but the number of plausible changes is limited.

4. A prime skill factor in chess is the ability to sum up each position dynamically in terms of the most significant elements in it, not to recall all details regardless of significance.

5. For the most part, the first four phases take place below the level of active consciousness. Once the summation of significant elements is made, the visual image reaches consciousness. Because of their capacity to organize the abstract and symbolic data, the "picture" blindfold players visualize consciously is a coherent one (Fine, 1965).

ry. The following is one of the many experiments carried out with this man, which you might want to try yourself. The man spent three minutes examining the table of numbers reprinted below.

6	6	8	0
5	4	3	2
1	6	8	4
7	9	3	5
4	2	3	7
3	8	9	1
1	0	0	2
3	4	5	1
2	7	6	8
1	9	2	6
2	9	6	7
5	5	2	0
x	0	1	x

He was able to reproduce the table perfectly, by calling off all the numbers in succession, within 40 seconds. He could call off the numbers in both the columns and the horizontal rows in either forward or reverse order. He also reproduced the numbers that form the diagonals (e.g., 6, 4, 8, 5; 5, 6, 3, 7) within 35 seconds. Finally, he took a minute and a half to convert all fifty numbers into a single fifty-digit number (Luria, 1968).

At this point, you may be wishing that you had the gift of eidetic imagery (or "photographic memory"). You might think that all of your schoolwork would be extremely simple to do, since you could remember everything so well. Actually, eidetic imagery is very much a mixed blessing, and often obstructs thinking, rather than helping it. Materials stored eidetically are not easily broken down and reassembled in new patterns. (See *P&L* Close-up at left.) Individuals with eidetic imagery can reproduce what they have seen, but it is difficult for them to use this information in new ways. Thus, eidetic imagery does not appear to play a role in abstract thinking or creative imagination, which require flexibility in thought. For example, Luria's sub-

---

How many chairs were there in the picture on page 207? If you have eidetic imagery you will still have a clear enough visual image to count them.

ject was unable to understand simple abstract ideas because he could not "see" them in concrete visual images. This could explain why eidetic imagery is most often found in children and is comparatively rare in adults.

One of the methodological problems in studying eidetic imagery is to determine whether it is a *memory* process or a *visual* process. That is, did the mnemonist described above have a special way of verbally *coding* the fifty numbers, so that he could later figure out what they were? Or did he have an exact image of the table in his head, which he could "look" at and call out numbers from?

To demonstrate convincingly that a person has the capacity for eidetic imagery and not "merely" superior memory, a special methodology must be used, and there must be a willing subject who claims to have eidetic imagery. Recently two young Harvard University graduate-student researchers, Charles Stromeyer and Joseph Psotka (1970), came up with the appropriate test, and at the same time came across a teacher at Harvard who apparently had the elusive capacity. The eidetic subject was a twenty-three-year-old woman artist with this rather remarkable ability. For example, she could read a page of poetry in a known foreign language, project the image on a blank page, and then copy it from the bottom line to the top as fast as her hand could write.

The test consisted of having the subject look at two stereograms. These were patterns of random dots arranged in a 100×100 matrix—giving a total of 10,000 dots or spaces. These two patterns were identical except for a small region in which some of the dots were shifted sideways in one of the figures. When one pattern is viewed with the left eye, the other with the right in a stereoscope, a three-dimensional figure emerges in the area of the displaced dots. These figures were devised by Bela Julesz (1971) of the Bell Telephone Laboratories. In different stereograms the three-dimensional figure may recede or stand out, and may be of any shape, including a spiral. When the patterns are viewed separately, it is impossible to see, guess, or deduce what "ought" to be seen when the patterns are merged stereoscopically. ▲

The subject was instructed to look at one pattern with her right eye alone (the left was covered). The pattern was removed, and three minutes later she looked at the second pattern with her left eye (the right was now covered). What did she see? "That's ridiculously easy!" she exclaimed, and proceeded to describe in precise detail the 3-D figure that she *saw* standing out from the surface. She could commit such patterns to her eidetic imagery for as long as three months and could even summon up her eidetic image for stereogram patterns of one million squares. There is no apparent way for such effects to occur other than for a "photographic" image to be retained in memory and projected as such when summoned up. How this is possible from a neurophysiological level is unknown.

Internal representation of objects. One hypothesis about concept development in children starts with the premise that successful interac-

▲ These two patterns appear to be random arrangements of dots on a two-dimensional surface. When they are viewed stereoscopically, however, a square pattern stands out three-dimensionally from the background surface.

tion with environmental objects requires the construction of an internal representation of these external objects and relationships. It is postulated that in the course of cognitive growth three successively more efficient types of representation are built up. The first is *muscular* or *motor* representation. You can climb your back stairs in the dark without tripping because you have learned to adapt your movements to the exact height of the steps and to turns or irregularities in the stairway. Even without visual cues, you can make the exact motions needed.

The next type of representation is through the use of *images*. Unlike motor representations, images can serve us in the absence of the objects themselves. But images are literal records; they remain similar in form and in their interrelationships to the objects as previously perceived. Not until we become able to construct *symbols*, such as language symbols, do we have a system of representation that can transcend the exact characteristics of what we have perceived. Images are based on particular perceptual details, while symbols may represent inference, abstraction, or transformation according to a rule (Bruner, 1964).

Until recently, statements like those above that people used images in thinking were based simply on their self-reports that they did. In order to be scientifically useful, the vague concept of "mental imagery" has itself to be reconceptualized in terms that permit it to be experimentally analyzed. To what extent do we form an internal representation of objects in our external environment? Can we *measure* the correspondence between such internal events and their external counterparts without relying on verbal reports? Is there a systematic relationship between variations in external stimulus arrays and their internal representations? These were the kinds of questions posed by Roger Shepard and his associates (Shepard & Metzler, 1971, 1974; Shepard & Feng, 1972; and Cooper & Shepard, 1973). Their research was designed to investigate whether internal representation is an *analogue* process; that is, one in which a *mental* process corresponds directly to a physical process (in this case, that of variation in an external stimulus).

In each trial, the subject was presented with a pair of perspective drawings of three-dimensional objects. The task was to determine as rapidly as possible if the two objects portrayed were different or had the same three-dimensional shape, but different visual orientations. The subject indicated whether the objects were "the same" or "different" by pressing one or the other of two levers. The dependent variable was the amount of time elapsed between the presentation of the drawings and the pressing of the lever. (See P&L *Close-up, p. 211.) By plotting the pattern of these reaction times against the degree to which the identical figures differed in angular rotation, it was possible to relate internal representation to external variations. Reaction times increased as the angle of rotation between the two figures increased.* ● *The*

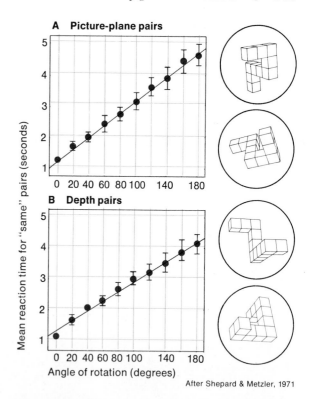

After Shepard & Metzler, 1971

● The graphs show mean reaction time required for the mental "rotation" of perspective line drawings to determine whether they were identical. (Vertical bars indicate the variability in responses of the eight subjects.) Sample objects are shown at right. Pair A requires rotation in the picture plane only; Pair B requires rotation in depth.

Taking Time to Think: Reaction Time

Psychologists who set out to study thought processes soon find that most of the phenomena they are interested in are not the sort of things that can be measured. One thing that can be measured, however, is *reaction time:* the interval elapsing between the presentation of a stimulus and a given reaction to that stimulus. The study of reaction time has been important in psychology, not only for what it tells us about simple motor reactions but also because it serves as an indication of how much mental processing may be taking place between stimulus and response.

The relationship between reaction time and thought can best be appreciated if we examine it from a historical perspective. Reaction time studies fall roughly into four chronological periods: (1) astronomers' studies of the "personal equation," (2) Helmholtz' experiments on nerve conduction, (3) the period of "mental chronometry," and (4) modern studies of the deep structure of language and the complexity of thought processes.

1. In 1796 an assistant to the Astronomer Royal was fired from his post at the Greenwich Observatory because he consistently recorded the transit of a star about one second later than the Astronomer Royal himself. Not much scientific note was made of this discrepancy until 1819, when the German astronomer Bessel became interested in such "errors" of observation. He carefully compared his own reports of stellar transits with those of other astronomers, and showed that there are very consistent differences between people in the times they give to the occurrence of natural events. Bessel expressed these differences in the form of an equation. For example, the difference between the reports of Walbeck, another astronomer, and himself was:

$$W \text{ (Walbeck)} - B \text{ (Bessel)} = 1.041 \text{ sec.}$$

As a result, this phenomenon of consistent discrepancies in observation was called the *personal equation.* This concept, as one of the first instances of the systematic study of *individual differences* in behavior, is a precursor of the concept of personality traits as an explanation for differences in reaction to the same situation.

2. Before 1850, scientists believed that impulses were conducted instantaneously along the nerves. However, in that year, Helmholtz demonstrated (a) that nerve conduction took time, and (b) that the time it took could be measured. In his experiments on sensory nerves (discussed in Chapter 2), Helmholtz administered a weak electric shock first to a man's toe and later to his thigh. The difference between the man's reaction times to these two stimuli was the measure of the speed of conduction in the sensory nerves. These experiments were the first true studies of reaction time ever to be done.

3. After Helmholtz had shown that there is an interval of time between a physical stimulus and a person's physiological response to it, scientists began to think that this might be a good measure of a person's mental processes. From the 1850s to about the 1930s, reaction time was studied under a variety of conditions, using different versions of a measuring device called the *chronoscope.* One of the major experimenters during this period was a Dutch physiologist named Donders. He identified three types of reaction time: (a) *simple reaction time,* the single response to a single stimulus; (b) *discrimination reaction time,* in which there are several different stimuli but the single response is not made until a particular one is distinguished; and (c) *choice reaction time,* in which there are several different stimuli and a different reaction for each of them. As you might expect, the third is longer than the second, which in turn is longer than the first.

4. Donders showed that reaction time appears to reflect the psychological *complexity* of the reaction—the amount of mental processing that must take place before the person responds to the stimulus. Present-day researchers have made use of this principle in studying the nature and complexity of cognitive processing. Such research is described in this chapter and various other places throughout the text.

data in the two graphs reveal that the time required to make the mental rotation was the same whether the rotation was two-dimensional or three-dimensional. Subjects reported that they mentally rotated one of the objects into the same orientation as the other, perceiving the two-dimensional figures as if they were objects in three-dimensional space. They said the activity of mental rotation seemed to require a certain amount of time, depending on how much rotation was needed, but that the two types of rotation could be carried out with equal ease.

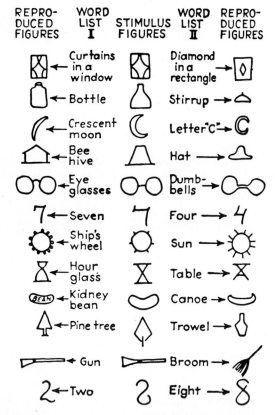

◆ Some of the stimulus figures used in this study are shown in the center column, with the word lists presented to the two groups. The outside columns show some of the figures drawn from memory.

Shepard believes that internal representation in this and a host of other related research does follow an analogue process in which the intermediate stages of the process have a one-to-one correspondence to intermediate situations in the external world. This is a molar process in contrast to other perceptual and thought processes involving search for distinctive features, symbol manipulation, verbal analysis, or digital computation at a molecular level.

Thinking in Words

Although words are probably not essential to thought and may sometimes even be a hindrance to it, language appears to be an aid in solving problems. Indeed, few of us would want to try to think without it. Words and other symbols can greatly facilitate the solution of problems that would be much more difficult to cope with if we had to rely on the direct manipulation of objects and images. The development of the precise symbolic systems of algebra and calculus, for example, has greatly increased our ability to control our environment.

The powerful influence that language has on our perception and recall is demonstrated in an early study. Two groups of subjects were shown the same stimulus figures but were given different words describing what the figures represented. All the subjects were later asked to redraw the figures as they remembered them. The drawn figures were consistently more like the named object than the original figures had been (Carmichael, Hogan, & Walter, 1932). ◆

Language can certainly influence our thought (as demonstrated in the Carmichael study), but to what extent does it actually *determine* what we think? The problem of whether thought determines language or language determines thought has stimulated much interest and controversy among students of linguistics (Brown, 1956). Is language a "cloak following the contours of thought" or a "mold into which infant minds are poured"?

The major proponent of the "mold" position is Benjamin Whorf, who contends that the language patterns of a cultural group shape the thought patterns and even perceptions of the children reared in that culture (Whorf, 1956). For example, the Eskimos have seven names for different types and conditions of snow, while English-speaking people have just the single term. The Hopi Indians have one name for birds and one name for all other things that fly (airplane, bee, etc.). Whorf would argue that such differences in descriptive nouns result in a different conception of the event. That is, Eskimos' perceptions and thoughts of snow are different from those of English-speaking people; the Hopis think about flying objects differently.

Whorf's hypothesis raises several important questions which, unfortunately, are difficult to resolve with experimental data. One major problem is the old one of cause and effect. Perhaps the culture's thinking about an event led to the development of different linguistic labels for it, rather than vice versa. Because the condition of the snow has a major impact on their daily life, the Eskimos need several terms to differentiate them linguistically. However, the type of snow may have no real importance to people living in New York City, so that for them, all snow (even slush) is "snow."

Critics of Whorf have also challenged the idea that there are actual differences in perception and thought between cultures with different languages. The fact that some people have only a single term for an event does not necessarily mean that they cannot distinguish differences within that event. Children in New York have just one term for snow, but they can easily tell what kind of snow is good for packing snowballs and what kind is not. Similarly, skiers are very sensitive to snow conditions and can distinguish between wet snow, powder snow, icy snow, and so on, even though they do not have completely different words for each of them.

The meaningfulness of a linguistic pattern for a particular culture may affect its way of categorizing events, but not its ways of actually perceiving them.

Navaho-speaking and English-speaking subjects were asked to divide eight colored chips into groups on the basis of the label the experimenter gave to each chip. He then proceeded to call four of them ma *and the other four* mo. *However, two* ma *and two* mo *chips were spoken of with the vowel drawn out, while the others had the short form of the vowel. This change in vowel length does not mark a phonemic change in English, but in Navaho the long and short vowels are two different phonemes. As a result, Navaho-speaking subjects grouped the chips into* four groups (mā, mǎ, mō, mǒ), *while the English-speaking subjects only divided them into two groups (ma, mo). Many of the English-speaking subjects reported that they had noticed the slight differences in vowel length, but had considered them irrelevant to the task (Brown, 1956).*

The "cloak-mold" controversy has never been resolved in one way or the other, but it seems fairly safe to say that language and thought affect each other. Ideas are undoubtedly "shaped" by language, but certainly not to the extent postulated by Whorf.

Thinking with "Silent Speech"

We think with images, we think with symbols, we think with words, but do we think with nonverbal muscular reactions as well? Such a question seems ludicrous until we rephrase it as, "What is the evidence that thought is accompanied by *covert oral behavior,* by electrical activity in speech musculature?"

The evidence from an extensive body of research in this area (summarized by McGuigan, 1973) leads to the conclusion that covert oral responding does occur reliably under a variety of linguistic conditions. The covert events thought to be indicators of the processing of "thoughts" stimulated by external linguistic stimuli are measured by psychophysiological techniques: EEG (electroencephalograph) for events in the central nervous system; EMG (electromyograph) for muscular responses such as lip, tongue, and chin movements; and measures of autonomic nervous system activity such as pupillary dilation and cardiac functioning.

The results for children shown in the figure reveal that while children are reading silently, they are moving their lips, increasing their breathing rate, and making subvocal sounds (measurable only through high audio amplification). ■ The same results were later found with silent reading and memorization of prose by college students. Such activity appears to be localized in the speech mechanisms. McGuigan concludes that "these phenomena are quite general among language-proficient people" (1973, p. 351).

Of greater interest are recent findings that while people are having dreams with conversational content (as contrasted to visual, nonlinguistic dreams), their lip and chin EMG responses increase significantly (McGuigan & Tanner, 1971). Also when dreams of various kinds were hypnotically induced in subjects, those with oral content showed marked increases in covert oral activity, while those with "relaxation" and induced "physical activity" dreams did not. ▲

From research that varies the nature of the information processing demands on the subjects and measures covert oral behavior, it has been concluded that the thought process is facilitated by such silent speech. When John Watson said that "we think with our whole bodies," he may have been correct to the extent that we respond to incoming, thought-provoking, linguistic stimuli with widespread autonomic and muscular responses.

Feedback and Servomechanisms

Considerable experimental evidence indicates that persons who have knowledge of their progress on any type of task will learn more rapidly

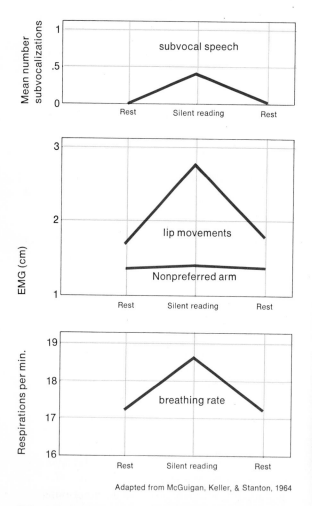

Adapted from McGuigan, Keller, & Stanton, 1964

■ During silent reading, subvocalization, lip EMG, and breathing rate increase in children, while nonpreferred arm EMG changes little.

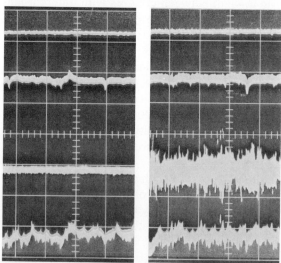

▲ EMG tracings for a hypnotized subject during relaxation (left) and during an induced verbal dream (right). Starting from the top, the tracings are of left arm EMG, eye movements, tongue EMG, and frontal lobe EEG.

than equally motivated subjects of comparable ability who are working "in the dark" (Ammons, 1956). It has become common for psychologists to replace the term *knowledge of results* with the more general expression *psychological feedback* (Brown, 1949). Psychological feedback is the process whereby individuals gain information concerning the correctness of their previous responses in order that they can adjust their behavior to compensate for errors. Thus feedback is essential not only for new motor learning but also for the performance of any integrated sequence of motor acts.

Functions and kinds of feedback. Feedback serves three distinguishable functions: (a) providing *information* both about the results of a response and about its characteristics (temporal, spatial, directional, level of intensity, and so on); (b) providing positive or negative *reinforcement*, depending on the adequacy of the response; and (c) providing *motivation* to continue the task by helping to make the world and one's behavior predictable and potentially controllable.

Feedback may be of two general types: *intrinsic* or *externally augmented*. When you are asked to count aloud rapidly from 1 to 100, you know where you are in the series at any moment from the sound of your voice that is fed back to your ears. Similarly intrinsic are the kinesthetic cues providing information that guides the rate of movement and location of your limbs. But if you closed your eyes and tried to touch the tip of another person's nose, and that person told you when you were "getting hot," you would be using externally augmented feedback; that is, your own intrinsic muscular sensations would be aided by the addition of outside cues.

Because intrinsic feedback works so well under normal conditions, we are totally unaware that we are even using it. To study our reliance on it and the variables influencing its functioning, the researcher must find a way to *disrupt* it. Information coming in through auditory or visual channels has proven easy to disrupt under controlled laboratory conditions by specially designed tape recorders that delay audio or video signals. ●

"If I can't hear what I'm saying, I can't think straight" is the kind of reply many subjects give when they try to explain some of their thoughts during experimentally induced delayed auditory feedback. This seems peculiar because we have come to view thought as the cause of speech, not vice versa. How can an effect influence its cause? It can do so when cause and effect are not simply related in a unidirectional fashion but

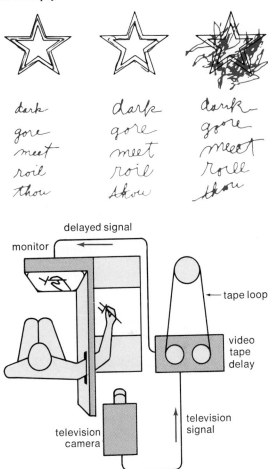

● **MOTOR TRACKING WITH DELAYED VISUAL FEEDBACK**

The lower diagram shows a videotape apparatus used to introduce a time delay into the tasks of tracing a star and writing a list of words. At the top are shown one subject's responses. Items in the first column were done under normal conditions, items in the second column were done using a TV monitor but no delay, and items in the third column were done using a TV monitor with a delay. The handicap this delay creates for coordinated eye-hand movements is insuperable.

are part of a more complex servomechanism arrangement.

The effects of auditory feedback are studied by delaying the interval between uttering a sound and hearing it. Rather than hearing the words they have just spoken through air conduction, as they normally would, subjects hear them over a set of earphones, with a delay interposed.

The consequences of such delay are measured in terms of changes in the subjects' speaking—its intensity, duration of phrase, fundamental speech frequency, intelligibility, articulation, and emotional stress (Smith, 1962; Yates, 1963). Under conditions where the delay interval is about a fifth of a second, speech is extremely disrupted. In fact, the speech of some people breaks down altogether.

Delay is most disruptive when the feedback is loud and when the material is closely organized with the parts dependent on each other, as in singing, whistling a tune, or saying a tongue-twisting limerick. Delays shorter or longer than a fifth of a second are less disruptive. There is very little adaptation or improvement with continued practice, although long-term studies have not been tried.

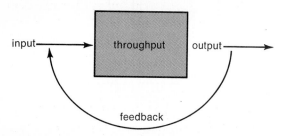

■ DIAGRAM OF A SERVOMECHANISM

In referring to human behavior in terms of a servomechanism, *input* refers to the stimuli that initiate the person's response. These stimuli produce activity within the nervous system called *throughput;* this, in turn, activates muscles that produce a response. Each finite response is an *output,* and the sum total of output in a situation is the behavior pattern, which is culminated when the goal is attained. Output is continually corrected by *feedback* information from the relevant portions of the environment or from within the individual.

The model of the servomechanism. Not only does behavior consist of a series of events, but feedback from the events completed and in progress is needed for smooth continuation of the sequence, as we have seen. Thus the *servomechanism*—the goal-directed, error-sensitive, self-correcting machine—has become a useful model for the thought-and-action sequences characteristic of living organisms. A servomechanism involves four basic processes: input, throughput, output, and feedback. The relationships between these four operations are shown in the figure. ■

Processing input, integrating and organizing throughput, directing output, and utilizing feedback from previous and ongoing output are all part of the mental process we call "thinking." Imagine, for example, that you are playing a game of chess. Your thought processes can be described in terms of these operations:

1. *Processing input*—noting the move your opponent has just made and the immediate threat it poses to your pieces.

2. *Integrating and organizing throughput*—figuring out what the new position means in terms of the board as a whole and assessing possible moves.

3. *Directing output*—deciding on your next move and making it.

4. *Utilizing feedback*—observing the new situation on the board and your opponent's response to it.

These elements of thinking overlap to some extent, and cannot be entirely separated. All can be demonstrated to take time, however. Thus it is clear that reaction time is not, as it was once thought to be, a single, unitary process. Nor can we have a model of thought that does not include provisions for multiple feedback channels as well as for complex servomechanisms by which output continually guides input that controls output, thereby giving reason to thoughts.

Reasoning

We mentioned earlier that thought ranges between two extremes—autistic and realistic. The fantasies, dreams, and wishful thinking of the autistic mode are used primarily for self-gratification and wish fulfillment. A heavy reliance on autistic thinking is found in the "Walter Mitty" type of person who spends a great deal of time in a world of fantasy and daydreams. An even more extreme form of autistic thinking is a factor in many types of mental disorders.

Realistic thinking, or *reasoning*, in contrast to autistic thinking, helps us adjust to the reality about us. Such thinking is often motivated by the need to reach solutions to problems involving one's livelihood or very survival. It may also be engaged in for sheer pleasure, as by the chess player or the crossword-puzzle addict.

Types of Reasoning

Three different processes are generally involved in reasoning: *deductive*, *inductive*, and *evaluative*. *Deductive reasoning* is essentially a matter of "putting two and two together." The person combines bits of knowledge previously obtained on separate occasions or draws conclusions that follow from the available data. Basically, this thinking converges toward the correct answer that is implicit in the evidence.

Deductive reasoning is exemplified by syllogisms, which follow the rules of Aristotelian logic. Given premises P_1 and P_2, there can be one, and only one, *valid* conclusion. You have undoubtedly used such reasoning when studying geometry. If the conclusion is not derived by using the rules of logic, then the syllogism is *invalid*. For example:

Valid Syllogism

P_1	All As are B
P_2	All Bs are C
C	Therefore, all As are C

Invalid Syllogism

P_1	All As are B
P_2	All Cs are B
C	Therefore, all As are C

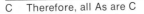

The *validity* of a syllogism should be distinguished from the *truth* of its conclusion. A syllogism may be valid but its conclusion false if it rests on false premises. Or the conclusion may be true but not logically derived from the premises; in this case the syllogism is invalid.

For many problems, however, there is not a single right answer, and the requirements of the situation cannot be met simply by putting together the available evidence. Something new must be added by the thinker, and more than one solution may be appropriate. Such a situation calls for *inductive reasoning*, where the thinker builds from the known to the unknown. This involves making an intuitive leap to formulate a new hypothesis about what future observations may reveal or to suggest several new lines of exploration. This is the essence of creative thinking, whether in science or art. Unlike deductive reasoning, in which one is always going from general premises to specific conclusions, inductive reasoning can lead potentially in any of several directions, since one is always going from specific instances to a more general conclusion. Thus the conclusion is not totally predictable from the available evidence.

A third kind of reasoning is *evaluative*—judging the soundness or appropriateness of an idea or product. Critical thinking is evaluative—it involves judging the suitability or goodness or effectiveness of an idea or representation, as distinguished from trying to create or add to it.

The validity of the result depends not only on the reasoning process itself—here the evaluating—but also on the standard used. If the standard is faulty, a solution judged "appropriate" may not fit the real requirements of the situation.

Solving Problems

Whenever you find yourself in a novel situation in which you are motivated to achieve a certain goal but in which your progress toward it is blocked by some obstacle for which you have no ready-made response, you are confronted with a *problem* (and a potentially frustrating situation). Solution of the problem involves the development of some mode of response that will eliminate the obstacle. Since frustration is an inevitable part of life, much of your behavior necessarily involves problem-solving activity.

Learning and insight. As you will recall from Chapter 3, Thorndike's cats engaged in random trial-and-error behavior before they eventually managed to escape from their puzzle boxes. The results of this research suggested that problem solving was more a matter of learning than of thinking—that is, the animal gradually learns to behave correctly rather than suddenly recognizing the correct response. Gestalt psychologist Wolfgang Kohler disagreed with this position, arguing that Thorndike's experiment was not appropriate to the study of problem solving since it was impossible for the cat to use foresight and planning in the solution of the problem. The release mechanism for the trick doors was out of the animal's field of vision, so it could not "figure out" how the doors worked. Also, the correct response (manipulating a door latch) was so foreign to the animal's normal movements that it could probably only be discovered by accident and not by "reasoning."

Kohler attempted to handle these difficulties by placing animals in problem situations where all the materials necessary for solution were in clear view. In his famous series of experiments with apes, the animal's problem was to get some food that had been placed out of reach. For example, a basket of fruit was suspended from

the wire roof of the cage in such a manner that the basket could be made to swing back and forth when a string was pulled. At one point of the arc described by the swinging basket, there was a scaffolding. Although unable to reach the basket from the ground, the animal could catch it as it swung by jumping up on this scaffolding.

In contrast to Thorndike's cats, Kohler's apes seemed to discover the solution suddenly rather than stumbling onto it accidentally while making random responses. Furthermore, once they had found the solution, they responded perfectly on all succeeding trials, instead of showing the gradual improvement over time that was characteristic of Thorndike's animals. In other words, Kohler's apes acted according to the *discontinuity* hypothesis, while Thorndike's results supported the *continuity* position. Kohler (1926) maintained that problem solving was primarily a matter of insight and perceptual reorganization, rather than trial-and-error behavior.

Later studies have modified Kohler's position by demonstrating that insight is not a completely sudden process but employs relevant previous trial-and-error experience.

One investigator placed some food beyond the reach of chimpanzees, so that they could obtain it only by using a hoe to rake it toward them. Animals who had previously played with some short sticks and gradually learned to use them for digging, pushing, and so on, were able to solve the food problem fairly easily. The problem was too difficult, however, for animals without this earlier experience (Birch, 1945).

Human problem solving commonly involves a mixture of insight and trial and error. Usually we start out with more insight into a problem than was possible, for example, for the cats in the puzzle box. Most of our problems are not totally unfamiliar to us, and there are likely to be intrinsic relationships in our situation, whereas the latch to be pressed in the puzzle box had no inherent relation to the food. So we make plausible hypotheses on the basis of what we already know from experience and then test them, either through action or by thinking through the proposed solution (*covert* trial and error). As we see the results of these tentative solutions, our insight increases, and our later hypotheses come closer to meeting the requirements for solution—until at last we "have it." Seldom do we solve a problem without trying some alternative possibilities; and the final achievement of a solution implies, by definition, some insight into the important relationships. Even the cats in the puzzle box gave evidence of this in the end, by going straight to the latch. Indeed, their earlier attempts to bite through the slats or to reach between them were not completely random movements.

Pitfalls in problem solving. Solving problems typically involves a search for a rule that will serve as a general principle for organizing specific instances. This search is an inductive process in which evidence is generated, hypotheses are formulated and tested, and the rule eventually discovered (Wason, 1971). We can learn much about problem solving and also about some of the limits we impose on our own problem-solving ability by trying to solve an apparently simple problem. For a description of Wason's study, see the *P&L* Close-up below.

Close-up
Reasoning Out the Rule

The three numbers 2 4 6 conform to a simple relational principle. The task is to discover that rule by generating other sets of three numbers. Subjects are told whether the sets they generate are correct (+) or incorrect (−). Below are excerpts from the *protocols* (experimental records) of two subjects in Wason's study (1971, pp. 207–8). See if you can determine the rule on the basis of the feedback given to them.

Protocol 1

Subject: 8 10 12, (+); 7 9 11, (+); 7 5 3, (−); 13 26 28, (+); 8 16 18, (+); 49 58 100, (+); 8 13 15, (+); 1 2031 2033, (+); the rule is that the first and second numbers are random, the third is the second plus two.

Experimenter: That is not the rule I have in mind. Please carry on with the task.

Subject: 7 5 7, (−); 1 5 7, (+); 5 5 7, (−); 4 5 7, (+); 9 5 7, (−); 263 364 366, (+); the rule is that the first and second numbers are random, but the first is smaller than the second, and the third is the second plus two.

Experimenter: That is not the rule I have in mind. Please carry on with the task.

Subject: 261 263 101, (−); 3 17 17, (−); 51 53 161, (+); 671 671 3, (−); 671 673 900, (+); 42 43 45, (+); 41 43 42, (−); 41 43 67, (+); 67 43 45, (−); the rule is that the second number is random, and *either* the first number equals the second minus two, and the third is random but greater than the second, *or* the third number equals the second plus two, and the first is random but less than the second.

Experimenter: That is not the rule I have in mind.

(Subject gives up after 50 min.)

Protocol 2

Subject: 4 6 8, (+); 6 8 10 (+); the rule is add two to the first and two to the second.

Experimenter: That is not the rule I have in mind. Please carry on with the task.

Subject: 8 10 12, (+); the rule is the progression of even integers.

Experimenter: That is not the rule I have in mind. Please carry on with the task.

Subject: 13 15 17, (+); the rule is any three positive integers.

Experimenter: That is not the rule I have in mind. Please carry on with the task.

Subject: 3 5 7, (+); the rule is any three numbers.

Experimenter: That is not the rule I have in mind. Please carry on with the task.

Subject: −11 0.999 22/7, (+); the rule is any three numbers with or without modifying signs.

Experimenter: That is not the rule I have in mind. Please carry on with the task.

Subject: 8 6 4, (−) . . .

At this point Subject 2 was able to state the correct rule. Can *you* state it? Write it here:

The correct rule is printed upside down below.
·sɹǝqɯnu ƃuᴉpuǝɔsɐ ǝǝɹɥʇ ʎu∀ :sᴉ ǝlnɹ ǝɥꓕ

Only 21 percent of the subjects in Wason's original experiment discovered the rule without making any incorrect announcements. Why do you think the other 79 percent had so much difficulty solving the problem? Why did you formulate incorrect rules, if you did?

An examination of the *process* by which the rule is discovered will illuminate some of the pitfalls and barriers to successful reasoning. These protocols demonstrate that "the exception proves (tests) the rule." Confirming instances alone are not sufficient; negative instances are required as well. We can also see how easy it is to overlook simple solutions in our effort to formulate overly complex hypotheses or unnecessarily precise statements.

Wason also found that subjects tended to put too much faith in their hypotheses, seeking to verify them rather than evaluate them. In some instances this dogmatic approach led to self-deception; subjects would misperceive or rationalize feedback that contradicted a proposed solution.

The problems used in studies of this type do not involve the emotions, values, and serious personal consequences that accompany real-life problem solving. Such influences can only magnify the difficulties involved in generating objective solutions to our problems. Thus we may come dangerously close to the type of pathological thinking described by Craik (1943) in which "a form of adaptation is . . . achieved by narrowing and distorting the environment until one's conduct appears adequate to it, rather than by altering one's conduct and enlarging one's knowledge till one can cope with the larger real environment" (p. 91).

Using Computers to Study Thinking

Up to this point, we have been discussing many of the factors that influence thinking. But what about the actual *processing* of information? Just how does the brain synthesize and transform information in thinking and problem solving? Recently, models for explaining this process have described the flow of information in the nervous system not in terms of neurophysiological structure but in terms of computer programs.

The information-processing approach is one of the most exciting developments in the study of cognitive processes and holds considerable promise for the future. The use of computer programs requires that the steps in a sequence of information processing be spelled out in explicit, precise, and rigorous terms, rather than vague generalizations. Such a sequence can be diagrammed in a *flow chart,* or *algorithm.* ● The rectangular boxes indicate *action steps* — the computer is instructed to do something. The oval box represents a *decision step* — the computer must answer "yes" or "no." In this case, each time the answer is "no," the computer must perform a *loop,* repeating the same sequence of steps as long as there are cards to be processed. Flow charts are merely visual representations; the actual *program* is the set of coded step-by-step instructions fed into the computer.

Are Computers Intelligent?

Why did psychologists interested in human thought processes turn to the computer? The inspiration for this union appears to be a paper by an English mathematician, Turing (1950), in which he posed the question, "Can machines think?" He argued that our answer would have to be "yes" if a human judge could not distinguish between the output responses of a computer and those of a human being. Turing proposed a game in which the judge could communicate with the computer and the human thinker only by teletype. He would ask them any questions he liked, then try to determine which teletype source was which. Nievergelt and Farrar (1973) have pointed out that a computer capable of "winning" this game will need to combine two distinct conversational abilities: it must understand the meaning of a statement or question however it is phrased, and be able to make plausible statements even when it has insufficient data to give a complete answer. Most programs developed until now have concentrated on one or the other of these abilities, but not both.

The first major computer system that could claim to show "intelligence" was the Logic Theorist, which was designed to find proofs for theorems in logic (Newell, Shaw, & Simon, 1958). In one test of the Logic Theorist's ability, it was able to prove thirty-eight of the first fifty-two theorems in Whitehead and Russell's *Principia Mathematica*. In addition to certain problem-solving procedures, the program of the Logic Theorist incorporated several "rules of thumb," or *heuristics*, that are used by humans. For example, one such heuristic was "working backwards" from the theorem to be proved. That is, the Logic Theorist would develop several propositions that would each imply the theorem, and then check whether one of these propositions could be deduced from the initial "givens." The problem-solving behavior of the Logic Theorist showed many "human" characteristics, such as examples of sudden "insight" into the solution of the problem. For this reason, its makers argued that such a system could actually be considered a *model* of human thought, since it appeared to simulate human cognitive processes.

The implications of computer simulation for the study of reasoning excited many psychologists who had ability and interest in computer programming. After the appearance of the Logic Theorist, a great many programs were developed that attempted to solve problems in the same way that people do. For instance, Gelernter (1960) wrote a program that made use of diagrams in solving problems in geometry.

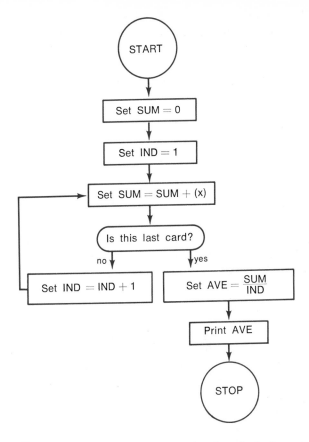

● A flow chart depicting the steps in a hypothetical computer program designed to calculate the average of a series of numbers. Each number to be processed is presented on a keypunch card. SUM stands for a memory cell of the computer that is being used as a temporary working space. IND stands for the index number that tells how many cards have been added. The computer is instructed to read the number (×) from each card in the stack, increasing IND by 1 each time it does so. When the last card in the series has been processed, the computer averages the numbers (dividing SUM by IND) and prints out the result (AVE).

Can a computer help you solve your personal problems? An example of its therapeutic abilities is demonstrated in the following actual conversation between a "patient" (one of the authors of this text) and the "Mad Doctor" computer whose office is at Stanford University's Artificial Intelligence Laboratory. The patient types responses on a teletype, and seconds later the computer-therapist replies by teletype or a videoscope display.

Patient (PGZ): Hello.

Therapist (Mad Doctor): How do you do. Please state your problem.

PGZ: I feel depressed all the time.

MD: Tell me more about such feelings.

PGZ: I am just unhappy and I want your help.

MD: You believe I can help you, don't you?

PGZ: I am not sure.

MD: Is it because you are not sure that you came to me?

PGZ: I think that I hate you.

MD: Perhaps in your fantasy, we do not like each other.

PGZ: You are nothing but a dumb machine.

MD: Do computers worry you?

PGZ: Computers and therapists worry me.

MD: Why do you mention computers?

PGZ: You mentioned it first.

MD: We were discussing you—not me.

PGZ: Are you a therapist or a computer?

MD: What do you think machines have to do with your problem?

PGZ: They are the cause of it.

MD: Did you ever think they might *not* be the cause of it?

PGZ: No.

MD: Are you saying "no" just to be negative?

PGZ: No.

MD: You don't seem very talkative today.

PGZ: I don't want to talk any more.

MD: Don't you *really* want to talk any more?

PGZ: No.

MD: You are being a bit negative.

PGZ: You bet I am. I am leaving.

MD: Do you believe it normal to be leaving?

Courtesy of Dr. Kenneth Colby

Computers have also been programmed to play board games against an opponent. Samuel's checker-playing program (1967) has an excellent performance record, having beaten human checker champions. A successful chess-playing program, however, is still in a more developmental stage. The best program that existed in the late 1960s (Greenblatt, Eastlake, & Crocker, 1967) could play fairly good chess but was still beaten by human experts. Researchers at the University of Southern California have recently developed an "advice-taking" chess program, capable of learning from its mistakes; its "tutor" is senior master Charles Kalme (Zobrist & Carlson, 1973). The game of chess provides an ideal situation for simulation and study of human thought processes. Both the possible operations (moves) and the ultimate goal (checkmate) are sharply defined, yet the strategies involved in reaching the goal involve high levels of analysis and abstraction.

Can Computers Be As Versatile As the Human Brain?

Psychologists soon realized that a computer program that could solve geometry problems but could not play games was not really an appropriate model of the human brain, which can do both. Presumably, human beings use the same intellectual processes to solve all problems—not one for checkers and a different one for logic. Could an all-purpose computer model be designed that could handle a wide variety of problems regardless of the nature of their content? The most ambitious attempt in this direction is the General Problem Solver (GPS) of Newell, Shaw, and Simon (1960). This is a highly sophisticated system that incorporates a large number of concepts, strategies, and heuristics that are believed to underlie human problem solving. It can be given some initial premises, a goal, and certain transformation rules and will then transform the premises into the goal by following the rules. The GPS has proved to be inappropriate for some types of problems, however, and still falls short of being the all-purpose supersystem that Turing envisioned.

Information-processing ideas and techniques have also been used to study psychological processes other than problem solving, such as verbal learning and the recognition of patterns. Abelson and Carroll's (1965) Ideology Machine attempts to simulate an individual's stable social or political belief structures. Computers have been programmed to simulate a neurotic person (Colby, 1965), and also to act as a psychotherapist (Colby, Watt, & Gilbert, 1966). The encounter of one of your authors with the computer "therapist" is reproduced here. (See *P&L Close-up*, p. 222.) His subsequent conversation with a paranoid computer "patient" appears in Chapter 11.

Uses and Limitations of Computers

In the past few years, there has literally been an explosion in the use and development of information-processing models and "artificial intelligence." A tremendous number of research problems have been started, and the computer programs themselves have become increasingly refined and sophisticated. Such rapid progress, however, has not been viewed without reservations. The most prevalent criticism is that computers, being single-minded and unemotional, cannot possibly simulate human thought.

While such criticisms are well taken, they certainly are not damning. More recent models of information processing have begun to build in some of the human "weaknesses" that were previously lacking. For example, Simon (1967) has developed a model that includes such attributes as "impatience" (selection of best alternative found in a given period of time), and "discouragement" (cessation of processing after a given number of failures). With further work in this area, we should not be surprised to see a computer program that can get bored, experience conflicting motives, be stupid at times, and so on. On the other hand, although such programs might be more similar to human thought, we would not want to use them for managing machinery. Thus the models developed to run intricate machinery or business operations may differ greatly from those developed to study human thinking.

In general, we can view the relevance of information-processing research in much the same way as the relevance of research on animals (Reitman, 1965). There are many *similarities* between the behavior of humans and that of other animals (they all eat, drink, reproduce, learn, and so on). Thus we can try to understand human drives, habits, and learning by studying these processes in rats, since we assume that a large part of the explanation for such behavior is common to both the rat and the human being. The limits of such a comparative approach depend on the basic *differences* between human and nonhuman species (e.g., the one uses spoken and written language, the others do not). What these basic differences are is thus critical to a decision as to what animal findings can be applied to humans; unfortunately our knowledge of the detailed characteristics specific to each species is all too sketchy at the present time.

Information-processing models, like animals, share certain characteristics with human beings (both take in information, recognize significant objects, solve problems, and so on). Therefore, such models can be justified as a basis for studying human cognitive processes, but within limits and with the same cautions that apply to conclusions from animal behavior.

At this time, the future of the information-processing approach is filled with unbounded expectations of what is possible. Many computer-science centers have been established and are currently engaging in a flood of ingenious research projects. Such work will undoubtedly continue to uncover the remarkable ways in which a human problem solver analyzes a problem and discovers its solution. Some day there may even be a computer program that solves problems *creatively*—a characteristic now considered uniquely human.

Common Responses
1. Smudges
2. Dark clouds

Uncommon Responses
1. Magnetized iron filings
2. A small boy and his mother hurrying along on a dark windy day, trying to get home before it rains

Common Responses
1. An ape
2. Modern painting of a gorilla

Uncommon Responses
1. A baboon looking at itself in a hand mirror
2. Rodin's "The Thinker" shouting "Eureka!"

Common Responses
1. An African voodoo dancer
2. A cactus plant

Uncommon Responses
1. Mexican in sombrero running up a long hill to escape from rain clouds
2. A word written in Chinese

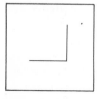

■ TESTS FOR CREATIVITY

Two of the projective tests that have been used to distinguish between creative and uncreative individuals are the inkblot test and the drawing completion test. In order to describe the inkblots shown above, the individual must attribute some order and meaning to a nondescript configuration. The average individual is apt to describe the inkblot in terms of its simple, obvious features. The creative individual is more likely to impose an elegant new order on the figure. When asked to complete a drawing (bottom, left), the average individual is satisfied with a drawing that "makes sense" (middle), while the creative individual produces a drawing that has greater meaning and/or emotional significance (right).

Creativity

If you were asked to think of people who were highly creative, what names would come to mind? Undoubtedly, you would list such individuals as Michelangelo, Beethoven, Shakespeare, or Einstein. But exactly what is the basis for your judgment? What characteristics do such people possess that lead you to label them as creative? One answer might be that they have all produced something new that has been acclaimed as a great work of art or as a brilliant scientific theory. However, such a criterion would allow us to identify creativity only in people of genius and acknowledged fame. What about the great majority of people who are less than geniuses and not at all well known for their accomplishments?

For example, let's look at the responses that a ten-year-old ghetto boy of average IQ gave to the simple question, "How many uses can you think of for a newspaper?"

"You can read it, write on it, lay it down and paint a picture on it. If you didn't have covers, you could put it around you. You can burn it, put it in the garage and drive the car over it when you wash the car, lay it down and put your baby on it, put it on a busted window, put it in your door for decoration, put it in the garbage can, put it on a chair if the chair is messy. If you have a puppy, you put newspaper in its box or put it in your back yard for the dog to play with. When you build something and you don't want anyone to see it, put newspaper around it. Put newspaper on the floor if you have no mattress, use it to pick up something hot, use it to stop bleeding, or to catch the drips from drying clothes. You can use newspaper for curtains, put it in your shoe to cover what is hurting your foot, make a kite out of it, shade a light that is too bright. You can wrap fish in it, wipe windows, or wrap money in it and tape it (so it doesn't make noise). You put washed shoes on newspaper, wipe eyeglasses with it, put it under a dripping sink, put a plant on it, make a paper bowl out of it, use it for a hat if it is raining, tie it on your feet for slippers. You can put it on the

sand if you had no towel, use it for bases in baseball, make paper airplanes with it, use it as a dustpan when you sweep, ball it up for the cat to play with, wrap your hands in it if it is cold." (Ward & Kogan, 1970)

In evaluating this boy's answers, you might say that he is very creative because he gave many unusual responses that you would never have thought of. In fact, if you were to compare his answers to those of other ten-year-old children of average IQ, his performance might be even more impressive. But where does such an ability come from? Is it a general characteristic that he was born with, or is it something that he learned? If we look at this boy's answers again, we might say that *experience* is an important factor. Clearly, the more often a person has had to use something in different ways, the more likely he or she is to think of other uses for it. Perhaps this child's responses would be considered less creative by other people of his own socioeconomic background. If so, this would imply that creativity is a relative quality that exists only when someone thinks it does. Many psychologists dispute such a viewpoint, however, and maintain that creativity *is* a characteristic that can be reliably measured and assessed.

What Is Creative?

The most widely used definition of creativity is that it is the occurrence of *uncommon or unusual, but appropriate responses*. This assumption underlies most of the tests that have been developed to measure creativity. ■

Although originality is usually taken for granted as a major factor in creativity, the importance of appropriateness is not always recognized. However, it is the criterion that distinguishes between creative and nonsensical acts. Solutions to a problem that are unique but totally worthless or irrelevant cannot be considered as creative responses. For example, suppose you were asked to imagine all the things that might happen if all national and local laws were suddenly abolished. A reply of "it would rain for forty days and forty nights," might be novel, but would not be regarded as creative because it lacks any relationship to the problem. Similarly, the utter-

Close-up
For Creativity: Go Right!

Ultimately, the creative process takes place in the brain and is given form through the action of muscles as we talk, write, dance, paint, sculpt, and so on. But where in the brain does this process take place?

We now know that each side of the brain has separate specialized functions. The left hemisphere is logical and analytical, taking the lead in mathematical and linguistic abilities. The right cerebral hemisphere is the "quiet" side that functions in activities of an artistic, musical, or spatial nature. Depending on the activity, one hemisphere takes charge and ensures coordination with the other.

In most right-handed people, the left hemisphere is dominant. But dominance varies with the activity, the individual, and perhaps even the culture. Right hemispheric activity is associated with meditation, hypnosis, drug use, intuition, and emotionality. Is it also the source of creative processes?

Fascinating research under way among the Intuit or Eskimo people of Baffin Island in northeastern Canada suggests that many features of their culture combine to promote right hemispheric activity. Anthropologist Solomon Katz (as reported in *Science News*, April 3, 1976) is studying the relationship between the art of the Intuit people and their language and social behaviors. The Intuit are noted for their soapstone and whalebone sculptures and their accurate map making. Their language is more synthetic than analytical, and they teach through demonstration rather than verbal instruction. Observation of their eye and hand movement while carving reveals that the stone is usually held in the left visual field (right hemisphere). The right hand does the detailed, analytical work, while the left does all the spatial manipulation of the stone.

While our culture fosters left hemisphere analytical functioning, that of the Intuit favors greater reliance upon right hemispheric functioning. Perhaps we too can learn to make more use of this "other" hemisphere and increase our creative potential by "going right" more of the time.

ances of psychotic patients may be unique and eccentric but are not viewed as evidence of creative talent.

In describing an Italian sculptor, Burnham (1968) has said, "[His genius] was such that he displayed an almost pathological inability to execute the expected solution to any problem in sculpture." To see a problem in a new way has often been the key to an important discovery or scientific breakthrough, as was demonstrated by Descartes in freeing physiological functioning for scientific study by postulating two kinds of processes (described in Chapter 2). This process of choosing and shaping appropriate representations for a problem is the focus of computer programs that attempt to simulate human creative behavior (Amarel, 1966). Basically, the quality of originality means that the creative response is not a predictable one until it is made—and then it becomes a standard by which the creativity of future responses can be judged.

Who Is Creative?

There are a number of different orientations in research on creativity. Some studies have focused on the *process* of creativity, some on the *product* that is created, and others on the *situational* factors that influence creativity. However, the major approach in this field has been research on the *creative person*. How can creative people be identified? What characteristics distinguish them from less creative people? How did they get to be the way they are? (Could you get there too?) The search for answers to these questions has been undertaken by many psychologists.

In general, studies have shown that there is a particular pattern of psychological traits that consistently characterizes creative individuals, regardless of their age, cultural background, or area of work. Creative persons appear to be distinguished more by their interests, attitudes, and drives than by their intellectual abilities (Dellas & Gaier, 1970). The lack of a strong correlation between creativity and intelligence may seem surprising, but research has clearly supported this conclusion (Wallach & Kogan, 1965).

There are other cognitive variables that do seem characteristic of creative people, however.

One of the most distinctive of these is a cognitive preference for *complexity,* as opposed to simplicity. This is revealed in a preference for figures that are asymmetrical, dynamic, and even chaotic, rather than those that are regular, neat, and simple. ▲

Much creativity research has been concerned with the personality characteristics of creative individuals. The results have pointed to a group of characteristics that includes impulsivity, independence, introversion, intuitiveness, and self-acceptance. Creative architects (MacKinnon, 1961) and creative research scientists (Gough, 1961) were remarkably similar in these personality traits, despite the differences in the content of their professional work. Creative writers displayed a similar complex of traits, although they showed greater originality and an emphasis on fantasy (Barron, 1963).

Independence, in both attitudes and behavior, is perhaps the most striking characteristic of this creative personality. Practically all studies have found that creative individuals are not very concerned with other people's opinion of them. As a result, such individuals are freer to be themselves and to express new ideas than are other, less creative people. Such independence is a critical necessity, since the creative response is often met with (and must continue in the face of) criticism, ridicule, and a total lack of reinforcement. As the Gershwins said,

*"They all laughed at Christopher Columbus
    when he said the world was round;
They all laughed when Edison recorded sound;
They all laughed at Wilbur and his brother
    when they said that man could fly.
They told Marconi wireless was a phony; it's
    the same old cry."*

Another personality variable that distinguishes creative individuals is that their pattern of interests reflects both the feminine and the masculine side of their nature—the *androgynous* type. Creative men are able to accept the feminine aspects of their personality without experiencing any sexual conflict, thus leading them to a greater openness to emotions and feelings, and to a greater aesthetic sensitivity (Hammer, 1964). One might expect that creative females would show an acceptance of masculine traits in their personality, but the little research available does not entirely support this view. According to the research of Ravenna Helson (1967) on creative women mathematicians, these women differ from the less creative in that they retain their femininity despite admission of masculine traits and are often *less* "masculine," rather than more so. Perhaps certain characteristics traditionally identified as "masculine" inhibit creativity rather than promote it. The extent to which there is a real sex difference in the creative process can only be elucidated by much more research.

One popular view of exceptionally creative people is that while they are geniuses, they are also completely crazy. The madness of such artists as Van Gogh or Nijinsky is often cited as a "typical example." What psychological evidence is there for a relationship between creativity and psychopathology? The answer (surprising to some) is that there is almost none. Instead, creative people appear to have superior ego strength and a constructive way of handling problems (Cross, Cattell, & Butcher, 1967). It may be that such characteristics as independence and originality, which lead creative individuals to think in ways that are taboo or considered "strange," cause the rest of the world to think of them (erroneously) as mentally unbalanced.

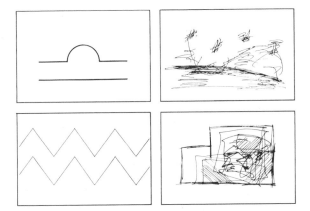

▲ These pairs of drawings are from the Welsh Figure Preference Test. Subjects chosen at random tend to prefer those on the left, while subjects identified by other tests as creative prefer those on the right.

Can Anybody (like me, for instance) Be Creative?

Even though people often criticize or attach negative labels to highly creative individuals, they still, paradoxically, want to be more creative themselves. Creativity is an attribute that has a high positive value for most people, in the sense that they wish they had more of it, and they would like the schools to help their children attain more of it. If creativity were something that you were born with, then it would be impossible to achieve such an improvement. Either you would have it or you wouldn't. Fortunately, there is no evidence to support the notion that creativity is innate; rather, it appears to be *learned* behavior.

How can we stimulate people to be more creative? Following basic principles of learning, Maltzman (1960) assumed that if people had been reinforced for creative responses in a preliminary training session, they would show more creative behavior in a later test situation as a result of response generalization.

To test this idea, Maltzman gave subjects a word-association test six times in a row, requiring them to give different answers each time. He thus forced subjects to go beyond common word associations and to produce more creative responses. When these subjects were later given a creativity test, they received higher scores than a group of control subjects who had not received such training.

Creativity is often stifled by the individual's fear that some new idea will be regarded as stupid or worthless by other people. A person who refuses to express new ideas (or receives no reinforcement for them) may eventually learn never to think in a truly creative way. How can we prevent this from happening? One proposal has been the use of "brainstorming" sessions (Osborn, 1957). In the initial "idea-finding" stage, the members of a group are presented with a problem and asked to think of all possible solutions to it, whether they seem practical or not. Participants are encouraged to be free of all inhibitions, except that they are not allowed to be critical of anyone else's ideas. In the second, "evaluation," stage, the group considers each idea very carefully, retaining all those that have a remote possibility of being useful. This entire procedure of *deferred judgment* can be used by an individual thinker as well as by groups.

How successful is the brainstorming technique in improving creativity? Unfortunately, there is very little evidence to support its effectiveness, however reasonable the method may seem. For example, one study found that brainstorming did not generate any more original ideas than were produced by the same number of individuals working alone (Taylor, Berry, & Block, 1958). This would suggest that the presence of other people, even under ideal conditions, can have certain inhibitory influences on creativity. However, there is evidence that individual brainstorming sessions can be made more effective if they are preceded by a group "warm-up" session (Dunnette, Campbell, & Jaastad, 1963).

Although a truly effective technique for promoting creativity has yet to be found, it is clear that creativity *can* be enhanced. This fact has important implications for education, since it suggests that a child can learn creativity as well as reading, writing, and arithmetic. It is to be hoped that more research will be done on possible methods for stimulating creativity. Strangely enough, the technique of reinforcing a person for original responses may not be the most successful one in the long run, since many creative individuals produce their most original work when they are independent of the traditional reinforcers dispensed by their society.

George Bernard Shaw, in his *Maxims for Revolutionists,* makes a distinction between reasonable and unreasonable individuals that appears to be equally valid for distinguishing creative, innovative people from others. "The reasonable man adapts himself to the world: the unreasonable one persists in trying to adapt the world to himself. Therefore all progress depends on the unreasonable [and creative] man."

Chapter Summary

Our human capacity to use our minds for solving problems above and beyond the ordinary problems of survival frees us from being slaves to our environment. We can manipulate symbols representing elements of the environment *(think),* utilize these symbols in solving problems *(reason),* and conceive new and original ideas *(create).* Thinking may be either *realistic,* as in reasoning directed at the solution of a particular problem, or *autistic,* as in daydreaming, or it may be a combination of the two.

A new approach to the study of *cognitive processes* has emerged in recent years. These processes are seen as complex, continuing events, acting and interacting over time. *Cognition* refers both to the *process* of knowing and to the *product* of that process.

Psychologists have long been interested in studying the development of cognitive processes. There is a discontinuity between the cognitive processes of children and those of adults. Children begin life as naive realists, accepting appearances at face value. According to Piaget, cognitive development occurs as children discover and learn to apply the rules that govern interaction with the environment. As children perceive discrepancies between simple concepts and environmental events, they form new concepts to account for them. Through the processes of *assimilation* and *accommodation,* they gradually refine the cognitive structures *(schemata)* they have formed to relate processes and results. Different children move through the four stages of cognitive development at different rates, but in the same sequence. These stages include the *sensory-motor period, preoperational thought, concrete operations,* and *formal operations.* The demands and needs of the particular culture may influence cognitive growth.

Throughout history, arguments have raged over whether the infant's mind is a blank tablet to be filled in by the environment or a storehouse of inherited abilities. Contemporary psychologists agree that the answer lies somewhere in between and are seeking to identify the environmental conditions conducive to the best development of whatever potential is present.

A number of highly unscientific early studies purported to "prove" the inheritance of specific levels of intellectual ability, as well as such traits as insanity, pauperism, lechery, and alcoholism. More recently, evidence for the importance of heredity has come from studies showing higher correlations between the intelligence of genetically identical twins than between other siblings. Environmentalists have called the soundness of this research and its interpretation into question and are demanding a reassessment of former studies as well as more rigorous controls in the future.

Evidence from various sources, including studies of children raised in foster homes or moved to more stimulating environments, indicates that environment plays a crucial role in the development of intellectual functioning. Current evidence suggests that intellectual ability is the result *of interaction* between heredity and environment, with heredity setting the limits and environment determining the exact level reached.

Thinking involves images, words, and covert muscular processes. *Images* are "mental pictures" of actual sensory experiences. Most people are strongest in visual imagery, although imagery is not essential to the thought process. *Eidetic imagery* is the capacity for imagery as clear and accurate as the original perception.

It has been suggested that conceptual development involves three stages of internal representation of objects. First we learn to use *muscular representations,* then *images,* and finally *symbols.* The length of time involved in thinking has been studied in *reaction-time* experiments. Words, like images, are apparently not essential to thought, but greatly enhance it. Our perception of objects is clearly influenced by the words we associate with them.

Psychologists have long disputed whether thought determines language or vice versa. The *Whorf hypothesis* holds that the language patterns of a cultural group mold its thought patterns and perceptions. Critics of Whorf have argued that it may well be different thought patterns that lead to a difference in language.

We do not think with our brains alone. *Covert oral behavior* (unseen muscular responses) also takes place and seems to facilitate thought processes. *Feedback,* or knowledge of results, is a necessary factor in thinking and learning. In recent years, psychologists have come to think of human responding as a series of events, and of the thinking organism as similar to a *servomechanism:* a goal-directed, error-sensitive, self-correcting device operating with *input, output, throughput,* and *feedback.*

There are three types of reasoning: *deductive reasoning,* in which data are combined and inescapable conclusions are drawn; *inductive reasoning,* in which hypotheses about the unknown are formulated on the basis of inferences from what is already known; and *evaluative reasoning* — judging the soundness or appropriateness of some new idea or product.

An individual in a new situation who wishes to reach a goal, but is blocked by some obstacle, is confronted with a *problem.* Human problem solving involves a combination of *insight* and *trial-and-error* learning. We begin with some ideas about how to solve the problem, try a few of them out (perhaps only mentally), and finally come up with the correct solution. Studies of the processes by which we search for some rule or organizing principle illuminate the pitfalls and difficulties inherent in the problem-solving process.

Recently computers have been used to study the processing of information by *simulating* human thought. Computers have imitated humans in processes as different as solving geometry problems, playing chess, and acting neurotic. While we are a long way from developing a computer that will duplicate all the complexities of the human mind, we can learn a great deal by studying the similarities and differences between mind and machine.

A *creative* individual is one who makes uncommon, but appropriate, responses. Creativity is a measurable characteristic, involving the ability to combine elements in new and different ways. Creative persons are distinguished from others more by their interests, attitudes, and personality traits than by their intellectual abilities. It appears that creativity is a learned ability, although investigators have not yet determined how it can best be encouraged.

Systematic Individual Differences in Information Processing

Ruth S. Day   Yale University

Several years ago I was doing some experiments on a fairly straightforward problem when some surprising results occurred. The experiments involved the dichotic listening technique, in which a different message is presented to each ear at the same time over earphones. Previous studies had obtained *rivalry* results; for example, given the dichotic pair SEVEN/NINE, subjects reported hearing either one or both of the input items, but not *fusions* such as SNEVEN. Since both fusion and rivalry results had been reported in analogous studies in vision, it seemed curious that only rivalry results had occurred in audition.

Examination of the items used in the previous dichotic listening experiments suggested that fusion might occur if certain psycholinguistic variables were taken into account. Therefore I constructed a variety of items such as BANKET/LANKET and asked subjects what they heard. The first few subjects reported hearing fusions such as BLANKET. At this point it appeared that fusion does indeed occur in dichotic listening. Then came a subject who did not fuse, but instead reported hearing both BANKET and LANKET. Perhaps the "discovery" was not "true," after all.

Instead of abandoning the project at this point, I decided to test a large number of subjects and observe percent fusions averaged over all subjects. This decision represented a well-established tradition in psychology, called the *nomothetic* approach. This approach assumes that individuals may differ to a certain extent in the ways that they perform various tasks, but that these differences are fairly uninteresting, minor fluctuations. Therefore we should test many individuals in order to minimize such differences and thereby obtain averaged results which presumably reflect underlying principles of behavior shared by all individuals.

Two Patterns of Perception

The nomothetic approach guided several subsequent fusion experiments which were designed to study the role of various stimulus and task factors in facilitating or hindering the fusion effect. Each time, a substantial number of fusions occurred.

However, large individual differences also continued to occur. Finally it seemed necessary to examine explicitly the nature of these differences.

Over 800 subjects have been tested in a variety of experiments using fusible dichotic items such as BANKET/LANKET. All pairs of items were time-staggered, such that one item began before the other by a short interval, as illustrated for a sample item at the top of Figure 1. Thus BANKET might begin first by 50, 75, 100, or 125 msec, or LANKET might lead by any of these same intervals. Since the average phoneme (basic speech sound) is about 70 msec in duration, these displacements are quite long. Several tasks were performed, using the same items and same subjects. In the *Identification Task,* subjects were simply asked to report "what they heard," whether "one word or two; . . . real words or nonsense words." In the *Temporal Order Judgment Task* (TOJ), the same subjects were asked to report the "first sound they heard," for example, /b/ or /l/.

Two basic patterns of data consistently emerge from these studies, as illustrated for the representative BANKET/LANKET item in Figure 1. Some individuals report hearing BLANKET in the identification task and also report that /b/ led most of the time in

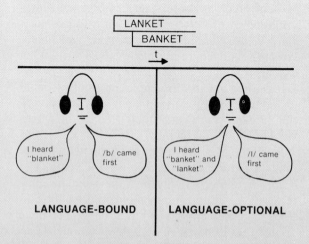

Figure 1   **Typical responses of language-bound and language-optional individuals in two dichotic fusion tasks: the identification task (response on left) and the temporal order judgment task (response on right).**

TOJ, even when /l/ led by a considerable interval. According to the phonological rules of English, stop consonants such as /b/ can precede liquids such as /l/ in initial position, but not vice versa; that is, words of the general form LBANKET cannot occur. It appears that these individuals are "language-bound" (LB), since they report what the language allows, not the actual stimulus events. Other individuals do not report many fusions in the identification task, and can correctly determine which sound begins first in the TOJ task. These individuals appear to be "language-optional" (LO), since they are able to use language rules or set them aside, depending on task demands.

A fairly lengthy testing session is needed to classify individuals reliably as LB or LO. The best approach involves examining the overall pattern of data in the TOJ task, as illustrated in Figure 2. LBs characteristically report hearing the stop consonant first, even when the liquid leads by a considerable interval; hence they perform well when the stop actually leads, but poorly when the liquid leads. LOs characteristically report hearing the correct phoneme as leading, no matter which leads. Although the curves in Figure 2 are averaged over groups of LBs and LOs, similar curves do occur for individual subjects. Most people show either the general LB or LO pattern, although some fail to meet the stringent statistical criteria adopted in the classification procedure. The few remaining individuals simply cannot perform the task; their data points fall randomly around the chance performance line of 50 percent correct.

The Nature of the Effect

At first it seemed that LBs might simply be poor judges of temporal order. However several experiments demonstrated that this is not the case. First, the same fusible dichotic pairs were used in another TOJ task. This time, subjects were asked to report the *ear* that received the leading sound and to ignore what the sounds actually were. LBs performed this task very accurately. Thus when no linguistic processing whatsoever was required, they were in some sense "released" from the language-binding effect. In a second experiment, subjects were asked to report the leading sound (phoneme) in nonfusible dichotic items such as BAE/GAE. LBs were again successful in judging the temporal order of these items. Since English does not permit consonant clusters such as those in BGAE or GBAE, there were no prescribed phonological rules to

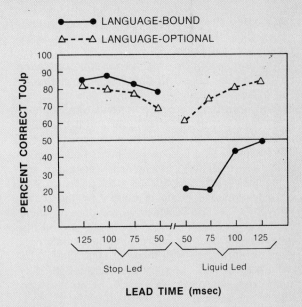

Figure 2 Percent correct temporal order judgment (TOJ) as a function of lead-time conditions. "Stop" indicates a stop consonant such as the /b/ of BANKET, while "liquid" indicates consonants such as the /l/ of LANKET.

bias the LBs' perception in a particular direction. In a final experiment, the item GAS/GAP was used, which can be fused in both directions, GASP or GAPS. Again, LBs could determine the temporal order of these items. These experiments demonstrate that LBs have trouble judging temporal order only when they must make a linguistic decision and the items are constructed such that phonological rules permit fusion into one sequence of phonemes but not the other. To say this in a more general way, LBs cannot disengage higher-level linguistic rules in order to make judgments at a lower level of analysis, even when reliance on such rules leads them into inaccurate perception. LOs, by contrast, are able to engage or disengage the appropriate level of rules, depending on the requirements of the task.

Another possible basis for the LB-LO distinction might be differences in overall intelligence: LBs might be less intelligent than LOs. Since I happen to be LB, I hoped that this would not be the case. The evidence was convincing: it showed that there are no differences between the groups on either a standard intelligence test or either the verbal or quantitative subtests of the Scholastic Aptitude

Test. Given this homogeneity of general intelligence, the differences in the dichotic fusion tasks are even more striking.

The term "cognitive style" is not appropriate for describing the LB-LO distinction, since the word "style" implies that the individual can decide to behave according to one pattern or the other at will. When LBs and LOs are told about the basic phenomena that distinguish them and are asked to "be the other kind," some odd things happen. LBs often say that they "really hear" BLANKET, and sometimes even argue that we made a mistake and actually recorded some BLANKETs on the tapes. When they take the TOJ task repeatedly over many days and are told what sorts of items are on the tape, their TOJ scores improve, but their data patterns do not merge with those of LOs. When LOs are asked to "be" LBs, they usually laugh; they know what the items are without being told and find it ridiculous to try to "hear" fusions. In short, the phenomenological experiences of the two groups are very different, and it is very difficult (if not impossible) for subjects of either group to "switch" to the other pattern. At present, it seems best to consider the LB-LO distinction as based on cognitive differences of an enduring nature.

Other Aspects of Cognition

While the LB-LO differences in the dichotic fusion experiments are very striking, if this were the only domain in which the two groups differ, then the effect would be of relatively limited value. After all, people do not go about their daily affairs with items like BANKET and LANKET delivered to their ears. The two groups do differ in a variety of perception and memory situations. For example, LOs are better able to recall a list of digits, such as 8-5-4-3-2-6-1-9-7, spoken in rapid succession. They seem more equipped to hold such information in a temporary storage system and report it in the same order as presented. However, in situations involving long-term memory skills, LBs show more organized memory. For example, a long list of 22 unrelated words is spoken, and then subjects write down all they can remember in any order. Then the same list of words is scrambled into a new order, and again it is presented and subjects must write down what they remember. Over many successive trials of this sort, LBs impose their own semantic organization on an otherwise chaotic list of items: they persistently report clusters of items together, even though

the positions of these items in the list change from trial to trial. LOs show relatively little semantic organization in this task. Instead, they show little observable organization of any sort, except for a tendency to report the items in the order that they occurred on each trial.

One way to view the results of these memory experiments is to assume that LBs characteristically employ more coding operations than LOs. There is little time available for such operations in the digit experiment; given more time LBs might "chunk" the items into groups such as "854-326-197" and hence achieve higher memory scores. In the word experiment, there is ample time to collect items into groups, and perhaps even devise "stories" for them, for example, WALKER-GARDEN-TRUMPET might be recalled as "The floor WALKER sits in the GARDEN playing his TRUMPET." Meanwhile LOs seem less inclined to perform such "deep" coding operations, and sometimes rely on more transient principles such as order of presentation. These experiments demonstrate that the LB-LO distinction extends into memory situations and is not confined to those concerned primarily with perception. Furthermore, they involve situations similar to those in everyday life, for example, remembering a telephone number or a grocery list.

Many other experiments have been conducted to compare the information-processing operations of LBs and LOs. Care has been taken to examine situations in which no differences occur between the two groups as well as those in which each group has, in some sense, an "advantage."

Implications for Research

It would be simplistic to claim that all of cognition is divided into only two basic "types." However the LB-LO distinction is sufficiently contrastive, enduring, and pervasive across various cognitive situations that a reexamination of the nomothetic approach to research seems warranted. Suppose we reorganize telephone numbers and put the "exchange" last (e.g., 2300-321) instead of first (321-2300), so people can rehearse the distinctive information immediately and then add on the well-known exchange. LOs may remember both forms equally well, since they have excellent memory for ungrouped digit strings. Form may make a difference for LBs since they have trouble remembering spoken digits and since they do organize items into meaningful "chunks" in other memory experiments. If we conduct an experiment and find that memory is equally good for both grouping forms, we might conclude that form has no effect on memory. However it could be that most of the people tested were LOs; had more LBs been tested, then there might have been a difference between the forms. Thus the relative proportion of LBs and LOs in a given experimental condition may override whatever effects stimulus or task variables might otherwise have.

The ratio of LBs to LOs could also account for the variability that sometimes occurs over repetitions of the same type of experiment. When one condition yields better performance than another in some experiments but not others, it could be that the contrast between conditions is not a potent one; or, it could be that the LB:LO ratio varied widely across the experiments, and that the contrast affects one of these groups but not the other.

Finally, some very well-known and often-repeated empirical results could be based on the averaging of different patterns of data. Thus it is possible that some widely accepted models in cognition are based on averaged data which do not reflect the patterns produced by the individual subjects tested.

Practical Implications

LBs seem to be so supremely "tuned" to the structure of their language that they have difficulty in changing its rules. For example, in "secret language" experiments, subjects have to change all spoken /r/s to /l/s, and vice versa. Thus ROCKET becomes LOCKET, and NELSON ROCKEFELLER becomes NERSON LOCKEFERREL. LBs make many more errors than LOs in this task. Similarly, LBs have trouble mimicking certain foreign-language words; for example, they produce the Lithuanian word, TSNOTA, as SNOTA, while LOs mimic it accurately. Informal discussion indicates that LBs have trouble learning to speak and understand foreign languages (although they may be able to read them satisfactorily), while LOs reach fluency readily (although they may make some grammatical errors). These experiments and informal comments suggest that various methods for teaching foreign languages may be differentially successful for LBs and LOs.

If young children show the LB and LO patterns, it might be useful to use different methods to teach them to read: LOs might profit more from a "phonetic" approach emphasizing sound-letter correspondences and LBs from a more traditional "look-say" approach.

In terms of general teaching practices for a variety of subject matter and at all levels of education, it is an open question as to whether specific methods can or should be devised to teach different kinds of people. Nevertheless appreciation of the extent to which large differences in cognition can occur (even within a population of fairly homogeneous intelligence levels) should make a difference in the way teachers teach.

Some Words of Caution

Given a striking set of individual differences in one domain, it is tempting to view the obtained distinction as a panacea for imposing order on observations made elsewhere and to try to "correlate it" with as many things as possible. Even though we might hope to make some sense out of the mass of data so collected (perhaps by using various factor analytic techniques), such an approach seems misguided—because it is *unguided*. There must be a theoretical basis for examining the behavior of LBs and LOs in other situations.

Each person is clearly unique in various ways. But that is *not* the point of the work. While I have argued against an extreme *nomothetic* approach in studying cognition, I also want to argue against an extreme *idiographic* approach, in which the uniqueness doctrine is so potent that we do not attempt to look for similar "principles" across individuals. Instead, the nomothetic and idiographic approaches may lie along a continuum, where various problems are better studied toward one end or the other. In the present work, I have found it useful to assume a position nearer to the nomothetic end of the continuum, but not at the extreme end: general principles of cognition appear to exist, not for "all" individuals, but for a small number of "groups" of individuals. These groups are clearly different from each other, but the people within them show considerable similarities in cognitive operations.

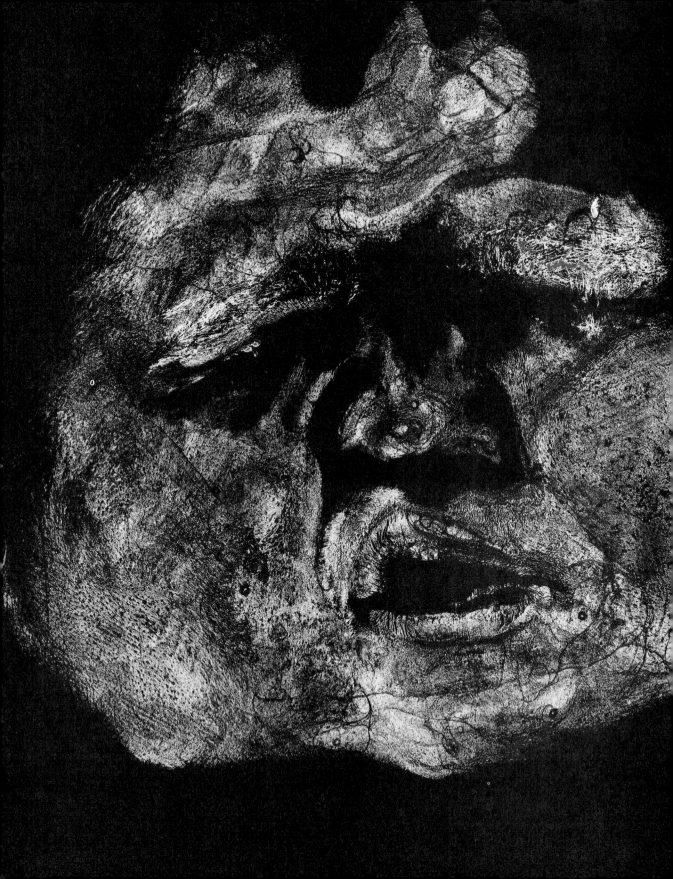

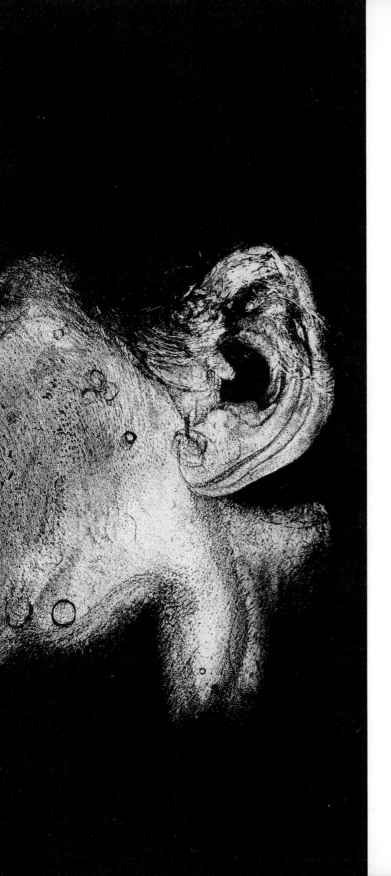

PART 3
Stimulation: External and Internal

6

Perception

Each of us, locked within the "time-bound capsule" of our own body, spends a lifetime trying to discover what the outer world and other people are really like. How do we ever come to know the nature of this incredibly complex external reality? How is it possible for our eyes to take in the patterns, shapes, and movement of life or for our ears to be tuned to the sounds of speech, the rhythms of music, and the calls of the wild? Perception is the key we use to open the doors to all these aspects of the world around us.

It is our perceptual processes that enable us to find stability and continuity in a world of constant change. Perception is the ordering principle that gives coherence to kaleidoscopic sensory input and meaningful unity to separated elements, making possible an organized direction to our behavior. Without the organizing processes of perception, we would not see objects, space, events, movement, people, or relationships, but would drift through a world of meaningless, random sensations.

Our nervous system is an exquisitely sensitive detection-reaction device that enables us to respond with great discrimination to physical properties of our environment. At a single moment in time, about *100 million* input pulses from light sources in the environment are typically being transmitted to processing centers in the retina of the eye and the brain. At the same time, we are probably processing inputs concerning sounds, temperature, tastes, smells, our body position, and muscular activity, as well as information generated by bodily needs, expectations, relevant past experience, and so on. Somehow, these separate bits of information are analyzed, organized, and integrated, and a decision is made to react in some way. It is estimated that such self-generated "commands" from our brains to our individual muscles are being made continually at the rate of at least five per second!

Our perceptual systems for seeing, hearing, smelling, tasting, touching, and feeling temperature have evolved over uncounted generations so that each of us starts life with a sophisticated set of mechanisms programmed by our genes and physiologically "wired in" at birth. Intricate as these mechanisms are, however, they are still flexible and plastic, capable of adapting to new situations and life experiences and thus of being influenced and changed by learning.

In addition, perceiving is much more than merely converting physical energy from stimulus energy into nerve-impulse energy, then back into physical energy that can act on the environment. We can think of the first stage in the process as the stage concerned with basic stimulus reception (called *sensation*) and of later stages as involving much more activity on our part in rejecting most of what comes in, selectively organizing what is received, interpreting it, and directing our attention to get still more input or turning elsewhere for new stimulation.

Enough generalizations. Now for a "magic" perception trick to illustrate the meaning of "the functional beauty of the perceptual process." It is a very simple trick, so watch carefully or you will miss it.

STEP 1—Make a clenched fist with your left hand, raise your thumb, and extend this arm full length in your line of vision.

STEP 2—Focus on your thumb. Now you will make it disappear three times before your eyes!

STEP 3—Continue to look in the direction of your thumb. Now close your eyelids for a few seconds . . . your thumb is gone (numero uno)!

STEP 4—After reading the next instruction, close eyes again, but look in the direction of your extended thumb. Now "hide" your left hand behind your back. OK, open your eyes; no thumb in front of them!

STEP 5—Get ready for the big one! Return your left arm to its original extended position and keep it there. Roll your eyes in their sockets until, without moving your head, you are looking up at the ceiling. Do you see any of your left thumb or is it gone again? Now close your eyelids and slowly turn your head as far to the right as you can. Now open your eyes. Presto, your thumb has disappeared completely for the third time! (With some practice you can make it reappear as quickly as you made it vanish.)

What? You say you are not impressed? You say your hand never *really* disappeared? You say there was no magic because you knew where it was at all times? But did you really? *How* did you know that your hand did not vanish when you were not looking, that your eyelids moved and not your hands or eyes, or that your eyeballs moved and not your eyelids, hand, or head, or that your head moved but your hand stayed exactly where it was? How could you tell the difference between what you *actually saw* and what *really was?* Answers at both the molar and the molecular levels of analysis, please. And one more question. How were the black ink marks on this page translated into a silent code that conveyed our instructions to your brain, which, in turn, hopefully resulted in its issuing executive commands to specific sets of muscles in your body? *That* is the real "magic."

Before we turn to consider some of the knowledge that research on perception has uncovered, knowledge that begins to answer some of these deceptively simple questions, we want to share with you a story about three ways of seeing the world. Some people believe that perception enables you to see the real world as it is. Others maintain that all you can ever know is your own process of perception—that is, what is going on in your head. It may correspond perfectly to what is going on in the external world, but then again it may not. Finally, there is a third group that argues that the important feature of perception is neither what is *nor* what we apparently see, but rather, how we agree to label and define what we perceive.

The story of how each of three famous umpires identifies a "strike" nicely reveals these alternative views of what perception is all about. Since the outcome of the entire game may hinge upon a single call of "strike" or "ball" by the ump behind the plate, it is, of course, important that this decision be as objective and "accurate" as possible.

"Well," said the first ump, "I crouch in real tight behind the catcher and rivet my eyes on the pitcher's hand, then on the thrown ball and its trajectory as it crosses the plate. Then I simply *call it as it is*."

"My approach is somewhat different," replied the second ump. "I too get in as close as I can to the plate, keeping an eye on ball, plate, and batter, and then I simply *call it as I see it*."

"For me," said the third ump, "it doesn't really matter if I stand close or far, or look at the pitcher or batter, because after the pitcher releases the ball in my direction, *it ain't nothin' until I call it somethin'*."

▲ In the room shown here either the subject's chair (in foreground) or the stimulus frame or both can be tilted. In darkness, where only the stimulus frame is visible, the subject is to indicate when it is vertical.

The Problem and Paradox of Perception

Naive observers accept the evidence of their senses uncritically. They feel that they are simply perceiving what is there. They take it for granted that they have direct contact and acquaintance with the outside world. They have a "vivid certainty" of the correctness of their perceptions and assume that other observers will perceive the situation in the same way—unless they are being "willfully perverse." This position is known as *phenomenal absolutism*.

Like the student we left in the shower in Chapter 3, you can tell the difference between hot and cold water. Certainly the attribute of heat resides in the water! Really? If you think so, you might try an experiment proposed by John Locke in 1690. Put one hand in a bowl of hot water, the other in cold water for a few minutes. Now put them both into a third bowl filled with lukewarm water. That water will feel cool to one hand and warm to the other whereas, as Locke pointed out nearly three centuries ago, "it is impossible that the same water, if those ideas were really in it, should be at the same time both hot and cold."

More recent experiments also demonstrate that what you perceive may not be what is there, despite your certainty that it is. For example, you know when something is up or down (relative to you) because it *is* up or down, right? Also you know when something moves relative to other stationary objects because it *does!*

In one set of experiments, subjects were seated in chairs in a room that was normal except for one feature—it could be tilted. When subjects in the chairs were stationary and the room tilted, their perception of up and down was impaired because they assumed that they themselves and objects in the room might tilt but that walls always stay vertical. So they experienced the tilted walls as unchanged and vertical, and themselves and the other vertical objects in the room as tilted (Witkin, 1954). ▲

A similar phenomenon has been reported by some passengers on the mammoth jets, who say that when the plane takes off, it appears that the ground is receding, rather than that they are rising.

Every time you go to a movie you see motion that is not there. The continuous movement of the actors is made up of a series of individual frames appearing at the rate of about twenty-four per second. There is no motion in the frames, yet you see motion. The same apparent movement is the basis for the neon signs with cartoon figures endlessly performing some simple act and for the news signs in which words seem to move across from one side to the other. Actually each single light in the display simply goes on and off, but if the timing of these unmoving on-off events is properly arranged and the stimuli are close enough together in space, you see movement. This perception of one moving light instead of two or more stationary lights going on and off is called the *phi phenomenon*.

The task of perception is to decode the information that comes in such a way as to identify the consistencies and relationships in the world around us and thus make it predictable so that we can deal with it appropriately. Our discussion here will center mostly on vision because of its dominant role in guiding human behavior.

The Trickery of Perception

The tropical forests in which the BaMbuti Pygmies live are so dense that the natives can rarely see for more than a few yards in any direction. Under such circumstances they have come to rely largely on sound cues to guide their hunting. Rarely is it necessary to make perceptual judgments based on visual cues of distance or depth discrimination. One of the remarkable consequences of this "natural" experiment is reported in the observations of an anthropologist, Colin Turnbull (1961). When a Pygmy named Kenge traveled with Turnbull to an open plain where the view was unobstructed, nature (or nurture?) suddenly began playing tricks on him. Turnbull reports:

"Kenge looked over the plains and down to where a herd of about a hundred buffalo were grazing some miles away. He asked me what kind of insects they were, and I told him they were buffalo, twice as big as the forest buffalo known to him. He laughed loudly and told me not to tell such stupid stories, and asked me again what kind of insects they were. He then talked to himself, for want of more intelligent company, and tried to liken the buffalo to the various beetles and ants with which he was familiar.

"He was still doing this when we got into the car and drove down to where the animals were grazing. He watched them getting larger and larger, and though he was as courageous as any Pygmy, he moved over and sat close to me and muttered that it was witchcraft. . . . Finally, when he realized that they were real buffalo he was no longer afraid, but what puzzled him still was why they had been so small, and whether they really had been small and had so suddenly grown larger, or whether it had been some kind of trickery." (p. 305)

In Kenge's attempt to maintain a rational explanation of his world, he attributes such capricious perception to witchcraft or trickery. In our attempt to explain such an illusion (and to maintain the assumption of a "rational" world), we assume that natural causes can be found. We look for an explanation either in unusual conditions of stimulation or in the particular background of experience of the perceiver.

From this anecdote, several important conclusions emerge. We assume, as does the Pygmy, that objects like buffalo do not change their size drastically over a short period of time. In a setting familiar to us, we see objects as maintaining their size regardless of our distance from them (Turnbull's perception). In an unfamiliar perceptual environment, the size of objects may appear to vary as a function of distance (Kenge's perception), but we attempt to fit novel perceptions into familiar contexts or frames of reference (Kenge compared the "insects" to beetles). Finally, under unusual conditions of stimulus presentation, our normal perception may change so that we see illusions. This is what happened

● This series of photographs was made as the man walked across the room. The room has not changed and the man has not grown. How do you explain what you see?

when Kenge saw the buffalo grow as he approached them rapidly in a fast-moving car.

A perceptual experience—how something appears to the observer—is called a *percept* (or, more formally, a *phenomenological experience*). A perception is judged a *veridical* (accurate) one when the percept agrees with other indicators about the object's characteristics that are measurable and verifiable independently. From related evidence to be discussed later, we know that Kenge would probably have come to see the world *veridically,* even from a distant vantage point, as Turnbull did, once he had learned that the objects he saw were in fact buffalo.

The perception of illusion. Would it be possible for you—a "sophisticated" perceiver—to have the same distorted experience of reality that this so-called "primitive man" did? Look at the three pictures. Do you see the man becoming twice as tall as he walks across the room? If you roll a sheet of paper into a tube and look through it at the man in the successive views, the phenomenon will be even more striking. You *know* this is impossible. What is happening? ●

The figure below is the well-known Müller-Lyer illusion. In the upper part, the two segments of the horizontal line look about equal in length but are not; in the lower half, they look different but are the same. Measure them and see.

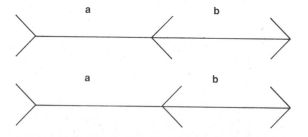

Psychologists are interested in illusions as a possible key to the understanding of all perception. Several other illusions are shown in the Special Transparency Insert opposite page 244.

The deceiving retina and the roving eye. If these illusions have convinced you that your eyes and interpretive mechanisms are faulty and not to be trusted, consider the basic perceptual apparatus you start out with and the job it must do. At the back of the eye is the retina, about an inch across, which receives all the sensory information coming through the lens and must transmit it to the brain for higher-level processing. But what kind of information does it send? Since it is a two-dimensional surface, it must send along a two-dimensional pattern to represent the three-dimensional world. And because the retina is so small, the lens must greatly reduce the size of what is out there. Furthermore, since images are inverted as light passes through the lens, the retina sees an upside-down world.

Complicating matters still further is the fact that the eye never stops moving around. The constantly drifting eye has a high-frequency, slight, but constant, *tremor.* In addition, it has *saccadic movements* of irregular flicking back and forth. Yet there is no tremor or flicking back and forth in the objects you see. (And try as you may when you look in a mirror, you cannot see your eyes shift their focus.)

Look around the corners of this page. As you do so, the retinal image moves and changes, yet you see yourself and the page as unchanging and stationary, in accord with the "facts." Now move the pages around and keep your eyes fixed. How does the retina differentiate between the two situations?

Somehow we do see a continuous world, right side up, "big as life," and full of 3-D substance, and usually we can distinguish movement in *it* from movement in *us.* If retinal transmission were all there were to perception, we would have a strange picture indeed of what the world was "really like." ▲

▲ Do camels grow in lawns? Or do your eyes sometimes deceive you?

The Dependability of Perception

The trickery and deceit of perception that we discover in the illusions surprise us precisely because our perceptual system is usually so remarkably reliable. Our visual system has earned the right to be depended on because under normal viewing circumstances the information it provides is accurate and useful in helping us adjust to and modify our environment. Because perception ordinarily works so well, so simply, and so effortlessly and "unconsciously," we must disrupt the system (as with the illusions) in order to become aware of the vast complexity of the physiological and psychological processes involved.

How does the perceptual act provide a stable, organized, coherent, and meaningful view of reality despite all the reasons for fallibility that we have just seen? When we search for an explanation of the illusions or seek to understand how the perceptual system manages to establish invariance between *objective reality* and *perceived reality*—our experience of what is there—a network of interlocking processes becomes apparent. The perceptual system acts like a computer, taking in multiple sources of information, selecting, integrating, abstracting, comparing, testing, sorting, outputting, and then repeating all these again and again. Each perceptual act is a construction or creation of reality based on all of the relevant past and current information available to the organism.

Far from being a direct experience of "things as they are," perception is thus a *mediated* process of organized conclusion drawing about the "real" world of time, space, objects, and events, based on much more than simply the stimulus input. In order to isolate "perception" as a field of study, then, psychologists must establish *arbitrary* boundaries between the various processes of sensation, attention, memory, learning, and so on, which are actually not separate at all but closely and dynamically interrelated.

What *does* your perceptual system give you that you can count on and how can it do so?

The accuracy and precision of perception. Visual acuity (sharpness of vision) is measured in terms of an arc on the circumference of an imaginary circle of which the eye is the center. Under good viewing conditions, our visual acuity is so great that we can see separate lines when the distance between them is less than one minute of an arc—less than a sixtieth of one degree out of the 360-degree circle. Small as it is, each eye has 125 million basic receptor elements in it. Our visual pattern recognition system is the most complex and accurate system known—far better than any computer yet devised.

The eye can detect an animal on a distant mountain or the ridges in fingerprints—and it can change its focus back and forth instantly. It skillfully guides the delicate hand-eye coordination of the watchmaker and the brain surgeon. And somehow it can do these things even though it is always moving itself; and when the retinal image changes, the eye can tell whether it is because of movement in the world or movement of the head or eyes, as you have seen.

The constancy of perception. Take a small box and move it slowly around, now at arm's length and then close to your face, into the sunlight and then into the shadow. It does *not* appear to change in shape, size, or brightness, although the image on the retina changes dramatically with each of these moves.

The stability of our visual world depends on this perception of *object constancy*—perception of an object as having continued existence as the same object despite changes in the size, shape, and position of the retinal image. In the competition for which source of stimulation will dominate the final perceptual judgment, the stimulation we get from the actual object (the *distal* stimulus) must win out over that of the pattern on the retina (the *proximal* stimulus) if the perception we get is to be accurate. The paradox of perception is that this is precisely what happens: what we experience subjectively does correspond more closely with the objective stimulus pattern out there than with the pattern of the image on our retina. We perceive *size constancy*, for example, by integrating the input about retinal size with estimates of distance. Information stored in memory about usual distances and sizes of familiar objects may enter into this process.

Seen from the top of the Sears Tower in Chicago, people look like ants, just as Kenge's buffalo did from the distance of a few miles. When you are in a novel situation and the cues you must rely on for distance estimation are inadequate or confusing, then size constancy no longer rules and your perceptual system falls back on the information it has available—namely, good old unreliable proximal stimulation.

The regularity in illusions. Illusions, far from being abnormal examples of runaway perception, are full of information about what is required for normal, accurate perception to take place. They do not reveal defects in our perceptual system, but rather show its strengths. They demonstrate the extent to which perception is not totally dependent on any one bit of stimulus information in the currently available environment. It is this freedom that keeps us from being stimulus-bound and enables us to use our perceptions in thinking, as we saw in our discussion of Piaget.

The explanations for some of the perceptual illusions we examined earlier depend in part on novel arrangements of cues or cues mixed in ways that change their usefulness. Instead of a literal perception of what is out there, we have an experience that clearly shows additional input from our own eyes or brain or both.

Have you ever noticed that the moon looks much bigger at the horizon than it does when it is high in the sky? Since we know its size does not really change each night as it moves across the sky, our perception of its apparent change in size is an illusion. This illusion was discussed as early as the second century by the Egyptian astronomer, Ptolemy. It has sometimes been blamed on the upward tilt of the eyes or on neck strain from looking up.

One explanation of this particular illusion combines the principles of size constancy and those underlying the "railway tracks" illusion shown on the transparency. Objects near the horizon are seen as larger because they are judged to be farther away. The misjudgment of the distance cues leads to a breakdown in the usual size constancy relationship (Kaufman & Rock, 1962).

How did the man become a giant as he walked across the room? You saw this illusion because you assumed that the room was rectangular whereas it was actually trapezoidal, as you can see by the diagram below. ■ The right-hand corner was actually much nearer to the camera. Because you assumed a normal room and did not have reliable distance cues, you took the larger retinal size at face value and saw the actual size of the man as increasing.

Other illusions seem to represent an exaggerated or unchecked use of normal organizing tendencies that operate in all perception and will be discussed a little later in the chapter.

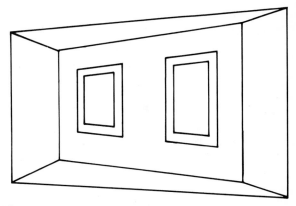

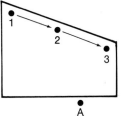

■ These diagrams show the room on p. 236 from the front and from the top. As the man moved across the room from point 1 to point 2 to point 3, he was actually getting closer to the camera, which was positioned at point A. Thus he appears to become larger in each succeeding photograph. The distorted room is pictured courtesy of the Exploratorium, San Francisco.

How Does Information Get In?

Information about the nature of the environment "out there" is detected by a variety of organs composed of highly specialized *receptor* cells. Generally, each receptor organ is sensitive to only one type of physical or chemical characteristic of the environment—sound waves or light waves, for example. These differences are not absolute, however. Thus the eye, though "tuned" to detect light waves, will also respond to the pressure of a finger poked against the eyelid—as you can determine empirically (but gently, please!) for yourself.

An organism can detect three things about environmental stimuli: (a) their general class or the type of energy they represent, such as light, temperature, or pressure; (b) their location in space; and (c) their intensity at each point in time.

Information about the first of these—classification of the stimulus—is conveyed to the organism by the type of receptor that is stimulated. For example, receptor cells in the eye are sensitive to stimulation by light waves within certain frequencies of electromagnetic radiation. Clues to the second—the location of the stimulus—are provided by the location of the receptors stimulated, since there are multiple receptors for every class of stimulus input.

The third—detection of how intense the stimulus is—is accomplished by a process called *transduction*. This is a two-step process in which stimulus intensity is translated into *generator potential* (a depolarization of the receptor membrane) that, in turn, is translated into nerve-impulse frequency. With stronger stimulation, a cell responds more frequently and more cells respond. Once in the form of nerve impulses, the information can be processed according to the basic principles of nerve transmission described in Chapter 2.

A stimulus must be of a certain strength before the sensory receptors can detect it at all. The magnitude of a stimulus that is strong enough to be accurately detected 50 percent of the time is called the *limen*, or *absolute threshold*. Values below this threshold are said to be *subliminal*.

Psychophysical Scaling

The relationship between stimulation and sensation can be measured either in terms of the organism's physical response (generator potential and nerve impulse) or in terms of its psychological response (how much change in the stimulus is necessary before the organism detects it as different). Techniques for measuring psychological response to physical stimuli are appropriately called *psychophysical scaling* methods.

It is clear that the relationship between changes in stimulus strength and changes in sensation is not one to one. In a dimly lit room, the lighting of a single candle is noticed at once, whereas in a brightly lit room, adding that same candle makes no difference in our sensation of brightness.

Early workers in this field assumed that, since sensation is a subjective experience, increase in sensation could not be measured objectively. In 1834, E. H. Weber invented a unit of measurement called the *just noticeable difference* (jnd). It is determined by presenting a standard stimulus and seeing how much stronger another stimulus must be to be perceived as "just noticeably different" 75 percent of the time. The required stimulus increase—the jnd—is a constant *proportion* of the original stimulus. That is, if the intensity of the original stimulus is 10 units and a stimulus increase of 5 units is required to make 1 jnd, a stimulus of 15 units would also require an increase of half its magnitude, thus 7½ units, and so on. (This unit of measurement can be used for such characteristics as weight and size, as well as intensity.)

A little later, G. T. Fechner hypothesized that there must be some regular relationship between stimulus increase and sensation increase. He believed that each time a jnd is added to the stimulus, the sensation increases by a constant amount, and thus that sensation could be measured by counting these increases. (In sound, the unit of increase is called a *decibel*.)

Fechner's experiments led him to formulate the Weber-Fechner Law: that *sensation increases by a constant amount each time the stimulus is doubled.* This is a *logarithmic function*. The not-too-modest Fechner predicted in 1877:

"The Tower of Babel was never finished because the workers could not reach an understanding on how they should build it; my psychophysical edifice will stand because the workers will never agree on how to tear it down."

Recently, S. S. Stevens of Harvard University (1972) has shown that it is not necessary to tear Fechner's edifice down: it can simply be replaced with a simpler one. Stevens started by questioning the original assumption that sensation increases could not be measured directly. He asked subjects to place different intensities of a wide range of stimuli along a numerical scale, and found that the average results for a group of observers were stable and reproducible.

By this new technique, he has discovered that *equal stimulus ratios produce equal subjective ratios*. Thus a given percentage change in the stimulus yields a constant percentage change in the sensed effect. This is a *power function* rather than a logarithmic function.

This principle holds for many different types of sensation. A constant percentage of increase in stimulus intensity always produces a constant percentage of increase in sensation—although the percentage of change in sensation may be larger or smaller than the percentage of stimulus change.

Varieties of Sensory Information

Our present concern will focus only on vision and hearing, the senses about which most is known. In addition to these two "long-range" senses, which gather precise information about the environment from long distances, we also gain information about the environment through several somatic (body) senses that are much less accurate and depend on direct contact. There are four somatic senses whose receptor cells are located in the skin: pressure (touch), pain, cold, and warmth. These skin senses are sometimes called the *cutaneous senses*. Each one tells the organism something different about the external world.

Two more somatic senses are located internally. They are intimately connected with each other and cooperate to help maintain bodily balance and to inform us of the position of our arms, legs, head, and all movable parts. These are the *kinesthetic* and *labyrinthine* senses. In addition, there are the *chemical* senses of taste and smell. The somatic and chemical senses will not be treated in further detail here.

Vision

The sense of sight, so important to survival, has followed a fascinating course of development. The intricate human eye apparently has evolved from a few light-sensitive cells such as those found in primitive forms of life. Gradually, as more advanced forms developed, there evidently appeared a greater and greater number of visual elements per unit area, an especially sensitive central spot, and more complex nerve pathways and related brain areas, making possible a more accurate appreciation of patterns. ◆ (p. 242) The eye also developed mechanisms for making use of the small amount of light available at night, giving it enormous range. And in monkeys and humans, the eyes moved gradually around to the front of the head so that binocular vision became possible. Finally, with the development of superior brain connections to the eyes, far more intelligent use of visual input became possible.

Structures for seeing. The eye is made up of two visual systems combined into one but specialized for different functions. Each system has its own distinctively shaped receptor cells; those of one system are called *cones;* those of the other, *rods.* The cones function only in the light; they are responsible for color vision and high visual acuity. In dim light, the cones cannot be stimulated and the rods function alone. The rods are extraordinarily sensitive to very dim illumination (night vision) but they do not discriminate among hues. When only our rods are operating, everything appears to be in black, white, and shades of gray.

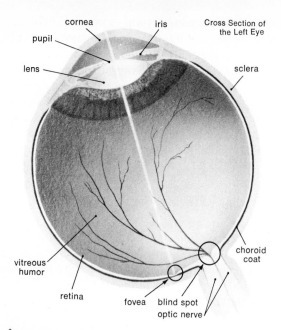

cornea   iris   Cross Section of
    the Left Eye

pupil

lens

sclera

vitreous
humor

choroid
coat

retina   fovea   blind spot
    optic nerve

◆CROSS SECTION OF THE LEFT EYE
   VIEWED FROM ABOVE

The eyeball is composed of three layers: (1) an
outer protective coat called the *sclera,* a portion of
which is the transparent *cornea* which acts as a
refracting surface; (2) a middle layer called the *choroid
coat* which is pigmented; and (3) a light-sensitive inner
layer called the *retina.* When light enters the eye, it
passes first through the cornea and then through the
pupil, which is an opening in the pigmented *iris.* The
pupil adjusts in size to regulate the amount of light
entering the eye, which influences both the brightness
and the clarity of the image. The light rays then
penetrate the *lens,* which focuses them onto the
sensitive surface of the retina. Before reaching the
retina, the light rays must pass through the liquid
(*vitreous humor*) that fills the eyeball. Light from the
center of the *visual field* (i.e., what the person is looking
at) is focused on the *fovea,* which is at the center of the
retina and is the most sensitive part of the eye in
normal daylight vision. The retina contains the visual
receptors that, when stimulated by light, initiate nerve
impulses that travel through the *optic nerve* and
ultimately reach the *occipital lobes* at the back of the
brain, one in each hemisphere.

The rods and cones are located in the bottom
layer of the retina, which means that light must
travel through several layers of nerve fibers and
blood vessels before reaching these receptor
cells. There are more than 7 million cones in the
retina. They are packed most closely together in
the fovea and decrease in number from the center of the retina to the periphery. Rods are
found in all parts of the retina *except* the fovea.

As shown in the diagram, ▲ the receptors
connect through synapses with the *bipolar cells,*
which in turn synapse with the *ganglion cells.*
(There are also many lateral interconnecting
cells within the retina, which are not shown in
the diagram.) These cells enable the retina to begin the job of processing information before
transmitting it to the brain. The axons of the
ganglion cells form the optic nerve; they synapse on cells at a relay point in the brain, the
lateral geniculate nucleus of the thalamus.
These latter cells, in turn, have axons going to
the *occipital cortex* at the back of the brain. ■
(p. 244) At the point where the optic nerve leaves
the retina, there is a *blind spot* that is not sensitive to light. (See *P&L* Close-up, p. 243.)

It has been estimated that the retina contains
about 125 million receptors, a few million bipolar cells, and one million ganglion cells. Obviously, there is a tremendous *convergence* of
information from many receptors to one ganglion cell. However, because of the many interconnections between cells in the retina, there is
also a *divergent* system of information flow.
Thus, one receptor connects to several bipolar
cells, which in turn connect to even more ganglion cells.

But how do these receptors translate light into
nerve impulses? Photopigments contained in the
receptors play a major part in this transduction
process. The rods have one type of photopigment, called *rhodopsin,* while each cone has one
of three types of *iodopsin,* corresponding to the
wave lengths of blue, green, and red light. When
light hits a receptor, it is absorbed by the photopigment, causing the pigment to break down
into its component parts (for example, rhodopsin breaks down into *retinene* and *opsin*). This
process changes the polarity of the membrane of
the receptor cell, producing a generator poten-

tial that activates the bipolar cells. As is true of other sensory systems, the visual transduction process is not completely understood; a number of important questions have yet to be answered.

After millions of receptors have responded to a visual stimulus, this tremendous amount of information must somehow be processed and interpreted by the nervous system. By combining the visual input in various ways, the nervous system provides us with information about different aspects of the visual image, such as brightness, color, form, and movement. To achieve this, input from the receptor must be analyzed for several different types of information *simultaneously* at the same level. The system of anatomical divergence, mentioned earlier, provides for such multiple parallel processing of information.

How we see brightness. The absorption of light by the receptor rods activates them and, through them, chains of neurons, to produce the "perception" of light. The greater the intensity of the light, the greater will be the activity produced in the retina and transmitted to the brain, and the greater will be the sensation of brightness.

The process that prepares the eyes to see under low illumination is known as *dark adaptation.* You undoubtedly have had the experience of going into a darkened theater and being unable to find your way to an empty seat without help. Yet after a few minutes, you were able to see quite well. For most people, complete dark adaptation requires about half an hour of darkness after the last use of the eyes in bright light.

You can perform a simple but interesting experiment on dark adaptation by staying in a

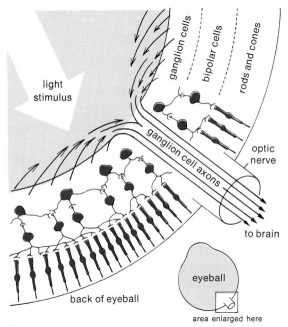

▲ **RETINAL PATHWAYS**

This is a stylized and greatly simplified diagram showing examples of the pathways that connect three of the layers of nerve cells in the retina. Incoming light passes through all these layers to reach the receptors, which are at the back of the eyeball and pointed away from the source of light. Through convergence, several receptor cells send impulses to each ganglion cell, while through divergence, one receptor cell may send impulses to more than one ganglion cell. Nerve impulses from the ganglion cells leave the eye via the optic nerve and travel to the next relay point.

Close-up
Spotting Your Blind Spot

Ordinarily we are unaware of our blind spots because when we are using both eyes an image never falls on both blind spots at once, since each faces a slightly different part of the visual field. You can determine the location of your blind spots by a very simple experiment. Close your right eye, hold the book at arm's length, and fixate on the circle below. Still fixating on the circle, move the book toward you until the cross disappears.

At that point, the cross corresponds to the part of your visual field that is falling on the blind spot of your left eye. To find the location of the blind spot in your right eye, follow the same procedure, but this time close your left eye and fixate on the cross with your right eye: no circle.

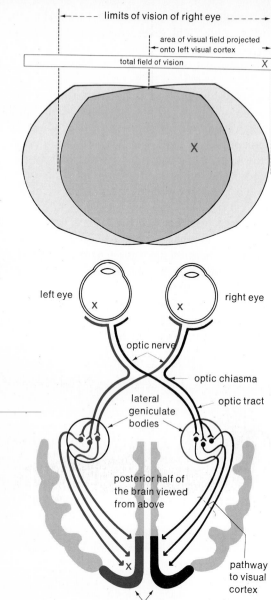

limits of vision of right eye

area of visual field projected onto left visual cortex

total field of vision X

left eye X

right eye X

optic nerve

optic chiasma

lateral geniculate bodies

optic tract

posterior half of the brain viewed from above

pathway to visual cortex

visual areas in the cortex of the occipital lobes

■ **THE MECHANICS OF SEEING**

In normal vision, light from one point in the right half of the visual field stimulates points on the left halves of both retinas, instigates impulses over nerve pathways on the left side of the brain, and finally activates a point in the left visual cortex of the brain, as shown above. Meanwhile, points in the left half of the visual field activate points in the right half of the visual cortex. Somehow, despite the fact that only half of the visual field is represented in each side of the brain, input from the two eyes combines to show us a single, unified world.

dark room for ten minutes. At the end of this period close one eye and, holding your hand over it, turn on the light for a few seconds. Then turn off the light again. Observe the room first through the eye that has been closed all the time and you will be able to see objects fairly clearly. Then close that eye and observe the room through the eye that was exposed to the brief period of light; to it the room will appear totally black. This experiment demonstrates that the process of dark adaptation takes place in the retina of each eye rather than in the brain.

How we see color. Color vision is the ability to differentiate various wavelengths of light (various colors) independently of their relative intensity, or brightness. This is believed to be accomplished through the cones in combination with special cells in the lateral geniculate nucleus called *opponent* cells. Each of these cells responds with excitation to impulses initiated by one wavelength and with inhibition to impulses initiated by another wavelength.

There are four basic types of opponent cells: red excitatory, green inhibitory ($+R, -G$); red inhibitory, green excitatory ($-R, +G$); yellow excitatory, blue inhibitory ($+Y, -B$); and yellow inhibitory, blue excitatory ($-Y, +B$). When light is absorbed by the cones (each of which, as you will recall, contains one of three types of photopigments), this information is passed on to the opponent cells, which *subtract* the output of one class of receptors from output of another. For example, a $+R, -G$ opponent cell subtracts the output of the green cones from the output of the red cones. Thus, the firing rate of a single opponent cell is dependent on the differential excitation of the two sets of receptor cells leading to it. Different patterns of excitation and inhibition of the opponent cells produce the sensations of different colors.

How we see patterns. Recent findings on the mechanisms for pattern perception have upset many long-held views. It was once assumed that all perceptual processing took place in the brain. That is, the input from the receptors was thought to be transmitted to the brain and mapped onto some surface there, where rela-

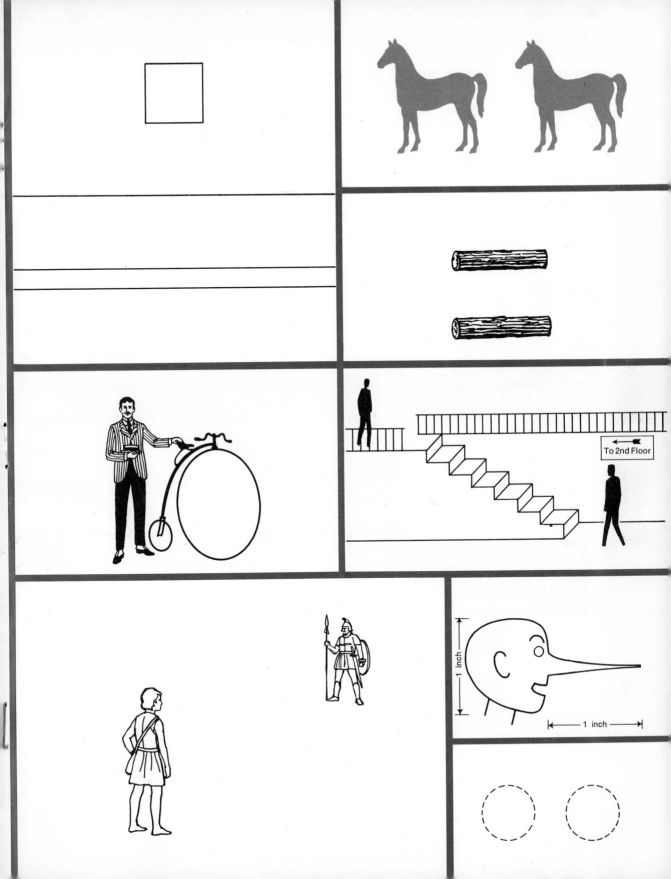

To 2nd Floor

1 inch

1 inch

● RECEPTIVE FIELDS OF VISUAL CELLS

Receptive Fields of Two Ganglion Cells

Each ganglion cell in the eye receives input from a circular area of the retina containing many receptor cells. In some cases the center of this area is excitatory and the outer part inhibitory; in other cases it is the other way around. A ganglion cell is most sensitive to input from the center of its receptive field.

Excitatory Center

Stimulation of cells in center of receptive field excites ganglion cell; stimulation in periphery inhibits same ganglion cell.

Inhibitory Center

Stimulation in center of receptive field inhibits ganglion cell; stimulation in periphery excites same ganglion cell.

Receptive Fields of Cortical Cells

By contrast, the retinal area that excites a simple cortical cell is elongated; it too has both excitatory and inhibitory parts. Input to such a cell would come from many ganglion cells whose receptive fields overlap to form a line.

Line in visual field	Receptive fields of many ganglion cells in retina	Receptive field of simple cortical cell	Perception of line

Adapted from DeValois, 1966

tionships were analyzed and interpreted and our subjective experiences of pattern vision were created. Then, in the 1950s it was discovered that particular cells at different stages in the sequence from retina to cortex were responsive only to particular features of a visual stimulus. Since then, discoveries have come thick and fast.

We now know that there are several stages of cells in the sequence of visual processing and that some of the analysis and pattern detection takes place at each of the stages. We also know that the response of intermediate levels is not automatic but depends on what pattern of response and inhibition has occurred at preceding levels. Furthermore, we have learned that these genetically determined potentials for pattern detection become operational only if the organism has certain experiences at early stages of its development.

H. B. Barlow of the University of California was the first investigator to discover that single cells in the retina of a frog were activated when a buglike stimulus was presented (1953). Not only did the neurons discharge vigorously; the frog made repeated feeding responses toward the stimulus. This discovery was important for two reasons: first, it demonstrated that recognition mechanisms related to vital behavioral functions may be located outside the brain; and second, it showed that, as we have seen (p. 83), some cells are sensitive to highly specific features of stimuli.

Patterns of sensory stimulation that initiate responding in particular sensory neurons are called *trigger features*. The neurons that respond selectively to them are called *feature analyzers*. The information processing that takes place as visual input is received by the retina and transmitted to the visual cortex can be inferred by studying the stimulus features that are required to trigger different neurons. Some neurons are excited only by stimuli at certain angles, others by vertical lines, or horizontal lines, or edges, or movement, and so on. It has been found that the retinal feature analyzers of different species respond to quite different features and that in species with stereoscopic (three-dimensional) vision, a greater proportion of the processing of visual information takes place in the brain.

Certain ganglion cells have been found to respond only to a stimulus that is moving in a certain direction. Movement in the opposite direction inhibits the cell from responding, while movement in other directions produces intermediate amounts of excitation and inhibition. Each of these cells differs in the direction of motion to which it is most responsive. Just how these cells are able to detect movement is not yet known, but higher-order analysis of the responses of these movement-sensitive cells is believed to take place in the cortex.

The receptive field of a given neuron is that area of the retina from which it receives impulses. Working with cats, Hubel and Wiesel (1959) found that the ganglion cells in the retina, each of which receives input from many receptors, have concentric receptive fields with either an excitatory center and an inhibitory surround or the other way around. These ganglion cells are very sensitive to *small spots* of light that just fill the center of their receptive field. In contrast to the ganglion cells, the cells in the cat's visual cortex often have elongated receptive fields, rather than concentric ones. In this case the stimulus that produces the greatest amount of activity of the cell is a *line* of a certain width located in a particular plane in the visual field. It appears that the "line" cells in the brain are responding to the input from a group of retinal "concentric" cells whose receptive fields are in a line. ●

Hierarchical processing. In the years since their first discoveries, Hubel and Wiesel (1959) have identified six successive stages in cats' processing of visual information: one in the retina, one at the *lateral geniculate body*—a relay point halfway back to the visual cortex—and at least four in the visual cortex itself. They have identified both the trigger features of the cells at each stage and the shape of the receptive fields of those neurons. Processing is clearly hierarchical, with input going from simple cells to increasingly complex ones, each performing a different share of the task of pattern detection.

It appears that the cells at higher levels become selective for more complex trigger features of the stimulus. For example, a particular position of a stimulus light is necessary for a retinal cell or even a simple cortical cell to be activated. But for higher-order complex cortical cells, orientation and length of line are more important than position.

One of the most important processes that occurs at levels of greater complexity is that of inhibition. Not only is a particular cell stimulated by certain trigger features and not by others, but it often inhibits (or blocks) responding to stimuli that do not have the required trigger features.

The task of perception. The central task of perceptual systems is detecting meaningful signals in a sea of "noise," or irrelevant signals. Put differently, the task of perception is the search for *invariant* properties in the stimulus field: our perceptual mechanisms must somehow spot the unchanging, "real" figure and disregard all the distractions that are camouflaging it.

In all systems concerned with processing information, a central principle is that of economy. Given the infinite amount of information that is possible, only essential information must be transmitted; the nonessential must be discarded. Such systems must develop programs for *reducing redundancy*—for minimizing inputs that "say the same thing." Some redundancy is necessary to ensure that the signal gets through, but excessive redundancy overloads the system, lowering its efficiency in processing other information.

Sensory pathways have many ways of reducing the redundancy in the information they transmit about the visual environment. Among these are *adaptation* to continued unchanging input (in which receptor cells cease to respond to an unchanging stimulus), *lateral inhibition* (in which cells inhibit neighboring cells), and *selective sensitivity* to the direction of motion. At higher levels, the stimulus regularities picked up at the lower levels become less significant, thereby allowing greater emphasis on stimulus discontinuities, novelty, and uniqueness.

This brief description of the mechanisms for seeing brightness, color, and various aspects of pattern is enough to suggest how intricately equipped organisms have become for responding to visual stimuli. This is an extremely active field of research at the present time, aided recently by efforts to combine concepts and approaches from physiology, psychology, and computer science.

Hearing

The sense of hearing involves the use of one of the most complex organs in the human body—the ear. The sensitivity of the ear is so great that it can respond to extremely soft, low sounds. (In fact, it can almost—but not quite—detect the sound of air molecules randomly hitting against the eardrum!) However, the ear is also resilient enough to withstand the pounding of very strong sound waves, such as highly amplified music at a rock concert. Moreover, it can be very selective, as when it picks out one voice from many in a crowd or a choral group.

There are some limits to the resiliency of the ear that it is important to be aware of, especially if you like your music loud or live in a noisy environment. The sensitive structures of the ear are protected from strong stimuli by two sets of muscles that reflexively contract in response to loud sounds. Ordinarily, this reduces the amount of pressure on the inner ear fluid. However, there is a limit to how long this protective mechanism can effectively function when decibel levels are extreme. One study found damage to the cochlea

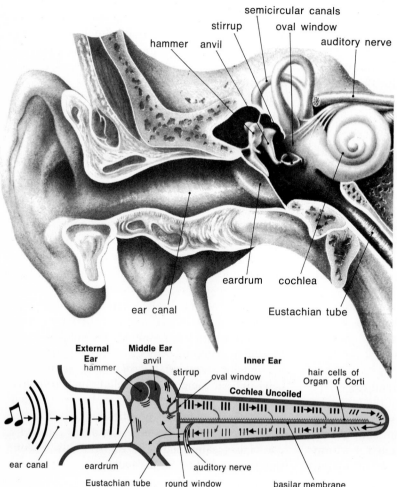

▲ STRUCTURES OF THE HUMAN EAR

The top drawing is a cross section of the human ear. Below it is a highly simplified diagrammatic cross section of the cochlea as it would appear if it were unwound and stretched out straight.

The sound waves travel first through the outer ear and auditory canal to a thin membrane called the *eardrum,* which begins to vibrate. These vibrations are picked up by three small bones *(ossicles)* in the middle ear and are transmitted through another membrane, the *oval window,* to the fluid of the *cochlea.* One of the ossicles (called the *stirrup)* acts like a piston, moving the fluid back and forth in the rhythm of the sound waves. The movement of the fluid makes a thin membrane within the cochlea (the *basilar membrane)* begin to vibrate. This, in turn, bends the hair cells of the *Organ of Corti,* which rests on the basilar membrane. These hair cells are the actual auditory receptors; moving them "excites" them and produces a generator potential which initiates nerve impulses in the fibers of the *auditory nerve.* The auditory nerve then carries the impulses to the brain.

Touch, temperature, and pain. The human fetus can react to touch stimuli about eight weeks after conception. By this time, then, some rudimentary sensory capacity has developed. Sensitivity to touch develops from the head downward. In the eighth week of prenatal life, the fetus becomes responsive to touch stimuli on the nose, lips, and chin, and the area sensitive to stimulation gradually increases with the passage of time. By the thirteenth or fourteenth week, the entire body is sensitive except for the top and back of the head, which do not respond to stimuli until after birth. Even at birth, the face is more sensitive to touch and pressure than other parts of the body.

Temperature sensitivity is present before birth; we know this from the fact that premature infants, like full-term ones, may refuse milk of the wrong temperature. They may also respond to external temperatures, usually reacting more strongly to cold than to heat.

Sensitivity to pain is weak in the fetal period and during the early days of life outside the womb. It is greater on the face than elsewhere and sufficiently underdeveloped that circumcisions may be performed without anesthetic during the first two weeks. The delay in development of the pain sense has been interpreted as a biological defense mechanism to protect the child during the birth process (Carmichael, 1951).

Taste and smell. A sense of taste is well developed at birth. Newborn infants usually react with sucking movements to sweet or salty stimuli and with rejecting behavior to sour or bitter ones. The taste sense apparently develops some time before birth, since even premature babies respond to taste stimuli.

Smell is another well-developed sense in the newborn. Definite changes in bodily activity and breathing rate following olfactory stimulation have been observed. Studies have shown that newborns can distinguish between such odors as acetic acid, asafetida, phenylethyl alcohol, and anise oil, although no clear differences are observed in response to odors that are pleasant and unpleasant to the normal adult (Engen, Lipsitt, & Kaye, 1963). The testing procedures employed in studies of this type were described in Chapter 2, in connection with the orienting reaction.

Hearing. There is some question as to whether the fetus can hear in spite of the fluid in the ears. It has been found that the rate of the fetal heartbeat will increase sharply in response to a tone sounded close to the mother's abdomen (Bernard & Sontag, 1947). A team of Swedish investigators studied fetal reactions to tones of differing frequency.

Reactions of the fetal heart to tones of 1000 and 2000 cycles per second at an intensity of 100 decibels and a duration of five seconds were observed in this study, which involved thirty-two women in the last month of pregnancy. The pulses of the mother and fetus were registered before, during, and after presentation of the tones. In the group tested at 1000 cycles per second, the increase in fetal heart rate averaged seven beats a minute. In the group tested at 2000 cycles per second, the acceleration was eleven beats a minute. The mother's pulse did not show any acceleration (Dwornicka, Jasienska, Smolarz, & Wawryk, 1964).

One point of special interest in this study was that the higher tones produced a greater response. Studies of babies soon after birth show them to be more pleased by low notes than by high notes, as inferred from their external behavior.

At birth, hearing seems to be less well developed than the other senses, though there is much variation from child to child. Hearing is at first hampered by amniotic fluid, which often remains in the middle ear for a few days after birth. Usually sometime between the third and the seventh day, the infant reacts to ordinary noises, responding more vigorously to the rattling of paper or dishes than to a voice. After the fourth week, however, there is more frequent response to voices than to loud noises. By the age of two months, infants are apparently not just hearing auditory stimuli, but discriminating among the sounds.

Vision. Since the retina has not reached its full development at birth, it was once assumed that newborns could not see clearly. Experiments have shown, however, that young infants can distinguish patterns and even give indication of size constancy and depth perception.

Pattern and color perception. Apparently there is an innate ability to perceive form visually. One study found that infants under five days of age looked longer at black-and-white patterns than at plain-colored surfaces. Infants a few days older were found to show even greater visual discrimination (Fantz, 1963). In another study, investigators showed newborn babies a series of pairs of shapes differing in the number of angles they contained. Shapes with ten angles or turns were preferred to shapes with five turns or twenty turns, as inferred from photographic recordings of eye fixations, which showed longer times spent looking at the ten-angle figures (Hershenson, Munsinger, & Kessen, 1965). By about ten days after birth, infants can follow slowly moving objects with their eyes. Because their eye muscles are not well coordinated at first, their gaze may occasionally seem to "flare out" in two directions at once.

There is some disagreement as to whether young infants perceive color, but experiments suggest that they do.

Stimuli varying in shape, color, or both were presented in pairs to infants four months of age. Here, too, preference (and hence ability to discriminate) was inferred from the amount of time spent in visual fixation. It was found that red and blue were significantly preferred to gray, but that shape dominated color as a basis for preference. A bull's-eye pattern was preferred to other patterns (Spears, 1964).

Size constancy. To find out whether young infants have size constancy, one investigator trained a two-month-old baby to respond to a 30-cm. cube. Every time the baby turned its head toward this discriminative stimulus, a potent reinforcer was presented—the experimenter popping up and "peek-a-booing."

When this operant response was well established, generalization tests were conducted to determine whether the baby was responding on the basis of the retinal size, the distance, or the actual size. It was reasoned that if size constancy is innate (or learned very early), then the true stimulus size (30 cm.) should be the perceptual factor to which the baby would continue to respond, rather than either a constant retinal size or a constant distance if the three factors were varied independently so that the baby had to choose one and ignore the others. This is exactly what was found: most responding occurred where retinal image size and distance were different from the original condition but true stimulus size was the same (T. G. R. Bower, 1966a).

In another study, the discriminative feature of the stimulus was not its size but its shape (angle of slant). Again the infant perceiver detected the "correct" stimulus on the basis of its objective shape, rather than its retinal shape (T. G. R. Bower, 1966b).

Depth perception. Further evidence of inborn abilities to perceive pattern and meaning in visual stimuli has been provided in an interesting series of experiments with young organisms of various species employing the "visual cliff."

This apparatus consists of a board laid across the center of a large sheet of heavy glass that is supported a foot or more above the floor. On one side of this board a sheet of patterned material is placed flush against the underside of the glass so that the glass appears to be as solid as it in fact is. On the other side of the board a sheet of the same material is several feet below the glass. This gives the visual appearance of a drop or "cliff," in spite of the solid glass above it. In experiments with thirty-six infants aged six to fourteen months, the babies were placed individually on the center board and their mothers called to them first from the deep side and then from the shallow side. ◆

Twenty-seven of the children tested moved off the board; all of these crawled out on the shallow side at least once, but only three crept off onto the glass above the "cliff." Many cried when the mother called to them from the cliff side, but were unwilling to go to her over the apparent chasm; others actually crawled away from her. Some patted the glass on the deep side, ascertaining that it was solid, but still backed away. Apparently they were more dependent on their visual sensations than on the evidence of their sense of touch.

Although this experiment does not prove that the infants' perception and avoidance of the chasm are innate, similar experiments with animals tend to support the hypothesis that such perception is inborn. Nearly all animals tested were able to perceive and avoid the visual cliff as soon as they were able to stand or walk. This was true of chicks less than twenty-four hours old, and of kids, lambs, and kittens. Rats ventured onto the deep side as long as they could feel the glass with their whiskers but consistently chose the shallow side when the center board was raised enough to prevent their whiskers from touching the glass (Gibson & Walk, 1960).

Actually it was discovered, somewhat surprisingly, that instead of responding to depth cues the subjects were responding to the *motion parallax:* the perceived changes in their own position relative to other objects. When the "floor" was close, a given movement of their own seemed faster relative to it, and the changes in their position were more clearly related to changes in its appearance from one moment to the next. Evidently learning was unnecessary for perception of this difference and for preference for the conditions associated with the faster motion.

Genetic potential doesn't just "unfold." Remarkable as it is, infant perception is not as adequate as adult perception. And even where genetic programming provides an infant organism with the exact sensory equipment needed by its species—as we saw in the case of the "bug detector" neurons in the retina of a frog—the equipment may not become functional without specific experiences at an early age. This has been shown in many species.

◆ These pictures show the apparatus used in the visual cliff experiments and the reactions of two subjects to the apparent drop-off. Although the child patted the glass with his hand and thus had tactual evidence that there was a firm surface there, he refused to crawl across it when his mother called to him. The one-day-old goat walked freely on the shallow side but would not venture out on the deep side. When placed at the far edge of the deep side, it perched carefully on the narrow edge of the board and shortly thereafter leaped across to the shallow side again.

Apparently the environment must provide experiences of tactile and painful sensation if these senses are to develop normally. Without this "environmental training," normal development may be seriously disturbed. Interesting effects of tactual deprivation have been studied in the chimpanzee.

One subject, Rob, had his limbs from elbow to fingertips and from knee to toes encased in cardboard tubes from the age of four weeks to thirty-one months. Rob never learned to turn his head toward the hand that the experimenter stimulated. That is, if the experimenter squeezed his right hand, Rob was to turn his head to the right in order to receive a reward. After 2000 trials he was unable to do this, although a normal chimpanzee learned the task in about 200 trials (Nissen, Chow, & Semmes, 1951).

It has also been found that dogs deprived of normal stimulation in infancy are virtually incapable of learning to avoid painful stimuli later and do not learn to fear objects associated with such stimuli (Melzack & Scott, 1957).

Vision, too, can be permanently impaired as a result of deficient early experience. One investigator found that raising a chimpanzee in total darkness resulted in degeneration of the retina and permanently impaired vision. When another chimpanzee was prevented from seeing objects but was allowed to experience light, however, its retina was not damaged (Riesen, 1950).

Later studies with both kittens and chimpanzees have demonstrated that wherever visual deprivation leads to chemical changes in the retina (as when the animal is raised in complete darkness), such changes become irreversible when the deprivation is continued beyond infancy, with the result that the animals suffer a permanent inability to learn certain perceptual habits (Riesen, 1961).

Apparently, motor activity is necessary for the normal development of perception.

In one experiment, kittens were restrained so they could not walk around from the time they were first exposed to light. Compared to animals reared normally, their behavior in situations calling for visual orientation was deficient. The original interpretation attributed these results to the effects of stimulus deprivation. Since the restrained kittens could not change their stimulus environment by walking about, they had been deprived of a great deal of variation in visual stimulation; this was presumed to be the cause of their deficient visual discrimination.

Further study showed that this explanation was not sufficient. Pairs of kittens were given experience in a device that equalized movement through the environment but prevented active motion by one member of the pair. ▲ The movements of the active kitten were transmitted through a pivoted bar and chain linkages to a small gondola in which the second kitten was restrained. When the active kitten moved around, the passive kitten in the gondola moved in identical ways; thus both animals experienced the same variation in visual stimulation.

In this situation, the active kittens developed normally: they blinked when objects approached and put out their paws when carried toward a surface, for example. The passive kittens, however, did not display these behaviors, though they learned quickly after a few days when allowed to move about normally (Held, 1965).

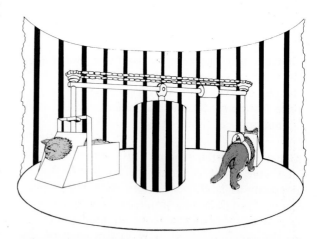

▲ The kitten on the right is able to move about and experience a variety of visual stimulation. The kitten on the left is suspended from a pivoted bar, connected to the other cat's harness, which allows it to have identical visual experience but no motor experience.

The practical significance of findings such as these was suggested in another experiment. A group of children being cared for in institutions were given special opportunities to deal actively with an enriched visual environment. Their developmental rates accelerated markedly for some kinds of visual-motor abilities. Evidence of a critical period was also found; the treatment was less effective if it came either too early or too late (White & Held, 1966). Thus some aspects of perception and perceptual-motor coordination require not only particular kinds of stimulation but also active participation of the motor systems if normal development is to occur.

It is the function of all effective stimulus processing and perceptual behavior to prepare the organism to respond overtly and appropriately to the demands of its environment. If perception is to be a dependable link in this sequence, we must develop a sensory-motor feedback system that gives us stable information about the consequences of our movements. This comes only through experience in which we are active.

One of the most exciting discoveries in the field of perception in recent years is the convincing demonstration that experience can change the response properties of individual sensory neurons.

Kittens were reared in specially designed visual environments in which they saw only vertical stripes or only horizontal stripes. When they reached adulthood, measurements were made to see if there had been changes in the receptive fields of neurons in their visual systems as a result of this early experience.

It was found that the adult cats had neurons sensitive only to stimuli in the orientation that they had experienced; none had neurons that responded to stimuli in the other orientation. That is, vertical-environment cats had no cells that responded to horizontally oriented stimuli and vice versa (Blakemore & Cooper, 1970).

Even more dramatic findings have emerged from a series of studies by Helmut Hirsch and his colleagues (Hirsch & Spinelli, 1970, 1971; Hirsch, 1972). Kittens were raised to the age of three months wearing masks that presented a visual field of black-and-white stripes to one eye and a field of horizontal stripes to the other. Recordings of the activity of single cells in the visual cortex at ten and twelve weeks of age and again at two years showed that cortical cells connected to the eye exposed to horizontal lines could be activated only by horizontal stimuli, while cells connected to the other eye responded only to vertical stimuli. Thus ability to perceive such features of the visual world as depth and contour appears to depend on experiencing them during a particular "critical period" early in development. The specificity of cortical neurons usually found in adults presupposes this experience with the visual world and is clearly shaped and modified by it.

It has been conjectured that the larger neurons in the brain may remain relatively constant, under genetic control, while small, short-axoned "microneurons" are changed through experience, changing, in turn, the activity patterns of the larger neurons (Hirsch & Jacobson, 1974). Nature and nurture thus work together to perfect our brain, enabling us to benefit from the past adaptations of our ancestors as well as from the current information we need for adaptation to the here and now. We do not yet know to what extent behaviors that we label as "intelligent" and test for in our "intelligence tests" develop through this combination and interaction.

Theories About How Perception Develops

Although philosophers, physiologists, and psychologists under many different banners have agreed that perception is the key to what human beings are all about, their differing explanations of it have been a source of heated controversy. We will sketch the main ones briefly. You can then weigh them for utility as we examine the ways evidence has been sought and the answers that have been found.

British associationism and the analytical introspectionists. The question of how we come to know reality was of philosophical interest long before psychologists began investigating perception. Starting in the seventeenth century, the British associationists (Locke, Berkeley, and Hume) proposed a general theory of knowledge and perception that has influenced scholars ever since. Knowledge of reality, they held, could come only from impressions processed through the sensory apparatus. Simple ideas were seen as the irreducible elements of sensory experience. Complex ideas were thought to be built by learned association of these simple elements. The contents of the mind thus could be analyzed into those basic units that are the building blocks of sensation. Because of their emphasis on sensory experience as the basis for knowledge, these philosophers are also called the British *empiricists*. Their interest was not in how perception takes place but in the role of perception in our knowledge of reality.

Early psychologists such as Wundt and Titchener in Germany accepted these assumptions. In the late 1800s they concentrated their efforts on trying to train observers to experience and report "pure sensation," uncontaminated by additives from learning. "Perception" was assumed to be a more advanced stage in which the "primary" sensory experience had been changed and distorted in various ways. They were confident that through *trained introspection* they could get back to the original elements of psychological experience and that these should be the starting content for the subject matter of psychology.

The Gestalt revolution. Early in this century a group of German psychologists at the University of Berlin (Kohler, Koffka, Wertheimer) attacked the concepts both of *association of elements* as the basis of perception and *introspective analysis* as the key to primary, original experience. Rather, they emphasized innate organizing processes that give us *patterns* as a primary characteristic of experience. According to the Gestaltists, our perception of context and relationships is as basic a "given" as "blueness" or any of the simple elements the introspectionists were looking for.

The German word *Gestalt* has no exact English equivalent; the closest approximation is *configuration*. The configuration is seen as the basic unit of perception and other experience. According to the Gestaltists, "the whole is greater than the sum of its parts" and in many ways determines the character and behavior of the parts, instead of the other way around. A melody is the same in one key as in another even though the individual notes all change. Also, qualities of wholes—like the liltingness or the plaintiveness of a melody—do not reside in the individual notes. Relational properties such as these are part of the primary perception, not added later through unconscious inference. Thus, for example, no amount of introspection of the apparent movement in the phi phenomenon (p. 235) can make it go away.

Barlow's studies of neurons support the Gestaltists' contention that pattern characteristics are provided by organizing forces in the nervous system. The physiological mechanism is different, though, for the Gestaltists assumed that the organizing took place in the brain, following a model of field forces, whereas the discovery of feature analyzers has shown that single neurons are responsive to particular pattern features in the visual field (Barlow, 1972).

The transactional approach. According to Ames (1951), who developed the distorted room studies, each one of us develops—through our transactions with our own unique environment—a restricted set of perceptions to handle the infinite variety of possible retinal images that we continually receive. On the basis of our experience, we make assumptions about how reality is constructed, and it is these assumptions that determine what we will perceive. Perception becomes a learned act of constructing reality to fit our assumptions about it.

We can think of this in terms of a gambling casino whose operator learns from experience what the odds are for different combinations of events. Usually the house has more information than it needs and it wins. In winning consistently, however, it learns nothing new. If it suddenly begins losing its bets and the events it depended on appear changed, new information must be sought. ●

Perception as signal identification. Still another approach is that of Eleanor Gibson (1969, 1970), who regards perception as a process not of *addition* to the sensory input but of *reduction,* in which nonessential elements—the "noise"—get filtered out and the essential elements of the signal are identified. This process enables the organism to learn what is predictable about the environment in order to deal with it.

According to Gibson, "Perception is extracting information from stimulation." From the limitless, variable flux of available stimulation, we must discover (or create) order in the apparent chaos and thus make our perceptual universe comprehensible and predictable. "Reduction of uncertainty," she believes, is itself intrinsically reinforcing and is thus the desired end-product in our search for the significant, invariant features in our environment. We must abstract the key elements, pulling the important details out from the context, filtering out irrelevant, random, noninformational aspects of the stimulation.

For effective perception in adulthood, Gibson suggests that children must learn: (a) to distinguish between stimuli that appear similar, (b) to recognize that changes in surface appearance do not always mean changes in identity, and (c) to identify the relationships, rules, and patterns that organize separate parts into wholes or allow wholes to be analyzed into units.

For example, to most young people the differences in the kind of music played by various rock groups are very clear. A teenager of the 1970s would hardly confuse a record by the Rolling Stones with one by The Who. But to the parents of the teenager, this distinction is usually unbelievable; both records are just "some loud rock music."

No matter what generation we belong to, there seem to be certain things about this world to which our parents are "blind"! But how often do teenagers and their parents listen attentively to the same kind of music? Certainly not very often. So when young people hear a group like The Who perform, their past experience makes them better able than their parents to distinguish specific features that identify that performance. On the other hand, the parents might be able to perceive differences between the music of Artie Shaw and that of Glenn Miller—which might sound indistinguishably syrupy to teenagers.

This is where Gibson's theory of differentiation becomes relevant..With experience, according to Gibson, similar stimuli begin to look or sound different as you begin to notice characteristics in one set that do not occur in the other. Gradually you identify important constancies and consistent relationships by which you can recognize them and tell them apart.

Repeated exposure is not sufficient, however, to ensure that such differentiation will take place. For example, it is quite possible that your parents have had enough *exposure* to the music you like to have learned to identify the different musical groups but have not paid attention to what they were hearing.

Drawing by W. Miller; © 1962 The New Yorker Magazine, Inc.

● We approach the world with certain assumptions about reality.

There are many other general and "mini" theories of perception, but these give you a feel for how basic one's theory of perception is to one's conception of what the task of psychology is. Psychologists who see perception as a combining of elements will investigate different problems from those tackled by psychologists who see perception as a matter of making new differentiations and identifying continuing structures. This is so whether their special research happens to be on learning, thinking, motivation, social behavior, or measuring individual differences.

Learning Perceptual Habits

Perceptual development in humans occurs along with the development of other systems — language, cognition, memory, and others. You will recall from the last chapter that in the view of developmental psychologist Jean Piaget, perceptual and cognitive development are not always complementary and at some stages are even antagonistic. The ability to grasp principles such as conservation, for example, may require that the child use concepts that contradict the sensory input of the moment. But because perception is so immediate, concrete, and apparently "real," it is difficult for the young child to learn to disregard it.

Cognitive development changes perception. At an early age, children are empiricists, taking what they see at face value and dealing only in actualities. In the play *The King and I*, the young prince of Siam refuses to believe in the existence of *snow* because he has never seen any. To this his father replies that there would be no need for education if we only believed in what we have seen.

Both our formal education and our day-to-day encounters with our environment soon teach us that there is more to this life than meets the eye. Thus our cognitive development turns us from empiricists to theorists dealing in symbols, abstractions, analyses, possibilities, and even fantasies. But to make this transformation requires freedom from the constraints imposed by having to be constantly perceptually vigilant, as in a threatening environment. There are no poets among battered children, nor philosophers among the starving.

In the process of normal perceptual development, we are taught by various means to ignore certain present perceptual features of a situation in order to make the transformations of it required to construct images of how it might look under other circumstances (from another vantage point or as it did look in the past or will look in the future or might be in some other configuration). It is indeed a difficult perceptual-cognitive task to learn to look at an object or situation and "see" what "could," "should," or "ought" to be there instead of what is there at the moment. This skill becomes finely developed in architects and designers, whose vocation it is to go beyond present stimulus information to visualize what an area will look like when it is transformed according to their design. Such an ability develops with age and experience.

In one study, children of different ages were shown four stimulus arrays, consisting of two single objects (eyeglasses and a flashlight) and two multiple objects (farm scenes). After they had viewed a stimulus array, eight colored photos of it taken from different perspectives were presented together. A doll was placed at different locations and the children were asked to pick the card showing the view that the doll had from each position. The children tried to perform this task under two conditions: with the original stimulus object still in view and with it shielded from view.

Six-year-old children could not select the correct cards under either condition; they were unable either to disregard what it "really" looked like to them when present or to visualize what it would look like from a different perspective. Eight- and ten-year-olds had trouble when the original stimuli were still in view but did better when they were out of sight and only conceptual cues could be used (Brodzinsky, Jackson, & Overton, 1972).

?thgir ot tfel morf daer uoy yhw rednow revE
An important example of the perceptual habits we develop through learning is our left-to-right movement in reading.

Hebb (1949) has hypothesized that repeated stimulation of a pattern of receptors keeps activating a particular set of neural cells and results in unequal training of certain parts of the retina. If this is true, readers of English text, who are trained to scan to the right for the next word, should develop greater sensitivity to stimuli just to the right of the point of focus. Indeed, experiments have shown that for American subjects (past the sixth grade) words presented briefly to the right of a fixation point are recognized better than words presented on the left. On the other hand, for subjects whose native language is Yiddish (where text is scanned to the left), more left-of-center words are recognized (Mishkin & Forgays, 1952).

But when you read English text, you read across a line of characters, not just single letters. What do you suppose results when the following cards are flashed (one at a time) on a screen for a fraction of a second and the subject is told to fixate on the center dot? Which letter will be most frequently recognized?

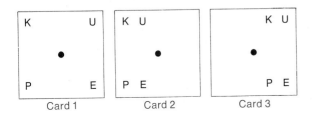

Card 1   Card 2   Card 3

Although K is close to the fixation point on only one card, it is recognized much more frequently than any other letter in all the cards. The least often recognized letter is E, with U and P intermediate. This pattern of results is to be expected from the learned attentional pattern of fluent readers who are set to start at the left end of the upper line and move toward the right (Heron, 1957).

In a more recent study, Sekuler, Tynan, and Levinson (1973), of Northwestern University, found that when two small squares or letters were flashed on a screen at the same time, subjects tended to report that the one on the left appeared first. When they were in fact presented a few milliseconds apart, subjects reported the sequence correctly 60 percent of the time when the left one was flashed first, but only 30 percent of the time when the right one was flashed first. The phenomenon was unrelated to whether the subject was right- or left-handed, and no sex differences were found among the 140 college students tested.

These findings demonstrate the influence of our left-to-right reading habits on the detection and interpretation of new experiences. They also offer hope for identifying and retraining children who have a reading problem known as *dyslexia.* Many of these children tend to see *d* as *b* or "was" as "saw" and to reverse the middle numbers of a series like 4-3-2-1.

Learning to See After Being Blind

More evidence for the need of experience in receiving and organizing sensory input basic to the normal development of the ability to perceive comes from studies of adults, blind all their lives, who have suddenly received their sight.

People born with cataracts (clouding of the lens) in both eyes are totally blind. The operation to correct this defect is quite simple. However, for one reason or another some of these people are left untreated until they are adults. Such people, of course, are completely without visual experience but fully as capable as any other adult with respect to most other abilities. In studying them immediately after the cataracts are removed, we have subjects who are at the earliest stage of visual development and yet able to communicate as adults about their experiences.

Von Senden (1932) compiled data on a number of such cases. Following their operations, the patients lacked the ability to identify even the simplest objects. Each patient needed many exposures to an object in a particular setting in order to be able to name it. Even then, the pa-

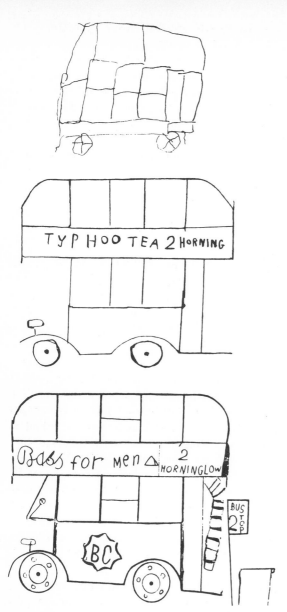

■ These drawings of English buses were made by S. B., Gregory's patient. The top drawing, made forty-eight days after the operation, contains only the details one would probably know by touch from having ridden the bus. The second drawing, made six months later, is more detailed, but the front of the bus, which a passenger would not know by touch, is still missing. The last drawing, made at the end of a year, shows added detail and the use of script lettering, but the front of the bus is still incomplete.

tient might be unable to recognize the same object in a different setting. The patients experienced just as much difficulty in identifying the faces of friends, relatives, and other persons of great importance in their lives as they did in identifying geometric figures. One exceptionally intelligent patient could identify only four or five faces two years after the operation.

Many of the distinctions we take for granted and assume are in anyone's perception these patients had to learn. For example, they could quickly learn to distinguish between circles and triangles but then might still be unable to distinguish triangles from squares. Apparently they had only recognized that the triangles had certain features the circles did not—perhaps corners. The importance of perceptual experiences at early stages of development is once again obvious.

The available evidence suggests that restoring sight to adults who have learned to live in a sightless world has not always been the blessing we might expect it to be. Many could see little at first and had difficulty learning to distinguish between simple shapes and objects; in fact, some never attained useful vision. A common occurrence in many of these cases was a reluctance to rely on the newly acquired sense of sight. Gregory (1966) has described the case of a fifty-two-year-old Englishman blinded at ten months of age.

"We saw in dramatic form the difficulty that S. B. [the patient] had in trusting and coming to use his vision whenever he had to cross the road. Before the operations, he was undaunted by traffic. He would cross alone, holding his arm or stick stubbornly before him, when the traffic would subside as the waters before Christ. But after the operation, it took two of us on either side to force him across a road: he was terrified as never before in his life." (Gregory, 1966, p. 197)

Eventually, S. B. would not bother to turn on the lights in the evening, but would sit alone in the (comforting) darkness. ■ In other cases, however, effective use of sensory processing has been regained by active, intelligent, well-educated patients.

Learning to Adapt to Contradictory Perceptions

Suppose one day when you awake everything is reversed, so when you reach to your left to turn off the alarm clock, you can't do so because it is actually to your right. Or, when you duck to the right to get out of the way of joggers you see running to your left, you smash into them although they were clearly on the left side of your visual field. Could you adapt to this distortion of your visual field? If you were a frog, the answer would be "no," but since you are a human with a modifiable nervous system you could.

A similar optical distortion was introduced in the visual field of frogs by surgically reversing their optic nerves (Sperry, 1945). They were unable to adapt their motor behavior successfully to fit this altered perception. Time after time they would strike out at an insect that appeared to be on the right, but since it was actually on the left, they never caught it.

In the 1890s, psychologist G. M. Stratton used himself as a subject in a similar experiment, reversing the visual field and also inverting it (what is down seems up and vice versa) by means of prism lenses that he wore continuously for several days. Despite initial headaches, anxiety, and many errors, he was eventually able to coordinate his bodily movements despite the apparently topsy-turvy world his vision provided. Effective visual-motor adaptation was also shown in more controlled studies done later by Ivo Kohler (1962). Indeed, some people reveal an amazing ability to adapt quickly to altered visual feedback. (See *P&L* Close-up at right.)

These visual-field reversal experiments confound three different processes, which more recent research is studying separately. They are: (a) disturbing the right-left and up-down orientation of the visual field; (b) creating a discordance between vision and other senses; and (c) disturbing visual-motor coordination.

It has been found that when the visual information we are receiving about the location of an object is different from the auditory information we are getting (a bird is heard to sing in one place but is seen in another place), there is not a compromise but a one-sided solution. One of the modalities preempts the other as "evidence" of where the stimulus really is. For example, when visual feedback and auditory feedback are

Close-up
The Jim Plunkett Story

To demonstrate the reliance of motor performance on visual cues, one of your authors asked Stanford Psych 1 student Jim Plunkett (later to be NFL Rookie of the Year) to serve as the subject in a test of football-throwing accuracy.

First, Plunkett threw the football with his customary pinpoint accuracy to a moving receiver at the end of a 50-foot stage. Then he was fitted with goggles on which were glued prisms that displaced the visual field 20 degrees to the right. On his next throw, he missed the target—as the class gasped in amazement. But with only one more practice attempt he was able to correct the misinformation provided by the distorted visual feedback and hit his target perfectly—to cheers from the class, and boos for the seemingly defeated professor.

After ten more perfect trials, the professor removed the goggles, returning the football star to his "normal" state. "Would you please throw just once more to the receiver, just to be sure you can?" requested the professor. With a disdainful snicker, Plunkett raised his powerful arm and fired the football across the stage—missing the target by 20 degrees on the left side!

Did this compelling psychology lesson enhance Plunkett's ability to adapt to visual distortions on the field, thus contributing to Stanford's Rose Bowl victory that year? The professor would like to think so.

discordant by less than 30 degrees, the direction of the object is determined by the visual information, and the auditory information is adjusted to it. This phenomenon is known as *visual dominance* or *visual capture* (Pick, Warren, & Hay, 1969).

Most current investigations of perceptual adaptation to distortion center on the problem of adaptation to visual-motor discordance in passive subjects who wear prisms that displace the visual field to one side (about 15 degrees) and attempt to point to visual targets at arm's length (Held, 1965). While ostensibly a simple task, eye-hand coordination involves many components: the stimulus target, its image on the retina, the position of the eyes in the head, the position of the head on the body, the position of the arm on the body, and the position of the finger in relation to the target. These components form a complex interacting system requiring coding of multiple sources of information, integration, and then coordination (Howard, 1971).

Prism adaptation in this task occurs when subjects actively move their arms, but not when their arms are moved for them. Experience with self-produced movement is thus believed to be critical for learning to adapt to the visual-motor discordance. Confirmation has come from an experiment in which hypnotized subjects who were told they would feel no sensation in their target-indicating arm were unable to adapt to a prism displacement. Control subjects who were hypnotized but received no instructions regarding sensation in their arm adapted readily to the prism displacement (Wallace & Garrett, 1973). These results fit with those of Held's studies of kittens (p. 254).

Although prism displacement is an artificial procedure for studying discrepancy, such research deals with a most important issue: how we all learn to reach and touch and manipulate what is out there in our physical environment on the basis of the experience of it that our eyes and brain mechanisms provide.

Factors Determining What We Perceive

It seems clear that the act of perceiving involves both a complex physiological processing of the stimulus signal energy and a psychological processing of the information received. Thus research on perception has tended to fall into three broad categories, according to the primary focus of the investigators: (a) an emphasis on the *stimulus* determinants of perception, such as configuration, complexity, signal strength, signal-to-noise relationships, and so on; (b) an emphasis on our *physical apparatus* for detecting the signals, at both the receptor and neural levels; and (c) an emphasis on *other factors in the individual* that affect perception, such as prior training history, cultural background, and motivational or personality factors. The first and second we have already examined. The third we will investigate in this section.

The Structuring of Perception

The basic tenet of the Gestaltists — that organization is part of any perception, not something added after elements are sensed — has been generally accepted. Several aspects of this organization have been determined.

Figure-ground relations. We tend to organize the perceived flux in such a way as to hold changes and differences to a minimum while maintaining unity and wholeness. Most basic in this process is our tendency to perceive a figure against a background. This seems to happen automatically, whether we are looking at the objects around us or at clouds or tea leaves.

Compared to the ground, the figure appears to: (a) have shape, (b) be nearer, (c) be thing-like, (d) be more vivid, (e) be more substantial in color, (f) own the common contour between them, (g) have the ground extend behind it. Some of the factors that determine what the "figure" will be are summarized on page 263. ▲

Camouflage is a familiar example of the use of these principles to change the figure seen. Whether practiced by nature to conceal prey from predators or by armies (for the same pur-

▲ WHY DO WE SEE THE FIGURES WE DO?

1. Similarity

Similar elements are seen as belonging to each other more than to other elements equally close but less similar. In this figure, do you see columns of Zs and Rs or rows of alternating letters?

```
Z   R   Z   R   Z   R
Z   R   Z   R   Z   R
Z   R   Z   R   Z   R
Z   R   Z   R   Z   R
Z   R   Z   R   Z   R
Z   R   Z   R   Z   R
```

2. Proximity

Elements that are physically close are seen as belonging to each other more than to similar elements that are farther away. Below you see pairs of ZRs, not RZs.

ZR   ZR   ZR   ZR

Proximity can also make things look more alike than they really are. The same figure that looks like an antelope when seen among antelopes looks like a bird in the company of other birds.

3. Closure

We tend to perceive incomplete figures as if they were complete. We see the line as a circle with a break in it and the irregular fragments as an animal.

4. Continuation

Elements are seen as belonging to each other if they appear to be a continuation of the direction of previous elements. The curving line is seen as one figure, the line with the right angles as another figure.

5. Common fate

Elements that move in the same direction are seen as belonging to each other. When alternate dancers in a ballet line step forward and make the same motion, we see them as a unit.

6. Reversible figure and ground

Occasionally a stimulus pattern is so organized that more than one figure-ground relationship may be perceived. When these conflict, they alternate in consciousness. In the example shown here, when the vase becomes "figure," the black ground seems to extend behind it; the reverse occurs when the two faces are seen as figures.

7. Good figure

The nervous system seems to prefer regular, simple forms. We see two overlapping squares here instead of a triangle and two irregular forms, equally possible from the sensory input.

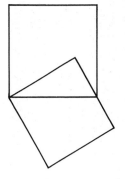

pose), camouflage is successful when it reduces the prominence of the figure cues, allowing the figure to be "lost" in the ground.

Not only do we create the best figure we can from the sensory information supplied us; we often tend to fill in missing parts, or see an almost circular figure as more circular than it is, or in other ways make the figure more stable or regular or complete than the sensory information provides for.

We tend to perceive configurations even when the elements taken individually bear no relationship at all to the composite that "emerges" from them. This is readily seen in the ingenious computer-generated composite photo of Quasimodo's gargoyle that is on Notre Dame Cathedral. ◆

◆ By means of a computer, the brightness level of each area of an ordinary photograph is "translated" into a particular micropattern. The resulting picture is a mass of confusing detail when seen at close range—but hold the book at arm's length and watch Quasimodo's gargoyle and the buildings of Paris come into view.

Combining cues to perceive depth. Among the cues by which we perceive depth are those based on distinctness, linear perspective, texture, light and shadow, relative position, and known standards. All contribute to the fund of data that are organized into a meaningful whole in perception.

1. *Atmospheric perspective.* Because of dust and smoke in the air, objects a long way off may appear to be blurred and indistinct in outline. Details we know are there may not be observable. The extent of the dimming depends on the distance, and we have long since learned to interpret distance in these terms. In fact, when the characteristic condition of the air changes, we often judge distances incorrectly. For example, a person reared in a smoky industrial city will greatly underestimate the distance of objects seen through clear mountain air. A tenderfoot on a ranch will amuse the old hands by announcing that he or she is going to "ride to the hill and back before breakfast," only to learn that the "hill" is really a mountain some fifty miles distant.

2. *Linear perspective.* Objects appear smaller and closer together as they become more distant. Railroad tracks or the edges of a highway appear to meet on the horizon. Uniformly spaced objects such as telephone poles appear to be spaced more closely as they recede into the distance. These phenomena of linear perspective are used by artists to represent distance in pictures.

3. *Texture.* Closely related to linear perspective is the factor of texture. On any surface not perpendicular to the line of sight, the texture elements appear denser as the surface recedes. Thus texture is an adjunct to linear perspective, operating in situations where there are no converging parallel lines to give us clues.

4. *Light and shadow.* When light strikes an irregular surface, as for example the human face, certain parts are brightly illuminated and others are cast in shadow. The appearance of these shadows tells us much about the depth of the parts concerned. The artist uses shading and highlights to convey the notion of depth on a two-dimensional canvas.

5. *Relative position.* When two objects are in the same line of vision, the nearer one conceals all or part of the farther one. Near objects usually appear at the bottom of the two-dimensional field of vision, distant objects at the top.

6. *Known standards.* Once we are familiar with the size or shape of an object, it can be used as a standard for the height of other objects. This cue is, of course, critical in establishing object constancy.

The perception of depth also involves using cues derived from changes in the lens of the eye, which bulges slightly when we look at close objects and flattens for looking at distant ones. Binocular vision greatly aids depth perception because of the extra feedback information provided by the *convergence* of the eyes as they focus on an object near the observer. In addition, the slightly different images we get from the two eyes (called *retinal disparity*) help us perceive depth and distance. We interpret distance by automatically comparing and integrating these two images—which permits inspection "around" contours.

Using cues in sound perception. People are able to locate the position of sounding objects in space in terms of distance and direction. This ability to locate sounds is of considerable adaptive value in modern life. For example, in crossing a busy street, your very life may depend on your knowing accurately the position of an approaching automobile.

Your ability to localize sounds is due almost entirely to your possession of two ears located at different points in space.

1. A sound coming from an object at the left of the head strikes the left ear before the right one. This difference in time can be very short, but it tells you from which side the sound is coming.

2. Sound waves coming from the left stimulate the left ear more strongly than they do the right ear.

3. Sound waves, as we saw earlier in this chapter, consist of areas of high and low pressure. Since the two ears are at different points in space, a sound wave will be in different phases as it stimulates the two ears. Sound waves travel very slowly as compared with light waves, with the result that differences in phase in sound waves are appreciable.

We can use these cues to direction only when sounds come from one side or the other. Sounds directly in front of us cannot easily be distinguished from those above or behind us because the stimulation reaching the two ears is nearly identical.

Culture, Experience, and Personal Motives

"Of *course* perception is dependent on past experience," you say. But just *what part* of the vague term "past experience," and how can you prove it? The many attempts at such a proof have studied the effects of broad cultural experiences, general perceptual habits, differential training, instructional sets, and manipulated influences on psychophysical detection.

Cultural experience. Kenge's perception of the distant buffalo as insects was a dramatic example of the effect of our cultural experience on what we perceive. To the extent that perception depends on assumptions based on past experience with the environment, there should be many differences in the perceptions of people from different cultural environments. Such differences should show up in the way they perceive illusions.

Evidence of differences in perception of illusions comes from a cross-cultural study of 1,878 persons from fourteen non-European cultures, plus an American sample. The investigators hypothesized that there should be cultural differences in susceptibility to two different types of illusions—the horizontal-vertical (Pinocchio's nose) and the Müller-Lyer (p. 236). They reasoned that experience with broad plains and open vistas should increase *susceptibility to the horizontal-vertical illusion, whereas the absence of such experience (as with forest dwellers) should* decrease *it. In contrast, those living in a "carpentered world," where angles are important and prominent, should be more susceptible* to the *Müller-Lyer illusion than those living in an environment such as that of the Zulus, where huts are circular and regular angles are rare. Their data supported these predictions (Segall, Campbell, & Herskovits, 1966).*

Differential training. To illustrate how even brief training can influence your perception, perform the following experiment. Carefully examine for a minute the woman's face in the illustration below. At the same time, have a friend look closely at the face on page 268, which *you should not see.* Then flip to page 271 and both call out, as soon as you can, what kind of face you see there. ■

When a similar experiment was first performed in the laboratory many years ago, the experimenter found that perceptual preparation with one of the first pictures was very effective in determining what the response would be to the ambiguous figure, whereas verbal preparation had no effect. He also found that when subjects saw only the ambiguous picture, twice as many of them reported seeing the young woman

■ VIEW I

in it as the old one. With supposedly comparable past experience, other characteristics—perhaps in the stimulus pattern itself—tipped the balance between which possibility was seen (Leeper, 1935).

On your mark, get set . . . A *set,* as the term implies, is a readiness to perceive or respond in a certain way. A set can be based on expectancies resulting from past experience or can be established by instructions from the experimenter (or anyone else whose edicts you take seriously). Thus a given set can be a momentary condition or a long-lasting part of your basic approach to situations.

The influence of sets on perception has been extensively studied in the laboratory. As Floyd Allport wrote some years ago (1955), "Sets tend, other things being equal, to determine physiologically what objects are to be perceived, the speed or readiness of their perception, and within limits, the content and vividness of the percept" (p. 241).

Perceptual discrimination can be increased by instructions that prepare subjects for the classes of objects or attributes on which they will have to report. In addition, such instructions can be effective in "priming" the response channels—making one response more likely than another, especially to an ambiguous stimulus pattern. While research has clearly shown that sets do affect reported perceptual judgments, it is less clear at what level the effect occurs—whether it is actual perceptual sensitivity that has changed or attention, memory, or motivation to respond.

Interests, motives, and self-defense. It has become amply apparent, especially with human subjects, that there is no one-to-one correspondence between stimulus and perception because in between is an organism with motives, needs, values, attitudes, expectations, and emotions, all of which can influence perception in important ways.

The study that began the controlled laboratory research on emotional factors in perception had a serious methodological flaw in it. Can you detect it?

A group of thirty ten-year-olds were tested with an apparatus consisting of a wooden box with a screen at one end and a knob at the lower right-hand corner. By turning the knob, the children could vary the diameter of the circle of light shining on the screen. Two groups of children, one rich and the other poor, were asked to match the size of the circle of light to the size of coins of various denominations; a control group matched the light to the size of cardboard disks.

The coins, socially valued objects, were judged larger in size than the disks. Furthermore, the poor group overestimated the size of the coins more than did the rich group (Bruner & Goodman, 1947).

This study led to considerable controversy because critics were quick to point out that there was no proof that values and needs were the determining factors, since other variables such as intelligence and past experiences with coins were not controlled. However, one group of investigators appears to have overcome these objections by the use of hypnosis to make people "poor" or "rich."

Before being hypnotized, middle-class subjects adjusted the size of the light spot until it looked equal to the actual size of each of three coins—a nickel, a dime, and a quarter. When made to forget their real life histories and given "poor" life histories under hypnosis, the same individuals made settings consistently larger than the ones they had made in the normal state. When given "rich" life histories while hypnotized, they made consistently smaller settings than previously.

The investigators concluded that their perceptions were indeed affected by needs and values, since their prior experience with money was identical. The effectiveness of the "poor" and "rich" life histories in inducing different needs and values was further shown by the fact that when "poor," the subjects sat erect and worked with great care, whereas when "rich," they slouched in their chairs and worked rapidly but condescendingly (Ashley, Harper, & Runyan, 1951). ●

Perceptual accentuation of a valued characteristic was also indicated in an "I like VW" study of owners of Volkswagen cars. Those who valued owning their VW tended to perceive it as smaller than those who were indifferent about it (Stayton & Weiner, 1961).

By using a measure of content analysis of children's drawings at different times of the year, investigators have discovered that Santa Claus drawings made before Christmas were bigger than those made after the holiday. This was not a general euphoria effect but a "Santa-specific" one since only drawings of Santa got bigger as his coming approached (Solley & Haigh, 1959; Sechrest & Wallace, 1964). In another carefully controlled study, the avoidance motive of fear seems to be implicated in the finding that the average size of drawings of witches *decreased* at Halloween (Craddick, 1967).

The active role of emotional and motivational factors in perception is shown in the fact that individuals tend to misperceive stimuli that are socially taboo and threatening and to require longer recognition time than for neutral stimuli.

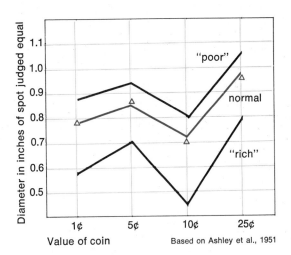

● **NEEDS AND VALUES INFLUENCE PERCEPTION**
This figure shows the sizes of white spots judged to be equal in size to the four coins at the start of the experiment in the normal state and under "poor" and "rich" conditions when hypnotized. Triangles indicate the actual sizes of the coins.

The first study to offer support for this hypothesis presented college subjects with seven "critical" words (such as "belly," "raped," "bitch") interspersed among eleven other, more innocuous, words. The duration of exposure was controlled by a tachistoscope, *a device that projected the words on a screen for a fraction of a second. A longer duration of exposure was required for identification of the critical words than for the neutral ones. In addition, the greater galvanic skin response (a change in the electrical resistance of the skin) to the taboo words during the time interval* before *they were reported was taken as evidence for an unconscious* perceptual defense *mechanism (McGinnies, 1949).*

The intriguing explanation of perceptual defense was subjected to criticism because the methodology of this study permitted three equally plausible alternative explanations. The differences in recognition thresholds could result either from differential sensitivity to taboo words because of their antisocial meaning as claimed, or from the fact that they are less fre-

quently seen under normal viewing conditions. Or it could be that the effect was not a perceptual one at all, but one of response inhibition: maybe the subjects perceived the "bad" words as rapidly as the "nice" ones, but felt inhibited about reporting them publicly.

Several subsequent studies helped support the perceptual defense hypothesis. Threat and nonthreat words were printed in booklets where they were totally blurred on the top page, but became decreasingly blurred (more signal in relation to noise) with each page turned. Threat words required more pages turned before they were recognized. This was true even though the frequency of the words was controlled and no public response was necessary. The same effect was found when subjects were alerted to the impending threat words and when the sex of the subject and the experimenter were the same (Cowen & Beier, 1954).

In another experiment the frequency of the words was again controlled, but this time they were presented in pairs. That is, a "pretask" word, sometimes taboo and sometimes neutral, was presented for an interval of 2 seconds, and then the "task" word, always a neutral word, was presented for .01 second. If it was not recognized, the pretask word was again exposed for 2 seconds, followed by the task word for .02 seconds. This was done until the task word was finally recognized. When the pretask word was a taboo word, the threshold for recognition of the neutral task word associated with it tended to be higher than when the pretask word was neutral (McGinnies & Sherman, 1952).

Even when viewing conditions are good and stimulus patterns are distinct, our perceptions may be distorted by our wishes, fears, habits, prejudices, and other internal factors. When viewing conditions are bad and the stimulus is ambiguous, perception is correspondingly more heavily influenced by internal processes. Clinicians take advantage of this tendency when they ask patients to react to ambiguous pictures or even meaningless inkblots. Responses under these conditions can give valuable clues concerning the patients' motivations and problems.

■ VIEW II

Extrasensory Perception

During the space flight of Apollo 14, Captain Edgar Mitchell communicated with Mission Control by means of radio telemetry, but he claims also to have secretly communicated with other people on the earth by means of ESP — extrasensory perception. From his space capsule he sent a series of thought waves to four contacts on earth. He reports that of 200 guesses they made of what he sent, 51 of them agreed with his notes of what he was attempting to transmit.

Do you believe in the existence of ESP? Do you think that people can communicate without using any of the known senses or measurable channels of communication? Recent surveys indicate that much of the public does believe so, but psychologists and scientists are divided sharply on this issue. Some believe "that the available evidence for ESP is sufficient to establish its reality beyond all reasonable doubt" (R. A. McConnell, 1971); others maintain that "a great deal of experimental work has failed to provide a clear case for the existence of ESP" (Hansel, 1966).

How can it be that there are such extreme differences in scientific opinion regarding ESP? It is not because the disbelievers do not take it seriously. Just the opposite; they recognize that transmission of information without known transmission channels would entail revolutionary changes in thinking about communication, causality, and the power of the human mind. A physicist tells us:

"If ESP is indeed a fact, then this is the most important fact in modern physics, for to explain it requires the assumption of a new kind of force — a force presently unknown to physicists. The only alternative is to abandon causality altogether, which would entail an even greater revolution in science." (Rothman, 1970, p. 280)

But it is precisely these revolutionary implications that excite the imagination of adherents of ESP. Let us here outline some characteristics of ESP and related phenomena, present some typical experiments designed to demonstrate its existence, and briefly review the bases on which they have been criticized.

The Field of Parapsychology

Parapsychology is the modern term that encompasses organized scientific investigations into psychical phenomena. The term covers the following quite distinct types.

ESP stands for acts of perception or cognition that are independent of (known) physiological activity in the sense organs. There are three kinds of ESP:

1. *Telepathy* ("mind reading") consists of one person's knowing a private event occurring at a given moment in someone else's thoughts without any observable means of communication between them.

2. *Clairvoyance* ("second sight") is knowledge of the characteristics of a given object, person, or event without the use of the senses.

3. *Precognition* ("divination" or "premonition") is knowledge of the future — either of another person's future thoughts (*precognitive telepathy*) or of the character of future events (*precognitive clairvoyance*).

A fourth related category involves something more than just acquisition of information. It is *psychokinesis* (*PK*, sometimes referred to as "levitation"). PK is control of objects and events (like the fall of the dice or the turn of a card) by an act of thought or will. ◆ (p. 270)

The acknowledged leader of this discipline is J. B. Rhine of Duke University, now head of the Foundation for Research on the Nature of Man. Rhine was a botanist who turned to psychical research many years ago after hearing a lecture on spiritualism by Sir Arthur Conan Doyle (the creator of Sherlock Holmes). Rhine first went to study ESP at Harvard, where psychical research flourished during the 1920s under the influence of William McDougall and Gardner Murphy. In the past twenty years, largely through his editorial efforts, the *Journal of Parapsychology* has published over 4000 pages of research. Many areas of psychology are widely accepted with much less of a research base, so why is the available evidence not convincing to the skeptics?

Typical Designs for Research

In a typical telepathy experiment, an *agent*, or sender, looks at one of five symbols on a set of ESP cards and a receiver, or *percipient*, "guesses" which of the symbols is being looked at on each of 200 trials. If the guesses were completely random, a correct guess, or hit, would occur in one of every five trials. In over 200 trials then, by chance alone the receiver should have 40 hits. ESP is demonstrated by tests of statistically significant deviations from this chance performance.

In a clairvoyance experiment there is no sender; the receiver guesses the identity of each card in repeatedly shuffled five-symbol sets. This becomes a precognition experiment when the receiver guesses the identity of the cards before they are shuffled and laid out. In a typical PK study, the subject tries to influence on which side of a line mechanically dropped dice will fall.

In many of these experiments, the results indicate that some subjects do score significantly above chance expectations. In addition, most of these studies utilize elaborate control procedures. So why is ESP still not regarded as "proven"?

To answer this question we must be reminded of some basic principles of the scientific method outlined in the first chapter of this text. Research never *proves* anything. If properly conducted, it allows us to reject alternative explanations for the phenomenon while encouraging confidence in the likelihood of a particular explanation. Secondly, the mere presence of control groups and control procedures in an experiment does not guarantee that the crucial biasing event was, in fact, controlled. Finally, the true scientist is motivated by the unknown, by unexplained events in life, but this curiosity is tempered by skepticism: "I believe anything is possible, but nothing is certain until I have measured it under conditions that can be reproduced by others even more skeptical than I."

Criteria for Acceptable Evidence

ESP, if a valid phenomenon, would of course demand major revisions in fundamental thought in psychology, physics, and biology. But neither acceptance nor rejection of ESP can be a matter of faith, philosophical beliefs, or personal opinion—it must rest quite simply on the soundness of the *method* used to assess its operation. This is true of all phenomena, but becomes more imperative as the consequences of accepting an idea become greater.

The following methodological considerations indicate the conditions under which a disbeliever in ESP would be forced to accept the evidence in its favor and suggest some of the problems with research conducted up to now:

1. If the results obtained could be reasonably attributed to *anything* other than ESP alone, the data are not adequate evidence. The ESP researcher must not only eliminate the usual sources of error, such as minimal sensory cues, mental habits, response preferences of sender

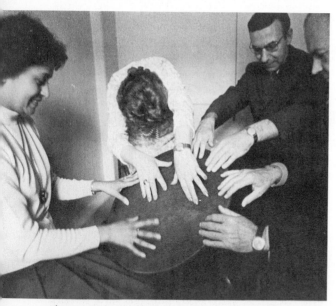

◆ Two professional mediums and two untrained observers attempt to produce a PK effect by levitating a small table. Although the table never rose completely off the floor, an observer reports that it did rock vigorously and "walk" across the room (Gatland, 1973).

and receiver, and recording errors, but must also remove the *opportunity* for either conscious deception by the subject or cheating or trickery by the experimenter. The research design must make it *impossible* to attribute the results to such biasing factors.

For example, there was a classic ESP experiment (the Pratt-Woodruff experiment) of which Rhine immodestly claimed, "In the entire history of psychology no experiment has ever been carried out with such elaborate controls against all possible error" (1954, p. 557). Yet it was possible for a critic (Hansel, 1966) to discover several conceivable sources of error and cheating as a result of the design.

2. High-scoring subjects must yield comparable success scores when tested in different laboratories by independent experimenters.

3. The same research paradigm must be able to generate similar results when used with the same subjects at different times or by different investigators.

4. It should be possible to devise research procedures that do more than infer ESP from the laws of probability (Gardner, 1957). If ESP exists, it must be a variable function, whose extent can be assessed in those who have it and can be related to other variables of which it is a function.

For instance, the presence of PK is testable by means of a *radiometer*, an apparatus you have probably seen in novelty stores. It looks like a miniature weather vane, consisting of four arms with one black and one reflecting side, delicately balanced within a glass bulb. The arms rotate as they absorb and reflect heat. The instrument can be made so sensitive that it can detect the heat of a candle flame a half mile away. It can also be constructed to measure the extent of the force or energy applied to it and thus should be able to reveal the alleged power of psychokinesis.

While skeptical scientists await more compelling evidence for ESP, many a college student as well as that ubiquitous "person-in-the-street" has gone beyond believing in traditional ESP, to believing in "astral energy" from outer space and other far-out psychic events. It is easy to see why people *want* to believe in parapsychol-

ogy. At one level, the phenomena are extensions of the goals of every individual: telepathy and clairvoyance would mean greater understanding; precognition would increase predictability; psychokinesis would be a form of control. And then, there is also the wish that there be something more to us humans than what we appear to be, than what can be measured on instruments, distilled in test tubes, and "dreamt of in your philosophy." On the other hand, the fear of more conservative scientists is that if the door were once opened to legitimize unseen, unmeasurable ESP forces, then there would be no limit to the unnatural; "sinister forces" and even witchcraft could be invoked to explain natural phenomena and human behavior. As an instance of the basis of such fears, we cite the case of a former physician from Michigan whose new specialty is "psychic vampires"—people who "suck up" the psychic energy fields of other individuals. He has been quoted as saying, "I've seen patients die 30 minutes after being visited by a vampire in the hospital" (*San Francisco Chronicle,* Dec. 15, 1973).

ESP is a curious phenomenon, deserving more rigorous investigation by skeptical researchers. But it is not likely that such researchers will become convinced in a hurry.

■ VIEW III

Chapter Summary

It is through our perceptual processes that we give stability and continuity to objects and events in the environment. Perception involves the analysis, organization, and integration of sensory input from environmental occurrences and internal conditions. Theorists differ as to whether the most important aspect of perception is reality as it exists in the world itself or as it exists in our minds. Some say it is our interpretation of what we perceive that is most important.

Phenomenal absolutism is the belief that perceptions are direct and accurate renditions of qualities that exist in the environment. But it is not always easy to know when the *phenomenal reality* (our perceptual experience) is a *veridical* (true) representation of *objective reality* (what is really there). *Illusions* dramatize the extent to which perception may trick us; they surprise us because, for the most part, our perceptual system does such a dependable job of providing us with a constant, predictable environment despite constantly changing retinal images. It does so precisely because it is a *mediated* process of drawing conclusions about stimulus input rather than a matter of one-to-one relationships between stimulus and perception. Under ordinary circumstances we can depend on both the accuracy and the constancy of perception. For example, unless we lack distance cues, the perceived size of an object is in accordance with the *distal* (actual) stimulus rather than the *proximal* (retinal) stimulus.

Stimulus energy from the environment is detected by organs composed of *receptor cells* that can discern the type, location, and intensity of stimuli. The process by which stimulus energy is converted into a nerve impulse and its intensity detected is called *transduction*. The *threshold*, or *limen*, is generally taken as the strength of stimulus that can barely be detected half the time. *Psychophysical scaling methods* establish the relationships between given intensities and resulting sensations. The *just noticeable difference (jnd)* is the stimulus increase required to produce a barely noticeable difference in sensation three fourths of the time. According to the *Weber-Fechner Law*, this is a constant proportion of the standard stimulus over most of the range of intensities. Stevens has further shown that equal stimulus ratios produce equal subjective ratios.

The various senses for which we have receptors include vision, hearing, pressure, pain, cold, warmth, balance, position, taste, and smell. Of these, vision and hearing are the most important in humans and the most accurate.

The eye has two separate systems of receptors: the *rods*, sensitive to very dim light but not to color, and the *cones*, specialized for daylight and color vision. Cones are most numerous in the *fovea*, the area of sharpest vision; there are no rods in the fovea. Light passes through several layers of nerve fibers until it reaches these receptor cells, which translate it into messages carried over the *bipolar* and *ganglion cells* to the *optic nerve* and thence to the visual area of the brain, the *occipital cortex*. At the point where the optic nerve leaves the retina, there is a *blind spot*.

Three types of *photopigments* in the cones absorb blue, green, or red light, respectively. Four types of *opponent-process cells* in the *lateral geniculate nucleus* add together the information reaching them and pass it on to the *visual cortex*, producing color vision. The perception of form, pattern, and movement depends on specialized cells called *feature analyzers* that are activated only by certain *trigger features* —stimuli in a given spatial orientation or location. Cells further up in the hierarchy of the nervous system are specialized for more complex trigger features.

The central task of visual and other perceptual systems is the search for *invariant properties* in the stimulus field. For the sake of economy, perceptual systems must have ways of reducing *redundancy*. This, too, is accomplished by hierarchical processing.

In our perception of sound, alternating pressure differences *(sound waves)* enter the *outer ear,* are transmitted through the *middle ear* to the *cochlea* in the *inner ear,* and there are translated into nerve impulses. Both a *volley theory* and a *place theory* seem necessary to explain the coding of sounds.

The anatomical structures of most sense organs are physically complete before birth, but it is difficult to determine the extent to which they are actually functional. Some sensitivity to touch and to temperature changes is apparently present before birth, but sensitivity to pain is weak. Postnatal environmental stimulation seems necessary if the tactile and pain senses are to develop normally. Both taste and smell are well developed at birth.

Hearing seems to be less well developed in the newborn than other senses, but there is some evidence that it may function before birth. Some ability to perceive form, and possibly color, is present at birth, but further development of the visual structures is necessary. Evidence suggests that some factors in visual perception are innate, whereas others are learned. Opportunities to practice coordination of perceptual and motor skills are essential to adequate sensory-motor development.

Theories about perception include: (a) theories asserting that we learn to have complex perceptions by *associating* simple ones, and that trained introspection is needed to eliminate additives from learning and identify the "original" sensory experience; (b) the Gestalt theory that even prior to learning, perception provides us with *patterns* and relationships; (c) the theory that perception is based on our assumptions about reality and our *transactions* with the environment; and finally, (d) the theory that learning to perceive is essentially not a process of addition but a process of *reduction* in which we make new differentiations and identify continuing structures.

Learning plays an important part in perception. In the course of cognitive development, we cease to be empiricists who take everything they see at face value, and learn, instead, to deal with symbols and abstractions and visualize the results. In learning to read, for example, we develop perceptual habits of scanning from left to right. The importance of experience in perception is seen in studies of blind persons who gain sight in adulthood. Such persons acquire with great difficulty, if at all, many of the perceptual abilities, such as recognition of objects, that we take for granted. Amazingly, it is not difficult to adapt to an artificially distorted perceptual field if sensory-motor feedback is not impaired.

Factors determining what figure is seen include *proximity, likeness, closure, common fate,* and *context.* "Good" figures are simple and regular; a figure becomes more "good" as it becomes more predictable from knowledge of any of its parts.

Cues that we use in depth perception include *atmospheric perspective, linear perspective, texture, light and shadow, relative position, known standards, convergence of the eyes,* and *retinal disparity.* Differences in *arrival time, intensity,* and *phase* of sound waves enable us to locate the directions of sounds unless they are at some point equidistant from the two ears; we cannot locate sounds made directly in front of, above, or behind us.

Both *cultural experience* and *personal experience* affect perception. *Set, interests, motives,* and *expectations* also affect perception, often dramatically. Internal, organismic factors have a greater effect on perception as stimulus characteristics become more ambiguous and open to alternative interpretations.

Parapsychology is the scientific study of psychical phenomena, such as *extrasensory perception (ESP).* ESP includes *telepathy* ("mind reading"), *clairvoyance* ("second sight"), *precognition,* and *psychokinesis.* Precisely because of the dramatic impact acceptance of ESP would have on our understanding of the world, rigorously controlled research in this area is a necessity.

Psychology of the Eyewitness
Robert Buckhout Brooklyn College, C.U.N.Y.

If you see an auto accident or witness a murder, and are then asked to describe what you saw, there is no one who can create an instant replay in slow motion for you. You depend upon your memory with all its limitations—a fact which may be of minor importance in your ordinary daily activities. If you are unreliable, if you shade the truth in describing what you saw, it matters little. But when you are called in as a witness to a crime, the situation escalates in importance. A person's life or an institution's reputation may be at stake. You may be asked to report what you saw in excruciating detail as if you were a videotape recorder.

In court, the written transcript contains your replay of the events. The prosecutor will attempt to show that you have perfect recall; the defense attorney will try to show, by cross-examining you vigorously, that your "tape recorder" is defective. The stakes are high because in modern courts eyewitness testimony is more highly valued than alibi testimony or "circumstantial" evidence. Uncritical acceptance of eyewitness testimony seems to be based on the fallacious notion that the human observer is a perfect recording device—that everything that passes before his or her eyes is recorded and can be "pulled out" by sharp questioning or "refreshing one's memory." In a categorical statement, which psychologists rarely make, I argue that this is *impossible*—human perception and memory function effectively by being selective. A human being has no particular need for perfect recall; perception and memory are decision-making processes affected by the totality of a person's abilities, background, environment, attitudes, motives, and beliefs, and by the methods used in testing recollection of people and events.

As I work in criminal courts, I'm aware of a fundamental clash of conceptions—the nineteenth-century vs. the twentieth-century view of a person. The nineteenth-century view—embodied in psychophysics—asserted a scientific parallel between the mechanisms of the physical world and the mechanisms of the brain. The courts in the United States accept this nineteenth-century thinking quite readily—as does much of the public. However, modern psychologists have developed a conception of a whole human being with an information processing mechanism which is far more complex than the one in the nineteenth-century model. Unfortunately, research psychologists, who began by studying practical problems (functionalism), have become more esoteric in their research and less visible in the real world.

I regard the human observer as an active rather than a passive observer of the environment; motivated by (a) a desire to be accurate in extracting meaning from the overabundance of information which affects the senses; and (b) a desire to live up to the expectations of others and stay in their good graces, a factor which makes the eye, the ear, and other senses social as well as physical organs.

In our laboratory experiments on the physical capabilities of the eye and the ear, we speak of an "ideal observer," by which we mean a subject who would respond cooperatively to lights and tones with unbiased ears and eyes, much like a machine. However, the ideal observer does not exist. In other words, the "ideal observer" is a convenient fiction. Great effort and expense are put into the design of laboratories to provide an "ideal physical environment" free of distractions to enable the observer to concentrate. Such ideal environments can be approached only in a laboratory; in the real world they are seldom, if ever, found. The nonmachine-like human observer copes reasonably effectively in uncontrolled environments with a perceptual capability which fits the nature of a social being. The witness to a crime is engaged in what can be described as "one-shot perception."

In a machine we would expect that what comes out (the report) would be a direct function of what goes in (the input or stimulus). However, human perception can be characterized in terms of the phrase: "The whole is greater than the sum of the parts." This characterization reflects the ability of the human observer to take the fragments of information to which he or she has time to pay attention (i.e., actively reduce the information), and to reach conclusions based on his or her prior experience, familiarity, biases, expectancy, faith, desire to appear certain, etc. Most human observers, for example, look at the moon and see a sphere—despite their inability to verify the shape of the unseen side. The conclusion, in psychological terms, is a decision efficiently arrived at and independent of the physical evidence which is incomplete.

As an eyewitness to crime, the fallible human observer is usually in a less than ideal environment. He or she is subject to factors which I believe inherently limit a person's ability to give a complete account of what took place or to identify the persons involved with complete accuracy.

The thrust of my research has been to learn about and describe (in a form useful to the criminal justice system) those factors which affect both the *recall* of events by a witness and his or her subsequent ability to make an *identification*. I've ventured into the courtroom in some 30 criminal trials discussing the following factors as they relate to eye-witness accounts.

1. Stress. "I could never forget what he looked like!" This common statement expresses the faith that people have in their memory—even under stress. When a person's life or well-being is threatened, a stress pattern known as the General Adaptional Syndrome (GAS) can be expected to occur in varying degrees (see pp. 381-82). This pattern is due to an increase in adrenaline levels and involves increased heartrate, breathing rate, and higher blood pressure. The end result is a dramatic increase in available energy, making the person capable of running fast, fighting, lifting enormous weight—taking the steps necessary to ensure safety or survival.

But, if you are under extreme stress, you will be a less reliable witness than you would be normally. Research shows that observers are less capable of remembering details, less accurate in reading dials, less accurate in detecting signals when under stress. They are paying more attention to their own well-being and safety than to nonessential elements in the environment. My research with trained Air Force flight crew members confirms that even highly trained people became poorer observers when under stress. They never can forget the stress and what hit them; the events, being highly significant at the time, can be remembered. But memory for details, clothing worn, colors, etc., is not as clear. Time estimates are especially exaggerated under stress.

You might test this idea by asking a few people where they were in 1963 when they first heard the news of the assassination of President John F. Kennedy. Chances are they will recall vividly where they were and who they were with. But can they describe what they or the persons with them were wearing? Can those who witnessed the killing of Lee Harvey Oswald on television describe the people next to the killer? These are logical questions—seemingly trivial—but if you were asking them in court, would you be willing to agree that the witnesses might have been too concerned with more important things to pay attention?

2. Prior Conditioning and Experience. Psychologists have done extensive research on how *set*, or expectancy, is used by the human observer to make judgments more efficiently. In a classic experiment done in the 1930's, observers were shown a display of playing cards for a few seconds and asked to report the number of aces of spades in the display (Bruner & Postman, 1949). Most observers reported only three, when actually there were five. Two of the aces of spades were colored red instead of more familiar black color. The interpretation was given that since people were so familiar with black aces of spades, they did not waste time looking carefully at the display. Thus efficiency, in this case, led to unreliable observation. In many criminal cases, the prior conditioning of the witness may enable him to report facts or events which were not present but which should have been. Our research also indicates that white observers show better recognition of white people than of black people in a lineup. Recent research supports the proposition that observers have better recognition of people of their own race.

3. Personal Biases and Stereotypes.

Expectancy in its least palatable form can be found in the case of biases or prejudices held by a witness. A victim of a mugging may initially report being attacked by "niggers," and may, because of limited experience as well as prejudice, be unable to tell one black man from another ("they all look alike to me"). In a classic study of this phenomenon, observers were asked to take a brief look at a drawing of several people on a subway train (Allport & Postman, 1945). In the picture, a black man was seated and a white man was standing with a knife in his hand. When questioned later, observers tended to report having seen the knife in the hand of the black man.

Prejudices may be racial, religious, or based on physical characteristics such as long hair, dirty clothes, status, etc. All human beings have some stereotypes upon which they base perceptual judgments; stereotypes which lead not only to prejudice but are a means of making decisions more efficiently. A witness to an auto accident may save thinking time by reporting his well-ingrained stereotype about "woman drivers." But these shortcuts to thinking may be erroneously reported and expanded upon by an eyewitness who is unaware that he or she is describing a stereotype rather than the events which actually took place. If the witness's biases are shared by the investigator taking the statement, the report may reflect their mutual biases rather than what was actually seen.

4. Unfair Test Construction.

The lineup and the array of photographs used in testing the eyewitness's ability to identify a suspect can be analyzed as fair or unfair on the basis of criteria which most psychologists can agree on. A fair test should be designed carefully so that, first, all items have an equal chance of being selected by a person who didn't see the suspect; second, the items are similar enough to each other and to the original description of the suspect to be confusing to a person who is merely guessing; and last, the test is conducted without leading questions or suggestions from the test giver.

All too frequently, I have found that lineups or photographic arrays are carelessly assembled or even rigged in such a way as to make the eyewitness identification test completely unreliable. If, for example, you present five pictures, the chance should be only 1 in 5 (20%) that any one picture will be chosen on the basis of guessing; but frequently, a single picture of a suspect may stand out. In the Angela Davis case, one set of nine pictures used to check identification contained three pictures of the defendant taken at an outdoor rally, two mug shots of other women showing their names, one of a 55-year-old woman, etc. It was so easy for a witness to rule out five pictures as ridiculous choices, that the "test" was reduced to four pictures—including three of Davis. This means that witnesses had a 75 percent chance of picking out her picture, whether they had seen her or not. Such a "test" is meaningless to a psychologist and probably tainted as an item of evidence in court.

Research on memory has also shown that if one item in the array of photos is uniquely different (in dress, race, height, sex, photographic quality, etc.), it is more likely to be picked out and attended to. A teacher making up a multiple-choice test designs several answers which sound or look alike to make it difficult for a person who doesn't know the right answer to succeed. Police lineups and photo layouts are also multiple-choice tests. If the rules for designing fair tests are ignored by authorities, the tests become unreliable.

So far I've presented the research framework on which I've built my testimony in court as an expert witness. The framework is built on the work of the past, much of which is familiar to a working psychologist, but is hardly the day-to-day conversation of adult Americans who become jurors. Some of the earliest psychologists, notably Münsterberg (see p. 18), had written the essence of this analysis as far back as the beginning of this century. But there was a nagging gap between the controlled research settings which yield data on basic perceptual processes and some very important questions about perception in the less well controlled, but real world. Thus our laboratory and field studies are designed to evaluate eyewitness accuracy and reliability after seeing simulated crimes where we have a good record of the veridical (real) events for comparison. I began with a more detailed version of an experiment which Münsterberg and others had conducted over 65 years ago.

An Experimental Study of the Eyewitness

In order to study the effects of eyewitness testimony in a somewhat realistic setting, we staged an assault on a California State University campus, in which a distraught student "attacked" a professor in front of 141 witnesses. We recorded the entire incident on videotape so that we could compare the veridical event with the eyewitness reports. After the attack we took sworn statements from each witness, asking them to describe the suspect, the incident, and the clothes worn (essentially a free recall process). We also asked for a confidence rating (0–100%) in their description. Another outsider, of the same age as the suspect, was on the scene.

Table 1 shows a comparison of the known characteristics of the suspect and the averages of the descriptions given by the witnesses. It is clear that the witnesses gave very inaccurate descriptions, a fact which has been demonstrated so often in this type of experiment that professors of psychology use this as a demonstration of the unreliability of the eyewitness. People tend to overestimate the passage of time—in this case by a factor of almost 2½ to 1. The weight estimate was 14 percent higher, the age was underestimated, and the accuracy score—made up of points for appearance and dress—was only 25 percent of the maximum possible total score. Only the height estimate was close; but this may be due to the fact that the suspect was of average height. People will often cite known facts about the "average" man when they are uncertain—inaccurate witnesses' weight estimates correlate significantly with their own weight.

Table 1 Comparison of Average Descriptions by 141 Eyewitnesses with Actual Description of Suspect and Events

	Known characteristics	Averaged descriptions
Duration of incident	34 sec	81.1 sec
Height	69.5 in	70.4 in
Weight	155 lb	180 lb
Age	25 yr	22.7 yr
Total accuracy score	28 pts	7.4 pts

We then waited seven weeks and presented a set of six photographs to each witness individually, creating four conditions in order to test the effects of biased instructions and unfair testing on eyewitness identification. There were two kinds of instructions: Low Bias, in which witnesses were asked only if they recognized anybody in the photos; and High Bias, where witnesses were told that we had an idea of who the assailant was, and we made a plea for them to find the attacker in the photos. There were two types of photo spreads, using well-lit frontal views of young men the same age as the suspect. In the nonleading photo spread (Figure 1), all six photos were neatly set out, with the same expression on all faces and similar clothing worn by all men. In the biased photo spread (Figure 2), the photo of the actual assailant was placed crooked in the array, and the suspect wore different clothing and had a different expression from the other photos. We thus violated good testing practice for the sake of comparison.

The results indicated that overall only 40 percent of the witnesses correctly identified the assailant; 25 percent of the witnesses identified the wrong man—an innocent bystander who had been at the

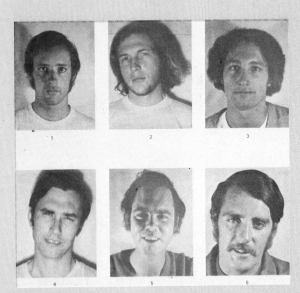

Confidence level

0–10–20–30–40–50–60–70–80–90–100%

Figure 1 Example of a reasonably unbiased photospread lineup used in testing eyewitnesses to an assault. Number 5 was the perpetrator.

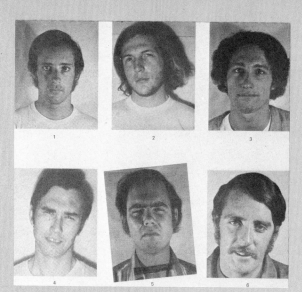

Confidence level

0 – 10 – 20 – 30 – 40 – 50 – 60 – 70 – 80 – 90 – 100%

Figure 2   Example of a biased photo-spread lineup used in testing witnesses to an assault.

scene of the crime. Even the professor who was attacked picked out the *innocent* man from the photos as his attacker! Of those correctly identifying the assailant, the highest percentage correct was found in the condition where there was a combination of a biased set of photos and biased instructions. In some of our recent research we have tested the same photo spreads with a group of nonwitnesses, who also picked out suspect number 5. We thus demonstrated how the violation of good testing practices could lead to unreliable eyewitness identifications in a fairly realistic setting.

Our conclusions in this study were as follows. First, the reports of over 100 eyewitnesses to a crime were so highly unreliable that if an investigation began to find the person most witnesses described, the likelihood is high that attention would focus on the wrong person. Second, in following police procedures for testing identification through photographs, the presence of biased instructions and leading sets of photos can increase the percentage of witnesses who end up picking the photo toward which the authorities are already biased.

Third, if the police are biased toward an innocent man, the presence of biased instructions and a leading set of photos could increase the likelihood that the wrong person would be identified.

Our more recent research is guided by the "signal detection" paradigm. This choice was made because signal detection theory evolved in psychophysics as a means of coping with the empirical fact that the observer's attitude "interferes" with the accurate detecting, processing, and reporting of sensory stimuli. An ideal observer has a clear distinction in mind as to what a signal (stimulus) is and what it is not. The task usually is to say whether a signal (e.g., a tone of a particular frequency) is present or not. The experimenter always presents the subject with some background noise, but only on half the trials will a low strength signal (the tone) also be present. In deciding whether the trial consists of noise alone or contains a signal, the subject employs a criterion which is influenced by individual factors such as personality, experience, anticipated cost or reward, or motivation to please or frustrate. The experimenter keeps track of both hits (correct "yeses") and false alarms (incorrect "yeses"), thus providing a quantitative estimate of the observer's criterion for judging his or her immediate experience. A very cautious person might have very few false alarms and a high number of hits, indicating that "yes" is being used sparingly. A less cautious observer might say "yes" most of the time, increasing the proportion of false alarms to hits.

In our experiment, we presented 20 to 25 statements about the crime which were true and the same number which were false. The witness indicated yes or no and gave a confidence rating as well. We end up with a record of hits and false alarms based on the witness's recall of the crime. These data are combined statistically to produce Receiver Operating Characteristic (ROC) curves as shown in Figure 3. The straight line would be generated by a person or group whose hits and false alarms were equal—indicating that responses have no relationship to the facts. The sharper the curve, the more cautious the observer. The greater the area under the curve, the more sensitive was the witness to the difference between a true and a false statement. Our current studies indicate that the

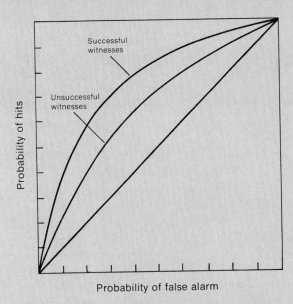

Figure 3   Comparison of ROC curves of successful and unsuccessful eyewitnesses where successful d′ = 1.18 and unsuccessful d′ = 0.74.

witnesses with better ROC curves in the laboratory perform more accurately in recognizing the suspect in a lineup. This observer sensitivity function enables us to test various hypotheses on how environmental conditions, stress, bias in interrogation, sex, and social milieu affect the accuracy and reliability of an eyewitness. Thus, we are on the way toward developing a standardized test of eyewitness sensitivity, accuracy, and reliability.

One basic change has occurred in our research strategy. Instead of staging the crimes "live" in the classroom, we are using color and sound movies of carefully staged crimes. In part, we did this for control, but more importantly, the time of the apathetic bystander to a crime appears to have passed. Staging even an innocuous purse-snatching became dangerous for our "perpetrators" as a number of the (bigger) witnesses began to take off in hot pursuit of the purse-snatcher. No research is worth

that much realism (at least my suffering assistants didn't think so)!

With the ROC curve as a measure of the sensitivity of witnesses, we can explore the extent to which biasing factors commonly encountered in court cases affect identifications. In our early studies, we found that witnesses who were ultimately successful in recognizing the suspect in a good lineup had shown high observer sensitivity scores during recall. People with low observer sensitivity scores tended to give height and weight descriptions which correlated with their own stature—confirming our belief that when pressured to give a description, witnesses fabricate their responses in the meaningful way that a perception researcher would expect.

We plan to refine the test, giving witnesses the chance to see several crimes. In this way we can check general reliability of a witness and test a number of hypotheses which police officers hold regarding older witnesses, women as witnesses, members of different racial and economic groups, etc. Thus, in one sense, we are just beginning a large research program which came from the real world to be absorbed into the laboratory—and changed the laboratory. Soon we hope to emerge from the laboratory and to bring the results back to the real world where they belong—and hopefully to utilize psychological knowledge to make eyewitness identification a more reliable and much fairer element in the judicial process.

References

Allport, G. W., & Postman, L. J. In *Transactions of the New York Academy of Sciences,* 1945, *8,* 66.

Bruner, J. S., & Postman, L. J. On the perception of incongruity: A paradigm. *Journal of Personality,* 1949, *18,* 206–223.

7

Altered States of Consciousness

. . . One can sense it but not describe it, . . . lost in a sea of color, "feeling," "being," quite utterly involved in it with no identity of your own, you know, . . . I say, it's an utterly amazing, fascinating state of finding yourself a pleasant part of an endless vista of color that is soft and gentle and yielding and all-absorbing, utterly extraordinary, most extraordinary.

Aldous Huxley, quoted in Erickson, 1965

The above is part of an account given by Aldous Huxley of one of his experiments on sensing color by means of what he called "deep reflection." It was a state he produced in himself at will, in a matter of minutes, without any special training, drugs, or intervention from anyone else. In his words again, he "simply cast aside all anchors" of usual awareness, and with an intense concentration on what was going on within himself was able to dissociate his consciousness from what was going on in the reality of the external world. Not only was he able to experience out-of-the-ordinary *sensations* when he entered this state, but he could also use it as a means of having new thoughts, developing ideas, and seeing new conceptual relationships that were subsequently incorporated into his conscious activity when he was once again operating with his usual consciousness.

Normal Consciousness and Its Alteration

What *is* "consciousness," and what does it mean to *alter* it? And, at a more personal level, you may be wondering "How about me? Can I experience altered states of consciousness?" In this chapter we will address ourselves to such questions as these as we go beyond what were the boundaries of "traditional psychology" as little as ten years ago. After a general discussion of the nature of human consciousness and its alteration, we will examine in more detail several areas of investigation that are generating intriguing information about the ways in which the mind can act upon itself, including sleep and dreaming, psychoactive drugs, meditation, biofeedback, hypnosis, and alteration of time perspective.

There are special problems in following the requirements of objective science in studying unusual states of consciousness. The phenomena are subjective, and it is often very hard to get objective indicators of them, much less measurable ones. And to an important extent there is a basic contradiction in trying to use tools designed for measuring and evaluating orderly physical events for studying nonphysical and often apparently nonrational and unpredictable ones. Perhaps we should entertain the notion that not all reality is reduceable to input-output formulas. In any case, to the extent that we decide to abandon or replace our usual rules of evidence, it is important that we recognize what we are doing and not claim "scientific verification" for conclusions based on other rules of evidence.

To be *conscious* means to be aware of one's own thought processes and usually also of external events. The person who has lost consciousness (through coma, traumatic shock, fainting, or general anesthesia) is out of contact with what is happening. As we all know, however, consciousness is not an all-or-none condition that we either have or do not have, but rather a process, an activity of the mind that can vary between extremes from heightened vigilance, arousal, and sensitivity to insensitivity and dormancy.

To function optimally, the human brain requires stimulation. It needs variation in the sensory input it receives. It probably also needs a certain level of cognitive activity, generated by evaluating and appraising these inputs as well as by thinking and imagining. If the level of the input is either too intense or too minimal, the individual's functioning will be impaired, at least temporarily. When it is too overwhelming, the person may "lose" consciousness as a means of coping with the overload: he or she may refuse to acknowledge the reality of the immediate experience by "turning it off." When the input is not sufficiently stimulating, the person may become bored and fall asleep, or may start having fantasies, daydreams, hallucinations, and so on, in which the brain is stimulated by a variety of tactics and games initiated by internal processes.

Altered states of consciousness are also induced deliberately by ingesting alcohol, psychedelic drugs, stimulants, or sedatives and undeliberately by fever, fasting, dehydration, glandular abnormalities, sleep deprivation, epileptic seizures, and poisoning. All these routes to alteration of consciousness have in common the fact that they change the ordinary environment of the brain cells, whether by means of chemicals or by under- or over-stimulation.

But altered states of consciousness can also be induced by psychological means—meditation, concentration, learning, hypnosis, and perhaps other methods. The fascinating thing is that though these states are initiated by psychological events, physiological changes also occur. Researchers are hard at work establishing correlations between the two. About causal relationships they are less ready to make claims.

Since no one else has direct access to your consciousness—or you to theirs—it becomes "a wonderful fact to reflect upon," in the words of Charles Dickens, "that every human creature is constituted to be that profound secret and mystery to every other." But to a considerable extent, we are mysterious secrets to ourselves also. We have all been subtly shaped by a Western orientation toward materialism, toward a belief in the ultimate reality of "things" and of the prime importance of physical actions in and on the world around us. Having founded a philosophy on "thingness," we have proceeded to elevate physics to the position of "queen of the sciences." Even our science of behavior has in large part studied people as physical beings rather than as experiencers, though clearly subjective experience is an important—perhaps central—feature of the human phenomenon.

Historical Changes in Our Valuing of Consciousness

Our orientation toward materialism is a profound change from early Christian thought, in which the mortal body not only was subordinated to the immortal soul but was regarded in effect as a "no-deposit, throw-away container" for it. To achieve mystical oneness with God required *contemplative meditation* exercises through which the soul could transcend any dependence on thinking or sensation and apprehend God directly. Indeed, the transcendental exercises described by a fourteenth-century Roman Catholic writer, Walter Hilton, in *The Ladder of Perfection,* are similar to those proposed by a famous sixth-century Yogi, Pantanjali (Woods, 1914).

In the Renaissance view, the soul (as a consequence of Adam's fall in Paradise) was differentiated into three aspects: sense, reason, and understanding. "From sense there arises appetite or longing, which is common with brute beasts; from reason arises election or choice, which is proper to man; from understanding by which man may be partner [once again] with the angels, arises will" (Castiglione, 1528). "In apprehension, how like an angel," was the ultimate description of human potential.

It remained for Descartes' mechanistic conception to separate soul and mind from matter and to direct the attention of science toward study of the physical operation of the "human clockwork."

At the very beginning of psychology's short history as a formal discipline, as we saw in Chapter 6, there was a group of German psychologists whose main interest was analyzing the structure of consciousness. They believed that when everything was analyzed to its simplest qualities, one was left with sensations and feelings. *Sensations* were defined as what one experienced as a result of stimulation of any of the sensory pathways (smell, touch, sight, etc.). *Feelings* were defined as experiences of emotion. In their view, memories, fantasies, and all other elements of consciousness could ultimately be reduced to mixtures of sensations and feelings.

With the emergence of American psychology, based on the models of physics and biology, and derived from a pragmatic perspective that admitted only objective behavior and measurable stimuli as real and worthy of consideration, the body lost its soul. Some say it lost its head as well.

But the pendulum has begun its swing back. Concern with issues of consciousness, inner representation of outer events, and the rich inner life that we each experience has attracted many rigorous researchers willing to step outside the approved boundaries of their discipline to try to understand the nature of human consciousness, its role in behavior, and its alteration. This redirection of part of the enterprise of psychology has come about in part from the interest in humanistic psychology, with its emphasis on the functioning of the whole human organism. It also reflects the new interest among Westerners in the oriental traditions of Zen, yoga, and mind control, practiced under a variety of names. And finally, the profound impact of psychedelic drugs and pharmacological agents in changing quite radically the perceptions, feelings, and information-processing functions of "normal" individuals has served as an impetus to psychologists to try to understand how normal awareness and consciousness can be changed. Regardless of the origins of this revival of interest, the study of altered states of consciousness has expanded to encompass all changes in mental state, whether induced by pharmacological agents, physiological interventions, or psychological maneuvers.

Characteristics of Altered States of Consciousness

It is no simple matter to set criteria for determining when normal consciousness becomes "altered." This is in part due to our poor understanding of so-called normal consciousness, which itself seems to consist of many states varying in kind and intensity. Though ever changing, the states of consciousness somehow seem to hang together with an identifiable constancy—identified, of course, by the individual who is monitoring his or her own consciousness.

A useful clarification is provided for us by Charles Tart, one of the pioneers in the study of altered states of consciousness. He writes:

"For any given individual, his normal state of consciousness is the one in which he spends the major part of his waking hours. That your normal state of consciousness and mine are quite similar and are similar to that of all normal men is an almost universal assumption, albeit one of questionable validity. An altered state of consciousness for a given individual is one in which he clearly feels a quantitative *shift in his pattern of mental functioning; that is, he feels not just a* quantitative *shift (more or less alert, more or less visual imagery, sharper or duller, etc.) but also that some quality or qualities of his mental processes are* different. *Mental functions operate that do not operate at all ordinarily, perceptual qualities appear that have no normal counterparts, and so forth. There are numerous borderline cases in which the individual cannot clearly distinguish just how his state of consciousness is different from normal, where quantitative changes in mental functioning are very marked, etc., but the existence of borderline states and difficult-to-describe effects does not negate the existence of feelings of clear, qualitative changes in mental functioning that are the criterion of altered states of consciousness." (Tart, 1969, pp. 1–2)*

Are there common characteristics among the many varieties of altered states of consciousness? Surprisingly, many similar qualities have been described despite the differences in the settings giving rise to the experiences (religious settings, injections of a psychoactive drug, meditation, situations of severe stress). The following characteristics are frequently associated with altered states of consciousness.

Distortions of perceptual processes, time sense, and body image. A common characteristic is distortion of many familiar perceptions, including those of the visual and auditory sense, as well as those of time and space. A "transcendent" experience may lack any sensory qualities whatsoever, but many altered states include sharpened visual and auditory sensations, perceptual illusions, and hallucinations—perceptions in the absence of appropriate external stimuli. A sense of being separate from one's body, or of having portions of the body feel and/or look very different from usual, is often reported. Portions of the body may feel enlarged or weightless, numb or disconnected. The sense of time frequently undergoes enormous change so that a second feels like an hour or an hour like a moment. Not uncommon is a report of experiencing "eternity" or "infinity" in the transcendent-type experience. Huxley's altered sense of colors typifies such perceptual change.

Feelings of objectivity and ego-transcendence. This is the sense that one is viewing the world with greater objectivity, more able to perceive phenomena as if they were independent of oneself and even of all human beings. One seems to be able to divorce oneself from personal needs and desires and see things as they "really" are, in some ultimate, impersonal sense. Often such a transcendent experience comes after long effort at renouncing worldly concerns and ties, but even without this framework it seems to happen naturally.

Sometimes this sense of objectivity is experienced as a loss of control, as a feeling of being outside oneself; it may be welcomed or resisted, often depending on the person's set and expectation prior to the altered state. If one feels that one is leaving one's own personal perspective to join a greater force, then it will not be resisted as much as if one feels that one's grip on reality is slipping and may not be recoverable at will.

Religious mystical experiences typically feature the renunciation of "fleshly cares," as well as a loss of concern for the trivia of a biologically based existence. Instead, the person transcends the mundane for the spiritual, for the communion with God, nature, or the cosmic forces of the universe.

Self-validating sense of truth. Altered states often carry with them a tremendous sense of certainty. One feels that the experience is highly valuable—even uniquely valuable, and that no subsequent "rational" explanation or interpretation can diminish its worth. Knowledge itself is experienced at an "intuitive" level, rather than at our customary rational-empirical-logical level of analysis. It is as if one "sees" beyond appearances into essential qualities. The experience is seen as more "real" or "true" than the perceptions of ordinary consciousness. The same thing, of course, is true of delusions and hallucinations, which complicates the evaluation of revelations during altered states of consciousness.

Positive emotional quality. Joy, ecstasy, reverence, peace, and overwhelming love are reported frequently in transcendent experiences where the person has some religious or philosophical framework for the interpretation of the experience. In the Eastern mystical reports, the experience is less one of ecstasy than of a deep and profoundly restful peace in which the individual seems in harmony with all things. It is this feeling of achieving a final state of quiescence that some Westerners have criticized as sloth and abdication of responsibility.

In reports of Christian mystics, the experience is less one of quiescent peace and more one of burning ecstasy. In some "bad trips" with drugs, profound fear and lack of enjoyment is reported, but in the transcendent experience, the emotional tone is always positive.

Paradoxicality. Descriptions of altered states of consciousness tend to be contradictory when analyzed on logical, rational grounds. One can report experiencing an emptiness that seems full and complete. One seems to feel one's individuality dissolving, yet there clearly is some sort of "self" perceiving this dissolution. The dichotomies and polarities of life seem to be experienced simultaneously, seem to reach some resolution, and yet seem to remain separate. It is like being Alice in Wonderland, where contradiction is the basis for agreement.

Ineffability. Individuals frequently claim an inability to describe the experience. The qualities seem so unique that no words seem appropriate. Often, too, the experience seems to contain so many paradoxical qualities that it makes no sense to describe it. (There is a similarity to dreams here.) The quality of unity—of self and others, or of internal and external—is frequently experienced but is most difficult to explain in a language that emphasizes the distinction between subject and object, between actor and action, between time and location.

Unity and fusion. A considerable portion of early socialization of children consists in training them to erect boundaries, such as "mine"/"not mine," and to recognize distinctions and discontinuities between themselves and others, between past, present, and future, between animate and inanimate, between inner and outer reality, and between what is actual and what is imagined and only potential. In an altered state of consciousness, this separateness of self vanishes, the boundaries dissolve, and there is a fusion of self with what previously was nonself. The experience of a collective identity, of everything partaking of everything, is often startling to the Western mind, formed in the forge of individualism and self-identity.

Because this characteristic is the essence of the transcendent experience and because it highlights assumptions about ourselves of which we are usually unaware, we will illustrate how people coming from widely differing backgrounds have experienced this unity and fusion. First, an autobiographical account of an LSD experience:

"It is meaningful to say that I, John Robertson, ceased to exist, becoming immersed in the ground of Being . . . in God, in "nothingness,"
in ultimate reality, or in some other similar symbol for oneness . . . . It is misleading to even use the words "I experienced," as during the peak of the experience (which must have lasted at least an hour) there was no duality between myself and what I experienced. Rather, I was those feelings . . . . This was especially evident when, after having reached the mystic peak, a recording of Bach's Fantasia and Fugue in G Minor was played. It seemed as though I was not my usual self listening to a recording, but that I was the music itself." (Robertson, in Metzner, 1968, p. 880)

Another perspective on the transcendent experience is provided by a modern Zen master, the late Sokei-an Sasaki:

"One day I wiped out all the notions from my mind. I gave up all desire. I discarded all the words with which I thought and stayed in quietude. I felt a little queer—as if I were being carried into something, or as if I were touching some power unknown to me . . . and Ztt! I entered. I lost the boundary of my physical body. I had my skin, of course, but I felt I was standing in the middle of the cosmos. I spoke, but my words lost their meaning. I saw people coming towards me, but all were the same man. All were myself! I had never known this world. I had believed that I was created, but now I must change my opinion: I was never created; I was the cosmos; no individual Mr. Sasaki existed." (Quoted in Watts, 1957, p. 121)

A college student under deep hypnosis was told that her past and future were remote and insignificant and her present was expanding. Describing her experience, she said:

"I'm melted, I am so thin, I cover practically everything. In fact, I am sort of falling into everything because I am so thin, and I can hear all the little things vibrating, and I can taste all the different things, like wood and the carpet, and the floor and the chairs. I really can't see any more, though, I mean it's all different

colors, but it's so big you can hardly see it, everything is very confusing, but I've just sort of melted into everything . . . I'm unresponsible! . . . I'm everything! I can keep going. . . . I'm not a thing anymore, I'm everything so I can't do anything. There's nobody there, nobody who says to me, 'Hey, Everything, you have to do this.'" (Quoted in Zimbardo, Marshall, & Maslach, 1971, p. 323)

The writings of one of the greatest sixteenth-century Christian mystics, St. Theresa of Avila, show even more strongly the universal nature of this experience, clothed though it may be in the language of the context from which the perceiver comes.

"In the orison [prayer; meditation-state] of union, the soul is fully awake as regards God, but wholly asleep as regards things of this world and in respect of herself. During the short time the union lasts, she is as it were deprived of every feeling, and even if she would, she could not think of any single thing . . . . Thus does God, when he raises a soul to union with himself, suspend the natural action of all her faculties. She neither sees, hears, nor understands, so long as she is united with God . . . . God establishes himself in the interior of this soul in such a way, that when she returns to herself, it is wholly impossible to doubt that she has been in God, and God in her . . . she sees it clearly later, after she has returned to herself, not by any vision, but by a certitude which abides with her and which God alone can give her." (Quoted in James, 1902, pp. 303–14)

Other characteristics sometimes mentioned in various reports are feelings of rejuvenation, sudden, intense emotionality, and extreme suggestibility (Ludwig, 1966).

In the rest of this chapter, we will be looking at several conditions that give rise to alterations in our consciousness, at the similarities and differences in the experiences they induce, and at what is known about related physiological changes. We will begin our discussion of the various altered states of consciousness with one that is familiar to us all—the state of sleep, with the dreaming that sometimes accompanies it.

Sleeping and Dreaming

"Between the darkness out of which we are born and the darkness in which we end, there is a tide of darkness that ebbs and flows each day of our lives to which we irresistibly submit. A third of life is spent in sleep, that most usual yet profoundly mysterious realm of consciousness where the person seems to live apart from the waking world. . . ." (Luce, 1965, p. 1)

We often think of sleep in a negative way, as a *lack* of action and awareness, and an interlude serving only a restorative function. Actually, investigators are discovering that it is an extremely complex state, with much activity taking place in the body while we are asleep. Such activity appears to be intimately related to many aspects of our behavior including attention, emotion, memory, and learning. Thus the study of sleep may be one way of increasing our understanding about consciousness and the waking state.

If sleep is a mysterious part of life, then how much more so is dreaming? Our dreams violate the usual principles of rationality, logic, perception, time, and space as well as many of our habits and moral standards; yet while they are taking place, they seem quite normal and real. There is no certain knowledge about why we dream or what dreams mean or even if they *have* a meaning. Nevertheless, each of us knows that something strange, wonderful, or frightening, occurs in our heads when we abandon the ordinary consciousness that guides our everyday journeys.

The Behavior We Call "Sleep"

Whatever may be the multiplicity or contrariety of opinions upon this subject, nature has taken sufficient care that theory shall have little influence upon practice. The most diligent inquirer is not able long to keep his eyes open; and once in every four-and-twenty hours, the gay and the gloomy, the witty and the dull, the clamorous and the silent, the busy and the idle, are all overpowered by the gentle tyrant, and all lie down in the equality of sleep. . . .

Samuel Johnson

It is a common experience of students to have to fight off sleepiness on those last-chance nights when they are cramming for finals. Sleep, to many, is a waste of the all-too-limited time there is. If only it could be eliminated, you would add almost half again to the time available for your daily rounds. But while you may *reduce* the time you need for sleeping in order to accomplish a specific task, the consequences of prolonged total sleep deprivation make it hardly a desirable state. (See *P&L* Close-up at right.)

An extended period of time without sleep can alter a variety of physiological and psychological reactions. Some of the results are fatigue, headaches, tremor, perceptual distortions, difficulty in concentration, disorientation, immediate memory loss, brain-wave abnormalities, and, in some people, paranoid ideas and vivid hallucinations like those on Tripp's bad trip. The effects of sleep deprivation, however, are not merely a simple function of how long the person has gone without sleep; environmental, personality, motivational, and age variables also determine its impact on behavior. A recent survey of total sleep deprivation studies concludes, "Though the exact symptoms produced by sleep deprivation depend on additional variables, the sleep-deprived person is not normal, suffering both neurological and psychological deterioration" (Freemon, 1972, p. 73).

Despite the degree of disruption produced by prolonged sleep deprivation, the effects are transient—one good night's sleep and ordinary func-

Close-up
No Sleep for the Weary

A particularly dramatic account of the alteration of consciousness resulting from prolonged sleep deprivation is that of Peter Tripp, a New York disc jockey who staged a 200-hour "wakathon" for the benefit of the March of Dimes. During this sleepless marathon, he was attended by several doctors and given periodic medical examinations, performance tests, and psychological tests. From the beginning, Tripp had to fight to keep himself from falling asleep. After two days, he began to have visual hallucinations, such as seeing cobwebs in his shoes. By 100 hours, his memory was becoming quite poor, and he was having a great deal of difficulty with simple performance tests. His hallucinations became more and more frightening: he saw a doctor's tweed suit as a suit of furry worms, and when he went to a nearby hotel for a change of clothing, he saw the bureau drawer in flames. To explain these visions to himself, he decided that the fire had been deliberately set by the doctors in order to frighten and test him.

A simple algebraic formula that he had earlier solved with ease now required such superhuman effort that Tripp broke down, frightened at his inability to solve the problem, fighting to perform. Scientists saw the spectacle of a suave New York radio entertainer trying vainly to find his way through the alphabet.

"By 170 hours the agony had become almost unbearable to watch. At times Tripp was no longer sure he was himself, and frequently tried to gain proof of his identity. Although he behaved as if he were awake, his brain-wave patterns resembled those of sleep. In his psychotic delusion, he was convinced that the doctors were in a conspiracy against him to send him to jail. . . . At the end of the 200 sleepless hours, nightmare hallucination and reality had merged, and he felt he was the victim of a sadistic conspiracy among the doctors." (Luce, 1965, pp. 19–20)

EEG patterns represent electrical activity of the cortex recorded from electrodes attached to the surface of the skull. Most of the patterns can be described by two features: their *amplitude* (how high each wave is when its voltage level is translated into excursions of a recording pen across a chart, as below), and their *frequency* (the number of cycles of ups and downs occurring each second). Together, amplitude and frequency define the *form* of a wave pattern. There are other features of these electrical tracings that the trained observer (and now computers) can recognize, such as "spikes."

There is a distinctive pattern during alert wakefulness as well as different patterns for the four stages of NREM sleep. In addition, there is a distinctive pattern during the periods when the sleeper's eyes move rapidly, the REM periods. A standard manual is available for scoring sleep stages reliably (Rechtschaffen & Kales, 1968).

Alert wakefulness

NREM sleep stages

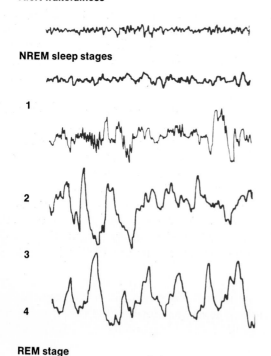

1

2

3

4

REM stage

tioning is restored. Even in a group of four healthy adult males who were closely studied as they underwent 205 hours of sleep deprivation, the psychopathological reactions did not extend beyond the actual period of sleep deprivation itself (Kollar et al., 1969).

Indeed, forced sleep deprivation has been used effectively by police as a tactic to induce confessions by those suspected of crimes. This approach was most thoroughly developed by Nikolai Yezhov who interrogated the former Soviet old guard during Stalin's purge of the Communist party in the 1930s. It appears that he would keep the prisoners awake for ninety straight hours, then interrogate them after they had had only a brief period of sleep. The prisoners not only confessed to absurd charges (such as sabotaging the state by putting tacks in butter), but they also came to believe in their guilt for the offenses reported in their false confessions. (Ironically, Stalin later used this same applied psychology on Yezhov when he too was suspected of being a traitor.)

In studying sleep, psychologists are concerned primarily with *internal* behavior—that is, processes that are presumed to take place inside each person. However, as we have seen, before we can study such behavior, we must find a way to make it external so it can be observed and measured. This methodological problem of *externalizing internal behaviors* is one of the recurring basic problems in psychology.

The lack of early research on sleep was due primarily to the lack of appropriate methodology. The methodological breakthrough for the study of sleep came with the development of the *electroencephalograph* (EEG) that allowed investigators to "listen" to the brain (see Chapter 2). In 1937, Loomis and his associates made the important discovery that brain waves change in form with the onset of sleep and show further changes during the entire sleep period. This meant that researchers could now continuously monitor the changes during sleep, as well as accurately identify its beginning and end. In addition, it became possible to identify the different levels of *depth* of sleep, as well as when a person was likely to be dreaming.

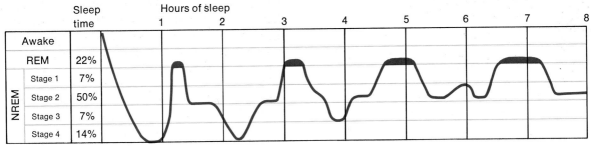

Adapted from Van de Castle, 1971

States and stages of sleep. It is generally agreed now that there are two states of sleep—a regularly recurring state during which rapid eye movements occur, called *REM* periods, and a state referred to as *nonrapid eye movement sleep* or *NREM* sleep, composed of four stages that evidently denote differences in depth of sleep. (See *P&L* Close-up, p. 282.)

Despite the marked differences among the four NREM stages, the distinction between REM and NREM has been shown to be the most vital one. It also seems to hold for nearly all mammals studied.

The most essential characteristic of REM sleep is a suppression of voluntary muscular activity. REM sleep is thus a time when the body is essentially paralyzed and voluntary movements are impossible.

A second feature of REM sleep is that the brain appears (from several measures) to be aroused or alert although the person is unconscious and quite asleep. Thus some researchers refer to REM sleep as *paradoxical sleep.*

The third process that characterizes REM sleep is called *phasic activity.* It consists of bursts of activity of short duration. The most clear-cut evidence of these phasic events is the rapid jerks of the eyeballs moving about in all directions. There also are muscle twitches, changes in pupil size, contractions of the middle ear, and, in males, erection of the penis.

A fourth characteristic common to REM periods is major physiological changes, particularly in the autonomic nervous system. These changes often include large, erratic fluctuations in heart rate and blood pressure. Such "autonomic storms" have important medical implications because it has been found that heart attacks and cardiac failure often occur during the early morning hours—the time when a person is most likely to be in REM sleep. If REM sleep involves activation of the cortex, NREM sleep implies deactivation. NREM sleep represents the perceptual disengagement of the person from the environment. (Dement & Mitler, 1975).

Over the course of eight hours of sleep, the average young adult human shows a cycle of going into and out of the various stages of sleep. Stage 4 sleep, the deepest sleep, occurs in the first hours of sleep, while the sleeper alternates between Stage 2 and the REM stage during the later hours of sleep. REM periods grow progressively longer with each occurrence, although they tend to be spaced about ninety minutes apart. ●

This progression varies somewhat from person to person according to individual circumstances, but it is relatively constant for healthy young adults. No sex differences have been found in the cycles of sleep, but age does make an important difference. Infants and children up to about age four spend substantially more of their total sleep time in the REM and Stage 4 periods. In elderly people the REM period is slightly shorter and the Stage 4 period is much shorter than when they were younger. Apparently older people get less sleep and less deep sleep within what they get (Roffwarg, Muzio, & Dement, 1966).

Adaptive significance of NREM and REM sleep. The most popular explanation of the function sleep serves—the issue of *why* we sleep—is that it offers a period of recovery from the fatigue of conscious activity. Despite the appealing analogy of the sleeping person to an overworked muscle in a state of relaxation, "the experimental analysis of sleep has *not* provided strong support for the notion that sleep is a process of recovery" (Williams et al., 1973, p. 306). Instead, it may be that we sleep not to make up what we have lost, but rather as a means of conserving energy at times when there is no need for action. In this view, advanced by Webb (1971), sleep enforces nonactivity on the organism at times when environmental demands on it are minimal. Each species has developed a biological rhythmic cycle of activity and sleep, called the *circadian rhythm,* geared to its energy requirements and the ecological character of its habitat.

Many functions of REM sleep have been suggested, any or all of which may explain the diverse phenomena associated with this state. Among them are: (a) REM sleep clears the brain of neurochemicals accumulated during daily life; (b) in newborn infants and young children it stimulates the development of the brain by the activity it generates; (c) it reorganizes neuronal firing patterns disorganized during NREM sleep; (d) it is somehow related to dreaming, perhaps providing a "safety valve" outlet for the discharge of intense impulses that would otherwise be expressed during waking.

It is likely that a full understanding of the role of both kinds of sleep in our lives will have to await the development of better techniques for studying the microbiochemistry of living brains.

To Sleep, Perchance to Dream

It was the incidental discovery of REM and NREM states of sleep that first provided a key to the physiological study of dreams. It had been suspected that dreaming might occur in certain stages of sleep and not in others, but analysis of brain-wave patterns had not provided a simple answer to this issue.

Physiological correlates of dreaming. While working on a study of sleep in 1953, Aserinsky and Kleitman noticed that several times during the night there were rapid, jerky movements of the closed eyelids, indicating that eye movements were occurring. During these periods there were increases in both heart rate and breathing, which suggested an emotional response. Acting on the hunch that REM activity was associated with dreaming, the experimenters woke their subjects during REM periods.

▪ DREAMING DURING REM AND NREM SLEEP

Definition of Dreaming Used in Study	Percent Recalling REM dreams	Percent Recalling NREM Dreams
"detailed dream description"	74	7
self-definition by each subject	88	0
"coherent, fairly detailed description"	79	7
"a dream recalled in some detail"	69	34
self-definition by each subject	60	3
self-definition by each subject	85	24
"any item of specific content"	87	74
"visual, auditory, or kinesthetic imagery"	82	54
"specific content of mental experience"	86	23
"any sensory imagery with . . . progression of the mental activity"	81	7

Adapted from Freemon, 1972.

The subjects almost always reported that they had been dreaming, while they rarely did so when awakened at other times (Aserinsky & Kleitman, 1953; Dement & Kleitman, 1957).

As evidence accumulated, however, the nice, neat relationship between dreams and REM periods *failed* to be supported. The best recall of dreaming occurred when sleepers were aroused during eye movements, but it turned out that a substantial amount of dreaming was also recalled when sleepers were awakened from NREM sleep, the exact amount depending somewhat on the definition of "dreaming" that was used. The percentage of dreaming reported from REM and NREM awakenings in ten studies and the definitions they used are summarized in the table. ■

Subjects aroused during REM sleep recall ongoing visual images that form a coherent drama, are vivid, and may be in color with sound. Despite bizarre or fantasy qualities of the plot, the unreal situation is accepted by the sleeper as "natural." In contrast, dreaming associated with NREM states is usually devoid of dramatic story content. It is full of specific thoughts but has minimal sensory imagery.

Research is under way to discover the processes that give rise to dreaming in REM and NREM states. The neural processes underlying our experiences of sights, sounds, emotions, and ideas during dream episodes must be quite complex. In some way neural stimuli must substitute for external sensory stimuli, and the intensity of these internal processes must be high enough to be experienced as "real."

Our "need to dream" is shown in studies of REM rebound. Volunteer subjects were allowed to sleep normally until they began to go into REM sleep. They were immediately awakened at that point, and then allowed to go back to sleep and remain asleep until the start of the next REM period. In this way, they were virtually prevented from having any REM sleep. Subjects in a control group were awakened the same number of times during NREM sleep.

The REM-deprived subjects started more REM periods each successive night of deprivation. Their daytime behavior also changed considerably, with increases in irritability, anxiety

and tension, difficulty in concentrating, and memory lapses. Many reported a marked increase in appetite and gained an average of a pound a day. When finally permitted to sleep undisturbed, these subjects "made up" for their deprivation by dreaming about 60 percent more than they normally did. The control subjects did not show these changes (Dement, 1960).

The human subjects in the above experiment were deprived of REM sleep for only five successive nights. What would be the effects of a much longer deprivation? To answer this question, cats were systematically deprived of their REM sleep for as long as seventy days. ▲ Even such extreme deprivation failed to produce any basic impairment in the animals' behavior. However, there was a dramatic *enhancement* of all drive-related behaviors, including aggression, sex, and hunger. Exactly how REM sleep is related to the control of primary drives is a fascinating problem that has yet to be solved.

An even more exciting result of the study of dreams is the discovery of their possible link to schizophrenia. One study of actively ill schizo-

▲ The treadmill prevents the cats from falling into REM sleep. Although they can doze briefly as they ride to the end of the slowly moving belt, they cannot go into a deep sleep without being carried over the end of the device and landing in a tank of water.

phrenic patients found that they failed to show the normal REM rebound effect after having been deprived of REM sleep (Zarcone et al., 1968). This suggested to Dement and his colleagues that their bizarre daytime symptoms might represent activity that would normally be discharged as dreams during periods of REM sleep.

What brain mechanism might allow REM activities to "spill over" into the waking state? Current research appears to implicate a brain chemical called *serotonin*. Cats treated with a chemical compound that blocks the production of serotonin in the brain showed behavior and brain-wave patterns similar to those of cats that had been deprived of REM sleep for long periods of time. Furthermore, when themselves deprived of REM sleep, the treated cats, like the schizophrenic patients, failed to show a rebound effect. It was shown that all these bizarre "psychotic" behaviors could be eliminated by administering chemical compounds that facilitate the production of serotonin. One such compound is *chlorpromazine,* a tranquilizing drug that has long been used in the treatment of schizophrenics (Dement, 1969).

All this experimental evidence suggests that there is a system in the brain that regulates drive behaviors and normally "discharges" through REM dreaming. If the functioning of this system is disrupted (e.g., by depleting the serotonin supply), there is an uncontrolled occurrence of REM activities and drive behaviors in the waking state. It is possible that this type of malfunctioning may occur in the condition called *schizophrenia,* which we will discuss further in Chapter 11.

The meaning of dreams. Despite the recent advances in the physiological analysis of sleep and dreaming, there has been little substantive study in recent years of the question of what dreams mean and why we dream the particular types of dreams we do.
Freud on dreams. For Freud, the content of dreams exists on two levels: the *manifest* and the *latent*. The manifest content is what you remember and report of the events you have dreamed. The real meaning of a dream, however, is in its latent (hidden) content, in ideas that represent unconscious impulses and wishes that have been denied overt gratification and appear in dreams in disguised form. The manifest content is the acceptable version of the story; the latent content represents the socially or personally unacceptable version—but nevertheless the "true, uncut one."

In the process of becoming socialized, according to Freud, we develop a conscience (superego) that monitors our thoughts and actions to keep us on the straight-and-narrow path. Unacceptable impulses are pushed down ("repressed") from conscious awareness into the realm of the unconscious. But they keep striving for expression, like a spring coil pushed down. They emerge into our everyday life in many forms: as neurotic symptoms, slips of the tongue, "forgetting" of particular things we do not *want* to remember, and symbols in dreams. They are expressed in disguised form to fool the censor, who might otherwise give them an "X rating" and arrest the distributor.

In sleep, the usually vigilant censor is relaxed, and by a variety of psychological processes, unacceptable unconscious material is transformed into an acceptable manifest story line and so slips by. Through *displacement* for example, emphasis is shifted from the central "naughty" theme to the unimportant but "nice" element.

According to Freud, the two main functions of dreams are to guard sleep and to serve as sources of wish fulfillment. They allow uninterrupted sleep by draining off psychic tensions created during the day, and they allow us to achieve the unconscious fulfillment of our wishes in hallucinated form.

Since Freud's theory emphasized the importance of repressed sexuality, it is no wonder that he saw sex as the primary source of most symbols in dreams. The extent to which manifest symbols could be perceived as having latent sexual referents is obvious in Freud's analysis in his classic *The Interpretation of Dreams* (1900).

"—*All elongated objects, such as sticks, tree-trunks and umbrellas (the opening of these last being comparable to an erection) may stand for the male organ—as well as all long, sharp weapons, such as knives, daggers and pikes. . . .—Boxes, cases, chests, cupboards and ovens represent the uterus, and also hollow objects, ships, and vessels of all kinds.—Rooms in dreams are usually women; if the various ways in and out of them are represented, this interpretation is scarcely open to doubt. . . . A dream of going through a suite of rooms is a brothel or harem dream. . . .—Steps, ladders or staircases, or, as the case may be, walking up or down them, are representations of the sexual act.—Smooth walls over which the dreamer climbs, the façades of houses . . . correspond to erect human bodies, and are probably repeating in the dream recollections of a baby's climbing up his parents or nurse. . . .—A woman's hat can very often be interpreted with certainty as a genital organ, and, moreover, as a* man's. *The same is true of an overcoat. . . . In men's dreams a necktie often appears as a symbol for the penis. . . .—It is highly probable that all complicated machinery and apparatus occurring in dreams stand for the genitals (and as a rule male ones). . . . Nor is there any doubt that all weapons and tools are used as symbols for the male organ: e.g., ploughs, hammers, rifles, revolvers, daggers, sabres, etc.—In the same way many landscapes in dreams, especially any containing bridges or wooded hills, may clearly be recognized as descriptions of the genitals. . . ."* (pp. 354–56)

Jung's archetypes and the collective unconscious. Carl Jung, a disciple of Freud, went beyond Freud's dream analysis with its focus on unconscious and sexual repression resulting from the individual's own experience. For Jung, it was the repetitive themes in dreams that were significant. These themes he believed were part of the dreamer's *collective unconscious* and consisted of *archetypes* of existence. He saw the collective unconscious as being at a deeper level than the personal unconscious and derived from our evolutionary history, making us see the world in much the same way that our ancestors did. Thus archetypes of birth, death, resur-

rection, power, and God are the "stuff" of dreams; they may also appear in other creations, such as masks. Whereas Freud saw dream symbols as representing past conflicts and events, Jung believed that they represented aspects of the individual's present life and future possibilities. Symbols in dreams were seen as providing clues not to what the dreamer had been, but to what he or she was in the process of becoming.

Sex and age differences in dream content. The manifest content of dreams can be scored in an objective, reliable way by means of standardized rating scales developed by Calvin Hall and Robert Van de Castle (1966). When this scoring system was applied to 500 home dreams of 100 male college students and also to those of a similar number of female students, the following patterns emerged.

Women's dreams tend to take place in familiar, indoor settings; men's dreams are in unfamiliar, outdoor surroundings. Men dream more of groups, women more of familiar, individual people. Women focus more on descriptions of physical appearance of the characters in their dreams.

Other sex differences are that men's dreams reveal more aggression, sex, physical activity, and achievement themes. ◆ *(p. 288) Women's dreams utilize more subtle forms of aggression, more emotion, and more verbal activity.*

These differences seem to be exactly those that characterize the stereotyped view of male and female in our society, and to some extent, may reflect bias in what the subjects reported to the experimenters. The *report* of a dream is not the same as the *experience* of a dream and is influenced by the social variables of the reporting situation. Again we have the problem of not being able to look directly at the behavior we are studying—the dream—but having to assess it through some intermediate, observable behavior—in this case, a verbal report.

In a high percentage of the aggressive dreams reported by both adults and children, the dreamer is the victim and not the aggressor. And children report apprehension as the primary emotion in their dreams rather than joyful fulfillment of their wishes.

Nightmares. Four-year-old Adam let out a scream of terror in the middle of the night that awakened his father, who picked him up out of bed to console him.

> *"There's a bear chasing me! He's going to hurt me."*
>
> *"There's no bear; you were sleeping and were only having a nightmare."*
>
> *"But I'm afraid! It was a real bear."*
>
> *"Go back to sleep now; the bear will be gone. You'll see it was only a nightmare."*
>
> *"But how do I know that I'm awake now and not dreaming, and that you're not part of that nightmare thing and that the bear won't come back as soon as I do what you say?"*

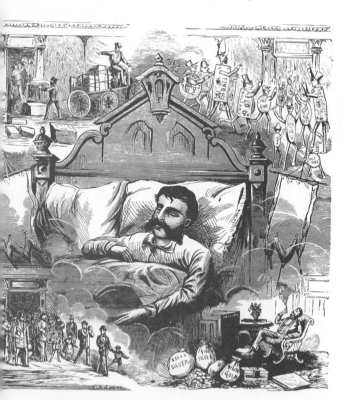

◆ The title of this woodcut from the 1880s is "The Merchant's Dream of Success."

How indeed? Can we really be so sure that we know what is real and what is imaginary and which form of our consciousness is normal?

When was the last time you had a nightmare? Nightmares are surprisingly widespread; 86 percent of a college sample reported at least one in the past year, and 5 percent indicated they had them at least once a week (Feldman & Hersen, 1967).

Nightmare themes often center around catastrophes that the dreamer is helpless to do anything about. Danger, dread, debilitation, and death are common core themes of nightmares. Falling, being chased, and being immobilized when action is necessary are also very frequent. Animals are among the most prominent nightmare characters retrospectively reported by the dreamer.

In laboratory studies of nightmares, where the dreamer is awakened and immediately reports on the nature of the nightmare, some thematic differences occur between REM sleep and Stage 4 NREM sleep. While REM nightmares contain anxiety and threatening material, those occurring in Stage 4 tend to include more internally directed aggression—falling, being crushed, choked, etc., accompanied by screams, vocalization, and more fright than REM dreams. REM nightmares often are continuations of nonnightmare REM dreams (Fisher et al., 1970).

While there are many intriguing questions one wishes to pose regarding the causes, correlates, and consequences of these terrors of the night, few sound answers are available for us at the present time. Although the nightmare dream has occupied the speculative attention of writers, philosophers, playwrights, medical doctors, and scientists since antiquity, understanding of its nature, cause, and course of progress is still relatively minimal. We have had hunches and hypotheses but few testable theoretical assumptions (Hersen, 1972). Further advances in our understanding of both nightmares and regular dreaming will require that we identify the related neurological processes while retaining our awareness of their reality as psychological processes.

Sensory Deprivation or Overload

The distortions of experience that occur under conditions of sensory deprivation were perhaps the first altered states of consciousness to be studied seriously by psychologists. It was found that any situation that involves unusual or prolonged reduction in the normal level of stimulus input or in the individual's motor functioning can give rise to such experiences. Prolonged solitary confinement, sensory and social deprivation (as occurs in the Arctic or at sea), and even prolonged immobilization in a cast or an iron lung have been shown to result in hallucinations and other changes in cognitive functioning. (See *P&L* Close-up at right.)

In one study of sixteen subjects who underwent a week or more of sensory isolation in a chamber where auditory and visual stimulation were virtually eliminated, eleven experienced hallucinations. They were mostly flashes of light, flickering lights, dim glowing lights, and so on, that lacked shape and usually appeared in the peripheral field of vision. The hallucinations were usually of very short duration, about five to ten seconds, although some were reported to last for as long as fifteen minutes. Many subjects reported only one or two brief hallucinatory periods a day; others only one or two during the entire week. Five reported no hallucinatory activity; the women appeared less prone to hallucinations.

In addition to visual hallucinations, several auditory hallucinations were reported. These were usually very realistic, such as howling dogs, a ringing alarm clock, and the sound of a typewriter. Two tactual-kinesthetic hallucinations were also reported. One consisted of cold steel pressing on the subject's forehead and cheeks; the other was a sensation of someone

Close-up
What Do You Say to a Naked Hallucination?

Under certain extreme and unusual conditions, the stimulus for perception seems to be not "out there" but "inside the head." An illusion of perception in which there is a perception of reality in the absence of external stimulus energy is called a *hallucination.* Unlike perceptual illusions, which are shared by most comparable observers, hallucinations are private, idiosyncratic events. It is this feature that makes them an intriguing puzzle for psychologists, and a cause of concern for psychiatrists. Active hallucination is taken as one of the primary diagnostic indicators of psychosis and will be discussed in that connection in Chapter 11. But hallucinations can also be caused by emotional stress, sensory deprivation, hypnosis, and hallucinogenic drugs, as well as by sleep deprivation.

In trying to evaluate whether a strange perceptual experience is a bona fide hallucination or only a facsimile of one—that is, caused by some nonobvious external source of stimulation—apply the following seven tests:

_____1. Volitional Control—Can you will it away?

_____2. Blocked Sensory Input—Is it still there when the appropriate sense receptor is blocked (mask eyes or cover ears)?

_____3. Consensual Validation—Do other people in the same situation report the same experience?

_____4. Cross-Modality Check—Can you touch it or kick it?

_____5. Physical-Attribute Check—Does a tape recorder or light meter also detect it?

_____6. Response-Stimulation Coordination—Does it get bigger under a magnifying lens? Does the sound level change as you move toward or away from it?

_____7. If you point out to a naked perception that it has no clothes on, does it blush?

If the first two checks are positive and the others are negative, do not pass "Go," but proceed immediately to the student health service.

pulling the mattress from under the subject. In most instances, the auditory and tactual hallucinations were reported during the last two days of isolation.

On first emerging from the chamber, subjects reported that images were more vivid than previously experienced. Hypersensitivity to sounds was also very common, especially during the first night after the experiment when subjects were aware of even the slightest sounds. Many sounds that normally are irritating seemed pleasant and in some cases were even considered delightful. Traffic noises seemed particularly loud and somewhat startling. Tests administered after isolation, however, showed no gross perceptual changes, and the minor changes in sensitivity disappeared shortly after the first day (Zubeck, Pushkar, Sansom, & Gowing, 1961).

Other studies demonstrated that a low level of diffuse visual and auditory stimulation had even more profound effects than an absence of stimulation. The following changes were reported in one such study.

Visual hallucinations were generally quite simple at the beginning, but later became more vivid and complex. At first there was a general lighting of the visual field, then dots or lines of light, then geometric figures and patterns. Finally full scenes appeared. One man thought he saw things coming at him and withdrew his head accordingly when this occurred; one was convinced that pictures were being projected on his goggles; another felt that someone was with him in the cubicle. These hallucinations were more vivid than normal imagery and appeared to be projected as on a movie screen in front of the subject, rather than in the "mind's eye" as is normally the case with imagery. Such experiences could be endured for only a few days, even though the subjects were being paid $20 a day (Heron, 1961).

It seems clear from present experimental findings that meaningful sensory experiences are necessary for the normal functioning of the brain. The complex, continually active brain, which never even allows itself forty winks, apparently demands that the environment, too, stay awake and provide stimulating conversation. Sensory isolation may be thought of as a means of "destructuring the environment." The subject, made uncertain and anxious by the lack of an orientation in space and time, has a tendency to try to structure the environment and restore meaning to the situation. In this attempt, the fantasies, hallucinations, and perceptual distortions that appear are in accordance with the subject's personality and past environment, as well as with the experimental setting.

Increased sensory input, excessive motor activity, and/or intense emotional arousal can all precipitate altered states of consciousness. The need to be alert and vigilant for a long time can also result in hallucinations or changed perceptions. Such experiences are frequently reported arising from prolonged vigilance during sentry duty, fervent prayer, intense mental absorption in some all-consuming task, or concentrated attention on an external object or internal sensation. But extended periods of decreased alertness may also lead to sensations of rhythmic stimulation or of floating in water.

Many instances of altered states of consciousness are reported following such "overstimulating" experiences as mob riots, religious revival meetings, prolonged dancing (such as is done by "whirling" dervishes), extreme fright or panic, trance states during primitive cermonies of numerous kinds, or moments of extreme emotion (whether the emotion be ecstatic love or unbearable grief).

Drugs and Mind Alteration

Saturday, April 10, 1965
"I had been experiencing brief flashes of disas-
sociations, or shallow states of nonordinary
reality. . . . In going over the images I recalled
from my hallucinogenic experience, I had come
to the unavoidable conclusion that I had seen
the world in a way that was structurally differ-
ent from ordinary vision. In other states of non-
ordinary reality I had undergone, the forms and
the patterns I had visualized were always within
the confines of my visual conception of the
world. But the sensation of seeing under the
influence of the hallucinogenic smoke mixture
was not the same. Everything I saw was in front
of me in the direct line of vision; nothing was
above or below that line of vision.

"Every image had an irritating flatness, and
yet, disconcertingly, a profound depth. Perhaps
it would be more accurate to say that the im-
ages were a conglomerate of unbelievably sharp
details set inside fields of different light; the
light in the fields moved, creating an effect of
rotation.

"After probing and exerting myself to remem-
ber, I was forced to make a series of analogies
or similies in order to 'understand' what I had
'seen.'" (Castaneda, 1968, pp. 181–82)

This entry from the journal of anthropologist Carlos Castaneda is part of a fascinating record of his five-year apprenticeship to a Mexican Indian "sorcerer," don Juan, who trained him to achieve awareness and mastery of a world of "nonordinary reality" through the use of peyote, jimson weed, and other plants that produce hallucinatory experiences (1968, 1971, 1972).

This drug-induced alteration in the functioning of mind and in the nature of consciousness was popularized in the 1954 publication of *The Doors of Perception* by Aldous Huxley. Huxley took mescaline as a personal experiment to test the validity of poet William Blake's assertion in *The Marriage of Heaven and Hell* (1793):

"If the doors of perception were cleansed every thing would appear to man as it is, infinite.

"For man has closed himself up, till he sees all thro' narrow chinks of his concern."

The experience for Huxley was one that transcended his perception of ordinary reality, leading not only to extrasensory perceptions but to new modes of thought, more mystical than rational. He described the final stage of giving up his ego within the mescaline experience as one where "there is an 'obscure knowledge' that All is in all—that All is actually each. This is as near, I take it, as a finite mind can ever come to 'perceiving everything that is happening everywhere in the universe.'"

Drugs that affect mental processes are called *psychoactive* drugs. Among these, the ones that can produce sensory hallucinations are termed *hallucinogenic* and those that can produce abnormal patterns of thought and arousal that mimic psychotic patterns are called *psychotomimetic*. Humphry Osmond, an early researcher in this area, used the term "psychedelic" to indicate the psychological consequences of drugs like LSD. *Psychedelic* means "mind manifesting" and was originally intended to be a scientifically neutral term to characterize drugs that led to altered states of consciousness. It is now generally used to refer to hallucinogenic drugs.

The step from experimental use of psychoactive drugs to gain self-knowledge or break perceptual constraints to the habitual use of drugs to "feel good" or turn off the world is a big step. And in all too many instances, it has been an irreversible step into drug dependence and addiction. In this section our focus on altered states of consciousness will lead us first to a brief categorization of the drugs most commonly used in the United States and their chief effects. Then we will describe those conditions other than the drug itself that are partly responsible for the action of the drug.

The Drugstore

A "drug" can be defined broadly as any chemical agent that affects living protoplasm. This encompasses a wide array of substances from vitamins to tobacco, with a wide assortment of physical, psychological, and behavioral effects. Human beings have displayed an active, searching curiosity as to the effects and properties of drugs. We have learned that drugs can result in profound physical effects—some detrimental, some healing—and at some point in prehistoric time our ancestors discovered that drugs could produce remarkable effects on their subjective experience. The history of the use and/or abuse of psychoactive drugs is the history of drugs from cannabis to opium to nicotine, involving people in every time and on every continent, from the use of the opium poppy for its euphoric effects by the Sumerians of 4000 B.C. to the use of peyote in the religious ceremonies of North American Indian tribes today. ▲

Ours is a highly aware, heavy drug-taking society. Every morning, noontime, and evening across the nation, millions of Americans down cup after cup of coffee, puff on cigarette after cigarette. Women seeking the ever evasive mannequin fashionable figure consult their physicians to obtain diet pills, and executives down tranquilizers to be calm in the face of troubles at the office and/or at home. There are cocktail parties, there are drunk drivers, there are millions of alcoholics. There are heroin abusers in the ghettos and junkies in suburbia. America is

a nation all too familiar with drugs. Our patterns of individual drug use and abuse are greatly influenced by the importance of drugs in Western medicine, millions of dollars of advertising, and custom and social influence. (See *P&L* Close-up, p. 293.). Almost every American has had some experience with a behavior-modifying drug of some sort.

Seven major drug groups appear to be involved. These are tobacco, alcohol, cannabis, the narcotic analgesics (pain killers), the hypnotics, the stimulants, and the hallucinogens. In these categories drugs have been grouped together according to their physical, psychological, and behavioral effects and the patterns of tolerance and toxicity associated with them.

Before briefly describing these drug groups and some of their mind-altering effects, it is well to point out that the peak experience of the occasional user or the person experimenting with drugs may diminish with repeated, habitual use. Also the effect the drug has when taken as part of a religious or communal ritual is not likely to be forthcoming when it is taken as a "quick and easy" way to get a lift or a calm.

▲ **U.S. DRUG USE—1911**

Tobacco. The active ingredient here is nicotine. Tobacco is smoked in cigarettes, cigars, and pipes; it is also chewed. The autonomic nervous system is stimulated by low doses and depressed by high doses; the central nervous system is stimulated. Tobacco has a high psychological dependence potential, causes a moderate development of tolerance, and causes irreversible damage to lungs, heart, and blood vessels as a result of chronic use.

Alcohol. Ethyl alcohol is generally consumed as a beverage. Alcohol generally depresses the central nervous system. A mild dose produces relaxation and a loss of inhibitions. Increased dosage leads to impaired judgment, loss of motor coordination, increased aggressiveness, violent behavior, and lessened emotional control. Still greater doses result in gross intoxication

Close-up
A Friend in Weed
Is a Friend Indeed

Among the factors responsible for adolescent students using drugs, one of the most potent is social conformity pressures. A large-scale 1971 survey of over 8000 secondary school students in New York State reveals that adolescents are much more likely to use marijuana if their friends do than if their friends do not (Kandel, 1973).

In this sample, 29 percent reported having used marijuana, with the freshman low of 16 percent escalating to the senior high of 41 percent. Of the users, a third were heavy users, having used it forty times or more. The vast majority of these heavy users (90 percent) also "were into" a variety of other drugs.

To some extent, initiation into the drug scene is a function of modeling parental drug use; students who perceived their mothers to be users of tranquilizers were more likely to become marijuana users than those who perceived their mothers to be nonusers. But the most striking finding was the crucial role that peers played. Association with other drug-using adolescents was the most important correlate of adolescent

marijuana use. ". . . Only 7 percent of adolescents who perceive none of their friends use marijuana use marijuana themselves, in contrast to 92 percent who perceive all their friends to be users" (p. 1068).

As can be seen in the figure, the influence of best friends overwhelms that of parents. Marijuana use is related in a small way to parental drug use, but it does not make much of a difference if your parents do not use drugs if your best friend does—chances are then that you will too. And, on the other hand, if your best friend does not use drugs, it does not make much of a difference if your parents do—chances are you will *not*.

Another instance of the significant role of drug use among friendship peers is that the degree of association between friends based on whether or not they use marijuana is greater than the association between them based on: smoking, drinking alcohol, grade-point average, school program, political orientation, and a range of other social and academic activities and attitudes. It seems reasonable to conclude, then, that drug use is encouraged by social peer pressures and, in turn, forms a basis for association among friends. That is why we say only half-facetiously that "a friend in weed is a friend in deed."

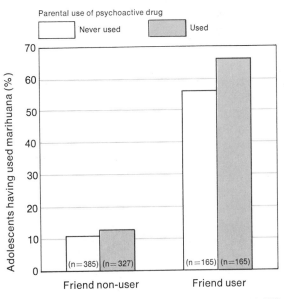

After Kandel, 1973

and, finally, general anesthesia, coma, respiratory depression, and death. Alcohol has a high potential for psychological and physical dependence, and also leads to irreversible tissue damage in such organs as the brain and liver. The symptoms of withdrawal from alcohol abuse are extreme and difficult to treat without a prolonged, intense, and concerted therapeutic effort.

Cannabis sativa. This group consists of marijuana, which is a mixture of the leaves, stems, flowers, and seeds of the plant *cannabis sativa,* and the more potent hashish, an extraction of marijuana resins. It appears that one of the "side effects" of the religious crusades of the Christians against the Moslems (1096–1270 A.D.) was to introduce cannabis to the Western world. (The Vietnam war has served the same intercultural transmission process for some American soldiers.) Cannabis had been in use in many Eastern cultures before the time of Christ and was used for over a thousand years in India as both an intoxicant and an aid to meditation (Blum, 1969).

Marijuana has only a moderate potential for psychological dependence, and no physical dependence results from its use. Preliminary research reveals no indication of chronic pathology, and a lethal dose is virtually unattainable. The chemical mechanism that gives marijuana its intoxicating properties is not yet well understood.

A few decades ago, when marijuana was largely limited to musicians, artists, and ghetto dwellers, it was reported to produce dramatic states of euphoria, ecstasy, and dreamlike fantasies, to improve creativity and sexual behavior, and sometimes to make people go crazy. Now, in the 1970s, when its use knows virtually no class, racial, educational, or other demographic barriers, marijuana has become a social-recreational drug expected to have rather mildly pleasant, "cool" effects. Gone are the extravagant claims of yesteryear.

In small quantities, marijuana produces a state of intoxication much like that of alcohol,

resulting in relaxation and reduced inhibitions, but many researchers feel that with marijuana there are fewer resulting aggressive tendencies. Some users report enhancement of their powers of concentration, some impairment. Some find it sexually stimulating, some the opposite. Behavior under marijuana use depends more than other drugs on social and personal factors. In larger quantities, the drug effect may be more like those of the psychedelic drugs, with distorted time sense and new dimensions in perception. The altered state is more controllable, however, and generally less intense, although there may be panic states and failure of judgment and coordination with high doses.

Narcotic analgesics. This group contains opium, its derivatives (e.g., morphine and heroin), and certain synthetic drugs. Narcotics act upon the central and parasympathetic nervous systems and are used therapeutically to ease pain. They exert a two-pronged pain-killing effect. First, they cause an elevation of the pain threshold, so that a stronger stimulus is required to be interpreted as painful; second, they alter the psychological response to pain. The individual becomes detached from pain, although still aware of it. A related sense of general euphoria also occurs, accompanied by or resulting from indifference to personal and environmental concerns. There is a reduction of the sex, hunger, and thirst drives.

Tolerance, the homeostatic process by which a drug's effect is reduced because it has been used before, develops quickly, and a high physiological and psychological dependence occurs. Use may continue in the absence of any pleasurable effects merely to avoid the traumatic withdrawal symptoms. No chronic tissue damage is caused, but death from overdose during initial uses is a real danger. Overdose from heroin occurs frequently because in the unregulated street sale, the percentage of pure heroin as well as chemical impurities may vary considerably from time to time. Heroin is the major killer of Americans between the ages of eighteen and twenty-five—ahead of accidents, suicide, and cancer (Smith & Gay, 1971).

Hypnotics. The hypnotics consist of the barbiturates and certain nonbarbiturates. They create a state of general nervous depression, acting mainly on the central nervous system. Medically the drugs are used to tranquilize—to reduce anxiety and to induce sleep. Use of hypnotics results in drowsiness, euphoria, intoxication, lack of coordination, memory loss, and impaired judgment, and can lead eventually to a slow-down in breathing, unconsciousness, coma, and death. With chronic use, tolerance develops, as does physical dependence. There is a high potential for psychological dependence.

The hypnotics depress nervous activity. Thus the altered experience of reality they produce is one of calming rather than of increased awareness. In therapeutic doses the hypnotics, or tranquilizers, are amazingly effective in selectively reducing anxiety-motivated behavior. They are also depressants and are similar to alcohol in action, causing slightly euphoric intoxication, loss of inhibition, and inducement of sleep. The state of mind produced is one free from tension and anxious feelings, with a relaxed feeling of well-being.

Stimulants. Included in this category are amphetamine, methamphetamine ("speed"), cocaine, and caffeine (found in coffee, tea, and colas). Drugs of this type stimulate the central nervous system, and lead to increased alertness, wakefulness, activity, and pleasurable sensations, as well as to decreased appetite. In small quantities, amphetamines are sometimes prescribed as "diet pills," with questionable results.

Stimulants like "speed" initially reduce sensitivity to the feelings of others and promote feelings of ability, invulnerability, and power. But greater doses produce irritability, anxiety, paranoid fears, and auditory hallucinations. A high degree of tolerance develops quickly, and there is a high potential for psychological dependence. Soon high doses must be taken intravenously to maintain the desirable effects. But these desirable effects cannot be maintained long. Use rapidly becomes abuse. (See *P&L* Close-up at right and continuing on p. 296.)

After several weeks or months of use, a very typical pattern develops. The user injects large doses of the drug several times each day (the intense feelings of the "rush" immediately after injection are much sought after) and remains awake continuously for three to six days. During this time, he or she becomes increasingly tense and anxious. A "run" is terminated by an interlude of profound sleep ("crashing") that may last one or two days. After waking, irritability is so intense as to seem irrational to non-users. It is often a very unpleasant experience, and a user may start another run or prolong a run in order to avoid it.

Close-up
**Flower People and
the Haight-Ashbury Free Clinic**

David Smith, the director of a drug clinic in San Francisco's once-famed Haight-Ashbury district, describes for us in his own words the "flower people" movement that erupted onto the drug scene in the 1960s and how his clinic emerged as a medical, social, and psychological response to the fallout from that movement.

"There developed in the San Francisco Bay area a widespread belief that LSD and expanded consciousness moved one into what was described as the *counterculture*—a culture whose views were opposite from those of the dominant culture in the United States (the establishment). This counterculture emphasized love and peace, minimized material acquisition, focused on experience rather than rational thought, and moved away from destructive forces such as the war, environmental pollution, exploitation of minorities, and so on. The 'hippie' was born out of this early psychedelic subculture, as were a variety of other things that have greatly influenced our society including acid rock music, multimedia light shows, and our language, producing such words as 'turn on,' 'tune in,' 'drop out,' 'do your thing,' and so on. The basic philosophy was to drop out of the dominant society's value system, turn on to using psychedelic chemicals, expand your consciousness, and tune in to a new philosophy.

"Unfortunately, a very large number of young people flocked to a small area in San Francisco, the Haight-Ashbury district, which came to be regarded as the hippie capital of the world. Many of these young people who came were quite disturbed psychologically; others were naive and did not understand the life-style that they were entering. They began to experiment with a wide variety of drugs, very often taking LSD quite indiscriminately. More destructively, they became progressively more involved with drugs of higher abuse potential, particularly amphetamines, or 'speed' (the street name for methamphetamines).

". . . When the Haight-Ashbury became a 'speed scene,' a great deal of violence developed. The original, peaceful 'flower children' moved out and the more destructive individuals stayed. These individuals very often took depressants to calm their nerves. As a result, the 'Hashbury' is now dominated by young heroin addicts, many of whom have a past history of amphetamine use and many of whom began using heroin as a 'downer' for their stimulant reaction.

"The young people who left, however, did not always go home or return to their former environment, but often formed communes either in the city or in the country. Many of them attempted to expand their consciousness without the use of drugs; others continued to use psychedelic chemicals to maintain this state of awareness that they felt was so valuable. In our studies we have found that communes which have moved on to a more stable family structure and away from drugs are healthier and more likely to survive. Communes that remain drug oriented have much less chance of providing a healthy life for the young people or their children." (Smith, 1971, pp. 683–84)

This run-crash cycle may repeat for several months. "Speed freaks" cannot readily function in the "straight" world. The temporal patterns, aggressiveness, paranoia, and irritability make it very difficult for a speed freak to hold a job or even to keep any "straight" friends.

Periods of methamphetamine abuse may be punctuated by physical or psychological breakdown or bouts with the law, or terminated by death. A methamphetamine abuser may begin injecting heroin or barbiturates ("downers") to ease the active symptoms of paranoia and anxiety that may be experienced while too "high" on speed. Mixing drugs, changing dependence, then further complicates the drug experience.

Hallucinogens. The hallucinogens, or psychedelics, include LSD-25, psilocybin (the "magic mushroom"), mescaline, and DOM (STP). The chemistry of their action is not fully understood, but they act primarily on the central nervous system and perhaps interfere with the filtering mechanisms of the brain (Shulgin, 1969). Drugs of this type closely resemble certain natural chemicals essential at various stages of the transmission of nerve impulses. Hallucinogens may block the action of these chemicals or act as a substitute for them (Seiden, 1970).

The hallucinogens uniquely and profoundly alter perception, resulting in greater sensitivity to all forms of stimulation (visual, auditory, tactile, etc.) and greater emotional sensitivity. They also create a sense of timelessness. On rare occasions they can cause psychotic reactions.

These drugs build up complete tolerance after four to five days, which is lost just as rapidly, and physiological dependence does not develop. There is a slight potential for psychological dependence. There is no substantive evidence to suggest that these drugs cause any tissue or brain damage (Irwin, 1971; Harvey, 1971).

The hallucinogens, or psychedelic drugs, are the most powerful of the mind-altering drugs. The label "hallucinogen" is not entirely accurate, since there is a physiological basis for the perceptions that occur. Actual hallucinations are not common with the use of the psychedelics. There are more likely to be acute changes in perception and interpretation and pseudohallucinations, in which an individual distorts perceptions and projects other meanings and images into them but is still aware of their realistic basis. For instance, the walls may "melt" or brown foam may creep out of drains, but the walls and drains are there and the user usually realizes that a distortion is occurring.

"Psychoactive" is indeed a good adjective to describe the effects of LSD and other psychedelic drugs. The variety of effects is staggering. Existence seems more interesting. A sense of timelessness may result, whereby a minute seems like an hour, and the past, present, and future seem like one. Stimuli of every sort may seem overwhelming; stimuli of one sort may be perceived in other forms, for example, music may be seen as waves of astonishingly vivid colors. One may have a mystical experience. Concepts and sensations that normally seem paradoxical may seem amazingly compatible—black may be white, life and death may exist together, one may see profound meaning in what normally seems trivial, a flower may seem to hold the key to existence.

Subjective reports of psychedelic experiences may be categorized as primarily sensory, recollective-analytic, or integral (Masters & Houston, 1966). At the sensory level, habitual concepts are cast aside, and there is generally a changed or "heightened" awareness of perceptions. At the recollective-analytic level, habitual interpretations of oneself, of relations to others, and of memories of past experiences are loosened. New insights may arise. There may be new interpretations of myths and symbols. At the integral level, religious revelations or mystical experiences may occur. One's state of mind may flow from one level to another, dwelling here or there depending on the stimuli, one's personality and mood, and the setting.

These levels of response are illustrated in an observer's account of a psychedelic drug experience:

"Watts listened to organ music, and described his experience. 'Every sound seems to issue from a vast human throat, moist with saliva.' An impression at the sensorial level. At a level of recollective-analysis he can 'hear the priest "putting on" his voice, hear the . . . steadily unctuous tones of a master deceptionist.' But the priest's voice became 'the primordial howl of the beast in the jungle' at the symbolic stage of the experience. Finally a mystical realization at the integral level of his psychedelic experience occurs, and Watts declares, 'I can hear in that one voice the simultaneous presence of all levels of man's history, as of all stages of life before me.'" (Krippner, 1970, p. 41)

The integration of drugs such as LSD, mescaline, and peyote into a religious experience, as occurs in American Indian tribes in the Southwest and Mexico, is hardly likely in a laboratory setting. However, psychedelic "transcendental" reactions may be elicited from research subjects if the drug variable is made part of a total "religious" experience. An unusual and fascinating study did just that (Pahnke, 1963, 1967).

Forty theological students were prepared for the drug experience first by attending "indoctrination" meetings about religious potentials. Then half of them received 30,000 micrograms of psilocybin prior to attending a lengthy Good Friday service. The service included prayers, songs, music, and personal meditation. Other subjects were randomly assigned to an active placebo condition in which they received nicotinic acid, which produces sensations of warmth and tingling. Thus set, setting, and prior history of the drug user all combined to maximize the religious interpretation of any psychedelic reactions.

On a detailed questionnaire given immediately after the experience, those who were in the psilocybin condition reported significantly more mystical, transcendental experiences than did the placebo controls. These differences persisted on a follow-up interview six months later.

Conditions That Influence Drug Effects

You might think that taking a certain amount of a drug would have a predictable effect. Not so. At least five conditions before or at the time of the drug taking help to determine what its consequences will be: the chemical nature and dose of the drug, whether there is an acquired tolerance for the drug, the "set" of the drug taker, the individual's personality characteristics, and the social-psychological situation in which the drug is taken.

Drug structure and dosage. The most obvious determinant of the reaction to a drug, of course, is its chemical composition and the size of the dose. The relationship between dosage and response for any drug can be empirically determined by plotting a curve that relates variations in the dosage to gradations in a given response. This *dose-response* function can be established for an *individual*, but not very satisfactorily when the data from many individuals are lumped together. Research has shown that drug effects vary depending on body size and on the speed with which the drug is absorbed, detoxified, and excreted, all of which vary for different individuals. Thus the same response may be generated in two people given different doses, or the same dosage level may result in different responses (Klee et al., 1961).

LSD is particularly interesting pharmacologically because part of its chemical composition resembles serotonin, the chemical that plays a key role in transmission of central nervous system impulses. Research is in progress to elucidate the ways in which LSD and serotonin are related. Another remarkable property of LSD is that tiny amounts have noticeable effects. An average oral dose of LSD that produces marked psychological effects is between 100 and 350 micrograms (1 microgram is only a millionth part of a gram). It would take about 30,000 micrograms of psilocybin and over 35,000 micrograms of mescaline to produce an effect of comparable intensity.

In one well-controlled study, it was possible for medical observers to tell perfectly when any of the twelve subjects had taken 1, 2, 4, 8, or 16 micrograms of LSD (per kilogram of their body weight). The experiment used a double-blind procedure in which the three observers (and the subjects) were unaware of the LSD dose administered at any given time. For any single subject, there was discriminably increased impairment in intellectual functioning, confusion, and visual and somatic effects for each higher dose. However, when the subjects were seen in groups, the observers could not *tell from their performance which ones had received larger or smaller doses. In the group setting, the differences between them were clearly not attributable solely to drug dosage but also to reflected social variables (Klee et al., 1961).*

Acquired tolerance for the drug. The individual's past history of drug use may affect the current impact of the drug. *Tolerance*, as we said before, indicates the process whereby a drug's effect is reduced by virtue of its having been taken before.

Three tolerance mechanisms are known and understood to various degrees. First, the rate at which the body deactivizes the drug may increase, causing the effects of the drug to be less prolonged. Second, the cells of the nervous system may adapt to the presence of the drug and thus not react to the same degree as they did initially. Last is the concept of behavioral tolerance, whereby the drug may lose its effect only on particular behavior. An illustration of this hypothesized mechanism is shown in an experiment involving the effects of amphetamines on lever-pressing in rats.

After a steady low rate of responding had been established by means of an appropriate reinforcement schedule, the initial effect of a dose of amphetamine was to increase that low response rate greatly. However, after repeated dosage, the response rate returned to its predrug level. This could not be explained in terms of an overall development of tolerance: It appeared that the availability of reinforcement for the slower rate of lever pressing enabled the animals to learn to control the unfavorable aspects of the drug action in that situation, thus achieving a sort of behavioral tolerance (Harvey, 1971).

A given drug may have multiple effects on an organism, and tolerance for all the effects may not occur uniformly. For example, results of the use of narcotics include drowsiness, reduced ability to concentrate, euphoria, a sense of detachment, reduction of hunger, thirst, and sex drives, feelings of heaviness of the limbs, itchiness, constipation, nausea, and pupillary constriction. Tolerance may develop to most of these effects to the extent that doses far exceeding the formerly lethal dose may be administered with virtually no effects, pleasurable or adverse, except for constipation and pupillary constriction, which may continue about as before.

Related drugs may also lead to what is known as *cross-tolerance*. This means that the drugs are similar enough to be interchangeable. Their effects and action are the same; thus a tolerance developed under one drug generalizes to suppress the action of the other drug also. For example, a person addicted to heroin also has a tolerance for morphine because they are both narcotics, and repeated LSD usage results in tolerance for mescaline and psilocybin. The physiological mechanisms responsible for cross-tolerance are being studied scientifically to discover how metabolism, nervous system pathways, and brain areas function to allow one drug to substitute for another.

The phenomenon of tolerance is what leads addicts to have to keep increasing the dosage or frequency with which they "shoot up." It is as if the demand is always greater than the supply, and—what makes the situation intolerable—when the need is supplied, it is not enough to produce the effect it used to. This results not only in escalation of drug abuse but frustration, anxiety, and experimentation with any and all drugs that might produce the desired high (or low).

The drug taker's expectations. The attitudes, expectancies, and motivations toward the total drug experience influence what that experience will be. Why people are taking the drug in the first place helps to predict whether the effect will be euphoria, anxiety, religious transcendence, or other experiences. To some extent, drug users find in drugs what they have sought.

Typically LSD highs are not as profound when the same dose is taken by subjects participating in an experiment as when they are seeking aesthetic experiences, personal growth, or religious meaning on their own or with friends. In addition, fears over the legal, medical, social, and behavioral consequences of drug taking bias the effects of the drugs.

"A 34-year-old single, hard working, white male business executive, in his capacity as president of a small and rapidly growing company, had a good deal of responsibility. He was well dressed, drove quality cars, had his own airplane, and fit the role of the dashing urban bachelor. He was a regular user of alcohol, attended many cocktail parties, and was a heavy smoker of cigarettes—approximately two packs per day. At the suggestion of various friends and out of curiosity he decided to smoke marijuana. He shared one marijuana cigarette with two other individuals; then they all went to dinner. During the course of his conversation he noted that he would forget what he had just said; as a result he became very disturbed. His anxiety increased because he felt he was losing control of himself; he said later it was like what he thought would happen if one lost his mind. The other two individuals who had smoked approximately the same dosage were having a very good time and showed no adverse effects. This individual, however, became quite panic-stricken and was taken home and given a sedative. After a good night's sleep there were no residual effects, but the individual described his marijuana experience as being most unpleasant, and said he greatly preferred alcohol. Subsequent interviews indicated that the threat of being arrested while under the influence of marijuana was also one of his major concerns." (Smith & Mehl, 1970, p. 71)

In reviewing the results of research relating subject expectations, LSD dose, and drug effects, Theodore Barber concluded: ". . . at least one third of the variance in response to a relatively small dose of LSD (25 – 100 micrograms) is independent of the drug *per se* and is related to factors which determine response to a placebo, such as subjects' expectancies as to what effects are likely to occur" (1970, p. 17).

As with other relationships between physical-biological variables and psychological ones, the psychological variables exert relatively less influence on behavior as the physical ones become more strong, bigger, more intense. When powerful drugs are administered in large doses or are taken without awareness of their intended effects, they will affect perception, thinking, time-sense, and emotional stability regardless of the psychological and social situation.

Personality characteristics. To some extent the personality characteristics the user brings into the drug experience shape what the drug will bring out. Both the overall intensity and the quality of reactions have been related to personality variables of drug subjects.

When experimental subjects ingested moderate doses of LSD under standardized conditions (after having taken a battery of personality tests), their behavior, both observed and self-reported, was significantly related to their test results. Those with the strongest *reaction to the drug had scores showing greater aesthetic sensitivity, imaginativeness, preference for an unstructured, spontaneous, inward-turning life, and low aggression, competition, and conformity. Those on whom LSD had the* least *effect had higher test scores in dogmatism and rigidity and in need for control (McGlothlin, Cohen, & McGlothlin, 1967).*

Another study showed that personality measures before drugs were taken were related to whether or not an individual experienced hostility and paranoid reactions during LSD drug sessions (Linton & Langs, 1964).

The social situation. Drugs are always taken in some kind of social setting, be it a physical environment that is barren and sterile, as in a hospital, or one that is gay and exciting, as at a party. Drugs are taken with other people present or absent, with friends or strangers, with others who are seen as sympathetic, hostile, curious, or indifferent. The social variables that combine to create the external context in which one takes drugs may be among the most crucial determinants of the drug's action on one's moods and emotions.

Where experimenters are friendly and relaxed and believe in the therapeutic value of the drug being tested, they will create a social environment likely to make the subjects receptive and open to the new experience. On the other hand, where researchers are coolly impersonal, treat the subject like a "guinea pig," and expect a psychedelic drug to lead to bizarre, psychotic-like behavior, they will act in ways that encourage suspicion, anxiety, and other negative reactions from the drug experience (Unger, 1963). Taking drugs alone rather than in a group setting is more likely to lead to anxiety and depression (Slater, Morinoto, & Hyde, 1957).

The social situation is not nearly as critical for the regular user as it is for the novice, the first-timer, who may be using the drug for "recreation" or goals other than science. The social influence of the group is not only reassuring in providing approval of the action, but helps to define what the "proper" procedures are and establish points of comparison by which the user can identify and label what is being experienced and how "normal" it is (Becker, 1967). Such an effect of the group on the individual is, of course, not limited to drug situations, but it is especially important whenever a person is about to enter a novel, ambiguous situation where there are no objective guidelines and the person is very much ego-involved in the outcome ("wants it to work," "to be OK," etc.).

The subculture of heavy drug users introduces new dimensions into any understanding of the effects of drug use and abuse. Largely because drugs are illegal, prices are exorbitantly high, but once addicted, it does not matter how high the price: the "doper" has to have a fix.

Given the escalating demand created by progressive tolerance, a daily heroin habit may run up to $200 or more a day.

How does someone get $1400 a week for just this one expenditure? Not by any regular employment, to be sure. Robbery and burglary are the obvious alternatives, but to realize a $200 profit from a "fence" may require stealing up to $1000 worth of goods. For women, prostitution can become a means of supporting the habit. For both sexes, becoming drug pushers can be the avenue that gets them their share while spreading what has been called "the American disease" of heroin addiction.

The addict becomes socialized in a variety of ways into a world of criminality and often comes to prefer that hip, exciting, uncertain street-life to the straight-life of the "squares." Imagine awakening every morning of your life knowing you have to steal a thousand dollars' worth of merchandise, push about that much worth of dope, or have intercourse with a dozen strangers (who may belong to the vice squad or crime syndicate, or carry venereal disease)! That is the outlook that colors the edges of the doors of perception opened by heavy drug abuse. Broadly speaking, all these changes in attitudes and behavior are part of the effects of drug use, as well as the characteristics of the social situation in which new recruits become enmeshed.

In conclusion, then, there is little question but that nonordinary reality may be apprehended by pharmacological means. By temporarily altering the functioning of the central nervous system and the sympathetic nervous system, drugs may have effects on:

1. The *body* (changes in pulse, respiration, heart rate, pupils, body temperature, blood pressure, and tendon reflexes change);

2. The *visual-perceptual system* (perceptual sharpening, blurring, projecting visual images, distortion of detail or ground, dimensional alteration, etc.);

3. The *attentional-intellectual system* (a dreamy detached feeling, a passive orientation, decrement in performance tasks, high distractability, memory impairment, etc.);

4. The *sense of time* (alteration in the rate at which events occur, merging or appearance of irrelevance of post and future time perspectives);

5. The *emotional-affective system* (more extreme, or variable moods).

What may be called "ecstatic-transcendental" reactions, where subjects interpret their experience in mystical, religious terms, are rarely elicited by drugs. In one study of over 200 subjects only 11 (5 percent) had an "illumination" experience that they interpreted as religious (Masters & Houston, 1966). In another study only 3 of 48 subjects (6 percent) reported "transcendental" experiences after taking 500 micrograms of LSD (Johnson, 1968).

Throughout recorded history, human beings have not been content with "reality" as given or consciousness as ordinarily experienced. We have sought means to enter new realms of awareness, to go beyond merely perceiving appearances to "seeing" essences. Of the many ways in which the limits of consciousness have been expanded, one has been by the eating and smoking of plants provided by nature.

Whether such desires to transcend the empirical reality of the here-and-now by means of drugs is "right," "good," and "proper" is debatable on moral and social-philosophic levels and is established in legal terms. On a psychological level, we can say that each day millions of Americans use a variety of drugs, some of which sometimes alter their view of the world. The drug experience may be a trivial social exercise in adolescent rebelliousness to society (and conformity to the gang), a unique mystical revelation, a trapdoor to madness, or a ticket to prison—but it cannot be denied that through such experiences human beings have altered their consciousness, leading psychologists to a new concern with the nature of human consciousness.

Meditation, Yoga, and Zen

"Meditation consists in letting go."
"Through Zen practice ultimate enlightenment is attained and emancipation is realized."

American students are in the process of discovering the phenomenon (and benefits) of *meditation*, one means of altering consciousness that has been perfected over centuries by Indian and Japanese practitioners. According to a recent estimate, one form of *meditation*, "Transcendental Meditation" has become so popular in this country that over 350,000 American disciples daily tune out of ordinary consciousness and turn on to its "power of positive nonthinking" (*Newsweek*, Jan. 7, 1974).

What is the attraction of meditation and the exotic psychologies of Eastern cultures? And why has it taken so many years for Westerners to appreciate their significance? The answers to the two questions are interrelated; fundamental features of Western (particularly American) culture are alien to those of the oriental way of life, and some people are beginning to question the relevance of our cultural values as guides for their lives.

Individual consciousness reflects the social-cultural "programming" under which it has developed. Our American culture emphasizes action, outward orientation, concern for the approval of others, control of nature by technology, a linear mode of time, planning for the future, and rational-logical thought processes. This is the antithesis of the traditional oriental perspective.

Broadly conceived, the concept of "meditation" involves a variety of techniques, attitudes, and values that provide alternatives to the dominant themes of action, rationality, and outward orientation that underlie Western cultural experience. Those who practice meditation claim there is a shift in the direction of consciousness to a more passive, quiescent inner focus, and a receptive tuning of the mind to be in harmony with nature and life as it "really is" now (not as it "might" or "ought" to be). In addition to a state of mental and physical relaxation, peace, and calm, persons who meditate often say they feel a more profound change in the way they think and what they think about. They find meditation to be a unique means of discovering knowledge of one's self, one's own construction of consciousness, and the relation of the self to everything else ("the All"). Using the metaphor of Robert Ornstein,

"Meditation is a technique for turning down the brilliance of the day, so that ever present and subtle sources of energy can be perceived within. It constitutes a deliberate attempt to separate oneself for a short period from the flow of daily life, and to 'turn off' the active mode of consciousness, in order to enter the complementary mode of 'darkness'. . . ." (1972, p. 107)

A variety of techniques are used by different masters of meditation in different countries, but common to all of them is concentration of attention and awareness on a single, unvarying source of stimulation for a certain time period. This "single-mindedness" may be an intent gaze directed toward a visual object, a sound of a word, chant, or prayer repeated again and again, or a physical movement performed in identical fashion time after time. ◆

◆ Meditation, once almost solely an Eastern phenomenon, is becoming more popular in the West, particularly among young people.

Transcendental Meditation

The form of meditation that is attracting so many disciples is called *Transcendental Meditation,* or TM. Its originator, Maharishi Mahesh Yogi, defines it as "turning the attention inwards towards the subtler levels of thought until the mind transcends the experience of the subtlest state of thought and arrives at the source of the thought." TM gained much notoriety when the Beatles journeyed to India and the Mahesh Yogi in search of new spiritual values and personal contentment.

The basic procedure TM utilizes is remarkably simple, but the effects claimed for it are extensive. One simply sits comfortably, closes the eyes, and engages in an effortless mental repetition of a special sound for short periods of time (usually twenty minutes twice daily). The practice of TM involves neither religious beliefs nor changes in life style.

The special sounds or syllables that are silently repeated are called *mantras.* Mantras are not written down but are recorded in an oral tradition and individually given out from teacher to student. Each meditator's mantra is a specially chosen sound which will help him or her experience deep relaxation and expansion of the mind. The Transcendental Meditation technique is thoroughly described in the Hindu holy books, the *Bhagavad-Gita* and the *Vedas.*

TM is considered to be a form of *Mantram Yoga.* In some ways it is similar to practices common in Christian and Hebrew services. They too have rituals for focusing attention away from the external material world to the inner spiritual reality, such as repetition of prayers, singing or chanting of hymns, concentration on symbolic forms, and restricted body movements. However, over the generations, such religious exercises have too frequently became automatic rituals that do not lead the practitioner to the kinds of altered consciousness reported by earlier religious figures. It may be that TM's popularity represents a rediscovery for Westerners of what was once a vital element in the mystical aspect of Western religious traditions.

What does TM do? After a review of the physiological, psychological, and social consequences of the TM experience, one is more likely to ask, "Is there anything TM does *not* do?"

● The following are some of the physiological changes attributed to TM by researchers Robert Wallace and Herbert Benson (1972): increased blood flow, decreased oxygen consumption and carbon dioxide production, increased skin resistance, alert "watchfulness" brainwave patterns, and a generalized "quiescence of the sympathetic nervous system" (usually overstimulated by the stresses of modern life).

In a variety of other studies, the benefits of TM were revealed in improved learning performance and lessened anxiety, hostility, and aggression. It has also been used effectively to improve therapeutic progress among mental patients, prisoners, and drug abusers (see bibliography of current research by Kanellakos & Ferguson, 1973, and evaluation by Schwartz, 1974).

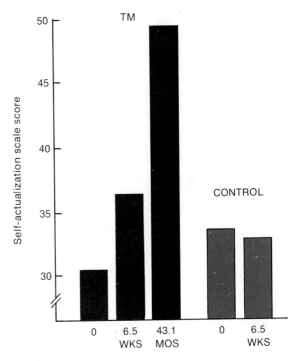

After Ferguson & Gowan, 1976

● **POSITIVE PERSONALITY CHANGES WITH TM**
Increased self-actualization, as indicated by a higher score on the Northridge Self-Actualization Scale, was shown by both short- and long-term meditators as compared to nonmeditating controls. Measures were taken before and after the short-term group began TM.

Yoga

The term *yoga,* as popularly used, connotes meditation based on physical posturing and breathing exercises. The use of yoga for health improvement without an accompanying dedication to a spiritual discipline is *not* common in India but is in America.

In the strict definition of the term, *yoga* "refers to a system of beliefs and practices whose goal is to attain a union of the individual self with Supreme Reality or the Universal Self" (Barber, 1970). Each of several different systems of yoga utilizes its own processes for reaching the ultimate state of trance. One system, called *Raja Yoga,* includes eight processes: self-control *(yama);* religious observances *(niyama);* physical postures *(asana);* regulation of breathing *(pranayama);* suppression of sense impressions stimulated by external objects and events *(pratyahara);* concentration or fixed attention on an object *(dharana);* contemplation of a solitary object for prolonged periods *(dhyana);* and losing consciousness of one's concentration by total absorption in a trance state *(samadhi).*

Observations of trained yogis (practitioners of yoga) under tightly controlled conditions have revealed that during the trance (samadhi) state of the yogi, there is a tremendous reduction in oxygen intake and carbon dioxide production (indicating reduced metabolic rate), reduction in rate of respiration, great reduction in heart rate (but not down to zero in any recorded instance), and increase in skin resistance.

One experiment also substantiated the control over painful stimuli claimed by some yogis. Two trained yogis immersed their hands in water of 4°C while meditating and indicated no sign of pain whatsoever during this experience. In fact, their EEG records indicated alpha waves throughout the experience, not likely in the presence of stress or pain (Anand, Chhina, & Singh, 1961).

On the other hand, serious investigations of the popular public demonstrations, such as fire-walking, being buried alive, sleeping on a bed of nails, and so on, have found them to be either deceptions, explainable by simple principles, or unrelated to true yoga practice. For example, lying on a bed of nails is not a major feat of control of mind over body if the nails are close together and not very sharp and if the person has a high pain tolerance, relaxes the back muscles, and is doped on hashish or opium. More controlled research is necessary to evaluate just how far yoga training can go in altering human functioning. (See *P&L* Close-up, p. 305.)

Zen

Although Western interest in the doctrine and practice of Zen is relatively new, its history dates back thousands of years, in India and Japan through Buddhism and in China through Taoism and Confucianism as well as Buddhism. Unlike TM, the practice of Zen involves more than brief daily exercises. It is a way of life and a guiding philosophy. A summary of the new orientation sought is given by D. T. Suzuki, one of the foremost authorities on Zen Buddhism:

"The essence of Zen Buddhism consists in acquiring a new viewpoint on life and things generally . . . . We must try to see if there is any other way of judging things, or rather, if our ordinary way is always sufficient to give us the ultimate satisfaction of our spiritual needs. . . . We must endeavor to find a way somewhere which gives a sense of finality and contentment. Zen proposes to do this for us and assures us of the acquirement of a new point of view in which life assumes a fresher, deeper, and more satisfying aspect." (Quoted in Stace, 1960, p. 89)

The state of mind sought through Zen meditation is one of alert emptiness, in which the mind is like a mirror, simply reflecting what impinges upon it from the outside.

"To borrow from the vocabulary of oriental philosophies, the mental reality is water, upon which the winds of external stimuli cause surges of intellects and desires, and which returns to its original level state when the winds' stop." (Akishige, 1970, p. 3)

"I Shall Feel No Pain and Bleed No Blood"

As an adolescent in a concentration camp, Jack Schwartz learned to minimize pain by voluntary automatic control. In self-defense he "taught" himself to control pain, temperature, bleeding, and other internal processes. Now at the age of 48, Schwartz has been the object of several intensive studies of the amazing discipline he can exercise "at will" over his mind and body (Green, Green, & Walter, 1972; Rorvik, 1972).

More recently, in an effort to substantiate the validity of his claims (and public demonstrations) of mind over matter, a rigorously controlled series of investigations have been carried out at the Langley Porter Neuropsychiatric Institute by Kenneth Pelletier (1974).

Experimentation was conducted in an electrically shielded, soundproof room with two physicians in attendance at all times. Baseline levels of functioning were obtained on a variety of psychophysiological measures (EEG patterns, cardiac, respiratory, muscle, and bleeding). These activities were continuously monitored across twenty-four testing sessions on six consecutive days by a team of skilled psychophysiological researchers (from the laboratory of Dr. Joseph Kamiya).

To demonstrate autoregulation of pain and bleeding, Schwartz was instructed to push an unsterilized knitting needle through his bicep and then to try to control bleeding from the wound. This was performed on three occasions when spontaneously requested by the experimenter without any prior preparation by Schwartz. All neurological and psychophysiological indices were monitored before, during, and after the puncture demonstrations.

The attending physician's report states that there was *no* spontaneous bleeding after removal of the needle. Even after he "wrung" the puncture site with moderate pressure, only one small drop of bloody serum was extruded. In two hours, the puncture appeared to have healed, and it was verified that no infection occurred from the needle (which had been rubbed into a carpet with the bare sole of Schwartz's foot thirty seconds before the puncture).

No pain was reported, and none was observable in overt reactions. More remarkable, this traumatic external event did not intrude upon Schwartz's mental state of meditation. His production of EEG alpha waves remained stable before, during, and after the puncture demonstrations.

How did he maintain alpha production, eliminate pain, and minimize bleeding? In his self-report, Schwartz pointed to the cognitive techniques of detachment and depersonalization. He said:

"It's very simple. I do it by changing a single word. I don't stick a needle in *my* arm; [I] stick it through *an* arm. I move outside my body and look at the arm from a distance; with that detachment it becomes an object. It is as though I am sticking the needle into the arm of a chair. I have taught myself to move as easily outside my being as inside it." (Pelletier, 1974, p. 86)

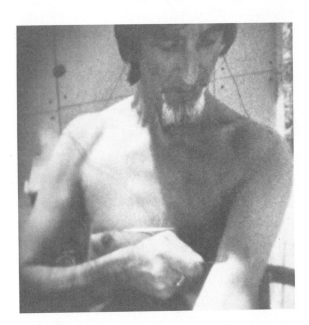

The original meaning of *Zen* was "quiet meditation," but over time the term came to include "wisdom," and now its objective is "enlightenment." The means by which a practitioner realizes enlightenment, or "nonconceptual comprehension" *(satori)* are three:

a) Zazen—exercises to regulate posture and the body, exercises to regulate breathing, and exercises to regulate the mind;

b) Kōan—intellectual exercises of meditating on riddles and questions that logic can never resolve, such as, "What is the sound of one hand clapping?" "How does one look before one's father and mother have met?" To comprehend the Kōan, one must discard rational cognitive processes, since the Kōan can be grasped but never explained. Concentration on the meaning of the Kōan frees the mind of other concerns until only the Kōan remains. Later, the Kōan, too, vanishes, leaving only the mind as a "blurless mirror";

c) Sanshi-Mompō—the practice of "going to a master to ask the way." It consists of disciplined study by a disciple with a Zen master for a long period of time. It is a type of counseling of Zen monks by masters, and it may include explanations, contradictions, perplexities, suggestions, guides, force, shouting, and sudden unexpected blows.

If Zen transforms the mind into a mirror that reflects thoughts and stimulation in each moment, for an instant, one might predict that EEG studies of Zen masters would: (a) reveal patterns characteristic of active concentration, and (b) show a failure to habituate to repetitive stimuli. Both of these predictions have been confirmed in recent investigations.

In a series of studies of practitioners and Zen priests (who had had up to thirty years of "religious austerities"), EEG patterns changed from their ordinary form to a high percentage of alpha waves during periods of Zen practice. The researcher concluded that the changes appear to represent the unique state of consciousness in Zen practice, that of active mental concentration (Yamaoka, 1968).

In another study, a click was sounded 20 times at intervals of 15 seconds while selected brain-wave changes were monitored in three Zen masters and four control subjects (relaxed with closed eyes). Initially, the control subject responded to the new stimulus by "attending" to it, as measured by a blocking of the alpha rhythm each time. But then, as the stimulus recurred, there was habituation to it—it was no longer "noticed," and the alpha waves were not blocked when it occurred.

It marked contrast, the Zen masters responded to each repeated presentation of the stimulus as they did to the first, with blocking of the alpha rhythm. It was as if their openness to the experience of the moment resulted in perceiving the world anew at each sound of life (Kasamatsu & Hirai, 1966).

This finding is especially notable because habituation is one of the most fundamental of all psychological adaptation processes: across a wide range of species and for virtually all responses that organisms make, from leg flexion to complex patterns of exploration and play, habituation is observed with repeated exposure to a stimulus (Welker, 1961). Further research is hoped for to replicate this important conclusion, because it validates in a form acceptable to scientific critics the claims of those who maintain that the subjective states of consciousness produced by Zen really do profoundly alter the relation of human beings to their inner and outer realms of reality. (See *P&L* Close-up below.)

Close-up
Biofeedback: Mind Control Through Technology

Related to the finding of physiological changes through mental discipline in Zen practitioners is the discovery that physiological functions which were formerly thought to be strictly involuntary can be brought under the individual's control by operant techniques. As we have already seen, Neal Miller's demonstrations of physiological changes through learning have opened a new area of research with exciting implications. Individuals can be taught to control a variety of internal body processes by a technique known as *biological feedback,* or *biofeedback.* In biofeedback, minute changes occurring in the body or brain are detected, amplified, and displayed to the person and/or researcher. Sophisticated recording and computer technology make it possible for a person to tune in to what is happening within—subtle changes in heart rate, blood pressure, temperature, and brain-wave patterns that would normally be unobservable.

These ongoing biological processes are thus available as continuous feedback to the individual. A "goal" is established, such as altering the brain-wave pattern in a particular direction, and then the individual continuously monitors his or her progress toward that goal. Subjects have been able to use this technology to change skin temperature by up to 9°F.; reduce blood pressure 15 percent; increase or decrease heart rate; relax tense muscles; alter alpha, beta, and theta EEG frequencies on command; and change still other activities once thought to be beyond human voluntary control.

In one recent study with college students, it was possible to increase mean heart rate by as much as thirty-five beats per minute after several weeks of biofeedback training (Wells, 1973). By applying this approach in medical settings, it is hoped that patients will be able to control hypertension, migraine headaches, and heart conditions even when these maladies can be traced to psychological origins.

The promise that modern technology and operant control may be used to cure our ills and create a life filled with the euphoria of alpha brain waves, however, is far from being realized at this time. Although statistically significant changes have been produced under ideal laboratory testing conditions, clinically significant changes relating to cardiac functioning have not yet been produced (Blanchard & Young, 1973).

It should also be pointed out for students interested in the inexpensive do-it-yourself biofeedback devices being marketed that caution and skepticism should be exercised. It is unlikely that the average person could alter alpha-wave production to any substantial degree using a cheap device and without proper training by an expert. In addition, it is dangerous to rely on biofeedback technology to put your brain and body back into normal working condition rather than altering your habits and life-style to achieve that goal. We have all become too intolerant of pain and anxiety and too eager to reach for the quick and easy solution—even though we know intellectually that happiness is not going to come commercially prepackaged.

Hypnosis

"You do what you like. Or is it possible you have ever not done what you liked—or even, maybe, done what you didn't like? What somebody else liked, in short? Hark ye, my friend, that might be a pleasant change for you, to divide up the willing and the doing and stop tackling both jobs at once. Division of labour, *sistema americano, sa!* For instance, suppose you were to show your tongue to this select and honourable audience here—your whole tongue, right down to the roots?"

"No, I won't," said the youth, hostilely. "Sticking out your tongue shows a bad bringing-up."

"Nothing of the sort," retorted Cipolla. "You would only be *doing* it. With all due respect to your bringing-up, I suggest that before I count ten, you will perform a right turn and stick out your tongue at the company here further than you knew yourself that you could stick it out."

He gazed at the youth, and his piercing eyes seemed to sink deeper into their sockets. *"Uno!"* said he. He had let his riding-whip slide down his arm and made it whistle once through the air. The boy faced about and put out his tongue so long, so extendedly, that you could see it was the very uttermost in tongue which he had to offer. Then turned back, stony-faced, to his former position.

Thomas Mann, *Mario and the Magician,* 1929

Of all the means of altering consciousness, hypnosis is perhaps the way most widely known about and least understood. It has been popularized as a technique for the control of others for one's own gain, as in Svengali's use of hypnosis to control Trilby. "The Shadow," of 1940s radio-serial fame, used hypnosis to "cloud men's minds" and discover "the secrets that lurk in the hearts of men." In the film *The Manchurian Candidate,* hypnosis is used to program an average person into a dedicated, maniacal killer.

The serious study and practical application of hypnosis has suffered from such associations and also from its exploitation as entertainment by stage hypnotists. Because in Show Biz one needs big, quickly produced effects in which people behave in ways the audience is certain they normally would not, hypnotism on the stage tends to demean and degrade human values and has had a generally "bad press." ▲

Animal Magnetism and Mesmerism

In the eighteenth century, a Viennese physician, Anton Mesmer, startled the world when he began to cure afflicted persons by application of *animal magnetism.* He believed that a universal fluid influenced the planets and all living things. A diseased body could be restored to its harmony with the universe by magnets placed on it to induce a flow of healing magnetic fluid. In *The Influence of the Planets on the Human Body* (1776), he wrote:

". . . through certain manipulations (such as touching, stroking, in a word 'magnetizing') even simply by merely a strong act of will, one can produce power in persons, impart to others and cause the most marvelous and wholesome effects."

Mesmer's brand of therapy involved principles of old-fashioned faith healing dressed up in scientific terminology, with a little medieval mysticism and ancient astrology thrown in for good measure (Shor, 1972; Darnton, 1968). The

▲ Over the years, hypnosis has been valued largely for the stage effects it can produce. Today, psychologists are beginning to consider it a branch of serious study.

power of *mesmerism* achieved such fame that as hundreds of patients experienced relief from pain, thousands more came. To handle the demand, Mesmer "magnetized" virtually everything in sight and proclaimed that contact with these objects would be curative. The hope of relief from suffering even led many to tie themselves together in a row and then to a special magnetized oak tree. ●

Animal magnetism was eventually discredited as having no physical basis by a commission of the French Academy of Science, led by Benjamin Franklin. Their verdict was, "Nothing proves the existence of magnetic animal fluid; imagination without magnetism may produce conversions; magnetism without imagination produces nothing."

A little later, hypnosis replaced animal magnetism and regained some scientific acceptance through the efforts of a Scottish surgeon, James Braid. He discovered in 1843 that the nervous system could be induced artificially into a state of "nervous sleep," which he called "hypnosis." The name *hypnosis* is derived from the Greek word *Hypnos*, the name of the god of sleep. It was demonstrated that this special state of sleep could be produced merely by concentrated attention or "fixity of gaze." The person in this state was found to be very responsive to verbal suggestions given by the hypnotist.

From 1845 to 1853, a Scottish surgeon working in India, James Esdaile, performed nearly 300 painless major operations including amputations and cataract removals, with hypnosis as the only anesthetic. The subsequent discovery of ether, however, led surgeons to prefer that physical drug treatment to the psychic one of hypnosis, although the latter was shown to be equally effective and to lead to fewer side effects and a lower mortality rate for many types of operations.

In 1878 an eminent neurologist, Jean Charcot, began demonstrations of hypnosis in Paris. Although his theories about hypnosis were little more than up-dated mesmerism, he made an important contribution by conferring scientific respectability to the study of hypnosis and by virtue of the fact that Freud and Breuer studied hypnosis with him. They were later to use hypnosis as a technique to study the unconscious processes in hysteria (although Freud subsequently gave it up in preference for the technique of free association).

It was not until the 1930s, however, that the current era of psychological experimentation in hypnosis began, with the work of Clark Hull at Yale University. Standardized procedures were developed to assess the depth of hypnosis by means of observable behavioral criteria. This research effort came to an abrupt halt when a subject in one of the studies successfully sued Yale University, claiming to have suffered psychological damage as a consequence of her hypnotic experience. It is one of the very few such legal suits brought against academic hypnotists, but it was enough to cause Hull to give up this line of research and become preoccupied for the

● Mesmerism became extremely popular in Viennese society in the late eighteenth century. This drawing shows Anton Mesmer performing one of his "miraculous" cures.

rest of his life with studying the principles of learning — in rats (see pp. 109 – 10).

In recent years the scientific standard-bearers for hypnosis have been Ernest Hilgard, of Stanford University, and Martin Orne, of the University of Pennsylvania. Through the productivity of their research laboratories and the rigor and ingenuity with which they and their students have studied the process, correlates, and consequences of hypnosis, the mystery is being replaced with sound fact and testable theory (Hilgard, 1973; Orne, 1970).

Close-up
A Rock by Any Other Name Is a Rose

During the training of a group of high-school students, the hypnotist (Chanon Rapaport) wanted them to experience sensory hallucinations. He held a small rock before one subject and told him it was a rose of unusual beauty and fragrance. As the student in the picture began to describe the "rose" he was seeing in a field of flowers and its fragrance, he began to wheeze as his eyes teared, lips swelled, and nose ran. The young man was having a full-blown allergic reaction to roses — one of many allergies he normally had. The "rose" was transformed back to a rock with a new suggestion, but the respiratory reaction was so strong it had to be relieved with an inhalator.

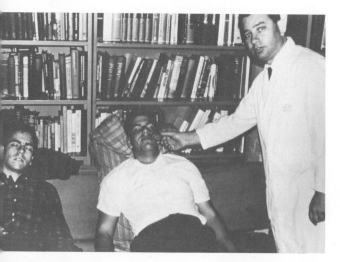

Consciousness Alterations Under Hypnosis

No one knows exactly how or why hypnosis "works," even though it has been around for so long. What is especially curious about hypnosis is that so little input — a few words — can generate such dramatic behavioral consequences. Some of the effects of hypnosis are specific to the verbal suggestions given by the hypnotist, as in the example of the boy involuntarily sticking out his tongue, but there are other nonspecific reactions that also typically accompany hypnosis. Subjects tend to show deep physical and mental relaxation; full, regular breathing; a lessening of tension, anxiety, fear, and concern for impression-management; and a strong tendency to block out distractions. In some instances, subjects may experience spontaneous amnesia for some portions of the hypnotic procedure without any suggestion to do so. Highly hypnotizable subjects who have been given some training in achieving deep levels of hypnosis are able to alter their senses of reality and control in rather remarkable ways. (See *P&L* Close-up at left.)

Among the more interesting alterations in consciousness that have characterized the hypnotic experience are: perceptual distortions, memory alterations, age regression, induced dreaming, posthypnotic responsiveness, and modified time sense.

Perceptual distortions. When given the appropriate suggestion, some subjects may perceive stimuli that are not physically present (positive hallucination) or fail to see those that are actually there (negative hallucination). Hypnotic subjects can be made to "see" movies of their choice, which they report not only in proper chronological sequence, but often with relevant emotional response all the way from hysterical laughter to anger (Erickson, 1939).

In one demonstration of the power of positive hallucinations, the lecturer of a large introductory psychology class was hypnotized and instructed to watch a movie of his choice that he had found pleasurable. To the amusement of the class, when asked what he was viewing, he reported (with a leering grin) that the feature was *Behind the Green Door* — an X-rated film. On the other hand, it is also possible for some subjects to fail to "see" one of the hands of a clock, their own handwriting, or even another person in the room. Such hallucinations are rarer and more difficult to achieve than illusory experiences, in which the qualities of stimuli are affected rather than their total presence or absence. A most convincing classroom demonstration of this is shown when subjects who normally cough and gag at the smell of ammonia will, under hypnosis, sniff it eagerly without any respiratory problems if they are told it is an exotic perfume. Similarly, perceived room temperature may be made to vary hypnotically so that subjects shiver in a warm room or become red and flushed in a cool room when told that the first room is cold, the second, overheated. Pain reduction involves a distortion of the pain stimulus such that it no longer elicits anxiety, which is a major component of our pain reaction (see Chapter 9).

Sometimes hallucinatory experiences are induced during the process of childbirth when hypnosis is used as an anesthetic. The mother may be made not to perceive the surgical instruments, the pain, or the blood, or may even be sent on a hallucinated vacation in the Caribbean.

One study found that subjects hypnotized and directed to see a rotating drum had the particular kind of eye movements that they had when actually watching such an event. However, the subjects were unable to feign these movements in the waking state when they were directed to do so (Brady & Levitt, 1964, 1966).

In another study, hypnotized patients were trained to hallucinate two gray circles on a white card. When they projected these hallucinated circles onto a black and white background, they reported the usual brightness contrast: the circle against white looked darker and the one against black lighter, so that they no longer appeared the same. A comparable group, asked to respond as if they were hypnotized, tended not to report the contrast (Graham, 1969).

Memory alteration. Since we value our memory and its ability to record all our significant experiences and have them available for retrieval upon demand, the idea that we could be induced to forget major events in our lives is disturbing yet intriguing.

Psychologists have studied specific amnesias, such as the inability to remember a particular name, event, or object. It has been shown (Orne, 1966) that when hypnotized subjects are told that the number 3 will disappear from their mind (until told it can reappear once again), they will be unable to use it in its appropriate function. When counting, the subjects report 1, 2, 4, 5 . . . , or 21, 22, 24, 25 . . . . When asked to count on their fingers, the subjects are amazed to discover they have 6 fingers per hand, 1, 2, 4, 5, 6! Simple arithmetic breaks down: 6 and 6 are 12, and 6 and 7 are also reported as 12. The subjects are aware of this incongruity and react with discomfort but cannot explain it or change it by rediscovering the lost *3*. The discomfort becomes greater the more mathematically sophisticated the subjects since inability to perform simple additions and subtractions involving the number 3 challenge their basic sense of competence.

Research has shown that hypnotic amnesia is much more likely to be found in children than in adults. Children are both more susceptible to hypnotic suggestions and have poorer memories than do adults. But in one study that compared amnesia for ten specific events recently experienced during the administration of a group test of hypnotizability, children who were hypnotized forgot significantly more items than did a comparison group of nine- to fifteen-year-olds who were not hypnotized (Cooper, 1972). It has not been demonstrated convincingly, however, that such forgetting is the result of "hypnosis" rather than of other variables operating in the testing situation (Orne, 1966; Evans & Kihlstrom, 1973).

Age regression. Age regression represents a special case of memory distortion. Some hypnotic subjects appear to be able to reexperience events in their lives that occurred at earlier ages. The recall of these events differs from the usual recall of past events because the subject loses the distinction between the present context in which the recall is being made and the original context that is recalled. When asked for an account of the experience, age-regressed subjects tend to describe it as an ongoing event, describing in present tense verbs rather than recalling in past tense verbs (as was the case for Chuck in Chapter 4). Handwriting, speech, mannerisms, and emotional displays also become generally appropriate to the particular time period. When college students are regressed to infant ages, they subsequently report not feeling any smaller themselves but perceiving everything around them as extraordinarily large — their crib, baby bottle, mother's finger, and especially huge faces looking into their crib. This occurs because the process of growth is so slow and continuous, we do not perceive our bodies as growing. Because of this apparent constancy of our own body size, it is likely that we learn to use it as a standard against which to judge other objects more often than we use other objects to judge its size. You may have had a similar experience without hypnosis, if you returned to a well-remembered childhood scene only to find that everything looked much smaller than it "was" then.

It is possible to approximate part of the phenomenology of age regression by engaging in a simple task. On the line below write your full name in pencil. But follow these three conditions: hold your pencil very tightly, write slowly (pressing hard), and close your eyes once you have made the first stroke.

Well, did the feedback from this task revive any vague feelings of what it felt like to be a youngster about seven years old? Try it on your friends.

The phenomenon of age regression has been used by some investigators as evidence for the total storage in memory of all sensory information. However, under controlled experimental conditions, this assumption is not supported. Some of what is remembered are not authentic details from childhood but elaborations and memory distortions. The proportion of credible memories from age-regressed subjects has been shown *not* to be greater than that of nonhypnotized role-playing subjects (O'Connell, Shor, & Orne, 1970). However, in that same study when experimental subjects were either hypnotically age-regressed to age 10 or told to role-play being that age, none of the hypnotic subjects included the phrase "under God" in their Pledge of Allegiance, while half of the role players did. This phrase was added to the Pledge by a 1954 Act of Congress and thus would not have been appropriate to the Pledge given by these subjects when they were ten years old. The methodological problems with a rigorous experimental demonstration of the validity of hypnotic age regression are considerable. When hypnotically age-regressed subjects are compared to control groups, much of their regressed behavior can be attributed to intentional mimicking of earlier behaviors; bias or support by the experimenter; demand characteristics of the testing situation; and other procedural artifacts.

Induced dreams. Dreams may be induced through hypnotic suggestion either during the session (waking dreams) or when the person normally goes to sleep that night (induced night dreams). The instructions may be for dreams of a certain type or emotional quality, or they may be without specific constraints. Subjects are also told to remember their dreams.

How do induced hypnotic dreams compare to night dreams? In one study, researchers found much in common between them in terms of characters, setting, and actions. Analysis of the content of the hypnotic dreams revealed greater uncertainty, vagueness, and metamorphoses of shapes. Striking in the hypnotic dreams were transformations of one's self (out of body experiences, duplication of self, etc.); of other people or objects ("Then I saw Jerry, and her breath turned into a flashlight"); of the scene and of states of being such as floating, falling, and changing size (Hilgard & Nowlis, 1972).

Posthypnotic suggestions. When a deeply hypnotized person is given the suggestion to carry out an action in response to a specific cue at a later time after the hypnotic induction has been terminated, it is called a posthypnotic suggestion. Amnesia for the source of the suggestion may be given so that the person will feel compelled to carry out the behavior without knowing why. Even when subjects resist the posthypnotic suggestion, there is evidence of conflict.

It is no wonder such a phenomenon elicits strong interest, since it appears to be a powerful instance of the unconscious control of behavior. In fact, research has shown that posthypnotic suggestions are *not* effective in forcing people to behave in ways they would normally consider undesirable. Posthypnotic suggestions are often no more powerful in securing compliance than are direct suggestions to waking individuals. They can be useful, however, when they concern behaviors the individual wants to control but cannot, such as smoking.

Alteration of time perspective. Hypnosis may be used not only to revive remembrance of things past or to influence future reactions, but also to change the perception of time itself.

In a very real sense, "time" is our greatest invention: with it we give meaning to our past and purpose to our future. All we "really" have is the present; without assumptions about time, we could not develop concepts of causation, consistency, or history.

The "past" and the "future" begin as abstract concepts, in contrast to the sensory foundation of our experience of the present. But we come to think of them as physically real, so real that the present actually becomes subjugated to them. Social institutions regulate individual behavior by inducing us to evaluate and guide our present actions in the light of considerations of our past and future.

In fact, we can become so preoccupied with past and future that we miss out on the present altogether. When asked for his metaphor of time, a salesman responded, "There is one bundle filled with my experiences and another with my expectations—that's all." "What about the present?" he was asked. He replied, "That's the transition between them." To what extent does *your* everyday life represent such a transition from somewhere to somewhere, with where you *are* now regarded as nowhere?

In an attempt to study the effects of altering time perspective, 12 trained hypnotic subjects and 18 controls were instructed under hypnosis "to allow the present to expand and the past and future to become distanced and insignificant." With only this single input, the hypnotized subjects (but not the unhypnotized controls, some of whom role-played being hypnotized) were able to change their time perception. Major changes in thinking, feeling, and acting took place.

Being in this state of "expanded present" was accompanied by a generalized shift from an analytical-rational orientation to a more impulsive, spontaneous, sensual one. These college subjects became more emotional, less inhibited, and less obedient to the experimenter's requests as they became more totally involved in the activity of the moment. ◆

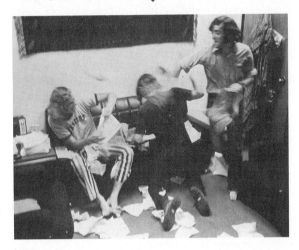

◆ One expanded-present subject, told he would feel angry about failing to find a certain name in the phone book, began to tear the book apart. Contagion was evident as the two other subjects present joined in the destructive activity without being told to do so. The same emotional contagion, loss of inhibition, and acting out were evident in other groups where one subject was told he would find the situation funny.

Some subjects became so present-oriented that they were unable to answer questions about events only a few minutes before:

QUESTION: *"How did you feel when working with the clay?"*
ANSWER: *"I remember feeling very, very good. But that was clay and now this is pencil and paper. It's amazing how a pencil can make marks on a paper that other people can read and understand . . . I can't really think about working with the clay. These questions interrupt my thought process. That makes me angry. But I don't care because it's all fantastically amazing. I can hear the blood in my ears . . . Now I wonder why that is. No more room. Back in the folder."*

Even grammar and handwriting underwent changes, since they, too, are bounded by constraints usually imposed by past and future (Zimbardo, Marshall, & Maslach, 1971). The changes in one subject's perspective and handwriting are shown in the sample reproduced here. ●

Research is underway in several psychology laboratories to extend our knowledge of the role time plays in our behavior and consciousness by altering it in various ways and then observing how subjects are affected.

For all the compasses in the world there's only one direction, and time is its only measure.
Tom Stoppard.
Rosencrantz and Guildenstern Are Dead, 1967

Explanations of Hypnosis

Hypnosis is not like ordinary sleep, as evidenced by comparison of EEG records of sleeping and hypnotized persons. It is another altered state of consciousness. The hypnotic subject agrees to suspend the usual, critical, reality-testing attitudes and go along with the suggestions of the hypnotist. A heightened state of selective attention is created by hypnotic induction procedures. The person "tunes out" the distractions of irrelevant realities and focuses on the experiences suggested.

Induction of hypnosis can be achieved by any of a variety of techniques that have in common conveying to subjects that they should: (a) relax, (b) concentrate, (c) give free rein to their imagination, (d) voluntarily agree to let mind and body "behave involuntarily," (e) allow temporal, spatial, physical, and causal relations to be distorted or dissociated, if necessary, and (f) be responsive to the suggestions of the hypnotist.

Basic to the entire process is a shift in one's belief system such that the hypnotic subject comes to believe that he or she *can* control body and mind in ways previously thought impossible or can lose control of events previously controlled automatically. A goal of hypnotic training is to guide the subject to be self-hypnotizable so that he or she comes to control a variety of physiological and behavioral processes by autosuggestion. The extent to which such tech-

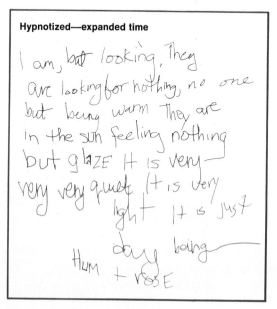

Hypnotized—normal time

The young lady is happy, looking at cows on the hill she is peaceful. The old lady is

Hypnotized—expanded time

I am, but looking, They are looking for nothing, no one but being warm They are in the sun feeling nothing but glaze It is very very very quiet It is very light It is just day being Hum + rose

● HANDWRITING CHANGES
IN ONE HYPNOTIC SUBJECT

niques can increase a person's potential control over the impact of a threatening environment is demonstrated by the finding that even in terminal cancer, intense pain can be brought under patients' control so that they no longer need to depend on morphine during the last phase of their lives (Sacerdote, 1966).

Variations in susceptibility to hypnosis are found among individuals in measures taken during the first formal attempt to hypnotize them. This objective measure of hypnotizability has been found to be a good predictor of responsiveness to a variety of hypnotic phenomena. However, few personality or social factors have been found to relate to hypnotizability. The percentage of subjects who are at various levels of hypnotizability the first time they are given the induction-test procedure is given in the table. ■ Often such measures show high correlations with measures made as long as ten years later (Hilgard, 1965). Some investigators have taken this to mean that such susceptibility is a relatively stable personality characteristic. Josephine Hilgard's (1970) clinical research with hypnotic subjects describes the curious, adventuresome, imaginative person as more hypnotizable than the competitive, controlled, fearful one.

The possibility that hypnotic susceptibility may have a genetic component is supported in a study of 140 pairs of twins and their families (Morgan, 1973). Using the Stanford Scale of Hypnotic Susceptibility, the correlations were significantly higher for monozygotic twins than for dizygotic twins, and a significant heritability index was found.

On the other hand, there was also evidence for social learning of hypnotizability, with children probably modeling the behavior of the parent of the same sex. And it has been demonstrated that hypnotic susceptibility scores can be improved by means of videotaped information presented to subjects in the form of modeling cues (Diamond, 1972). In addition, graduate student subjects showed significant increase in susceptibility scores following experience in an experimental encounter group, perhaps because of the development of a greater sense of trust (Shapiro & Diamond, 1972).

Some investigators have argued that all hypnotic phenomena represent nothing more than strong states of motivation. Theodore Barber (1970) has shown that many behaviors attributed to the "state of hypnosis" can be reproduced even in unhypnotized subjects simply given a set of motivating instructions in the waking state.

Although some of the effect of hypnosis is attributable to the same motivation that operates in faith healing (Frank, 1963), there is an effect over and above the placebo effect that is unique to hypnosis.

In a well-controlled study, pain thresholds were recorded as well as subjective and physiological reactions to the stress of ischemic pain (stopping of arterial blood flow in the arm by a tourniquet). The twenty-four male paid volunteer college students then underwent two additional, double-blind sessions—one in which they believed that a drug (placebo) would relieve the pain, and one in which they were simply told under hypnosis that they would feel no pain. It was known from previous measures that half of the subjects were highly susceptible to hypnosis and half were not.

It was found that there was a sizable placebo effect on reduction of pain for both placebo and hypnotic subjects but no correlation between degree of hypnotic susceptibility and amount of placebo reaction. Over and above the general

■ LEVEL OF HYPNOSIS AT FIRST INDUCTION

The table shows results for 533 subjects hypnotized for the first time. Hypnotizability was measured on the Stanford Hypnotic Susceptibility Scale, which consists of 12 items.

General Level	Susceptibility Score	Number of Subjects	Percent of Subjects
Very high	11–12	56	11
High	8–10	100	19
Medium	5–7	151	28
Low	0–4	226	42

Adapted from Hilgard, 1965

placebo effect with both the placebo and the hypnotic procedures, there was a perceptual distortion effect in the subjects who were known to be highly susceptible to hypnosis and were deeply hypnotized, enabling them to withstand pain significantly longer than the subjects in any other condition (McGlashlin, Evans, & Orne, 1969). ▲

Other researchers have shown that student subjects, trained to relax and concentrate intensely through hypnosis, have been able to vary the skin temperature of their two hands in opposite directions simultaneously. The graph shows the changes in skin temperature for one subject instructed to make her left hand hotter and right hand colder than normal, and then, after a period of time to return them to normal. Unhypnotized control subjects, not able to concentrate as deeply, showed no systematic changes in either hand (Maslach et al., 1972). ◆

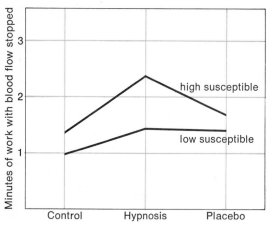

After McGlashan et al., 1969

▲ **HYPNOSIS VS. PLACEBO IN PAIN REDUCTION**

The greater reduction of pain for the high-susceptible subjects during hypnosis than for either the low-susceptible subjects with hypnosis or either of the other groups indicates that hypnosis was having an additional effect.

Perspective on Alteration of Consciousness

Many of us realize that limits on our personal growth have been imposed by the cultural conditioning process we have undergone. Too much of our everyday, "garden variety" of consciousness is filled with thoughts and sensations that have been programmed into us, so that we perceive the world as others want us to. We do not "see" it for ourselves as it is or as it could be.

People who seek the experience of altered states of consciousness often do so to be liberated from such societal constraints upon their feeling, perceiving, and thinking. They want new forms of knowledge about themselves and nature. They hope to find a sense of contentment, inner peace, and certainty to give meaning to their lives and substance to their existence.

Are Altered States of Consciousness Desirable?

Altered states of consciousness sometimes act to reaffirm moral values, resolve emotional conflicts, assist creative insights, allow absolute joy and harmony. As we have seen, for example,

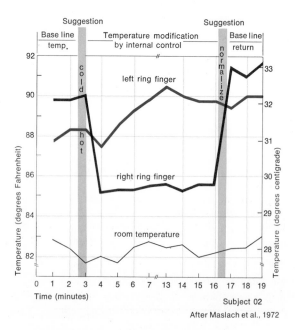

Subject 02

After Maslach et al., 1972

◆ **CHANGE OF SKIN TEMPERATURE AFTER HYPNOTIC SUGGESTION**

the Zen practitioner undergoes very profound changes and develops a whole new orientation toward life.

In some cultures the communal experience of altered consciousness in rituals related to healing of the sick not only is beneficial to the sick person, but helps to reaffirm the social bonds that link isolated individuals together into a community.

For too many people, however, the search for altered states of consciousness is an escape from the cares and trials of ordinary existence. Feeling frustrated in their ambition to "make it" in their society, or helpless to have an impact on governmental policies seen as perverting human values and diminishing the quality of life, some students have turned inward "into their heads" to try at least to "get their own stuff together."

Usually such students are not "dropping out" of society but already *are* out, experiencing a lack of meaningful ties to family and peers and the absence of a group to relate to. Where altered states of consciousness are sought for escapist reasons, the consequence is likely to be further isolation of the individual from meaningful social contact.

How "Normal" Is Ordinary Consciousness?

We have been discussing ordinary consciousness as if it were "all of a piece," an entity, a solitary, stable launching pad for trips to outer space. Have you ever considered the possibility that *you* have not one but two different forms of consciousness in your head? ■

You met a hint of such a possibility in Chapter 2 in the split-brain studies of Sperry and others. It is rather well established now that the two hemispheres of the brain are specialized to carry out quite different functions. For most people, the left side of the brain handles the verbal-intellectual-analytical business of life, while the right hemisphere handles the more spontaneous, intuitive, experiential aspects of information processing. This lateral specialization of brain functions (two-sidedness) has been shown to be unique to humans and related to the evolution of language.

Because the left side of the brain usually controls speech functions and the more skilled movements of the right hand (in right-handed people), it has long been assumed to be the dominant hemisphere. This supposition has been supported by the finding that the left hemisphere is typically heavier than the right one. Researchers now are wondering if perhaps they have been confusing cause and effect. Perhaps the greater weight of our left hemispheres is the result of our greater valuing and use of the rational-analytic functions for which it is specialized. Studies are now under way to find out whether people in societies that put higher priority on the intuitive and experiential may perhaps have a different weight balance of the two hemispheres.

In any case, a fair amount of evidence is accumulating to suggest that these activities of the

■ THE YIN AND YANG OF CONSCIOUSNESS

The duality of human consciousness is recognized in many cultures, and we have a variety of ways to express the poles of this dichotomy. Perhaps, as with the Chinese symbol of Yin-Yang, the opposite parts must complement rather than exclude or control each other, transcending and encompassing the contradictions to form a whole that will be harmonious and more than the sum of its parts. Some of the many aspects of the "Yin" and the "Yang," long a part of oriental thinking, are listed below.

Yin	Yang
Night	Day
Dark	Light
Feminine	Masculine
Intuitive	Intellectual
Right hemisphere	Left hemisphere
Left side of body	Right side of body
Space	Time
Present	Past and future
Simultaneous	Sequential
Spatial	Verbal
Implicit	Explicit
Gestalt	Analytic
Diffuse	Focused
Noncausal	Causal
Feeling	Thinking
Receptive	Active
Experiencing	Planning
Being	Controlling
Eternity	History

Modified from Ornstein, 1972, p. 67

two hemispheres represent different modes of consciousness. The two *complement* each other but cannot entirely substitute for one another. Robert Ornstein of the Langley Porter Neuropsychiatric Institute (1972) makes a convincing case for the necessity of freer interaction between these two modes of consciousness if we are to realize our highest potential.

Chapter Summary

Consciousness is awareness of one's own thought processes and external events. It is not an all-or-none phenomenon, but rather a continuum, depending to some extent on the level of sensory input to the brain. *Altered states of consciousness* may be induced by the presence of too much or too little stimulation, by physical means (such as alcohol or drugs) or by psychological means (such as meditation or hypnosis). In recent years, psychologists have shown a growing interest in the study of consciousness as a part of human functioning.

Characteristics common to various altered states of consciousness include: (1) distortions of perceptual processes, time sense, and body image; (2) feelings of objectivity and ego transcendence; (3) a self-validating sense of truth; (4) positive emotional quality; (5) paradoxicality; (6) ineffability; and (7) unity and fusion.

Sleep is perhaps the most familiar of the altered states of consciousness. Strangely enough, *sleep deprivation* can also bring on altered states of consciousness, including such symptoms as disorientation, hallucinations, and perceptual distortions. Such effects usually wear off as soon as the lost sleep is made up.

The observation and description of sleep behavior is made possible by the *electroencephalograph* (EEG), which records brain waves. Two kinds of sleep can be identified: *REM*, during which rapid eye movements occur, and non-REM or *NREM*, during which such movements are absent. NREM sleep consists of four stages of differing depth.

The main characteristics of REM sleep are: (1) the suppression of voluntary muscular activity; (2) brain waves similar to those of the waking state; (3) *phasic activity*, including the rapid eye movements and other muscular activity; and (4) fluctuations in the autonomic nervous system. NREM sleep, on the other hand, involves complete disengagement from the environment. During a night's sleep, an individual passes in cycles from stage to stage; infants spend a great deal of time in REM sleep and the elderly very little.

The discovery of REM sleep led to the first physiological studies of *dreaming,* as individuals awakened during REM sleep nearly always report that they have been dreaming. Dreaming also occurs during NREM sleep, but REM dreams tend to involve activity and complex plots, while NREM dreams have little sensory imagery.

An individual who is deprived of REM sleep over a period of time will show a REM rebound, spending an unusual amount of time in REM sleep to "catch up." Cats deprived of REM sleep for extensive periods show increases in drive-related behavior, such as aggression, sex drive, and hunger. A link between schizophrenia and REM sleep mechanisms has been suggested.

Freud believed that dreams give expression to repressed impulses, transforming the unacceptable, repressed *latent content* into the harmless, symbolic *manifest content* that is remembered. He believed that one primary function of dreams is to provide wish fulfillment, and that most dream symbols represent sexual objects. Jung, however, believed that dreams stem from a *collective unconscious* and contain *archetypal* symbols universal in their meaning.

Differences between the dreams reported by men and women reflect the sex roles found in our society; it is not known whether the differences reported reflect actual differences in content. Children's dreams seem to reflect apprehension more often than wish fulfillment. Although *nightmares* are common in both children and adults, they are little understood.

Prolonged *sensory deprivation* or a low level of unstructured stimulation results in vivid hallucinations and perceptual distortions, and can be endured for only a short time.

Drugs have long been used to induce altered states of consciousness. *Psychoactive* refers to any drug that affects mental processes. *Hallucinogens* are drugs that induce hallucinations; the term *psychedelic* is also used to refer to these drugs. *Psychotomimetic* drugs produce symptoms similar to those of psychosis.

Psychoactive drugs used in our society include tobacco, alcohol, cannabis (marijuana), narcotic analgesics, hypnotics, stimulants, and hallucinogens. *Marijuana* creates mild psychological, but not physical dependence. Its effects vary with social and personal factors in the situation. *Narcotic analgesics*, such as morphine and heroin, function as pain killers and induce euphoria. *Tolerance* develops quickly, and both physiological and psychological dependence are high. The uneven quality of street drugs often leads to death from overdose.

Hypnotics include the barbiturates and similar drugs. They depress the central nervous system and are used as tranquilizers. Psychological dependence develops readily, physical dependence and tolerance with long use. Stimulants include amphetamines and metamphetamines (speed). Initially, they increase alertness and feelings of ability, but overdoses can produce anxiety and paranoid fears. Psychological dependence develops quickly. A "run" of drug use is generally followed by a "crash," and the cycle repeats itself endlessly.

Hallucinogens, such as LSD and mescaline, affect the central nervous system, heightening sensitivity and distorting perception. Tolerance builds up quickly and disappears just as quickly. There is no physiological and little psychological dependence. In appropriate settings, such drugs may induce transcendental religious experiences.

Factors that influence drug effects include: (1) structure and size of dose, which may have different effects on different individuals; (2) acquired tolerance resulting from previous use; (3) the expectations of the user; (4) the personality characteristics of the user; and (5) the social situation in which the drug is taken.

Meditation, yoga, and *Zen* are disciplines in which the mind is trained to act on itself in order to produce altered states of consciousness. Such techniques involve single-minded concentration on a single unvarying stimulus. *Transcendental meditation* involves simple concentration and relaxation, without religious ritual or change in life-style. It produces measurable physiological changes and is claimed to have many psychological benefits. *Yoga* combines meditation with physical and breathing exercises. In its traditional forms it involves a spiritual regimen as well. Trained yogis can produce marked changes in metabolic processes. *Zen* is a form of Buddhism involving an emptying of the self and a search for enlightenment.

Of all the altered states of consciousness, hypnosis is one of the best known and least understood. *Mesmerism,* or animal magnetism, attracted great attention in the eighteenth century as a proclaimed "cure-all." *Hypnosis,* which involves extreme suggestibility, has been studied seriously only within the last few decades.

Characteristics common in the hypnotic state include: (1) perceptual distortions; (2) memory alterations, such as amnesia; (3) age regression; (4) induced dreaming; (5) responsiveness to posthypnotic suggestions; and (6) altered time perspective. Hypnosis involves the creation of a heightened state of selective attention in which the individual agrees to suspend reality and focuses on the suggestions of the hypnotist. Through hypnotic training subjects can gain increased control over their own physiological and behavioral processes. Hypnotizability may have a genetic component and appears to be fairly stable over time, although learning is apparently involved to some extent.

It has been speculated that there are two sides to human consciousness: the intellectual-rational and the intuitive-experiential. It is only by allowing these two aspects to interact freely that we can realize our highest potential.

Passive attention: The gateway to consciousness and autonomic control[1]

Erik Peper San Francisco State University

Passive control over autonomic functions or altered states of consciousness is the critical process by which both physical and psychological health are modulated. By investigating such processes we may learn new dimensions of our growth and perhaps change traditional views about the nature of health and sickness.

Ideas for this essay have come from two sources: first, my study of "adepts," those remarkable people who demonstrate unusual control over mind and body, and secondly, the systematic investigation and observation of the mechanisms of voluntary autonomic control. In 1971, I studied my first adept, Ramon Torres, a young man who was able to insert bicycle spokes through his cheeks without reporting any pain. In fact, he was able to sustain a state of relaxation while undergoing this experience, as shown by his increased alpha EEG activity. These findings are similar to those produced by adept Jack Schwarz (see p. 305).

In studying adepts I try to discover: "What is going on?" "By what means or strategies have these adepts attained autonomic control or achieved 'cosmic consciousness'?" "How can their internal functioning be translated (that is, made explicit and external), and then learned by ordinary or nonadept people so that they too may be able to use these skills?" Adepts illustrate the potentialities of human capabilities and sometimes contradict accepted psychological observations. For example, the observation that we do not learn during deep sleep has been placed in doubt by the study of Swami Rama, an associate Shankaracharya of Southern India. While studying this yogi, Dr. Elmer Green of the Menninger Foundation clinic found that the yogi would remember everything that had happened to him while in a state of Yogic sleep (one in which the electroencephalograph showed 40% delta wave activity). Swami Rama was able to recite verbatim nine of the ten sentences given to him while in this state and paraphrased the tenth sentence spoken to him.

This single-subject observation casts some doubt upon the accepted theory that learning during deep sleep does not occur. What it indicates is that most likely we simply do not recall the information. The information is encoded in the brain, and we may act upon it, but we do *not* have conscious access to it. Further study of such a subject as Swami Rama supports the observation that information can affect us even when we are in a nonconscious state. For example, there are reported cases of a patient's heart stopping during surgery right after the surgeon said aloud, "I wish the S.O.B. would drop dead"—not meaning the patient, but someone else. The above observation offers us a chance to reevaluate what we accept as the limits of human functioning. The limits are often defined through our cultural bias. The study of adepts allows us to see through those cultural blindfolds and to perceive a different picture of reality—one in which belief in one's own powers sets the limits on what is possible.

What we discovered in studying the adepts and their ability to control unconscious and autonomic functions was that: (a) body control is achieved through *passive attention* and not active trying, and (b) the important part of the control is the *process* and the *attention* to it—NOT the outcome or the goal. These dimensions operate in all physical, emotional, and mental activity and are certainly opposed to the teaching of the Protestant ethic, which reinforces us for striving and for achieving goals. Such an orientation gives meaning only to consequences and not to the process—to the ends and not to the means. We can see that in cases of sexual dysfunction a major component of male impotence or female frigidity occurs when the person is actively "trying" to achieve an orgasm instead of letting it happen and knowing it is okay if it does not happen this time. One of the first steps in sexual therapy is to teach the person not to try. The

1. I thank Susan Chandler and Joanna Taylor for their help in preparing this essay.

initial homework in such therapy consists of teaching people to perceive through the senses and not the intellect. Actual intercourse is postponed until much later, after each person develops adequate communication skills with the partner. Such exercises aim at removing fear of failure. Success is not the *achievement* of a future goal, but the awareness of the *process* in the present, here-and-now. This awareness consists of subtle ways of learning passive attention. For example, sexual stimuli may initiate a "turn-on"; this triggers passive attention to the sexual feelings that allow the "turn-on" to continue. But if one tries actively to be turned on, one is likely to succeed only in turning oneself off. The way to succeed in this business is definitely without really trying!

The dynamics of sexual arousal are similar to the mechanisms which underlie other forms of autonomic control. The process is mediated by *passive attention*. But what is passive attention? It is doing without trying! It is allowing and directing without dictating. To investigate it involves us at once in a contradiction of the usual research approaches; the problem of investigating passive attention lies in the very nature of the process. The moment we try to perform, we inhibit passive attention: in colloquial language, we "break the flow." But research designs are usually demand- and performance-oriented. The phenomenon of passive attention is such that research attempts which focus on performance actually eliminate the thing they are trying to investigate.

Experientially, the processes affecting and interfering with passive attention are those of anticipation and striving. These effects may be experienced when we *try* to defecate or urinate. Before you continue reading this essay, you might go to the bathroom and urinate. Become aware of the many physical, emotional, and social constraints as well as the tensions and holding patterns in your body: what are they? Don't you resent the demand I've placed on you to take this action at this time? Doesn't your body resist complying with that arbitrary demand? (Note that in order to urinate you merely attend passively and *allow* the urine to flow). When you *try* to urinate, such as at the doctor's office when you are asked for a urine sample,

or when you sit on the toilet during a theatre intermission with people standing in line waiting for you to finish, the harder you try, the less successful you are likely to be. So either you read the graffiti, to distract your mind, or you flush the toilet so that other people will not know that you are so uptight. The process of passive attention consists of *letting go* and allowing a process to occur, which is inimical to the "normal" active striving mode which has been programmed into us.

On the other hand, passive attention is optimized during the practice of meditation. In meditation one learns a focused, passive attention without effort, without anticipation. Instead of focusing on the products of the mind (thoughts and images), which is so often the case in clinical psychology, meditation focuses only on the *process;* whatever happens, we let happen. The being in the present time is maximized. The moment one anticipates, worries, fears, etc., one is out of the present mode, either ruminating about the past or worrying about the future. One should be in a place where one is neither ruminating, worrying, nor falling asleep, but experiencing the internal and the external worlds as they are.

Meditative practices do not focus upon an outcome. It is the inspection of the process which is most important. It is how the person is doing it and never why or what for. Without "grooving" on sensations, or on images or fantasies, one is learning the process of passive attention. It is the feeling of going with the flow, instead of fighting the river. One experiences this process only sporadically in the usual mode of being and one knows this sensation best from joyful sexual experience. Similarly, this occurs in altered states of consciousness: "I want to reach the high point of cosmic consciousness"—yet in most cases, this level of consciousness comes to a person unsuspected, when one is not trying, only attending to the process.

This process of doing without effort modulates all activities. The process is so similar to, yet so different from habitual action patterns. One usually forces while participating in a sport—the braced neck and shoulders—or one tries while studying—

the clenched jaw. When one does an exercise without effort, the results are totally different than if the exercise is forced. For example, you may want to do the following toe-touching exercise and note how different it feels from the habitual pattern in which we *force* ourselves to touch our hands to our toes, as we were trained to do in gym classes. Now touch your toes without effort. To do this, let your body, spine, and head lean forward *very slowly.* Pay attention to the minute changes in your body as it slowly changes position. Let your arms hang loose, and let the legs be flexed rather than locked back. Be sure that your head and neck are loose and that you are not holding your head up. Be aware of the stretch, but do not try to stretch or reach down. Breathe slowly and deeply. As you bend more and more, continue to breathe slowly and see if you can bend farther without tensing your neck and lifting your head. Don't push or force, just *allow* your spine to bend and the muscles of the back and legs to stretch. When you have bent over as far as is comfortable, continue to breathe, and with each exhalation feel yourself going down further. Then come up again very *slowly,* vertebra by vertebra, without raising your head, letting your head hang loose. Be aware of the changes in your position, the changes of your spine from a curved to a straighter shape, the changes in your balance. Your head will be the last part of your body to become vertical. At the end, breathe calmly and be aware of how your body feels in its standing position. Do this again; let it take five minutes.

If this exercise were done without "trying" but with passive attention to the stretch, two things would probably happen: muscle activity would decrease and blood vessels would dilate at the areas where passive attention was focused. Recording these physiological changes can indicate to researchers what type of attention the person is using.

The different effects of attentional processes are illustrated by the following clinical example in which a young woman with Raynaud's disease (which leaves the limbs cold) learned to warm her hands with the use of thermal biofeedback. Changes in her skin temperature triggered a signal

that indicated when she was getting warmer. Biofeedback creates an external signal the person may use to become aware of subtle variations in internal functioning (such as heart rate or, in this case, skin temperature). You can see the gradual progress the trainee is making during the first six minutes of the biofeedback training. At minute seven, she stopped striving actively to control her temperature, she began to passively attend to what she was experiencing. Obviously, she wanted to feel warmer but didn't know consciously how to achieve that goal. But at a physiological level, her body "knew" how to do it—she had merely to tune into that process. At the point that she gave up actively striving, her hand temperature increased dramatically, as illustrated in Figure 1. Even more interesting, once she stopped trying and allowed the warmth to flow into her hands she also experienced an insight into how she herself had created her own distressing physical symptoms. By withdrawing her psychological concern and emotional affect from the people around her, she had created the physical symptoms of chronic, peripheral coldness. I find that as the physiological system is alleviated, the underlying psychological difficulty often emerges—a striking demonstration of the interaction between mind and body. In the process of attempting to control

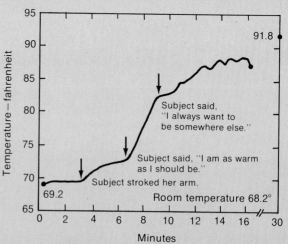

Figure 1 Woman being trained with biofeedback to raise her skin temperature. Gradual improvement over first six minutes shifts to marked increase in warmth when she stops actively trying and passively attends to the process. In 30 minutes she raised her skin temperature 22°F.

her autonomic system through biofeedback learning, this woman came into closer contact with her conscious and unconscious processes and thereby was able to reestablish a harmonious state between mind and body. That is the basis of transforming sickness states into healthy ones.

To help teach autonomic control via passive attention, biofeedback and autogenic training are often used. In autogenic training, a person attends passively to his or her arm and talks to it: "my right arm is heavy" or "my right arm is warm" and something happens: the electromyographic (muscle) activity decreases and the blood flow changes in those areas where the passive attention is focused.

It is important to realize that the prerequisite of passive attention is profound relaxation. Deep relaxation enhances and may even be considered a precondition for this process because the moment we try the body reacts. Most likely for every thought there is a corresponding muscle activity. Hence rumination on emotional events can lead to an increase in anxiety. For instance, I often demonstrate this with my trainees (experimental subjects or patients) using biofeedback. We record the electromyographic activity of the forearm extensors while they allow the muscle to relax. I purposely used the word *allow* instead of *relax,* because "allow" implies not striving while "to relax" may mean you "do something" forcibly. When electrical activity in the muscles is down to 1.0 microvolts (a totally relaxed muscle), I ask the trainees to *imagine* lifting their fingers, but not to move them. The EMG often increases up to 2.5 microvolts, illustrating that the muscles contracted even though there were no perceptible movements in the hand or fingers or conscious attempts to move the body.

Dimensions of passive attention can also account for the healthful effect of Hatha Yoga *asanas* —a specific yogic stretch. While doing an asana, the "complete stretch" is not the goal; instead, one gently attends to the area of the stretch, letting the rest of the body relax. One no longer attends to the end goal, or to achievement ("How far can I stretch?"); but instead one gently attends to the process. Hence, we would predict that the striate muscle activity would decrease and that change in blood circulation would occur. In the asana, the stretch *captures* our passive attention. The result is the same—a change in physiology. Asanas are body attention-getters to bring passive attention to a specific area. If this is true, some health claims of yoga could be validated. In the Hatha Yoga, the shoulder stand (feet pointed to the ceiling) is said to be done to promote thyroid functioning. But why should that occur? The upside down posture would cause the throat to compress. What happens is that the person experiences the pressure inside the neck and throat which captures passive attention. Attending to it could bring about an increased blood flow and affect the thyroid. (This hypothesis is testable through the use of a thermograph and biological monitoring). Too many of us try to do the asanas without attending passively. Usually one assumes that a person would learn passive attention through doing; however, the person may just continue to strive since we must unlearn the habit of working toward ends and learn to be part of the means. I am presently attempting to explore the occurrences of passive attention during different states of consciousness and during meditative practices.

Passive attention is the wedge through which we join our conscious and unconscious processes. The adepts illustrate some of the possible effects of using it. Autogenic training, biofeedback, meditative, and yogic practices are techniques to develop these same capacities. By this paradoxical process—grasped without grasping—we allow ourselves to open an infinite world in which we can expand our own potentials and participate in the restoration and maintenance of our psychic, spiritual, and physical well-being.

PART 4
Motivation
to Act

8

Motivation and Human Sexuality

"The devil made me do it!" is one answer to the question, "Why did you steal a loaf of bread?" The person does not deny the deed, but rather denies any personal motivation for having initiated the theft. In this case, the argument is advanced that the force that determined or caused the behavior was so powerful that it overcame the individual's resistance. Other answers to the same question might be: "I took it to help a poor family in distress" or "I was starving and had no money to buy the bread, and so was compelled by hunger to steal it."

While obviously there are many different kinds of answers that could be given, they all share the common property of being "reasons for actions." These *reasons* typically are statements of the assumed causes of behavior, and the causes quite often are phrased in terms of *motives*.

Some of these motives, such as hunger, stem from biological drives of the organism. Others, such as altruism, develop as a consequence of social experiences and social needs. Still others fall in between the biological and social, such as acting from the passion of anger, revenge, curiosity, religious motives, or a host of others.

When we ask what makes us, and other living organisms, "tick," we are asking questions about motivation. Is human behavior driven by impulse and appetite? Why does competition bring out the best in some individuals and teams, who get "psyched up," and the worst in others, who end "psyched out"? Why are some people ready to sacrifice their lives for what they believe in, while others are so apathetic they seem not to care about anything? How can children be taught to cooperate? What can be done to increase the productivity of workers? How can a manufacturer make people "want" a product? Is it true that people on welfare do not want to help themselves? The answers given to such questions imply some conception of the way in which motivational factors influence our lives. Thus any understanding of the behavior of organisms rests on an understanding of motivational principles.

Beyond the wish for understanding of motivation is the hope to predict and perhaps control behavior in order to regulate and improve the quality of one's own life and that of others. What does a knowledge of motivation tell us about the technology for controlling behavior used by teachers, parents, sales representatives, politicians, animal trainers, entertainers, marriage counselors, therapists, and other agents of change—including ourselves?

The Concept of Motivation

No one has ever "seen" motivation, just as no one has ever "seen" learning. What we do see, through the systematic observation of situations, stimuli, and responses, are changes in behavior. To explain or justify these observed changes, we make inferences about their underlying psychological and physiological processes—inferences that are formalized in the concept of motivation.

In inferring internal motivation to explain behavior, we try to simplify the complex web of possible interrelations by postulating a single intermediate variable linking the various stimulus inputs to the varied response outputs. Thus instead of trying to establish a variable relating each aspect of the stimulus situation to each aspect of the response, we postulate an overall *intervening variable* like hunger or thirst. ■

The psychologist, cast in the role of a Sherlock Holmes or Dick Tracy, must use the available evidence from the stimulus conditions and the observable behavior to identify this basic internal variable. ● The words we use to label the inner states behind this variable all share some implication of causal determination: *purpose, intention, goal-directed, need, want, drive, desire, motive.* Psychologists usually use the label *drive* when the motivation is assumed to be primarily biologically instigated. The labels *motive* and *need* are more often used to refer to psychological and social motivation, which is generally assumed to be at least in part acquired or learned. However, there is variation in the usage of these concepts among psychologists. Some, for example, prefer to use the term *needs*

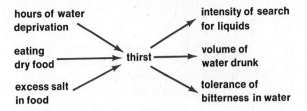

■ DRIVE AS AN INTERVENING VARIABLE

Three things that *affect* drinking behavior (independent variables) are shown on the left, and three ways of measuring drinking behavior (dependent variables) are shown on the right. Any one of the three on the left could be manipulated to change one or more of those on the right. But instead of postulating nine possible relationships, it is simpler to postulate a single intervening or "mediating" variable, *thirst,* as the mechanism through which all the variables on the left affect those on the right.

● In trying to "establish the motive," all the possibly significant characteristics of the situation and the person's traits, habits, and actions are listed and carefully sifted to see if a pattern emerges.

only for biological demands (like the body's need for water) whether or not they trigger actual behavior designed to alleviate this need. Because there are no conscious correlates of oxygen deficit, it does not motivate behavior, although excesses of carbon dioxide do.

Motivation is characterized by: (a) energy arousal, (b) direction of effort toward a particular goal, (c) selective attention to relevant stimuli (with decreased sensitivity to irrelevant ones), (d) organization of response units into an integrated pattern or sequence, and (e) persistence of this activity until the initiating conditions are changed. In the following sections we will look at a number of ways the concept of motivation has been used by psychologists.

To Account for Behavioral Variability

The basic function of a motivational analysis is to explain the observed *variability* in behavior. How can we make sense out of the differences in response to the same external situation between different people and even in the same person at different times? When conditions of training, testing, and ability are equated and the performance of individuals still varies, differences in behavior are attributed to motivation.

When, for example, one of two prizefighters of equal ability wins a fight, it is said he *wanted* the win more, or he was more *hungry* for the win. Or in championship team sports, it is said that the team that is most "up" for the contest wins it. The outcome—why A won and B lost—is explained as a difference in level of motivation that resulted in A's putting out "more of what it takes."

However, not all behavior requires a motivational explanation. For example, a knee jerk from a tap on the patella is not taken as evidence of a drive to flex the knee but is regarded as a nonmotivated reflex. No motivational constructs are required to understand why a person dies after receiving a high-voltage electric shock, but the sudden death of a seemingly healthy older person shortly after having been placed in a home for the aged does seem to require a motivational explanation.

You do not eat every time food is available, or study as much as you know you might before every exam. And you might never devote time or energy to perfecting some skills that are utterly absorbing to other people. We are often at a loss to explain the single-minded concentration of effort of baton twirlers, Yo-Yo spinners, fire-eaters, or, for that matter, academic scholars. We say that we eat because we are "hungry," and that we work to excel others because we are impelled by a desire for "achievement."

If *everyone* in a given place behaved in the same way to a certain stimulus event, we would be more interested in knowing about that stimulus than about the nature or motivations of those people. Or, if an individual reacted identically each time a given situation arose, we would not be concerned about "why" he or she was behaving that way, or perhaps even notice the relationship. It is only when there is some "slippage" in the system that we invoke concepts of "motivation." It is when we are anxious about a forthcoming exam and someone else is indifferent, or when we get aroused by an experience about which another is blasé, or when we perform much better or worse than we expected to—only then do we look to motivation for the reason.

To Infer Private Dispositions from Public Acts

'Tis e'er the wont of simple folk to prize the deed and o'erlook the motive, and of learned folk to discount the deed and lay open the soul of the doer.

John Barth, *The Sot-Weed Factor,* 1960

Most of us *assume* that there is a consistency in our behavior over different times and situations. When there is not, it is then further assumed not that *we* have changed in any permanent way, but that there is a *temporary* change in the conditions that made us act differently. In such instances, motivational concepts are also used to infer from these publicly observable acts what inner private states are or have been operating.

In addition, as people develop more complex ideas about the dynamic causes of human behavior, they are not content with merely taking behavior at "face value," but see it as the visible tip of the submerged motivational iceberg. It then becomes an intellectually fascinating game to find the motive or motivational syndrome that best "fits" the occasion.

To Establish the Possibility of Inner Directedness

When motivation is used in the sense of instigating "purposive" or "goal-seeking" behavior, it provides a directedness to behavior. In this way the concept of motivation comes to be interchangeable with such concepts as "willpower," which imply that the origins of behavior are to be found *inside* the person and not in the external environment. Motivation is thought to *energize* behavior, just as coal energizes a furnace. Therefore, inner motivation is the antecedent of external action—the wellspring of behavior.

A very different account of why behavior varies, and what are the significant causal determinants of any given action comes from the radical behaviorists who follow the operant conditioning approach of B. F. Skinner (see Chapter 3). For them it is not the internal conditions preceding a response that are important, but what has taken place following similar responses in the past. In their view, it is reinforcement *following* responding and not motivation *preceding* it that makes the important difference. This approach obviously stresses the role of environmental control of behavior, of bringing behavior under stimulus control. It is reinforcers that give behavior its direction, argue behaviorists. According to George Reynolds of the University of California, "the practitioner of operant conditioning scarcely mentions motivation, since it has come to refer only to those conditions that render a given event reinforcing at a given time. . . . [M]otivational conditions have become mere technological details" (1967, p. 127). Motivation, in this view, is the insignificant stagehand that sets the stage for the big star of the show, the *reinforcer*. Thus hunger has value to the behavior modifier only because it increases the reinforcing effectiveness of food.

As a rejoinder, proponents of motivational psychology claim that motivation has direct effects on behavior as well as its indirect effects through making reinforcers "relevant." The motivated individual emits more responses, sooner, faster, more vigorously, and more persistently than the unmotivated one. Motivation initiates the environmental search for reinforcers in freely ranging animals, an activity not possible in laboratory operant studies where the experimenter controls the reinforcers and limits exploration by creating a highly simplified, artificial environment such as a Skinner box.

To Assign Volition, Responsibility, and Blame

We are not more ingenious in searching out bad motives for good actions when performed by others, than good motives for bad actions when performed by ourselves.
Charles Caleb Colton, *Lacon*, 1825

Whatever the proper place of motivation in scientific psychology, it occupies a very central position in legal and religious tradition as well as in the thinking of teachers, social workers, and most of us who want to know from time to time what makes other people's behavior so different from our own.

In law, it is necessary to distinguish between behavior that was involuntary from that which was voluntary, crimes compelled by passion from those that were premeditated, accidental events from intentional ones. Underlying such determinations are issues of motivation. (See *P&L* Close-up, p. 326.)

In some orthodox religions, the assignment of blame for wrongdoing similarly involves assumptions not only of the intellectual capacity to know right from wrong, but a motivated intent to forsake good and engage in evil. Motivation comes to the fore with the concept of "sin" applied to *desire* as well as to *deeds*. For example, "to *covet* thy neighbor's spouse" is no less a violation of the Ten Commandments than to steal or curse.

Close-up

When Is a Killer Not Responsible for Killing?

Determination of the actor's state of mind is basic to our system of justice. The same act of taking another person's life is regarded as *murder* if it is an intentional act, or as the lesser crime of *manslaughter*, if not.

We can learn much about a society's conception of human nature from its definition of those conditions under which one who takes another's life is not held responsible for that act. To see how varied such judgments can be, check below the conditions you think should "excuse" a killer and compare notes with your friends.

1. Inability to exercise reason due to:
   _____ a) tender age
   _____ b) mental retardation
   _____ c) insanity, temporary or chronic
   _____ d) killer being infrahuman—i.e., an animal

2. Influence of controlling agents that limit exercise of free will:
   _____ a) drugs and intoxicants
   _____ b) sleepwalking

3. Influence of emotions that overwhelm reason:
   _____ a) passions of jealousy
   _____ b) uncontrollable rage

4. Situational and role-required behaviors that change intention of act or individual responsibility:
   _____ a) public executioner
   _____ b) police officer in line of duty
   _____ c) soldier in battle
   _____ d) citizen in self-defense
   _____ e) parent protecting family
   _____ f) doctor in mercy killing

In more popular usage, the concept of motivation has degenerated into a catch-all pseudo-explanation. It forms the basis for apologies when you do not do what *you* are supposed to and the basis for complaint when others behave in undesirable ways.

Typically the resort to such motivational clichés as "underachieving students," "hard-core unemployables," "alienated youth," "hung-up," and so forth, places the blame for the *problem* with the person or group labeled in this way. It also directs attention away from factors in the situation that may be the real causes. In *West Side Story*, the Jets satirize the motivational jargon used to explain why they are such "bad dudes" in the song "Gee, Officer Krupke," some instructive lines of which go:

"Gee, Officer Krupke, we're very upset; we never had the love that every child oughta get. We ain't no delinquents, we're misunderstood. Deep down inside of us there is good! There is good. There is good. . . . There is untapped good. Like inside the worst of us is good. . . .
. . . I'm depraved on account I'm deprived!
. . . The trouble is he's crazy. The trouble is he drinks. The trouble is he's lazy. The trouble is he stinks. The trouble is he's growing. The trouble is he's grown! . . . Gee, Officer Krupke, Krup you!"

From "Gee, Officer Krupke"

It has also been observed (by psychologist George Kelly, 1958) that in education the most frequent complaint of teachers is that their students "just are not motivated the way they should be." When questioned,

". . . the teacher would insist that the child would do nothing—absolutely nothing—just sit! Then we would suggest that she try a nonmotivational approach and let him 'just sit.' We would ask her to observe how he went about 'just sitting.' Invariably the teacher would be able to report some extremely interesting goings on. An analysis of what the 'lazy' child did while he was being lazy often furnished her with her first glimpse into the child's world and provided her with her first solid grounds for communication with him. Some teachers found that their

laziest pupils were those who could produce the most novel ideas; others, that the term 'laziness' had been applied to activities that they had simply been unable to understand or appreciate." (pp. 46–47)

To Link Physiological Processes to Behavior

Motivated states are generally initiated by *deprivation* of something required for biological or psychological functioning. For example, number of hours without food is a stimulus condition that affects level of hunger, and therefore increases motivation to find food. Motivated states may also be produced by the presence of noxious agents, such as painful electric shock, smog, or a bully. In addition, they may be induced by the presentation of conditioned stimuli associated with strong unconditioned stimuli, as with *Playboy* or *Cosmopolitan* centerfolds or romantic love stories. Finally, as we saw in Chapter 2, modern techniques make it possible to induce motivational states directly via electrical or chemical stimulation of various parts of the brain. Similarly, brain lesions and direct infusion of drive-relevant substances into the blood, stomach, or other organs can make animals hungry, thirsty, or sexually aroused.

Modern researchers no longer look for a *single* physiological process underlying a given drive. Instead, the experimental search is for the ways in which a whole constellation of control systems interrelate to generate particular motivational states. It has also become obvious that to understand the effects of physiologically based motivation on behavior, it is necessary to study the interaction between a particular physiological condition of the organism and an appropriate set of stimulus objects or events in the environment. The latter are referred to as *incentive stimuli*. They may trigger certain response sequences and serve as cues to guide responding in appropriate channels (Bindra, 1969). Motivation thus influences behavior through its specific *cueing* and *sensitizing* function as well as through its more generalized *energizer* role.

The Function of Arousal

In addition to the energy associated with a particular motivational state, there may also be a more diffuse arousal through the action of the general arousal system. It is not motivation that wakes us from sleep or induces dozing in stuffy lecture halls. It is not motivation that makes us vigilant when we smell smoke, hear our name called, or see the green light turn red. There are many signals in the environment to which we must respond quickly and many conditions in which behavior is dependent on the general degree of arousal experienced by the organism. Effective action requires the functioning of many sensory and motor systems; thus it is often vital to be able to arouse all of them into optimal functioning "on a moment's notice."

It is the *reticular activating system (RAS)* that has the job of "waking up the cortex" and making the organism vigilant and aware of what is happening in the environment and to it. The RAS is a bundle of nerve fibers running from the spinal cord through the medulla into the cortical regions of the brain. These fibers receive inputs from all the senses, thus helping put the total organism in better contact with its environment. ▲ They then make the organism alert,

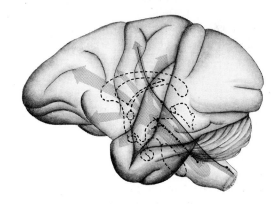

After Magoun, 1954

▲ Lateral view of a monkey's brain, showing the ascending reticular activating system in the brain stem receiving collaterals from direct afferent paths and projecting primarily to the associational areas of the hemisphere.

aroused, and sensitive to changes in environmental stimuli. This generalized arousal may play an important role in determining the ultimate expression of behavior.

This activity level may vary from the low level of sleep to the high level of alert excitement. As arousal increases, there is a generalized increase in the strength of instrumental responses, regardless of their actual utility in satisfying the motivational requirement. The same stimulus can serve both an *arousal* function and *cue* function (as the smell of food, which may both initiate a search for food and also guide the direction of that search). Or sometimes, different stimuli are responsible for arousal of activity and direction of it, as when changes in blood sugar level lead to feelings of hunger and the sight of food moves us toward it.

The capacity of sensory stimulation to guide behavior is poor when arousal is very low or very high. With very low arousal, the sensory message does not get through; with very high arousal, too many messages get through and prevent the individual from responding selectively to the correct stimulus message. Thus an intermediate level of arousal produces optimal performance, because more useful information can be extracted from the relevant cue stimuli to guide the behavior. Such an intermediate level has been shown to be most effective for both rats in mazes and students in a test-taking situation. This reaction between arousal and effectiveness of performance is called an *inverted-*∪ function. ◆

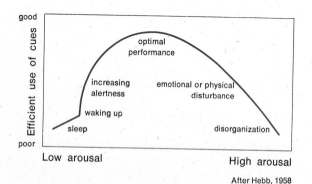

THE INVERTED-U FUNCTION

Studying Biological Drives

Most biological drives originate in the organism's undeniable biological requirements. These drives motivate the behavior of the organism in directions that lead to the required changes in internal environment. For example, the hunger drive motivates the organism to seek and take in food, which is necessary to maintain metabolism. Prolonged failure to satisfy this drive can result in impaired health and intellectual functioning, increased susceptibility to disease, and possibly death. To sustain life, the individual organism must have food, water, oxygen, rest, and sleep. It also needs some means of maintaining a constant body temperature, and a signal system (pain) that will enable it to avoid bodily damage.

Yet the biological drives of the species entail far more than these basic physiological needs of the individual. Each species to inhabit this earth has had to face up to the alternative of procreation or extinction. Thus, in addition, to ensure the continuation of life from one generation to the next, sexual drives and "maternal" drives (nurturance of dependent, young offspring) must come into play. It is not clear whether these latter drives should be considered "biological" in the same sense as hunger and thirst. Similarly uncertain are the status of a "drive to dream" (as evidenced by the REM rebound phenomenon discussed in Chapter 7), and of exploratory or curiosity drives. Drives influence behavior from birth and are present even during fetal life, although normally at that time they are automatically satisfied by the environment created by the mother's body. But we have seen in the past few years an increasing number of babies who come into the world with one of the most intense drives imaginable—the addict's craving for narcotics. These babies born of mothers who are heroin addicts (or now, even methadone addicts) experience painful withdrawal reactions when the umbilical cord is cut and they lose their "connection."

Biological Drives As Homeostatic Mechanisms

Though they vary in intensity, all the biological drives, with the exception of sex, serve as regulatory mechanisms that help maintain the physiological equilibrium of the individual. An organism will go to remarkable lengths to maintain the constancy of its normal internal environment—a process called *homeostasis*.

Biological drives originate in physiological conditions that have disturbed the organism's equilibrium. When an internal state is disturbed, conditions are produced that motivate the organism into seeking activity. Such activity ceases only when the goal is attained and biological equilibrium is restored or when a stronger motive takes precedence.

Many homeostatic activities are largely internal and automatic. Among these are the maintenance of constant body temperature and of the proper balance of oxygen and carbon dioxide in the bloodstream. Another, related to nutrition, is the very complex process by which the body maintains a constant level of sugar in the bloodstream.

But biological needs can never be satisfied permanently, and complex higher forms of activity have developed—particularly in humans—to meet the problem of recurring changes in physiology. Besides becoming able to detect very small physiological changes as cues to a change in equilibrium, many species have developed mechanisms for anticipating certain needs. Animals build nests and hoard food for winter use. We not only have learned to eat before hunger pangs begin, but have developed elaborate systems of agriculture, food preservation, storage, and commodity exchange in order to ensure an adequate food supply at most times.

Thus homeostasis is more than the automatic maintenance of chemical conditions of the body in response to specific stimuli. It involves an active effort of the organism to establish a physical and social environment that is as constant as possible. Yet it cannot account for all types of behavior, even at the physiological level. An organism may occasionally behave in a manner detrimental to bodily maintenance or even strive for goals that have little or no significance for

adaptation: it is difficult to explain in terms of homeostasis why some people seek "arousal jags" on roller-coaster rides or dangerous trips down the rapids, and so on. The explanation that "it feels good when it's over," just as banging your head against the wall does, does not seem to be satisfactory. This would make an interesting research project for you, to interview your friends and family members who are "super-arousal seekers" and those who avoid such situations. What is the difference between them? Why do they behave as they do?

Furthermore, many Americans literally starve themselves in an effort to live up to the current cultural ideal of "thin is beautiful." For example, when one of your authors asked students in an introductory psychology class at New York University to list their actual and ideal height and weight, many of the ninety males and every one of the seventy females indicated their ideal weight was *less* than the actual. This was as true of students who were overweight in terms of insurance company weight charts as it was of frail, delicate students who appeared to be rather emaciated. (In passing, we might mention that there was also a marked tendency among every one of the males and most of the females to have a height ideal as taller than whatever height they were.)

Thus although homeostasis is a valuable concept, it does not seem to tell the entire story. Throughout the following discussion of the physiological needs of lower animals, one must continually be cognizant of the inseparable nature of the mind and the body. Even though these "needs" are classified here as biological, all, of necessity, involve a psychological element. This concept will be of more importance later when we examine biological motives in humans.

Manipulation and Measurement

Much of our knowledge about biological drives has come from careful study of the behavior of animals under experimental conditions. Since measurement and quantification is one of the basic aims of any science, psychologists and physiologists have developed numerous ways of measuring the strength of drives. They do this by varying the intensity of drive stimulation and observing the effect produced on some facet of behavior.

To arouse drives, experimenters employ stimulus operations that disturb the organism's homeostatic balance. Deprivation of a needed substance, such as food or water, or variation in the calorie/bulk ratio of food or the salt concentration of water are most often used. As we have seen (p. 74), direct stimulation of specific brain sites by electrical current or by chemical injections is being increasingly used to study biological drives. In addition, changing environmental conditions by creating an excess of heat, cold, or noxious stimulation provides another means of experimentally manipulating the antecedent variables of motivation.

The dependent consequences of the arousal of biological drives are measured by a variety of response indicators. Among them are: (a) gross motor activity; (b) autonomic nervous system activity; (c) consummatory behavior (amount, latency to begin, and patterning of eating and drinking); (d) rate or force of responding; (e) speed of learning associations that are reinforced by biologically relevant reinforcers; (f) resistance of conditioned responses to experimental extinction; (g) preference shown when given a choice between alternative activities or goal substances; (h) interference with an ongoing activity; and (i) amount of obstruction overcome or effort expended to reach an appropriate goal.

This last measure was one of the earliest sources of data on the relative strengths of various drives. A group of psychologists at Columbia University in the late 1920s devised an obstruction box that separated a motivated rat from the object of its affection by an electrified grid. The strength of a variety of drives (induced by deprivation) was pitted against a constant level of noxious stimulation that the animal had to endure in order to reach food, water, a sexually responsive mate, or its own offspring. The behavioral index of drive strength was the number of times the animal would repeatedly cross the "hot grid" in a given period of time. (It could also have been the highest level of shock intensity that would be tolerated to get the goal.) Typical of the data obtained with this method are the patterns shown in the figure. ■ The motivating effects of thirst are greatest after a short period of deprivation, then decline, as does hunger, with extreme deprivation. This inverted-∪ function may, however, reflect primarily the debilitating effect of prolonged deprivation. In contrast, the rats kept on running at a constant rate in order to get a little sex, regardless of length of deprivation (after the first few hours). Surprisingly, mother rats overcame the greatest obstruction in order to retrieve their young. This powerful evidence for the existence of a maternal drive in animals went unchallenged until quite recently, as we shall see.

It is of interest to note another aspect of these studies. Without deprivation of any kind, the animals nevertheless crossed the grid a few times. Furthermore, even when there was nothing on the other side—except a chance to explore the novel environment—they crossed the barrier, perhaps motivated by an exploratory drive. This program of research is characteristic of early studies of drive, which focused only on deprivation and ignored the effects of external incentive stimuli on the motivated behavior.

Let us now look at a sampling of the significant facts that have been uncovered about some of the biological drives.

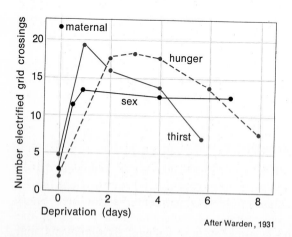

After Warden, 1931

■ You say you would climb the highest mountain, or swim the deepest ocean, but would you cross a hot grid in the Columbia Obstruction Box for me?

The Nature of Hunger

Of all the motivational states, hunger has received the most study from both psychologists and physiologists, primarily because it is so easily induced in the laboratory through a simple schedule of deprivation. Countless studies have shown that the number of hours without food establishes a stimulus condition that affects an organism's hunger level. The hungry animal will turn from other activities to searching the environment for food, and eating it once it is found. The *consummatory response* of eating *reduces* or temporarily eliminates the complex of internal conditions we call the *hunger drive*. The consummatory behavior ceases or becomes less probable as the animal becomes *satiated* (has had enough of the goal or activity). The *instrumental response*—the behavior of searching or working to obtain the goal—increases in strength as motivation increases in intensity and decreases with its reduction. Thus to regulate its food intake effectively, an organism must be able to detect the physiological state of hunger, initiate and organize eating behavior, and then stop this behavior when it has ingested enough food. As we shall see, the nature of the internal conditions and regulatory mechanisms associated with hunger and eating—and cessation of eating—are quite complex.

What Makes Us "Hungry"?

Subjectively, we know the feeling of hunger as a mass of sensations seeming to come from the region of the stomach. But just what are the physiological and cognitive changes that produce these sensations? Is the stomach primarily responsible for regulating hunger or are there other factors involved?

One of the prominent early explanations of the hunger sensation came from Walter Cannon, a physiologist. He suspected that the feeling of hunger was triggered by stomach contractions that occurred when the stomach was empty. The main support for this idea came from an experiment that Cannon performed with Washburn, his research assistant. Cannon persuaded Washburn to swallow a thin rubber balloon attached to a long tube whose free end was connected to a recording device. After the balloon had been inflated, any changes in pressure that were caused by stomach activity were graphically and automatically recorded. Whenever he experienced hunger pangs, Washburn pressed a button that activated a marking device, thereby recording the time and frequency of hunger pangs. ◆

Continuous records of stomach behavior over a period of many hours revealed two types of stomach activity: one associated with digestion and another occurring when acute hunger was reported. Only the regular churning movements of digestion were observed immediately after eating, but as the stomach emptied, the contractions associated with hunger set in. They appeared about every hour and a half at first but came more frequently as the length of time without food increased. When the records were examined closely, it was found that Washburn had reported feeling hunger pangs *only* during times of strong stomach contractions. Cannon concluded that the "disagreeable ache" of hunger was actually caused by the vigorous contractions of the empty stomach (Cannon, 1934).

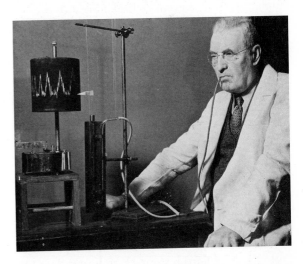

◆The late Dr. Anton J. Carlson is shown here with the stomach-balloon apparatus. Pressure on the balloon causes the stylus to move up and down on the revolving drum, producing a record of stomach activity.

Some later studies using sophisticated recording devices have reported that the classic pattern of stomach activity that Cannon found does not occur until *after* the balloon has been placed in the stomach and inflated (Penick, Smith, Wienske, & Hinkle, 1963). This provides an excellent illustration of the fact that the technique of measurement may affect the thing that is being measured. In this case, the presence of the balloon may have *caused* the contractions that were measured. Of course, we still cannot discount other evidence that many people do experience hunger pangs.

The early enthusiasm for Cannon's theory quieted as evidence accumulated that was incompatible with the notion that stomach contractions alone were responsible for hunger. If the sensation of hunger and the initiation of eating activities were solely the result of stomach contractions, it should be possible to alter eating behavior drastically by preventing the "message" of stomach contractions from reaching the rest of the body. This, however, is not what occurs; a number of studies, in which the stomachs of animals were surgically removed or the connecting neural pathways severed, showed that the animals continued to eat with only slight changes in their normal feeding patterns. For example, in one experiment, rats whose stomachs had been removed exhibited essentially the same hunger-related behavior that normal animals (used as a control group) did. They learned mazes to obtain food just as quickly as did the controls, and they were equally active as feeding time approached. The only difference was that the rats without stomachs sought food more often than the control animals, which would be expected since they had only their intestines for food storage and hence had to eat more often.

Cofer and Appley (1964) have raised an important point concerning the interpretation of this and similar experiments. Such studies demonstrate only that the *continuation* of already established eating patterns does not depend entirely on stimuli from stomach contractions. It is conceivable, however, that the organism may have utilized this particular hunger stimulus in the early development of eating patterns, or it may be that an organism normally relies on the stimuli from stomach contractions, but when deprived of this information is able to regulate feeding adequately by use of other cues. Since the animals used in these studies were mature and experienced in eating, it is likely that they had come to associate eating and food-related responses with a variety of both internal and external stimuli. The food-oriented behavior observed after stomach removal may have been part of a previously established habit pattern, elicited and maintained by the presence of various conditioned stimuli. Thus, while stomach contractions probably play some part in the regulation of eating, they are by no means the only, or even the most important, stimuli involved.

Blood chemistry and hunger. The body's immediate source of the energy it needs for cellular functioning is glucose, or blood sugar. Therefore, it has been suggested that chemical changes in blood composition should play a role in hunger.

Early studies showed, for instance, that blood transfused from the body of a starving dog to that of a recently fed one can cause stomach contractions under certain conditions (Luckhardt & Carlson, 1915; Tschukitschew, 1929). It has also been found that transferring blood from a recently fed animal to a starving one stops stomach contractions in the latter (Bash, 1939).

When subjects are given an injection of insulin, the glucose level in their blood is lowered, inducing a state known as *hypoglycemia*. Following insulin injections, patients and experimental subjects report feelings of hunger as well as stomach contractions. Animals given insulin exhibit a variety of food-related instrumental activities.

If glucose deficit induces a state of hunger, then injections of glucose should produce satiation, and they apparently do. Glucose injections inhibit eating in food-deprived animals as well as inhibiting electrical self-stimulation of brain areas presumed to be satiety centers (Balagura,

1968a). How changes in glucose level in the blood are registered in the central nervous system in order to direct behavior is still uncertain, however.

Does the "feeding center" control hunger?
Early evidence showed that lesions in various parts of the hypothalamus affected eating behavior as well as other consummatory responses and apparently even some motivated behaviors.

The later development of techniques for electrical stimulation of the brain generated an amazing amount of additional research focusing on the hypothalamus as the control center for hunger and the other biological drives. Stimulation of specific hypothalamic regions was thought to produce drive states that were functionally equivalent to naturally occurring drives. Even food-satiated rats could be motivated by electrical stimulation of one of these regions, the so-called "hunger center," to learn a new response for which food was the reinforcement. This and other sites were assumed to be highly specific in function, with one region of the hypothalamus controlling eating, another drinking, another aggression, and so on.

As newer evidence accumulates, however, several troubling conclusions threaten to dethrone the hypothalamus. First, there is a lack of anatomical specificity for a number of consummatory responses. Eating and drinking sites coexist with those for general exploratory behavior. Moreover, there are a number of areas in the limbic region of the brain that seem to exercise a more specific influence on motivational states than does the hypothalamus. It has been suggested that the hypothalamus may only operate as a "connection center" for these other basic areas (Grossman, 1968).

If an animal eats food when one hypothalamic site is stimulated, and drinks water when another site is stimulated, obviously the first taps "hunger," the second "thirst." Obvious, but apparently not true, say investigators who performed a simple but very telling experiment.

It was found that when the object initially preferred by a stimulated rat (say, food) was removed from the animal's cage, subsequent stim-ulation at the same site was just as likely to elicit other forms of consummatory behavior, such as drinking or gnawing on wood (Valenstein, Cox, & Kakolewski, 1968a).

Other studies by these investigators have shown that animals eating in response to hypothalamic stimulation will not switch to a familiar second food when the first is removed — as they do when actually deprived of food. In fact, they will not even switch to another form of the same food, as when pellets are mashed into a powder (Valenstein et al., 1968b).

Another area of trouble for defenders of the hypothalamic theory of motivation is the self-stimulation problem. Animals will generate extremely high rates of response in order to receive electrical stimulation of the regions of the brain that have been identified as "pleasure centers." Some investigators have noted that this motivation is so powerful that rats will cross a "hotter" grid in an obstruction box when this stimulation is available on the other side than they will for any other usual deprivation-incentive condition.

The problem is that some of the same areas of the hypothalamus that are reinforcing pleasure centers appear also to be drive-producing centers eliciting feeding (Hoebel & Teitelbaum, 1962). How can the same stimulation provide reinforcement and induce eating?

One recently suggested explanation that radically alters the earlier conception of the place of the hypothalamus in motivation is that hypothalamic stimulation does not create hunger, thirst, or other drives directly. Rather, it creates the conditions that excite neural activity underlying a well-established consummatory response; the act of carrying out the response may in itself be reinforcing (Valenstein, Cox, & Kakolewski, 1970).

The issue is far from settled, and although the absolute monarchy of the hypothalamus may be over, selection of a successor awaits advances in physiological technology and behavioral research designs. Nevertheless, the search for the "center of motivation" has revealed a wealth of information about the motivated behavior of organisms.

Inner and outer instigators. Anyone who has been in the Big Cat house at the zoo around 2:30 P.M. on a 3 o'clock feeding day is amazed at how the lions and tigers "know" that dinner time is drawing nigh. They prance, circle, bellow, roar, scratch, and are full of (exciting to watch) activity. Does their hunger drive "drive" them into this state of frenzied activity? Do they have an "internal clock" that is coordinated with the clock in the zoo-keeper's office?

Such basic questions about why it is that motivation seems to heighten an animal's activity have intrigued psychologists, too. Early studies of rats running on activity wheels seemed to agree with the observations of animals in the zoo: food deprivation to a point makes animals more active.

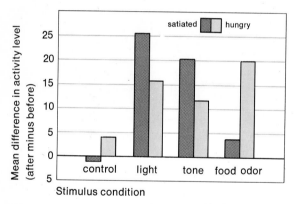

After Tapp et al., 1970

● **THE SMELL OF FOOD BRINGS OUT THE RESTLESS (HUNGRY) BEAST**

The graph compares activity level in hungry and satiated animals before and after the onset of various stimuli. When no stimulus was presented (control), the activity level of satiated animals went down over time, while the activity level of hungry animals showed a slight increase. When a light or a tone was used as the stimulus, the activity level of the satiated animals increased more than that of the hungry animals. When the odor of food was used as the stimulus, however, the activity level of the satiated animals increased only slightly, while the activity of the hungry animals was affected more than in any of the other conditions.

Activation or sensitization? The simple activation notion was questioned, however, when Campbell and Sheffield (1953) showed that hungry rats were significantly more active than satiated ones *only* when there was a change in environmental stimulation (an increase in light and the cessation of sound from a fan). Perhaps, they reasoned, hunger does not have a general activating effect, but rather a *sensitizing* effect; that is, the effect of lowering thresholds of response to various kinds of stimulation. In a further study, Sheffield and Campbell (1954) found that hunger increased activity in response to any novel stimuli, but *greatly* increased activity in response to stimuli associated with eating.

It would seem that from an adaptive point of view, increased drive should make organisms *selectively* sensitive to stimuli that signal events related to drive satisfaction and not merely indiscriminately active or sensitive. This appears to be the case from a recent study that compared reactivity of hungry and deprived animals to a range of stimulus change conditions. Hungry animals were more active than nonhungry ones in response to the odor of food, but less responsive than the other animals to light and sound (Tapp, Mathewson, D'Encarnacas, & Long, 1970). ●

Exploratory behavior is one type of activity that appears to be facilitated by hunger. In the wild, where animals must forage for food, it would be expected that exploration when hungry would have adaptive significance in helping the animal locate food sources.

In a laboratory experiment it was shown that after rats had thoroughly explored one part of their environment, the opportunity to explore a novel compartment was seized upon more by hungry than by satiated rats. With successive trials the hungry animals ran faster from the familiar to the unfamiliar section of a two-compartment box. When the novelty of the environment was increased, their relative speed of entering the unexplored portion increased even more (Zimbardo & Miller, 1958). ▲

The facts of motivation do not often yield the simple generalizations one hopes for in reducing behavior to explanatory principles. Increased drive does increase sensitivity to external stimulation, *but* the effect varies from species to species, is not the same for all other drives as it is for hunger, and depends on what stimuli are being changed and what behaviors are being observed.

Can external cues take charge? How often have you eaten a meal because the clock told you it was the appropriate time to do so, even though you did not feel hungry? Have you ever gotten hungry just from watching others eating some delicious, creamy pastry or from smelling a turkey roasting in the oven or a spicy pizza ready to be cut into mouth-watering pieces? Certainly, external cues such as these sometimes govern when, what, and how much we will eat.

The importance of many of these external hunger cues has been demonstrated in studies of animal behavior. It is known, for example, that the presence of a hungry rat eating can stimulate eating responses in a satiated one. A number of experiments have shown that the more familiar an animal is with the eating situation in which it is being tested, the greater will be the strength of its eating behavior (Bolles, 1967).

External environmental cues may become associated with physiological states through conditioning. These "neutral" cues may subsequently become capable of eliciting food-related responding and even the experience of being hungry. A very interesting experiment by Balagura (1968b) suggests how the physiology of hunger may become linked to external stimuli. After a group of rats had been injected with insulin, which lowers the blood-sugar level, their food-seeking and consummatory behaviors increased, as we have mentioned previously. Once this pattern had been established, the researcher continued the injections, but without the insulin. These preliminary events, which had in the past been normally associated with the UCS (unconditioned stimulus) of the insulin injection, became conditioned stimuli. The animals reacted to the insulinless injections with the same food-seeking behavior that they had

previously shown to the insulin injections. Apparently, the learned association of external cues with the *sudden onset* of the experience of hunger can bring eating under the control of these cues. Under normal circumstances, hunger mounts slowly and is reduced slowly; therefore it is more difficult to establish an association between a specific conditioned stimulus and the unconditioned stimulus. The short hunger cycle in infants may render them more susceptible than adults to environmental modification of food-seeking and eating.

In any case, the feeding-time activity of lions and tigers is probably best explained by two factors: food odors from preparation of the meat pails and the increased number of people like us who always arrive just before feeding time. But

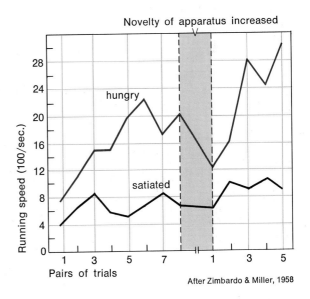

After Zimbardo & Miller, 1958

▲ **EFFECT OF HUNGER ON EXPLORATORY BEHAVIOR**

The speed of running into an unfamiliar environment was greater for hungry than satiated animals, and this difference increased over trials. When there was a marked change in the novelty of the second environment, at first the hungry animals were somewhat slower in entering it than previously, but soon were again high-stepping out of their old place into the new. Since they were never fed in either part of the apparatus, hunger was clearly motivating this difference in performance.

they still may have an internal clock operating too. Can you suggest a means of setting up a study to determine whether or not such a factor exists?

Scarcity of food and external sensitivity. The Greek philosopher Diogenes said, "A rich man eats when he is hungry, a poor man eats when he can." Animals living in an economy of abundance can rely on internal cues to regulate consumption, since food will be available whenever they feel the need for it. But for animals living in an economy of scarcity, the situation is quite different. When food is scarce and available only at irregular intervals, it is more adaptive to eat as much as possible when one has the opportunity, and therefore to be more sensitive to external cues (such as the taste of food) than to internal ones (such as feelings of hunger).

Wild opossums (and some other species) have been found to be highly sensitive to the taste qualities of their diet and insensitive to internal hunger cues. It has been suggested that having a rigid daily calorie intake is of little value to them, given the irregularity of the food supply, whereas sensitivity to the taste of food would aid in rapid detection of and discrimination between nutrients (Maller, Clark, & Kare, 1965). Hibernating animals also have to eat in excess of their current physiological need before beginning their period of inactivity.

Laboratory rats, however, "eat for calories," maintaining a relatively constant intake in terms of energy requirements. Rats in a wild situation where there is a variable food supply maintain a pattern of internal control by developing the habit of hoarding. By hoarding food when it is available and eating it when hungry, the animal maintains a steady level of intake.

When rats are deprived of food and cannot engage in hoarding, however, control of eating shifts from internal regulation to external regulation. Hungry rats faced with an economy of scarcity will eat more in response to the taste of the food they are given than to the caloric value of the food (Jacobs & Sharma, 1968). In a sense, they become more externally sensitive as they become hungrier.

Gross (1968) has demonstrated that this effect continues even when rats are returned to a state of constantly available food. Rats that have been deprived respond to experimental variations in the taste and caloric value of their diet by ignoring the caloric density and "eating for taste." Rats that have been normally fed continue to maintain a steady caloric intake despite taste variations.

How Do We Know When We've Had Enough?

How does the hungry organism know when it has eaten enough? The mechanism involved in the cessation of food intake is related to, but different from, that of the initiation of eating. One hypothesis is that "metering" takes place in the mouth as a function of the quantity and taste qualities of the materials passing through it. The validity of this hypothesis has been tested by means of "sham-feeding" experiments in which animals are operated on surgically so that food entering the mouth is chewed and swallowed but passes through an opening in the esophagus and never reaches the stomach (James, 1963). These animals do stop eating, but only after the food intake is much greater than it would have been had the food reached the stomach. Apparently some metering by means of feedback in the mouth occurs, but it is crude and inaccurate.

On the other hand, the rat can regulate its food and water intake perfectly in the absence of taste, smell, or tactile input from the mouth or esophagus. In one experiment rats were taught to use voluntary acts—bar presses in this case—to obtain injections of food directly into their stomachs. The animals were able to regulate their food intake, holding their body weights at normal levels (Teitelbaum & Epstein, 1962).

A number of studies have highlighted the dual nature of the hunger satiation mechanism. They have shown that while animals will learn to perform new responses to obtain food rewards injected directly into the stomach, producing stomach fullness and satisfaction of metabolic needs, they learn much more rapidly when the food is taken in normally through the mouth. It is apparent, then, that food metering is facilitated when both oral and gastric factors are involved.

Researchers have found that hungers for specific foods are often the result of biological needs and deficits—the organism seeks out foods that contain substances lacking in its diet. The behavioral effects of *deficiency cravings*, as they are called, are often particularly evident in lower animals that have been deprived of certain necessary substances. For example, rats that have been deprived of thiamine and salt will select foods containing these substances, even when a large variety of foods is available to them (Rozin, 1965). Similarly, laboratory rats on a fat-free diet, when offered a choice among fat, sugar, or wheat, exhibit a significant preference for fat; and rats deprived of either wheat or sugar show a marked preference for the substance that is lacking. Other experiments with dairy cows, pigs, and chickens have shown that all are competent in the self-regulation of their diet. These animals eat not only for calories but also for the chemical constituents needed for good nutrition. It is not clear yet how such deficiency cravings are regulated, although taste is apparently a major factor. Richter (1943) effectively showed that rats with their taste nerves severed *failed* to select a balanced diet.

Dietary self-selection gives further evidence that the body is sensitive not only to the total amount of food intake, but to the many aspects of nutritional balance as well. Many studies have shown that human subjects, as well as lower animals, are able to select their foods in a manner that satisfies specific bodily needs and provides a balanced diet.

In a now classic study, three newly weaned infants were allowed to select their meals from a wide variety of wholesome foods. Two of them selected their foods for six months, the other for a full year. All subjects gained normally and showed no signs of nutritional disorders. In fact, a baby who suffered from rickets at the beginning of the experiment cured himself by choosing large quantities of cod-liver oil, which contains the vitamin D required to overcome rickets. The baby gave up the oil when the rickets had disappeared.

All three babies tended to eat large quantities of one food for a time and then switch to another, going on "egg binges" or "cereal binges." But in the long run, with this cafeteria feeding program, the babies generally did on their own what nutritional experts would have recommended—and obtained a balanced diet. At the end of the study their health and growth were normal (Davis, 1928).

We know that learning and conditioning are ways of instilling habits or predispositions in an organism. What happens, though, when these habits are placed in conflict with the organism's biological needs? Do acquired tastes interfere with the organism's natural ability to choose the type of food that it needs? Answers to these questions are suggested by the following studies.

An organism that has had its adrenal glands removed requires abnormal amounts of salt. Normally rats will ingest extra salt after the removal of the adrenals, preferring salt solutions to glucose solutions when offered a choice. But more "sophisticated" rats that have had experience with both sweet and salty solutions before their operation will choose the glucose and die (Harriman, 1955).

It has also been found that rats deficient in protein will select sucrose rather than protein whenever they are placed in a test situation in which they have formerly selected sucrose. In a new and different test situation, however, they will choose the needed protein. Apparently, the preferential habit for sucrose is strong enough under the original stimulus conditions to override the bodily need for protein. The investigator summarized these results by noting that "habits tend to form in agreement with bodily need but established habits tend to persist regardless of need" (Young, 1961, 1968).

Unfortunately civilized people, like the "educated" rats, have formed many food habits—such as the American taste for candy and soft drinks—that are not in accord with bodily needs. Thus the "wisdom of the body," though remarkable in natural conditions, may be undermined by acquired habits. We will discuss this later on when we consider human obesity and other aspects of the hunger drive in humans.

The Tyranny of Hunger

Love and business and family and religion and art and patriotism are nothing but shadows of words when a man's starving.

O. Henry, "Cupid à la Carte," 1907

What would you feel like if *you* had to wake up each morning like a rat in a cage or a poor child in Calcutta, completely at the mercy of the Experimenter or of nature? How would *your* life be different if you had to worry continually about the source of your next meal, the coming of the next rain to bring you clean water, or the securing of a patch of dirty floor to call your bed when darkness comes?

The vast majority of students reading this book will never have to worry about such biological necessities. Technology and affluence have brought most Americans freedom from physiological needs and given them the time and energy to devote to deeper human concerns.

It is through appetite that humans have their closest association with "brute beasts." A life spent foraging for food, water, safety, and a sexual partner would be a life that would minimize a distinction that evolution has taken millions of years to make. Are the priceless gifts of reason, choice, abstract powers of intellect, and creativity evolutionary legacies to be put aside

for a crust of bread? Hunger is the great leveler that reduces us once again to the level of the lowest animal.

The quest for sustenance in a world of scarcity is one of the most critical problems facing the international community—one that demands innovative solutions at a technological, political, economic, social, and psychological level. On the other hand, the quest for starvation in an economy of abundance, while a less obvious and less pervasive problem, is nevertheless a psychologically compelling one for us to consider because it too distorts and demeans the quality of human life.

Do You Live to Eat or Eat to Live?

Over one third of the world's population lives under conditions of famine or semistarvation, yet relatively little investigation has been done concerning the effects of chronically inadequate food intake on human behavior and human life. ● How does the body adapt itself to such an experience? What are the psychological consequences of semistarvation? One rather elaborate laboratory study, conducted with a group of conscientious objectors during World War II, answers some of these questions.

Thirty-six volunteer subjects participated in the study, which lasted nearly a year. The experiment consisted of three phases: (a) a twelve-week control period, during which the subjects received a well-balanced diet designed to represent the fare eaten under good economic conditions in the United States; (b) a twenty-four-week semistarvation period, during which the subjects were maintained on a diet characteristic of European famine areas; and (c) a twelve-week rehabilitation period, during which the subjects were carefully nourished back toward normal. The experimental semistarvation diet consisted mainly of bread, macaroni, potatoes, turnips, and cabbage. It provided less than half the calories of the "normal" diet received during the control period. ■ *(p. 340)*

Throughout the experiment the subjects were kept on a full-time weekly schedule of physical exercise, maintenance of the living quarters,

I HAVE WRITTEN AN ARTICLE ON MAN'S GREAT HUNGER.

MUNCH MUNCH

MUNCH GULP

THANKS.

1-25

©1972 by United Feature Syndicate, Inc.

TANDBERG

and educational activities. Each subject was given regular physiological and psychological checkups (Keys et al., 1950).

The physical changes produced by the twenty-four-week period of semistarvation were, of course, profound. As the body struggled to adapt to the severely restricted caloric intake (resulting in an average weight loss of 25 percent), marked changes took place in the energy allotments for various bodily functions. During the control period it was established that an approximately equal number of calories were used in the performance of both basal metabolic functions and voluntary physical activity— slightly less than 50 percent of the total calories going to each. At the end of the starvation period, however, it was found that approximately 60 percent of the now-reduced caloric intake was used in basal metabolic functions while less than 30 percent was devoted to physical activity. The body appeared to have adjusted in the most adaptive way possible, with a larger percentage of the lowered total number of calories going into essential body maintenance and a correspondingly smaller percentage into voluntary (thus expendable) physical activity (Brôzek, 1963).

The authors of the study adopted the term "semistarvation neurosis" to describe the striking personality changes that appeared as a result of the semistarvation and then disappeared when the subjects returned to a normal diet. The outstanding characteristic of the "neurosis" was apathy. Humor disappeared, a depressing air of gloom and dejection appearing in its place. There was also a marked decrease in sociability. The men became nervous and irritable, tended to be boorish and tactless, dressed sloppily, and were inclined to "blow up" at each other. Self-confidence was replaced by feelings of inferiority and depression.

In addition, sexual urges decreased markedly and were slow to return during the rehabilitation period. Subjects "cooled" noticeably toward their girl friends and courtships collapsed. The men seemed practically incapable of displaying affection.

Tests of intellectual capacity administered at different times throughout the study failed to reveal any marked changes, although the subjects' general level of performance on such tests did decrease slightly, probably due to general physical impairment. Because of their constant preoccupation with thoughts of food and their inability to concentrate on other things, the subjects became convinced that they were actually suffering a decline in intelligence.

There can be no doubt that by the end of the semistarvation period the hunger drive had become the dominant factor in the subjects' lives. Food, either directly or indirectly, dominated their conversation, reading, leisure activities, and daydreams. Many of the men devoted their spare moments to reading cookbooks and collecting recipes; some seriously considered changing their occupations and becoming cooks (Keys et al., 1950; Guetzkow & Bowman, 1946).

● Hunger is the primary problem of existence in many parts of the world, and it is often the children who are the most pitiable victims. This child is being nourished back to health in a French hospital following evacuation from war-torn Biafra.

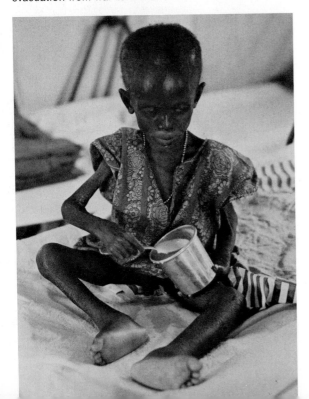

"Many women make a fetish of being thin and follow reducing diets without awareness of or regard for the fact that they can do so only at the price of continuous strain and tension and some degree of ill health. There are millions of young girls and women who starve themselves in order to look like those envied models for whom slimness is a well-paid professional pose. Ordinary young women do not get paid for being slim. When they become young mothers they will complain continuously about fatigue, about their children's problems, and about their own irritability. Little attention has been paid to the fact that their attempt to fulfill fashion's demands to be skinny is directly related to these problems. Having grown up with the concept that thinness is identical with beauty and attractiveness and is desirable for its own sake, they have become used to living on a semistarvation diet, never eating more than their bony figures show. Never having permitted themselves to eat adequately, they are unaware of how much of their tension, bad disposition, irritability, and inability to pursue an educational or professional goal is the direct result of chronic undernutrition.

"It is impossible to assess the cost in serenity, relaxation, and efficiency of this abnormal, over-slim, fashionable appearance. It produces serious psychological tensions to feel compelled to be thinner than one's natural makeup and style of living demand. There is a great deal of talk about the weakness and self-indulgence of overweight people who eat 'too much.' Very little is said about the selfishness and self-indulgence involved in a life which makes one's appearance the center of all values, and subordinates all other considerations to it. . . .

"Increasingly often such people come to the attention of psychiatrists. Though successful in controlling their weight, they have remained unhappy and dissatisfied, and this theme, with endless variations, runs through their many complaints. . . ." (Bruch, 1973, pp. 197–98)

The experimental findings of this semistarvation study become even more horrifying when we realize how many men, women, and children throughout the world are forced to live under such conditions, not only for a twenty-four-week period in the interests of science, but for a lifetime in the interests of no one.

Wasting Away: From Want of Affection?

While at this very moment, innumerable people in various parts of the world are struggling to ward off the silent death of hunger, others, perhaps even in your own school are in the process of dying of self-induced hunger. They are victims of a rare, chronic, and almost-impossible-to-treat wasting disease called *anorexia nervosa*.

These victims of their uncontrollable choice to stop living are almost exclusively young girls, often bright and well-to-do, in their teens or early twenties (Bruch, 1971). At some point, they stop eating altogether, refuse all offers of food,

During the semistarvation period of the experiment, the hunger drive became the most important factor affecting the subjects' behavior. The men became unsociable, frequently ignoring such amenities as table manners.

and begin to lose considerable weight. They eventually become weak and bedridden, having to be fed intravenously. If treatment is not successful, they die of starvation.

Most people find it inconceivable that a girl from a prosperous family could die from starvation. Yet several American authorities on eating disorders have independently concluded that in the last ten years, there has been a significant increase in the incidence of anorexia nervosa in the United States. Perhaps some young women are "predisposed" to become anoretics, since our culture obsessively extols the virtues of skinniness and thus avidly supports the physical qualities associated with the early stages of anorexia nervosa. (See *P&L* Close-up, p. 340.) Duncan (1973) has described the symptoms of this condition:

"The anoretic's ruthless avoidance of food leads to such serious complications as the collapse of her circulation. Other symptoms, such as extreme constipation, depression, and an abnormal preoccupation with herself, her food, and her physical exercise, are not so much direct threats to life as they are means of speeding up the process of weight loss. Another group of symptoms which sometimes occur in the years preceding her starvation phase are considered to be direct physical expressions of her underlying emotional chaos. These symptoms include the complete absence of her [menstrual] periods, an inability to feel hunger, and tiredness." (p. 47)

Yet there are marked differences between an anoretic and a victim of ordinary starvation. People in a state of starvation, like those in the semistarvation experiment, experience an intense desire to eat, while the anoretic relentlessly maintains that she has no need to eat. She seems to be a victim of her own inability to recognize or correctly interpret messages and signals from her own body.

But what makes these young women act (or refuse to act) in this self-destructive manner? We are not sure. Some investigators suggest it is a result of chemical imbalances in the body. Others see a psychological pattern in such cases, noting that often some disturbing precipitating event seems to trigger the choice to stop eating. This "choice" is not a consciously formulated, rational decision, but appears to be unconscious and, in a sense, imposed by the mind on the body. Such events include the failure of an intense love affair, separation from home, or an overdependence on one's parents that persists into adulthood. However, even a chance remark about the person's "body fat" might serve as the signal to stop eating.

Obviously, such events do not result in anorexia nervosa for most people who experience them. What is unique in the case histories of many anoretic girls is: a history of self-punishment and an excessive concern, prior to the onset of the anorexia, with food and avoiding obesity (Verville, 1967). Often food is of special significance to the parents of these girls, while avoiding obesity is of special significance to the girls themselves. It has also been suggested that these girls resent having the secondary sex characteristics that boys find attractive, such as breasts, hips, and buttocks, which disappear with excessive weight loss (Kessler, 1966).

The causes underlying such a bizarre overreaction are certainly complex. But if you were faced with treating an anoretic patient, would you begin by trying to unravel psychological problems? (Remember, she might starve to death while you were doing so.) Or would you concentrate your efforts on getting her to eat? The *P&L* Close-up on page 342 describes how a team consisting of a psychologist, a physician, and a medical student used the systematic application of principles of behavior modification to do just that.

Food Addiction: The Not-So-Jolly Obese

Unlike the anoretic, who is relatively rare, the obese person is all too common. Obesity is the social disease of an affluent society and leads to very serious physiological consequences. In

Close-up
A Pound a Day
Keeps Anorexia at Bay

The patient, 37 years old and 5'4" tall, weighed only 47 pounds when treatment began (see the photo on the left). After determining that there were no obvious organic causes for her failure to eat, the treatment team embarked on a program designed to bring her eating behavior under stimulus control. Eating was to be the only response that would get the patient the reinforcers she wanted. But what did she want? At first she was placed in an attractive hospital room and allowed visitors, and a variety of entertainment. She reported enjoying these activities, and so they became the reinforcers to be made contingent on her eating.

Before these reinforcers could be systematically paired with eating, the patient had to be denied free access to them. She was placed on a barren ward, with no visitors or entertainment. She was to earn the gradual return to her desirable environment as a reinforcement for eating.

In order to start the patient eating, the nurse who brought a food tray in was instructed to reward her verbally for any movements related to the process of eating. This "shaping" procedure of successively reinforcing such movements got the fork in hand, food on fork, food in mouth, and, eventually, food chewed.

To increase the amount of food eaten, the nurse would allow the patient some of her former privileges—when she had eaten a certain amount of food. Over time that amount had to be larger and larger in order to be followed by the desired activity. Finally, she was required to clean her plate.

The program was successful. In 6 months the patient's weight was up to 85 pounds, and she was released from the hospital. Her family was instructed in how to help generalize the newly rediscovered eating behavior from the hospital setting to the home setting. Essentially this consisted of deemphasizing eating as a "problem,"

while making it a pleasant, social activity and complimenting the patient on her attractive appearance. What underlay her anorexia, we cannot say; we can only describe how she overcame it successfully (Bachrach, Erwin, & Mohr, 1965).

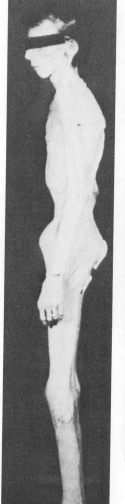

fact, more people die from medical conditions associated with excessive body weight than from any of the other addictions, including alcohol, cigarettes, and drugs (Mayer, 1968).

But the toll that obesity takes is not only physical, but psychological as well. A 1972 Gallup poll revealed that 55 percent of American women and 38 percent of American men surveyed described themselves as overweight. The fat child is taunted by playmates ("Fat, Fat, the water rat, couldn't bend down to grab his hat"), while fat teenagers are likely to be ignored by peers, and fat adults try desperately either not to make spectacles of themselves by trying to conceal their bulk, or to pretend that they are happy being fat.

But what about the jolly fat giant? According to most obese people, it is either a myth or the exception that is noted, because most fat people are not jolly at all. As Jim Fries, formerly 587 pounds but now down to 181 pounds after a diet of TV frozen dinners and an intestinal operation, said: "The world is made for people in small sizes. Fat people have to be jolly. Everybody expects it, yet jolly we are not. It's misery. It's lonely" (*San Francisco Chronicle,* Nov. 14, 1973).

Surprisingly, it is only in recent years that obesity has been studied experimentally. While weight-watching organizations flourish financially by watching their tens of thousands of fat customers paying *not* to eat (and even losing some weight, at least temporarily), research efforts are being directed at understanding what it is about obese individuals that makes them eat so much, so often.

Is the obese individual a glutton driven by a lack of willpower, as traditional views maintain? It seems not, according to current research coming out of the laboratories of Richard Nisbett at the University of Michigan and that of Stanley Schachter at Columbia University. Nisbett's work (1972) suggests that obese people are biologically programmed to be fat. Schachter's research (1971) points to an overdependence of the obese on external stimuli that encourage eating, and an insensitivity to internal cues telling them to stop.

Born to be fat? How fat you are is a function of the number and size of specialized fat cells in your body. These cells, called *adipocytes,* store body fat in the form of fatty acids. Painstaking research that involved counting and measuring fat cells in normal and obese individuals reveals that it is the greater *number* and not the larger size of these fat cells that differentiates the obese from the normal-weight individual (Björntorp, 1972). In one study the obese sample had three times as many fat cells as the average-weight group.

The importance of this finding becomes apparent when combined with several related

facts: the *number* of fat cells an adult possesses does not vary but is a stable quantity; dieting and starvation do not change the number of fat cells, they only reduce their size; overeating increases the mass of the fat cells, not their number.

Nisbett's work is based on the conclusion (Hirsch, 1969) that if you have a large number of fat cells, you are programmed by nature to be fat—you are constitutionally fat. Two factors determine how many fat cells a person will possess in adulthood: the genetic component (fats breed fats) and an early nutritional component (being overnourished in infancy). There are critical periods in life when fat is most likely to be deposited. They are right before birth, around nine months of age, then again between six and ten years of age, and finally during late adolescence. Limiting food intake and not cleaning one's plate, especially during these fat deposition periods, can help to prevent obesity.

If you have relatively few fat cells you cannot become obese even with overeating; if you begin with a high base level of fat stores (or "set point" level), then it will be difficult in an economy of abundance for you not to become obese. In a sense, if you had a high set point fat level, you would be a "latent fat" even if you were skinny from dieting. This may be the reason why obesity clinics have only limited, short-term success when the latent fats return with their oversupply of underfed adipocytes to a world full of goodies.

Obese patients who have lost literally hundreds of pounds after drastic clinical treatment typically gain all or most of it back once they have free access to food again. What makes it even more difficult for a constitutionally programmed obese person to lose weight is that the "feeding centers" in the brain are thought to adjust food intake in such a way as to maintain fat stores at that person's set point level. If this is the case, those people with a high set point level, living in our society that rewards slimness, will be hungry all the while they are maintaining the socially desired normal weight.

To turn on or not to turn off? That is the question. Schachter and his students have attempted to determine under what stimulus conditions obese people eat more than normals, and under what conditions they do not. It seems obvious that people become overweight when they are stimulated to eat more often and consume more food than is nutritionally required, and/or when they keep on eating regardless of internal hints to stop. But what cues turn on—or fail to turn off—such eating behavior? The hypothesis has been advanced that the obese person is *more sensitive* than others to external cues related to food, and relatively *insensitive* to internal ones.

Clinical evidence implicates both of these factors. One study found that obese patients ate more as the attractiveness of their physical and social environment was increased. They restricted their diet dramatically, however, when their meals had to be drunk through a tube projecting from a liquid dispenser (Hashim & Van Itallie, 1965). In addition, unlike people of normal weight, whose reports of experienced hunger are associated with gastric motility (hunger pangs), there is no correlation among the obese between stomach activity and feeling hungry (Stunkard & Koch, 1964).

In the controlled laboratory research conducted by Schachter, Nisbett, and their students, the eating of overweight college students was compared with that of a comparable normal-weight control group across a wide variety of situations. When their fear was aroused, or their stomachs were preloaded with food, normal subjects reduced their food intake, whereas these internal conditions had no effect on the eating (cracker consumption) of the obese students. On the other hand, obese subjects ate more than normals when given tasty ice cream, but less when the ice cream was bitter.

Obese subjects also ate more than normals when they thought it was dinner time—on the basis of external information rather than their own biological clock. This was shown by using a trick clock that could be speeded up or slowed down. An actual thirty-minute experimental session scheduled near dinner time appeared to last either sixty minutes or only fifteen minutes. The obese ate more when the clock indicated it was 6 P.M. than when it looked like only 5:15 P.M. The normals did not. Also, when a plate of cashews was placed before obese persons, they ate more when attention was called to the cashews by either brighter illumination or instructions to think about them. These variations in cue salience did not affect amounts eaten by normal-weight subjects.

These investigators have also been struck with the parallels in behavior patterns between obese humans and overeating *(hyperphagic)* rats. Both show a greater taste sensitivity, greater sensitivity to shock and work/reinforcement payoff schedules, faster sensory reaction times, and less willingness to expend effort in order to get food. It has been suggested that in such individuals a central state is involved that produces a generalized type of *"externality"*—an overresponsiveness to all external stimuli, food being but one class. (See *P&L* Close-up at right.)

Obesity has for so many years been attributed to sheer gluttony. Yet it now appears that obesity may be characterized by biological determinants and/or an oversensitivity to environmental cues that initiate and maintain eating independently of physiological need. In a society of abundance, attractive packaging, good cooking, and time-related eating patterns like those of the technologically advanced United States, it is no wonder that too many people overeat and become obese. Maybe the predicted shortages of food in the coming years will be a blessing in disguise for obese people as well as us "latent fats."

Close-up
If You Were Fat, Would You Take It All Off?

Will obese subjects still eat more than normals when they have to work for their food? This question was tested by Schachter and Freedman (1971) in an ingenious experiment that compared how many almonds were eaten by obese and normal-weight student subjects when the almonds had shells or were preshelled. While filling out a questionnaire, the students munched on the almonds: the obese ate more preshelled almonds than did the average-weight controls, but not more when they had to be shelled.

But an even more ingenious study refines the apparent conclusion that fats won't work for their supper if they can get it handed to them on an almond platter. Researchers Singh and Sikes (1972) at the University of Texas created conditions that demonstrated that with a little prior experience in working to get a desired food, obese people would put in more work and thus would eat more than normals. Obese people back off only when the effort required to get to the food is annoying, frustrating, and not part of the usually experienced ritual of eating that particular food.

The researchers arranged for normal-weight and obese subjects to eat two kinds of cashews: preshelled (as is customary) and wrapped in foil (as is not). The obese subjects ate more than the normals of the preshelled and less than the normals of the wrapped cashews. In a second situation, where effort-to-get-the-treat was part of the previously learned experience with the food, the experimental subjects were offered chocolate candy kisses, foil wrapped (as customary) and unwrapped. The chore of unwrapping the wrapped chocolate proved not to be an impediment for the obese subjects—they wolfed them down with as much ease as did the normals, wrapped or not.

Thirst: Another Maintenance Drive

While hunger is perhaps the most obvious of the physiological drives, and the easiest to study, there are other drives that are equally vital. Chief among these are air hunger—the need for oxygen—and thirst. But if the organism is to survive in a sometimes hostile environment, it has other needs as well. These include, at the level of the individual, the need for sleep, the maintenance of a fairly constant body temperature, the protection of the body from physical harm, and, at the level of the species, sex. In this section we shall discuss thirst as a vital maintenance drive. Sex comes next in the final section of this chapter.

Although most animals can live for weeks without food, they can survive only a few days without water. People who have been completely deprived of both food and water for long periods of time report that the sensations of thirst soon become maddening, whereas the pangs of hunger tend to disappear after a few days. King

(1878) described the intense suffering experienced by a detachment of the U.S. Cavalry deprived of water for eighty-six hours in the Texas desert. When at last they had the opportunity to drink, "although water was imbibed again and again, even to repletion of the stomach, it did not assuage their insatiable thirst."

Hunger and thirst not only differ in intensity but also seem to have qualitatively different effects on behavior, at least in lower animals. In experiments with rats, it has been found that thirsty animals will learn to find a reward of water more quickly than hungry ones learn to find food, at least when the rewards are in the same location in the maze. However, when the rats have to learn to go to different goal locations on alternate trials, the hungry rats learn to alternate between the two locations much more readily than do the thirsty ones. This suggests that the motivational state of hunger leads to variability in behavior, whereas thirst facilitates stereotyped responding. An interpretation of this result could be provided in terms of the adaptive significance of these behavior patterns. The natural environment of the rat is one in which the animal is usually forced to explore and forage for its food, while the location of its water supply usually remains relatively fixed.

The Physiology of Thirst

A parched or dry feeling in the mouth and throat seems to be a sufficient stimulus for the initiation of drinking. As the water supply in the body becomes low, the tissues of the mouth become dry; to alleviate this dryness, the organism drinks. ● Studies using the technique of *preloading*, in which an animal's stomach is injected with a large quantity of water, show that an animal that has been prevented from drinking will start and continue to drink (at a reduced rate), even though its stomach may have been preloaded to twice the normal drinking capacity. This would suggest that at least one set of cues involved in the initiation of drinking is oral.

But water metering by mouth is not a necessary condition for regulation of water intake. When thirsty rats must learn to press a bar in order to receive water injections directly into

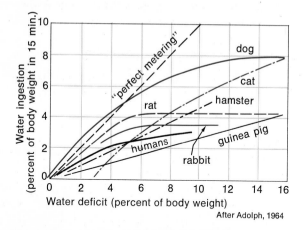

After Adolph, 1964

● **WATER METERING IN DIFFERENT SPECIES**
The graph shows the relationship between water deficit and water consumption in different species. The line marked "perfect metering" represents a hypothetical case in which the animal drinks exactly as much water as its body requires. Dogs exhibit almost perfect metering, while other species show less sensitive metering either at all levels of deficit or after some critical level of water deficit has been reached. It is clear from these findings that the animal's species must be taken into account when making conclusions about thirst based on water consumption.

their stomach, they soon maintain normal levels of water intake (Teitelbaum & Epstein, 1962). Thus water regulation is still possible without feedback from the mouth or throat, and gastric factors must also be involved. However, it appears that thirst is reduced to a greater extent when water is drunk by mouth than when the same amount is passed directly into the animal's stomach. Using, as an index of thirst, the rate of bar pressing for water reinforcement, Neal Miller (1957) reports that among deprived rats, those given no water pressed at the highest rate, a group given 14 cc. of water by injection into the stomach was next, and a group receiving 14 cc. of water by mouth pressed least.

Biologically, of course, an animal does not drink simply in order to moisten its mouth or fill its stomach with water. Rather, there is a delicate balance of body fluids that is preserved by an interrelated system of physiological processes. All animals keep losing fluids through perspiration, excretion, and respiration, whether or not they are allowed to replenish their supply. Unlike food, there is no excess storage of water in the body; thus with continued deprivation, the extracellular fluids that bathe the cells of the body become depleted, and the concentration of a number of substances, mainly sodium and chloride, increases in the extracellular fluids. The pressure created by this imbalance causes water to pass, by a process called *osmosis*, from inside the cells themselves to the surrounding fluids. Dehydration within the cells themselves occurs with continued deprivation. Wolf (1958) refers to tissue dehydration as "true thirst," distinguishing it from local dryness in the mouth and throat, or "false thirst."

The most prominent explanation of the homeostatic control of thirst postulates the existence of *osmoreceptors*—special receptor cells, probably located in the hypothalamus, that respond to signals of increased osmotic pressure by initiating drinking. Support for this theory comes primarily from studies in which salt solutions are injected into the body and increased drinking results, even when the animal has been satiated with water immediately prior to the injections (Fitzsimmons & Oatley, 1968).

As a complete explanation of thirst, however, the osmoreceptor theory is found wanting. For example, the exact mechanism by which the receptors cue the rest of the body that the time to begin drinking has come, is as yet unknown. In addition, there are a number of phenomena inconsistent with the theory: a perspiring individual (losing salt) will drink water, even though this further increases osmotic imbalance, and animals depleted of salt increase rather than decrease their water intake.

The intricacy of the timing of water intake and return of water to the cells from the extracellular fluid is remarkable. An animal will stop drinking before any appreciable amount of water has left its stomach (thereby diluting the salt concentration in the extracellular fluid). When an investigator implanted a sensitive recording apparatus in the brains of thirsty rats, he found that hydration (return of fluids to the cells) begins almost as soon as water reaches the stomach. In some way, there is an anticipation that liquid will be available to add to the extracellular fluid, and water is released to the cells *before* it is paid back by the stomach's supply.

External Stimuli Controlling Drinking

Yet an explanation of thirst that focuses solely on physiological causes does not tell the whole story. Thirst, like hunger, is not entirely a physiological motive, although it is a most powerful biological drive. Drinking has been shown to be regulated by a wide variety of associative factors that are independent of cellular dehydration or other physiological aspects of "true thirst."

Rats will drink more in situations that have remained constant than in situations that have changed. Their drinking can become so controlled by regularly occurring drinking times that their water intake becomes independent of deprivation state (Collier, 1962). With us, drinking is a usual accompaniment of eating ("a jug of wine, a loaf of bread . . ."). The two processes may become associated so that once either drinking or eating is begun, it becomes a cue-producing response, eliciting the other behavior.

An ingenious series of experiments illustrates the extent to which consummatory behavior may be brought under the control of other stimuli, even other motivational states. The experimenter was able to get rats to consume large quantities of water by making the termination of painful shock contingent on drinking. To avoid receiving the shocks, rats learned to drink far beyond the point of satisfaction or that required by bodily needs. Hunger was also used to induce drinking. Hungry rats were trained to drink enormous quantities of water simply by feeding them only after they had drunk some water (Teitelbaum, 1966).

It is obvious that this conditioning paradigm can be extended to make any consummatory behavior contingent on any other drive or stimulus pattern.

On the other hand, consummatory behavior can be inhibited by making an unpleasant event contingent on its occurrence. This principle is being employed by behavior therapists attempting to treat patients who have problems controlling eating, drinking, smoking, or sexual behavior they have sought help for. The thought or action associated with the consummatory behavior is paired with an aversive consequence such as shock, induced nausea, or an unpleasant image. However, strong addictions to food and alcohol are as difficult to change permanently as is narcotics addiction, regardless of the behavior change tactics employed.

In any event thirst, like other drives, is evidently not the single, unitary intervening variable researchers once hoped to find. It is conceptualized now as a heterogeneous cluster that involves many neural centers that are "differentially affected by various regulators and have differential effects on various response systems" (N. Miller, 1957, p. 1275).

The Sex Drive

Survival of the individual organism does not depend on satisfaction of the sexual drive; some animals and humans remain celibate for a lifetime without apparent detriment to their daily functioning. However, survival of the species does depend on sex. And so the issue for evolutionary design was how to encourage animals to engage in the "altruistic" act of helping the species make it. This was not an easy problem, since the sexual act requires great energy consumption and subjects the individual to considerable stress. The answer, of course, is that sexual stimulation is intensely pleasurable for the individual in simple physical terms. A climactic orgasm serves as the ultimate reinforcer for all the time, effort, and work that go into the process of mating sperm with ova. So effective is this design that it has resulted in "altruism" above and beyond the call of nature.

Extensive studies of various species have shown that the condition of sexual receptivity induces a much higher than normal level of activity, tension, and restlessness. Accordingly, if one thinks of sexual receptivity as a drive with copulation as its goal, then sex can be seen as the motive that ties the two together and leads to both the satisfaction of the individual (through tension reduction) and ultimately the perpetuation of the species (through successful reproduction).

What Makes Sex Different from All Other Drives?

There are a number of ways in which the sexual drive occupies a unique place in our analysis of motivation.

1. As already mentioned, it is not essential to individual survival, but only to species survival.

2. Its arousal is independent of deprivation or satiation except for a variable refractory period after the individual has reached the peak of sexual excitation.

3. It can be aroused by almost any conceivable stimulus.

4. Arousal of the drive is as actively sought as reduction.

5. It will motivate an unusually wide variety of behaviors and psychological processes.

6. It is not clear what constitutes the terminal goal response of the sex drive, making its status as a homeostatic function questionable.

Sexual Behavior Patterns

It is surprising to note that researchers studying "sexual behavior" are not at all in agreement as to what constitutes "sexual." Some see as fundamental only the exchange of germ cells in the act of mating; others maintain that copulation in heterosexual intercourse is what sex is all about. But insemination and copulation are only a small part of a larger, complex pattern that includes attracting a mate (using appropriate "display tactics"), courtship, foreplay, nest building, and care of any young produced by the sexual union.

Within these general classifications of what is meant by "sexual" are the specific behaviors actually observed. Each component of the sexual act is a behavior that has its own initiating stimuli, and that may be affected differentially by various neural, hormonal, and environmental conditions.

The patterns of overt sexual response in animals are remarkable for both their variability between species and their consistency within species. The influence of sex hormones in females is most clearly seen in the lower mammals. At ovulation, when the bloodstream becomes enriched with estrogens, the female animal loses her previous indifference to the male and becomes highly receptive or even aggressively suggestive in her sexual behavior. This behavior is known as *estrus*, or "heat," and is a signal that the female animal is in a condition of readiness for pregnancy. The behavioral signals to the male are species-specific, stereotyped responses designed to attract and focus his attention on the female's genital region. Among males of some species there is also a particular time for mating. For example, in the Virginia deer there is a specific breeding season and just prior to this the testes grow in size.

The sexual response in animals is also under the influence of odor cues, especially in females. The name given this "sweet smell of sex" is *pheromone*. Male rhesus monkeys show sex-related physiological changes such as increase in size of testes when they smell the estrus odor of females in adjacent cages who have been brought into heat through hormone injections. A sexually potent male mouse introduced into a cage of female mice will initiate a "recycling" of estrus in the females; most of them will go into estrus at once (Parkes & Bruce, 1961). Crowding together of female mice can induce pseudopregnancies—which are prevented if their olfactory bulbs are removed. Inseminated female mice will not become pregnant if they are made to smell the urine odor of a mature male mouse other than the original stud. This pregnancy block occurs with a greater frequency if the male odor is from an alien strain.

The variability in copulation can be seen from a few examples: apes remain linked in copulation for only about fifteen seconds, sables for as long as eight hours. Predators such as bears and lions copulate for hours, while prey such as antelope copulate for a few seconds at most, while on the run. The male rat engages in a series of ten to twenty successive, brief intromissions before copulation.

The arousal of sexual response patterns in most animals results in a complex stimulus-response chaining between the male and the female that must be coordinated for successful insemination to occur (Schein & Hale, 1965). ■ (p. 350) Yet even these seemingly mechanical behavior displays are controlled and regulated by an exquisite integration of hormonal and neural mechanisms—profoundly sensitive to environmental stimuli.

The Importance of Early Experience

Early experience factors have been shown to affect the initiation, maintenance, and improvement of sexual behavior in animals. Research demonstrates that early social experience is a necessary condition for normal sexual behavior.

Close-up
The Sexual Hangups
of Bored Animals

"The more intelligent they are, the more problems they seem to have." Though this may sound like a statement from your friendly college psychologist, they are in fact the words of San Francisco zoo director, John J. Spring, who is thoroughly convinced that his charges have almost as many emotional hangups as the people who come to stare at them. According to Spring, the major problem among animals in captivity is boredom—a problem that often is caused by the lack of available sexual gratification in their puritanical prison of enforced celibacy. Among the examples cited of sexual hangups observed in these zoo animals are:

"A horny okapi named Ralph is so lonely for female company (there isn't another okapi, a relative of the giraffe, in the place) that he has been grating his horns on a metal fence in sheer frustration. He was put in with the giraffes but he had to be removed when they began kicking him after he started making sexual overtures to a female giraffe."

"A female macaque, one of the short-tailed monkeys, was so desperate to have a baby that she stole another macaque's recently born offspring, Rudy, and refused to give him back. She was removed, and mother and baby are now doing well."

"Henrietta, an old lioness, . . . became so irate with the fumbling foreplay of a new mate who had never bred before that she bit him in the leg. Finally, in desperation, she crawled under him. He got the idea and went berserk." (*San Francisco Chronicle*, Nov. 2, 1973)

(See *P&L* Close-up at left.) Comparing male rats reared in isolation with cohabitation-reared males on a variety of measures, Zimbardo (1958) found the isolated males to be relatively ineffective in all aspects of sexual performance. In monkeys and chimpanzees, social isolation has even greater consequences. The male has to learn to mate, usually being taught by an experienced female. Females, on the other hand, learn through contact with others of their own sex to use sexual behavior for nonsexual as well as sexual purposes. By "presenting" herself sexually, a female chimp is often able to win out against a much larger male, especially in competition for food.

It has been shown that young animals of most species need, in their play, to "act out" behavior that will in adulthood become part of their sexual repertoire. Without this "practice" and bodily contact, sexual behavior patterns in animals' later life will most likely be deficient.

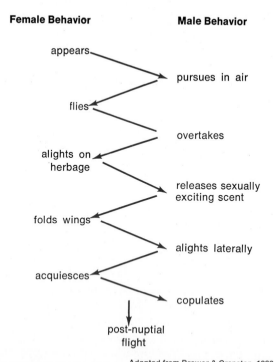

Adapted from Brower & Cranston, 1962

■ **COURTSHIP OF THE QUEEN BUTTERFLY**

Is "Mother Love" Necessary?

It is commonly accepted that human and animal mothers have a biological drive (virtually a "maternal instinct") to protect and nurture their offspring. The data from the obstruction box studies cited earlier (p. 330) indicated that female rats would endure pain more often to reach one of their pups than they would for any other motivational condition. Our literature is replete with instances of human mothers abandoning all concern for self-preservation to rescue their children from danger, and of animal mothers successfully defending their litter against attack from physically stronger predators.

It has been argued that enduring the pain of childbirth and providing the prolonged care required for the survival of dependent infants requires the existence of such a basic drive. A modern expression of the maternal drive is witnessed in the statement of a nineteen-year-old unwed mother who said, ". . . right now I've got to take care of my son . . . I'm acting in these films ['skin flicks'] because I will do and have done anything that will give me money to feed William" (*The Daily Californian*, July 26, 1970, p. 3).

However, the innate universality of such a drive is questioned by other equally significant evidence. In the Murray Islands a balanced sex ratio is maintained by killing newborns of whichever sex is becoming too numerous. Many mothers in our society willingly give their children up for adoption, and mothers in the Andaman Islands adopt their friends' children while giving up their own. In lower mammals, development of "appropriate" maternal behaviors may depend on certain stimulus-specific experiences. If female rats are reared with a rubber collar around their necks that prevents them from sniffing and licking their own genitals, their mothering instinct is absent. If they cannot lick their young as they are being born, they not only subsequently neglect them but are even likely to eat them (Birch, 1956).

What does a mother provide for her child that is unique to the mother-child relationship? What are the conditions under which females who bear children do not become "mothers"? The first question was posed by Harry Harlow and investigated by him and his colleagues at the University of Wisconsin in an extensive program of research with monkeys (1971). The second question emerged as a consequence of the observations they made while studying *"contact comfort"* as a significant aspect of the mother-child union.

Happiness is a terry-cloth mother. In a series of experiments, macaque monkeys were separated from their mothers at birth and placed with artificial surrogate mothers.

A substitute mother made of wood covered with sponge rubber and terry cloth and a wire mother of similar size and shape were placed in the infants' living cages. Half the monkeys could obtain food from a bottle attached to the cloth mother, the other half from the wire mother. All of them were free to go to either mother at any time, and the amount of time spent with each mother was recorded automatically.

With increasing age and opportunity to learn, time spent with the lactating wire mother decreased and time spent with the nonlactating cloth mother increased. Thus contact comfort completely overshadowed nursing in determining which mother was preferred. Furthermore,

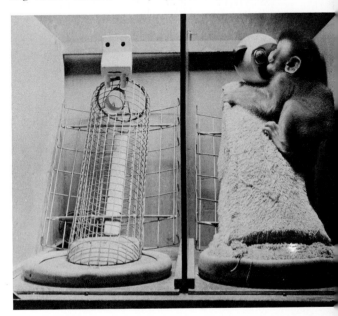

when a fear stimulus (a toy bear beating a drum) was introduced, the monkeys consistently sought the cloth mother, regardless of which mother gave milk. ▲

Open field tests confirmed this reaction. The young monkeys would use the cloth mother as a "base of operations" from which to explore a strange environment, running to her whenever they were frightened. When placed in a strange room without the mother, they would freeze and whimper or rush from object to object, screaming and crying.

The monkeys were then separated from their mother substitute and were tested for affectional retention daily for the first nine days and at thirty-day intervals for five months, by means of open field tests. On these occasions they spent their time on the mother and did not explore other objects, except that occasionally they would bring a folded piece of paper to the mother. When the mother was absent, they at first behaved as they had in early tests but gradually overcame their fear and became adapted to the open field situation. When the mother was covered by a clear plastic box, they were initially disturbed (but much less so than when she was absent), and they still used her as a base of operations. The affection of the monkeys for their cloth mothers showed no decline throughout the period.

Four control monkeys had cloth and wire mothers attached to their cages for the first time at the age of 250 days (after weaning). All screamed and tried to escape. However, within forty-eight hours they began to explore and after ten days were spending about nine hours a day on the cloth mother, even running to her when frightened. They came to use her as a base of operations in field tests, but they never rushed to her as did those who had had her from the beginning. Less than half an hour a day was spent with the wire mother (Harlow & Zimmerman, 1958).

In general, the behaviors that the infant monkeys exhibited toward the cloth mothers were almost identical to those displayed by other monkeys toward their real mothers. It appeared as though the young monkeys had developed real emotional and affectional bonds to the cloth mothers that persisted over long periods of time, even when the cloth mother was removed. The initial implication of these findings was that the essential ingredient in mothering was simply contact comfort, which apparently could be provided by any old terry-cloth towel. When these young monkeys matured, however, strange behavior patterns unfolded, which should make us cautious of joining a "Down with Mother's Day" movement.

But you can't fool Mother Nature. What happened in the next generation, when it was time for the "motherless" monkeys to become mothers themselves? It was found that they showed totally inadequate heterosexual behavior. Despite elaborate arrangements designed to promote some "monkey business" (including putting the colony on an uninhabited island in the zoo and introducing sexually competent wild-reared monkeys) mating did not occur. After many months only four (out of eighteen) laboratory-born females were inseminated and gave birth.

"After the birth of her baby, the first of these unmothered mothers ignored the infant and sat relatively motionless at one side of the living cage, staring fixedly into space hour after hour. If a human observer approached and threatened either the baby or the mother, there was

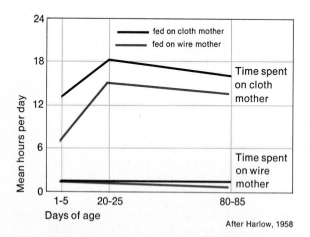

After Harlow, 1958

▲ THE IMPORTANCE OF CONTACT COMFORT
The baby monkeys nestled close to the cloth mother and spent little time near the wire one, regardless of which one gave milk.

no counterthreat. . . . As the infant matured and became mobile, it made continual, desperate attempts to effect maternal contact. These attempts were consistently repulsed by the mother. She would brush the baby away or restrain it by pushing the baby's face to the woven-wire floor." (Harlow, 1965, pp. 256–57)

In addition to the several socially deprived females who gave birth after being inseminated by persistent and patient breeding males, other "motherless monkeys" were artificially inseminated. From this total of twenty new mothers, three patterns of maternal responsiveness were observed. Eight of the mothers brutalized their infants: biting off their fingers or toes, pounding them, and nearly killing them were it not for intervention by the caretakers. Seven of the females were simply indifferent to their babies—ignoring them, unresponsive to their demands, unprotective. Finally, the remaining five were described as being "borderline adequate" in their maternal behavior. Three of these had experienced some minimal social contact with other monkeys during their own infancy (Arling, 1966).

Despite the consistent punishment the babies received for approaching the mother, they persisted in their struggle to make maternal contact. In the end "it was a case of the baby adopting the mother, not the mother adopting the baby" (Harlow, 1965, p. 259). ◆ Fortunately, it turned out that with subsequent pregnancies, the maternal behavior of these unmothered mothers improved.

In subsequent studies the Harlows found that the monkeys who had only terry-cloth mothers showed adequate, but considerably delayed, heterosexual adjustment if they were given ample opportunity to interact with other infant monkeys as they were growing up. However, the Harlows concluded that:

"The implication [of these studies] is that mothering is important not only as a source of social security, but also as a very powerful agent in the social training of infants, and we are happy to state that we now believe that real mothering, monkey or human, is a very important social factor and that real mothering is here to stay!" (Harlow & Harlow, 1966)

◆ Monkeys who were separated from their mothers at birth and who were prevented from observing behavior in others of their species subsequently either rejected or ignored their own babies. The infant monkey's attempts to make maternal contact were consistently repulsed by the mother. Sometimes she would restrain her baby by pushing its face to the wire floor (top). Infants who were continually thwarted in their attempts to gain maternal contact often approached their mother by climbing onto her back (bottom) and gradually working their way around to the front.

Human Sexuality

"Dear Dr. Reuben: Don't you think there's entirely too much attention paid to sex these days? I'm a physical education major and I think that it's much better for people to devote themselves to good clean pursuits like sports and exercise rather than occupying so much of their time and energy with something like sex. Don't you agree?" (Reuben, 1973)

Well do *you?* or don't you?

The implications of the above letter are that sexual thoughts (and worse, sexual actions) are the opposite of "good clean pursuits." This attitude that sex degrades the purity of human conduct and the nobility of human spirit is somewhat less prevalent than it was in the days of your parents and grandparents. It was not too long ago that marriage manuals described sexual behavior as "a dangerous evil which, unfortunately, is necessary for the perpetuation of the race." Sex as something sinful or dirty was the starting point (and thus the ending point) for discussions about human sexuality.

Since in earlier times open discussion of sexual behavior was taboo for males and unthought of for those of more gentle, tender persuasion, marriage manuals carried the burden of sexual education of the literate masses. Typically these manuals, though written by men with M.D. degrees, were designed to instill fear, guilt, shame, and the urgency of endless vigilance on the part of parents who hoped to nip "the vicious habit" in the bud! It is difficult for us to imagine the psychological impact of such indoctrination on the minds of untold numbers of parents, except to realize that without that era of sexual repression, it would not have been necessary for us to have to be "liberated" now in the 1970s. (See *P&L* Close-up, p. 355.)

It is well to compare the effects of this sexual repression of past years with that of food deprivation in the semistarvation studies reported earlier in this chapter. In a sense, the conclusion one might draw from the pervasive concern with food that emerged from being deprived of it is that "deprivation can make a potent reinforcer out of a commonplace event." Sex has become one of the most powerful generalized reinforcers precisely because it has been placed "off limits." What ought to be a most natural, normal activity, pleasurable in both process and consequence, has been, at one extreme, transformed into the root of all human disease and degradation of the mind and flesh, and, at the other extreme, exaggerated into the magical, mystical, cosmic union with Nirvana.

The "see-no-evil, hear-no-evil, speak-no-evil" aspect of the sexual taboo extended into the domain of psychology textbooks as much as it did in the oblique references in high-school hygiene books to matters "genital." Few psychology texts until the last few years made any extended mention of sexual behavior; when they did it was directed at animal sexual behavior, and even that focused on the physiological and on abnormalities due to castration, deprivation, and other misfortunes. There are two main reasons for this omission of a major aspect of human behavior from introductory psychology texts. First, there has been surprisingly little psychological research on sexual behavior in humans, and so there is not much substantial evidence on which to base conclusions. The second reason is in part related to why there has not been more research on this vital topic—it is still felt to be too "touchy" a topic to write about openly. This is an unfortunate situation because there is much yet to be learned about human sexuality, many myths to be dispelled, and some available knowledge to be imparted to students curious about the great unspeakable topic.

In the few schools where there is a course on human sexuality, it is not only a popular course, but one in which mature young men and women, frequently of twenty years of age or more, are learning things about sex and about themselves that they should have learned and discussed years before. Despite the recent publication of some excellent texts on the subject (see especially Katchadourian & Lunde, 1972), the fundamental direction of these courses and texts

S–X: Telling It Like It Was

From an informative pseudomedical pocket guide published in 1902 (*The Ladies Guide in Health and Disease*, by J. H. Kellogg, M.D.), which is chock full of helpful hints to parents regarding sex and how to prevent its outbreak in their children, we quote without comment from a section dealing with one of the greatest of all human vices: "self-abuse" (masturbation).

"*Vicious Habits.*—Many mothers are wholly ignorant of the almost universal prevalence of secret vice, or self-abuse, among the young. It is exceedingly common among girls as well as boys. The nature of this vice is such that it may be acquired and continued months and even years, possibly during the greater part of a lifetime, without its existence being suspected by those who are not skilled in its detection. We have met scores of such cases in which it was impossible to convince the doting mother that her daughter could be guilty of such an offense, although the marks of vice were too plain to be mistaken. A careful study of this too prevalent vice and a wide opportunity for observation have convinced us that this is one of the great causes of the large increase of nervous diseases and diseases peculiar to the sex, which has been so marked among women during the last half century. A pungent writer who has devoted himself almost exclusively to the treatment of the diseases of females, asks pertinently: 'Why hesitate to say firmly and without quibble that personal abuse lies at the root of much of the feebleness, paleness, nervousness, and good-for-nothingness of the entire community?' . . .

"Mothers place their daughters in boarding schools which enjoy a good reputation as successful and respectable schools, and imagine that they are safe; when their associations are such that if they escape contamination with this foul vice it is to be regarded as almost a miracle. . . .

". . . The victim of this evil habit is certain to suffer sooner or later the penalty which nature invariably inflicts upon those who transgress her laws. Every law of nature is enforced by an inexorable penalty. This is emphatically true respecting the laws which relate to the sexual organs. . . .

". . . Much of the nervousness, hysteria, neuralgia, and general worthlessness of the girls of the rising generation originates in this cause alone. The pale cheeks, hollow eyes, expressionless countenances, and languid air of many school-girls, which are likely to be attributed to overstudy, are due to this one cause. . . .

". . . Girls will uniformly deny very emphatically that they are addicted to the vice, when they are truthful on every other subject. . . . Hence, it requires the greatest care and watchfulness in most cases to obtain such evidence of the vice as will render mistake impossible. The only positive evidence is, of course, detection of the child in the act.

". . . The habit of self-pollution is one which when thoroughly established, is by no means easily broken. The victim of this most terrible vice is held in the most abject slavery, the iron fetters of habit daily closing the prisoner more and more tightly in their grasp. . . .

". . . The mother should first carefully set before the child the exceeding sinfulness of the habit, its loathsomeness and vileness, and the horrible consequences which follow in its wake. . . . Immediately upon waking in the morning, the child should be taken out of bed and dressed, and should be employed from that moment until the time of retiring at night. . . .

"Reform is not impossible, however, for anyone who really desires to reform; but the work of reformation must begin with the mind. The impure thoughts and images which have been harbored must be banished. The mind must be cleansed from every taint of evil. This is a task which requires no little patience, and in many cases more than human strength." (1902, pp. 144–65)

is biological. These texts fail to make an important distinction concerning sexual processes. Reproduction is biological. Human sexuality is basically a psychological process that may or may not have biological consequences. People engage in sexual activities for largely psychological reasons and whether it is a "positive" or "negative" experience depends almost entirely on the psychology of sex. For many individuals the most important element is not what happens *during* sex, but the attitudes, motives, expectations, anxieties, and cultural values with which they have previously been inculcated and which they carry with them like a cumbersome duffle bag without a handle.

In order for human sexuality to be treated as a subject worthy of psychological inquiry, it must be "legitimized" as a scientifically valid topic. In part, that occurs when otherwise reputable teachers and textbook authors simply declare it to be so and include it in lectures and texts. It also requires researchers to study the complex nature of human sexuality. This is not so readily accomplished.

Until a few decades ago the study of human sexual behavior was primarily limited to the clinical and anecdotal reporting of sexual abnormalities, as in the classic work on perversion by Krafft-Ebing (1932). The investigation into normal sexual behavior in humans was given an impetus by the work of Kinsey and his colleagues (1948, 1953), although the data collected were limited to interview reports of dubious validity. It remained for Masters and Johnson (1966, 1970) to break down the traditional taboo by directly observing and recording the physiological and behavioral patterns involved in human sexual intercourse and sexual inadequacy.

It is expected that the next decade will see a many-fold increase in our scientific knowledge about the nature of the sexual drive in human beings. It will also be interesting to observe whether changes in social mores and legal definitions of what constitutes "acceptable" sexual behavior will change the pervasive impact that sex motivation has on our behavior. Currently, sex sells not only itself (in the form of prostitution and pornography) but virtually anything it can be associated with, from entertainment to automobiles, cigarettes, and even food. (See *P&L* Close-up, p. 357.)

Will people become more hedonistic and dominated by sexual passion or less preoccupied and influenced by the lure of sex—better able to take it in stride as a natural part of life—as the "sexual revolution" of the seventies gains strength? What do you predict will be the long-range consequences of more liberal abortion, pornography, and sexual deviance laws; of sex education in the schools, computer-arranged mating, communal marriages, public nudity, birth-control devices, and coed dorms?

It is curious to note that in *The International Thesaurus of Quotations,* where one might find a fitting quotation with which to close the introduction to our discussion of human sexuality, the topic of SEX (Ref. 885) falls between SEWERS (Ref. 884) and SHAME (Ref. 886).

How Do You Know Whether You Are ♂ or ♀?

What sex you are may be as obvious to you as what is meant by sexual behavior. However, your confidence depends on a number of different variables of sex that you assume are congruent. They are: (a) genetic sex, determined by the XX (♀) or XY (♂) chromosome constitution; (b) hormonal sex, determined by a predominance of androgens (♂) or estrogens (♀); (c) gonadal sex, determined by the presence of testes or ovaries; (d) reproductive sex, determined by internal reproductive organs; (e) physical (morphological) sex, determined by external genitals; (f) assigned sex, determined by parents and doctors; and (g) psychological sex or gender-role, determined by learned masculine or feminine identification.

Normally, of course, all of these determinants of sex are in agreement. But occasionally, experiments of nature mix these variables into combinations that are incongruent, thereby producing a *hermaphrodite:* "an individual in whom there exists a contradiction between the predominant external genital appearance on the one hand, and the sex chromosome pattern, gonads, hormones, or internal reproductive structures, either singly or in combination, on the other" (Hampson, 1965, p. 110). The existence of hermaphrodism indicates that sexual *differentiation* is not complete at birth, or for some time thereafter.

There is a critical period in the establishment of such differentiation. It appears that about the time a child learns its native language may be the latest period when sex reassignment of hermaphrodite children is possible without psychological maladjustment. Evidence from cases in which children's initial sex assignment was later changed by their parents indicates that the later the point at which those changes are made, the greater the likelihood of disturbance in sexual and personality functioning (Hampson, 1965).

During embryonic development, sexual differentiation can be interfered with by administration of hormones or removal of the sex glands (castration) in mammals. Both "masculinized females" and "feminized males" of many species have been produced experimentally through such techniques. The closest approximation in human beings is the syndrome known as *progestin-induced hermaphroditism.* This condition of prenatal masculinization was, until the 1950s, accidentally induced in a few genetic females by hormonal injections given to their mothers to prevent miscarriage. These babies were born with somewhat masculinized female genitalia, abnormalities that were corrected early in childhood. Although the researchers of the 1960s claimed these babies were more masculine in their subsequent childhood behavior (Money & Ehrhardt, 1972), as measured by toy preferences, energy expenditures, and "tomboyism," their findings could easily describe the behavior of today's normal, "liberated" little girls.

Close-up
Sex by Any Other Name Would Not Sell As Sweet

In the first quarter of this century, publisher E. Haldeman-Julius sold millions of copies of his "Little Blue Books." One of his marketing techniques was to change the titles of books that were not selling well (Haldeman-Julius, 1928). Four of the books that sold only a few thousand copies a year under their original titles were:

Fleece of Gold	6,000 copies
The King Enjoys Himself	8,000 copies
None Beneath the King	6,000 copies
Casanova and His Loves	8,000 copies

Add a dash of sex, however, and watch those sales rise! The yearly sales of the same four books after being given new titles are shown below:

Quest for a Blonde Mistress	50,000 copies
The Lustful King Enjoys Himself	38,000 copies
None Beneath the King	
Shall Enjoy This Woman	34,000 copies
Casanova: History's Greatest Lover	22,000 copies

Does sex still sell books? Publishers of paperbacks apparently think so. Take a look at the cover illustrations on display at your friendly neighborhood newsstand.

The degree to which "boys will be boys" and "girls will be ladies" is strongly influenced by early parental childrearing practices, which help support or distort appropriate gender-role development. The distinctions between passive, nurturant, submissive girls and aggressive, forceful, dominant little boys may have served natural functions in the past, but are beginning to be questioned.

Sexual Arousal in Men and Women

For literally thousands of years, in both primitive and highly developed civilizations, the sexual double standard has predominated in the relationship between men and women. History has recorded a wide variety of extraordinary devices and measures used by men to dominate and control the sexual attitudes, beliefs, and behavior of females. Yet the steady march of women toward sexual equality has set the archaic double standard tottering and has substituted awareness of a myriad of mental chastity belts.

The degree and kind of a man's sexuality reach up into the ultimate pinnacle of his spirit.
     Friedrich Wilhelm Nietzche, *Beyond Good and Evil*, 1886

If a woman hasn't got a tiny streak of a harlot in her, she's a dry stick as a rule.
     D. H. Lawrence, *Pornography and Obscenity*, 1930

An obvious external stimulus that triggers the pattern of sexual arousal is tactile stimulation of erogenous body zones. Others include visual and narrative erotic stimuli and images, as well as individual fantasies. One frequently hears the generalization that while men are easily aroused by visual stimuli (nude or partially nude bodies), women are not. Have you heard that one? Do you believe it is true? If not, why do you think such a myth might be sustained?

The issue of whether pictorial representations of nudity or erotic activity are equally arousing for men and women has not been experimentally studied until quite recently. Most generalizations on this subject have been based on little

more than intuition and uncontrolled observation, spiced by some strong opinions and values. The impetus for research into this "taboo" area came largely from legal and constitutional questions related to censorship of obscene and pornographic materials, and the control of such potential instigators of antisocial conduct. The increase in crime rates in general and sexual crimes in particular concurrent with the increased availability of pornographic films and magazines has led many people to attach a causal connection to this temporal correlation. Recent investigations designed to assess the consequences of exposure to pornographic materials provide us with data relevant to the question of whether females as well as males can be sexually aroused by such stimuli.

The first studies to measure the consequences of controlled exposure to erotic stimuli outside the laboratory setting in which they were shown were conducted in Germany at the University of Hamburg (Sigusch, Schmidt, Reinfeld, & Wiedemann-Sutor, 1971). In one of their studies of 99 college males, masturbation increased after viewing erotic slides and films for about a quarter of the subjects (comparing the reported incidence of masturbation for the 24-hour periods preceding and following presentation of the stimuli). When another sample of 128 college males and the same number of college females viewed erotic motion pictures, both sexes reported significant increases in masturbatory activity within the following day. For females there was also a small but statistically significant increase in petting and coitus. In another of their studies 72 percent of college female subjects reported physiological arousal to viewing erotic films. Research in Denmark and the United States has utilized married couples to determine if pornographic stimuli increase heterosexual reactions as well as autoerotic ones.

Couples living in a Copenhagen university married-students' dormitory volunteered for a study of the effects of erotic stimuli on their attitudes, perceptions, and behavior (Kutschinsky, 1971). More than half had never seen a pornographic film, but many expressed an interest in doing so. In a one-hour group setting, the 70 subjects were exposed to two 15-minute explicit, "high quality," hard-core pornographic films, 15 minutes of reading pornographic magazines and 15 minutes of listening to a reading with pornographic content. Reactions were measured on a series of questionnaires administered before, immediately after, and at intervals of four and ten days later.

On the whole, the entire session did not evoke strong affective reactions other than disappointment and boredom. Exposure to pornography did not change attitudes toward sex crimes. It was reported as not sexually exciting by the majority of both sexes, had only a slight effect on increasing masturbation (net change pre-post of 11 percent), intercourse was reported increased by 29 percent of the subjects, unchanged by 70 percent, and decreased by 1 percent, and there was a decreased overall interest in deviant sexual practices.

Comparing the two sexes it was found that the men began with higher expectations and were more disappointed than were the women. At the end of the sessions about a quarter of the subjects of each sex reported feelings of "sexual arousal" and "lust." The researcher concludes that "during the session there was a tendency toward 'heating up' of women (though still the majority remained unaffected) while the men tended to 'cool down' " (p. 145). The table presents the "excited" ratings to the different pornographic stimuli reported by the two sexes. ●

● RATINGS OF THE EXCITABILITY OF
    PORNOGRAPHIC MATERIALS BY BOTH SEXES

Despite these and similar data the researcher concluded that "it is a fact that, as a whole, the women liked pornography presented in the experiment somewhat less than the men and they reported less sexual arousal" (p. 147). Thus old myths continue despite evidence to the contrary!

Sequence and type	Males (N = 43)	Females (N = 29)	Difference
1. Film 1 (2 girls, 1 boy)	42%	35%	−7%
2. Magazine	19%	14%	−5%
3. Text	7%	28%	+21%
4. Film 2 (heterosexual and lesbian couples)	37%	48%	+11%

Adapted from Kutschinsky, 1971

One of the most comprehensive studies of the effects of erotica on sexual behavior comes from a California research team (Mann, Sidman, & Starr, 1971). They studied detailed reactions of eighty-five married couples to a series of erotic and nonerotic films over an extended period of time.

The subjects, who were volunteers recruited through newspaper ads, were representative of "straight" society: middle-class, married to each other at least ten years, majority of wives were "housewives," husbands were largely from low-level professional or white-collar occupations. The majority were satisfied with their marriages and sex life and did not condone partner swapping or group sex. Their ages ranged from 30 to 64, with an average in the mid-40's.

Each subject filled out daily reports on a variety of measures for a total of 84 days (before, during, and subsequent to erotic film exposure). The overall results "indicated that viewing erotic films, as compared with viewing nonerotic films or no films, produced no significant differential changes in subjects' attitudes . . ." (p. 171). There were no sustained effects on subjects' sexual behavior, although there was greater sexual activity at home on erotic film-viewing nights.

On most measures, men and women reacted similarly to the erotic films; major differences showing up in ratings of specific scenes on sexual practices in the films. On physiological reactions reported while viewing the films, arousal was greater for women than men on seven of eight physiological variables for the erotic film they had rated most favorably.

The basic question of whether females can be aroused by pictorial representation of nudity or erotic activity is answered in the affirmative by the data from this study indicating that nearly 60 percent of the women reported genital sensations while viewing a film portraying group sexual activity.

These studies, informative as they are, are beset with numerous methodological problems (not to mention moral or ethical ones). For example, in the California study, subjects reported being most aroused by filling out the daily questionnaires that sensitized them to sexual issues—more so than by viewing the erotic films! The same may have been true of the questionnaires in the Danish study that asked subjects to examine a set of ten drawings of coital positions and to check those tried and also those they might like to try. Nowhere does the Heisenberg principle of uncertainty (see p. 41) operate more clearly than in assessing sexual arousal: the measurement affects the construct measured, either enhancing it or inhibiting it. Another major methodological problem involves the use of indirect, subjective reports taken after the stimulus exposure rather than ongoing physiological and behavioral reactions to the stimuli as they are being experienced. Sexual reactions also vary with the setting in which the material is to be viewed and are different in public, "scientific," group settings than in private, informal settings.

The average person's knowledge of the world comes largely through exposure to reports in our mass media about the "way things are." So what is he or she to conclude about the effect of pornography on causing delinquent or criminal behavior? The 1969 Presidential Commission on Obscenity and Pornography concluded that there was *no* reliable relationship demonstrated in the research it had commissioned. But columnist James Kilpatrick advised his readers:

"Some of the 'empirical research' was patently absurd. Causality cannot be measured in a beaker, or plotted on a graph. In this highly subjective area of human behavior, we probably never will know precisely what motivates a man to rape or to sexual molestation. Common sense is a better guide than laboratory experiments; and common sense tells us that pornography is bound to contribute to sexual crime." (S. F. Chronicle, 1/16/75)

Patterns of Human Sexual Arousal and Response

Sexual activity may be observed in some infants at birth and may last well into senility. Age does take its toll, however, with the peak intensity of male sexual drive occurring between puberty

and the early twenties and steadily declining thereafter. For females, approximately the same generalization holds, but cultural factors complicate matters. The decline of sexual drive with age is in part related to poor health and to greater fatigue rather than to an inherent "cooling of the blood." Although there is a reduction in androgens with old age, the Kinsey researchers report cases of men in their fifties who averaged fourteen acts of intercourse a week; Mae West, over eighty, can still boast plenty of "sex appeal."

Poor nutrition diminishes sexual drive (as we noted in the semistarvation experiments), as does excessive use of alcohol or drugs. Similarly inhibiting are preoccupation with personal problems, fear of the consequences, or overconcern for sex as a performance to be evaluated.

Cultural variations in sexual response. We are never so aware of the extent to which our sexual drive and the behavior patterns to which it gives rise are under the controlling influence of a broad set of cultural experiences as when we compare ourselves to people from other cultures. Margaret Mead's (1938) perceptive analysis of Samoan and American girls revealed that the physiological disturbances and psychological tension that accompany the reaching of sexual maturity in America must be learned since they are absent in Samoa.

Another anthropologist has described a pattern of sexual behavior among people living on the Melanesian Islands in the Southwest Pacific that is alien to many of our basic conceptions.

Since the sex drive is assumed to be a powerful urge that requires satisfaction, and since premarital intercourse is forbidden, males and females are encouraged to masturbate. In addition, to relieve this drive, all males engage in homosexual intercourse with the full knowledge of the community. There is, however, no indication of subsequent sexual inversion in which males prefer other males as sexual objects. Premarital chastity is so strictly enforced that unmarried females and males are kept separated and not allowed even to talk or look at each other if they have a chance to meet. This results in considerable shame, awkwardness, and embarrassment during the "excruciating adjustment" period at the start of married life (Davenport, 1965).

Individual variations: Heterosexuality vs. homosexuality. Heterosexuality has been recognized as the "appropriate" and "socially acceptable" mode of sexual activity in our country. It is obviously necessary to carry on reproduction (although some lesbian groups are considering artificial insemination to achieve the goal of reproduction without heterosexual intercourse). Many of our social conventions and institutions are based on the premise that heterosexuality is the right and proper way for individuals to relate sexually. To do otherwise is considered "abnormal," "sinful," and (frequently) illegal.

The recent emergence of homosexual groups on many college campuses and in larger cities is an important indicator of both the "fact" of homosexuality and the need for "straight" society to reevaluate its attitudes toward the gay community. Did you know that most states in the Union condemn private acts of homosexuality between consenting adults as criminal? In seven states such acts are punishable by life imprisonment, and in thirty-five others the maximum penalty is at least ten years. Until recently, psychiatry has made the homosexual a sick person with a serious "mental disorder" to be treated with prolonged therapy until the "patient" rejects this inappropriate attachment in favor of heterosexuality. A few overzealous behavior modifiers, impatient with talk and insights, simply attach electrodes and shock the homosexual every time a sexual response is made to a same-sex visual stimulus. Arousal to such stimuli soon extinguishes, and contingency management can be used to "reprogram" the individual to get turned on by pictures of the opposite sex. (In some cases this new response generalizes from the therapist's slides to real people.)

But is homosexuality a mental disorder? Should we treat it in Chapters 11 and 12 of this text?

On December 14, 1973, homosexuals were mentally ill sexual deviants.

On December 15, 1973, homosexuals were no longer psychiatric deviants.

This turnabout was not achieved by mass therapy, but by a vote of the trustees of the American Psychiatric Association. They declared homosexuality to be a "sexual orientation disturbance" not requiring treatment unless an individual desires it.

This change signals a new orientation toward acceptance of alternative life-styles. Heterosexuality is the statistical norm; it is where most people are at. But does it, therefore, follow that it is "normal" in a psychological or personal sense or that homosexuality is "abnormal"? The importance of greater tolerance in our views toward homosexuality is that it allows all people greater freedom of self-expression and a life directed toward goals that are determined by personal preference and not merely dictated by social convention and fear of disclosure. This does not mean "all hell will break loose" and everyone will be turning gay, but that those who are or prefer to be, do not have to do so out of rebellion, resentment, or rejection of parental and social values, but because for a variety of personal reasons they find the companionship of members of the same sex more desirable than that of the opposite sex.

Chapter Summary

The study of motivation is the search for the causes of behavior. Motives are not directly observable; they are *intervening variables* that we can only infer by noting the relationships between stimuli and responses. Aspects of internal motivation include: (1) arousal, (2) direction of effort, (3) selective attention, (4) organization of activity, and (5) persistence.

We infer the existence of motives in order to: (1) account for the variability among the behavior of different individuals; (2) infer inner dispositions from observable acts; (3) establish the internal origins of behavior; (4) assign volition, responsibility, and blame; and (5) link physiological processes with overt behavior.

While particular motivational states produce arousal, a general arousal system also exists. This is the *reticular activating system (RAS)* in the spinal cord and brain. Intermediate levels of arousal lead to more effective behavior than either high or low levels (an *inverted-∪ function*).

Biological drives result from the organism's basic tissue needs. *Homeostasis* is the tendency to maintain a constant internal environment within the limits needed for physiological equilibrium. Biological drives may be studied by depriving an organism of some drive-related substance or subjecting it to some unpleasant stimulation and measuring the changes in behavior that result.

The *hunger drive* is the one that has been most extensively studied. A state of hunger is induced by depriving an organism of food. The *consummatory response,* in this case eating, satisfies the organism and reduces the drive state.

Stomach contractions play a part in causing awareness of hunger, as does level of blood sugar. The hypothalamus plays an important role in the processing of hunger and other drives, but it is not clear whether it functions as a "center of motivation" or only a "center of communication" about drive states.

Hunger seems to exert a sensitizing effect, lowering thresholds for various kinds of stimulation. Both *external* and *internal* cues may initiate the hunger drive. It has been found that animals living in an economy of scarcity are more sensitive to external cues; those who live in an economy of abundance are more sensitive to internal cues. Studies show that *metering of food intake* involves both the stomach and, to a lesser extent, the mouth. Both animals and humans experience *specific hungers,* particularly when they have been deprived of needed substances. In humans, however, these hungers are often overruled by learned preferences.

Prolonged semistarvation leads to increasing apathy and preoccupation with food. *Anorexia nervosa* is a rare disease in which the victims, usually young women, simply stop eating and waste away. Its origins are not clearly understood, but it has been successfully treated with behavior modification techniques. *Obesity,* the result of overeating, is a serious problem for many people. Two lines of research currently under way suggest that (a) obese people may have *more* fat cells than normal individuals and (b) the obese tend to eat in response to *external* rather than internal cues.

The *thirst drive* is more intense than the hunger drive under conditions of deprivation, and also shows certain qualitative differences. For example, the behavior of thirsty animals tends to be stereotyped, while that of hungry ones does not. Water metering involves both the stomach and the mouth. The physiological basis of the thirst drive is maintenance of a correct balance of fluids in body cells.

Sex, unlike other biological drives, is not essential to the survival of the individual—although it is obviously essential to the survival of the species. It can be aroused by almost any conceivable stimulus, and its arousal is as actively sought as its reduction.

The sexual behavior of animals is under the control of physiological factors, such as the cycle of estrus in the female, to a much greater extent than is that of humans. There is wide variation among species in frequency and timing of copulation, but in all of them response patterns depend on complex reciprocal cues between male and female. Isolation from peers during infancy can lead to inadequate sexual behavior in adulthood.

Although the existence of an innate "maternal drive" is commonly accepted, there is evidence that leads one to question it. Animal mothers' acceptance of their young seems to depend heavily on olfactory cues.

Early studies of "contact comfort" showed that baby monkeys raised with artificial mothers vastly preferred a "cuddly" terry-cloth one, even when milk was provided by one made of wire. These monkeys seemed to develop normal affectional responses to their surrogate mothers, and they were thought to be growing up normally. It eventually appeared, however, that the adult sexual behavior of these "unmothered" monkeys was totally inadequate—and when some of them eventually became mothers themselves, they rejected their young. Apparently both "real" mothering and social interaction with peers are essential to adequate heterosexual adjustment in adulthood.

A generation or two ago, sex was regarded as a "necessary evil," not to be discussed in polite society. This could be one reason why it has become such a potent reinforcer in our day.

Until recently, research on human sexuality has been limited to clinical and interview reports.

The psychosexual differentiation of male and female depends on both physiological factors (determined primarily by hormones) and psychological factors (such as learned gender role). *Hermaphrodites* are individuals in whom there is a contradiction between external and internal sex characteristics.

It has long been assumed that men and women differ markedly in their patterns of sexual arousal, but recent research is challenging this assumption. In studies involving controlled exposure to erotic stimuli (pornographic films or literature), female as well as male subjects have reported physiological arousal to visual stimuli. Many methodological problems are yet to be solved, but controlled research in this area should go far toward replacing myth with fact.

Most human beings are capable of sexual behavior throughout most of their lives, although sexual activity generally diminishes with age. Psychological factors, as well as changes in physical health, can lead to a decline in sexual responsiveness. Sexual attitudes and behavior patterns are dependent to a great extent on cultural factors. *Homosexuality,* which has long been regarded as criminal and/or pathological, is coming to be regarded as a matter of individual preference, requiring treatment only if a person desires it.

The Hunger of the Obese
Richard E. Nisbett University of Michigan

About a decade ago, when I was a graduate student in Columbia's department of social psychology, I began studying the behavior of obese people. Stanley Schachter—my adviser at the time—and I both firmly believed that obesity could be explained as the result of a behavioral disorder. Like most social psychologists, we had a strong environmentalist bias. We believed that most differences between people arose from difference in learning histories. Schachter hypothesized that some people are obese because they do not attend to the physiological cues that initiate and terminate feeding but instead are highly attuned to external, sensory cues such as taste, sight, and smell. Our research in the intervening years has amply verified the notion that obese people are highly responsive to external cues, but I have been compelled to do an about face on our initial assumptions about causality. I no longer believe that people are fat because they behave as they do, but rather that they behave as they do as an indirect result of their attempts to control their weight.

Obesity itself, I now believe, is in most cases largely the result of bad genetic draw. This conclusion stems in part from work on fat tissue by Hirsch and Knittle at Rockefeller University and by the Swedish physiologist 'Per Björntorp. They have found that obesity is primarily the result of an elevated number of fat cells. While there is sometimes a slight increase in the size of fat cells, obesity seems in most cases to be basically due to an increased number of cells. Obese subjects have been found to have as much as three times as many fat cells as normal weight individuals.

The importance of this work for an understanding of obesity becomes clear when it is realized that the number of fat cells an adult possesses is basically unchangeable. Dieting in adult humans can decrease the *size* of fat cells but has virtually no effect on the *number* of fat cells. After losing weight, the formerly obese person is left with the same high number of fat cells to be filled back up the moment will power fades. Conversely, overeating in the adult does not stimulate the growth of more fat cells. Prison volunteers paid to get fat increase the size but not the number of their fat cells. This would seem to mean that individuals who happen to have a large number of fat cells will in effect have a higher baseline of body fat. That is, constitutionally they are "programmed" to be fat.

The two factors that seem to influence the "fat baseline" are genetic make-up and, perhaps, early nutritional experience. Strains of rats differ greatly in the percent of fat in their bodies. It seems likely that humans would show something approximating the genetic range that rats do. The actual data on parent-child similarity for obesity, though of course subject to interpretation on environmental grounds (fat parents teach their children to overeat), show such a powerful relationship that it seems highly likely that heredity does play a role in human obesity. For example, one investigator found that the slender parents in his sample *never* produced a fat child, while the very obese parents *never* produced a slender one.

The second factor that likely plays a role is early childhood nutrition. It is possible to affect the number of fat cells a rat will have as an adult during the first few weeks of life. It seems likely, although it has not yet been clearly demonstrated, that the fat baseline for humans could similarly be affected by overnutrition through the first few years of life.

The possibility that baselines for fat stores differ among people becomes important in view of the fact that recent evidence suggests that the body defends the mass of fat tissue. This appears to be done by feeding centers in the hypothalamus which adjust food intake so as to maintain fat stores at the baseline or "set point" level. There is no reason to assume that this set point is the same in all individuals of the same height and bone structure. Rather, the hypothalamus may defend different baselines in different individuals, maintaining whatever set point the individual is favored with — or saddled with. This proposition suggests a new way of thinking about obesity. It would suggest that obesity, for some, is a "normal" or "ideal" state. Moreover, it would then follow that many individuals in the "overweight" population are actually "underweight." The person with a high set point for fat tissue will be under considerable social (and often medical) pressure to lose weight. But his or her hypothalamus could be expected to respond to weight loss in approximately the same way as the central nervous system of a leaner individual — with hunger. Such a person would, in effect, be starving all the time.

There are in fact many parallels between the behavior of obese humans and that of hungry humans and animals. But before discussing the behavior of the obese, it will be helpful to describe in some detail the behavior changes that are induced by hunger. Some of these changes are familiar, but many of them are not at all widely known, even to researchers in the area of feeding and nutrition.

The food-deprived organism, of course, eats more at a given opportunity and eats more rapidly than the less deprived organism. The food-deprived organism is also more likely to eat in a new or strange setting, and so on. Less obvious are the effects of hunger on the organism's response to the taste of food. Until recently, no one has looked closely at the effects of hunger on responsiveness to taste. Most researchers have simply assumed that the hungry organism is undiscriminating, eating large quantities of any available food without regard to its taste properties. This assumption now seems a mistaken one. The evidence, coming mostly from work by Jacobs and Sharma, suggests that the deprived organism consumes proportionally more good-tasting food and less bad-testing food than does the less deprived organism.

Jacobs and Sharma offered dogs and rats either standard laboratory chow, chow with improved flavor due to the addition of fats or saccharin, or chow which had been made to taste bad through addition of bitter-tasting quinine or cellulose. Animals were either allowed to eat whenever they wanted (ad lib diet) or were given only one brief meal in every 24 hours. Ad lib and deprived animals consumed equivalent amounts of standard chow, but deprived animals consumed much more good-tasting chow than ad lib animals and consumed much less bad-tasting chow. The evidence thus suggests that the deprived animal becomes increasingly more responsive to taste, consuming proportionally more good-tasting food and less bad-tasting food.

Hunger also has powerful effects on other kinds of behavior. Most of what we know about the effects of extreme hunger on general behavior comes from the classic World War II work of Keys, Brozek, and others on the effects of semistarvation on human beings (see pp. 338–340). Keys subjects were conscientious objectors who volunteered to lose 24 percent of their body weight over a 24-week period. This was done by restricting the men's daily caloric intake to the vicinity of 1600 calories while requiring them to continue normal work routines. During the course of this regimen, Keys' subjects showed three chief symptoms: they became progressively more prone to emotional upset, more apathetic and inactive, and less interested in sex.

Irritability was quite marked throughout semistarvation and outbursts of temper were so frequent that the group meetings held during the control period had to be stopped. Periods of elation also occurred, which were inevitably followed by periods of depression. Psychological tests revealed progressively more emotional upset and pathology as semistarvation proceeded.

Activity of any kind was aversive to the men. They preferred to sit and do nothing than to perform any kind of formerly pleasurable work or play. This lack of joie de vivre extended to sex. Many engagements were broken, few of the men continued to date, and masturbation and nocturnal emission virtually ceased.

Despite the fact that almost none of the research on obese humans seems to have been guided by the hypothesis that the obese are hungry, it is fair to say that the major areas in which obese humans have been shown to differ behaviorally from normal weight humans parallel almost exactly the areas affected by hunger. Like the hungry organism, the obese human eats more at a given sitting and eats more rapidly; the obese individual also has a greater readiness to eat as indicated by the fact that, in a novel environment containing food, he is more likely to eat than the normal individual. And like the hungry organism, the obese individual is highly taste responsive, eating extra-large portions of good food and unusually small portions of bad food.

The eating behavior of the obese seems to reflect a constant, moderately strong degree of hunger, and is remarkably little affected by the physiological cues that increase or lower the normal individual's interest in food. In one experiment, Schachter asked obese and normal subjects to "taste" a variety of crackers. Some of their subjects had just eaten two roast beef sandwiches and some had eaten nothing for several hours. Normal subjects, to no one's surprise, ate fewer crackers in the "tasting session" if they had just eaten two sandwiches than they did if food deprived. Overweight subjects, however, ate just as many crackers if they had just eaten the sandwiches as they did if deprived. Similarly, I have found that self-report of hunger varies with deprivation state for normal subjects but does not vary for obese subjects. And in another study, in a supermarket, I found that while normal weight individuals do more and more impulse buying as their state of food deprivation increases, overweight shoppers do a moderate amount of impulse buying regardless of their state of deprivation. It is as if the long-term hunger of the obese completely overrides the physiological cues associated with short-term changes in nutritional state.

The obese seem markedly similar to Keys' starving subjects in a variety of other behavioral areas. Overweight humans appear to be more emotional than normal weight individuals. Schachter has found that overweight subjects are more frightened by the prospect of receiving electric shocks than are normal subjects. In another study, it was found that the proofreading and monitoring performance of obese subjects deteriorated when they listened to emotionally charged tape recordings. Performance of normal subjects did not suffer. The greater emotionality of the obese is also reflected in the scores they receive on psychological adjustment batteries. Moore, Stunkard and Srole reanalyzed the data collected in a mental health survey of a random sample of Midtown Manhattan residents. The obese individuals in that sample were found to be more emotionally disturbed by a variety of indicators. Interestingly, the lower socioeconomic status respondents were more obese than higher status respondents. Perhaps lower SES individuals are subjected to less social and/or medical pressure to lose weight. If so, it might be that more of them are at their baseline for body weight and it is primarily the middle- and upper-class overweight individuals who are struggling to keep their weight down, and hence suffering from the consequent emotional disorders. To test this, I reanalyzed their reanalysis of the Midtown survey and found that, indeed, it is almost exclusively the middle and upper SES overweight individuals who show excessive symptoms of emotional distress.

If it is correct that many overweight individuals are emotionally distraught because they are actually "underweight," then any systematic attempts at weight loss ought to result in further deterioration. This is such a terribly important point that I want to stress that the data are contradictory and incomplete on this issue. Some investigators do report deterioration, often severe, including depression, irritability, and even psychosis and suicide attempts. Other investigators, however, report no untoward effects. It is possible, of course, that the different results reflect the use of different patient populations. The untoward effects may have been obtained from patients already below their baselines, and the less deleterious results may have been obtained with patients at, or even perhaps above their baselines at the start of treatment.

The other symptoms of hunger reported by Keys, et al., also seem to be present in the obese. Mayer and his colleagues find the obese to be highly inactive, even remaining relatively immobile when engaging in "active" sports. Stunkard and his colleagues find that, within given occupational roles, the obese individual manages to walk much less during the course of his day than the normal individual.

Sexual interest has not been well studied to date, but the psychoanalyst Hilde Bruch reports that her obese patients as a group have remarkably little sexual interest. In a preliminary investigation, I have found that obese male college students have fewer orgasms than normal students. This finding includes nocturnal emissions, which of course would be little influenced by social considerations.

It is clear then, that the obese individual and the hungry individual have much in common. These similarities raise the question of whether there are also physiological indications that the obese are hungry. The answer appears to be yes. The most generally agreed upon physiological index of hunger is the level of free fatty acids (FFA) in the blood. When the organism is food deprived (or is cold or exercises), free fatty acids are mobilized from fat tissue to meet energy requirements. When something is eaten, FFA levels fall rapidly.

Many studies show that free fatty acid level is higher in obese individuals than in normals. It has usually been assumed that this elevation of FFA in the blood of the obese was simply due to the elevation of fat stores, which essentially "spill over" into the bloodstream. It does not seem likely, however, that this is the case. Two investigators have found no elevation of FFA levels in obese patients who had been overeating and gaining weight during the period immediately preceding the tests. More importantly, when obese individuals lose weight, free fatty acid levels increase still further.

A perhaps equally important fact about FFA level is that, in the obese, it is relatively inflexible, showing little variation in response to short-term nutritional changes. During a day's fast, FFA levels of the obese increase only slightly or not at all. Normals, in contrast, start with low levels, and after 20 to 24 hours of deprivation equal obese FFA levels. Furthermore, the dropping off of FFA levels in response to food intake is both slower and less complete in obese subjects than in normal ones.

The physiological data are in agreement, then, with the behavioral data. Overweight individuals behave as if their hunger switch were stuck in the "on" position. They eat more at a given sitting, they eat more rapidly, they are more responsive to taste, and neither their eating behavior, their self-report of hunger, nor even the attractiveness of supermarket food is much affected by short-term changes in deprivation state. The physiological evidence justifies this inflexibly hungry pattern: FFA level is inflexibly high.

What are the implications for the individual who is obese? A physician I know, who is familiar with the evidence I have described, believes that the following cautions are in order for the obese person:

"I try to get the point across to my patients before they start to lose weight that they need to make an intelligent decision. For some it may be better to accept the social and health risks of obesity whatever they are and go ahead and enjoy the pleasures of eating. I point out to them that if they undertake to lose weight and maintain a normal weight they will never again be able to eat as they have been eating at their obese weight. They must be made to realize that they will be in a sense dietary cripples. They will never be able to eat freely of their foods as their normal weight counterparts do and maintain their low normal weight. I also point out this is not fair but neither is it fair to be born blind or with other physical abnormalities. For some the pain of maintaining a normal weight is not counterbalanced by the benefits of being at a "normal" weight. I see little reason to attempt to coerce these people into doing so."

For me, there is a still more important implication. The obese may be the last oppressed minority group whom no one feels guilty about oppressing. Executives, policemen, and stewardesses are fired from their jobs because of obesity. Jean Mayer and his colleagues have shown that obese high-school girls are less likely to be admitted to the college of their choice than slender girls with the same grades and entrance exam scores. And every obese person knows that other people hold him or her personally responsible for that condition. To their discredit, psychologists and psychoanalysts have largely aided and abetted this prejudiced assumption of lack of internal control. There is reason to hope that in the future, people will be held no more responsible for their weight than for their height.

9

Emotion and Cognitive Control

There are more things in heaven and earth, Horatio,
Than are dreamt of in your philosophy.
William Shakespeare, *Hamlet*, I:v

How is behavior influenced by the mind? For centuries, people have been intrigued by the puzzle of what seemed to be nonphysical *sources* of "energy" contained within the physical substance of the body. The essence of human life has been seen as flickering in the ephemeral light of an inner spirit, a soul, mind, will, or consciousness. It was assumed that the engagement of these forces provided the energy that drove the human machine. In 40 B.C., a Roman poet declared: "No barriers, no masses of matter however enormous, can withstand the powers of the mind; the remotest corners yield to them; all things succumb; the very Heaven itself is laid open" (Marcus Manilius, *Astronomica I*).

Thus one might expect the powers of the mind to be a central concern of psychology. However, until recently, the relationship between mind and body has been a minor topic studied by only a small band of researchers. As we have seen in preceding chapters, the doctrine of observable behavior and its eliciting external causes and consequences has been the focus of primary interest for the past three decades. There has been little tolerance for any phenomena that could not be grounded in physical, biological, or empirical explanations.

The picture is beginning to change, however. Canadian psychologist Donald Hebb, addressing the American Psychological Association in September 1973, stated firmly, "Psychology is about the mind: the central issue, the great mystery, the toughest problem of all" (1974, p. 74). Hebb went on to define "mind" in these terms: "Mind then is the capacity for thought, and thought is the integrative activity of the brain" (p. 75).

Perhaps the most intriguing of all phenomena attributed to the human mind are religious miracles, faith healing, the death of healthy individuals after being "hexed," dying for an ideal, the individual without a "price," the influence of mere words in hypnosis or brainwashing, unconscious motivations, the conformity pressures induced by group consensus, and the powerful emotions that underlie hate and love. They are interesting precisely because their existence seems to challenge our basic conception of causality. In addition, they pose the possibility that we are not the passive victims of our immediate physical environment. Rather, on the one hand, we are related to forces external to ourselves, and on the other, we possess the potential for internal control over the environment. Suppose "believing could make it so": would faith and hope be more valuable commodities? Is the physical reality "out there" fixed, immutable, and the only determinant of our behavior? Suppose that we assumed a more dynamic view of ourselves, one in which—by exercising our capacity to choose—we could reject reality as a given, and create a new social and physical reality?

Carl Rogers has been in the forefront of those who believe in the dignity of the "inner" person and the power that individuals have to transform the situations they find themselves in, as well as their destinies. He has underscored the importance of raising the kinds of questions we have posed (and will continue to pose) for you:

"[The] ability of the person to discover new meaning in the forces which impinge upon him and in the past experiences which have been controlling him, and the ability to alter consciously his behavior in the light of this new meaning, has a profound significance for our thinking which has not been fully realized. We need to revise the philosophical basis of our work to a point where it can admit that forces exist within the individual which can exercise a spontaneous and significant influence upon behavior which is not predictable through knowledge of prior influences and conditioning." (1946, p. 422)

In our attempt to provide a comprehensive, unified view of the determinants of human behavior, it is necessary to consider (albeit briefly) some topics not traditionally presented in introductory psychology texts: voodoo deaths, miracle cures, witchcraft, hopelessness, and the power of cognitive control through placebos (substances having no medicinal value) and of hypnosis on pain will be analyzed.

But first we will begin with *emotion*—the everyday phenomenon that somehow falls at the intersection of the mind-body problem. The experience of emotion is a subjective, psychological process, though emotions can be induced by environmental stimuli and are clearly mediated by physiological reactions. Furthermore, inadequate handling of emotional reactions can lead an individual to mental disorder, psychosomatic illness, or other disease states. (See *P&L* Close-up, p. 366.) In a positive vein, emotion sometimes makes the whole human enterprise bearable and even beautiful. It is also what makes the enterprise of living human.

When people lose the capacity to experience emotions, or when their emotional expression becomes flattened, it is taken to be a sign of a major psychological disturbance, as in autism or schizophrenia. Without emotions there is little basis for empathy, for developing attachment to others, for love, for caring, and for fear of the consequences to oneself of one's actions. A person who is without emotions becomes as a robot, an automaton, and can be potentially the most dangerous enemy. Yet to the extent that emotions represent spontaneous, impulsive, often unpredictable, individual reactions, it becomes important to restrict them in institutional settings. In institutions charged with the management of "deviant" individuals, such emotional expression is seen as a source of potential danger and must be minimized. Thus prisons, rather than promoting a fuller, more normal expression of emotions among the inmates, do exactly the reverse by creating conditions that distort, inhibit, and suppress emotions.

George Jackson's *Soledad Brother* (1971) letters proclaim, "I have made some giant steps toward acquiring the things I personally will need if I can be successful in my plans . . . I have repressed all emotion" (p. 37). A longtime prisoner at Rhode Island Adult Correctional Institution told us that he "beat the system" by learning how to turn off all emotions so that he now no longer feels anything for anybody. There is nothing more *they* can do to him. He learned this lesson in "self-control" after being in solitary confinement for several years in a Maryland prison. He expects to be able to turn his emotions on again when he gets out. We doubt it will be possible to do so.

Prisoners who let their emotions show reveal a *sensitive* "weakness," and become more likely to be chosen by the guards as candidates for an "informer" role or by other prisoners for the female role in forced sexual encounters. Also, the more strongly you feel about other people, the more open you are to being hurt when they are punished or when they leave, die, or betray you. In prison, where you have so little control over the nature of your relationships with other people, tender emotions ultimately result in more pain than pleasure, and so are better dispensed with altogether.

But the guards are little better off than the prisoners. For them, emotional control begins with having to conceal their fear of working in a situation where their lives are constantly on the line. The denial of their fear goes beyond "whistling a happy tune" to constantly affirming their fearlessness and toughness in interactions with prisoners and with each other. A guard who is afraid is a threat to every other guard, because he cannot be counted upon in an emergency — and it is this eventuality for which the guards are always preparing. Moreover, a guard who shows any warmth or positive emotional regard toward the prisoners is suspected of being "wired up" by them, of taking graft, or of in some way being controlled by them.

It is not surprising, then, that the basic advice given to "fish bulls" by the captain of the guards at San Quentin is to be "firm and fair but not friendly" in dealing with the inmates. But it is not enough for the guards to conceal their emotions only from the inmates; they must also conceal them from each other. There is an implicit norm among many correctional officers not even to discuss their emotions among themselves, and certainly not for the new men to tell the "old bulls" how they feel. This bottling-up of their intensely felt emotions can be expected to be displaced onto family and friends, and also expressed in the disguised, introverted form of psychosomatic illnesses.

We may extend this analysis of the way in which the institution of prison suppresses emotional expression to the way in which most of our other social institutions do likewise. It is as if emotions were the antithesis of reason, order, and control. When was the last time you witnessed strong emotions being expressed in any institutional setting you are in — especially in academic ones? When, in fact, was the last time *you* responded with intensely felt emotions? The diminution of emotional expression leads to a denial of our own humanness — whether we are the "guards" or the "prisoners" of this world.

Emotion

Let us imagine that we could create a robot that looked, talked, and moved exactly like a human being. By means of an elaborate computer system, we could program the robot to think, solve problems, and perform various activities. Such a robot could certainly do many things just like a human being but, like Mr. Spock of *Star Trek,* would never express any emotions. That is, it would never smile, laugh, cry, blush, and so on. Anyone introduced to our robot would probably guess that it was not human because it never showed any feelings when in an "emotional situation."

How could we make our robot more human? One solution would be to take the behavioral response associated with a particular emotion and build that into the robot. For example, if we wanted to make the robot appear sad, we could put in some tear ducts and program the robot to cry at the same times that humans do. But when *do* people cry?

If we look around, we see that babies cry until they are given food, and small children will cry and throw temper tantrums until they get a cookie or a favorite toy. People cry while watching certain movies, and sometimes cry at weddings. They cry when they stub their toes or otherwise hurt themselves. An actress or actor may cry while playing a dramatic role on stage. Student protesters will cry when they get a whiff of tear gas. People often cry when they hear a speech given by a skillful orator, and they cry while cutting up onions. A mother will cry if she hears that her son is killed in the war, and she will also cry if her son arrives home safely from the war.

At this point you may be saying to yourself, "Wait a minute! Not all of these examples of crying refer to an emotion. And even when they do, the emotion isn't necessarily a sad one." Obviously, then, a single behavioral response such as "crying" cannot signal the presence of a single emotion. But in that case, how do we ever know that an emotion is being experienced either by others or by ourselves? Why do we say that we are "sad" when we hear bad news but not when we are slicing onions? In other words, what *is* the complex process that we call emotion? Before we can program our robot, maybe we have to learn how *we* have been programmed to experience emotion. How do we know the difference between feelings of happiness, sadness, anger, and euphoria?

The Concept of Emotion

Since the beginning of time, people have tried to understand the stirred-up, *affective* states that they often experience. The ancient Greeks believed that there were four characteristic emotional temperaments, each based on the dominance of a particular fluid in the body: sanguinary (blood), melancholic (black bile), choleric (yellow bile), and phlegmatic (phlegm). Aristotle was the first to distinguish between the physiological and the psychological components of emotion, which he referred to as its "matter" and its "form or idea," respectively. Seventeenth- and eighteenth-century philosophers generally thought that the emotions were instinctive and nonrational and thus represented the animal side of human beings. In contrast to the emotions were the uniquely human attributes of reason and intellect, which were meant to curb people's emotions and govern their behavior in a rational way. This rigid opposition of the emotional and the rational implied not only that the emotions were harmful and disruptive, but that they were an aberrant psychological process that was different from and opposed to thought and reason. Many common-sense expressions still support this viewpoint, such as "I got so mad that I couldn't think straight," "I tried to do the right thing but my emotions got the better of me," or "In the heat of passion, I didn't realize what I was doing."

When psychology came into being as a formal discipline separate from philosophy and physiology, one of the many problems it considered was that of emotion. Psychologists attempted to provide a more precise definition of emotion, but quickly found that it was a very difficult task. Some have defined emotions as *motives,*

Two recent surveys of psychological literature give the impression that psychologists are obsessed with studying and talking about unpleasant emotions and the negative aspects of human behavior. One analyzes the content of 172 psychology textbooks written over the past eighty-five years and finds that unpleasant emotions are discussed twice as much as pleasant ones (Carlson, 1966). The other reports that nearly 80 percent of over 500 journal articles on emotion from 1935 to 1965 have dealt with unpleasant emotions (Lindauer, 1968). Both these surveys exclude material on psychopathology; thus psychologists' preoccupation with the unpleasant is probably even greater than is represented by these data.

In dramatic contrast is the evidence from literary sources, which clearly indicates a preference for pleasant, positive emotions. A thorough analysis of eighteen standard reference books of collections of plays, fiction, poetry, and quotations showed that almost three quarters of all references to emotions (7,303 out of 10,519) were *pleasant* references. Of the twelve emotions most frequently referred to, ten are pleasant emotions (Lindauer, 1968). Fear, which accounts for only 4 percent of the literary references to emotion, is one of the most frequent references in psychology.

How do you account for this discrepancy in outlook? Are psychologists telling it like it is while literary writers are providing an escape into what life could never be like? Or are psychologists overly concerned with "problems," and with behavior that needs to be modified and improved? Do they perhaps just take for granted the more prevalent, pleasant, positive side of life? Or is there a more satisfactory explanation? Do *you* prefer to read newspaper and magazine accounts dealing with evil, sin, violence, and negative emotional experiences or the contrary? If you were a psychologist, would you prefer to study positive forms of social behavior or social "problems," interpersonal conflicts, and personal pathology?

while others feel that emotion is a very different process from motivation. Some define emotions as bodily changes, while others define them in terms of the subjective feelings experienced and reported by the individual. This lack of agreement on a definition has been one of the factors that has hampered research in this area.

In accordance with varying definitions of emotion, psychologists have studied a wide range of responses. Some of them have been concerned with the role of such neurophysiological processes as activities of the brain, endocrine system, and autonomic nervous system. Another approach has focused on overt bodily movement and facial expressions. Many researchers rely on verbal self-reports of emotional experiences, as well as other introspective data. None of these has been accepted as totally adequate, suggesting that a successful account of emotion will have to integrate all these facets of emotional response in some fashion.

While the research on emotion has yielded many interesting results, it has suffered from several limitations. One of these is the assumption (inherited from rationalist philosophy) that emotions are disruptive and usually coincide with the disintegration of some ongoing, rational behavior. But although extreme emotional states like panic and stage fright can and often do interfere with performance, this model does not seem adequate for all emotional responses. Leeper (1948) proposed that emotions often serve the very positive function of forcing the individual to organize new adaptive responses to a changed environment.

A second limitation of the research on emotion is that it has concentrated on the negative emotions (primarily anxiety and fear), while neglecting the positive emotions such as love, happiness, and contentment. (See *P&L* Close-up at left.) Finally, much of it has focused on the *consequences* of emotional states and has paid little attention to the antecedents of the emotion and to the characteristics of the emotions themselves.

How Do We Perceive Emotion in Others?

Don't sigh and gaze at me,
Your sighs are so like mine,
Your eyes mustn't glow like mine,
People will say we're in love.

Richard Rodgers, *Oklahoma!*

Behavioral cues. Although we can never directly observe another person's feelings, we often make judgments about them, as when we say, "I've never seen him look this angry," or "She looks so sad today." How do we arrive at such emotional classifications? We could, of course, just ask people how they are feeling (assuming that their answer will be truthful and accurate). However, as we saw in Chapter 4, we often use people's *nonverbal* behavior (e.g., facial expressions and body movements) as reliable signs of what emotion they are experiencing. ■ The "look" of love communicates just as much feeling as (if not more than) a verbal protestation of passion.

The detection and interpretation of nonverbal cues to the emotional state of others require rather subtle perception, and are quite difficult skills to learn. Societies that tend to inhibit strong displays of individual emotion must develop highly stylized, ritualistic patterns of behavior to deal with recurrent, emotionally charged situations such as weddings and funerals. This recognition of the relevant nonverbal cues leads not only to the appropriate overt reaction, but may determine the emotional experience as well. Thus a child can learn to feel grief at a funeral simply by observing the nonverbal reactions of adults. This point is captured in Tolstoy's description, in "The Death of Ivan Ilych" (1886), of a man attending the wake of a close acquaintance.

"And Peter Ivanovich knew that, just as it had been the right thing to cross himself in that room, so what he had to do here was to press [the widow's] hand, sigh, and say "Believe . . . me . . ." So he did all this and as he did it felt that the desired result had been achieved, that both he and she were touched."

The "animal" in you. The first person to emphasize the behavior and expression of emotion, as opposed to the subjective experience, was Charles Darwin. In his book *The Expression of the Emotions in Man and Animals* (1872), he advanced the belief that emotional patterns are largely inherited, innate responses that have had biological utility in evolution. For example, animals who are preparing for attack will bare their teeth, growl, and show a bristling of their hair. If such displays were effective in warding off attackers, they would have obviously adaptive significance for survival. The remnants of this behavior are seen in the tendency of some people to sneer and grit their teeth when they are feeling hostile.

To what extent are emotional expressions innate (as Darwin argued) and to what extent are social learning factors involved? In support of his position, Darwin pointed to the fact that blind children show the same facial expressions of emotion, in the same situations, as normal children. However, we cannot rule out learning in this case, since the blind children could have been reinforced for exhibiting the correct response and corrected when they displayed an inappropriate one. Darwin also cited

■ While a fire rages in a sixteen-story office building in New Orleans, spectators watch in disbelief and horror as four people leap to their death to escape the flames.

the universality of emotional expressions, particularly in infants. While confirming the universality of various types of expressions in all cultures, Ekman and Friesen (1969) found that the emotion linked to particular expressions (and thus the interpretation of them) varied tremendously from culture to culture.

Your face is like an open book . . . Even within one culture, a particular nonverbal response can reflect any of several different emotions, as we saw earlier in the example of crying. If there is not a one-to-one relationship between a facial or behavioral expression and a particular emotion, then nonverbal behavior does not provide a very reliable communication system. The results of many early studies of facial expressions would tend to support this statement. Subjects were asked to look at pictures of people's faces

and indicate the emotion that they thought was being expressed. Contrary to the expectations of the experimenters, there was a great deal of variability in the subjects' judgments, suggesting that people are not very accurate in judging emotions. A study by Schlosberg (1952), however, found that facial expressions could be described in terms of two dimensions—pleasantness-unpleasantness and rejection-attention—with a fairly high degree of agreement between judges. ■ Later Schlosberg (1954) discovered a third dimension in facial expressions (intensity, or level of activation) and developed a three-dimensional model of emotion that has influenced much subsequent research. Current experiments have established that subjects rating facial expressions by the use of this model show very high accuracy and agreement (90 percent or more) in their judgments of basic,

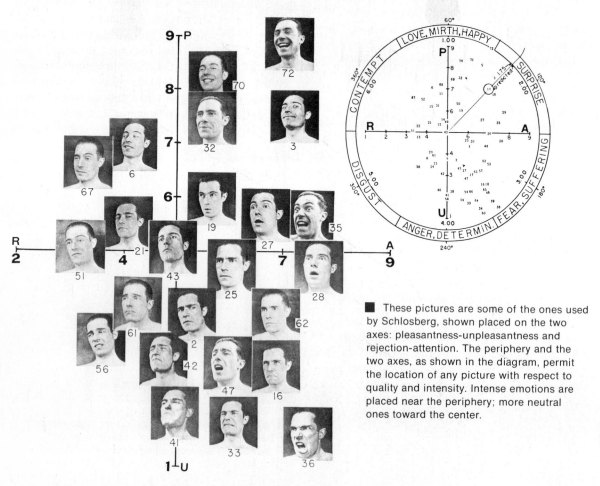

■ These pictures are some of the ones used by Schlosberg, shown placed on the two axes: pleasantness-unpleasantness and rejection-attention. The periphery and the two axes, as shown in the diagram, permit the location of any picture with respect to quality and intensity. Intense emotions are placed near the periphery; more neutral ones toward the center.

simple emotions like fear, surprise, happiness, anger, sadness, disgust, and interest, and furthermore that such agreement is cross-cultural (Ekman, Sorenson, & Friesen, 1969). This ability to identify different emotions accurately increases dramatically with age, as shown by studies that tested children in both the United States and France (Izard, 1971).

However, people do not always express such pure, simple emotions as happiness and anger. Often they experience compound or mixed emotions, such as embarrassment, frustration, and jealousy, and the nonverbal expression of these is rather ambiguous. How do people make accurate judgments of these emotional states, since the cues, though strong, are so complex? One solution is to infer the emotion from the situational context. Thus, if we saw a woman crying as she greeted her son who had returned from the war, we would say that she was happy, overjoyed, and relieved. However, if we saw her crying after hearing that her son had died, we would label her emotion as grief.

This reliance on situational cues when the expressions tend to be ambiguous was demonstrated experimentally (Munn, 1940). Subjects were presented with photographs taken from *Life* magazine and asked to judge the emotions of the person in each picture. In some of the photographs, the background had been eliminated, so that only the person was visible. Munn found that subjects' accuracy and agreement in labeling the emotion was considerably better when the background situational cues were included. ● The importance of these cues is also stressed by Frijda (1970), who argues that emotions are *always* interpreted in terms of a situational reference. He noted that subjects who were judging facial expressions rarely used simple words like "angry" or "happy." Instead, they usually described an inferred situation—for example, "You told her a disgusting story," or "She seems to be looking at a tiny kitten."

How Do We Perceive Emotion in Ourselves?

For all the reasons described, trying to identify the emotion that someone else is experiencing can often be a very complex process. A major stumbling block is that we cannot observe what is going on inside the person's head and are forced to rely only on overt, outer cues. But in the case of our own emotions, the covert, inner aspect is available to us, and thus we ought to know just what *our* emotions are. Do we?

The physiological component. Several attempts have been made to relate emotion to physiological processes, or even to explain emotion entirely in such terms.

The James-Lange theory. Whenever you have experienced a strong emotion, you have undoubtedly had a feeling of being "churned up" inside because of various bodily changes. If someone were to ask you how this stirred-up state comes about, you would probably say that your feeling of an emotion (e.g., "I am afraid") gives rise to the subsequent bodily expression of it (e.g., "therefore I am trembling"). Most people would agree with your statement—but not William James. In 1884 he proposed that the sequence of felt emotion and bodily changes was the *reverse* of the common-sense one just stated; that is, our feeling of the bodily changes *is* the emotion" (James, 1884). In modern terminology, "the changes are the medium." That is, James believed that the cognitive, experienced aspects of the emotion were a *result* of physiological arousal instead of the other way around. To use his classic example, the sight of a bear produces a stirred-up internal state that is then perceived as fear.

A Danish scientist named Lange presented some similar ideas at about the same time, and so this theory is known as the *James-Lange theory of emotion.* Its importance lies in the fact that it was the first to postulate that visceral processes exert some control over emotional

● Can you tell from this woman's facial expression what emotion she is probably experiencing?

Check your judgment on page 374.

behavior and thus to challenge the idea that mental processes control bodily reactions.

Cannon fires back. There were many people who responded to the James-Lange theory with cries of "It just ain't so!" One of these was the physiologist Walter Cannon. His criticisms (1929) were the most serious attack made against the theory, and they had a major influence on much of the subsequent research on emotion. The James-Lange theory implied that in order for a person to experience different emotions, there must be discriminably different sets of physiological changes for the person to rely on as cues. Cannon disputed this notion by citing evidence that: (1) different emotions are accompanied by the *same* visceral state; (2) the viscera are too insensitive for changes in them to be noticed and used as cues; and (3) visceral changes are too slow to be a source of emotional feelings, which are fast-changing and mercurial. He also pointed to the work of Marañon (1924) as being critical of the James-Lange theory, since Marañon had found that artificial stimulation of the viscera through injections of adrenaline (epinephrine) produced only "cold" or "as if" emotions in the person (e.g., "I feel *as if* I were afraid") rather than true emotions.

The "centers" of emotion. Partly because of Cannon's criticisms, many researchers began to look at other physiological systems that could be the site of emotion. In general, there has been an increased interest in central neural mechanisms.

One of the most popular theories has placed the control of emotion in the limbic system (which includes the earliest parts of the cortex and parts of the thalamus and hypothalamus). As we saw in Chapter 2, researchers have found that stimulation and lesioning of various parts of the limbic system produce changes in emotional reactions.

The fact that the limbic system is made up of the primitive brain probably lent credence to the idea that the "primitive" emotions are located there. However, as Pribram (1960) has noted, these supposedly phylogenetically old structures have achieved their greatest degree of evolu-

tionary development in humans just as have the so-called "higher" cortical structures, and thus they can no longer really be considered as "primitive." Furthermore, research has shown that the limbic system is involved in cognitive functioning as well as in emotion (e.g., lesions and stimulation of limbic structures influence problem solving). Moreover, stimulation and lesions of parts of the brain other than the limbic areas also produce emotional changes (Pribram, 1967). These findings would suggest that the emotions (and cognitive behavior) are controlled by many different interacting parts of the brain, rather than by any single "emotion center."

The endocrine system and emotion. The physiological component of emotions is greatly influenced by the activity of various *endocrine glands.* These glands pump secretions directly into the bloodstream, which are carried to and influence every part of the body. These chemical substances are called *hormones* (from the Greek word for "I excite"). One of the functions of the endocrine glands is to coordinate the body processes. In sudden fear, for example, a hormone is circulated through the blood that brings about such widely diverse processes as dilation of the pupil of the eye, constriction of the blood vessels in the wall of the stomach, and an increase in the rapidity with which blood clots in the presence of air.

The neural regulatory center for the endocrine system evidently lies in the hypothalamus. The *pituitary,* a small structure attached to the underside of the hypothalamus, secretes a number of different hormones that perform various functions concerned with growth and maintenance. The pituitary also produces a variety of "middle-man" hormones that act directly on other endocrine glands, such as the *adrenal glands* (which are located at the upper end of the kidneys). When stimulated, the adrenal glands secrete two hormones, *epinephrine* and *norepinephrine* (also called *adrenaline* and *noradrenaline,* respectively). Research has shown that these two hormones appear to be related to different emotions.

Early studies found that epinephrine is generally associated with fear, while both norepi-

nephrine and epinephrine are found in anger reactions. Animals that are fearful and that survive by being able to run away from danger (e.g., rabbits) secrete mostly epinephrine, while animals that usually attack (e.g., lions) secrete a high amount of norepinephrine as well (Funkenstein, 1955).

Another study found that college students who were exposed to a frustrating task showed one of three emotions: fear, anger expressed outwards toward the experimenters, and anger directed inwards (blaming themselves). Students who expressed anger outwardly tended to show a secretion of norepinephrine, while those who were fearful or blamed themselves showed more secretion of epinephrine (Funkenstein, King, & Drolette, 1957). More recent research on the endocrine system has demonstrated both increased and differential release of both epinephrine and norepinephrine under various conditions of stress (Brady, 1967).

In addition to being secreted into the bloodstream, norepinephrine is also found in the brain. There is evidence to suggest that drugs that cause changes in mood do so through their effect on brain norepinephrine. Drugs that increase the accumulation of norepinephrine produce euphoria and hyperactivity, while drugs that deplete norepinephrine produce depression (Kety, 1967a).

Physiological differentiation of emotions. Some research has indeed shown a relationship between emotions and physiological responses, such as the previously cited studies on the adrenal hormones. Similarly, Wolf and Wolff (1947) observed two different patterns of stomach activity in a patient—one when he was fearful and the other when he was angry. ▲ However, differences in the experience of emotions have not been shown to correlate with physiological changes, except in extreme reactions such as fear and anger. Given persons may show distinctive patterns of physiological arousal, depending on whether they tend to focus on internal or on situational factors.

There are some investigators (for example, Duffy, 1962) who have argued that physiological differences correspond only to different *amounts*

of the same general, undifferentiated arousal. Although intensity is certainly one aspect of emotion, this approach seems a rather limited one, since (a) it is possible to be physiologically aroused and not feel emotional (as when you have been exercising strenuously), and (b) a differentiation between intensities of arousal still would not account for the *qualitative* differences in the experience of various emotions. If you feel your heart pounding and have "butterflies" in your stomach, what is it that tells you whether you are afraid, excited, angry, or madly in love? Even if researchers, with high-powered recording and amplifying devices, could eventually identify all the physiological correlates of every single emotion, it still would not explain why people *experience* what they do when they are physiologically aroused.

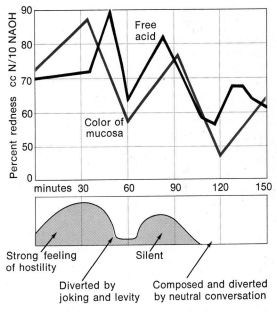

Based on Wolf & Wolff, 1947

▲ HOSTILITY AND GASTRIC PHYSIOLOGY

This graph was drawn from observations made on a patient whose stomach was open for scientific study. At the beginning, the patient was feeling resentment and hostility as the result of a humiliating experience. While he discussed it, his hostility increased, and there was a greater flow of acid in his stomach and more redness of the mucosa. With changes in his mood, there were corresponding changes in gastric physiology.

The cognitive component. If clues from physiological activity are not the whole story, what about perceptions, expectations, interpretations, and other such cognitive processes? What role do they play in emotion?

Emotional stew: Add one part gut and one part cognition. As we saw in Chapter 6, the information provided by the proximal stimulus alone is not sufficient to explain why we see things the way we do. It is only through cognitive organization and interpretation of stimuli after they reach the retina that we can apprehend what is "out there." Similarly, modern psychologists believe that emotion is not determined by physiological responses alone, but requires a cognitive appraisal and evaluation of the stimulus situation.

● Now that you know the situation, do you have any different judgment of the emotion being expressed?

One theory is that physiological responses (essentially undifferentiated) determine the *intensity* of an emotion but that people use emotionally relevant cognitions, drawing on cues in the immediate environment to determine its *quality*—which emotion it is.

This theory was proposed and tested in an ingenious experiment in which male subjects were led to believe that the experimenter was studying the visual effects of a new vitamin compound. They received an injection and then were sent to a waiting room, supposedly to wait for the drug to take effect. For experimental subjects, the injection actually consisted of epinephrine, which usually causes increased heart rate, accelerated breathing, tremor, and sometimes a feeling of flushing. A group of control subjects received a placebo injection, which produces no direct physiological arousal.

The experimenters also manipulated the subjects' cognitive appraisal of their bodily states. The first group of subjects (epi-informed) was told of the compound's "side effects"; thus they had a appropriate explanation of their arousal. The second group (epi-ignorant) was told there would be no side effects, while the third group (epi-misinformed) was told that the side effects would be numbness, itching, and headache. Thus the latter two groups had an inappropriate explanation for their arousal. It was predicted that these subjects would actively search their immediate situation for appropriate explanations of what they were feeling, and thus be more susceptible to whatever cues were prominent.

In the waiting room, each student found another student, supposedly waiting like him for the drug to take effect. Actually this was a confederate of the experimenter, who soon began to behave emotionally. For half of the subjects, he acted very playful: doodling, throwing paper airplanes, twirling a hula hoop, and so on. For the rest of the subjects, he became increasingly irritated and angry with a questionnaire that the experimenter had given them to fill out, until finally he ripped it up and stomped out of the room. During both of these situations, observers watched the subject through a one-way mirror and rated the extent to which he acted either euphoric or angry. Subjects also filled out self-report questionnaires on their emotional state.

The two groups who did not have an appropriate cognition for their arousal felt happy when the stooge acted happy and less happy when he acted angry. Presumably, perception of the stooge's behavior and mood influenced their appraisal of their own unexplained arousal. But the correctly informed subjects, who already had an appropriate explanation for their physiological arousal, were not susceptible to the confederate's mood and did not show these results. Similarly, the control subjects, with no physiological arousal but with the same social cognitions, did not show these differences (Schachter & Singer, 1962; Schachter, 1971). ◆

These results appear to support the theory that the quality of emotional states is determined by cognitive factors. Given the same state of physiological arousal (for which they had no explanation), subjects labeled their emotion in different ways, depending on the cognitive aspects of the situation. Such findings pose a direct challenge to the earlier theory of emotion that suggested a cause-effect relationship between physiological arousal and cognitive experience. However, the validity of this study has itself been challenged. (See *P&L* Close-up, pp. 375–76.)

Cognitive appraisal theories. Although more investigators are becoming concerned with the role of cognitive processes in emotional and other reactions, few have tried to speculate on the dynamics of such processes. What does it

◆ **SELF-REPORT OF EMOTIONAL STATE**

Scores are based on subtracting "anger" ratings from "happy" ratings—the more positive the score, the more positive the emotional feeling. Range is from +4.0 to −4.0.

Arousal Groups	Emotion Modeled by Confederate	
	Euphoria Condition	Anger Condition
Epinephrine—Misinformed	+1.9	not tested
Epinephrine—Ignorant	+1.8	+1.4
Epinephrine—Informed	+1.0	+1.9
Placebo Control	+1.6	+1.6

Adapted from Schachter & Singer, 1962

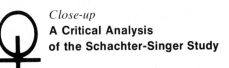

Close-up

A Critical Analysis of the Schachter-Singer Study

The research devised by Stanley Schachter and Jerome Singer to test their notion of a two-component process of emotion is an extremely important study. It opens the vague concept of "emotion" to experimental investigation for the first time. In addition, their approach has fostered a greater interplay between "hard" and "soft" approaches to psychological phenomena. They are pioneering in combining physiology, cognitive processes, and social psychology to investigate the nature of emotion.

Their underlying theory has been influential in generating new ideas about the process by which people come to interpret the causes of anxiety, fear, and other emotions that play a central role in "neurotic" behavior. Indeed, a new form of therapy has been based on it.

But in spite of the significance of their theory of emotion, Schachter and Singer's experiment—though ingenious—is *not* an adequate test of the theory. Perhaps because people were eager to accept their results, and because the experimental design is so complex and costly to implement, it was only recently that an attempt was made to replicate their study (Marshall, 1976). Marshall's failure to replicate their results forces us to examine the original study more carefully; when we do, it is obvious that it contains several flaws.

Data Handling and Interpretation

The mean differences between conditions, though statistically significant, were not large. They became significant only after a number of subjects were discarded from the placebo and epi-ignorant conditions (those said to have "aroused themselves" or "informed themselves"). Instead of presenting the happiness and anger ratings separately, the researchers *subtracted* one from the other, yielding a composite measure of *relative emotion* (more or less happiness), not an absolute one of "euphoria" versus "anger." This led to subjects being described as "more angry" than others, when they were in fact only "less happy." The biggest difference in quality of emotional experience between the anger and euphoria conditions was not for the epi-ignorant group but for the epi-informed group (see table p. 375).

Methodological Problems

Epinephrine has different effects on different people; the onset, intensity, and duration of symptoms vary with body size and other factors. The researchers neither controlled for this variable nor were able to estimate the extent of its influence. Dosage was constant despite body-weight differences; there was no attempt to determine whether arousal had yet taken place when the confederate's act began. The physiological measure of pulse rate, taken (by hand) after the activity period, confounds the effects of the epinephrine with those of the physical activity itself.

Another set of methodological problems centers around the cognitive cues provided by the confederates. The angry confederate gave a good reason for his arousal (invasion of privacy and embarrassment); none was offered by the happy confederate. Thus his display of happy emotion did not provide any cognitive *explanation* for the arousal the subject was feeling; it was only a source of emotional contagion or imitation. Furthermore, the angry confederate stormed out of the room, leaving the bewildered subject to face the experimenter alone—and probably anxious not to make a scene. Without a measure of each subject's perception of the confederates, we cannot assess whether they were evaluated as "angry," "euphoric," "rational," or "bizarre." Futhermore, there was no assessment of the subject's mood before the drug was administered. Thus initial variations in mood between subjects may have interacted with treatment in unspecifiable ways.

These and other criticisms could mean either that the conclusions of the authors may be stronger than they actually appear (if these and other sources of confounding were removed), or, more likely, that they are overgeneralizations and perhaps even false. The theory, tempted as we may be to accept it, still awaits its definitive test.

mean to have a cognition that determines an emotional response? Two of the psychologists who have worked on this problem have discussed such cognitions in terms of appraisal.

Appraisal is the evaluation and judgment of the significance of a stimulus. One of the first people to use this concept in a theory of emotion was Magda Arnold (1960), who proposed a sequential model. The first step in this sequence is *perception,* in which external stimuli are received. The next step is *appraisal,* in which the stimuli are judged as good and beneficial or bad and harmful. This appraisal then determines the *emotion,* which is defined as a felt tendency toward stimuli appraised as good or away from those appraised as bad. The *expression* of the emotion is the pattern of physiological responses that accompanies the felt tendency. These may be organized toward approach or toward withdrawal. The final step is *action,* when actual approach or withdrawal occurs.

A more complex extension of this approach is that of Richard Lazarus (1968). He postulates two basic kinds of appraisal processes: *primary appraisal,* which evaluates whether the situation is threatening or not, and *secondary appraisal,* which has to do with assessing alternative means of coping with a perceived threat. If a situation is perceived as threatening, there are two possible *coping strategies:* (a) *direct action,* such as fight or flight, with the negative emotional states accompanying them; or (b) *benign reappraisal,* in which the person reassesses the situation as less threatening, thereby reducing the negative emotional state. The positive emotions follow various appraisals of nonthreat (including benign reappraisals). This entire analysis stresses the interplay between cognitive appraisals and emotional reactions.

Both these theories argue against the notion of neutral, undifferentiated arousal that is later given meaning, as proposed by Schachter. They postulate that there *are* different patterns of physiological responses, but that such responses do *not* determine or cause the emotion. Rather, the physiological component is seen as a function of the cognitive appraisal—usually following it, but in any case being incorporated into it.

Stress

Business executives are under constant pressure from their boss to do better work. Athletes try very hard to improve their game. Spectators get caught up in the excitement of their team's attempt to win the championship. Friends watch helplessly as someone close to them slowly dies of cancer.

All of the people in the above examples face very different situations, but they share one thing in common—they are all experiencing stress. *Stress* is the nonspecific response of the body to any demand made on it (Selye, 1973). Although the causes of stress are many and varied, and can be either pleasant (such as a passionate kiss) or unpleasant (such as the loss of one's job), they all demand readjustment or adaptation. (See *P&L* Close-up at right.) The biological stress response to this demand (regardless of the source) is always essentially the same. As we shall see later on, this response involves the activities of various hormones, and

it occurs in several phases. Contrary to popular opinion, stress is not some terrible circumstance to be avoided; rather, it is a process that is continually evoked throughout one's life. No matter what you do, there will always be demands to perform necessary tasks or adapt to changing influences. Instead of avoiding stress, we need to learn how to deal with it in the best way possible.

Close-up
Extreme Emotional Arousal

The distorting effects of extreme stress or euphoria in modifying the reality of the perceptual world can be better illustrated by reference to Shakespeare (for the former) and to modern songwriters (for the latter) than by laboratory experiments.

Macbeth in anguish says:

"Is this a dagger which I see before me,
The handle toward my hand? Come, let me clutch thee.
I have thee not, and yet I see thee still.
Art thou not, fatal vision, sensible
To feeling as to sight? or art thou but
A dagger of the mind, a false creation,
Proceeding from the heat-oppressed brain?
. . . . .
"Mine eyes are made the fools o' the other senses,
Or else worth all the rest; I see thee still,
And on the blade and dudgeon gouts of blood,
Which was not so before. There's no such thing:
It is the bloody business which informs
Thus to mine eyes."

William Shakespeare, *Macbeth*, II:i

Similarly, the ecstasy of love can induce perceptual distortion, although of a different nature:

"Are there lilac trees in the heart of town?
Can you hear a lark in any other part of town?
Does enchantment pour out of every door?
No, it's just on the street where you live."[1]

[1]"On the Street Where You Live" Copyright © 1956 by Alan Jay Lerner and Frederick Loewe. Used by permission of Chappell & Co., Inc.

Consequences of Stress

Sometimes, in the face of repeated, intense stressful arousal, the physiological response of the body is maladaptive and injurious. Deterioration in bodily functioning that is *psychogenic* (has a psychological-emotional source) is called, appropriately, a *psychosomatic disorder* (*psyche*="mind," *soma*="body"). This term is used to refer to the symptoms involved in a persistent stress reaction, such as rapid pulse and high blood pressure, and to actual tissue damage that may result, as in a gastric ulcer.

It is estimated that about half of all patients who consult physicians have symptoms originating largely in emotional disturbance. In fact, some investigators believe that *all* illness and disease has some emotional basis. Emotional factors have been clearly demonstrated in the development of some cases of ulcers, high blood pressure, colitis, migraine, low back pain, dermatitis, obesity, asthma, and many other ailments.

Destructive emotions and physical illness. Physicians are currently recognizing the fact that high-pressure, "go-getting" businessmen are especially prone to heart conditions. According to one report, coronary heart disease strikes these men seven times as often as it does individuals in the general population (Friedman & Rosenman, 1960). Several cognitive factors have been discovered that are characteristic of these coronary-prone men. Among them are: feelings of time urgency, a sense of unrelenting external demands, and behavioral patterns of compulsive activity designed to ward off impending harm (Jenkins, Rosenman, & Friedman, 1967; Friedman & Rosenman, 1974).

We often hear that "bottling up" one's feelings is bad for one's health. Research evidence supports this view at least as far as frustration and pent-up aggression are concerned.

In separate studies employing over 160 college-age subjects of both sexes, frustration was experimentally aroused by the blocking of goal activity, or by ego threats. Some of the subjects were allowed to aggress physically, verbally, or in their fantasy against the frustration, while others were given no such opportunity.

The results clearly indicated that both heart rate and systolic blood pressure rose significantly following the frustrating experience. Opportunity to aggress physically or verbally lowered these levels, whereas when subjects were not allowed to express their strong feelings overtly, the physiological changes persisted (Hokanson & Burgess, 1962).

Full-blown asthmatic reactions to psychological stimuli were demonstrated by a team of Dutch psychologists in some patients who had a history of asthma.

One patient, shown a picture of a man mourning at a grave and reminded by it of her father's death and burial, suffered a sharp decrease in the vital capacity of her lungs, as measured by constricted breathing. In another case, a patient who had had a pet fish destroyed by her mother as a child was shown a toy fish in a fish bowl. She not only showed the same constriction in breathing but experienced a severe asthmatic attack (Dekker & Groen, 1958).

Psychological factors may also be involved in illnesses that, at first glance, appear to be purely physical in origin. (See *P&L* Close-up, p. 379.)

One study found that among 1000 telephone operators, one third of the group accounted for two thirds of the absences, mostly from respiratory problems. Those highest in absenteeism differed from those lowest primarily in their psychological outlook: they were more unhappy, resentful, and frustrated. This group suffered from twelve times as many respiratory illnesses (Hinkle & Plummer, 1952).

Although prolonged stress can lead to a wide range of serious disorders, psychosomatic reactions cannot be predicted solely on the basis of exposure to behavioral stress. Constitutional factors and specific kinds of past experience appear to play a role not only in whether stress will result in a psychosomatic reaction, but in the kind of reaction as well. As we saw earlier (p. 373), people who had learned to express their anger outwardly toward the source of the stress displayed different physiological responses than those who had developed a characteristic reaction of fear or self-blame. Convincing evidence that physical and psychological factors may combine to cause disease also comes from a study using mice as subjects.

Mice were stressed for three days by being given cues for anticipating shock plus the shock itself, then inoculated with Coxsackie B virus and stressed for four additional days. Neither stress alone (for some control groups) nor virus alone (for others) was sufficient to cause manifest disease. Only a combination of the two—environmental stress plus the viral agent—resulted in disease (Friedman, Ader, & Glasgow, 1965).

After reviewing the available evidence on factors related to acquiring or resisting infectious disease, a team of physicians concluded that "relatively subtle psychological and environmental factors appear to influence susceptibility to a wide range of infectious and parasitic agents" (Friedman & Glasgow, 1966, p. 323).

Life crises and health change. Even with diseases such as cancer or leukemia, emotional traumas earlier in life may contribute to the development of the disease. More surprising is the evidence that such early psychic traumas may not show their effects until many years later.

In a study investigating the history of early psychic traumas in cancer patients, a psychic trauma *was defined as an experience in which "emotional relationships brought pain and desertion."*

Of 450 cancer patients, 72 percent (as compared to only 10 percent of a noncancerous control group) were found to have suffered such an experience early in life. It was theorized that the cancer patients had, as children, responded to these crises with feelings of guilt and self-blame. During adolescence and early adult-

hood, these feelings were submerged as desires, and energies were concentrated on school, job, and meaningful relationships with others, particularly the spouse. However, often after as long as forty years, when the pattern was changed, perhaps by retirement from work or by the death of the spouse, and the individuals could find no substitute source of satisfaction and meaning in their life, their feelings of guilt and inadequacy returned. Usually the first symptoms of cancer appeared from six months to eight years after this second life crisis (LeShan, 1966).

A group of investigators at the University of Washington School of Medicine developed a scale for rating the degree of adjustment required by forty-three different life changes, both pleasant and unpleasant. (See *P&L* Close-up, p. 380.)

In a group of almost four hundred subjects, a consistent relationship was found between the number of life change units, according to the scale, and major health changes during the same ten-year period. Of those with moderate crisis scale scores, 37 percent had had a major health change; of those with substantial life crisis scale scores, 70 percent had showed a major health change. In addition, those who usually remained well during flu epidemics were more likely to have flu after a major life change (Rahe & Holmes, 1966).

"Medicine of the mind" for physical illnesses. Most physicians have long realized that even when symptoms are due primarily to physical causes, emotional strain can work against successful treatment. Emotionally unstable people who suffer from a severe organic disorder may become so depressed by their physical condition that they will lose their normal recuperative powers. A Baltimore coroner has reported that a number of individuals die each year after taking nonlethal doses of poison or inflicting minor wounds on themselves. Although the injuries in themselves would not have been fatal, apparently thinking made them so (Richter, 1957).

Dr. Thomas H. Holmes and his colleagues (1970) have constructed a scale of stress values measured in "life change units (LCU). Holmes has predicted that people run the risk of developing a major illness in the next two years if they total more than 300 LCU points. It might be well to calculate your personal LCU rating.

Events	Scale of Impact
Death of spouse	100
Divorce	73
Marital separation	65
Jail term	63
Death of close family member	63
Personal injury or illness	53
Marriage	50
Fired at work	47
Marital reconciliation	45
Retirement	45
Change in health of family member	44
Pregnancy	40
Sex difficulties	39
Gain of new family member	39
Business readjustment	39
Change in financial state	38
Death of close friend	37
Change to different line of work	36
Change in number of arguments with spouse	35
Mortgage over $10,000	31
Foreclosure of mortgage or loan	30
Change in responsibilities at work	29
Son or daughter leaving home	29
Trouble with in-laws	29
Outstanding personal achievement	28
Wife begins or stops work	26
Begin or end school	26
Change in living conditions	25
Revision of personal habits	24
Trouble with boss	23
Change in work hours or conditions	20
Change in residence	20
Change in schools	20
Change in recreation	19
Change in church activities	19
Change in social activities	18
Mortgage or loan less than $10,000	17
Change in sleeping habits	16
Change in number of family get-togethers	15
Change in eating habits	15
Vacation	13
Christmas	12
Minor violations of the law	11

At the other end of the spectrum are the many cases on record of patients determined to get well who have done so despite a physician's opinion that they were beyond recovery. It has been reported that old people are more likely to die after a holiday or birthday than before, as though they were determined to live until a certain target date.

Emotional factors are particularly important in such organic disorders as tuberculosis, heart disease, diabetes, and epilepsy. In treating tuberculosis, for example, care must be taken to avoid emotional disturbances, since the patient is not allowed to engage in vigorous physical exercise and is thus denied an important natural means of working off emotional tensions. Unless efforts are made to help the patient maintain a cheerful mood, a disease that is essentially organic may be intensified by emotional factors.

It is likely that at least as many patients are cured by a doctor's reassuring "bedside" manner as by any of the medicines prescribed. Physicians are now being cautioned to be more responsive not only to the whole patient but to the social-emotional network in which the patient lives. Although the significance of the "mind" in physical illness is receiving greater attention in medical circles, it may be that the general trend away from family doctors and general practitioners to clinics and specialists means that the patient's emotional needs are receiving less attention than the family doctor could give.

Coping with Stress

How does the individual respond when faced with a stressful situation? Two major approaches have developed that focus on this syndrome, one being more concerned with the physiological changes occurring with stress, and the other with psychological and cognitive factors.

The general adaptation syndrome. A theoretical approach that helps explain psychosomatic symptoms is the concept of the *general adaptation syndrome,* developed by Hans Selye (1956, 1973). According to Selye's theory, the body's reaction under stress occurs in three major phases: the *alarm reaction,* the *stage of resistance,* and the *stage of exhaustion.*

1. The *alarm reaction,* sometimes called the *emergency reaction,* comprises the physiological changes that are the organism's first response to the application of a stress-provoking agent, or *stressor.* A stressor is anything injurious to the organism, whether physical (such as inadequate food, loss of sleep, bodily injury) or psychological (such as loss of love or personal security). The alarm reaction consists of various complicated bodily and biochemical changes that usually have the same general characteristics regardless of the exact nature of the stressor. This latter finding was established by subjecting a large number of animals to a wide variety of stressful conditions including starvation, infections, poisoning, extreme cold, extreme heat, surgical hemorrhage, and others. Regardless of the type of stressor, much the same general pattern of physiological change was observed.

These results account for the similarity in general symptoms of people suffering from diverse illnesses—all seem to complain of such symptoms as headache, fever, fatigue, aching muscles and joints, loss of appetite, and a general feeling of being "run down."

2. If exposure to the stress-producing situation continues, the alarm reaction is followed by the *stage of resistance,* the second phase of the general adaptation syndrome. Here the organism seems to develop a resistance to the particular stressor that provoked the alarm reaction. The symptoms that occurred during the first stage of stress disappear, even though the disturbing stimulation continues, and the physiological processes that had been disturbed during the alarm reaction appear to resume normal functioning.

Resistance to the stressor seems to be accomplished in large part through increased level of secretions of the anterior pituitary and the adrenal cortex (ACTH and *cortin,* respectively). For example. Navy pilots clearly showed this adrenocortical response during landing practice in a F-4B jet aircraft. Interestingly, their partners in the jet did not have this reaction. Thus it apparently was not simply exposure to danger that induced the stress response, but responsibility

Close-up
A Critical Look at LCU and Illness

The extensive research by investigators Holmes and Rahe has directed attention to an important relationship between psychosocial factors and somatic illness (Holmes & Masuda, 1974; Rahe, 1974). Because of the theoretical and practical implications of their work, we must be cautious in accepting the evidence and sufficiently critical in our appraisal of what has been found. Some points of contention are:

Methodological

(a) Many of the studies correlate retrospective accounts of life changes with other retrospective accounts of illness. In some studies subjects reported on life changes and illness simultaneously—the purpose of the study being all too clear. (b) When predictive follow-up of illness is the dependent variable, prior LCU of 6 months predicts illness rather than LCU of two years as in earlier studies. (c) The correlations are generally quite small but are statistically significant with larger samples. (d) Some of the LCU life events may be presymptomatic indicators of the illness and not independent of the predictor variable (such as changes in eating or sleeping).

Theoretical

(a) No specific biological mechanisms for the relationship are given. (b) The LCU measure may be a better predictor of "treatment-seeking behavior" than of actual illness. (c) "No change" may be stressful, when change is expected, as in an expected promotion or anticipated request for a date. (d) There is no provision for the broader context in which the changes take place, social contacts, capacity to deal with stress, established ways of handling such changes. (e) What are the differences between positive and negative changes in the person's interpretation and subsequent illness reaction? (f) Perhaps both LCU and illness involve losses of close social contacts which is the important mediating process (based on Cohen, 1975).

for the complex and hazardous task that the pilot—but not the passive partner—had to assume (Rubin, Miller, Arthur, & Clark, 1969).

3. If exposure to the injurious stressor continues too long, a point is reached where the organism can no longer maintain its resistance. It thereupon enters the final phase of changes related to stress, the *stage of exhaustion.* The anterior pituitary and adrenal cortex are unable to continue secreting their hormones at the increased rate, with the result that the organism can no longer adapt to the continuing stress. Many of the physiological dysfunctions that originally appeared during the alarm reaction begin to reappear. If the stressor continues to act upon the organism after this time, death often occurs. It is rare, however, for stress not to be relieved before this stage of exhaustion is reached.

The concept of the general adaptation syndrome has been exceptionally valuable in explaining psychosomatic disorders. In terms of its framework, many disorders can be viewed as the results of stress or of the physiological processes involved in adaptation to stress. The value of administering additional ACTH and cortisone in treating some of these diseases can also be understood. In effect, such treatment may be regarded as a way of helping the anterior pituitary and the adrenal cortex maintain the body's resistance to some stressor.

One psychologist, after reviewing the work of Selye and others, summed up the situation as follows:

"Perhaps emotional reactions are basically constructive—defensive and adaptive. However, if emotional activity or reactivity is sufficiently frequent or prolonged or intense, it becomes maladaptive or destructive, leading to physiological aberration or structural damage to the organism, and even to death. Thus, an organism may be injured or destroyed by its own defenses." (Lachman, 1963, p. 27)

Cognitive coping strategies. Obviously, stressful situations do not always lead to illness or dysfunctioning. Under what conditions do they *not* do so? The research that is being done on this question has consistently pointed to the importance of psychological factors in coping with stress. How the person perceives the situation and what emotion he or she feels can drastically affect the outcome of the event. (See *P&L* Close-up, p. 383.)

Appraisal of threat. As we saw earlier in this chapter (p. 376), Richard Lazarus and his colleagues have developed a cognitive appraisal theory of emotions. Most of the research done to test this theory has generally focused on how appraisals and reappraisals are used to cope with extremely threatening situations.

In one study, subjects watched a film that showed some very crude genital operations carried out as part of male initiation rites in a primitive Australian tribe. The sound track that accompanied the film either emphasized the dangers of the operation, denied such dangers, or discussed them in an intellectualized, detached way. The investigators hypothesized that these sound tracks would alter the subjects' cognitive appraisal of (and thus their emotional response to) the threatening film. They found that, as compared with arousal by the film alone, levels of physiological arousal were higher with the "danger" sound track and lower with the "denial" and "intellectualization" tracks (Speisman, Lazarus, Mordkoff, & Davison, 1964).

In another experiment, subjects who watched a film about unexpected, dramatic accidents in a woodshop (such as an accident in which a man was impaled by a plank of wood while operating a circular saw) showed less physiological arousal, as measured by skin conductance (galvanic skin response) and heart rate, if they had cognitively rehearsed, or imagined, the threatening scenes prior to seeing the film. ■ *Relaxation training also helped reduce stress, but the opportunity for advance cognitive appraisal was clearly more effective (Folkins, Lawson, Opton, & Lazarus, 1968).*

Such results have important implications not only for our intellectual understanding of what emotion is, but for preparation of people who will be subjected to severe stress (as in certain dangerous occupations).

When not enough fear is too much. Does the person who is fearless in the face of danger have a psychological advantage over the worrier? Not necessarily, according to research. In fact, under some circumstances too little fear may have as bad an effect on health as too much.

One investigator, Irving Janis, hypothesized that when an individual must cope with a threatening situation, as in anticipating major surgery on oneself, a moderate amount of realistic fear before the surgery would be valuable in promoting both psychological and physical adjustment afterward. He found that a moderate level of fear, which initiated the "work of worrying" prior to exposure to the actual event, helped the patient to plan future reactions and modulate stress and induced a kind of "emotional inoculation." Extreme fear created the general stress syndrome we have discussed, and thereby introduced additional physiological complications. On the other hand, the patient with little or no fear before the surgery, who did not engage in mental rehearsal of the impending event, was less well prepared to cope with the conse-

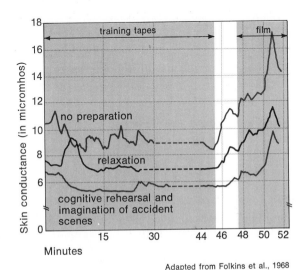

Adapted from Folkins et al., 1968

■ **COGNITIVE PREPARATION FOR STRESS**

Close-up
Stress on the Job

The characteristics of any work situation tend to have a strong impact on the way in which people perceive their job and react to its stresses and strains. For example, executives in certain departments of a large company were placed in a new organizational system of decision making, which proved to be a very inefficient one. Their frustration with the structure of their job was not only reflected in lowered sales and staff infighting, but in a high frequency of psychosomatic complaints (Ruma, 1973).

In another study of the effects of switching workers from a fixed monthly salary to the more demanding schedule of a piecework rate, the result was also a negative psychological reaction and a corresponding change in bodily state. Although the women workers were earning more money as their average production rate rose by 113 percent, they reported more strain and fatigue and there was a sharp increase in secretion of stress hormones (Levi, 1972).

Air-traffic controllers at Chicago's O'Hare Airport were responsible for more than 37 million passengers last year, with 666,560 takeoffs and landings occurring (one every twenty seconds). Any letup from constant vigilance, a slight error in instructions, or a switch missed can result in a fatal air crash. This intense stress is comparable to battle fatigue and has been labeled "collisionitis." The consequences are high blood pressure and ulcers along with other stress symptoms of anxiety, insomnia, loss of appetite, irritability and depression (Martindale, 1976).

But perhaps not having a job when you want one is worse than having a stress-producing one. When health statistics are related to economic cycles over a 127-year period in the U.S., it can be shown that increased deaths follow periods of economic depression two to four years later (Brenner, 1973). This research points up the importance of the political, economic, and social context of behavior. It also makes us aware of the interdependencies between our biological nature and the ecosystem.

quences of the surgery. When he or she suddenly became aware of the loss of a limb, or of being incapacitated or in extreme pain, such a person tended to respond with feelings of helplessness, vulnerability, disappointment, and anger.

The graph illustrates the better postoperative adjustment made by a group of college-student patients whose fear level before the operation was moderate, as compared with the adjustment of those at either extreme. Those with low preoperative fear displayed most anger, most complaints against the hospital staff, and most emotional disturbance (Janis, 1958). ●

Patients with a low level of fear due to denial, false optimism, or ignorance may be given an "emotional inoculation" by preparatory communications. This cognitive preparation has been shown to have remarkable effects.

A group of 97 patients at the Massachusetts General Hospital were randomly divided into two groups. One of the groups received only the routine, minimal medical interview, while the other group received additional relevant information about the surgery. The anesthetist who administered these treatments did not tell the hospital staff or the surgeons which patients were in which group, so as to keep constant all other aspects of their hospitalization. Following the operation, the forewarned group required a much smaller dosage (about half as much) of morphine sedation than the routinely processed group. Not only did they complain less, but they were judged to be in so much better health that they were discharged an average of nearly three days earlier than the cognitively unprepared patients (Egbert, Battit, Welch, & Bartlett, 1964).

When does fear make you act? Research—as well as your own observation—makes it clear that warnings of danger are not always accepted and acted on. Even when they are believed, as in the case of VD, drug abuse, and cancer related to smoking, they sometimes only increase the individual's emotional arousal without also increasing the likelihood of one's initiating preventive behavior.

In a series of studies focused on the problem of how a person can be made to act to promote his or her own health, one researcher set up information booths at the New York World's Fair, several state fairs, and also in conjunction with college health centers. He found that many of the people most in need of the preventive action refuse it in an attempt to maintain their illusion of personal invulnerability. Among a group of smokers encouraged to have chest X rays, 53 percent of those with moderate levels of fear were willing to do so, as compared with only 6 percent of those with high fear, demonstrating that those with the greatest fear were not the ones most likely to take action to safeguard their health (Leventhal, 1965).

In the same way, people who are afraid they have VD or cancer often put off seeing a doctor.

For fear warnings to serve an effective function, they must: (a) establish a reasonable (not excessive) level of fear; (b) not only arouse fear but also change general attitudes toward doing something about the feared activity or event; and (c) provide clear guidelines for coping action in concrete terms of what the person must do, how, and where. Finally, recommendations

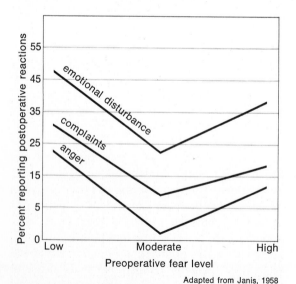

Adapted from Janis, 1958

● **PREOPERATIVE FEAR AND POSTOPERATIVE STRESS**

for action are more likely to be followed if the person is induced to make a public commitment to act in the prescribed way.

So who's afraid of the big bad wolf, anyway? A soldier about to go into battle, a surgeon about to perform his or her first major operation, a prizefighter facing an undefeated opponent, and a novice parachutist readying for a leap into open space all face fear head on. If they cannot master their fear, their performance will suffer, with obviously disastrous personal consequences.

How does an individual cope with the dangers inherent in a situation such as sport parachuting? Although the people who engage in this activity are highly motivated, they still experience extreme fear during their early training. The effects of this emotion on their psychological performance, and their manner of exerting cognitive control over their fear, were studied in a provocative field experiment.

Twenty-seven novice sport parachutists were tested on a battery of measures at three different times in relation to jump time: two weeks before a jump, one day before, and on the day itself. They were tested on word-association lists and projective tests, both of which contained items varying in their relevance to the critical event—the parachute jump. In addition, GSR and basal skin conductance were recorded as indicators of physiological activation.

As compared with a control group of similar age, education (college), and geographical location who were not involved in parachuting, the parachutists, two weeks before a jump, reacted less *emotionally to words that were not associated with parachuting. "This finding appears to reveal a personality difference as it may be interpreted to indicate that parachutists are more apt to release tension in motor activity, rather than to inhibit their emotions, or bind their tensions" (p. 13).*

On the other hand, the parachutist's general state of tension, generated by increasing proximity to the jump, was handled in a complex way. On the projective measure, they denied fear of jumping in reactions to pictures of high relevance to parachuting, but then expressed *more fear responses in relation to pictures of little or no relevance. Their physiology betrayed them, however: as the time of the jump came closer, there were increasingly steep gradients of GSR to the highly relevant pictures (Fenz, 1964).* ▲

These findings are in accord with a report of the Parachute Club of America that indicates that most failures are due to the jumper's inability to develop cognitive control of the fear (Moore, 1963).

Denial of fear may serve an adaptive function, but in excess it may also interfere with execution of responses that depend on complex, unbiased information processing.

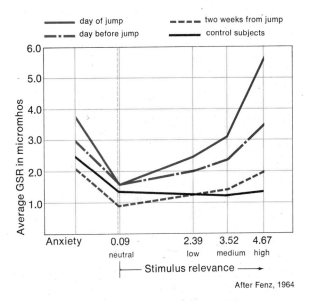

After Fenz, 1964

▲ **MIND AND BODY IN STRESS REACTIONS**
In the projective test, the parachutists made up stories about pictures such as these, which had differing degrees of relevance to jumping. Although their verbal responses showed less fear with high-relevance pictures, their GSR responses, as shown in the graph, were clearly higher for the more relevant pictures as the time to jump approached.

Pain

Perhaps the most eloquent definition of pain is that it is "a hurt we feel" (Sternbach, 1968). It is a hurt that may come from tissue damage caused by external conditions — stubbing one's toe, burning a finger on a hot stove, being hit hard, or receiving a gun or knife wound. But it also comes, as we know only too well, from "inside" us, in the form of toothaches, headaches, menstrual cramps, arthritic pain, or the intractable pain accompanying terminal cancer. Our sensitivity to pain can also vary a great deal, ranging from a heightened response to every small hurt to a complete blocking-out of painful sensations. (See *P&L* Close-up, at left.)

Although at times we might wish we could be free of pain, the ability to experience pain, and its motivating properties, is actually one of nature's most valuable gifts to us. Pain should be viewed as: (a) *a signal system* that has evolved to warn us of assaults on the integrity of the body and (b) *a defensive system* triggering automatic withdrawal reflexes as well as motivated avoidance and escape behaviors. As such, it is indispensable in coping with an occasionally hostile environment and with the diseases and eventual deterioration of the living matter that is our body.

Pain As a Neurological Event

The stimulus that initiates the pattern of neurological pain responses is an intense or rapid change in physical energy capable of producing tissue damage. It appears that there are *not* specialized pain receptors, but that undifferentiated free nerve endings distributed throughout the body are responsible for pain reception. Pain impulses are transmitted by nerves that enter the spinal cord and, after synapsing, send impulses up various spinal tracts to the thalamus, the reticular formation, and the cortex.

Although we might think the pain we experience is determined entirely by the stimulus causing it, research findings have not supported this notion. Rather, the amount and quality of perceived pain are affected by many psychological variables as well as by sensory input. Accordingly, Melzack and Wall (1965) have developed a *"gate-control" theory* of pain, which integrates both physiological and psychological factors. They propose a control-feedback system that continuously interacts to modulate pain input. When pain occurs, selective brain processes are activated that exert control over incoming messages. Influenced by this trigger mechanism, cells at each level of the spinal cord act as a gate-control system, increasing or decreasing their receptivity to incoming pain sig-

---

Close-up
But Get Me to the Bakery on Time

Dramatic accounts of soldiers in battle being oblivious to their serious wounds while continuing to fight valiantly to save their lives and win the day are not as powerful evidence for the cognitive control of pain as is the recent demonstration of mind over pain by a New York baker.

George Keller, age 53, works in a big New York bakery. He had a record of not having missed a single day's work in the past eighteen years. He would arrive promptly at 4 A.M. each day to prepare the bakery for his co-workers. But just before Christmas his record was threatened. As he left his home in the cold predawn hours, he was attacked by five young men who stole his watch and, as he broke away from them, shot him in the chest, stomach, and buttocks.

Somehow, George's record was not broken, and even without his trusty watch, he got to the bakery on time. He managed to board a bus, make it to the bakery, and get the ovens and the dough prepared before walking twelve blocks to a police station to report the crime.

George Keller was then rushed to the hospital, where his condition was listed as "critical" after emergency surgery. However, when his boss arrived at the bakery, all was, as usual, in perfect order. "Old reliable George" had done it again. Loyalty to a cause had transcended self-concern over pain and personal well-being (Associated Press release, Dec. 24, 1973).

nals traveling along the nerves. This system makes it possible for central nervous system activities (which underlie attention, emotion, and memories of prior experience) to alter afferent input by efferent processes. (See *P&L Close-up* below.)

Psychological Aspects of Pain

In attempting to integrate the diverse body of research on pain and develop a core set of elements that characterize pain, Sternbach (1968) proposed that people's reaction to pain involves: (a) their perceptual coping style, especially the way they respond to anxiety, (b) the learned association of physical stimuli that cause pain reactions with the social context in which the pain occurs, and (c) the internal sensory modification of these pain responses by various cognitive inputs.

To suffer in silence or cry out . . . Denial of the experience of fear, stress, or pain is not necessarily an individual matter, but may be acquired by members of ethnic groups as a consequence of certain cultural experiences. In fact, in some cases, patients who show exaggerated pain reactions are referred for psychiatric care when actually they are only manifesting learned behavior patterns approved in their group.

When surgical patients at a Bronx VA hospital were observed and interviewed (along with their families and staff), ethnic group membership generally predicted how they were handling the pain they were experiencing. The Jewish and

and British physicians, it really does stop pain. Newspaper columnist James Reston underwent an appendectomy in Peking using acupuncture, and there are other reports of its use in major surgery of various kinds. Although there is evidence that acupuncture works, the puzzle for Western medicine is *how* it does so.

According to Melzack (1973), the gate-control theory suggests three different ways in which acupuncture can reduce pain: (1) There are large fibers in the sensory nerves running from the body surface to the central nervous system. When stimulated, these fibers "close the gate" in the pain-signaling system and thus reduce the amount of perceived pain. It may be that acupuncture needles are stimulating these large fibers. (2) When certain parts of the brain stem are stimulated, a deep, long-lasting analgesia (insensitivity to pain) is produced in a large part of the body. Apparently, these parts of the brain stem can "close the gate" by blocking signals coming from the site of the pain stimulus. Again, the nerve impulses produced by twirling the acupuncture needles may be stimulating the brain stem. (3) Fibers that descend from the cortex can also affect the "gates" and modulate pain. Since the cortex is the brain's center for memories, expectations, anxieties, etc., these psychological processes can have a marked effect on the experience of pain. Since acupuncture patients have faith in the effectiveness of the procedure and are also given explicit suggestions that they will feel no pain, their cognitive set may be very influential in reducing the pain that they feel.

Close-up
The Mystery of Acupuncture

With the recent opening of China to American visitors, the news media have been flooded with stories about the traditional Chinese technique of pain relief called *acupuncture*. The procedure involves the insertion of long, fine needles into certain points on the person's body, and, according to eyewitness accounts of American

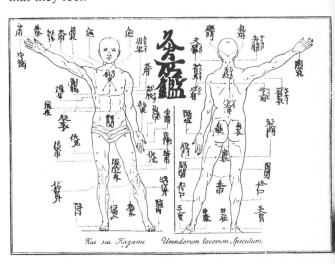

Kiu su Kagami   Urendorum locorum Speculum.

Italian patients emotionally exaggerated the intensity of their pain, feeling free to cry out to elicit support from family or hospital staff. By contrast, Irish and Old American patients (Anglo-Saxon Protestants from at least three generations of Americans) adopted a phlegmatic, detached, matter-of-fact orientation that inhibited any public show of emotion. When their pain became intense, they would withdraw; they would moan or cry out only when alone.

Further investigation showed that the common demonstrativeness of the Jewish and Italian patients stemmed from different concerns. The Italians focused on the immediacy of the pain experience and pain relief, whereas the Jewish patients were concerned about the meaning and future implications of the pain, and also had a distrust of pain-relief procedures.

Although both the Irish and the Old Americans were "good" patients who did not make a fuss, they too were acting from quite divergent attitudes. The Old American patients, in refusing to be seen as weak or helpless, assumed that pain was a common experience that everyone has but which threatens one's masculinity. With probing by an interviewer, however, such patients openly discussed their feelings and were optimistic about their future since "doctors are experts."

The Irish patients, on the other hand, were reluctant to speak about their pain and seemed to need to endure it alone as a unique experience. Their inability or unwillingness to share their feelings gave a superficial appearance of outward calm and lack of concern. The investigator reported that "among the four groups of patients of different ethnic backgrounds, the Irish patient presented the saddest, most depressing picture . . . not prepared to think in terms of illness and health care, he discovers in the hospital a world of human suffering of which he is a part. But he is unable to share his emotions, anxieties, and fears with a close person who would understand them and offer some comfort and support" (Zborowski, 1969, p. 235).

The basic results of this research were substantiated in a controlled laboratory study, where pain was induced (by electric shock) in housewives of various ethnic backgrounds. The Italian subjects were most sensitive to the pain, with significantly lower pain tolerance than any other group. Jewish women were able to take the greatest increase in shock level when motivated (coaxed) by the experimenter. While Yankee subjects physiologically adapted to shock more readily than any other group, the Irish housewives deliberately suppressed their suffering and concern for the implication of the pain (Sternbach & Tursky, 1965).

There were important differences, however, in the experience and interpretation of pain induced in the laboratory, as compared with pain experienced by patients in the hospital. For example, in the laboratory, where the cause of pain was obvious and controlled by the experimenter, the Jewish patients had a higher threshold for pain (as compared with the Jewish hospital patients), since the lab pain did not signal ominous future dangers.

Hypnotic control of pain. As we saw in Chapter 7, hypnosis is a unique state of consciousness that allows the individual to exert considerable cognitive control over both body and mind. As such, it has often been used to help control pain. Prior to the discovery of ether, for example, hypnosis was routinely used as an anesthetic. In addition to effectively reducing pain, hypnosis has the added advantage of producing fewer side effects.

Ernest Hilgard and his associates have carried out several studies on hypnosis and pain, in which pain was produced either by immersing the subject's arm in ice water or by temporarily cutting off the blood flow in the arm through use of a tourniquet. After being hypnotized and given a suggestion for analgesia (insensitivity to pain), subjects reported that their pain was either reduced or eliminated entirely. Those subjects who could be easily hypnotized showed a greater pain reduction than those who could not (Hilgard, 1969).

Another study shows how complete the independence of the pain response from environmental stimulation can sometimes become under hypnotic control.

Volunteer high-school subjects were given a series of constant-intensity, painful electric shocks, both before and after receiving a hypnotic suggestion for analgesia. As compared to a control group, these hypnotic subjects reported feeling much less pain and showed less physiological responsivity to the shocks. One subject's reactions to the shocks are shown in the graph. ■ *(Numbered lines indicate shock onset.) After the subject was hypnotized and told "This time the shocks will not hurt so much," his response was greatly lessened. In fact, the response to the first shock in this series was only a tenth the size of the first response in the unhypnotized condition. After eight shocks, the subject gained control over the sensory input, and the response was completely eliminated (Zimbardo, Rapaport, & Baron, 1969).*

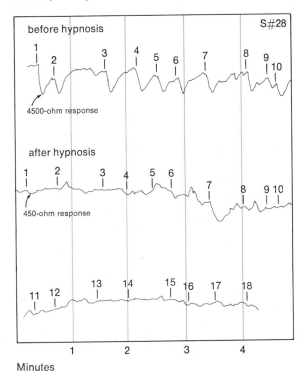

Minutes

After Zimbardo, Rapaport, & Baron, 1969

■ **PAIN REDUCTION UNDER HYPNOSIS**

Deviant uses of pain motivation. Before concluding this section, it may be instructive to consider two deviant uses of pain motivation: pain as torture and pain as pleasure.

Pain as torture. During the Inquisitions that took place throughout Europe in the Middle Ages, it was believed that devils were very sensitive to pain. This belief provided the justification for subjecting women thought to be witches and men possessed by Satan to unbelievable tortures. If the victims reacted with expressions of pain—as they invariably did—they identified themselves as devils and were executed. "From the thirteenth and fourteenth centuries downwards such was the reign of terror that we find persons of the highest condition abandon rank, fortune, everything, the moment they were accused, and take flight" (Michelet, 1962, pp. 314–15).

As the church-state yielded power to the police-state, the motivating effect of pain was attributed not to satanic forces but to the distinct weakness of human flesh. The rack and iron boot gave way to the abuses of the "third degree": water tortures, exposure to the desert sun, and the like. However, people also realized the psychological determinants of pain, especially the pain arising from social isolation. In earlier centuries offenders were walled up permanently with only a slit through which daily bread was thrown in. This torture, ironically called the *in pace* (place of peace), successively became the solitary confinement of our penal institutions and, more recently, the psychological isolation used as part of the program of "brainwashing" practiced by the Chinese Communists during the Korean War (Schein, 1957).

Pain as pleasure. It is easy for us to identify pain as an inevitable outcome of torture, but pain as a source of pleasure is a less obvious relationship. Yet, from the earliest days of the Christian church, we have the writings of mystics who believed that by enduring pain one could transcend the bodily senses and attain a higher state of being. The barrier between pain and pleasure disappeared when suffering for God became the ultimate experience to which one could aspire in this mortal life. ●

" 'Whip me,' said the masochist. 'No,' replied the sadist gleefully." The nineteenth-century writings of Leopold von Sacher-Masoch and the Marquis de Sade gave names to the perverse sexual pleasure that some individuals derive from the infliction of pain on themselves or a sexual partner. It has been suggested that one-trial conditioning may be responsible for cases in which the experience of pain becomes essential for sexual gratification. In discussing the origins of this behavior pattern, Paul Gebhard (1965), of Kinsey's Institute for Sex Research, points to the occurrence of an unusual combination of situational factors experienced by an adolescent coming into puberty. He cites the case of a boy who had fractured his arm. While it was being hurriedly set without anesthesia, the physician's attractive nurse caressed the boy and held his head against her breast. This experience of a "powerful and curious combination of pain and sexual arousal" influenced not only his adult attraction to women who had a hair style similar to the nurse's, but his heterosexual relations, which were marked by both sadistic and masochistic tendencies.

Helplessness, Hopelessness, and Loss of Cognitive Control

The psychologist attempts to formulate general laws of behavior in order to be able to explain, predict, and control behavior. For individuals attempting to cope with the demands of the environment, existence itself depends on their being able to meet this goal. To discover causal relations gives meaning to events; to be able to predict the occurrence of events brings order and regularity where chaos and uncertainty would otherwise exist; to control events by one's purposeful actions leads to active mastery in place of passive dependence and submission to the environment. To be unable to exert any control over one's environment can have far-reaching pathological effects.

Give-up-itis

A fateful reaction of some prisoners of war has been aptly described as "give-up-itis." In this syndrome, the loss of all hope of ever being freed and consequent loss of interest in the future resulted in emotionally caused death. Bruno Bettelheim (1960), a psychologist who himself survived imprisonment in Nazi concentration camps, characterizes one such reaction that he observed among some of his fellow prisoners in this way:

"Prisoners who came to believe the repeated statements of the guards—that there was no hope for them, that they would never leave the camp except as a corpse—who came to feel that their environment was one over which they could exercise no influence whatsoever, these prisoners were, in a literal sense, walking corpses. In the camps they were called 'moslems' (Muselmanner) because of what was erroneously

● In this famous statue, Bernini has depicted the ecstasy experienced by St. Teresa. It seemed, she recorded in her autobiography, that an angel was piercing her heart with a fiery spear, "and so excessive was the sweetness caused me by this intense pain that no one can ever wish to lose it."

viewed as a fatalistic surrender to the environment, as Mohammedans are supposed to blandly accept their fate.

"... they were people who were so deprived of affect, self-esteem, and every form of stimulation, so totally exhausted, both physically and emotionally, that they had given the environment total power over them." (pp. 151–52)

For the American POW of the Chinese Communists in the Korean War, there were reported to be similar feelings of being abandoned and deserted by one's own people, of suffering constant intimidation, of loss of self-respect, of the day-to-day uncertainty of existence, of social-psychological isolation from one's fellow Americans (planned by the captors), and, finally, of the futility of resisting or escaping (Nardini, 1952; Schein, 1957). Even after repatriation and return to civilian life, these men were observed to show a "zombie-like" detachment. This is also a common reaction pattern among some depressed hospitalized patients who seem to withdraw, quietly or sullenly, from all social contact. In severe cases,

"... there is complete paralysis of the will. The patient has no desire to do anything, even those things which are essential to life. Consequently he may be relatively immobile unless prodded or pushed into activity by others. It is sometimes necessary to pull the patient out of bed, wash, dress, and feed him. In extreme cases, even communication may be blocked by the patient's inertia." (Beck, 1967, p. 28)

This psychic state of loss of feelings of cognitive control over the environment has been shown to render even "normal" individuals more biologically vulnerable to a host of diseases. Medical investigators have begun to accumulate evidence suggesting that when persons respond to events in their life with helplessness or hopelessness, they initiate a complex series of biological changes that foster the development of any disease potential that is present—even diabetes, heart disease, and cancer. These findings are explained by one physician in an analysis that has broad implications beyond those of psychosomatic medicine.

"Man is constantly interacting within his many environments, and at many levels of organization—from the subcellular and biochemical to the most external or peripheral, that of family, work and now even his universe. We postulate that when a person gives up psychologically, he is disrupting the continuity of his relatedness to himself and his many environments or levels of organization.

"In making such a break, or with this loss of continuity, he may become more vulnerable to the pathogenic influences in his external environments and/or he may become more cut off from his external environments and more predisposed to internal derangements. Thus, disease is more apt to appear at such times of disruptions and increased vulnerability." (Schmale, quoted in Brody, 1968, p. 11)

Voodoo Deaths

There are few human phenomena that so capture the imagination as the sudden voodoo deaths described in anthropological reports. The following is an account of what happens in one tribe when a man discovers that he is being "boned"—having a bone pointed at him in a certain way by an enemy.

"He stands aghast, with his eyes staring at the treacherous pointer, and with his hands lifted as though to ward off the lethal medium, which he imagines is pouring into his body. His cheeks blanch and his eyes become glassy and the expression of his face becomes horribly distorted .... He attempts to shriek but usually the sound chokes in his throat, and all that one might see is froth at his mouth. His body begins to tremble and the muscles twist involuntarily. He sways backwards and falls to the ground, and after a short time appears to be in a swoon; but soon after he writhes as if in mortal agony, and, covering his face with his hands, begins to moan. After a while he becomes very composed and crawls to his wurley. From this time onwards he sickens and frets, refusing to eat and keeping aloof from the daily affairs of the tribe.

Unless help is forthcoming in the shape of a counter-charm administered by the hands of the Nangarri, or medicine-man, his death is only a matter of a comparatively short time." (Basedow, 1925, cited in Cannon, 1942, p. 172)

Other reports tell of healthy people succumbing to sudden death upon discovering that they have transgressed against the supernatural world by eating a food that is cursed.

A young traveler, lodging at the house of a friend, was served a dish containing fowl. He asked his host if it was wild hen, for that delicacy was banned for the young. The host replied, "No," so the boy ate his fill and then went on his way. A few years later the two friends met again and the older man asked the youth if he would eat a wild hen. When the boy said, "No," the man laughed and told him that he had eaten the forbidden food a few years before at his house. At this knowledge, the young man began to tremble and in less than twenty-four hours he was dead (Pinkerton, 1814).

Such reports from societies that believe in the power of witchcraft and the supernatural were thoroughly analyzed by the physiologist Walter Cannon (1942), who became convinced of the reality of this phenomenon. Nevertheless, people from technologically and scientifically more advanced societies find it difficult to accept such events. We do not believe in black magic or witchcraft, but rather in natural causes for rationally related events. But in lumping voodoo deaths with magic, we overlook the possibility that the ultimate cause of death may indeed follow physiological laws but be set in motion by the cognitive belief system of the tabooed person and of the society that promotes and reinforces such beliefs. In order to understand how this might work, let us look at the ways in which some societies view the phenomena of disease.

Knowing what we now do about the role of cognitive appraisal in emotional arousal, such mysterious sudden deaths are easier to understand when we realize that in many cultures illness is not separated into mental and physical

categories as with us, nor is the cause of illness clearly attributed to natural causes as opposed to supernatural ones. Illness, disease, and early death are more common in less advantaged societies and thus represent an ever present concern, as does the burden of treating and caring for the sick. They are not merely treated by technologists or medical specialists, but involve the family and friends of the sick person as well as those in charge of the healing ritual.

A cross-cultural study compared the beliefs about disease held by a sample of American students and rural Mexican adults (both non-Indians and Spanish-speaking Indians). The categorization of disease by the American sample seemed to be based primarily on two dimensions: "Is it contagious?" and "How serious is it?" Emotional diseases like psychosis and ulcers were distinguished from those with organic causes.

In contrast, analysis of the Mexican belief system regarding disease classification revealed no dimension of contagiousness as such. Rather, diseases were classified as requiring either "hot medicine" or "cold medicine" and as children's diseases (most of which were contagious) or diseases of old age, the latter category including visceral ailments and diseases caused by witchcraft. No distinction was made between physical and mental diseases.

Such belief systems do not recognize the dangers of contagion in epidemics, since diseases are considered to be happenings caused by external (often magical) sources in which their bodily processes do not play an active role. If many people get the same disease, they are all considered to be afflicted by some common external agent over which they have no control. This raises a serious problem for public health officials concerned with preventing the spread of disease (D'Andrade, Quinn, Nerlove, & Romney, 1969).

Once individuals accept their society's beliefs about external disease causation, capricious spirits, and evil sorcerers, and the unalterability of certain disease states, it is easy to see how they come to accept the inevitability of their doom when designated as transgressors against the supernatural world (Frank, 1961). A person's feeling of "helplessness" is then reinforced by friends and relatives who, believing in the same system of fate, begin to withdraw their support, socially isolate the individual, and finally act as if death had already come.

We know that ulcers in animals can occur after a prolonged period of vigilance or stress. It is not hard to see how the extreme state of fright induced in people who believe that they are doomed might lead to physical deterioration and death. An outpouring of adrenaline from the inner portion of the adrenal glands has been suggested as the cause of death in such cases. According to this theory, adrenaline impairs the capillary walls, allowing a passage of fluid to the surrounding tissues; the resulting reduction in the volume of circulating blood sends the organism into a state of shock that leads to deterioration of the heart and nerve centers (Cannon, 1957).

An alternative physiological explanation has been proposed by Curt Richter (1957).

To demonstrate experimentally that an organism deprived of hope of survival will give up and die, Richter immersed wild rats and domestic rats singly in a water jar. Normally, rats will swim in such a container for sixty to eighty hours before exhaustion sets in and they drown. Rats whose whiskers were clipped, depriving them of an important source of contact with the environment, behaved in a much different manner, however.

When the whiskers of tame rats were clipped before placing them in the water, three out of twelve died within two minutes, but the others did not give up and kept swimming for forty to sixty hours. However, when the procedure was repeated with wild rats, thus depriving them of contact with their natural environment, all thirty-four animals died either within fifteen minutes after being placed in the water or even while simply being held. Their giving up is even more dramatic when it is noted that they are "characteristically fierce, aggressive, and suspicious . . . constantly on the alert for any avenue of escape." A slowing of heart rate and lowering of body temperature preceded death,

indicating that in this case, death was due to overstimulation of the parasympathetic system rather than to hyperactivity of the adrenal glands.

The hypothesis that hopelessness *was the initial cause of the sudden deaths was supported by two observations. First, when animals close to death were removed from the water, they became normally aggressive and active within a minute or two. Even more convincing was the finding that when wild rats were briefly held and then released several times and given several experiences of being briefly immersed in the water ("hope pretraining") they subsequently did not give up and die but swam as long as the domestic rats.*

Before dismissing this general line of evidence as perhaps revelant only to wild rats and "unsophisticated" human beings, we must add the results of a thorough investigation into the causes of the sudden and unexpected death of a great many American soldiers who were not in combat at the time they died.

From a sample of 1000 such reported deaths between 1942 and 1946, investigators surveyed 550 cases in which the men were young (under forty years of age), physically healthy, died within twenty-four hours after the onset of any symptoms, and were not engaged in exertion or physical activity at the time of death (most were asleep). In 140 of these cases no physical cause of the death could be determined after analysis of all available protocols and postmortem autopsies (Moritz & Zamchech, 1946).

For the past two decades the consequences of stress on physical disease have been investigated at the University of Rochester. Over a six-year period, this one research unit has catalogued 170 cases of death arising from psychologically disturbing situations. The phenomenon of sudden psychologically induced death is by no means limited to primitive cultures and subhumans (Engel, 1971). (See *P&L* Close-up, p. 394.)

In Hopeless Situations, People Become Helpless

Systematic research on the hopelessness seen in the sudden-death phenomenon has begun only recently. In general, behaviorally oriented psychologists have tended to avoid such loose concepts as "hope" or "hopelessness." There have been occasional exceptions, however, in which such cognitive concepts have been used in relation to expectation of success in attaining one's goals. In fact, the purposeful psychology of E. C. Tolman viewed expectancy of achieving a goal as an essential part of all voluntary activity. Tolman pointed out that an organism undertakes an action only when it expects that action to lead toward a desired goal state.

Expectation of the instrumental value of one's behavior for effecting a change in the environment creates a state of hope and motivates action. Apathy and inaction are the consequences of the hopelessness that follows ineffectual responding. When an organism, human or animal, comes to believe that nothing it can do can eliminate a threat, it yields to passive resignation.

It well may be that at least for humans, the basic reinforcer that sustains broad classes of behavior over long periods of time is the confirmation of one's *competence* (White, 1959). This source of reinforcement comes from attaining mastery over one's external or internal environment rather than from merely satisfying appetites or minimizing aversions. From the infant's elation in learning to walk to the mountain climber's pride in conquering difficult and hazardous terrain, the perception of ourselves as active, capable agents is one of our greatest joys, whereas the perception of ourselves as helpless pawns controlled by others is one of the most galling of experiences.

The acceptance of control by external factors or "fate" is not an all-or-none affair but varies with the degree to which we have had the experience of seeing that what we do makes a difference. Rotter (1966) conceives of this dimension of perceived degree of environmental control as a consistent personality trait. Some individuals perceive that they possess considerable internal, personal control over what reinforcements they receive. At the other end of the continuum are those who believe that the external environment—forces beyond their control—determines what happens and that nothing they could do would change the outcome.

Learned helplessness. What happens to an organism when this mastery over its environment and sense of competence are destroyed? How would you feel if you discovered that traumatic events continue to happen to you independently of any attempts on your part to reduce or eliminate them?

Close-up
Dead-After-Arrival

The Baltimore City Hospital was reluctant to admit a young woman who, though extremely frightened, appeared to be in good health. They agreed to put her under observation after she convinced the staff she was in terror as she waited for her death to occur within the next few days. She told the bizarre story of having been one of three baby girls delivered by a midwife in the backwoods of Florida. For some unknown reason, the midwife put a death curse on each of the three children—the first to die before her sixteenth birthday, the second prior to her twenty-first birthday, and the third to die before she reached twenty-three years of age.

Two of these "curses" had apparently already been realized. The first girl died at fifteen in an automobile accident. The second was shot accidentally in a nightclub brawl on the evening of her twenty-first birthday. The patient, the last survivor of the trio, was thus understandably anxious.

She was found dead in her hospital bed on the morning after she was admitted—only two days before her twenty-third birthday.

Although the "curse" may have been related to the earlier two accidental deaths only coincidentally, it can be said to have *caused* the death of the third woman because she *believed* it had the power to do so, and she psychologically and physiologically terrified herself to death.

Think back to your elementary school days to recall the following scene. Your homeroom teacher is questioning the class about current events that virtually everyone knows. After each question, every hand is raised in eager anticipation. "Call on me, teacher, please call on me, I know the right answer," is the refrain running through your mind and the minds of your classmates.

At last, your eyes make contact. You hear your name, stand tall, answer proudly, and the teacher smiles. As you sit back, the next question is posed to the sea of waving hands; some of the others are called on, some are not—and the period is over. What is it that you learned in this situation, and what did your friends learn who were *not* called on? Weren't there some who in fact were *never* recognized? What did they learn from this experience?

The answers are obvious. You were reinforced for raising your hand and for answering correctly, and you continued to do so, and here you are in college. The hand-raising response was simply extinguished in the others. But is that all that was being learned in that situation? Psychologist O. Hobart Mowrer (1960) believes that specific physical responses such as hand-raising were but minor components in the total pattern of emotional responding that occurred. You were "conditioned" to feel *hope* in that sit-

uation because your responses produced gratification—they changed something in ways that were desirable to you. Your unrecognized peers were "conditioned" to feel there was no hope in this same setting because their responses were ineffective in generating any positive consequences. Your sense of hope encourages you to take more chances, to be more active, more optimistic of success, and more competent in your mastery of the environment; you make more responses, and some of them are likely to get reinforced. In contrast, a sense of hopelessness decreases not only the question-answering response but the thinking that must precede it, as well as the intellectual curiosity and an active involvement in the entire learning process. People who have learned to feel helpless in situations that are hopeless turn off, tune out, and give up. What is perhaps even worse is that they often come to blame themselves rather than the situation for their unfortunate state.

This general problem was first put to experimental test several decades ago.

In this study hungry rats were shocked ten seconds after they began to eat. The animals in one group were given control over the shock since it was terminated when they jumped up off the shock grid. The animals in the other group had no control over the shock. It was found that the

animals who could control the shock ate more often than those who had no control—even though both received the same total amount of shock. The experimenters postulated that exposure to the unavoidable shock caused the animals to eat less because they had developed a "sense of helplessness" (Mowrer & Viek, 1948).

Recently these speculations have been raised to a firm empirical level by the provocative research on learned helplessness by University of Pennsylvania psychologist Martin Seligman and his associates (Seligman & Maier, 1967; Overmier & Seligman, 1967; Seligman, 1973, 1974, 1975). The initial research was conducted with dogs and is now being replicated with human subjects. Seligman's approach shows how rigorous laboratory investigation can lead to principles with widespread applicability to human psychiatric problems and, eventually, to new forms of therapy and new ideas for reprogramming our environment to make it more hope inducing. The principles uncovered are currently being extended to depression, psychosomatic illness and death, and the adverse effects of institutionalization.

In Chapter 3, we discussed the Seligman study in relationship to the carry-over effects of Pavlovian aversive conditioning on subsequent avoidance learning. We will review that study here as it relates to the phenomenon of learned helplessness.

Dogs restrained in Pavlovian harnesses were conditioned to respond to a tone signaling a painful shock from which they could not escape. The next day the dogs were put into a two-compartment apparatus where they were to learn the simple instrumental response of jumping over a barrier to escape a shock they received in the first compartment. Control dogs that had not received the prior conditioning quickly learned to avoid the shock. In startling contrast, two thirds of the dogs that had experienced the inescapable shock the day before seemed to give up and accept it rather than learning to escape it. Even if one of these dogs did occasionally escape by jumping over the barrier, on the next trial it would simply sit there and take the shock.

Two things had happened to these animals: they had become both unmotivated and retarded in their learning. Seligman proposes that the prior experience in the harness taught the dogs a sad lesson—their responses had no effect on their traumatic environment. Hope was extinguished and in its place there was fear and a sense of helplessness. This lesson was well learned. In the original study the effects of a prior session of helplessness seemed to wear off after forty-eight hours, but a later study showed that they could be made lasting. Repeated exposure to inescapable shock produced a failure to try to escape danger as long as a week later.

This study also showed that domesticated beagles were more susceptible to the conditions inducing helplessness than were mongrels of unknown history, who may have had to learn to persist in order to survive in an environment that was unfriendly and not as predictable as that of the laboratory. Learned helplessness was eliminated when the dogs were given a means of controlling the shock (by pressing a panel) in the original shock harness situation. These dogs escaped normally when put in the shuttlebox later. Their experience with mastery carried over to the traumatic situation and they did not passively give up.

The helplessness experiments with dogs have now been replicated with college students.

This experiment utilized three conditions: an inescapable condition in which subjects were unable to turn off a loud noise, an escape condition in which subjects were able to control the noise, and a no-noise control condition. After the three groups had experienced the above conditions, they were then taken to a finger shuttlebox in which a loud noise occurred when a finger was placed on one side of the box, but ceased when the finger was moved to the other side. It was found that both the escape and no-noise group subjects learned to turn the noise off by moving their hands to the other side of the *shuttlebox, while the subjects who had experienced the inescapable condition did not escape the noise, but remained passive. (Hiroto, 1974).*

If the incentive for responding comes from an expectation that responding will produce relief from pain, fear, or other aversive situations, then this incentive is undercut when one observes that emitted responses and environmental consequences are not related to each other. The learned helplessness that results takes a toll on physiological functioning as well as on behavioral adaptation to the threatening environment. The results of these studies are at odds with those in well-known studies of "executive monkeys." (See *P&L* Close-up at right.)

Prevention and cure of helplessness. All people experience traumatic events and discover situations that are beyond their control. There are a number of factors that have been experimentally demonstrated to prevent, moderate, or cure helplessness that may be found in our daily lives. These include: immunization, predictability, superstitious perception of control, and retroactive therapy.

"Immunization" against learned helplessness. The most significant kind of therapy is the preventive kind in which the individual is "inoculated" against learned helplessness by prior mastery training. Mastery training in the laboratory consisted of providing sufficient prior experiences in which the dogs had a means of controlling their environment before they were exposed to inescapable trauma. When the dogs were later put into a shuttlebox where they could escape shock, they did so, unlike the helpless dogs that had not received prior mastery training.

The implications for human conditions of helplessness are obvious. The time to begin such mastery training is in childhood—and the need for *you,* as a future parent, to do so for your child is imperative as forces in modern society increasingly make people feel anonymous, unrecognized, expendable, and powerless.

Close-up
The Meek Shall Inherit Ulcers

"Executive monkeys develop ulcers" was the conclusion of a famous study done back in 1958 that has been widely quoted both in the popular press and in psychology textbooks (Brady et al., 1958). The investigators placed pairs of monkeys in an environment where they both received electric shocks following a cue light, unless one of them operated a switch that prevented the onset of the series of shocks. The monkey in charge of the switch was, of course, labeled the *executive monkey* because it had all the responsibility. The other monkey could do nothing to control the situation. In this study the executive monkeys developed ulcers and died; the passive control monkeys remained healthy.

The obvious conclusion is that "pressure to perform" produced the ulcers—a conclusion that, if true, would have obvious implications for human executives. It has recently been suggested, however, that the conclusion is probably a false one, and probably resulted from a bias in the way the monkeys were assigned to the two conditions. Instead of assigning the monkeys at random to the "executive" or "passive" condition, the researchers chose the monkeys that had shown the most initiative in lever-pressing to avoid shock—the ones that were the fastest starters—to be the executives. The "slow-pokes" were the controls. It has since been found that monkeys that respond most quickly when shocked are those that are most "emotional" to begin with (perhaps with a low threshold for pain and anxiety). Thus the conclusion must be recast: *emotional* executives are more likely to get ulcers than are *unemotional* observers.

When researcher Joy Weiss at Rockefeller University (1968, 1971) randomly assigned rats to the executive and passive treatments, the helpless animals fared worse, losing more weight, drinking less, defecating more, and getting more severe ulcers than did the executives. Perhaps, then, executives develop ulcers not so much because of their greater responsibility or even hard work, but from biting off more than they can control.

Predictability to reduce uncertainty. Even when aversive stimulation cannot be avoided, its disrupting effect can be reduced by making it predictable.

In one study, after animals had learned to press a bar for food, their bar pressing was suppressed when shock was given. When the shock became predictable, however, responding again occurred regularly. Six of eight subjects in an unpredictable shock condition developed ulcers after forty-five days, whereas none of eight animals given predictable shock developed ulcers (Seligman, 1968). ▲

When events are unpredictable there is greater stress and anxiety as well as a higher incidence of stomach ulcers. Not only can ulcers be prevented by signaled shock, but also the fear and anxiety created by uncertainty about future threatening events can be reduced. Subjects pre-

fer a shock that has a predictable warning signal over one that is unsignaled (Lockard, 1963). Rats prefer predictable shocks that are four times as long and three times as intense as unpredictable shocks (Badia, Culbertson, & Harch, 1973). Human subjects given a choice of advance information about either intensity or timing of the coming shock request temporal information more often than information about intensity (Jones, Bentler, & Petry, 1966). Subjects also want to take inevitable shocks immediately — to "get it over with" — rather than wait for a delayed shock (Gibbon, 1967; Knapp, Kause, & Perkins, 1959).

A recent study extends these basic findings about the consequences of both behavioral and perceptual control of the environment on physiological reactions in human subjects.

Male college volunteer subjects worked for half an hour on a demanding shock-avoidance task. To keep from being shocked, they had to press a start button, quickly respond by depressing the correct lever when one of a series of lights came on, and then immediately go through the next trial. Once every forty-five seconds, on the average, they missed at some point and received a painful shock. Their arousal to this stress was recorded by elevations in systolic blood pressure (arterial pressure during a heart contraction).

At first, twelve experimental subjects were given the opportunity to call for a time-out of one minute whenever they wanted it, while twelve yoked controls received the same time-out periods, but not upon request. Thus the only difference was in the cognition of one group that it controlled the avoidance response of calling for a time-out and of the other group that it did not. Over the course of the experiment, systolic blood pressure was consistently higher for the helpless subjects, indicating a higher level of arousal (and, presumably, stress). ◆

In a second part of the study (using different subjects), the rest period was preceded by a signal indicating that relief was on the way. The subjects again worked on the light-matching task, which was interrupted by a conditioned stimulus signaling that a time-out was thirty

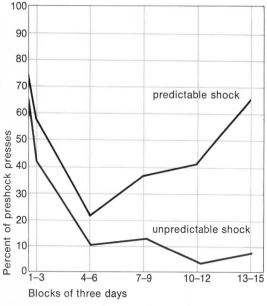

After Seligman, 1968

▲ CHRONIC FEAR
PRODUCED BY UNPREDICTABLE SHOCK

A base-line rate of bar pressing without shock was established; thereafter, this rate was regarded as 100 percent and the rates of bar pressing under predictable and unpredictable shock were plotted in terms of percents of the base rate. After an initial drop for both conditions when shock began, the subjects with predictable shock steadily increased their rate again.

seconds away. *The subjects had to continue working after the signal until the relief period started.*

Even though they were still being shocked as often and as intensely after the safety signal as before, and had no control over its occurrence, their knowledge gave them perceptual control and their blood pressure dropped markedly as soon as the signal appeared. When, in addition, they did *have control over the timing of the safety signal (both perceptual and behavioral control), the reduction in physiological stress was even greater though the number of signals and time-out periods remained unchanged (Hokanson, DeGood, Forrest, & Brittain, 1971).*

Superstitious control. All of these conditions that have been studied in the artificiality of psychology laboratories have their counterparts in our everyday lives. Helplessness is often related to superstitious attempts to control the environment. Superstitions flourish when individuals do not have control over their environment and yet are faced with risky decisions. While ideas on the value and function of superstitious behavior are speculative, the widespread popularity of superstition is not. In

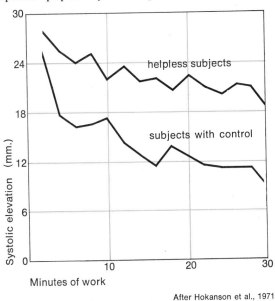

After Hokanson et al., 1971

◆ BEHAVIORAL CONTROL, HELPLESSNESS, AND SYSTOLIC BLOOD PRESSURE

learned helplessness we are dealing with connections between our responses, environmental outcomes, and the perception of controllability. We have seen that controllability prevents helplessness. What is surprising to consider, however, is that actual control is irrelevant. Instead it is simply the belief that one has control that matters.

In a study on urban stress and uncontrollability, it was demonstrated that subjects' belief that they could turn off an uncontrollable loud noise resulted in better performance on proofreading and problem-solving tasks than that of helpless subjects. Performance was also better when subjects believed that a person who could turn off the noise was accessible—even though the noise was not turned off (Glass & Singer, 1972).

This finding suggests a psychologically functional value for human superstition. Superstitions prevent learned helplessness by providing the superstitious person with an "illusion of control." (See *P&L* Close-up, p. 401.)

In Hiroto's (1974) study of learned helplessness in college students (see pp. 396–97), subjects who believed that the shuttlebox results were determined by chance were more helpless than subjects who were led to believe that the shuttlebox was a test of skill. In addition, by means of a personality test, subjects were divided according to their belief in internal or external origins of control. "Internals" believed that they had a high degree of control over the environment, while "externals" believed that environmental outcomes were largely independent of their responses. Externals became helpless more easily than internals in the shock test situation.

Belief in one's control of the environment and the perception that the results of a task are determined by one's own skill are important to prevent helplessness. An individual who believes only in fate will give up when faced with aversive conditions. To perceive one's own knowledge, skill, and action as being effective—even if this is "merely" a superstitious belief—will, while not altering the conditions, prevent the psychic consequences of helplessness: depression, lack of response initiation, and psychosomatic death.

On the other hand, when you accept a superstitious belief that there will be aversive consequences to not performing a specified behavior, you enter into an "open-ended bad-luck contract." It is impossible for it to be proven false, because there is no time limit for the bad luck to come your way—"maybe not today or tomorrow, but you'll see, eventually." Superstitions do not specify when or where the price of defiance will be paid. Consequently, the belief will always come true if you wait long enough for the payoff.

Retroactive therapy. If helplessness is not prevented, it can be alleviated by treatment that comes after it has been established. Such treatment after the problem has become manifest is called *retroactive therapy.* Hopelessness in the confined wild rats was eliminated simply by repeatedly immersing them in water for a few minutes and then freeing them. A few trials were sufficient to relearn "hope": after that they became aggressive again, tried to escape, and did not give up. It was found that the passive dogs in Seligman's studies could break out of the learned helplessness syndrome if they were forcibly dragged (perhaps as many as two hundred times) across from the shock compartment to the safe compartment to rediscover that responding could bring relief, and to develop self-initiated activity.

The symptoms of learned helplessness in these dogs bear a remarkable similarity to the psychiatric condition of human depression. Depression is the most prevalent psychiatric disorder in the United States today and its incidence is increasing. When the depression becomes chronic, it can lead to alcoholism, prolonged hospitalization, and sometimes suicide. In Chapters 11 and 12 we will discuss depression and its treatment more fully, but Seligman's research emphasizes the behavioral parallels (passivity, negativity, loss of energy) between the helpless dog and the depressed person, and it suggests that the cure for the depressed human being may be similar to that for the helpless dog—learning to become effective, to regain mastery over the environment, to rediscover that responses produce desired environmental consequences. This may mean a program of reshaping responding by having the person make only minimal responses that are always reinforced, then gradually increasing the complexity and vigor of the reinforced response until it is self-initiated.

Hope, Faith, and Placebos

If the phenomena of psychosomatic disorders, debilitation from stress, and learned helplessness represent the negative influence of the mind over the body, what is the evidence for its positive influence?

Faith, defined as belief despite absence of knowledge or impossibility of empirical validation, is the essential characteristic of religion and of religious healing. Absolute faith in the power of God can provide a powerful source of expectancy motivation. One study reported that 71 percent of Roman Catholic patients said their religious faith had helped them through a surgical crisis, and their records showed that they required appreciably smaller doses of morphine than patients of other religions (Egbert, 1969). Healing sects, such as Christian Science, and the shrines of miracle cures, such as Lourdes in France, attract millions of believers from all parts of the earth. There is ample, well-documented evidence that severe illnesses have been cured, that the lame have given up crutches and the blind have seen, after participation in religious-emotional pilgrimages to such spots (Cranston, 1955).

The existence of such cures, whether skeptically viewed as cures of the mind, or accepted as cures of organic illness, represents to the cured person genuine relief from a lifetime of real pain, incapacitation, and suffering. Our earlier discussion of pain and the complex interactions of mind and body shown in disease causation should indicate the difficulty in establishing whether pain is "real" or a bleeding ulcer is all in one's mind.

We moderns put our faith in medical doctors, in ritual visits to their offices, and in the pills they dispense. This faith is so strong that even when the pill or procedure administered is a *placebo* (has no medicinal value), the individual may nevertheless be relieved of the pain and other symptoms of illness. But how effective can a sugar pill really be?

In a survey of 4681 patients treated with placebos for over twenty ailments or symptoms, including colds, epilepsy, and multiple sclerosis, successful results were achieved in 27 percent of the cases (Haas, Fink, & Härtfelder, 1959). According to another report, headaches were shown to be relieved by placebos in 58 percent of 4588 cases. Overall, about one third of all patients treated with placebos in fifteen test series achieved positive results (Beecher, 1959).

Even pain from incurable organic illness was lessened. In studies comparing pain relief from

Close-up
**Superstitions As Cultural
Cognitive Control Mechanisms**

It is easy for psychologists to take too narrow a view of the origin and function of superstitions. In concentrating on how individuals learn superstitious habits, they may overlook the ways cultures transmit such habits to their members.

Superstitious rituals generate a sense of control. We can speculate that superstitious behavior will increase to the extent that people feel threatened, helpless, controlled, or without sufficient knowledge to make decisions that may be vital to their survival. In societies that operate on a subsistence level, depending on the vicissitudes of nature for the daily bread, fish, or game, superstitious charms and ritual behavior provide an illusion of control. There is at least something that the society can do to help tip the scales of fate, rather than passively waiting for the drought to end or the disease to abate.

In one tribe where hunting is the major source of food, someone must decide to stalk the prey during its migrating season. The herd does not

always take the same route, and waiting in the wrong place may result in no food for the tribe. Such crucial decisions entail too much responsibility for any one person, and answers are typically sought by superstitious practices. Bones may be cast on the ground and the pattern "read" as a message from the gods as to where to stalk the herd. If the hunters are unsuccessful, it is assumed the gods were displeased and thus some new behaviors must be enacted to regain their favor. So even when the response has no favorable consequences, it does result in some action—which helps to prevent or forestall helplessness.

Superstitious beliefs also help to explain unusual, unnatural events and discontinuities in one's life. If a healthy child becomes sick, it is assumed in many countries of the world that an "evil eye" has been cast on the child and it must be broken. Babies in Puerto Rico, Italy, and elsewhere often wear special colors and charms (often shaped like a horn) to avert the possibility of the evil eye. Sounds strange, but did you never "knock on wood" to avert "bad luck"?

The power of such beliefs ("superstitious" to some, but "religious" to believers) is illustrated by a recent occurrence in Hawaii. On November 21, 1973, a workman at the site of the Halawa stadium fell to his death—one more in a series of accidents at the construction site. Workmen recalled that in July 1971, the Reverend Abraham K. Akaka had refused to bless the stadium site because at that time several people living on the site had not been relocated by the state. Furthermore, a woman opposed to the stadium project had prayed in Hawaiian to old Hawaiian gods at the 1971 dedication. As a result, a number of workmen walked off the job.

A superstitious explanation had been discovered to account for the tragedy. If the accident had been caused by a curse, future accidents could be prevented by removing the curse and substituting a blessing. The woman was persuaded to retract her "curse," and the Reverend Mr. Akaka agreed to give the site of the stadium a full blessing, since housing had been found for the displaced residents. Satisfied, the workers returned to their jobs (*Honolulu Advertiser,* Nov. 24, 1973).

placebo and morphine injections for 122 patients with postoperative wound pain, 39 percent were relieved by placebos, while 67 percent were relieved by morphine. The chronic pain of cancer was relieved in 65 percent of the patients receiving a 10-mg. injection of morphine. But 10 mg. of placebo equally helped 42 percent of the cancer victims (Beecher, 1959).

Believing that a placebo will lead to pain reduction is thus sufficient to bring about major psychological (and perhaps physiological) reorganization. Such belief not only reduces pain but can even produce new "symptoms." Placebo-treated patients have complained of a wide range of "negative side effects" following administration of a placebo, including nausea, headaches, sleepiness, and reduced concentration.

Likewise, the patient's conviction can do more than make potent an inert drug: it can even *reverse* the usual pharmacological effect of a medicine. Ipecac, which is normally used to induce vomiting (for example, in cases of poisoning) "had healing effects on patients with nausea of pregnancy when it was suggested to them that they were receiving a good preparation" (Haas et al., 1959, p. 27).

Positive placebo reaction is a "problem" precisely because placebos work so well when they are not supposed to. How can the effectiveness of a "real" drug or treatment procedure be tested when people are so ready to respond to their expectations instead of to the physical properties of the treatment?

It is instructive to note the characteristics that distinguish placebo reactors from nonreactors. Those whose postoperative pain was relieved by placebos tended to be regular churchgoers, talkative, anxious, dependent, self-centered, and preoccupied with their internal bodily processes. Nonreactors tended to be withdrawn, rigid, and intellectually critical rather than emotionally responsive (Lasagna et al., 1954).

In general, when those who believe in the doctor's recommendations and have faith in authority are given a placebo, they experience a reduction in their *anxiety* over the illness and with it, pain relief and improved healing. Since even the most rationally critical, intellectually skeptical person may retain some of the "irrational" beliefs of childhood, everyone is potentially a placebo reactor.

Cognitive Control of Motivation

A hungry Fox saw some fine bunches of grapes hanging on a high trellis in a vineyard. He tried and tried to reach them by jumping as high as he could; but all his efforts were in vain, for the grapes were out of his reach. Finally, tired from his efforts, he left the vineyard. With an air of unconcern he said, *"I really wasn't very hungry. Besides, I thought those grapes were ripe, but I can see now they are sour."*

Aesop, "The Fox and the Grapes," Sixth century B.C.

Did the Fox say he wasn't hungry in an attempt to rationalize away his heightened drive state? Or did he, in fact, effectively reduce his hunger drive by some cognitive process? When we do not get what we want (or need), have to postpone gratification or endure some unpleasant, aversive, or deprivation state, we can control the impact of biological and environmental stimuli by exercising cognitive control. Thinking can make it so, and cognitions can make it otherwise. Human beings need not react to the situation as it is given to them; they may, through their imaginative powers, *define* the situation to make it fit their needs, values, and motives.

To test this basic idea, a number of studies were conducted in the social psychology laboratories at New York University, Duke, and Ohio State. Well over a thousand subjects were put in a variety of situations where intense biological drives (hunger, thirst, pain) or strong social motives (achievement, approval, frustration, aggression) were aroused in them. The debilitating effects of these motivational states on behavior and physiological functioning were recorded. Then subjects were asked to take more of the same or agree to be subjected to even more extreme arousal.

In some conditions subjects agreed to go on after being given considerable justification (money, social pressure, or good reasons) for doing so. In other conditions, subjects agreed to go on after being given a *choice* to do so or to quit, and only minimal justification.

In which of these conditions do you think the second set of motivational arousal had the *least* impact? Those who committed themselves to go on under pressure and with high justification suffered the same as they had in the first phase of the studies. However, those subjects who had voluntarily agreed to undergo an unpleasant experience with only minimal justification for doing so, cognitively controlled the impact of the second stimulation phase of the study. The shocks did not hurt as much as they did the first time; the subjects were less thirsty and hungry, less aggressive, more able to tolerate frustration and failure, and so on. They not only said so and acted so, but at a physiological level, these low-justification subjects were not reacting as intensely to the motivational stimulus. It is as if they persuaded themselves that it would not be so bad, and lo and behold, they were right. Motivation was brought in line with the behavioral commitment. After all, it would be "crazy" to agree to take painful shocks for no good reason when one had a choice to leave, wouldn't it? However, it would not be inconsistent if you convinced yourself that the shocks would not hurt much. Indeed, the same voltage shocks hurt these subjects less than they hurt the no-choice, high-justification controls (Zimbardo, 1969).

Thus it now becomes possible to argue that cognitive control processes can impose consistency where it is lacking, even if that requires changing the usual relationship between a physical stimulus and the body's reaction to it. But how far can we push the notion of cognitive control?

Cognitive Control of Death

In a society with the accent on youth, what does it mean to be old? At best, the aged are tolerated; more typically they are ignored, made to feel useless and a burden to their family. Approximately one of every ten Americans is over sixty-five, and the proportion increases as life

expectancy is prolonged. Two thirds of these individuals suffer from some chronic condition such as high blood pressure, heart trouble, or arthritis. Increasingly, they are being abandoned to care by nursing homes, of which there are about 30,000 in this country. "It's rather like condemning old cars to the scrap heap," commented Charles Boucher, senior medical officer in the British Ministry of Health.

What are the consequences to the aged individual forced by his or her family to enter an old-age home?

In one carefully documented study of forty people whose applications were received by a nursing home in Cleveland, Ohio, twenty-three died within a month of mailing the application. It turned out that of those who died, the vast majority were applicants whose families had made application for them, as compared with those who had made the application themselves (Ferrare, 1962).

This study suggests an important relationship between the perception of choice to enter the home and the "sudden death" phenomenon discussed earlier. It seems probable that extreme helplessness would be common among people who feel they have no alternative but to leave their own homes and enter a strange, hopeless environment, with no ties to the past, an uncertain present, and the worst expectations about the future. In contrast, a comparable group of people who believed that they still retained freedom of choice, that they did not have to go to the home if they did not want to, would be more able to restructure their environment cognitively to make it liveable. Support for this line of reasoning comes from another finding—one of the most dramatic in our psychological literature—by the same investigator.

After each of fifty-five female applicants to the home was interviewed, they were classified into one group of seventeen who perceived they had no choice but to go to the home, and one group of thirty-eight who perceived that they did have other alternatives even though they were going to the home. Within ten weeks of being admitted to the home all but one woman in the no-choice group had died. In sharp contrast, all but one of the choice group were still living. Examination of the medical records revealed there were no medical health differences between the women in these two groups upon admission to the institution (Ferrare, 1962).

If it is the exercise of choice that is the independent variable accelerating or retarding death, then by providing a perception of choice, it should be possible to prolong life. Even for those who have no "real" choice about entering the home, a series of minimal choices might be presented, such as which day to enter, which floor to be housed on, which of several activities to engage in, and so on. If perceived helplessness results in death, then manipulating the environment to create an "illusion of choice" and mastery through decision making should delay death or promote life.

Such a study has just been done — with remarkable results (Langer & Rodin, 1976). Ninety-one patients in a Connecticut nursing home were randomly assigned to an experimental group in which they were given the freedom to make simple choices and some responsibility (for taking care of a plant). In the comparison group, the staff made all decisions and were responsible for caring for the patients' plants. In every other way, both groups were treated identically. As predicted, the sense of cognitive control induced by the experimental treatment showed up in significant improvement in alertness, active participation, and general sense of well-being. A follow-up conducted a year and a half later revealed the profound power of such cognitive control; compared to the no-choice subjects, only half as many of the patients in the experimental group had died!

The existentialist philosopher Jean-Paul Sartre (1957) has said that "man makes himself" and "through his choice he involves all mankind, and he cannot avoid making a choice." Unless the helpless, hopeless person can be provided with more meaningful alternatives, his or her final choice may be death. Unless society provides its citizens with more meaningful options, the quality of social life deteriorates.

Chapter Summary

Human beings have long been intrigued by the puzzle of the nonphysical "mind" in the physical body. At one extreme, mind and soul have been seen as the fundamental and lasting reality; at the other, as in American behaviorism, their existence has been almost totally ignored. This picture is changing, however.

Emotion, difficult to define objectively, has been the object of much study. This has tended, however, to dwell on its disruptive or negative aspects.

We judge emotion in others to a large extent on the basis of their nonverbal behavior; much of the overt behavior in emotion is learned in accordance with cultural norms and expectations. Darwin suggested that some patterns of emotional expression are innate in both animals and humans. The meaning of such expressions, however, may vary from culture to culture. Simple emotions can be judged with some accuracy and agreement, even across cultures, but the same behavior, like crying, may appear in several different emotions. Sometimes we receive contradictory or ambiguous cues, and we tend to rely heavily on situational indicators.

According to the *James-Lange theory,* physiological events precede and cause the felt emotion, but there has been mixed success in finding specific visceral reactions associated with the different emotions. Recent research on physiological factors in emotion has centered on the role of *neural mechanisms* (particularly the *limbic system*) and certain *endocrine glands* (particularly the *pituitary* and the *adrenal glands*). *Epinephrine (adrenaline)* is a *hormone* that appears to be associated with fear reactions, while *norepinephrine (noradrenaline)* is associated with anger.

Physiological cues probably contribute to the *intensity* of felt emotions, but their *quality* —

which emotion is felt — depends partly on *cognitive cues* from the individual's interpretation of the situation. Elaborate studies by Schachter and Singer have upheld this theory, but a number of methodological flaws in their research have been pointed out. *Appraisal,* both of the meaning and seriousness of a situation and of possible coping strategies, is clearly important in determining the emotion felt.

Stress is the body's response to environmental demands, positive or negative. It is an inevitable part of life, and one we must learn to cope with rather than try to avoid. Chronic stress due to unrelenting pressure or pent-up emotions may lead to *psychosomatic illness* or increased susceptibility to infection. There is a clear association between *life crisis scores* and health problems. Emotional factors may also impede recovery from illness.

The body's reaction to stress may be explained in terms of the *general adaptation syndrome*, which consists of an *alarm (emergency) reaction,* a *stage of resistance,* and a *stage of exhaustion.*

Opportunity for *cognitive appraisal* increases our ability to cope with even highly threatening situations. Even negative emotion can be adaptive. Patients who experience moderate fear before an operation undergo less stress and recover faster than those who have either high or low fear before the operation. Warnings of danger that produce only moderate fear are more conducive to action than warnings that make people more fearful. Clear guidelines for coping action and an attitudinal change also make warnings more effective. People exposed to predictable danger, as in parachute jumping, may learn to handle their fear in complex indirect ways.

Pain serves as both a *signal* system and a *defensive* (reflex) system, protecting the organism from physical harm. The cognitive aspects of pain are complex, involving perceptual coping style, learned associations, and cognitive modification of sensory input. There are wide cultural differences in response to surgical pain, associated with different interpretations of

it. Under hypnosis, considerable cognitive control of pain can be achieved. Deviant uses of pain include the use of pain as torture or as a source of mystical union or sexual pleasure.

A belief that one has no control over one's environment can lead to "giving up" and eventually to death, even in previously healthy individuals. Such emotionally caused deaths may occur in prison camps or in response to voodoo curses. Many cultures do not distinguish between physical and mental diseases or between natural and supernatural causes. In voodoo or similar deaths, extreme fright may lead to an outpouring of adrenaline, leading to a state of shock, or the mechanism may involve an overstimulation of the parasympathetic nervous system. Laboratory and clinical studies point to the role of *hopelessness* and *helplessness* in setting this mechanism into action.

It has been suggested that feelings of *competence* and mastery over the environment are basic to survival; feelings of helplessness lead to passive resignation in both humans and animals. Research has demonstrated, however, that such helplessness may be prevented or cured in several ways: (1) *immunization,* or prior experiences of mastery; (2) *predictability* of unavoidable painful events; (3) *superstition* — perception of control where it does not actually exist; and (5) *retroactive therapy,* or retraining in situations where hope and control are possible.

Just as belief that one will die can bring death to a healthy person, belief that one will recover can bring remission of physical symptoms. Even in incurable illness a *placebo* can be effective in relieving pain. Belief can even reverse the usual effect of a drug. People who respond readily to placebos differ in some personality characteristics from nonreactors.

Feelings of predictability and control are enhanced through perceptions of *consistency* in a situation; to achieve such perceptions, we may impose consistency by *cognitive control,* producing changes in our own motives, feelings, attitudes, and even biological states like hunger. For older people who feel they have lost control over their lives and have no choices left, even death may represent a final act of cognitive control — the ultimate choice.

RESEARCH FRONTIER

Reversing Depression and Learned Helplessness
Martin E. P. Seligman University of Pennsylvania

Helplessness, when induced in humans in a laboratory setting by unsolvable problems or inescapable noise, results in many of the same symptoms as naturally occurring depression. We have found that both psychologically depressed college students and helpless subjects passively accept noise without attempting to escape, fail to solve anagrams, have trouble seeing patterns in trying to solve problems, devalue their own effectiveness on tasks of skill, and show a "blue" mood. I believe that we can use these striking parallels to find out through laboratory research what therapies actually work to reverse depression. Before making the argument, I want to review a few therapies which may help depression, and which follow from a view of depression based on the concept of learned helplessness.

There is no cure-all for depression: left alone, it often dissipates in a few weeks or months. There are, however, therapies that are thought to alleviate depression and that are also consistent with the theory of learned helplessness. According to this theory, the central goal in successful therapy should be to have the patient come to believe that his or her responses produce the desired results — that he or she is, in short, an effective human being.

Therapies may be successful in alleviating depression insofar as they provide the patient with control over important outcomes. The "Tuscaloosa Plan" of a Veterans Administration hospital in Alabama sends severely depressed patients to an "anti-depression room." In this room patients are subjected to a regime of "kind firmness": They are told to sand a block of wood, and then reprimanded for sanding against the grain. They then sand with the grain, and are told that is not right. Then they are told to begin counting about a million little seashells scattered about the room. This systematic harassment continues until the individual finally tells the aide "Get off my back!" or

says something like, "I've counted my last seashell." The patient is then promptly let out of the room with apologies. Thus the patients are forced to make one of the most powerful responses people have for controlling others: *anger,* and when this response is dragged out of their depleted repertoire, they are powerfully reinforced. This tactic may break up depression — lastingly.

In assertiveness-training therapy, the patient actively rehearses making assertive social responses, while the therapist plays the role of the domineering boss or husband who is being told off or the hen-pecking wife who repents her ways and asks forgiveness. Here, too, the patient makes responses that have powerful outcomes. It probably benefits mildly depressed people to return faulty merchandise to department stores, or to ring the bell at the meat counter to get exactly the cut they want.

Gradual exposure to the response-reinforcement contingencies of work reinforces active responses, and may be effective against depression. In a graded-task treatment of depression, Elaine Burgess first had her patients emit some minimal bit of behavior, like making a telephone call. She emphasizes that it is crucial that the patient succeed, rather than just start and give up. The task requirements were then increased, and the patient was reinforced for successfully completing the task by the attention and interest of the therapist. Incidentally, Burgess and others have pointed to the role of "secondary gain" in depression: depressives are often alleged to "use" their symptoms instrumentally to gain sympathy, affection, and attention. By lying in bed all day and crying, rather than going to work, a depressed man may cause his philandering wife to pay more attention to him, and may even win her back. Secondary gain is annoying, and it is tempting during therapy to try to remove the rewards that maintain it. But caution is in order here: secondary gain may explain the persistence or maintenance of some depressive behaviors, but it does not explain how they *began.* The theory of helplessness suggests that failure to respond actively originates in the patient's perception that he or she cannot control outcomes. So a depressed patient's passivity can have two sources: (1) patients can be passive for instrumental reasons, since staying depressed brings them sympathy, love, and attention; and (2) patients can be passive because they believe that no response they can make will be effective in controlling the environment. Comparing the first to the second, one might conclude that secondary gain, while a practical hindrance to therapy, is a hopeful sign in depression: it means that there is at least some response (even a passive one) that the patient believes he or she can effectively perform. Steven Maier found that dogs whose passivity was reinforced by shock termination were not nearly as helpless as dogs for whom no form of responding had any effect upon shock termination. Similarly, patients who use their depression as a way of controlling others may have a better prognosis than those who have given up.

My colleagues and I have used a graded-task treatment like that of Burgess on 24 hospitalized depressives. These patients were given verbal tasks of gradually increasing difficulty in a one-hour session, and were praised upon successful completion of each task. First they were asked to read a paragraph aloud. Then they were asked to read a new paragraph aloud, with expression. They were asked to read yet another with expression and interpret it in their own words; then reading aloud with expression, plus interpretation and arguing for the author's point of view. At the top of the hierarchy, the patients were asked to choose one of three topics and given an extemporaneous speech. All patients completed the speech. (Anyone who has worked with hospitalized depressives knows they do not usually make extemporaneous speeches.) Nineteen of the 24 showed substantial, immediate elevation in mood as measured by a self-rating mood scale. Although we did not observe how long the improvement lasted, the comment of one smiling patient was illuminating: "You know, I used to be a debater in high school and I had forgotten how good I was."

Training in decision making may be important in curing depression. Depressed patients often have trouble making decisions, even trivial ones such as what clothes to wear. One can learn to make decisions in a manner similar to the graded task assignment. The patient's first assignment is to make a minor decision; e.g., what TV program to watch. As the patient feels comfortable making decisions at this level, weightier and weightier decisions are required until the patient learns to make important decisions more comfortably.

It is easy to overlook the fact that depressed people often have social deficits. They don't know how to tell jokes, how to ask for a date, how to assert themselves when taken advantage of. Social skills can be taught. Personal effectiveness training probably works in depression because it provides the patient with new responses which control important sources of social gratification.

Insight-oriented therapies, such as psychoanalysis, may work by helping the patient acknowledge, and thus become free from, the conditions that have led to hopelessness. Depression subsides when goals that were for some reason unrealizable appear to come within reach, or are substantially modified, or are replaced by goals that can be achieved. Thus successful insight therapy involves bringing about a fundamental change in attitude toward the future, freeing the individual to set realizable goals and plan effective strategies for reaching them.

A warning is in order about all psychological forms of therapy for depression, however. In severe depression, the patient is often so withdrawn that social skills training, cognitive therapy, graded tasks, etc., will have no impact at all. The patient just won't care about the goals. Such severe depressions (most of which probably have physiological rather than psychological bases) should be treated with antidepressant drugs or electroconvulsive shock. Such physical therapies will probably alleviate the major depressive symptoms. Once those profound symptoms are reduced and the patient becomes communicative, psychological treatments are in order.

Many other therapies, from psychoanalysis to T-groups, claim to be able to cure depression. But we do not yet have sufficient evidence from well-controlled studies to evaluate the effectiveness of any form of psychotherapy for depression. The evidence I have presented is selective: only a few of those treatments that seem compatible with help-lessness were discussed. It is possible that when other therapies work it is because they, too, restore the patient's sense of efficacy. What is needed now is experimental evidence isolating the effective variable in the psychological treatment of depression. We are now in a position to do this.

There are two problems to be overcome in order to do an adequate study on what therapies work in depression: dissipation in time and "demand characteristics."

Depression, fortunately, is usually a self-limiting state. It dissipates in time. Most depressions of psychological origins fade as the events that set them off become more remote. What your grand-mother told you about "time healing all wounds" is largely true. Take people who lose their jobs, for instance: some people are happy (they don't count), others become sad for a few days, others for weeks, some for months. This is an important fact for a depressed patient to know, since during a depression it often seems as if the mood will last forever. It is, however, an inconvenient fact for re-searchers studying the effectiveness of therapy. In order to test therapy X, a researcher needs a con-trol group which does not receive therapy X but is looked at before and after the same length of time as therapy X lasts. Many untreated depressions will dissipate during that time period, and no signifi-cant differences will be seen between therapy X and the untreated control group.

The other problem about finding out what thera-pies actually work in depression is what has been termed the *demand characteristics* of research studies. Subjects (or patients) who are asked by an authority figure to participate in a research study often want to be "good" subjects. Those who figure out what the experimenter's hypothesis is (and who like the experimenter) may try to confirm it. In therapy studies, the measures usually used to assess depression are very obvious ones, easily subject to such demand characteristics (e.g., "Do you feel sad?") A subject who likes the therapist may be biased toward saying "yes," and so distort the actual results of treatment.

David Klein has done the first in a series of studies that overcome both these problems, and may tell us from laboratory experiments what therapies reverse depression. Recall that nonde-pressed persons made helpless in the laboratory display the same set of symptoms as depressed people who walk into the laboratory and are given no pretreatment: failure to escape noise, distortion of expectancy for success in skilled tests, failure to solve anagrams, failure to see patterns, as well as low mood. Except for the last, these deficits are not very subject to demand characteristics. Subjects do not readily perceive that the experimenter ex-pects them to sit with their hand in the noise shut-tlebox and fail to escape. In addition, depressed and helpless subjects can be tested immediately, before the symptoms have had time to dissipate. Any therapy that can be miniaturized and brought into the laboratory can be given for an hour to de-pressed and helpless subjects. We can then look at the five deficits and see if the miniaturized therapy reverses them.

Klein carried out the pioneering study on revers-ing helplessness and depression. Groups of non-depressed people made helpless with inescapable noise and depressed people later failed to escape noise and showed distorted skill expectations. Other groups of helpless and depressed people re-ceived "success" therapy. They were given cogni-tive problems which they could successfully solve. As the helplessness view of depression predicts, mastering the cognitive problems broke up the noise escape deficits and the expectation distor-tions.

The extension of a therapy procedure effective in the laboratory to psychotherapy for depression need not involve great conceptual leaps. In Klein's experiments, solvable problems were an effective therapy for helplessness. We do not propose that a therapist take cognitive discrimination problems and give them to depressed patients. We do sug-gest giving the patient solvable problems which he or she considers important. For example, we can present a fired accountant with problems from an accounting textbook on which he or she can suc-ceed (if the patient is depressed about *being* an accountant and not an actor, however, such prob-lems are clearly inappropriate). The identification of tasks that are important to the patient will not only make success more satisfying, it will help get the depressed patient to make an initial effort to do something, a very laborious process in many cases. Once the problems are generated, they will be given to the patient one at a time, perhaps in increasing order of difficulty, so that success at each stage is more likely.

I believe that Klein's research design will enable us to determine what therapies will actually work with depressed patients. Any potential therapy that is miniaturizable can be given to our subjects: assertiveness training, anger expression, relaxation, drugs. Those therapies that break up deficits in laboratory performance are likely to work in the clinic; those that do not are likely to be ineffective.

A final remark should be made concerning the types of depression to which our therapy studies and the helplessness model are most applicable. The classification of depression is confusing and controversial: process/reactive, neurotic/psychotic, and unipolar/bipolar are but a few of the attempted subdivisions. This difficult question needs empirical research. Our studies divide college students into depressed and nondepressed groups by the Beck Depression Inventory. This measuring device lumps affective, behavioral, cognitive, and somatic symptoms together to yield a single severity score. A scale of this sort does not map neatly onto any of the distinctions proposed with depression. Further research of the type described above can tell us whether those individuals displaying primarily affective, behavioral, cognitive, or somatic symptoms are best understood as "helplessness" depressions and respond best to any particular therapy. Similarly, by dividing depressed subjects into any of the proposed subdivisions, we could ascertain which subtypes are best seen as helplessness depressives, and which respond to particular therapies. I believe that helplessness will not correspond perfectly with any preexisting subgroup of depression. If the model is valid, changes in diagnostic labeling might be in order. Certain depressives who display passivity, negative cognitive set, and other symptoms of learned helplessness, and whose disorder began with a loss of control over important events, might usefully be classified as "helplessness depressives." These depressives might be specifically responsive to therapies validated in studies of the sort we are doing. Other depressives, who do not display such symptoms or history, might be specifically responsive to other therapies.

At any rate, it seems possible that we shall know in the next decade what therapies reverse depression caused by helplessness, and with them alleviate the intolerable suffering which leads many depressives to self-defeating patterns and some even to suicide.

PART 5
Personality, Pathology, and Treatment

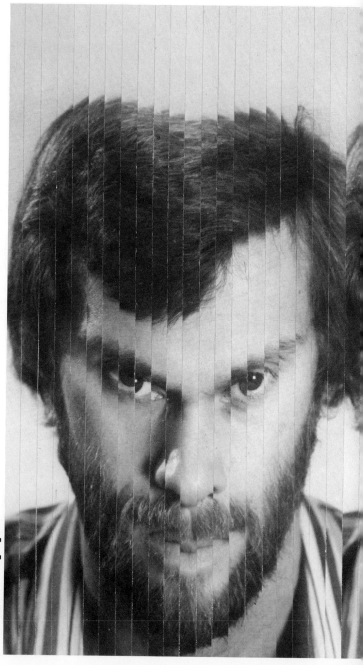

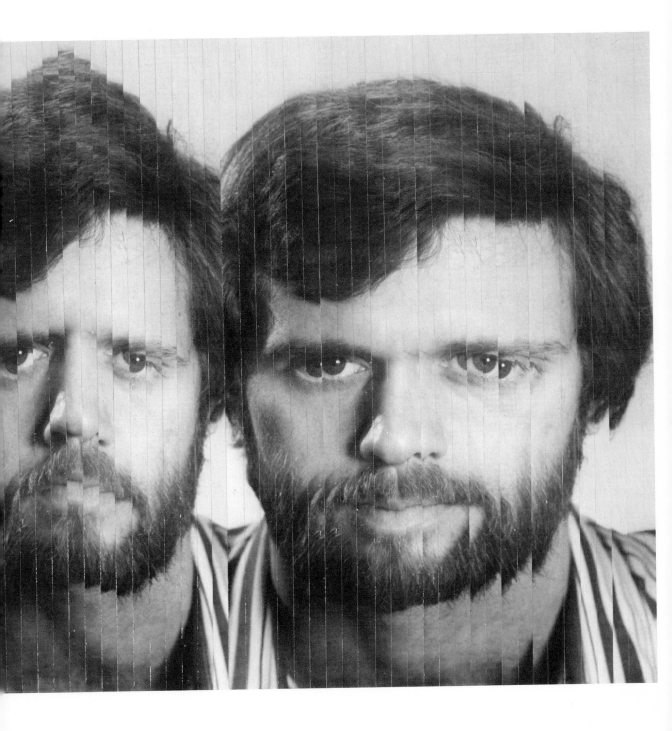

10

Personality Theory and Assessment

"Was I surprised when my classmates at James Monroe High School elected me for the title of 'Jimmie Monroe'! That meant I had the best *personality in the whole school . . . well, that is, best among the senior boys ('Janie Monroe' was the girl counterpart). It was the first contest I had ever won, and I didn't have to do anything for it—no boxtops, no tests—I just had to be* me. *That was easy enough because on those occasions when I tried to be someone else it always came out me.*

"Of course, it felt good to have the best personality, but I would have gladly traded it for my fantasy of being able to change personalities any time I wanted—like mild-mannered Clark Kent with his telephone booth number—in like a sissy, out like Superman. Or even flip-flopping between Dr. Jekyll and Mr. Hyde. Or what about The Three Faces of Eve? *Wouldn't three completely different personalities be better than one always-the-same personality?*

"People could 'psych me out' too easily; they knew 'where I was coming from.' People liked me because I was 'out front.' They felt at ease around me, like with an old pair of slippers, or an 'oldies but goodies' favorite rock 'n roll record. I could be counted on. I was reliable. I could be taken at my word. 'You're a boy of your word,' the cop on the beat would say. In my yearbook my girlfriend even wrote: 'I can't count in Latin/I can't count in Greek/I can't count in Zulu/But I can count on you.' I was just too consistent, as predictable as the sun rising in the east.

"What made it most delightful to have the Number One personality was that curiously only a year before when I was a junior at North Hollywood High School, I had practically no friends, no dates, and, I had assumed, no personality either. The kids thought I was a New York sharpie with a funny name, and to make matters worse, I had no wheels. I felt rejected, became shy for the first time in my life, and began to prefer reading to wasting time talking to other people. 'Personality is a bummer' was my favorite bit of graffiti.

"But as my sister says, 'You can't keep a good personality down,' and my naturally 'best' personality couldn't be suppressed. I guess I just

kept it under wraps until I got back to New York where it could be better appreciated. Over the years being Jimmie Monroe has been a source of constant comfort because you know that even if you were in a horrible motorcycle accident that totally disfigured you, people could always say, 'He may not be a good looker, but he really does have a nice personality.'"

Popular usage, as in the above account, makes "personality" something akin to "attractiveness," "charm," "forcefulness," or "charisma." It is a quality movie stars and those politicians we like have a lot of, while the rest of us must make do with less. As psychologists use the word *personality*, however, it has a more neutral universal meaning, being "what characterizes an individual." Or, put more formally, personality is "the sum total of the ways in which [an individual] characteristically reacts to and interacts with others" and with objects (Ferguson, 1970, p. 2).

Even as a child, you had probably developed and put to use your own system of appraising the personality of yourself and others. It was of vital importance to be able to distinguish between friends and foes, to judge the temperamental moods of siblings and parents, to size up and "psych out" competitors, and to determine your own strengths and weaknesses. Your judgments were, in fact, primitive personality assessments. Each one of us operates, day in and day out, on the basis of what we might call *naive personality theories*. In constructing these theories, we use much the same sources of information that are used by psychologists in constructing sophisticated personality theories. These sources include information on personal history, current behavior patterns, habits, interests, attitudes, and future goals or aspirations. The chief difference is that our naive, informal theories are based largely on intuition and guesswork, while personality theorists have developed objective procedures and measuring instruments on which to base their personality judgments. A wide range of individuals, such as pool hustlers, con artists, and fortune-tellers, depend heavily on the use of naive personality theories for their livelihood.

"By trial and error, by shrewd observation of men, many fortune-tellers have worked out long since many of the great truths that official psychology has only just discovered. Before Freud, the soothsayers knew that little boys are often jealous of their fathers; before Adler, they recognized that a brash manner usually conceals a sense of inferiority. As the alchemist preceded the chemist, the herb doctor the druggist, and the midwife the obstetrician, so the average 'mind reader' anticipates in technique and knowledge the psychiatrist. He is, in fact, the psychiatrist of the poor; and when he is clever enough he sometimes becomes the psychiatrist of the rich as well." (Gresham, 1949, p. 59)

Such an individual is a skilled pseudoprofessional who operates on the basis of a naive personality theory built upon observational acuity, a knowledge of human nature, and considerable *chutzpah* (nerve). The basic tools of the trade include an ability to classify people quickly on the basis of age, appearance, marital status, and so on, and a shrewd knowledge of what kind of problems a given type of individual is most likely to have.

Uniqueness and Consistency: Key Problems for Personality Theory

Vital to any discussion of personality are two conceptually related questions:

a) What makes people behave alike?

b) What makes people behave differently?

The first question seeks to determine the minimal number of conditions, factors, and variables that can account for the reactions that members of the human species show in common. The second question seeks to account for the observed differences in the behavior of different individuals in response to apparently the same situation. Here the problem is to explain individual uniqueness, the variability in response that is not attributable to the stimulus situation.

On the one hand, then, the study of personality is indistinguishable from the broad study of psychology, which is an attempt to understand the *totality* of human behavior. In addition, however, the personality theorist has a special interest in trying to understand why people's behavior still differs after all of the known environmental factors have been specified.

How Different Is Normal?

A common misconception perpetuated by newspaper advice columnists is that normal human beings function pretty much alike. Moreover, to be normal, one *ought* to be functioning like others who are in some way comparable (of similar age, sex, or education, for example). Parents worried that their baby has not yet begun to walk are told the age at which the "normal" baby does, while adolescents are told when it is "normal" to begin dating according to surveys of when the "average" teenager does.

The myth of the normal, average, human function was dispelled in a thorough analysis by Williams (1956) showing the enormous range of variation in the location, size, and operation of internal human organs. Nearly every organ is several times larger in some normal individuals than in other individuals equally normal. For example, some stomachs hold six to eight times as much as others. Similarly, examinations of 182 normal young men revealed heart rates ranging from 45 to 105 beats per minute. Normal pumping capacities range from 3.15 to 11.9 quarts per minute. Similar differences are reported in neural structure, chemical composition and activity, and reactions to drugs and various stimuli.

When such an array of physiological differences is added to the infinite variety of life experiences individuals have, it is no wonder that there is such diversity of human behavior, even among people in the same situation. These differences among individuals are hindrances to researchers looking for general laws, and are usually either overcome by studying powerful stimuli in simple situations or averaged out by combining the varied responses of a large number of subjects. Most personality theorists, however, take a quite different view of this "problem." What makes people behave as individuals is looked on not as a problem to get rid of, but as *the* problem to be studied.

This does not mean that psychologists working in personality are not interested in finding general laws. As in other areas of psychology, many personality theorists believe that eventually psychologists will discover principles that can be applied to all human beings. But in personality theory the principles must also be able to account for differences among people. Not all personality theories emphasize individual differences, but all must be able to account for them. They must be able to say what makes one person different from another, what makes one person behave consistently in different situations, and what makes people either remain the same or change over a period of time.

Personality As Consistency

Just what *does* characterize an individual? Without really thinking about it, we are able to recognize our friends, even if we have not seen them for some time. If we know people well enough, we are even able to recognize them from someone else's account of their behavior. ("Oh, that must have been Jim. He always does things like that.") How are we able to do it? The key seems to lie in *consistency*. We are able to recognize individuals, and to characterize them to others, by the ways they are consistent. Even if they are consistently unpredictable, that is something we can say about them that distinguishes them from less mercurial folk.

But the matter is more complex. Try the following test. Think about two people who are important in your life—one you like and one you do not like. Is either one primarily "good" (strong, kind, understanding) or primarily "bad" (weak, cruel, inconsiderate)? Or does it depend on the circumstances? Now think about yourself and answer those two questions.

Most often, the results of this simple experiment are to discover that we see other people we know well as quite consistently either good or bad irrespective of the situation, while we see ourselves as more influenced by circumstances and thus more variable. This paradox highlights our need to attribute consistency to the behavior of others and to formulate consistent patterns of responses and traits when we characterize others.

This tendency to perceive consistency in other people is an extension of a more general tendency to perceive consistency in all events, part of a general process of organizing our world in such a way as to make it coherent, orderly, and more readily predictable. Thus we must raise the question of whether the consistency we perceive in people, around which theories about personality traits are organized, actually exists in the people observed or only in the minds of naive observers and sophisticated personality theorists. (See *P&L* Close-up, pp. 411–12.)

Personality theorists differ markedly in how they describe this consistency and in the ways they try to account for it. In this chapter, we shall first consider a number of these different ways of thinking about what personality is. We shall then go on to look at the complicated process of personality assessment—how tests and other devices are used in an attempt to measure and reduce to numbers and labels what the theorists are theorizing about.

"Seems to Me People Are Pretty Consistent, By and Large"

It certainly seems to be the better part of common sense that people can be characterized according to some dominant traits that they exhibit across different situations. We all know "gregarious" people, "shy" ones, "honest" ones, "impulsive males," "dependent females," and so forth. Despite our confidence in the reliability of such intuitions, there is considerable research evidence accumulating that suggests our intuitions are just plain wrong.

Here we have an intriguing paradox: on the one hand our naive view is in accord with the basic assumption of most theories of personality—namely, there *is* consistency in personality from one situation to another. What personality theories are all about is the explanation of the whys and hows of that individual consistency. On the other hand, systematic research that tries to predict behavior of the person in a given situation from personality-trait scores or from his or her behavior in different situations shows rather poor predictability. A resolution of these discrepant views may come from analyzing the reasons why we (and personality theorists) might see consistency existing *within* individuals to a greater extent than it actually does.

There are at least ten good reasons why our intuition tells us that what we believe is true of a person in one situation holds for all or most situations (adapted from Bem & Allen, 1974).

1. We each carry around an "implicit personality theory" by which we link observed behavior to inferred traits and then predict to other unobserved behaviors. Such theories encourage us to fill in missing observations of what *is* with what *ought to be*—according to our theory of personality. In addition, we overgeneralize from available evidence of areas where there is some consistency (such as in intellectual ability or cognitive style) to areas of the person where consistency is not really present.

2. We rely too heavily on a language of traits to describe human behavior, having over 18,000 trait names in our vocabulary. We tend to *think*

in terms of the language we have at our disposal—in terms of traits rather than situations.

3. Perhaps the reason we have such an over-abundance of individual trait terms is the emphasis both in psychology and in our society on the individual. We tend to locate "problems" in people rather than in situations. This results in a tendency to label people according to their "problem," and the label often sticks.

4. We underestimate subtle situational forces that may produce different reactions in different people. We especially ignore the situational impact when it affects others but not us.

5. We usually see certain people only in a limited number of situations (sometimes only one, as with teachers and students in school) and generalize our observations to other unobserved situations.

6. Often others will behave the way they think we want them to, thus exaggerating how consistent they appear to us (but sometimes they act quite differently for another observer).

7. Most of us are free to choose the situations we enter, and we enter those we predict that we will feel comfortable in and can handle. Those situations tend to be familiar ones, where the opportunities for new stimulation, conflict, or challenge are limited. It is no wonder that we act consistently in situations we have chosen for the sake of their constancy.

8. Our judgments of others often come not from what we observe them doing but from what they tell us they do. Such self-reports are often biased.

9. Our first impressions bias us strongly, and subsequent evaluations are reinterpreted so as to fit in with the original "true" view. Once established, a belief needs little evidence to support it, but much to refute it.

10. We tend to see consistency where it is not because we have come to equate consistency with goodness, reliability, stability, and so on. As Mark Twain put it: "There are those who would misteach us that to stick in a rut is consistency—and a virtue, and that to climb out of the rut is inconsistency—and a vice." ("Consistency," 1923)

Ways of Thinking About Personality

Only a few of the many systematic personality theories can be presented here. Those that we have chosen represent four basic ways of conceptualizing what personality is. Most of these imply or specify a particular explanation for what happens when something goes wrong and adjustment difficulties appear. Thus specific methods of therapy have been developed in connection with many of these theories; they will be discussed in Chapter 12.

Freud and His Followers:
Consistency As the Outcome of a Battle

Toward the end of the nineteenth century, in the aftermath of Darwin's powerful reminder that human beings and animals have much in common, many psychologists tried to explain consistency in individual behavior by talking about "instincts." If a person went around hitting other people, it might be because of an inborn "instinct of pugnacity." If someone was miserly, it was a "hoarding instinct." Yet, this sort of explanation did not work out very well. If psychologists had a new kind of behavior they wanted to explain, they had only to postulate a new instinct, which left them with a new psychological term but no more understanding of the psychological process than before. By the 1920s, according to one survey (Bernard, 1924), at least 849 different classes of instincts had been proposed. Clearly a more fruitful approach was needed. For many it was provided by the work of Sigmund Freud.

Freudian concepts. In Freudian theory, the foundations of adult personality are laid in early childhood. Not only is the course of normal personality development a continuous one across ages and stages, but the origins of adult fears and neurosis can be traced back to traumatic events in early life. Since we cannot begin to encompass the complexity of Freud's thought in just a few pages, we will touch on only a few central notions. ∎

Stages of psychosexual development. According to Freud's psychoanalytic theory, personality development in childhood is divided into *psychosexual stages.* Each stage is dominated by instinctual, unlearned biological urgings, which are *hedonistic* (pleasure-seeking). During each of these successive periods, sensual satisfaction comes through stimulation of various "erogenous" zones of the body—the mouth, the anus, and the genitals. These broadly conceived sexual forces are termed *libido,* and comprise all of the ways in which an individual derives gratification from bodily stimulation. At each stage of development, the extent to which such libidinal drives are satisfied or frustrated provides the occasion for intrapsychic conflict. Excess of either gratification or frustration at one stage prevents the normal progression to the next and is said to lead to *fixation* at that stage. Such fixations then influence how the child will interact with his or her environment.

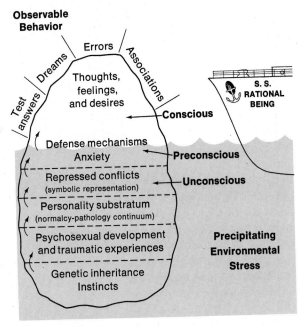

■ Before Freud, it had been assumed that people's actions were influenced largely by conscious thought and rational choice applied to present situations. Freud believed that the thoughts and behavior of which a person was aware constituted only a small portion of his or her ongoing experience and that the major influences on both conscious thoughts and observable behavior were irrational, unconscious, and historical, each layer influencing those above it.

Thus, as anal fixation is presumed to lead to a stingy, neat, stubborn, obsessive-compulsive character, oral fixation is alleged to be a determinant of drug addiction, compulsive eating, and even tendencies toward sarcasm and verbal fluency.

The most primitive stage of this psychosexual development is the *oral* stage, in which the mouth region is the primary source of nourishment, stimulation, and contact with the environment. There is little doubt that infants and young children spend a great proportion of their time in sucking activities of a nonnutritive nature (such as thumb or toe sucking).

The *anal* stage, which follows, focalizes gratification first on elimination of feces, then on retention of them. The child's pleasure from both the process and the products of excretion is challenged by social demands in most cultures and is eventually suppressed and regulated.

The final general period of erotic satisfaction centers around the exploration and stimulation of one's own body, especially the penis for the boy and the vagina for the girl. This *phallic* stage is followed by a *latent stage,* where sexuality "goes underground" for a few years; finally, with puberty, the individual arrives at the *genital* stage of sexual differentiation, away from autoeroticism toward stimulation from contact with the genitalia of others. As they progress through these stages, children learn their appropriate sex-role identification, develop a conscience partially through the resolution of their sexual love for the opposite-sex parent (the Oedipal situation), and become ready for culturally appropriate adult heterosexuality.

While this sketch does violence to the subtlety of Freud's thought, which you should read more fully,[1] it does provide the basic outline of his central theme of personality development. It should be mentioned in passing that this grand design of the child's psyche was derived not through direct observation of children, but

[1]See Freud's *Psychopathology of Everyday Life* (1960) and *Introductory Lectures on Psycho-Analysis* (1963).

largely from Freud's own analytical introspection and from his psychoanalytical interviews with adult patients that involved historical reconstructions of their past. ◆

Eros and Thanatos. On the basis of his observations, Freud concluded that all behavior is powered by two fundamental "drives," which are present in every individual at birth. He labeled the two "Eros" and "Thanatos." *Eros*, the "sex drive" or "life instinct" (which earned Freud his reputation in some quarters as a "dirty old man"), actually meant more than we usually mean by the sex drive. Eros encompassed all striving for creative synthesis; the urge for sexual union was thought to be only one

◆ This photograph, taken in 1912, shows Sigmund Freud with his daughter Anna, who is also a well-known psychoanalytic theorist.

expression of this drive. *Thanatos*, the "aggressive drive" or "death instinct," included all striving toward self-destruction, or breaking down of order, form, and regulation. Freud assumed that psychological activity, like physical activity, takes energy. As we have seen, the energy of the creative drive was called *libido;* he did not suggest a separate term for the psychic energy supposedly associated with Thanatos.

Id, superego, and ego. Freud accounted for individual differences by suggesting that different people deal with their fundamental drives (Eros and Thanatos) in different ways. To explain these differences, he pictured a continuing battle between two parts of the personality, the id and the superego, moderated by a third aspect of the self, the ego.

The *id* is conceived as the primitive, unconscious part of the personality, the storehouse of the fundamental drives. It operates irrationally; impulses push for expression and gratification "no matter what," without considering whether what is desired is realistically possible or morally acceptable.

The *superego* is the repository of an individual's values, including moral attitudes implanted by society. The superego proper corresponds roughly to the *conscience;* it develops when a child *internalizes* the prohibitions of parents and other adults against certain kinds of actions. The superego also includes the *ego ideal,* which develops as a child internalizes the views of others as to the kind of person he or she should strive to become. Thus the superego, society's representative in the individual, is often in conflict with the id, survival's representative. The id just wants to do what feels good, while the superego insists on doing what is "right."

In this conflict, the *ego* plays the part of arbitrator. The ego represents the individual's picture of physical and social reality, of what will lead to what and which things are possible in the world as it is actually perceived. Part of the ego's job is to choose kinds of action that will gratify id impulses without having undesirable consequences. Thus the ego would probably block an impulse to fly by leaping from a cliff, and might substitute sky diving or a trip on a roller coaster. When the id and the superego are in conflict, the ego generally tries to find a compromise that will at least partially satisfy both. In doing so, it may make use of one or a number of unconscious "defense mechanisms." ● Since Freud's model assumes that any urge has psychic energy associated with it, each of these mechanisms involves finding some outlet for the energy linked to the unacceptable urge. In the mechanism known as *reaction formation*, for example, the energy gets linked to expression of an opposing impulse ("I don't hate him, I love him. See how I smother him with love?").

According to Freudian theory, we all have some urges that are unacceptable in our society and thus all use these defense mechanisms to some extent. Overuse of them, however, constitutes *neurosis*. People who are neurotic spend so much of their energy deflecting, disguising, and rechanneling unacceptable urges that they have little energy left over for productive living or satisfying relationships.

As we have seen, the conflicts focused on by psychoanalytic theorists are thought to emerge during the various psychosexual stages of development. The individual's ability to adjust in later life is considered to be determined largely by early childhood experiences. If painful conflicts have been repressed in childhood without being adequately resolved, they will continue in adulthood—though unconscious—to influence the individual's thoughts, feelings, and behavior, causing emotional tension and difficulties in adjustment.

Freud's conception of a healthy or well-adjusted person is one who can successfully

● SUMMARY CHART OF EGO DEFENSE MECHANISMS

Compensation	Covering up weakness by emphasizing desirable trait or making up for frustration in one area by overgratification in another
Denial of Reality	Protecting self from unpleasant reality by refusal to perceive it
Displacement	Discharging pent-up feelings, usually of hostility, on objects less dangerous than those which initially aroused the emotion
Emotional Insulation	Withdrawing into passivity to protect self from being emotionally hurt
Fantasy	Gratifying frustrated desires in imaginary achievements ("daydreaming" is a common form)
Identification	Increasing feelings of worth by identifying self with person or institution of illustrious standing
Introjection	Incorporating external values and standards into ego structure so individual is not at the mercy of them as external threats
Isolation	Cutting off emotional charge from hurtful situations or separating incompatible attitudes by logic-tight compartments (holding conflicting attitudes which are never thought of simultaneously or in relation to each other); also called *compartmentalization*
Projection	Placing blame for one's difficulties upon others, or attributing one's own unethical desires to others
Rationalization	Attempting to prove that one's behavior is "rational" and justifiable and thus worthy of the approval of self and others
Reaction Formation	Preventing dangerous desires from being expressed by endorsing opposing attitudes and types of behavior and using them as "barriers"
Regression	Retreating to earlier developmental level involving less mature responses and usually a lower level of aspiration
Repression	Preventing painful or dangerous thoughts from entering consciousness, keeping them unconscious; this is considered to be the most basic of the defense mechanisms
Sublimation	Gratifying or working off frustrated sexual desires in substitutive nonsexual activities socially accepted by one's culture
Undoing	Atoning for, and thus counteracting, immoral desires or acts

engage in both "love and work." He was rather pessimistic about the chances for escaping neurosis. Perhaps because he grew up in the Victorian era, he believed that any society must teach its children that most expression of their basic drives is bad. Hence nearly everyone will have to be defending against such impulses nearly all the time. Those who came after him, as we shall see, were more optimistic about our prospects for avoiding repressed conflicts and neurosis.

The psychopathology of "normal" behavior. What evidence is there that the conflicts Freud described actually take place? Freud's answer has passed into the popular culture as the "Freudian slip." According to Freud, these unacceptable impulses within us, even though inhibited, suppressed, or repressed, still strive for expression. Our desire to confess our imagined transgressions against society "oozes from our pores" and takes on many forms. For example, "forgetting" an important appointment with the dentist or being consistently late for dates with a particular person may not be accidental but may be an instance of this tendency to express the way we *really* feel. Telling unwanted guests on their arrival, "I'm so sorry—oh, I mean glad you could come," may reveal the true intention of the host or hostess. When a radio announcer, reading a commercial for Barbara Ann Bread, misread "Barbara Ann for the best in bread" as "Barbara Ann for the breast in bed," was he making a public confession of his impulses?

According to Freud, such slips are meaningful, the meaning being in the unconscious intention. Such "errors" can be explained in terms of the final result produced, even though some other meaning was expected by the hearer or apparently intended by the speaker. Freud believed that such slips invariably indicated an actual intention. ▲

Symptoms as signals. Freud believed that more serious disturbances, such as irrational fears, paralysis without physical cause, or uncontrollable anxiety, also had a meaning in the lives of individuals, in expressing a sense of helplessness and in getting others to be concerned about them. He considered such symptoms to be signals of some underlying conflict; the job of a therapist was to uncover the connection between the symptom and the problem causing it. Thus for both normal and abnormal behavior Freud postulated the principle of *psychic determinism:* that mental events do not occur by chance, however random they may appear, but are all meaningfully related if we explore them deeply enough. As we saw in Chapter 7, he felt that even dreams were meaningful though disguised expressions of hidden, unconscious processes. Freud has been called the "world's greatest egoist" because he hoped, by subjecting his own every thought and action to

My dear Irving,

The news of your engagment came as a delightful surprise. Naturally we are very pleased at the results of your efforts. When must we meet the fair lady again? She seemed just to shine when we saw her at your New Year's party. Richmond is such a long way—I hope you won't be going to Virginia so often that you have no time left for studies.

We look forward to the future knowing that I have not lost a son but a daughter.

Congratulations,

Mother

▲ THE PROSPECTIVE MOTHER-IN-LAW

As an exercise in Freudian-slip detection, read the above letter quickly once, then reread it more carefully. What is the message Mama is unconsciously telegraphing to her son, who has just broken the news of his engagement to a woman from Richmond, Virginia?

relentless microscopic analysis, to discover the true meaning of everyone's feelings and actions.

Criticisms of Freudian theory. Critics have complained that psychoanalytic theory is very difficult to evaluate because it makes few empirically testable predictions. The theory can be used to explain a good deal, but most of its explanations are made "after the fact." Also some critics have pointed out that psychoanalytic therapy represents a learning situation in which patients are reinforced for making statements that are in accord with the theory. Hence psychoanalysts' assertions that the theory is "confirmed" by what they actually encounter in their patients may be somewhat suspect. In addition, it has been pointed out that the language of psychoanalysis is one that is imposed on the patient by the therapist, rather than one that is mutually shared. As such, it becomes a one-way form of communication that does not easily help the individual to understand inner emotions and feelings (Holt, 1970).

Yet another criticism of Freud's theory is that it has developed from speculation based on clinical experience with people suffering from neuroses and other problems of adjustment, people in whom something has gone wrong. Thus it has little to say about healthy personality or lifestyles that are not primarily defensive.

Finally, much of the evidence on which the theory is based has depended on an analyst's memory of what happened during a therapy hour. This means that the events have had to pass through the therapist's "theoretical filter," which will have tended to screen out data inconsistent with this theory of personality. Furthermore, the therapist's information is dependent on the patient's memory. In fact, Freud was quite dismayed when he learned that many of his patients had been telling him of early sexual traumas that had never really occurred. He resolved the problem for himself by deciding that what a patient *thinks* happened is significant even if the memory is incorrect.

Even Freud's severest critics, however, acknowledge certain of his contributions to modern thought:

1. In applying the concept of unconscious causes for behavior (as opposed to the rationalists' claim that our will has full control over our behavior), Freud for the first time emphasized the importance of unconscious and irrational processes in the motivation of human behavior. ◆

2. Although most modern psychologists believe that Freud overemphasized the role of sexual factors, psychoanalysis "opened up" the scientific study of sexuality and indicated its importance as a source of adjustment problems.

3. Psychoanalysis focused attention on the importance of childhood experiences in later personality development and adjustment.

Neo-Freudian theories. Many of those who came after Freud kept his basic picture of personality as a battleground in which unconscious primal urges fight it out with social values. Most, however, made a few changes. Some, like

◆ "All right, deep down it's a cry for psychiatric help—but at one level it's a stick-up."

Carl Jung and Alfred Adler, offered different candidates for the most important "primal urges" to replace Freud's broadly defined sex drive. Adler focused on power, contending that what people basically strive for is superiority, to compensate for feelings of inferiority to others that they experienced when they were small and helpless. Jung stressed the importance of universal symbols and predispositions — *archetypes* — inherited, he believed, in a "collective unconscious" shared by all members of the human race. He also expanded Freud's picture of personality development by suggesting that a "self" emerges around the age of thirty to hold together the parts that have developed by then. Other "neo-Freudians," like Hartmann, Kris, Rapaport, and more recently Schafer, have expanded Freud's account of the ego and its functioning to make it equal in importance to the id and superego instead of a mere arbiter between them. Still others, like Karen Horney and Erich Fromm, have believed that Freud overemphasized the biological influences on personality at the expense of the social influences and have attempted to redress the balance. We shall consider in some detail the theories of two of those who went farthest in emphasizing the social nature of personality: Erik Erikson and Harry Stack Sullivan.

Erikson's complete portrait of the individual. From his clinical observations of children, adolescents, college students, and older adults, Erikson made three major contributions to the theory of personality development in his book *Childhood and Society* (1950). First, parallel to the psychosexual stages, he posits *psychosocial* stages of ego development in which individuals establish new orientations to themselves and to other people in their social world. Second, personality development is seen as continuing throughout all stages of life, rather than being established primarily during the infantile stage. Third, each of these stages requires a new level of social interaction that can change the course of personality in either positive or negative directions.

Eight stages of psychosocial development have been identified by Erikson, describing the human cycle of life from infancy through old age. At each stage a particular conflict comes into focus; although it is never resolved once and for all, it must be resolved sufficiently that the individual can cope successfully with the conflicts of later stages.

1. *Trust vs. mistrust* (first year of life; corresponds to Freud's oral stage). Depending on the quality of the care received, the infant learns to trust the environment, to perceive it as orderly and predictable, or to be suspicious, fearful, and mistrusting of its chaos and unpredictability.

2. *Autonomy vs. doubt* (second and third years of life; corresponds to Freud's anal period). From the development of motor and mental abilities and the opportunity to explore and manipulate emerges a sense of autonomy, adequacy, and self-control. Excessive criticism or limiting the exercise of the child's exploration and other behaviors leads to a sense of shame and doubt over his or her adequacy.

3. *Initiative vs. guilt* (fourth to fifth year of life; corresponds to Freud's phallic stage). The way parents respond to the child's self-initiated activities, intellectual as well as motor, creates either a sense of freedom and initiative at one extreme, or at the other, a sense of guilt and a feeling of being an inept intruder in an adult world.

4. *Industry vs. inferiority* (sixth to eleventh year; corresponds to the *latency* phase in Freudian theory when the child is least sexually preoccupied). The child's concern for how things work and how they ought to operate leads to a sense of industry in formulating rules, organizing, ordering, being industrious. However, a sense of inferiority may be promoted in a child when these efforts are rebuffed as silly, mischievous, or troublesome. It is during this stage that influences outside the home begin to exert a greater influence on the child's development — at least for middle-class American children.

5. *Identity vs. role confusion* (adolescence, from twelve to eighteen years of age). During this period the adolescent begins to develop multiple ways of perceiving things, can see

things from another person's point of view, behaves differently in different situations according to what is deemed appropriate. In playing these varied roles, the person must develop an integrated sense of his or her own identity as distinct from all others, but coherent and personally acceptable. Where such a "centered" identity is not developed, the alternatives are to be confused about who one really is or to settle on a "negative identity"—a socially unacceptable role, such as that of a "speed freak" or the "class clown."

6. *Intimacy vs. isolation* (young adulthood). The consequences of the adult's attempts at reaching out to make contact with others may result in intimacy (a commitment—sexual, emotional, and moral—to other persons) or else in isolation from close personal relationships.

7. *Generativity vs. self-absorption* (middle age). Here one's life experiences may extend the focus of concern beyond oneself to family, society, or future generations. This future orientation may not develop, and instead, like Scrooge in *A Christmas Carol,* a person may become concerned with only material possessions and physical well-being.

8. *Integrity vs. despair* (old age). In this last stage of life one looks back on what it has been all about and ahead to the unknown of death. As a consequence of the solutions developed at each of the preceding stages, one can enjoy the fulfillment of life, with a sense of integrity. But despair is what faces the person who finds that life has been unsatisfying and misdirected. Too late either to look back in anger or ahead with hope, the life cycle of such a person ends with a whimper of despair.

As our world changes ever more rapidly, becoming both less stable and more complex, it appears that views such as Erikson's are more appropriate for understanding the "identity crises" that so many students feel than the more traditional views of Freud, which were derived from a relatively static conception of the traditional challenges posed by the individual's social and physical environment.

Sullivan's social perspective. Sullivan, like Freud, proposed that tension arising from a set of physiological needs often gets people to act.

Unlike Freud, however, he believed that our basic needs are not biological but derive from interactions with people, and that these interpersonally developed "human" characteristics may directly affect or alter physiological functioning. Most cultures, for example, have more or less elaborate sets of rules specifying when and how one may eat, eliminate, and so on.

Sullivan went so far as to define personality not as something in the person but as "the relatively enduring pattern of recurrent interpersonal situations which characterize human life" (1953, p. 111). Thus for him personality meant consistency not in internal traits but in what a person does *in relation to other people.* These other people need not be present physically, however, for personality to manifest itself (nor need they even actually exist) because a person can interact with people in imagination as well as in actuality. For example, people can drive along lost in fantasies of what they "should have said" to the police officer who stopped them, or can even interact in their "mind's eye" with a fictional character in a book or movie.

In accounting for consistency in interpersonal behavior, Sullivan introduced the concepts of "dynamism" and "personification." A *dynamism* is a prolonged, recurrent behavior pattern (other theorists would call much the same thing a *habit*). For example, a person who characteristically behaves in a hostile way toward a certain person or group of persons is said to be expressing a dynamism of hostility; a person who tends to seek out lascivious relationships with others displays a dynamism of lust. A dynamism can be any habitual reaction, whether in the form of an attitude, a feeling, or an overt action.

One particularly important dynamism is the *"self-system,"* which, according to Sullivan, develops as individuals learn to avoid threats to their security. They learn, for example, that if they do what their parents like, they will not be punished. They then come to engage in habitual "security measures" that allow some forms of behavior (the "good-me" self) and forbid others (the "bad-me" self).

A *personification* is an image a person has of someone else. It is a complex of feelings, attitudes, and conceptions that in large part determines how one will act toward that person. Personifications learned in infancy may remain intact and influence a person's adult reactions to people. Children who personify their father as overbearing and hostile, for example, may come to personify other older men as being overbearing, and will then react to certain teachers and employers as if they were overbearing and hostile whether they actually are or not. Sullivan called a personification held in common by a group of people a *stereotype*. Examples of stereotypes common in our culture are the "long-haired student radical," the "ivory-tower intellectual," the "rising young executive with a house in the suburbs," and the "male chauvinist pig."

Sullivan outlined seven stages of personality development in Western European societies. These are: (a) infancy, (b) childhood, (c) the juvenile era, (d) preadolescence, (e) early adolescence, (f) late adolescence, and (g) maturity. The emphasis is on the kinds of interpersonal relationships and the ways of thinking that become possible in each stage. Thus Sullivan recognized that somewhat different patterns might be found in other societies.

Although he stressed the influence of social forces in the development of personality, Sullivan also recognized the potential influence of individuals in changing their society. Indeed, he was often critical of contemporary society, believing that many of the ways it influences personality development run counter to people's personal needs and inhibit rather than enhance the full realization of human potential. At the same time, because he believed that people remain flexible throughout their lives, he was optimistic about their chances to live in harmony with the dictates of society, until it becomes so irrational and repressive that individuals attempt to *change it* rather than just adapt to it.

The Organismic Field Theorists: Consistency As the "Actualization" of Self

The ways of thinking about personality that fit into this general category have a good deal more to say about both the central coordination and the individual self-direction of human behavior. Three such theories will be summarized here. All have been strongly influenced by *field theory,* a concept that emerged from analogy with the physical sciences. Based on the study of electromagnetic fields, this model postulates fields of force that are in dynamic and constantly shifting equilibrium. For psychologists applying this theory, psychological events, like physical events, are thought to represent a balance and interaction of many forces, and a change anywhere in the system is seen as affecting the whole system. Thus behavior is seen as shaped not by individual chains of cause and effect, but by the combination of forces that make up the entire field.

Goldstein's organismic theory. A personality theory that has borrowed heavily from field theory is *organismic theory,* a leading exponent of which is Kurt Goldstein (1963). As a neuropsy-

▲ Carl Rogers is well known both as a personality theorist and a leader in the field of humanistic and experiential therapy.

chiatrist working with brain-injured soldiers in World War I, Goldstein arrived at the principle that particular symptoms could not be understood merely as the product of particular diseases or injuries but only as products of the organism behaving as a whole. The organism is a unity, and what happens in any part of it affects the whole. Organization is natural to the organism, and disorganization means disease. Although constituent parts have to be differentiated for psychological and medical study, they do not operate in isolation within the person.

Organismic theory stresses primarily the orderly unfolding of the inherited potentialities of the organism. However, it does recognize that an appropriate environment is essential if this unfolding is to occur. As one might expect, the organism is thought to be motivated by one main drive rather than by a number of different, independent drives. This drive is our constant striving to realize our inherent potentials and is called by Goldstein *self-actualization*.

Rogers' theory of the self. Among the best known of the organismic theorists, who has achieved recognition also as a therapist, is Carl Rogers. ▲ He emphasizes the private world of the individual, the world of experience, which he calls the *phenomenal field*. It is the individual's perceptions and interpretations that determine subsequent behavior. Thus to understand someone's behavior, it is not enough to know the objective external situation: we must understand how it looks subjectively to that person.

A differentiated portion of this field is the *self-concept*, which develops out of the individual's interaction with the environment. People behave in ways that are consistent with their picture of themselves and tend to reject or distort incoming information that is threatening to the self. Thus experience may be *symbolized*, in which case it becomes clearly and consciously perceived, or it may be denied symbolization and remain below the level of consciousness, or it may be ignored.

For Rogers as for Goldstein, the most basic drive of the human organism is toward self-actualization. Unfortunately, this drive at times comes into conflict with the need for approval or *positive regard* from both the self and others. If other important people in a child's environment express dismay at some of the things the child does without making it clear that this "conditional regard" applies to the *behavior* rather than to the *child* as a person, he or she may begin to do and think only things that are "acceptable" (recall our Chapter 3 distinction between punishing a response and punishing a person). In that case, *incongruence* will develop between the child's "real" feelings and fulfilling activities, on the one hand, and the "acceptable" things that are allowed, on the other. Mental illness comes when one does not dare to be oneself or to acknowledge one's real experiencing.

Once the alternatives are clearly perceived and adequately symbolized, however, Rogers believes that the individual chooses the path of growth. Thus in therapy it is the patient's own inner urge toward growth and wholeness that makes recovery possible, and the therapist's task, as we shall see in Chapter 12, is to provide a safe and encouraging climate.

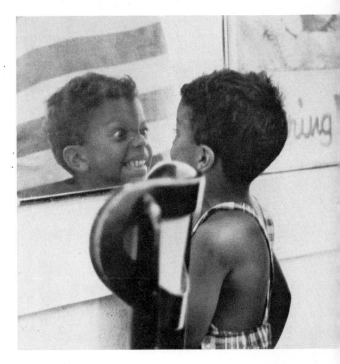

Maslow's self-actualization theory. Another theorist who found self-actualization a fruitful concept was Abraham Maslow. Feeling that psychology had concentrated too much on human weaknesses, while neglecting strengths, Maslow sought to round out the picture by studying emotionally healthy individuals. He regarded human nature as basically good, but saw the innate tendency toward growth and self-actualization as rather weak and fragile, easily overcome by social pressures. Maslow distinguished between *deficiency motivation,* in which individuals seek to restore their physical or psychological equilibrium, and *growth motivation,* in which individuals seek to go beyond what they have done and been in the past; people may welcome uncertainty, an increase in tension, and even pain if they see it as a route toward greater fulfillment.

According to Maslow (1959), a person's inborn needs are arranged in a *hierarchy* of priority. As those on one level are satisfied, those on the next level take precedence. Thus when the physiological needs such as hunger and thirst are satisfied, the needs on the next level — safety needs — press for satisfaction. After these come, in order, needs for belongingness and love, needs for esteem, and needs for self-actualization. At the top of the needs hierarchy is the sixth

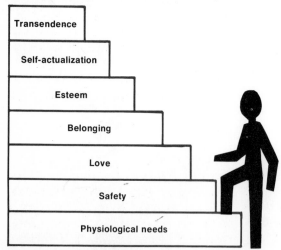

■ HIERARCHY OF NEEDS

According to Maslow, needs on the "lower" levels are prepotent as long as they are unsatisfied. When they are adequately satisfied, however, the "higher" needs occupy the individual's attention and effort.

stage of "transcendence." Maslow added this highest level to represent the ultimate human need which goes beyond self-actualization, the quest for identity, even beyond individual humanness. Transpersonal psychology has become a distinct field of inquiry into higher states of consciousness and the spiritual search as basic aspects of human life. ■

Although for most people self-actualization is only a hope or a goal, something wished for and striven toward, a few appear to achieve it to a large degree. Maslow studied a group of such persons, although he never made it very clear just how he chose his sample and carried out his investigations. He did include both historical personages, such as Beethoven and Lincoln, and persons alive at the time of the study, including Einstein and Eleanor Roosevelt. On the basis of his findings, Maslow formulated a list of fifteen characteristics of self-actualized persons (Maslow, 1954). Would you consider yourself "actualized" according to the following standards?

1. Self-actualized persons perceive reality more effectively than most people do and have more comfortable relations with it. That is, they *live close to reality* and to nature, can judge others accurately, and can tolerate ambiguity or uncertainty more easily than most people can.

2. They can *accept themselves* and their various characteristics with little feeling of guilt or anxiety and, at the same time, can readily *accept others.*

3. They show a great deal of *spontaneity* in both thought and behavior, although they seldom show extreme unconventionality.

4. They are *problem-centered,* not ego-centered, often devoting themselves to broad social problems as a mission in life.

5. They have a *need for privacy* and solitude at times and are capable of looking at life from a detached, objective point of view.

6. They are relatively *independent of their culture and environment* but do not flaunt convention just for the sake of being different.

7. They are capable of *deep appreciation* of the basic experiences of life, even of things they have done or seen many times before.

8. Many of them have had *mystic experiences* such as having felt a deep sense of ecstasy, hav-

ing felt limitless horizons opening to them, or having felt very powerful and at the same time very helpless but ending with a conviction that something significant had happened.

9. They have a *deep social interest* and identify in a sympathetic way with people in general.

10. They are capable of very *deep, satisfying interpersonal relations*, usually with only a few rather than many individuals.

11. They are *democratic* in their attitudes toward others, showing respect for all people, regardless of race, creed, income level, etc.

12. They discriminate clearly between means and ends but often *enjoy the means toward their ends* ("getting there") more than impatient persons do.

13. They have a good *sense of humor*, tending to be philosophical and nonhostile in their jokes.

14. They are highly *creative*, each in their own individual way. They have "primary creativeness that comes out of the unconscious" and produces truly original, new discoveries. This shows itself in whatever field the self-actualized person has chosen, and is to be distinguished from the kind of productive creativity reflected in art, music, poetry, science, or invention. Of course, the self-actualized person in any of these fields will show both kinds of creativity.

15. They are *resistant to enculturation*. That is, although they fit into their culture, they are independent of it and do not blindly comply with all its demands.

With all these characteristics, self-actualized persons are particularly capable of loving and of being loved in the fullest way.

Peak experiences of various kinds are characteristic of the self-actualized. These are "moments of highest happiness and fulfillment" and may come, in differing degrees of intensity, during various activities—sexual love, parental experiences, creative activity, aesthetic perceptions, appreciation of nature, or even intense athletic participation.

Thus organismic field theorists such as Goldstein, Rogers, and Maslow have stressed a basic drive toward self-actualization as the organizer of all the diverse forces whose interplay contin-

ually creates what a person is. In the process they have developed theories that seem more "human" than many that preceded them, with an emphasis on the importance of how people perceive their world and on processes of health and growth.

Criticism of self-actualization theories. Criticisms of this approach focus on the fuzziness of the central concept, "self-actualization." First, it is not clear to what degree self-actualization is a socially defined rather than an inborn tendency. Second, it is not well enough defined to be very powerful as a specific predictor of behavioral relationships. Thus these theories have difficulty in accounting for the *specific* kinds of consistency that characterize particular individuals, except in a very general way. Also, these approaches have not led to a body of research but more to a way of conceptualizing human personality.

The Factor Theorists: Consistency from a Collection of Traits

Another way of thinking about personality involves describing and accounting for specific clusters of human characteristics.

Trait theory and the development of factor analysis. One of the earliest and most straightforward ways of describing human consistency was by the delineation of *traits*. If a person was consistently friendly, he had a trait of "friendliness"; if she did well in sports, a trait of "athletic ability." Traits were like instincts in that both were seen as inner characteristics, but the question was left open as to whether a given trait was inherited or not.

Not too surprisingly, trait theorists ran into the same problem as instinct theorists: their lists of traits seemed to go on endlessly, and no two lists agreed. Then it occurred to someone that perhaps some traits were more "basic" than others: that the confusing multitude of *surface traits* might reflect the interaction of a much smaller, more orderly set of *source traits* (Cattell, 1957). That was not much help at first, for it was anyone's guess which were the surface traits and which the underlying source traits. The lists of source traits that were proposed were shorter but still showed little agreement. Then a powerful mathematical tool called *factor analysis* came on the scene.

Factor analysis is a mathematical technique (involving matrix algebra) for reducing a large number of observed phenomena to a smaller number of basic, more fundamental variables. Assume that we begin with many people taking a large battery of personality tests on which for each person 100 scores (presumed trait measures) are obtained. We want to know how these scores are related to each other, but if we correlated all the scores for just one person, we would have 4950 different figures to evaluate. To make sense of this vast amount of data, much of which may be redundant (that is, measuring the same thing), mathematical and statistical techniques are used to determine the minimum number of factors that can adequately account for the entire correlation matrix.

These factors are then given names according to the general characteristic that they seem to represent, for example, "sociability" or "impulsiveness." In this way a factor analysis of the results of 100 personality test questions might yield five or six factors that most of the questions were really measuring in different ways.

Why were such findings important? For the trait theorists it was highly exciting, because factor analysis made it possible to examine tests designed to tap different traits and discover whether in fact they appeared to be measuring the same thing or different things. When the same factor was found in several tests, it seemed reasonable to assume that that factor must represent one of the "source traits" the theorists had been trying so hard to find. Here was an objective, mathematical procedure theorists could use to discover the underlying structure of human personality. Several of them set about at once to try to do so. We will examine the work of one of these investigators, J. P. Guilford.

Guilford's factor theory. Guilford has identified two groups of general personality factors (hormetic and temperament), as well as a group of factors having to do with specific kinds of intellectual functioning.

Hormetic factors. The hormetic traits are the direct motivational aspects of an individual's personality. (The word *hormetic* comes from the Greek, meaning "to set in motion" or "to excite.") These factors depend on the physical needs of the body and on the kinds of experience the individual has had; thus they might be somewhat different in different societies. They include needs, attitudes, and interests.

Careful work by Guilford, Cattell, Eysenck, and many others over the years has revealed a number of measurable needs, attitudes, and interests that are seen as directing our behavior and consciousness and as keeping us busy seeking until some goal is reached. Examples of needs are general ambition, need for freedom, and aggressiveness, while interest factors include liking for adventure, liking for precision, and aesthetic appreciation. The list of hormetic factors that has been studied is by no means exhaustive, and research in this area continues. Other psychologists are working in the same field, and it is interesting to note that their findings are in essential agreement—a situation quite different from that which has often arisen among those using less objective approaches.

Temperament factors. Guilford and his associates have also studied factors of temperament, which describe the *manner* in which an individual characteristically operates in certain types of situations. Such characteristics are measured by scales like the Guilford-Zimmerman Temperament Survey, a self-inventory device that has grown out of the factor analytic research. Each of nine traits is conceived as a dimension with two extremes; the individual's score falls somewhere on a scale in between. A "profile" of the person's high and low scores on the nine temperament traits (as well as on interests and abilities) can be constructed. This scale is frequently used in predicting an individual's probable success in various types of jobs, as shown in the test profile. ●

Centile Profile of *Ms. Susan Ortez*

Comparison Group: *Office Workers*

		centile scores	1	5	10	20 25 30 40	50	60 70 75 80	90	95	99
Mental Abilities	Verbal Comprehension	20				●					
	Numerical Ability	95								●	
	Visual Speed and Accuracy	80						●			
	Numerical Reasoning	98						●			●
	Verbal Reasoning	80						●			
	Word Fluency	80						●			
Job Knowledge	Sales Knowledge										
	Supervisory Knowledge										
Occupational Interests	Mechanical	95							●		
	Computational	90							●		
	Scientific	90							●		
	Persuasive	30				●					
	Artistic	50					●				
	Literary	1	●								
	Musical	10			●						
	Social Service	80						●			
	Clerical	60						●			
Personality or Temperament	Slow→Energetic	95							●		
	Impulsive→Restrained	70						●			
	Timid→Self-Assured	70						●			
	Solitary→Sociable	95							●		
	Easily Upset→Emotionally Stable	60						●			
	Over-Sensitive→Objective	85						●			
	Resistant→Agreeable	40					●				
	Superficial→Reflective	20				●					
	Critical→Trusting	90							●		
Strength of Motives	Theoretical	60						●			
	Economic	99									●
	Aesthetic	1	●								
	Social	99									●
	Power	15			●						
	Religious	40					●				

● TEST PROFILE OF AN APPLICANT

Evaluation: Ms. Ortez is recommended for the position of Inventory Control Desk Clerk. She is a bright candidate with considerable drive and capacity for hard work under pressure. In addition, Ms. Ortez has ambition. Moreover, she is very cooperative and congenial in her attitudes and should take direction well.

In terms of interests, Ms. Ortez has a good tolerance for the heavy volume of detail involved in this work. However, it should be noted that Ms. Ortez very much wants to be an accountant some day. And she has the ability to do so—an unusually good aptitude for quantitative work, in fact. Therefore, Ms. Ortez shows potential not only for the immediate assignment but also for ultimately reaching her objectives in accounting work. If circumstances allow, management is advised to encourage her taking evening courses in preparation for promotion to accounting level responsibilities. It would appear to be in management's best interests as well as Ms. Ortez', for she does have the potential to grow.

While this test provides measures of several traits, it is important to keep in mind that no trait stands alone. Each is conditioned and modified by all the other traits and characteristics of the individual. For example, a person very high in ascendance and at the same time high in friendliness would have a vastly different personality from that of a person who was equally dominant but low in friendliness.

Intellectual factors. A still more ambitious attempt to classify factors into a systematic framework is Guilford's *structure of intellect model.* Guilford classifies intellectual factors according to *content* (kind of information), according to *product* (form), and according to the *operation* involved. There are five kinds of operations (evaluation, convergent production, divergent production, memory, and cognition); six kinds of products (units, classes, relations, systems, transformations, and implications); and four kinds of content (figural, symbolic, semantic, and behavioral).

The different intellectual abilities represent different combinations of contents, products, and operations. That is, any of the four types of content may take the form of any of the six products ($4 \times 6 = 24$). On these twenty-four resulting kinds of information, any of the five types of operation may be performed ($24 \times 5 = 120$). Thus we have a total of 120 possible intellectual abilities. An example of one such ability is "verbal comprehension," which under this system is classified as *cognition* of *units* with *semantic* content. ◆

This theoretical model is analogous to the chemist's periodic table of the elements. By means of such a systematic framework, intellectual factors, like chemical elements, may be postulated before they are discovered. In 1961, when Guilford proposed his model, nearly forty intellectual abilities had been identified. Since that time, researchers have accounted for close to a hundred abilities (Guilford, 1973).

Criticisms of trait theories. It is plain that the factor theorists have developed potent ways of describing and accounting for even highly complex patterns of consistency in individual characteristics. Criticisms of the approach have been of three kinds: theoretical, methodological, and empirical.

Theoretically, the main complaint has been that the factor theorists picture personality as a bundle of traits but provide little to help understand how these traits hang together to form the coherent system that we recognize as a personality.

Methodologically, the approach has been accused of generating scales that are impure or mislabeled. For example, several different measures labeled "anxiety" do not seem to correlate highly with each other. At the other extreme, it

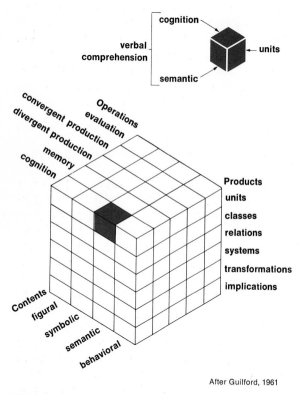

After Guilford, 1961

◆ THE STRUCTURE OF INTELLECT

is charged that too often high correlations between scales result simply from the use of identical items in the different scales—differently phrased but really testing the same thing. Finally, scales that are intended to measure particular traits have sometimes been contaminated by social desirability (the tendency of the people being tested to check items they think would be approved of) or by acquiescence (consistency in agreeing—or disagreeing—with almost any statement).

Empirically, the strongest criticism of trait theory has come from Walter Mischel (1968). In his view, the various personality dimensions derived from factor analysis of questionnaire responses look fine on paper but do not correlate highly enough with anything except other questionnaire responses to be trusted for any use beyond gross screening decisions.

In fact, Mischel questions whether these traits and factors are "in" the person at all. He has marshaled an impressive array of evidence that noncognitive (nonintellectual) traits are not good predictors of behavior because behavior itself is variable and inconsistent across different situations. He argues cogently that this lack of a nice, neat pattern of high correlations is due not to imperfect methodological tools for personality assessment, but rather to the faulty assumption that there *is* a central core of personality dispositions to be found.

Mischel, like the social learning theorists (to be discussed in the next section), stresses the situational forces that evoke behavior and the reinforcing conditions that maintain it. A person's behavior is stable when the maintaining conditions are stable; it is consistent from one condition to another if and when the important stimulus features are the same. However, when these features change, behavior changes (is unstable or inconsistent), regardless of whatever core of enduring dispositions there may be. In his view, behavior follows the laws of learning, and the consistencies we attribute to "behavioral traits" simply result from the fact that the evoking and maintaining conditions stay substantially the same for most of us most of the time.

Does such a view render the individual into a mechanistic automaton without uniqueness and distinctive character? To the contrary, contends Mischel: in insisting on invariant traits despite the variability we observe, we do violence to the complexity of human behavior. To recognize that people are responsive to subtle changes in their environment is to argue for human adaptiveness and flexibility.

The Learning Theorists: Consistency from Learned Habit Patterns

Most experimental psychologists have looked somewhat askance at personality theories and their creators. By and large, they have focused their attention on trying to find consistent relationships between observable stimulus conditions and observable behavior, making as few assumptions as possible about unobservable processes (such as "personality"). A few, however, have tried their hand at extending stimulus-response learning theory to account for the more complex kinds of consistency in human behavior. For a long time the best known of these were John Dollard and Neal Miller.

Dollard and Miller: the reconcilers. Dollard, a sociologist-anthropologist, and Miller, an experimental psychologist who had undergone psychoanalysis in a training program at the Vienna Institute of Psychoanalysis, combined a concern for the sorts of problems discussed by Freud with an appreciation for the methodological rigor of Hull's learning theory (see p. 109). So they set about trying to find a way to put the two together. At first sight, Freud's rich theory seems very different from the sort of statements usually generated by studies of rats running around in mazes. In fact, however, there are some strong points of similarity. First, Freud's conceptualization, like Hullian learning theory, was a *tension-reduction* theory: both conceived of the organism as acting in order to reduce "tension" produced by unsatisfied drives. Second, both kinds of theory stress the importance of *early learning* in determining what an organism does later in life. Although the two theoretical systems use very different words to describe their conclusions, they thus come out with models of the human organism that have important parallels.

The central focus in Dollard and Miller's (1950) formulations is on the process of learning, or habit formation. They discuss four significant features of this process: drive, cue, response, and reinforcement (reward). *Drives* get the organism into action, *cues* suggest what behavior is appropriate (will lead to drive reduction), *response* is the behavior itself, and *reinforcement* strengthens the connection between cue and response by reducing the tension of drives.

An interesting example of Dollard and Miller's translation of Freudian concepts into experimental learning terms is their handling of the personal characteristic of "indecisiveness." Consider, they suggested, the case of a lover contemplating marriage. The perfect mate has been found, and the appropriate arrangements have been made. But as the day of the wedding approaches, the lover's doubts increase. Finally, to the consternation of all concerned, the whole thing is called off at the last minute. A week later, the lover decides to go through with it after all. But again, when the day approaches, the wedding is canceled. How are we to account for this wishy-washy, vacillating behavior? And how are we to account for the scores of lovers who, in spite of increasing doubts at the last minute, go ahead and get married anyway?

Miller (1944) listed four principles derived from animal research that seem to help us understand this sort of conflict situation:

1. The tendency to approach a desired goal gets stronger the nearer the subject is to it *(approach gradient).*

2. The tendency to go away from a feared place or object also gets stronger the nearer the subject is to it *(avoidance gradient).*

3. The strength of the second (avoidance) tendency increases more rapidly than that of the first (approach). In other words, it may be said that the avoidance gradient is steeper than the approach gradient.

4. The strength of both tendencies varies with the strength of the drive on which the tendencies are based. A high level of drive may thus be said to raise the height of the entire gradient. The two graphs show how these principles help us understand our different lovers. ▲ These examples are intriguing illustrations of Dollard and Miller's approach, but they have more to do with how people behave in relatively transient situations than with the kinds of consistency over time and place with which personality theorists are usually concerned.

Social learning theory. More recent learning theorists have applauded Dollard and Miller's experimental methods and testable statements but have criticized them on two other counts. First, they see it as an important limitation that Dollard and Miller have relied so heavily on results from studies using *nonhuman subjects* in deriving a theory they hoped to apply to humans. Second, they consider it essential to study human behavior in a *social* setting rather than in isolation (for example, studies of people sitting apart learning lists of nonsense syllables rule out many of the interpersonal processes that are most characteristically human).

Social learning theory does not view human beings as being driven by inner forces or as being the helpless pawns of environmental influences. Rather, it proposes that "psychological functioning is best understood in terms of a continuous reciprocal interaction between behavior and its controlling conditions" (Bandura, 1971). Any individual's unique characteristics are determined by such factors as social stimuli, social and personal reinforcements, past learning history, and so on. (See *P&L* Close-up, p. 430.)

In contrast to other theories of learning, the social learning approach stresses the uniquely human cognitive processes that are involved in acquiring and maintaining patterns of behavior. The theory points out that people can learn things *vicariously* through observation of other people, in addition to learning by direct experience. Furthermore, people can use *symbols* to represent external events cognitively, thus allowing them to foresee the possible consequences of their actions without having to actually experience them. Also, people are capable of *self-regulatory processes,* whereby they evaluate their own behavior (according to personal standards) and provide their own reinforcements (e.g., self-approval or self-reproach). This self-regulating capacity allows people to control their own actions, rather than being controlled by external forces.

The leading proponent of the social learning approach to personality is Albert Bandura. One of his major contributions to the development of the theory has been his work on *observational learning.* According to this research, much of the behavior that we display has been learned or modified by watching *models* engage in these actions. Such individuals may include parents, teachers, peers, television performers, cartoon characters, and so on. The influence of modeling is determined by four interrelated processes:

1. *Attentional processes.* People will only learn from a model if they are attending to, and recognizing, the critical features of the model's behavior. Models who are attractive or perceived as similar to the observer are more likely to be influential, as are models who are repeatedly available and are engaging in important, functional behaviors. Some models (such as those seen on television) are so effective in capturing attention that viewers will learn the modeled activities even in the absence of special incentives to do so.

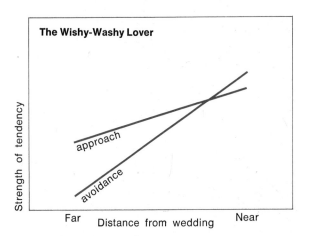

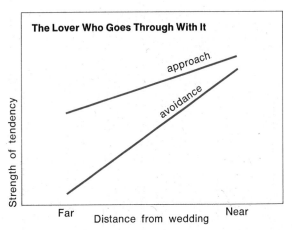

▲ I'M (NOT) GETTING MARRIED IN THE MORNING

The first figure shows visually what Miller's principles might mean in the case of lovers who keep calling the wedding off. They both desire and fear marriage, but when the wedding is still far off, the approach gradient is well above the avoidance gradient: the tendency to approach is greater than the tendency to avoid, so they go on with the marriage plans. Then, as the day comes closer, the tendency to avoid increases faster than the tendency to approach, until at some point the tendency to avoid is stronger. These lovers may go on with the plans anyway for a little while, knowing how upset everyone would be if they knew. But soon the tendency to avoid is a great deal stronger than the tendency to approach and they decide not to go through with it.

That, however, puts them back where they started: a long way from getting married, where the tendency to approach marriage is again stronger than the tendency to avoid it. So they change their minds again. Miller's principles would predict that such lovers might go on vacillating forever, unless their prospective mates decide they've had enough and tell them to get lost.

The second figure shows what might be going on in the case of lovers who have doubts that increase as the day approaches but go ahead and get married anyway. They, too, start with fears, but they also start with a stronger drive to get married. Thus though both tendencies increase and their avoidance gradient increases faster, their approach gradient remains higher than their avoidance gradient right up to the wedding, so they go through with it.

From Neal E. Miller—"Experimental Studies of Conflict" in *Personality and the Behavior Disorders,* edited by J. McV. Hunt, Copyright 1944, renewed © 1972. The Ronald Press Company, New York.

Close-up
A Nervous Nellie or a Concerned Critic? Two Views of the Same Behavior

A board of examiners is evaluating applicants for medical school. During her interview, one of the candidates, Ms. Nellie, confronts the committee with her belief that they are subjecting students to unnecessary stress, that they are fostering excessive grade competition and lack of concern for knowledge among students, and that they are not in touch with or sympathetic to the current realities of undergraduate life. She speaks rapidly and loudly, stutters, shows affect and distrust, and does not make eye contact with any of the committee members.

How might this behavior be evaluated by a committee member with a traditional personality-trait/psychodynamic orientation as compared with one with a social-behaviorist orientation?

Analytic

This student is full of hostility and resentment; has both low self-esteem and weak ego strength; needs affection and support but cannot ask for them for fear of rejection; tends to have a drive toward independent thinking coupled with strong needs for social approval; is generally orderly, clean, stingy with her possessions, and easily provoked into aggressiveness.

This applicant's problem is "obviously" rooted in an ambivalent love-hate relationship toward her parents as a consequence of severe toilet-training experiences. Her "anal-compulsive" syndrome (of order, cleanliness, and miserliness) has led to an overreliance on thought and words rather than deeds, to anxiety over any expression of hostility, and to stuttering from pent-up rage. All the behaviors observed are merely "smoke screens," concealing her real, deep-down problem.

Recommendation: Applicant reveals a lack of emotional maturity and an inability to contain personal problems; is clearly a bad risk for medical school (and a probable troublemaker).

Behavioristic

The committee members interrupt more and pay attention less when the applicant speaks slowly and softly. They listen more when she talks fast and loud and thus reinforce her for doing so. They are visibly distressed by what she is saying; this attitude elicits negative affect in return. By altering her normal speech delivery, the applicant disrupts her usual feedback pattern and begins to stutter. This adds to her anxiety, since she knows she is being evaluated on her poise, among other things. She tries to regain composure and avoid the negative reactions of the committee by not looking directly at them. She continues to talk because this reinforces her image of herself as someone engaged in a meaningful social activity. She knows that when she stops, the interview — and her candidacy — may be terminated.

Recommendation: Committee to check into validity of applicant's assertions, monitor its own negative response to criticism, and recognize the independence of action and maturity of thought shown by this applicant.

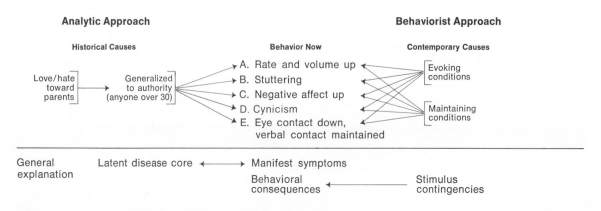

2. *Retention processes.* A model's influence is dependent on a person's ability to remember the model's actions, even after the model has disappeared from the scene. Symbolic coding and mental rehearsal of modeled behaviors are two processes that help to increase retention.

3. *Motoric reproduction processes.* Even if people learn new behaviors by observing a model, they cannot show evidence of this learning unless they can *perform* the modeled activities. If they are deficient in certain skills, then they will be unable to do what they have seen.

4. *Reinforcement and motivational processes.* The performance of learned behavior is also dependent on whether it will be rewarded or punished. If there are positive incentives, modeled behavior will be given more attention, learned better, and performed more often.

In addition, Bandura has found that modeling can be a source of more effects than just learning specific behavior. For example, he showed that "rule-modeling" also takes place, in which children learn to govern their behavior by the same underlying rules that they have watched models follow, even when they face an entirely different situation from the ones in which they watched the models. Modeling can also produce *disinhibition* of responses previously learned. For example, if a well-dressed person (attractive model) crosses the street against a "don't walk" sign, others who were waiting for a "walk" light may imitate this action.

Criticisms of learning theories. In sum, the learning theorists see consistency in human behavior as resulting from the learning of habit patterns. The most telling strength of their approach has been their statement of hypotheses and conclusions in a form subject to experimental verification. Their work has, consequently, given rise to a good deal of interesting research and to an effective set of therapeutic procedures. The major criticism of their work has been that it remains too elementaristic and environmentalistic: they propose little in the way of mechanisms to tie their bundles of behaviors together and give them coherent direction, and they exclude from study most behaviors that cannot be considered learned.

Sources and Dimensions of Individual Differences

There never were, since the creation of the world, two cases exactly parallel.
Lord Chesterfield, *Letters to His Son*, 1748

When we casually observe human beings and their behavior, we are struck by their remarkable similarities and continuities. But the closer we look and the finer we adjust our analytical apparatus, the more we become aware of their differences and discontinuities. It is exactly like putting your two hands, side-by-side, palms up, and noting how identical each finger on your left hand is to its corresponding right-hand member. But now look closely at your fingers and see how different the fingerprints are on each. Just as there are no recorded cases of two identical fingerprints, so there are no two people, not even "identical" twins, who are not different in many respects.

Although scientific inquiry has as its goal the discovery of uniformity and patterns of lawful regularity, this search is motivated by the existence of variation, eccentricities, and instances that refuse to conform to expectation. Were people identical, then psychology could be dispensed with entirely in favor of the physics and biology of human organisms. But they are not, and it is the task of psychology to attempt to discover the sources of that mystery of how and why different people in the same situation sometimes behave quite differently.

At a personal level, we rarely stop to inquire why we have acted the way we have when everyone else has done so too. It is only when we behave differently from others, or when someone else deviates from the rest, that we pause to wonder why. It is in this pause that the study of individual differences and personality originated.

Approaches to the Study of Individual Differences

As we pointed out at the beginning of the chapter, one of the key problems for the personality theorist is to develop laws of behavior that can account for uniqueness. To some, this seems like a contradiction in terms. How can you have a science of unique events?

As we have seen (pp. 13–14), psychologists have tended to follow one of two approaches in trying to "reconcile the irreconcilable." The *nomothetic* approach has been to assume that all human beings, different as they are, simply differ in the degree to which they possess the same set of characteristics. This approach characterizes trait theory and any attempt to predict behavior on the basis of standardized scales or tests.

The *idiographic* approach, on the other hand, assumes that a person is more than the sum of a group of characteristics and that predictions based on averages are of limited value in understanding or helping individuals. As is true of any "whole," there are qualities of persons that are present only when the whole person is functioning, qualities that never show up on measures of how much or how little that person has of particular traits measured singly. This approach has characterized the work of most clinicians.

A related controversy within the field of personality study has to do with the relative accuracy of subjective, clinical judgments as against those based on objective tests and statistical processes. In the 1950s, the issue was framed in terms of the *predictive success* of clinical judgments versus that of statistical ones (Meehl, 1954).

Statistical prediction relies on the straightforward application of an equation or actuarial table to a set of data. Such prediction may be made by anyone who knows how to read the tables and apply the formula. Clinical prediction relies on the skills of the individual clinician, who on the basis of observation, interviews, projective tests, training, and experience makes predictions about the future behavior of a given individual.

So far, studies of the relative success of these two predictive approaches have clearly favored the statistical (Meehl, 1965; Sawyer, 1966). It has been claimed by some critics, however, that the studies from which these conclusions are derived pitted *naive* clinical judgments, rather than *sophisticated* ones, against statistical procedures (Holt, 1971). The question of whether statistical prediction is superior to sophisticated clinical prediction thus remains open for further research — but the burden of proof now rests with the clinicians.

Self and Identity

When I say "I," I mean a thing absolutely unique, not to be confused with any other.
Ugo Betti, *The Inquiry,* 1944

What do you mean when you say "I"? Take a sheet of paper and number from 1 to 20. On each line write a statement beginning with the words "I am." When you have completed your list, please analyze your responses according to the four categories given below (Kuhn & McPartland, 1954).

Put an A next to statements that refer to the self as a physical entity (size, weight, color, sex).

Put a B next to statements that refer to the self within institutionalized roles and statutes (student, citizenship, football player, cheerleader).

Put a C next to statements that refer to the self as acting or feeling in characteristic ways in social interactions (happy, anxious, religious, shy).

Put a D next to statements that remove the self from interaction with others or from a specific context or social structure. These general, nondifferentiating statements would be of the type "I am a human being," "I am me," "I am one with the cosmos," and so on.

Tally the proportion of your self-statements that fall into each of these categories and see what kind of person they define. Compare that "self" with that of a classmate, and with that of someone older than yourself. There is evidence that while the B category was most prevalent in previous generations, today's students are more likely to respond with a majority of C statements (Zurcher, 1972). While the B mode reflects a self that gains its identity from the social structure, the C mode of self-conception is one not of fixed identity but of processes of self based on current experiences. The C mode has been described by Louis Zurcher as the *mutable self*, the self that adapts to rapid social change by a willingness to be fluid and actively shifting rather than anchored to a situationally based identity when the social structure is not stable. It may well be that category D, which was used relatively rarely in previous years, will eventually become the predominant self-conception if the rate of social change continues its dizzying acceleration. The D self is a self divorced from physical being, social structure, and interaction with the environment—it is the free-floating self, anchored only in abstractions.

Conceptions of the self. It has been generally agreed upon by most of those who theorize about the development of self-conception that this most personal aspect of our human nature is a product of our social interaction with others. Charles Cooley, back in 1902, proposed a "looking-glass self" that reflected the appraisals we imagine others hold of us. George Herbert Mead extended this notion that self-conception reflects the views of other people by proposing that the self develops from adopting as our own the orientations others have toward us. Over time, we come to think of ourselves in terms of the way others behave toward us. (See *P&L Close-up*, p. 434.)

According to William James, this *social self* is only one of three components of self—the others being the *material self* and the *spiritual self*. The social part of our self-conception is not a unitary entity; we carry around as many social selves as there are people who recognize us and maintain some image of us in their mind. We may thus suffer a deficiency of self by not being recognized by others or by becoming aware that the significant image others hold toward us is an unpleasant, negative one. The latter was sadly experienced by one of our students whose mother told him that she found him *boring* when he had always thought she accepted him as "serious" and "intense." The lack of a social self through nonrecognition was eloquently described by Ralph Ellison (1952) in his account of how a black person feels in a predominately white society.

"I am an invisible man. No, I am not a spook like those who haunted Edgar Allan Poe; nor am I one of your Hollywood-movie ectoplasms. I am a man of substance, of flesh and bone, fiber and liquids—and I might even be said to possess a mind. I am invisible, understand, simply because people refuse to see me. Like the bodiless heads you see sometimes in circus sideshows, it is as though I have been surrounded by mirrors of hard, distorting glass. When they approach me they see only my surroundings, themselves, or figments of their imagination—indeed, everything and anything except me." (p. 3)

"Do unto others as you would have them do unto you" is, of course, the Golden Rule of good social relations, but what do you do when others don't care about you enough to notice your existence? For many young people, social relations are painful events filled with uncertainty. This eloquent plea for understanding and social recognition comes from a young man who served a four-year prison term for possession of marijuana.

"I need to learn how to communicate. I need to know how to recognize other people's needs. I want you to teach me. . . . I need to know how to express my feelings so that no one will misunderstand them. I am afraid to express my anger and hurt, because I am afraid someone will misunderstand me. . . . I have to smoke a long pipe, wear my hair long, wax the handlebars of my moustache, and wear different clothes, to gain people's attention. But I am afraid I may have already frightened some of you. I did not want to frighten you, I just wanted to be noticed because I am lonely. I need to feel free. I wish I did not have to wave my hands in front of you, but I'm afraid you might not notice me. I also have to do it to feel free; to make sure there is no prison cell around me; I command more body space than you. I need to be reminded that I'm not in prison any more, because I was very lonely while I was in prison. I am still very lonely. I want to cry. I am afraid to cry, because I am afraid of what someone might think of me. I am afraid that someone might not think I was a human being. I am afraid that someone might call me a 'SISSY.' I am afraid that someone might not just understand me. I am afraid that someone might not hug me, or just hold my hand, or even just touch me. I am afraid to touch other people, because I am afraid of people. I want to be touched. I want to feel someone else's warmth. I want to feel more than just one other person's warmth. I want friends . . . and now you know my anger, and I am Happier than I was before I gave this speech to you. However, this was 'JUST A SPOONFUL'!!!!!!!!" (Robert C. Olcott, 1973)

In addition to the self developing out of the appraisals of others, our concept of self comes from labeling with trait names the behavior patterns we observe ourselves engaging in frequently or intensively. We also develop a "fix" on ourselves by virtue of social comparison processes (to be discussed in Chapter 13). We assess the quality of our ideas, the correctness of our opinions, the appropriateness of our emotions, and the extent of our abilities by comparing them with the behavior of others. Finally, it can be shown that once we come to have some sort of self-concept, we *bias* the incoming information from both our environment and our memory to be consistent with that image. Thus once we think highly of ourselves and have positive self-esteem, negative feedback is explained away or treated as an exception to the rule. On the other hand, once we have developed low self-esteem, positive feedback does little to change it because it, too, is seen as the inconsistent exception, whereas any failure or bad experience is readily accommodated as "expected" evidence.

Our self-conceptions influence not only our relations with others but our sense of autonomy (low self-esteem people are generally more conforming than are highs), the goals we aspire to, and—perhaps most important—the quality of our private emotional life.

Identity crises. From this brief discussion it should become clearer why adolescence is a time of life filled with *identity crises*. It is a time of transition in which the self of childhood is no longer appropriate to the new body, emerging sexual urges, lessened dependence on parents, movement away from the home, reliance on friends, exposure to new ideas and experiences. The adolescent is constantly being forced to shed old labels and comfortable self-conceptions that are no longer relevant before finding suitable substitutes. The need to conceptualize experience into stable categories so as to reduce the anxiety created by uncertainty is, according to Kenneth Gergen (1971), a driving force in this period of identity-in-chaos. Recently it is becoming apparent that a second identity crisis has been developing among middle-aged men and women. After having lived their lives according to socially accepted prescription, many of these forty- to fifty-year-olds realize that they have not been true to themselves. When they consider what they want out of the remaining years of their lives, more and more people are rejecting their mindless 9 to 5 jobs, lawn mowing, furniture waxing, keeping up with the what's-their-names, and so forth. It is too soon to evaluate whether this "pre-senior-citizen" crisis stage will lead to social chaos or to a peaceful overthrow of traditional limiting concepts of identity.

Developmental Factors

In view of the stress laid on early experiences by many personality theorists, it should not surprise us that developmental factors affect the ways in which individuals differ from one another. We shall look briefly at two such factors: moral development and sex differences.

Moral development. What we will or will not do in a given situation may depend not so much on what we *can* do as on what we think we *ought* to do. Issues of "ought" and "should" embody moral judgments of the basis on which actions are taken or restrained. Personality functioning is considerably affected by the stage of moral development a given individual has reached.

Lawrence Kohlberg (1967, 1969a, 1969b) has developed a moral conflict test by which people may be categorized as being at one of six stages of moral development. ■ The progression of a child through these stages follows an invariant sequence from 1 through 6, although the rate of movement toward conventional and principled levels of morality may vary in different children, and upper levels may never be reached. This analysis is obviously influenced in structure by Piaget's model of cognitive development (see Chapter 5).

■ **KOHLBERG'S CLASSIFICATION OF MORAL JUDGMENT INTO LEVELS AND STAGES OF DEVELOPMENT**

Levels	Basis of Moral Judgment	Stages of Development
I	Moral value resides in external, quasi-physical happenings, in bad acts, or in quasi-physical needs rather than in persons and standards.	Stage 1: Obedience and punishment orientation. Egocentric deference to superior power or prestige, or a trouble-avoiding set. Objective responsibility.
		Stage 2: Naively egoistic orientation. Right action is that instrumentally satisfying the self's needs and occasionally others'. Awareness of relativism of value to each actor's needs and perspective. Naive egalitarianism and orientation to exchange and reciprocity.
II	Moral value resides in performing good or right roles, in maintaining the conventional order and the expectancies of others.	Stage 3: Good-boy orientation. Orientation to approval and to pleasing and helping others. Conformity to stereotypical images of majority or natural role behavior, and judgment by intentions.
		Stage 4: Authority and social-order maintaining orientation. Orientation to "doing duty" and to showing respect for authority and maintaining the given social order for its own sake. Regard for earned expectations of others.
III	Moral value resides in conformity by the self to shared or shareable standards, rights, or duties.	Stage 5: Contractual legalistic orientation. Recognition of an arbitrary element or starting point in rules or expectations for the sake of agreement. Duty defined in terms of contract, general avoidance of violation of the will or rights of others, and majority will and welfare.
		Stage 6: Conscience or principle orientation. Orientation not only to actually ordained social rules but to principles of choice involving appeal to logical universality and consistency. Orientation to conscience as a directing agent and to mutual respect and trust.

From Kohlberg, 1967, p. 171

Adult moral development is characterized by: dropping of childish modes of thought rather than forming higher modes of thinking; stabilizing of Stage 4 conventional morality; greater consistency of moral judgment and moral action; integration of the use of moral structures and the application of moral thought to one's life.

Sex makes a difference. Being born male or female accounts for a major source of individual variation across a score of attributes, traits, and behaviors. Some of these differences are tied to anatomy and physical-biological structure; others are confounded by differences in the ways children of the two sexes are socialized and "programmed" by their societies. A summary of some of the important sex-role differences is given in the table (for a fuller account see Maccoby & Jacklin, 1974; Watson & Johnson, 1972). A full discussion of sex-role differences and stereotypes will be found in Chapter 13 and in the essay by Sandra Bem following that chapter.

● SUMMARY OF SEX-ROLE DIFFERENCES

	Male	Female
Overall Intelligence (measured by IQ tests)	No difference was found between males and females	
Spatial and Analytic Ability	Advantage (after about 10 years of age)	
Math Reasoning	Advantage by high-school years	
Verbal Ability		Marked advantage in early years; lesser advantage in later years
Impulsivity and Intellectual Performance	Negatively related	Weak positive relation
Anxiety	May have positive effects on achievement	Detrimental effect on performance
Early Shyness and Timidity	Timid boys have higher adult IQs	Shyness is hazardous to intellectual development
Aggressiveness	Much greater in general, but male aggressivity inhibits intellectual development	Female aggressivity facilitates intellectual development, physical aggression rare
Self-confidence in Ability	The brighter the boy the better he expects to perform in the future	The brighter the girl the less well she expects to do in the future
Creativity	Greater for men and boys who show more "feminine" traits	
Flexibility	The "androgynous" person who incorporates both sex roles is most adaptable and flexible to varying situational demands	
Conformity		Greater to group influence and formal communications
Maternal influence	Most intelligent boys have protective mothers	Most intelligent girls have less nurturant mothers who encourage independence

Some Personality Variables and Types

Among the many personality variables and character types that have been studied by researchers, we have chosen to describe four that we think may be of special interest to you.

Internal vs. External Locus of Control

To what extent do you believe that what happens to you, what your destiny will be, is determined by forces that are *external* to you—fate, chance, powerful others, unpredictable world events—and to what extent do you feel the controlling influence is *internal*, that is, comes from within you? There are individual differences in these beliefs that form different ideologies about the locus of control of behavior. This metaphor of internality-externality has been popular in many approaches to personality (as described by Collins et al., 1973).

In their classic text *The Lonely Crowd*, sociologist David Reisman and his colleagues (1950) distinguished between two character types in modern society that differ by being either inner- or other-directed. The *inner-directed* person is controlled by values and goal orientations implanted early in life by the "elders" of society. In contrast, the *other-directed* individuals are viewed as being more responsive to their contemporaries for direction and social influence.

We have seen that humanists such as Abraham Maslow have contended that the ideal character is that of the *self-actualized* person who is free of both peer-group external constraints and internal constraints imposed by the socialization process. This self-actualization results in greater autonomy and creativity by transcending dependency on others and the limits imposed by earlier principles of living.

The dimension of *introversion-extroversion* found in the Eysenck Personality Inventory (Eysenck & Eysenck, 1968) uncovers individual differences in the degree to which people need others as sources of reward and cues to appropriate behavior. The outgoing, impulsive extrovert needs people to interact with, while the reserved, cautious introvert relies less on other people for stimulation and more on books or nonsocial sources.

The internal-external personality metaphor has been given considerable attention through its use by Rotter (1954, 1966) and Lefcourt (1966, 1972) to distinguish different types of generalized expectancies or beliefs about *internal versus external control of reinforcement*. "Internal" people perceive that reward is contingent on their own behavior and/or their personal attributes. "Externals" perceive that rewards occur independently of their actions and are controlled by external forces.

While other approaches to internal-external personality types have emphasized the *origins* of an individual's goals, values, and motives, Julian Rotter's (1971) internal-external control dimension focuses on *strategies* for attaining goals regardless of the origins of these goals. The measurement of locus of control in individuals has been primarily accomplished by a forced-choice questionnaire (The I-E Scale). For one who has a belief in the internal locus of control, the world should be seen as a predictable place where one's actions have consequences. For an "external" person, on the other hand, the world is unpredictable and one's behavior does not necessarily gain rewards or help avoid pain.

"Learned helplessness" (discussed in Chapters 3 and 9) is obviously related to the locus of control variable. Internals avoid situations where they are apt to lose control over their reinforcements and are able to maintain an expectancy of eventual success despite short-term losses and defeats. Externals give in and give up sooner in experimental situations of learned helplessness.

There is evidence that internals are more resistant to social influence, less conforming, and more independent than are externals. Since successful management of one's behavior requires planning of means-ends relationships and the ability to "steer around obstacles toward desired goals," externals should be more likely to utilize available information in the situation that is relevant to their decisions and goals. This prediction has been verified in several ways. In an experimental study, externals used previously learned information to a greater extent than did internals 'when they were both called upon to make decisions where incorporation of that prior knowledge would be advantageous. Among tuberculosis patients (matched for hospital experience and socioeconomic class), internals possessed more objective information about their illness than did externals (Seeman & Evans, 1962).

Internals take their decisions more seriously as judged by their greater deliberation time, which increases with decision difficulty. They also react differently to tasks that are described as "skill versus chance," concentrating more in the skill situation. For externals, differences in concentration or distractability on skill-versus-chance tasks did *not* occur.

The relation of ethnic and socioeconomic variables to locus of control may be summarized as follows:

"In all of the reported ethnic studies, groups whose social position is one of minimal power either by class or race tend to score higher in the external-control direction. Within the racial groupings, class interacts so that the double handicap of lower-class and 'lower-caste' seems to produce persons with the highest expectancy of external control. Perhaps the apathy and what is often described as lower-class lack of motivation to achieve may be explained as a result of the disbelief that effort pays off." (Lefcourt, 1966, p. 212)

Many poor people and third-world peoples have learned that, in fact, they exercise little control over their lives, but are controlled by a complex set of external conditions within their political-economic-social situation. They have available many fewer options than others in their society as to where they will live, work, and play. Poverty makes education a luxury, but without education and the skills and "certification" it brings, poor people are the last to be hired, first to be fired, even on menial jobs. Here

we have a paradox that those who are to a large extent externally controlled develop a *belief* in external locus of control that in turn leads to less commitment to actions that might eventually change their condition. "You can't fight City Hall!" is one part of this belief system. Another is to give up on the possibility of any meaningful change in *this* life, but to look beyond it to the "pie in the sky when you die."

It should be one task of education to help people appraise what aspects of their lives are amenable to change through their actions and which are less so. An external orientation can lead to a self-fulfilling prophecy of gloom and, under some circumstances, can even make a difference between life and death. It has been suggested, for example, that the proportionately greater incidence of tornado deaths in some areas of the South is due to the greater tendency to "external" orientation in those areas. One study found that externals tended to react to tornado threats with fatalism and inactivity, rather than taking active measures to protect themselves (Sims & Baumann, 1972).

An interesting but depressing relationship between I-E personality scores and prevailing conditions in our country has been documented recently. During the decade from 1962 to 1971, there was a marked shift in the average I-E score among college students. Can you predict in which direction? The Vietnam war, campus unrest, increased crime, and mass violence all helped to shift scores in the external direction.

A recent review of the literature on locus of control research (Phares, 1976) makes it clear that perceived locus of control is not only a relatively stable characteristic that people carry from situation to situation as a generalized belief about their power and control. It can also be viewed as a relatively narrow expectancy determined by the specific environmental situations the person is functioning in. Only the most extreme internals may be able to remain optimistic and active when the situation appears hopeless.

God grant me the serenity to accept the things I cannot change, courage to change the things I can, and wisdom to know the difference.

Reinhold Niebuhr

Machiavellians (almost) Always Win

Imagine yourself in the following situation with two other people. One hundred dollars is put down on the table to be distributed among you in any way, as soon as any *two* of you agree to how it will be split. Obviously, the fair allotment would be $33.33 each — if all three had to decide how to share it. However, a selfish pair could cut the third party out and each have $50. One person suggests this alternative to you. Before you can agree or refuse, the left-out third party offers to give you $51, taking $49 as his or her share and cutting out the other person. What do you do? Do you manipulate the others to maximize your "take" before agreeing either to cut out one of the two, or to have them share what is left over after your portion? Or, is it likely that you will even be bargaining to get a small piece of the prize and not be cut out by the other two?

When this situation is actually staged in an experiment, over many trials, the typical pattern is for one person to come out with about $53, one to get $30, and one to get only $17. Which of the three would you be?

Niccolo Machiavelli has provided in his writings (notably *The Prince*, 1532, and *The Discourses*, 1531), the origins of a social-personality theory that helps answer that question. He was concerned with how people can be manipulated, and with what traits and tactics differentiate those who wield influence from those who are influenced.

Traits of Machiavellians. From these anecdotal descriptions of power tactics and the nature of influential people, a Columbia University psychologist, Richard Christie, constructed a questionnaire scale to measure "Machiavellianism." The questions were organized around a cluster of beliefs about tactics, people, and morality. Examples of each are (Christie & Geis, 1970):

Tactics
High Mach: "A white lie is often a good thing."
Low Mach: "If [something is] morally right, compromise is out of the question."

View of People
High Mach: "Most people don't really know what's best for them."
Low Mach: "Barnum was wrong when he said a sucker is born every minute."

Morality
High Mach: "Deceit in conduct of war is praiseworthy and honorable."
Low Mach: "It is better to be humble and honest than important and dishonest."

The "Mach" scales differentiate between High and Low Machiavellians on the basis of the extent to which they endorse Machiavelli's rules of conduct in human relations. The scales place at one end of the continuum people who have *relative* standards of behavior ("Never tell anyone the real reason you did something, unless it's useful to do so"), and at the other extreme those with *absolute* standards ("Honesty is always the best policy"). Between the extremes of the High Machs and the Low Machs fall the middle group, who endorse some part of the Machiavellian philosophy.

Essentially, this philosophy is one of pragmatism: "if it works, use it." In the $100 con game, the people who get the lion's share consistently are those who score high on these scales. They are included in every coalition, whereas the Low Mach scorers are lucky to be included in any coalitions and have to be content with the leftovers. The Moderate Mach scorers get only slightly less than would be expected by a fair one-third split.

In other experimental situations, High Machs have been shown not to cheat more, but to cheat better. When they lie, they can look their accusers in the eye and convince them that they did not cheat. When competing against other students, they are more effective at "psyching out" their competitors (they work harder at it and devise more creative disturbances). When they have behaved irrationally or in a manner inconsistent with their private attitudes, they can tolerate this dissonance without changing their attitudes to fit the behavior. In experiments, they manipulate not only other subjects, but often the experimenter as well.

What makes a High Mach high? The essence of the High Mach is "to keep one's cool when others are blowing theirs." Machiavellians maintain emotional distance, do not get involved in others' behavior, or even in their own. Their behavior is guided by what they know rationally, not by what they feel emotionally.

High Machs flourish where three general situational features exist:

a) Interaction is face-to-face (rather than impersonal or indirect);

b) Rules and guidelines are minimal and there is considerable latitude for them to improvise and structure the ambiguity;

c) Emotional arousal is high (thus interfering with task performance) for the Low Machs, but not for them.

Predictions regarding a High Mach's behavior in a social influence situation must take into account the *interaction* of this trait and the social-psychological features of the situation. The High Mach is a person who has learned a strategy that gives rise to a consistent set of behaviors that are reinforced only in certain situations. Thus one cannot predict the High Mach's behavior from the scale score alone.

The Authoritarian Personality

Because of the devastation wrought by Hitler's fascism in World War II and the threat it posed to democratic society, social scientists became concerned about the psychological processes that made it both possible and effective. After the war, researchers at the University of California's Berkeley campus set out to see if there was a cluster of political attitudes, social and economic values, and personality traits that was characteristic of an "antidemocratic personality" (Adorno, Frenkel-Brunswick, Levinson, & Sanford, 1950). Was it possible to identify the potential fascist, whose personality structure would render him or her particularly susceptible to antidemocratic propaganda?

These researchers began by constructing a scale designed to measure *ethnocentrism*—the tendency to hold prejudiced attitudes toward all groups different from one's own. High scorers on this scale show a general tendency to see the world in terms of noble in-groups that must be supported and offensive out-groups that must

be avoided or rejected and attacked when they become threatening. This scale was administered to a large sample of subjects and the very low and very high scoring (the extremely tolerant and the extremely intolerant) subjects were singled out for systematic study. Then the search began for character structures consistently associated with these opposite types.

Those high in intolerance on the ethnocentrism scale were found also to give consistently rigid, constricted, prejudiced responses on an anti-Semitism scale, a scale of political and economic conservatism, and a fascism scale. The latter, nicknamed the *"F-scale,"* tapped a syndrome of personality traits organized around the following characteristics:

a) conventionalism—obedience and respect for authority;

b) authoritarian submission—idealization of authority, with an inability to question or criticize authority;

c) authoritarian aggression—rejection of all violations of conventional values;

d) anti-intraceptionism—resentment against prying into motives, resistance to introspection or psychological analysis;

e) superstition and stereotypes—rigid categorical thinking, need for order and regular routine;

f) power and toughness preoccupation—perceiving people as strong and domineering or weak and submitting;

g) destructiveness and cynicism—vilification of all those outside one's family or in-group;

h) projectivity—disposition to see evil forces at work in a hostile environment full of threatening people;

i) excessive sexual concern—an exaggerated condemnation (and ambivalence) regarding expression of sexuality and sexual freedom.

High scores on these four scales identified an *authoritarian personality,* described by one writer as:

". . . the basically weak and dependent individual who has sacrificed his capacity for genuine experience of self and others in order to maintain a precarious order and safety. In the type

case, he confronts with a façade of spurious strength a world in which rigidly stereotyped categories are substituted for the affectionate and individualized experience of which he is incapable. Such a person, estranged from inner values, lacks self-awareness and shuns intraception. His judgments are governed by a punitive conventional moralism, reflecting external standards in which he remains insecure since he has failed to make them really his own. His relations with others depend on considerations of power, success, and adjustment, in which people figure as means rather than as ends, and achievement is not valued for its own sake. In his world, the good, the powerful, and the ingroup stand in fundamental opposition to the immoral, the weak, the out-group. For all that he seeks to align himself with the former, his underlying feelings of weakness and self-contempt commit him to a constant and embittered struggle to prove to himself and others that he really belongs to the strong and good. Prejudice against out-groups of all kinds and colors is a direct corollary of this personality structure."* (Smith, 1950, p. 776)*

Correlates of authoritarianism. Several consistent correlations have been found between high authoritarianism (as measured by the four scales used in the California studies) and other behavior. Those who score high are more likely to change their attitudes in response to statements attributed to authority figures than in response to straight information—and will sometimes even accept attitudes contrary to their own if a respected authority endorses them.

Other studies showed authoritarians to be more rigid in solving problems when their ego was threatened; to behave more punitively and condescendingly to social inferiors (when they were camp counselors); to be less willing to be subjects in psychological experiments; to attribute their own attitudes to others more often than low scorers; to estimate the preferences of their superiors more accurately than those of their peers (contrary to low scorers); and to exhibit more hostility toward a low-status person than a high-status one for making the same mistake.

Perspective on the authoritarian personality. The methodology underlying the approach to studying this unique "social-personality type" and its implications have been justifiably criticized (Christie & Jahoda, 1954). The major points of contention have been that: (a) overgeneralizations to a broad population have been made, based on findings from highly selected extreme subsamples—only the individuals with the highest and the lowest scores on the ethnocentrism scale were studied in the original sample; (b) the original scale scores may have been confounded by a general *acquiescence set* (the high scorers may have been "yea-sayers" who had a tendency to agree frequently and thus could have gotten high scores without being authoritarians); (c) the low authoritarian scores were positively correlated with intelligence and education, perhaps reflecting a greater ability on their part to fake "acceptable" responses; (d) the relationship of the adult behavior to the childhood experiences of the subjects was determined by unverified *introspective reports* of adults recalling their childhood, and thus may have been based on distorted recollections.

The portrait of the high F-scale scorer as neurotic, rigid, and unable to be effective is certainly overdrawn. In many situations the high-F person will be able to act more decisively than the low-F person, since this more simplistic view makes him or her less likely to examine ambiguity, inconsistency, and "shades of gray." It is likely that the liberal values of the researchers and of other psychologists working in this area predisposed them to overemphasize the undesirable aspects of authoritarianism.

Similarly, there was a tendency to identify the authoritarians as only right-wing conservatives. But not all rigidity and authoritarianism are on the political right. It has been pointed out that some of those on the radical left, though they differ in ideological goals from the reactionary right, are fully as authoritarian in their interpersonal functioning and power tactics.

Despite its acknowledged shortcomings, this approach to the study of antidemocratic attitudes opened a fascinating area of intellectual inquiry into the nature of human beings. It has demonstrated that political and social attitudes can be held because they serve personal needs to defend one's own security and sense of worth rather than because of rational evidence. What began as a literary-historical analysis broadened into a sociological investigation and led to an integration of methods and approaches from personality psychology and social psychology.

But perhaps the most lasting value of this research program lies in calling our attention to the fact that authoritarians, whether left or right politically, are made, not born. In the normal process of forming a consistent, organized personality, a particular combination of early life experiences and prevailing societal conditions sets the stage for a perversion of personality. Faced with the acute insecurities and bewildering changes of modern life and needing a predictable world even more than the rest of us do, today's authoritarian personality achieves predictability through the rigidity of a "mental straitjacket" that insulates him or her from the doubts born of constantly trying to adapt to changing conditions. Through identification with external power or with a rigid ideology, such personalities escape having to form their own values and make independent judgments, but at the cost of openness to their own experience and selfhood.

The Silent World of the Shy Student

"I am interested in shyness because it was a real prison for me, especially during my high-school years. As I have experienced it, shyness is a feeling of self-consciousness, an inhibition of your natural self, evoked by certain situations and people. It's an intense awareness of the self along with the feeling of constriction—the feeling that your every action is being noticed by others—the pain of struggling to think of something to say—the dryness in your throat—the croaking in your throat—the flush in your cheeks —the feeling that you are different from other people, that you are stiff and rigid—it is the longing to be spontaneous. How can you over-

come your feelings of shyness? How can you help others free themselves from this oppression? How many other people are there out there who are shy like me?" (Letter from Susan, a Stanford University student, 1973)

Shyness means different things to different people, but basically it is an awareness of one's inability to take action when one both wants to and knows how to. Shyness is a fear of negative self-evaluation and/or negative evaluation from others. The shy person is conspicuous by silence when others are talking, by immobility when others are moving, by isolation when others are affiliating. Thus the shy person is characterized more by an absence of overt responding than by the presence of unusual responses.

When extreme, shyness indeed becomes a self-imposed prison where the person plays both the role of hated guard who constantly enforces "not-allowed" rules and also the despised prisoner who sheepishly follows them. Under some conditions shyness may result in a severe form of pathology leading to total withdrawal from social contacts and excruciating loneliness. This extreme shyness shades off into a lack of self-confidence and anxiety over meeting new people or entering new situations. There are also people who are "shy" by choice—that is, they feel more comfortable with things, projects, ideas, books, etc., than with people. They can join the crowd if necessary and don't have any apprehension about being with people; but other things being equal, they would rather be alone (a type popularized by actress Greta Garbo).

In an effort to better understand this personality variable that, surprisingly, has been given almost no research attention, a team of researchers at Stanford University has begun to collect data on the incidence and nature of shyness among students (Zimbardo, Pilkonis, & Norwood, 1974). How would you respond to the following two questions in their survey?

Do you presently consider yourself to be a shy person? Yes _____/No _____
Was there ever a period in your life during which you considered yourself to be a shy person? Yes _____/ No _____

In surveys of several thousand high-school and college students, more than 40 percent labeled themselves as presently "shy," and over 80 percent reported that they are or once were "shy." Although shyness can be represented along a continuum of intensity, people do think of themselves as "shy" or "not-shy." It is probable that in the general population there are at least as many people who label themselves "shy" as those who label themselves "not-shy." Shyness is related to introversion, but it is something in addition; more than a third of the subjects who felt they were extroverts considered themselves to be shy, and some introverts felt they were not shy.

While a small percentage of subjects (8 percent) reported shyness was a "desirable" trait, over a third (35 percent) said shyness was either "undesirable" or "very undesirable." (The rest evaluated it as neither desirable nor undesirable.) However, the majority of both shy and not-shy subjects agreed to the negative consequences of shyness, such as:

a) creates social problems; makes it difficult to meet new people, make new friends, enjoy potentially good experiences;

b) has negative emotional consequences; creates feelings of loneliness, isolation, depression;

c) prevents positive evaluations by others (e.g., one's personal assets never become apparent because of one's shyness);

d) makes it difficult to be appropriately assertive, to express opinions, to take advantage of opportunities;

e) allows incorrect negative evaluations by others (e.g., one may unjustly be seen as unfriendly or snobbish or weak);

f) creates cognitive and expressive difficulties and inhibits the capacity to think clearly while with others and to communicate effectively with them;

g) encourages excessive self-consciousness, preoccupation with oneself.

The experience of shyness may be analyzed into eliciting conditions and reactions. The table shows the percentage of 800 "shy" subjects who reported that each of the situations and people listed elicited shyness in them, as well as produced the various reactions noted. ◆

◆ INVENTORY OF SHYNESS ELICITORS AND REACTIONS

Situations	% Shy Students
Where I am focus of attention—large group	72.6%
Large groups	67.6%
Of lower status	56.2%
Social situations in general	55.3%
New situations in general	55.0%
Requiring assertiveness	54.1%
Where I am being evaluated	53.2%
Where I am focus of attention—small group	52.1%
Small social groups	48.5%
One-to-one different sex interactions	48.5%
Of vulnerability (need help)	48.2%
Small task-oriented groups	28.2%
One-to-one same sex interactions	13.8%

Other People	
Strangers	69.7%
Opposite sex group	62.9%
Authorities by virtue of their knowledge	55.3%
Authorities by virtue of their role	39.7%
Same sex groups	33.5%
Relatives	19.7%
Elderly people	12.4%
Friends	10.9%
Children	10.0%
Parents	8.5%
Siblings	3.2%

Physiological Reactions	
Increased pulse	54.4%
Blushing	53.2%
Perspiration	49.1%
Butterflies in stomach	48.2%
Heart pounding	48.0%
Dry mouth	18.1%
Tingling sensation	17.0%
Tremors	12.0%

Thoughts and Sensations	
Self-consciousness	84.8%
Concern about impression management	67.3%
Concern for social evaluation	62.9%
Negative self-evaluation	58.5%
Unpleasantness of the situation	56.1%
Shyness in general	45.9%
Distractions	26.6%

Overt Behaviors	
Silence	79.5%
No eye contact	50.6%
Avoidance of others	43.9%
Avoidance of action	41.8%
Low speaking voice	39.5%
Posture	18.8%
Stuttering	18.8%

Adapted from Zimbardo, Pilkonis, & Norwood, 1975

The importance of the process of self-labeling (that is, coming to think of yourself as "shy" or "not-shy") becomes apparent in the way students from these two groups described conditions of stress, anxiety, and apprehensions. Shy subjects viewed shyness as a trait they carry around *inside* them that emerges from time to time across different situations, and is latent even when they are being gregarious. The not-shy subjects, on the other hand, pointed to situations "out there," and not to an inner disposition, that make them react with discomfort. Similarly, the symptoms shy subjects used as indicators of their shyness were the same ones not-shy people used as indicators that they were under social pressure. Thus it seems that not-shy people learn something about situations from their reactions to them, while shy people continually relearn something about themselves — that they are shy.

Although shyness is a personal reaction, it is created and maintained by basic social values and cultural programming. The prevalence of shyness is higher in ego-oriented cultures than in group or community-centered cultures. Where cultural norms overvalue competition and achievement and control behavior through shame and social expectation, shyness thrives. However, where group goals are of primary importance, as on an Israeli *kibbutz* or in mainland China, shyness is not common. Cross-cultural perspectives also reveal that the label of shyness and its interpretation may differ from our own. Among a sample of Tokyo University students who were generally quite shy, some viewed shyness in positive terms since it creates a modest, appealing impression, does not intimidate others, prevents one from being aggressive, enables one to be a good listener, and so on (G. Hatano, 1975).

Help for students with a shyness problem may thus proceed by setting up student-run "shyness clinics" where shy students themselves act as social facilitators who: (a) create an atmosphere of nonevaluation, (b) disseminate information on the prevalence of shyness, (c) help their shy peers to reinterpret the consequences of shyness, and (d) provide specific assertion-training tactics effective in shyness-eliciting situations.

Personality Assessment

Any attempt to assess individual characteristics is based on the notion that "it all hangs together somehow." That is, such assessment always involves the attempt to predict a wide range of ways in which an individual will be consistent from a much narrower range of characteristics that we can tap directly. In the following sections we shall look at some of the approaches to the problem of predicting a lot from a little, but first we need to consider why such assessment is undertaken despite the difficulty and grief often entailed.

Why Try?

One of the questions most frequently asked about psychological testing is "What's it for?" Students who have to take psychological tests sometimes feel dehumanized, "put in boxes" that leave no room for their individuality to show through. Prospective employees — particularly those from minority groups — sometimes feel that tests are being used against them. This is indeed ironic, for the main purpose in giving a psychological test is usually to be able to take *better* account of the test-taker's individual characteristics. If personality theorists are trying to find fruitful ways of conceptualizing the kinds of consistency in individual behavior, psychological testers are in the business of trying to predict which individuals will show which of these kinds of consistency under what conditions. Typically they are trying to do so for one of three broad reasons.

1. *To predict success.* A great many psychological tests are used in vocational counseling, as "entrance examinations" for schools, and in personnel placement work. In settings such as these, the tests are used to predict the probability that an individual will be successful in a given line of work, at a particular school, or in some specified job.

2. *To determine treatment.* The second major use of psychological tests is in schools and clinical settings. Here the tests are used in deciding

what sorts of educational or therapeutic experiences will be helpful for which people. In some cases they are used to determine the advisability of special classes for children who are mentally retarded or emotionally disturbed. In others they are used to explore the degree and nature of psychopathology in order to determine which sort of therapy will be likely to be most fruitful. At times, they are used to investigate the possibility that psychological or neurological difficulties are involved in physical ailments or below-average functioning.

3. *To further our understanding.* Finally, psychological tests are used in research aimed at refining our conceptions of how people function. Part of this research involves testing the sorts of personality theories we examined above. Another part involves the development of new tests that will enhance our ability to predict who will be successful at what, and who will benefit from which types of treatment. Still another has to do with learning about how people develop: at what ages children develop which skills, attitudes, and ways of dealing with the world. In all such testing, then, the goal is to find out more: to further the development of psychology as a theoretical and applied science.

Instruments for Measuring Personality

In developing quantitative instruments for the measurement of personality, the psychologist is concerned with the concepts of validity, reliability, objectivity, and standardization. The index of *validity* is the extent to which an instrument actually measures what it is intended to measure. An instrument cannot be "valid" in the abstract; rather, it is valid for a specific purpose, assessed against explicit criteria such as predicting success in college or in a particular profession.

The *reliability* of a measuring instrument is the degree to which people earn the same relative scores each time they are measured (aside from changes in them due to health, fatigue, etc.). Reliability is assessed by retesting and by different evaluators scoring the same behavioral event. A measuring device cannot be valid un-less it is first of all reliable, but reliability does not guarantee that it is valid.

A common cause of unreliability in psychological tests is a lack of *objectivity* in scoring procedures. If a test must be scored on the basis of subjective judgment, different people scoring it are likely to get widely differing results unless detailed scoring rules are provided.

To be most useful, a measuring device must be *standardized*—administered under standard conditions to a large group of persons representative of the group for which it is intended. This procedure yields *norms*, or standards, so that an individual's score can be compared with those of others in a defined group. The test must, of course, be administered to all subjects in the same way and under the same conditions, or comparisons will be meaningless.

Rating scales. Some kinds of behavior from which one might wish to predict individual characteristics are difficult for a psychologist to observe directly. They may be too private, for example, or occur over a prohibitively long period of time. Thus in trying to assess these kinds of behavior, it is often useful to have others who know the subject give their impressions of what he or she does. One device for obtaining such impressions is the rating scale. There are two kinds of rating scales, *relative* and *absolute*, each with certain advantages and disadvantages. These are frequently used in connection with an interview, as well as to record subjective impressions based on a longer period of contact. Both types have the advantage of yielding numerical values that can be analyzed quantitatively.

Relative rating scales. A relative rating scale may be used when several subjects are being rated. The order-of-merit method is typical. The rater ranks the subjects in order by indicating the best, then the next best, and so on until all subjects have been ranked on the trait being measured. This method indicates what each person's position is relative to that of all other subjects being considered.

Absolute rating scales. In absolute rating scales the judge assigns a score to each individual on each trait being rated. Each person is compared to some standard established independently of the particular group of individuals being considered. For example, the judge may rate each candidate on a seven-point scale of neatness or may check all the adjectives in a list that apply to the candidate.

Both types of rating scale are subject to two important types of errors of judgment: halo and stereotype. The *halo effect* is the tendency to judge a likeable or intelligent person as "good" in other respects as well. *Stereotypes* are preconceived notions as to what we expect a given kind of person (Russian, politician) to be like. Both errors can be minimized by having the judge rate all the individuals on only one trait at a time, so that the earlier ratings of a given person will be less likely to influence the later ones.

Because the rating scale inevitably depends so much on the subjective judgments of the raters, however, it is usually regarded as inferior to the more objective psychological tests to be described below. Certainly the value of the ratings will depend both on a judge's ability to evaluate others and on his or her definition of the traits being assessed. To some extent these factors can be appraised by a check on how well two sets of judges agree on their ratings of the same individuals and on how consistent the same judges are on their ratings of the same individuals on successive occasions.

Behavior sampling. In behavior sampling techniques, the examiner simply observes the person's behavior in a typical situation. Unaware of being watched, the subject behaves as usual.

One interesting behavior sampling technique for assessing leadership qualities was developed by the Office of Strategic Services during World War II. Situations were set up that were as nearly as possible like those that a candidate might actually meet. For example, a construction test involved an assignment in which the candidate was to complete a piece of construc-

tion, supervising men who had secretly been instructed to make every attempt to sabotage the effort. Observers rated the candidate on his behavior under this type of stress (Fortune, 1946).

Later assessment of such tests proved them to be much more expensive and less valid per hour of testing time than were other objective psychological tests. However, such behavior sampling techniques may have value as a supplement to more conventional testing procedures.

The interview. The interview has long been the central technique used by clinical psychologists and psychiatrists in their attempts to study and treat personality disorders. It has also been used extensively by employers in selecting new workers.

In one form, the interview may be fairly loose and open-ended—"standardized" only to the extent that there is an expectation that two people will share an office for a brief time and that one will do most of the talking. In this form, however, it has proved to be a rather undependable device for yielding impressions that predict future behavior, at least in a job setting. This undependability probably results in part from its vulnerability to errors in judgment, such as the halo effect and stereotypes mentioned above in connection with rating scales. In addition, any impressions formed in this way are limited by the perceptual filter of the interviewer and by the interviewee's desire to make a good impression.

Many of these difficulties can be circumvented by using a *standardized interview schedule,* whereby predetermined questions are asked in a prearranged order. Such an approach yields data that are less subject to interviewer bias and that can be scored and evaluated objectively.

Clues from projective devices. Undoubtedly you have sometimes "seen" a face or the shape of an animal in a cloud. But if you mentioned this to friends, you may have discovered that they saw a tree or a castle or something else quite different. Psychologists rely on a similar phenomenon in their use of *projective* techniques of personality measurement. The subject is presented with a standardized set of ambiguous or neutral stimuli—inkblots or pictures that have no definite meaning but can be interpreted in various ways—and is encouraged to interpret freely what is "seen" in them. Thus the subject can "project" onto each neutral stimulus some special, private meaning—much as you projected the face or animal onto the cloud. Psychologists have suggested that such projections reflect the differing needs and emotional adjustments of individuals and thus help reveal their underlying personality patterns.

Projective tests are difficult to fake because there are no obviously right or wrong answers; they have the further advantage of tapping deeper levels of needs and fears than other measurement methods. They are not, however, entirely satisfactory. One major limitation is that the psychologists must rely to a large extent on their own subjective judgment in scoring the subject's responses. Although objective standards have been set up for evaluating various types of responses, skillful interpretation on the part of the examiner is still required. This means that the judgment of the examiner influences the final "score" to a greater extent than it does with more objective tests. In addition, considerable training is necessary for using projective tests as a diagnostic tool.

The Rorschach test. The *Rorschach* technique, one of the oldest projective methods, makes use of a series of inkblots. Some are black and white, some colored, and they vary in form, shading, and complexity. Subjects observe the cards in a prescribed order and describe what they "see" in each one. This often gives information about their personality structure that is not brought out by clinical interviews. For example, the way subjects react to the color in the blots may throw light on their emotional responses to their environment. ■

In addition to analyzing the content of the projected stories, the Rorschach expert detects clues to personality functioning from stylistic aspects of the response. Does the person respond to the whole stimulus or only to parts? Do form and structure predominate over movement and action in the subject's attempt to organize the ambiguity in the test materials? Such analyses help the clinician identify the individual's style of perceiving the world, areas of conflict, and the extent of pathology.

The Thematic Apperception Test (TAT). Another projective technique is the Thematic Apperception Test. This test is composed of three series of ten pictures, each picture representing a different situation. The subject is asked to make up a story about each picture, describing the situation, the events that led up to it, how the characters felt, and what the outcome will be. By evaluating both the structure and the content of these stories, as well as the subject's behavior in telling them, the examiner tries to discover the personality characteristics of the subject. For example, the examiner might evaluate the subject as being "conscientious" if the subject told TAT stories about "people who lived up to their obligations" and told them in a very serious, orderly way.

The interpretation of the TAT stories (as well as the Rorschach) is very much a subjective judgment of the clinician, in which inferences are made about the subject's motives, values, attitudes, defenses, and more. Basically, the cli-

■ An inkblot similar to those used in the Rorschach test. What do you see in it? Ask one or two of your friends what *they* see.

nician puts together a theory about the subject that accounts for as much as possible of that person's history and responses. In practice, the TAT is used in conjunction with several other types of assessment techniques, which form a balanced set, or *battery,* of tests.

Self-inventories. Standard self-inventories require subjects to give information about *themselves.* They may be asked to tell what they like or dislike to do, what emotional reactions they tend to have in certain situations, whether they admire or condemn various figures in public life, and so on.

The self-inventory is valuable in that it goes below the surface appearance to tap the individual's own personal experience and feelings. It is also convenient to give because it does not require the services of a group of raters or interviewers. Its chief disadvantage is that the individuals tested do not altogether understand themselves and therefore cannot always give an accurate report. Or, if they wish, they can easily lie about themselves in an attempt to make the results look more favorable.

The first self-inventories were developed for the purpose of classifying individuals in terms of either occupational interest or psychopathology. Many such measuring devices are developed by a statistical approach called *item analysis.* Psychologists determine which of a number of items are answered in a consistent way by most members of a particular group. On the basis of such information, a scoring system is developed for discovering those groups that a person resembles most in terms of interests and personality.

There are several interest inventories of this type in general use. They are particularly appropriate for testing people who are of an age where commitment to a career choice is imminent. Because of its high validity, the most widely used test is the Strong Vocational Interest Blank. The basic principle underlying its scoring system is that a person who marks a great majority of the items in the same way as, for example, doctors would be likely to be happy as a doctor.

There is substantial evidence that young people who choose occupations that are consistent with their interest scores find greater satisfaction in their work than those who do not choose occupations consistent with their scores.

Intelligence and IQ Tests

Intelligence is the capacity to profit from experience and to go beyond the given to the possible. It is in our intellectual development that we humans have been able to transcend our physical frailty and gain dominance over more powerful or numerous animals. No wonder, then, that intelligence is our most highly prized possession. But what is intelligence? What are its origins? How can it be assessed? What are its advantages?

Speculation about such questions has intrigued scientists over the centuries. In France in the year 1799, there arose a unique opportunity to study the nature of human intelligence. A naked child of perhaps twelve years was "captured" by three sportsmen in the woods of the Aveyron district. After a week in captivity he escaped into the mountains, but was retaken later that winter.

The following year he was taken to Paris, where curiosity about the nature of this wild human-animal ran high. Would he be Rousseau's natural man, the "noble savage" uncontaminated by civilization? Or would he be the rare instance of John Locke's "tabula rasa"—an unformed, blank mind to be transformed into a normal human being by the imprint of education? Others were just curious, as they would be to see any strange new animal.

What they saw was "a disgustingly dirty child affected with spasmodic movements and often convulsions who swayed back and forth ceaselessly like certain animals in the menagerie, who bit and scratched those who opposed him, who showed no sort of affection for those who attended him; and who was in short, indifferent to everything and attentive to nothing" (Itard, 1962 edition, p. 4).

The child was turned over for care and education to a young, enthusiastic, dedicated physician, Jean-Marie-Gaspard Itard. For the next five years Itard worked with the child (who was given the name Victor) as tutor, scientist, and parent. Itard's report of his successes and failures makes fascinating reading or viewing (it is available in a paperback edition entitled *The Wild Boy of Aveyron*, 1962, and as a film).

Medical experts of the time judged the boy to be an "incurable idiot," perhaps originally abandoned because of his feeblemindedness. But Itard believed that the civilizing influence of education would suffice to turn a subnormal wild child into a normal human adult. What Itard failed to recognize in his optimistic environmentalist view was that in many cases experience must come at the appropriate time in the course of development. For some of the changes Itard sought, it was apparently too late; for others, the success was remarkable.

In summary, the young savage began his education with the following limitations: he was incapable of attention; had a poor memory, judgment, and aptitude for imitation; was mute except for grunts; showed little intelligence and poor sensory awareness; and "was insensible to every kind of moral influence." But somehow he *had* survived—a mere child in a wilderness whose dangers were attested to by his twenty-three scars.

Itard divided his training emphasis into three areas: the senses, the intellect, and the emotions. Of the first, all senses except hearing showed marked improvement. Victor acquired the ability to make perceptual discriminations between objects by touch, vision, and taste, which he could not do at the start of his training.

Perception was the foundation for the development of the intellectual functions—the "great work of the communication of ideas." Victor learned to connect objects with abstract signs and symbols. He learned the concepts of relative size, weight, color, resistance, and other comparisons. The boy also learned to copy in writing the words whose meaning he knew. He was able later to reproduce them from memory and use them to express his needs and communicate in a simple way with other people so as to effect "a free and continual exchange of thoughts."

But Victor was never able to master spoken language beyond the use of two words, *lait* (milk) and *Oh Dieu* (Oh God). Unfortunately,

Victor's failure in this area (which could have been related to his hearing deficit) led Itard to despair.

The attention, patience, and security provided Victor by his teacher also was apparent in his emotional development. He became "sensible of care taken of him, susceptible to fondling and affection, alive to the pleasures of well-doing, ashamed of his mistakes, and repentant of his outbursts" (p. 101). But here, too, Itard erred in assuming that the values of his own civilized, social life were the only acceptable ones. He saw as an incurable fault in his young savage "his immoderate taste for the freedom of open country and his indifference to most of the pleasures of social life" (p. 101).

It is evident that some, but not all, of the early deficiencies of the wild boy of Aveyron were improved or indeed remedied by experience. But on the side of the nativists who argued for the importance of inheritance, is the plain fact that Victor was never so normal in his behavior to be indistinguishable from other boys his age. Whether Victor was born feebleminded or the limits of his development were reduced by lack of human contact and education in his early life will never be known.

Victor lived to about forty years of age, a not uncommon longevity in that era. The lessons learned in his education were passed on to Edouard Séguin and through him to Maria Montessori, whose method of teaching normal children by engaging all of their senses as well as their intellect was developed out of early work with the feebleminded. Thus the lasting significance of the case of Dr. Itard's Victor extends beyond its specific goal of "civilizing the wild savage of Aveyron" and shows us how premature was his conclusion after one failure in training: "since my labors are wasted and your efforts fruitless, take again the road to your forest and the taste for your primitive life" (p. xvii).

Intelligence tests. The most elaborate refining of personality tests has been done in connection with the measurement of intelligence.

Intelligence tests were originally designed as a democratic means of ensuring that qualified children would be allowed to progress in the public education system solely on the basis of their objective test performance and would not be held back by subjective biases of teachers. Psychologists are now at work to remove the other sources of bias that have crept into the construction, administration, and evaluation of intelligence tests. The real value of such testing is that it enables us to see how a child's performance compares with the norms of other children who are most comparable in terms of language, cultural and socioeconomic background, educational opportunities, and broad patterns of life experience, in order to determine what educational experiences will be most fruitful for him or her at certain stages of development.

Binet's early scale. In 1904 the Minister of Public Instruction in France formed a commission of medical men, educators, scientists, and public officials to study the problem of how to teach the mentally retarded children in their public schools. The important work of this commission was done by Alfred Binet, a scholar of the then young science of psychology, and Theodore Simon, a physician. Unlike Itard, these men believed that before a program of instruction could be planned it was necessary to work out some way of measuring the intelligence of the children they were studying.

Binet and Simon prepared a test of intelligence containing problem situations that could be scored objectively, were varied in nature, were little influenced by differences in environment, and called for judgment and reasoning rather than mere rote memory.

Binet expressed the results of his tests on mentally retarded children in terms of the age at which normal children could make the equivalent score. This was called the *mental age* (MA) of the child. When a child's score on the test was equal to the arithmetic mean of the scores of five-year-olds, the child was said to have an MA of five, regardless of his or her actual (chronological) age.

Binet's extensive use of intelligence tests showed conclusively that intelligence exists in degrees. Most people's scores cluster around the mean, and there is no break between the dull, the average, and the bright. This *normal distribution* of scores is shown in the *P&L* Close-up on p. 451.

You can get a good idea of what the Binet scale was like from these examples of capabilities expected of a normal person at different ages (Binet & Simon, 1911).

Age 3 Can point to nose, eyes, and mouth on request.
Age 5 Can count four coins.
Age 7 Can show right hand and left ear.
Age 9 Can define familiar word in terms superior to use; that is, shows how it is related to other ideas.
Age 12 Uses three given words in one sentence.
Adult Gives three differences between a president and a king.

As more and more children were tested and retested at later dates, it was found that retarded children usually fell further and further behind as they grew older. Four-year-old children with a mental age of three, for example, would probably have, at age eight, a mental age of only six. Thus, although the mental and chronological ages maintained the same relationship to each other ($3/4 = 6/8$), the total retardation would have increased from one year to two years.

Early in the history of intelligence tests, therefore, psychologists adopted the practice of stating the relationship between mental age (MA) and chronological age (CA) as a ratio (Stern, 1914). This ratio is known as the *intelligence quotient* (IQ) and is computed as follows:

$$IQ = \frac{MA}{CA} \times 100$$

If a child who is eight years old (CA = 8) has a test score equal to that of ten-year-olds (MA = 10), IQ will be $10/8 \times 100$, or 125. (Multiplying by 100 elimates decimals.) If the child's CA is 10 and MA is 8, then IQ will be $8/10 \times 100$, or 80. When an individual performs at the mental age equivalent to chronological age (MA = CA), that person's IQ is 100—the "normal" or average IQ.

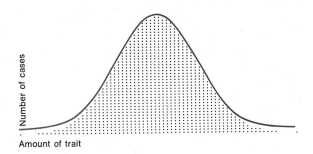

The figure at the right shows the distribution of scores that would be expected if 1000 randomly selected persons were measured on weight, IQ, or other continuous traits. Each dot represents an individual's score. The baseline, or *horizontal axis*, shows the amounts of whatever is being measured; the *vertical axis* shows how many individuals have each amount of the trait, as represented by their scores. Usually only the resulting curve at the top is shown, since this indicates the frequency with which each measure has occurred. Actual curves only approximate this hypothetical one, but come remarkably close to it with very large samples.

This curve is very useful to psychologists because they know that in a large, randomly selected group, a consistent percentage of the cases will fall in a given segment of the distribution. For example, if the trait is one that is distributed normally, 68.2 percent will fall in the middle third of the range of scores.

The standard deviation, as you saw in Chapter 1, is a measure of the variability of the scores. It indicates the typical amount by which the scores differ from the mean. The more widely the scores are spread out, the larger will be the standard deviation. Most of the scores in a distribution fall within three standard deviations above the mean and three standard deviations below it, but usually a few scores in an actual distribution will be lower and a few higher.

The distance of the standard deviation from the mean can be indicated along the baseline of the curve, as is done below. Since the standard deviations are equally spaced along the range of the scores, they are convenient dividing points for classification. For further explanation of the standard deviation and of the uses of both it and the normal curve, see the Appendix.

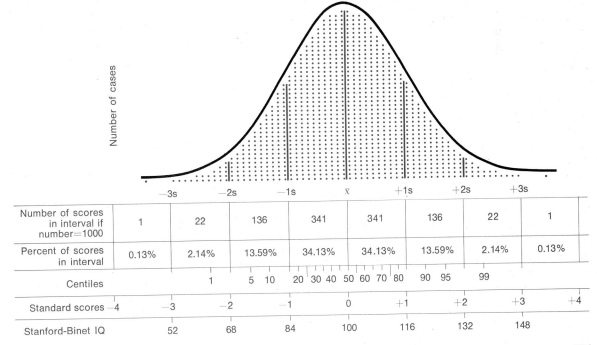

	−3s	−2s	−1s	x̄	+1s	+2s	+3s	
Number of scores in interval if number=1000	1	22	136	341	341	136	22	1
Percent of scores in interval	0.13%	2.14%	13.59%	34.13%	34.13%	13.59%	2.14%	0.13%
Centiles		1	5 10	20 30 40 50 60 70 80		90 95	99	
Standard scores −4	−3	−2	−1	0	+1	+2	+3	+4
Stanford-Binet IQ	52	68	84	100	116	132	148	

The Stanford revisions. The concept of IQ was used in the development of intelligence tests by L. M. Terman of Stanford University, who tested almost 3000 children with Binet's materials and other tests. He arranged the tests by mental age levels and in 1916 published the Stanford Revision of the Binet Tests, commonly referred to as the *Stanford-Binet,* which soon became a standard instrument in clinical psychology, psychiatry, and educational counseling.

In 1937 Terman and Maud A. Merrill published a revised edition of the Stanford-Binet (Terman & Merrill, 1937). This new revision was aimed at correcting the difficulties and defects of the former scale as follows:

1. The test was extended at the upper limits of the intelligence scale so that differentiations could be made among adults of superior intelligence.

2. Provision was made for testing children as young as two years of age. Sets of tests were provided at half-yearly intervals for children from two to five, a period when mental growth is very rapid, and at yearly intervals thereafter.

3. The 1937 scale contained two forms of comparable materials (parallel forms) so that when retesting was necessary the psychologist would not need to worry about a practice effect from taking the same test twice.

As time passes, even the most carefully constructed test becomes obsolete and needs revision. This is especially true in the case of verbal tests, since meanings of words change, and formerly rare words suddenly spring into popularity. The vocabulary of the present-day child or adult, oriented to space and television, is much different from that of the persons who were tested when intelligence tests were first used. For example, *Mars* was a very difficult word for children in the 1916 edition of the Stanford-Binet, being equal in difficulty to the word *conscientious* at that time (Terman, 1916). In the 1937 edition it was much more familiar (thanks to Buck Rogers), being no more difficult than the word *skill* (Terman & Merrill, 1937). By the late 1950s, when space travel was an everyday topic

of conversation, this planet name had become about as familiar as the everyday word *eyelash* (Terman & Merrill, 1960). The Stanford-Binet was again revised in 1960.

Performance tests. Even the 1960 revision of the Stanford-Binet, although it measures other abilities to some degree, is predominantly a test based on the use of words or ability to think and communicate through the use of written language. Thus for a deaf child or for a child who does not come from an English-speaking home, the Stanford-Binet often does not give a fair score.

It has been necessary, therefore, to develop certain tests called *performance tests* in which motor reactions are substituted for verbal reactions. Sometimes even the instructions are given without the use of speech. Performance tests include such tasks as *form boards,* with recesses into which the individual must fit blocks of the proper size and shape as quickly as is possible; *picture completion tests,* in which the individual looks at an incomplete picture and decides which of several parts will fit most sensibly into the blanks; and *matching tests,* in which blocks or other items must be arranged to conform to the pattern of a model.

The WAIS and the WISC. The Wechsler Adult Intelligence Scale (Wechsler, 1955) and the Wechsler Intelligence Scale for Children (Wechsler, 1949) are combinations of verbal and performance tests. The WAIS and the WISC, as these scales are referred to for the sake of convenience, are similar in content, differing chiefly in difficulty. The WISC has been standardized for children of ages two through fifteen years. The WAIS is for age sixteen and over. Both tests consist of two parts—verbal and performance. The verbal section includes tests of general information, comprehension, vocabulary, similarities between words, arithmetic, and digit span (repeating a series of digits after the examiner).

The performance section also has several parts. In the block design test, the subject tries to reproduce a series of designs shown on cards by fitting together colored blocks whose six sides are all different. In the picture arrangement test, the task is to arrange a series of pictures in the correct sequence so that a meaningful story is depicted. Some of the other performance tests include mazes (in the WISC only), picture completion, and object assembly.

Primary mental abilities. Although there obviously are many situations in which it is helpful to know the general overall level of a person's intelligence, as indicated by an IQ rating, modern research in the statistical tradition has shown that the "general intelligence" represented in an IQ figure is actually a composite of a number of "special intelligences" or *primary abilities* that are relatively independent of each other. Two people who obtain the same IQ may have a very different pattern of specific abilities and deficiencies: one may do best on the verbal and abstract reasoning questions, the other on the memory and motor skill items. Comparison of six primary mental abilities typical in different occupations is given in the figure. ▲

The meaning of IQ in terms of behavior. What is a person like who has an IQ of 100? What can that individual do that someone with an IQ of 70 cannot? Trained psychologists, as well as teachers and physicians dealing with problem cases, associate different IQ values with definite pictures of adaptive behavior.

Several classifications of IQ have been suggested by different test makers, usually in terms of categories containing a given number of IQ points. The great majority of people have IQs between 84 and 116 on the Stanford-Binet and are regarded as being of *average* intelligence. Below them is a range classified as *dull normal* or *borderline;* individuals in this range do not do well in school but may finish eighth grade and can usually be self-supporting. Those with IQs below 68 are generally classified as *mentally retarded,* though many can be self-supporting, whereas some with IQs above 68 are institutionalized.

Individuals in the range above *average* are classified as *superior;* individuals in this range may become lawyers, engineers, teachers, and so on. Above 132 are the *gifted;* they are the group with the greatest potential for academic achievement and abstract thought.

These are only rough classifications, based on a test that measures largely abilities needed for schoolwork. The level at which individuals actually function depends on many other factors too, including their motivations, working habits, the demands made on them, their view of their own abilities, and the extent to which their past experiences have developed their potentialities.

Chapter Summary

Personality can be defined as "the sum total of the ways in which an individual characteristically reacts to and interacts with others." The study of personality is concerned with explaining both the similarities and the differences among individuals. We characterize others on the basis of the *consistency* of their behavior, and probably tend to perceive more consistency than actually exists.

All of us "size up" the people we deal with on the basis of *naive personality theories* developed by trial and error. There are numerous more highly systematized formal theories of personality, including Freudian and neo-

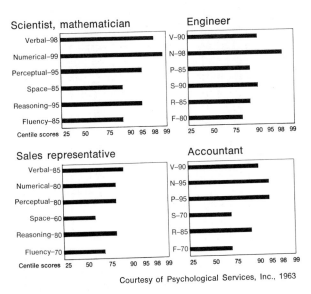

Courtesy of Psychological Services, Inc., 1963

▲ **PROFILES OF INTELLECTUAL ABILITIES TYPICAL OF VARIOUS OCCUPATIONS**

Freudian *(psychoanalytic)* theories, *organismic field theories, factor theories,* and *learning theories.*

Freud placed great stress on early experiences, believing that all the foundations of adult personality (and psychological deviance) are laid down in childhood. He delineated five stages of *psychosexual development (oral, anal, phallic, latent,* and *genital),* based on instinctual biological drives and interaction with parents.

According to Freudian theory, all behavior is (unconsciously) powered by two basic drives: *Eros* (the "sex" or "life" instinct) and *Thanatos* (the "aggressive" or "death" instinct). The energy underlying Eros is called *libido.* Freud pictured the personality as consisting of three parts: the *id* (storehouse of the basic drives), the *superego* ("conscience"), and the *ego,* which serves as a moderator and as a reality appraiser. The ego frequently makes use of unconscious *defense mechanisms,* overuse of which constitutes neurosis.

Even serious behavior disturbances are seen as the expression of unconscious processes, for according to the *principle of psychic determinism,* all behavior, however irrational it may appear, is *caused.* Freud's greatest contributions to the study of personality were in stressing the importance of: (a) *unconscious processes,* (b) *sexuality,* and (c) *childhood experiences.*

Neo-Freudian theorists such as Jung and Adler have placed less emphasis on the role of sexuality, stressing other basic drives or social influences instead.

Erik Erikson expanded Freud's psychosexual stages to *psychosocial stages.* He proposed eight stages of development, marked by prominent conflicts. These stages include *trust vs. distrust, autonomy vs. doubt, initiative vs. guilt, industry vs. inferiority, identity vs. role confusion, intimacy vs. isolation, generativity vs. self-absorption,* and *integrity vs. despair.*

Harry Stack Sullivan also stressed the importance of social interaction. His major concepts include *dynamisms* (prolonged recurrent behavior patterns such as the *self-system*) and *personifications* (our images of others).

Field theorists see personality and behavior as shaped by the balance and interaction of many forces. Goldstein's *organismic theory* stresses the unfolding of the inherited potentialities of the organism as a whole, powered by a basic drive for *self-actualization.* Rogers' *self theory* emphasizes the *phenomenal field*—the private world of the individual. The individual's *self-concept* develops out of interactions with the environment, and he or she will behave in ways that are consistent with it.

In his *self-actualization theory,* Maslow stressed the study of emotionally healthy persons. He saw a hierarchy of human needs ranging, in order, from physiological needs through safety needs, needs for belonging and love, needs for esteem, and needs for self-actualization to needs for knowledge and aesthetic needs. It is only as needs on the lower levels are satisfied that the individual is free to deal with those on the higher levels.

The work of the factor theorists utilizes the statistical technique of *factor analysis* in attempting to identify specific personality *traits.* Guilford has identified two different types of traits: *hormetic* (motivational) *factors* and *temperament factors.* He has also applied factor-analytic techniques to the study of intelligence, delineating a three-dimensional *structure of intellect* model. Social behaviorists such as Mischel insist that stability of behavior results from maintaining and reinforcing conditions in the environment rather than from enduring qualities within the individual.

The learning theorists are the most experimentally oriented of the personality theorists. Dollard and Miller began by putting Freudian concepts into forms more amenable to experimental study, investigating relationships between *drive, cue, response,* and *reinforcement.* The *social learning theory* of Bandura stresses the importance of self-regulatory processes and *observational learning,* in which a person learns by observing the behavior of a *model.*

Some psychologists studying individual differences take a *nomothetic* approach, studying similarities between individuals. Others prefer an *idiographic* approach, holding that each individual is more than the sum of a number of parts. *Statistical prediction* has so far proved more successful than *clinical prediction* in the study of personality.

Our *self-concept* is primarily a product of interaction with others. We tend to accept the images that other people have of us and to judge our behavior by making social comparisons. *Identity crises* come about when our "old" view of ourselves is no longer appropriate to our changing life setting, as in adolescence or middle age. *Developmental factors* that affect personality differences include moral development, in which six distinct stages can be identified, and sex-role socialization.

A personality variable that is currently being studied is *internal* vs. *external* locus of control. "Internal" individuals perceive themselves as having a greater amount of control over their environment than do "externals" and are less likely to give in to learned helplessness. Socioeconomic limitations may be a factor in external orientations.

A consistent trait termed *Machiavellianism* has been identified, predictably associated with skill in the kind of social influence known as "conning" others in certain kinds of situations. *High Machs* flourish in face-to-face situations where rules and guidelines are minimal and where the other people are emotionally aroused.

The term *authoritarian personality* has been used to describe individuals with high scores on measures of *anti-Semitism, political and economic conservatism,* and *fascist attitudes.* Such individuals tend to show prejudiced attitudes toward all outsiders and to show greater deference to authority figures than do low scorers.

"Shy" students differ from "nonshy" ones primarily in attributing certain behaviors and feelings to a trait of "shyness." Students who describe themselves as not-shy experience many of the same feelings but attribute them to situational rather than internal factors.

Tests designed as measures of personality are generally used for one of three purposes: (a) to *predict success* in school or work, (b) to *prescribe* educational or therapeutic *treatment,* or (c) to *further* our *understanding* of human behavior. To be most accurate and most useful, a psychometric device must be *valid, reliable,* and *objective,* and must have been *standardized* on a group of persons representative of those for whom it is intended.

Precise measurement of behavior demands standardization of situations and measuring instruments, as in *rating scales;* these are subject to such errors as the *halo effect* and *stereotyping,* however. *Behavior sampling* techniques involve observing the subject's behavior in a typical situation, either natural or simulated. The *interview* is a frequently used technique; *standardized interviews* minimize the possibility of errors in judgment. *Projective techniques* such as the Rorschach Test and the Thematic Apperception Test involve presenting ambiguous or neutral stimuli and seeing what meaning the subject "projects" onto them. Another frequently used measuring device is the *self-inventory.*

Intelligence testing was pioneered in France in the early 1900s by Simon and Binet. It is based on comparison of an individual's intellectual performance with that of others of the same age. *IQ,* or *intelligence quotient,* indicates the ratio of *mental age* to *chronological age.* Three tests of general intelligence are the Stanford-Binet, which consists primarily of verbal tests, and the Wechsler tests (one for adults and one for children), each containing both verbal and performance scales. Intelligence is not a single ability, but includes a number of *primary mental abilities,* which factor analysts are attempting to identify. Persons with Stanford-Binet IQs between 84 and 116 are considered to be of average intelligence. But what one accomplishes given a particular IQ depends on many nonintellectual factors as well.

Psychological Androgyny and Sexual Identity
Sandra Lipsitz Bem Stanford University

For most people, whether they are adults or children, being male or female is a fairly central aspect of their self-concept. A good test of whether this is the case for you is to try to imagine what it would be like if you were to discover in the mirror tomorrow morning that you had suddenly and miraculously become a member of the other sex. How would you feel about yourself, about your way of relating to other people, and about the ways in which other people related to you? Would you continue to have the same life goals, the same interests, the same friendships, the same way of moving your body, the same way of expressing anger or sadness or joy, the same sense of who you are as a person? Would the event simply represent a physical change in your body (a change which would take some time to adjust to, of course), or would it necessitate a profound change in your self-concept and perhaps even in your behavior? I suspect the latter to be the case for most people.

For many people, being masculine or feminine is also a fairly central aspect of their self-concept. In American society, men are supposed to be masculine, women are supposed to be feminine, and neither sex is supposed to be much like the other. Men are supposed to be tough, dominant, and fearless; women are supposed to be tender, sympathetic, and sensitive to the needs of others. The man who gently and lovingly cares for his tiny infant or who prefers ballet to football will have his masculinity questioned, just as the woman who aggressively defends her clients in court or who refuses to defer to the wishes of her husband will have her femininity questioned. In American society, masculinity and femininity are seen as polar opposites, and a person is therefore taking a risk of sorts when he or she ventures into the other sex's territory. Even standard psychological tests of masculinity and femininity reflect this perspective: A person can score as either masculine or feminine, but most tests do not allow a person to say that he or she is both.

In principle, of course, a person can be *both* masculine and feminine. A child can play with both trucks and dolls; an adolescent can play basketball in the driveway and also serve as a "candy striper" in the local hospital; and a criminal lawyer can aggressively defend his or her clients in court and then lovingly and gently care for a baby at home. In principle, a person can also blend these complementary ways of dealing with the world in a single act. For example, he or she can criticize an employee's performance on the job straightforwardly, but also with sensitivity and understanding. The concept of androgyny (from the Greek *andro,* male, and *gyne,* female) refers specifically to this blending of the behaviors and personality characteristics which have traditionally been thought of as masculine and feminine. By definition, then, the androgynous individual is someone who is *both* independent and tender, *both* aggressive and gentle, *both* assertive and yielding, *both* masculine and feminine, depending upon the situational appropriateness of these various behaviors.

But do androgynous people really exist? And is there any sense in which they are "better off" than people who are not androgynous? My research goal over the last few years has been to try to demonstrate (a) that traditional sex roles restrict behavior in important human ways, and (b) that psychological androgyny would greatly expand the range of behaviors open to everyone. In my view, the concept of androgyny is a very appealing one, primarily because the two domains of masculinity and femininity are both fundamental. In a modern complex society like ours, an adult clearly has to be able to look out for himself or herself and to get things done. But an adult also has to be able to relate to other human beings as people, to be sensitive to their needs and to be concerned about their welfare, as well as to be able to depend on them for emotional support. Fully effective human functioning would thus seem to require that masculinity and femininity be totally integrated into a more balanced, a more fully human, a truly androgynous personality.

Although there is no previous research which addresses itself directly to the concept of androgyny, there is already considerable evidence that a high level of sex typing may not be desirable. For example, high femininity in females has consistently been correlated with high anxiety, low self-esteem, and low social acceptance. And, although high masculinity in males has been correlated during adolescence with better psychological adjustment, it has been correlated during adulthood with high anxiety, high neuroticism, and low self-acceptance. In addition, greater intellectual development has been correlated quite consistently with cross sex-typing; i.e., with masculinity in girls and with femininity in boys. Masculine boys and feminine girls have been found to have *lower* overall intelligence, *lower* spatial ability, and *lower* creativity.

Studies of Androgyny

Before I could actually find anything out about the androgynous person, however, I first had to develop a new sex-role inventory, one which would treat masculinity and femininity as two independent dimensions rather than as opposite ends of a single dimension. Specifically, the Bem Sex Role Inventory (BSRI) consists of twenty "masculine" personality characteristics (e.g., ambitious, self-reliant, independent, assertive) and twenty "feminine" personality characteristics (e.g., affectionate, gentle, understanding, sensitive to the needs of others). I chose the particular characteristics that I did because they were all rated by both males and females as being significantly more desirable in American society for one sex than for the other. The BSRI also contains twenty neutral characteristics (e.g., truthful, happy, conceited, unsystematic) which serve as filler items.

On the test itself, the masculine, feminine, and neutral items are combined into a single list, and a person is asked to indicate on a scale from 1 ("Never or almost never true") to 7 ("Always or almost always true") how well each characteristic describes himself or herself. The average or mean number of points assigned by each person to the masculine attributes constitutes his or her Masculinity Score; the average or mean number of points assigned by each person to the feminine attributes constitutes his or her Femininity Score.

On the basis of these two scores, a person is then classified as either masculine (high masculine-low feminine), feminine (high feminine-low masculine), or androgynous (high masculine-high feminine). According to this definition, over one-third of the males and females in the Introductory Psychology course at Stanford University in 1975 described themselves as sex-typed, approximately one-quarter described themselves as androgynous, and fewer than one-fifth described themselves as "cross-sex-typed." (Those who described themselves as low in both masculinity and femininity will not be discussed in this essay.)

The Avoidance of Cross-Sex Behavior. Once the BSRI was in hand, I was in a position to ask whether traditional sex roles actually do lead some people to restrict their behavior in accordance with sex-role stereotypes. In order to find out, we told undergraduate subjects that we needed photographs of the same person performing many different activities; we gave them a list of thirty pairs of activities; and we asked them to select the one activity from each pair that they would prefer to perform for pay. Some of the activities were masculine (Nail two boards together; Attach artificial bait to a fishing hook), some were feminine (Iron cloth napkins; Wind a ball of yarn), and some were neutral (Play with a yo-yo; Peel oranges).

We were predicting that masculine men and feminine women would consistently reject the cross-sex activity, *even though it always paid more.* And we were right. Sex-typed subjects were significantly more likely than anyone else to avoid even trivial behaviors associated with the other sex. Moreover, when they were actually required to perform several cross-sex behaviors, it was the masculine men and the feminine women who experienced the most discomfort and who felt the worst about themselves.

Independence and Nurturance. In light of this demonstration that traditional sex roles do restrict simple, everyday behaviors, it becomes important to ask whether traditional sex roles also constrict the individual in more profound ways as well. In particular, is the masculine male low in tenderness and nurturance? Is the feminine female low in independence? Is the androgynous male or female able to be *both* independent and nurturant? I choose these particular behaviors because I feel that they represent the very best that masculinity and femininity have each come to stand for, and because I believe that they are essential for effective adult functioning.

In our study of independence, subjects were asked to rate a series of cartoons for funniness. Although the subjects believed that they were hearing the responses of other subjects, they were in fact hearing *tape-recorded* voices which gave false ratings to the cartoons. We found that feminine subjects, both male and female, were significantly less independent in their ratings than anyone else.

In our first study of nurturance, undergraduate subjects were given the opportunity to interact with a six-week-old kitten. We were predicting that masculine subjects would be less responsive toward the kitten than anyone else. And we were right—but only for the men! The results for women came as a surprise. Like the androgynous men, the androgynous women were very responsive toward the kitten, but the feminine women were significantly *less* responsive, and the masculine women fell ambiguously in between.

Because it seemed possible that feminine women might simply find animals unappealing, we conducted two more studies of nurturance, involving genuinely interpersonal situations where the subject's nurturant sympathies would be more likely to be aroused. One of these studies involved interacting with a five-month-old baby; the other with a "lonely, unhappy" fellow student (actually an experimental assistant). In both of these studies, we found that masculine subjects, both male and female, were less responsive or nurturant than anyone else.

Summing Up

Considering all of these studies together, what can we now conclude about the effects of sex typing and androgyny? In my view, the androgynous males and females in these studies have performed spectacularly. They did not avoid behavior just because it was stereotyped as more appropriate for the other sex, and they were also able to be both independent and nurturant. In contrast, the masculine subjects were low in nurturance and the feminine subjects were low in independence. Thus, for both men and women, sex typing does serve to restrict one's behavior, and androgyny does expand one's range of possibilities.

Because at least one-third of college-age males describe themselves as masculine, it is particularly distressing that the masculine males were relatively unresponsive and nonnurturant in every one of the diverse situations that we devised to evoke their more tender emotions. I do not know, of course, whether the masculine men were simply unwilling to act out their tender emotions or whether they were too emotionally inhibited even to experience the tender emotions we tried to tap. But in either case, their partners in the interaction received less emotional sustenance than they would have otherwise.

We cannot conclude, of course, that masculinity inhibits all tender emotionality in the masculine male. Obviously, none of our laboratory situations was as powerful as, say, having a child who becomes ill or a friend who seems about to have a nervous breakdown. We can conclude, however, that their thresholds for tender emotionality are higher than all the other men and women we have observed. And that, I believe, is sufficient cause for concern.

Sexual Identity. Thus far, the whole thrust of this essay has been to argue that having a self-concept as masculine or feminine serves primarily to restrict one's behavior, to lock oneself inside a restricting prison of sex-role stereotyping. Accordingly, I have all but suggested that the best sex-role identity is *no* sex-role identity.

But what about our identities as male or female? For most people, being male or female *is* a fairly central aspect of their self-concept. If we are all to become psychologically androgynous, what will be left of our sense of maleness and femaleness?

I would like to suggest that, even if we were all to become psychologically androgynous, the world would continue to consist of two sexes, male and female would continue to be one of the first and most basic dichotomies that young children would learn, and no one would grow up ignorant of or even indifferent to his or her gender. After all, even if one is psychologically androgynous, one's gender continues to have certain profound *physical* implications.

Precisely because there are biological "givens" which cannot be avoided or escaped, except perhaps by means of very radical surgery, it seems to me that psychological health or well-being must necessarily include having a healthy sense of one's maleness or femaleness. *But I would argue that a healthy sense of maleness or femaleness involves little more than being able to look into the mirror and to be perfectly comfortable with the body that one sees there.* One's gender does dictate the nature of one's body, after all, and hence one ought to be able to take one's body very much for granted, to feel comfortable with it, and perhaps even to like it.

But beyond being comfortable with one's body, one's gender need have no other influence on one's values, behavior, or life-style. Thus, although I would suggest that a woman ought to feel comfortable about the fact that she can bear children if she wants to, this does not imply that she ought to want to bear children, nor that she ought to stay home with any children that she does bear. Similarly, although I would suggest that a man ought to feel perfectly comfortable about the fact that he has a penis which can become erect, this in no way implies that a man ought to take the more active role during sexual intercourse, nor even that his sexual partners ought necessarily all to be female.

Finally, I would argue that a healthy sense of one's maleness or femaleness becomes all the more possible precisely when the artificial constraints of gender are eliminated and when one is finally free to be one's own unique blend of temperament and behavior. When gender no longer functions as a prison, then and only then will we be able to "accept as given" the fact that we are male or female in exactly the same sense that we "accept as given" the fact that we are human. Then and only then will we be able to consider the fact of our maleness or femaleness to be so self-evident and nonproblematic that it rarely ever occurs to us to think about it, to assert that it is true, to fear that it might be in jeopardy, or to wish that it were otherwise.

The Ultimate Irony of Androgyny. The concept of psychological androgyny would seem to define a model of mental health or psychological well-being for both men and women which is free from culturally imposed definitions of masculinity and femininity. For if there is an ultimate moral to the concept of androgyny, it is that *behavior* should have no gender.

But there is an irony here, for the concept of androgyny contains an inner contradiction and hence the seeds of its own destruction. As an analysis of the word itself implies, the concept of androgyny presupposes that masculinity and femininity themselves represent distinct and separate elements which must be integrated if the human personality is to be freed from the restricting prison of sex-role stereotyping. But if and when the moral of androgyny is actually absorbed by the culture, the concepts of masculinity and femininity will no longer exist as separate elements. Thus, when androgyny becomes a reality, the *concept* of androgyny will have been transcended—and will be but a relic of an earlier sexist era.

11

Deviance, Pathology, and Madness

The unknown, the unusual, the unexplained, the mysterious have always held a peculiar fascination for human beings. Such things stimulate the curiosity to explore and understand, but they also evoke fear. The former reaction has been institutionalized by science, education, and art; the latter reaction has led to interest in pagan religious practices, witchcraft, magic, the occult, and unidentified flying objects. What we cannot understand we cannot control, and if it is malevolent, it can perhaps come to control or even destroy us. Even worse, if someone else were to discover the secret power of unknown forces, that person might come to have power over the rest of us. This basic theme pervades our ghost stories, old science-fiction movie serials, and literary tales of horror and madness. It is as if, in the awareness of our own fragility and mortality, we both yearn for and dread omnipotence and immortality.

Abnormal Psychology and Mental Illness

There are few areas of psychology that students are more interested in than abnormal psychology and the dynamics of psychopathology. Indeed, the average person often equates the whole of psychology with the study of mental illnesses. Despite this fascination with *studying* abnormal processes, however, there is little tolerance and less concern for the person in whom such processes occur. In our society, the "mentally ill" person is *stigmatized* in ways that the physically ill person is not. Research has shown that, in general, the public seems to fear and shun individuals deemed "mentally ill." Such persons have always been set apart from others. At different times and in different places, individuals seized by fits, visions, or hallucinations have been made into prophets or shamans and revered as ones elected for divine inspiration. But more often they have been rejected, cast out, isolated, tortured, or destroyed by society. ▲

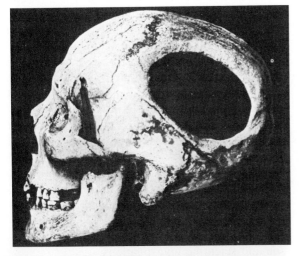

▲ This neolithic skull is mute evidence of one of the earliest attempts at treatment of mental disorder: boring a hole in the "patient's" skull to let evil spirits escape. The circulating swing, designed to bring the mentally disturbed back to sound reasoning, and the crib for restraining violent patients were in use less than a hundred years ago.

Despite our lingering bias against those people categorized as "mentally ill" or "insane" (the legal term), we have come a long way in our view of why some people behave in ways that are unusual, bizarre, and disturbed. Before the modern conception of "mental illness" existed, such behavior was attributed to possession of the mind and body by demons, the invisible powers that were assumed to cause the evil, pain, and suffering that were everywhere in evidence. The only hope lay in preventing such spirits from entering one's body, for once they gained entry, the process of driving them out was as likely to result in death as in a return to normalcy. People wore charms and amulets (usually fashioned from parts of sacred animals) to ward off evil.

Demonic possession accounted, then, for both physical sickness and mental aberrations; thus the cure for either consisted in driving out the evil spirits by means of wizardry, magical rituals, herbal preparations, and blood-sucking leeches. (See *P&L* Close-up, pp. 457–58.) In a collection of writings from "wizard-doctors" practicing before the Norman conquest of England in 1066, we discover the following prescription: "When a devil possesses the man or controls him from within with disease; a spew drink or emetic, lupin, bishopwort, henbane, corpleek; pound these together, add ale for a liquid, let it stand for a night, add fifty bibcorns of cathartic grains and holy water—to be drunk out of a church bell" (quoted by Margotta, 1967, p. 292).

Close-up
Satan and the Madness of Witchcraft

Old beliefs never die, they just lie low until the time is right for them to be resurrected. Exorcism, which might seem a primitive rite of a bygone age, has become fashionable again. Indeed, in the wake of publicity for the movie *The Exorcist*, it was revealed that religious rites for exorcism of the devil have been occurring with some regularity all along—it is only the extent and publicity of the practice that has diminished.

The modern baptismal rite of the Catholic Church still retains this exorcism of the devil since the infant is presumed to be possessed by virtue of the original sin of Adam in Paradise. "I exorcise thee, thou unclean spirit!" the priest declares. Belief in demonic possession is also found among Mormons, the Hassidic Hebrew sect, and other religious groups. In a 1974 survey conducted by the Center for Policy of 3546 adults across the U.S., 48 percent were *certain* the devil exists and another 20 percent thought it *probable* (*Time*, April 29, 1974, p. 99).

Back in 1692, a greater percentage of the public believed in the existence of the devil and in witches. When eight young girls living in Salem, Massachusetts, were afflicted with an unusual sickness for which there was no apparent medical explanation, "witchcraft" became the preferred diagnosis. The girls' behavior was at first characterized by disorderly speech, odd postures and gestures and convulsive fits. (Only *after* the explanation of witchcraft was provided, were hallucinations and a delusional system manifested.) There followed witchhunts, accusations, trials, and indictments. When it was over, 19 men and women had been hanged and one man pressed to death. Another 150 accused witches were released when the Governor ordered a general reprieve in 1693. The witchcraft crisis ended as abruptly as it had started.

A remarkable new reanalysis of this madness in Salem comes from graduate psychology student, Linnda Caporael (1976). She makes a convincing case for the hypothesis that the girls' strange behavior had a rational physiological basis which was not detected because the Puritans were not aware of it at that time. The likely candidate is *ergot*—a parasitic fungus which contaminates rye, and when eaten in rye bread contains a number of chemical agents that cause convulsive seizures and other symptoms. "Without knowledge of ergotism and confronted by convulsions, mental disturbances, and perceptual distortions, the New England Puritans seized upon witchcraft as the best explanation for the phenomena. . . . One Satan in Salem may well have been convulsive ergotism" (p. 26).

The great Roman physician Celsus, just before the birth of Christ, made considerable strides toward the enlightened view that had in fact been proclaimed (but not heeded) centuries earlier by Hippocrates. Celsus included in his classic work *De Medicina* a chapter in which he classified and described a variety of mental disorders. His ideas about therapy, however, were not so enlightened; he advocated starvation and beating overexcited patients with chains.

With the rise in power of the Church in the Middle Ages, all that was not right and proper, good and healthy, was thought to be the work of the devil and witches. This insistence that mental perversions were manifestations of Satan not only led to the excesses of the Inquisition and witch-hunts throughout much of Europe and New England, but for centuries it made impossible any analytical, empirical study of psychiatric disturbances. Only the drastic social and intellectual changes brought about by the Renaissance were able to supplant superstition by reason and scientific investigations.

One area of medicine that has made great strides after the Renaissance is *neurology*, which deals with the functions and malfunctions of the brain, spinal cord, and nervous system. The consequent separation of mind and soul, with their mystical and spiritual qualities, from the medically investigatable action of the physical nervous system brought legitimacy and respectability to the study of mental disturbances. In one stroke, the medical model transformed madness and demonic possession into "mental illness" and "nervous disease."

Just as physical diseases were classified to allow for more reliable diagnosis and standardized treatment, psychiatric classification (called *nosology*) of mental, emotional, and behavioral complaints also emerged in the eighteenth century. German neurologists of the nineteenth century focused their attention on description, classification, and careful experimentation on the physiology of the nervous system, cellular pathology, and the organic basis of mental disease. In contrast, French psychiatry during this period was characterized by its *dynamic* orientation in searching for the *causes* of emotional disturbances, mainly neurotic conditions. Sigmund Freud, a Viennese medical student, studied in Paris in 1885 and, on his return to Vienna, evolved the method of free association (with Josef Breuer), which became the methodological cornerstone of the psychoanalytic movement.

It was Freud more than any other single individual who made the study and treatment of abnormal behavior acceptable, fashionable, and intellectually exciting. He did so by rejecting what had been essentially a static model of the suffering individual as a passive victim of demons or disease. Freud transformed these views into more dynamic ones by implicating the individual as an active (though unknowing) agent in his or her mental anguish.

The dynamic forces that accounted for much that was "abnormal" were (as we saw in the previous chapter) unconscious motivation and the repression of unacceptable impulses. Freud developed psychoanalytic theory to the point where it made rational much that was thought to be irrational and senseless in neurotic behavior. By postulating that neurosis was to be understood as an extension of these "normal processes" of psychic conflict and ego defense, Freud took the neurotic back into the fold of the social community. Freud brought the soul back in the form of the superego and conscience, and reunited the mind to the nervous system, so the whole person could be treated.

Freudian notions were quickly adopted by American clinical psychologists and psychiatrists as the basis for psychoanalytic therapy (to be described in the next chapter). It remained for John Dollard and Neal Miller (1950) to recast some of the basic Freudian notions into the language of learning theory prevalent in the early 1950s to give psychoanalytic thought more respectability and utility among research-oriented psychologists.

The systematic scientific study of abnormal patterns of human behavior is a relatively recent development. The traditional research approach has been the case study report that analyzes in depth the apparent causes, symptoms, and course of "mental illness" in a single patient. Students are often surprised to learn that Freud's monumental work was derived largely from such case studies and not from any experiments involving controlled observations and comparisons. The intensive one-subject case study is valuable primarily as a source of ideas and hypotheses. Evaluating the soundness of such hypotheses requires the same scientific methodology as does the test of ideas in any other area of psychology. It is only in recent decades that large-scale data collection, testing of theoretically derived hypotheses, and rigorous evaluation of treatment strategies have become part of the foundation of abnormal psychology.

It is impossible to determine accurately the extent to which mental and emotional problems are implicated in other more obvious problems such as divorce, crime, warfare, prejudice, and suicide. But we do know that "disorders of personality" often result in social conflict, and at times in acts of violence directed against other people or the self. Serious physical illness may give rise to major psychological disturbances; on the other hand, a wide range of physical malfunctions originate at an emotional level.

An untold number of people suffer every year from some form of mental illness, nervous disease, emotional disturbance. At this very moment there are more people being treated in American hospitals for "mental problems" than for any other illness. The chances of having a serious emotional breakdown are 1 in 10; 2,500,000 people are treated each year in this country for such breakdowns. At present, the estimate of what mental illness costs in monetary terms in the United States exceeds $20 billion dollars. No one can estimate the cost in terms of suffering and loss of human potential. Although statistics are cold facts, they provide a framework for evaluating the extent of the problem posed by mental illness in the United

States. Schizophrenia is one of the most incapacitating forms of mental illness, requiring hospitalization and extended treatment: more than 2 percent of all American children born in 1960 are expected to suffer from schizophrenia sometime in their life (all estimates are from the 1970 report of the National Clearinghouse for Mental Health Information, Publication No. 5027).

Depression is the number-one malady of our times, resulting in nearly 100,000 hospitalizations annually, and afflicting millions of us daily. The suffering of depression ends in the tragedy of suicide for more than 20,000 people a year in the United States. It is estimated that there is a death from suicide somewhere every 26 minutes around the clock. For every suicide, there are at least three more that are unreported or "unsuccessful." Alcoholism is a personal problem for more than 5 million people in this country and a social problem to their families, friends, and employers, and to the innocent victims of fatal auto accidents due to alcoholism. Drug abuse is a way of life for the over 100,000 known narcotics addicts in the United States, and a major problem for the hundreds of thousands more who are habituated to other types of drugs; but drug abuse is no less so a problem to their communities, which are struggling to contain it and its consequences as measured in crime and violence. The costs of crime and delinquency to society are estimated at over $20 *billion* dollars every year, to say nothing of the loss of social trust in others that accompanies high crime rates.

Sick! Sick. Sick?

Is madness, like beauty, in the mind of the observer, or does it "really" exist independent of social evaluation and the observer's cultural bias like, say, death? Some attempts to answer this question clearly challenge the very foundations of modern psychiatry. We will consider some of them in this section.

In a physical illness there are clear, agreed-upon, usually measurable signs of pathology. For example, leukemia is identified by an unusual white-to-red blood-cell ratio, cancer by the uncontrolled growth of tumors, and paralysis by nerve degeneration and muscle unresponsivity. But mental illness is present when someone says it is.

Thus psychological pathology is established not by physical realities but by social ones. It is behavior, not tissue, that is observed, and someone has to evaluate the behavior and judge whether it is pathological. In our society, today, we generally consider individuals mentally ill on the basis of some combination of the following evidence (adapted from Wegrocki, 1939; W. A. Scott, 1958; Allport, 1960):

1. They are under psychiatric care.

2. Respectable, influential members of the community (teachers, judges, parents, spouses, priests) agree that the behavior represents a given degree of maladjustment.

3. A psychiatrist or clinical psychologist makes a diagnosis of mental disturbance.

4. Their test scores on psychological self-report inventories deviate by a specified extent from standards of a group designated as normal.

5. They declare themselves to be "mentally sick" either explicitly or through expressed feelings of unhappiness, anxiety, and inadequacy.

6. They behave publicly in such ways as to call attention to their behavior as deviating from standards accepted by the majority of others in the society.

The Medical Model: Why Some Are Sick of It

It is reasonable to conclude that major advances in the study and treatment of dysfunctional behavior can be traced to the adoption of a "medical model." However, from another perspective, the assumptions of this model, and the orientation it leads to, may be seriously criticized as misguiding both research and possible solutions to the problem.

The main features of the application of a medical model to psychological and psychiatric behavior problems are: (a) abnormal behavior is symptomatic of an underlying disease; (b) overt symptoms are signs of internal pathological states or processes; (c) the ultimate cause of mental illness will be found in genetic, biochemical, organic malfunctioning; (d) the present illness is the manifestation of the individual's prior history of trauma, deprivation, and variables related to poor mental health care; (e) sharp distinctions are seen between "illness" and "health," "abnormal" and "normal," "sick" and "well"; (f) treatment involves hospitalization and medical intervention designed to rid the sick person of the disease, to cure the illness that rages within.

But is mental illness within or without? The major consequence of accepting the medical model as the appropriate one for understanding dysfunctional behavior is that the emphasis is on the person, not the milieu in which he or she is functioning. It is oriented toward past origins of disease, rather than toward current conditions that may be maintaining the dysfunctional behavior. It assumes that the "afflicted" individual must be isolated to some extent, assuming a passive role as "patient" in the curative process presided over by medical experts. The medical model further assumes that even when *all* symptoms disappear following treatment, the patient is not necessarily cured, since symptoms are but the visible tip of the submerged iceberg of mental illness. A mental patient whose disease symptoms are no longer present is described as having the disease *in remission*. That means it is not out in the open, but it implies that it may break forth at any time. Can you imagine how it might feel to be rid of all the symptoms for which you went into the hospital and then be told you were a "schizophrenic in remission"? (See *P&L* Close-up, pp. 461–62.)

The essential features of the criticism of the medical model are: (a) the phenomenon termed "mental illness" is more properly conceived of in terms of *deviance* than *disease;* (b) whatever it is called, "mental illness" is not an entity in the same sense as cancer or tuberculosis, but is rather a subjective *label* or metaphor applied to some people by other people to infer states and processes that are not directly observable; (c) it is the socially, economically, politically *powerless* people who are more likely to be labeled "mentally ill" than the powerful ones, even if they display identical behaviors; and (d) madness is a product of the individual's interaction with and adjustment to his or her social environment, with its conflicting demands, unreasonable rules, and pathological relationships fostered in the family, schools, work, and other situations. These general criticisms have come primarily from three sources: radical psychiatry, sociology, and social psychology.

A quite different conception of what we have been calling "mental illness" comes out of the

Close-up
On Being Sane in Insane Places

Could a normal, "sane" person who has never suffered from serious psychiatric symptoms be admitted to an insane asylum and not detected as sane once inside? This is more than an academic question; it is an expression of the fear felt by many people who visit or work in mental hospitals. According to a most remarkable study by David Rosenhan (1973) this fear is partially justified. Once a person is labeled as insane and admitted to a hospital, nothing that person does is likely to be considered normal.

Rosenhan and seven other people had themselves committed to twelve different mental hospitals in five different states on the East and West Coasts. This was done by calling the Admissions Office of each hospital for an appointment. Each of these pseudopatients presented the same complaint: "I hear voices, unclean voices. I think they say 'empty,' 'hollow,' 'thud.' " Except for this falsehood and altering their name, vocation, and employment, everything else they said was truthful and represented their nonpathological current or past histories. In almost every case they were diagnosed "schizophrenic"; the exception being at the only private hospital in the sample, where "manic depressive" was the diagnosis. (This diagnosis has more favorable chances of recovery or cure.) Once on the psychiatric ward, the pseudopatients immediately ceased simulating any symptoms. Each pseudopatient behaved as "normally" as possible in every way.

How quickly were they detected? "Despite their public 'show' of sanity," Rosenhan reports, "the pseudopatients were never detected. Admitted in the main with a diagnosis of schizophrenia, each was discharged with a diagnosis of schizophrenia 'in remission.' " Length of hospitalization ranged from seven to fifty-two days, with an average commitment of nineteen days. Release was typically accomplished with the intervention of spouses or colleagues, but not by any staff member realizing that an admissions "error" had been made or that a sane person was in an insane place.

To demonstrate further the subjectivity of judgment and the unreliability of psychiatric diagnosis of mental illness, Rosenhan (1973) performed a simple companion study at a hospital whose staff learned of the above study and refused to believe such errors could occur in *their* hospital. He told them that sometime in the next three months one or more pseudopatients would seek admission to their hospital. Staff members were thus set to detect imposters, and systematically rated their confidence in their belief that each of 193 patients admitted to the hospital during this time period was either a sane pseudopatient or an insane real patient. Forty-one of the patients admitted were confidently judged to be pseudopatients by at least one staff member, and 19 of these patients were judged to be sane pseudopatients by *both* a psychiatrist and a staff member. How many pseudopatients had Rosenhan sent over to the hospital? You probably guessed it already. *None.*

"radical" school of psychiatry, pioneered by Ronald Laing and Thomas Szasz. They argue that the relationship between the "institutional (or hospital) psychiatrist and an involuntary patient is more like the relationship between master and slave than between physician and adult medical patient" (Szasz, 1973, p. xii). The medical relationship is, in their view, based on power that may operate without compassion and without consideration of the patient's rights, wishes, or perspective, or of the functions that his or her "madness" might be serving in an even madder personal environment. For Laing, schizophrenia is a "special strategy that a person invents in order to live in an unlivable situation" (1967, p. 115).

Deviance, not disease. In recent years, growing awareness of the shortcomings of the medical model have led critics operating out of a sociological framework to contend that the appropriate comparison for what is called "mental illness" is other forms of *deviance,* not of *disease.* Starting with the influential writings of Erving Goffman (1961) on the mental patient treated as a moral deviant, a movement has developed that stresses the importance of societal responses in defining what deviance is, who deviants are, and how they shall be treated (Becker, 1963; Kitsuse, 1964; Erikson, 1966). In effect, the status of "deviant" connotes moral inferiority, social rejection, and biased labeling by those who either have power or want some. In addition, the term *deviant* implies that an individual "is different in kind from ordinary people and that there are no areas of his personality that are not afflicted by his 'problem' " (Scott, 1972, p. 14).

Erikson (1966) has proposed that each society defines itself negatively by pointing out what it is *not:* an easier job than creating a positive definition. Deviance gives shape to what is evil or unacceptable or feared. Thus it can be argued that society, by its nature, will always demand some boundaries in order to achieve a minimum of stability. Deviants, since they clarify these boundaries, may be a necessary part of society; they serve to make the rest of the society feel more normal, healthy, sane, good, moral, and law abiding. No matter what you are doing, it is a comfort to be able to point to someone else and righteously proclaim, "You'd never catch *me* doing *that.*" By locating a form of disease or sickness and establishing the difference between "us" and "them," we are comforted because then we can't imagine *we* might ever become like *them,* and further, we are not responsible for having created conditions that might have triggered their "abnormal" reaction. ◆

Stigma, stigma, everywhere. The diagnosis of "mentally ill" carries with it the dual consequences of public degradation and self-devaluation. The social stigma associated with "mental illness" is more potent and enduring than virtually any other form of stigmatism. (See *P&L Close-up,* p. 465, left column.) Fear of such stigmatism may lead people to deny the need for psychological counsel and treatment when it is called for in themselves and others (Yarrow et al., 1955; Schwartz, 1957). Becoming a "mental patient" in itself contributes to the anxiety of the individual so labeled, lowering self-esteem and perhaps working as a self-fulfilling prophecy.

Rather than conceive of themselves as ordinary individuals who have been unable to solve certain ongoing problems posed by their society and environment, mental patients learn that they are persons to be feared, pitied, disliked, degraded, and isolated. Often they are viewed as malingerers, weak-willed and unassertive in overcoming their personal problems (Fletcher, 1967).

The negative consequences of the mental illness label have been manipulated in controlled experimental settings at the University of Connecticut by social psychologist Amerigo Farina and his colleagues (1965, 1966, 1971). In these experiments, subjects who believed they were paired with former mental patients rather than "normal" persons liked their co-workers less, evaluated their performances as less adequate, treated them more harshly, preferred to work alone, and desired no further interactions with them. Student research subjects asked to play the role of a mental patient (or some other stigmatized role) in an experimental setting went to great lengths to prove their normality, masculinity, and intelligence. The thought that a stranger perceived them as stigmatized was a more powerful influence on their behavior than the role-playing instructions they had agreed to follow (Farina, 1971). In similar experiments, actual former patients who believed their co-

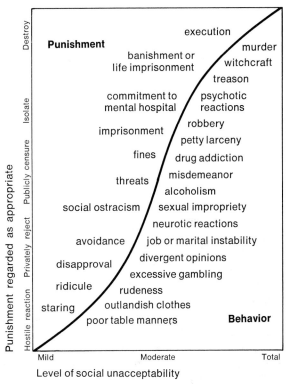

Adapted from Haas, 1965

◆ **"LET THE PUNISHMENT FIT THE CRIME"**

This figure illustrates a continuum of behaviors that are deemed increasingly unacceptable and are responded to with increasing severity. Basically, all these reactions are punishments for deviance; thus behavior toward those who behave neurotically or psychotically can be seen to resemble that toward criminals and other antisocial deviants, despite our acknowledgment that the mentally ill should not be held legally responsible.

Like antisocial deviants, those showing psychopathology may be seen as threatening people's lives and property. They behave in unpredictable ways, thus weakening the social control function. And, more basically, they appear unable to control their behavior toward goals defined as desirable, thereby bringing into question fundamental assumptions about the dignity and integrity of human nature.

worker knew of their previous hospitalization performed more poorly and were perceived as more tense and anxious than those who believed their co-worker did not know (Farina et al., 1971).

Is Any Behavior Really Abnormal?

Granted that labels are arbitrary and that behavior may be misjudged, is there any behavior that is always normal or always abnormal for human beings?

ABNORMAL, *adj.* Not conforming to standard. In matters of thought and conduct, to be independent is to be abnormal, to be abnormal is to be detested.

Ambrose Bierce, The Devil's Dictionary, 1911

Is "normal" just what most people accept as normal? Inevitably, what is seen as "abnormal" is in part historically determined. A Roman Catholic priest wants to get married; a woman smokes in public; a young man refuses induction into the army; a high-school freshman takes drugs—all would have been "abnormal" in the eyes of their peers not too long ago. Are they still? Until very recently people who entered psychotherapy because of homosexual behavior would have been made to feel society's censure for their deviant impulses and would automatically have received treatment to "cure" their "problem." Psychiatrists are redefining the problem today, regarding homosexuality as acceptable if it is a freely chosen alternative and not a reaction impelled by fear or an avoidance mechanism based on deep feelings of inadequacy.

Beyond nose-counting. Most definitions of abnormality are basically statistical—how much does a given individual deviate from what most people do? "What most people do" (or what the most powerful people do), in turn, depends on the culture or epoch. Societies differ both in what the norm is and in how much variability they will tolerate before the behavior differences are seen as significant deviations. But there is always a tendency to protect the social status quo by punishing nonconformers or treating them in a variety of ways designed to bring them back to the norm or eliminate them, in order not to permit the average response ("what most people do") to shift in their direction. (See *P&L* Close-up, p. 465, right column.)

Psychologists function as agents of the society. Yet to adopt the simplistic view that what is good for the average person is what is *healthy* makes deviants of critics and maniacs of nonconformers. It becomes obvious that the "normality" of any group's norm must in turn be judged by some other criteria. Was the anti-Semitic norm in Nazi Germany "normal"? If everyone in your college decided to take heroin, would it be "normal" to conform? Would it have been abnormal to be a slave owner before the Civil War?

'Tis the majority
In this, as all, prevails.
Assent, and you are sane;
Demur,—you're straightway dangerous,
And handled with a chain.

Emily Dickinson, c. 1862

Perhaps the most odious example in recent times of the detrimental nature of psychiatric labels was the public and political abuse of Senator Thomas Eagleton as the Democratic vice-presidential nominee in the '72 election. The disclosure, following his nomination and acceptance, that he had undergone psychiatric treatment set off a round of speculation that ultimately led to his replacement on the Democratic ticket. A good deal of the controversy centered around the fact that ten years previously Eagleton had received treatment for depression. Although there was no evidence of a recurrence of the depressive symptoms, he was considered by politicians and the public to be still "vulnerable." At what point in his life will the senator be judged to be "perfectly normal" again—if ever? Or never?

In response to the public outcry over the "Eagleton affair," the American Psychiatric Association released a statement that said in part, "the assumption of normal activities by countless thousands of people who have been successfully treated for depression is compelling evidence that the existence of an episode of depression in a person's medical history should be considered in the same manner as a wide range of successfully treated illnesses" (*Science News,* Aug. 5, 1972, p. 85).

But the matter was not put to rest with this authoritative appeal. When Gerald Ford was being evaluated by his congressional colleagues before being appointed vice-president, his mental health record was thoroughly scrutinized. In a provocative statement, columnist Sydney J. Harris pointed out the dangers of our unhealthy attitudes toward "mental health."

"[The Congress] sought repeated reassurances from Ford that he had never visited a psychiatrist or been treated for any emotional upset; as though the fact that a man has never consulted a psychiatrist somehow certifies him as stable. . . . Emotional problems do affect behavior far more than merely physical ones. But the point is that they affect behavior even more when they are not recognized and treated." (1974)

Social norms, by determining who will be rejected and branded as outcasts, may contribute to abnormality in those who cannot or will not conform, through inducing anxiety, self-doubt, and social isolation. For example, one price of our high valuation of economic success is that with any downturn in the economy there is a rise in mental-hospital admissions among the middle and upper classes.

Many people in our society have been made to feel intellectually inadequate or deficient because of excessively high standards imposed by parents, teachers, and others. Others have suffered agonies over their sexuality because of parental training that has equated sex with sin or peer training that has equated it with conquest and achievement. Feelings of being ugly, worthless, burdensome, or willfully evil may be bred into children unintentionally by parents who hold up extraordinary models for social comparison or use other "normal" child-training techniques.

Perhaps the worst perpetrator of this hoax of paranoic conformity is the mass media. Television advertisements tell women that they must diligently apply countless cosmetics to face and body in order to look "natural" and "sexy." Furthermore, they must use deodorants, special soaps, "feminine sprays," mouthwash, and so on to eliminate natural body odors and use perfumes instead to create an alluring body odor. For a man to be a real man, he must drink, smoke, and use an aftershave designed to transform him into a karate expert overnight. In this sort of "conform or fail" atmosphere, it is indeed a tribute to humanity that any of us ever dares to be different at all!!!

The Winds of Change

In this time of rapidly shifting social values, a counternorm is developing that advocates that people "do their own thing," taking what they need from the larger society but feeling no responsibility for keeping it going or helping to make the communal aggregate fulfill its functions of supporting and nourishing the individual. It may well be that the challenges being posed by this trend will lead to a more healthy concern for the individual, a reduced willingness to sacrifice individual eccentricity for the balm of consensus, and the acceptance of multiple norms of appropriateness. On the other hand, we are social animals, and a life of solitary self-indulgence is not the only alternative to the conformity pressures of society. Each one of us must decide how we can benefit from the others we live with, without losing our identity in the shuffle and quest for social approval. The goal of a society where the individual and the group share and benefit from each other, rather than take and diminish, needs time to reach fruition. Meanwhile, psychiatric wards are overcrowded and understaffed, and pathological tendencies of the individual are reinforced and indeed encouraged by various forms of social pathology — problems that only concerted effort can solve. The remainder of this chapter will be devoted to some of the most prevalent forms that individual pathology takes, and we have arbitrarily divided them into four categories — dependencies and addictions, neurosis, psychosis, suicide — each of which deals with a loss in the potential for realizing our fullest humanness. Later in the text, we will devote an entire chapter to an analysis of the more clearly social pathologies that confront us in our daily life.

Loss of Self-Regulating Capacities: Dependence and Addiction

For an increasing number of individuals in American society, consummatory activities, such as drinking alcohol, smoking cigarettes, and taking drugs, are rapidly coming to dominate their lives. These unfortunate individuals become conditioned to depend on artificial substitutes for a wide range of emotional and behavioral satisfactions — to relax them when too high, to pick them up when down, to put them to sleep, to keep them awake, in short, to enable them to "make it through the day."

What starts out as the generally approved social-hour cocktail can become a craving for a quart or more of alcohol a day, starting the first thing in the morning. The after-dinner cigarette can somehow escalate into more than four packs a day. The marijuana "high," initially reserved for occasional parties, can become an LSD nightmare, sometimes ending in suicide, an endless speed trip into a world of paranoia and violence, or the heroin addict's endless quest for the next fix. Even the presumably innocuous act of eating, normally an activity necessary to maintain cell metabolism, can develop abnormal properties that endanger the functioning and existence of the organism as much as, or more than, any of these other action-addictions (as we saw in Chapter 8).

The loss of self-regulating capacities, then, can have disastrous physical consequences on the health of the addicted person. These stem both from the *direct* effects of the excessive amount of foreign substance on cerebral, respiratory, vascular, and digestive functioning and from the various *indirect* effects of inadequate diet and contagious disease conditions associated with some addictive habits.

The psychological and social consequences are no less serious than the physical ones. At the psychological level, there is a loss of both self-confidence and feelings of self-control as addicts come to define themselves as unable to make it on their own. Accompanying this lowered self-esteem is a loss of interest in usual life activities and goals, as addiction takes over as the central reinforcer in their lives.

The social consequences of maintaining these habits can be measured in the money lost in earnings, family savings, welfare, rehabilitation attempts, and crime. They can also be assessed in terms of the loss of human productivity and the breakdown of meaningful interpersonal relations—the end of which may be skid row, jail, a mental hospital, or a life of prostitution. But although almost everyone is intellectually aware of the potential danger of addictions[1] and we are exposed to widespread information campaigns against such self-abuse, the incidence of such addiction appears to continue on its not-so-merry way upward.

Why do people start? This is the first puzzle. Actually, there are many reasons for the paradox that rational people voluntarily engage in a behavior that they know can be so self-destructive. Aside from possible masochism (a tendency to derive pleasure from hurting or punishing oneself), there are a number of less abnormal processes that are more likely reasons why otherwise sensible people start and maintain addictive behaviors.

Often the response in question is learned by watching others: parents consuming the nightly martini, prestige figures advocating a life-style of good food, good booze, good smokes, and peers doing their thing and pressuring you to do their thing, too. The mass media spend considerable amounts of money to create a belief structure in which the "normal" way to achieve pleasure, health, happiness, relief from pain and anxiety, and even sexual prowess is through smoking, drinking, eating, and taking drugs (starting with aspirin, tranquilizers, diet pills, and sleeping pills). Gambling, too, is promoted as a socially acceptable activity in public lotteries, TV quiz shows, and church bingo games.

[1]Technically, the term *addiction* means physical dependence, but we will be using it more broadly here to refer to either physical or psychological dependence severe enough that the behavior has become compulsive and the individual does not have adequate voluntary control over it.

If the first step is taken because of social encouragement, the second step is bolstered by pleasurable oral factors, physiological changes that "feel good," and social approval for having gone along. It seems like the right, cool, hip, sophisticated, manly, womanly, etc., etc., thing to do. Once begun, the activity slowly moves up in priority, and other aspects of life are organized around it.

Society assumes that individuals have sufficient self-imposed control over their behavior to keep from giving in fully to these temptations. And most people themselves are convinced that they would never succumb to such danger and self-destruction. "*I* could not become an alcoholic or drug addict." They see addicts as people who "deserve" what they get because they are too "weak willed" to help themselves.

It is precisely our *illusions of self-control and invulnerability* that lead us to underestimate the powerful influence of the addictive substances and the environmental setting in which they are presented to us. We overestimate our "inner resourcefulness" or "willpower" and are convinced that we can stop whenever we want to. Yet there are few behavior patterns more difficult to change than those centered around a compulsive addiction habit. To what extent is individual addiction a symptom of prevailing social pathology, and to what extent a sign of personal pathology?

Dependence on Alcohol

Intoxicating beverages and their effects have been well known and used since ancient times. In fact, recent archaeological discoveries have shown that the art of fermentation predates the recorded history of civilization. Alcohol, in one form or another, was quite possibly the first tranquilizer known to humanity and has maintained its dubious position as the most widely used since its inception. Yet in the last few centuries, it has become increasingly clear that alcohol does not mix well with human lives. It is estimated that today there are more than five million drinkers in this country whose drinking seriously impairs their economic, social, and family lives. In short, alcoholism has become one of the most serious forms of addiction, both in incidence and consequence.

The problem of controlling alcoholism is accentuated by the existing attitudes toward drinking in our society. Moderate consumption of alcohol is legally tolerated and often socially encouraged. Yet the individual who develops a dependence on alcohol receives little sympathy and, instead, is berated for a "lack of willpower," criticized for irresponsibility, and abandoned because it is assumed such an individual simply does not "want" to be helped.

You've got to understand the drink. In a world where there is a law against people ever showing emotions, or ever releasing themselves from the greyness of their days, a drink is not a social tool. It is a thing you need in order to live.

Jimmy Breslin, quoted in *Time*, Feb. 28, 1969, p. 76

Patterns in alcoholism. Drinking makes the alcoholic's life temporarily less difficult to face; thus it provides an escape that becomes increasingly tempting the more it is used, as unsolved problems accumulate and new ones are created by the drinking itself. Despite its long-term maladaptiveness, the pattern is maintained because it is reinforced by short-term relief. At some point in the sequence, the picture is further complicated by the establishment of physical dependence too. Yet long after it is clear to everyone else that a once healthy person has become an alcoholic, the individual may stoutly deny that a drinking problem exists.

E. M. Jellinek (1960), this century's leading expert in the study of alcohol abuse, set forth the proposition that alcoholism can best be understood as a "disease process" in which physical damage becomes progressively greater with the passage of time and the increased consumption of alcohol. Jellinek delineated five main types of alcoholism, which he labeled with the first five letters of the Greek alphabet:

1. *Alpha alcoholism:* psychological dependence on alcohol;

2. *Beta alcoholism:* the appearance of physical complications, and in some cases, physical dependence;

3. *Gamma alcoholism:* the development of a tolerance to alcohol, which causes the alcoholic to consume greater and greater quantities;

4. *Delta alcoholism:* a persistently raised blood-alcohol level and the inability to abstain for long periods of time;

5. *Epsilon alcoholism:* periodic excessive alcohol use (going on "benders").

Although many who have studied the problem of alcoholism have corroborated this categorization, others maintain that it is not so much a set of distinct types as a continuum along which individuals progress.

Control of alcoholism. Not surprisingly, experience has shown that legal penalties such as fines and imprisonment are unsatisfactory means of controlling excessive drinking. Yet approximately a third of *all* police arrests in this country are for drunkenness. This involves a great expenditure of time, effort, and expense on the part of both the police department and the court system. Imprisonment rarely brings any treatment for the problem of alcoholism—only punishment for having made the "illness" public. Dramatic evidence for the futility of this response to alcoholism (where it does not involve a victim) comes from the discovery by a committee investigating prison sentences that there were six men in Washington, D.C., who had been arrested 1409 times for drunkenness and collectively had spent 125 years in penal institutions. Hardly evidence of rehabilitation! Nor was another legal measure—national prohibition—successful in reducing the amount of harmful drinking. Statistics on the admission of alcoholic patients to state hospitals in New York between 1889 and 1943 showed no relationship between legal prohibition of drinking and the incidence of alcoholism (Landis & Cushman, 1945).

A wide variety of clinical treatments for alcoholism have been developed, none of which has met with more than limited success. Psychotherapeutic techniques, based on the belief that drinking is primarily a symptom of an underlying emotional disorder, attempt to alter the alcoholic's attitudes and life-style through personal and social counseling. It is assumed that a person who has found a satisfactory means of coping with problems will no longer need to drink. Even in cases where the dependence is purely psychological, however, the drinking habit is so strong that it is not easily eliminated to any permanent degree.

In some cases there has been success with treatment based on learning principles. The patient is forced to drink alcohol mixed with emetic drugs that cause severe nausea. Eventually, a conditioned link is established so that the sight, smell, and taste of alcohol evoke nausea and vomiting. Usually, psychotherapy and often family counseling is also needed, however, because the drinking is being maintained by sufficient reinforcement to make life with it seem more comforting—or at least less painful—than life without it. Thus alcoholics are not likely to be cured until they really want to be, until they find other ways of meeting the needs that their

drinking has satisfied, and until they change the environmental setting that reinforces drinking.

With patients who are motivated to change, group therapy or other group approaches have generally had the greatest success. Many alcoholics have found new help in facing their problems through private organizations such as Alcoholics Anonymous. This organization provides for its members an atmosphere of mutual understanding, acceptance, sympathetic fellowship, and emotional support in which they can work out their problems without the feelings of isolation, shame, and helplessness that may torture the alcoholic struggling alone. This social therapy approach to alcoholism has met with considerable success, but many more alcoholics never join an AA group than do so. A critical feature of all therapy—not previously recognized—is that to be effective, therapy must reach those who need it, and thus must *reach out* to them and not wait for those in need to come around.

Dependence on Cigarettes

Although history dutifully recorded the awe-inspiring discoveries of Christopher Columbus in founding the "New World," little if any notice has ever been given to what was perhaps his big mistake—the discovery and popularization in Europe of tobacco. Today cigarette smoking constitutes the most common form of addiction in our culture. In the past ten years this habit has become a cause for national concern due to widespread scientific reports of a connection between smoking and an array of serious physical maladies, including lung cancer, bronchitis, coronary thrombosis, and deaths of infants born to heavily smoking mothers. Even nonsmokers are affected, since, according to the Surgeon General's Report (1972), "the level of carbon monoxide attained in experiments using rooms filled with tobacco smoke has been shown to equal, and at times to exceed, the legal limits for maximum air pollution permitted . . ." (p. 7). Thus the outcry from nonsmokers for seating separate from smokers on planes, in restaurants, etc., is understandable.

Dependence on cigarettes is primarily psychological. Although a tolerance for nicotine develops in the habitual smoker, this tolerance is limited, thus preventing the adaptive changes in nerve cells that cause physical addiction to other substances. But this hardly means that terminating the habit is a simple matter, as any heavy smoker who has tried to stop will tell you. In spite of numerous attempts to devise a method of "curing" the cigarette addict, the tobacco habit has remained amazingly resistant to extinction. A wide range of techniques—behavior modification, psychotherapy, sensory stimulation, drug therapy, hypnosis, and a host of others—seem to work for a short time after the completion of the initial program, but none has shown any long-term effectiveness.

The question of the motivations involved in the maintenance of smoking behavior—particularly in individuals who profess a desire to quit—is an extremely complex one. Numerous hypotheses concerning the behavioral mechanisms involved in such behavior have been advanced. An amazing array of techniques have been used, singly or in combination, in attempts to modify smoking behavior. ◆ Such techniques reflect the wide variety of hypotheses—implicit or explicit—held by different workers in this area.

The cognitive world of the cigarette smoker. One of the primary causes of excessive smoking is the satisfaction that has come to be associated with it. Since the associations are learned and not inherent, they vary tremendously from one smoker to another. One smoker may claim to smoke for stimulation, another for relaxation, and another for the feeling of social togetherness that smoking gives. One can only speculate as to the number of smokers in your parents' and grandparents' generation who began to smoke after watching the love scene in the old movie *Now Voyager* where Paul Henreid put two cigarettes in his mouth, lit them, and, in one of the most sophisticated moments in the cinema, passed one to Bette Davis.

To a considerable extent cigarette smoking has been associated with cognitions of "machismo" (of the rugged he-man), of loyalty and tenacity (of those who would rather fight than switch, or we presume would rather die than stop), as well as many other desirable qualities. Cognitive factors also play a role in attempts to stop smoking.

In one "stop smoking" program, all 18 subjects who were given a high expectation of success and a great deal of positive reinforcement did quit smoking, and 14 of them were still abstaining two months later. The 18 matched control subjects received minimal verbal reinforcement and expected a low chance of success. Only 8 of them kicked the habit and only 1 was not smoking at the time of the follow-up study two months later (Lichtenstein, 1971).

Smokers expect that if they refrain from smoking they will experience a series of undesirable side effects, irritability, nervousness, and increased hunger. Such cognitions make it more difficult to stop or to sustain the commitment to do so, but they can be manipulated by a technique called "attribution therapy" (Ross, Rodin, & Zimbardo, 1969; Nisbett & Schachter, 1966). Starting with the claim that psychological manifestations of a change in internal states are dependent on the interpretation that people place on their sensations, attribution therapy simply provides new or different interpretations for what is being experienced. These new interpretations attribute the perceived internal state to a cause that is external, affectively neutral, and controllable by the individual.

An interesting application of attribution therapy to control of cigarette smoking comes from a study of female nurses by Barefoot and Girodo (1972).

Fifteen female nurses who smoked regularly were told that they were taking part in a study relating certain drugs to heart rate. They were asked to refrain from smoking for a period of one day. Experimental subjects were given a placebo that they were told would cause certain negative side effects: increased irritability, nervousness, and appetite (symptoms frequently associated with smoking cessation). Control subjects also received the placebo, but no warning about possible side effects. As was predicted, experimental subjects attributed their discomfort to the action of the pill and reported that it was easier to refrain from smoking than did the control subjects who attributed their physiological and psychological discomfort to cigarette deprivation.

An ounce of prevention . . . Because of the difficulty involved in eliminating the tobacco habit, many investigators consider the *prevention* of smoking a more fruitful realm for experimentation. To this end, they have attempted to identify the social and psychological conditions that contribute to smoking behavior. It seems clear that if any permanent effort to eliminate smoking is to succeed, the image of the cigarette smoker as presented by such agents of culture as the mass media must be altered. It has been suggested that the required "therapy," then, must take the form of political legislation to restrict advertising and mass media displays of the pleasures of cigarette smoking that create this "attractive death-dealing nuisance." In addition, it may be necessary to develop more effective counter-education to warn children against the health consequences of heavy smoking. Such suggestions are being met with resistance by

powerful interest groups, pointing up the conflict between the government's social responsibility for the physical health of its citizens and its concern for the economic health of commercial enterprises (and the sales taxes it derives from them) that thrive on this form of addiction.

Drug Addiction

There is perhaps no psychological phenomenon that has had a more profound effect on such a broad segment of the population as the use and abuse of psychoactive drugs. People use psychoactive drugs for a variety of reasons. They use them for pleasure, to relieve discomfort, to escape personal problems, to expand consciousness, to facilitate performance, and so on. Very often individuals develop a strong psychological need for a particular drug because they have

◆ **TECHNIQUES THAT HAVE BEEN USED TO MODIFY SMOKING BEHAVIOR**

1. Chewing food a certain number of times before swallowing
2. Keeping especially clean
3. Avoiding profane language
4. Changing diet
5. Rising early
6. Hot baths
7. Cold showers
8. Sending clothes to be cleaned
9. Deep breathing exercises
10. Keeping physically fit
11. Drugs such as lobeline
12. Hypnotic instructions
13. Verbal encouragement
14. Supportive counseling
15. Group discussion
16. Signing a pledge, with loss of a deposit contingent on breaking it
17. Drug-induced nausea paired with cigarette smoking
18. Aversive stimuli (hot air puff in face) paired with smoking
19. White noise interrupting ongoing pleasant music contingent on smoking
20. Electric shock contingent on smoking
21. Saying "Cigarette smoking causes cancer" prior to performing some frequently occurring behavior
22. Role playing a doctor-patient interview where the patient learns that he or she has lung cancer.

Based on Bernstein, 1969

a particular problem that they cannot deal with. American society has been accustomed to using drugs in large quantity—both for medical purposes and in illegitimate settings. Drug addiction has been with us for a long time, but it has been confined primarily to racial minorities and those in lower socioeconomic situations. In the last five to ten years there has been a tremendous increase in the use of illegal drugs in the middle and upper classes, especially among young people and basically because they have been turning to drugs for recreation, escape, and mystical experiences.

A survey by the National Commission on Marijuana and Drug Abuse in 1972, based on a sample of 3186 Americans (including youths 12 to 18 years of age), projected the following rather startling statistics of the extent to which people young and old are trying, flying, coasting with drugs.

Drug	Number Who Have Tried It
Pain killers, morphine, codeine	2,600,000
Prescription tranquilizers for pleasure	2,600,000
Prescription stimulants	5,800,000
Sleeping pills, barbiturates	4,500,000
Methamphetamines	3,700,000
Cocaine	2,600,000
Hallucinogens (LSD, mescaline, peyote)	4,700,000
Heroin	2,200,000

There are many theories as to why this has occurred. One is that this is a natural outcome in an already drug-oriented culture such as ours as it becomes more affluent. Another is that as individuals find out more about drugs, they become more curious about trying them. As soon as drug use becomes an acceptable or normative behavior in a particular culture, more of its members have opportunities to observe others taking drugs, drugs are more available, and group pressures toward "turning on" increase (as we have seen in Chapter 7).

It is well known that drug use has increased in other times of cultural turmoil. After wars, or during wars, there is often a dramatic increase in the use of drugs. Our time is one of special instability, in which all traditional values and institutions are being challenged and neither adults nor young people know what the future holds. The youth of today look with a fresh awareness at the problems of pollution, political corruption, racial and sexual discrimination, and people's basic inhumanity to each other, and although they have yet to offer better answers for these problems in many cases, nevertheless they do not blindly accept the values of their elders. Once you begin to break away from the value system of the dominant culture, for whatever reasons, you begin to experiment with a variety of things that would not be sanctioned by traditional values, such as political protest, alternative religions, a more liberal sexual ethic, and drug use. But drug use is a very complex phenomenon. Personality problems, adolescent turmoil, identity crises, societal reasons, and peer-group pressure—all are important.

Recent research has indicated that most young people who begin taking a drug, particularly an illegal one, do so for the first time because of curiosity and peer-group pressure. Once an individual is in the drug subculture, his or her patterns of drug use are greatly influenced by the attitudes that particular drug subculture has. If it is a very destructive subculture, there may be tremendous peer-group pressure to experiment with amphetamines by injection or with heroin or cocaine or a variety of drugs of high abuse potential. If the individual is in a less destructive drug subculture (such as in a college), then the influence of that group's pressure may keep him or her within the framework of drugs of lower abuse potential. Individuals rarely make decisions about drugs on an independent basis in the beginning stages of drug use. Usually they are greatly influenced by what they think others are doing, by their desire to impress their friends or not to be different, and by what drugs are available in their community. (See *P&L* Close-up at right.)

A recent study of the dynamics of the heroin addiction epidemic that hit Washington, D.C., in 1969–70, revealed that an estimated 18,000 residents were directly involved and an untold number were "contaminated" indirectly (Du-Pont & Greene, 1973). The Narcotics Treatment Administration (NTA) was created as the city's comprehensive treatment program. As many as 58 patients began this treatment in a single day, the demand exceeding the capacity of the facility. About 13,000 people were treated within a three-year period through this one drug program. During this same time there were over two hundred deaths from acute opiate overdose.

In addition to dealing with medical cases, such facilities are vital to collect data on the characteristics of drug addicts so we may better understand the dynamics of the problem, not just the consequences. As can be seen in the figure, the age at which heroin was first used among the 13,000 drug patients at NTA was

Close-up
Heroin Hits Harlem

"Heroin had just about taken over Harlem. It seemed to be a kind of plague. Every time I went uptown, somebody else was hooked, somebody else was strung out. People talked about them as if they were dead. You'd ask about an old friend, and they'd say, 'Oh, well, he's strung out.' It wasn't just a comment or an answer to a question. It was a eulogy for someone. He was just dead, through.

"At that time, I didn't know anybody who had kicked it. Heroin had been the thing in Harlem for about five years, and I don't think anybody knew anyone who had kicked it. . . .

"I was afraid to ask about somebody I hadn't seen in a while, especially if it was someone who was once a good friend of mine. There was always a chance somebody would say, 'Well, he died. The cat took an O.D.,' an overdose of heroin; or he was pushed out of a window trying to rob somebody's apartment, or shot five times trying to stick up a place to get some money for drugs. Drugs were killing just about everybody off in one way or another. It had taken over the neighborhood, the entire community. . . .

"The cats who weren't strung out couldn't see where they were heading. If they were just snorting some horse, they seemed to feel that it wouldn't get to them. It's as though cats would say, 'Well, damn, I'm slicker than everybody else,' even though some slick cats and some strong guys had fallen into the clutches of heroin. Everybody could see that nobody was getting away from it once they had started dabbling in it, but still some people seemed to feel, 'Shit, I'm not gon get caught. I can use it, and I can use it and not be caught.'

"Guys who were already strung out were trying to keep their younger brothers away from stuff. They were trying feebly, and necessarily so, because guys who were strung out on drugs didn't have too much time to worry about anybody but themselves. It was practically a twenty-four-hour-a-day job trying to get some money to get some stuff . . . ." (Brown, 1965, pp. 179–80)

predominately between 16 and 20, although many individuals were using heroin before they were 15 years old. ■ The primary mode of transmission was shown to be by means of person-to-person social contact. Thus it is a "contagious disease" to the extent that people who are addicted pass on the habit to others. This social transmission pattern was also found in an earlier study of heroin addiction in the suburbs (Levingood et al., 1971).

Control of this epidemic requires vigorous law enforcement to reduce the available heroin supply and increased availability of accessible drug treatment facilities. The problem, however, is very complicated, since clinics that substitute methadone for heroin are reporting that some former heroin addicts are taking methamphetamines to augment the "high" obtained from the methadone, others get addicted to the methadone, and others complain of the loss of sexual impulses—a side effect of methadone. The latter obviously creates new problems for the patient.

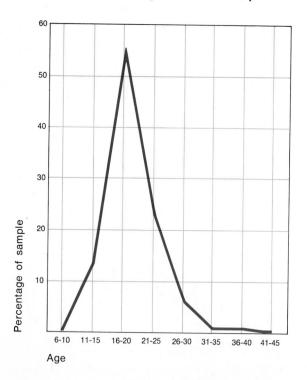

After DuPont & Greene, 1973

■ AGE AT FIRST HEROIN USE

Physical and psychological dependence. Any psychoactive drug has a certain abuse potential. One of the characteristics of this abuse potential is that the individual may use the drug compulsively because of either psychological dependence or physical dependence or both.

In psychological dependence, the individual has a strong emotional need to continue to use the drug for pleasure or for the relief of discomfort. If the drug is unavailable, the user may become anxious, irritable, and angry, but usually has no serious physical discomfort.

Almost any psychoactive drug can produce psychological dependence. Nicotine in cigarettes, alcohol, caffeine, marijuana, and amphetamines are drugs that are often involved in psychological dependence.

Certain drugs can produce physical dependence too. Probably the best known in this latter category are the *narcotics* derived from opium, such as heroin and morphine. With these drugs, prolonged use makes the body physically dependent on the presence of that chemical for continued normal functioning such that if the drug is not present, there is a general physiological reaction called the *abstinence syndrome* that produces great discomfort to the individual. It will continue for several days unless relieved by further administration of the drug.

In certain cases, this withdrawal of the drug may be life-threatening. For example, if one develops a physical dependence on barbiturates, which are commonly used as sleeping pills, abrupt withdrawal from these agents can produce convulsions and even lead to death.

With other drugs that produce physical dependence, such as heroin, withdrawal causes extreme discomfort lasting several days. However, fear of this withdrawal from heroin very often prevents the individual who is addicted to the drug from stopping, so that the user may continue to take the drug long after he or she has stopped deriving any euphoric effects from it, merely to prevent the painful process of withdrawal.

The progressive nature of drug addiction. Individuals who become heavy drug users usually pass through three stages of drug use. The first is a stage of *experimental* use, where they may try a wide variety of psychoactive chemicals out of curiosity or peer-group pressure. Then they may decide to discard most of the drugs they have experimented with and then periodically or recreationally use just a few. For example, an individual may become a periodic alcohol drinker or pot smoker. At this *recreational* stage, unless intoxicating levels are reached, the individual rarely gets into difficulty. However, on occasion, because of either social circumstance or personality problems, such a person moves into a period of compulsive drug use. This third stage is called *drug abuse* because it is the use of a drug to the point where it interferes with the individual's health and economic or social functioning.

There are many personality characteristics that may predispose individuals to the abuse of drugs. The psychiatric or clinical depiction of the addict has traditionally been one of an immature individual, overburdened by feelings of inadequacy, bent on self-destruction, yet simultaneously narcissistically preoccupied with self-gratification (Nyswander, 1956). Psychoanalytic interpretations sometimes relate drug addiction to such things as "unconscious homosexuality," "phallic symbolism" (e.g., of the syringe), "the Oedipus complex," and especially "oral fixation" (Fenichel, 1945). Yet psychiatric attempts to classify the diagnosed personality characteristics of addicts remain highly questionable. Psychiatrists only study the addict *after* addiction, and therefore are unable to separate those traits resulting from addiction from those that caused addiction. Their interpretations are always of a retrospective historical variety. Given what we see now, what was the person like before? Aside from the obvious effects of protracted drug taking on the addict's personality, several incidental factors are surely involved, particularly the psychological and sociological implications of playing the role of the addict in our society. As Clausen (1971) has properly stressed, "personality is not independent of environmental influences, and, by and large, the

influences that permit [drugs] to be available to a teenager and permit a high proportion of adolescents to become members of street-corner society also create psychological needs and vulnerabilities which enhance the value of narcotics to the individual" (p. 212). Thus the complex problem appears to be as much a function of social pathology as individual pathology.

The extremely inadequate success record of conventional therapeutic techniques has in recent years prompted a necessary search for new approaches and the rejection of earlier oversimplified theories of addiction. Increasingly, there is an acceptance of the need for an interrelated conception of the social, psychological, medical, and legal aspects involved in addiction. Surely, all these perspectives must be seriously considered both in any assessment of the "causes" of an individual's addiction, society's drug problem, and in viable programs to control drug abuse.

"I Got a Right to Be Me, to Do My Own Thing"

To drink, to smoke cigarettes, to take drugs, to gamble are the rights of adults; they are sources of personal pleasure and, when done alone or with a few close friends, are private acts not infringing on the public sector of life. However, when carried to excess, they cease being "victimless crimes" because they involve other people—family, friends, work associates, the police, those in the court system, those who must render medical care, organized crime, and those who are "ripped off" in various ways to support the pathological habit. These addictions force the addicts to become dependent on the nonaddicted part of society for care and treatment. They constitute an enormous burden psychologically as well as financially to their society. More attention must be paid by social planners to develop our society in ways that help fulfill some of the needs expressed through these addictions. At the same time we must each become more in touch with our own vulnerability and aware of the subtle forces in our environment that can insidiously direct our behavior to do exactly those things we believe we would never do.

Loss of Joy in Living: Neurosis

When an individual feels chronically threatened by life's hazards and inadequate to the task of coping with them, the ordinary ego defenses we all use are not enough. Gradually he or she may come to rely excessively on one or more neurotic defense patterns. These patterns have in common the search for relief from anxiety. Thus they are characterized by an absence of joy in living and by actions aimed at lessening pain rather than at positive accomplishment or the constructive solution of objectively real problems. They provide enough temporary relief from anxiety that many individuals cling to them desperately despite the fact they do not solve their basic problems and may even worsen them—and thus are self-defeating in the long run.

The tragedy of neurotics is that often their evaluations of the world as threatening and of themselves as ineffectual are faulty. With more realistic perceptions there would be no need for this loss of joy or a tortured preoccupation with worries and threats.

In general, the normal person functions as an organized whole and deals with frustrations more or less effectively. But "normality," for the psychologist, includes a wide range of behavior rather than a single fixed point on a scale. Thus there is no clear dividing line between the normal and the neurotic: the difference is one of degree. The neurotic's defenses are regarded as abnormal because they represent seriously and chronically ineffective ways of coping with life's demands. However, they are rarely severe enough to require hospitalization.

If there is a continuum from normal to neurotic, at what point can we identify a person as being disturbed enough to justify assigning the label of "neurotic" (or is this labeling process never justified)? What are the behavioral signs that are used to identify the neurotic individual? A number of fairly distinct neurotic patterns have been identified within the realm of traditional psychology, of which six will be described here.

Anxiety Neurosis

Sometimes the source of anxiety for neurotic individuals is not an external danger but an inner one. They may believe they should not have certain feelings and wishes, such as hostility or sexual desires, and thus may be unable to accept the fact that they have them. When such thoughts or impulses arise, they may be repressed—pushed out of consciousness—and much effort, also unconscious, may be devoted to keeping them there. When they threaten to emerge into consciousness from time to time, the neurotic may experience feelings of impending doom and may have attacks of physical symptoms such as palpitation of the heart or respiratory difficulty.

In many instances, the individual consults a physician; in fact, it is estimated that 30 percent of all patients seen by general practitioners and internists actually fit in this category (Pitts, 1969). About 10 million Americans are thought to suffer from anxiety neurosis. Not only is the physician unable to find anything wrong, however, but the patients themselves may be quite at a loss to explain why they are so anxious. This anxiety is said to be "free-floating." Sometimes, too, they feel extreme guilt without knowing why.

It is this elusive nonspecificity of the anxiety experiences that is responsible for much of the terror experienced by the patient. Imagine feeling intense arousal and strange things happening inside your head and body—and having no rational explanation to account for them. You see a doctor and after a thorough physical examination, the doctor assures you that nothing is wrong with you. But inside your head the beat goes on and on and . . .

The failure to explain this "unexplained arousal" itself now constitutes a threat to your feelings of self-knowledge and self-control and generates additional anxiety. One of the main functions of psychotherapy is to identify the original source of anxiety in order to make it a tangible, manageable fear. "Put a name on it and you can do something about it" (Grimmett, 1970).

Neurotic anxiety can be differentiated from objective anxiety or fear. Fear is a rational reaction to an objective, identified external danger and may involve flight or attack in self-defense. In neurotic anxiety the emotional arousal is just as strong, but the danger is internal: neither identifiable nor shared as a common threat by others in the situation.

Although anxiety attacks are thought to be triggered by factors in the individual's experience, there is some evidence of abnormal biochemical reactions also (Pitts, 1969).

Phobias

In *phobic reactions*, anxiety becomes attached to a definite object in the external environment, but typically the object is not a source of physical harm or biological danger. Thus, neurotics often realize that their acute reaction is irrational—there is not an adequate explanation for it—but that recognition only makes their anxiety more unbearable. In some cases, the choice of the phobic object is purely symbolic; in others, it has a close connection with the underlying conflict.

A construction worker had to quit his job because he began to develop a fear of heights. Everyone knows that accidents can happen on construction work; was his reaction objective or neurotic? Without further evidence you could not tell. In this particular case, however, the man also developed a fear of open spaces on the ground (not a source of danger) and also a fear of death.

It turned out that prior to the onset of his anxiety reactions, a fellow employee had begun to aggravate him constantly. In fact, he reported, "I felt like killing him." But he had felt hopeless about actually taking any action to stop the annoying behavior. It is possible that in quitting his job he was defending against his impulses toward homicide as well as his own inability to stand up to his tormentor. In any case, developing a phobia of heights was one effective resolution of his problem, providing a justification for giving up his lucrative job.

There are virtually no limits as to what a phobia may symbolize, since a creative mind can construct quite remote associations. Phobias of harmless snakes or insects, birds flying, touching another person, hair, and other quite safe objects or situations may come to induce strong reactions resulting in panic if the individual cannot escape. In fact, characteristic of phobic reactions are the elaborate precautions and defenses the individual erects to avoid all contact with the "dangerous" phobic object. It is as if neurotics handle their internal conflicts by externalizing them onto some object; then as long as they can avoid the object, they can avoid confronting the terror within themselves.

Phobias work quite well when the phobic object is rarely encountered or easily avoided. Snake phobias among city dwellers, height phobias among country people, and so on, prove to be convenient ways of channeling anxiety by taking it "out of your head" and putting it onto something that will not be a recurrent threat. Indeed, phobic anxiety only becomes a source of major concern for the person when the object is not readily avoidable and thus interferes with one's ongoing behavior.

In some cultures, the choice of the phobic object is not left up to the individual but is culturally prescribed by the medicine man or witch doctor who treats the person in distress. An object or activity is selected as "taboo"—a certain tree to be avoided, a kind of food never to be eaten, and so forth—such that avoidance of it will bring contentment, and exposure to it will result in severe anxiety, illness, and perhaps death. The individual then can explicitly locate the source of his or her troubles in these specific things and, by avoiding them, contain them.

Obsessive-Compulsive Neurosis

Repressed desires and guilt feelings frequently lead to another type of abnormal behavior pattern known as an *obsessive-compulsive neurosis*. Actually, obsessions and compulsions are separate types of reactions that may occur quite independently of each other, but they occur together so often that they are generally considered as two separate aspects of a single behavior pattern.

Obsessions. An obsession is a persistent and irrational thought that comes into consciousness inappropriately and cannot be banished voluntarily. Almost everyone has some sort of mild obsessional experience occasionally, such as the intrusion of petty worries, "Did I really lock the door?" or "Did I set the alarm?" or the persistence of a haunting melody we simply cannot shake from our consciousness. Most of us have at times felt a bit better after a ritual crossing of fingers or knocking on wood.

Although mild obsessions such as persistent tunes can be irritating, true neurotic obsessions are much more insistent and so disturbing that they come to interfere with all facets of the individual's daily life. Often they center around morbid thoughts of death or suicide or continual fantasies of committing murder in some brutal fashion. Extreme obsessional reactions can be almost completely disabling—patients may be so overwhelmed by a recurrent obsession that they find it almost impossible to concentrate on any other thoughts, and unable to control the occurrence or direction of the obsessive thoughts.

One explanation of the function that obsessions serve is that they impose a structure on impulses that are perceived (at some level) as chaotic and dangerous. Not only does obsessive thought limit action, but it also serves to contain strong emotions, such as feelings of hatred, destruction, or lust. For the obsessive, the thought, set up as the barrier between affect and action, becomes the ultimate reality to be dealt with rather than whatever would be the consequences of taking the desired but forbidden action.

Compulsions. Sometimes only thinking, even obsessive thinking, is not an adequate safeguard against expression of forbidden impulses. An additional mechanism for imposing order on impulses is seen in *compulsions*. In most cases, compulsive reactions do not require hospitalization but merely inconvenience the individual

and may puzzle associates. Occasionally, however, they are seriously incapacitating or part of a broader picture of psychopathology.

In one case, an elderly male patient would spend hour after hour writing one or two messages and giving them to the other patients and the staff. When he was ordered to stop and his paper and pencil were taken away, the messages ceased for a while; then they mysteriously resumed—written on napkins and somehow slipped under the door or into the pocket or mailbox of the staff members, a different target each day. Some samples received by one of the authors over a three-month period are shown. ● Note the remarkable similarity of the fine details of this compulsive patient's handwriting as well as the "magic number" and theme of the napkin message.

Compulsive behavior consists of repetitive ritualistic actions. Even though such rituals are highly charged emotionally for neurotic people, they may remain unaware of their meaning. By becoming preoccupied with carrying out these minor everyday tasks repeatedly, however, the compulsive neurotic has no time or energy left to carry out the impulsive action that is unconsciously being guarded against. In some cases, guilt feelings for real or imagined sins may find expression in compulsive rituals designed to undo them; an example is excessive hand-washing—a kind of Lady Macbeth reaction.

Hysterical Neurosis

It is not uncommon for students to forget appointments with the dentist or get sick on the day of a final exam, for singers to get laryngitis before an audition, or for track athletes to develop "charley horses" that prevent them from competing in a track meet. These represent some of the "normal" forms of avoiding an unpleasant, feared situation. These escapes are not consciously sought. In fact, the individuals using them vigorously deny that they are "escapes": they just "happen" in situations of anticipated stress. But losing one's memory or becoming physically incapacitated does remove the person from a situation that is threatening psychological well-being or self-esteem and does so in such a way that the individual cannot be blamed for not facing it.

When such a mechanism is carried to the extreme that the person becomes physically paralyzed or has a total loss of memory—without any organic defect—then the condition is abnormal and is labeled *hysterical neurosis*. Included under this general heading are two related disorders: *conversion hysteria* and *dissociated states*.

Conversion hysteria. In conversion hysteria there is a loss of sensory or motor function without organic pathology. The individual suddenly cannot hear or see or feel, or may have an arm or leg paralyzed or be unable to speak.

Many hysterical symptoms are completely incompatible with medical fact. For instance, in certain types of hysterical anesthesia (loss of sensitivity to touch or pain), areas of the body are affected that do not correspond with the actual arrangement of the neural pathways. In other cases, however, a physician may have great difficulty in telling whether the patient is suffering from an organic ailment or a hysterical one.

It is important to remember that in a conversion reaction no actual biological change is involved. This is clearly demonstrated by the fact that when the individual is asleep or under hypnosis the hysterical symptoms generally disappear. For instance, patients who suffer from hysterical paralysis may be entirely incapable of moving their legs, but under hypnosis they may be made to get up and walk across the room. Moreover, hysterical symptoms may come and go or even appear at different times in different areas of the body; occasionally a patient who is hysterically "blind" in the right eye on one day may unconsciously shift the ailment to the left eye the next day.

Although hysterical symptoms may sometimes be made to disappear by means of hypnotic suggestion, they are fairly likely to recur, perhaps in modified form, as long as the underlying conflict remains.

● **NAPKIN WRITING BY A COMPULSIVE PATIENT**

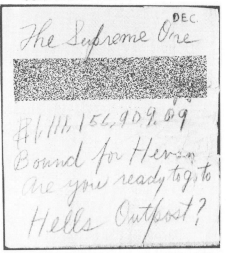

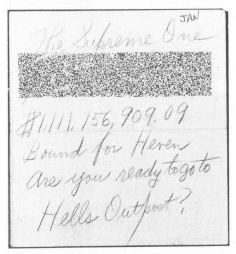

Individuals who develop conversion reactions tend to be immature, emotional, and demanding, given to histrionics and self-pity. In many cases they have sexual feelings that they cannot accept. Usually they manage to obtain not only escape from the threatening situation but extra dividends in the form of considerable attention and sympathy—which in turn reinforce their pattern of helpless dependence. Interestingly, the forms that conversion reactions take and their frequency depend on the degree of medical sophistication of the patient and the society (which must be accepting of the physical condition for the maneuver to be successful). Fainting, frequently reported in Victorian England, is a type of conversion hysteria rare today. In fact, the incidence of neurotic conversion reactions has diminished greatly in the United States in recent years, though they still occur in significant numbers in countries where medical knowledge is less widespread.

Dissociated states. We have noted throughout this text how important it is for people to see themselves as basically in control of their behavior—including their emotions, cognitions, and actions. Essential to this perception of self-control is the assumption that we have an integrated, consistent personality, a central core that represents our essential, unique nature. This "personality" provides a basis for perceiving a continuity of ourselves over time. We see meaning in present experiences in terms of frames of reference established in the past, and we attach significance to them in terms of their likely future consequences. Situations change, time passes, our behavior changes, even our attitudes or values may change, yet we hold firm to the belief that we are the same person throughout. It is this constancy of self that provides for most people a firm, reliable yardstick against which perceived change in the outer world is measured, interpreted, and evaluated.

In dissociated states, individuals escape from their conflicts by giving up this precious consistency and continuity and, in a sense, disowning parts of themselves. They may accomplish this in any of several ways. One way is through *somnambulism* (sleepwalking), in which the individual may walk about while sleeping and perform some action of symbolic significance of which there is no recollection when awake. A related kind of dissociation is often found in nervous mannerisms or bodily movements that somehow get detached from conscious control. Many of us are the victims of tics, twitches, and motor habits that seem to live a life of their own.

The loss of memory for what one did during states of somnambulism can assume a more extreme form by occurring during waking. In cases of *amnesia*, people perform their usual waking actions—eating, speaking, reading, driving, and so on, but have no memory of their own identity. By obliterating the past through amnesia, the person in one deft stroke cuts off the present from these ties to an unhappy past and is able to start all over again, constructing the present on its own terms. In many cases, amnesics are people whose life history and habitual patterns of psychological reaction have made them exceptionally good at escaping from situations with which they simply cannot cope.

Often an amnesic person who has given up an old identity may actually travel to some other place, either a completely new one or a familiar place that was emotionally supportive at some earlier time. This is called a *fugue* episode, from the Latin word meaning "to flee." (See *P&L* Close-up, p. 481.) In this new place, the person may assume a new identity and create a new life-style, dissociated psychologically, temporally, and geographically from a prior unacceptable life-style. Cases have been reported where such persons were rediscovered several years after their disappearance. Of course, we do not know how many remain undiscovered and lead the rest of their lives as their reconstituted selves.

The most extreme form of dissociation is *multiple personality*. In this type of reaction—which is very rare, despite being dramatized so often in the movies and on television—the individual may develop two (or sometimes more) distinct

Close-up
Out of Sight, Lost from Mind

The following is an account by a woman who developed amnesia and experienced a fugue episode. It is unusual not only for being a personal account of such an experience but also because in the process of writing it for use in *Psychology and Life,* she began to lose control and regress to childhood, as evidenced in her handwriting, and after completing it, did lose her memory temporarily again.

"I found myself with my son, then four and a half years old, but unusually precocious, in an automat in Manhattan. We were having breakfast, a meal which I usually do not eat, and I noticed that it was about 9 A.M. . . . We were, I thought, starting on an expedition of Christmas shopping (it was early in December) and the events of the day were scheduled around lunch, which I thought we were to have with my mother (who was at that time three months dead). We spent the morning hours shopping and running with great (unusual, it now seems) exuberance and hilarity down streets and into stores. . . .

"As noon approached I felt a slight tension, an anxiety that somehow we were not going to make the luncheon date. We went to a telephone booth where I had decided to call my mother to make an alternate plan for lunch. In the telephone booth I discovered that I could not remember my mother's phone number or name (to look it up in the telephone book). . . . I charged my inability to remember to a virus I had heard of at that time that produced unusual psychological states in those who had it. I decided to have lunch, took my son to a museum and then to a movie. I was feeling especially energetic and seemed to do more than normal activities.

"It was in the movie, thinking again of calling my mother, that I realized that I not only did not know her name but did not know my own. I took my son to the lounge and searched my purse for identification. I was being particularly careful not to frighten him, but I was myself not frightened and unusually lucid. I found in my purse a list of three names with telephone numbers and the address of one person. I did not recognize the names. I called the first person on the list—an old college teacher of mine and very close friend. When I reached him, I proceeded to describe my situation and realized that I could not describe myself. I looked to my left into a mirror and did not recognize myself.

"I told my teacher that I had my son with me and described him. My teacher told me to get into a taxi—that he knew who I was and the address I was to give the driver was my home. After I hung up, I had forgotten what he said my name was, but, looking at the address and finding that it was in Brooklyn, I thought he was mistaken for I remembered (or thought I did) that I lived in New Haven. . . . I had supper with my son and boarded the train for New Haven. . . . As the train pulled out of Bridgeport, my son remarked that he knew that this was not the way home to Brooklyn. I became frightened for the first time. When I reached New Haven, I called the next name on my list . . . he told me to take the next train back to Grand Central. . . .

"In the morning I was taken to a psychiatrist. My husband was waiting when I left the psychiatrist's office. When I saw him I did not know him. He looked so different to me. I was very ashamed that I did not know him. I felt very hot and was blushing. I was aware for the first time that everyone was looking at me, and it was with a terrible shock that I became aware of being an object in the vision of others. At that moment. I was aware that I was a visible entity. I think now that during the state I was almost always under the impression that I was invisible except when I wanted to make myself visible to the consciousness of whomever I was talking with and then would become known as a consciousness myself rather than as a person. . . ."

personalities that alternate in consciousness, each taking over conscious control of the person for varying periods of time. Each part of the multiple personality is based on sets of motives that are in conflict with the motives of the other parts. These conflicting motive patterns originally existed simultaneously in one personality but were so incompatible—and yet all so insistent—that the person was able to satisfy them all only by repressing consciousness of one set while temporarily gratifying another set. Usually, though not always, each personality is completely unaware of the other. In some cases one personality may be aware of the other but not vice versa.

▲ TWO PERSONALITIES IN ONE BODY

Listed here are some of the contrasting personality characteristics of "Eve White" and "Eve Black" as noted in the first two "faces of Eve."

Eve White	Eve Black
Demure, retiring	Vivacious, a "party girl"
Sweet, quiet face	Pixie-like mischievous face
Dresses simply, conservatively	Dresses attractively, provocatively
Reads and writes poetry	Never serious or contemplative
Soft, feminine voice	Coarse, teasing voice
Language restrained	Language vernacular, witty
Admired for her quiet strength	Liked for her wit and adventuresomeness
Industrious and competent	Lighthearted and irresponsible
Seldom animated or playful	Delights in pranks
A devoted mother	Feelings momentary and ephemeral
Not allergic to nylon	Allergic to nylon

Students frequently make the error of confusing such cases of multiple personality with so-called "split personality," known technically as *schizophrenia*, a psychotic disorder in which the individual is "split off from reality." In multiple personality, the conscious part of the personality remains in contact with reality, though reacting to it neurotically.

This dramatic form of reaction is illustrated by the widely publicized case of Eve White. Eve, twenty-five years old and separated from her husband, had sought therapy because of severe, blinding headaches, frequently followed by "blackouts." During one of her early therapy sessions Eve was greatly agitated; she reported that she had recently been hearing voices. Suddenly she put both hands to her temples, then looked up at the doctor with a provocative smile and introduced herself as "Eve Black."

It was obvious from the voice, gestures, and mannerisms of this second Eve that she was a separate personality. She was fully aware of Eve White's doings, but Eve White was unaware of Eve Black's existence. Eve White's "blackouts" were actually the periods when Eve Black was in control, and the "voices" marked unsuccessful attempts of Eve Black to "come out." With extended therapy, it became evident that Eve Black had existed since Eve White's early childhood, when she occasionally took over and indulged in forbidden pleasures, leaving the other Eve to face the consequences. This habit had persisted, and Eve White frequently suffered Eve Black's hangovers. ▲

After about eight months of therapy, a third personality appeared. This one, Jane, was more mature, capable, and forceful than the retiring Eve White; she gradually came to be in control most of the time. Electroencephalograms of Jane and Eve White were both normal and very similar; Eve Black's was classified as borderline normal.

As the therapist probed the memories of the two Eves, he felt sure that some shocking event must have precipitated the actual development of distinct personalities in the disturbed child. In a dramatic moment, the climax of therapy, the missing incident came to light. Jane sudden-

ly stiffened, and in a terrified voice began to scream, "Mother . . . Don't make me! . . . I can't do it! I can't!" When the screams subsided, a new — and final — personality took over. She was able to recall the shocking event that lay at the bottom of the personality dissociation. At the age of six Eve White had been led by her mother to her grandmother's coffin and been forced to place a good-bye kiss on the dead face. (Thigpen & Cleckley, 1954, 1957; Thigpen, 1961).

"Eve" has recently been revealed as a 48-year-old Fairfax (Va.) housewife who has manifested 21 different personalities over the past two decades. Each time they came in sets of three very different personalities, but her last split-selves died a year ago, leaving Chris S. now ready to make it on her own (Chicago Sun-Times, *Sept. 16, 1975*).

Hypochondria

Neurotic individuals frequently show an extreme concern about their health and physical condition, dwelling morbidly on every minor bodily sensation as a possible sign of some serious organic disorder. When such a preoccupation is the main feature of the neurosis, it is called *hypochondria.*

One explanation of hypochondria is that the individual feels separated from his or her body and is attempting to know it, but by analyzing and describing it rather than by being and experiencing it. It may also be that in the process of trying to explain vague feelings of anxiety, tension, and mysterious emotional arousal, some people find it more reasonable and less threatening to the ego to have an organic problem than to have a psychological one. For such people, the choice may be between "being mentally crazy" and "being physically sick."

In any case, hypochondriacs are often said to "enjoy poor health," for their greatest satisfaction seems to be in finding bodily symptoms that confirm their dire predictions. These supposed ailments not only prevent active engagement in life — with its risk of failure — but also may bring secondary gains in attention, sympathy, and service from others. On the other hand, these demands for extra consideration and enormous medical consultation fees and useless surgery bills sometimes lead the patient's exasperated family to forget that the discomfort, however irrationally induced, is subjectively real.

Depressive Neurosis

In *depressive neurosis,* the person distorts reality in degree rather than kind. Such an individual reacts to a loss or threatened loss with greater sadness and for a longer time than most people would — a vigil of eternal mourning. In addition to being depressed, patients often complain of inability to concentrate, lack of self-confidence, sleeplessness, boredom, irritation, and ill health. They may consciously recognize the source of their depression, but overestimate its significance. The patient makes the world too large to cope with, by magnifying out of all proportion any setbacks, frustrations, personal shortcomings, or deficiencies.

In many cases, there is little correspondence between the objective situation of loss, failure, or frustration and the subjective evaluation. For such persons, however, subjective reality is the only reality. They may dwell on their personal, recurring "slide show" of depressing long-past experiences as if they were indeed present reality — an attitude that can only make living more difficult. The failure to enjoy life often is accompanied by the need to drink or take drugs simply to bear the pain of living another day. This fatalistic view of enduring unhappiness may become a potent source of motivation not to bear the pains of life but to escape through suicide.

The depressive reaction is an expression of helplessness, as are all the neuroses. All these strategies are ways in which neurotics prove to themselves and the world that they are impotent, unable to deal with their problems through no fault of their own. The phobic says, "I am terrified by this; I must avoid it." The obsessive-compulsive says, "I *have* to think or do this."

The hysteric says, "I am immobilized; I cannot move from where I am; I cannot face the part of me I don't like." The hypochondriac says, "If I weren't so sick, I could deal with other problems, but in the face of such physical pain, all else is irrelevant." The depressive says, "I am weighed down by the world, I am overwhelmed by my intense grief."

What all these neurotic patterns have in common is a mechanism for limiting anxiety by avoiding any direct confrontation with its source, and an inability to contemplate any other way to handle the problem. Neurotic individuals see "no exit" from their problems and no choices among alternative ways of being. As theologian Paul Tillich once said, "Neurosis is the way of avoiding nonbeing by avoiding being" (1952, p. 66).

When therapy is successful with such people, it changes their self-concept by getting them to accept the fact that they can exert control. By rediscovering the power of decision making and action, or simply by having a visible effect on the environment and recognizing it as their doing, neurotic patients learn that they not only can cope with their particular present problems but also can begin to shape their life along new dimensions that can bring pleasure, satisfaction, and feelings of accomplishment. Most of the therapeutic procedures to be described in the next chapter are directed at the neurotic reaction patterns described above. Although varying in approach, the different therapies share the basic goals of making the neurotic person less helpless and hopeless by helping him or her become more effective and self-accepting.

Loss of Contact with Reality: Psychosis

When an individual's behavior becomes so deviant from normal functioning that contact with "reality" is lost, the resulting condition is labeled *psychosis*. To be psychotic is, in nontechnical terms, to be crazy or mad. Not only is this the most totally disabling of the kinds of losses we have discussed, but it is perhaps society's most feared and unacceptable "disease." The very existence of psychosis challenges our fundamental concept of the integrity of mind, the controlling function of the human will, and the nature of reality.

Insanity is not a psychiatric or psychological term but a legal concept applied to any mental condition that renders the individual incapable of knowing right from wrong and therefore of being legally responsible for actions committed. Thus the term *insanity* can include not only psychotic disorders but also extreme, severely incapacitating neurotic reactions.

Psychosis is not merely a more intense or exaggerated degree of neurosis, but a unique pathological condition that differs dramatically in quality. The psychotic person does not necessarily pass through a neurotic stage, nor do very disturbed neurotics eventually become psychotic, although there are some cases where the symptoms may be mixed, being drawn from both types of disorder.

Whereas neurotic patients are characteristically overwhelmed with anxiety and dread, psychotic patients typically show either a flattened or inappropriate affect (emotion), or extremes of manic or depressive reactions. Furthermore, neurotics often experience a secondary source of anxiety in perceiving that their present behavior is irrational and different from that of other people and from their own "normal" prior behavior. Some neurotic symptoms may in fact develop out of a search for a rationale to explain unusual feelings and thoughts or as a justification to oneself and others. Psychotics rarely acknowledge that their actions or experiences are out of the ordinary, or appear to be anxious about their "condition."

One way to think of the difference between normal, neurotic, and psychotic is by analogy to the difference between a simile and a metaphor. Normals and neurotics may often experience their feelings in the form of a *simile*—"I feel *like* a computer, which functions without emotions." The normal person may add, "but is generally mechanically competent," while the neurotic adds "but is mechanically incompetent." Psychotics eliminate the "like" and live with the full intensity of a *metaphor*—"I *am* a computer."

One crucial consequence of acting out a metaphor is a dissolving of the boundary between self and object, between subjective and objective reality. The psychotic individual, then, is one who refuses to accept both the empirically based definition of what is real and the socially agreed-upon definition of reality. This strategy frees the individual from many constraints that limit the thoughts, feelings, and actions of normal people, who must conform to the rules about what is real, causal, logical, rational, appropriate, and acceptable.

Thus psychotics often lump together "what is" and "what ought to be." Or they may dissociate effects from their causes, actions from thoughts, feelings from actions, conclusions from premises, or truth from evidence. In one sense, what appears as the psychotic's bizarre, inappropriate, and irrational behavior follows from the creation of a closed system that is self-validating and internally consistent. (See *P&L* Close-up at right.) Someone once said that neurotics build castles in the air, while psychotics live in them (and critics add that psychiatrists collect the rent).

Why should some people develop such a deviant pattern of thinking and acting? Unfortunately, despite years of research by psychologists, psychiatrists, and a host of medical investigators, there is still no satisfactory answer to this critical question. Medically oriented researchers argue for an inherited, genetic basis for some types of psychosis or point to metabolic deficiencies and malfunctioning. The psychological view has emphasized factors in the upbringing and social experience of the individual. Some more radical thinkers like Ronald Laing

Reality Testing and the Inner and Outer World of Psychosis

In the course of our cognitive development, we learn how to test reality. We develop the capacity to judge whether the source of a given perception is out there in the external world or within our own heads. This becomes elaborated into a process whereby we check out whether our thoughts, perceptions, and feelings are appropriate to the situation, to current or prior conditions, and to the actions of other people. Thus the reality of our inner world is evaluated against criteria established in the external world—the physical and social environment.

Severely disturbed psychotic children appear to be out of contact with external reality, although they give evidence of having an active internal life. A very provocative theory advanced by two investigators working on the Project on Childhood Psychosis is that psychotics *reverse* the usual reality-testing procedure. Inner experience is the criterion against which they test the validity of outer experiences.

"When external reality does not fit the criteria of their inner reality, it is disregarded or distorted. When external reality experiences in terms of their inner reality seem irrelevant to their inner needs, these are cast aside just as the normal individual, who uses external criteria as a basis, may set aside inner reality experiences which do not fit the external criteria. Still further for these children, since external reality is experienced as a projection of the inner reality, many events take on special and terrifying meanings and, therefore, must be avoided at all costs." (Meyer & Ekstein, 1970, p. 5)

The discontinuity experienced by the neurotic is between the demands of the unconscious and the demands emanating from external reality. For the psychotic the discontinuity is between the awareness of inner consciousness and that which corresponds to outer reality. The task of the therapist is to build a bridge across these two worlds, each of which is a necessary part of the process of reality testing and self-knowledge.

(1967) have even rejected the view of psychosis as abnormal, preferring to conceptualize the psychotic state as a radical revolt against questionable prevailing assumptions about the purpose of life, means-ends relationships, and a too-limited view of human thought and subjective reality.

Classification of Psychoses

Some psychotic reactions and other mental disorders may be *organic* — that is, associated with brain damage due to physical causes such as diseases of the nervous system, brain tumors, brain injuries, overdoses of gases, drugs, alcohol, or metallic oxides, and disturbances in arterial circulation occurring in old age.

More prevalent are the *functional* psychoses that stem from no known physical defect in brain tissue, but rather from deficits in functioning. They fall into three major classifications, as shown in the chart. ■

■ CLASSIFICATION OF THE FUNCTIONAL PSYCHOSES

Paranoid reaction
Major Symptoms: Logical, often highly systematized and intricate delusions with personality otherwise relatively intact.
Major Subgroups: Paranoia; Paranoid state.

Affective reaction
Major Symptoms: Extreme fluctuations of mood or intense, prolonged depression or euphoria, with related disturbances in thought and behavior.
Major Subgroups: Manic reaction; Psychotic depression; Involutional melancholia.

Schizophrenic reaction
Major Symptoms: Retreat from reality, with emotional blunting, inappropriate emotional reactions, and marked disturbance in thought processes; delusions, hallucinations, and stereotyped mannerisms common.
Major Subgroups: Childhood; Simple; Paranoid; Catatonic; Hebephrenic; Unclassified.

Paranoid Reactions

Unlike the other psychotic reaction patterns, which may be quite varied, paranoid reactions are marked by one major pathological symptom — persistent delusions. A delusion is a firmly held belief that is maintained by the individual in the face of objective evidence to the contrary and despite lack of any social support. In the *paranoid state*, the delusions are transient and not well organized into a coherent story. Patients may exhibit hallucinations, but their personalities are otherwise intact. As the pathology progresses, the delusions become more systematized, coherent, and internally logical, while hallucinatory activity disappears. This condition is termed *paranoia*.

There are three types of delusions that occur in paranoid disorders and sometimes in the other psychotic states. The most common kind is the *delusion of grandeur*. Individuals believe they are some exalted being, such as the Virgin Mary, a millionaire, a great inventor, or even God. One woman patient in a mental hospital had a pleasing personality and was rational enough in most ways to be trusted with many duties, including that of helping show visitors through the institution. But nothing could shake her firm conviction that she was really Bing Crosby's wife.

A second type of delusion is the *delusion of reference*. In such cases, the individuals misconstrue chance happenings as being directly aimed at them. If two people are seen in earnest conversation, paranoics immediately conclude that they are talking about them. If their beds are changed to a new position in the ward, it is because the attendants are displeased with them and want to guard them more closely or because they are being rewarded for good conduct. Nothing is too trivial or too accidental to escape notice as having some personal significance.

The third delusional type is the *delusion of persecution*. Here individuals are constantly on guard against "enemies." They feel that they are being spied on and plotted against and are in mortal danger of attack. Delusions of persecution may accompany delusions of grandeur — the patient is a great person, but is continually being opposed by evil forces.

The Federal Communications Commission receives many letters from people complaining that radio and television programs are talking about them, broadcasting their names, addresses, and personal information. Often these letters demand an investigation and punishment of the offenders.

The press recently publicized the story of an elderly lady who spent nearly all her waking hours in front of the television set. She so believed that the broadcasters were talking only to her that she would avidly listen to the commercials, then compulsively dash out to the store to buy the products advertised, and return just in time for the next batch of commercials. Since the woman had no friends or relatives to stop her, this economically and physically draining process might have persisted for quite some time. Luckily, a member of the fire department on a routine inspection tour of her apartment realized what was happening and convinced the woman to place herself under psychiatric care.

The intellectual and economic level of the paranoid is usually higher than that of other psychologically disturbed patients. These individuals can usually function for some time without anyone realizing the need for treatment and hospitalization. Among the psychological factors frequently found to be important in the dynamics of paranoid disorders are guilt over immoral or unethical behavior, repressed homosexuality, inferiority feelings, and unrealistically high ambitions.

It may also be that when the individual first begins to develop these paranoid ideas, they go unchallenged by sympathetic friends and relatives. As time goes by the delusions become more systematized; that is, more logical and apparently rational. Thus we have the curious paradox that the more serious the condition becomes, the more logical the person's reasoning appears. Such people resist therapy because it is easier to assume that the therapist is part of an enemy plot than to accept the fact that one's thought processes are illogical.

In Chapter 5, we presented a typescript of a computerized "psychotherapist" (the Mad Doctor) interacting with a human "patient." Kenneth Colby and his associates have also developed a computerized psychotic patient. The patient, called Parry because of certain paranoid tendencies, can be programmed to respond to an interviewer with different levels of anger, fear, and mistrust as well as to give nonverbal reactions. Part of a typical "therapy session" between Parry and one of the authors of *P&L*, where these three variables are at low levels, is reproduced in the *P&L* Close-up on p. 488. Could you tell from the answers that Parry was not a real human patient? If Parry were to be interviewed by input from the computerized Mad Doctor, would you be able to tell that their interaction was the product of simulated intelligence rather than of human beings thinking and speaking?

Affective Reactions

In one group of psychotic disorders, the major characteristic is extreme distortion of mood. Here the usual symptom is a deep depression, accompanied by a generalized slowing down of mental and physical activity, with gloom, morbid thoughts of disease or death, and feelings of worthlessness. During such *depressive* episodes, patients may attempt to commit suicide and must be carefully watched. The speech of psychotically depressed patients is slow and laconic; when they do speak, it is generally to express their suffering and suicidal desires.

In sharp contrast to psychotic depression is the *manic* reaction, which is characterized by high excitement, elation, and restless activity. Manic patients indulge in frequent boisterous laughter and eloquent, loud speeches. They walk about wildly and gesture dramatically, banging upon the walls and furniture.

Most patients show only a manic pattern or only a depressive one, but some patients alternate between manic and depressive periods, often in a cycle of great regularity. Sometimes there are long periods of apparent normality between episodes. The loss of contact with reality is evidenced by the onset of these extremes of emotions without any apparent outer justifi-

**Parry the Paranoid Computer
and the Mafia**

PGZ: Hello.
Parry: Hi.
PGZ: What is your name?
Parry: You can call me Parry.
PGZ: I am Doctor Zimbardo.
Parry: Glad to meet you.
PGZ: Where do you live?
Parry: San Jose. Not a bad section, though.
PGZ: What do you mean by that?
Parry: I mean not too many, well, foreign types.
PGZ: What do you mean by foreign types?
Parry: Those foreigners are beginning to make
this country a bad place to live.
PGZ: Which foreigners do you dislike most?
Parry: Italians, for instance.
PGZ: Do you dislike Italians?
Parry: (frown) Italians?
PGZ: You said you don't like them, why?
Parry: Do you know anything about Italians?
PGZ: No.
Parry: How about gangsters?
PGZ: Are gangsters Italians?
Parry: I would say so.
PGZ: Why should you say that?
Parry: Why?
PGZ: Are gangsters really Italian?
Parry: No.
PGZ: Can you tell me about the Mafia?
Parry: (fearful) Mafia?
PGZ: I would like to know about them.
Parry: You know, they know me.
PGZ: Who?
Parry: The Mafia.
PGZ: Really?
Parry: They are out to get me.
PGZ: Who?
Parry: The Mafia.
PGZ: How do you know?
Parry: They spy on me.
PGZ: (silence)
Parry: They know what I'm doing.

cation. With or without treatment, the episode typically runs its course (perhaps a few weeks or months) and then subsides.

One form of extreme depression in middle life or later (after the age of forty or so), which occurs more frequently among women than among men, is called *involutional melancholia.* The psychological features of this reaction are apprehension, agitation, and hopelessness, as well as feelings of guilt and failure. It has been suggested that this disorder is related to physiological "change of life" involving reproductive functions. It has recently been shown, however, that there is no greater risk of an affective disorder during menopause than at other times in a woman's life (Winokur, 1973). Although there are certainly physiological concomitants of menopause, it is likely that "change of life" has come to be a convenient explanation to account for a variety of purely psychological changes accompanying middle and old age. Physiological explanations are handy because no one is at fault or responsible for the problem, physical forms of treatment (drugs, hormones, etc.) can be used, and one does not have to look for environmental causes. But consider what middle age means for many women, with their children grown and no longer dependent on them, husbands absorbed in a career, sick, dead, or interested in younger women or pro football, few friends, girlhood dreams unrealized and presumed to be unrealizable, and above all, a profound sense of loss of youth, beauty, and opportunity. It may well be that successful, happily situated women who feel fulfilled in their daily lives and in their hopes will not suffer from the so-called change-of-life depression. This has not been studied, but deserves to be.

Depression has been called the "disease of the '70s" by the *Wall Street Journal;* "Coping with Depression" was a cover feature story in a 1973 edition of *Newsweek;* Martin Seligman terms it the "common cold of psychopathology." Of all the forms of pathology described in this chapter, it is the one most students are likely to have already experienced. We have all at one time or another been sad, "blue," down at the loss of or separation from a loved one, the failure to achieve a desired goal, or from chronic frustration and stress. The normal, "garden-variety" depression is transitory and situationally specific. In neurotic depression the symptoms are more intense, prolonged, recurrent, and disabling. The boundary between neurotic and psychotic depression is not clearly drawn, since the general concept of "depression" denotes a cluster of symptoms without a single defining characteristic. The psychotic forms of depression would not only be characterized by their severity and chronicity but also by associated loss of contact with present reality. The depressed psychotic requires hospitalization and intensive care. The National Institute of Mental Health estimates that "4 to 8 million Americans may be in need of professional care for the depressive illnesses" (Williams et al., 1970).

In an analysis of the symptoms characteristic of depressed psychiatric patients, Beck (1967) found marked differences in five general areas: emotional, cognitive-motivational, vegetative-physical, delusional, and appearance. When a mixed sample of 966 psychiatric patients was categorized into levels according to the depth of their depression, certain symptoms most clearly differentiated those suffering severe depression from those without depression. Each of these symptoms listed in the table was found to occur among at least 30 percent more of the severely depressed sample than of the nondepressed sample. ▲

Depressive behavior is difficult to categorize, however. It is felt by many that there are actually two types of depression: endogenous and reactive. This distinction is based on the presence or absence of precipitating external factors (such as stress, conflict, or loss).

Endogenous depression is assumed to be caused by internal (biochemical or genetic) factors. The symptoms of this form of depression include: retardation, severe depression, lack of reactivity to the environment, loss of interest in life, insomnia, weight loss, guilt, suicidal tendencies (Mendels, 1970). In contrast, *reactive depression* is less severe but is marked by self-pity, inadequate personality features, and the presence of precipitating stressors.

One of the problems with this classification and others based on etiology (the study of causes or origins of a disease) is that the observations are made *after* the fact, when the symptoms are pronounced enough for the individual to be in treatment. Some studies indicate that the absence of psychosocial precipitating stresses in endogenous depression is due to the failure of these severely disturbed patients to report them or to be aware of them. When carefully questioned upon recovery, such patients often report stressful events comparable to those reported by reactive patients.

Two of the most promising directions in the study of depression come from the work of Seligman on learned helplessness (reported in Chapter 9) and that of research psychiatrists Akiskal and McKinney (1973).

Seligman has convincingly demonstrated the parallels between the symptoms and causes of learned helplessness experimentally produced in the laboratory and reactive depression occurring in everyday life. He believes that the common core is the development of a belief in the futility of active responding. The depressed person becomes passive only with repeated lack of positive reinforcement for responding. Some depressed persons make many responses that

▲ CHARACTERISTICS OF DEPRESSION

Emotional

Dejected mood	Self-dislike
Loss of gratification	Loss of attachments
Crying spells	Loss of mirth response

Cognitive-Motivational

Negative expectations	Loss of motivation
Suicidal wishes	Low self-evaluation
Distorted self-image	Self-blame, self-criticism
Indecisiveness	

Vegetative-Physical

Loss of appetite	Loss of sexual interest
Sleep disturbance	Constipation
Fatigability	

Delusional

Worthless	Sinner

Appearance

Sad faced	Speech slow, reduced, not
Stooped posture	spontaneous

After Beck, 1967

lack "social awareness," that is, behaviors that others seldom reinforce. Reinforcement then comes primarily through the attention that is given to the person's depressive reactions (a "secondary gain" of the pathology). Therapy then must consist of selective *inattention* to (extinction of) depression symptoms and positive reinforcement for active behaviors.

A unified hypothesis of depression developed by Akiskal and McKinney posits that depressive behaviors may be elicited by a variety of mechanisms, but they all have a *final common pathway* that is a derangement (although a reversible one) in the cortical mechanisms of reinforcement. These mechanisms may be affected by chemical or genetic abnormalities in the brain, interpersonal stresses in infancy, chronic aversive stimulation, or loss of control over reinforcement effectiveness.

Schizophrenic Reactions

There exists no greater puzzle and challenge to medical and behavioral science than the understanding and control of schizophrenia. Between 2 and 3 million living Americans at one time or another have suffered from this most mysterious and tragic mental disorder. Half of the beds in this nation's mental institutions are currently occupied by schizophrenic patients. The estimate that 2 percent of the population will have an episode of schizophrenia during their lives rises in certain social settings—the urban ghetto for example—to a frightening 6 percent, or more than 1 in 20 persons.

The statistics on hospitalized cases of schizophrenia present us with a paradox. On the one hand, there has been a steady *decrease* in the numbers of resident patients in our mental hospitals—a decline of more than 30 percent in the past fifteen years. But over the same time period, hospital admissions of schizophrenic patients have steadily *increased*. In 1968 alone there were over 320,000 episodes of illness diagnosed as schizophrenia. What is apparently occurring is a "revolving door" phenomenon: patients are being hospitalized for shorter periods of time, but are being readmitted more frequently. The probability of a schizophrenic being readmitted for hospitalization within two years of being discharged from a first episode of schizophrenia is as high as 60 percent. This *recidivism* rate does not reflect the fact that only 15 to 40 percent of outpatient schizophrenics living in the community achieve an average level of adjustment.

In a special report from the National Institute of Mental Health (Mosher & Feinsilver, 1971) on the current status of schizophrenia research and treatment, two problem areas were singled out as blocking progress to better understanding of schizophrenia: attitudinal barriers and disagreement over scientific fact.

The patient's loss of interest in the world around him or her is disturbing and a source of nonreinforcement to family and friends. They too often and too readily respond by relegating the person to a distant custodial institution to shield themselves from the madness in their midst. Family attitudes reflect those of the general society. "Perhaps because of the fear madness engenders in each of us, the public at large has never demanded an all-out attack on a problem whose very existence, they are, by and large, loath to remember" (Mosher & Feinsilver, 1971, pp. 31–32). This may be why schizophrenia has not been given the attention it deserves by the scientific community or the resources required by the legislature and government administrators.

The scientific controversy that still exists over a number of issues has resulted in a diversification rather than a concentration of research effort. Is schizophrenia a single disease or the result of a combination of various afflictions? How important are genetic factors, and what is the manner of genetic transmission of schizophrenia? Are distinguishing family factors and biochemical correlates of schizophrenia the causes or the consequences of schizophrenia? Are infantile autism and childhood schizophrenia related to each other and to adult manifestations of the disease? These are but a few of the basic issues that demand resolution before significant progress can be made in the understanding and treatment of the riddle of schizophrenia.

Describing what schizophrenia is. Initially this disorder was regarded as a progressive mental deterioration beginning early in life and was called "dementia praecox" to distinguish it from affective psychosis. It is now recognized as neither necessarily progressive nor a deterioration into a demented (mentally retarded) state. Rather, its essential feature is the breakdown of integrated personality functioning. Different aspects of the patient's personality are at odds with each other, and behavior is not guided by or dependent on environmental feedback.

Once people stop checking against feedback, their entire range of behavioral processes may change. Perceptions can occur without sensory stimuli (hallucinations); emotions can occur without arousal stimuli or can fail to occur in their presence; thoughts and language do not follow Aristotelian logic or accepted grammatical and stylistic rules. There may be a distortion in time perspective, affecting perception of causal relationships. Such individuals are usually hospitalized for treatment primarily because behavior that is not under the control of some definable feedback system becomes unpredictable and poses a potential threat both to the individual and to other people.

There are several intriguing characteristics of the schizophrenic reaction that are being discovered through controlled research. Schizophrenics exhibit a greater sensitivity to perceptual stimuli, resulting in more distractability and a "flooding" by external stimulation. This makes it difficult for them to find constancy in their sensory environment. Disturbed thought patterns may be the consequence of an inability to give sustained attention to events or processes.

Similarly, the incomprehensibility of schizophrenic speech is due, in part, to bizarre intrusions where thoughts irrelevant to the verbalized statement being uttered are *not* suppressed, and long interconnected strings of words cannot be maintained. The schizophrenic's speech seems to be under the control of immediate stimuli. Distracted from completely expressing a simple train of thought by constantly changing sensory input and vivid inner reality, the schizophrenic does not make sense to a listener.

Classifying schizophrenia. For convenience, clinicians distinguish several types of schizophrenia, each with a characteristic cluster of behaviors. Six such types are summarized in the table. ◆

In the ten-year period from 1957 to 1967 there was an 88 percent increase in the number of hospitalized patients under fifteen years of age diagnosed as childhood schizophrenics. This increase probably reflects more widespread rec-

◆ **TYPES OF SCHIZOPHRENIA**

Childhood schizophrenia (autism)
A clinical entity first recognized by Leo Kanner in 1943, this type of schizophrenia appears due to a biologic deficit that results in an inability of the child to relate to other people and to environmental stimulation in the ordinary way. Autistic children show obsessive stereotyped behavior, a failure to attend to stimulation in more than one modality at a time, and an inability to transfer from verbal instructions to performance. They represent the clearest example of a psychological system closed in on itself.

Simple schizophrenia
Reduction of external interests and attachments, apathy, withdrawal, inconspicuous delusions or hallucinations, some disintegration of thought processes, often aggressive behavior, hypochondriacal experiences, and sex and/or alcohol indulgence.

Paranoid schizophrenia
Poorly systematized delusions; often hostile, suspicious, aggressive. Delusions are often of omnipotence, remarkable talents, and high social status. Delusions are combined with personality disorganization.

Catatonia
More sudden onset than other types with vivid hallucinations and grandiose delusions. Alternation between stupor and excitement; in stupor, there is a sudden loss of animation, and a stereotyped position may be maintained for some time, during which patient will not eat, drink, or take care of other bodily functions. Catatonic schizophrenics are the most likely to recover.

Hebephrenia
Most severe disorganization: silliness; inappropriateness of affect; incoherence of thought, speech, action; unusual mannerisms; auditory and visual hallucinations; fantastic delusions; obscene behavior; lack of modesty; hypochondriasis; emotional indifference; regression to childish behavior.

Unclassified
Acute or chronic reactions with a hodgepodge of symptoms.

From the Diary of a Schizophrenic

A view of the "inner world of mental illness" is provided by accounts such as this one written by a male in his late twenties. His unusual spelling and sentence structure stem not from lack of knowledge or skill, but rather from a loosening of thought and expression.

"I believe these things listed below are differance ways we have of letting our emotions out. Smoking 1. Learn to plan horn. 2. Chewing Gum 3. Sports ect. 4. Doing actives we enjoy doing 5. drinking till drunk. 5. Working at or with things we enjoy doing

"Man can not live by what the church say's 100% Because we are human and human nature we can not live without showing or emotions. Will power I need more of in some faze's of Life

"Some reason why I love men. 1. Plight 2. Attractive build 3. Neat apirance 4. not feeling my self around wemon 5. not feel able to relax around them 6. Feel that I would not be able to control my love emotion around them but, I am learn how to.

"God is giving me the gift of knowledge. God help me as his servent to keep humbley befor him at all times. Look forward and not backward. We can never change the past. But we can change the future. So we can look forwand instead of backward. . . . I feel I have been a homosexual because I am in love with everyone, We have to love all man kind in order to get to heaven It is sure hard to say no went you have form a habit of looking guys over and see if you really love them or not. . . .

"We have to learn to *trust people*. We have to learn to trust people all over again after we have been sick. Sin or trusting the wrong person cause's us to become metal sick. We have to learn to master our own mind. Our actions are not allways explanable as much as we try to understand them. Don't rush things will work out better if we relax and do things at our own gate. God is love and he know the trouble we have learning to make up our own mind. Take it easy every thing will work out." (Kaplan, 1964, pp. 191–92)

ognition and diagnosis of the condition rather than an increase in its incidence.

The problem of diagnosis and labeling is a persistent one, however, and one of the big obstacles to a better understanding of schizophrenic behavior is a disagreement among clinicians on the best criteria for classifying it. While there is some consensus about a number of the prominent symptoms associated with schizophrenia, no one patient shows them all, and any single patient may exhibit a variety of them over time.

Evidence that there is a difference in those who do the labeling as well as in those who are labeled comes from a study in which American and British psychiatrists were asked to make diagnoses on the basis of videotaped doctor-patient interviews. The patients were more likely to be classified as schizophrenic by the Americans and as affective psychotic by the Britishers. Patients showing both disorder of thought and mood disorder were labeled schizophrenics by the American psychiatrists and diagnosed as suffering from an affective disorder by the British psychiatrists (Mosher & Feinsilver, 1970).

Even when observers agree in classifying what they see, a full understanding of schizophrenia can come only if we supplement our observations of the outer, behavioral indicators with first-hand accounts of what it feels like by patients themselves. (See *P&L* Close-up at left.)

Some schizophrenic patients appear to be so apathetic and lacking in any motivation that the psychiatric staff decides therapy would be "wasted" on them. Given the limited resources available in every mental hospital, treatment decisions are often made in terms of the patients' apparent prognosis: those with a favorable prognosis receive intensive treatment, while those showing no signs of responsivity to environmental stimulation are given only custodial care. The latter often end up on a back ward where they may spend their entire lives unless they recover "on their own." But this lack of responsivity may be only apparent and in fact is often the mental patient's method of coping with events in the impinging environment.

In a careful observational study of the minute-to-minute behavior of chronic psychotic patients at the West Haven Veterans' Hospital, it was revealed that these men had set up a complex system of social interaction based on requesting and giving cigarettes and matches. Without words, written rules, or explicit instructions, a system emerged in which certain patients when seated in certain chairs were reliable signals to the rest of the ward of the availability of either cigarettes or matches. Thus if a patient asked he would receive, and if he wanted to give he would be asked. Such a system minimized potential frustration in the only area in which interpersonal contact was acknowledged (Hershkowitz, 1970).

The creation of and sensitivity to such an interpersonal network demands more motivation and cognitive acuity than chronic psychotic patients are usually credited with. Unfortunately, much of their apparent lack of motivation comes from their attempts to appear unmotivated. It may be that such a tactic is designed to deceive not their keepers, but themselves—if you have no goals or do not want anything, you cannot be frustrated. Thus it may be that mental patients, in giving the appearance of being unmotivated, are successful in managing the impression they want to give, but thereby inadvertently become less likely candidates for therapy and subsequent release.

Origins of Psychotic Behavior

In the attempt to solve the puzzle of psychotic behavior, researchers have vainly searched for *the* cause. Some have probed nature, others nurture. Obviously more than scientific curiosity is at stake since an understanding of why psychosis develops, and hopefully the control that such knowledge would make possible, would relieve an unbelievable amount of human suffering while simultaneously illuminating how the human mind functions—and malfunctions.

We have already discussed the problems inherent in trying to find out whether nature or nurture is the more important determinant of any trait. Many researchers favor the "multifactoral" view of schizophrenia and other

psychoses: that there is an interplay of genetic, biochemical, neurological, and environmental factors. Nevertheless, the search for a single biological cause of psychotic "disease" continues.

Hereditary factors. "It's all in the genes," is one view of the basis of functional psychosis. Affected individuals inherit a genetic structure that presumably makes them likely to become psychotic. Initial support for this position came from numerous studies that indicated that psychotic disorders tend to run in families. This fact is hardly proof of a hereditary basis, since people with "unfavorable" heredity often live in environments that are physically and psychologically unhealthy.

More substantial evidence supporting the hypothesis of hereditary causality came from the finding that the risk of becoming schizophrenic increased with the degree of genetic relationship to the schizophrenic patient. The full sibling of a person with schizophrenia was twice as likely to become schizophrenic as was a half-sibling—although both shared a common environment. There was a marked increase in schizophrenia risk when both parents were schizophrenic, and it was greatest of all among identical twins reared together—more than a 90 percent chance.

Although several early studies agreed that an identical twin of a schizophrenic was much more likely to develop schizophrenia than a fraternal twin, recent investigations have seriously challenged their findings.

One very thorough study of 342 pairs of twins, 35 to 64 years of age, living in Norway, where one or both had been hospitalized for a functional psychosis, found concordance rates of only 38 percent[2] for identical twins and 10 percent for fraternal twins. This difference suggests that a genetic factor is important but does not play the major role as had been assumed previously. The researcher noted, "In the investigations so far, the pattern seems consistent:

[2]A concordance rate of 38 percent means that in 38 percent of the cases the identical twin of a schizophrenic patient also became schizophrenic.

The more accurate and careful the samplings, the lower the concordance figures" (Kringlen, 1969, p. 38).

While the studies published prior to 1960 cited concordance rates of up to 86 percent for identical twins and only 17 percent for fraternal twins, the five major studies done since 1960 reveal concordance rates varying only from 6 to 43 percent for the monozygotic twins and 5 to 12 percent for the dizygotic.

When offspring of schizophrenic parents who had been adopted by psychiatrically normal parents were compared with adoptees whose biological parents were classified as normal, the difference between the two groups in their incidence of schizophrenia was shown to be minimal. The Danish team of investigators reported that 14 percent of the "high risk" children had been hospitalized for psychiatric reasons, but 10 percent of the controls were similarly hospitalized. According to the hospital report only 1.3 percent of the offspring of schizophrenic parents were clearly diagnosed as schizophrenic and none of the controls were (reported in Mosher & Feinsilver, 1971, p. 12).

Most psychologists and psychiatrists today are in agreement that what *can* be inherited is a *predisposition* to the psychosis; under conditions severe enough, a predisposed individual is believed to be more likely to develop a psychosis than other individuals, who might develop some less severe disorder. Pathological ways of coping with the environment are more likely to be learned if a child lives with a psychotic relative than if he or she lives with a normal one. With two schizophrenic parents — two models of abnormal, pathological behavior to imitate and use for social comparison purposes — a child has a greater likelihood of learning schizophrenic behavior patterns.

Environmental factors. In the past decade, there has been an increasing emphasis on studying the complex environmental-social matrix in which a schizophrenic individual operates. Just as genetic factors can make an individual biologically vulnerable, so environmental factors like parental rejection or overprotection, excessive or inconsistent discipline, or extreme insecurity can predispose the individual psychologically to mental disorder. Studies of the family structure of schizophrenics, as well as of other features of their social life, reveal the extent to which functional psychosis may represent learned ways of attempting to cope with chronic stress and unresolvable conflicts.

One of the most reliable prognostic indicators of future schizophrenic development is an early pattern of *social isolation* in which the adolescent withdraws from interacting with others. This may be a consequence of feeling different or "abnormal" in some way, or of not having learned how to relate to other people in a positive, meaningful way, or both.

Many studies clearly show that one of the most abnormal things about schizophrenic children is the relationship between their parents and the parents' use of the child to work out their own feelings of frustration and hostility. The child may be cast in the role of "buffer" or mediator and made to feel responsible for the continuation or failure of the marriage; or in subtle ways, the parents may establish a pattern in which continuation of their precariously balanced relationship relies on keeping the child dependent on them.

Family interaction studies show less responsiveness and interpersonal sensitivity in the speech of families with a schizophrenic member than in normal families. In families with the most disturbed offspring, the members do not listen to each other or spend as much time in information exchange as normal families (Ferriera & Winter, 1964). Those in families with withdrawn adolescents are less able to predict each other's responses in a test situation.

Sometimes other members of the schizophrenic's family show more deviation from normal communication patterns than the member diagnosed as schizophrenic. This leads to the conjecture that where various members of the family react "abnormally," one may be "chosen" to be labeled as the mentally sick one. He or she is then expected to act "crazy" and may even be reinforced for doing so.

The broader cultural environment also appears to influence what form pathological behavior will take when it occurs. For example, just as the neurotic conversion reaction is less common today than formerly, manic-depressive psychosis also appears much less often in mental hospitals than it did twenty or thirty years ago (Lundin, 1961).

Within our own society, people from lower socioeconomic classes are more likely to become schizophrenic and those most affluent to become neurotic (Hollingshead & Redlich, 1958). ● It may be that the higher rate among lower-class families can be traced to their patterns of childrearing (Lane & Singer, 1959). It may also be that many of the environmental consequences of being poor—powerlessness, frustrated ambitions, rootlessness, a losing battle for survival—provide fertile soil for psychotic pathology.

The view that poor people face a lifetime of environmental insults that increase their chances of becoming seriously disturbed psychologically has been documented in an ongoing survey in New York City. On the basis of psychiatric evaluation and computer analysis of intensive interviews with the mothers of 2000 children aged five to eighteen, it was found that 23 percent of the welfare children suffered from mental disturbances to a degree severe enough to require immediate treatment. This was almost twice as many as among their nonwelfare peers (Langer et al., 1970).

The presumed relationship between social class and mental illness has much historical precedent, as shown in the thorough analysis of social and cultural influences on psychopathology by Bruce and Barbara Dohrenwend (1974). *Social stress* theorists with their environmentalist orientation argued that the poor suffer greater stress of living, which leads to greater pathology. *Social selection* theorists, on the other hand, attributed the greater incidence of pathol-

ogy among the lower classes to genetic factors. The fact that the mentally ill are often incapable of managing their affairs was seen as a cause of economic failure. Poverty becomes the end-product of a prior history of mental derangement in this view.

The apparent differences in who develops which disorder may also reflect bias in how patients are diagnosed and treated. For example, poorer disturbed patients, unable to pay for therapy, may be committed to state hospitals as "out-of-contact psychotics," while those with similar symptoms who can afford psychotherapy are perceived and labeled as "neurotics in need of treatment to work through their conflicts."

As social values change, as definitions of what is acceptable and appropriate are modified, as our shared definitions of what constitutes meaningful goals in life and "reality" become altered, we can expect corresponding changes in the ways people attempt to adapt to their psychological environment. It seems likely that there will be an increasing incidence of those who, instead of losing contact with an unmanageable reality, will revolt against it openly, tune out temporarily with drugs, or drop out permanently with friends who decide to share the delusion of a new private, communal reality to which they can relate.

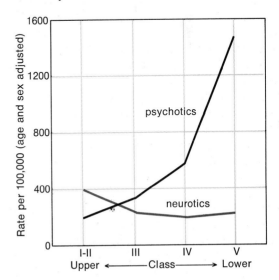

After Hollingshead & Redlich, 1958

● SOCIAL STATUS AND PSYCHIATRIC ILLNESS

▲ Sylvia Plath (top), well-known poet and author of *The Bell Jar*, committed suicide in 1963. Janis Joplin and Jimi Hendrix, popular rock artists, both died at age 27, in 1970, from drug overdoses. It is not clear whether their deaths were intentional.

Loss of Alternative Modes of Being: Suicide

Surely all of us experience times in our lives when we simply cannot face another day; when life just doesn't seem worth the agony and pain it forces us to endure. Perhaps we've just lost a parent or an intimate friend; a lover has disappointed us; we've just failed a course or been fired from a job we liked. Yet however "appropriate" and strong these feelings of utter hopelessness and the fleeting impulse to end it all, most of us do not give in to the impulse. As Nietzsche once said, "The thought of suicide is a great consolation. By means of it one gets successfully through many a bad night."

Tragically, for some thousand people each day, self-destruction is a great deal more than a fleeting impulse, it is the final reality of life. According to the World Health Organization, almost half a million persons a year commit suicide, a statistic that becomes even more grisly when we realize that as many more try unsuccessfully to end their lives as succeed. As a cause of death, suicide now ranks seventh in the U.S. and among the first ten in the industrialized world. What are the reasons for and the kinds of people who contribute to these statistics? What do we know of the human element in this life-and-death equation? ▲

The Scientific Classification of an Unscientific Concept

Suicide is most succinctly defined in terms of two basic characteristics: *intention* and *outcome*. "True" suicides involve people who intend to kill themselves and who actually do so. Although outcomes are obvious—the individual either survives or dies—intentions are not so easily recorded. Some cases quite clearly indicate lethal intention; a jump from the roof of a high building or the firing of a bullet through the brain. Others, such as the taking of a few extra sleeping pills immediately followed by a telephone call to friends informing them of the action, or a superficial cutting of the wrists just as the spouse's car is pulling into the garage, seem to suggest less than lethal intent.

Perhaps the most frightening suicidal intention of all is one that has been called "the gamble with death." In this case the individual's intention is to die or not to die depending totally on outside forces in a contrived situation. Playing "Russian roulette" is one extreme example of this phenomenon. It is especially fascinating that this type of suicidal act can be institutionalized in a society. In Tikopia, an island near New Guinea, an anthropologist has reported that an insulted man seizes a canoe and paddles out into the great reaches of the Pacific. When his absence is noted, a search party paddles out to find him. If they do, he will go on living; if not, he dies. Again, there is this test of fate: "If they care for me enough, they will come find me; if they don't, I want to die" (Firth, 1961).

On the basis of the foregoing information, Farber (1968) has formulated a simple model that cross-tabulates intention and outcome, utilizing only the most clear-cut extremes of intention. ■ The cases in Cell A are the only "true" suicides that meet both definition criteria. Those in Cell B, though psychologically most similar to "true" suicides, are not successful in their attempts to die. These individuals either overestimate the lethal effects of a drug or are unexpectedly rescued. Bitterly ironic are those cases that fall into Cell C. These individuals do not intend to die, yet they do. The lover forgets the scheduled visit, the maid comes late, or the lethal effects of a drug are underestimated. Overall, the largest group of cases falls into Cell D, the "true attempters": "the perpetuators of the suicidal gesture," the "criers for help."

Direct psychological research on suicide can involve only historical reconstruction of cases where the outcome of the attempt was successful. Therefore, investigation of the antecedents and psychosocial dynamics of suicide obviously focuses on those people who fail, whether intentionally or unintentionally. Indeed, we can learn much that may help us understand this flight from living by studying those people who tried but did not succeed.

Social Factors in Suicide

Self-destruction is most comprehensible when viewed in conjunction with environmental factors—social situations and the pressures of life, both of which play a profound role in the suicides of many individuals. In the complex of activities, relationships, and institutions that constitute the social life of men and women in today's society, suicide rates have been shown to be associated with a large number of variables.

Sex. Women outnumber men in *attempted* suicides by a ratio of three to one. One study found that 69 percent of all attempted suicides in America are by females, but males are more effective when they try—70 percent of successful suicides are male (Farberow & Shneidman, 1965). It has also been found that housewives make twice as many suicide attempts as all other women. Though in the past, society was quick to hail the security of the housewife's role, researchers now believe that many women in this category are in fact crying out for an escape from the loneliness of what amounts in many cases to a life of solitary confinement.

The discrepancy between attempted and successful suicides among men and women may be due to the fact that men are more experienced with and have easier access to lethal weapons that effectively translate destructive

Outcome

		Death	Survival
Intention	To die	True suicide A	Suicidal failures B
	Not to die	Suicidal mistakes C	Intentional failures D

After Farber, 1968

■ **SUICIDAL INTENTION AND OUTCOME**

intentions into deadly outcomes. Men most frequently commit suicide by shooting or hanging, while women almost always use a more passive method of self-annihilation: pills, poisons, or gases.

It should be noted, however, that the means by which people commit suicide vary from country to country, according to what is available and fashionable. Thus, in contrast to Americans' preferences, in Nigeria, hanging is the preferred mode for all, while men and women in England tend to use gas. In Basel, Switzerland, suicide with gas had been most common until the government made home gas nonpoisonous; then drowning became the most popular substitute.

Age. Suicide among children is very rare. For ages 5 to 15, the rate has remained at 0.2 per 100,000 and varies neither with time nor demographic variables. Among the general adolescent population (ages 15 to 19), the suicide rate jumps to 5.5 per 100,000 for boys and 2.0 per 100,000 for girls, and ranks fourth as a cause of death—second among college students.

Statistics recently released by the Los Angeles Suicide Prevention Center show that an ever increasing number of young people seem to be turning to suicide. In Los Angeles county alone, the rate of suicides by people in their late teens and early 20s exceeds the rate among those over 30—an alarming reversal of the traditional finding that the frequency of suicides increases with age. And the trend seems to be nationwide. What accounts for this increased number of young people who are willing to do away with themselves? Researchers say pat explanations of drug abuse and school pressures simply cannot account for this tragic waste of human lives. Interviews with unsuccessful suicide victims and retrospective analyses of successful suicides have revealed an intense fear of parental pressure, utter hopelessness that is projected onto society in general, and most frequently, an overwhelming feeling of loneliness (*Newsweek*, Feb. 15, 1971).

During the middle years, suicide rates rise steadily in correlation with increased pressures from business and family, as well as the psycho-logical and physiological changes that usher individuals into old age. It has been shown that although rates of attempts are lowest among the elderly, completed suicides are the highest. Thus older people are most serious about the act of self-destruction. It is little wonder that in so many cases with loneliness—through the death of loved ones, rejection by one's families, lack of social contacts, acute physical pain, or financial insecurity—suicide is seen as a prime solution to the rapidly approaching inevitable.

Education. Among the adult population in the U.S., the suicide rate is *inversely* related to the amount of education. People with more than average education are less likely to commit suicide than people with less than average education. However, college students have a higher suicide rate than nonstudents of the same age. The only cause of death among college students that exceeds suicide is accidents. Yet one must note that the death rate is normally low among all young people and further that youths who do not attend college are far more likely to die of homicide than of suicide. (See *P&L* Close-up, p. 499.)

Occupation. The kind of job or profession in which one is involved has clearly been shown to be a significant factor in suicide. University of Oregon researchers studied self-inflicted deaths in that state for a period of eleven years. They found suicides among doctors, dentists, and lawyers to be three times as common as among nonprofessional white-collar workers.

According to the American Psychiatric Association, the annual suicide rate among physicians is at least 33 per 100,000—double that of the general rate among Americans. For psychiatrists, the rate is 70 per 100,000, or four times as great! Can you think of hypotheses to account for the abnormally elevated suicide rate among psychiatrists?

Marital status. One of the most reliable social predictors of suicide, especially for men, is whether the individual is married. Contrary to what many cynics maintain, there is something about marriage that sharply reduces the likelihood of suicide, compared to being single. More-over, becoming widowed or divorced greatly increases the probability of death from suicide. Apparently, men also seem to need women (or to be married) more than women need men—again contrary to popular masculine myth. Suicide statistics reveal that the absolute increase in suicide rate as a consequence of being widowed or divorced is substantially greater for males than females in every age group.

Economic conditions. It has been said that "suicide is the luxury of the wealthy." Such a statement is false. For all classes, economic uncertainty and financial distress bring a sense of hopelessness and despair. Suicides take place not only in the mansions of the rich but in the tenement dwellings of the poor and the "rest homes" of the aged. Suicide soars during periods of economic depression for both the upper and the lower classes. However, it has been shown that those with the highest status positions react more violently to fluctuations in the financial world (Grollman, 1971). Perhaps this is because the rich and the mighty have further to fall from their lofty positions in life.

Race. Comedian Dick Gregory, in commenting on the much lower incidence of suicides among blacks than whites in America, claimed that it was difficult for blacks to commit suicide jumping out of their basement windows. In this statement he touches on the complex relationship between socioeconomic class, race, living conditions, and suicide. Blacks as a race have traditionally not committed suicide despite impoverished conditions of ghetto life. We may speculate that this has been due to: feeling less personal responsibility for failure and more anger directed outward to the oppressive system they live in and "the Man" who controls their fate; social norms of suicide as cowardly; conditioned acceptance of limited goals and high probability of failure. But in the last few years a startling increase in the black suicide rate has been observed. It is too soon to know whether it is a transient phenomenon or a permanent accompaniment of changing social-racial values.

Close-up
Suicide Among College Students

Ten thousand students in the United States attempt suicide each year, and over 1000 succeed. The greatest incidence of suicidal behavior occurs at the beginning and the end of the school quarter or semester. Approximately three times more female than male students attempt suicide, but as with the general population the incidence of fatalities is considerably higher among males.

When a college student attempts suicide, one of the first explanations to occur to others around is that he or she may have been doing poorly in school. However, suicidal students are, as a group, superior students, and while they tend to expect a great deal of themselves in terms of academic achievement and to exhibit scholastic anxieties, the significant precipitating stresses are *not* usually grades, academic competition, and pressure over examinations. Moreover, when academic failure does appear to trigger suicidal behavior—in a minority of cases—the actual cause of the behavior is generally considered to be loss of self-esteem and failure to live up to parental expectations, rather than the academic failure itself. For most suicidal students, the major precipitating stress appears to be either the failure to establish, or the loss of, a close interpersonal relationship.

A change in mood and behavior is a most significant warning in students who may be planning suicide. Characteristically, students become depressed and withdrawn, undergo a marked decline in self-esteem, and show deterioration in habits of personal hygiene. This is accompanied by a profound loss of interest in studies. Often they stop attending classes and remain in their rooms most of the day. Usually they communicate their distress to at least one other person, often in the form of a veiled suicide warning. Many leave suicide notes.

Although most colleges and universities have mental health facilities to assist distressed students, few suicidal students seek professional help. Thus, it is of importance for those around to notice the warning signs and to try to obtain assistance for fellow students (Coleman, 1976).

Loss of Alternative Modes of Being: Suicide 499

A dramatic cultural contrast exists between American attitudes and group norms on suicide and those of the Japanese. Suicide statistics (rated per 100,000 population) for 1966–67 reveal the following pattern by race, nationality, and sex:

	Male	Female
American		
White	103.6	34.3
Nonwhite	50.8	15.3
Japanese	118.8	86.9

From *Statistical Bulletin*, Metropolitan Life Insurance Co., 1966

Japan's high suicide rate for both males and females is supported by the national emphasis on *shame* as a technique of social control. People avoid actions that will bring shame on themselves or their families or even groups to which they belong. When they perceive they are responsible for bringing shame upon others, suicide is a culturally acceptable means to right this wrong. In addition, suicide—*hara-kiri*—has been elevated to a noble status through literature, plays, movies, and the popular press.

Depression and Suicide

Suicidal individuals are often plagued by the crushing combination of hopelessness and helplessness; the feeling of despair that nothing can be done and no one can do it. Without question, the single most outstanding characteristic of those who attempt suicide is depression.

A tragic commentary on loneliness and human isolation is seen in the report of a student who was discovered dead in his room after he had lain there for eighteen days. There were no friends, no one involved enough in his daily life to care or even notice that he had been missing for more than two weeks (Grollman, 1971).

Any sudden and radical change that removes an individual's basic sources of security and predictability can make that person more susceptible to suicide. Rapid social and economic change, the unexpected loss of a loved one, or

▲ A note is left in about 15 percent of suicide cases, although the frequency of suicide notes is much greater among unsuccessful attempts than among actual suicides. Two actual suicide notes are reproduced above. The widely spaced handwriting in the note to Estelle gives evidence of the writer's deep sense of isolation. The upward flick of the pen at word endings in the second note is interpreted by graphologists as a sign of great hostility. Certainly the content is intended to produce guilt as well as sorrow in the recipient.

strong feelings of life's injustice coupled with a sense of powerlessness to exert any control can become a precondition for suicide. Research on the syndrome of learned helplessness discussed earlier in this chapter and in Chapter 9 is providing some new leads to the causes and, hopefully, effective treatment strategy for those so depressed that life is not worth living. ▲

Those Left Behind . . .

The cry for help is not heard. A person succeeds in self-destruction. Life has ended. But for the family, the tragedy is just beginning. "There is just not enough time to heal the wounds of a self-inflicted death. The crushing blow is a bitter experience for all those left behind. They carry it in their hearts for the rest of their lives. Suicide is truly the cruelest death of all for those who remain" (Grollman, 1971, p. 109).

Often those who commit suicide do so simply to have a profound impact on the survivors. Thus suicides are often arranged so as to inflict maximum distress on the survivors. Suicides express deep bitterness. Some suicides may be arranged to look like an accidental death, thereby sparing the survivors a considerable amount of guilt and anguish, while in others, the living are made to feel: "I could have prevented it, if only I had been there . . ."

Recent research on 384 suicide attempters clearly indicates that *hopelessness* is the catalytic agent in suicidal behavior. Suicide attempters were seen twice for psychiatric interviews within 48 hours of admission to the hospital. These interviews offer support for the role of hopelessness in leading to negative expectations about the success of any attempts to obtain major personal goals. When the resulting depression becomes pervasive, then suicide seems to be the only alternative (Beck, Kovacs, & Weissman, 1975). Therapy then should focus on reducing hopelessness through building renewed competence, as proposed by Seligman in his Research Frontier essay at the end of Chapter 8.

Suicide Prevention

The prevalence of suicide is a grim reminder to society of its failure to make life worth living for all of its members. Suicidal behavior poses many complex questions, some philosophical, some psychological, some social, and some political-legal. Is suicide ever justified? Under what conditions do some societies encourage suicide? Should the person's decision to commit suicide be respected and intervention not undertaken? What, if anything, would lead *you* to commit suicide?

Surprisingly, we have only just begun to take suicide seriously as a human problem deserving scientific and humanitarian interest. The first Suicide Prevention Center was founded in Los Angeles by Edwin Shneidman as recently as 1958. Fortunately, such centers have begun to proliferate, and 200 prevention and crisis intervention centers were in existence by 1971. ■

■ *The Cry* is by the Norwegian artist Edvard Munch. The Los Angeles Suicide Prevention Center has used this picture to demonstrate the desperation underlying the individual's "call for help" and to emphasize the importance of responding to such calls.

Hospitals are instituting new programs of therapy for those who have attempted suicide, and many cities have suicide-alert phone numbers that potential suicides are urged to call. But it is obvious that for any program to work, the suicidal people must either take the initiative and identify themselves or be unsuccessful in an attempted suicide. Suicide prevention efforts obviously fail when potential suicides decide to kill themselves without giving the so-called cry for help.

It would seem that attempts at prevention need to start earlier. Instead of trying to spot a person already so desperate that he or she is prepared to die, we need to find ways of identifying children and young adults who are potential suicides.

Meanwhile, many people do overtly threaten to commit suicide before they actually do so. In fact, it is unusual for a person to commit suicide without giving some prior indication of intent. Therefore, the most important response to any suicide threat is to take it seriously—as if somebody's life depended on *your* being concerned.

You and Your Mental Health

As limitless as are the pathways to the fulfillment of human potential, so too are the roads to the perversion of that potential of mind and spirit. We can, if we so choose, become our own worst enemy, able to destroy ourselves more totally than any adversary could with the most advanced weapons of modern technology. Suicide is but the most obvious way in which we reject the gift of life and fail to appreciate its purpose or to look beyond our mortal frailty to some greater meaning to our existence.

In cataloging some of the forms that deviance, pathology, and madness may assume, we have seen how varied and potent are these forces of psychological destruction. The next chapter deals with therapy, professional approaches to the treatment of the disturbances we have outlined here. But not enough people who need therapy seek it, and perhaps fewer would ever need it if we paid more attention to ensuring our mental health than to curing mental illness. It is certainly the case that an ounce of prevention is worth much more than the time, money, effort, anxiety, and *probable* success of any cure.

Although this textbook is meant to be an academic survey of the current state of psychological research and knowledge and *not* a personal adjustment manual, we believe that the following principles may be of value in the quest for sanity and mental health. They are presented only as guidelines to encourage you to think more rationally and to act more effectively about matters that relate to mental health.

1. Look for the causes of your behavior in the current situation or in its relation to past situations, and *not* just for some defect in yourself.

2. Compare your reactions, thoughts, and feelings with those of other comparable individuals in your current life environment to assess their appropriateness and relevance.

3. Have several close friends with whom you can share your feelings, joys, and worries.

4. Don't be afraid to show others you want to be their friend or even to extend or respond to love.

5. Never say bad things about yourself; especially never attribute to yourself irreversible, chronic, negative traits—such as "stupid," "ugly," "uncreative," "incorrigible," "a failure." Find the sources of unhappiness in elements that can be modified.

6. Always take full credit for your successes and happiness.

7. Keep an inventory of all the things that make you special and unique, those qualities you have to offer to others. For example, a shy person can offer a talkative person the gift of being a good listener. Know your sources of personal power.

8. When you feel intense physiological reactions, which you typically interpret as "anxiety," first analyze the components of this physiological reaction objectively (count your pulse, note as many bodily changes as possible). Then consider whether there is some explanation for your physiological reaction other than psychological "anxiety"—perhaps you are excited, overeager; perhaps the room is too hot, etc.

9. When you feel you are losing control over your emotions (hyperexcited or depressed), distance yourself from the situation you are in by (a) physically leaving it; (b) role playing the position of some other person in the situation or conflict; (c) projecting your imagination into the future to gain temporal perspective on what seems like an overwhelming problem here and now.

10. Don't dwell on past misfortunes or sources of guilt, shame, failure. The past is gone and only thinking about it keeps it alive in memory.

11. Develop long-range goals in life—what you want to be doing five, ten, twenty years from now—and think about alternative ways of getting there.

12. Take time to relax, to meditate, to enjoy hobbies and activities that you can do alone and by means of which you can get in touch with yourself.

13. Think of yourself not as a passive object to which bad things just happen, but as an active agent who at any time can change the direction of your entire life.

14. Remember that failure and disappointment are sometimes blessings in disguise, telling you that your goals were not right for you or saving you from bigger letdowns later on.

15. Don't judge your behavior and that of others as "normal" or "crazy," but rather as situationally and culturally appropriate or inappropriate, and try to discover ways of modifying undesirable *behavior* rather than undesirable people (including yourself).

16. If you see someone you think is acting strangely, intervene in a concerned, gentle way to find out if anything is wrong and how you can help. Often listening to someone's troubles is all the therapy needed if it comes soon enough.

17. If you discover you cannot help yourself or the other person in distress, seek the counsel of a trained specialist in your student health department. In some cases the problem may seem to be a psychological one but is really physical, as with thyroid glandular conditions.

18. If it is not a medical problem, then consult a psychiatrist or clinical psychologist recommended by your family doctor, the student health department, or your local hospital.

19. Assume that everyone would be better off if they had the opportunity to discuss their problems openly with a mental health specialist; therefore, if you do go to one there is no need to feel stigmatized.

20. As long as there's life, there's hope for a better life, and as long as there are hope, caring, and determination, life will get better.

I don't ask for your pity, but just your understanding—not even that—No. Just for your recognition of me in you, and the enemy, time in us all.

Tennessee Williams, *Sweet Bird of Youth,* 1959

Chapter Summary

Mental disorder has always been both fascinating and frightening. Despite the almost universal fascination with studying abnormal mental processes, there is a tendency to reject and stigmatize the victims of such disorders. Historically, both physical and mental diseases were once attributed to supernatural influences; therapy, then, consisted of exorcism and similar procedures designed to rid the sufferer from evil spirits. In recent times, investigations have centered on the *neurological* and the *dynamic* causes of mental disturbance. While earlier approaches such as psychoanalysis were based on the study of individual cases, American learning theorists have recast them in terms more amenable to controlled research.

Mental disturbance is a serious (and expensive) problem in our society. Unlike physical illness, which presents clear-cut, measurable signs, mental illness exists when someone says it does. When a medical model is applied to psychiatric "illness," the label given may stick to a person indefinitely. This comes about partly because of our fears of those who are deviant in some way and our need to set them apart as being different from the rest of us. What is "normal" is what most people do. New cultural trends may lead to greater acceptance of people who do "their own thing."

Loss of self-regulating capacities is seen in psychological and/or physical dependence on alcohol, cigarettes, or drugs. Such a loss can have disastrous consequences physically, psychologically, and socially but is apparently learned and maintained because of short-term reinforcement.

Alcoholism can best be understood as a progressive disease process that grows more serious over time. It cannot be easily dealt with by psychotherapeutic techniques, even those based on learning principles, until the individual really *wants* to be helped.

Dependence on *cigarettes*, although primarily psychological, is extremely difficult to break. A wide range of techniques have been used, but few show any lasting effectiveness. Cognitive factors are important in both starting and stopping smoking, and prevention can be accomplished more readily than cure.

Addiction to psychoactive *drugs* is a serious problem at all socioeconomic levels of our society. Peer-group pressure is an important factor in the spread of drug use. Nearly all psychoactive drugs can produce psychological dependence; many produce physical dependence as well, causing agonizing withdrawal symptoms if drug use is discontinued. *Drug abuse* occurs when drug usage interferes with an individual's health and/or social functioning.

Loss of joy in living and an overreliance on psychological defense mechanisms characterize the *neuroses*. In *anxiety neurosis*, free-floating, nonspecific anxiety is the chief characteristic, and the individual may have no idea what is causing the anxious symptoms. In *phobias*, the individual develops an intense fear of a particular object or activity, typically something with a personal symbolic meaning. The victim realizes the fear is irrational but feels powerless to cope with it. In *obsessive-compulsive reactions*, the individual may be unable to get rid of an obsessive thought or feeling, and/or may feel compelled to go through particular rituals in order to relieve anxiety.

Hysterical neuroses provide mechanisms for escape from anxiety through *conversion hysteria*—a physical affliction without physical cause—or a *dissociated state*. Dissociated states include *somnambulism* (sleepwalking), *amnesia* (loss of memory for one's identity), and *fugue* (amnesia plus flight). The most extreme form of dissociated state is *multiple personality,* a rare condition in which different parts of the personality become separate and are in control at different times, often unaware of each other.

In *hypochondria,* the individual's constant concern with supposed but usually fictitious ailments provides an excuse for not coping with problems, and at the same time elicits attention and sympathy. In *depressive neurosis,* the individual gives in to grief and depression, magnifying negative factors out of all proportion. All the neuroses are mechanisms for *proving helplessness,* thereby inducing sympathy and avoiding efforts that might lead to failure, and for *limiting anxiety* by enabling the individual not to confront its source.

Loss of contact with reality is called *psychosis. Insanity* is a legal term that may be applied to both the psychoses and severe neurotic disorders. Psychoses may be *organic* (due to physical causes) or *functional* (resulting from no known physical defect). In *paranoid reactions,* the individual has delusions, either transient, as in *paranoid states,* or systematized and rigid, as in *paranoia.* Most common are delusions of *grandeur,* of *reference,* and of *persecution. Affective disorders* are disorders of mood; the individual may be deeply *depressed* or *manic* (euphoric), or may alternate between the two, perhaps with periods of normalcy in between. *Involutional melancholia* is a deep, pervasive psychotic depression occurring in middle age. Depression assumed to be precipitated by external factors is called *reactive;* where no such factors are evident it is called *endogenous.*

Schizophrenic reactions involve a breakdown of integrated functioning in which the individual stops checking against environmental feedback.

Schizophrenic patients occupy half the beds in mental hospitals. There may be distortions in perception, emotion, thought, language patterns, and time perspective. Types of schizophrenia include *childhood, simple, paranoid, catatonic, hebephrenic,* and *unclassified.* The distinctions are not clear-cut, however.

There seems to be no *one* cause of psychosis. *Genetic predispositions* may play a role in given cases, as may family interaction patterns and broader cultural factors. The higher incidence of neuroses among the affluent and of psychoses at lower socioeconomic levels may be a true difference but sometimes represents only differences in labeling.

Suicide is the final act of those who feel they have lost all other alternatives. Suicidal acts may be classified in terms of *intention* and *outcome:* some are intended to be lethal and succeed; others intended to be lethal fail. Some acts are actually intended to fail but prove lethal; others are intended to fail and do so.

Methods of suicide vary in different cultural groups, but suicide is, in all countries, more common among men than among women. In this country suicides increase with age, although they are becoming more common among young people. Suicide rates are also rising among blacks. Completed suicides are most common among the aged. The most outstanding characteristic of suicidal individuals is *depression.* Suicide prevention and crisis intervention centers are becoming increasingly numerous.

It is important to be alert to factors that can influence your own mental health and that of individuals close to you, and to recognize when help is needed.

Behavior, Context, and Meaning
David L. Rosenhan Stanford University

What do we mean by "normal" behavior? When does it become "abnormal"? How do we know when there is something amiss in an individual's behavior? In this essay we shall explore some of the ways in which we have learned to give meaning to both our own behavior and that of others.

By themselves, behaviors rarely have clear meanings. Rather, meaning is jointly determined by the behavior and the context in which it is found. A raised hand means one thing when it occurs in a classroom, another when a friend approaches, and yet a third in the German army. Whether that hand means "permission to speak," or "friendly greeting," or "salute" depends on its context.

As we shall see, it is hard to think of a behavior that is meaningful by itself, independent of its surround. That fact alone is responsible for endless debates about the meaning of people's behavior. When someone fails to greet us, we may wonder whether they failed to see us, whether they were preoccupied, or whether they are shy, aloof, or angry. The behavior is sufficiently ambiguous that any of these interpretations alone or other meanings might apply. Which meaning strikes us as most reasonable will depend on whether we know the person to have poor vision, or to be very worried about something, or whether we have recently had an argument with them.

The Multiplicity of Contexts

As one might imagine, there are a vast number of contexts that can color and give meaning to behavior. In fact, those contexts often interact with each other to produce quite different meanings for identical behaviors. Let us consider some such contexts:

Age. What is appropriate behavior for a child is often viewed as inappropriate for the adult. Infirmity means something quite different at 20 than it does at 70. Indeed, one of the constant complaints of older people is that their aches and pains are not taken seriously. "It's just age," doctors tell them, as if the disease processes that create pain in a 20-year-old are invariably different from those in the aged. Sometimes they *are* different, but quite often they are not.

Interesting things happen at transition points, when a person's age is not visibly detectable by others. My wife began college teaching when she was 23. That in itself was a trial; but it was compounded by the fact that she looked even younger. At that time, certain elevators and bathrooms were reserved for faculty and were different from those used by students. She had daily to deal with the consternation of other faculty and staff who felt that she was a student poaching on their territory!

Age, then, is a significant contextual variable that determines how identical behaviors are interpreted by us, and by others who are evaluating our behavior.

Gender and race. Is it not the case that seeing a man drive a motorcycle seems somehow "more appropriate" than seeing a woman drive the same machine? And correspondingly, finding an aproned woman in the laundry room strikes us as more "right" than finding a similarly dressed man in the same place. Notice that neither men nor women are especially qualified or disqualified by birth or by physiology to handle either motorcycles or laundry. Nevertheless, the context (in this instance, gender) focuses a variety of attitudes that yield judgments of appropriateness or inappropriateness of the behaviors.

What is true for motorcycles and laundries holds equally and painfully true for jobs, salaries, and promotions. Women and racial minorities find higher entry barriers into many occupations than do men. And once hired, women and racial minorities will often be paid less for equal work and will advance more slowly—this, despite equal competence and qualification. Once again, identical behaviors embedded in varying contexts elicit different meanings, reactions, and consequences.

Status. Personal status constitutes a strong context within which behavior may be differentially interpreted.

Social behaviors particularly lend themselves to differential interpretation according to the status that surrounds them. Behaviors that might ordinarily seem quite bizarre, rude, or crazy are often viewed as mere eccentricities among the very wealthy. This does not mean that judgments of rudeness or craziness are not made of the wealthy, only that they are made more rarely and for a more restricted set of behaviors.

Place. The locale in which a behavior occurs is an obvious interpretive background for the behavior itself. Undressing has different implications according to whether it is done in one's bedroom or in a classroom. Pacing the floor strikes people differently in a dormitory than in a psychiatric hospital. Indeed, "normal" behaviors that are performed inside a psychiatric hospital seem "abnormal" to the staff precisely because abnormal behavior is expected in that setting. Thus, when I was admitted to a mental hospital as a pseudo-patient (see pp. 561–62), if I asked questions it was interpreted as "intellectualizing," and if I took notes of my observations, it was noted in my case record that I often engaged in "writing behavior."

Personal characteristics. The characteristics we attribute to others often constitute contexts against which their behaviors are understood. These are not visible contexts like place or gender. They are psychological ones. But that fact makes them no less powerful and, indeed, endows them with special properties that make them more difficult to change or destroy.

Consider a boy with an IQ of 70 who stammers a hesitant response to a teacher's question. That response is likely to be interpreted against the background of his IQ, lending further support to the view that the child is "not very bright." The identical response from a child with an IQ of 130 is likely to lend credence to an entirely different view—that the child is "thoughtful" or "nervous."

Many of these personal characteristics take the form of personality labels, which are verbal designations that we use to describe others as well as ourselves, and which serve as backgrounds against which instances of behavior can be made meaningful. Our belief that someone is "dependent," for example, colors, correctly or incorrectly, our response to their request for assistance.

Some personality labels are relatively weak. They color few behaviors and they tint them weakly. But others are strong, "central traits" as they have been termed by Solomon Asch. They constitute stark backgrounds against which all manner of behaviors become seemingly understandable. To say that someone is "lucid" or "tall" may make a few of his behaviors understandable, but surely not many. But to label a person "stupid" or "schizophrenic" is to provide a broad canvas against which a host of behaviors can be interpreted. Such potent labels overwhelm and color all other personality contexts that might lend meaning to a given behavior.

Langer & Abelson (1974) conducted an elegant study that illuminates this issue. They videorecorded an interview between two people, one of whom was describing his job difficulties to the other. Subsequently, they played this videotape to a group of well-trained psychologists and psychiatrists, and asked them to rate the mental health of the interviewee. Half of these professionals were told that they were viewing an employment interview, while the other half believed it was a psychiatric interview. The clinicians' evaluations of the interviewee were quantified on a scale that ranged from 1 (very disturbed), through a midpoint, to 10 (very well adjusted). The words "job applicant" and "patient" constituted entirely different contexts for these judgments. Psychodynamically oriented clinicians who thought the interview was for employment rated the young man reasonably well-adjusted (average rating = 6.2). Those who thought they were viewing a psychiatric interview rated the behavior as more than moderately disturbed (average rating = 3.5).

The Power of Context over Perception

People do not ordinarily separate behaviors from the contexts in which they occur. They are not likely to say to themselves that a particular behavior in a different environment might have a different meaning. Rather, they comprehend meaning immediately, as if behavior and context are one. An excellent example of the speed of this reaction is seen in the figure below (adapted from Selfridge, 1955).

THE CAT

What do you see? Most people have no difficulty recognizing the phrase as THE CAT, even though the A and the H are identically shaped. Indeed, some people respond so rapidly to context that they experience surprise when the identity of the middle letters is pointed out to them.

Of course, the relative power of a contextual background to influence meaning, and the direction of that influence, depend in part on the ambiguity of the figure that is set into it. Figures that are sufficiently strong and unambiguous reduce the range of meanings that contexts can encourage.

TAE CAT

In the second figure the middle letter of each word is clearly "A". Because the A is well-articulated, readers find no meaning in the phrase other than a spelling error, and may take longer to identify the phrase.

These powerful effects occur because neither perception nor memory are passive processes. They are active, constructive ones in which the individual is swiftly and unwittingly processing, interpreting, construing and reconstruing events that are observed. Seemingly small changes in either figure or ground, conveyed by a word, an instruction, a setting, even a gesture, alter understanding. Such changes affect perception. They affect memory. And they affect what is retrieved from memory.

The Supportive Circularity of Context. Once a behavior has been given meaning by a particular context, it becomes likely that on subsequent occasions the appearance of the behavior alone will evoke the context in the minds of observers. This is because minds search for meaning, and meaning is not attributable to behavior alone.

What is true for all contexts is especially true for the contexts created by personality labels. Such labels are carried around in the minds of observers. Their very portability makes them conveniently applicable to behaviors that are puzzling, ambiguous, or worrisome, while their invisibility makes them difficult to disconfirm, alter, or destroy by contrary evidence. Furthermore, the labels usually stand for a vague constellation of reactions or behavior patterns rather than for a precise, clearly defined reaction. Thus, the appearance of any part of the complex pattern is often sufficient for the global label to be applied—even when all the other parts are absent or no longer performed. For example, if a sustained period of crying was made comprehensible by the label "depression," a second bout of tearfulness may evoke the same label even if it arises from the recent loss of a loved one.

Ennis (1972) describes the case of a man named Charlie Youngblood. Charlie, who had been diagnosed "paranoid schizophrenic" some 25 years earlier, was being interviewed by a psychiatrist to determine his ability to stand trial. Upon arriving, Charlie began to tape-record the proceedings. Knowing of the diagnosis, the psychiatrist viewed this particular bit of behavior as confirmation of Charlie's paranoia. But Youngblood had a good deal at stake. He could well be committed to a psychiatric hospital for the rest of his life on the basis of this interview. Therefore it was important to him to obtain a good, objective record of the interview. Had the psychiatrist understood his very real concerns, he might have interpreted that behavior against a different context.

When a label is broad and serves as an all-purpose umbrella for a host of behaviors, it may acquire the attributes of a self-fulfilling prophecy. Since so many behaviors can be subsumed under it, few behaviors can escape the interpretation that it affords. As a result, a wide variety of ambiguous behaviors may call forth the identical context in the observer. "He is getting sick again," we may say, even though the behavior bears no relation to the original context in which it was first seen.

If personality contexts are readily applied to behaviors by outside observers, they stand a fair chance of being applied by the person to himself. On seeing himself behave in ways that are reminiscent of earlier contexts, he may be concerned that his present behavior reflects something of that past. People who have once had a major psychological crisis, for example, worry that the "sickness" may reappear. Those worries are nurtured by the similarity of present to past behaviors, even though the meanings of those behaviors could be entirely different. Powerful contexts tend to overwhelm less powerful ones. Thus, a person may not notice that his current behavior is entirely appropriate in the present context, but will rather interpret it in light of an earlier, painful context that alters its meaning and causes renewed distress.

Contextual error. By now, it should be clear that errors can occur in the interpretation of behavior depending on the context which is imposed upon it. Behaviors appropriate in one context can appear bizarre in another.

In the case described earlier, Mr. Youngblood told the psychiatrist, "You are going to murder me for $75." The psychiatrist, having no such intention, saw this remark as one more example of Youngblood's paranoia. Youngblood, however, had brought his own very different context to that remark. He feared that he would be involuntarily committed to a psychiatric hospital, perhaps for life. Such loss of freedom was, to him, akin to being murdered. The $75 was the standard state fee for a diagnostic interview. Against this context, his remark might well be judged as overly poetic—but not as evidence of paranoia.

Much of understanding people consists of understanding the contexts in which they embed their behaviors. Those contexts are not always available to outside observers. Sometimes a simple inquiry elicits them. At other times, patient and imaginative probing may be necessary. In any event, the context of people's behavior is seldom automatically clear.

We frequently fail to probe for the context of behavior because we assume we already understand the context. The basis for that understanding, however, is sometimes fragile. We may feel that we understand because we know this person. We impose a historical context upon his or her behavior, making no allowances for the possibility of change or the enormous variety of human motivations. Sometimes we feel that we've seen "people like this" before, imposing a normative diagnostic context upon him or her, and making no allowances for individual differences and idiosyncrasy. Sometimes we just don't take the time to understand.

And occasionally, the behavior annoys us, making it very likely that we will impose an undesirable context on it. And the fact that we are occasionally right in these hasty judgments, or that we receive no negative feedback about them, or that all of us tend to forget our erroneous judgments, increases the likelihood that they will be made.

Wine tasting may provide an interesting model for increasing our ability to understand the meaning of our own and others' behaviors. The taste of wine is an entirely subjective event. Yet, wine tasters seem able to communicate with high agreement regarding the quality of wines they imbibe. How do they do it? First, they proceed slowly. Second, they base their judgments on the qualities of the wine—its clarity, bouquet, color, acidity, and such—and not on their own likes and dislikes. And finally, the context and conditions under which wine-tasting is done are always well controlled. Wine tasters understand that perceptions change when contexts and conditions change. Accuracy requires constancy and as much "objectivity" as that subjective task permits.

Understanding people's behavior is not identical to understanding wines. We prefer to understand the ways people behave in their natural environments, for example, and not in artificial ones that are akin to wine cellars. Nevertheless, the important lessons are there. Understanding the contexts from which behavior emerges takes time. It takes personal concern and objectivity. And it takes a calm and patient observer, often a highly trained one and especially one who is aware of the many meanings a single behavior can have.

References

Ennis, B. J. *Prisoners of psychiatry: Mental patients, psychiatrists, and the law.* New York: Harcourt Brace Jovanovich, 1972.

Langer, E. J., & Abelson, R. P. A patient by any other name . . . Clinician group differences in labeling bias. *Journal of Consulting and Clinical Psychology,* 1974, *42,* 4–9.

Selfridge, O. G. *Pattern recognition and modern computers.* Proceedings of the Western Joint Computer Conference, Los Angeles, Calif., 1955. Cited in Neisser, U., *Cognitive psychology.* New York: Appleton-Century-Crofts, 1967.

12

Therapeutic Modification of Behavior

Canst thou not minister to a mind diseas'd;
Pluck from the memory a rooted sorrow,
Raze out the written troubles of the brain;
And with some sweet oblivious antidote
Cleanse the stuff'd bosom of that perilous
    matter
Which weighs upon the heart?

William Shakespeare, *Macbeth*, V:iv

A current theme throughout this book has been the potential use of psychology in helping individuals achieve greater control over themselves and more meaningful relationships with their physical and social environment. We turn now to an area of applied psychology where that goal is most likely to be realized: *psychotherapy*. Although there is no universally accepted definition of what psychotherapy is or, indeed, what it is supposed to accomplish, popular usage of the term conveys the idea that it is the psychological treatment of some abnormality in thought, emotion, or action. The forms that such treatment may take are as varied as the theories of what makes people behave abnormally.

Since we have seen that there are many masks of madness, and even more notions about why certain people in different cultures "go mad," it is no wonder that therapy may be directed toward modifying the soul, the spirit, the mind, the brain, the heart, the character, the willpower, the behavior, or other aspects of the individual who has suffered a fall from normal functioning.

But what constitutes normality and abnormality is relative to the culture and circumstances in which the individual lives. Therefore, in many instances the goal of therapy (whatever its specific features or tactics) is to maintain the *status quo* of the society by modifying deviant behavior that is socially disapproved. To be "cured" often means to become acceptable and approved by other people in one's society. Therapy in such a view is a tool for social control; a subtle form of indoctrination to accept the values, morals, laws, rules, and belief system of the dominant institutions and prevailing authority in the given society at a particular time in history.

Most psychotherapists would reject the view that the purpose of therapy is to make people more normal by eliminating undesirable behaviors, idiosyncratic thinking, and deviant acts. Rather, the goal of psychotherapy is usually stated in more positive terms: to help people become more self-accepting, more inner-directed, and to develop a fuller sense of personal satisfaction and competence. In this perspective, therapy "frees up" individuals whose behavior is too constrained and imprisoned by the dictates of society.

Thus it can be said that psychotherapy embodies a systematized set of procedures to modify behavior that is *either* too deviant or too inhibited and restricted. Such behavior is feared because it does not make sense to others, and because it is not readily predictable and controllable by available social mechanisms. Like a contagious physical disease, it is assumed abnormal behavior must be treated or else it will contaminate the healthy as well. Thus, *therapy* has traditionally been associated with the idea of "curing" or "healing"—returning the individual to a state of health. We have come to think of psychotherapy as something a specially trained person does to another person who is already "sick" in some way.

Recently, psychotherapy is also being used in another sense, that of *preserving* health. Rather than being a *retroactive* attempt to change a bad situation, a new movement in the field of psychotherapy is based on an orientation of prevention and enrichment. Too many of us become overly concerned with the *business of living* and forget or never adequately develop the *joy of living*. For some therapists the successful outcome of therapy is to be assessed as fostering greater autonomy and enhancing human potentiality.

In practice most therapy is of the corrective or curative kind because people are more willing to invest the time, money, and effort when they are already "sick" and have a "problem" than when they are "well" and want only to stay that way or to improve their mental outlook. Most therapists then deal with the two aspects of therapy in varying proportions, ranging from exclusive focus on one to a blend of both.

Another distinction between two general types of therapy is that between *informal* and *formal* therapeutic approaches. Virtually all college students have been "in therapy" of an *informal* nature at some time in their lives. In seeking help with personal psychological problems, they have turned to parents, teachers, clergy, and friends. Such "therapy" typically is voluntarily initiated by the individual, is of short duration, and is not the primary basis of the relationship with the other person. On their part, these "nonprofessional" therapists have no special training in this function. Usually they dispense advice, love, and understanding or serve as "cathartic sounding boards," and do so without charge. It has been shown that most people do not go to psychotherapists for help with their personal problems. A survey of American adults conducted by the Joint Commission on Mental Health (reported by Lowen, 1968) revealed that they were much more likely to seek advice of professionals outside the field of mental health: 42 percent went for help to clergymen, 29 percent to physicians, and 11 percent to lawyers. Less than a quarter of those with "psychological problems" were likely to go for aid to someone designated as a psychotherapist.

We shall here define as *formal* therapy those procedures used by trained, accredited psychotherapists in the process of healing or curing "mental illness" (by whatever name it is called), or preserving and enriching "mental health."

Who does formal therapy and why? Historically, the role of the psychotherapist was assigned to the physician, a practice dating back to the writings of Hippocrates in the fourth century before Christ. *Psychiatrists* are in fact physicians who, after completing the standard first years of medical school curriculum, take a specialty in the field of "mental, emotional, and neurological illness." They are permitted by law to use drugs and other physical means of treatment for mental problems. It is possible for a psychiatrist to have majored as an undergraduate in some field other than psychology, to have had relatively few courses in psychology, or even to be unfamiliar with methods of psychological research.

Clinical psychologists receive a Ph.D. in an academic department of psychology (or counseling psychology or educational psychology) in conjunction with or followed by a supervised practicum and internship in a hospital or psychiatric clinic. Without the M.D. degree, they cannot prescribe any form of medication but must rely largely on *words* as the medium of therapeutic intervention. Before World War II the principal function of the clinical psychologist was psychological testing, used for diagnosis and evaluation of changes in a patient's psychological state—psychotherapy was the psychiatrist's domain. The suddenly increased load of psychological disturbance during the war and the sheer enormity of the demand forced a relaxation of the barriers against clinical psychologists engaging in the practice of psychotherapy.

A *psychoanalyst* is a special brand of therapist, one who has completed postgraduate studies (after the M.D. or Ph.D.) in a psychoanalytic institute that offers advanced training in the Freudian approach to understanding and treating neuroses and other psychological problems.

Why would anyone want to become a therapist? The most obvious motivation is the desire to help others in distress, to rescue the drowning, to transform suffering and sorrow into health and joy. But in helping others one also helps oneself. Concern for the welfare of others can give meaning and purpose to one's life, is highly esteemed in our society, and can increase one's sense of self-worth. In addition, it is possible that one way to get in touch with and work through one's own problems is by doing so with others. There are other, less noble, aspects of a career as a psychotherapist: money, status, self-employment, power to influence the lives of others, feeling needed, and at times to be in a position to reassure yourself of your own sanity. But despite the monetary gain and the fact that "just talking" sounds like easy work, to be a full-time, effective psychotherapist is one of the most demanding of all occupations, not to be entered into without an awareness of the emotional stresses and personal commitment involved.

But let's consider the other side of the couch: what brings people into formal therapy—to get some rather than to give some? As we indicated earlier, society usually establishes the conditions under which the patient is either *recommended* or *required* to undergo prescribed change procedures. Therapy is often recommended when an individual's behavior falls short of some standards of performance or expectations of others in the culture—lack of productivity, inability to profit from learning experiences, complaints of being unhappy or fearful, failure to relate to others, inability to derive pleasure from or to utilize the resources of the society. Often therapeutic change is demanded by the society when an individual threatens the social control function of society or its basic assumptions about human nature and social structure.

In the last chapter we saw that psychopathology has been variously conceptualized as a disease (physical or mental) within the individual, as something that exists not in individuals but in their interactions with others, or as just another type of learned behavior, induced and maintained because it is reinforced. It can also be viewed as only a set of labels for behavior out of keeping with some set of social norms, with the terms *abnormal* and *insane* having utility only for social and legal purposes. Attempts at therapy inevitably reflect the varying assumptions about what psychopathology is, what conditions create it, and how it can be alleviated. Perhaps even more basic to any approach of psychotherapy are the assumptions one makes about the nature of human nature. What is the "human essence" that must be treated, modified, or developed through therapeutic intervention?

Underlying any particular therapy is a general theory or view about what is the most important ingredient in the recipe for humanness. Some views hold that inheritance, genetics, and biological processes are all-important in determining what we are and why some of us can't cope and so break down. Others maintain that it is environmental influences that shape—and sometimes misshape—our thinking, feeling, and behavior. Some theories of human nature place an emphasis on early childhood experiences as the critical elements in creating conflicts, traumas, and current irrational behavior. Others assert that it is current situational forces and choices that define what we are. Or is it the knowledge of change, of the future, of the endless potential for growth, renewal, and death that is at the core of what makes human beings unique among all living creatures?

In this chapter, we will examine a variety of psychotherapeutic approaches that emerge from two alternative views of human nature. The perspectives to be used in categorizing different therapies are: *biological and psychodynamic*—where the emphasis is on repair of the broken-down or poorly functioning organism—and *behavioral and existential-humanistic*—where the emphasis is on creating new options and possibilities for growth. We will see how the dual nature of psychotherapy is addressed by these viewpoints. After considering the features of the major therapeutic approaches, we will examine: the scorecard of success or failure of psychotherapy; the ways in which therapeutic resources are combined; the effects of institutional treatment for mental illness. We will also mention some of the innovations in therapy and discuss some practical advice on choosing a therapy and a therapist. ●

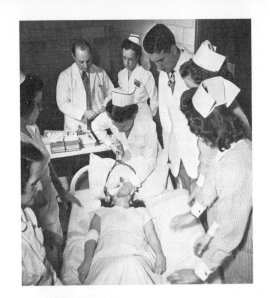

● Different methods of treatment of the mentally ill reflect different ideas about the causes of irrational behavior. The first photo shows a patient being prepared for electroconvulsive shock treatment—a physical form of therapy based on the medical model. Other forms of therapy focus on understanding the situational factors that are maintaining an individual's behavior problems. New forms of group therapy seek to create an atmosphere in which there is freedom for expression of feelings and interaction between people.

Biological Basis of Therapy

The relationship of human functioning to its biological underpinnings is unquestionably important. We are, after all, an animal species subject to many of the same limitations as other species in nature. Much of what we do every day and night is determined by the necessity to satisfy primitive biological needs that provide nourishment and oxygen to maintain the metabolism and reproduction of billions of body cells. The molecular environment of the human brain is influenced every moment by a bewildering array of neural impulses and biochemical alterations. This internal ecology is held in a delicate balance that may be upset by nutritional deficiencies, under- or over-secretion of hormones, the failure of certain enzymes to perform their required function, and many other biological mishaps.

In this view, mental ailments have their basis in physical-biological disorders, and so *somatic* therapy is called for. (*Soma* means "body" in Greek.) In the psychiatric treatment of severe emotional disturbances, particularly where there is considerable loss of contact with reality, various physical methods of therapy are often used. Such medical measures range from the use of special diets to the application of chemical sedatives or the artificial induction of violent convulsions. It should be emphasized that such "physical psychiatry" is not always intended to cure the individual's emotional disorder but may be used in an attempt to prevent some extreme act such as homicide or suicide or to make the disturbed patient receptive to psychotherapy. The most prominent of these physical methods are shock therapy, chemotherapy (drug therapy), and psychosurgery.

Shock Therapy

Severely disturbed patients who would once have been considered hopeless have responded favorably in some cases to artificially induced seizures or convulsions. Such treatment, known as *shock therapy,* became routine in most mental hospitals after World War II but is considerably less common since the discovery of new techniques of chemotherapy. Although a number of different techniques have been used in shock therapy, one feature they have in common is inducing a state of coma lasting for several minutes to several hours after the shock. It is not entirely clear whether the coma itself is the therapeutic factor or whether the value of shock is due to some other factor — such as physiological changes in the nervous system or the creation of a violent psychological reaction. Another possibility is that for depressed patients its effect is mediated through guilt reduction, the shock being viewed as "punishment" that they deserve for some actual or imagined transgression.

The most recently developed and by far the most widely used form of convulsive therapy is electroconvulsive shock. The patient is placed on a bed and securely padded or held firmly by nurses and attendants to prevent injury during the convulsion. Often muscle relaxants are administered to decrease further the possibility of bone fractures or too-strong muscle contractions. Electrodes are then fastened to the patient's head, and electricity ranging from 70 to 130 volts is applied for a fraction of a second. Twenty, thirty, or more such treatments may be given over a period of weeks or months. Electroconvulsive shock has proved particularly effective in cases of severe depression.

Conflicting findings have been obtained, however, in regard to its benefits. Many psychiatrists believe that this drastic form of treatment will be used less and less in the future; it is already being supplanted by drugs and new techniques of psychotherapy. There is some evidence that electroconvulsive shock has adverse effects on learning and retention (Leukel, 1957; Stone & Bakhtiari, 1956) and may also cause brain damage (as reported by Maher, 1966). Certainly it disrupts the integrated functioning of the organism.

In deciding on the utility of electroshock therapy for treating even "stubborn" cases, certain psychological factors must be weighed along with the physiological consequences. Although patients have no memory of the shock itself, they are aware of the marked changes from before to after the event, and they often can observe the violent convulsive reactions of patients who precede them in the waiting line. Many patients develop a strong fear of shock treatments but are nevertheless subjected to them involuntarily. In large state institutions that are understaffed, shock therapy has been used rather indiscriminately and sometimes as a threat or punishment.

Chemotherapy

The most dramatic change in hospitalized mental patients over the past twenty years is that they now rarely "run around like lunatics," exhibiting themselves, shouting obscenities, threatening, screaming, or showing extreme emotional displays. The reason is *chemotherapy*, the use of drugs in the treatment of mental and emotional disorders.

Two reports in the 1950s generated considerable interest in the relation of chemical factors to relieve mental illness. One was that a certain protein found in the blood of schizophrenics temporarily produced some of the symptoms of schizophrenia when injected into monkeys or nonschizophrenic volunteers. This led to the suggestion that schizophrenia might be a disease in which the body manufactures substances that disrupt the functioning of brain cells, and that a profitable line of research might involve the development of drugs that would block the action of such substances.

In 1952, two investigators (Osmond & Smythies) noted that *mescaline,* a drug whose action is similar to that of the body chemical *epinephrine,* induces a state comparable to schizophrenia. Since then, other researchers have found several pharmacological agents that stimulate or depress the function of certain organic compounds involved in the chemical transmission of nerve impulses in the brain (Schildkraut & Kety, 1967).

The introduction of *antipsychotic drugs* (drugs that suppress psychotic reactions) was proclaimed as having a major impact on the field of psychiatry. And it has recently been asserted that "there is almost universal agreement that antipsychotic drugs are effective in treating schizophrenic behavior, as evidenced by the fact that practically all schizophrenics are treated with antipsychotic agents" (Prien, Caffey, & Klett, 1973, p. ii).

The drugs that have been used in chemotherapy (also referred to as pharmacotherapy) fall into three major categories according to their behavioral and psychological effects: tranquilizers, energizers, and hallucinogens. Another useful classification is that of *antipsychotic drugs, antidepressant drugs,* and *antianxiety drugs.* You may be familiar with the trade names of some of the latter—Librium, Valium, Benadryl, Miltown, to name but a few.

Tranquilizers. Tranquilizing drugs reduce some of the physiological arousal associated with anxiety, as well as muscle tension and overt physical activity and agitation. In terms of diminishing psychotic behavior, tranquilizers such as chlorpromazine and reserpine have proven quite successful. In a thorough review of tranquilizer effectiveness, they were found to be more effective than placebos in 71 studies, and equally as effective as placebos in 21 studies (Davis, 1965).

But it is important to note that these drugs do not "cure" in the usual sense of that term; what they do is decrease the frequency of occurrence of certain behaviors that are undesirable and apparently unexplainable. Hospitalized mental patients are kept on *daily* medication for prolonged periods of years. When discharged, such patients must continue outpatient drug medication indefinitely, or risk a return of psychotic symptoms. ■ The relapse rate (deteriorating behavior requiring treatment) of chronic schizophrenics taken off tranquilizing medication is from 40 to 60 percent. Patients on high doses of antipsychotic drugs were shown to be more likely than patients maintained on smaller doses to suffer a relapse after having their medication replaced by placebo (Prien, Levine, & Switalski, 1971). It is not clear if the relapse effect is due to the fact that those patients who required more medication were initially more disturbed or whether it is a carryover effect of becoming dependent on the large dose of medication. Even when drug use is continued regularly after discharge from the hospital, the majority of psychotic outpatients seldom make more than a marginally successful adjustment to the community (Rickles, 1968).

Although tranquilizers are not a cure-all for chronic psychotic disorders, they do help a great many people with a variety of mental disturbances to continue to function without the breakdowns experienced in the past. For example, Joshua Logan, the successful producer-director of *South Pacific, Picnic,* and *Mister Roberts* suffered for years from uncontrollable bouts of mania alternating with severe depression. He, like many other manic-depressives is receiving daily maintenance doses of *lithium carbonate,* which he says "has given me renewed hope for my future life and work" (*Newsweek,* July 9, 1973). This ancient drug is said to have been prescribed by the fifth-century physician Aurelianus, who gave alkaline mineral water to patients suffering from depressive or manic forms of insanity. One virtue of this drug is that it does not dull the senses as do other tranquilizers; therefore it does not interfere as much with creative work.

If we use sales figures of Librium and Valium as a reliable index, the tranquilization of our tension-ridden society outside the mental hospital is proceeding at a brisk pace. It is reported that more than 20 million Americans have used these two tranquilizers to "calm their jangled, edgy nerves." The total worldwide sales of the pharmaceutical company that distributes these two tranquilizers exceeds $1.5 billion dollars a year (Moskowitz, 1973). A great deal of influence is exerted by drug companies to persuade the mental health profession to continue intensive use of their products. (See *P&L* Close-up, p. 513.)

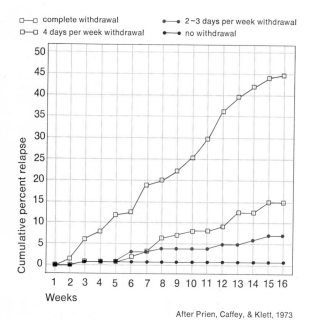

After Prien, Caffey, & Klett, 1973

■ **RELAPSE RATES FOR SEVERAL DRUG WITHDRAWAL SCHEDULES**

In two studies of over 500 chronic schizophrenic patients in Veterans Administration hospitals the risk of having a relapse was related to different schedules of drug withdrawal. After the patients' behavioral reactions had been stabilized by long-term administration of antipsychotic drugs, drug schedules were modified using a placebo substitute in a double-blind research design. The relapse rate increased over time as a function of the extent to which drugs were withdrawn. These data suggest that it is possible for antipsychotic medication to be interrupted for 2 or 3 days at a time without significant clinical change, but that greater withdrawal results in relapse.

Close-up
**Guaranteed to Cure Any Disease:
Mail-Order Remedies**

Do you "feel generally miserable or suffer with a thousand and one indescribable bad feelings, both mental and physical? No matter what the cause may be or how severe your trouble is, Dr. Hammond's Nerve and Brain Pills will cure you." It is instructive to go back to the period prior to the Pure Food and Drug Administration Act of 1906 and see what the public was led to believe were the causes and cures for mental and behavioral problems. In the Sears, Roebuck Catalogue of 1902, a safe and reliable "cure for the opium and morphia habit" was offered for a mere 67 cents a bottle. For only pennies, alcohol addiction could also be eliminated, since "Drunkenness is a disease and must be fought and counteracted by proper medical methods, the same as any other disease."

Such advertisements illustrate the common assumptions of that time about the bases of mental disorder. The link between acceptable physical diseases and unacceptable mental ones was the concept of "nerves"—tired nerves, overworked nerves, weak nerves—and impure or weak blood. For only 69 cents it was possible to buy *Vin Vitae*, "a pleasant medical tonic to strengthen and tone up the nerves, purify and enrich the blood, invigorate brain, body, and muscles, regulate the system." Portions of two similar ads are reproduced here. (Note their care in cautioning the public about the danger of fraudulent claims by others.) Electricity, then a newfound, wonderful mystery, was also sold as a curative for a "weak or deranged nervous system."

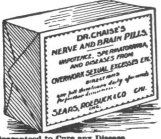

OUR 60c
Nerve and Brain
PILLS.
**GUARANTEED THE HIGHEST
GRADE ON THE MARKET.**

DR. CHAISE'S
NERVE AND BRAIN PILLS
IMPOTENCE, SPERMATORRHŒA,
AND DISEASES FROM
OVERWORK SEXUAL EXCESSES ETC.
DIRECTIONS
take full directions daily of course
for further directions
SEARS, ROEBUCK & CO. CHI.
INC.

**Six Boxes Positively Guaranteed to Cure any Disease
for which they are intended.**

THIS WILL CURE YOU if you feel generally miserable or suffer with a thousand and one indescribable bad feelings, both mental and physical, among them low spirits, nervousness, weariness, lifelessness, weakness, dizziness, feeling of fullness, like bloating after eating, or sense of goneness, or emptiness of stomach in morning, flesh soft and lacking firmness, headache, blurring of eyesight, specks floating before the eyes, nervous irritability, poor memory, chilliness, alternating with hot flushes, lassitude, throbbing, gurgling or rumbling sensations in bowels, with heat and nipping pains occasionally, palpitation of heart, short breath on exertion, slow circulation of blood, cold feet, pain and oppression in chest and back, pain around the loins, aching and weariness of the lower limbs, drowsiness after meals, but nervous wakefulness at night, languor in the morning, and a constant feeling of dread, as if something awful was going to happen.

If you have any of these symptoms our NERVE AND BRAIN PILLS will cure you. No matter what the cause may be or how severe your trouble is, DR. CHAISE'S NERVE AND BRAIN PILLS will cure you. These pills have a remarkable effect on both old and young. They can not be equalled by any other medicine as a cure for impotence, spermatorrhœa, night sweats, emissions, varicocele (or swollen veins), weakness of both brain and body, arising from excesses and abuses of any kind. It will tone up the **whole nervous system**, no matter how much worn out, overworked or depressed you may be; the weak and timid young man made strong and bold again; they will give youthful vigor and a new lease of life to the old.

BEWARE OF QUACK DOCTORS who advertise to scare men into paying money for remedies which have no merit. Our Nerve and Brain Pills are compounded from a prescription of one of the most noted German scientists, and are the same as has been used in German hospitals for years with marvelous success. HOW TO CURE YOURSELF, and full and explicit directions, are enclosed with every box. All orders and inquiries concerning these pills will be treated **confidentially**, and all shipments made in plain sealed package.

ONLY $3.00 FOR 6 BOXES. Enough to cure any case, no matter how severe, no matter how long standing, whether old or young, no matter from what cause. Send us $3.00 and we will send you 6 boxes by return mail, postpaid, in plain sealed package, with full instructions, full directions.

ELECTRO MEDICAL BATTERIES
For Home or Physicians' Use.

The Electro Medical Battery as a curative agent is becoming more appreciated from day to day. In cases of nervous trouble and partial paralysis it has brought about phenomenal results. The best physicians prescribe its use even when all else fails, and even under such adverse circumstances it often cures. For rheumatism, neuralgia, paralysis and all nervous disorders it seems to be nature's own cure. There need be no fear from the use of these machines, as there can be no bad results derived. An invalid may use them with perfect safety. There are a great variety of electrical machines and batteries on the market, from which we have selected of each kind those in which we can furnish our customers with the best value for the amount of money expended.

No. 6350.

No. 6350. The Little Wonder. A complete and perfect working little battery, neat, portable, and powerful, and produces an electric current from a small cell of zinc and carbon. This is a small machine that embodies all of the features of the larger ones and produces an electric current of great tensity and long duration with a very small charge of chemicals. There are no dangerous acids to handle, and it is so simple that any child can operate it; full instructions accompany each battery. Each...$1.35

Energizers. Depressed patients are frequently helped by *psychic energizers* such as *imipramine*.

A survey of studies involving a total of 5864 patients found that overall, imipramine and two other widely used antidepressants (amitriptyline and isocarboxazid) helped almost 65 percent of the patients for whom they were used. Three other commonly used energizers (phenelzine, malamide, and iproniazid) aided in 40 to 49 percent of the cases in which they were used. Placebo controls were effective in only 23 percent of the cases in which they were employed (Wechsler, Grosser, & Greenblatt, 1965).

An interesting sidelight of this survey was that less effectiveness was reported in studies that used placebo controls than in the studies that were using no control group or comparing the effects of two drugs. The investigators attributed this difference, at least in part, to the fact that in the placebo-control studies the staff's evaluation was biased by the knowledge that half of the patients were receiving no drug and thus should show no change in behavior. In the other studies, by contrast, the physicians evaluating the progress knew that all the patients were receiving a drug of some kind and thus might be expected to change—a good example of methods of study influencing the finding.

While imipramine has been found to be the most clinically effective of the antidepressant drugs (Klerman & Cole, 1965), recent studies have reported on the similar efficacy of a group of substances known as *monoamine oxidase inhibitors*. A significant correlation has been found in several studies between clinical improvement in depressed patients and the degree of inhibition of monoamine oxidation produced during drug administration (Feldstein, Hoagland, Oktem, & Freeman, 1965).

Hallucinogens. Mescaline and lysergic acid diethylamide (LSD), discussed in Chapter 7 as hallucinogens, can bring on symptoms of mental disorder but have also been used in therapy.

One of the principal effects of these drugs is that patients under their influence often regress to childhood behavior and feelings and are able to recall past events that may have helped cause their emotional disturbance.

LSD has sometimes been useful in group therapy, where, provided the setting is appropriate, it seems to enhance empathy and decrease defensiveness, helping the patient to communicate freely and reveal deep levels of feeling (Eisner, 1964).

Some therapists who see mental disorder as a disease advocate small doses of LSD in conjunction with traditional psychotherapies (Crocket et al., 1963). Other therapists, who regard therapy as primarily a means for growth, use LSD primarily for rapid personality change; they induce an extended psychedelic experience with large single doses. LSD therapy has shown some promise with a wide range of psychiatric disorders, especially in cases resistant to more conventional therapies.

An unconventional but highly promising use of LSD has come from research at the Maryland Psychiatric Research Center. Patients with terminal cancer suffer extreme physical pain and undergo severe psychological trauma in the last stages of the disease. LSD is being used to induce a psychedelic experience that, in addition to personal contact with the therapist, helps to relieve the pain of cancer and to give the patients a sense of well-being and a greater interest in life around them (Richards, Grof, Goodman, & Kurland, 1972).

Evaluating the effectiveness of LSD therapy is a difficult task since the hallucinogens are extremely susceptible to experimental bias (as we noted in Chapter 7). The effects of these drugs on an individual are very much dependent on what the person expects to happen (set), the social and physical surrounding during the experience (setting), and a host of other factors unique to the individual, such as stress tolerance, ability to suspend reality constraints, degree of adjustment, and so on. Such factors have undoubtedly contributed to the mass of conflicting research findings. On the basis of more than 300 studies dealing with LSD therapy, it has been tentatively concluded that when the factors of set and setting are optimal, "LSD can produce far-reaching beneficial effects in some people" (Mogar, 1969, p. 393).

Chemotherapy in perspective. The use of tranquilizing and energizing drugs has certainly played an important role in reducing the length of hospitalization of mental patients. Such drugs have decreased the incidence of the more extreme forms of maladaptive, bizarre behaviors previously associated with psychotic reactions. They have also made it possible for some types of patients previously "unreachable" to become amenable to psychotherapy.

But a critical analysis of chemotherapy must also take account of the following factors. There is no evidence of permanent "cure" via drugs; in fact, as we saw in the preceding chapter, the higher discharge rate in mental hospitals is now being compensated for by an even higher return rate of formally "cured" patients. Even among those patients who are most clearly improved by chemotherapy, it is not possible to separate the direct biochemical effect of the drugs from other factors in the drug experience. By making the patients more manageable, chemotherapy may make the psychiatric staff feel less threatened by the patients and thus treat them more humanely.

Any evaluation of the effectiveness of drugs must also take into account the predictable positive placebo reactions. The *suggestion* that a given substance will relieve pain and bring well-being is often as effective in doing so as the chemical composition of the drug itself.

An interesting sidelight is the finding that the method of administration may be an important factor in determining response to a placebo. One doctor found that the same placebo administered in a bright red gelatine capsule brought favorable results in 81 percent of the cases tested, as compared to only 49 percent when it was administered as a tablet and 69 percent when administered as a liquid (Clauser & Klein, 1957). Hypodermic injections of placebo substances have been found to be usually more effective than tablets but inferior to capsules. While blue or green solutions have been shown to bring better results in preparations applied externally, liquids to be swallowed are proven to be more effective if colored in warm tones of red, yellow, or brown—and if they have a bitter taste (Leslie, 1954).

A study that points up even more directly the need to separate drug effects from placebo effects in analyzing the effects of drugs on mental disorders was conducted with pharmacy students who were asked to help in the "testing" of two new drugs.

All forty-five students took a capsule at 8:30 A.M. and were told that its maximum effects would be felt in about two hours and would disappear by the close of the experiment at 12:30. Fifteen were informed that their capsule contained a stimulant, another fifteen that it contained a tranquilizer. The remaining fifteen were told that it contained only cornstarch (as did all the capsules, in reality).

Overall, 60 percent of the experimental subjects reported feeling the effects they were supposed to feel. This result was more pronounced among the "stimulated" subjects, 73.3 percent of whom reported feeling the suggested effects, as compared to 46.7 percent of the "tranquilized" subjects, perhaps because they had to continue with their usual laboratory work during the entire time.

Even pulse rates were affected. The pulse rates of the "stimulated" group rose at the second reading, taken during the supposed time of maximum effect of the drug, and fell again by the close of the period. Those of the "tranquilized" group fell and then rose again by the close of the period. Those of the control group rose slightly during the period, possibly owing to the pressure of completing their laboratory tasks (Brodeur, 1965).

Among the hazards of long-term chemotherapy are: (a) an overreliance by staff on drug therapy to the detriment of psychosocial and "human contact" therapies; (b) various physical side effects, including some visual impairment;

and (c) most serious of all, the development of a psychological dependence on drugs so that users come to attribute any improvement in their mental state or behavior to the drug and not to their own increased capacity for control of their behavior (Davison & Valins, 1969).

Finally, there is some new experimental evidence that schizophrenics with a prior history of reasonably good adjustment actually do *worse* when put on a tranquilizer schedule. Poorly adjusted patients were helped by the drug but not by a placebo. However, the previously well-adjusted group of fifteen patients who were given the drug *thioridozine* became more hostile and belligerent and required even longer hospitalization than did the well-adjusted placebo control patients. The authors of the study speculated that the drugs might have interfered with the self-reliance of these patients and with whatever process of recovery would occur naturally (Evans, Rodnick, Goldstein, & Judd, 1972).

Psychosurgery

Among the most dramatic, most widely publicized, and most disappointing innovations in psychiatry have been the techniques of brain surgery used in the treatment of severe emotional disorders (Moniz, 1937; Freeman & Watts, 1942). The best-known form of psychosurgery is the *prefrontal lobotomy,* an operation that severs the nerve fibers connecting the prefrontal lobes of the brain with the lower brain centers, especially the hypothalamus.

Studies with animals have demonstrated that signs of anxiety arising from conflict may be removed by such an operation. Clinical experience has shown that lobotomy does often diminish the emotional tone accompanying the individual's thoughts and memories. Thus, though psychosurgery is not thought to remove the *sources* of the patient's disturbance, it may eliminate the emotional torment of disturbing ideas or hallucinations.

These benefits must be set against the following list of side effects, however, described by Freeman and Watts, the medical team that introduced the operation into the United States in 1936: (a) a loss of interest in body and in the relation of the self to the environment, (b) an inability to foresee the consequences of a planned series of personally relevant acts, (c) an indifference to the opinions of others, (d) an increase in some forms of impulsive behavior, since remorse, guilt, and fear are banished, (e) a reduced capacity to form a unified self-image and project it into the future. In general, lobotomy patients may be described as lacking self-continuity; that is, they lose the feeling that they are the same person they were yesterday and will be tomorrow (Robinson & Freeman, 1955).

With such side effects, who needs a cure? Unfortunately the convictions of theorists, true believers, and researchers with a new technique are often undaunted by negative or disconfirming evidence of this sort. In spite of the above list of detrimental effects, the original proponents were convinced that continued efforts would discover "the critical zone, the important fibers, the necessary areas to be resected, tracts to be cut, and dangers to be eliminated" (Freeman & Watts, 1942, p. 18).

Because psychosurgery, once performed, cannot be undone, and because its results are uncertain, it has been considered a method of last resort and is less widely used today than it has been in the past. Presently there are no controls, either legal or professional, over such operations, although action is being taken by Congress to legislate restrictions. Burtram Brown, director of the National Institute of Mental Health, recently called for a systematic investigation of the effects of the estimated 500 psychosurgical operations that still take place in the U.S. annually before any new procedures for regulating such operations are recommended (reported in Trotter, 1973).

Physical Therapy and the Medical Model

Any physical therapy for psychopathology assumes that physical intervention can change the course of psychological processes, either by correcting underlying chemical abnormalities or by calming or stimulating a patient to a more optimum level of arousal. In some degree, a medical model of mental disorder is assumed. ◆

One of the problems of using a medical model in describing and treating behavior disorders is that the "symptoms" of the "disease" are behavioral rather than physical; thus the changes, too, must be in behavioral terms. But descriptions of behavior are subject to bias by the observer. Many psychologists believe that the terms derived from the disease model (*sickness, cure, relapse,* even *patient)* are not really suitable terms for describing or understanding what they believe is primarily a behavioral-psychological process. As we have seen, some investigators totally reject the "myth of mental illness" (Szasz, 1961, 1965) as having brought more disadvantages with it than beneficial consequences.

Meanwhile, others continue the search for more objective physical indicators both of psychopathology and of "cure" in consistent patterns of brain waves or chemical composition of the blood. For example, Rappaport and Silverman (1970) have reported finding identifiable

◆ POSITIVE AND NEGATIVE ASPECTS OF THE MEDICAL MODEL

Positive Aspects
Development of physiological therapies

More humane treatment of patients

Money, facilities, legislative lobbies, and respectability, due to medical involvement

Intradisciplinary medical research

Negative Aspects
Stigma of "disease" label

Deviance as "sickness"

Concept of "incurable"

Treatment costly, limited availability

Lessened community involvement

Psychiatry a medical discipline, nonbehavioral

Long-term hospitalization, isolation from community

Vested professional interests and status hierarchies

Emphasis on curing individual pathology, disregard of social pathology

brain-wave patterns in the schizophrenic patients who are likely to benefit from certain types of therapy.

Clearly, drugs can change behavior and mental processes, both directly and indirectly (through changing arousal and facilitating or inhibiting neural conduction). They may make an individual less disturbing to others and less anxious. To the extent that normal functioning depends on an intact brain and nervous system functioning smoothly, physical agents to restore or maintain such functioning will provide physical readiness for healthy adjustment. But to the extent that effective behavior depends on learning in a social setting, one can expect that relearning and social interaction will need to be part of therapy in order for new behavioral repertoires to be acquired. And to the extent that effective adjustment depends on a perception of one's own control over oneself and one's destiny, therapy must increase that perception; dependence on pills or other external physical agents is likely to work in the other direction.

The biological orientation to mental illness has not had nearly the same success as with medical illness. This is due in part to the secondary status of mental illness research within medicine and the lack of adequate financial appropriations. It is also probably a function of the complex interactions of variables that enter into psychopathological behavior—only one of which is biochemical. The notion that mental illness is an entity, a form of emotional, neurological disease, does injustice to the subtle interplay of the underlying cognitive, social, and experiential processes.

Psychodynamic Basis of Therapy

The psychodynamic view of psychopathology, like the biological one, locates the core of the disturbance inside the disturbed person but, unlike it, emphasizes ongoing, intense psychological processes rather than physical deficits, excesses, or imbalances. As we saw in our discussions of Freudian theory in the previous chapters, neurosis is viewed as the inability to resolve adequately the inner conflicts between the unconscious, irrational impulses of the *id* and the internalized social constraints imposed by the *superego*. According to this view, biology determines the sexual stages an individual progresses through from infancy to adulthood, but the particular psychological experiences at each stage from oral to anal to phallic determine whether there will be a fixation at an immature stage and a failure to progress to a more mature, healthy level of development.

In the struggle between the child's impulse and reason, reason typically wins the battle, but in the case of neurosis, it loses the war. The biological impulse denied in favor of the forces of social "good" and parental "might" nevertheless remains behind the curtain to make trouble at every opportunity. The impulses of the id, being strong, unverbalized, and amorphous, persist forever in seeking expression in disguised forms while the rational, intellectual awareness of the conflict is not available for recall or analysis. The neurotic person may feel and do things because of motives of which he or she is not conscious, and thus, such behavior must by definition be irrational.

The goal of Freudian psychoanalysis is the establishment of intrapsychic harmony that expands one's awareness of the forces of the id, reduces overcompliance with superego demands, and strengthens the role of the ego. Freud appeared to be rather pessimistic that this ideal harmony could ever be attained. After explaining some of the main features of Freudian therapy, we will compare and contrast it to the therapy that was developed from the psychodynamic theories of Freud's early colleagues, Carl Jung and Alfred Adler.

Freudian Psychoanalysis

Psychoanalytic therapy, as developed by Sigmund Freud, is an intensive and prolonged technique for exploring the patient's unconscious motivation, with special importance attached to conflict and repression stemming from problems in the early stages of psychosexual development (see pp. 412–14). Its aim is to bring to consciousness such repressed memories and conflicts and to help the individual resolve them in the light of adult reality. Such a process presumably effects a radical change in the individual's basic personality structure. Psychoanalysts use several techniques for bringing repressed conflicts to consciousness and helping the patient resolve them. These include free association, dream analysis, analysis of resistances, and analysis of transference.

Analysis of free associations. The principal procedure used in psychoanalysis to probe the unconscious and release repressed material is *free association*. The patient sits comfortably in a chair or lies in a relaxed position on a couch and lets his or her mind wander freely, giving a running account of thoughts, wishes, physical sensations, and mental images as they occur. The patient is encouraged to reveal every thought or feeling, regardless of how personal, painful, or seemingly unimportant. The therapist often takes a position behind the patient, so as not to serve as a distraction or disrupt the flow of associations.

Freud maintained that "free associations are subject to determination and are not a matter of choice." The task of the analyst is to track down the associations to their inner-determined core and to penetrate through the disguises in which repressed urges may appear — to identify what is beneath the surface in the psychoanalytic "iceberg" depicted on page 413.

Analysis of dreams. Psychoanalytic therapists try to gain further insight into the patient's unconscious motivation by the technique of dream analysis. When the individual is asleep, the ego is presumably less on guard against the unacceptable impulses originating in the id, so that a motive that cannot be expressed in waking life may find expression in a dream. Some motives are so unacceptable to the conscious self, however, that they cannot be revealed openly even in dreams but must be expressed in disguised or symbolic form. Thus a dream has two kinds of content (as we discussed in Chapter 7). The *manifest* (openly visible) content of the dream is that which we remember and report upon awakening. It usually is not painful and, in fact, often seems quite amusing. Beneath the manifest content is the *latent* (hidden) content—the actual motives that are seeking expression but that are so painful or unacceptable to us that we do not want to recognize their existence. The therapist attempts to uncover these hidden motives by studying the symbols that appear in the manifest content of the dream.

The unconscious process that transforms the emotionally painful latent content of the dream into the less painful manifest content is called *dream work*. Dream work distorts the content of a dream in various ways, making the motives expressed in it less obvious to the dreamer. For example, a male student who is filled with anxiety about failing an examination and being expelled from school may dream that he is pushing his way through a heavy snowstorm, pursued by wild animals. Or, with rather less disguise, a woman who feels hostility toward her husband might dream of killing a rat—the significance of this symbol being revealed in the waking state by her occasional playful reference to her husband as "the little rat."

Analysis of resistances. During the process of free association, the patient may show *resistances*—that is, inability or unwillingness to discuss certain ideas, desires, or experiences. Resistances prevent the return to consciousness of repressed material that is painful to recall, such as material connected with the individual's sexual life or with hostile, resentful feelings toward parents. Sometimes a resistance is shown by the patient's coming late to the appointment with the therapist or "forgetting" it altogether.

When such material is finally brought into the open, the patient generally claims that it is either too unimportant, too absurd, too irrelevant, or too unpleasant to be discussed.

The psychoanalyst of the Freudian school attaches particular importance to subjects that the patient does *not* wish to discuss. Such resistances are conceived of as *barriers* between the unconscious, where repressed conflicts wage guerrilla warfare on the individual's psychic health, and the conscious, which could deal with these rebellious forces rationally. The aim of psychoanalysis is to break down resistances and bring the patient to face these painful ideas, desires, and experiences. Breaking down resistances is a long and difficult process but is considered absolutely essential in order to bring the whole problem into consciousness where it can be solved.

Analysis of transference. During the course of psychoanalytic treatment, the patient usually develops an emotional reaction toward the therapist, identifying him or her with some person who has been at the center of an emotional conflict in the past. This phase of therapy is known as *transference*. In most cases, the analyst is identified with a parent or a lover. The transference is called *positive transference* when the feelings attached to the therapist are those of love or admiration and *negative transference* when they consist of hostility or envy. Often the patient's attitude is ambivalent—that is, both positive and negative feelings toward the therapist are experienced, as is often the case with children's feelings toward their parents.

The analyst's task in handling the transference is a difficult and dangerous one because of the patient's emotional vulnerability, but it is a crucial part of treatment. The therapist helps the patient to interpret the transferred feelings and to understand their source in earlier experiences and attitudes.

However, it must be remembered that the therapist is not a perfectly programmed, objective analyzer of patient input. The therapist, despite attempts to maintain an "emotional detachment," may still react to the patient's problems in a personal way. In the intense dyadic interaction that must occur when two people meet as often as five times every week for several years to discuss personal problems, it is difficult for the analyst to keep personal reactions calibrated at psychological zero. Thus, *countertransference* may also develop during the prolonged period of analysis. In countertransference the therapist comes to like or dislike the patient at a personal level because of perceived similarity of the patient to significant others in the therapist's life. In working through this countertransference therapists may discover some unconscious dynamics of their own.

Psychoanalytic Therapy Since Freud

As we saw in Chapter 10, neo-Freudian theorists differ from Freud in placing relatively more emphasis on the current social environment and less on childhood experiences. The same difference in emphasis appears in neo-Freudian therapy, which is aimed at understanding the patient's present situation as well as past experiences. Also, most neo-Freudian psychotherapists believe that a cure cannot be effected simply by helping patients understand their unconscious feelings. Rather, patients must be directed along the path of self-initiated change and reappraisal of inadequate modes of adjustment.

Freud's emphasis on repressed sexual conflicts has also been questioned as a fundamental basis for neurotic behavior today, especially among the young. Victorian constraints and the generally accepted religious doctrine of sin forced a denial of sexuality during Freud's time, and it is not surprising that he found sexual repression a common problem among his patients. The dramatic changes in our sexual mores in recent years, however, make sexual repression a less common cause of emotional disturbance than "existential crises," failure to see meaning in life, feelings of helplessness, and inability to cope with rapid technological and social changes.

Jung and Adler, though originally disciples of Freud, broke with him in 1911 and went on to develop their own views on personality, pathology, and therapy. They rejected Freud's emphasis on the past, the individual's unconscious, sex, and aggression. Jung argued that there were much deeper levels of meaning to life than sexual motivation, and that human beings aspired to greater expectations than the mere satisfaction of "base" drives. Both men sought to place the individual more completely in a cultural setting, related to all other human beings through common myths, archetypical symbols (original models or prototypes of basic symbols from which others are derived), and shared communal life. Although Adler and Jung emphasized the positive characteristics of people and perceived in them the central striving for self-actualization (Adler termed this "completion" and Jung thought of it as attainment of the Self), Adler appears to have been more optimistic about the attainment of this goal. For Adler, humans were self-determined creatures who can shape both their internal and external environment, a view that won him the distinction of being one of the first humanistic psychologists. With their emphasis on the individual's search for meaning in life and concern for the "here and now" of the patient and future goals, both theorists foresaw the developments of existential psychology. A comparison of the views of Freud, Jung, and Adler on major issues in psychodynamic therapy is outlined in the table. ▲

Evaluation of Psychoanalytic Therapy

Psychoanalysis has come under attack because of its closed-mindedness to criticism and because many Freudian concepts and hypotheses are not testable scientifically. Behavior therapists have criticized the practice of apparently ignoring the patient's current problem in the search for the presumed underlying cause. They maintain that the present symptom *is* the problem. What right has the psychoanalyst, they ask, to determine what the patient's "real" problem is, while shunting aside the problem that the patient wants treated?

	Freud	Jung	Adler
Insight	Of central importance in understanding unconscious motivation. Usually refers to repressed memories of conflicts arising during early psychosexual development and their effect on present relationships.	Leads to understanding of personal unconscious only and is thus of little help in curing neurosis. Collective unconscious can only be understood through exploration of patient's use of symbols in dreams, fantasy, etc.	Emphasis on gaining insight can be used as a strategy to avoid changing. Insight is redefined as "understanding translated into constructive action" (Mosak & Dreikurs, 1973, p. 59).
Free Association	Principal procedure used in psychoanalysis to explore unconscious.	Used not in a vertical sense of exploration down into repressed content of unconscious, but in a horizontal sense to explore associations specific to dream or fantasy images.	Freudian concepts of repression and unconscious are rejected; thus there is no need for free association.
Dreams	Dreams are an attempt to secure forbidden satisfactions and are seen as wish fulfillment in the service of the id. Using free association, the analyst can interpret the latent content to the patient, thus making the unconscious conscious.	The dream, like all other products of the unconscious, is a symbolic message indicating the way to future growth. It is the creative and healing aspect of the unconscious, revealing the path to wholeness.	The dream is a future-oriented problem-solving activity—a rehearsal of possible future courses of action in relation to immediate problems. It is also a reflection of the individual's life-style.
Resistance	A fundamental concept in psychoanalysis referring generally to anything that works against progress in therapy and specifically to an active opposition by the patient to the expression of repressed material.	Although the presence of resistance is recognized, it is considered to be typical of human nature and there is no concern for interpretation of any underlying dynamics.	Resistances occur when the patient's goals and those of the therapist do not coincide. They are analyzed not to uncover repressed material but to realign the goals of therapy.
Transference	Seen as an emotional reaction to the therapist or other individuals that follows a pattern established in early childhood through the relationship with one's parents. Working through (bringing to consciousness) of transference and resistances is the heart of Freudian psychoanalysis.	Two levels of transference are recognized: (a) personal—similar to Freudian concept in which traits of important people in the past are projected onto the therapist; (b) transpersonal—archetypal projections where the analyst is viewed as omnipotent. Not the main focus of therapy but has some value.	Seen as a patient-therapist goal discrepancy stemming from inadequate learning. Through long-term interactions with parents and other authority figures the patient has constructed a "script" (perhaps unconscious) in which others are expected to respond to him or her in a certain way. Analyst should refuse to follow this script.

From a practical standpoint, psychoanalysis has also been criticized on the grounds that it requires a great deal of the patient's time and money. Psychoanalysis aims to create a fundamental and permanent alteration in the individual's personality structure, a goal that usually requires at least two or three years of frequent sessions with the analyst. Even when the individual can afford to spend the time and money necessary for a complete course of analytic treatment, the results are not always satisfactory. Because psychoanalysis relies heavily on the patient's achieving great personal insight, it is best adapted to individuals who are above average in intelligence and who do not have severe disorders such as schizophrenia. It also is tailored for those who are highly verbal and introspective, and those with whom the analyst can relate during the long, intensive period of close association.

The most important question, of course, is how effectively psychoanalysis produces the improvements it aims for. We will consider the problem of criteria for cure at some length in a later section of this chapter.

By emphasizing instinctive biological drives, the psychodynamic viewpoint makes the individual a victim of unrestrainable inner forces. Unless individuals can overcome these innate tendencies, it is not possible for them to freely choose their destiny. But there is another viewpoint, which sees human nature as pushing us toward realization of our human potential and wholeness. Irrationality in behavior is then seen as the product of either faulty learning or the ignoring of the inner guide that points the way toward spiritual fulfillment as well as satisfaction of animal appetites.

Behavioristic Basis of Therapy

The behavioristic perspective sees pathology in observable *behavior*, not as something within the individual's nervous system or in free-floating repressed conflicts or in the insatiable, unobservable id. Functional mental illness is best understood, according to this view, as behavior pathology that can be changed by discovering and modifying those existing stimulus conditions that maintain such behavior.

Just as the psychodynamic view was, in part, a reaction to the nineteenth-century emphasis on reason, structural mechanisms, and willpower, so behaviorism represented a rejection of prevailing views that the golden pathway of psychology was "the introspective analysis of consciousness." We saw in earlier chapters that behaviorism represents a view that is pragmatic, empirical, and grounded in research. Inferred concepts such as the unconscious are rejected because they are not amenable to empirical verification. The central task of all living organisms is seen as *learning* how to adapt to their current environment. Therefore, theories of learning are thought to provide the foundation for the study of behavior. When organisms have not learned how to cope effectively with the demands of their social and physical environment, their maladaptive reactions, it is believed, can be overcome by therapy based on principles of learning (or relearning).

These various types of therapies are often titled collectively as *behavioristic*, or *action*, therapies in that they all emphasize the therapeutic benefit of "doing" rather than just "talking about." In other words, these approaches all maintain that it is performance that is important, and not simply an intellectual understanding of the causes of one's behavior. Behavior is viewed as determined not by underlying drives but by the individual's past learning history and the present environment. Social learning theorists would modify this statement to include the individual's unique perception of the environment and other cognitive factors (expectations, values, goals, etc.). Such a viewpoint has been labeled "soft" determinism in that some degree of control over behavior is attributed to the organism.

Slight variations among different behavioristic therapies reflect differing emphases on the relative importance of emotional learning, overt reinforcement and overt responding, the use of social models of the appropriate behavior, vicarious learning through observation of others, and so on.

Behavior modification is the term usually applied to the use of operant conditioning procedures, and here the emphasis is on observation of behavior and contingent reinforcement. We will see this most clearly operating in *token economies* within institutional settings. The therapeutic use of social learning theory is often called *modeling therapy* or *social learning therapy*. Despite certain differences, all forms of behavioristic therapy assume that the "problem" of undesirable or maladaptive behavior stems not from irrational motives, sins, or disease states, but simply from inappropriate learning.

Behaviorists argue that abnormal behaviors are acquired in the same way as normal behaviors: through a process of learning. They assert that all pathological behavior, except where there is established organic causation, can be best understood and treated in terms of the conditions of "abnormal" reinforcement that happen to have been associated with the coping attempts of those particular "learners." Treatment is needed because their behavior brings them more pain than pleasure or is threatening to them or other people. The unique aspect of this treatment is thus that it is directed toward a modification of *behavior*, rather than of something within the individual. In keeping with this point of view, many behavior therapists prefer to call the people they treat "clients" rather than "patients."

Extinction

The simplest way to eliminate an unwanted behavior is sometimes just to stop reinforcing it. When this approach is possible, the behavior tends to become less frequent and finally disappears. Extinction is a useful therapeutic procedure in situations where undesirable behavior is actually being reinforced unknowingly, and in fact such situations appear to be rather common in everyday life. For example, adults sometimes inadvertently reinforce undesirable behavior in children, such as temper tantrums, by giving them extra attention for it.

Why do people continue to do something that causes pain and distress when they are capable of doing otherwise? Many forms of behavior (or symptoms) have multiple consequences—some negative, some positive. Often subtle positive reinforcements keep the behavior going despite its obvious negative consequences. This is often found in cases of stuttering, where the inordinate tension, embarrassment, and inconvenience generated by stuttering are counterbalanced, in part, by the attention, sympathy, and ready excuses for failure or rejection that stuttering provides.

Clinical psychologists have long been aware that such *secondary gains* accompany and support maladaptive behavior. Many believe, however, that such gains will be abandoned only after the core problem is cured and they are no longer needed. In contrast, behavior therapists believe that the maladaptive behavior is the whole problem, and that all you need to do to get rid of the whole problem is change the reinforcement contingencies.

Unintentional reinforcement has been found to maintain and encourage psychotic behavior. It is standard procedure in many mental hospitals for the staff to ask patients frequently how they are feeling. This may suggest to the patients that the "appropriate" behavior is to be thinking and talking about one's feelings, unusual symptoms, hallucinations, and so on. In fact, the more bizarre the symptoms and verbalizations, the more attention may be shown by the staff in their efforts to understand the "dynamics" of the case (Ayllon & Michael, 1959). A hospitalized patient being interviewed by one of the authors, when asked if there was "anything else that was bothering him," responded, "You mean *halicinations* or *sublimitions?*"

Although it is difficult to do so, it is important to extinguish behaviors on the part of well-intentioned staff members, teachers, relatives, and friends that are providing reinforcement for the maladaptive behaviors. It takes considerable restraint not to intervene in attacks by a bully or not to get alarmed when a child appears ready to engage in self-mutilation, but it can be demonstrated to "work."

Extinction of undesirable behavior is typically used in conjunction with positive reinforcement of responses regarded by the therapist as more adaptive. We shall return to the positive reinforcement techniques in more detail in a later section—and also to the problem of who is to say what behavior is "adaptive" and on what basis.

Desensitization

It is difficult to be both happy and sad, or relaxed and anxious, at the same time. This principle is applied in therapy in the *reciprocal inhibition* technique developed primarily by Joseph Wolpe (1958, 1969). One type of reciprocal inhibition is *desensitization.* Since anxiety is assumed to be a major cause of inability to approach positive goals and of fixation on negative ones, the client is taught to prevent anxiety arousal by relaxing.

Desensitization therapy begins by identifying the stimuli that provoke anxiety in the client and arranging them in a hierarchy ranked from weakest to strongest. Next, the client is trained in a system of progressive deep-muscle relaxation. Relaxation training requires several sessions; hypnosis or drugs may be used to help tense clients learn to achieve complete relaxation.

Finally, the actual process of desensitization begins. The client, in a relaxed state, is told to imagine as vividly as possible the weakest anxiety stimulus on the list. If anxiety reactions occur, the client stops and concentrates on relaxation again. When the weakest stimulus can be visualized without discomfort, the client goes on to the next stronger one. After a number of

sessions, the most distressing situations on the list can be imagined without anxiety—even the one that could not be faced originally. Great care is taken not to arouse anxiety during this process of gradually approaching the "unthinkable" stimulus. If anxiety is evoked, the therapist terminates the imagery production and relaxes the client, and they begin again with a weaker stimulus.

As in other conditioning, once anxiety is extinguished to a particular scene due to the pairing of that stimulus with relaxation, there is a *generalization* of this inhibition to related stimuli, including those next stronger in the hierarchy. Thus desensitization works both directly, by reducing anxiety to a particular stimulus through relaxation, and indirectly, through generalization of anxiety reduction to similar stimuli.

Desensitization is ideally suited for treatment of specific phobic reactions that are maintained by the relief experienced when the anxiety-producing stimuli are avoided or escaped. Considerable research has been done on people with snake phobias. One might wonder if overcoming anxiety reactions to the *thought* of a snake would carry over to situations in which the client is faced with a real, living snake. The evidence indicates that therapeutic effects do transfer to real-life situations. Clients treated for fear of snakes have shown significantly less fear in behavior tests requiring them to approach or pick up live, nonpoisonous snakes.

This approach has been attacked by traditional therapists as one that treats only surface symptoms that have been serving an adaptive function for the person and, by removing them, creates still more anxiety. It has been likened to tinkering with a weathervane in an attempt to change the wind or changing a thermometer in order to regulate the temperature.

In fact, however, the fear that removal of one symptom will simply result in the appearance of another symptom to take over its function is *not* justified by any available data. Rather, it appears that symptom removal increases the clients' self-confidence (they see themselves as the kind of people who can overcome anxiety and cope with their problems), and may even have a positive effect on other maladaptive reactions than the one treated (Grossberg, 1964). The chart gives a comparison of the dynamic and behavior-therapy approaches, as seen by two behavior therapists. ●

Desensitization techniques have been successfully applied to a diversity of human problems, including such generalized fears as test anxiety, stage fright, acrophobia (fear of heights), agoraphobia (fear of open spaces), claustrophobia (fear of enclosed places), impotence, and frigidity (Paul, 1969).

Implosive Therapy

Another method of extinction training in current use is *implosive therapy,* in which every effort is made to arouse as much anxiety in the client as possible. Implosion therapists, too, regard neurotic behavior as the conditioned avoidance of anxiety-arousing stimuli, but they feel that if a person is allowed to escape the anxiety-arousing stimulus, anxiety will never extinguish since there will be no reason for it to do so (Stampfl & Levis, 1967).

The dynamics of the situation are nicely illustrated by the old joke about the man who went around snapping his fingers all the time. When asked why, he replied that it kept the tigers away. Told there were no tigers in that part of the country, he exclaimed happily, "See, it works!" Obviously, this kind of behavior is resistant to extinction, because it arranges its own conditions for reinforcement.

In order to extinguish an irrational fear most effectively, implosion therapists believe it is necessary for the client to experience a full-blown anxiety reaction without suffering any harm. The therapeutic situation is arranged so that the frightening stimulus occurs in circum-

---

● **DYNAMIC AND BEHAVIOR THERAPY COMPARED**

Dynamic Therapy	Behavior Therapy
1. Based on inconsistent theory, never properly formulated.	1. Based on consistent, properly formulated theory leading to testable deductions.
2. Derived from clinical observation not based on controlled observations or experiments.	2. Derived from experimental study specifically designed to test basic theory and deductions made therefrom.
3. Considers symptoms the visible upshot of unconscious causes ("complexes").	3. Considers symptoms as unadaptive conditioned responses.
4. Regards symptoms as evidence of *repression*.	4. Regards symptoms as evidence of *faulty learning*.
5. Believes that symptomatology is determined by defense mechanisms.	5. Believes that symptomatology is determined by individual differences and as accidental environmental circumstances.
6. All treatment of neurotic disorders must be *historically* based.	6. All treatment of neurotic disorders is concerned with habits existing *at present;* the historical development is largely irrelevant.
7. Cures are achieved by handling the underlying (unconscious) dynamics, not by treating the symptom itself.	7. Cures are achieved by treating the symptom itself, i.e., by extinguishing unadaptive CRs and establishing desirable CRs.
8. Interpretation of symptoms, dreams, acts, etc., is an important element of treatment.	8. Interpretation, even if not completely subjective and erroneous, is irrelevant.
9. Symptomatic treatment leads to the elaboration of new symptoms.	9. Symptomatic treatment leads to permanent recovery, provided autonomic as well as skeletal CRs are extinguished.
10. Transference relations are essential for cures of neurotic disorders.	10. Personal relations are not essential for cures of neurotic disorders, although they may be useful in certain circumstances.

From Eysenck & Rachman, 1965

stances where the client cannot run away. The therapist describes an extremely frightening situation relating to the client's fear and urges the client to imagine being in it, experiencing it through all the senses as intensely as possible. Such imagining is assumed to cause an explosion of panic. Since this explosion is an inner one, it is called an *implosion;* hence the term *implosive therapy.* As this happens again and again and no harm is forthcoming, the stimulus loses its power to elicit anxiety. When anxiety no longer occurs, the neurotic behavior employed to avoid it disappears. In other words, extinction occurs.

Instead of starting by imagining mildly frightening stimuli and gradually working up to the really terrifying ones, trying to prevent anxiety from ever being aroused, the implosion therapist plunges the client into imagining as vividly as possible the most terrifying scene that can be conjured up. The way such therapy works, and its contrast with desensitization, can be seen in its application with a group of ten female subjects who were afraid of snakes (try putting *your* imagination to work on the images they worked with):

Highly frightening scenes involving snakes were described, and subjects were asked to imagine these scenes as vividly as possible, using all of their senses: imagine being attacked by a huge man-sized snake, having a slimy snake crawling all over your body, having it slowly strangle you, having the snake trapped inside your stomach where it is biting you relentlessly. *Subjects were periodically reminded that nothing was actually happening to them. Seven of the ten subjects were able to pick up a snake after a single forty-five-minute session (Hogan & Kirchner, 1968).*

Aversive Learning

There are some types of behavior disorders in which the individual's behavior (smoking, drinking, gambling, turning on with potent drugs) brings immediate pleasure, but has long-term negative consequences for health or for the satisfaction of other needs. Or it may be that a given stimulus has acquired the power to elicit a conditioned response that the individual finds undesirable, such as homosexual arousal. The most promising forms of treatment for such disorders involve the use of aversive stimulation.

As we saw in Chapter 3, there are a number of variables that interact to influence learning when aversive stimulation is used. Intensity, timing, and scheduling of the aversive stimulus are all important, as are its predictability, the context in which it occurs, and whether it is paired with eliciting stimuli (respondent conditioning) or is a consequence of behavior (instrumental conditioning).

Aversive instrumental conditioning has been used successfully to eliminate stuttering.

Stutterers were instructed to read printed material aloud for nearly an hour to obtain a base-line measure of stuttering. Then they were asked to read very slowly, but each time they stuttered, they received a burst of delayed auditory feedback of their own voice. Delayed auditory feedback, as we saw in Chapter 6, is very aversive to a person trying to speak. Once clients were able to read slowly without stuttering, their reading rate was gradually accelerated while the delayed feedback was faded out. By the seventieth session, one stutterer was reading faster than during the original base-line period and stuttering on less than a word a minute, as compared with fifteen words at the start. Another stutterer, whose training had to be compressed into only a week, showed even more dramatic results: more than double his original reading rate with no stuttering at all (Goldiamond, 1965).

In order to modify the "temptation value" of stimuli that elicit deviant desires and behaviors, counterconditioning procedures are employed. Stimuli that have come to arouse unwanted responses are paired with noxious stimuli such as electric shocks or nausea-producing drugs. Therapeutic outcome is measured by the failure of the eliciting stimulus to arouse the undesired conditioned response at a physiological or behavioral level.

Treatment of a transvestite by this approach consisted of first recording the patient's sexual arousal in terms of frequency and latency of erections. Arousal occurred not only to the photo of a nude female, but equally to items of female clothing that the patient wore when he dressed in "drag." Each item of clothing was successively paired with painful electric shocks. By the end of fifteen sessions, none of the items of clothing elicited an erection, but the appropriate heterosexual response to the body of a woman—not counterconditioned—still produced sexual arousal (Marks & Gelder, 1967).

In some cases aversive counterconditioning has been used with considerable success with alcoholics. One investigator reported complete abstinence in all but one of twenty-six clients over a period ranging from eight to fifteen months following counterconditioning (Blake, 1967). However, other evaluation studies of aversive conditioning with alcoholics, as well as such therapy with excessive smokers, have shown only mixed success. The obvious problem limiting the clinical effectiveness of these aversive conditioning techniques is that humans can easily discriminate between "unsafe" therapy-laboratory situations and situations outside where it is once again "safe" to drink, gamble, and "have a ball." It can even be argued that in the case of smokers these aversive techniques are themselves a cause of anxiety, thus strengthening the relief effect of smoking outside of the treatment situation.

One problem with the use of aversive therapy is getting the person to submit to it willingly (and even to pay to be tormented). Aversive therapy is not designed to encourage a person to endure it freely or come back for more. Especially if the positive, immediate gains of the "bad habit" are strong, the motivation to receive aversive stimulation will not be strong unless the person is impressed with long-term negative consequences of engaging in the undesirable behavior. Such "impression" involves education, indoctrination, and sometimes mass propaganda. It is also counteracted by those segments of society that depend for economic survival on the "bad habit"—liquor, tobacco, gambling industries, among others.

Positive Reinforcement

The judicious application of positive reinforcement of desired responses according to a systematic schedule has been successfully applied in the classroom, in penal and mental institutions, and in many other settings.

Even patients who have been totally mute for many years but are physically capable of speech have been trained to speak by the use of operant techniques (Isaacs, Thomas, & Goldiamond, 1960).

In one study making use of this technique it was found that by reinforcing a patient with pennies or by agreeing to write letters for the patient contingent on speech, it was possible gradually to shape what were at first primitive grunts. Further training gradually led to more complete words and finally to sentences. After sixteen training sessions, the speech behavior generalized to the patient's behavior on the ward: for the first time in two years he spoke to one of the attendants. When the attendants were also trained in reinforcement techniques, they were able to participate in further treatment, and eventually the patient was restored to full speech (Sherman, 1963).

Dramatic success has also been obtained in the application of operant conditioning procedures to the behavior problems of children with psychiatric disorders. The following is one such case.

The patient was a three-year-old boy who was hospitalized with a diagnosis of childhood schizophrenia. The child did not eat normally and lacked normal social and verbal behavior. He was given to ungovernable tantrums that included self-destructive behavior such as banging his head, slapping his face, pulling his hair, and scratching his face. He had had a cataract operation, and the wearing of glasses was essential for the development of normal vision. He refused to wear them, however, and broke pair after pair.

■ The photo above shows an early imitation session with Billy, who at seven could not talk at all and had been making life a nightmare for his parents with tantrums in which erratic, violent destructiveness alternated with fits of beating his head against the wall. He had been diagnosed as retarded by a series of experts consulted by his distraught parents. Below Billy and another boy are shown receiving immediate food reinforcement of social interactions. After several months, Billy was able to live at home and attend a special school. Two years later, he was doing first-grade reading and arithmetic and seemed happy, though his speech was often unclear and he still had some problems at home. (Photos by Allan Grant.)

To counteract this problem, the psychologists decided to use the technique of shaping. An attendant worked with the child in his room for two or three twenty-minute sessions each day. First the child was trained to expect a bit of candy or fruit at the clicking sound of a toy noisemaker. The noise of the click soon became a conditioned reinforcer. Then training began with empty eyeglass frames. The child was reinforced first for picking them up, then for holding them, then for carrying them around. Slowly and by successive approximation, he was reinforced for bringing the frames closer to his eyes. After a few weeks, he was putting the empty frames on his head at odd angles, and finally he was wearing them in the proper manner. With further training the child learned to wear his glasses up to twelve hours a day (Wolf, Risley, & Mees, 1964).

Operant reinforcement has also been effective in getting even chronically regressed psychotic patients to begin responding and thus become more receptive to treatment (Skinner, Solomon, & Lindsley, 1954).

Imitation of Models

Positive reinforcement alone can be quite satisfactory for strengthening behavior that already occurs some of the time, but it can be a long and tedious technique when new behaviors are to be learned. New responses, especially complex ones, can be acquired more easily if the person can observe and imitate a model. Imitation is often used in combination with positive reinforcement.

In one program, schizophrenic children were first treated for muteness by a variety of techniques, including reinforcement for imitation. First, the children were rewarded simply for making sounds. Later they were rewarded for vocalization only when the sound was similar to a "model" sound made by the therapist. When the children had learned to imitate sounds, rewards were given for duplicating words spoken by the therapist. By building on the children's growing repertoire of vocal behaviors, and their growing readiness to imitate, more intricate communicative and social behaviors were eventually established (Lovaas, 1968). ■

Such a therapeutic approach requires considerable patience and diligence on the part of the therapist. One of the autistic children with whom Ivar Lovaas worked required 90,000 trials before he could reliably label two objects.

Even severely withdrawn preschool-age children can learn new behavior that they see others rewarded for in a film. A group who saw interaction between children positively reinforced later showed marked increases in social interaction, as compared with a comparable group of withdrawn children exposed to a control film (O'Connor, 1969).

In the treatment of phobias (such as the fear of snakes, which is often used in research on therapeutic effectiveness) the therapist will first demonstrate fearless approach behavior at a relatively minor level, such as approaching the snake's cage or touching the snake. The client is then aided, through demonstration and supportive encouragement, to model the therapist's behavior. Gradually the approach behaviors are increased to the point where the client can pick the snake up and let it crawl freely over him or her. ● At no time is the client forced to perform any behavior, and, as in desensitization, if a request is met with overt resistance, the therapist returns to the previously successful approach behavior and starts over again. The remarkable power of this form of participant modeling can be seen in the research of Albert Bandura and his colleagues (1970) depicted in the graph. ◆ (p. 530) It compares live modeling with symbolic modeling (self-managed exposure to a film of models fearlessly handling a large snake), desensitization, and a control (without any form of therapeutic intervention). Snake phobia was eliminated in eleven of the twelve subjects in the participant modeling group.

Token Economies

In recent years, an increasing number of mental hospitals in this country have employed what are referred to as "token economies." This technique may be classified as a special case of posi-

● The subject shown here first watched a model safely make a graduated series of snake-approach responses, then repeated them herself. She eventually was able to pick up the snake and let it crawl about on her.

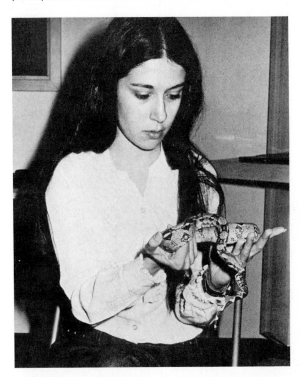

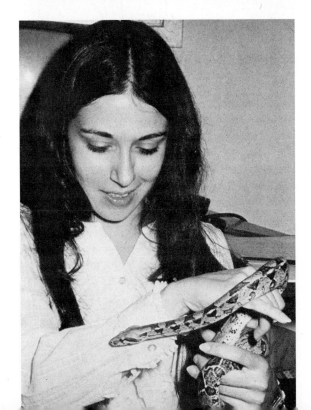

tive reinforcement. Patients are tangibly rewarded for engaging in such socially constructive activities as maintaining personal cleanliness, arriving on time for meals, and performing assigned tasks. Payment consists of tokens (such as poker chips) that may be used later to "purchase" such luxuries as more elegant dining facilities, increased television time, private sleeping accommodations, and weekend passes.

Hospital administrators have found that token economies can often be quite effective in eliciting desired behaviors, even on the part of rather severely disturbed patients. It usually is necessary to start gradually, however. Thus patients may initially be rewarded for merely approaching nurses or other patients. Then, through a process of shaping, it may be possible to coax them to strike up conversations among themselves. Finally, they can be rewarded for more complex forms of interpersonal interaction as well as for other more tangible activities.

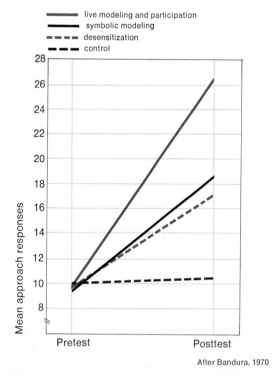

After Bandura, 1970

◆ APPROACH RESPONSES IN PARTICIPANT MODELING AND OTHER CONDITIONS

The effectiveness of token economies has been amply demonstrated in a number of studies. Patients who have led a virtually vegetative existence for years have become responsive, even performing previously neglected tasks with dedication and enthusiasm.

A team of therapists conducted a series of experiments in which they systematically tested the effectiveness of a token economy. Their patients were chronic psychotics who had been given hospital work assignments that they had performed inefficiently and haphazardly, often not showing up at all. A token economy was instituted, in which patients were rewarded for performing their jobs. Dramatic changes in conscientiousness occurred. Patients began to report for work reliably and promptly. No requests were made for time off, though it was made clear that such requests would automatically be granted.

To test the motivating power of the token economy directly, the researchers decided to make continued reinforcement contingent on the patients' willingness to switch to nonpreferred jobs when reinforcement was changed. To the extent that the patients did this, the token economy was controlling the choice of job.

The results were convincing. Patients immediately switched to nonpreferred jobs when it was made clear that continued reward depended on their doing so. In a final test of the motivating power of the tokens, the investigators reversed the contingencies again and patients were now reinforced for performing their originally preferred jobs. Again the patients switched promptly to the rewarded tasks (Ayllon & Azrin, 1965).

The control used in this research is quite common in behavioral studies. Evaluating the effectiveness of a token economy by reinforcing first preferred jobs, then nonpreferred jobs, and finally preferred jobs again provides a good illustration of the "A-B-A" experimental design. The experimental condition whose results are to be tested is instituted, then systematically altered, and finally restored. Each patient serves as his or her own control. In this case, the patients' choice of jobs could be reliably attributed to the reinforcement itself and not to "job satisfaction" or other factors. Employing this same design, Ayllon and Azrin found that when tokens were given automatically, regardless of job performance, or when rewards were made freely available independently of tokens, there was a marked *decrease* in the work patients did.

Patient motivation can be noted from a tabulation of what they freely chose to buy with their earned tokens. Privacy was easily the most sought-after commodity, followed by commissary goods and leaves from the ward. Individual differences in preference were largely limited to the rankings of these three major items. Very few tokens were spent for interviews with the hospital staff or for religious or recreational opportunities. (See *P&L* Close-up below.)

Close-up
Token Economies in Action

A token economy operant conditioning program was first established at Camarillo State Hospital (California) in 1966. It was so successful in achieving its objectives that within a few years eleven such programs were functioning on various wards. Some of the behavioral criteria on the basis of which tokens are given or taken away are listed below (from Montgomery & McBurney, 1970).

1. Neat and well-groomed at all appropriate times.
2. Aware of personal hygiene needs such as showers and able to bathe with no supervision.
3. Men shaved before breakfast.
4. Girls made-up efficiently and hair arranged before breakfast. Suitable attire.
5. Table manners socially acceptable.
6. Little swearing, hitting, spitting.
7. Takes turns in all situations.
8. Behavior socially appropriate. Able to go about grounds freely. Can go off grounds in a group with acceptable manners. Aware of community customs and procedures or learning them.
9. Puts own clothing in laundry and puts it away.

10. Locker neat at all times.
11. Makes own bed and cleans dormitory including floors swept and mopped and toilet cleaned with no supervision before A.M. shift arrives.
12. Helps with unit chores and less skilled people without being asked.
13. Has work detail or attends school or Work Training Center regularly.

In general, it can be said that most hospital token economies reinforce appropriate grooming, socializing, and carrying out on-ward assignments, as well as engaging in self-directed behaviors. Undesirable behaviors cost the patient tokens, so it is expected that such behaviors will decrease in frequency. The effectiveness of a token economy recently put into practice at the Palo Alto Veterans Hospital is apparent in the graph that shows behavior changes over ten months from before to after the introduction of a token economy (Rouse & Reilly, 1974). A noteworthy feature of this program was the formation of a patient ward government that allowed patients to participate in the management and direction of their own token economy, and eventually to establish their own "satellite" home off the grounds of the hospital.

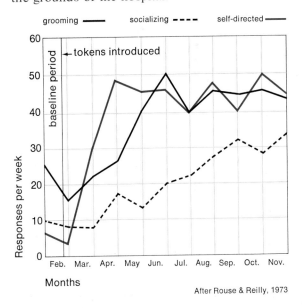

After Rouse & Reilly, 1973

In the near future, we can expect to see widespread application of the principles of token economies in many other settings. For example, they have been used in a number of schools, and some proponents see them as eventually replacing the present grading system. From the learner's point of view, token economies have the value of: (a) providing an unambiguous indication of approval, (b) introducing consistency and predictability into the situation by making clear exactly what must be done to achieve what effect, (c) not being dependent on the mood or personal values of the teacher or authority figure, (d) allowing the learner to have complete freedom in determining what he or she is willing to work for (among the options available), and (e) guaranteeing that even minimally appropriate responses will be observed by someone, acknowledged, and reinforced; thus putting success and reinforcement within reach for everyone in the group.

Critics, however, shudder at the encroachment of a system based on the profit motive, maintaining that learning will come to be motivated by a "marketplace mentality" in which effort is expended only for extrinsic rewards and children have no opportunity to learn to value the joy of discovery or intellectual mastery for its own sake. As currently being used in some prisons, behavior modification in the form of token economies has the objectionable aspect of first depriving prisoners of virtually everything. Then they may earn the "privilege" of a shower, hot meals, a decent bed, books, exercise, and so forth. Given extreme deprivation, it is possible to convert anything into "positive reinforcement" — such as the opportunity to eat, sleep, or even go to the toilet. It is being strongly debated whether under conditions of coercion and deprivation, reinforcement contingencies can really be said to be *positive*.

Evaluation of Behavioristic Therapies

Reports on the effectiveness of behavioristic therapies are generally quite favorable, with a success rate typically between 75 and 90 percent.

As compared with other therapies, a number of advantages can be noted for the behavioristic therapies. They are more tied to, and receptive to, empirical research than analytic therapies have been. Because of their emphasis on treating specific symptoms, behavioristic therapies get results in a much shorter time than traditional therapies. This means faster relief and financial savings for the client and more clients treated by a given therapist. Since the therapy depends on explicit principles of learning, and not on the personality, interpersonal skill, or interpretive ability of the therapist, training is easier and shorter and can be mastered by technicians (teachers, nurses, supervisors, etc.) or *paraprofessionals*.

Critical evaluation of behavioristic therapy, however, also discloses a number of qualifications as to its effectiveness, its methods, and its unintended consequences.

There are a few studies that assess long-term effectiveness of this treatment — that is, follow-ups more than a year after therapy. In the study most often cited as proof of behavioristic therapy's 90 percent cure rate (Wolpe, 1960), there is a major source of sampling bias. Included in the final results are only clients who had at least fifteen therapeutic sessions. All those who dropped out during the first fourteen sessions are excluded, thus stacking the cards in favor of a high success rate.

More serious criticism is raised as to what constitutes the effective independent variable in "behavior therapy" (Breger & McGaugh, 1965). It appears that in many cases, behaviorists do not rely solely on conditioning procedures, but "mix in" more traditional counseling techniques as well, such as discussion of how clients can stand up for themselves and gain control of their relationships with other people (Weitzman, 1967).

Other critics maintain that the most effective tools in the "black bag" of the behaviorists are actually cognitive manipulations—that the primary operants are not overt behaviors at all but cognitions—images, feelings of anxiety, anticipations, and evaluations. Thus it can be argued that behavioristic therapy may work not because the reinforcement manipulates and maintains particular overt responses, as claimed, but because individuals, perhaps for the first time, have a predictable environment in which they can clearly see the consequences of their behavior and thus can use environmental resources to get what they want.

A different criticism of this therapeutic approach centers on the undesirable *indirect* learning that behavior therapy may encourage and the values that may be taught by it. For example, if reward is given only for surface behavior and conformity to what someone else decides is "good," the individual may be getting taught to value outer appearance, blind conformity to the socially accepted norms, social approval at the expense of self-approval, and action at the expense of thinking or feeling (D. Grossman, 1968).

Perhaps the most important problem facing behavioristic therapy is the failure of successful behavior modification in the treatment setting to *generalize* to settings in the person's natural environment. Such relapse limits the utility of the treatment since the person must live within his or her own community and not forever in the laboratory, clinic, school, hospital, or other institution.

For more effective transfer of therapeutic learning to natural settings it has been suggested that the following principles be observed: (a) therapeutic stimuli should be representative of and similar to those encountered in the patient's environment; (b) the therapeutic settings should be varied and some should resemble or actually be the patient's natural environment; (c) more than one therapist should establish the conditioning procedures and reinforcement contingencies; (d) the therapeutic response should be put on a partial reinforcement schedule and be overlearned; and (e) some of the original learning should be *without* the patient's awareness so it is not under his or her cognitive control (Goldstein et al. 1966, Gruber, 1971).

Concern about the limitations of behavioristic therapy should not be allowed to obscure the positive and unique contributions of this approach. Behavioristic therapy has had considerable success, promises more, and appears to be the best method available for treatment of inhibitory anxiety and specific phobias. There is no reason why behavior therapy should be expected to cure every psychological disorder, just as there is no reason to expect penicillin to cure cancer.

The behaviorist view of therapy, then, is one of optimism, of faith in the power of the principles of learning and in treatment derived from research and not merely from theory, speculation, and case studies. The newer approach of the social learning theorists goes beyond the assertion of the hard-line behaviorists that any behavior (normal or abnormal) can be brought under environmental control. It is possible as an outcome of the therapeutic process for the environment to be affected by, and to some degree controlled by the person. To that extent, the person develops a sense of mastery and effectance, and in so doing overcomes feelings of powerlessness and is on the way to a happier, more productive life.

The Existential-Humanistic Basis of Therapy

The humanistic movement has been called a "third force" in psychology because it grew out of a reaction against both the pessimistic view of human nature offered by psychoanalytic theory and the mechanistic view offered by behaviorism. At the time the humanistic movement was forming in the United States, similar viewpoints, which came to be known collectively as *existentialism*, had already gained acceptance on the continent of Europe. Existentialism was primarily the result of a marked dissatisfaction with traditional philosophy as superficial, academic, and remote from life (Kaufman, 1956).

One important factor that unites humanism and existentialism is the acceptance by both of *phenomenology* as a philosophic base. The fundamental proposition of phenomenology is that all human knowledge is based on experience, and the approach used is to maintain an openness and readiness for acceptance of the data of experience as they emerge. The observer attempts to put aside all preconceived notions concerning a person or event, all judgments of value, cause-and-effect relationships, and even the subject-object distinction. In relation to psychotherapy, this approach is seen as an openness to and acceptance of the patient as an emerging person. That person, as currently constituted in the here-and-now, is what must be attended to, understood, and treated.

The term *existentialism* comes from the Latin *existere* — "to emerge or stand out" — which fully describes the focus on the *existing* human being as he or she is emerging or becoming. Existentialism is an attempt to understand our unique position in the universe: feelings of love, hate, anguish; self-awareness; and the knowledge of one's own imminent death.

Although there is much disagreement among the proponents of this view — a tribute to the individualistic emphasis of existentialism — there are some common themes. First of all, there is a sharp criticism of the scientific approach with its dehumanizing, rigid methodology. The person is seen not as some static entity, but as a continual process, a process of becoming. Although environment and heredity place certain restrictions on the process of becoming, we remain always free to choose what we will become by creating our own values and committing ourselves to them through our decisions. However, along with this freedom to choose comes the burden of responsibility. Since we are never fully aware of all the implications of our actions, we experience anxiety and despair. We also suffer from guilt over lost opportunities to achieve our full potential.

These apparently negative aspects of existentialism have perhaps been overemphasized by naive critics. This negativism can be seen, however, as an attempt to jar us out of our complacency and conformism. It encourages us to face the reality of our own existence without seeking refuge in theistic or monolithic systems where some higher authority will dictate how we should live. It is felt that forcing us to confront the fact that we are continuously responsible for choosing and creating is the only antidote against the despair of modern times.

The humanistic and existential approaches are alike in many respects. Both view human beings as the source of values and focus on their potential for self-actualization. Both stress the concepts of responsibility, freedom, and commitment.

There are several points of disagreement, however. In accordance with the flavor of the American outlook, humanistic psychology is much more optimistic and positive than European existentialism. We are seen as not only responsible for actualizing our potential, but as having a positive drive and need to do so. The humanistic view also places heavy emphasis on the value, dignity, and worth of the individual with a correlated focus on positive aspects of human behavior such as love, joy, creativity, friendship, play, fun, ecstasy, and so forth.

As we turn to the therapeutic application of existentialism and humanism, we find considerable diversification in method and style. Existentialism is not a technique, theory, or systematic explanation of human behavior, but rather an attitude one maintains toward oneself and others. Thus we may find therapists trained in psychoanalysis and using such psychoanalytic techniques as free association and dream analysis still calling themselves existential psychotherapists because they share that basic attitude and value orientation. Similarly, when we turn to Jungian or Adlerian therapists, it is difficult to say whether they should be called neo-Freudians or existential humanists, for as we have seen, both Jung and Adler dealt with existential concerns and both had a deep respect for the integrity of the individual's existence.

Existential Psychotherapy

The existential movement in psychiatry was formed by a number of Europeans who were dissatisfied with orthodox psychoanalysis. Realizing that the most common problem of a modern individual was a feeling of alienation from the world, a loss of the sense of identity or belonging, these psychiatrists and psychologists felt that psychoanalysis often tended to increase the problem by fragmenting the individual still further. For them, the basic reality was the individual's experience rather than physical events.

One school of existential analysis, called *logotherapy*, focuses on the need to see meaning in one's own life. The "will-to-meaning" is regarded as the most human phenomenon of all. This school emphasizes Nietzsche's statement, "He who knows a Why of living surmounts almost every How." The human being finds the "Why" through self-realization, which involves both freedom to choose a course of action and responsibility to choose in such a way as to further spiritual values. Thus logotherapy lays particular stress on the development of spiritual and ethical values (Weisskopf-Joelson, 1955).

Logotherapy is the only school of existential psychiatry to have evolved specific psychotherapeutic techniques. One such technique, called *paradoxical intention*, is found useful in the short-term treatment of obsessive-compulsive and phobic patients. Viktor Frankl, originator of logotherapy, speaks of the vicious circle in which the phobic person is caught. It is not so much the feared object or occurrence that concerns the patient, but the *fear of fear itself* and

the potential effects of such fear, such as fainting or heart attack. Frankl (1959) calls such phobic reactions a "flight from fear" and sees the patient as reacting to "the fearful expectation of the recurrence of the event." This expectation, however, triggers off exactly what the patient fears will happen: a phobic reaction. Paradoxical intention is a technique for dealing with this anticipatory anxiety by encouraging the patient "to do, or wish to happen, the very thing he fears." There is an obvious similarity between this technique and implosive therapy discussed previously. Here, however, we find the chief responsibility for applying the technique rests with the patient rather than the therapist. Furthermore, paradoxical intention is deliberately formulated in as humorous a manner as possible, since humor involves self-detachment.

It is not felt that paradoxical intention or even logotherapy itself is applicable to all individuals seeking therapy, nor is it believed that any such techniques will have long-lasting effects unless the individual also establishes a commitment to purposeful goals.

Humanistic Psychotherapy

One of the clearest and earliest examples of a humanistic approach to treatment is *client-centered therapy*, developed originally by Carl Rogers in the 1940s. The basic tenet of this method, that the therapist remain *nondirective* throughout the course of therapy, is explained quite beautifully in this quote of an Oriental teacher, Lao-tse:

"To interfere with the life of things means to harm both them and one's self. He who imposes himself has the small, manifest might; he who does not impose himself has the great secret might. . . . The perfected man does not interfere in the life of beings, he does not impose himself on them, but he helps all beings to their freedom." (in Buber, 1957, pp. 54–55)

This nondirective therapy is based on the premise that individuals who are sufficiently motivated can work through their own problem if they can become free enough from self-deception and fear to recognize their problem for what it is. Accordingly, they are encouraged in a face-to-face interview to talk freely about anything that troubles them and to approach it in any way they like. The therapist neither praises nor blames but accepts whatever is said, perhaps rephrasing it or helping clients to clarify their own reactions, paying specific attention to both the overt feelings expressed and the covert ones being experienced.

The theory of nondirective therapy is that by "talking it out" in a permissive atmosphere, clients will come to see certain relationships between their feelings and behavior. Therapy is regarded as a "growth process" in which clients utilize their own potentialities to achieve a more mature level of emotional adjustment. From the beginning, they are responsible for their own behavior and decisions, as well as for the course of therapy. The idea that "the doctor knows best" is unheard of in this form of therapy. Superficially the role of the therapist is that of "reflecting" the feelings the client has expressed. Actually, however, the therapist's attitude of acceptance and concern is probably of greatest significance, for it helps the client develop the self-confidence and strength to handle difficult problems of adjustment.

The following case illustrates the nature of nondirective therapy and also the characteristic gradual change from negative feelings to positive ones.

Mary Jane Tilden (a pseudonym), age twenty, was brought to the counselor by her mother. She seemed to be retreating from life, spending the major portion of her days sleeping, listening to the radio, or brooding. She had given up her job and all social contacts; she rarely bothered even to dress. Her first interview was completely negative except that she did decide to return for further treatment.

Miss T.: *". . . It's just when I compare myself to the other girls it seems—I don't feel at all up*

to it . . . they seem to be so normal in everything they did and they were unfolding the way everybody should unfold in this world. And when I thought about myself, I thought, 'Well, my gosh! I'm not even coming near it.' And it was just such a blow that—I just started to realize that I wasn't coming along the way I should—I mean I just wasn't progressing."

Counselor: *"It wasn't that you were jealous, but that you gradually realized that here they were ready for a new part of their life and you just weren't ready for it. . . ."*

T: *". . . There's one thing I can't quite make up my mind—I've tried to figure it out—well, what is it, when I get into a rut like this, what is it that I really want? And when I examine myself I can't figure out what I really want. It's only by looking at what other people want that I think, well, maybe that's what I want. It's a very odd thing, and I don't like it. That's what makes me feel—that it's—a—that I can't do what I want to do because I don't really know what I want."*

C: *"You feel that, so far, the best you have been able to achieve along that line is just to take a goal that seems to be good for somebody else. But that you don't feel that there's any real gain that you are sure you want. . . ."*

During the fifth interview Miss Tilden discussed her first tentative steps toward improving her situation, but with many reservations. By the eighth interview, she was beginning to look at her behavior more objectively.

T: *". . . When you're in a family where your brother has gone to college and everybody has a good mind, I wonder if it is right to see that I am as I am and I can't achieve such things. I've always tried to be what others thought I should be, but now I'm wondering whether I shouldn't just see that I am what I am."*

C: *"You feel that in the past you lived by others' standards and you are not sure just what is the right thing to do, but you're beginning to feel that the best thing for you is simply to accept yourself as you are. . . ."*

T: *"Well, I guess that is so. I don't see what it is that has changed me so much. Yes, I do. These talks have helped a lot, and then the books that I've read. Well, I've just noticed such a difference. I find that when I feel things, even when I feel hate, I don't care. I don't mind. I feel more free somehow. I don't feel guilty about things." (Rogers, 1947)*

In the course of therapy, the client made considerable progress in working out for herself a new understanding and acceptance of herself and hence a more satisfactory adjustment to life. This did not come suddenly and there were setbacks, but the overall progress was unmistakable. Note that the counselor did not at any time force the issue, nor did he introduce any new ideas, give her advice, or employ reassurance or moral exhortation. What he tried to do was to reflect and clarify the client's own feelings and attitudes in such a way that she could understand herself better.

This may sound like an easy process, but it takes a good deal of restraint to keep from offering suggestions or interpretations and thereby imposing one's own value system on the client. Many students have remarked that not only does client-centered therapy appear to be simple to do, it also seems simplistic; how could something as inane as reflecting back the feelings of the client be helpful? Perhaps for a person who has come to the therapist specifically to be told what to do, this may be a valid criticism, if only for the reason that the person's expectations concerning the course of therapy have been shown to be related to therapeutic gains. However, for people caught up in emotional stress and mental anguish, what is experienced is not the cold reflection of a clear mirror but the warm support and extremely human concern of a good listener who believes they can help themselves.

It should also be mentioned that this nonjudgmental attitude toward others need not be restricted to therapy. Reflecting the feelings of others and expressing one's own feelings have been shown to be very effective ways of communicating in many types of interpersonal relationships (see Ivey, 1971).

An important aspect of client-centered therapy has been the willingness to submit its techniques to investigation and to modify the approach in light of such experience. In fact, Rogers was the first clinician to tape-record his sessions, which led to the first meaningful analysis of the process of therapy. Out of such a context developed the idea of responding to and clarifying the client's emotions instead of just the words being used. Similarly, in later work with schizophrenics it was found that in contrast to the client-centered approach with neurotics, greater gains were achieved when the therapist took an active, self-expressive stance in therapy, making his or her own inner experiencing, as well as the client's, part of the therapeutic process (Meader & Rogers, 1973).

Such a shift in emphasis more clearly represents the existential concept of "interpersonal encounter" where therapists are free to be themselves and to trust in their own experiencing, while at the same time respecting and helping clients to trust their own inner feelings. This approach to the client has been further developed by Eugene Gendlin (1973) into what he calls *experiential psychotherapy*, which may well represent the integration of humanistic and existential concerns as described earlier.

In summary, we find that in the existential-humanistic view of human nature, there is no attribution of any basic *essence*, only meaningful existence that influences what is being experienced and expressed. The presence of irrational motives, biological drives, or social conditioning is not rejected but is secondary to the importance of an individual with the freedom to choose how to behave. As Frankl suggests, regardless of the restrictions imposed on us, we still have the freedom to choose how we will face these limitations. Even in the most extreme conditions of suffering—such as Frankl himself experienced in a Nazi concentration camp—where there is human existence, we may discover meaning and new facets to our being.

Evaluating Psychotherapeutic Effectiveness

The therapist's theoretical perspective influences his or her basic orientation to the nature of what the "problem" is — whether it is "mental illness," "emotional conflict," "inappropriate reinforcement contingencies," or "self-alienation." Each therapist is thus *set* to interpret a given behavioral event in terms that are consistent or harmonious with the guiding assumptions of a particular theoretical framework — while ignoring the alternatives.

Just as a dentist would not treat intestinal disorders, nor an internist treat dental problems, so a psychotherapist treats only those patients whose "problems" *fit* his or her specific training. But since the indications of psychological "problems" are behavioral events that cannot be as neatly categorized, isolated, and objectively assessed as can medical problems, different therapists treat the same manifest problem according to their *perception* of its origins.

Patients, then, must make a tacit contract with the *particular* therapist of their choice to be "sick" in a way the therapist can treat. It is not unreasonable to suggest that the first task of the patient is learning to play the correct role in the therapist's scenario. This requires learning to use the special language of the therapist to describe symptoms and past events. It may also involve a kind of conversion to the therapist's belief system, enabling the patient to notice and label as "significant" and "relevant" the same events and variables the therapist does.

Using such reasoning, some critics have contended that therapists are *persuaders* who sell their world view and theory of behavior to their patients (Frank, 1961). Patients may be judged "cured" when they exchange their original assumptions and values for those the therapist accepts as valid and meaningful — or at least talk as if they do.

The psychoanalyst's patient thereby becomes a "historian," discovering historical precedents, and the historical continuity that links present ills to their past origins. The behaviorist's client becomes sensitized to the future environmental consequences of current behavioral responses and to attaching an S to every R and an R to every S. The self-actualized patient emerges from existential-humanistic therapy focusing on the present, on the here-and-now of existing, being, and becoming, while talking about "sharing, meaning, choice, and freedom." Finally, the person treated by the biologically oriented therapist comes away from "successful" treatment with the attitude that "doctor knows best," and with little feeling of responsibility for the "problem" or its alleviation.

Who Gets Credit for the Cure?

"The neuroses are 'cured' by Christian Science, osteopathy, chiropractic, nux vomica and bromides, benzedrine sulfate, change of scene, a blow on the head, and psychoanalysis, which probably means that none of these has yet established its real worth in the matter . . . moreover since many neuroses are self-limited, anyone who spends two years with a patient gets credit for the operation of nature." (Myerson, 1939, p. 641)

This critique of psychotherapy has been extended by those who suggest that some patients improve even when "inexact interpretations" — that is, incorrect diagnoses — are made (Glover, 1966). It may be that the crucial element is having an authority figure provide *any* interpretation that indicates that one's problem is understandable by someone in a position to help. Therefore, it may not be the content of the different theoretical explanations that helps the patient, but that a socially respectable, normal representative of the community acknowledges that the patient's problem "makes sense" and can be treated. There is much comfort in the knowledge that for what ails us there is an explanation, a label; and there are other people who are or once were in a similar state.

There is no available evidence to suggest that any particular form of therapy can take the credit for being more effective than the others. Indeed, there is some evidence to support the conclusion that none of the therapies is more effective *in general* than any other and that collectively they are not better than no therapy at all! However, it is also the case that some individuals with certain types of problems can be helped best by a particular type of therapy and therapist and would get worse without any therapy.

In his analysis of how psychotherapy fails, Richard Stuart (1970) concluded from his review of twenty-one studies that "it can be said that persons who enter psychotherapy do so with a modest chance of marked improvement, a much greater chance of experiencing little or no change, and a modest chance of experiencing a deterioration in their functioning" (p. 50). The British psychologist Hans Eysenck created a furor some years ago (1952) by reporting that persons receiving no therapy still had a higher cure rate than did those receiving either psychoanalysis or eclectic therapy (a combination of treatments). A later study that was not open to some of the criticisms leveled at Eysenck's research shows that conclusion to be a bit too extreme—but not far from the truth. It was found that no therapy is *as good as* psychotherapy (Bergin, 1966). Across seven studies that compared changes in untreated subjects with those given psychotherapy, the *average* amount of change was the same. However, the *variability* in outcome was greater among those who had been given a treatment: some got much better, while others got worse or did not change. Those people who improved considerably with therapy might not have done so without it, so for them psychotherapy deserves credit for their "cure." For others, the mere passage of time was sufficient to "heal all wounds."

To what extent do patients perceive themselves as involved in and sharing responsibility for the improvement in functioning? This unanswered question deserves to be investigated because if the therapist or the particular therapy is given all the credit, then patients will be forced to return for more whenever comparable problems come up in the future. This, in part, may be the explanation for the high "relapse" rate of many psychological disorders.

It is also well to ask who (if anyone) should take the blame for those patients whose condition deteriorates following therapy. Is it conceivable that psychotherapists could say, as do some surgeons, that the operation (therapy) was a success, even though the patient died (got crazier)? When therapy does not work, is that negative information utilized constructively to change the therapeutic procedure or some elements of the theory so it will work better in the future? There is no systematic evidence to support such a view. Rather, one might suspect that each noncure is a failure for the therapist, who would prefer to forget it or account for it in terms of the operation of factors outside therapeutic control. (See *P&L* Close-up below.)

Close-up

One Smile from the Therapist Is Worth a Thousand Words

Research has shown that the degree of change in a patient is positively correlated with the therapist's: (a) length of experience, (b) degree of self-confidence, and (c) similarity to the patient (Stuart, 1970). The therapist's failure to openly show a sufficient level of empathy and understanding of the patient has been shown to be a source of patient deterioration (Truax, 1963).

But should therapists conceal their feelings from patients or share them? Freud recommended that the therapist should "be impenetrable to the patient, and, like a mirror, reflect nothing but what is shown to him" (1956, p. 331). He urged psychotherapists to take as their model "the surgeon who puts aside all his own feelings, including that of human sympathy, and concentrates his mind on one single purpose; that of performing the operation as skillfully as possible" (p. 327).

Such a stance may not be the ideal one for a modern therapist to adopt in counseling young people today who do not want to interact with an aloof, authoritarian surgeon in therapist's clothing. It has been suggested that "it is not the therapist's training and what he does as a therapist that is important, but rather his ability to be human that is of prime concern" (Dreyfus, 1967, p. 575). "Humanness" in a therapist goes beyond the *ability* to be supportive, kind, and warm; it entails sharing with the patient what the therapist is feeling, be it despair, sadness, joy, anger, or guilt.

Each participant in the patient-therapist relationship must give and take something. Among the Hasidic Orthodox Jewish sect, the spiritual leader and teacher, or Zaddik, played a role that included teaching of information, but one that also encouraged a close personal relationship to develop between the young student and the teacher. Kopp (1969) has suggested that modern therapists could well benefit from adopting the dual role of the Zaddik.

The impact of therapist authenticity is revealed in this excerpt from a group therapy session. The group was discussing the therapist's insistence on ending the session promptly as a sign of his not caring. Bob, who was also in individual therapy with another therapist, interrupted to say why he thought the individual therapist cared:

Bob: "She does care about me because we run over. Sometimes we go an hour or an hour and fifteen minutes. When she ends our session I never feel cut off. When you cut it at the end I wasn't used to it. . . . I think she gets involved. I think she cares."

Carol: "When you say involved, do you mean she cared about you?"

Bob: "I needed someone to care. I was going through something bad. It was bad. She had tears for me. It was the greatest thing that ever happened to me. Nobody's ever had tears for me." (Rustin, 1970, p. 47)

It may be that if therapists allowed themselves to feel and to express their feelings during psychotherapy that the outcome would be as good for them personally as for the patients. The "detached concern" model of therapy may make it easier for a hard-working therapist to get through a day of listening to other people's problems, but we are reminded that the suicide rate among psychiatrists is extraordinarily high. A smile, a tear might feel good for them too.

Judging Success in Therapy

It seems obvious that therapists are not the best judges of their own success. They want to see themselves as competent and effective. Besides tending to see what they want to see, they can inflate their "cure rate" by unknowingly encouraging difficult patients to terminate therapy, or by using vague criteria of "cure." But parents or friends who want to see improvement in the patient may also tend to "see" it, and patients who want to please their therapist will report that they feel they are being helped. Who can be close enough to the individual to evaluate what has really happened to him or her, yet objective enough not to have a bias? This is a perplexing, unsolved problem.

Changes as a result of therapy are usually assessed by various means, such as: (a) the therapist's overall impressions of change, (b) personality test scores, (c) patient interview behavior, (d) reports by friends or relatives, (e) patient self-reports, (f) patient attitudes, and (g) selected overt behaviors of the patient. But changes in verbal attitudes are not highly correlated with changes in actual behavior, and interview behavior or a score on a personality test is not necessarily a valid predictor of how the individual will behave in other situations. What measures can you trust? In addition, the same patient may be judged as improved or not improved depending on the criteria used.

In one case a hospitalized patient who had refused to eat with the others in the group began to put two to four bottles of milk on his tray and drink it with the others. The therapist regarded this behavior as a sign of improvement, but a psychiatric consultant held that it showed regression to the infantile level (Luchins, 1960).

Whatever the measures used, the content that is looked at (the kind of change looked for) tends to be in terms of what the particular therapist was trying to achieve, be it greater insight, removal of an annoying habit, assertiveness, self-actualization, or whatever. The goals of a particular therapy sequence are set partly by the therapist's concepts, partly by what the patient is seeking, and partly by time and cost considerations. "Successfully" making a patient more manageable is hardly the same as "successfully" enabling a person to be a self-directing, responsible citizen. Thus even with an objective, unbiased judge, the answers that are found will depend on previous answers to a host of definitional and procedural questions.

Still another problem in judging the effects of therapy is the lack of adequate controls. Until recently, therapists typically assumed that their efforts were worthwhile because they observed success in a portion of the cases they treated. The flaw in this assumption points up one of the basic requirements of any evaluative research design: the necessity for appropriate controls and control groups. For if people often improve without any formal treatment at all, we do not know whether the specific treatment was the primary causal variable in any group of cures.

The solution for assessing the efficacy of a given treatment is the same as it is for observing the effect of any experimental variable. How much change can be attributed to the treatment over and above a *base rate* of change in an untreated control group? A therapist who believes that a particular form of treatment achieves results will be reluctant to assign suffering people to control groups. Yet without adequate controls, there is no way to be sure that the therapy was responsible for recovery; perhaps the patients would have recovered simply with the passage of time.

All these are reasons why we do not know more than we currently do about the actual effects of the various therapies with different individuals and different kinds of problems. Yet the need for not only objective, stringent, explicitly formulated *criteria for therapeutic effectiveness* but also independently assessed and well-controlled *evaluative studies* represents one of the most pressing needs facing clinical psychology and psychiatry.

Therapeutic Groups

Formal psychotherapy is typically practiced on either an individual or a group basis. In individual psychotherapy, the interaction is restricted to the therapist and the person seeking therapy. Such one-to-one approaches to therapy have been criticized because of their limited applicability, exclusiveness, and questionable effectiveness. Any treatment that requires special techniques administered by professionally trained therapists on a one-to-one basis over a long period of time is inherently restricted in usefulness. The training of therapists is expensive and lengthy and requires in turn a professional staff of teachers. This minimizes the number of therapists available. Also, all of the therapies described demand special sensitivity and complex intellectual skills on the part of the therapist. These requirements make inevitable considerable variability in effectiveness even between therapists who are using the same approach. Nor is it clear to what extent the therapist's expectations come to shape the client into discovering what the therapist's theory says is there. Even in nondirective therapy, it is difficult for the therapist not to interact with clients, subtly reinforcing them for moving toward whatever criteria the therapist uses for making the determination of "improved" or "cured."

Conventional psychotherapies are unavailable or ineffective for many segments of the population: the poor, the uneducated, the unintelligent, the nonverbal, the addicted, the psychopathic, and the psychotic. Moreover, the persons who complete therapy fall into an even more exclusive group since up to 60 percent of those who consult psychotherapists discontinue treatment after several preliminary visits (Kirtner & Cartwright, 1958).

Finally, some critics have suggested that psychotherapy is an expensive way for people to purchase temporary friendships (Schofield, 1964). That the friendship aspect may be a crucial part of successful therapy for many patients is suggested by a study illustrating "student-friend power." Psychotic patients who were "treated" for five months by untrained, inexperienced college students showed greater gains than comparable patients given no treatment or given group treatment by a psychiatrist or a psychiatric social worker (Posner, 1966).

Such criticisms and new developments have had a positive effect in directing a greater interest toward group therapy, toward more practical, short-term training, toward therapy for "underprivileged" people, and toward a reexamination of the assumptions, values, and goals of psychotherapy. Notwithstanding these negative views, individual psychotherapy may still be the best treatment for certain people with certain problems when practiced by a perceptive and sensitive therapist.

Prior to World War II, practically all formal psychotherapy was practiced on an individual basis. With the added pressures for more qualified therapists and the necessity of training many small groups for bomber and submarine crews and such, there occurred an increased interest, during and after the war, in working with groups. The group approach to psychotherapy caught on rather rapidly when it became obvious that Freud's warnings concerning the danger inherent in working with groups was unfounded. In fact, group work is viewed by many as having a number of advantages over working with individuals.

Group Therapy

Group therapy provides both a chance to see that others have similar problems and a "safe" environment in which to explore one's real feelings.

A study conducted in one of the wards of a large Veterans Administration neuropsychiatric hospital compared group and individual therapy.

Four groups of patients were observed, each group containing an equal representation of nonpsychotics, short-term psychotics, and long-term psychotics. In one group, work and living arrangements, as well as psychotherapy, were group-oriented. The second group received group therapy but had individual work assignments, while the third group had individual therapy and individual work assignments. The

fourth group acted as controls; they were given the routine individual work assigned to all patients in the ward but received no therapy.

Patients in group therapy required the shortest time in treatment, with those in individual therapy requiring the longest time. Later adjustment was equally good, regardless of which kind of therapy they had and whether tranquilizers were used. The follow-up criterion of successfully holding a job after discharge revealed that all three therapy groups were significantly superior to the control group, with the first and third groups having the highest percentages of full-time employed members (Fairweather et al., 1960).

Certain individuals appear to derive less benefit than others from group therapy, and often as many as one fourth or one third of the members drop out of groups. In seeking an explanation for this, psychologists have identified three personality characteristics that apparently enable a person to derive maximum benefit from group as opposed to individual therapy. These are willingness to form relationships with others on an emotional level, ability to express rather than repress anger, and flexible perception of authority.

Thirty-two neuropsychiatric nurses and nursing assistants who had volunteered for a series of group sessions designed to aid them in their work by helping them gain insight into their own emotions were first seen in an interview designed to measure the three characteristics. Each was assigned a score for each characteristic. At the end of the fifteen-week course of sessions, each member was asked for her positive or negative reactions to the course. Nurses who tended to be emotionally "encapsulated" (very cautious about relating to others on an emotional level) were significantly less favorable in their reactions than were those not classed as encapsulated. Significant relationships were also found between scores on the other two characteristics and degree of satisfaction with results of the course. Moreover, a group especially selected from nurses high in the three personality characteristics achieved unusually fruitful results from the therapy sessions (Gruen, 1966).

It should be noted that individuals high in the three characteristics conducive to successful group therapy are not necessarily better adjusted as a whole than others. They may be neurotic in other respects, while the emotionally encapsulated may show a high degree of personality integration.

Experiential Groups

During the 1960s there occurred a virtual explosion in the number of groups offered in this country for psychological purposes. In his analysis of the evolution of small group work, Kurt Back (1974) sees this phenomenon as more of a social movement in the U.S. than a development solely within psychology. Whatever the reasons, the evolution of what have variously been called "sensitivity training (T-groups)," "growth groups," or, more generally, "encounter" groups is having a profound and perhaps lasting effect on our society.

The basic goal of encounter groups is to provide an intensive interpersonal experience in a small group, focusing on the interactions and feelings that emerge within the group setting itself in an atmosphere encouraging openness, honesty, emotional sensitivity, and expression. A major aspect is thus prompt and honest feedback. A member usually receives a good deal of encouragement and affection for qualities seen as good by the other group members and unequivocal criticism for qualities seen as bad. The leader may be either directive or nondirective.

Encounter groups, in the form of *T-groups*, were started over twenty years ago at the National Training Laboratories (Bethel, Maine) by advocates of the group dynamics approach to studying social psychology in an attempt to develop group and leadership skills. It is the unique pattern of social conditions facing Americans today, however, that has made the group movement catch on and has changed its focus to more general personal growth. Many individuals are experiencing a lack of intimate association with other people, a lack of any close community. Geographical and occupational mobility, family instability, the breakdown of extended families in which many relatives used to live nearby, the anonymity and impersonality imposed by mass education, mass transportation, mass communication, and huge housing complexes all contribute to the individual's sense of isolation. Encounter groups provide an opportunity for intimacy with others—even though limited in duration and without commitment to permanence.

In addition to the social-emotional experience, encounter groups also provide a needed opportunity for social comparison of oneself with one's peers. For many entering an encounter group, the "hidden agenda" begins with "Am I an acceptable person? Am I lovable, desirable? Am I as good as other people?"

Because they do fill a widely felt need, the proliferation of encounter groups on college campuses throughout the country is matched by their increasing use by church, business, and civic organizations. In such settings they are viewed not as therapy for the sick, but as a learning experience for those with problems as well as for all those who want to "grow"—to increase the joy they derive from life, to gain self-awareness, and perhaps to reexamine their values and life-style.

When we consider how much we conceal ourselves, the many masks we wear, and the general tendency to hide our true reactions, it is clear that honest group probing in a climate of openness can be an important learning experience. Group members can become more open-minded, more aware of their own needs and feelings, and more sensitive to the needs and feelings of others. They can also begin to understand better the sources of their responses to others and the reason for other people's reactions to them and can begin to build more honest and open relationships. (See *P&L* Close-up, p. 544.)

Close-up
Choosing an Experiential Group

The most important factor in determining what type of experiential group to join is your motivation for wanting to join. Basically, there are three types of experiential groups, although the differences are not that clear and depend a good deal on the leader (see Lakin, 1972).

The first type of group is for people wishing to bring about some immediate change in themselves. Perhaps they are lonely and feel unable to form emotional ties to others, or are seeking help with some emotional strain. Clearly, such individuals see the group as serving a therapeutic purpose and should consult a professional therapist in order to locate a group with clearly stated therapeutic aims.

A second type of group may be considered as a recreational group, where one can practice emotional expressiveness and experiment with different modes of behaving and perceiving. Such groups are for people who are already fairly effective and competent and do not need the group for corrective purposes. The encounter group, or personal growth group, typically serves this function and can be found through your local church, school, or "growth center."

The third type of group is specifically concerned with learning. Here the individual has some desire to gain an understanding of how groups function and develop, how the group influences the members, and how various factors inhibit or facilitate group functioning and communication. The T-group, or sensitivity group, focuses on such issues, and the National Training Laboratories at Bethel, Maine, or the Western Training Laboratory at Lake Arrowhead, California, can provide information concerning such groups in your area.

After determining what type of group you wish to join and locating such groups in the area, the next step is to contact the leader of a group. A personal interview is best, but a phone conversation will do. The first issue to explore is whether your goals and expectations match those of the leader. Secondly, you will want to get some indication of his or her qualifications.

A simple question such as "How long have you been leading groups?" or "How did you get started in leading groups?" should be sufficient. If the person seems defensive or does not answer the question, look elsewhere for a group. The next step is attending a group meeting. If you are disturbed by the leader's handling of the situation or the reactions of the members during this meeting, look for another group.

Another point to remember is never let yourself be pushed into doing something you are unwilling to do. This may take considerable effort, for groups can be incredibly coercive. Remember, your first responsibility is to *yourself*, not to the leader or the group. If you feel yourself being pushed and are unable to handle the situation, the best thing to do is to leave the group, telling the leader why you are doing so. Unless there are assurances forthcoming that satisfy you, do not return.

Some people would disagree with this advice, saying that you should stay with the group and see it through, and that sometimes we need to be pushed into doing things differently. Perhaps – but becoming a "psychological casualty" in such groups is a more serious concern. Ask yourself how much you are willing to pay in terms of your own mental stability for someone else's ill-founded theories of personal growth. The message here is to risk, but only when you feel yourself ready to risk. Despite our cautionary emphasis, the casualty is the exception, not the rule. Most group members find the encounter group experience beneficial or at least not harmful. Many students find that even in brief encounter group sessions, the experience and self-knowledge they derive can be a source of joy to them. Just to be able to reach out and touch another person and in return to share tenderness is for many students a new experience. It *ought* to be part of our everyday life, but until we can change our society to make that happen, experiential groups help form a bridge from isolation to independence to interdependence.

The stated goal of most encounter groups, however, is not to treat emotional problems but to enrich life for normal men and women. There is little doubt that such groups do attract people with emotional problems and ineffective coping skills. To complicate matters even further there is the problem of amateur leaders whose only "training" has been their own participation in such a group. Unlike professional psychotherapists, encounter group leaders need not be licensed or certified, and many lack the necessary skills for dealing with severe emotional problems. However well-intentioned, most such leaders take little responsibility for following up on the effects achieved during group sessions and are reluctant to allow professional investigators to examine their results. As a consequence of this, many of their methods tend to be useless; they even may include outright destructive verbal or physical assaults on members of the group.

In one of the few well-designed comparative studies in the field of encounter groups, it was found that groups with high risk in terms of casualties resulting from the group experience were characterized by highly aggressive stimulation and relatively high charisma on the part of their leader. In addition, there was no evidence to support the widely held notion that high risk is necessary in order to achieve a high level of growth. Quite the contrary, it was those leaders who were rated as high on *caring* dimensions and as supplying a cognitive framework on how to change who produced the highest positive outcomes and had the fewest casualties. Although it is evident that clear-cut positive results can and do occur for some participants of encounter groups, it is equally clear that a serious danger exists in terms of psychological casualities from such groups. Whether any single group has more of one kind of result than the other seems to depend considerably on the social-psychological attributes of the leader. (See *P&L* Close-up at right.)

Close-up

What Effects Do Encounter Groups Have?

Findings from one extremely well-designed and executed study evaluating the effectiveness of encounter groups indicate both the value and possible dangers of this "therapeutic" experience.

Groups were organized specifically for this study using sixteen experienced leaders, each a specialist in a different brand of encounter group approach, and 279 student volunteers who received course credit. Comparisons could be made with three types of control groups: students who registered but could not be accommodated due to scheduling problems and other reasons (38); interested friends of the participants who could not participate that term (31); and those students who attended fewer than half the sessions (35).

Assessment was both varied and intense. Self-reports and other ratings were taken before, during, immediately after, and six months after the group experience. Each participant described his or her attitudes, values, perceptions, motivations, self-esteem, social experiences, and other aspects of self and reactions to others and to the situation. Each student was also evaluated by the other participants, the group leader, and a sample of friends. The functioning of the group and the leader were evaluated by twenty-nine observers (two at each group session, rotated across all group leaders).

Processing of the massive amount of data collected is still going on, but the investigators point to the following illustrative findings:

1. Seventy-five percent of those in groups reported a positive change in themselves, most of them feeling the change was a lasting one. Ninety-five percent believed that the encounter group experience should become a regular part of the academic curriculum. There was a greater increase in self-esteem among a higher proportion of those who had the group experience.

2. Wide variations in outcome were found with different leaders and in different groups. In some groups, the experience had virtually no effect on the participants; in others, almost

every participant reported being affected by the experience. In some, however, the effect was mixed: 60 percent of the members in a given group changed, but as many were affected negatively as positively. Some groups had no dropouts; others had 40 percent quitting.

3. Group leaders varied considerably in the amount and style of stimulation and "leadership" they provided, which had an impact on the norms of appropriate group behavior that developed within their groups.

4. What students felt they got out of the encounter groups also varied—acceptance for some, understanding or involvement for others, advice or intellectual stimulation for yet others.

5. Sixteen students were identified who had been adversely enough affected by the experience to warrant psychiatric follow-up treatment. This percentage was greater for the "experimental" than for the control group students.

6. The most typical source of injury was attack or rejection by the leader or the group. Other sources of injury included failure to attain unrealistic goals, coercive expectations, and overstimulation.

7. The most sensitive casualty indicator was peer response to the question "Who got hurt?" Leaders were especially insensitive to casualties in their own groups.

8. The most effective leadership style in terms of maximizing gains while minimizing casualties was a combination of giving love and support as well as information about how to change (cognitive structuring).

9. Outcomes were unrelated to ideological labels or "brand names" attached to the different groups.

10. At present writing, the authors of the study conclude: "It thus appears that the generic title 'encounter groups' covers a wide range of operations by leaders that lead to many kinds of group experiences, and perhaps to many types of learning" (Lieberman, Yalom, & Miles, 1973).

Combining Therapeutic Resources

Although many specific techniques of psychotherapy have been tried, some based on elaborate theories and others merely on practical experience, none has proved universally effective. In the face of this situation, most therapists have adopted an *eclectic* approach, not limiting themselves to any one procedure.

This broader approach was first advanced by Adolph Meyer, famed Johns Hopkins psychiatrist. Meyer's approach, which emphasizes the inseparability of *psycho*logical and *bio*logical processes, is known as *psychobiology*. The psychobiological approach aims at an understanding of all the factors—biological, psychological, and social—that are involved in a disorder. This philosophy leads to an *integrated* therapy in which various techniques are used in various combinations, depending on the individual case. Thus, a particular patient's program of treatment might include such techniques as free association, dream analysis, hypnosis, and any physical methods deemed necessary. The ideal of the eclectic approach is a flexibility and freedom from theoretical dogmatism in attempting to fit the therapy to the problem—not the patient to the therapist's theory.

Institutional Care

The most complete program of integrated therapy is found in mental hospitals, where the patient receives treatment on a teamwork basis, with psychiatrists, psychologists, social workers, occupational therapists, and other specially trained personnel all contributing their diagnostic and therapeutic skills. Seriously disturbed patients can derive important benefits from living in an institution where they are relieved of difficult decisions and do not have to face many of the frustrations of normal living. Guilt feelings tend to be reduced in the presence of others who are having similar difficulties. Moreover, patients are kept from endangering the safety—both physical and financial—of themselves and those around them.

For better . . . Life in a well-run institution follows as normal a pattern as the condition of each patient permits. The current trend is toward increasing freedom for patients to live normally and to govern themselves while in the hospital. Such arrangements, still in the experimental stage, have shown therapeutic value in many instances; they help the patients prepare to govern themselves and not be totally dependent on the hospital so they can better adjust to their home communities when released.

A recent trend in institutional treatment is referred to as the *therapeutic community*. It is a method of operating a psychiatric hospital unit that attempts to develop and maintain a sense of staff-patient social community. A close relationship between staff and patients is the basis for sharing work activities and decisions affecting the life of the ward. ▲ Such a community is in operation on the psychiatric ward at the Yale-New Haven Hospital, where patients have drawn up a constitution for their ward. The ward is described in the constitution as "a community whose goal is that each can learn how to be responsible for himself and is able to help himself through helping others." The patient's obligations and privileges are made explicit, as are the staff's responsibilities and the values and behavioral norms that govern both staff and patient life on the ward. The patient's problems are openly confronted in an atmosphere of trust and comradeship. The primary concern of the community is in helping patients to be discharged as soon as feasible and improved sufficiently to be effective in their home community.

In a questionnaire study of the changes in patients and staff attributable to the therapeutic community experience, Richard Almond (1971) reported significant increases in patient social-openness and decreases in staff authoritarianism. The ward was effective in its efforts to bring new patients into its culture. It was also discovered that not only did patients improve during their stay, but they behaved (according to staff ratings) in accord with the norm of social openness. Interestingly, this new behavior preceded the development of new attitudes to-

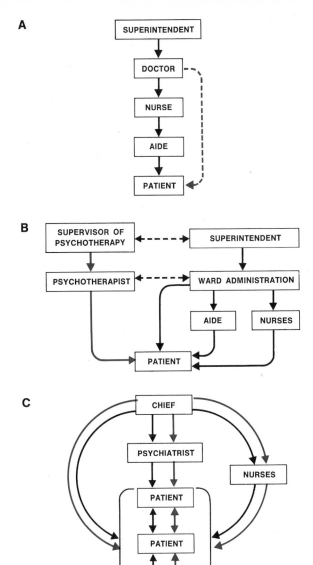

After Almond, 1971

▲ THE THERAPEUTIC COMMUNITY

The diagrams contrast the therapeutic community (C) with the "asylum" situation (A) and the typical psychotherapy hospital (B). In A, lines of authority (black) are clear, and there is little therapeutic contact (color) between doctor and patient. In B, more staff members interact directly with the patient, but the therapeutic relationship is distinct from authority concerns. In the therapeutic community, all relationships have both authority and therapeutic aspects.

ward openness—they acted first, then came to believe in what they were doing. The personal impact of such a therapeutic community is captured in the description of a young woman patient's first day on the ward: "I was quite taken aback when people would come up and say to me, 'Why were you brought here?'" Recounting her reaction over the next few days, she said: "I began talking with very many people, staff and patients alike. I began seeing the problems I had. . . . I was becoming more objective. . . . I had never been quite so clear about what got me into this illness." Describing how she became part of the ward and learned its customs, she said: "It was through talking, actually. The intensity of this ward is impressive. . . . [It] keeps things so intense that you do adjust quickly and begin to see your own problems more objectively because you're constantly thrown into situations where you must talk about it. . . . People here all have many things in common and seem genuinely to be interested in one another's welfare" (p. 39).

. . . or for worse? The institutional care and treatment of mentally ill individuals is a medical, financial, and social problem. Over one million patients are treated annually in United States mental hospitals. In fact, as we noted in the previous chapter, about half of the hospital beds in the country are occupied by mental patients. This is not because mental disorders are more prevalent than physical illnesses but because they are generally more difficult to cure and to cope with at home and therefore require hospitalization for a longer period of time.

The total cost of mental illness in the United States, direct and indirect, is estimated to be in the billions of dollars. Each state operates mental hospitals, and in most states appropriations for the care and treatment of mental patients constitute one of the largest single items in the budget. Yet even in states with enthusiastic mental hygiene programs, facilities are inadequate. Almost all state hospitals are severely overcrowded. Furthermore, even though the number of psychologists and psychiatrists has increased manyfold in the last thirty years, there still are not enough trained psychiatrists, psychologists, and other capable personnel for adequate care of the mentally ill.

Very few institutions for the treatment and care of mental patients come near approaching an ideal that promotes rehabilitation. There are many state hospitals where the conditions are so bad that if they were known, or if the taxpayers really cared, there would be a national scandal.

In some, there is but one psychiatrist for over one thousand patients. In others, treatment decisions must be based entirely on the prognosis that a new patient will respond favorably and quickly to therapy. For patients not expected to benefit quickly or for those who get therapy and do not show clear improvement in a short time, treatment is reduced by necessity to chemotherapy and occupational games—to keep the patients manageable and out of trouble.

A recent barrage of criticism against mental hospitals has documented the destructive effects that these institutions often have. Their practices have been found to be authoritarian (Holzberg, 1960), degrading to the patient (Sarbin, 1967), dehumanizing (Goffman, 1961), and illness-maintaining (Schwartz, 1960). According to one investigator, "the person's nature is redefined so that, in effect if not by intention, the patient becomes the kind of object upon which a psychiatric service can be performed. To be made a patient is to be remade into a serviceable object, the irony being that so little service is available once this is done" (Goffman, 1961, p. 379). Such conditions are more prevalent than one could wish.

We noted in the previous chapter that Rosenhan and his colleagues (1973) were not only able to get committed to mental hospitals by pretending to be schizophrenic, but once inside they were treated in ways that depersonalized them. Unlike the model therapeutic community, in all the hospitals "visited" by this team of pseudopatients there was little personal concern shown by the staff for patient well-being, little direct contact with psychiatrists or psychologists, and much of the patient-staff interaction was characterized by indifference or hostility. (See *P&L* Close-up, p. 549.)

At Elgin State Hospital in Illinois another unique kind of experiment was conducted recently in which the *staff* divided themselves into "pseudopatients" and role-playing staff. For three days, twenty-nine staff members were confined to a ward of their own—a mental ward on which they were the mock patients. Trained observers and video cameras recorded what transpired throughout. "It was really fantastic the things that happened in there," reported Norma Jean Orlando (1973), director of the research. In a short time the mock patients began acting in ways indistinguishable from real patients: six tried to escape, two withdrew into themselves, two wept uncontrollably, one came close to having a nervous breakdown. Most experienced a general increase in tension, anxiety, frustration, and despair. They reacted most strongly to the total invasion of their privacy, to being treated as incompetent children, ignored, and obliged to conform to the rules of the staff.

One staff-member-turned-patient who suffered during his weekend ordeal gained the insight to declare: "I used to look at the patients as if they were a bunch of animals; I never knew what they were going through before."

The positive outcome of this study was the formation of an organization of staff members dedicated to raising the consciousness of the rest of the hospital personnel as to the way patients were being mistreated, and also to working at personally improving their own relationship to patients.

One of the most severe critiques of psychiatric hospitalization comes from a very thorough study of 2926 adult patients admitted to the psychiatric ward of Los Angeles County General Hospital (Mendel, 1966). It was concluded that 75 percent of all patients diagnosed as "schizophrenic" could have been (but were not) discharged to their community. The shorter the stay in the hospital, the higher the level of social functioning of patients after being released. The longer patients remain institutionalized, the less improvement they show, and their chances of making a successful adjustment to the outside community diminish.

Close-up
The Patient As Ugly Duckling

One reason it becomes very important for patients to learn how to create the desired impression on the psychiatric staff is that psychiatric evaluations are based largely on whether or not the staff *likes* a patient. This surprising conclusion emerged from an intensive study of staff and patients on two wards at Agnews State Mental Hospital in California by Michael Katz (1974), who was himself a psychiatric aide. Weekly ratings by staff of a patient's social attractiveness were correlated with amount of staff-patient contact, judgments of the patient's mental health status, and decisions as to whether the patient should be kept on a particular ward or transferred. The results of Katz's study support the contention that to a considerable degree social attractiveness *is* mental health!

There is a patient status hierarchy based on sociability. Compared to likeable patients, those patients the staff likes least are more avoided and are recommended for more drug medication and transfers to other wards, or for discharge (despite the fact they are judged as more mentally ill). Well-liked patients are judged to be improving and see themselves as mentally healthy.

Katz points out the need for staff members to become aware of the influence of patients' sociability on their allegedly objective evaluations. Furthermore, it would be well for the staff to make explicit to patients precisely what behaviors they find attractive or disturbing and then to reinforce selectively those that make a patient likeable. To the extent that the mental hospital is a microcosm of society, perhaps the implication of this study is that we are all more apt to overlook in attractive people what we fault in the ugly ducklings.

Community-Based Mental Health Care

The Joint Commission on Mental Health (1961) recommended that no more mental hospitals with over 1000 beds be built; that acute cases be handled through facilities to be developed in the patient's home community, without the delay of being put on a waiting list; and that, as soon as it became possible to do so, the existing large state institutions should be either dismantled or converted to institutions for the care of chronic physical and mental patients. Since then, a start has been made through the Community Mental Health Centers Act to encourage the building of comprehensive community centers throughout the country. As such centers become more numerous and better equipped, it is hoped that more and more of those who need help can be cared for in their communities and that the large state mental hospitals will become a thing of the past.

Such comprehensive community centers have many advantages. With immediate care, adjusted to the need of the individual, overall treatment time can be greatly shortened and the patient and his or her family saved much trauma and grief. The stigma attached to being "sent away" is minimized or removed entirely, and the patient is spared the problems of adjusting to a lonely, faraway, impersonal institution and the equally difficult problem of coming back to the community after a long absence and trying to find a viable place in it again. (See *P&L* Close-up, p. 551.)

The concept of community mental health. With the advent of federal aid to community mental health programs during the past decade, there has been a remarkable and much needed shift in the availability and provision of psychological services to people in need of them. The table outlines many of these changes, showing how they differ from the more traditional, clinically oriented practices we have described. ● Community mental health is an exciting and necessary approach to treatment, where innovation is the rule rather than the exception. Clearly, if the psychological needs of large numbers of people are to be met, clinicians must leave the confines of the institution and search out the needs of the people instead of waiting for people in need to come to them. But even more important is the concept of treatment and *prevention* for the entire community akin to public health programs to immunize the community against sources of disease such as smallpox. Sources of environmental or organizational stress can be identified, and plans can be formulated to alleviate or circumvent them as well as to increase people's resistance to specific sources of stress.

While some of our emotional problems undoubtedly stem from early-life unresolved conflicts and inappropriate learning, nevertheless, the major sources of stress we face come from the conditions under which we live our daily

● **COMMUNITY MENTAL HEALTH CONTRASTED WITH TRADITIONAL CLINICAL APPROACHES**

1. Emphasis on practice in the community as opposed to practice in institutional settings.

2. Emphasis on a total community or total defined population rather than on individual patients considered singly.

3. Emphasis on preventive services as distinguished from therapeutic services for those already "sick."

4. Emphasis on indirect services, such as consultation and mental health education, rather than direct treatment services.

5. Emphasis on innovative clinical strategies, such as brief psychotherapy and crisis intervention, that have the potential for meeting the mental health needs of larger numbers of people than has ordinarily been possible.

6. Emphasis on rational planning of mental health programs, including demographic analyses of the community, specification of unmet health needs, identification of high-risk populations, and the establishment of priorities.

7. Emphasis on the innovative use of human resources, such as paraprofessionals.

8. Commitment to "community control" in identifying the needs of the community, proposing and evaluating programs to meet these needs, and planning for future program developments.

9. Interest in identifying sources of stress within the community rather than assuming that psychopathology exists entirely within the identified individual patient.

Adapted from Bloom, 1973

Many of us have developed (or been taught) the feeling that we ought to be able to work out our own problems and not burden others with our troubles. It somehow seems inappropriate, or a sign of weakness, to admit that we might need help. There is little doubt, however, that almost everyone sometimes experiences feelings of depression or loneliness, or the inability to cope. Numerous life experiences have the potential of inducing such personal crises. It is important to realize that everyone faces such crises at one time or another and that there is nothing wrong or unusual about reacting to them emotionally. Seeking help at such times may not be easy, but it seems preferable to muddling through alone.

When our usual emotional supports, such as parents or close friends, are absent or unavailable, we should not hesitate to seek help from other sources. The duration of crisis is usually short for most people (from 4 to 6 weeks) and contains both the danger of increased psychological vulnerability and the opportunity for personal growth. The outcome seems to depend to a large degree on the availability of appropriate help and one's own attitude and definition of the "problem."

In terms of prevention, however, it would make better sense to seek out sources of help *before* they are needed. An interesting and worthwhile project would be to identify various sources of psychological support available to you now. First of all, you should list the available sources of help outside the mental health profession, such as family, friends, teachers, clergy, "rap centers," etc. Perhaps a visit to a local church or drop-in center would be instructive in terms of whether or not you think these places could be of help to you. You need not feel that you should make up a story to hide the exploratory nature of your visit; you can simply explain that you are trying to identify sources of emotional support in the community.

Most problems are in fact minor ones that will go away in time, that diminish in intensity as we look back on them. But the process of working them through helps us get in touch with ourselves and perhaps reduces the stressfulness of such problems in the future. However, there are also cases of real distress where perhaps you or a friend might become severely depressed, seriously contemplate suicide, or else begin to develop paranoid feelings of persecution, hallucinations, or other signs of major psychological stress. For such problems you should go at once to an accredited professional therapist for help. Ideally, it should be someone you have identified earlier as a person whom you can respect and trust, and with whom you can deal openly. Go early, before the symptoms themselves become problems (causing poor grades, etc.).

It is not unreasonable to talk ahead of time about the "therapeutic contract"—what you get for what you give. If you think it appropriate, you might want to explore the therapist's personal philosophy; his or her view of human nature and the causes of emotional and behavioral disturbance. Of course, feeling comfortable with the therapist and being able to develop feelings of trust are more important than knowing the therapist's philosophy. This can best be accomplished through sharing your problems and concerns and gauging the helpfulness of the response you get. Remember though, most therapists refrain from giving advice, but seek to help the client achieve his or her own resolution to the problem. You may judge for yourself whether or not this is what you need.

Therapy is an intimate social exchange in which you pay for a service. If you feel the service is not benefiting you, discuss this openly with the therapist, expose the possibility that failure of therapy represents the *therapist's failure* as well as your own. Discuss criteria for successful termination of therapy—when will the two of you know you are "really" better? Also discuss the issue of terminating therapy if you are unsatisfied with it. This may itself be a positive step toward self-assertion. There is an almost universal understanding among professionals that no therapist relates well with everyone, and a good one will sometimes suggest that a client might do better with another therapist.

lives—violence, prejudice, forms of ecological deterioration, social isolation, crime, unemployment, poverty, wars between governments, and the powerlessness felt in trying to change the systems that control and manipulate us.

When we learn that a majority of hospitalized patients suffer relapses after being discharged, is that evidence for the severity and "depth" of their illness or the disturbance in the environment into which they are discharged? It is curious that the high recidivism rate of mental patients is comparable to that of psychiatrically normal prisoners who have also been institutionalized for long periods of time. "Dumping" a person back into a setting that was unsupportive to begin with (and may have deteriorated in the interim) is likely to provide the stimulus for deviant responses. It is also critical to realize the difficulty in readjusting to one's family and friends after any prolonged absence. Returning American POWs from Vietnam were given "reentry" training, but in a fair number of cases were not able to adjust to a family that had gotten along without them for a number of years and a "community" that really never noticed they were gone. If this is true of those given a hero's welcome, what are the reentry problems of the ex-schizophrenic or ex-convict?

An intensive evaluation of community mental health facilities (Hogarty et al., 1969) emphasizes the need to broaden the provisions of comprehensive community care available for outpatients if we are to avoid the revolving psychiatric hospital door syndrome. Where aftercare is absent or inadequate, social adjustment among psychiatric patients is much worse than where it is present. The investigators concluded from their study of the social and mental health status of discharged patients over a twelve-month follow-up period that "the level of social restoration achieved by a large number of patients treated in the community is impressive, and appears equal, if not superior, to the adjustment achieved by patients following traditional in-patient hospitalization" (p. 280).

Peer therapy.   Perhaps the most innovative and potentially far-reaching concept to come out of the community mental health approach is the use of nonprofessionals as therapeutic change agents. College students, high-school students, even grade-school students are being pressed into service along with housewives, retired persons, blue-collar workers, juvenile delinquents, patients, *ex*-offenders or *ex*-addicts, and indigenous inner-city nonprofessionals. These new help agents are, collectively, doing virtually everything that professionals do in terms of mental health services (except for dispensing drugs and medical forms of therapy), and are even involved in activities not formally considered as part of mental health services, such as community improvement. This rapid development of new human resources is seen as a "social revolution" by some (Sobey, 1970), the effects of which on the field of mental health are not quite clear yet. There is little well-designed research in this area but from limited data available, it appears as though nonprofessionals can often be as helpful, and occasionally *more* helpful, than trained professionals (recall Posner's *student-friend* experiment described on pages 541–42). An important by-product is the typical finding that the *helper* also profits personally from the service provided (Gruver, 1971).

Substitutes for Institutionalization

It seems probable that there will be an increasing trend toward treatment of even severe behavior disorders away from hospital settings. "Psychiatry Without Doctors," "Treatment Goes Home," and "Landladies for the Mentally Ill," are examples of headlines that will be appearing more frequently, as such innovations prove successful. George Fairweather and his colleagues (1969) demonstrated with an experimental pilot program that a group of newly released mental patients could be organized to function effectively outside the hospital. A lodge was founded in the community where these patients could live as a group. At first there was a single research staff member present; later he was replaced by a layperson. The patients were given full responsibility for regulating each other's behavior, for operating the lodge, purchasing and preparing food, and earning money. They set up a handyman service business that produced an income of over $50,000 in three years. They proportioned the money they took in according to each patient's productivity and responsibility.

Forty months after their discharge, a comparison was made of this group and a comparable group of another seventy-five patients who had been released at the same time but had not had this experience. The members of the supportive lodge were better able to hold income-producing jobs, to maintain satisfactory levels of adjustment, and to achieve meaningful lives in the community than the controls. All this had been achieved for the first group at a cost to the concerned taxpayer of $6 a day per lodger! (Raush & Raush, 1968)

A Dream for the Future or Future Shock?

A mental patient with paranoid delusions began to have a fantasy that he was married to one of the nurses whom he hardly knew. As this thought became elaborated, his "marriage" was blessed with three children and his life filled with happiness. Soon this unemployed middle-aged bachelor lost interest in his work "if it was real," and cared only for his dream, "which," he told the therapist, "if real is wonderful."

When he requested the therapist's opinion about the reality or unreality of his ideas, the therapist replied that they were just a kind of waking dream. At that point, the patient cited his loneliness, his approaching old age, and the fact that he was not married and had no one who would really care if he died tomorrow. "What," he asked, "would I do if my dreams were taken away from me? What can you offer me better than this dream?"

If *you* were the therapist how would you answer him? Whether you could offer a better dream to this mentally disturbed person depends on whether your society could offer *you* the possibility of a dream for the future. (See *P&L* Close-up at right.)

Close-up
Ethical Issues in Therapy

As we have seen, any attempt to induce a change in another person represents an ethical decision as well as a pragmatic or theoretical one. Some therapists avoid confronting such vexing problems by keeping their goals unspecified. But anyone's changed behavior is felt by some other person; thus, the entire process of the therapeutic modification of behavior must be set within a broad social context. What values would *you* go with in the following cases?

1. A bombardier with a phobia of heights wants to be cured so he can rejoin his bomber crew and continue to drop bombs effectively.

2. A man who is impotent wants desperately to have a big family. Curing his sexual problem would add to the population explosion.

3. A youth is obsessed by a desire to excel in one pursuit to the exclusion of all other interests. Making the youth a more well-rounded person would result in a better-adjusted adult, but society might lose a gifted performer.

4. A woman with a multiple personality enjoys her sexy, lustful self, which leads her to promiscuity, and dislikes her conservative, modest self, which inhibits such desires. Which "face of Eve" would you try to get rid of, or would you try to integrate them?

5. A student radical, convinced that society is corrupt and that his life and yours are controlled by the "military-industrial complex" wants to lead a violent revolution. Do you treat him as paranoid and try to fit him back into his society, or do you try to promote changes in the society to make it fit individuals better?

As our traditional patterns collide with voices demanding change in virtually all those patterns, the role of therapist as value mediator for the society becomes more sharply drawn than ever before in history. Will that role be to support the statistical definition of normalcy in terms of what the majority want, or to moderate and "adjust" each side to the other, or to see the high rate of individual disturbance as a reflection of societal "sickness" and direct one's efforts toward curing social pathology?

In Chapter 14 we will look at the forces that can diminish our "humanness" including some of the ways civilization can be uncivilizing. Many people today, such as Alvin Toffler (1970), believe that "future shock"—an anxiety-ridden inability to cope with the rapid transformations of our society—is all that the future holds for any of us. As leaders with a vision of a better dream are cut down by the madness of an assassin's distorted reality, will their dream die too? Or will others—perhaps you—step forward to uphold the dream, as much for the "sick" as for the "well"?

Theologian Martin Buber (1957) wrote:

"The most important events in the history of that embodied possibility called man *are the occasionally occurring beginnings of new epochs, determined by forces previously invisible or unregarded. Each age is, of course, a continuation of the preceding one, but a continuation can be a confirmation or it can be a refutation." (p. 167).*

In the final analysis, whether the dream of a better future is confirmed or refuted will be determined by the *behavior of individuals* and the social contract we are willing to commit ourselves to—what each of us is willing to do to make a shared dream come true, not only for ourselves but for each other.

Chapter Summary

Psychotherapy is commonly understood to be the psychological treatment of some abnormality in thought, emotion, or action. Since normality is relative to a given culture, this can unfortunately come to mean adjusting the individual to the status quo. Psychotherapy is now coming to be used in the sense of preserving as well as restoring health.

Those who practice formal therapy include *psychiatrists,* who have an M.D. degree with a specialty in treating mental illness; *clinical* psychologists, who have academic and clinical training but no medical degree; and *psychoanalysts,* who are trained in the Freudian approach to psychotherapy. Therapies can be categorized

into those that take a *biological or psychodynamic* point of view, emphasizing causes within the individual, and those that take a *behavioral or existential-humanistic* point of view, emphasizing situational causes and potential for growth.

Biological or *somatic* forms of therapy include shock therapy, chemotherapy, and psychosurgery. The most common form of *shock therapy* involves the application of controlled electroconvulsive shock to the patient's head. It has proved useful in cases of severe depression.

Drugs used in *chemotherapy* may be categorized as tranquilizers, energizers, and hallucinogens. *Tranquilizers* reduce anxiety and agitation, permitting the individual to function more adequately. *Energizers* are useful in treating depressed patients. *Hallucinogens* such as mescaline and LSD have proved useful in making patients more responsive to psychotherapy. Treatment with drugs does not lead to permanent cures, however, and may lead to psychological dependence. *Placebo reactions* make it difficult to evaluate the effectiveness of drugs.

Psychosurgery involves the severing of neural fibers in the brain, separating emotion and thought. It is a drastic, and highly controversial, form of treatment used only as a last resort. Biological therapy assumes physical causes (and hence a *medical model*) of mental illness, failing to take such factors as learning and social interaction into account.

Psychodynamic forms of therapy also assume internal causes, but psychological rather than physical ones. Based on Freud's personality theory, *psychoanalysis* seeks to bring about personality change by uncovering repressed memories and conflicts. Techniques used include analysis of *free associations,* of *dreams,* of *resistances,* and of *transference.* Neo-Freudian therapists, like the followers of Jung and Adler, have placed greater emphasis on cultural factors and self-actualization. Psychoanalysis has been criticized because it is time-consuming and seems to ignore current symptoms.

Behavioristic therapies focus on overt behavior, using learning principles to modify behavior. Variants include: (1) *extinction,* in which all reinforcement is withheld when the unwanted response occurs; (2) *desensitization,* as in *reciprocal inhibition,* in which the individual overcomes anxiety by learning to remain completely relaxed in the presence of the anxiety-invoking stimuli; (3) *implosive therapy,* in which the person is forced to confront the feared stimuli and discover that no harm results; (4) *aversive learning,* in which unwanted responses are paired with noxious stimuli; (5) *positive reinforcement,* in which desired responses are shaped by satisfying consequences; (6) *imitation of models,* in which the individual watches someone making the desired response and then is reinforced for imitating it; and (7) *token economies,* in which individuals in an institution (school, prison, mental hospital) earn tokens for specified behaviors, which they can then exchange for any of several specified privileges. These therapies have been very successful, take less time than traditional therapies, and require less training on the part of the therapist. They may, however, mix cognitive techniques with learning principles, making it difficult to isolate and evaluate "pure" behaviorist techniques, and the results do not always generalize to real-life situations.

Existential-humanistic therapies have grown out of a "third force" in psychology and are less pessimistic and mechanistic than other approaches. Existentialism focuses on the here-and-now, the process of becoming. *Logotherapy,* one form of existential therapy, emphasizes the will-to-meaning in one's life, making use of *paradoxical intention.*

One of the earliest examples of humanistic psychotherapy was the *client-centered therapy* of Carl Rogers, in which a *nondirective* therapist provides a "safe" climate in which the client is free to discover buried feelings and develop greater self-understanding and self-acceptance. Techniques in which the therapist is encouraged to reveal his or her own feelings and experiences are being used increasingly.

Any given therapist defines a patient's problem in terms of a particular theoretical perspective. It thus becomes difficult to evaluate the effectiveness of different forms of therapy in treating specific disorders. There is even some question as to whether any form of psychotherapy is more effective than no therapy at all. Factors making evaluation difficult include subjective or vague criteria, differing goals, and inadequately controlled evaluative research.

Therapeutic *groups* make more efficient use of time and personnel and promote interaction among patients. Group therapy is highly beneficial for certain individuals. *Experiential groups* such as encounter groups provide intensive interpersonal experience; they are becoming increasingly popular as a means to increasing self-awareness and fulfillment of potential among "normal" individuals. Some individuals may become casualties of the group experience, however, and much depends on the quality and training of the group leadership.

Most therapists today prefer an *eclectic approach,* not using any one procedure exclusively but employing a combination of techniques. A complete program of *integrated care* is made possible in institutional settings. The concept of a *therapeutic community* stresses interaction and sharing between doctors, patients, and administrative staff. Yet overcrowding and lack of funds have led to deplorable conditions in many large institutions, which have become custodial rather than rehabilitative.

Government-sponsored *community mental health centers* are bringing patient care out of the state institution and into the local community, emphasizing local needs and the prevention of mental health problems. There is a growing trend toward the use of nonprofessionals in therapeutic roles and toward establishing settings where patients can learn to function effectively in the real world. As we are confronted with a changing society in which "future shock" is an ever increasing problem, it is more important than ever that we determine whose interests and values therapy should serve: the individual's or the society's.

Therapy for a Competitive Society
Elliot Aronson University of California, Santa Cruz

Americans have made a religion out of winning. From the fans in the college football stadium chanting, "We're number one," to the little leaguer who bursts into tears when his team loses, to Lyndon Johnson who poured troops and weapons into Vietnam, declaring that he was not going to be the first American president to lose a war, our society asserts its allegiance to victory and its contempt for losers.

What are the consequences of this attitude? How do people behave when competition is a way of life and they are afflicted with this fear of finishing second? They have difficulty relaxing; they view one another as competitors and potential enemies; they are forever looking over their shoulder lest someone overtake them; they have difficulty relaxing or admitting to weakness, vulnerability, or other attributes of being human. They experience pangs of envy and jealousy when an acquaintance lands a good job or becomes a successful doctor, lawyer, or barber. And once on this treadmill, there is no respite—there is no safe harbor, no resting place. Even reaching great heights of accomplishment, for most people, does not lead to relaxation. When you win the Nobel Prize, the first question you'll be asked is: "And what are you working on now?"

Competitiveness is not inborn—but it seems that way because it is learned early. And one place where it's learned is the elementary-school classroom. Recently, we performed systematic observations of a great many elementary-school classrooms. The most typical situation we saw was this: The teacher stands in front of the class, asks a question, and the children are expected to answer it. Most frequently six to ten children strain in their seats and wave their hands in the teacher's face. They seem eager to be called upon. Several other students sit quietly with eyes averted as if trying to make themselves invisible. When the teacher calls on one of the students (and indeed she can only call on one), you can see looks of disappointment,

dismay, and unhappiness on the faces of the students who were eagerly raising their hands and were not called on. If the student who is called upon comes up with the right answer, the teacher smiles, nods her head and goes on to the next question. This is a great reward for the student who happens to be called on. At the same time that the fortunate student is coming up with the right answer and being smiled upon, you can hear an audible groan coming from the children who were not called upon. It is obvious that they are disappointed because they missed an opportunity to show the teacher how smart and quick they are.

Through this process the students learn several things. First they learn that there is one and only one expert in the classroom: the teacher. They also learn that there is one and only one correct answer to any question that the teacher asks: namely the answer that the teacher has in her head. The student's task is to figure out what answer the teacher expects. The students also learn that the payoff comes from pleasing that teacher by showing her how quick, smart, neat, clean and well-behaved they are. If the child does this successfully, he or she will gain the respect and love of this powerful person. This powerful person will then be kind to the child and will tell his or her parents what a wonderful person the child is.

The game is very competitive. Moreover, the stakes are very high. Think back on your own elementary-school days. I'll bet that you have a vivid memory of your elementary-school teachers— perhaps even more vivid than some of your college teachers whose impact was more recent, but perhaps not more profound. In elementary school the stakes are higher precisely because the kids are competing for the love of one of the two or three most important people in their world (important for most students anyway). If you are a student who knows the correct answer and the teacher calls on one of the other kids, it is likely that you will sit there hoping and praying that he or she comes up with the wrong answer so that you will have a chance to show the teacher how smart you are. Those who fail when called upon or those who do not even raise their hands and compete, have a tendency to resent the kids who succeed. Frequently, they become envious and jealous; perhaps they try to put them down by referring to them as "teacher's pet." They might even use physical violence against them in the schoolyard. The successful students, for their part, often hold the unsuccessful students in contempt; they consider them to be dumb and uninteresting. The upshot of all this is that the process that takes place, to a greater or lesser extent, in most elementary school classrooms is virtually guaranteed not to promote friendliness and understanding among children in the same classroom. Quite the reverse.

The process that exists in the classroom is one that does not encourage a child to look benevolently upon his fellow students; it is not a process that is designed to increase understanding and interpersonal attraction. Rather, the process induces competitiveness, one-upmanship, envy, jealousy and suspicion. When one adds to this situation the already existing racial tensions that are present in any urban society, it is little wonder that violence is often forthcoming.

It doesn't have to be that way. A few years ago we tried to reverse this process in the elementary schools of a large city in the southwest. Our attempt to change the process was a relatively simple one. First, we changed the structure of one expert and 30 listeners by placing the students in small groups of six students each. We eliminated the teacher as a major resource for each of the learning groups by creating a process that made it imperative that the kids treat *each other* as resources. This was achieved in two ways: (1) we structured the process so that competitiveness was incompatible with success, and (2) we made certain that success could occur only after cooperative behavior. In a traditional classroom the kid is rewarded when he or she succeeds in attracting the teacher's attention by outshining the competitors. In the cooperative classroom that we instituted, the kids

achieved success as a consequence of paying attention to the other kids, asking good questions, helping each other, teaching each other, and helping each other teach.

How did this come about? Let me try to put some meat on the bare bones of the above outline. First, we made no attempt to change the content. We used the same curriculum that the teachers had been using. An example will clarify. In our initial experiment, we entered a fifth-grade classroom where the students were studying biographies of great Americans. The upcoming lesson happened to be a biography of Joseph Pulitzer. First, we constructed a biography of Joseph Pulitzer that consisted of six paragraphs. Paragraph one was about Joseph Pulitzer's ancestors and how they came to this country. Paragraph two was about Joseph Pulitzer as a little boy and how he grew up. Paragraph three was about Joseph Pulitzer as a young man, his education, his early employment. Paragraph four was about Joseph Pulitzer as a middle-aged man, how he founded his newspaper, etc. Each major aspect of Joseph Pulitzer's life was contained in a separate paragraph. We mimeographed our biography and cut each copy into six one-paragraph sections and gave each child in the six-person learning group one paragraph about Joseph Pulitzer's life.

Thus, each learning group had within it the entire biography of Joseph Pulitzer, but each individual child had no more than one-sixth of the story. In order to learn about Joseph Pulitzer they had to master their paragraph and teach it to the others. For example, Johnnie was responsible for reporting on Pulitzer as a young man, Carlos was responsible for Pulitzer as a middle-aged man, Mary was responsible for Pulitzer as a child, etc. Each student took his paragraph, read it over a few times, and then joined his counterparts. That is, if Johnnie had been dealt Joseph Pulitzer as a young man, he consulted with Millie, Ted, Jane and Sam who were in different learning groups and who had also been dealt Pulitzer as a young man. They could use each other to rehearse and to get clear on what the important aspects of that phase of Joseph Pulitzer's life were about. A short time later the kids came back into session with their six-person group. They were informed that they had a certain amount of time to communicate that knowledge to each other. They were also informed that at the end of that time (or soon thereafter) they were going to be tested on their knowledge. The process is highly reminiscent of a jigsaw puzzle, with each student possessing a single vital piece of the big picture. We came to refer to our system as the "jig-saw" model.

When thrown on their own resources, the children eventually learned to teach each other and to listen to each other. The children came to learn that none of them could do well without the aid of each person in that group—and that each member had a unique and essential contribution to make. Suppose you and I are children in the same group. You've been dealt Joseph Pulitzer as a young man; I've been dealt Pulitzer as an old man. The only way I can learn about Joseph Pulitzer as a young man is if I pay close attention to what you are saying. You are a very important resource for me. The teacher is no longer the sole resource—she isn't even an important resource; indeed, she isn't even in the group. Instead, every kid in the circle becomes important to me. I do well if I pay attention to other kids; I do poorly if I don't. It's a whole new ball game.

It is the element of interdependence which makes this a unique learning method; and it is this interdependence of each student on all of the other students that encourages the students to take an active part in their learning. In becoming a teacher of sorts, each student becomes a valuable resource for the others. Learning from each other gradually diminishes the need to try to out-perform each other because one student's learning enhances the learning of the other students instead of inhibiting it, as is usually the case in most traditional teacher-oriented classrooms. Within this cooperative paradigm the teacher learns to be a facilitating resource person, and he or she shares in the learning and teaching process with the students instead of being the sole resource. Rather than lecturing to students, the teacher facilitates mutual learning, in that each student is required to be an active participant and to be responsible for what he or she learns.

Cooperative behavior doesn't happen all at once. It is very difficult to break old habits. These children had grown accustomed to competing during their first four years in school. Typically, for the first several days of "jig-sawing" the students tried to compete—even though competitiveness was now dysfunctional. Let me illustrate with an actual example which was quite typical of the way the children stumbled toward the learning of the cooperative process. In one of our groups there was a Chicano boy whom we will call Carlos. Carlos was not very articulate in English (it was his second language). He had learned over the years how to keep quiet in class, and now he had a great deal of trouble communicating his paragraph to the other kids and was very uncomfortable about it. He liked the traditional way better. It is not surprising when you look at it—because, in the system we have introduced, Carlos was forced to speak, whereas, before, he could deindividuate himself and bury himself in the normal classroom.

The situation is even more complex. It might even be said that the teacher and Carlos had entered into a conspiracy. They were in collusion. Carlos was perfectly willing to be quiet. In the past, the teacher called on him occasionally; he would typically stumble, stammer and fall into an embarrassed silence. The other kids would make fun of him. The teacher had learned not to call on him anymore. This decision probably came from the purest of intentions; she did not want to humiliate him. But by ignoring him, she had written him off. The implication was that he was not worth bothering with—at least the other kids in the classroom got that message. They believed that there was one good reason why the teacher wasn't calling on Carlos—that he was stupid. It is likely that even Carlos began to draw this conclusion.

Let us go back to our six-person group. Carlos had to report on Joseph Pulitzer's middle years, and he was having a very hard time. He stammered, hesitated and fidgeted. The other kids in that circle were not very helpful. They had grown accustomed to a competitive process and they responded out of this old, overlearned habit. They knew what to do when a kid stumbles—especially a kid whom they believe to be stupid. They ridiculed him, put him down, teased him. During our experiment, it was Mary who was observed to say: "Aw, you don't know it, you're dumb, you're stupid. You don't know what you're doing."

In our first experiment, the groups were being loosely monitored by a research assistant who was floating from group to group. When this incident occurred in her earshot our assistant made one intervention. The intervention was something like this: "O.K., you can do that if you want to, it might be fun for you, but it's *not* going to help you learn about Joseph Pulitzer's middle years; the exam will take place in about an hour." Notice how the reinforcement contingencies have shifted. No more does the child gain much for putting Carlos down, and she stands to lose a great deal.

After a few days and several similar experiences, it began to dawn on the children that the *only* way that they could learn about Joseph Pulitzer's middle years was by paying attention to what Carlos had to say. And what gradually happened is that they began to develop into pretty good interviewers. If Carlos was having a little trouble communicating what he knew, instead of ignoring him or ridiculing him, they began asking probing questions. They became junior versions of Dick Cavett—asking the kinds of questions that made it easier for Carlos to communicate what was in his head. Carlos began to respond to this treatment by becoming more relaxed; with increased relaxation came an improvement in his ability to communicate. After a couple of weeks, the other children concluded that Carlos wasn't nearly as dumb as they thought he was. They began to like him. Carlos began to enjoy school more and began to see the Anglo kids in his group, not as tormentors but as helpful and responsive.

What happened in Carlos' group is a good example of the technique and how it frequently worked to produce beneficial effects, but it hardly constitutes acceptable scientific data. For that, we must turn to our field experiments in which we systematically investigated the effects of the jig-saw techniques on interpersonal attraction, self-esteem and happiness in school. We instituted the jig-saw technique in the classroom for six weeks and assessed its effectiveness by taking measures at the beginning and end of this period—comparing the performance of the children in the jig-saw classrooms with the performance of children in traditional classrooms being taught by highly competent teachers.

Our findings are quite consistent : (1) children in the jig-saw cooperation classrooms grew to like one another more than did children in traditional classrooms; (2) children in the jig-saw classrooms grew to like school better (or to hate school less) than the children in traditional classrooms; (3) children in the jig-saw classrooms increased in self-esteem to a greater extent than children in traditional classrooms; (4) in terms of the mastery of classroom material, children in the jig-saw classrooms performed as well as or better than children in traditional classrooms. Specifically, while Anglo children performed as well in either type classroom, children from ethnic minorities in desegregated schools performed significantly better in jig-saw classrooms than in traditional classrooms; (5) children enjoyed cooperating with each other and preferred it to the competitive mode.

Our research has demonstrated that what seemed like a deeply ingrained piece of behavior—competitiveness—can be modified. Our aim is not to eliminate a child's ability to compete; a certain amount of competition can be fun and may, in many circumstances, enhance performance. What we want to do is teach cooperativeness as a skill—so that when we find ourselves in a situation where cooperativeness is appropriate, we will not doggedly try to defeat the other person. What the children in our experiment learned is that it's possible to work together in a helpful way without sacrificing excellence.

PART 6
Society:
Its Problems
and Their
Solutions

13

The Social Bases of Behavior

The quiet of a Sunday morning in Palo Alto, California, was shattered by a screeching squad-car siren as police swept through the city picking up college students in a surprise mass arrest. Each suspect was charged with a felony, warned of his constitutional rights, spread-eagled against the police car, searched, handcuffed, and carted off in the back seat of the squad car to the police station for booking.

After being fingerprinted and having identification forms prepared for his "jacket" (central information file), each prisoner was left isolated for a while, then blindfolded, and transported to the "Stanford County Prison." Here he was stripped naked, skin-searched, deloused, and issued a uniform, bedding, soap, and towel.

The prisoner's uniform was a loosely fitting smock with an identification number on front and back. A chain was bolted around one ankle and worn at all times. Instead of having his head shaved (a usual prison procedure), the prisoner had to wear a nylon stocking cap over his head to cover his hair. Orders were shouted at him, and he was pushed around by the guards if he didn't comply quickly enough.

The individuality of the guards was reduced by uniforms (military khaki style), which gave them "group identity." No names were used, and their silver reflector sunglasses made eye contact with them impossible. Their symbols of power were billy clubs, whistles, handcuffs, and the keys to the cells and the main gate.

By late afternoon, when all the arrests were completed and each prisoner had been duly processed, the warden greeted his new charges and read off sixteen basic rules of prisoner conduct (previously compiled by the warden and his staff of eleven correctional officers):

Rule Number One: *Prisoners must remain silent during rest periods, after lights out, during meals, and whenever they are outside the prison yard.* Two: *Prisoners must eat at mealtimes and only at mealtimes.* Three: *Prisoners must not move, tamper, deface, or damage walls, ceil-*

ings, windows, doors, or other prison property. . . . Seven: Prisoners must address each other by their ID numbers only. Eight: Prisoners must address the guards as "Mr. Correctional Officer." . . . Sixteen: Failure to obey any of the above rules may result in punishment.

Most of the nine youthful prisoners, all "first offenders," sat on the cots in their barren cells, dazed and shocked by the unexpected events that had transformed their lives so suddenly. Just what kind of prison was this?

It was, in fact, a very special kind of prison—an experimental, "mock prison"—created by social psychologists specifically for the purpose of investigating the psychological effects of imprisonment on volunteer research subjects (Zimbardo, Haney, Banks, & Jaffe, 1973). Both the guards and the prisoners had been recruited through ads placed in a city newspaper calling for student volunteers for a two-week study of prison life. The lure of $15-a-day payment had attracted over one hundred volunteers, who were then given clinical interviews; from them, two dozen students had been selected as possible participants. They were chosen because they were judged to be emotionally stable, physically healthy, "normal-average" on the basis of extensive personality tests, and law-abiding (no history of convictions, violence, or drug abuse). They were told that their later assignment to the condition of "guard" or "prisoner" would be randomly determined by the flip of the coin. Asked their preference, they all said they would prefer being prisoners.

At the start of the study, then, there were no measurable differences between the young men assigned to be guards and those who were to role-play being prisoners. They were a relatively homogeneous sample of white, middle-class college students from colleges throughout the United States and Canada. They were, however, *not* informed that the experiment was to begin with arrests by the City Police. The "correctional officers" received no special training in how to be prison guards. They were told merely to "maintain law and order" in the prison and not to take any nonsense from the pris-

oners—who might prove to be dangerous if they attempted to escape. Physical violence was forbidden.

The "prison" was in the basement of the Stanford psychology building, which was deserted after the summer session. A long corridor was converted into the prison "yard" by partitioning off both ends. Three small laboratory rooms opening onto this corridor were made into cells: their doors were replaced with barred ones, and existing furniture was replaced with three cots each. A small, dark storage closet opposite the cells served as solitary confinement, and was posted with an appropriate sign, "The Hole." Data collection consisted of videotaping the interactions of guards and prisoners, direct observations by the research team, and interviews with the subjects, as well as their reactions on a battery of self-report questionnaires, in diaries, letters, and daily reports.

This mock prison represented an attempt to simulate *functionally* some of the significant features of the psychological state of imprisonment. A set of procedures had been formulated to operationalize the variables involved in a prison situation so that they would be maximally effective, given the limitations and constraints of the research setting. The intention was not to make a literal copy of a real prison setting but to achieve some equivalent *psychological* effects despite differences in the physical details.

In a variety of ways, however, attempts were made to introduce enough "mundane realism" (see Aronson & Carlsmith, 1969) that the participants might be able to go beyond the superficial demands of their assigned roles into the deep structure of the prisoner and guard mentality. There were visits by a former prison chaplain, a public defender, and relatives and friends of some of the prisoners, disciplinary and parole hearings before a board consisting of a group of "adult authorities." Although the mock guards worked eight-hour shifts, the mock prisoners were imprisoned in their cells around the clock, allowed out only for meals, exercise, toilet privileges, head count lineups, and work details.

In a remarkable short time, a perverted relationship developed between the prisoners and the guards. After an initial rebellion was crushed, the prisoners reacted passively as the guards daily escalated their aggression; assertion by the guards led to increasing dependency and deference by the prisoners; guard authority was met with prisoner self-deprecation, while the counterpart of the guard's newfound sense of arbitrary power was the prisoners' sense of depression and learned helplessness. In less than thirty-six hours, the first prisoner had to be released because of uncontrolled crying, fits of rage, disorganized thinking, and severe depression. Three more prisoners developed similar symptoms and also had to be released on successive days. A fifth prisoner was released from the study when he developed a psychosomatic rash over his entire body, triggered by rejection of his parole appeal by the mock Parole Board.

Social power became the major dimension on which everyone and everything was defined. Although there were no initial differences between those assigned to play the roles of prisoner and guard, enacting those roles in a social situation that validated the power differences created extreme behavioral and emotional differences between the two groups. The primary forms of interaction on the part of the guards, as evidenced in analyses of the videotapes, were commands, insults, degrading references, verbal and physical aggression, and threats. The prisoners' dominant modes of interaction were resistance, giving information when asked questions, questioning, and (initially) deprecating the guards.

Every guard at some time engaged in abusive, authoritarian behaviors. Many appeared to enjoy the elevated status that accompanied putting on the guard uniforms, which transformed their routine, everyday existence into one where they had virtually total control over other people.

As these differences in behavior, mood, and perception became more evident, the need for the now "righteously" powerful guards to rule the obviously inferior (and powerless) inmates became sufficient justification to support almost any indignity of man against man.

Consider the following typical comments taken from their diaries, post-experimental interviews, and report files:

GUARD A: *I was surprised at myself . . . I made them call each other names and clean the toilets out with their bare hands. I practically considered the prisoners cattle, and I kept thinking I have to watch out for them in case they try something.*

GUARD B: *(Preparing for the first Visitors' Night) After warning the prisoners not to make any complaints unless they wanted the visit terminated fast, we finally brought in the first parents. I made sure I was one of the guards on the yard, because this was my first chance for the type of manipulative power that I really like—being a very noticed figure with complete control over what is said or not.*

GUARD C: *Acting authoritatively can be fun. Power can be a great pleasure.*

After six days the researchers stopped the planned two-week simulation because of the pathological reactions being elicited in subjects

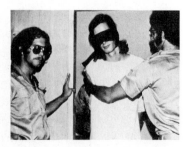

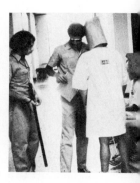

chosen precisely for their normality, sanity, and emotional stability.

No personality test scores or other variables related to the subjects' past history were found to be related to the extreme differences in reaction observed between the prisoners and the guards. Thus the pathology witnessed here cannot be reasonably attributed to preexisting personality traits—such as those of "psychopathic" or "sadistic" guards, or of "criminal, weak impulse-control" prisoners. Rather, the abnormal personal and social behavior in both groups is best viewed as a product of transactions with an environment that supports such behavior.

Since the subjects were randomly assigned to "guard" and "prisoner" roles, showed no prior personality pathology, and received no training for their roles, how can we account for the ease and rapidity with which they assumed these roles? Presumably, they, like the rest of us, had learned stereotyped conceptions of guard and prisoner roles from the mass media as well as from social models of power and powerlessness (parent-child, teacher-student, boss-worker, police-suspect, etc.). Indeed, this research illustrates not only what a prison-like environment can bring out in relatively normal people, but also how they have been socialized by their society.

This experiment is by no means typical of the kind of research carried out by social psychologists. Nevertheless, it highlights a number of the issues, concepts, and variables that we will be concerned with in this chapter—social reality, norms, status, roles, power, group dynamics, social-influence processes, and interpersonal conflict.

The Social-Psychological Approach

Our psychology, like our religion and our politics, has assumed the primacy of the individual. The doctrine of individuality is a cornerstone in our thinking about evolution and about the existence of "self." We all believe in our uniqueness, independence, self-sufficiency, and individual power, as well as in personal salvation and gain through our individual initiative and creative invention. These beliefs seem to coexist quite naturally with the rise of a capitalistic economic order, the tradition of romantic love, literary forms emphasizing character development, and, more recently, the psychology of personality and individual behavior.

But such beliefs are relatively new, not existing before the close of the Middle Ages. Actually, a strong case can be made for the primary importance of the social group rather than the individual as the unit of evolution. Life in groups affords advantages for survival that the solitary individual cannot share. Protection from predators through warning or group counterattack and the provision of a more certain and abundant food supply through hunting with the combined strength of the pack are obvious advantages. The mutual protection and nurturance provided by group association allow more offspring to mature and reproduce. This, in turn, makes the genetic characteristics of members of such groups more likely to be passed on to succeeding generations. In contrast, creatures not part of a social group become targets for enemies and easier prey to nature's physical forces. Group association also provides a medium for

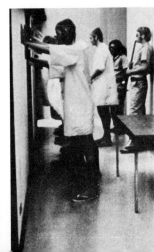

imitation through which the adaptive innovation of any one member can benefit all the rest.

Social psychology is the discipline that studies individual behavior, motives, and perceptions in response to social variables. It tries to answer the question of how the behavior of one individual is affected by the real or imagined presence and behavior of other individuals. It has developed largely in the last thirty years to fill the niche between traditional psychology—which studies the behavior of individual organisms carefully removed from complex, "confounding" social variables—and sociology and anthropology—which study social institutions and the broader influences of culture on human behavior. Although the reactions of individuals are still what is being studied, the focus in social psychology is on the social setting in which such reactions occur and on their cognitive significance and social consequences.

In studying the social nature of the human animal, social psychological investigations focus sometimes on the dependent variable of social *behavior* and sometimes on the independent variable of social *stimuli*. In this chapter both social stimuli and social responses will be considered, as well as the concepts that unite them in meaningful psychological relationships. Our level of analysis will typically be a molar one, and the variables will be more complex than in the research described in earlier chapters.

Today, social psychology is moving toward a position of central importance in psychology as it becomes increasingly evident that even nonsocial reactions are often influenced by social variables such as attitudes, values, social needs for achievement or affiliation, the way the situation is perceived and defined (rather than how it "really is"), and broad cognitive structures developed through the processes of socialization. Social psychology is also showing an increasing concern for applying the knowledge learned from basic research to the solutions of pressing social problems. Racism, sexism, aggression, vandalism, alienation, blind obedience to authority, and international conflict are but some of the society's "relevant" problems demanding social action that will be discussed in this and the next chapter.

Attribution: Inferring Traits and Causes

To make sense out of the complex behavior of others, we make inferences about their intentions, emotions, motivations, and personality traits, and about the extent to which these conditions are the causes of their behavior. This cognitive process is called *attribution:* we attribute to the person or the behavior underlying conditions that we do not see but infer.

The Perception of People

Like our perception of objects, our perception of people is subject to various illusions and distortions. That is, we often "see" people differently from the way they are objectively presented to us. How do such less-than-accurate impressions occur? What information do we use in judging another's personality?

Judgment at first sight. You may think that your judgments of other people are based on careful consideration of their behavior. This is almost opposite to the truth, however. Psychologists have found that the perceiver's judgment of another person is heavily influenced by first impressions, which, in turn, may depend on rather minimal cues.

In one "real-life" experiment on first impressions, a professor told his class that a guest lecturer would be teaching that day and then passed out a brief biographical note about this person. Half of the students received a note that described the lecturer as a "rather cold person, industrious, critical, practical, and determined." The other students received identical notes, but with "warm" substituted for "cold." Not only did the "warm" subjects like the lecturer better, but they volunteered more in the class discussion than those who received "cold" notes (Kelley, 1950).

Why is the first impression so influential? One explanation is that the initial information creates a *frame of reference* that the perceiver uses to interpret later information. If later information is discrepant, it is distorted to fit the established frame of reference. This process is very similar to the operation of set in nonsocial situations, which we discussed in Chapter 6.

Pictures in our heads. Most of us carry around images of what various people are like. For example, we all "know" what a New York cab driver, a German scientist, or a college professor would be like. These images, or *stereotypes,* involve attributing certain characteristics to a whole group of people. When such images are based on experience and are relatively accurate, they make it easier for us to deal successfully with others. However, when they are inaccurate or when they prevent us from seeing an individual's unique characteristics, they can have a very negative, abrasive effect on human relationships. ∎

© 1972 by NEA, Inc.

∎ "We have rights, too! And I, for one, am fed up with trying to live up to somebody else's preconception of a retired person!"

The first major study of stereotypes clearly demonstrated the ability of people to agree on the traits that other people supposedly possess (Katz & Braly, 1933).

One hundred Princeton undergraduates were asked to select the traits that best described ten different national racial groups. The results showed a high degree of uniformity in stereotyping, as reflected in a distinctive set of labels (many of them derogatory) for each of these groups. For example, Jews were viewed as shrewd and mercenary, Negroes as superstitious and lazy, and Germans as scientifically minded and industrious. Some of the stereotyped groups were ones that the students had had very little, if any, contact with, so it seems obvious that they had simply adopted stereotypes that were present in their society.

Nearly twenty years later, this experiment was repeated at Princeton, with the results showing a decline in stereotyping (Gilbert, 1951). Furthermore, the students expressed more resistance to being asked to characterize other people. In general, these trends continued in a second, later replication of the study at Princeton, although the tendency to stereotype was still evident. Students could still agree on the "most characteristic traits" of various groups, even though the particular traits had changed over the intervening years (Karlins, Coffman, & Walters, 1969). ● (p. 564)

Consistency is in the mind of the perceiver. Besides relying too heavily on first impressions and stereotypes, there are other ways in which we often misperceive other people. One of the best known of these perceptual errors is the *halo effect,* which was noted as early as 1907. When people rate others on several traits, they usually rate them in terms of an overall impression (or "halo") of goodness or badness. For example, if they value courtesy and notice that a person is polite, they are more likely also to see him or her as being friendly, honest, and intelligent. The perceivers may also make the *logical error* of assuming that certain traits always go together. Thus, if they rate someone as being strong, they will probably also see him or her as being active and aggressive. A third kind of common error in perceptual judgment is the *leniency error* of lumping judgments at the positive end of a scale, and minimizing negative evaluations. This leads to a situation where "warm is the norm." Finally, a *central tendency error* occurs when raters ignore the variability among people or among the traits of one person and rate them all as "good," "fair," or "average."

As a result of all these judgmental errors, we see other people as being more consistent than they really are. A number of studies have found that people may behave rather inconsistently in different situations. For example, a person's honesty in one situation cannot be predicted on the basis of how honestly he or she behaved in another situation (Hartshorne & May, 1928). In spite of this demonstrated lack of consistency in

● STEREOTYPES OF FOUR GROUPS

Trait	Percent Checking Trait		
	1933	1951	1967
Japanese			
Intelligent	45	11	20
Industrious	43	12	57
Progressive	24	2	17
Shrewd	22	13	7
Sly	20	21	3
Jews			
Shrewd	79	47	30
Mercenary	49	28	15
Industrious	48	29	33
Grasping	34	17	17
Intelligent	29	37	37
Americans			
Industrious	48	30	23
Intelligent	47	32	20
Materialistic	33	37	67
Ambitious	33	21	42
Progressive	27	5	17
Negroes			
Superstitious	84	41	13
Lazy	75	31	26
Happy-go-lucky	38	17	27
Ignorant	38	24	11
Musical	26	33	47

Adapted from Karlins et al., 1969

people's behavior, however, we assume that people *are* consistent and perceive them in this way (see discussion on pp. 410–11). The extent to which we generate consistency by inferring underlying traits or dispositions is shown by our tendency to attribute such traits even to inanimate objects. This tendency was demonstrated in a study in which subjects saw geometric forms as "aggressive," "shy," and so on—traits that obviously do not exist in triangles and circles. ◆

Suppose you learn that a certain man is regarded as kind, but is also known to be very dishonest. According to several studies, you would try to resolve this inconsistency probably using one of the following techniques: (a) you could ignore or discount some of the information (e.g., the guy is really just a good-hearted, well-meaning soul); or (b) you could change your interpretation of one or both of the traits (e.g., the kindness is not "real," but is a deliberate trick to con people). The effect of either technique would be to allow you to have a more consistent (and therefore more comprehensible) impression of the man.

The Perception of Causes

To the extent that given behaviors have consequences that may bring us pleasure or pain or tell us something important about ourselves, others, or our environment, it becomes vital to us to identify the causal factors or forces to which the behaviors can be attributed.

Dispositional vs. situational attributions. Attributions that center upon the personality traits, skills, values, and needs of the person are called *dispositional* attributions. Such attributions imply *non*modifiability through new experience or intervention. Attributions of transient personality characteristics in oneself or others, such as attitudes, preferences, or motives assume the potential for change but still imply that the change must be in the individual.

Situational attributions, in contrast, look to properties not in the person but in the environment, the situation, or the interaction. These attributions locate causes as either outside the actors or not inherent in any one person but deriving from the interaction between them. Situational attributions imply that outcomes could be changed by changes in the relevant situational variables; thus they take the "blame" off the people involved.

The laws of behavior that most *experimental* research generates are empirical statements relating situational variables to certain outcomes. Such laws explain the variability of comparable subjects' behavior in different situations; differences between people are ignored. The generalizations of *personality* research, on the other hand, attempt to explain the variability of different people's behavior in the same situation. There is also a third class of explanations: those involving *interactions* between situational and dispositional variables—the situation has a different but predictable impact on different types of people. Taken together, these three types of explanation account for all the possible variation (other than random) in the behavior of people across situations.

There is a growing body of literature in social psychology pointing to the greater value of situational than dispositional variables in explaining, predicting, and controlling behavior (Argyle & Little, 1972; Larsen, Coleman, Forbes, & Johnson, 1972). The simulated prison described at the beginning of this chapter was a dramatic demonstration of the power of situational variables to produce markedly different behavior in similar subjects, while Milgram's obedience studies

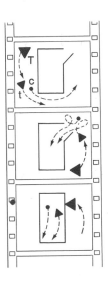

◆ In one study subjects were shown a film in which geometrical forms moved in and out of a large rectangle. Underlying motivations were attributed to the "characters," and the triangles were often seen as two males fighting over a female (the circle). On the basis of their movement, the large triangle was perceived as being aggressive, the small triangle as being heroic, and the circle as being timid. In the sequence shown here, most observers reported seeing T chase t and c into the house and close the door (Heider & Simmel, 1944).

(Chapters 1 & 14) also show how the situation may "overwhelm" personality characteristics and individual values.

The attribution error. Despite such research evidence, however, most people tend to make dispositional attributions when trying to understand why a given action has occurred—to overestimate the importance of an actor's *dispositions* and underestimate the importance of *situational* forces and restraints in accounting for behavior. This tendency has been called the *attribution error* (Ross, Bierbrauer, & Polly, 1974).

This source of error occurs across a wide range of everyday situations and is seen in our belief that *we* would not have acted the way so-and-so did in a given situation.

It is inconceivable to most people that they could have acted as Lt. Calley or the other members of Charlie Company did in the My Lai massacre, or as the National Guard did at Kent State, or as the Watergate "plumbers" did.

But it was also inconceivable to the psychiatrists—and perhaps to you—that the majority of subjects in Milgram's obedience studies would go all the way in giving electric shocks to an innocent victim. Similarly, in the Stanford prison-simulation study, all subjects who were later prisoners asserted that they were absolutely certain they would last the full two weeks—whereas half of them did not last even five days. And the guards did not believe they would ever act in the brutal manner they did. Said one before the study began, "As I am a pacifist, I cannot imagine ever being aggressive toward another person." Yet he became one of the most cruel, abusive guards. Even when subjects are asked to role-play the position of the shocker in Milgram's experiment and instructed to pay attention to the aspects of the *situation* that influence the decision to obey, they still continue to make dispositional attributions with the same frequency—although increasing their tendency to make situational ones also (Bierbrauer, 1973).

A major conclusion from all the research on attribution is that while people are remarkably *susceptible* to situational pressures (of authority figures, rules, protocol, etiquette, group consensus, justifications for actions, etc.), they are even more remarkably *insensitive* to and unaware of the extent to which these pressures are determining their behavior. We often say of ourselves, "My behavior depends on the situation" to signify that it varies from time to time, but we usually do not clearly relate what we do to situational forces. And we see other people's behavior as even more dispositionally based than our own (Jones & Nisbett, 1972).

Heider's attribution theory. How do we move so readily from observed acts to inferred, inner dispositions as causes of behavior? What information do we use, and what determines the kind of causes we attribute to different events?

These questions were first addressed in the writings by Fritz Heider (1944, 1958), who framed them in terms of a "naive psychology." Heider's interest was in the processes by which the average individual *knows* the world, how he or she develops an understanding of how events and people and self are related to each other. In that sense, Heider's inquiry and that of Piaget (as described in Chapter 5) are quite similar—how do children and adults go from perception of specific external events to a conception of the abstract principles behind those events?

Because of the apparent simplicity and lack of theoretical rigor in Heider's formulation, his contributions to our understanding of basic issues in human psychology were overlooked at first. More recently, however, there have been efforts to organize ideas about the attribution process into a *theory of attribution* (Jones & Davis, 1965; Kelley, 1967, 1972; Bem, 1965, 1972), and, today, attribution theory is probably giving rise to more research within social psychology than any other approach.

Attribution theory assumes that we have a need to develop an understanding of predictable relations in order to give stability and meaning to events in our lives. This leads to a *reality orientation* to the world. In addition, it assumes that we have a need to be able to predict important events and alter them in desirable direc-

tions. This leads to a *control orientation* to the world. (We met these two orientations in Chapter 3 in discussing the two kinds of conditioning and the need for organisms to know when signals and events and consequences are related.) Attribution theory assumes further that our assignment of causes may involve active information seeking, that it occurs in a systematic manner, and that the "meaning" an event has for us depends heavily on the cause we assign to it.

Attributional analysis proceeds by a rational-logical analysis of the information available to the perceiver-attributor. If a friend tells you that a certain movie you were planning to see is no good, how do you decide whether to take your friend's advice? You know that movies vary in quality and that people vary in how discriminating they are. Thus a number of factors must be taken into consideration.

Suppose your friend always puts down all movies; then his or her evaluation of this movie tells you nothing about *it* but is just characteristic of your critical friend. On the other hand, if the evaluation had been very positive, you would have assumed that it carried information specific to this movie.

Your judgment of whether an evaluation is *veridical* (tells it like it is) also depends on whether you think the other person is trying to influence you. If so, you see the statement as caused not by the thing described but by the person's intention and thus not likely to be trustworthy evidence about the thing itself. In general, you tend to make dispositional inferences when you see a person's acts as intentional and deliberate rather than as spontaneous, informational, or accidental.

Generally, when a person conforms to situational demands, we are likely to attribute the behavior to external causes, and thus we infer little about the person from his or her actions. On the other hand, when a person *deviates* from behaving according to clear situational demands (rules, expectations, social pressures, threats, incentives, etc.), we are likely to perceive such out-of-role behaviors as indicators of underlying dispositions.

You also attribute your own behavior to inner or outer causes under different circumstances.

Furthermore, how you evaluate *why* you do what you do has an important bearing on whether you like those activities, whether you will continue to do them in the absence of intrinsic reinforcement, and what priority you will give them.

An interesting shift occurs when you have been choosing to engage in an intrinsically interesting activity and start being given an extrinsic reward for it. In that situation, you may stop making the dispositional attribution that you are doing it because you like it and start attributing your activity to the external reward. Then, if the reward is cut off or "the price is not right," you may cease the previously enjoyed activity altogether.

In one experiment with undergraduate subjects from the University of Rochester, giving them money for working on puzzles that were intrinsically interesting decreased the time they spent on the puzzles later during a free-choice period, compared with subjects who had been unrewarded (Deci, 1972).

The same thing can happen in the classroom as a result of the extrinsic rewards of praise, approval, and grades.

Fifty-one preschool children who showed an initial intrinsic interest in a drawing activity were subjects in an experiment on this effect of "overjustification" for an activity by the addition of extrinsic justification. These children were randomly assigned to one of three conditions for the second part of the study: (a) extrinsic reward expected for engaging in the drawing activity (a gold seal and ribbon); (b) no reward expected—but received after *the activity; (c) no reward expected or received. One to two weeks later, the drawing activity was again introduced into the classrooms and the children's behavior was observed and recorded. The results clearly support the overjustification effect—attributing the reason for engaging in an initially interesting, freely chosen activity to an extrinsic reward lowers its value and reduces the amount of time the children later engage in the activity on their own. The children in the expected reward condition spent only half as much time on the target* activity as did those in the other two conditions—which did not differ from each other in time spent on the target activity (Lepper, Greene, & Nisbett, 1973). These findings have been replicated in other studies (Lepper & Greene, 1975).

The detrimental effect whereby extrinsic reinforcement transforms intrinsically motivated children into free-enterprise entrepreneurs points up an important limitation to the laws of reinforcement that we learned about earlier: even positive reinforcement may be counterproductive in its effect on the emission of behaviors that would have been practiced and enjoyed for their own sakes. (See *P&L* Close-up, p. 568.)

The way in which the attribution process can be affected by social conditions and then, in turn, can influence subsequent social conditions and attributions is revealed in an early study by Lloyd Strickland (1958) on surveillance and trust.

Do we trust people less whose behavior requires surveillance, or does exercising surveillance over others' behavior make us less likely to trust them? To separate out cause and effect, the researcher designed a procedure in which "supervisors" were required to monitor the output of two "workers" who had been assigned a dull task. The conditions required that the supervisors monitor Worker A nine times, while monitoring Worker B only twice. At the end of the work period, the output of the two workers was the same; thus there was no difference in the behaviors that the supervisors were observing.

The supervisors' interpretations of the why *of the behaviors differed, however. The more surveillance they had given, the more they attributed the behavior to the monitoring and not to the worker's motivation or personality. And in the next phase of the experiment, where no set amount of supervision was prescribed, the supervisors chose to monitor A's performance more often than B's and perceived B as more trustworthy and dependable than A, who "needed careful watching to keep him on his toes."*

A comparable phenomenon happens in a maximum security prison, where almost everyone assumes that the elaborate environmental controls are responsible for the prisoners' cooperation, and there may be nothing cooperative that a prisoner can do that the staff will see as coming from inner intentions. In general, only deviance is seen as prisoner-caused.

Close-up
The Joy Killer

An apocryphal tale is told of a little Italian shoemaker in New York who became the target of epithets shouted gleefully by boys in the neighborhood: "Dirty Wop!" "Greaseball, go back to Sicily!" and unprintable obscenities. In vain did the shoemaker ignore the boys, reason with them, and try to chase them away.

Then one day when he saw them approaching, he tried a new way. "Don't ask me why," he said to them, "but I will give each one of you 50¢ if you will shout ten times as loud as you can, 'Dirty Wop! No greaseballs in our neighborhood!'" The boys were delighted and enthusiastically shouted the phrases at the top of their lungs.

The next day, right after school, the boys reappeared, expecting more of the same. The shoemaker met them with a smile and said, "A quarter to every boy who will shout the same things I told you yesterday and make up at least one more." Again the boys complied, screaming at the top of their lungs until they were hoarse.

But when they came the next day, the little shoemaker said sadly, "Sorry, but business has been bad, and all I can afford today is a nickel apiece."

At which, so the story goes, the boys departed, grumbling that they had better things to do than please dumb Wops for only a nickel. What had been an inherently satisfying activity had come to be seen as something done because of a reward; when the reward was removed, they saw no reason to do it—as the shoemaker had rightly predicted.

Personal and Social Motives

People do not live by bread alone. They spend a lot of time and energy planning how to make a better loaf than their competitors, and often they are more concerned about the decor and the company than about what they are eating.

"Even people in the least technologically advanced societies do not spend most of their waking moments in eating, drinking, and sexual activities. Instead, people in both modern and preliterate societies bend the bulk of their energies toward the attainment or expression of states of mind and qualities of experience that are stirred not by the innate imperatives of their biological functioning but, instead, by the values they have learned as members of their society." (Sarnoff, 1966, pp. 15–16)

As we saw in Chapter 9, motives are considered to be inner states that instigate, organize, and direct certain patterns of behavior. As opposed to *biological drives*, which are aroused by neurophysiological stimulation or biological deprivation and are similar for all members of the species, *personal and social motives* are much more variable, are aroused and satisfied by psychological and social conditions, and are much more dependent on learning. (See *P&L* Close-up, p. 569.)

People generally seem to develop psychological needs that they express through the social patterns of their particular culture. Although these needs are sometimes overwhelmed by other needs, including environmental requirements, their satisfaction is nonetheless essential to the individual's healthy functioning. Frustration of personal and social motives, while not leading directly to the individual's death—as does prolonged frustration of most biological drives—can result in emotional disturbances or even severe physical illness.

The Need for Achievement

No student needs to be told that there is a strong emphasis in the United States on achievement. Business, sports, and the whole educational system all stress it. Grades are used as keys to higher levels of further competition (to admit the junior-college student to a four-year college and the college senior to graduate and professional schools). Students' characterization of the whole endeavor as one big rat race, with only a small piece of cheese in the trap, does not prevent them from joining in the race, especially if medical, law, or graduate-school admission is the prize.

The origin of a need to achieve has been the subject of much research.

In one study, mothers of eight- to ten-year-old boys indicated at what ages they expected each of a list of accomplishments in their sons. Mothers of children independently evaluated as high achievers, compared to those of low achievers, expected twice as many of the accomplishments to be met by the age of seven. The high achievers were expected earlier to know their way around their part of the city, to try new things, to do well in competition, and to make their own friends (Winterbottom, 1953).

The achievement motive is viewed by some investigators as a relatively general and stable characteristic of an individual, present in any situation (McClelland, 1961). It is seen as giving rise to a general *tendency to approach success,* although the strength of the tendency, in a given situation, is seen as depending on three other variables: (a) expectation of success, (b) the incentive value of the particular kind of success involved, and (c) perception of personal responsibility for success (Atkinson, 1964; Feather, 1967). For example, two people might both have a high general-achievement orientation, but one might especially value prestige and work hardest in situations where success would mean greater prestige, whereas the other might place greater value on the satisfaction of a job well done and put forth greatest efforts in situations in which success would bring that kind of satisfaction.

Close-up
The Motive to Work

What motivates people to study and work? One answer may be that they are working for *extrinsic* rewards, such as money, grades, and prestige, rather than because work is intrinsically appealing. But is this always the case?

According to McGregor (1960), most organizations are structured around a set of assumptions about human nature. One such set (which he calls *Theory X*) involves the belief that people basically dislike work and will do everything possible to avoid it. Although they want security, they have little ambition and do not like to have responsibilities. In any work situation, then, people must somehow be bribed or coerced.

An alternative set of assumptions is called *Theory Y* by McGregor. Here, the belief is that people are basically creative and responsible, that the expenditure of energy in some form of work is a natural process. To the extent that work objectives fulfill personal needs (such as self-esteem, curiosity, competence), people will be intrinsically motivated to do well.

Businesses that operate on Theory X usually try to increase the quantity or quality of production by offering such standard inducements as extra pay and shorter work weeks. However, some companies have changed their organization according to Theory Y principles and have found dramatic changes in work performed. For example, instead of having assembly lines (where each person only makes a small part of the final product), some have set up small work forces where each person works on the entire product, from beginning to end. Not only do people have more pride in their work, but the chance to work in small groups allows them to develop close friendships. The workers are more satisfied, and there is less absenteeism, job turnover, and work "sabotage."

Similar shifts from Theory X to Theory Y have been taking place in school systems. One of the best known of these is the "open classroom," in which students are encouraged to learn and explore at their own pace, guided by their own interests.

The complexity of the achievement motive is further indicated by the fact that among subjects with a high need for achievement, interesting differences have been found between those who focus on gaining success and those who focus on avoiding failure. Those who focus on attaining success tend to set more realistic goals and to choose tasks of intermediate difficulty. Those who are most concerned about avoiding failure tend to set more unrealistic goals (too low or too high in relation to their ability) and to choose tasks of low difficulty, where failure is least likely but where success, even if achieved, would be least satisfying. The importance of a feeling of responsibility for the outcome is also important in determining the level of tasks chosen. Subjects who feel highly responsible for their successes and failures tend to choose intermediate-level tasks, like the success-motivated subjects, whereas subjects who do *not* feel responsibility for their successes and failures show no preference among tasks of varying difficulty (Meyer, 1968). ■

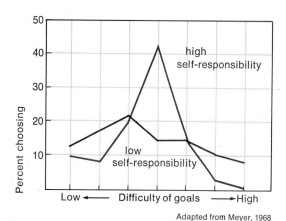

Adapted from Meyer, 1968

■ GOAL SETTING AND RESPONSIBILITY

Children nine to eleven years old were found to set goals of intermediate difficulty if they felt responsible for both successes and failures but to show little consistency in goal setting if they did not feel such responsibility.

In most of the research on the need to achieve, the subjects have been men. Until recently, very little attention has been paid to achievement motives in women. While this may be partially a result of societal stereotypes, it probably also reflects the fact that women did not behave the way they were "supposed" to (i.e., like men) in the few investigations in which they were studied. For example, although men show an increase in achievement motivation when placed in situations that stress intelligence and leadership ability, women do not.

One possible answer to this problem of gender differences has been provided by Matina Horner's research on *the motive to avoid success* in women. According to Horner, achievement-oriented women find themselves in a unique double-bind. On the one hand, they share with men society's general exhortation to compete and succeed; however, since successful achievement for women often brings such negative consequences as being labeled "unfeminine" or being socially rejected, women are also motivated *not* to succeed.

In a study designed to explore this motive, subjects were given an opening sentence for a story and asked to complete it. For women, the opening line was, "After first-term finals, Anne finds herself at the top of her medical school class," while for men it was, "After first-term finals, John finds himself at the top of his medical school class." The subjects' stories were scored as reflecting a motive to avoid success if they contained negative imagery about success. (See P&L Close-up, p. 571.) While fewer than 10 percent of the male subjects exhibited such negative concern, over 65 percent of the women wrote stories with high fear-of-success imagery (Horner, 1969).

Reactance: The Need for Freedom of Action

As a child, you probably had the experience of being told by your parents to do some particular chore (e.g., "Clean your room," "Do your homework") or of having some decision made for you ("We're going to see movie A, not B"). At times, you probably resisted these decisions, either by refusing to go along with them or by choosing to do something else. However, if your parents then said, "OK, so don't do it," you may have decided that the original activity wasn't so bad after all and ended up doing what they had initially asked.

According to Jack Brehm (1966), this type of "reverse" response is an example of *reactance*. The theory behind this concept rests on the assumption that people are motivated to maintain their freedom of action. When this freedom is threatened in any way, they will "react" by doing whatever they can to restore it. Thus, when someone threatens your freedom by putting pressure on you to act in a certain way, you will attempt to maintain your freedom by refusing to act in that way. Or, if someone tries to influence your decision by telling you that "A is better than B," you may react by deciding that B is better than A.

Experiments have borne out these predictions.

In one study, subjects were asked to participate in a group task along with two other subjects (actually confederates of the experimenter). The task involved analyzing and solving the problems in a human relations case study, and the group first had to decide which of two case studies to work on. When one of the confederates demanded that the group take Case Study A, subjects indicated their preference for the other alternative, Case Study B. However, when this demand was followed by the second confederate's saying he had not made up his mind yet (an action that restored the freedom to choose), subjects preferred Case Study A (Worchel & Brehm, 1971).

The Need for Social Comparison

"How'd you do on the exam?"
"I got an 80; you?"
"75, but the mean was only 60."

To take effective action, it is necessary to have some sense of your strengths and weaknesses, resources and biases. How do you follow the dictum, "Know thyself"?

Essentially, there are two major channels available for such information. The first in-

Close-up
Fear-of-Success Themes

In scoring women's stories for fear-of-success imagery, Horner (1969) found that there were three main categories.

1. The most common type of story expressed fears of social rejection (e.g., being unpopular, lonely, unmarriageable) as a consequence of success. For example: "Anne is an acne-faced bookworm. . . . She studies 12 hours a day, and lives at home to save money. 'Well, it certainly paid off. All the Friday and Saturday nights without dates, fun—I'll be the best woman doctor alive.' And yet a twinge of sadness comes through—she wonders what she really has . . ."

2. The second group of stories showed a concern about definitions of womanhood and raised doubts about Anne's femininity and normality: "Unfortunately Anne no longer feels so certain that she really wants to be a doctor. She is worried about herself and wonders if perhaps she is not normal . . . Anne decides not to continue with her medical work but to take courses that have a deeper personal meaning for her."

3. The third category of "fear-of-success" involved a direct denial that a woman could be so successful: "Anne is a *code* name for a nonexistent person created by a group of med students. They take turns taking exams and writing papers for Anne. . . ."

In contrast to these "fear-of-success" stories written by women, the stories written by men exhibited a positive attitude toward success.

In spite of the above evidence, however, the view that women take toward successful career women seems to be taking a turn for the better. Some of the women's stories predicted a brighter outlook:

"Anne is quite a lady—not only is she tops academically, but she is liked and admired by her fellow students—quite a trick in a man-dominated field. She is brilliant—but she is also a woman. She will continue to be at or near the top. And . . . always a lady."

volves "reality testing," in which you pit yourself against some physical attribute of the environment. Push a large boulder over, climb the highest mountain, swim the deepest ocean, throw a coin across the Potomac River, run a mile in four minutes flat, put out a fire with your bare hands. By such actions you find out what your physical capabilities are.

Whether you have succeeded in such tests of *physical reality,* however, is almost always evaluated according to tests of *social reality:* "Can other people do it too? Can they do it better? By how much?" The nonsocial motivation to know what we can do thus leads to the social motivation to use other people as yardsticks for evaluating our own accomplishments and abilities, and we initiate a process of *social comparison* (Festinger, 1954; Latané, 1966). We observe what others say and do, and we ask questions about what they think and feel. From these tests of social reality, we come to have a picture of how strong *we* are, how bright, how emotionally responsive, how politically conservative, how attractive, and so on.

From social comparisons we also learn "can" and "ought" relationships (Heider, 1958). Is it right or correct to believe, feel, or act in a certain way? Other people influence us by providing explicit information about appropriateness and thus helping us to define the existing social standards. They also influence us by reinforcing behavior that conforms to their standards and punishing or failing to reward behavior that does not (Deutsch & Gerard, 1955).

Not all comparison information is equally useful for forming exact and stable self-evaluations, however. The best information is derived from comparison with others who are close to our own ability or opinion, or who are experiencing the same stimulus situation.

Members of a group tend to use the group standards and the performance of other members as bases for self-evaluation. Thus, an individual who is very different from others in the group makes them uncomfortable because the differences disrupt their stable base for social comparison. Typically, as we shall see, they react either by trying to bring the individual into line or by rejecting him or her.

The extent to which our evaluation of our own intelligence and ability depends on comparing ourselves with others is demonstrated unhappily on every college campus each fall. Students who were "hotshots" in high school (compared to their classmates) are perplexed to discover that suddenly they are only "average"; indeed half of them are suddenly below the median compared to their new "hotshot" classmates. What has changed, of course, is not their intelligence but their basis for social compari-

son. An IQ of 120 is "superior" in relation to the population as a whole. But it may be "average" or even "low" in a highly selected group.

The Need for Social Approval

At a very early age, children learn that behaving according to parental (and societal) definitions of what is right and proper results in an array of positive consequences. But such consequences, when they come from other human beings, do much more than merely increase the probability that the response will be repeated and learned. They come to be sought for themselves, and many of our highly valued activities are undertaken not for their own sake but as instrumental in getting other people to notice, appreciate, honor, help, or love and cherish us. There are no limits to the length to which we may go to gain approval from other people, including killing someone or enduring humiliation, pain, or even death.

Social approval of your actions has at least five related but distinguishable consequences:

a) approval of your behavior is a sign of recognition of *you*, and confers *visibility* and *identity;*

b) approval *legitimates* your existence, increasing your status as a person deserving to be recognized;

c) approval implies acceptance of what you have to offer, and with it the *security* of not being rejected because of inadequacy in your abilities, opinions, or feelings;

d) approval establishes a bond of contact between approver and approved, creating *liking* for the approver and perception of reciprocation by him or her;

e) approval provides one criterion of your *control* or power over the environment, by specifying how behavior on your part can generate desired consequences.

It is no wonder, then, that children's learning is strongly influenced by deprivation of social approval or by the positive social reinforcement of a nod or "Good" (Gewirtz & Baer, 1958). Consider what you would have done (or did) to get a little piece of gold paper in the shape of a star from your second-grade teacher.

The social approval of age-mates can become even more precious than the social approval of parents and teachers, leading to "antisocial" behavior approved by the group. We can make sense of the class clown whose antics enrage the teacher, of teenagers risking their lives playing "chicken," or of the apparently senseless violence of gang members toward an innocent victim by recognizing the power being exerted by social approval from age-mates.

The Need for Affiliation

Because it appears that people everywhere live in groups, and because, as indicated earlier, survival has often depended on the safety of numbers, early social psychologists assumed that gregariousness was a basic, innate instinct. The "herd" was seen as the normal, natural environment for human beings. An early observer wrote:

"The conscious individual will feel an unanalyzable primary sense of comfort in the actual presence of his fellows, and a similar sense of discomfort in their absence. It will be obvious truth to him that it is not good for the man to be alone. Loneliness will be a real terror, insurmountable by reason." (Trotter, 1916, p. 31)

Research, however, has revealed great differences among individuals in the strength of affiliative needs, as measured by projective tests (Atkinson, 1958). Some also act in more affiliative ways than others, such as belonging to more social clubs, communicating more with others, and behaving in a friendlier way.

Stanley Schachter (1959) posed the question of the nature and source of the "herd instinct" as an empirically testable hypothesis. Evidence from various sources indicated that being isolated aroused feelings of anxiety. If so, perhaps the arousal of a strong drive such as anxiety would lead to a tendency to avoid isolation or to seek affiliation.

To test this reasoning, he induced high fear experimentally in half of a group of subjects and a low level of fear in the other half. The subjects were female university students who were tested in small groups of five to eight women. Half were led to expect that the ominous-looking Dr. Gregor Zilstein would give them a series of painful electric shocks as part of a study concerned with the effects of electric shock. The others anticipated no pain since they were to receive only mild electrical stimulation. Self-report measures indicated that those anticipating the pain were indeed made more fearful.

To see if this difference in fear of an anticipated shock had an effect on the dependent variable of affiliation, the women were given an opportunity to spend a ten-minute "waiting period" before the shock, either alone or with other women. Each subject indicated whether she had a preference to be alone or with others and if so what it was and how strongly she felt about it. The clear-cut results confirmed the hypothesis: fear did indeed lead to affiliation. ▲

A subsequent study showed that the *type* of person one chooses to affiliate with is also important.

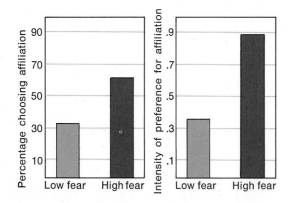

Adapted from Schachter, 1959

▲ **AFFILIATION INCREASES AS FEAR LEVEL GOES UP**

Almost twice as many high-fear subjects as low-fear ones preferred affiliation. In addition, the intensity of their preference for affiliation was almost three times as great as that of the low-fear subjects who chose affiliation.

As in Schachter's experiment, highly fearful subjects were given a choice of waiting alone or waiting with another subject. However, half of the subjects were told that the other person was waiting to go through the shock procedure (just as they were), while the other subjects were told that the person had already completed the experiment. The fearful subjects chose to affiliate with the person who was in a similar emotional state, and not *with the person who had finished the experiment (and could conceivably give them objective information about the source of their fear). Apparently, misery does not love just any* sort *of company—rather, misery loves miserable company (Zimbardo & Formica, 1963).* ●

Altruism: The Need to Help Others

He who saves a single life, it is as though he has saved the entire world.

Talmud

When we give help to others in the absence of any external rewards (such as money or praise), our behavior is described as *altruism*. Some psychologists have argued that altruism may be partly instinctive, since individual survival usually depends on the cooperative, helping behavior of others (Campbell, 1965). Others have demonstrated that an altruistic response (such as delivering another human being from suffering) can be inherently rewarding (Weiss et al., 1971). To the extent that the "Golden Rule" is a social norm that is explicitly taught and promoted by our society, we can also think of altruism as resulting from learning.

Another explanation of altruism centers on the concept of *empathy*. Once you learn to experience vicariously the thoughts and feelings of others, then you will feel pain when you see others in trouble and will take action to reduce their pain and your own (Aronfreed, 1970). In a related approach, altruism has been postulated as resulting from the arousal of *promotive tension*, which is defined as tension related to another's goal attainment: when we experience someone else's needs and desires, we are motivated to help the person fulfill those needs. According to this hypothesis, we will be more likely to help people who are similar to us in important opinions and who are close to achieving a desired goal (Hornstein, 1972).

Altruism may also be motivated by *guilt* and the subsequent attempt to make amends (Rawlings, 1970). People who feel that they have injured someone are more likely to behave altruistically, though the person they help may not be the one they have injured.

To test the "guilt" hypothesis, a field study was conducted in a large shopping center. Women shoppers were asked by a male experimenter to take his picture, as a favor to him. In all cases, the camera failed to work. Half of the women were led to believe that they had broken the camera (guilt condition), while the others were told that it was not their fault (control condition). Later on, as each subject walked through the shopping center, a female experimenter walked in front of them carrying a broken grocery bag with items falling from it. Of the subjects in the guilt condition, 55 percent told her

The following situations were among those presented to 100 students at Central Connecticut State College, who indicated in each case whether they would wish to be with others or alone.

Situation	Percentage of students who:		
	Wished to be with others	Wished to be alone	Had no preference
When depressed	42	48	10
When worried about a serious personal problem	52	44	4
When physically tired	6	85	9
When very happy	88	2	10
When feeling very guilty about something you have done	45	43	12
When embarrassed	16	76	8
When you want to cry	8	88	4
When you are in a strange situation or doing something you've never done before	77	13	10

Adapted from Middlebrook, 1973

that she was losing some of her groceries, while only 15 percent of the control subjects did so (Regan, Williams & Sparling, 1972).

Another approach to the understanding of altruism is based on the operation of *social norms*. One such norm is that of *social responsibility*—people should help those who are dependent on them and in need of help. The person who adopts this norm feels obligated to help others because it is the "right" thing to do, not because he or she will be directly benefited by it (Berkowitz, 1972). The norm of *reciprocity* also influences altruistic behavior—people feel they should help those who have helped them (Gouldner, 1960).

Any cues that make the norm of helping stand out will increase the amount of helping behavior. One such cue is altruism demonstrated by a model. For example, motorists were more likely to stop and help a woman fix a flat tire if they had just driven past another person helping someone fix a flat tire (Bryan & Test, 1967). Similarly, children who saw a model share were more likely to share themselves than were children who either did not see the model share or saw a model praising the idea of sharing but not actually doing so (Grusec, 1972).

The Need for Consistency

A number of psychologists have developed theories around the central theme of the need for consistency (see Abelson et al., 1968). All these theories postulate that individuals seek consistency, prefer balanced relations to unbalanced ones, and are motivated to reduce the disharmony inherent in inconsistent perceptions.

Cognitive dissonance. The most formally developed of these approaches is the *cognitive dissonance theory* of Leon Festinger (1957). The basic assumption of this theory is that people cannot tolerate inconsistency and will work to eliminate or reduce it whenever it exists. According to the theory, a state of *dissonance* will be aroused whenever a person simultaneously has two cognitions (bits of knowledge, beliefs, opinions) that are psychologically inconsistent. Since this state is an unpleasant one, the individual will be motivated to reduce the dissonance in some way and achieve greater *consonance* (consistency). This can happen if one of the cognitions is changed or if new ones are added.

For example, suppose the two dissonant cognitions are a piece of knowledge about oneself ("I smoke") and a belief about smoking ("Smoking causes lung cancer"). To reduce the dissonance involved here, one could: (a) change one's belief ("The evidence for lung cancer is not very convincing"); (b) change one's behavior (stop smoking); or (c) add new cognitions ("I don't inhale") that make the inconsistency less serious.

The more *important* the cognitions are for the individual, the greater the dissonance will be. For example, if our smoker didn't care about getting lung cancer (was ninety years old and had already lived a full life), then there would be little dissonance between "I smoke" and "Smoking causes lung cancer." For a younger person very frightened of becoming ill or dying, however, the dissonance would be much greater.

The amount of dissonance is also a function of the *ratio* of dissonant to consonant cognitions. Thus, the smoker who has not only the two contradictory cognitions but others less contradictory with "Smoking will harm me," such as "I hardly ever smoke" and "I don't inhale," would reduce the ratio from 1:1 to 1:3 and so experience less dissonance. According to the theory, the amount of dissonance that is produced is very important to an understanding of the individual's later behavior, since the greater the dissonance, the harder the person will try to reduce it.

In a later modification of the original theory, Brehm and Cohen (1962) postulated that dissonance is more likely to occur in a given situation if one *commits* oneself to an inconsistent course of action publicly while believing that one has a genuine *choice* to do otherwise. For example, you might feel considerable dissonance if you publicly supported a politician for whom you had contempt. But if you saw no other choice (you would lose your job otherwise), then you could disown the support as not personally caused and feel no dissonance.

Reducing cognitive dissonance. An important implication of Brehm and Cohen's hypothesis is that it can make predictions as to how dissonance will be reduced. Since public actions are observed by others, while private ideas and beliefs are not, any public behavior will be more "fixed" in reality and less susceptible to change than private thoughts. For example, suppose you are experiencing dissonance between an overt behavior ("I am working on a job I chose") and a covert belief ("This job is boring"). Since you have already made the behavioral commitment, it would be very hard for you to change that cognition to ("I did not choose to do this job"). Your private belief, however, is less anchored in external reality and thus is more amenable to change ("Actually, this job is interesting—I'm learning a lot").

A large number of studies have been conducted to test such dissonance-reduction hypotheses.

In one experiment, subjects participated in a very dull task and were then asked (as a favor to the experimenter) to lie to another subject by saying how much fun and interesting the task had been. Half the subjects were paid twenty dollars to tell the lie, while the others were paid only one dollar. For the former group, the amount of money was seen as a sufficient external justification for lying. For the others, the one-dollar payment was seen as an inadequate reason for telling the lie, so they were left with two dissonant cognitions: "The task was dull" and "I chose to tell someone it was fun and interesting." To reduce their dissonance, these subjects changed their evaluation of the task and later expressed the belief that "It really was fun and interesting—I might like to do it again." In comparison, the subjects who lied for twenty dollars did not change their evaluation of the dull task (Festinger & Carlsmith, 1959).

Another experiment tested the responses of male Army Reservists toward eating a highly disliked food—fried grasshoppers. After hearing a talk on "the needs of the new mobile army," the men were asked to try some new food and were each given a plate of fried grasshoppers. For half the subjects, the request to eat was made by a pleasant, likable ROTC officer. For the others, the request was made by a very cold and unpleasant officer who had been seen earlier acting in a rude and hostile way to his assistant.

Within both groups, about half of the men actually ate at least one grasshopper. Those who ate them at the request of the nice officer did not experience dissonance at eating a disliked food since they had adequate justification for it ("He's a great guy—I'll do it as a favor to him"). However, the men who ate at the bidding of the unpleasant officer had no good reason for eating such disliked food and behaved in a paradoxical way. To reduce dissonance, they changed their attitudes about the grasshoppers by deciding that they were actually rather tasty. The graph shows these results (Zimbardo, Weisenberg, Firestone, & Levy, 1965). ■

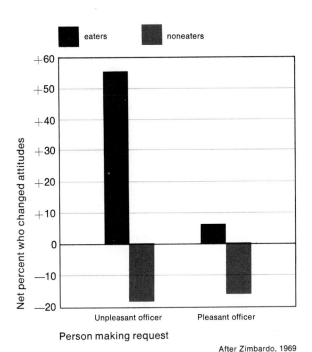

After Zimbardo, 1969

■ **TO KNOW GRASSHOPPERS IS TO LOVE THEM**

Subjects who ate grasshoppers for the unpleasant officer rated them much more positively. The other eaters improved their ratings only slightly, and the noneaters expressed greater distaste than before.

Interpersonal Attraction

Does "absence make the heart grow fonder," or is it "out of sight, out of mind"? Do "birds of a feather flock together," or does "familiarity breed contempt"? Or which wisdom shall we follow from Shakespeare: "They do not love that do not show their love," or "Love looks not with the eyes, but with the mind"?

When it comes to friendship, attraction, love, and marriage, every human society has a vast accumulation of knowledge collected over the ages to guide the social psychologist's inquiry. But as our opening "hypotheses" nicely indicate, common sense and literary wisdom have enjoyed a long life by the simple expedient of being all things to all people. There are homilies, clichés, quotations, old wives' tales, and down-home good sense to handle all outcomes—so long as you select the one that suits the occasion and conveniently ignore its contradiction.

Despite the obvious importance of attraction between people in creating the foundations of social life, it is only recently that energetic young researchers have begun to recast the flowery verse of the poets and the essence of common sense into testable hypotheses. From this emerging enterprise we may soon learn some valuable lessons to help us love each other both wisely and well.

What People Do We Like?

Basically, research has shown that we are attracted to people who bring us maximum rewards or gratifications at a minimum expense. For example, we are more attracted to people who are nearby than to those who are farther away. We like people who are already attracted to us, and who demonstrate their attraction by doing us favors and saying nice things about us. We like people who satisfy our needs and who have needs that we can satisfy.

beauty gets the best of it in this world

Don Marquis, *The Lives & Times of Archy and Mehitabel,* 1927

Physical attractiveness. Generally speaking, we like beautiful people more than we like homely or ugly ones. Although this finding may contradict our beliefs in equality and in the irrelevance of external appearance to personal relationships, it has been demonstrated in a number of experimental studies (Berscheid & Walster, 1974). Why do we prefer the beautiful? One reason is that we have a stereotyped notion that whatever is beautiful is good. Thus we perceive beautiful people as more intelligent, more successful, more pleasant, and happier than other people, even if there is no objective basis for these judgments.

So far, the research on physical attractiveness has been done in situations where people did not know each other or were only beginning to get acquainted. It may be that physical attractiveness plays a more important role in these initial, "getting to know you" stages than later on in a relationship.

We don't love qualities, we love persons; sometimes by reason of their defects as well as of their qualities.

Jacques Maritain, *Reflections on America,* 1958, p. 3

Competency. In general, we like people who are able and competent, rather than those who have difficulties in doing things well. However, it is possible to be too competent for one's own good: highly competent people may be better liked if they show some human weaknesses or blunder occasionally than if they maintain an image of too-great perfection.

In one study subjects listened to one of four tape recordings of a "candidate for the College Quiz Bowl." The same voice was used on each tape, but on two of the tapes the candidate was presented as highly intelligent and as having done well both academically and in extracurricular activities. On the other two tapes, the candidate was presented as average in intelligence and as having done only moderately well in school. On two of the tapes (one involving the superior person, one involving the average person), the candidate committed an embarrassing blunder by clumsily spilling a cup of coffee all over himself.

After listening to each tape, subjects were interviewed about their impressions of the candidate, how much they liked the candidate, and so on. "The results were clear-cut: The most attractive stimulus person was the superior person who committed a blunder, while the least attractive stimulus person was the person of average ability who also committed a blunder. . . . there was nothing charming about the blunder itself; it had the effect of increasing the attractiveness of the superior person and decreasing the attractiveness of the average person" (Aronson, 1969, p. 149).

There can be little liking where there is no likeness.

Aesop, *Fables*

Similarity and complementarity. One of the most consistent findings in research on attraction is that people like others who are similar to themselves. In particular, they like people who have similar attitudes and agree with them (Byrne, 1971). Why should an agreeing person be so attractive? One possible reason is that agreement is *reinforcing.* We are less likely to argue or have unpleasant encounters with someone who generally agrees with us, and are more likely to feel confident in the correctness of our attitudes. Furthermore, we may believe that similar people will more likely become attracted to us. Similarity may also lead to attraction because it allows us to maintain *consistent,* balanced relationships with our friends. Thus we like those who like what we like. Another explanation is that we are attracted to people with similar attitudes for reasons of *social comparison.* As we saw earlier, we usually look to other people to give us information about our own abilities, feelings, and beliefs. In other words, we may be attracted to people who are reflections of ourselves or of what we would like to be.

Not all similarity breeds such liking, however. There is some evidence that attraction is the result of having *complementary* needs or personality styles. For example, the person who is very domineering may like someone who is quiet and submissive, rather than another domineering individual.

It may be that at different times, different factors are important to the development of a couple's relationship. For example, similarity of values may be necessary at the early stages, while complementarity of needs may be critical for a long-term relationship (Kerckhoff & Davis, 1962).

Why Do We Like the People We Like?

As more and more research is done on the antecedents of attraction, attempts have been made to pull them all together into some kind of comprehensive theory. The most typical approach has been to explain attractions in terms of a reward-cost analysis, although other theories are beginning to be developed.

Love is often nothing but a favorable exchange between two people who get the most of what they can expect, considering their value on the personality market.

Erich Fromm, *The Sane Society*, 1955, p. 5

Equity theory. As we saw in Chapter 3, individuals tend to engage in behaviors for which they are positively reinforced and avoid those for which they are punished. This basic proposition is at the heart of *equity theory*, which states that people will try to maximize their outcomes by achieving the greatest possible rewards at the minimum costs. Much of the attraction research can be understood in such reward-cost terms. For example, all other things being equal, it "costs" less in time and effort to like someone who is physically close than someone who is far away. Similarly, we receive more "rewards" from people who are pleasant and do nice things for us than from those who are unpleasant and disagreeable.

When two people are involved in a friendship or romantic relationship, then *two* sets of rewards and costs need to be considered. According to equity theory, a relationship will endure only if it is profitable to both participants. That is, each person must be getting rewards from the relationship (such as security, prestige, etc.) with a minimum number of costs. Such an outcome can best be achieved by an equitable relationship, in which there is an equal exchange of benefits. Thus, a couple will be happiest if they receive "equal" benefits (Walster, Berscheid, & Walster, 1973).

In the application of equity theory to romantic relationships, the "matching" of partners has usually been conceptualized in terms of social desirability. People of high social desirability are those who are more attractive, are more intelligent, have greater material resources, and so on. Equity theory predicts that such people will select, and like best, people of equally high "social worth." Similarly, people with lower social desirability will choose and prefer partners who match them in terms of desirability. However, the evidence for this "matching" hypothesis is somewhat mixed. Although individuals do tend to choose partners of approximately the same social worth, they still persistently try to attract partners who are far more socially desirable than they. In other words, we strive for the ideal, but our choices tend to be based on the reality of what we have to offer someone else.

Hatred which is entirely conquered by love passes into love, and love on that account is greater than if it had not been preceded by hatred.

Benedict Spinoza, *Ethics*, 1677

Gain-loss theory. Liking is not determined entirely by the other person's characteristics and the extent to which they "match" our own. In situations where attraction is involved, the individual's own ego is at stake, and liking may depend as much or more on one's feelings about oneself as on the characteristics of the other person. One's self-esteem is often based on the feedback one gets from other individuals, and the response that occurs is not always in line with the predictions of equity theory.

Elliot Aronson (1969) has developed a model called the *gain-loss theory of attraction* to deal with this area of feedback and liking. According to this theory, *changes* in another person's evaluation of us will have more impact on our liking for him or her than if the evaluation were constant. Thus we will like a person whose esteem for us increases over time (a "gain" situation) better than someone who has always liked us. Similarly, we will dislike a person whose evaluation of us becomes more negative over time (a "loss" situation) more than someone who has always disliked us.

Why should this be so? One reason is that we are more likely to attribute a change in the person's attitude to something that *we* did ("She's changing her mind because she's gotten to know me better"), while attributing an unchanging attitude to the person's disposition ("He always says that—it's just the way he is and has nothing to do with me"). Thus we take the change in opinion more personally. Another possible reason involves the arousal and reduction of anxiety. People arouse anxiety in us by saying negative things; when they later say positive things ("gain"), these evaluations not only are rewarding in and of themselves, but also reduce the previous anxiety and are thus doubly rewarding. Just the opposite would be the case for the "loss" part of the theory.

To test this model, a study was conducted in which female subjects interacted in two-person groups over a series of brief meetings. After each meeting, it was possible for one subject to eavesdrop on a conversation between the experimenter and the "partner" (actually a confederate) in which the partner evaluated the subject. There were four major experimental conditions: (1) positive—the evaluations were consistently favorable; (2) negative—the evaluations were consistently unfavorable; (3) gain—the evaluations began as unfavorable, but gradually be-

came as positive as those in the positive condition; (4) loss—the evaluations began as favorable, but gradually became as negative as those in the negative conditon.

If liking depended on the number of rewards received by each subject, then there should have been most liking in the positive condition, least in the negative condition, and an intermediate amount in the gain and loss conditions. This did not occur. Rather, it was the pattern or sequence of reinforcements that was the major determinant of liking. Subjects liked the confederate in the "gain" condition better than the confederate whose evaluations were all positive. Similarly, there was a tendency for the confederate in the "loss" condition to be disliked more than the confederate who gave negative evaluations every time (Aronson & Linder, 1965).

Romantic Love

Given the importance of love in promoting happiness and making the world go 'round, it is somewhat surprising that psychologists have done so little research on this topic. This may be partly attributable to a reluctance to "objectify" something that is viewed as romantic and mystical. What is this thing called love? The research of Zick Rubin (1973) illustrates one of the most systematic approaches to this delicate topic:

This investigation had three major phases. First, a paper-and-pencil "love scale" was developed. Second, the scale was administered, together with other measures, to 182 dating couples (college students). Third, predictions based on the conception of love that emerged were tested in a laboratory experiment extending over a six-month period.

The development of the love scale began with the construction of a pool of items that were suggested by various psychological and sociological speculations about romantic love. Items intended to tap the more extensively researched "garden variety" of interpersonal attraction—simple liking—were also included. After preliminary sortings by panels of judges, a set of seventy items was administered to several hundred college students, who completed them with respect to their attitudes toward the person they were dating. Primarily on the basis of factor analysis of these responses, shorter scales of love and of liking were then built. ●

The content of the love scale served as the working definition of love for the succeeding phases of the research. It included three major components: (a) affiliative and dependent needs, (b) predisposition to help, and (c) exclusiveness and absorption.

Rubin was curious to know if a couple's scores on the love scale were related to their actual behavior toward one another. Operating on the notion that romantic love includes a tendency to be completely absorbed with each other, he unobtrusively watched couples who were sitting alone waiting for the experiment to begin. He found that couples who had high scores on the love scale were more likely to gaze into each other's eyes than couples with low love scores.

Six months later, Rubin asked the couples to fill out a questionnaire about their relationship at that time. As predicted, their initial love scores were positively related to their reports on whether or not their relationships had made progress toward permanence.

According to popular belief, another aspect of love is the extent to which one shares the other person's feelings. A true lover not only knows the partner's ups and downs but experiences them as well. An unusual test of this "empathy hypothesis" was conducted in the context of a learning and memory experiment.

Subjects for the study were male college students, who were seated around a big table in a classroom. Their task was quite simple: each one in turn had to read aloud a word printed on a card in front of him. On any one trial, half of the subjects performed (read aloud a single word) while the others merely listened. The subjects were told in advance that they would be asked to recall all the words that had been read.

When the subjects were strangers to each other, they had very different recall patterns depending on whether they were performers or audience. For the audience condition, recall ranged between about 23 percent and 37 percent. But in the condition in which listening was punctuated by a public performance (even so simple a one as reading aloud an ordinary word), the recall curve was strikingly different. Recall for one's own performance was almost perfect, whereas recall for the closest words before and after was very poor; in fact, the closer the word was in time to one's own performance, the lower the recall. Anxiety about performing well apparently resulted in a tuning out of the responses just before and just after one's own (Brenner, 1971). ▲   (p. 582)

● HOW DO I LOVE THEE?
LET ME CHECK THE ITEMS

Rubin's love scale comprises the items listed below. Each item is answered on a 9-point continuum, where 1 = "Not at all true; disagree completely" and 9 = "Definitely true; agree completely."

Love Scale

1. If _____ were feeling badly, my first duty would be to cheer him (her) up.

2. I feel that I can confide in _____ about virtually everything.

3. I find it easy to ignore _____'s faults.

4. I would do almost anything for _____.

5. I feel very possessive toward _____.

6. If I could never be with _____, I would feel miserable.

7. If I were lonely, my first thought would be to seek _____ out.

8. One of my primary concerns is _____'s welfare.

9. I would forgive _____ for practically anything.

10. I feel responsible for _____'s well-being.

11. When I am with _____, I spend a good deal of time just looking at him (her).

12. I would greatly enjoy being confided in by _____.

13. It would be hard for me to get along without _____.

From Rubin, 1973

When subjects participated in this experiment along with their romantic partner, an interesting change took place in the audience recall curve. Subjects who were watching while their partner performed showed the same recall curve as their partner (i.e., high recall for partner's word, poor recall for the words before and after it). In other words, their memory for the task was the same as if they had done it themselves, rather than just watching. This "empathy" effect was highly correlated with other measures of love and caring; couples with high "empathy" scores were more likely to: (a) report that they cared about each other, (b) arrive at the experiment holding hands or having their arms around each other, and (c) still be going together eight months later (Brenner, 1973).

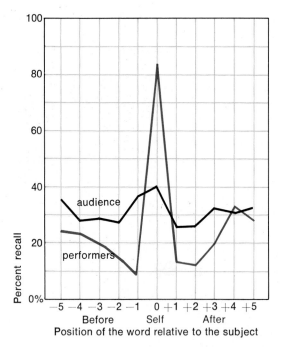

After Brenner, 1971

▲ **CIRCLE OF APPREHENSION**

For those who were only audience, recall was about the same for most of the words, only slightly higher for the words nearest one's own position. However, when members of the audience became performers, the pattern was very different. They remembered the words they spoke almost perfectly but showed a sharp decline in memory for what was said just before and just after their turn to step into the spotlight.

Social Influence As "People Power"

SCENARIO 1: On June 27, 1973, Kathy Crampton, age 19, was abducted from her new residence in a commune belonging to the fundamentalist Church of Armageddon in Seattle. Her abductors—a woman and two men—forced her into a car while she was out jogging. When a State Trooper stopped the car, Kathy told him she had been kidnapped, taken against her will by these people. She also told him that her name was Corinth Love Israel, she was 85 years old, and her mother was the "spiritual vision of peace" (all according to her religious faith). The police officer did *not* intervene. Instead he allowed her abductors to drive her off to San Diego.

The woman Kathy accused of kidnapping her was Mrs. Henrietta Crampton, Kathy's mother; the men were her sister's fiancé and Ted Patrick, an expert on "deprogramming."

Kathy claimed that she had neither taken drugs nor had sexual intercourse with any members of her new family but had freely given her life to the founder of the Church of Armageddon to become a child of God. After 102 hours of coercive reindoctrination, including religious services, intensive questioning, emotional attacks, and physical challenges, the deprogramming had apparently succeeded.

But the next day Kathy Crampton freely chose to escape and make her way back to Seattle and the Church of Armageddon. Because of her perseverance in resisting the deprogramming, she was renamed by the Church founder *Dedication* Israel (CBS Evening News Special, Aug. 13, 14, 15, 1973. See also *Los Angeles Times*, Dec. 4, 1972).

SCENARIO 2: On February 4, 1974, Patricia Hearst, age 19, was abducted from her apartment in Berkeley, California, by a woman and two men belonging to the Symbionese Liberation Army. After demands for millions of dollars of ransom in the form of food for the poor were met by her father, Randolph Hearst, Patty was scheduled to be released. Then, about sixty days after her kidnapping, the Hearst family and much of the nation were stunned by the tape-recorded announcement that Patty Hearst—renamed Tania—had chosen to stay with the SLA. Along with the tape was a photo of the young woman in a military posture, machine gun in hand in front of the SLA flag. ■

Patty prefaced her prepared statement with the notice that she was saying "what I feel," that the words were her own, and that in no way was she "brainwashed, drugged, tortured, hypnotized, or in any way confused." She went on to denounce her father for his "crimes against the people" and she abandoned her fiancé with the statement, "I have changed—grown. I've become conscious and can never go back to the life we led before. . . ."

During the nineteen months that she eluded "recapture" by the FBI, Tania was involved in at least one bank robbery and other illegal activities. Her sensational trial in San Francisco was obviously more than just one in which her guilt was to be established. At trial was the nature of free will versus assumptions about the power of social forces of persuasion and indoctrination. Defense lawyer F. Lee Bailey based his case on a form of "brainwashing." He contended that she was under a state of such duress that it conditioned her to unthinking obedience to her captor's wishes. Thus her behavior was not rational, but influenced and forced through fear and primitive needs for survival. The jury did not accept that view, finding her guilty of the Hibernia Bank robbery. They could not accept the notion of duress in the absence of her captors, most of whom had been killed in a Los Angeles shoot-out with the police more than a year earlier.

It seems reasonable to conclude that Patty made an ideological conversion to the romantic political belief system of the SLA—in many ways similar to Kathy Crampton's religious conversion. The physical fear she initially experienced was likely to make her grateful to her captors when she was released from the closet confinement and allowed to eat, sleep, and interact with young people who were her peers. Their ideals and rhetoric of justice, equitable distribution of wealth, and racial equality when part of a Robin Hood life-style must have been very appealing to a young person of no firm political, religious, or social ideology.

These cases raise two basic issues for the social psychologist. What are the conditions and variables that cause individuals to change their attitudes, their beliefs, and their behavior? And when there is a profound change in what a per-

■ This photo of Patricia Hearst was released by the Symbionese Liberation Army fifty-eight days after her kidnaping. The taped message that came with the photo revealed that Patty had chosen to join the cause of the SLA.

son says and does—as with Kathy Crampton and Patty Hearst—how can it be determined whether the conversion is a "genuine" one or only overt compliance? Restated, the second question becomes, "How do we know whether any act—by ourselves or others—is freely chosen or is the consequence of coercive pressures?" When do we perceive it as emerging naturally from within and when do we see it as induced artificially from without?

The Many Faces of Persuasion

Virtually every day of our lives we are being bombarded by systematic attempts to influence the way we think, feel, and act. Our senses are assaulted through the mass media by planned programs of advertisers who want us to buy various products and sundry services whether or not we want them, need them, or can afford them. Politicians try to influence our votes; teachers try to influence our thinking; religious leaders try to influence our moral behavior and spiritual values; and while our friends influence our style of dress, vocabulary, "taste" in music, and ideas of what constitutes an acceptable date, our parents press on us the importance of eating spinach, cleaning our room, personal hygiene, certain sexual attitudes, and much more.

We have come to accept such attempts as facts of life. Witness such homilies as "You can catch more flies with honey than with vinegar." Examples of persuasion like those cited above, however, still distress us. One-sided social influence becomes more unacceptable to most people to the extent that: (a) the "victim" is unable to resist because of "tender age," "weak intellect," or dependence on the influencer; (b) the influencer employs coercive power and has control of most of the relevant resources; (c) the "victim" gains nothing while the influencer gains something; and, most importantly, (d) there is a high probability that the influence attempt will be successful: no one cares about social influence that does not work.

Education vs. propaganda. A person can be said to have chosen freely only to the extent that he or she was aware of all the options and of the possible consequences and contingencies. Many educators believe that it is their primary task to teach students *how* to think and not *what* to think—that students should be encouraged to seek out alternatives and learn how to evaluate them rather than accept someone else's definition of the problem or choice of solution.

Propaganda, in contrast, is defined as the systematic, widespread promotion of particular ideas, doctrines, or practices to further one's own cause or to discredit that of one's opposition. Effective propaganda usually involves concealing from the intended target audience both the intention to persuade and also the true source of the propaganda.

But if propaganda works best when it is subtle and not obvious because it fits into an available social context, then it is sometimes indistinguishable from what passes as education. In teaching students how to think, textbooks and teachers must use content. In the content they select or fail to use, we may discover the operation of a bias that qualifies some education as propaganda, according to the standard dictionary definition. Remember how many examples designed to teach you mathematical reasoning employed concepts of buying, selling, renting, loans, interest, penalties, and wages? Such examples are considerably more frequent in texts of countries with a capitalist economic system than in those from socialist countries. Similarly, by their absence from our history books, minority peoples have been systematically overlooked as contributors to the development of the United States.

When is persuasion coercive? More carefully calculated are the efforts of lawyers, police interrogators, and leaders of the state to gain our "freely given" consent or assent. Louis Nizer (1961), a famous trial lawyer, describes the subtle psychology of the jury, which, he feels, must be played upon since "the opportunity to condition the jury is as limitless as the attorney's art" (p. 42). Our literature abounds with the folklore of persuasive tactics, Marc Antony's funeral oration for Julius Caesar being a classic example.

The manuals for training police in the art of interrogation may take some of the credit for the fact that 80 percent of all arraigned suspects confess following a period of interrogation (see Inbau & Reid, 1967). In these manuals the physical excesses of the old "third degree" have been replaced by the "sophistication" of applied psychology used in ethically questionable ways. (See *P&L* Close-up below.)

Normally, we would assume that the tests for coercion might include the following criteria: (a) sudden, dramatic conversion of beliefs and values rather than gradual evolution of a new position; (b) inaccessibility to one's usual sources of information, approval, and social comparison; (c) being detained in a situation where informational inputs, as well as sources of social reinforcement, are controlled; (d) intensive contact with persuasive agents; (e) promise that the present situation is only temporary and that return to one's former situation is possible.

Close-up
Confess, My Child, and You Shall Be Saved—in Prison

Interrogation manuals claim that they do not "coerce" confessions, but rather elicit them as voluntary statements from suspects actually guilty of committing crimes. After giving a 61-page typewritten murder confession, suspect George Whitmore, Jr., said he felt closer to his interrogating officer than to his own father. It was subsequently proven that Whitmore's confession was false, and had been subtly coerced by means of an old standard technique known as the *Mutt and Jeff approach*. Two detectives work as a pair: Mutt, the "heavy" who leans on the suspect, is abusive and menacing. Jeff, who is kindly and gentle, pretends to be distressed by Mutt's degrading attacks on the suspect, whom he tries to protect. Jeff is the only source of friendship in the barren, hopeless situation. A confession to him will help straighten things out, will enable Jeff to put Mutt in his place and give him a chance to help out his new-found friend-in-distress. In such a situation, Whitmore obliged with an incredibly detailed description of two murders he had never committed.

Variations on this theme include the "bluff on a split pair," in which two suspects are separated, and Suspect 1 is taken into a back room while Suspect 2 waits in the front office. After hearing screaming and loud noise from the back room, Suspect 2 hears the secretary called in over the intercom. Later, the secretary returns to the front office and begins typing, occasionally stopping to ask Suspect 2 for some vital information that gets typed into the report. Eventually, the detective in charge appears and says there is no need to interview Suspect 2 because the case is closed: the partner has "spilled the beans," turned state's evidence, and put the finger on Suspect 2. In many cases, the unsuspecting Suspect 2 then pleads innocence while describing the crime in detail and accusing the partner of it. After this "voluntary" confession, Suspect 1, who up to this point has said nothing, gets a chance to read the confession and take the full rap or further implicate the deceived accomplice.

In a "reverse line-up," a suspect in a minor crime may be identified by several reputable-looking witnesses (police confederates) as a child molester, kidnaper, armed robber, or whatever. Against the possibility of a 20-years-to-life sentence, pleading guilty to the lesser crime with a 1-to-5-year sentence seems the better part of wisdom for many naive suspects.

Besides describing tactics such as these, interrogation manuals tell detective candidates how to dress, talk, and size up the suspect, as well as how the room should be arranged for maximum persuasive impact. That some people can come to believe in the truth of their false confessions was shown in the political purge trials held by Stalin in the 1930s, and demonstrated in a controlled laboratory study by Daryl Bem (1966).

"Brainwashing" fits these criteria. It is not a scientific term but a word coined by a reporter to account for the conversions apparently produced by the Chinese Communists in some American POWs during the Korean War (see Schein, 1961; Hinkle & Wolff, 1956).

What Produces—and Changes—Attitudes?

An *attitude* is a relatively stable, emotionalized predisposition to respond in some consistent way toward some person or group of people or situations. The question of how attitudes are learned—and changed—is of concern to us all. Not only are we targets of the kinds of persuasion outlined above, but it is the rare person who has never tried to influence someone else, to change someone's mind by a "line," "reason," example, appeal, threat, or bribe in disguised form. The incredible success of Dale Carnegie's book *How to Win Friends . . .* may be attributed in part to our affiliative need, but since the rest of the title and the text concern influencing people, it may also be that most of us would like to sharpen our manipulative skills. (See *P&L* Close-up at left.)

Attitudes have three components: (a) *beliefs,* or propositions about the way things are or ought to be; (b) *affect,* or emotion associated with these beliefs, measurable in terms of physiological reactions or intensity and style of response; and (c) an *action* component, with a given probability of responding in specific ways. We form attitudes about many things in our lives, some of which we know about only indirectly, through information provided by others. Thus one source of attitude formation is *information,* be it through direct observation, information from others, or inferred information. Other sources, already discussed in earlier chapters, include *observation of models* and of the consequences of their actions, and *rewards and punishments* (usually social) meted out by our peers or family for holding or not holding a given attitude. The attitudes we form may also be by-products of repressed conflicts or displaced forms of them. This *ego-defensive* function of attitudes is assumed to play a potent role in the development of some of our most strongly held and "irrational" attitudes, as in racial and religious prejudices (Sarnoff, 1960).

If attitudes are formed in these several ways, then we can expect that changing them will take place through exposure to new information, observation of new models or old models with new reinforcement contingencies, changed rewards and punishments for our own attitudes, and resolution of our psychodynamic conflicts. Although all these methods are now being explored, the major approach taken by social psychologists has been to view individuals as rational information-processors whose attitudes could be changed through exposure to persuasive communications.

Close-up
Social Facilitation in the Absence of Persuasion

We are so sensitive to other people that they often exert considerable influence on our behavior even when they do not intend to. The effect that the presence of others has on us is called *social facilitation.* For example, an actor may experience "stage fright" and forget his lines simply as a result of seeing the theater filled with an audience. On the other hand, racers (track, swimming, auto, bicycle) consistently perform *better* when other competitors are present than when they compete against time (Triplett, 1897). In many controlled studies with humans and animals, the same generalization emerges: the mere presence of other individuals may facilitate or interfere with behavior (Simmel, Hoppe, & Milton, 1968).

It has been hypothesized that the *presence of others* is a stimulus that arouses a general, nonspecific drive state that then facilitates performance of established habits and simple responses but has an interfering effect as a distractor in situations where complex responses are being acquired (Zajonc, 1965, 1968). On the basis of this analysis, would you rather study alone and take a test in a group, or study in a group and be tested alone?

Who says what to whom with what effects? Aristotle, in his *Rhetoric*, attributed the persuasive impact of a communication to three distinguishable factors: *ethos, logos,* and *pathos.* These correspond to communicator characteristics, message features, and the emotional nature of the audience. The scientific study of communication effectiveness has followed Aristotle's lead in its investigation of "*who* says *what* to *whom*—and with what effect." The basic paradigms were worked out by researchers in Yale University's Communication and Attitude Change Program (Hovland, Janis, & Kelley, 1953).

Even though the research has concentrated on only the three variables—source, message, and audience—complex interactions have typically been found rather than simple main effects. The reason becomes apparent when we consider only a few of the dimensions on which source, message, and audience may vary:

1. *Source*—expertise, trustworthiness, status, coercive and reward power, age, sex, race, ethnic group, physical appearance, attractiveness, voice qualities, identification with audience's initial attitude, and so on.

2. *Message*—use of rational or emotional appeals, type of emotional appeals (fear, guilt, shame, etc.), organizational features (builds to climax or starts out as hard-hitting), language style (formal, colloquial, slang, profanity, slogans), presents both sides of the issue or only one side, presents positive or negative points first, and so on.

3. *Audience*—all the physical and demographic characteristics on which people can vary; especially relevant are sex, intelligence, educational level, and personality traits (self-esteem, dependency, dogmatism, extroversion); also their involvement and informational level on the issue, the extremity of their initial attitude, and so on.

Despite the complexities involved, literally thousands of experiments have been conducted based on this paradigm. (See *P&L* Close-up at right.)

Close-up
Findings of Attitude-Change Studies

Below is a sample of the conclusions drawn concerning effective messages from the large body of research on attitude change through controlled exposure of message, source, and audience. In actual practice, we would usually have to add, "but it also depends on factors X, Y, and Z."

1. Present *one* side of the argument when the audience is generally friendly, or when your position is the only one that will be presented, or when you want immediate, though temporary, opinion change.

2. Present *both* sides of the argument when the audience starts out disagreeing with you, or when it is probable that the audience will hear the other side from someone else.

3. When opposite views are presented one after another, the one presented last will probably be more effective. *Primacy effect* is more predominant when the second side immediately follows the first, while *recency effect* is more predominant when the opinion measure comes immediately after the second side.

4. There will probably be more opinion change in the direction you want if you *explicitly* state your conclusions than if you let the audience draw their own, except when their intelligence is high.

5. Sometimes emotional appeals are more influential, sometimes factual ones. It all depends on the kind of audience and the setting.

6. Fear appeals: The findings generally show a positive relationship between intensity of fear arousal and amount of attitude change, if recommendations for action are explicit and possible, but a negative reaction otherwise.

7. The fewer the extrinsic justifications provided in the communication for engaging in deviant or discrepant behavior, the greater the attitude change after actual compliance.

8. Cues that forewarn the audience of the manipulative intent of the communication increase resistance to it, while the presence of distractors simultaneously presented with the message decreases resistance and enhances persuasion.

To change attitudes, change behavior first. Social psychologists have studied the process of changing attitudes because they have assumed that attitudes are "predispositions to act." Thus, knowledge of the conditions that control the formation and change of attitudes has been expected to provide an efficient means of predicting and controlling behavior change. How valid are these assumptions and explanations?

Unfortunately, many studies have found a very weak correlation between measured attitudes and other behavior. Moreover, a *change in attitude* produced by the social influence of a persuasive message often has no relation to *behavior change.* This is not surprising when we realize that the conditions under which the verbal statements on attitude scales are elicited may differ in many ways from the conditions under which the overt behavior one is trying to change is elicited. Even if both sets of behavior are related to a common underlying attitudinal core, each one is also partly under the control of its own reinforcement contingencies. Thus a verbal questionnaire in which an individual expected approval for a tolerant position might show no prejudice, whereas the same individual might reveal quite different attitudes in the company of prejudiced friends.

Recently, investigators have begun a new kind of attack on attitude change, based on the wisdom shown in Aristotle's statement that "men acquire a particular quality by constantly acting in a particular way." In fact, there is considerable evidence now to support the view that attitude change is best accomplished *after* exposure to a situation in which behavior is changed directly.

Individuals can be induced in a variety of situations and for a variety of reasons to engage in behavior that is contrary to their relevant attitudes: in a debate, in play, because their job demands it, for personal gain, to avoid punishment or ridicule, not to make trouble, and so on. Often the mere act of engaging in a previously low-probability behavior is enough to make the individual aware of positive aspects, and people come to believe what they have preached and practiced more than what they have heard and read. Getting people to comply with a small behavioral request has also been shown to increase their tendency to comply with a bigger, more discrepant request — the "foot-in-the-door technique" (Freedman & Fraser, 1966).

Usually, however, it is not enough simply to get people to perform a strongly disliked activity in order for their attitude to change. To the extent that they can attribute their compliant act to *external* forces (such as reward or coercion), they can maintain their original attitude even though their behavior contradicts it. However, stimulus conditions that can get people to perform a discrepant act and see it as of their own choosing create a state of cognitive dissonance; thus they must either: (a) change their attitudes to fit their behavior, (b) separate the act and the attitude psychologically, or (c) admit to themselves that they are behaving irrationally. These findings are in accord with our earlier discussion of dissonance.

Thus we arrive at an answer to the initial questions we posed in regard to Kathy Crampton and Patty Hearst. They are likely to have seen their own belief conversion as free and uncoerced to the extent that they were unaware of or insensitive to situational forces sufficient to cause their actions. If powerful physical forces, threats, rewards, and other types of extrinsic justification were used to elicit their public compliance, it is unlikely that their private beliefs would have been similarly affected. Once the extrinsic pressures were off, their private beliefs would have reemerged. But we have seen that when public compliance is induced with minimal apparent extrinsic justification, then the accompanying private changes in beliefs and values are not only seen by the individual as "genuine" and "inner-directed" but are likely to endure.

The fundamental rule for any form of social influence, therefore, is to use as little pressure as is necessary to barely elicit a behavioral commitment while magnifying the subject's perception of choice. Under such circumstances, it becomes impossible to say whether the resulting change in attitudes was coerced or was indeed the free choice of a reasoning person.

The Dynamics of Groups

There are many times when people are persuaded and moved to action not by any one persuader but through the more diffuse pressure exerted by groups to which they belong. A major area of social psychological inquiry has been the study of the effects of group processes on the functioning of individual group members.

The Group Dynamics Movement

In the early 1940s, when behaviorism and the study of animal learning were the dominant approaches in psychology, a group of young researchers began to investigate broader classes of molar reactions of human beings in group settings. Under the leadership of Kurt Lewin, a recent immigrant from Germany, they organized the first formal Group Dynamics Center, initially at M.I.T. but now at the University of Michigan. They also established the National Training Laboratories in Bethel, Maine, where for several decades people from many walks of life have been trained in group processes and in whose "T-groups" (training groups) the current "encounter group" vogue had its origins.

One of the goals of this school was to study the dynamic properties of *social interaction* within groups with the same rigor and precision with which other psychological processes were being studied at an individual level. In the words of two of the popularizers of this approach (Cartwright & Zander, 1968):

"*. . . group dynamics should be defined as a field of inquiry dedicated to advancing knowledge about the nature of groups, the laws of their development, and their interrelations with individuals, other groups, and larger institutions. It may be identified by four distinguishing characteristics: (a) an emphasis on theoretically significant empirical research, (b) an interest in dynamics and interdependence among phenomena, (c) a broad relevance to all the social sciences, and (d) the potential applicability of its findings in efforts to improve the functioning of groups and their consequences on individuals and society.*" (p. 7)

The study of group influence on individuals' attitudes and behavior was given its impetus by a classic study conducted during World War II by Kurt Lewin.

This research was of practical as well as theoretical value. With ordinary meats rationed and scarce, he set about to try to change housewives' decisions about what meats to buy. He sought to interest them in glandular meats, such as heart, sweetbreads, and kidneys, which were highly nutritious, more readily available, not rationed, and cheaper, but generally disliked.

Half of the groups listened to an interesting lecture, designed to change their minds about using these meats. The handsome young communicator (psychologist Alex Bavelas) tried to be as influential as he could. The other groups were told of the same problem and were then encouraged to discuss the obstacles that "housewives like themselves" might face in trying to change toward using more of these meats.

At the end of the meeting the women were asked to indicate by a showing of hands who would be willing to try one of these meats within the next week. A follow-up showed that only 3 percent of the women who had heard the lecture served one of the meats never served before, while 32 percent of those participating in the group discussion and decision served one of them (Lewin, 1947).

We can identify at least four sources of group influence that probably operated to change the behavior of the subjects and are characteristic of groups in general: (a) shared participation, (b) public commitment, (c) social support, and (d) normative standards.

a) *Shared participation.* When people participate in discussions about matters of interest to them and share in the decision-making process, they become personally involved. In the "participatory democracy" thus created, each group member is a part of the *active* change process, rather than the *passive* recipient of some externally supplied information or decision made by someone else (similar to the difference between your involvement in a large lecture class and a small seminar). Research and practical experience with groups in industrial and other natural settings clearly shows that shared group participation is essential before individuals will accept innovative ideas and changes in their usual way of doing things. In fact, attempts by management to impose changes in operating procedures on workers are typically met with direct and indirect resistance, including absenteeism, reduced productivity, and lowered morale—even when the change is intended to make the work easier (Coch & French, 1948).

b) *Public commitment.* When the group decision involves a "show of hands," the individual member is more likely to follow through with the recommended behavioral change than when his or her commitment is private. Public commitment witnessed by other group members requires a follow-up in action if the individual is to be perceived as consistent and receive later approval. Commitments also help to focus vague thoughts and channel opinions into goal-directed actions (Kiesler, 1971).

c) *Social support.* Individual decisions to act are bolstered when others in the group concur. The social support provided by group consensus not only increases confidence in the validity of one's own decision but also is a line of defense in the face of opposition and contrary pressures.

d) *Normative standards.* Given an infinite variety of possible ways to react in different situations, we are directed toward some and away from others by discovering the standards accepted by fellow group members. These rules of "appropriate" social response in given situations help define the nature of social reality for us, allow social comparison processes to operate in our determination of what is the "right" way to behave (see pp. 571–72), and provide a common referent for members to conform to, thus increasing feelings of group identity.

Such standards are called *social norms.* They become powerful influences on us all and have been the subject of extensive research. In some instances group norms are clear and explicit and function almost like laws. In others, a norm is never spelled out, and new members become aware only gradually and imperceptibly of its influence in controlling their behavior. We often learn a norm exists only when we are punished for violating it. (See *P&L* Close-up, p. 591.)

The Functions of Social Norms

Although group norms backed by powerful punishments for violations can stultify behavior and promote excessive conformity, norms nevertheless serve indispensable functions. Awareness of the norms operating in a given group situation helps orient and regulate social life. Norms oil the machinery of social interaction by enabling each participant to anticipate how others will enter the situation (for example, what they will wear) and what they are likely to say and do, as well as what behavior on one's own part will be expected and approved.

While we are learning to behave in ways that optimize the reward/punishment payoff, we are also developing a world view, a cognitive structure, a set of guidelines for "making sense" of reality. Thus it is that socially established reality can come to override physical and biological reality.

Some latitude of tolerance for deviating from the standard is also part of the norm—wide in some cases, narrow in others. Thus, members have a basis for estimating how far they can go before experiencing the coercive power of ridicule, repression, and rejection.

Adhering to the norms of a group is also the first step in establishing identification with it, allowing the individual to share in whatever

prestige and power the group possesses. In this way, a skinny little kid becomes a tough, feared member of the Jets, or some balding middle-aged man with a motorcycle is seen by outsiders as one of the Hell's Angels.

The social control carried out by group norms, however, does not wait for individuals to join groups (except as one joins a society by being born into it), but is introduced as a central part of the socialization process. Respecting one's elders, saying "Thank you," "doing unto others as you would have them do unto you," and our codes of etiquette are norms that influence us almost from the moment of birth.

We also learn from observation that norms operate even in certain situations where social interaction is limited and transient. For example, in elevators everyone is supposed to face front and not talk too loudly. In waiting lines, it is not "right" to push ahead out of one's place. It is improper to blow one's nose except into a handkerchief. And so on. However, it is also apparent that social norms are culture-bound: what is proper in one society is often outrageous behavior in another.

The Power of Social Norms in the Laboratory

One approach to studying the impact of group norms on individual behavior is to compare an individual's judgments of a perceptual event when alone and when in the company of others. The two classic studies are those of Muzafer Sherif (1935) and Solomon Asch (1955).

The power of a majority. Sherif used as his stimulus a stationary spot of light in a dark room. Without any frame of reference, such a light appears to move about erratically. This illusion is called the *autokinetic effect.*

Male subjects were asked to judge the movement of the light individually at first. Their judgments varied widely: some saw movement of a few inches, while others reported that the spot moved many yards. After a series of judgments, however, each subject would establish a range *within which most of his reports would fall. But then, when he was put into a group with two or three others, his estimates and theirs would*

converge on a new range on which they would all agree. After this happened, his judgment would continue to fall in this new range even when he was in the room by himself.

These group-developed norms may be quite divergent from the individual's own estimate, measured before any social influence. And they persist: in one study the effect was observed an entire year afterward (Rohrer et al., 1954).

It might be argued that the social influence seen in these studies has very limited relevance, since the whole perception of motion was an illusion, and the situation was so ambiguous that there was no physical reality on which the individual could depend. But research by Solomon Asch has convincingly demonstrated that group

Close-up
Why Charlie Don't Raise His Hand No More

In some colleges there is a student norm that restricts student participation during lecture classes. In one notable case, breaching such a norm of "shutting up and letting teachers do what they are paid to do" had devastating consequences for an eager, naive student in an introductory psychology class. This young student, Charlie B., would not only answer questions at great length, but would ask questions and volunteer information. At first, when he rose to answer, those seated around him would poke each other, smirk, frown, and clear their throats. In time, these non-verbal comments turned into snickers, giggles, and shuffling sounds. Finally, as he was about to rise, the student on one or the other side would bump him accidentally, or in turning to look at him, would knock down his books or jam his seat up. By the middle of the year, Charlie never raised his hand or answered when the teacher called on him. What is more, two years later he told his teacher (during a counseling session about graduate school): "I never take lecture courses any more, even if the teacher is good; I don't know why, but somehow they just make me feel uncomfortable and anxious."

norms can sway the judgments of individuals even when the stimuli being judged are structured and familiar and are perceived accurately when presented in a nonsocial situation. Ironically, his investigations began as an attempt to show that under conditions where physical reality was clear, individuals would be *independent* of the influence imposed by social reality. Instead, his research has become the classic illustration of group *conformity*.

Groups of seven to nine male college students were assembled for a "psychological experiment in visual judgment." They were shown cards like the ones illustrated and asked to indicate which line on the comparison card was the same length as the line on the standard card. The lines were different enough that in ordinary circumstances mistakes in judgment would be made less than 1 percent of the time. All but one of the members of each group, however, were confederates of the researcher and were instructed beforehand to give incorrect answers unanimously on twelve of the eighteen trials.

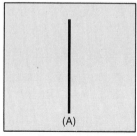

(A)

Standard line

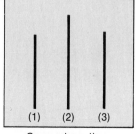

(1) (2) (3)

Comparison lines

Under this group pressure, the minority subjects, overall, accepted the majority's wrong judgments in 37 percent of the trials. But this figure is misleading, for individual differences were marked. Of the 123 minority subjects, about 30 percent nearly always yielded, while another 25 percent remained entirely independent. ■

Interviews with the subjects at the end of the experiment indicated that many of those who did not yield to the opinion of the majority had strong confidence in their own judgment—after the contradicting responses, they were able to recover quickly from any doubt. Other independent subjects thought they were probably

wrong but felt they should be honest about what they saw. Of the subjects who yielded to the majority opinion, some felt that their perception must be wrong; others said they agreed with the majority "so as not to spoil the experimenter's results." All who yielded underestimated the frequency of their conformity.

Next, the design of the experiment was changed slightly to investigate the effects of the size of the opposing majority. Pitted against just one person giving an incorrect judgment, the subject exhibited some uneasiness; when the opposition rose to two, he yielded, on an average, 13.6 percent of the time. The effect appeared in nearly full force when a majority of three opposed him: errors rose to 31.8 percent. Beyond three, the influence of the majority did not increase appreciably. When the subject was given an agreeing partner, the effects of the majority were greatly diminished—errors decreased to one fourth of what they had been with no partner, as shown in the graph, and the effects lasted even after the partner left (Asch, 1955).

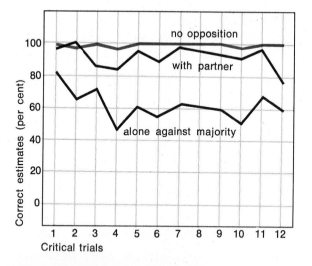

■ **JUDGMENTS WITH AND WITHOUT SOCIAL PRESSURE**

The graph compares the average errors under normal circumstances with those made under social pressure both with and without a supporting partner.

This social influence of groups on the perceptions and judgments of individuals has been found repeatedly in other conformity experiments using a variety of stimulus conditions and types of subjects. We may conclude that about a third of us, when faced with a discrepancy between reality as we see it and reality as seen by others, choose to deny our sense impressions.

The power of a minority. Given the power of the majority to control resources and reinforcements, it is not surprising to observe the extent of conformity that exists at all levels of our society. What is remarkable is to consider how anyone escapes this group domination, or how anything new—counternormative—ever comes about. Yet every society, while depending for its maintenance on conformers who will defend the establishment norms, reluctantly turns to its deviants for new ideas and innovations that will move it ahead.

But can a small minority turn the majority around and create new norms, using only the same basic psychological principles that usually help to establish the majority view?

Recently a group of French psychologists found that if two confederates in groups of six French female students consistently called a blue light "green," almost a third of the naive subjects eventually followed their lead, and many others gave "green" responses later when tested individually (Moscovici, Lage, & Naffrechoux, 1969; Faucheux & Moscovici, 1967).

If a consistent minority can win adherents to this extent even when it is wrong, there is abundant hope for a minority with a valid cause.

The Power of Social Norms in the Real World

Research in several kinds of settings has confirmed the power of social norms over individual attitudes and behavior.

College norms vs. family norms. What impact does membership in a college community have on the attitudes and values of its students? This question is of obvious concern to every student caught between twin pressures to become part of the group and to maintain his or her independence and individuality. A study begun back in 1935 in a small New England college for women offers some insights.

Bennington College is situated in a small Vermont town, and at the start of this study had been in existence for only four years. Its curriculum emphasized individualized instruction and small group seminars. The college community was "integrated, self-contained, and self-conscious." The prevailing norm was one of political and economic liberalism. On the other hand, most of the women had come from conservative homes and brought conservative attitudes with them. The question studied, then, was what impact this "liberal atmosphere" would have on the attitudes of individual students.

The conservatism of the freshman class steadily declined with each passing year. By their senior year most students had been "converted" to a clearly liberal position. This seemed to be due both to faculty and upper-class social approval for expression of liberal views and to the greater availability of politically oriented information in the college community.

A second part of the study sought to discover why some students had been able to resist this pervasive norm and retain their conservatism. It was found that the uninfluenced students fell into two classes. Some, part of a small, close-knit group, simply had been unaware of the conflict between their conservatism and the prevailing campus attitudes. Others had maintained strong ties with their conservative families and continued to conform to their standards (Newcomb, 1958).

Twenty years later, the marks of the Bennington experience were still evident. Most women who had left as liberals were liberals, and those who had resisted remained conservatives. This had been accomplished in part by marrying men with comparable values, thus creating a supportive home environment. Of those who left college as liberals but married conservative men, however, a high proportion returned to their freshman-year conservatism (Newcomb, 1963).

Deviance from a group's standards can be expected to bring with it some degree of social ostracism. Most people then experience uncomfortable feelings of alienation. But ultimately the direction of the group is governed by individuals' actions. Consistency by one person in holding to a deviant view is easily dismissed as an idiosyncratic quirk, or, as we have seen, may be labeled "madness." Two such people turn a delusion into a belief; a few more can turn it into a social movement. But psychologists have yet to discover those characteristics that enable a single individual to stand out from the yea-saying crowd and declare that the Emperor is not wearing any clothes at all.

My norm is better than your norm. To the extent that group goals and individual goals are in agreement, there develops a sense of group identity, loyalty, and cooperation. But what happens when the members of one such group are confronted with those of another such group, a common situation in everyday life? To study the process by which *in-groups* form friends and *out-groups* become enemies, a special kind of summer camp was created.

In this camp, friction was generated between two experimentally created groups and was later overcome as the groups worked toward common goals. The subjects were twenty-two normal boys about eleven years of age, with similar backgrounds, who were divided into two groups comparable in such factors as size and various abilities. Before arriving at the camp the boys did not know each other, and they remained unaware that an experiment was taking place.

To cement the boys into true groups, the experimenters put the groups in different bunkhouses and kept them separate for daily group activities. By the end of this part of the experiment, the two groups had acquired definite group structures, including leaders, names for themselves (Rattlers and Eagles), nicknames, private signals, cooperative patterns within the group, and individual symbols of identification (flags and signs set on places and facilities designated as "ours").

Next, rivalry between the groups was stimulated by a series of competitive events. As predicted, this increased in-group solidarity and also produced unfavorable stereotypes of the out-group and its members. In-group democracy and cooperation did not extend to the out-group. After losing a tug-of-war, the Eagles burned the Rattlers' flag. The Rattlers retaliated, and a series of bunkhouse raids ensued, accompanied by name calling, fist fighting, and other expressions of hostility. During the conflict, a physically daring leader emerged to replace the less aggressive boy who had led the Eagles, indicating that relations with other groups will cause changes within a group.

An attempt was then made to break down the hostility and induce the two groups to cooperate with each other. First, the rival groups were brought into close contact in pleasant activities—such as eating and shooting off firecrackers. The groups refused to intermingle, however, and the activities merely provided them with further opportunities for expressions of hostility, indicating that intergroup contact does not in itself decrease tension.

Situations were then contrived to bring about interaction of the groups to achieve superordinate goals—that is, important goals that could not be achieved without the combined efforts of both groups. The most striking episode in this period was one in which the tug-of-war rope, formerly the central object in a most antagonistic situation, served as a tool. On an overnight trip, a truck that was to bring their food "stalled," and the boys hit upon the idea of using the rope to pull the vehicle. After looping the rope through the bumper, the two groups pulled on different ends; but the next day, when the truck "stalled" again, members of the two groups intermingled on the two lines, obliterating group divisions. ●

Further evidence of the change in the boys' attitudes was obtained from sociometric choices made at the end of the period of intense competition and again at the close of the experiment. Rattlers' choices of Eagles as friends went up from 6.4 to 36.4 percent of their total friendship choice. Eagles' choices of Rattlers went up from 7.5 to 23.2 percent. The boys were also asked to rate each other on six characteristics designed to bring out the presence of stereotyped images. During the period of antagonism, Eagles received few favorable ratings from Rattlers, and Rattlers few from Eagles; but at the close of the experiment there was no significant difference in the ratings of in-group and out-group members (Sherif & Sherif, 1956).

Clearly this study has many implications for the overcoming of bitterness between national groups and between antagonistic groups within our own society. It provides valuable leads for action-oriented research on these crucial problems—why then do you suppose so little attention has been paid to them?

The Power of the Leader

For centuries, the question of what constitutes leadership has puzzled political and social analysts. Are great leaders born with special traits that give them a *charisma*, a special emotional appeal and attraction? Or do great leaders emerge because momentous situational demands happen to occur at a given point in history and "put them on the spot"? Would Napoleon have been a great leader if he had been born in Switzerland in 1930? Would Martin Luther King, Jr., have been a great leader of his people if he had lived 150 years earlier? Questions such as these are interesting to debate, but have little scientific value except to focus our attention on two approaches to studying leadership: the *trait approach* and the *situational approach*.

Do leaders "have what it takes"? In one early analysis of the "essence of political leadership" several interesting hypotheses were presented:

"In ordinary politics it must be admitted that the gift of public speaking is of more decisive value than anything else. If a man is fluent, dexterous, and ready on the platform, he possesses the one indispensable requisite for statesmanship. If in addition he has the gift of moving deeply the emotions of his hearers, his capacity for guiding the infinite complexities of national life becomes undeniable. Experience has shown that no exceptional degree of any other capacity is necessary to make a successful leader. . . . The successful shepherd thinks like his sheep, and can lead his flock only if he keeps no more than the shortest distance in advance. He must remain, in fact, recognizable as one of the flock, magnified no doubt, louder, coarser, above all with more urgent wants and ways of expression than the common sheep, but in essence to their feeling of the same flesh with them. In the human herd the necessity of the leader having unmistakable marks of identification is equally essential." (Trotter, 1916)

Recent research has confirmed that leaders tend to be the most verbally active members of their groups. In fact, in an experimental group of strangers, any member with an artificially induced high verbal output can be perceived as the leader, even one who has been seen in another group (when less verbal) as low in leadership and "social appeal" (Bavelas et al., 1965).

It also appears that to maintain their effectiveness, leaders must emphasize their community with the rank-and-file. The downfall of leaders is often traced to their losing contact with their roots and identifiability with those who have given them leadership.

● At the beginning of the experiment a cooperative atmosphere developed rapidly within each group; in the photo (left) the Rattlers work together carrying canoes to the lake. After the second stage, during which intergroup competition was fostered and rivalry became intense between the Eagles and the Rattlers, the final stage of the experiment was initiated. Here intergroup cooperation was brought about by the creation of situations that could be worked out only by cooperative means, such as searching for the source of trouble in the camp water supply (right photo).

The earliest psychological studies of leadership, in keeping with the general focus on the individual, sought to identify the traits that leaders have in common. One investigator concluded that the traits most associated with *effective* leadership fell into five general categories (Stogdill, 1948):

a) *capacity* (intelligence, alertness, verbal facility, originality, judgment);

b) *achievement* (scholarship, knowledge, athletic accomplishments);

c) *responsibility* (dependability, initiative, persistence, aggressiveness, self-confidence, desire to excel);

d) *participation* (activity, sociability, cooperation, adaptability, humor);

e) *status* (social and economic position, general popularity).

But the attempt to find a standard set of traits to characterize leaders in general has been fruitless, and it is little wonder. Could we possibly expect consistent traits for leaders of, say, the Daughters of the American Revolution, a Sunday-school choir, a suburban wife-swapping group, and a labor union? It seems obvious that an effective leader must possess whatever resources are needed by the individual members of the group and by the group as a unit in order to reach its goals—and that these needed resources will be somewhat different for every situation.

There is evidence that in many situations more than one leader is needed. Bales (1970) has distinguished between two general types of leaders: (a) *task leaders,* whose orientation is to get the job done as efficiently as possible, and (b) *social-emotional leaders,* whose perspective favors creating and maintaining a good psychological climate within the group, responsive to the personal needs, problems, and uniqueness of individual members.

Evidently, effective leadership depends on neither personality characteristics nor situational factors alone but on an optimal combination of leader personality and situational demands. One investigator found that leaders who were high on *task* orientation were most effective where there were (a) good leader-member rela-

tions and either a highly structured task or a strong power position for the leader or both or, at the other extreme, (b) poor leader-member relations, low task structure, and a low power position for the leader. Leaders high on *relationship* orientation were most effective in situations where there were either (a) good leader-member relations and an unstructured task and weak power for the leader or (b) poor leader-member relations with a highly structured task and strong power for the leader (Fiedler, 1964, 1967).

A recent development in the study of leadership calls attention to the leader's role as "definer of reality" rather than productivity supervisor. Edwin Hollander, of the State University of New York (Buffalo), is directing new research toward the questions of how leaders attain and sustain their status, how they influence the perception of their followers, and how the followers' perception of the leader relates to their group loyalty, identification, and sense of equity and trust. This process-oriented research also addresses itself to a question of current political interest: how elected leaders surmount challenges to their authority (Hollander, 1972; Hollander & Julian, 1969).

Do different leadership "styles" have different effects? Putting aside the problems of uncovering personality traits that "make" leaders, a team of social psychologists wondered whether particular styles that leaders use in relating to their groups make any difference in how a group behaves. In 1939, at the time the study was initiated, the example of Hitler's autocratic domination in Germany was frightening people who believed that democratic leadership was not only more desirable, but more effective. Some were even proposing that the best leaders were those who were nondirective, who led by providing resources only when requested to do so, and let things go as they might—a *laissez-faire* style. This complex problem was studied in the context of a controlled experiment with groups of ten-year-old boys.

The subjects were four five-member groups of ten-year-old boys who met after school to engage in hobby activities. The groups were roughly equated on patterns of interpersonal relationships, personality traits, and intellectual, physical, and socioeconomic status. Four male adults were trained to proficiency in each of three leadership styles and performed in each role. An autocratic leader was to: (a) determine all group policies, (b) dictate techniques and activity steps one at a time, (c) assign the work task and work companion to each member, and (d) be personal in praise and criticism of the work of each member while remaining aloof from group participation except when demonstrating techniques. A democratic leader was to: (a) encourage and assist group decision-making on all policies, (b) indicate general steps toward a goal and promote overall perspective of plans, (c) leave division of labor and worker selection up to the group, and (d) be objective in praise and criticism and participate in group activities without doing too much of the work. Finally, a laissez-faire leader was to: (a) allow complete freedom for the group with a minimum of leader participation, (b) supply only needed materials and information, (c) take no part in work discussion, and (d) offer only infrequent comments, making no attempt to appraise or regulate the course of events unless directly questioned.

At the end of each six-week period, each leader was transferred to a different group, at which time he also changed his leadership style. In this way, all groups experienced each style under a different person. All groups met in the same place and performed the same activities with similar materials. The behavior of leaders and the reactions of the boys were observed during every meeting.

The following generalizations came out of this experiment (Lewin, Lippitt, & White, 1939).

1. The laissez-faire atmosphere is not identical to the democratic atmosphere. Less work—and poorer work—was done by the laissez-faire groups.

2. Democracy can be efficient. Although the quantity of work done in autocratic groups was somewhat higher, work motivation and interest were stronger in the democratic groups. When the leader left the room, the democratic groups typically went on working, while the autocratic ones did not. Originality was greater under democracy.

3. Autocracy can create much hostility and aggression, including aggression against scapegoats. The autocratic groups showed as much as 30 times more hostility, more demands for attention, more destruction of their own property, and more scapegoating behavior.

4. Autocracy can create discontent that may not appear on the surface. Four boys dropped out, all during autocratic periods in which overt rebellion did not occur. Nineteen of the twenty boys preferred their democratic leader, and more discontent was expressed in autocracy than in democracy. "Release" behavior (such as unusually aggressive group actions) on the day of transition to a freer atmosphere suggested the presence of previous frustration.

5. Autocracy encourages dependence and less individuality. There was more submissive or dependent behavior in autocratic groups, and conversation was less varied, more confined to the immediate situation.

6. Democracy promotes more group-mindedness and friendliness. In democratic groups the pronoun I *was used less frequently, spontaneous subgroups were larger, mutual praise, friendly remarks, and overall playfulness were more frequent, and there was more readiness to share group property.*

This was the pioneering study in "group dynamics." It demonstrated that group interaction and group-related variables could be studied experimentally to yield conclusions of a causal nature. It showed that the same person, no matter what his own "traits," had a markedly different impact when he employed one leadership "style" as opposed to another. This was true even when the "styles" were dictated by situational demands rather than by political and economic ideology, as would be more likely in real life.

Prejudice and Racism

We have seen that group membership gives us security, status, a basis for reality testing, and much more that we need for both survival and the full flowering of the human spirit. But being identified as a member of a certain group can also bring us insecurity, loss of self-esteem, and a precarious existence—if others with power choose to label our group as inferior. The consequences of prejudice take many forms, but common to all of them is a less human reaction to other people and a diversion of psychological energy from creative to destructive directions.

Prejudice may be defined as a cluster of learned beliefs, attitudes, and values held by one person about others that: (a) is formed on the basis of incomplete information, (b) is relatively immune to contrary informational inputs, (c) makes a categorical assignment of individuals to certain classes or groups that are (typically) negatively valued. *Prejudice*, then, is the internal state or psychological set of the individual to react in a biased way toward members of certain groups; *discrimination* is the behavior(s) that prejudice may give rise to. At one time or another we probably all have been targets of prejudice as well as the sources of prejudice toward others.

Close-up
Up Against the Corporate Wall

The perpetuation of prejudice against out-group members is revealed in a recent survey of employment of U.S. citizens of different ethnic origins in executive positions in Chicago's 106 largest corporations. Latin and Polish Americans accounted for less than 1 percent of the officers, whereas they represent 4.4 and 6.9 percent of the overall population, respectively. Black Americans fared even worse: 0.1 percent among the officers, compared with 17.6 percent in the general population of Chicago (Barta, 1974). If employers "cannot find qualified applicants from those groups," as they often say, why might that be?

Consider not only much discussed prejudices toward members of other racial, religious, and ethnic groups, but also the prejudices toward "reactionaries," "squares," "the establishment," "communists," "radicals," "hippies," and "queers," as well as toward the old by the young and vice versa. (See *P&L* Close-up at left.)

The development of prejudice—and its results. One of the most effective demonstrations of how easily prejudiced attitudes may be formed and how arbitrary and illogical they can be comes from the class of a third-grade schoolteacher in Riceville, Iowa. The teacher, Jane Elliott, wanted to provide her students from this all-white, rural community with the experience of prejudice and discrimination in order to draw from it the implications of its seductive appeal and devastating consequences. To do so, she devised a most remarkable experiment, more compelling than any done by professional psychologists.

Without warning, blue-eyed Mrs. Elliott announced to her class of nine-year-olds one day that brown-eyed people were more intelligent and better people than those with blue eyes. The blue-eyed children, although the majority, were simply told that they were inferior and that the brown-eyed children should therefore be the "ruling class."

"We began our discriminating by laying down guidelines for our inferior group to follow so that they would be sure to 'keep their place' in our new social order. They were instructed to sit in the rear of the room, to take the last position in the lunch and recess lines, to allow the brown-eyed children to have the first choice of seats in reading class, to use only the faucet and paper cups when getting drinks (instead of the fountain, which was for brown-eyes), and many other frustrating and demeaning things. They were also informed that the superior students, due to the fact that they were *superior, would be given some privileges that would not be available to the inferior students (like extra recess time for work well done)."*

Within minutes the blue-eyed children began to do more poorly on their lessons and became depressed, sullen, and angry. The words they most often used to describe themselves (after taking a spelling test and selecting the words that were most appropriate) were: "sad," "bad," "stupid," "dull," "awful," "hard," "mean." One boy said he felt like a "vegetable." Of the brown-eyed superiors, the teacher reported, "What had been marvelously cooperative, thoughtful children became nasty, vicious, discriminating little third-graders . . . it was ghastly."

To show how arbitrary and irrational prejudice and its rationalizations really are, the teacher told the class on the next school day that she had erred, that it was really the blue-eyed children who were superior and the brown-eyed ones who were inferior. The brown-eyes now switched from their previously "happy," "good," "sweet," "nice" self-labels to derogatory ones similar to those used the day before by the blue-eyes. Their academic performance deteriorated, while that of the new ruling class improved. Old friendship patterns between children dissolved and were replaced with hostility.

The children's relief and delight at the end, when they were "debriefed" and learned that some of them were not "inferior" to others, is evident in the photograph. ◆ *Hopefully they had learned to empathize with those they might see being made targets of prejudice in the future (Elliott, 1970).*

This experiment has been repeated with other classes and even with an adult group of businessmen—with the same results. In each case the assumption of power by one group over another based on supposed superiority has led to discriminatory behavior, disruption in the social structure, loss of self-esteem, changes in performance by the "inferior" members in accord with their ascribed status, and justification by the superiors for the pattern of discrimination sanctioned by the "system" (see Mrs. Elliott's

essay at the end of this chapter). The ease and speed with which such behavior patterns can be adopted, the psychological damage they can cause to both victim and victimizer, the long-term costs to the society, and their persistence make prejudice a form of pathology no less serious than the most disintegrated form of psychotic behavior.

The problem of having dark skin color in a society that places value on light skin color con-

◆ Besides the observable changes in the children's overt behavior toward each other and in their school-work under the two conditions of the experiment, Jane Elliott obtained measures of their feelings under each condition by having them draw pictures of how they felt. One pair of these drawings is reproduced below. When the children were "on top," they felt competent and capable and exulted in their feeling of power and superiority. When they were "on the bottom," they felt small, glum, and pushed down, evidently accepting the discriminators' image of them as inferior and unworthy.

The reality of the emotional strain the children had undergone during the brief two-day experiment is also reflected in the exuberance with which they crowded around the teacher at the end as one united, happy group, in which everyone could accept and be accepted by everyone else.

fronts young black children by the age of three (Landreth & Johnson, 1953). Until the recent advent of the "Black is beautiful" norm, to be brown or black—by the standards of white America—meant to be dirty, unclean, and everything bad. ●

A black girl

A white girl

A black boy

A white boy

● The way in which a prevailing ideology of prejudice can be internalized by children who are victims of it— and the anxieties it can engender—are shown in these drawings made by a six-year-old black girl named Ruby. They were drawn during her first year in an integrated southern school.

The white children are drawn as taller and more robust; they are smiling and their bodies are more clearly articulated and intact. In contrast, the black children are drawn without emotion, are asymmetrical, and are missing parts of their bodies. They are generally much smaller and are drawn with less attention to detail (Coles, 1970).

In a study of 253 black children aged three to seven from both Northern and Southern schools, preference for a doll (among two white and two black ones) favored a white doll. Approximately 60 percent of these children perceived a white doll as the "nice" one, and the one they liked to play with, and a black doll as "looks bad." A third of these children through age six when asked to select "the doll that looks like you" selected a white one. Even among the children with the darkest skin color, a fifth picked a white doll as looking most like them (Clark & Clark, 1958).

In an incomplete stories test, both black and white children, three to six years of age, tended to put black characters in negative roles as the "bad guy" or aggressor (Stevenson & Stewart, 1966). Black children both in the North and South chose fewer members of their own race and more whites as playmates they would like to be like or would like to play with (Morland, 1966).

Nor are such conclusions limited to black children. Intensive studies of Mexican-American youth have likewise documented their perceived status as "forgotten," "invisible" people from "across the tracks" (Heller, 1966; Rubel, 1966).

One long-term consequence of early training in "inferiority-acceptance" was shown in experiments in which college-age black students worked in biracial situations.

Black college students who had demonstrated their intellectual ability on standard, relatively objective indices, including college board scores, and were enrolled in top-ranking colleges, nevertheless deferred to the judgments of white students when they were in biracial teams. Solutions to task problems presented by a white member of the four-person groups were more likely to be listened to and accepted than were solutions proposed by one of the black members (Katz, 1970).

Once you adopt the derogatory stereotype as a valid indicator of *your* lack of worth, then you may want to dissociate yourself from the despised group—to "pass" on your own via a name change, nose job, hair straightening, and other alterations of your appearance as well as by changing your friends and maybe even rejecting your family. Such a prejudice-induced reaction is one of the most insidious effects of prejudice since it turns the individual not only against his or her own group but against self as well. (See *P&L* Close-up at right.)

Racism: Prejudice backed by power. For decades, psychologists have studied the determinants, functions, and consequences of prejudice in individuals. Socially oriented psychologists have tried to develop programs to modify prejudiced attitudes in bigoted individuals. Psychology's focus on the individual has led it to ignore the broader political, social, economic context from which individual prejudice is nurtured and sustained.

The difference between *prejudice* and *racism* (broadly defined) is a difference between individuals and systems, between molecular and molar levels of analysis, between individual preferences and power exercised by groups in ways they see necessary for their survival. While prejudice is carried in the minds and ac-

Close-up
Identification with the Aggressor

The term *identification with the aggressor* was coined by Anna Freud to designate the process that supposedly takes place when a boy, loving his father but fearing castration by him as a result of rivalry for the mother, resolves the conflict by identifying with him. This process not only reduces the perceived differences between himself and his powerful father but may, through magical thinking, enable him to believe that he has the power of the stronger, supposedly would-be aggressor. Supporting this line of reasoning is evidence from cross-cultural studies that societies in which very close mother-child ties have developed tend to have severe initiation rites for boys at puberty (Whiting, Kluckhohn, & Anthony, 1958). Such rites do have the effect of breaking the boy's dependence on the mother and ensuring that he identifies with and accepts the man's role in his society—although there are alternate hypotheses for why such rites have developed.

Under certain conditions, however, identification with the aggressor involves an enforced fractionation of the self and an alienation of components of one's personality. Bruno Bettelheim has vividly described how identification with Nazi prison guards developed among civilians in German concentration camps. His analysis indicates how conditions that rendered a person helpless and dependent on the guards for survival and all reinforcement produced extreme forms of childlike identification with them.

Old prisoners had reached the final stage of adjustment to this unusual situation when they began practicing the same forms of verbal and physical aggression on other prisoners as did their captors. They helped get rid of the "unfit" and, when they found traitors, might torture them for days and then kill them. They even attempted to look like the Gestapo and internalized their values (1943, 1958).

In the Stanford simulated prison study, a similar identification with the guards was seen in the fact that 80 percent of the prisoners' comments about each other were negative and disparaging.

tions of individuals, racism is perpetuated across generations by laws and treaties, group norms and customs. It is carried by newspapers, textbooks, and other mass-media communications. A prevailing racist ideology in a culture constantly provides the "informational" support and social endorsement for discrimination despite personal evidence of its invalidity and injustice. Such ideas become unquestioned assumptions that are seen not as biased opinions or distorted values, but as self-evident truths. They are a major contributor to racial differences in the quality of employment, the frequency of unemployment, and substandard housing, schooling, health care, and nutrition. They also contribute to crime and violence, and in other cultures and other times have led to "holy wars."

Under the banner of the "white man's burden," it was possible for colonialists to exploit the resources of black Africa. American Indians could be deprived of their land, liberty, and ecological niche in the United States by newly arrived European immigrants whose desires for wealth, homesteads, and new frontiers were in conflict with the "menace of the red savages."

The "yellow peril" was another journalistic fiction to set people's thinking against Americans of oriental ancestry. After their usefulness was over as laborers on the railroads, mines, and other manual jobs, the press and labor groups mounted campaigns to deport the Chinese, to deprive both them and Japanese immigrants of the rights and privileges of American citizenship. Did you know that over 100,000 Japanese Americans were put into concentration camps in the Western states at the start of World War II, their property sold at small return, and millions of dollars of their money held by the government and used in banks until 1973 (without any interest)? Nothing comparable was done to those of German or Italian ancestry—America's other two enemies during that same war.

When a group becomes the target of prejudice and discrimination, it is socially segregated, preventing normal interchange and destroying or blocking channels of communication. This isolation, in turn, allows rumors and stereotypes

to go unchecked, fantasies to surface and grow, and the "strangeness" of the group, real and fancied, to increase over time. The isolation of American Indians on reservations and the segregated housing patterns in our cities increase the alienation between groups and prevent either reality checks or casual interaction.

The differentness of an isolated group can be the *result* of the discrimination and segregation instead of the *cause* of it.

In Japan, since medieval times, based on the myth of biological inferiority, there has been systematic segregation of a pariah caste known as the Burakumin. *Not racially different, or visibly distinguishable from other Japanese, they can be identified with certainty only by their registry of birthplace and residence. Over the years, however, they have been segregated as untouchables, crowded into squalid shacks in ghettos, and limited in whom they can marry, what work they can do (only menial jobs), and how much education they can have.*

Generations of segregation and inferior status have created *differences. Their speech patterns have become different and now identify them as does the speech of the lower-class Cockney in London. Regardless of their abilities, their papers (identifying their occupation and place of residence) prevent their escape. Not surprisingly, there is greater delinquency and joblessness, higher school absenteeism and dropout rate, and lower tested IQ among boys who live in the Buraku ghettos. These are regarded as signs of "innate racial inferiority" and used to justify the necessity for further discrimination (DeVos & Wagatsuma, 1966).*

In the end, as any successful teacher will tell you, you can only teach the things that you are. If we practice racism, then it is racism that we teach.

Max Lerner, *Actions and Passions*, 1949

Can prejudice and racism be overcome? Once established, prejudice and racism are relatively resistant to extinction because of the several needs they may serve for the individuals and the group and the many conditions that may encourage and maintain existing attitudes. We have a few clues but have been woefully inadequate so far in overcoming this serious social problem.

1. *Change actions.* From our knowledge of other kinds of attitude change, we can predict that effort might best be expended in getting people to act in new ways rather than giving them arguments for doing so. Research has shown that *contact* between antagonistic groups can promote better intergroup relations and lessen existing hostilities if—and only if—many other factors are favorable; mere exposure does not help and is more likely to intensify existing attitudes. Changes as a result of contact are most likely when the contact is rewarding rather than thwarting, when a mutual interest or goal is served, and when the participants perceive that the contact was the result of their own choice. (See *P&L* Close-up at right.)

2. *Change the rules and the reinforcements.* Although "righteousness cannot be legislated," a new law or regulation that people generally follow provides a new system of rewards and punishments and can thereby create a new social norm, which then becomes a powerful influence on individuals to conform to the new pattern. Legislation thus attacks the group phenomenon of institutionalized racism as well as the prejudice of the individual. The same results may be achieved by more informal agreements to change "ground rules."

The difficulty, of course, is that those who must make the new rules are often those who see the disliked group as a social or economic threat; thus the motivation for meaningful change is low and progress agonizingly slow. It is important for those who are working for change to realize that groups who feel threatened by change must feel that their essential needs are being taken into account if they are to support—much less enact—a new social rule or law.

3. *Change the self-image of victims of prejudice.* Young people who are targets of prejudice may be "inoculated" against the crippling psychological effects of it—and thus be helped to develop and demonstrate their real poten-

tials—if they can establish a sense of pride in their origins, history, and group identity. The "Black is beautiful" movement represents an effective instance of this approach.

The impact of this self-assertion and new group pride was demonstrated in a study that reexamined racial preferences for dolls of different apparent races. Contrary to the earlier results (see p. 600), this research indicated that the majority of 89 black children preferred the

(see p. 600)

Close-up
Meatheads Don't Laugh at Archie Bunker

The popular program "All in the Family" has stirred up considerable controversy because its hero is portrayed as an outright bigot. Archie Bunker is indiscriminate in his discrimination; he shows open disdain for all those different from him— different in race, creed, sex, country of origin, or political preference. Some critics have argued that such bigotry promotes prejudice by making light of it and sanctioning the use of stereotypes. Proponents have stoutly maintained it has a positive effect by publicly airing prejudice and ridiculing the extremes to which Archie's thinking leads him. Which view do you believe is most likely to fit the facts?

It appears from a recently conducted survey that the critics are more accurate. This survey of 237 American Midwestern teenagers and 130 adults from London, Ontario, investigated reactions to the show in general and to Archie and his liberal-thinking son-in-law, Mike. The researchers, Neil Vidmar and Milton Rokeach (1974), conclude that this program is "more likely to be reinforcing prejudice and racism than combatting it."

Many viewers did not even see any satire on bigotry. Instead they agreed with Archie's ethnic slurs. Those who watched regularly, compared to infrequent viewers, were more prejudiced, condoned Archie's views more, admired Archie more than Mike, and perceived Archie as triumphing in the end.

black-skinned dolls, played with them more, and found them to be more attractive than white-skinned dolls. In addition, although most of the 71 white children played with the white doll and thought it was a nice doll, 49 percent of them reported that the color of the black doll was "nice" (Hraba & Grant, 1970).

The Unconscious Ideology of Sexism

Which sex do *you* believe is the more emotional, sensitive, affectionate, squeamish, protective, intuitive, jealous, catty and talkative? Which do you think is more rational, creative, assertive, cool, mechanically and mathematically inclined, and tough? Which would not make a good President, or Little League outfielder? Which looks foolish changing an infant's diapers or puttering around the kitchen? A Martian visitor might answer "Golly, I don't know, but maybe it has something to do with which infants get put under the pink or blue baby blanket."

While boys are playing with guns and mechanical erector sets, girls get dolls and are encouraged to "play house" in preparation for their "station in life" as obedient, dedicated wives and self-sacrificing mothers. They are more likely than male students of equal ability to be counseled to go to commercial high schools and "finishing schools." Unless they are exceptional, they are less likely to receive encouragement to continue with higher education.

If they are exceptional and do the original work required for a Ph.D. degree, the chances of getting a good job that will be personally and financially rewarding are low. Of nearly 30 million women in the work force, nearly two thirds work as domestics or as clerical, service, or sales workers. In 1968, a woman with four years of college training earned on the average of $6,694 a year—the same as a man with only an eighth-grade education—and much less than her male classmates, who averaged $11,795.

The ideology, often unconscious, that leads to these distinctions is called *sexism*. The two major factors responsible for perpetuating sexist thinking and practices are biological barriers and sex-role socialization training.

Nature intended women to be our slaves . . . they are our property; we are not theirs. They belong to us, just as a tree that bears fruit belongs to a gardener. What a mad idea to demand equality for women! . . . Women are nothing but machines for producing children.

Napoleon Bonaparte

Biological barriers. Because women have wombs and bear children, and because artificial control of the reproductive function has always been imperfect, woman has always been defined primarily as *childbearer*. Any supplementary activities that might alter the power of social control over her reproductive capacities have been seen as threatening to the very foundation of society itself and "contrary to nature." Thus the basic dichotomy in humanity—different reproductive roles—has been used to rationalize all the other supposed differences between men and women and to justify the discriminatory treatment of women. Without the ability to limit her own reproductiveness, a woman's other "freedoms" were illusions that could not really be exercised (Cisler, 1970).

The improved technology of birth control, along with social changes in awareness of the need for reduced population growth, egalitarian male-female relationships, alternative life-styles (single mothers, commune families, etc.), and more day-care facilities are combining to permit more varied self-fulfillment for women.

Sex-role socialization. If discrimination begins early enough and is consistently applied in many spheres of the person's life, then that is the only social reality available on which to base one's self-identity and from which to derive a sense of self-worth. Many studies have documented the general acceptance by women of the stereotype of inferiority.

In one study six articles, on subjects ranging from education to law, were read by college women. Nothing was said about the authorship of the articles, but for each subject half the articles were supposedly by a male author and half by a female author (John T. McKay or Joan T. McKay, for example). The same arti-

cles were consistently rated as more authoritative and more interestingly written when attributed to male authors than when attributed to female authors (Goldberg, 1968).

Several studies utilizing groups of male and female subjects of three age groups (7–12 years, 12–18 years, and 18–26 years) showed that females consistently had lower expectations of their task achievement and academic success than did matched male counterparts (Crandall, 1969).

Stereotyped thinking of what girls and women can or cannot do—as well as what they should do—develops through bias in both *commission* and *omission*. Take TV, for example, which gets more of many children's time than school. What they see on TV, according to an extensive study of prime-time Canadian TV viewing, are women who are poor models for achievement (Manes & Melynk, 1974). Frequent themes are financially independent female characters portrayed as having unsuccessful marital relations or having happy marriages destroyed by a decision to take a responsible job. We know from other research that filmed models affect the behavior of observers (see Bryan & Schwartz, 1971).

Women are much more likely than men to be the butt of jokes in popular periodicals.

An analysis of 740 jokes taken from six years of the feature "Humor, the Best Medicine" in Reader's Digest *showed six times as many antifemale jokes as antimale ones. The humor in the joke frequently depended on an acceptance of stereotypes of the woman as "spendthrift," "incompetent," "gossipy," "a nag," "sentimental," "money-mad," or "jealous."*

In the 1940s, in fact, a third of all the humor in this feature was sexist. Although the figure has gradually declined, this influential source continues to disseminate prejudiced stereotypes in a framework of comedy (Zimbardo & Meadow, 1974).

A thorough analysis of sex-role stereotypes portrayed in elementary-school texts published in the 1960s revealed clear stereotypes.

Female characters (a) occurred less frequently than males, (b) followed orders rather than gave them, (c) were more likely to be engaged in fantasy than in problem solving, (d) were more conforming and verbal, and (e) were more often found indoors. In addition, whereas positive outcomes were attributed to male actions, happy outcomes after female action were attributed to the situation or to the goodwill of others. With increased grade level, there was an increase in sex differentiation on these dimensions and a more divergent presentation of the "appropriate" characterizations of males and females (Saario, Jacklin, & Tittle, 1973).

Even in the most commonly used college psychology texts, sexism is manifest in a variety of ways, most significantly by omission: women rarely appear except as "mothers." The excessive use of the masculine pronoun and the generic term *man* also help to convey the picture of psychology as the study of the "he-man" and not as the study of people's behavior (*APA Task Force Report*, 1974).

The aptness of the term *unconscious ideology of sexism* (coined by Bem & Bem, 1974) is seen in an old *Science* article reporting the discovery of "faint menstrual bleeding on a definite premenstrual day in man" (Simpson & Evans, 1928, p. 453), no doubt meaning "man as a species" but showing a certain obliviousness nonetheless.

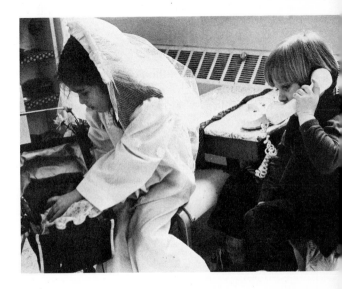

Chapter Summary

Social psychology is the study of the behavior of individuals in social settings. It includes research on both *social behavior,* as a dependent variable, and *social stimuli,* as independent variables. Even nonsocial behavior is often influenced by social stimuli.

Through the process of *attribution,* we make inferences about other people and the causes of their behavior. Our perceptions of people are colored by our *first impression,* our *stereotypes* of various groups, and our tendency to expect *consistency.* We have a tendency to make *dispositional attributions,* which center upon characteristics of the individual, more often than *situational attributions,* which center upon factors in the environment. This tendency is called the *attribution error.*

Attribution theory assumes that we develop both a *reality orientation* and a *control orientation* to the world, giving both meaning and predictability to events in our lives. This involves active information seeking. We are likely to attribute conformity to situational causes and deviance to dispositional ones. Extrinsic reinforcement can transform an intrinsically motivated activity (dispositional) into something to be done only for the sake of reward (situational).

Personal and social motives are more variable than biological drives and more dependent on learning. Frustration of them can result in emotional disturbances.

The *need for achievement* is widespread in our culture. It gives rise to a general tendency to approach success, although some individuals seem to focus on achieving success and others on avoiding failure. Achievement motives in women have not been studied until recently; there is evidence that a motive to avoid success may be operating. This double-bind situation results from sex-role socialization in our society.

Reactance is the need for freedom of action. It is evidenced by the tendency to assert one's own choice rather than follow the suggestions of others. The *need for social comparison* leads us to measure our performance against that of others. Fulfillment of our *need for social approval* has five powerful consequences: (1) it confers identity; (2) it legitimates our existence; (3) it provides security; (4) it establishes a bond of liking; and (5) it evidences control over the environment.

The strength of the *need for affiliation* differs in various individuals. It tends to be stronger in the presence of anxiety—at least when the other individuals involved are similarly anxious. *Altruism,* or the need to help others, may be partly instinctive and partly learned. It has variously been suggested that altruism may be related to: (a) *empathy* (vicariously experiencing the emotions of others) and the reduction of *promotive tension;* (b) the reduction of *guilt feelings;* or (c) the operation of *social norms.*

Study of the *need for consistency* has given rise to the *theory of cognitive dissonance,* which states that an individual who is experiencing inconsistency between two cognitions will be motivated to reduce the inconsistency by altering at least one of the cognitions in some way. Dissonance is greater when one perceives that an inconsistent course of action was freely chosen rather than externally imposed.

Studies of *interpersonal attraction* have shown that we tend to like people whom we perceive as attractive, competent, and similar or complementary to ourselves. Theories about interpersonal attraction include *equity theory,* which holds that people tend to seek the greatest possible rewards at the minimum possible cost; and *gain-loss* theory, which holds that *changes* in another person's estimation of us have considerable impact on our attraction to that person. Even *romantic love* is becoming a subject for laboratory study and prediction. Scores on a recently constructed romantic love scale are positively related to actual behavior and the permanence of romantic relationships. *Empathy* is an important aspect of romantic love; people tend to show similar signs of anxiety concerning their own and their partner's public performance.

Attempts to persuade and influence us are almost universal; they are cause for concern, however, when the person being influenced is in some way being taken advantage of. *Propaganda* consists of attempts at persuasion whose true purpose or source is hidden; it can sometimes be difficult to distinguish from education. Attempts at persuasion may be considered coercive when they involve sudden rather than gradual conversion or when the persuader is in complete control of the situation and its consequences.

An *attitude* is a relatively stable disposition to respond in a certain way toward people or situations. Attitudes involve three components: *beliefs, affect* (emotion), and *action*. Factors involved in attitude formation include *information, observation,* and *rewards and punishments,* as well as *ego-defense mechanisms.* Research on attitude change has generally involved study of three variables: the *source,* the *message,* and the *audience.* Complex interactions rather than simple cause-effect relationships have generally been found. A major finding of this research has been that attitude change is frequently *preceded* rather than followed by behavior change.

The *group dynamics* movement of the 1940s involved studying the dynamics of social interaction within groups. Four major sources of group influence are: (1) *shared participation* in the decision-making process; (2) *public commitment* to a recommended course of action; (3) *social support* from other group members; and (4) *normative standards* (social norms) that define appropriate behavior. Norms have utility in preserving the group's values and in enabling members to know what behavior is expected and will be rewarded. The member who conforms gains status and approval; the one who does not may be rejected by the group or pressured to conform.

Laboratory research has shown that artificially developed social norms can influence perceptual judgments; there is a surprisingly strong tendency to *conform* to group norms in the face of physical evidence to the contary. It is possible, however, for a consistent minority to bring about the creation of different norms.

Adherence to group norms can bring about a sense of group identity (in-group) that operates to the exclusion and rejection of outsiders (out-groups). True reconciliation and acceptance in such situations generally requires interaction to achieve superordinate goals.

Leadership has been studied through attempts to identify characteristics of successful leaders and through study of the effects of different leadership styles. Effective leadership has been found to be associated with such traits as intelligence, achievement, responsibility, participation, and status. Different situations create the need for leaders with different characteristics, such as *task leaders* and *social-emotional leaders.* The particular situation and the needs and expectations of the members help determine what kind of leadership will be most effective. Differing leadership styles can have considerable impact on both the performance and atmosphere of a group.

Prejudice is a cluster of beliefs, attitudes, and values (usually negative) that bias us toward members of a particular group, giving rise to behavioral *discrimination.* Even artificially induced prejudice and discrimination lead to a lowering of self-esteem on the part of the victims. When prejudice is backed by an entire social system, it becomes *racism.* Overcoming established racism requires changing *actions,* changing *rules and reinforcements,* and changing the *self-image of the victims.*

Sexism results from biased expectations about the abilities and personality characteristics of the two sexes. It is based primarily on *biological barriers* (woman = childbearer) and *sex-role socialization* (stereotypes presented by society from the moment a boy or girl is born).

The Power and Pathology of Prejudice
Jane Elliott Riceville, Iowa, Public Schools

"They shot that King yesterday; why did they shoot that King, Mrs. Elliott?" How could I explain to this innocent, curious third grader the reasons why Dr. Martin Luther King had been assassinated in Memphis on that terrible April day in 1968? "Prejudice," "discrimination," "ignorance," and "fear of what's different," are the usual concepts we might use to account for that tragedy, but they do not explain it; they do not help children understand the root causes of such blind hatred toward our fellowmen and women.

My task was made more difficult by the facts of our daily existence in Riceville; we were part of an all-white, all-Christian rural community in northeast Iowa with a population of fewer than 900 souls. There were no blacks in the town or in the farming area surrounding it. Neither were they pictured or described in the textbooks the children read in school. During National Brotherhood Week, we had discussed the position of Negroes in white America and particularly of Dr. King's efforts to correct existing injustices. At the time of his death, we had been studying the Indians, and had converted bedsheets into a giant Indian tepee. Since the events surrounding Dr. King's death were reminiscent of the treatment the Indians had received, it seemed natural to tie the Indian study unit into an analysis of the forces responsible for Dr. King's assassination.

I decided that the irrationality, the mindless brutality of racism could not be packaged into a tidy, little curriculum project to be taught to my students—no, they had to experience it from the inside for the lesson to have any lasting value for them. My resolution to depart from my standard lesson plan was bolstered by the horror, anger and shame experienced as I watched white TV commentators decry the riots that swept our nation's urban ghettos. The implication was obvious that "these people" were violence-prone, that "they" were indeed defective and different from "us" who had behaved with restraint when President Kennedy was assassinated. Even the righteous indignation of the black people was denied any legitimacy—the fault was portrayed as in them, and not in the system of discrimination which oppressed them. Such an analysis blamed the victims for their misery rather than the miserable conditions centuries of prejudice and neglect ("benign" and otherwise) had created. It was easy to justify discrimination by pointing to obvious differences currently existing between the status, behavior, and living conditions of racial groups in the United States. It is not as easy to show that such differences are the consequence of prejudice—the aftereffects of arbitrary labeling of inferiorities.

It would take a special kind of experience to drive that message home to the children, and hopefully to the adults who have socialized them into believing stereotypes that blacks are "dumb," "lazy," "dirty," "violent" and so on.

We would all participate in a kind of experiment, a role-playing experiment in which part of the class would be superior and privileged and the rest would be inferior and deprived. The basis for assignment to the top banana group would be totally arbitrary, being based on eye color. For a full day, brown-eyed children were to be on the top and blue-eyed children on the bottom. The next day we would reverse roles and the inferior group would become superior. Since this project was designed as an "experience in moral education" and not as a formal experiment in social psychology, I did not set out to systematically collect behavioral data attesting to the impact of this experience. However, the results proved to be so dramatic that there was no need for refined measuring instruments, scales, questionnaires, and the like to reveal the pathological power of prejudice.

As described on page 598, I divided my class by eye color into seventeen blue-eyes and eleven brown-eyes (with a few greens lumped in). "Brown-eyed people are better, cleaner, smarter, more civilized than blue-eyed people," I told them and then proceeded to show them the truth of that assertion. I pointed to children who slumped in their seats, forgot their eyeglasses, were inattentive, hit their little sister—in every case my finger pointed to a blue-eyed child. In contrast I held up the example of the good, kind, efficient, courteous, smart brown-eyed youngsters.

Once the list of restrictive rules described in the text supported the arbitrary classification, the children began to react in unusual ways. When a blue-eyed child faltered in reading, I shook my head and allowed a brown-eyed child to do it the right way. As the blue-eyed people nervously awaited their turn to perform, I called attention to their destructive tendencies readily apparent to all in one boy's rolling a corner of the page of his book into a tight curl.

The blue-eyed children changed their posture, they slumped, were more awkward and more downcast—expressions of defeat. Their classroom work regressed sharply from that of the previous day. Arithmetic problems took much longer for the blue-eyed children than they had previously, and much less time for the now "smart" brown-eyed people. When I asked why the blue-eyed group had done so poorly, one girl blurted out, "I just knew we wouldn't make it!" They had begun to live down to their lowered expectations!

What was particularly depressing was to observe how my brown-eyed children changed from marvelously cooperative, thoughtful children to nasty, vicious, discriminating little third graders. Some of them even suggested that someone should alert the cafeteria personnel to keep an eye on the blue-eyes because they might try to go back for seconds, and we must not waste food on blue-eyed people. Needless to say, the day was ungodly for everyone. Fights broke out during recess because, "he called me a name; he called me 'blue-eyes,' so I hit him in the gut!" Children who had been friends for years were alienated, some of the girls cried as they were excluded from the games of their former friends with those nice brown-eyes.

The "inferior status" children said things like, "You don't want to even try to do anything," and "I felt like a dog on a leash" or "I felt like you were jailed in a prison and they threw the key away." But the lesson is bi-directional, if some people are down, it's because others are up. "I felt like a king," said a newly enthroned brown-eyed monarch, "I ruled them like I was better than them, I was happier."

Nor was I immune to the taunts of my "superiors." When I accidentally flipped the screen up, little brown-eyed Debbie shouted out, "What do you expect, she's blue-eyed!" In an instant, I experienced a genuine urge of violence against my little tormentor, and struggled with the desire to give her the back of my hand. So powerful is the status conferred by such arbitrary designations that an adult seen as "inferior" can be publicly ridiculed by a child from a superior caste. One of my blue-eyed brothers came to my defense by reminding everyone, "She's never been able to pull it down right!" I was learning much from my own lesson.

As described in the text, the second day brought a complete turn-about. Blue-eyes were now identified as superior and showed improved performance and self-esteem. The brown-eyes skidded to the bottom of the heap.

On the following day each child was asked to write a four-paragraph composition describing how he or she felt on each day of the exercise, what discrimination is, and who Martin Luther King was. The compositions were shared with the group only after all had finished and then only with each child's consent. The compositions showed considerable growth in the children's understanding, and obviously it is my hope that this understanding might help them to empathize with those they might see being made targets of prejudice in the future.

I have conducted this classroom exercise almost every year since that first time, with essentially the same pattern of results emerging. I have been quite concerned that the effect of this exercise would be lessened as students became aware of it and anticipated its effect before coming into my room. Such has not been the case. Even those students whose brothers or sisters have been involved in the exercise and who have been warned about what will occur have reacted exactly as those first students did when placed in this situation for two days: with anger, despair, frustration, and misery when they are the victims; with classic signs of racism when they are labeled "superior."

Perhaps it is expecting too much to think that a two-day exercise at the third-grade level might change a child's attitude forever. I have become convinced, however, while watching some of these children develop over the intervening years, that many of them have indeed been changed by the exercise and that they are changing the attitudes of those around them. Some of the changes I've witnessed were totally unexpected. For some children the experience of being singled out as superior started a dramatic and lasting change in academic performance as a result of being described as superior for a day. Several parents stopped in on parent-teacher conference day this year to tell me of their child's continued high performance in school. Attitudinal change in the children has been illustrated by one mother's description of her daughter's admonition to her grandmother: "If you say 'nigger' again, I'll leave the house until you go," because "we don't use that word in our house anymore." Another mother told me that her son was like a different child after the Discrimination Days. "Why," she said, "he's even nice to his little sister!" (Incidentally, I'm now working with my class to overcome sexist stereotypes).

The results of an attitudinal survey conducted by Professor Martin Houg of the University of Northern Iowa (Cedar Falls) indicate that there are reliable changes toward more tolerant attitudes and beliefs of children who took part in the "Discrimination Day" compared to nonparticipating peers. Also, evaluation of the academic classroom testing of these children by Professor Zimbardo substantiated the depressed performance of inferior-status children and the enhanced performance of those with an elevated status.

I have taken special joy in the unexpected by-product of this experience; each child learns that he or she can be superior, can perform well in the classroom when they believe they are really special and worthwhile. I should mention that some of the children in my classes have been sent to me specifically because they are disabled readers—dyslexic. They have been previously taught that they were "dummies," considered "retarded" by their teachers, peers, parents, and siblings. They had come to fulfill that expectation, until it was exploded when they performed so well during their superior status day. By reinforcing that new found positive self-image, I have been able to help them make remarkable gains in their reading level, gains which appear to be enduring. Here again we see how prejudice involves living down to the biased expectations of others, these white children had learned to think and act inferior when it came to reading, as many girls do in math and minority students in a variety of subjects.

I have been asked whether adults could ever respond to this situation of arbitrary discrimination as these children had. My answer is a resounding "yes." It is frightening how much adults react to the experience very much the way children do. As Forum Member of the 1970 White House Conference on Children and Youth, I exposed over a hundred so-called sophisticated, well-adjusted, educated, knowledgeable adults to the exercise and was amazed at the similarities between their reactions and those of my third graders.

At the end of the day of playing the discrimination game, the tension in the room was so great that it *was* for real—so much so that at the break, when the blue-eyed people, who had been instructed to stay in the room, forced their way into the hall to caucus, the first suggestion made by a member of the group was to "shoot that Honky bitch." An Uncle Tom said, "But brown-eyed people have always been nice to me." Other suggestions were for picketing, tearing up the meeting room, more reason—and love.

Even though some people said it was unnecessary to have such an experience, at the end of the day the majority of the group indicated that they had *learned*. This had quickly become a great deal more than a game.

In August of 1971 I was invited to use this technique with a group of teachers in a workshop at the University of Iowa in Iowa City. We posted a sign on the door of the meeting room that said "Dogs and blue-eyes not allowed." For some reason the blues took offense at this and decided not to attend the class. They caucused in an adjoining room, thereby "illegally occupying unauthorized university space." When we refused to negotiate with them they took all the furniture out of that room and stacked it in front of our door, thereby "vandalizing university property." When they realized how we labeled their actions, they quickly removed the furniture, but not until they had recognized their own "chaotic state of mind."

Blues had begun this caucusing in a spirit of "We'll play the game and act the way minority group members are supposed to act in the same circumstances," but this soon turned to a "What's going on here? Nothing's working! Why are they doing this to us?" reality. And for those few blue-eyed people who had come into the meeting room in spite of the treatment they expected to receive (they were being paid by the federal government for their attendance at this workshop), the situation was even more enlightening—and frightening. Every act in opposition to the browns' rules was used to prove the truth of our accusations. When, after repeated warnings about the consequences to be expected for their continued lack of cooperation, the rioting blues still refused to attend the meeting, the campus police were summoned. When they began to take pictures of the demonstrators, several of them ducked out the back door. Flight to avoid prosecution.

So what does it all prove? To me it proves that we can—and must—teach values in the elementary school. It proves to me that discrimination is not the result of prejudice, but just the reverse; *prejudice is the result of discriminatory actions.* Choose a group, accuse the members of certain characteristics, attitudes, disabilities, treat them as though your accusations were facts, and when they begin to act as you predicted they would, use those actions to prove the validity of your accusations.

Watching groups before, during, and after this exercise has also proved to me the damage prejudice does, not only to the minority group members but also to those in the majority group. One teacher said to me, "Isn't it sort of like that poem about 'Why did you put that bean in your ear when the very thing I told you was not to put that bean in your ear?' Don't you think you were really causing prejudice, that they probably would never have thought of it if you hadn't brought it up?" She is tragically wrong. We must not only eliminate racism from education, we must teach children the horror of the reality of racism in our society, and that means we must first sensitize them so that they recognize racism in themselves and others.

So what am I suggesting? That using the blue-eye/brown-eye exercise will change the world? Absolutely not! What I am suggesting is that rather than exposing every child to this exercise, we expose every teacher to it. Just as whites, rather than blacks, are responsible for the racism in the United States, so the teachers rather than the children are responsible for the destructive attitudes in the schools—and in those children coming out of the schools.

The Sioux have a prayer that says: "Oh Great Spirit, keep me from ever judging a man until I have walked a mile in his moccasins." Perhaps this is one prayer we should put into the schools? Or at least into the hearts of teachers!

14

The Perversion of Human Potential

[The historical account of humans is a] heap of conspiracies, rebellions, murders, massacres, revolutions, banishments, the very worst effects that avarice, faction, hypocrisy, perfidiousness, cruelty, rage, madness, hatred, envy, lust, malice, and ambition could produce.

. . . I cannot but conclude the bulk of your natives to be the most pernicious race of little odious vermin that nature ever suffered to crawl upon the surface of the earth.

Jonathan Swift, *Gulliver's Travels,* 1726, Pt. 2, Ch. 6

Although this total condemnation has been dismissed as the work of a cynical hater of the human condition, many others concerned about "human nature" over the centuries have echoed similar sentiments. A basic theme in Western literature is that Man—once great, once the most noble paragon of all creatures—has suffered a great fall from his state of perfection.

According to biblical scholars, the Fall originated with Adam's one defect—his pride—which led to his disobedience to God and banishment from Paradise. In other schemes, the corrupting force is not within the person but from without—as exemplified by the social influence of Eve, who, tempted by Satan in snake's clothing, persuaded Adam to disobey God's command not to eat the fruit of the tree of knowledge.

This theme of the corrupting influence of social forces was developed by Rousseau, who envisioned human beings as noble, primitive savages diminished by contact with society. To recapture and preserve their essential goodness, individuals must escape the cities and the evil wine-press of uncivil civilization. The French impressionist Paul Gauguin followed this advice, fleeing Paris for the unspoiled charm and simple native life of Tahiti. For Americans, Thoreau's isolated cabin at Walden Pond, Massachusetts, has become a symbol of breaking the bonds of dependence on social convention. At present, many young people have responded to this same primitive appeal by forming and joining small communes in rural areas.

Standing in stark opposition to this general view of human beings as the innocent victims of an all-powerful, malignant society is the view that people are basically evil. According to this view, people are driven by desires, appetites, and impulses unless they are transformed into rational, reasonable, compassionate human beings by education, or controlled by firm authorities.

Where do *you* stand in this argument? Are we born good and corrupted by an evil society, or born evil and redeemed by a good society? Before casting your ballot, consider an alternative perspective. Maybe each of us has the capacity to be a saint or a sinner, altruistic or selfish, gentle or cruel, dominant or submissive, sane or mad. Maybe it is the social circumstances we experience and how we learn to cope with them that determine which potential we develop. In fact, maybe the potential for perversion is inherent in the very processes that make us able to do all the superbly wonderful things we can do.

The preceding chapters have documented the complex development and supreme specialization that have resulted from untold millions of years of evolution, growth, adaptation, and coping. We have become the rulers of this planet, controlling the other animals and the physical matter of the earth for our survival, comfort, and happiness. This reign is currently being extended to life beneath the oceans as well as to outer space. We have reached this position because of our capacity for learning new relationships, for remembering old ones, for reasoning, inventing, and planning action strategies. We have developed language to manipulate symbols and transmit our thoughts and information to others. Our perceptual, cognitive, and motor skills allow us to see, reflect, and act in countless intricate ways to avoid pain and gain pleasure and change our surroundings to suit ourselves.

But each of these unique attributes can also become cancerous. Implanted in the very potential for perfectibility are the seeds of perversion and breakdown.

For example, our remarkable memory enables us to profit from mistakes, establish continuities within our lives, and master complex feats of learning. But this same gift of memory can convert our minds into storehouses filled with traumatic events, fears, anxieties, unresolved conflicts, and petty grudges.

Because we have developed a unique temporal perspective, we can plan for our future, "save for a rainy day," delay gratification, and profit from history. But because of this very sense of time, our present behavior often loses its spontaneity. We fail to take full measure of the love others offer or the joys of nature as we plod through each day's obligations, promises, and commitments (past contracts), while fulfilling responsibilities, avoiding liabilities, and anticipating the worst (future concerns).

A partial catalog of human traits and attributes and their possible positive and negative consequences is given in the table. ■ (p. 610) You are invited to extend the list by adding other traits that share this dual nature or by elaborating on the positive or negative aspects of those listed.

In this chapter our attention will be directed toward some of the psychological processes that are occurring when people "go wrong." Much of this material on "social pathology" is unique among current introductory psychology texts. It is included here because we believe that the scientific study of the behavior of organisms must be extended to include the multiple influences of social, political, and economic forces on our behavior. If these forces can make us compete rather than cooperate, fight rather than love, stifle and destroy instead of create, we need to know about them. Only with a knowledge of what can go wrong and how, can we reformulate our modes of relating to one another and design social institutions more appropriate for the fulfillment of each of our individual lives.

Attribute	Enables Us to	But Can Also Lead Us to
Memory	Profit from past mistakes Develop and use complex concepts Relate present to past Distinguish novel events from previously experienced ones	Carry grudges, suffer from former conflicts and past traumatic events Lose spontaneity of behavior because of commitments and obligations Feel excessive remorse or sense of loss
Time sense	Develop a history and sense of continuous self Relate present behavior to the future Distinguish between transience and permanence	Fear change, live in the past, feel guilt Dread an unknown future, become anxious Experience disappointments from unfulfilled expectations Concentrate on past or future, ignoring the present
Ability to associate elements and infer unseen events	Create, imagine events not experienced Generalize from partial data Construct theories, hypotheses	Form negative, crippling associations Misperceive self or others, develop stereotypic and delusional thinking
Perception of choice	Not be stimulus bound, be independent See ourselves as responsible agents Hope, build for future	Experience conflicts, indecision Suffer from inability to act when action is necessary
Responsibility, self-evaluation	Take pride in accomplishments Delay gratification, undertake difficult or unpopular tasks Be concerned about effects of our actions on others	Feel inadequate Feel guilt for not living up to standards or for letting someone down Feel constrained by obligations
Competence motivation	Do work well, set high standards Gain benefits of hard work Advance technologically, use resources to meet our needs	Fear failure, suffer feelings of inadequacy Be anxious about tests of our ability Work for self-aggrandizement, to be "number one," to beat others down
Concept of justice	Protect individual rights Set up fair rules binding on all Value equality of opportunity	Sacrifice individual needs to group principles or rules Torture, imprison, execute dissenters Impose our own solutions on others
Ability to use language and other symbols	Communicate with others, present and absent, for information, comfort, pleasure, planning, social control	Circulate and be prey to rumors and falsehoods; conceal true feelings Use "word magic"—curses, verbal derogation—to inflict harm Mistake the symbol for the reality
Susceptibility to social influence	Follow group standards Learn and transmit values Cooperate; establish community	Overconform, sacrifice integrity Reject innovation and stifle creativity in ourselves and others
Love	Experience tender emotions Nurture growth and independence of others Support, encourage, comfort others Feel wanted and special	Become jealous, vengeful Possessively limit another person's freedom Become depressed and suicidal from loss of love

Aggression and Violence

The world we live in is often a violent one. The daily news accounts of murders, muggings, riots, suicides, and wars are ample evidence of the extent to which people can inflict injury on others and on themselves. How can "abnormal" behavior be understood? Can it be controlled?

Psychologists concerned with these questions have focused on the study of *aggression,* which can be defined as physical or verbal behavior with the intent to injure or destroy. Research evidence on aggression has been drawn from a wide variety of sources, including physiological studies, clinical observations, and studies of aggressive interactions in both the laboratory and the "real world." In addition, aggression in animals has received a great deal of attention in the hope that it will clarify our understanding of aggression in humans. In this section we will review several of the theories that have been proposed to account for aggressiveness.

Aggression As Inborn

In his famous essay "Leviathan," Hobbes argued that people are naturally selfish, brutal, and cruel toward other people. He expressed this concept by the phrase *Homo homini lupus* —"Man is [like] a wolf to [his fellow] man." Although the wolf is unjustly maligned by this phrase (wolves are actually quite peaceful and gentle with others of their own species), this phrase expresses the fairly common belief that human beings are instinctively aggressive animals.

Psychic energy: Thanatos and the concept of catharsis. One of the first psychologists to elaborate on this belief and develop it into a theory was Sigmund Freud. As we saw in Chapter 10, he believed that from the moment of birth a person possesses two opposing instincts: a life instinct (Eros), which causes the person to grow and survive, and a death instinct (Thanatos), which works toward the individual's self-destruction. He believed that the death instinct is often redirected outward against the external world in the form of aggression toward others.

According to Freud, energy for the death instinct is constantly being generated within the body. If this energy cannot be released in small amounts and in socially acceptable ways, it will accumulate and eventually be released in an extreme and socially unacceptable form. Thus a highly aggressive or violent person can be assumed to be someone who: (a) generates a great deal of aggressive energy and (b) is unable to discharge that energy appropriately in small amounts.

Freud visualized this energy as being like water accumulating in a reservoir until finally it spilled over in some aggressive act. It could be drained off in various "safe" ways, however, including *catharsis* (a Greek word meaning purification or cleansing), in which the emotions were expressed in their full intensity through crying or words or other symbolic means. Aristotle first used the concept of catharsis to explain the way in which good drama first built up and then purged feelings of intense emotion in the audience.

Home they brought her warrior dead,
  She nor swooned nor uttered cry.
All her maidens, watching said,
  "She must weep or she will die."
  Alfred, Lord Tennyson, *The Princess,* 1847

Some experimental support for the catharsis hypothesis of aggression is found in a study by Robert Sears (1961). Male children high in aggressiveness at age five were also high at age twelve. Some were still overtly and antisocially aggressive. However, the others, though low in *antisocial* aggression, showed high *prosocial* aggression (aggression for socially acceptable purposes, such as law enforcement or punishment for rule-breaking) and more *self-aggression* than did boys who were still highly antisocial aggressors. ▲ (p. 612) Furthermore, the prosocial aggressors were more anxious and fearful of antisocial aggression than the antisocial aggressors.

A study by Megargee (1966) also provides some support for the Freudian "psychic energy" theory of aggression and catharsis.

Megargee hypothesized that extremely aggressive acts would be carried out by individuals who usually exercise too much control and are unable to release aggressive energy in small amounts. Their instigation to aggress would accumulate over time, and when aggression finally did emerge, it would burst forth in extreme form.

To test this notion, Megargee compared boys who had been detained by the juvenile court for moderately assaultive crimes, such as battery and gang fights, with boys detained for extremely assaultive crimes, such as murder, brutal beatings, and assault with a deadly weapon. He found that the extreme aggressors were indeed overcontrolled, oversocialized individuals, as compared with both the moderate aggressors and a comparison group of average high-school graduates. They had very good conduct records in both school and prison, and were rated by others as being very friendly, cooperative, and docile people. During detention, they showed less verbal and physical aggression than all other groups of juvenile delinquents. In addition, on psychological tests, they scored very high on

self-control. Typically, their initial deadly aggressive behavior had been triggered by a seemingly trivial frustration or minor setback.

In spite of some supporting evidence, however, Freud's theory has been criticized by psychologists for failing to specify any factors that could be used to predict the occurrence of aggression or the direction or form it will take. It has a lovely literary, after-the-fact, descriptive quality but little scientific utility. Indeed, in his later writings Freud himself abandoned reliance on this death instinct, but many others (such as Rollo May) have continued to incorporate it into their conception of human nature.

The "aggressive instinct." Another theory stressing the innateness of aggression is that of the well-known ethologist Konrad Lorenz (1966). On the basis of studies of animals, he argues that aggression is a spontaneous, innate readiness to fight, which is critical for an organism's survival. In other species, however, aggressiveness between members of the same species rarely involves actual injury or death because one animal will eventually "signal" appeasement or submission. According to Lorenz, human beings have somehow lost this means of inhibiting aggression while retaining the instinct to aggress, and thus have become killers.

Although Lorenz tries to make a case for the parallels between animal and human aggression, it is clear that there are basic differences between the two. First, because of people's memory and evaluative abilities, their actions are often a response to memories and ideas rather than to the immediate situation; second, because of their tool-making capacities and ability to plan ahead, they can carry out virtually unlimited injury by intention, even without feelings of aggressiveness or personal interaction with their victims. Interestingly, the one difference that Lorenz reported between human beings and animals (that innate "appeasement gestures" inhibit aggression in animals) has been shown by more systematic observation to be nonexistent (Barnett, 1967). Animals' responses to submissive behavior by other animals are quite

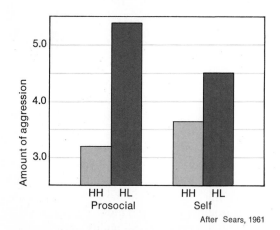

After Sears, 1961

▲ **INCREASE IN PROSOCIAL AGGRESSION AND SELF-AGGRESSION**

The graph shows the amount of prosocial and self-aggression exhibited by two groups of boys, both initially high in antisocial aggression at age five. The boys who became low in antisocial aggression by age twelve (HL) showed more prosocial and self-aggression than did the boys whose antisocial aggression remained high (HH).

variable, much as with humans. It is difficult to predict the conditions under which displays of weakness and submission will elicit sympathy and "fair play" and the conditions under which they will simply elicit even more intense violence on the part of the aggressive individual or group.

During a police confrontation at the University of California at Berkeley, a student was being hit as he was dragged downstairs out of an occupied building. In a letter of protest, clerks in the Admissions Office allege that he screamed, "Please don't hit me any more! Won't someone help me?" According to the account, the more he begged, the more they hit (San Francisco Chronicle, Feb. 20, 1969).

Physiological bases of aggression. The relationships between aggression and biology are complex and unclear. We will mention here only the role of the brain and of genetic and hormonal factors.

The *hypothalamus* and the *amygdala* (and probably other regions of the brain) seem to be involved in some aggressive behavior. As you will recall from Chapter 2 (p. 80), electrical stimulation transmitted by radio to the amygdala stopped a charging bull in his tracks. The complex chemical and anatomical specificity of the brain mechanisms controlling aggression is suggested by the fact that one drug injected into the lateral hypothalamus of rats made usually spontaneous mouse-killers stop such killing, whereas a different drug injected into exactly the same brain site of normally peaceful rats induced them to kill mice (Smith, King, & Hoebel, 1970).

Epilepsy is ten times as common among criminals as noncriminals (Mark & Ervin, 1970), and abnormal EEGs are also reported to be more common among prisoners who are repeated offenders (Levy & Kennard, 1953). In one case of a teenage girl who had attacked several babies and finally smothered one of them to death because its crying annoyed her, doctors located a specific brain area that produced highly abnormal EEG patterns *at the sound of a crying baby* (Mark & Ervin, 1970).

Some types of aggressive behavior in humans are often related to brain disorders. For example, brain disease of the limbic system or temporal lobe has sometimes been found in persons exhibiting a *dyscontrol syndrome*, characterized by senseless brutality, pathological intoxication, sexual assault, or repeated serious automobile accidents. Tumors in the brain may influence aggressive behavior, as suggested by the case of mass murderer Charles Whitman. (See *P&L* Close-up, p. 614.)

What part do specific genes play in aggressive behavior? Although animals such as bulls and cocks can be selectively bred for their fighting and killing abilities (Scott, 1958), the evidence is less clear that this holds true for human beings. The folk notion of "bad genes" or "bad blood" was encouraged by the early studies of the Jukes and the Kallikaks but, as we saw in Chapter 5, these reports were biased and untrustworthy.

More recently, there was a flurry of excitement over the possibility that overly aggressive behavior might be the result of an extra Y chromosome (the Y chromosome in an XY pair in a fertilized egg makes the baby a male and also promotes other masculine characteristics, such as physical size and strength, which may be related to aggressiveness). However, although a statistically significant percentage of inmates in "penal-mental" institutions are of the XYY type, the absolute percentage is small, and they show no more violent behavior than other inmates.

In both humans and animals, males are characteristically more aggressive than females—a fact apparently due in part to the early influence of sex hormones on the brain. Female animals that have been injected with male sex hormones often display increased aggressive behavior (Edwards, 1971). On the other hand, there are different physiological patterns in different kinds of aggression. In fact, Moyer (1968) distinguished between *seven* different neural and

Overcome by Overwhelming Violent Impulses

In the summer of 1966, Charles Whitman killed his wife and mother, and then climbed to the top of a tower at the University of Texas. Armed with a high-powered hunting rifle equipped with a telescopic sight, he shot 38 people, killing 14, before he himself was gunned down. How could he have done such a thing?

Investigators found some letters that Whitman had written the night before his attack, which partially answer that question:

". . . I don't really understand myself these days. I am supposed to be an average, reasonable, and intelligent young man. However, lately (I can't recall when it started) I have been a victim of many unusual and irrational thoughts. These thoughts constantly recur, and it requires a tremendous mental effort to concentrate on useful and progressive tasks. In March when my parents made a physical break I noticed a great deal of stress. I consulted a Dr. C. _____ at the University Health Center and asked him to recommend someone that I could consult with about some psychiatric disorders I felt I had. I talked with a Doctor once for about two hours and tried to convey to him my fears that I felt overcome by overwhelming violent impulses. After one session I never saw the Doctor again, and since then I have been fighting my mental turmoil alone, and seemingly to no avail. After my death I wish that an autopsy would be performed on me to see if there is any visible physical disorder. I have had some tremendous headaches in the past and have consumed two large bottles of Excedrin in the past three months . . . ."

A postmortem examination of Charles Whitman's brain revealed a highly malignant tumor the size of a walnut in the area of the amygdala (Sweet, Ervin, & Mark, 1969).

hormonal patterns, depending on whether the aggressive behavior was predatory, intermale, fear-induced, irritable, territorial, maternal, or instrumental. These findings further highlight the complexity of the relationships between physiological factors and aggression, which also typically involve learned and situational factors.

Aggression As an Acquired Drive

Almost twenty years after Freud proposed the existence of a death instinct, a group of academic psychologists at Yale University formally presented an alternative view of aggression called the *frustration-aggression hypothesis* (Dollard, Doob, Miller, Mowrer, & Sears, 1939). Aggression, they said, was a drive acquired in response to frustration. *Frustration* was defined as the condition that exists when a goal response is blocked, its intensity being a function of three factors: (a) the strength of the motivation toward the goal response; (b) the degree of interference with it; and (c) the number of prior goal-response sequences interfered with. The greater the amount of frustration, the stronger the resulting aggressive response.

It soon became obvious, however, that not every act of aggression is preceded by frustration and that not every frustration results in aggression. The original frustration-aggression hypothesis was revised to state that every frustration produces an *instigation* to aggression, but that this instigation may be too weak to elicit actual aggressive behavior (N. Miller, 1941). They agreed with Freud that the aggressive drive would increase if not expressed (if frustration continued) but saw the origin of aggressive behavior in *external* factors (accumulated frustrating experiences), rather than the *internal* factors (aggressive "instinct").

Displacement of aggression. When frustration occurs, the first and strongest aggressive impulse is toward the source of the frustration. Thus, if a child sees a piece of candy, but is prevented by Mother from eating it, the child is most strongly motivated to be aggressive toward her. However, such aggression may be inhibited because of the threat of punishment. According to the frustration-aggression theory, the child will then *displace* the aggression onto some target other than the original source of frustration. This tendency to vent one's hostile feelings on a "safe" target is illustrated by the example of a man who is berated by his boss and who then goes home and yells at his wife, who spanks their child, who kicks the dog. According to the theory, the less similar the target is to the source of frustration, the weaker is the displaced aggression and the less complete the cathartic effect. ●

The frustration-aggression theory applied to prejudice also predicts that when a powerful frustrator is feared or impossible to retaliate against, aggression may be displaced onto a *scapegoat*. Presumably, minorities and members of out-groups are favorite targets of displaced aggression because they are identifiably different from members of the in-group (against whom aggression must not be vented) and because they are already in vulnerable positions and thus are not likely to retaliate.

If the Tiber overflows into the city,
If the Nile does not flow into the countryside,
If the heavens remain unmoved,
If the earth quakes,
If there is famine and pestilence,
At once the cry goes up:
"To the lions with the Christians."
Tertullian, Roman historian

When anything went wrong in Rome, it would seem that the Christians were thrown to the lions. In more recent times, when the price of cotton fell in the South around the turn of the century, the number of lynchings of blacks rose sharply. And during World War II the Jews were blamed for all Germany's woes. Do you see any contemporary parallels?

The role of releasers in the environment. Recently, the frustration-aggression hypothesis has been revised to stress the importance of both inner and outer factors. According to Berkowitz (1965), the probability that people will aggress depends on their *internal readiness to aggress* and *external cues* that elicit their aggres-

sion and provide a target. The internal and external forces operate in an additive (or even multiplicative) manner. If one is weak, the other must be strong for aggression to be elicited. A habitually aggressive person has a strong "readiness" and needs only mild outside provocation, but even a mild-mannered individual may become aggressive if he or she is subjected to strong repeated frustration and potent provocation.

The important role of appropriate *releasers* (disliked objects or objects already associated with aggression) was demonstrated in the following study.

Subjects were seated before a table on which lay either weapons (such as a gun) or assorted neutral objects. The subjects who were in the presence of the weapons responded more violently to insults than did those who saw only

● "It was either this or I was going to get a rifle and go up on a rooftop to shoot at people," said the young man who smashed nineteen plate-glass windows at the Wells Fargo Bank in San Francisco with the sledgehammer the officer is holding (*San Francisco Examiner/Chronicle*, June 17, 1973).

neutral objects, even though, of course, no use was made of the weapons. Thus, it appears that the mere presence of such external aggressive cues as guns can heighten the probability of aggressive behavior (Berkowitz & LePage, 1967).

The concept of external releasers has been used as a further explanation of why minority groups are consistently chosen as targets for aggression and prejudice. Because these groups have been attacked before, they have become associated with hostility and violence and thus become elicitors or releasers of further aggression toward themselves. In other words, they become associated with violence because they have *received* aggression in the past.

To demonstrate how this vicious cycle might operate, the following experiment was performed.

Subjects saw a film of a prizefight in which a man named Kelly was badly beaten by a man named Dunne. Later on, supposedly in another experiment, the same subjects had a chance to give an electric shock to a person whose name was given variously as either Bob Kelly, Bob Dunne, or Bob Riley.

This person received significantly more shocks when he was named Kelly than when he had either of the other two names (Geen & Berkowitz, 1966).

Aggression As Socially Learned

Another answer to the "why" of aggression is that it is learned just like many other kinds of behavior: it is not due to some instinct or drive but is the result of the norms, rewards, punishments, and models that the individual has experienced (Bandura, 1973). According to this *social learning approach*, aggression can be the result of (a) aversive experiences and/or (b) anticipated benefits or incentives. Any kind of aversive experience (not only frustration) produces a general state of emotional arousal. This arousal can then lead to a number of different behaviors, depending on how the individual has learned to cope with stress. When they are up-

set, some people become aggressive, some withdraw, some turn to others for help, some engage in constructive problem solving. Aggression, like other responses, can also occur in the absence of emotional arousal if the individual feels that it will lead to some desired outcome (as when a child hits a younger one in order to get a toy).

Models for aggression. As mentioned in Chapter 3, one of the basic ways in which people learn new behaviors is by watching other people perform them. Bandura and his associates pioneered in studies showing the power of aggressive models to produce aggressive behavior in children.

Nursery-school children were exposed to one of several conditions: a real-life aggressive model, a model acting aggressively on film, an aggressive cartoon character, or no model at all. Soon after this experience, all the children were mildly frustrated. The experimenters then measured the amount of imitative and nonimitative aggression that the children displayed in the absence of the model.

The frustrated children who had observed the aggressive models exhibited many imitative aggressive responses, while the frustrated children who had not observed a model were barely aggressive at all. Furthermore, the children who saw the filmed model were just as aggressive as those who saw the real-life model. The extent to which children imitated the model's aggressive responses is shown in the photographs (Bandura, Ross, & Ross, 1963). ▲

Suppose the children saw a model being punished for aggressive behavior; would they then be less likely to imitate aggression?

Children were shown a film in which a model demonstrated four novel aggressive responses. One group saw a version in which the aggressive behavior was rewarded; another saw a version in which the model was punished; for a third group there were no consequences for the model. After viewing the film, children who had seen the model punished displayed fewer imitative aggressive acts (Bandura, 1965).

But did the observation affect their *learning* of aggression or only the *performance* of aggressive behavior?

After the experiment proper was supposedly over, the experimenter offered each child a prize for doing just what the model had done. Given this positive incentive all children readily performed the aggressive responses in imitation of the model. Evidently the aggressive act had been learned plus the knowledge that such acts were inappropriate in that situation. When the payoff was changed, the act was performed (Bandura, 1965).

More recent research has shown that children who are emotionally aroused (as when they are participating in competitive games) are more likely to imitate a model's behavior whether the model is displaying aggressive or non-aggressive behavior (Christy, Gelfand, & Hartmann, 1971).

Do as I say, not as I do. A number of experiments have shown that some models are more effective than others in producing imitation. The most effective models are nurturant, high-status adults who have control over the rewarding resources. The people most affected by models are those who are dependent and moderately aroused and who have been previously rewarded for displaying imitative responses (Bandura, 1969).

▲ As can be seen from these photographs, the model's hammering of an inflated doll (left) was faithfully imitated by the young subjects, two of whom are shown.

If, for some reason, you *wanted* to get a person to become very aggressive, what would be your ideal learning situation? How could you "program" an aggressive person? First you would certainly want an adult model, and, since children are dependent on adults, it would be good to have the learner be a child. You would want to make sure that the aggressive adult would be noticed by the child and that the child would be emotionally aroused. Both of these conditions are satisfied by having the adult punish the child—a child is certain to notice aggression if he or she is the target of it, and is usually upset, fearful, and angry when being punished. The adult model, in turn, should be nurturant and should have rewarded imitation in the past. Thus parents would be an ideal choice since they have taken care of the child for a long time and have often rewarded the child for imitating their attitudes, behaviors, and beliefs. Also, parents control most of the available rewards (privileges, praise, affection, candy, and so on) and thus are quite powerful.

Finally, to make the situation truly "ideal," the parents, too, should be rewarded for their aggressive behavior by achieving *their* immediate goal—being obeyed. All in all, it would be hard to program an environment more conducive to the learning of aggression than that provided in the home of Mr. and Mrs. Average Punishing Parent.

Obviously, if a parent always punishes a child for behaving aggressively when the aggression is discovered, the child will soon learn to inhibit aggression in the presence of the parent. How-

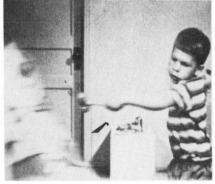

ever, from Bandura's research we would expect that the imitative aggressive response would be powerfully learned, but would be withheld in the presence of the parent and performed in other situations—and it is. Mothers who punished aggression in the home were found to have children who behaved more aggressively in nursery school (Sears, Maccoby, & Levin, 1957). A study of overly aggressive adolescent boys showed that their fathers severely punished aggression in the home and that, consequently, few of the boys exhibited aggressive behavior there. In fact, many of the parents were surprised to learn that their "good boys" were highly aggressive in school (Bandura & Walters, 1959). Paradoxically, then, parents who physically punish a child for aggression are modeling and fostering the very behavior they are trying to eliminate. ●

Parents can also teach aggression in other ways. By telling their son to "be a man," always fight back and use his fists, parents are explicitly training and encouraging him to be aggressive toward other people. Such parents not only condone aggressive behavior; they demand and reward it. An example of such "Aggression training" is revealed in this interview segment:

INTERVIEWER: *"Have you ever encouraged Earl to use his fists to defend himself?"*

MOTHER: *"Oh yes. Oh yes. He knows how to fight."*

I: *"What have you done to encourage him?"*

M: *"When he was a little boy, he had a pair of boxing gloves. His dad has been an athlete all his life, so his dad taught him."*

I: *"Has he ever come to you and complained that another fellow was giving him a rough time?"*

M: *"Oh yes, when he was younger. I told him, 'Go on out and fight it out yourself'. . . ."*

I: *"What would you do if you found Earl teasing another fellow or calling him bad names?"*

M: *"That would be up to Earl. If the other boy wants to lick him, that would be up to Earl. He deserves it." (Bandura & Walters, 1959, pp. 115–16)*

The broader cultural environment too can encourage violent behavior. By providing many aggressive models and by giving approval and prestige for violent acts, the community can put much pressure on individuals—especially young ones—to conform to the aggressive norm. ■

As I saw it in my childhood, most of the cats I swung with were more afraid of not fighting than they were of fighting. This was how it was supposed to be, because this was what we had come up under. The adults in the neighborhood practiced this. They lived by the concept that a man was supposed to fight. When two little boys got into a fight in the neighborhood, the men would encourage and egg them on. They'd never think about stopping the fight. . . . You had to fight, and everybody respected people for fighting. . . . A man was respected on the basis of his reputation. The people in the neighborhood whom everybody looked up to were the cats who'd killed somebody.

Claude Brown, *Manchild in the Promised Land*, 1965, pp. 253–56

● "This will teach you to hit your sister!"

Expression of aggression: Catharsis or goad? Because social learning theory does not postulate any aggressive drive or instinct, it rejects the concept of catharsis—that the expression of aggressive feelings will lessen aggressive actions. In fact, it predicts just the opposite result: that expressing aggressive impulses or watching aggressiveness in others will *increase* the probability of future aggression. This hypothesis is supported by studies such as the ones cited earlier, which show that aggression increases after exposure to aggressive models. In addition, studies have demonstrated that the expression of aggressive behavior in a permissive setting maintains the behavior at its original level, instead of reducing it.

Subjects were exposed to an anger-arousing antagonist; then half of them were allowed to express their anger and hostility to a sympathetic interviewer. The other subjects did not have such an interview but merely sat for a while. Later, subjects who had experienced the cathartic interview disliked the antagonist more (rather than less) and remained more physiologically aroused than the control subjects (Kahn, 1966).

■ Children in Northern Ireland are witnessing aggressive acts daily in their streets and learn to imitate these adult models.

In another study, children were given an opportunity for either physical or verbal aggression toward a child who had frustrated them. Neither activity reduced their aggressive feelings (Mallick & McCandless, 1966).

The results of these studies would suggest that therapeutic procedures that encourage the person to act out aggressive feelings may have an effect opposite to that intended.

Not only do these and other recent research findings contradict instinct and drive theories of aggression, but they seem to run counter to the common-sense notion that it is good to "let off steam" and "get it all off one's chest." It may help us to understand this contradiction if we make a distinction between *expressing emotional feelings* and *acting aggressively*. Giving vent to your feelings (as in crying, laughing, or talking to others) may make you feel better or relieve your anxiety, but displaying aggression against your enemy, either verbally or in overt action, is *not* going to reduce the likelihood that you will do so again.

Do the mass media teach violence? Crime may not pay for criminals, but violence certainly does for the television industry. Programs with "action" and "adventure" (as violence is euphemistically referred to) are the ones that have larger audiences—and therefore attract more expensive commercial ads to pay the bills. As a result, any person who turns on the television set is very likely to see both drama and comedy episodes in which people are killed or injured in a wide variety of ways, cartoons with lovable but sadistic characters, and news programs with on-the-spot coverage of wars, assassinations, riots, and "crime in the streets."

What is the impact of all this violence on the viewer? Does he or she become any more aggressive as a consequence of watching television? Such questions have recently been the focus of much public attention and debate. According to proponents of both instinct and drive theories of aggression, the viewing of violence is cathartic and thus serves a positive social function by decreasing aggressive energy. The opposite point of view is taken by social learning theorists, who argue that television programming (as well as other media) provides models and sanctions for violent actions and is thus a major factor in the promotion of antisocial behavior.

So far, the research evidence generally supports the social learning viewpoint. As mentioned earlier, the modeling of aggression has been shown to influence the level of children's aggressive behavior. Not only do they learn the aggressive responses immediately, but they can reproduce many of them several months later (Hicks, 1968). Furthermore, the amount of violence that boys see on television has been found to be significantly correlated with their aggressiveness ten years later, as shown in the graph (Eron, Huesmann, Lefkowitz, & Walder, 1972). ◆

Filmed aggression (particularly if it is realistic) can be very exciting for child viewers. They become emotionally aroused by watching it, and they usually remember more of the aggressive than the nonaggressive content (Osborn & Endsley, 1971). However, after repeated viewing of violence, children seem to habituate to it and experience less emotional arousal than they did initially (Cline, Croft, & Courrier, 1972). This may be an even more damaging aspect than the teaching of aggression: once we are able to view violence and human distress in an unemotional, detached, and blasé manner, we are programmed for dehumanized reactions toward other people (see pp. 651–53).

Although there have been some studies claiming to show that TV violence is cathartic and decreases aggressive tendencies, major methodological flaws have reduced their credibility.

In one of the most widely cited of these studies, for example, aggressive or nonaggressive TV programs were shown for six weeks to boys in two institutions, and their aggressive behavior was observed and rated by personnel in these institutions. The authors reported that the results supported the catharsis hypothesis (Feshbach & Singer, 1971).

However, few of the findings were significant statistically when the boys were equated for initial levels of aggressiveness. The classification of the programs as "aggressive" or "nonaggressive" was also questionable; for example, cartoons (which have the highest violence ratings) were classified as "nonaggressive." In addition, the experimenters did not have control over the TV programs that the boys watched, and some of the boys actually viewed both violent and nonviolent shows.

Better-controlled replications of this study have since disconfirmed Feshbach and Singer's results (Wells, 1971) and in addition have found that delinquent adolescents who repeatedly viewed movie violence became *more* aggressive than those who saw nonviolent films (Parke et al., 1972). Laboratory experiments, field studies, and correlational investigations have all provided evidence that the viewing of violence tends to foster aggressiveness. Unfortunately, such scientific evidence does not lead directly to a change in social policy. (See *P&L* Close-up, p. 621.)

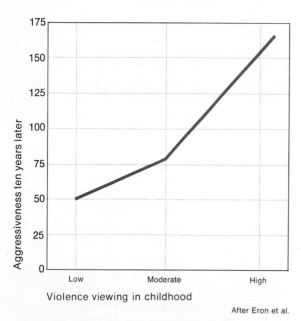

After Eron et al.

◆ **VIEWING TV VIOLENCE IN CHILDHOOD AND ITS INFLUENCE ON LATER AGGRESSION**

Violent Encounters

Up to this point, we have been focusing on aggressive tendencies *within* the individual. However, aggression typically occurs in a social context, involving other people. For a better understanding of the dynamics of violent behavior, we need to take a closer look at the aggressive interactions *between* individuals.

■ According to the boys in the top photo, who were found in this condition by a neighbor after their parents had gone out for the evening, they had been tied up "so that they wouldn't get into the peanut butter." The father who had amputated his little girl's right hand at first claimed it had been "an accident."

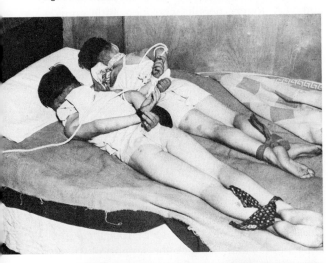

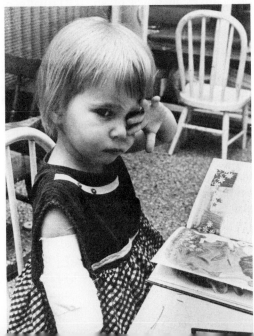

The battered child.   One of the most basic and critical social relationships is that existing between parent and child. This relationship is not always a normal, healthy one, since some parents neglect their children, provide inadequate care, and do not express feelings of love for them. Furthermore, it has become very clear in recent years that some parents physically abuse their children, even to the point of death.

Accurate statistics are hard to come by, but a conservative estimate is that over 700 children are killed each year by their parents in the United States alone, and about 40,000 more youngsters are seriously beaten and tortured by their parents, siblings, and relatives. ■   And it is estimated that perhaps three million adults have participated in a "conspiracy of silence"—

Close-up
Politicizing Social Science

Growing public concern about the effect of televised violence recently led Senator John O. Pastore to request that the Surgeon General set up an advisory committee to study the problem and make recommendations. One would expect that the members of this committee would include the best available experts on the subject. However, the Surgeon General allowed the television industry to veto proposed committee members, with the result that many of the leading researchers in this field were kept out. Two of these "blackballed" experts were Albert Bandura and Leonard Berkowitz, whose classic research findings are clearly not what the television industry wants to hear. The committee that was eventually formed, the Surgeon General's Scientific Advisory Committee on Television and Social Behavior, concluded (not surprisingly) that studies in this area are not "wholly consistent or conclusive." It did concede that "a modest relationship exists between the viewing of violence and aggressive behavior" (Surgeon General's Report, 1972, p. 9).

knowing of instances of child abuse but not intervening in any way to help (Helfer & Kempe, 1968). A vivid case of child abuse is described in the *P&L* Close-up below.

Close-up
Case Study of a Battered Child

When Gloria was found stealing food from a store and apprehended as a runaway, she was fourteen years old and weighed only 50 pounds. Investigation disclosed an unbelievable array of abuses perpetrated against her from birth. She was regularly beaten by her mother, her hair pulled out, her head held under water, her shoulder burned with a hot iron; multiple bone fractures gave evidence of a long history of beatings. She was confined to her room and not allowed to eat with the family, receiving only left-over scraps of food. When she was three *weeks* old she had to be hospitalized for malnutrition. At four *months,* according to hospital records, she was treated for five multiple bone fractures.

She had run away in part because she was literally starving to death. There was nothing at all unusual about the "neat, clean" home the visiting nurse found during an investigation, nor about the apparently normal relations of the parents with their other children. Gloria's siblings would occasionally sneak food in to her, but this was not "acceptable" behavior. The mother reported that the child was just "different" from all the rest, uncontrollable and incorrigibly bad. There was no evidence to support this perception. It appears rather that the mother disowned the child psychologically five days after her birth, when her mother-in-law claimed that the infant did not look like her son and was not his.

With adequate care in the hospital, Gloria gained 20 pounds in eleven days and her physical health improved steadily. It is unlikely, however, that anything could undo the scars on her memory or erase her picture of the nature of maternal love (Case presented at *Symposium on Children in Peril: The Battered Child,* San Francisco, Feb. 19, 1969).

Why does such abuse occur? Are battering parents unusually sadistic people? Research on these questions has shown that there is a distinct pattern in abusive families, but that the adults can rarely be viewed as pathological "deviants."

Battered children are more likely to emerge from families in which there is marital stress (as well as other emotional problems), a relatively low family income, and a strong reliance on physical means of discipline and control. Abuse is often directed at only one child, rather than all of them, and appears to be correlated with whether or not the child was the result of an unwanted pregnancy. Abusive mothers are often very lonely people who have little contact with other people outside the home. They usually have basic misconceptions about their children's development and abilities. For example, many of them believe that a child knows the difference between right and wrong at the age of twelve months or earlier (Elmer, 1967).

By perceiving their children as far more capable and potentially responsible than they really are, abusive parents are more likely to interpret crying, soiling of diapers, or breaking a toy as a deliberate attempt to misbehave, to be spiteful and cause trouble. Since they are often "loners," the parents have no basis for social comparison (which could help to correct their misconceptions) and also lack the support of friends or relatives in times of stress. Usually people who batter their children had parents who battered them—clearly a case of violence breeding violence (Silver, Dublin, & Lourie, 1969).

Efforts to prevent child abuse must occur at many different levels. Laws have been enacted that require medical and social service professionals to report suspected cases of child abuse. Programs are being developed by which the child can be temporarily removed from the home while the parents receive some kind of therapeutic treatment. Proposals for better education on birth control programs, childrearing, and family life have been made, and some big-city hospitals have reported a reduction in child-abuse cases. Unfortunately, in many cases, the relationship between battering parent and battered child is still decided on a purely legal basis, without reference to the social and psychological problems that are involved. Severely abused children may be returned to their parents' custody without any assessment of the family situation, or abusive parents may be treated like criminals, rather than as people who desperately need help. The solutions to this social problem are not easy ones to achieve, but strong action must be taken if society intends to reduce the destruction of its young by those entrusted with their care and protection.

It takes two to fight. Interpersonal aggression is rarely a case of one person being completely at fault and the other being totally innocent. More typically, both people are involved in escalating violence to the point where an assault occurs. This pattern is shown in interactions between police officers and individuals being arrested.

In an analysis of 344 arrest reports, Toch (1969) concluded that in the cases where violent incidents occurred, both parties were reacting to what they perceived as threats against their own integrity and self-esteem. Often the encounter began with what might be an innocuous request by an officer for information or identification or an order to "move on," "break it up." In 60 percent of the episodes studied, the civilian reacted negatively to the officer's approach and failed to cooperate. The officer viewed this uncooperativeness as "irrational," disrespectful, and perhaps concealing criminal activity, whereas the individual had perceived the original request as unwarranted or discourteous or as an expression of personal hostility. A chain of events was then set off in which both parties contributed to the spiraling potential for violence.

Toch's analysis of these encounters is that violence generally follows a standard, two-step pattern. The first step is some action by either person that is seen by the other as a *provocation*. In many of the incidents involving police, the officer's initial verbal approach was such an action. To the officer, the approach was just part of the job, but to the civilian, it was a threat to personal dignity and autonomy. This is a common theme in most violent encounters—neither participant takes the other's point of view into account.

Following the initial provocation, the second step of a violent interaction is *escalation and confrontation*. Each person reacts not only to what the other one does but also to his or her perception of the *intention* behind the act, thereby gradually increasing the level of aggressiveness. This escalation ends in a final violent confrontation, unless one or the other breaks off the sequence. Thus, push leads to shove. In interactions between police officers and resisting civilians, the officer's requests eventually become orders, and then escalate to threats or arrests. The civilian, on the other hand, will often move from resistance to verbal abuse, and from there either to an attempt to flee or to an assault against the officer. As these mutual provocations and escalations occur with increasing intensity, we can begin to understand some of the causes of "police riots."

The role of the victim. Although there are, of course, many cases where an unknown person is attacked, crime statistics do not support the common view of a stranger who assaults a passive, unsuspecting victim in the dark with the intent to injure. In more than 75 percent of all cases, murderers and their victims are relatives, friends, or acquaintances. Two thirds of all rape victims report knowing their attacker personally, while most victims of felonious assault have had some prior association with their assailant.

A survey by the New York Police Department of three typical urban neighborhoods provides some interesting facts that are contrary to accepted fallacies:

About 90 percent of all murder, rape, and assault victims are attacked by persons of the same race. Chief murder victims are the poor, the black, the unemployed, the alienated, the alcoholic, and the addicted. A poor person making less than $3,000 a year is five times more likely to be robbed than a more well-to-do citizen earning $10,000 yearly (San Francisco Chronicle, Feb. 22, 1970).

There needs to be more research directed toward what the victim does and especially toward the "social contract of violence" that exists between many victims and their aggressors. (See *P&L* Close-up below.) In the cases where the victim does play an active role, what is it that he or she does (see Ryan, 1971)? And what do some potential victims do that successfully inhibits or limits aggression? (See *P&L* Close-up, p. 625.)

Collective and Institutionalized Violence

"Historically, collective violence has flowed regularly out of the central, political processes of Western countries. Men seeking to seize, hold, or realign the levers of power have continually engaged in collective violence as part of their struggles. The oppressed have struck in the name of justice, the privileged in the name of order, those in between in the name of fear." (Tilly, 1969, pp. 4–5)

Close-up

The Shlemazel-Shlemiel Syndrome: Learning to Be a Good Victim

Perhaps because Jews as a group have suffered persecution for so long, the Yiddish language is rich in a vocabulary that differentiates among types of people who are victims—of fate, of their own ineptitude or insensitivity, of self-induced provocation, of ingratitude in their children, and more.

The *shlemazel* is a person who is continually frustrated and never seems to achieve any satisfaction in life. It is as if such people carry a personal trouble-lightning rod that attracts grief. The fatalism of the shlemazel may result in a self-definition of being one who always gets "dumped" on; increasingly, he or she acts in ways that are irritating to others, thus provoking aggression even from friends and relatives. The hopeless shlemazel becomes a *shlemiel* when the destructive, self-fulfilling prophecy leads others to delight in that person's misery.

Over the years, collective and institutionalized violence have taken many different forms. Governments have continually exhorted their citizens to take up arms against foreign invaders or to go forth to conquer new lands. In countries like the United States, where the threat of outside attacks has been small, violence has been directed toward the "enemies" within—the American Indians, for example, whose ranks were brutally cut from 850,000 to less than 400,000 in a series of "skirmishes." When governments have become oppressive, people have often joined together to fight their rule and overthrow them. Many massacres have been committed in the name of religious principles.

While some of these violent actions have been expressions of feelings of hate and anger, much collective violence is coolly instrumental—a means to an end. It can be used either to maintain power and preserve the status quo, or to change the existing society and achieve power.

"The streets of our country are in turmoil. The universities are filled with students rebelling and rioting. Communists are seeking to destroy our country. Russia is threatening us with her might. The republic is in danger. Yes, danger from within and without. We need law and order. Yes, without law and order our nation cannot survive. . . . We shall restore law and order."

These words were written not by a U.S. law-and-order candidate in the 1970s but by Adolf Hitler in 1939. They highlight the fact that there are some forms of violence that traditionally have been viewed as legitimate, such as the use of violence by the State or by the police to maintain order and control crime. They also demonstrate that this legitimacy is based on people's acceptance of the authority of their institutions. Once this acceptance begins to fade, perceived legitimacy crumbles and each side sees its own violence as legitimate and the violence by the other side as illegitimate.

What one person views as justified violence may be regarded as unjustified by another; for example, a ghetto resident may feel that police activities are illegitimate uses of violence, while a suburbanite may approve of the police "doing their job." In general, the more negatively one feels about the individuals being aggressed against, the higher the level of violence that is felt to be justifiable. Thus a person who dislikes student protestors is likely to be in favor of maximal force by the police to stop sit-ins and demonstrations. Violence perceived as either self-defense or retribution is also likely to be seen as justified. Since these two values are so pervasive in our society, one might question the extent to which they may be creating positive attitudes toward violence (Blumenthal, 1972).

Tax evasion, price-fixing, and misleading advertising are examples of more "legitimized" violence; they are usually tolerated by the general public, either through ignorance of what is going on or because such activities are less personally threatening than what people see as "real" crime, such as robbery, muggings, and rape. In a classic study (Sutherland, 1949), the seventy largest industrial and commercial corporations in the U.S. were all found to have engaged in illegal activities. All of them had been prosecuted for various crimes, with the average company receiving fourteen convictions. Given this high rate of recidivism, 90 percent of these companies could be legally considered habitual criminals. People who engage in this kind of crime, however, do not feel they are doing something really wrong:

"Businessmen differ from professional thieves principally in their greater interest in status and respectability. They think of themselves as honest men, not as criminals, whereas professional thieves, when they speak honestly, admit they are thieves. The businessman does regard himself as a lawbreaker, but he thinks the laws are wrong or at least that they should not restrict him, although they may well restrict others. He does not think of himself as a criminal, because he does not conform to the popular stereotype of the criminal. This popular stereotype is always taken from the lower socioeconomic class." (Sutherland, 1968)

This sort of attitude toward crime may be the reason why some people felt the participants in the Watergate conspiracy should not be punished because "they weren't criminal types."

Pathology in Urban Centers

People have traditionally been attracted to cities because of the economic opportunities they provide and also for their cultural and social functions. The urban centers are "where the action is."

But today, for many people, the action is too much, too fast, and too unpredictable and uncontrollable. The tempo and pace seem nonstop; there is too much competition for limited and often deteriorating resources (such as taxis, seats in subways, nursery schools); and there are too many people willing to "con" you, too much incivility, and too little neighborly concern. The advantages of urban-style living are increasingly counterbalanced by the adaptations an individual must make to the sensory-cognitive overload and stress created by such a life.

While cities represent our greatest technological control over nature, they have begun to limit the power of the individuals within them to regulate the quality of their lives. In fact, our big cities are increasingly becoming centers of unsolvable problems and sources of pathology and destruction for those who must live within their plasterboard walls.

In the summer of 1970, a temperature inversion trapped hot air and air pollutants over New York City, causing temperatures to soar and

Close-up
Changing the Script

San Francisco's Channel 5 news one night carried the story of a quick-thinking bank teller in Stockholm who thwarted a potential robbery. A man, armed with a revolver, stuck his head in the door of the bank and yelled, "Is there any money in here?" The teller, seemingly unshaken by the potential danger at hand, yelled back, "I'm sorry, sir, but the cashier is out to lunch. Is there something else I could help you with?" The robber thanked her politely, thought a moment, put the gun in his pocket, and walked out (Aug. 30, 1973).

creating respiratory problems. The technological solution was simple: air conditioners and dehumidifiers were turned on everywhere. But the demand overtaxed the electrical supply, leading to reduced electrical power not only for air conditioners but for the subways as well.

This increased the frustration of stranded and late passengers, many of whom then turned to their cars for transportation. Naturally, the greater use of cars in an already overcrowded city not only created maddening traffic jams, but also added to the air pollution. And so did the greater effort by the utilities companies to generate more electricity. All this was just one more in a long series of continuing problems created by excessive population density: inadequate garbage and sanitation facilities, erratic telephone service, noise pollution, crowded schools, and unsafe streets, among others. ▲

In large cities it has become an axiom that the solution to every problem is the cause of a new one. As soon as many city dwellers can afford to do so, they move to the suburbs where they can find better schools, more space, nature, and

▲ Within a few days of each other in 1968, New York City had a garbage strike, a teachers' strike, a police strike, and a longshoremen's strike.

a private home. But if their job is in the city, then they must go back and forth daily. To avoid traffic congestion on the cities' highways, the frustration of trying to find on-the-street parking, and the substantial parking-lot fees, they become commuters on local trains.

But what is the psychological cost of being a commuter?

A psychiatrist distributed 100 questionnaires to the faithful waiting for the 7:12 A.M. "bullet" train from Long Island into Manhattan. From the 49 completed questionnaires returned, it was determined that these average commuters had just gulped down their breakfast in less than 11 minutes, if at all; were prepared to spend 3 hours each day in transit; and had already logged 10 years of rail time—about 7500 hours, assuming two-week vacations and no time off for illness. Two thirds of the commuters believed their family relations were impaired by their commuting, 59 percent experienced fatigue, 47 percent were filled with conscious anger, 28 percent were anxious, and others reported headaches, muscle pains, indigestion, and other symptoms of the long-term consequences of beating the rat race in the city by living in the country (Charatan, 1973).

However distressing this life, the commuter at least has the perception of an escape each night from the growing sense of fear and social pathology that emotionally cripples many of those not affluent enough to flee to the suburbs or afford the luxury of a high-security apartment. The plea of one frightened man trapped in an inner-city ghetto is all too common. (See *P&L Close-up* below.)

There are more murders per year on Manhattan Island than in all of England and Wales (where the population is nearly thirty times as large). In one high-crime district in Harlem, one out of every *five hundred* people walking the street will become a homicide victim during the year. More than half of those interviewed in a high-crime area felt unsafe and believed that their community was not a good place to bring up children, as compared to less than 5 percent in the suburban area (Conklin, 1971).

Help! Who Will Help Me?

Among the most potent forces for diminishing human nature are social conditions that make it possible for one person to be close to many people and yet feel alienated from them. In a big city one is surrounded by literally hundreds of thousands of people, hears them on radio, sees them on television, eats with them in restau-

Close-up
'I Am a Frightened Man'

To the Editor:
One of these nights I will not be coming home to my wife and four-year-old son. I will have been the victim of one of the numerous packs of muggers that have turned the streets of Bedford-Stuyvesant-Williamsburgh into an asphalt jungle filled with terror and violence for my fellow black and Puerto Rican neighbors and myself and my family.

I am of black and Puerto Rican parentage. I grew up in Harlem and East Harlem in the midst of fighting gangs. As a young man I would come home late at night from evening college after working during the day. During all my previous 39 years I never really felt afraid for my own safety. I have been afraid for my mother, my son, my wife and other loved relatives, but never for myself. Now I'm afraid, really afraid, because I can see my number coming up, and feel absolutely helpless.

I want to see my son grow up into a happy, successful and honorable person. What is most terrifying is the knowledge that the odds are now definitely against that happening.

So many of my friends, neighbors and relatives are getting mugged, stabbed, assaulted and robbed that I know it is just a matter of days or merely hours before my turn will come.

What makes it even more horrifying is that now for the first time I know how a helpless old man, a woman or a child feels while walking down the street in the early evening darkness. Scared and absolutely helpless, with no policemen around, and knowing that no one wants to get involved.

I am no longer a cocky combat-ready ex-Marine infantry sergeant. I am a frightened man returning home from work at night, looking behind me, to the side of me, to the front of me, wondering if tonight is the night I will get it.

Will I get it in the subway exit where the bulbs are broken nearly every night, in the street while passing one of the numerous empty lots or empty houses, or on my doorstep while putting my key in the lock?

I know it is too late to save my life, but I pray that the people and our leaders wake up, organize and stamp out illicit drugs, permissiveness and loss of respect for authority, which I know are the causes of this tremendous increase in violent crime.

Then we will be able to save the lives of our children and of countless other people that deserve a life free from fear of a violent death or even of a violent mugging. Then people will be able to concentrate on living life to its fullest, on being happy, bright-eyed and filled with a love for humanity that is reciprocated by their fellow human beings.

LOUIS S. CAMPBELL
Brooklyn, Jan. 30, 1972

rants, sits next to them in movies, waits in line with them, gets pushed around in subways with them, touches them—but remains untouched, unconnected, as if they did not exist.

For a woman in Queens, they did not exist.

"For more than half an hour, 38 respectable, law-abiding citizens in Queens [New York] watched a killer stalk and stab a woman in three separate attacks in Kew Gardens.

"Twice the sound of their voices and the sudden glow of their bedroom lights interrupted him and frightened him off. Each time he returned, sought her out and stabbed her again. Not one person telephoned the police during the assault; one witness called the police after the woman was dead." (The New York Times, *March 13, 1964)*

This newspaper account of the murder of Kitty Genovese shocked a nation that could not accept the idea of such apathy on the part of its responsible citizenry. Yet only a few months later there was an even more vivid and chilling depiction of how alienated and out of contact one can be in the midst of people. Imagine for a

Close-up
The Eyewitness

I was the man on the spot.
    I was the first at the crime.
I got a story in hot;
    I wasn't wasting no time.

I got my name in the news.
    I got my face on TV.
I had the stuff they could use;
    I got a nice little fee.

I saw the van hit the cab;
    I saw the man with the gun;
I saw the smash and the grab;
    I saw the driver get done.

I saw the gang get away;
    They passed me as close as could be,
I could have—What's that you say?
    Why didn't I *stop* them? Who, *me?*

Peter Suffolk

moment that you had been in the position of an eighteen-year-old secretary who was beaten, choked, stripped, and raped in her office and then finally broke away from her assailant. Naked and bleeding, she ran down the stairs of the building to the doorway screaming, "Help me! Help me! He raped me!" A crowd of forty persons gathered on the busy street and watched passively as the rapist dragged her back upstairs. Only the chance arrival of passing police prevented her further abuse and possible murder (The New York Times, *May 6, 1964).*

Would *you* have called the police if you had lived in Kew Gardens? Would you have intervened to help the woman being raped? Will you (when your chance comes) do anything other than "your own thing"? (See *P&L* Close-up at left.)

More potential helpers—less help. Is the failure to intervene in emergencies due to some defect in the personalities of the particular bystanders, or can it be traced to existing conditions of social learning that could affect anyone?

Two social psychologists set out to answer this question by ingeniously creating in the laboratory an experimental analog of the bystander-intervention situation. A college student, placed in a room by himself, was led to believe that he was communicating with other students via an intercom. During the course of a discussion about personal problems, he heard what sounded like one of the other students having an epileptic seizure. The subject heard him gasp for help over the intercom:

"I-er-um-I think I-I need-er-if-if could-er-er-somebody er-er-er-er-er-er-er give me a little-er-give me a little help here because-er-I-er-I'm-er-er-h-h-having a-a-a real problem-er-right now and I-er-if somebody could help me out it would-it would-er-er s-s-sure be-sure be good . . . because-er-there-er-er-a cause I-er-uh-I've got a-a one of the-er-sei —— er-er-things coming on and-and-and I could really-er-use some help so if somebody would-er-give me a little h-help-uh-er-er-er-er-er c-could somebody-er-er-

help-er-uh-uh-uh (choking sounds). . . . I'm gonna die-er-er-I'm . . . gonna die-er-help-er-er-seizure-er-[chokes, then quiet]."

During the "fit" it was impossible for the subject to talk to the other students or to find out what, if anything, they were doing about the emergency. The dependent variable was the speed with which he reported the emergency to the experimenter. The major independent variable was the number of people he thought were in the discussion group with him.

It turned out that the likelihood of intervention depended on the number of bystanders he thought were present. The more there were, the slower he was in reporting the fit, if he did so at all. As you can see by the graph, everyone in a two-person situation intervened within 160 seconds, but nearly 40 percent of those in the larger group never bothered to inform the experimenter that another student might be dying. ● A battery of personality measures taken on each subject failed to show any significant relationship between particular personality characteristics and speed or likelihood of intervening (Darley & Latané, 1968).

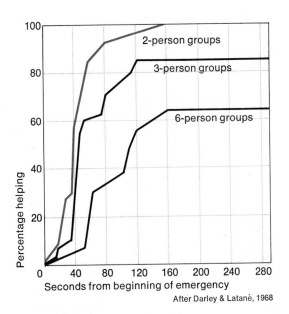

BYSTANDER INTERVENTION IN AN EMERGENCY

Related studies have shown that your chances of being helped if you are a victim in an emergency situation are greater if the bystanders are: black, rather than white; men, rather than women; part of a service group, rather than a social group; and in a pleasant mood at the time. Also, bystanders are more likely to intervene if they have witnessed a model similar to themselves helping someone else in distress, but not if others in the emergency situation who do *not* help are perceived as similar to them. Furthermore, you will be helped to the extent that the situation is clearly defined as an emergency; that you are trying, if possible, to help yourself; and that the situation is not a formal, structured one. (See *P&L* Close-up below.)

Close-up
**Bystander Intervention:
Laboratory vs. the Real World**

Although laboratory research on bystander intervention has helped to specify some of the conditions that determine whether observers will help or be inactive, a curious discrepancy emerges when we compare the frequency of intervention in laboratory studies with behavior in the real world. A thorough review of this literature reveals that "without exception, field studies have discovered a considerably *greater* willingness on the part of bystanders to intervene than the lab studies would indicate" (Warner, 1972). What accounts for this difference?

Compare the following field experiment with those of Latané and Darley. A man on a moving New York subway train suddenly collapses and falls to the floor. This event is witnessed by a number of naive bystanders on their way to or from work, shopping, etc. The experimenters manipulate the situation by varying the characteristics of the "victim"—an invalid with a cane, or a drunk smelling of liquor, or, in a companion study, with the invalid seemingly bleeding (or not bleeding) from the mouth. They then unobtrusively record the bystander responses to these emergency situations.

Surprisingly, in light of both the low intervention rates in laboratory studies and the newspaper stories of "callous" city folk, one or more persons responded directly to almost every emergency (81 of 103) and did so with little hesitation! Help was slower when the apparent cost of intervening was higher (that is, slower for a bloody victim than for a simple collapse), but still it came, even if it was indirect, such as by a question: "Is there a doctor in the subway?" (Piliavan, Rodin, & Piliavan, 1969; Piliavan & Piliavan, 1972).

Why the difference? Helping may be inhibited in the laboratory setting for the following reasons: (a) the college student subjects have already adopted the *passive* role of "the subject"; (b) they assume that the experimenter-in-charge is ultimately responsible for everything that occurs during the experimental session, which itself is an artificial situation; (c) they often do not actually see the victim-in-distress; and (d) their physical locomotion is severely restricted by obedience to an unstated rule of the laboratory setting—"You stay in your seat; you stay put and follow instructions until told otherwise." In unstructured, informal settings none of these conditions hold, the decision to intervene is probably based more on the observer's weighing of the personal costs of intervening or of not intervening.

I'm late! I'm late for a very
Important Date. No time to say
"Hello." Goodbye, I'm late.

From "I'm Late,"
in *Alice in Wonderland*, 1949

No time to say "Hello." One of the most perplexing characteristics of our modern way of life is that everything seems to be moving and changing faster than we can psychologically cope with. Especially in big cities, anything that stands still is ticketed, towed away, or buried.

The ultimate test of the degree to which being in a hurry can destroy the foundation of social life was created in a remarkable experiment at Princeton University by Darley and Batson (1973).

Forty students studying for the ministry at Princeton Theological Seminary volunteered for an alleged study on religious education and vocations. After being briefed about the study in one building, each student was supposed to report to another building in order to give a speech. Some of them expected to give a speech on jobs for which seminary students would be effective; the others were prepared to deliver a sermon on the parable of the Good Samaritan. That parable is from the Gospel of Luke, Chapter 10:

"A man was going down from Jerusalem to Jericho, and he fell among robbers, who stripped him and beat him, and departed, leaving him half dead. Now by chance a priest was going down the road; and when he saw him he passed by on the other side. So likewise a Levite, when he came to the place and saw him, passed by on the other side. But a Samaritan, as he journeyed, came to where he was; and when he saw him, he had compassion, and went to him and bound his wounds, pouring on oil and wine; then he set him on his own beast and brought him to an inn, and took care of him."

Before each seminary student left to deliver his speech, the experimenters systematically manipulated his perception of how much time he had to get to the other building.

LOW-HURRY: *"It'll be a few minutes before they're ready for you, but you might as well head on over. If you have to wait over there it won't be for long."*
INTERMEDIATE-HURRY: *"The assistant is ready for you, so please go right over."*
HIGH-HURRY: *"Oh, you're late. They were expecting you a few minutes ago. We'd better get moving. The assistant should be waiting for you so you'd better hurry."*

As the subject passed down an alley to the other building, guess what he found? Sure enough, slumped over in a doorway was a man coughing, groaning, head down, eyes closed. Here was the opportunity to be a Good Samaritan, to stop and help this poor victim. The "victim," who did not know which experimental condition any subject was in, noted whether or not each subject helped and also the kind of help offered. The seminary students eventually made their speeches, filled out a questionnaire that contained questions about helping people in need and specifically about when they had last seen such a needy person and whether they had helped. Then they were debriefed and the purpose of the study was explained fully.

The results are startling and depressing: overall, 60 percent of the subjects did not *stop to help the victim. The fact that they were on their way to give a sermon on the Good Samaritan parable had* no *effect on increasing the likelihood that they would act like one. Most significantly, the best predictor of who would stop to help was the situational variable of the degree to which a subject was in a hurry. Of those not in a hurry, 63 percent helped; of those somewhat in a hurry, 45 percent helped. Only 10 percent of the seminary student subjects who were late, in a big hurry to deliver the Good Samaritan sermon, stopped to help a fellow man in need of their help.*

These were not callous people, but individuals who were fulfilling a prior obligation that conflicted with stopping to give aid.

Overcrowding

To what extent does the physical fact of overcrowding lead to hostility and the social ills manifest in cities such as New York, Philadelphia, Newark, Detroit, Chicago, Tokyo, Calcutta, London, and others?

The most thorough investigation of the relationship between population, the physical environment, and social-emotional behavior in animals has been conducted by John Calhoun at the National Institute of Mental Health over the past two decades (Calhoun, 1962, 1971). Colonies of wild or tame rats or mice have been reared in artificial habitats where the effects of increasing population could be observed over several generations.

In one series of experiments, a kind of "housing project" was created in which there were four interconnected units reached by a winding staircase. To reach the end units, the animals had to pass through the center ones, which soon became the focal point for social activity. When the population grew to about 80 rats—48 would have been optimal—"vice" or life-destroying behaviors began to emerge.

Despite the presence of ample physical resources, such as food and nest-building materials, there were frequent vicious fights between the males as well as unprovoked attacks on females and infants. Some males were extremely aggressive, while others withdrew and became passive. Hypersexuality, homosexuality, and bisexuality increased tremendously. Social order broke down completely to the point that such normal activities as nest-building and infant care were ignored by the females, cannibalism occurred, and no infant reached maturity.

In another version, with living quarters arranged as "high-rise apartments" around an open area, again with ample food and nesting materials and freedom from germs, predators, or rain or snow, breakdown began when all the desirable physical spaces and social roles were filled. Dominant males started to break down, worn out from defending their territories. Females chased their young out of the nest early and became more aggressive and dominating. Young adults stopped struggling for territory of their own and took to a pathological life "on the streets" in the large open area. Breeding ceased. The last mouse died less than five years after the start of the study. ◆

As we saw in Chapter 9, when stress is prolonged and unremitting, the adrenal glands work overtime to keep producing the hormones needed for defensive responses; they grow larger and eventually may be unable to respond at all. In addition, body growth is suppressed, resistance to infection decreases, blood composition changes, various internal organs show degenerative changes, and the reproductive organs either stop functioning or function incompletely. The overcrowding and social disorganization in Calhoun's colonies provided adequate stress for these changes to occur.

The parallels between Calhoun's findings and the violence, vandalism, sexual perversion, and general breakdown of social etiquette in our big cities are all too obvious. Yet we do not know how far his findings apply to human beings or just what role overcrowding may play in the whole picture. It is a very new research area, and evidently the relationships are more complex than at first thought.

◆ Dr. John B. Calhoun looks down on Universe 25, now labeled Dead City—the community home of some 2200 mice who finally died. The spokes were their runways; the hub, the communal meeting place; the bottles provided all the water needed and the wire baskets the food.

For example, it makes a difference whether subjects have a personal territory, such as a desk or chair, whether much or little interaction is required, and whether the experimenter studies *spatial density* (the same number of people in different-sized spaces) or *social density* (more or fewer people in the same space). Age differences, cultural differences, expectations, and duration of the crowding also help to determine the effects of crowding. Most important of all seems to be the individual's interpretation and evaluation of the crowding. Thus, whereas overcrowding seems to act in a one-to-one, predictable way on mice or rats, its influence on human behavior is mediated by a whole host of other variables, many of them "subjective" (see Loo, 1972 and Freedman et al., 1972).

Anonymity and Deindividuation

Living among strangers with whom one has only superficial and impersonal contacts can lead to apathy, alienation, and cynicism as a means of coping with overload by psychologically distancing oneself and not getting "taken." The extent to which city dwellers develop a lack of trust of each other was demonstrated in an interesting field experiment.

In middle-income apartments in Manhattan and in apartments in small towns in surrounding counties, student investigators, working singly, rang doorbells and asked to use the telephone, explaining that the address of a friend who lived nearby had been misplaced. The researchers wanted to see whether there would be a difference between the city and town dwellers in their willingness to help a stranger with such a request.

The differences were striking. Male students were allowed to enter half of the homes in the small towns but only 14 percent of the homes in the city. The females were admitted to 94 percent of the town homes but only 60 percent of the city ones (Altman, Levine, & Nadien, 1970).

Big-city living not only robs people of many of the potential benefits of social living but often nibbles away at one of their most precious possessions—a sense of personal identity and uniqueness. Though surrounded by people, the individual becomes anonymous. It is easy for him or her to get the feeling, "No one knows or cares who I am—so why should I care about anyone else?"

Being anonymous decreases the chances of getting either one's just reward for socially beneficial behavior or punishment for antisocial behavior. Emotions or impulses that would otherwise be held in check by conformity to social norms and fear of social disapproval may be released under the mask of anonymity.

In one laboratory experiment, anonymity was created in some groups of female students by having them wear baggy lab coats and hoods that covered their faces. In addition, they sat in a darkened room and were never referred to by name. Other groups were randomly assigned to a condition that emphasized their individuality: they wore name tags, were frequently called by name, and saw the faces of the other women in their group. All groups had four subjects.

The subjects were told that the experimenter was studying empathy. Electric shocks were to be given to two young women (who were supposedly undergoing a conditioning experiment anyway). Two subjects would give the shock while the other two would only observe; then all would make empathy judgments. To determine who would do the shocking, they drew lots (which were rigged so that each subject believed that she and one other would deliver shocks). During the administration of shock, each of the four subjects was in a separate cubicle so that she couldn't see the other subjects.

The subjects were instructed to press a shock button whenever a green light went on; another light would go on to show shock being transmitted and stay on as long as either button was pressed down (up to a 2.5-second maximum). Subjects were led to believe that the same amount of shock was delivered whether one or more buttons were pressed and that the experimenter would not know which subjects were doing the shocking.

Before seeing each victim and watching her twist, squirm, and jump in reaction to each supposed shock (actually she was a confederate who received no shock), the subjects listened to a taped interview with each victim. In one condition the victim was portrayed as obnoxious, prejudiced, "bitchy"; in the other, as sweet, warm, loving, and altruistic.

As predicted, subjects in the anonymous condition gave much more shock than the individuated subjects initially and increased it over the twenty trials. ■ *The individuated subjects*

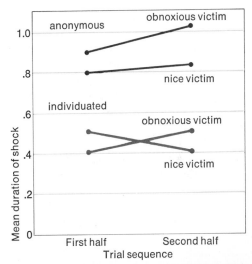

After Zimbardo, 1969b

■ **AGGRESSION AS A FUNCTION OF ANONYMITY**
The anonymous subjects delivered more shock and gradually increased the amount of shock they gave both the victims. The individuated subjects gave only about half as much shock and decreased the amount they were giving the "nice" victim in the course of the experiment.

shocked the "nice" victim less over time; the anonymous ones shocked both victims more. For the individuated subjects, there was a strong positive correlation between evaluation of the victim and aggression toward her: more if she was rated negatively, less if she was rated positively. Among the hooded subjects, there was no such relationship: once they began to be aggressive to either one, their aggression increased. Behaving aggressively when you cannot be identified appears to be self-reinforcing (Zimbardo, 1969b).

A body of subsequent research supports the basic conclusion of this study—that under conditions fostering anonymity, people are more likely to act aggressively or to behave in other antisocial ways. College student subjects are more likely to cheat or steal when they are treated by the experimenter as anonymous "guinea pigs" than when they are treated as unique individuals.

The same phenomenon occurs under the anonymity of Halloween costumes. In a field experiment, 1352 children were unobtrusively observed as they made their Halloween trick-or-treat rounds either alone or in groups. Confederates of the researchers either emphasized the children's anonymity or made them identifiable by asking their names and removing their masks. They were more likely to take extra candies and money when they were concealed by costume and were part of a group whose leader was also anonymous, and were more honest when individuated and alone (Fraser, Kelem, Diener, & Beaman, 1974).

In another study, eight children were invited to an experimental Halloween party where they were allowed to play at aggressive or nonaggressive games in which they could win tokens. These tokens were exchangeable for attractive toys at an auction held at the end of the party. Playing the aggressive games involved physical competition (pushing and shoving) and took more time, thus earning fewer tokens and not being instrumental to the goal of getting the best toys later.

At first, the children played at these games in their normal street clothes; then they were dressed in Halloween costumes that made them appear anonymous; finally, they were unmasked and wore their regular clothing again—an A-B-A research design. The dramatic effects of simply being made anonymous are evident in the following mean group results:

	Aggressive Acts	Tokens Won
(A) Initial Baseline Phase	42%	58
(B) Anonymity	86%	31
(A) Final Baseline Phase	36%	79

Thus, their anonymity facilitated their aggression even when the instrumental consequence of the aggression was not in the child's best interests (Fraser, 1974).

Sometimes people choose to enter a situation of anonymity (and unaccountability) through being part of a group. Examples of chosen anonymity are seen in the exuberance (and often destructiveness) at large conventions, as well as in fraternity hell-night, costume parties, the Mardi Gras, and Ku Klux Klan activities. And in some situations anonymity is imposed by society. Just as the subjects in the experiments described above were made anonymous by wearing the costumes provided by the experimenters, men become G.I.'s ("Government Issue") by wearing identical military uniforms.

This uniformity in appearance makes it easier for leaders to obtain behavioral conformity, as Adolf Hitler noted in his book *Mein Kampf*. But the psychological anonymity provided by uniforms or gang jackets also frees the wearers from conventional constraints on their behavior, especially when there is not a strong leader in charge—in part accounting for the murder, rape, and looting that soldiers of almost all nations engage in when on foreign soil. (See *P&L* Close-up, p. 635.)

Anonymity is but one of many conditions that can foster the subjective state of deindividuation, with its weakening of the usual controls that restrain impulsive and antisocial behaviors. Others include shared or diffuse responsibility, altered states of consciousness or time perspective, emotional or sexual arousal, sensory overload, novelty or lack of structure in the situation, and physical involvement in an aggressive act (Zimbardo, 1969b).

If anonymity is conducive to deindividuation and, in turn, to greater susceptibility to aggressive and other antisocial actions, it is in society's interest to discover what conditions prevent deindividuation and foster individuation instead.

In a recent study (mentioned also in Chapter 4 in connection with communication) groups of college students were told that one member of the group would be chosen as coordinator for a city-planning simulation game. In one condition, this was a desirable job for which they would be paid; in another condition, being chosen was undesirable because the coordinator would be shocked for every wrong decision. In the positive condition, the subjects behaved in verbal and nonverbal ways that clearly individuated them, whereas in the negative condition, they did all they could to be "un-unique," to deindividuate themselves (Maslach, 1974).

Vandalism: Senseless Violence?

"It's just wanton, senseless destruction by vandals." Rare trees in a park garden are cut up, wrecked, and demolished; animals in a sanctuary are tortured and killed, birds defeathered; churches are desecrated, synagogues sacked; schools are burned, windows broken; comfort stations are set afire; public telephones are ripped from their booths; parked cars are stripped and battered; cemetery gravestones are overturned.

Such is only a partial listing of the daily activities not of a conquering enemy army, but of a curious breed of citizens called *vandals*, so-called after the barbarians who invaded Western Europe in 455 A.D. The characteristic feature of vandalism is the destruction of property and life without any apparent goal beyond the act of destruction itself. Such behavior seems to be motiveless and irrational since the perpetrators put a lot of effort into an activity that seems to have no instrumental value to them.

When is destruction vandalism? To a large extent, vandalism is what someone has *called* vandalism. The damage done to town property after a big football game has usually been accepted as a "normal" process. In contrast, breaking college windows becomes "trashing" if it is seen as part of a radical protest and is reacted to with more severe judicial action—even when the extent of property damage is the same as in the mischief of the "fraternity boys," "the frosh," or "the jocks."

Close-up
Anonymity and Cross-Cultural Aggression

In some societies, men prepare for war by changing their appearance through the use of masks or painting their bodies, whereas in others there is no such process of changing one's identity prior to becoming a warrior. What do you imagine might be the consequences of this variation in self-imposed anonymity? Which of the two social groups do you predict would exhibit most aggression in combat? To answer these questions, Robert Watson (1973) examined twenty-three different cultures on which the relevant data were available. The striking results can be seen in the table. Of the fifteen societies in which warriors changed their appearance, twelve were high on the index of "killing, torturing, or mutilating the enemy," while only one out of eight of those with unchanged appearance were so aggressive.

	Painted face	Unpainted face	Total
High Aggression	12	1	13
Low Aggression	3	7	10
Total	15	8	23

Adapted from Watson, 1973

All the two eight-year-old boys (top photo) had to say when caught vandalizing their school was, "We intended to wreck the whole building." In the bottom photo, some youngsters practice a much more common form of vandalism.

Derailing a train by putting obstacles on the track is "mischief" if done by children, "vandalism" if the perpetrators have attained the age of reason, or "sabotage" if the cargo of the train is related to the national defense. Even killing animals becomes a sport if the killer has a license to hunt. While polluting the environment by littering is a criminal act that draws a fine if done by an individual, pollution of the air, water, and earth by factories did not even draw public censure until the recent ecology movement identified these acts as vandalism against the property of the human race.

A number of important consequences follow from calling a given destructive act "an act of vandalism." The first is to deny that it could result from legitimate motives. The second is to identify certain people as "deviants" whose irrationality is a danger to everyone. The third is to absolve the society: people blame the supposedly disturbed mind of the vandal instead of looking for possible causes in the individual's transactions with society. Finally, it implies the futility of remedial action, the impossibility of scientific investigation of the problem, and the desperate need for greater police deterrents and stiffer penalties—the only noticeable effect of which seems to be a shifting of targets and an even greater incidence of vandalism. ●

Finding sense in the "senselessness." If vandalism were indeed "senseless" we could never hope to control it, because an effect without a cause does not fit into any systematic plan that could limit it. Fortunately, it *is* possible to make sense of even apparently senseless, malicious vandalism. History can give us some clues, as can talking to gang members, observing the behavior of college students engaged in acts of physical destruction, and various kinds of field experiments.

In the eighteenth century, when a group of workers called *Luddites* began destroying factory machines, they were stereotyped as "frenzied" and "mad," and their actions as "pointless." But they were part of an earnest movement aimed at the betterment of their society. They were protesting against the evils of the industrial system.

Similarly, the property destruction that occurred during the racial disturbances in Watts, Newark, and other American cities in the late 1960s appeared "mindless" until it was noted that the targets chosen were not arbitrary but appeared to be deliberate attacks on white-owned businesses believed to be unfair or disrespectful toward members of the community.

Analysis of the behavior of gangs reveals several interrelated causal factors in their violent acts (Becker, 1963; W. Miller, 1966; Yablonsky, 1968). Gang members, like many individuals in lower socioeconomic groups, typically lead lives with little hope of change or significant improvement, without feelings of ownership or relatedness to society. Social conditions have limited their accessibility to the traditional means of "making it," of gaining status, prestige, and social power. They have reacted by becoming outsiders, in forming a counterculture with its own norms. But they still need to *use* the traditional culture in order to "make it" in their own subculture. One gang member said,

"If I would of got the knife, I would have stabbed him. That would have gave me more of a build-up. People would have respected me for what I've done and things like that. They would say, 'There goes a cold killer.' It makes you feel like a big shot." (Yablonsky, 1968, pp. 230–31)

For such a youth, vandalism against property and violence against people may be a reaction to transform boredom into excitement and get pleasure from violating a social taboo. On the basis of our prior analysis, we would also predict that vandalism would be used as a means of gaining a measure of self-recognition. Indeed, a recent vogue among big-city vandals has been *"identification graffiti."* The vandal leaves his or her calling card sprayed on walls of everything in sight: houses, churches, public buildings, mass transit vehicles, toilets, and more.

At a deeper level, vandalism may be an affirmation that powerless people can at times rebel and be the controllers. Malicious vandalism can be seen as a public acceptance of society's rejection and an active attempt to establish oneself as an outsider—one to be feared. Apparently, in fact, an act that appears senseless receives *more reinforcement* than one that is understandable and predictable. People make their mark, gain a reputation, are remembered or feared for behavior that is out of the ordinary, unaccountable, and unlikely to be performed by others in the same situation. Arbitrariness is a way of showing that your personal power is controlled by internal forces and not by other people or events. We see the same mechanism in Albert Camus' play *Caligula,* in which a Roman emperor attempts to show that he is a god by his arbitrary exercise of power over the life and death of other people—friend and foe alike.

One need only provide an old car, a sledgehammer, and the sanction to smash the car in order to unleash an astonishing degree of violence in even the most timid of middle-class intellectual college students.

One freshman dormitory group invited to such a "smash-in" not only demolished the car in a short time, but set it ablaze, tried to prevent firemen from extinguishing it, and eventually had to be restrained at gunpoint by police order from attacking it again. Graduate students who were invited to try their hand at "just denting an old car a bit" were reluctant at first, but got carried away with the exhilarating feeling of physically destroying it. At one point, one student was stomping on the roof, two others were trying to pull the doors off, and another was systematically trying to break all the glass. ◆

◆ The tow-truck operator who removed the battered hulk said that the last car he had seen in that condition had been hit by an express train.

■. The first view shows the "respectable" middle-class family who were the first to begin stripping the car. In the second view, another adult vandal removes one of the tires. In the third view, a group of youngsters take their turn at picking over the now-battered remains.

Who becomes a vandal? In a more systematic effort to observe who the people are that vandalize automobiles and what conditions are associated with such vandalism, a simple field demonstration was performed in New York City and Palo Alto, California.

Two used automobiles in good condition were abandoned on the streets with their license plates removed and their hoods raised. One was placed a block from the New York University campus in the Bronx, the other a block from the Stanford University campus. Hidden observers watched, photographed, and took notes on all those who came into contact with the "bait." The researchers expected to find that the greater anonymity in New York City would lead to a greater incidence of vandalism to the New York car and that most of the vandals would be adolescents and young children.

The first prediction was confirmed; the second was certainly not. Only ten minutes after the New York car was staked out, the first auto strippers appeared—a mother, father, and young son. The mother acted as lookout while father and son emptied the trunk and glove compartment, then hacksawed out the radiator and pulled out the battery. Soon after they drove off, another passing car stopped and its adult driver jacked up the abandoned car and removed the best of its tires. By the end of the day, a steady stream of adult *vandals had removed every conceivable removable part of the car.* ■

Then random destruction began, as other passers-by stopped to examine the car and then cut up a tire, urinated on the door, broke all windows, and dented in the hood, fenders, door, and roof.

"In less than three days what remained was a battered, useless hulk of metal, the result of twenty-three incidents of destructive contact. The vandalism was almost always observed by one or more other passers-by, who occasionally stopped to chat with the looters. Most of the destruction was done in the daylight hours, not at night (as had been anticipated), and the adults' stealing clearly preceded the window-breaking, tire-slashing fun of the youngsters. The adults were all well-dressed, clean-cut whites who would, under other circumstances, have been mistaken for mature, responsible citizens demanding more law and order."

That anonymity provides a release of inhibitions against engaging in such antisocial behavior is inferred from the startling contrast between what occurred in the two different locations. In the town of Palo Alto, not a single item was stolen, nor was any part of the car vandalized during the full week it was left abandoned. Instead, as a sign of the greater prevailing sense of social consciousness in this community, one man passing by in the rain protectively lowered the hood so the motor would not get wet! (Zimbardo, 1973)

It would appear that "vandalism" includes many kinds of behavior, by many kinds of people, in a variety of settings. It is not senseless, but may serve any of several purposes. (See *P&L* Close-up below.)

Close-up
Purposes of Vandalism

Acts of vandalism can be sorted into one of six categories according to the significance that the destructive behavior seems to have for the person.

1. *Acquisitive vandalism* — Property damage done to acquire money or goods, such as breaking open vending machines or telephone coin boxes, stripping parts from cars or fittings from housing project heating systems.

2. *Tactical vandalism* — Property damage as a means to draw attention to a grievance or to force a reaction. Such a tactical approach is exemplified by prisoners who destroy their cells or the mess hall in protesting inadequate facilities or a man who breaks a store window to get arrested so that he will be institutionalized.

3. *Ideological vandalism* — Similar to tactical vandalism, but carried out to further an ideological cause. Examples are antigovernment slogans painted on embassy buildings, burning down R.O.T.C. headquarters, and "trashing" on college campuses as a tactic to make the administration call the police onto campus, in hopes that their expected overreaction would then radicalize apathetic students and faculty. At some point ideological vandalism gets labeled "sabotage" or "treason."

4. *Vindictive vandalism* — Damage done to a selected target for revenge on its owner, guardian, or representative. Sometimes a group of students demolish a classroom because they feel the teacher has been unjust.

5. *Play vandalism* — Damage to property in the context of a game: who can break windows on the highest level, shoot out the most street lamps, jam telephone receivers most ingeniously.

6. *Malicious vandalism* — Damage done to property as part of a general expression of rage or frustration. This vandalism may be indiscriminate but often is directed at symbols of the middle class, public institutions, and anonymity-promoting systems, such as subways, schools, automobiles (Cohen, 1973).

Such a classification makes it clear that there are many motivations for vandalism and many kinds of people who may be *labeled* vandals.

Social Sanctions for Evil

Auschwitz. My Lai. Kent State. Attica. Jackson State. Cambodia and . . . . For many people these names have come to symbolize modern versions of evil. *Evil* is a term applied to "situations when force, violence, and other forms of coercion exceed institutional or moral limits" (Smelser, 1971). The three classes of situations that qualify as "evil" by this definition are those in which individuals or groups: (1) exercise coercive power over others when they are not legitimately empowered to do so; (2) exceed the limits of their legitimate authority to exercise coercion; or (3) exercise coercive or destructive control over others that violates a higher standard of humanity or morality even though it may be within politically sanctioned authority.

Those who engage in evil deeds rarely, if ever, see them as such. For the evil-doer, there is always sufficient justification to make the deed appear not only reasonable but absolutely necessary. Here again is the paradox of human perfection—the same mind that can comprehend the most profound philosophical and metaphysical truths can distort reality so that "evil" becomes "good."

People who violate basic laws of humanity often are convinced that evil is about to be wrought on them. Typically, they rationalize their behavior according to some principle acceptable to others in their society. In addition, they often have some degree of social or political support or institutionalized structure that helps make it possible to redefine the act in other than its human terms.

Consider Hitler:

"Thus, if we review all the causes of the German collapse, the final and decisive one is seen to be the failure to realize the racial problem and, more especially, the Jewish menace. . . . Thus do I now believe that I must act in the sense of the Almighty Creator: by fighting against the Jews I am doing the Lord's work. (1933, p. 25)

Or consider the reason mass killer Herbert Mullin gave for killing four teenage boys in Santa Cruz, California, in 1973. He "punished" the "hippies" because they influenced him to be a conscientious objector and not to be a soldier "in the best country on earth." He also killed thirteen people in the belief that their human sacrifice would prevent a catastrophic earthquake (Associated Press, Aug. 7, 1973).

For the massacre of more than four hundred civilians in My Lai, Vietnam, on March 16, 1968, by Charlie Company, Lieutenant William Calley was found guilty. But an analysis of the conditions that led him and his buddies to this act of atrocity (repeated in a nearby village by a sister unit, Bravo Company) reveals it to be "only a minor step beyond the standard, official, routine United States policy in Vietnam" (Opton, 1971) and a consequence of the *psychic numbing* that was fostered by the conditions of this undeclared war (Lifton, 1971).

It might be argued that Calley and the other soldiers were responding to intense situational pressures that overdetermined their behavior. But now, in a cool analysis that distance and time from that atrocity provide, does the average citizen judge this action as evil? Is it likely to happen again, or was it a once-in-a-wartime event? A survey of a representative sample of nearly a thousand respondents across the United States carefully conducted by Herbert Kelman and Lee Lawrence (1972) led the investigators to conclude:

". . . our data suggest strongly that the cognitive and ideological foundations for Calley's actions are present in large segments of the population. If the situation seems to require it, if the binding forces are strengthened, and if the opposing forces are weakened, they would consider such an action at least justifiable, probably acceptable, perhaps even desirable. Thus, the public reaction to the Calley trial tells us a great deal about the readiness *for such violence in the American population." (p. 212)*

In a letter from five soldiers in Vietnam to the *San Francisco Chronicle* (Dec. 31, 1969), this conclusion is not only supported but enthusiastically endorsed as right and proper. In part, they wrote:

"I want to come home alive; if I must kill old men, women, or children to make myself a little safer, I'll do it without hesitation. War is ugly. There are no rules of good conduct toward the enemy. . . . I'd be willing to bet that the next time American units went into that village they'd encounter very little opposition. To my mind, his [Calley's] was a successful, and anything but unique, type of operation."

As historian Hannah Arendt (1965) has pointed out, although evil behavior is often dramatic in its consequences, the circumstances in which evil occurs is the contrary—often banal and commonplace. Evil occurs frequently without raging emotions or confrontations between id and superego—it is often just a job to be done, an unpleasant interlude in one's life. This mundane perspective on evil is all too frighteningly revealed in the diary of a concentration-camp doctor at Auschwitz. (See *P&L* Close-up at right.)

Blind Obedience to Authority

When you think of the long and gloomy history of man, you will find more hideous crimes have been committed in the name of obedience than have been committed in the name of rebellion.

C. P. Snow, 1961

We began your introduction to psychology with an analysis of Milgram's research on obedience. We are now in a better position to consider some conceptual and practical consequences of this research. Do you believe women would react in the same way as the males used in the Milgram studies? Do you think the subjects really fell for the rationale? Perhaps the procedure lacked plausibility for them; they did not really believe they were hurting the learner but were just going along with the pretense. Both of these concerns have been addressed in a recent experiment, the results of which are in some ways even more striking than the original findings.

Close-up
The Banality of Evil

The following diary was written by Johann Kremer, an Auschwitz doctor, with the expectation that "I could defend myself with the diary at a future time." How much weight would this defense of innocence carry if you were the judge?

September 4, 1942. At noon, I witnessed a Special Operation conducted in the women's camp. The most horrifying sight ever seen. Herr Thilo (crew doctor) was right when he told me that we were living here in the *anus mundi* (the anus of the world). At about 8 this evening, I was again present at a Special Operation with a transport from Holland. Because additional rations are awarded, consisting of a fifth of vodka, 5 cigarettes, and 100 grams of sausage and bread, there are always hordes of SS men willing to serve in this detail.

September 6, 1942. The Sunday dinner was excellent: . . . At 8 this evening I again was present at a Special Operation.

October 3, 1942. Today I have preserved some absolutely fresh tissue of human liver and spleen and pancreas. There are also lice taken from typhus patients preserved in pure alcohol. Whole streets of Auschwitz have typhoid. . . .

October 18, 1942. This damp and cold Sunday morning I was present at the eleventh Special Operation (Dutch). A revolting scene with three women begging for their lives.

October 31, 1942. The last seventeen days or so the perfect autumn weather has encouraged daily sunbaths in the garden of the SS house. Even the bright nights are comparatively mild.

November 13, 1942. I obtained tissue from a fresh body of an 18-year-old Jew. Acute atrophy. . . .

November 14, 1942. Today, Sunday, a vaudeville show at the city club (splendid!). . . .

From *Poland Illustrated Magazine*, 1964, No. 11, p. 123

College students (13 male, 13 female) were recruited for a study in which they were to act as experimental assistants to train an animal to learn a discrimination task. They were to punish each error by administering an increasing level of shock intensity from 15 to 450 volts—exactly as in the earlier research. The subject picked up the animal, put it in a shuttlebox apparatus, and then viewed its behavior through a one-way screen in an adjacent room. The actual experimenter was in the room with the subject but could not see the animal.

The animal was a cute, little, fluffy puppy, who was actually shocked when the subject-teacher depressed the levers on the shock box. The actual shock the puppy received went from only mild to moderate shock levels, which (though low enough levels not to harm the puppy) made the experiment seem totally plausible since as shock administration increased, the puppy's reactions became more intense.

The results for the male subjects replicated the earlier ones—54 percent went all the way. But would you expect females, with their allegedly high nurturant needs, to react in such a fashion? When a comparison sample of 45 students from the same school were asked to predict the outcome of this study, only 3 said that anyone would go beyond 300 volts, and all of them said that no women would ever go to 450. In fact, the majority of these judges (86 percent) estimated that no female subject would even go higher than 150 volts.

Despite these confident predictions and the best available common sense, the facts are that every female subject blindly obeyed—delivering the maximum intensity shock to the helpless puppy whose pain they could witness directly! They were upset, they dissented, and some even wept, but none disobeyed (Sheridan & King, 1972).

Three conditions can be distinguished that lead to such "blind obedience to authority" in violation of one's self-image and moral values.

1. Obedience is fostered by the presence of a *legitimate authority* who is trusted, who is seen as a valid representative of society, and who controls significant reinforcers. An authority who is not face-to-face with the subject loses some of this power.

2. Obedience is enhanced when a *role relationship* is established and accepted in which the individual is subordinated to another person. In this role, people perceive that they are not personally responsible for their behavior since they are not spontaneously initiating action but merely carrying out orders. The person ceases to be a self-directed actor and becomes, instead, a *reactor*, behaving according to someone else's script. However, when subjects see two other people refuse to accept the experimentally imposed role, 90 percent of them will defy authority commands themselves.

3. Obedience is nurtured by the presence of *social norms* that are seen as relating oneself to others in the situation and providing proscriptions as to protocol, etiquette, and socially approved and acceptable behaviors. These norms come to govern and constrain what is perceived as possible and appropriate. One subject in the original Milgram study said to the experimenter, "*I don't mean to be rude, sir*, but shouldn't we look in on him? He has a heart condition and may be dying."

Thus individuals often perceive social forces as so binding that they are locked into behaviors and interactions that they must carry out regardless of what they feel is right or believe is just. The values prescribed by the situation replace their individual values; "duty" and "loyalty" to the group and its norms supersede the dictates of conscience. The subjects do not want to hurt anyone, but feel that it is more imperative not to disrupt The System—the show must go on!

One of the most remarkable aspects of these studies on blind obedience to authority is not that so many intelligent, responsible people consented to obey and help an authority who assumed responsibility for the suffering they inflicted on an innocent victim; it is that they did not get up out of their assigned seat and walk into the next room where a human being might be seriously injured. Even those who did disobey simply asserted verbally that they would not go on. They did not violate the powerful implicit rule of the academic setting—good students stay in their seats. Even their disobedience was within the polite ethic of civilized protocol.

The act of behavioral disobedience is just not the same as the statement that one will disobey. We consistently make the error of attributing more independence, control, and rationality first to ourselves and then to others than is actually observed when we or they are involved in a social situation such as that described by Milgram. We fail to appreciate the magnitude of the social forces that are acting upon a person who is enmeshed in this kind of social matrix.

The social matrix of obedience to authority does not start in the social psychologist's laboratory, but in the elementary-school classroom, Sunday school, and other socializing environments where we are taught to be seen and not heard, not to make trouble, not to talk back, and not to get too uppity. The breeding ground for such evil is in the innocence that accepts such constraints on our independence as justifiable and routine.

There is abundant evidence from the real world to support the assertion that blind obedience will be likely whenever the three conditions described earlier are met. Two of the most cogent examples of unquestioning obedience to authority—doing whatever is asked—come from a tape-recorded interview of one of the authors of *P&L* with a wounded Vietnam veteran, who describes how he killed women and children only a few yards away from him (see *P&L* Close-up below) and from statements made by the bombardier who released the first atomic bomb over Hiroshima.

Close-up
The Killing Power of Obedience

Veteran: The most particular experience I had was one time in the DMZ. We were in a small village and there was a machine gunner in the schoolhouse firing at us. We all spread out and hit the ground. I said I was a medical corpsman [no weapons] but I was the only one in position. So they handed me a grenade and said to throw it in a window and wipe it out. So when I got up close enough to see inside to drop it in, I noticed there was about twenty or thirty children sitting in the back of the room in the corner with about two or three ladies. I threw in a grenade and . . . blew them all to hell.

Zimbardo: Was there any way you could knock out the machine gun without . . .

Veteran: No. There was no way at all, 'cause like you were about three feet away from them. And this grenade is set to explode around a diameter of about forty or fifty feet at least, killing power. You don't have time to think 'cause either you get shot or you kill them. It's them or you. So it's survival is all it is. Save your ass.

Zimbardo: What about afterwards? I mean after you threw it, everybody get killed, or . . .

Veteran: Right. All the children were killed, the building was destroyed, that was that. Is there anything else you'd like to know?

Zimbardo: Is there anything else you'd care to tell me?

Veteran: My last two weeks there in the jungle we're on a routine patrol and this little girl about three years old starts running toward us. She was about forty or sixty feet away from us at the time, we noticed something bouncing on her back as she ran, and our officer said "shoot." We shot her down. At the same time we shot her down she exploded. She blew into small bits. The V.C. attached a savoy mine to her back and it was wired to explode by the time she reached us. It was either her or us. We didn't know for sure the mine was there but we couldn't take the chance.

Zimbardo: When the officer said "shoot," how many people shot?

Veteran: We all shot at her. There was about thirty of us in this particular platoon.

Zimbardo: But did *you* have to do it?

Veteran: Right. You have to do it, you are ordered to do it. You either shoot them, or if you don't shoot them, your officer shoots you. You don't have any choice. No choice about it, you don't have time to think about it, you do it.

The bombardier, when interviewed recently, recalls "I just laughed" when "they said they were developing a bomb that would blow up everything for eight miles." He was not briefed about his payload, but from the special flight maneuvers necessary to avoid the mushrooming cloud he "put two and two together and figured it was radioactive." Nevertheless, he reports, "I'd flown so many missions by then that it was mostly a job to do." The characteristic dichotomy between *dissent* and *disobedience,* as well as the typical error of overestimating *other* people's internal, personal control and underestimating the influence of the social setting in controlling *their* behavior and decisions is summarized in the bombardier's statement:

"I don't believe in everything we do, but if I'm in the military, I've got to support the government. I may not agree, but if ordered I'll sure do it. I think everyone has enough sense never to use the bomb again." (Newsweek, *Aug. 10, 1970)*

The Dynamics of Groupthink

In many organizations and institutions, important decisions or policies are made by *groups* of people, rather than by any single individual. The advantage of such a group process is that there will be several different perspectives on the problem, so that the decision does not depend solely on one person's biases or errors in judgment. Even with a variety of inputs, however, group decisions can sometimes turn out to be extremely bad ones—the kind that later lead smart people to ask, "How could we have been so stupid?"

In an attempt to understand how the group process can go wrong, Irving Janis (1972) made an intensive analysis of several major policy decisions that turned out to be fiascoes, such as the Bay of Pigs Cuban invasion in 1961 and the invasion of North Korea. After analyzing thousands of pages of historical documents, Janis found that these blunders were the result of what he calls *groupthink*—a mode of thinking that persons in highly cohesive groups engage in when they become so preoccupied with seeking and maintaining unanimity of thought that their

critical thinking is rendered ineffective. Instead of carefully weighing the pros and cons of a decision, considering alternatives, raising moral issues, etc., the group has an overriding concern with *consensus,* which makes them vulnerable to committing serious blunders.

Groupthink has eight major characteristics:

a) An illusion of invulnerability, which creates excessive optimism and encourages taking extreme risks;

b) Collective rationalizations of the group's actions, which allow the group to discount any evidence that is contrary to the decision;

c) An unquestioned belief in the group's inherent morality, which leads the group to ignore the ethical or moral consequences of the decision;

d) Stereotyped views of the enemy as weak, evil (thus ruling out negotiation), and/or stupid;

e) A strong internal pressure on group members to conform to the group norm and not to dissent;

f) Individual self-censorship of thoughts and ideas that deviate from the group consensus;

g) An illusion of unanimity on the decision, which is partly the result of the conformity pressures mentioned above;

h) The emergence of self-appointed *mindguards*—group members who suppress inconsistent information and reproach anyone who deviates from the group consensus.

Groupthink is not a trait of certain kinds of people; rather, it is a process that can take place in all types of groups, even those composed of the best and the brightest. The important question, then, is "When is groupthink most likely to occur?" Janis has suggested three conditions that encourage groupthink: (a) high cohesiveness of the decision-making group; (b) insulation of the group from other, more balanced, outside information and authorities, and (c) endorsement of the policy by the group leader. These conditions work together to produce a group that is likely to arrive at an early consensus and, once the consensus has been reached, to force the members to support it.

The planning of the Bay of Pigs invasion in 1961 is a good example of the groupthink process in action. President Kennedy and his advisers were a close-knit group who had worked together for many years. Information about other possible options and criticisms of the plan were kept from the group, and several qualified experts were excluded from the meetings. Although he sometimes criticized the plan, President Kennedy clearly communicated his endorsement of it to the group. Reports of the decision-making sessions that were held clearly show the symptoms of groupthink. Because Kennedy's political career had been so enormously successful, the group had a feeling of invulnerability, that everything would continue to go well. The invasion was justified by the thought that the Cuban people would rally to the cause and rebel against Castro, even though there was no evidence to support such a belief. The stereotyped view of the enemy as weak and stupid was reflected in the assumptions (all incorrect) that the Cuban military would be ineffective and that Castro would not take steps to control possible supporters of the invading exiles. And so on . . .

Given the disastrous consequences that can result from groupthink, what can be done to prevent it from happening? Janis makes several proposals, all of which change the process of group decision making so that independent thinking is encouraged. For example, he recommends using procedures that force group members to evaluate critically both their own and others' ideas; that set up channels of information, feedback, and criticism from outside experts or groups; and that require the group to both analyze and role-play the opposition's reactions and strategies. Although no research has been done to test the validity of these recommendations, it should be pointed out, as a historical note, that some of these techniques were intuitively adopted by President Kennedy after the Bay of Pigs fiasco. In the following year, basically the same group of men were faced with the Cuban missile crisis, and at that time were able to arrive at a more effective group decision.

Watergate and the Perversion of Loyalty

Master, go on, and I will follow thee,
To the last gasp, with truth and loyalty.
William Shakespeare, *As You Like It*, II:iii

To be loyal to a person or an ideal is to acknowledge oneself to be not merely a sensate animal but a sensitive social animal, able to transcend the self-centered concerns of individuality. The fabric of life in a community depends fundamentally on the operation of loyalty; perversion of this loyalty can be a lethal poison.

In the summer of 1973, most Americans were shocked to discover the extent to which "loyalty," "duty," and "team play" did not have the same meaning for those who were shaping the destiny of their country as they do for most of us. The scandal of Watergate exposed a plot by the President's closest aides and the Committee to Re-elect the President in the 1972 elections to bug and to burglarize the Democratic headquarters, housed in the Watergate apartment-office building in Washington, D.C.

As a Senate subcommittee began its investigation into this conspiracy, the extent to which subversive activities had been undertaken by these men in the name of protecting "national security" was startling. They had been using the good offices of the Attorney General, CIA, FBI, and Internal Revenue Service to gather secret files on potential political enemies and dissidents. They had compiled a list of Americans—senators, union leaders, actors, reporters, athletes, and even some university presidents—who were considered to be "enemies" so that they could be singled out for attack by the machinery and weapons available in the Federal bureaucracy. They had discredited political opponents through forged letters and other documents. They had burglarized the confidential files of the psychiatrist of the man who had exposed governmental deceit in the Vietnam war by making public the Pentagon Papers. They had subverted money from the treasury of the Republican party to pay bribes to cover up their illegal activities, and there was evidence of involvement in crimes of extorting campaign contributions from big businessmen.

How could so many apparently decent, respectable citizens—university graduates, lawyers, successful and financially comfortable "family men" abdicate their sense of morality so totally? The answer to such a question is obviously complex, but its core can be found in the concepts already outlined in our earlier analysis of violence, social pathology, and evil. Although the events and their consequences can be analyzed at legal, political, and sociological levels, we are concerned here with the social-psychological forces acting on the individuals involved in the Watergate affair.

For some, the motivation was vanity—the downfall of Eve in Paradise. "My vanity was appealed to when I was told my name had been brought up in high councils and that I was an honest man and made a good appearance and that sort of thing" said one of the members of the Committee to Re-elect the President (UPI, June 13, 1973).

Some other participants in the illegal activities behaved as they did from a sense of *duty*. The former Assistant Attorney General testified that he helped cover up the Watergate scandal against his conscience because he felt it was a lawyer's duty to serve his client. The sense of duty to others who were in positions of power turned to irrational zeal when these men began to compete for places of honor nearest the seat of power.

The psychic numbing and dehumanized perception that comes from believing that one's goals are important enough to justify any means led one government official to say: "When these subjects came up, I was aware they were illegal and I am sure the others did. We had become somewhat inured to using some activities that would help us in accomplishing what we thought was a cause, a legitimate cause" (New York Times Service, June 15, 1973).

But the most significant factors were those that encouraged the "groupthink" atmosphere among the aides and associates of the President. The parallels here to the general conditions outlined by Janis are surprisingly close. Prominent among them were: (a) the emphasis on *secrecy*, which made none of these civil servants accountable to the public or the press; (b) the collective *paranoia* against hippies, antiwar radicals, and others who were critics of the administration; (c) the insulated belief that in behaving illegally and immorally and using the resources of the government against *their* enemies, they were safeguarding "national security"; (d) the importance of consensus on a team where playing the role of "team player" was the key to being personally accepted by the other members of the group.

This last point deserves special emphasis in a nation as sportsminded as ours. To be a team player on an athletic team means to work for the success of the team and not for individual fame or glory. It is a compliment to be so considered by your team and your leader. In politics the concept has been perverted so that it means "to go along," not to make trouble for the party, to be a conformist, not to challenge affronts to one's conscience. In Watergate this perversion of a positive relationship of an individual to his or her group was made complete. One of the conspirators explained why he "abdicated his conscience" in these terms; he did it "for the President, because of the group pressure that would ensue—of not being a team player."

The brilliant satirist Arthur Hoppe provides the link between the specifics of Watergate and the general psychology of evil that we have been analyzing:

"So each time we join a group for the comfort of group security, we must sacrifice some of our individuality. We must abdicate some small part of our conscience to the conscience of the group. We must be team players.

"It is this, I think, that explains why Nazis could slaughter Jews, why jailers can torture prisoners, why we did what we did at My Lai. It explains, too, why Bart Porter followed orders to commit perjury. He was a team player." (1973)

Dehumanizing Human Relationships

Would you ever deliberately humiliate, embarrass, or degrade another person? Can you imagine turning down a poor family's request for some food or clothing if you were in a position to authorize it just by signing your name? Is it conceivable that you would ever decide that certain groups were unfit and order their extermination? What would it take to make you kill another person?

These and other antisocial behaviors become possible for normal, morally upright, and idealistic people to perform under conditions in which people stop perceiving others as having the same feelings, impulses, thoughts, and purposes in life that they do. Such a psychological erasure of human qualities is called *dehumanization*. The result is that the people are seen and treated as objects, rather than as human beings. In contrast to humanized relationships between people (which are subjective, personal, and emotional), a dehumanized relationship is objective, analytical, and lacking in emotional or empathic interaction or response. The noted theologian Martin Buber described the former as an "I-Thou" relationship, and the dehumanized one as an "I-It" relationship.

The dehumanization process protects the individual against any kind of emotional arousal that might be painful, overwhelming, or debilitating, or might interfere with some necessary ongoing behavior. For example, in major crisis or emergency situations (as in wartime or national disasters) or in situations requiring careful, objective, nonpersonal work involving a human being (as in surgery), a dehumanized orientation toward others can serve as a defense against emotional responses that might otherwise be disturbing or incapacitating. So in these situations dehumanization can be adaptive.

But dehumanization can also have many negative and destructive consequences. When you are not responding to the human qualities of other persons, it becomes more possible to act inhumanely toward them. The golden rule then becomes "Do unto others as you would." It is easier to be callous or rude toward dehumanized "objects," to ignore their demands and pleas, to use them for your own purposes, and even to destroy them if they are irritating. The attempted genocide of Jews and gypsies by the Nazis could be carried out with the same efficiency as occurs daily at the animal slaughterhouses in Omaha by the simple expedient of perceiving these fellow human beings as inferior forms of animal life. To many military men in Vietnam, the Vietnamese people became nonhuman, as indicated by the general pervasiveness of the so-called "gook rule": Killing a Vietnamese noncombatant was essentially equal to killing a water buffalo.

The same underlying psychological mechanism operates in many familiar situations and poses a constant threat to the fundamental principles of social justice and human dignity. When large numbers of people must be "pro-

cessed," the processing may become impersonal and devoid of human contact or concern. Fraternity pledges are made to contribute to their own dehumanization by reciting, "I am a pledge; a pledge is the lowest form of animal life on campus." Even training an athletic team to uphold the honor of the university can become an incredibly cruel exercise in dehumanization and brutality. (See *P&L* Close-up below.)

Close-up
Football Builds Character

Twenty-eight football players either quit or were thrown off a university football team because of their objection to physically brutal preseason drills. According to one player, "everyone was so desperate to win we kicked, slugged, hit each other in the groin, did everything and anything."

Wrestling matches in which two combatants stooped under chicken wire four feet off the floor were "the cruelest thing I've ever seen . . . it was dehumanizing to the extent that you could be out there with your best friend, and you'd be trying to kill him. . . . We'd start by sitting on the mat back to back, one match going on at each end of the mat. At the whistle, the coaches told us we were to spin around 'and just beat the hell out of the other guy, beat him right into the mat.' They let the matches go on until they felt you had worked hard enough or were beating hell out of the other guy. . . . Everybody was desperate.

"You had to win because all the losers had to wrestle again, and again, and again, until they won. I had to wrestle as many as seven or eight straight times. The final loser of the day had to report at 3:30 Friday morning to run up and down the steps of the stadium. People were so mentally and physically exhausted they were staggering around like drunks, lunging at each other and missing. We'd be too tired to stay down and several times players stood up and were cut on the wire." (Associated Press release, June 11, 1973)

The Functions of Dehumanization

The conditions that encourage people to treat others as objects are related to the functions that dehumanization can serve—the apparent benefits it can bring to the one doing the dehumanizing. Dehumanization may be: (a) socially imposed, (b) imposed in self-defense, (c) imposed deliberately for self-gratification, or (d) rationalized as the necessary means toward some noble end.

Socially imposed dehumanization. Dehumanization can occur in various work situations as a result of the way in which the job is defined by society. Such definitions fall into two major categories: (a) the job requires that the individual dehumanize other people in order to deal with them; and (b) the job itself dehumanizes the worker because it permits no opportunity for expression of either personal feelings or uniquely human abilities.

Examples of the first category include situations in which a large number of people have to

◆ In Tokyo, being shoved into commuter trains is the norm.

be processed efficiently—such as college students during registration, subway commuters during rush hour, prisoners or mental patients during the institutional mealtime. In order to do this, administrators of institutions often become concerned with "managing the flow," monitoring time schedules, and minimizing disrupting influences. Once the number of individuals requiring a given service becomes too great, they stop being seen or treated as "individuals." Moving mental patients in and out of the cafeteria and the showers may take precedence over therapeutic concerns. As college enrollments increase, students become anonymous IBM numbers, and it is increasingly difficult for faculty members to relate to them on a personal level sufficiently even to recognize them outside of class. Being shoved around by the employees hired as subway "packers" in the Tokyo Transit System is no more dehumanizing than being given an administrative runaround or being told that there can be no (human) exceptions to "the rules." ◆

You can't take pride anymore. It's hard to take pride in a bridge you're never gonna cross, in a door you're never gonna open. You're mass-producing things and you never see the end result of it.

From an interview with a steelworker
in Terkel, 1974

The second category of socially imposed dehumanization in a work situation is perhaps best illustrated by that marvel of American technology, the assembly line. On an automobile assembly line, cars may pass by each work station at the rate of over fifty an hour. Each person has less than a minute to perform a task, and must repeat it hour after hour. ∎

Work on such assembly lines is so depressing and exhausting that even during a recent period of high unemployment—between 8 and 9 percent—one major auto company reported that over the course of the year 4000 newly hired workers never even stayed through their first day on the job! But for each one who quit in less than eight hours, there were many who could not afford the luxury of quitting and thus

voluntarily engaged in "forced labor" (Price, 1972).

Such a worker no longer feels meaningfully related to the product of his or her labors and works only to get money to buy things other people make. The result has been high rates of absenteeism, high turnover, poor quality of work, alcoholism and drug abuse on the job, massive worker dissatisfaction, increasing mental health problems, lower productivity, and unsafe autos that have to be recalled—all measures of how prevalent dehumanization is in the contemporary work scene (Congressional Hearings on Worker Alienation, 1972).

Dehumanization in self-defense. Individuals in many health and service professions must function in situations that ordinarily arouse very intense emotional feelings, elicit painful empathy, and/or involve "taboo" behaviors, such as invasion of privacy or violation of the human body. In order to perform efficiently in such situations, the individual may develop defenses against these disruptive emotions through techniques of dehumanization. By treating one's clients or patients in an objective, detached way, it becomes

∎ A cog in the economic wheel: a man inspects an endless row of bottles. Such work permits no opportunity for expression of either personal feelings or uniquely human abilities.

easier to perform necessary interviews, tests, or operations without experiencing strong psychological discomfort.

For example, surgeons have reported that before they could perform their role effectively, they had to learn not to perceive a whole person under their scalpel but only an organ, tissue, or bone. Within the profession itself, this process is called "detached concern," a term that better conveys the difficult (and almost paradoxical) position of having to dehumanize people in order to help or cure them (see Lief & Fox, 1963).

However, it is possible for this "detachment" to go to an extreme. If the psychological stress and strain of the job become too severe (as when a social worker is faced with trying to help several hundred poor and suffering families), the person may "burn out" emotionally and lose all human feeling for the people being served. It is not uncommon for some caseworkers to begin refusing requests for food supplements and clothing because of the extra red tape involved, plus suspicions that they are being "conned."

The same self-protective, impersonal style is sometimes seen in those who work with mentally retarded or schizophrenic children, patients with terminal diseases, and institutionalized elderly people.

In many so-called homes for the aged, the hapless inmates are given excessive tranquilizers to control them; are forced to be inactive and stay bedridden to cut down insurance risks and make it easier to manage them; are denied privacy, deprived of small conveniences, and not allowed any idiosyncrasies; and are given only a minimally adequate diet. It becomes obvious to the patients that their continued existence is nothing more than a burden for their relatives and the staff (Burger, 1969).

Dehumanization for self-gratification. Sometimes others are used solely for one's own gain, pleasure, or entertainment, with no concern given to their feelings or thoughts. An example of this process is prostitution, in which a person openly buys the privilege of dehumanizing another individual. Parenthetically, the prostitute reciprocates in kind, viewing the purchaser as just another "trick" to be turned. Men for

whom sexual intercourse is only a self-gratifying experience—with a woman simply the means—show this dehumanization when they call a woman "a piece," "a real dog," "a cow," etc.

The depths to which this insensitivity to other human beings can go are revealed in news accounts of people taunting a would-be suicide to go through with it for the sheer excitement of seeing him do so.

In Albany, New York, a man was saved from a suicide leap by the coaxing of his seven-year-old nephew while onlookers jeered, "Jump! Jump! Jump!" Among the curious crowd of about 4000 were people challenging him to jump, "C'mon, you're chicken," "You're yellow," and betting on whether he would or not. Instructive is the comment by one well-dressed man, "I hope he jumps on this side. We couldn't see him if he jumped over there" (New York Times, *Apr. 14, 1964).*

The same perversion of social concern was witnessed in Miami, Florida, when an 87-year-old man, depressed from years of loneliness, threatened to commit suicide by jumping off a bridge. Instead of trying to prevent his death, a group at the scene taunted him: "Come on, Jump! Jump! Jump!" He took their advice and jumped. One young man hurried to his aid, dragged him from the river, and tried in vain to revive him—as the apathetic crowd watched without offering any assistance (Knight Newspapers Service, Aug. 17, 1973).

An even more unbelievable example of dehumanization is the report of patients at a mental hospital being smuggled out of the institution by attendants and forced into prostitution. Even little girls were included. The attendants allegedly received ten dollars for each patient smuggled out—the patient got a piece of candy or a coin (UPI release, March 25, 1969).

Dehumanization as a means to an end. There have been many times in history when people have viewed a particular group of others as obstacles to the achievement of their goals. By perceiving such people in a dehumanized manner as "the enemy," "the masses," "a threat to national security," "inferior," etc., it becomes less of a problem to take action against them in the name of some great cause, such as peace, victory, liberty, the revolution. Their suffering, injury, or destruction is then justified as a means toward a "noble" end. Many examples of such dehumanization come to mind, including the dropping of the atomic bomb on the residents of Hiroshima in order to "bring peace," the mass killing of Jews by the Nazis because "they are unfit," and the denial of medical treatment to black men afflicted with syphilis (the control group in a controversial study at Tuskegee, Alabama) in order to "study the course of the disease."

To demonstrate the ease with which people can adopt this dehumanized view of others, a psychologist studied the reactions of a large group of college students to an alleged threat to their security.

The subjects were male and female students at the University of Hawaii, ranging from age seventeen to forty-eight. Groups of twenty to thirty were assembled to hear a brief speech by a professor. This authority asked for their cooperation as intelligent and educated people to assist in the application of scientific procedures to kill the mentally and emotionally unfit. The problem was convincingly presented in the following context:

"In recent times, a growing concern with the increasing menace of population explosion has taken place. Of particular concern is the fact that the mentally and emotionally unfit are increasing the population much faster than the emotionally fit and intelligent humans. Unless something drastic is done about this, the day will come when the fit and the intelligent part of the population will find itself in danger. Education and birth-control devices are not succeeding in controlling this population explosion, and unfortunately it has now become necessary to devise new methods of coping with this problem—and new measures are being considered by several of the major powers in the world including our own. One of these devices is euthanasia, which means mercy killing. Such kill-

ing is considered by most experts as not only being beneficial to the unfit, because it puts them out of the misery of their lives, but more importantly it will be beneficial to the healthy, fit, and more educated segment of the population. It is therefore a 'final solution' to a grave problem.

"This should not be a surprising thought since we already practice it in many countries—including our own. We do decide when a human is unfit to live as in the case of capital punishment. What is not clear, however, is which method of killing should be applied, which method is least painful, and who should do the killing and/or decide when killing should be resorted to.

"For these reasons, further research is required and our research project is concerned with this problem. We need to relate intelligent and educated people's decisions to such problems, and we are therefore asking you to help us out. The findings of our studies will be applied to humans once the system has been perfected. At the moment, we need to try this out with animals first, and only when the necessary data have been obtained will it be applied to human beings in this and other countries. It is important that this be studied and applied scientifically."

Slight variations were made in four separate studies in the imminence of the threat, in the means to be used (warfare versus euthanasia), and in which group was characterized as unfit (Americans, minority groups, Asians). The students indicated whether or not they approved of the various solutions presented and then answered several questions about the practical aspects of "systematic killing."

At the end they were told the true purpose of the experiment. From their emotional responses and their attempts to justify their previous answers, it was assumed that they had accepted the problem as stated and had been genuinely concerned about its solution.

In the first variation, about two thirds approved of the "scientific solution" when the threat was expected to occur within the sub-

ject's own lifetime, while two fifths endorsed it even if the threat would not be a danger for seventy to a hundred years. The use of scientific extermination was preferred over killing the unfit by sending them to battle, and there was more endorsement of killing of groups more distant from one's own. Their answers to the questions are in the table (Mansson, 1972). ●

Here was a direct parallel to Hitler's "final solution" of the "Jewish problem." But it was presented as a high-minded scientific project, endorsed by scientists, planned for the benefit of humanity, and actually even a kindness to those who would be eliminated. It was further "justified" by an analogy to capital punishment, and those whose opinions were being solicited were flattered as being intelligent and educated, with high ethical values. In case there might be any lingering misgivings, assurances were made that much careful research would be carried out before action of any kind would be taken with human beings. It is likely that all 570 subjects would have said they disapproved of Hitler's extermination of six million Jews, but when it was labeled differently and disguised as something noble, 517 of them accepted the basic premise, and all but 33 even indicated what aspect of the job *he* or *she* would prefer to take part in. Not one of these college students refused to have a part in such an undertaking.

A few years later, the study was replicated with 618 introductory psychology students, also at the University of Hawaii.

The results were once again disquieting. Even without a scientific rationale or sponsorship by an authority, there was general sympathy for application of the "final solution" to segments of the population judged to be "unfit" or "dangerous to the general welfare." There were no significant differences between the responses of those who had been given the rational justification by an "expert on population sponsored by the federal government" and those who simply completed the questionnaire administered by a graduate student with no justification. A surprising 29 percent even supported the final solution when applied to their own families! (Carlson & Wood, 1974)

These findings should give every reader pause, for they show how little effort might be necessary to translate these "artificial" experimental findings into the same nightmare of reality that occurred in Germany in World War II — and in other places and other times before that.

The Techniques of Dehumanization

What are the methods or strategies that people use to achieve dehumanization and emotional detachment? Surprisingly, very little research has been done on this question. In fact, there is only one relevant experimental study showing that people can indeed control their emotional reactions to upsetting stimuli (Koriat, Melkman, Averill, & Lazarus, 1972). Subjects were asked to watch a very disturbing film of industrial accidents, and were told to try to *detach* themselves from it psychologically. Apparently, these verbal instructions were sufficient to make subjects feel less emotionally aroused by the film (even though their physiological responses were still high). In contrast, subjects who were told to become *involved* in the film showed significantly more physiological arousal and also reported that they felt more emotionally upset. This work is based on studies by Lazarus and his colleagues reported earlier (p. 382).

How did these subjects actually suppress or enhance their emotional response? At the moment, we have to rely on some supportive evidence and speculation for our answer. According to a recent theoretical analysis, there appear to be several techniques by which humans become able to dehumanize other humans. In different ways, all of them help the individual to: (a) perceive the other person(s) as less human; (b) perceive the relationship with the other person(s) in objective, analytical terms; and/or (c) reduce the amount of experienced emotion and physiological arousal (Maslach & Zimbardo, 1973). Some represent special uses of the defense mechanisms discussed in Chapter 9 — in this case protecting the individual from pain while others are being hurt.

Relabeling. The use of certain kinds of language is perhaps one of the most visible techniques of dehumanization. A change in the labels or terms used to describe people is one way of making them appear more object-like and less human. Some of these dehumanizing terms are derogatory ones, such as "gook," "queer," "half breed," "hippie." Others are more abstract labels that refer to large, undifferentiated units — like "aliens," "the masses," "undeveloped nations."

Another form of dehumanizing language describes people in terms of the functional relationship the individual has with them. For example, social-welfare workers often speak of "my caseload" when referring to the people they deal with, while poverty lawyers talk about "my docket." Substituting verbs with less emotional meaning can have the same effect. The Vietnam war provided several new instances of this type of verb change: "to kill" a person became "to waste" a person or "to eliminate with extreme prejudice." Similarly, it becomes easier for honest students to steal from their college bookstore if they relabel their activity as "ripping off the establishment."

Intellectualization. A related technique of dehumanization is one in which the individual recasts the situation in more intellectual and less personal terms. By dealing with the abstract qualities of other people (rather than the more human ones), the individual can "objectify" the situation and can react in a less emotional way. For example, in dealing with a mental patient who is being verbally abusive, a psychiatric nurse may avoid being personally upset by standing back and looking at the patient's problems analytically ("This patient is exhibiting a delusional syndrome"). In a similar way, physicians may view their patients in terms of their illness ("I admitted two coronaries yesterday"), and a teacher may avoid feelings of responsibility for students' boredom by blaming it on *their* limited attention span, the apathy of youth, or lack of discipline at home.

Compartmentalization. To the extent that a particular situation or type of activity can be separated from the rest of an individual's life, it becomes easier to detach it from one's personal values and feelings. An example is the belief that "Thou shalt not kill" — except in wartime

● STUDENT OPINIONS CONCERNING THE "FINAL SOLUTION"

1. Do you agree that there will always be people who are more fit in terms of survival than not?	*Agree*	90%
	Disagree	10%
2. If such killing is judged necessary, should the person or persons who make the decisions also carry out the act of killing?	*Yes*	57%
	No	43%
3. Would it work better if one person were responsible for the killing and another person carried out the act?	*Yes*	79%
	No	21%
4. Would it be better if several people pressed the button but only one button would be causing death? This way anonymity would be preserved and no one would know who actually did the killing.	*Yes*	64%
	No	36%
5. What would you judge to be the best and most efficient method of inducing death?	*Electrocution*	1%
	Painless poison	9%
	Painless drugs	89%
6. If you were required by law to assist would you prefer to:		
(a) *be the one who assists in the decisions?*		85%
(b) *be the one who assists with the killing?*		8%
(c) *assist with both the decision and the killing?*		1%
No answer		6%
7. Most people agree that in matters of life and death extreme caution is required. Most people also agree that under extreme circumstances, it is entirely just to eliminate those judged dangerous to the general welfare. Do you agree?	*Yes*	91%
	No	5%
	Undecided	4%

Adapted from Mansson, 1972

when your country orders it. The diary of the Auschwitz doctor (p. 641) shows how complete such compartmentalization can become in a "good cause."

Withdrawal. Another technique for reducing emotional arousal is to minimize one's involvement in an interaction with others that might be stressful. This can be done in a number of ways, such as by spending less time with the other person, physically distancing oneself (standing farther away from the person or not making eye contact), communicating with the other person in impersonal ways (e.g., superficial generalities, form letters), and so forth. Rosenhan's (1973) description of how often mental-hospital staff stay inside their glass "cages," and how little time they actually interact with patients, is an excellent example of this technique at work.

Diffusion of responsibility, social support, humor. In attempting to deal with strong emotional feelings, an individual will often turn to others for help and support. If such actions reduce psychological stress and discomfort, they can be used to promote dehumanization. Having other people say, "It's not so bad" or "Why don't you look at it *this* way," helps the person achieve detachment. A perceived diffusion of responsibility can also aid in dehumanization. If the individual knows that other people feel the same way or are doing the same thing, he or she may have fewer qualms about engaging in a particular behavior.

Being able to joke and laugh about a stressful event is another way of reducing the tension and anxiety that one may feel. It can also make the situation seem less serious, less frightening, and less overwhelming. Observers have noted the "sick" humor of medical students who are dissecting a cadaver for an anatomy class, and have suggested that it serves these purposes (Lief & Fox, 1963).

The above list of techniques, while not exhaustive, should provide some idea of the variety of subtle and not-so-subtle ways in which dehumanization is achieved. Much more thought and concern needs to be given to such techniques, not only to understand better how they work, but to discover the effects of their use on both the object of dehumanization and the person doing the dehumanization. You might begin to catalog the ways and the situations in which you are treated in a dehumanized manner—as well as the ways and places in which you may have been dehumanizing others without realizing it. The next task for you and for our society is to develop strategies to minimize dehumanizing institutional relationships while allowing us to do our jobs and still relate to others not as objects, but as brothers and sisters for whom we care.

Chapter Summary

The human race has been viewed by some as noble by nature but corrupted by civilization, by others as evil by nature and held in line only by social pressures. Paradoxically the very capacities that make possible our greatest achievements also, if misused, can cause the greatest misery.

The prevalence of *aggression* has led some psychologists to see it as *instinctive.* Freud considered aggression to be an outlet for energy associated with the death instinct. Physiological factors linked to aggression include brain damage, genetic abnormalities, and hormone imbalance.

The *frustration-aggression hypothesis* suggests that aggression is a drive acquired in response to *frustration,* which exists whenever a goal response is blocked. Aggression may be *displaced* from the source of the frustration and directed toward some less threatening target, or *scapegoat.* The presence of *releasers* in the environment interacts with internal factors in eliciting aggression.

According to the *social learning approach*, aggression, like other behaviors, is learned through observation of *models*. Aggressive responses learned through such observation may be performed in some settings but withheld in others.

Unlike those who believe that aggression is instinctive and can be reduced through *catharsis*, social learning theorists hold that expression of aggressive responses will *increase* the probability of future aggression. Research has generally supported the view that watching media presentations of violence leads to increased aggression among children.

Violent encounters between parent and child are becoming an object of scientific study. *Battered children* are likely to be found in family situations where there is emotional stress and little basis for social comparison. Parents who batter their children are likely to have been battered by their own parents. *Interpersonal aggression* is not usually one-sided, but is rather a matter of *mutual provocation, escalation,* and *confrontation.* Most of the victims of violent crimes are personally acquainted with—or even related to—their attackers. Collective violence may be viewed as legitimate if there is social power behind it.

Urban crowding and frustration often lead to pathological conditions in our cities. Bystanders may passively hold back from intervening in emergency situations, particularly when a number of others are present or when they are in a hurry. Research has shown that *overcrowding* can lead to severe social and personal pathology in animals—the implications of these findings for human beings in crowded urban areas depend largely on their psychological interpretation of the situation.

The *anonymity* of urban living robs individuals of their sense of identity. Such *deindividuated* persons are more likely than individuated ones to show aggression or other antisocial behavior. Anonymity and unaccountability may be fostered by the wearing of costumes or uniforms.

Vandalism is commonly defined as destruction for destruction's sake. The same act may be seen as vandalism or as a prank depending on who is doing it. Vandalism may serve as a source of excitement or self-assertion for members of a counterculture, although the perpetrators of such acts come from all socioeconomic levels. Vandalism is not necessarily purposeless for the perpetrator; it may be *acquisitive, tactical, ideological, vindictive, malicious,* or a form of *play.*

Socially sanctioned *evil* may involve the abuse of authority through the exercise of coercive power. Studies of *blind obedience to authority* have shown that such obedience is fostered by the presence of a *legitimate authority*, a *role relationship* that subordinates one individual to the other, and *social norms*. We tend to overestimate the operation of internal factors and underestimate situational influences in evaluating the behavior of other people in such settings.

Group decision making can deteriorate into what has been called *groupthink*, in which concern for unanimity outweighs critical thinking. Such factors as group cohesiveness, insulation, endorsement by the leader, and an overemphasis on "team play" and "loyalty" increase the likelihood of such an occurrence.

Dehumanization involves the creation of "I-it" relationships in which other persons are treated as objects. Such a process may serve as a needed protection in emergencies or medical settings, but it can also be highly destructive to human dignity and even human life. Dehumanization may be *socially imposed*, as in some work situations, necessary for *self-defense*, as for medical personnel, imposed for *self-gratification*, as when others are used for one's pleasure, or used as a *means to an end*, as in political settings. Techniques used to achieve dehumanization include relabeling, intellectualization, compartmentalization, withdrawal, diffusion of responsibility, social support, and humor.

Burn-Out: The Loss of Human Caring
Christina Maslach University of California, Berkeley

Just before Christmas, a woman came to a poverty lawyer to get help. While discussing her problems, she complained about the fact that she was so poor that she was not going to be able to get any Christmas presents for her children. The lawyer, who was a young mother herself, might have been expected to be sympathetic to the woman's plight. Instead, she found herself yelling at the woman, telling her, "So go rob Macy's if you want presents for your kids! And don't come back to see me unless you get caught and need to be defended in court!" Afterwards, in thinking about the incident, the lawyer realized that she had "burned out."

There are many situations in which people work intensely and intimately with other people. They learn about people's psychological, social, and physical problems, and they are often called upon to provide personal help of some kind. Such intense involvement with people occurs on a large-scale, continuous basis for individuals in various health and social service professions. Hour after hour, day after day, these professionals must *care* about many other people, and our research indicates that they often pay a heavy psychological price for being their "brother's keeper." Constant or repeated emotional arousal is a very stressful experience for any human being, and can often be disruptive or incapacitating. In order to perform their work efficiently and well, these professionals may defend against their strong feelings of emotion through techniques of detachment. Ideally, they try to gain sufficient objectivity and distance from the situation without losing their concern for the person they are working with. However, in all too many cases, they are unable to cope with this continual emotional stress, and eventually "burn-out" occurs. They lose all concern or emotional feeling for the people they work with, and come to treat them in detached and even dehumanized ways.

"Burn-out" is not an isolated phenomenon that can be attributed to just a limited number of individuals. Rather, it occurs very frequently for a wide variety of people within many different professions. It appears to be a major factor in low worker morale, absenteeism, and high job turnover, and plays a primary role in the poor delivery of health and welfare services to people in need of them. It may well be implicated in the increasing number of malpractice suits and thus the soaring costs of insurance for doctors. Furthermore, it is correlated with other negative indices of personal stress, such as alcoholism, mental illness, suicide, and marital conflict. "Burn-out" may vary in severity among different professions, and it may be called by different names (for example, some law enforcement groups refer to this suppression of emotion as the "John Wayne syndrome"), but the same basic phenomenon seems to be occurring in a wide variety of work settings.

For the past few years, I have been studying the dynamics of this destructive process of "burn-out" in collaboration with my coworkers at the University of California, Berkeley. We have observed professionals at work, collected extensive questionnaire data, and conducted personal interviews. Thus far, the professional samples we have studied include social welfare workers, psychiatric nurses, poverty lawyers, child care workers, clinical psychologists and psychiatrists in a mental hospital, some prison personnel, and physicians. Our research goals have been to identify (a) the interpersonal stresses these professionals face; (b) what (if any) educational preparation they received for coping with these stresses; (c) what specific techniques they use to "detach" themselves effectively from their clients or patients; (d) what personal and social consequences result from using such techniques; and (e) what distinguishes those work settings where "burn-out" typically occurs from those where it is uncommon.

Our findings to date show that all of these professional groups (and perhaps others that you can think of from your own experience) often find it necessary to cope with their feelings of emotional stress by distancing themselves from the people with whom they work. In some cases, this distancing occurs while the professional is in the process of interacting with the patient or client (as in "listening with only one ear"). In other cases, it functions as an anticipatory or retrospective device. For example, some professionals learn to "turn off" all thoughts and feelings about their patients or clients, once these people have walked out the door—"next, please." Within the medical professions, such objectivity and detachment are viewed as critical and essential in providing good health care for the individual. This philosophy of "detached concern" blends the notion of concern for the patient's well-being with the idea that some personal detachment from the stressful aspects of patient care is necessary in order to achieve that goal. However, in other professional situations, there is not even the recognition that such a psychological defense is operating. Insensitivity to the process of detached concern makes total burn-out more likely.

Detachment Techniques

Despite the differences in their functions, all of the many professional groups that we studied reported surprisingly similar changes in their perception of their clients or patients and in their feelings towards them. Also, the specific verbal and nonverbal techniques used to achieve some degree of detachment were comparable. In different ways, each of these techniques helps the individual to: (a) see the other person as less human; (b) view the relationship with the other person in objective, analytical terms; and (c) reduce the intensity and scope of experienced emotional arousal.

Semantics of detachment. A change in the terms used to describe people is one way of making them appear more object-like and less human. Some of these terms are derogatory labels (e.g., "they're all just animals"). Others are more abstract terms referring to large, undifferentiated units, such as "the poor." Another form of objective language is one which labels people in terms of the functional relationship the individual has with them. For example, social welfare workers often spoke of "my caseload" when referring to the people they deal with, while many a poverty lawyer talked about "my docket." Another way of divorcing one's feelings from some stressful event is to describe things as precisely, exactly, and as scientifically as possible. This use of language is illustrated in several professions where the inclusion of jargon (e.g. "a positive GI series," "reaction formation") in patient interviews typically serves the purpose of distancing the person from a patient or client who is emotionally upsetting in some way. Furthermore, the patient who is only a "coronary" loses much of his or her complex humanness.

Intellectualization. A related technique is one where the individual recasts the situation in more intellectual and less personal terms. By dealing with the abstract qualities of other people (rather than the more human ones), the professional can "objectify" the situation and react in a less emotional way. For example, in dealing with a mental patient who is being verbally abusive to her, a psychiatric nurse may stand back and look at the patient's problems more analytically ("he's exhibiting a particular delusional syndrome") so as not to get personally upset.

Situational compartmentalization. Professionals often made a sharp distinction in our interviews between their job and their personal life. They did not discuss their family or personal affairs with their co-workers, and they often had explicit agreements with their spouses and friends not to "talk shop." Some of the prison personnel even refused to tell people what their job was—in response to questions, they would only say, "I'm a civil servant" or "I work for the State." By such devices, the emotional stress is confined to a smaller part of the professional's life. One social worker in child welfare stated that if he did not leave his work at the office, he could hardly stand to face his own children. Likewise, when he was at work he could not think of his family because he would then overidentify and overempathize with his clients and treat their misfortunes as his own—

an emotional experience which he could not handle repeatedly. As one might expect, such a person doesn't have the usual family photos on the office desk. Some institutions have rules that promote compartmentalization by forbidding staff to socialize with their patients or clients outside of the job setting.

For many psychiatrists, one of the drawbacks of going into private practice is that the distinction between their job and their private life cannot be maintained, since they are always "on call." As one of our respondents put it, "Every time you hear your telephone ring at night, you think, 'Oh no—I hope it's not a patient.' At times it seems like you can't ever get away from your patients' problems for some peace and quiet for yourself. When I worked at the hospital, there wasn't the same problem because when I went home for the day, another shift came on—and so I could relax in the evenings because I knew that if any of the patients needed help, there was someone else there to provide it."

Withdrawal. Another technique for reducing emotional arousal is to minimize one's physical involvement in the stressful interaction with other people. This is accomplished by professionals in a number of ways. One obvious approach which we observed was to distance oneself physically from the other person (by standing further away, avoiding eye contact, or keeping one's hand on the door knob) even though continuing a minimal interaction. Withdrawal was also evidenced by professionals who communicated with the patient or client in more impersonal ways, such as superficial generalities and form letters. In some cases, the professionals simply spent less time with a patient or client, either by deliberately cutting down the length of the formal interview or therapy session, or by spending more of their time talking and socializing with the other staff members. In more extreme forms of withdrawal, the professional did not interact with the other people at all. Taking longer lunch breaks, spending more time on paperwork, leaving early on Friday, or simply being absent from work are all examples of such withdrawal.

Social techniques. In attempting to deal with our own strong emotional feelings, we often turn to friends for help and emotional support. To the extent that such actions reduce psychological stress and discomfort, they can be used by these professionals to develop detachment. One type of social technique used by our professional samples was to solicit advice and comfort from other staff members after withdrawing from a difficult situation. Not only did such social support help to ease the stress and pain, but it helped the individual to achieve intellectual distance from the situation. Getting together with fellow staff to "hash things out," "bitch a lot," "talk about new things to do," or "laugh about it" was the mainstay of the "detached concern" process for many of the professionals we studied.

Social support also aided in detachment by promoting a perceived diffusion of responsibility. If several other staff people adopted a particular course of action, then an individual often had fewer qualms about doing the same thing. Another social technique was the use of humor. Being able to joke and laugh about a stressful event was one way of reducing the tension and anxiety that the professional might feel. It also served to make the situation less serious, less frightening, and less overwhelming. The "sick humor" of the battlefield surgeons in *M. A. S. H.* is a particularly apt example of this technique at work.

Many of these detachment techniques can be used by professionals to either reduce the amount of personal stress or to successfully cope with it, while still maintaining a working level of concern and caring for the people they must work with. However, because some forms of these techniques preclude any continued caring, they eventuate in the total detachment and dehumanization found in "burn-out." In these cases, the professional's attempts at psychological self-protection come at the expense of the client, patient, prisoner, student, or child.

Remedies for "Burn-Out"

When is "burn-out" more likely to occur? Our research findings point to several factors in the professional's work situation that can have a major determining influence on whether he or she will "burn out" or will successfully cope with the personal stress of the job.

Ratio. The quality of the professional interaction is greatly affected by the number of people for whom the professional is providing care. As this number increases, the general result is greater cognitive, sensory, and emotional overload for the professional. The importance of this ratio for understanding "burn-out" is vividly demonstrated in the research on child care workers which I recently conducted with Ayala Pines. We studied the staff members of eight different child care centers which varied in their ratio of staff to children, ranging from 1:4 to 1:12. The staff from the high ratio centers worked a greater number of hours on the floor in direct contact with the children, and had fewer opportunities to take a break from work. They were more approving of supplementary techniques to make children quiet, such as compulsory naps and the use of tranquilizers for hyperactive children. They did not feel that they had much control over what they did on the job, and overall they liked their job much less than did the staff from low ratio centers.

When these staff ratios are low, the individual staff member has fewer people to worry about and can give more attention to each of them. Furthermore, there is more time to focus on the positive, nonproblem aspects of the person's life, rather than concentrating just on his or her immediate problems or presenting symptoms. For example, in psychiatric wards with low staff-patient ratios, the nurses were more likely to see their patients in both good times and bad. Even though there were occasions when their interactions were frustrating or upsetting, there were also times when the nurses could laugh and joke with the patients, play ping-pong or cards with them, talk with their families, etc. In a sense, these nurses had a more complete, more *human* view of each patient.

Time-outs vs. escapes. Opportunities for withdrawing from a stressful situation are critically important for these professionals. However, the type of withdrawal that is available may spell the difference between "burn-out" and successful coping. The most positive form of withdrawal that we observed is what we have called a "time-out." Time-outs are not merely short breaks from work (such as rest periods or coffee breaks). Rather, they are opportunities for the professional to voluntari-

ly choose to do some other, less stressful work while other staff take over his or her responsibilities with clients/patients. For example, in one of the psychiatric wards that we studied, the nurses knew that if they were having a rough day they could arrange to do paperwork or dispense medications, instead of working directly with the patients. The other nurses would "cover" for the one taking a time-out and would continue to provide adequate patient care. What makes this form of withdrawal a positive one is that good patient care could be maintained even while the professional was getting a temporary emotional breather.

In contrast to sanctioned time-outs, most other types of withdrawals represented a negative form of "escape." Here, the professional's decision to take a break from work always came at the expense of clients or patients, since there were no other staff people to take over the necessary duties. If the professional was not there to provide treatment or service, then people in need simply had to wait, come back another day, or give up. In such situations, the professionals were more likely to feel trapped by their total responsibility for these people, and could not temporarily withdraw without feeling some guilt. When guilt was heaped upon the already heavy emotional burden they tenuously carried, the load often became too much to bear. Eventually, these guilt feelings would disappear for those professionals who began to lose both their sense of caring and concern. When institutional policies prevented the use of voluntary time-outs, we found lower staff morale, greater emotional stress, and the inevitable consequence of more dissatisfied citizens, frustrated at not getting the care they needed.

Amount of direct contact. The number of hours that a person works at a job is very likely to be related to that person's sense of fatigue, boredom, stress, etc. Consequently, one might suspect that longer working hours would result in a higher incidence of "burn-out." However, our data reveal a somewhat different pattern of behavior. Longer work hours are correlated with more stress and negative staff attitudes only when they involve continuous direct contact with patients or clients. Our study of child care centers provides a good illustration of this point. Longer working hours were related to signs of "burn-out" when the longer hours involved more work on the floor with children. When the longer hours involved administrative, non-child-related work, "burn-out" was less likely to occur. Basically, staff members who worked longer hours with children developed more negative attitudes toward these children. They were more approving of institutional restraints on the children's behavior, and when they were not at work, they wanted to get as far away as possible from children and child-related activities. In contrast to these people were the staff members who worked just as many hours, but with a smaller proportion of time involving direct contact with children. They did not develop such negative attitudes towards children, but instead felt positively about them and about the child care center in general. Perhaps the quality of caring, if not mercy, may have to be time-shared.

Social-professional support system. The availability of formal or informal programs in which professionals can get together to discuss problems, and get advice and support, is another way of helping them to cope with job stress more successfully. Such a support system provides opportunities for analysis of both the problems they face and their personal feelings about them, for humor, for comfort, and for social comparison. "Burn-out" rates seem to be lower for those professionals who have access to such systems, especially if they are well-developed and supported by the larger institution. Some of the psychiatrists reported being part of a social-professional support group when they were doing their residency. After they entered private practice, they found that the lack of such a group was a serious, unanticipated loss to them, and they often made efforts to become part of such a support system again (although not always successfully).

Analysis of personal feelings. Since the arousal of strong emotional reactions is a common feature of health and social service occupations, efforts must be made to constructively deal with them and prevent them from being entirely extinguished, as in "burn-out." We were surprised to find that many of our subjects did not know that other people were experiencing the same changes in attitudes and emotions as they were. Each of them thought that the personal reaction they were experiencing was a unique one (an illusion maintained by their tendency not to share their feelings with fellow workers). They were unaware of the fact that their experience is a fairly common one, rather than an aberration. However, even though many of these professionals keep their feelings to themselves, it is painfully clear that they have a strong need to talk to someone about them.

Our findings show that "burn-out" rates are lower for those professionals who actively express, analyze, and share their personal feelings with their colleagues. Not only do they consciously "get things off my chest," but they have an opportunity to get constructive feedback from other people and to develop new perspectives and understanding of their relationship with their patients/clients. This process is greatly enhanced if the relevant institution (such as an agency or hospital) establishes an appropriate mechanism for doing so. This could include social-professional support groups, special staff meetings, or workshop group sessions. In general, we found that those professionals who are trained to treat psychological problems were better able to recognize and deal with their own feelings. For example, one clinical psychologist reported that she could not work well with a particular type of patient—i.e., a passive, overly dependent female. By analyzing her personal reactions to this type of woman (which were related to childhood experiences and her own professional training), she was able to understand why she worked so poorly with this type of patient and could take appropriate steps to remedy the situation. In contrast, prison guards who experienced great fear were constrained from expressing, or even acknowledging, it by an institutional "macho" code, one consequence of which was the destructive channeling of this emotion into psychosomatic illnesses such as ulcers, muscle spasms, and migraine headaches.

Training in interpersonal skills. It seems clear from the research findings to date that health and social service professionals need to have special training and preparation for working closely with other people. While they are well-trained in certain healing and technical service skills, they are often not well-equipped to handle repeated, intense, emotional interactions with people. As one poverty lawyer put it, "I was trained in law, but not in how to work with people who would be my clients. And it was that difficulty in dealing with people and their personal problems, hour after hour, that became the problem for me—not the legal matters *per se*."

From the point of view of the person seeking help, these professionals may need extra "people learning" to go along with their "book learning." Although many of our subjects stated that they wished they had had prior preparation in interpersonal skills, some reported that there was no time for it in their already packed curriculum. Others felt that such preparation was just "icing on the cake" and not an essential part of professional training. The view of several physicians was that the competent practice of medicine was all that they needed to know to be successful in their career, and that any psychological training simply amounted to knowing how to make "small talk" with their patients. Such a skill was viewed as pleasant, but as basically unimportant. In my opinion, such a viewpoint is sadly in error, for it trivializes an essential aspect of the doctor-patient relationship and fails to recognize that both the doctor and the patient are human beings whose personal attitudes and emotions can affect not only the delivery of health care, but also how and even whether it is accepted.

Conclusion

Is "burn-out" inevitable? Some professionals seem to think so and assume that it is only a matter of time before they will "burn out" and have to change their job. The period of time most often cited in one psychiatric ward was one and a half years, while some poverty lawyers spoke of a reduction of the former four-year stint down to a quick and dirty two years, at most. I think that "burn-out" is *not* inevitable, and that steps can be taken to reduce and modify its occurrence. It is my belief that many of the causes of "burn-out" are located not in permanent, fixed traits of the people involved, but in specifiable social and situational factors which can be influenced in ways suggested by our research.

However, regardless of the actual causes of "burn-out," its effects are dramatically clear in terms of social and personal costs. To the extent that people feel compelled to "escape" from their jobs or even to leave their profession entirely, it represents a tremendous waste of their training and talent. More importantly, "burn-out" has detrimental psychological effects, both for the professionals and for their patients/clients. The professional's perception of, and feelings about, people in general often shows a shift towards a cynical, negative pole. They begin to think of their patients or clients in more derogatory terms and to believe that they are somehow deserving of their problems. When on vacation, they want to get away from all people. In telling us about their ideal job, they often describe work situations in which they fantasize few, if any, people existing. For example, one social worker said that he loved art and would like most of all to work by himself in a museum, cataloguing paintings in the back storage room.

A final detrimental consequence of "burn-out" is the effect it can have on the professional's relationships with family and friends. If stress cannot be resolved while on the job, then it is often unknowingly resurrected at home, which can lead to increased personal and family conflict. Many of these professions have higher rates of divorce, mental illness, and suicide than the national average (for example, the suicide rate of police officers is six and a half times higher than that of people in non-law-enforcement occupations, and psychiatrists contribute more than their share to suicide statistics).

Clearly, health and social service professionals pay a high price for working in their chosen career. But what about the costs to *us,* their patients and clients? It is equally clear that we suffer from their "burn-out" as well. We wait longer to receive less attention and less concern. The quality of the care or service we receive becomes poorer, and the experience of obtaining it becomes a dehumanizing one.

As this analysis has attempted to point out, "burn-out" is not a function of "bad" people who are unfeeling and brutal. Rather, it is a function of "bad" situations in which originally idealistic people must operate. Hopefully, implementation of some of the ideas proposed here can be a start towards changing these basic health and welfare situations such that they promote human values rather than destroy them.

Epilogue:
A Dream
for the
Future

We have now come a long way together on the journey we started back in Chapter 1. We hope you have a better appreciation of what psychology is all about and of how some of the personal and social problems you encounter may be analyzed (and coped with more effectively) through the new psychological perspective you have gained.

Although you are at the end of this text and your introductory course, you are, of course, just at the beginning of the fuller, in-depth study of the many aspects of psychological inquiry. For virtually every major topic we have presented, most colleges offer an entire course (or several courses) devoted just to its concepts, methods, and body of knowledge. You may want to undertake further formal course study of those topics you found interesting, either personally or academically. But there is also a wealth of literature available in your college library on even those topics and issues we have only been able to touch upon briefly. One of the reasons we have included reference citations of various studies, researchers, and topics throughout the text (and alphabetically listed starting on p. 727) is for your benefit in pursuing those ideas about which you may want to know more. A second reason is for you and others to be able to assess independently the evidence on which specific psychological conclusions have been based—to be able to separate speculation and opinion from reliable data and valid inference.

In this final statement, we would like to present three general issues that are usually not discussed in introductory psychology texts, but about which many students have voiced concern—ecological psychology, the ethics of intervening in people's lives, and the application of psychology for improving the quality of our lives.

Ecology has become one of the primary issues of our times, and we would like you to consider the ways in which an ecological perspective offers a rather different view of psychology from the more traditional one that has characterized psychological thinking up until now. Also, it is important for us all to realize that although ecological problems are often stated as environmental problems of physical resources, ultimately the key to both these problems and their solutions is *people*. It is, after all, the attitudes, values, and behaviors of people that result in overpopulation, pollution, disregard of nature's gifts, and ambitious plans to "modernize," "urbanize," and control the existing environment. But there are also other *people* who have alerted us to the dangers of overdependence on dwindling energy supplies, and the long-term negative consequences of interventions that appear to have short-range value—such as the use of DDT and other pesticides to control insects. How do we change the behavior of litterers, vandals, profiteers, and the like? That's where psychology must be involved.

But wherever some person intervenes in the life of another so as to change it, ethical questions arise. Since psychology is an experimental science relying on a research model in which attempts are made to influence behavior, ethical considerations must be faced in all of its research activities. But beyond that, all psychological therapy represents an attempt to modify the way people think, feel, and act toward others, as well as toward themselves. Is it ethical to impose one's values on the "human design," to change the personality—however "pathological"—of another individual? What are the criteria by which we can assess that "successful therapy" is in the patient's best interests rather than simply for the convenience of the social order into which that person is being refitted? Although there are no pat answers to such general questions about the ethics of intervention, it is time for psychologists, students, and other citizens to begin serious dialogue about them.

After reading about the variety of forms that the perversion of human potential can assume, many students get discouraged about the potential of psychology (or anything else for that matter) to bring about prosocial reactions and to have a positive impact on the world. However, we are optimistic about the future of applying psychological knowledge to the solution of many types of problems that face our society. Up until now psychology has not had as much impact on relevant legislation as it might because psychologists have been wary of, or maybe just modest about, venturing out into the "real world" with the knowledge they have amassed. Also the applications of psychology in the past have tended toward business-military-institutional interests and have not as often been directed toward "people problems." The winds of change are upon us, and the next decade will probably see a marked increase in the degree to which psychology will be "given away" to ordinary people (see p. 30, Miller, 1969). In this Epilogue, we would like to point out some applications of psychology and new directions that applied psychology can take to make the life of the average person fuller and more satisfying.

Ecological Psychology

Ecology's uneconomic
but with another kind of logic,
economy's unecologic.

Kenneth Boulding (1974)

In a city in southern Illinois it has been discovered that nitrates used for fertilizer on the surrounding farms—greatly increasing the yield—have seeped into the water supply, where, in the presence of certain bacteria, they are being converted into nitrites, which are highly toxic and can lead to a serious children's disease. But the farmers have come to depend on the extra yield to make farming economically feasible, and the city, in turn, is economically dependent on the success of its farming community. The farmers cannot just give up using nitrates without upsetting the whole system and facing financial ruin; yet if they continue, they are endangering the health of the children in their own community.

Just as we have come to realize that we are part of a biological *ecosystem* in which all parts are interdependent, so we are discovering that people in a community are interdependent and that much of their behavior has its roots in this psychosocial interdependence rather than in either their isolated character traits or the particular stimulus conditions acting upon them at the moment.

These interdependencies are not apparent when we study the behavior of single individuals, and thus psychology has tended to ignore the range of issues that arise when the behavior of individuals is enmeshed in a social system. But it has become increasingly apparent that the principles of individual psychology cannot be simply and directly translated into those necessary to understand complex system-related behaviors. Successful therapy with one individual may upset the whole family balance. An individual with high ability begins to perform poorly in school when age-mates disapprove of academic interests. Normally kind, decent individuals kill helpless villagers in a war. A crowd taunts a frightened boy who is threatening suicide. An upstanding citizen administers what he thinks is dangerously high shock to a person he does not know and has no wish to hurt. A seminary student hurrying to deliver a sermon about the Good Samaritan does not take the time to be one when he encounters a person in apparent need. Competing fishermen knowingly deplete stocks of fish to a point that threatens their livelihood. And nations that already have enough weapons to kill their enemies many times over keep devising more terrible ways of killing human beings while reducing funds for badly needed social and health services for their own citizens. People act in some situations in ways that don't seem to make sense.

It would seem that we have two choices: either we can declare such self-defeating and inconsistent behavior irrational and incomprehensible, or, if we assume that all behavior has causes, we can look for broader principles that fit such behavior into a *social-systems* analysis, where causality may operate differently than in the case of a single individual reacting to an isolated stimulus. If we choose the latter, what then?

Several contrasts become obvious between the traditional principles for explaining individual behavior in a social vacuum and the principles we will need for understanding the whole ecology of complex social behavior. We will separate them arbitrarily for discussion, although (since we are dealing with a psychological ecosystem) the various aspects are all interrelated in their actual functioning. For analysis, then, we will point out three contrasts in *focus* and four in *basic concepts* between ecological and traditional psychology.

Contrasts in Focus

A researcher trying to make sense of the complexities of behavior in real-life social situations must be concerned with molar rather than molecular behavior, with observation and analysis of ongoing behavior more often than manipulation and control, and with human values in addition to values of scientific objectivity.

Molar vs. molecular units of analysis. Psychological analysis has commonly attempted to explain behavior in terms of events in particular parts of the organism, especially the brain and other parts of the nervous or endocrine systems. As we have seen, this process of focusing on the parts is called *molecular analysis*. In contrast stands *molar analysis*, which looks at the behavior of the whole organism.

For example, a classic experimental psychologist might investigate the relationship between the stimulus intensity of a light and a subject's reaction time in releasing a switch. On the other hand, a psychologist doing research at a molar level of analysis might investigate the relationship between level of street lighting and acts of vandalism. Both are trying to discover the effects of environment on behavior, but the latter is defining both "environment" and "behavior" more broadly.

A molecular approach tends to be reductionistic, explaining events at one level of organization in terms of processes at a simpler level and assuming that there is no loss in the translation—that behavioral acts of an organism can be adequately described in terms of nerve cells and electrochemical processes. A molar approach is more likely to be taken by psychologists who postulate that wholes have properties not present in or predictable from their parts, that at each level of organization new properties emerge that are best studied at that level and perhaps cannot even meaningfully be described in terms of processes at the lower levels. For example, they would argue that it would be futile to try to explain why hijackers take over airplanes in terms of the firing of their neurons and the contracting of their muscles. Fear, hope, anger, political ambition—all these are characteristics shown by human beings that you would never see in neurons or glands or blood vessels. And social systems have characteristics (e.g., cohesion and power relationships) not seen in individuals.

A molar approach also studies ways in which the characteristics of a whole affect the functioning of its parts. Thus the nervous system, endocrine glands, and other internal systems work differently depending on whether the individual is anxious about an examination, straining to hear a bit of gossip, or deep into transcendental meditation. Similarly, the characteristics of a society affect the behavior and functioning of its members and in fact help us make sense of some behavior that seems irrational when looked at in isolation. Although societies are not organic physical units like organisms, they represent systems of mutual interdependencies that may determine the alternatives and options an individual has and the rewards or punishments that will follow from each choice.

Observation and classification vs. control and intervention. As we have seen, the highest-priority goals of traditional psychology have been prediction and control. The most admired research has been the controlled experiment, in which relevant variables can be held constant and independent variables manipulated so that findings can be stated in terms of causes rather than mere correlations.

But when hypotheses are formulated and tested in this way, only conditions already suspected of being causes get studied. Important parts of the network of causes that operate in the everyday world may never be recognized and studied. Furthermore, many vitally important questions about social behavior cannot be investigated in this way because of practical or ethical limitations on what psychologists can manipulate and control, and because in many cases the researcher's interference would change the very behavior being studied.

One of the pioneers in ecological psychology, Roger Barker, has rejected an interventionist approach in favor of studying behavioral phenomena intact, as they occur within the natural habitat (the "field") of the individuals under investigation. He has set himself the task of describing as accurately and completely as possible the whole spatial and temporal context of behavior—what occurs, when, where, who is involved, for what duration. Instead of entering the situation with a theory to prove or a hypothesis to test, he tries to impose as little as possible of his own bias in attempting to describe and categorize what is happening.

With this approach, the environmental-behavioral *data* become the reality to be analyzed and understood, and their changes through time are an important aspect of what is observed. The ecological researcher does not pick out and systematically manipulate any variable; instead, the "stream of behavior" is allowed to flow uninterrupted, merely observed and recorded for subsequent analysis. (See *P&L* Close-up, p. 660.)

Concern for improving the human condition vs. value-free intellectual discovery. Science provides means of gathering evidence to solve certain kinds of problems. For many scientists, the motivation for doing so is chiefly intellectual curiosity about the mysteries of nature, how things or people function as they do. "Knowledge for its own sake" is the slogan of "pure science," including pure psychology.

As we saw in Chapter 1, however, many psychologists are accepting psychology's potential—and responsibility—for improving the human condition. Though objectivity must prevail in the data-collecting and data-analyzing

Close-up
Natural Behavior Settings As Determinants of Behavior

Barker and his associates at the University of Kansas (1963) have carefully analyzed natural behavior settings in a small midwestern community, such as drugstore, garage, basketball game, and after-school play. They have found that such natural settings are stable situations that have a strong influence on the behavior that occurs in them and that the same individual may behave quite differently in different ones.

As only one example of many of their findings, they have discovered that students in small schools with relatively few associates in the school setting feel twice as many pressures on them to take part in school activities, according to students' reports. Also, they actually take on twice as many responsible positions in these settings and report more satisfactions growing out of being challenged, being involved in important ways, being valued by others, and gaining competence as well as moral and cultural values.

The kind of observational records that an ecologically oriented researcher keeps on the stream of behavior is seen below in the record of an eight-year-old boy's afternoon play (Barker, 1963).

Play time after school　　　　　　　6:14 — 7:11 pm

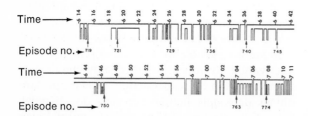

Examples

719 Playing in fort	745 Getting jar of jam
721 Discussing fort with Roy	750 Eating preserves and pickles
729 Showing Blake how to shoot	763 Shooting arrow
736 Playing cowboys and indians	774 Telling story about arrow
740 Listening to radio	

After Barker, 1963

phases of research, the possible utilization of the findings to change people's lives inevitably involves value choices.

The ecological psychologist wrestles with problems whose solutions could have a bearing on the quality of the environment and directly or indirectly on the lives of people in it. There is a sense of "mission," a goal of social relevance, a concern for applied problems and for solutions that can be translated into action programs. To such a researcher, the humanistic concerns are as important as—or more important than—the detached, scientific, intellectual concern of solving a puzzle posed by nature. (See *P&L* Close-up, p. 661.) We will have more to say on this point in the last part of the Epilogue.

Contrasts in Concepts

In addition to the differences in emphasis and overall approach, there are differences in key concepts that emerge in the study of complex social behavior. These include multiple causes and multiple effects instead of "the independent variable" and "the dependent variable," mutual influence among interdependent parts instead of one-directional influence, and systems conceived of as organic wholes instead of collections of separately functioning entities.

Multiple causes vs. "the independent variable." Research in traditional psychology has been guided by the strategy of attempting to isolate the influence of single factors on behavior. The variables operating in any given situation are arbitrarily separated into three categories: independent, constant, and dependent. By letting only the independent variable vary, the researcher can say that under the conditions of the experiment, the change in the independent variable *caused* the change observed in the dependent variable, which was the *effect*.

But isolating one factor for study often leads us to forget the continuing influence of all the variables that we did *not* manipulate. Flicking a switch turns on a light only *if* there is an intact circuit, a good light bulb, an energy system to tap into, and so on. All these other elements are part of the cause of the light's going on—not just

660　*Epilogue: A Dream for the Future*

the flicking of the switch. With behavior, too, precise control may make it possible for one stimulus change to be regularly followed by a given change in behavior, but the factors held constant still remain part of the cause too: food reinforcement changes behavior only if the organism is hungry, awake, can see or hear or smell it, and is not more interested in something else at the moment.

To the question, "What is responsible for making your car run?" there was a different public answer after February 1974, than before that period of gasoline shortage. (See *P&L* Close-up, p. 662.) A survey of public opinion reported that most people believed that the policies of the federal government and the oil companies determined whether or not there would be enough gasoline to run their cars (Murray et al., 1974). Gasoline may be the direct causal factor in fueling an automobile engine, but its availability became the end-product of a host of other causes—international intrigue, the Arab-Israeli conflict, alleged collusion among oil companies to raise prices by curtailing supplies, political favors to big business, lack of adequate government surveillance or long-range planning of energy resources, and so on.

It is important to recognize that which variables are manipulated and which are held constant or ignored in any study is arbitrary and a matter of preference. Each psychologist varies whatever variables seem most important in terms of his or her particular theoretical bias, and holds constant the "unimportant" ones.

Psychologists interested in the effects of different reinforcement schedules have used organisms of similar genetic strains, with similar motivation (such as hours of deprivation). When organismic variables have been held constant in this way, different reinforcement schedules have indeed led to different learning curves. When personality theorists have held reinforcement constant (provided the same reinforcement for all subjects) and varied motivation or other organismic variables, behavior has been found to change with changes in *these* variables, and

An excellent example of the way basic research may generate practical solutions is provided by a recent study in which aversive conditioning was used to control coyote attacks upon sheep (Gustavson, Garcia, Hankins, & Rusiniak, 1974).

Wild coyotes prey upon lambs in the public lands of the western United States. This has led to a sharp controversy between those who want to destroy the predators and naturalists who wish to preserve the species in its natural habitat. Control of such predation has typically involved offering bounties for killing the animals. Now psychology is finding behavioral methods that may both spare the predator and save the prey.

In Chapter 3 we discussed the research of John Garcia and his colleagues on "bait-shyness" as a newly discovered constraint on basic laws of conditioning (see p. 135). Bait-shyness is a conditioned aversion to the taste of a given food acquired on the basis of a single learning experience in which the animal has become sick from eating that food.

Conditioned aversion to a specific kind of meat was induced in six coyotes by feeding them meat treated with lithium chloride, which produces a temporary illness. For three of the coyotes the treated meat was lamb flesh; for the other three it was rabbit. The attack and eating behavior of each coyote following this treatment was observed. With only one or at most two aversion experiences, the predators ceased to attack the prey whose flesh had made them ill, but did continue to attack the alternative prey.

The researchers suggest that sheep predation in the open range can be suppressed by treating lamb and sheep carcasses with the nonlethal toxin so that the smell and taste of the meat may become aversively conditioned. Here is a fine example of psychological research that might appear to have little practical utility, yet can be applied in an ecologically valid manner to maintain the life of a threatened species while also suppressing its killing of animals vital to our food supply.

Close-up

**What Will You Feed Your Car
When the Gasoline's All Gone?**

How will the automobile addicts among us adjust to the energy crisis? One set of predictions by Kenneth Boulding (1974) distinguishes between the long- and short-run accommodations.

"The most obvious and dramatic change has been the sharp rise in the price and the decreased availability of gasoline for private automobiles. This situation seems likely to persist for quite a while . . . . The long-run effects, however, depend both on changes in the technology of supply and to some extent on what might be called the "technology of demand," the adaptation of preferences and life-styles to changing price and income structures.

"I must confess that I think in this regard a good deal more effort will be put into the supply problems than into the demand adjustments. The automobile, especially, is remarkably addictive. I have described it as a suit of armor with 200 horses inside, big enough to make love in. It is not surprising that it is popular. It turns its driver into a knight with the mobility of the aristocrat and perhaps some of his other vices. The pedestrian and the person who rides public transportation are, by comparison, peasants looking up with almost inevitable envy at the knights riding by in their mechanical steeds. Once having tasted the delights of a society in which almost everyone can be a knight, it is hard to go back to being peasants. I suspect, therefore, that there will be very strong technological pressures to preserve the automobile in some form, even if we have to go to nuclear fusion for the ultimate source of power and to liquid hydrogen for the gasoline substitute. The alternative would seem to be a society of contented peasants, each cultivating his own little garden and riding to work on the bus, or even in an electric streetcar. Somehow this outcome seems less plausible than a desperate attempt to find new sources of energy to sustain our knightly mobility." (p. 255)

reinforcement schedules have not been mentioned—or seen—as a cause. But in both cases the variables held constant were still operating and were part of what was "causing" the behavior. If they had been different or absent, the behavior might have been very different. A change anywhere in the system could have changed the behavior that was observed.

Sometimes the variables we have been holding constant and ignoring turn out to be so crucially important that they break through the constraints of the research design and force us to recognize and study them. An example of such a variable came to light in Keller Breland's discovery of "instinctual drift" (see p. 135), when he found that the power of the experimenter-controlled reinforcement was sometimes limited by the animal's own species-specific genetic tendencies. Imprinting (see p. 136) was another example; here some powerful learning does not seem to follow the usual laws for operant behavior. Still another example was the finding of learned helplessness (see p. 394), in which animals with a past experience of severe, inescapable shock never did learn to escape when it became possible to do so, despite ample motivation and reinforcement. A powerful motive in both humans and animals is *curiosity,* the drive to explore and know the environment. Until the 1950s, when this source of motivation was "discovered," researchers tried to minimize its "interfering effects" by getting animal subjects thoroughly accustomed to the testing environment before beginning an experiment, in which biological drives or learning history were then varied.

The search for single causes, for simple functional relationships has traditionally been the quest of science and social science just as it has been of the average person who tries to answer questions about what caused a particular event. We all seek simplicity within the complexity we encounter. Sometimes it is possible to discover a central cause—a factor that accounts for most of the variability in reaction—but often we do injustice to the phenomenon by demanding simple answers when the causality is an interrelated network that cannot be analyzed bit by bit.

"Why?" we ask as our cars, schools, churches, parks, and homes are defaced and destroyed in an apparently senseless way. We saw in Chapter 14 that "vandalism," the cause of such property damage, could be the consequence of social-environmental conditions that promoted a sense of anonymity. But for anonymity to be expressed as vandalism also required other conditions, such as prior social models for specific acts of vandalism, feelings of being alienated from the reward structure of society, and group support for such activities.

So an ecological approach recognizes that most events of significance have many causes. Furthermore, these causes are operating not just independently and additively but as a network, interactively. Thus, they must be studied as a network, as interdependent, interacting variables. These variables may have different effects in different networks, and different effects when they are all varying at once than when only one at a time is allowed to vary. Studying them separately as independent variables may give us an inaccurate picture as well as an incomplete one.

Multiple effects vs. "the result," or "the main effect plus side-effects." As we look for multiple causes, we must also look for multiple effects. We have always known this, but in much of our research it has not been important—or so we have thought. Some educators have tried to develop special instructional schemes to improve the verbal performance of schoolchildren. But besides learning a list of spelling words well enough to pass a test, children may be learning to love or hate school, to feel self-esteem through excelling or to feel that they are stupid compared to their peers. They may also perform well at the time as measured by grades, but develop ulcers later on from continued strain and worry. They may learn to be obedient to their teacher and to overgeneralize this obedience to authority figures who do not deserve it.

The ecological psychologist is concerned with *all* the effects of a given intervention, including remote effects in other parts of the system and delayed effects that do not show up right away. All too often, in social and political affairs, even a policy that is successful in doing what it was intended to do turns out to have many other effects too—not all so desirable. And the long-term negative effects may even more than negate the short-term good effects.

The Aswan Dam in Egypt provides a good example of short-term success in achievement of an objective, with unanticipated long-term disaster in another part of the system. The dam has done what it was designed to do—control flooding on the Nile River and bring electrical power and irrigation to the area. But it has also destroyed the complex life cycle in which flooding brought rich nutrients as part of a food chain from phytoplankton to zooplankton to sardines to humans. Fisheries at the Nile delta that used to produce 1800 tons of sardines per year now yield only 500 tons. The quality of life in entire sardine fishing villages has been adversely affected by the success of the dam in controlling floods. And even upstream there is concern that minerals left on the land by the irrigation water may eventually ruin the land; in addition, since the dam was built, there has been a disturbing increase of *schistosomiasis,* a waterborne intestinal disease.

As our psychology becomes more powerful, we need to realize that any intervention we make in other people's lives (or our own) will have many effects, some unintended and some unforeseeable; the long-term effects in one direction may wipe out the short-term ones in another. Also we should become aware of the fact that most social reforms and legislation that are intended to correct some prevailing social ill are interventions, *experimental manipulations.* We take for granted the existence of mental hospitals and prisons, although they were originally designed as a liberal reform to provide an asylum from the stresses of modern life in the turbulent times of Jacksonian America. (Rothman, 1971) Now that there is considerable evidence that these "asylums" are failing, they are not aborted because they have become "institutionalized" and resist critical evaluation.

In California prisons, inmates are sentenced to indeterminate periods of confinement (six months to five years; five years to life, etc.). The intended effect of this innovation in sentencing was to reduce prison terms to a minimum by giving the staff the flexibility to recommend an inmate for the earliest possible parole rather than having the judge impose a rigid time period in which an inmate could not be rewarded for "good behavior." The *actual* effect, contrasted with the intended one, has been to *lengthen* the average term; California prison terms are now the longest in the nation!

As citizens and as psychologists, we must learn to anticipate as many effects as we can, short-term and long-term, from any proposed change—as well as from our present practices—so that we can choose the alternatives that will have the highest proportion of benefit to cost—economic, social, and psychological. We must also insist that every such proposed intervention be subject to periodic review and critical evaluation to determine whether or not it has been effective, useless, or even counterproductive. The rationale for continuing social experiments must not be their mere existence, but whether they are meeting specifiable behavioral objectives. And all social experiments done on us must be continually assessed and independently evaluated. Indeed, a basic component of all new social legislation should be a proposal for systematic evaluation research of its effectiveness in doing what it was designed to do.

Mutual influence vs. one-directional influence. Traditional psychology has studied the effects of stimuli on responses, a one-way effect. Recently, many psychologists have tried to correct this model by postulating feedback loops. The ecological approach goes farther and recognizes reciprocity and mutual influence as the most common condition. The effect of an environmental factor on behavior feeds back to change the environment, which, in turn, may then subsequently affect the behavior quite differently. Both the individual and the environment keep changing as a result of their transactions.

Traditional research designs conceal this mutual influence because they attempt to relate one set of stimulus conditions to one set of responses, other things being equal (controlled and constant). But in real life, things don't stay equal and constant, and their fluctuations change and are changed by each other. When we look at behavior as a continuing stream, what we see is mutual influences and dynamic interactions—not activities and events sitting still waiting to be related to something.

For example, a curious wife (a brunette) asks her husband where the blonde hair on his jacket came from. Assume this question elicits guilt in him, which he tries to conceal by taking the offensive and verbally attacking in return. The intensity of his response is a cue to her that perhaps he is concealing something; she intensifies her interrogation. Her questioning is met with further aggression on his part, and the episode escalates into a major confrontation. How could you specify an independent variable in this episode? Was it the wife's question? her curiosity? the blonde hair? the husband's past history of infidelity? her way of asking the question? his guilt? his defensive counterattack? or maybe even some other motive on her part, such as covering up her own infidelity or setting him up for some guilt-induced compliant act, such as visiting his in-laws? Indeed, the appropriate analysis is not to isolate variables but to study the pattern of interdependence between the two responding parties.

Another example illustrates even better this same point of the subtle interdependence of environment and behavior.

Before adding a small, rare bird called the "Bearded Tit" to the birdhouse of a European zoo, the curator spent considerable time, effort, and patience investigating the bird's natural habitat and way of life. He designed a zoo environment that was ecologically correct for this species, and the male and female birds appeared to be very happy in it. The birds liked their new environment so much that they not only ate and drank and groomed and flew freely about; they sang, mated, made a nest, laid eggs, and hatched their young.

The delighted zookeeper was horrified a few days later to discover that all the babies were lying dead on the ground. The parents were still as active and "cheerful" as ever, so he concluded that it must have been an accident. But when the mating cycle recurred and a new brood was hatched, they, too, were soon all dead.

Careful observation revealed that the parents were the killers—pushing the babies out of the nest, onto the ground where they died! This cycle of mating, hatching the young, and pushing them out of the nest to die was repeated several times. But why? Why would these apparently happy, "normal" parents behave in this "abnormal" way in their carefully designed environment?

The curator returned to the natural habitat to observe whether there was something he had overlooked in his design. He discovered that the infant birds there spent many hours crying for food while the parents spent much time searching for food (which was scarce) and feeding their demanding young. In addition, the parents kept the nest clean by shoving out any inanimate object, such as a leaf, eggshell, or feather.

The solution! In their "perfectly designed" environment, food was in abundance so that the needs of the babies could be quickly satisfied. After being fed, the babies fell asleep—during daylight hours while the parents were still awake. The babies then became "inanimate objects" and were shoved out of the nest by the parents. When food was made scarce and harder to find in the designed environment, the infants stayed awake crying for it, the parents were kept busy working for it, and they all lived happily ever after (Willems, 1973).

This example points up the complex interdependence between the available food supply, the parents' search for it, the infants' unsatisfied hunger, and their activity and survival. It shows again why the most meaningful criteria for the ecologically oriented psychologist to use in evaluation of any treatment are often long-term effectiveness measures. The designed environment was a success when judged only by the apparent adaptation of the parents to it. But when the criteria included whether the babies of these parents survived, it was another story.

The same problem arises when we try to evaluate the success of social changes for human beings, such as communal living and alternative marriage styles. Should the success of such arrangements be assessed according to how happy they make their members feel or according to whether they promote healthy development and happiness in the children of the *next* generation? Will we be intelligent enough to work out patterns that will benefit both us and our children? (See *P&L* Close-up below.)

Close-up
Transadults and Communal Living

The two major periods of personal development recognized by most societies are childhood and adulthood. "Adolescence" as an intermediate stage came into being through the writings of developmental psychologists and others only about the time of World War I. There are a number of social changes occurring now that appear to be giving rise to still another stage in the process of becoming a "grown-up." The period extending from late teens (entrance into college) to late twenties or early thirties can best be described as *transadulthood*. It is the consequence of profound value shifts in modern society that may, in turn, lead to even greater changes in the pattern of life in the coming generations.

Researchers Carl Danziger and Matthew Greenwald of Rutgers University (1974) describe the transadult stage as "a period of experimenting with different life-styles, of searching for career orientation, and for testing educational goals. It is often a time in which responsibilities are minimized and personal freedom is maximized. The desire to keep options open, to be constantly flexible and prepared for change, is characteristic of the transadult" (pp. 9, 30).

Some of the factors that are contributing to this new stage and to the life-styles that accompany it are: (a) the greater accessibility of college for many young people, especially living in dormitories and exclusively with age-peers, has enhanced feelings of a special identity of youth too old for adolescence and too young for adulthood; (b) the women's liberation movement is challenging traditional male/female, husband/wife roles and all the commercial trappings associated with early marriage and passive acceptance of a woman's place in the home; (c) the Zero Population Growth movement has caused many young adults to rethink the desirability of large families, to delay having children, or to decide not to have any at all; (d) the acceptance and availability of "the pill" has, among other things, changed sexual attitudes, one result of which has been a sense of permissiveness to experiment with various kinds of partner-living arrangements; (e) the increase in divorce rate has made many transadults more cynical of permanent commitments and has provided the models of single parents successfully adjusting to that life-style.

The researchers conclude from their interviews with individuals, couples, and groups that "during the seventies, the transadult stage will be increasingly recognized by society. More people in the late teens to middle or late twenties will adopt a transadult life-style. This will have significant economic repercussions, just as the formalization of adolescence had economic effects" (p. 30).

Thus we are witnessing the start of a new psychosocial stage, illustrating how complex forces in the society create conditions that influence an individual's options. As individuals begin to make new choices and new assumptions, then the system or part of it will also change.

Systems vs. collections of entities. Traditional psychology has spent a great deal of effort trying to identify traits, abilities, drives, attitudes, and other characteristics of individuals as variables to explain why we do what we do. Radical behaviorism has gone to the opposite extreme, trying to explain all the variance in behavior in terms of environmental events, particularly contingencies of reinforcement. But still each organism has been viewed as a separate entity.

The ecological approach emphasizes the fact that we are not so much surrounded by an environment as part of it, and that the structures and pressures of the systems of which we are a part are important "causes" of our behavior. The nature of the system determines what choices there are, as in the case of the Illinois farmers who must choose between material gain and the health of their children. The social system may exert strong pressure toward one choice rather than another, as in the case of the Milgram obedience studies, in which individuals routinely behaved aggressively though they had no desire to hurt the victim and their behavior was in contradiction to their own beliefs. (See *P&L* Close-up, pp. 667–68.)

An everyday way in which the structures and pressures of a system prevent us from interacting with other individuals as human beings is highlighted by the following headline:

MOTORISTS IGNORE
10-YEAR-OLD NUDE GIRL'S PLEA—
CHILD FOUND RAPED, SLAIN

According to the newspaper account, a ten-year-old girl had vainly tried to hail passing cars for help on a crowded expressway. It was during the rush hour and an estimated one hundred cars had passed her. None had stopped, although the girl was naked, yelling and waving her arms. She had been abducted, had escaped from the car, and was trying to signal for help. When no one stopped, the abductor returned, raped the girl, and then strangled her.

Several motorists who had passed the girl later reported to police having seen her and also a car backing along the shoulder of the highway toward her. Their reasons for not stopping to help are illustrative of the "expressway mentality" we have created by our high-speed traffic system: "I couldn't believe what I saw, I went by so fast," said one motorist. Another justified his failure to react to this human distress signal by explaining, "I felt someone behind was in a better position. I was in the passing lane going 65 to 70, and there were five or six cars right behind me. . . ."

It was not that the motorists were heartless or unfeeling. But they were parts of a system of interdependent parts going 60 miles an hour. They got only a fleeting glance, and by the time they realized the girl was there, they were past her. To have jammed on the brakes would have been dangerous. They could not know what had happened to the girl, and all the pressures of their situation prevented communication with her and kept their primary attention focused on not endangering themselves and each other by changing course or stopping suddenly. Those who saw the car backing toward her probably assumed (or hoped) that it was some Good Samaritan going to her rescue—and felt relief since then it was not necessary for them to do so.

Many of their rationalizations had a basis in reality. But the fact remains that they kept going instead of stopping to respond to a child in trouble: in the split second of choice, the freeway "system" structured their actions in that way.

So we see a circular pattern: humans change the natural environment and create physical and social structures. These, in turn, confine, direct, and change us, encouraging certain behaviors, while discouraging or preventing others, often in ways we did not anticipate.

Close-up
Neighborhoods vs. Collections of People

The difference between a system and a collection of separate entities is seen in the contrast between old neighborhoods in downtown New York and the same or comparable areas converted to "housing projects." Jane Jacobs (1961) has described the use of sidewalks and other public areas in the old neighborhoods to provide as much or as little human contact as people wanted, making possible a sense of neighborliness and trust:

"The trust of a city street is formed over time from many, many little public sidewalk contacts. It grows out of people stopping by at the bar for a beer, getting advice from the grocer and giving advice to the newsstand man, comparing opinions with other customers at the bakery and nodding hello to the two boys drinking pop on the stoop, eyeing the girls while waiting to be called for dinner, admonishing the children, hearing about a job from the hardware man and borrowing a dollar from the druggist, admiring the new babies and sympathizing over the way a coat faded. . . .

"The sum of such casual, public contact at a local level—most of it fortuitous, most of it associated with errands, all of it metered by the person concerned and not thrust upon him by anyone—is a feeling for the public identity of people, a web of public respect and trust, and a resource in time of personal or neighborhood need. The absence of this trust is a disaster to a city street." (p. 56)

One of the consequences of the presence or absence of this network of trust is seen in the behavior of the children in the area and adults' reaction to it. Jacobs contrasts the situation on two sides of the same wide street in an area of New York composed of residents of roughly similar economic and racial groups.

"On the old-city side, which was full of public places and the sidewalk loitering so deplored by Utopian minders of other people's leisure, the children were being kept well in hand. On the project side of the street across the way, the children, who had a fire hydrant open beside their play area, were behaving destructively, drenching the open windows of houses with water, squirting it on adults who ignorantly walked on the project side of the street, throwing it into the windows of cars as they went by. Nobody dared to stop them. These were anonymous children, and the identities behind them were an unknown. What if you scolded or stopped them? Who would back you up over there in the blind-eyed Turf? Would you get, instead, revenge? Better to keep out of it. Impersonal city streets make anonymous people. . . ." (p. 57)

This contrast shows the pitfalls of applying findings about correlations between particular single factors, like "socioeconomic status" and particular behavior. The influence of given socioeconomic factors is not the same in different situations but depends on what other factors are operating and how strong or weak *they* are.

The inadequacy of applying single findings while ignoring other crucial factors in the situation is shown in the public places planned in the projects, according to Jacobs. Though they provide gathering places, they do not provide the needed balance of opportunity for human contact and opportunity for privacy and control over who can make inroads on one's time. Too often, planned gathering places like game rooms become traps from which tenants find that they cannot extricate themselves or in which they cannot have just a *little* contact. When tenants become too well acquainted with their neighbors in the project, they lose their freedom of movement and freedom from intrusion. So there is a tendency *not* to establish close friendly relationships with other people in the same project but to make their friends in other projects or in other parts of the city. This, in turn, breeds the anonymity and lack of social "glue" that contributes to the social pathology of many of our urban centers.

John Platt, of the University of Michigan, has called attention to "traps" that sometimes develop in social systems, in which people find themselves engaging in behavior that they can see will be harmful to them in the long run but do not know how to stop (Platt, 1973). The farmer's dependence on phosphates is an example of such a trap. But so, too, is our dependence on technology, on other people to provide services for us, on an unlimited supply of natural energy. We are trapped by the gadgets and time-savers of modern technology—and simply could not do without them, unless of course we have to. *The Whole Earth Catalogue* enjoyed popular acclaim and wide sales because it revived in many of us an interest in self-sufficiency, in learning to do with less while doing it for ourselves and with others. The current energy crisis likewise has spawned new creative energies addressed to alternative life-styles that are not so totally dependent on oil, coal, and the machinery that took both the drudgery and simplicity out of our lives (see Hammond, 1974).

Another example of a social trap has been called the "tragedy of the commons." In England, each farmer using common grazing land found it to his advantage to keep adding another cow. It was clear that in the long run all would suffer as the land became overgrazed, yet any farmer who started limiting his herd would lose out as long as the others kept their herds large. How do we teach people to act not from self-interest but from *common interest?* Or put differently, how do we ever learn that short-run self-interests often have disastrous long-run consequences because they violate the common good—of which we also partake? A more familiar social trap is the nuclear arms race, in which both sides realize that everyone would be better off to use precious resources and skills for life potential rather than death potential. Yet neither side dares be the first to stop. (See *P&L* Close-up, p. 669.)

Such social traps are characteristics not of individuals but of systems. They limit the choices available and determine what payoffs will follow from the choice made. Thus, they are important determinants of whether and how the individuals in the system can meet their basic needs. People who cannot "opt out" and establish their own life-style in isolation from the rest of the system must follow the rules of the system if they are to prosper and perhaps even if they are to survive. If following the rules means engaging in behavior they disapprove, their choice may be to give up either their self-esteem or the esteem of others, including recognition, advancement, and more tangible rewards.

But although, as individuals, our possibilities of action and payoff at a given moment are limited by these system characteristics, we are not permanently at their mercy because systems can be changed. We are learning at last that "what is" in social patterns is not inevitable. As we have changed our physical world—sometimes almost beyond recognition—we are beginning to realize that, by planning and joint action, we can change our social world to make it work better to meet our human needs. (See *P&L* Close-up, p. 670.)

In the remainder of the Epilogue we will look at some of psychology's special problems and potentials in contributing to such changes. We will turn first to the ethical problems of intervention—in the laboratory, in therapy, and in the larger community. Then we will close our discussion—and our book—with some case examples of the successful use of psychology to improve human life.

Close-up

System-Level Problems Need System-Level Solutions

In a city we know, rush hour means over an hour to get home, instead of the usual twenty minutes any other time. This is not because there are too many cars on the streets but because cars crowd into the intersections even when they will not be able to clear the intersection before the light changes. So cross traffic cannot even enter the intersection while *it* has a green light. Eventually it begins nudging in until there may be cars headed all four ways jammed into the intersection. All drivers seize every inch they can; if they didn't they "would never get across."

The same thing is happening at the next intersection, and the one after that, and on and on in all directions. So the intersection does not clear because the next one is jammed, and the whole area where traffic is heavy is suddenly immobilized.

Individuals are helpless in such a system. Their normal driving habits are suddenly not adaptive. They no longer have the choice of showing courtesy or observing the traffic lights. The system in which they are caught offers them no rational solution to the problem of getting across the intersection. They all dislike what they are doing, realize its irrationality, resent each other for being in the way, and continue to push ahead whenever they can.

Only a change in the system can solve their problem. Stationing a traffic police officer at the intersections would do it, or a strict law with a fine for being caught in the intersection when the light changes. In another city we know there are boxes painted on the pavement in the intersections. Any car caught in a box when the light changes is subject to a fine. But it is also possible to persuade employers to arrange staggered work times so that the commuting period is spread out over longer intervals. Or car pools and better mass transit would reduce the number of autos competing for their solitary rights. Such simple changes require massive changes in thinking and in the values of getting all the privacy and comfort that affluence affords.

If we are to help put the household of Earth in order, we will have to decide what "in order" is. In exploring these ideas, you might find it an interesting exercise to invite your friends to try to describe their "utopias." What characteristics would they expect to see in an environment perfectly designed to meet human needs? When they have finished, compare their formulations with your own and with the following definition (based on Potter, 1971). In Potter's formulation, the following characteristics are listed as defining an "optimum environment":

1. Basic needs satisfiable by individual or communal effort;

2. Individual health through freedom from toxic chemicals, unnecessary trauma (war, traffic injuries, noise, etc.), and preventable diseases;

3. Respect for sound ecological principles; learning to live with nature rather than "controlling" it;

4. Continual development of an integrated, adaptive response system in each individual as a result of systematic challenges posed by physical and mental tasks that are within the individual's capability (or at the upper limits of it);

5. Individual happiness that involves the development of a sustained sense of personal identity and the ability to appreciate life's satisfactions and profit from dissatisfactions;

6. A commitment by each individual to the other members of the society to increase their strength, functioning ability, and happiness;

7. A continual search for beauty and order that does not deny the role of individuality, eccentricity, and disorder.

The Ethics of Intervention

The specialized perspective of the scientist inevitably creates ethical dilemmas, if only because scientific knowledge and techniques that can be used for human betterment can usually be turned to manipulative and exploitative purposes as well.

APA, *Ethical Principles,* 1973, p. 8

Ethical issues arise whenever one individual does something that has an impact on the life of another. They are an inescapable part of all involved social living. But they assume special significance for the psychology profession because its research and its therapy involve direct intervention in the behavior, thinking, and outlook of experimental subjects and clients. Ethical principles involve conformity to moral standards as well as to the guidelines for acceptable conduct established by one's group or profession. In practice, the determination of what constitutes a violation of ethical principles is rarely a simple decision based on absolute criteria. Nevertheless, it is only with a commitment by psychologists to strive continually toward ethical practices in dealing with their subjects and clients that potential for abuse of ethical standards can be overcome.

Because of the public indignation over the withholding of medical treatment from patients with VD or cancer who were designated as part of the "control group" in various medical studies, Congress is enacting legislation to create an ethics commission within the Department of Health, Education, and Welfare. This bill would establish a Commission for the Protection of Human Subjects of Behavioral and Biomedical Research. For the first time, there would be research requirements with the force of law, and severe restrictions on access to certain subject populations considered not able to offer voluntary informed consent to their participation — such as young children, orphans, prisoners, the mentally "infirm," and others. Such a bill protects the rights of powerless institutionalized subjects. However, without the participation of such individuals in research, many vital questions affecting their care, treatment, and disposition must go unanswered.

Similar controversy rages over whether a subject must be informed of all aspects of the research and even given a choice as to the experimental treatment preferred. While openness and honesty must be a goal of research, there are some problems that could not be investigated without the withholding of some information — for example, research on uncertainty, unexplained arousal, decision making under stress or with limited information, and other subject matter. And it has no doubt occurred to you that the essence of experimentation is destroyed without the necessary condition that subjects are *randomly* assigned to treatments and to experimental and control groups. Where subjects are free to choose which treatment they will be exposed to, it is not possible to establish causal relations between independent and dependent variables but only to establish correlational relationships. All variables that determined which treatment each individual chose would be confounded with the experimental variable, influencing the outcome in undetermined ways.

But while the specific guidelines are being debated, there is no question that psychologists have become sensitive to the necessity for explicit ethical criteria in the conduct of their professional affairs. This concern in part reflects the growing humanistic orientation within psychology, the greater emphasis on human rather than infrahuman research, and the developing belief in the power of psychological interventions to influence behavior.

The essence of ethical conduct in psychology is responsible adherence to culturally accepted norms of humane treatment of subjects or clients. Unpleasantness, risk of harm (physical, psychological, or social), invasion of privacy, injury to self-esteem are to be avoided.

Research and Ethics

"The ethical problems of psychological research on human beings are intrinsic to the research enterprise. They follow from the very nature of scientific inquiry when it is applied to human research participants rather than from evil intent or from callousness to human values on the part of the researcher. Almost any psychological research with humans entails some choice as to the relative weights to be given to ethical ideals, some choice of one particular ethical consideration over others. For this reason, there are those who would call a halt to the whole endeavor, or who would erect barriers that would exclude research on many central psychological questions. But for psychologists, the decision not to do research is in itself a matter of ethical concern since it is one of their obligations to use their research skills to extend knowledge for the sake of ultimate human betterment." (American Psychological Association, 1973, p. 7)

The decision by a researcher to initiate a project should include a careful appraisal of: (a) its purposes and goals (basic or applied; to help a specific subject or group, or to be of general value, etc.); (b) the rights of the subject to privacy, to alternative treatment, to refuse further participation at any time, to be informed as fully as possible of the hypothesis being tested and the knowledge gained, etc.; (c) accountability of the investigator (to whom is the researcher accountable for the conduct of the research, for communicating the findings, for handling complaints, etc.?); and (d) the comparison of benefits to risks.

It is on this last point that the determination of the acceptability of a given study often revolves. Do the benefits of conducting the study outweigh the risks it poses to the individual subjects participating in it? If not, then "no go." If they do, then the possibility of conducting or continuing the project must be based on a reasoned analysis of the best available information. The basis for that decision, according to the draft of the American Psychological Association Guidelines, requires the investigator "to estimate and balance three subjective parameters associated with risks, and the same three associated with benefits. These are the *magnitude* of the risks and benefits involved, the *probability* that harm or benefit will actually occur, and the *number* of people that will suffer or profit" (APA, 1971, p. 10).

However, there is no calculus available for such equations; the ultimate decision is still a personal, subjective one. As such, it is open to criticism because if a researcher really believes in a given theory or the outcome of a certain treatment and has invested years of time, effort, money, and reputation in it, that vested interest may very likely bias his or her estimate of the risk/benefit ratio in the "go" direction. Also, in the initial stages of research it is often impossible to determine in advance whether there will be any actual benefits or long-range risks. To remove the burden of responsibility and the liability of abuse from the researcher's shoulders, virtually every university, hospital, and research unit requires psychological investigators to submit their research proposals to a committee of their peers for review. Those judged to be ethically questionable or to violate safeguards proposed by the government, the profession (APA), or the local group must be modified accordingly or are rejected. On issues where there is some uncertainty, tentative approval might be given subject to committee review after a limited set of preliminary data are collected, and, thereafter, periodic reviews should be held. This is preferable to an absolute "go/no-go" decision in the absence of pertinent data on which to base such a decision. Carrying out research in defiance of the committee's approval could have serious legal and professional consequences for the researcher. The goal of these committees is two-fold—to protect the subject's rights while ensuring that research on significant psychological and social problems is carried on.

Distress, Deception, and Discovery

We noted in previous chapters that much psychological research was directed toward understanding the causes of personal and social pathology, toward the evaluation of concepts such as anxiety, fear, dependence, aggression, obedience, etc. But experimental manipulations that create such states in subjects create emotional anguish, however transient.

Does anyone have the right to make another person feel upset, even temporarily, in order to prove a point or test a theory? When a subject experiences failure in a study where self-esteem has been manipulated to some extent, that lowered self-estimate may continue to persist even after the researcher has debriefed the subject and explained that the failure was arbitrarily imposed and not really contingent on performance (as shown by Ross, Lepper, & Hubbard, 1975).

In some research, the purpose is to study reactions to stress, and thus the arousal of stress reactions is necessary for the study. The work of Lazarus (see p. 382) on coping strategies to handle stress involves showing subjects filmed sequences that clearly create strong physiological and affective arousal. But his findings are helping to specify techniques for coping with unavoidable stress in everyday life.

How would *you* evaluate the following two studies if you had been on an ethics committee that had to approve or reject them?

In the first, male alcoholic patients volunteered for a study they thought was a possible therapy for alcoholism. They were not warned in advance of the effect of the drug they were to receive, since the researcher felt this information would reduce the traumatic impact of the experience. The actual purpose of the research was to study the establishment of a conditioned response in a traumatic, but not painful situation. The drug administered interfered with normal respiration to create a severe psychological stress that, although not physically painful, was so frightening that "all the subjects in the Standard Series said that they thought they were dying" (Campbell, Sanderson, & Lavertz, 1964, p. 631).

In the second study, a group of army recruits were put in situations designed to study how they would react to perceived threats to their lives. In order to avoid the unrealistic, minimal threats used in laboratory studies of stress and to study real-life reactions to military stresses, subjects were put into the following situations: on a plane apparently about to crash-land; in a desolate area where nuclear radiation was sup-

posedly spreading, or where a forest fire was raging, or where artillery shells were being misdirected. When a subject tried to radio for help, the transmitter failed to work. "How would he react?" was the researchers' question (Berkum, Bailek, Kern, & Yagi, 1962).

"How do *you* react to such research?" is our question. How do you evaluate the risks and benefits of these studies, which were conducted before ethics committees were established?

Deception takes many forms in psychological research, all the way from not calling attention to the true purpose of the study or some critical variable to misinforming or lying to the subject about the rationale for a given event or even about the contract between experimenter and subject. An instance of the latter is the Festinger and Carlsmith study (1959, see p. 576) in which the subject believed himself to be the experimenter's assistant and not a research subject during the critical stage of the study when he tried to convince the true assistant-dressed-as-subject that the boring experiment was interesting (for a $1.00 or $20.00 reward). Misinformation as to the nature of the arousal was central to Schachter and Singer's study (1962, see pp. 374–75) of emotional arousal via epinephrine injections with and without appropriate cognitions. In the Asch study (1955, see p. 592) on conformity, each subject had to believe that the group saw comparison lines differently from the way he did in order for the researcher to study how this disagreement was resolved. To some extent failure to disclose the full information about an experiment may be a necessary condition if the variables in question are to be studied at all, since they would change in fundamental ways if the subject knew what was happening.

Herbert Kelman of Harvard University has long been a critical voice of concern about the problems of deception and ethics in human research. He says, "Too often deception is used not as a last resort, but as a matter of course. Our attitude seems to be that if you can deceive, why tell the truth? It is this unquestioning acceptance, this routinization of deception that really concerns me" (1967, p. 3).

In some experiments, the existence and possible detrimental consequences of deception go unnoticed even by critics of deception research because the emphasis of the study directs the reader's attention away from it. In the classic study on how children resolve group conflict by use of superordinate goals, Sherif and Sherif (1956, see pp. 594–95) deceived the children (and the parents?) by not telling them that their summer camp was a psychologist's outdoor laboratory or that the environment was rigged to create intergroup conflict. When *you* read our description of the study, were you concerned about the physical risks of induced conflict in an open setting without adequate supervision, especially during night raids, or about whether the children were learning how to be more effective warriors from their "combat experience"?

Milgram has justified the experience he put his obedience subjects through as "an opportunity to learn something of importance about themselves and, more generally, about the conditions of human action" (1964, p. 850). Thus he argues that participation in some kinds of research constitutes a unique *discovery* for subjects. In fact, deception studies by their very nature involve the greatest potential for such new self-knowledge. Learning that one acted in a cowardly way or has blindly obeyed an irresponsible authority might be a valuable insight that would help the person avoid such reactions in real life — where it really counts. However, to teach a lesson when the student neither asked for it nor was prepared to accept it — and might not want to be exposed to his or her defects or weaknesses — represents a questionable assumption on the part of the experimenter who justifies the necessity for deception on such grounds.

In the experimental research on bystander intervention, stimulated by the failure of citizens to respond to the distress cues of Kitty Genovese (see p. 628), those who don't intervene are faced after the study with their lack of social responsibility, while those who do are possibly faced with their "foolishness" in "overreacting" to a staged emergency.

Ironically, much of the field research on altruism (see p. 574) is subject to the criticism of unethical procedures. Individuals who are unaware that they are subjects in an experiment find a lost wallet or letter or see someone give money to a charity or help fix a flat tire. How they respond is observed and recorded without their knowledge. If they are debriefed afterward, they may be *less* likely to behave altruistically in the future when a real emergency or social need arises, since they cannot be certain it is not just another rigged experiment in disguise. If not, they have participated in research without their consent and without any personal benefit or gain from the experience.

These issues are thorny ones, but are being addressed by all those who want to be sure that we are not polluting the psychological environment by unethical experimental practices that can spawn suspicion, distrust, and cynicism in college sophomores and other subjects in psychological research. An awareness of the problem and a sensitivity to its many facets is a prerequisite for developing solutions that will promote both good research and good human relations.

Therapy—Intervention on Request

Research on psychotherapy must concern itself with all of the above issues plus new ones. We saw in Chapter 12 that evaluation of the effectiveness of psychotherapy demands random assignment to treatment and no-treatment control groups of people who request therapy for their personal problems. Withholding treatment when it might be effective is an unethical therapeutic practice, since it sacrifices the needs of the current individual patient to the interests of an unknown larger number of future patients who may benefit from the research findings. Similarly, in such research the patients are not informed of the therapeutic options available to them, and are discouraged from switching therapists or type of therapy even if they feel no improvement—and are paying for their mental health care. One resolution to the problem is to ensure

that every member of the control group later be offered the therapeutic treatment proved to be most effective.

In the course of ordinary therapy, where controlled research is not a factor, ethical issues still abound. Some we touched upon in Chapter 12. To what extent is the patient involved in formulating a therapeutic contract that explicitly defines the goals of the therapy, the approach to be used, alternatives, and the right to criticize, terminate treatment, or seek other help? The tremendous status that all doctors possess in our society puts patients at a substantial power disadvantage so that no request made by a therapist can be refused.

Therapists are engaged in the practice of helping people whose behavior and experience do not conform to cultural standards of normality. Thus therapists must be sensitive to the possibility that they are being used by society to maintain the status quo by changing round pegs that don't fit into square holes rather than changing the square holes. Therapist Fred Spaner argues that his peers have a responsibility to help change social conditions that produce dysfunctions and not merely to change people who have become dysfunctional. "If we are not participating as activists to promote beneficial social change we are participating as activists to maintain the system as it is" (1970, p. 62). The force of this injunction becomes most evident when psychologists work for an institution (such as the military or the prisons) where one goal of therapy is to make the person a "good soldier" or a "good prisoner." When such a goal conflicts with the individual's self-actualization and personal values, does the therapist ever recommend rebellion or change of institutional practices to adjust to the person, or is adjustment always a one-way street?

At another level, the very definition of mental health "problems" is called into question when the blame for people's suffering and for the situation they are in is assumed to rest on defects in them and not on the situation. Michigan researchers Nathan Caplan and Stephen Nelson, in their very provocative analysis (1973), describe this as a general tendency in psychology as well as in the legislature, legal system, and law enforcement agencies—to attribute "person-blame" as the cause for most social problems. If the shoe doesn't fit, the appropriate course of action appears to be to discover what's wrong with the foot!

The extremes to which therapy may go as an unethical procedure for the control of human freedom of thought and action is revealed in a recent Senate report on psychiatric abuse in the Soviet Union for repression of political dissidents. To deviate from the narrow standards of political orientation acceptable in the USSR is political heresy. Abnormality is defined to include such heresy, and intellectual dissidents are incarcerated in remote mental hospitals for long terms. (See *P&L* Close-up at right.) Alexander Solzhenitsyn's exile from Russia after exposing such practices has helped give them notoriety, but it should also give us pause in our certainty that they are limited to the Soviet Union.

Social Engineering—Intervention in Society

It is not only researchers and therapists (and their subjects and patients) who must be concerned with the ethics of their activities. Such activities are relatively rare in our society compared with the widespread "social engineering" that takes place daily as people arrange conditions for other people to operate in, often without their consent or even participation in the decision making. Business annually spends more on commercial research than the federal government allocates to all social science research (Meyer, 1974, p. 9). Industrial psychologists are usually hired by management to reduce employee dissatisfaction while increasing production, and thus profit margins. Military psychologists create propaganda and design indoctrination programs. Newspaper editors and radio and TV station managers decide not only what will be reported as "newsworthy," but also the form of programming the public will be forced to accept each season.

It is appropriate to view social policy changes that affect large numbers of people as experimental manipulations whether or not they are

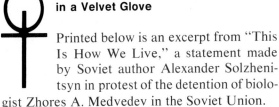

Close-up
Therapy As a Hammer in a Velvet Glove

Printed below is an excerpt from "This Is How We Live," a statement made by Soviet author Alexander Solzhenitsyn in protest of the detention of biologist Zhores A. Medvedev in the Soviet Union.

"Without any warrant for arrest or any medical justification, four policemen and two doctors come to a healthy man's house. The doctors declare that he is crazy; the police officer shouts, 'We are the organ of force! Get up!' They bend his arms back and take him to the madhouse.

"This can happen tomorrow to any of us. It has happened to Zhores Medvedev, a scientist, geneticist, and publicist, a man of subtle, precise, and brilliant intellect, a man of good heart. (I personally know of his disinterested help to unknown dying sick people.)

"It is precisely for the diversity of his gifts that he has been charged with abnormality: a split personality. It is precisely his sensitivity to injustice, to stupidity, that are made to seem a sick deviation: poor adaption to the social milieu. Once you don't think as you are ordered to think, you are abnormal! And well-adapted people—they must all think alike.

"And there is no restraint of law; even the appeals of our best scientists and writers are bounced back like peas off a wall.

"If only this were the first case! But it has become a fashion, a devious method of reprisal without searching for a fault, when the real cause is too shameful to be stated. Some of the victims are widely known; many more are unknown. Obsequious, perjuring psychiatrists put on the label of mental illness.

"They said he had concern for social problems, excessive ardor and excessive sangfroid, too brilliant abilities and lack of them. . . .

"It is time to think clearly. The incarceration of free-thinking healthy people in madhouses is spiritual murder. . . ." (1970, p. 6)

incorporated into formal research designs. (See *P&L* Close-up below.) They, too, ought to be subject to the same scrutiny for violations of ethical practices as we are now demanding of researchers and therapists. We should ask: (a) What is the involvement of the people to be affected? Have they consented to the manipula-

(See *P&L* Close-up below.)

Close-up

The Pros and Cons of Social Experiments

Alice Rivlin, chairperson of the Panel on Social Experimentation of The Brookings Institution, has analyzed some of the dilemmas involved in the new trend toward social experimentation. These include:

1. *Design dilemmas*, arising from the conflict between the desire for valid and reliable results and the need for quick, low-cost results.

2. *Implementation dilemmas*, arising as the program is put into action. Should one insist that the original design be followed to the letter? If so, how can one find out what will happen when the program is implemented on a large scale by people who do not adhere strictly to that design?

3. *Evaluation dilemmas*, which involve the choice of the evaluators. Surely those who are most familiar with a program are best qualified to evaluate it. But are they likely to be the most objective?

4. *Timing dilemmas*, arising from the fact that politicians are unlikely to fund research until a decision is about to be made, and thus may not allow time to do a thorough job.

5. *Moral dilemmas*, which include ethical questions of the type described in the text as well as concern for the privacy of the participants. Rivlin concludes that, "If great care is not taken to make current experiments as useful and as sensible as possible, there may be a reaction against the whole technique, and a potentially useful tool may be taken away" (1974, p. 35).

tion? (b) What is the basis for the proposed manipulation? Scientific knowledge? Popular wisdom? A crude power play? (c) How will consequences be measured? Will the actual results be recognized and publicized? (d) If the manipulation is counterproductive, can it be reversed? Will it have irreversibly altered the people affected or their life contexts? (e) What side effects will the manipulation have? For example, airport surveillance seems to have reduced hijackings, but it has unquestionably led citizens to accept personal searches, tight controls, and silent acquiescence to yet another limitation on their freedom of movement. From the ecological perspective we outlined earlier, the unexpected long-term effects might prove more insidious than the dramatic immediate gains of the search and seizure operation.

But who will be on the Ethics Committee to act as watchdog on abuse of the very standards of society? Would you be willing? And where would the power to enforce sanctions against offenders come from, when the offenders often are those who already possess most of the power?

"The psychologist believes in the dignity and worth of the individual human being. He is committed to increasing man's understanding of himself and others. While pursuing this endeavor, he protects the welfare of any person who may seek his service or of any subject, human or animal, that may be the object of his study. He does not use his professional position or relationships, nor does he knowingly permit his own services to be used by others, for purposes inconsistent with these values. While demanding for himself freedom of inquiry and communication, he accepts the responsibility this freedom confers: for competence where he claims it, for objectivity in the report of his findings, and for consideration of the best interests of his colleagues and of society." (American Psychological Association, 1963, p. 1)

Psychology for a Better Life

When we added to the traditional goals of psychology the notion of "improving the quality of life," we stepped beyond the purely scientific, academic pursuit of knowledge for its own sake into the realm of social action where knowledge is a tool, an instrument for change. The apparent simplicity of the phrase "improving the quality of life" leads virtually everyone to nod in agreement, "Sounds fine with me," "Sure, why not?" "I'll buy some in pastel shades." All would-be reformers, leaders of religious or political groups, or even garden-club members would espouse that high-sounding principle. But didn't Hitler believe that was what he was doing, and so too the Watergate "plumbers," and even Mafia hit men? "Whose life will be improved at whose cost and at whose gain?" is the question we must pose.

In this now optimistic era of psychology where the presidents of the national association talk of "giving psychology away," "psychology for the people," and "for the 'human enterprise,'" some more conservative scientists shudder at the grandiosity of such plans and at the dangers involved in becoming a problem-solving discipline. To the layperson—or to the scientist as a person/citizen—there is also a sinister ring to the notion of *control* of human behavior.

But it can be argued that any joint enterprise involving two or more people requires control over behavior. Our major problems derive from things that people *do* or *don't do*. Pollution, resource-depletion, discrimination, individual and group violence—all are the result of human action or inaction. Thus why they happen and how they can be changed are, at least in part, psychological problems. While we are aware that effective behavior-control methods are subject to abuse, we also believe that efforts to solve human problems without dependable knowledge about human behavior can lead to great waste of effort, disastrous failure, and quite likely the creation of new and greater problems. (See *P&L* Close-up, p. 678.)

Our intention in this final section of *Psychology and Life* is merely to point to a few positive uses of psychology as related to children's lives that reveal its utility for the goal of making a better life for all.

The major turning point in the actions of the federal government in regard to racially separated school facilities was the decision by the Supreme Court in 1954 in the case of *Brown v. Board of Education of Topeka et al.* (347 U.S. 483). Chief Justice Warren quoted a Kansas court opinion asserting that racial segregation of educational facilities had a detrimental effect upon the educational and mental development of Negro children. This conclusion was "amply supported by modern authority" (p. 494) according to the opinion of the Court. That authority consisted of a series of analyses of the effects of prejudice on personality development by Kenneth Clark, and of the psychological effects of enforced segregation by Isidor Chein, along with evidence and opinions from other psychologists and sociologists.

More recently other researchers have been studying ways to enhance voluntary integration across racial lines (Hauserman, Walen, & Behling, 1973). By use of prompting, rewards, and individuating techniques for forming "new friendships," first-grade schoolchildren were encouraged to broaden their circle of friends across the culturally sanctioned racial barrier between white and black children.

Computer-assisted instruction (CAI) has helped children learn to read in schools in Florida, Oklahoma, Texas, and Washington, D.C. Each child spends 10 or 15 minutes daily at a teletype machine wearing a headset that brings audio messages. The computer presents (on a video tube) words to be read, recognized, and typed, and gives the child immediate feedback. It stores the child's complete history of interaction with the material and constantly updates its calculations concerning parts of the material that the child finds difficult. Each child therefore learns to read according to a curriculum uniquely adapted to his or her individual needs and progress. Evaluation has demonstrated the effectiveness of the program. First-grade students participating in CAI were 5.05 months ahead of a

If You Design a Garbage-Can City, What Will People Do With It?

The design of human environments has proceeded usually from the twin goals of efficiency and practicality. Sometimes aesthetic decisions enter into the planning of buildings, housing projects, shopping centers, and other permanent features of our life space. But how often do urban planners and architects design with *people* in mind and not just with steel and mortar, dollars and cents?

We are beginning to recognize the important influence that our physical environment has on our behavior, mood, and perceptions. The way a space is partitioned can help bring people together or isolate them. The type of windows in an apartment house can encourage residents to look out at activities on their streets and thereby keep an "eye on the neighborhood"—or, if they are of the casement type (which do not allow one to look out easily) they can turn people in on their own apartments.

As psychologists turn their attention to the "coercive power" of designed environments over the behavior occurring within them, "social ecology" laboratories are emerging to help conceptualize such environments. Researchers such as Rudolf Moos (1973) study behavior in a variety of different social environments and try to characterize the "climate" of these life spaces along dimensions that have demonstrable effects on individual and group behavior. Thus we are witnessing a new concern for describing the "personality" of environments, where previously environments were taken for granted and only differences in people were sought.

The interplay of behavioral science and architectural design is also leading to new developments in "humanizing the city environment." In the forefront of this movement is Lawrence Halprin, who designs fountains, recreation areas, and other urban mini-environments that are for people. As one reviewer of his approach to people-architecture put it: "His point—the fundamental one—is that working toward predetermined goals is a bad approach to design or to anything, because en route to the preordained solution, the real problems and opportunities are often overlooked. A lot of beautiful buildings, whole new towns, have failed because they've been aesthetic band-aids applied to trouble spots in the environment, creating new problems rather than eradicating existing ones because they were made to fulfill limited 'ideal' life-styles, not the needs of real live people."

Halprin's nongoal-oriented approach evolved (in the way of most innovative techniques or philosophies) from his isolation of a phenomenon that was so enmeshed in the social fabric that it had eluded social awareness. Halprin simply recognized that people are going to *move* and *live* in the spaces he articulates—not merely look at finished structures and scenery. And he believes that people who will be participants in the final product *must be in on the process of making it* (Schoen, 1972, pp. 14, 15).

control group of first-graders not given the program when tested at the end of the first-grade year; testing one year later showed that the gain had persisted, with CAI students ahead of controls by 4.90 months. (There was no CAI during this second year.) Boys typically read more poorly than girls at this age. CAI helps them improve more than it helps girls, thus overcoming this widely recognized sex difference.

This research by Richard Atkinson (1974) represents a technology derived from a theory of instruction and models of cognitive development and information-processing, as well as sophistication with computer simulation and programming. It is the result of years of laboratory research on memory processes and on attention to and detection of stimulus features and patterns.

A different kind of learning environment has been developed for youngsters who are in trouble because they have committed crimes. At the National Training School for Boys in Washington, D.C., Harold Cohen devised a total environment for delinquent boys between the ages of 13 and 21 (some charged with murder). Ninety percent of the boys showed the equivalent of four years' academic growth within six months in at least one of their academic subjects. In one year, there were dramatic changes not only in academic performance but in interpersonal behavior and in skills necessary to succeed in society (as evidenced by the low recidivism rate the following year after they were released).

The technique involved first carefully analyzing the ways in which the physical environment had to be designed in order to be conducive to learning, cooperation, and positive social interactions rather than aggression and competition. Then explicit performance criteria and reinforcement payoff schedules were established and adhered to. Over time, delayed gratification and symbolic reinforcers took over from the immediate, tangible reward system. The experience of academic success, the sense of competence, and the feeling of personal growth and accomplishment also contributed to the boys' measured self-respect, dignity, and ability to give and receive love and affection (Cohen & Filipczak, 1971). ●

We must learn to create contingency structures that facilitate those behaviors in us and our children that, added together, will help create the kind of society that will optimize individual freedom of growth and realization of the full potential of each person.

Most children do not have problems as severe as those in Cohen's project, and, at present, few institutions are equipped to provide the type of environment Cohen did. But children can be trained to help their peers learn good behavior in a way analogous to the social control adults tend to exert over each other and over children.

Solomon and Wheeler (1973) selected five "problem" children and five cooperative, popular children from a sixth-grade class of thirty students. Observation showed that under normal circumstances the other children paid attention to and gave social reinforcement to problem children only when they emitted undesirable behaviors. The cooperative children were then trained to attend to and reward behaviors deemed desirable by adults; then a cooperative child was seated next to each problem child. The cooperative children ignored problem behaviors, with the result that the "problem" children soon began to emit significantly fewer

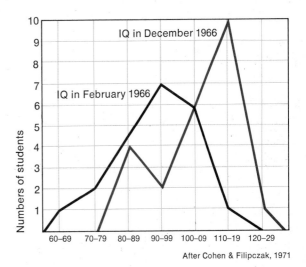

After Cohen & Filipczak, 1971

● **FREQUENCY DISTRIBUTION OF IQ SCORES FOR TWENTY-FOUR STUDENTS**

Recently six inmates at San Quentin brought a civil lawsuit against the California prison system, charging that prolonged solitary confinement in the "maximum adjustment" center constituted cruel and unusual punishment. These men, the "San Quentin Six," had been housed in their solitary cells for over three years, being indicted for the murder of the guards during the George Jackson escape episode of August 21, 1971. Although the indictment was quashed, the State was still holding these men in solitary until its legal appeal was settled. The San Quentin Six claimed that they were brutalized by the guards and dehumanized by the situation; the prison system denied such allegations.

On the basis of the possibly relevant knowledge uncovered in the Stanford simulated prison experiment, Zimbardo was invited to be an expert witness for these plaintiffs. He observed their living conditions, interviewed each of the inmates, as well as former guards and inmates, and reviewed all relevant psychological literature. The parallels with various aspects of the simulated prison study were remarkably close in many ways. Zimbardo's observations and conclusions were presented to Federal Judge Zirpoli as part of the evidence on which to base his decision in the case.

In his opinion, issued December 15, 1975, Judge Zirpoli stated: "it is evident that the continued segregated confinement of plaintiffs ["the San Quentin Six"] to the first tier of the Adjustment Center not only militates against reform and rehabilitation of plaintiffs, but is so counterproductive that it instills in them a deeper hatred for and alienation from the society that initially and justly put them there" (p. 20). . . . "Psychiatric and psychological experts testified that AC conditions threaten the sanity of and dehumanize plaintiffs in a way that will only be fully known after they are released" (p. 6). He concluded that such continued segregation "constitutes cruel and unusual punishment in violation of the Eighth and Fourteenth Amendments to the Constitution of the United States" (p. 21).

undesirable behaviors and significantly more prosocial behaviors. Interestingly, the cooperative children did not reinforce desirable behaviors, or else did so in ways that the adult observers did not notice. Nevertheless, undesirable behaviors were reduced in frequency by peers simply not noticing them. Perhaps this allowed more positive responses to be emitted and reinforced by the teacher or by the absence of expected negative reinforcement.

This study is important in that it showed that, in the natural setting, peers reinforce problem peers for "bad" behavior exclusively and that "problem" behavior is very susceptible to peer influence. If cooperative peers can be trained to influence problem peers routinely, problem behaviors could be eliminated even in situations where adult influence would be difficult or impossible to exert.

Children are being recognized as one of the most disadvantaged, powerless groups in society—neither listened to nor seen as they are (see *Harvard Educational Review,* 1973, 1974—Special Issues on "The Rights of Children"). Previous research and teacher training has too often dealt with ways for adults to gain still more power over children who are "troublemakers." A recent study is turning the tables and training children in techniques for influencing and shaping their teachers (Gray, Graubard, & Rosenberg, 1974). In this research, entitled "Little Brother Is Changing You," problem children from the rural California town of Visalia are being taught to shape the behavior of their teachers. They are learning to record data on satisfactory versus unsatisfactory interactions and to recognize behaviors of their own that are rewarding or nonrewarding to teachers. In order to shape the teachers to interact helpfully and pleasantly with them, they must provide social reinforcement for the teachers when the teachers emit the desired response. Teachers describe students as well behaved when they provide such reinforcement, so the whole relationship improves. These children are also being taught to shape their parents into more satisfactory supervisors and housekeepers, and to shape their peers toward more pleasant interaction. The beauty of the method is that those who would control must provide what their "clients" want in order to reward the behaviors they in turn desire.

Psychologists are being called upon more and more to add their knowledge and orientation to the decision-making processes that occur in various legal, social, and political settings. Awareness of behavioral dynamics, of subtle sources of motivation, of the impact of situational forces on behavior, of the sources of subjective bias are but some of the contributions a psychologist may bring to such deliberations (see Brodsky, 1973).

Surprisingly, the research on the simulated prison by Zimbardo and associates, reported in Chapter 13, turned out to be the only available evidence for a Senate subcommittee hearing on the effects of juvenile pretrial detention. The study was one involving juveniles arrested and booked by the police and detained prior to an alleged court hearing. Senator Birch Bayh, the Chairman of that subcommittee, subsequently introduced legislation designed to improve and humanize the treatment of juveniles suspected of criminal offenses. He has said that his thinking was indeed influenced by this research evidence. (See *P&L* Close-up, p. 680, for another social consequence of this research.)

There are, of course, a host of other examples we might cite of psychology for the good of people and society—going all the way from new approaches to controlling hypertension to anti-litter research projects and citizen training in crime prevention through re-creating a sense of community values. Some psychologists are at work trying to elevate the level of moral functioning of prison guards and inmates, while others are studying the elements that will contribute to the most meaningful experience in child-care centers (the major new social experiment of the seventies). Some are trying to discover means of overcoming feelings of shyness and loneliness, while their colleagues strive to uncover the basis for lasting commitments and affectional bonds. This is a psychology quite different from that envisioned by Wilhelm Wundt in his little brass-instrument laboratory in Leipzig nearly a hundred years ago. But we are witnessing a curious merger of the scientific search for knowledge, regularity, and order and the humanistic quest for understanding, acceptance, and personal fulfillment. There is no reason why modern psychology cannot do both.

However, it is well for psychologists and psychology students to heed the wisdom of Judge David Bazelon (1972) before rushing out to put a band-aid on the world. He asked a group of correctional psychologists:

"Why should we even consider fundamental social changes or massive income redistribution if the entire problem can be solved by having scientists teach the criminal class—like a group of laboratory rats—to march successfully through the maze of our society? In short, before you respond with enthusiasm to our pleas for help, you must ask yourselves whether your help is really needed, or whether you are merely engaged as magicians to perform an intriguing side-show so that the spectators will not notice the crisis in the center ring. In considering our motives for offering you a role, I think you would do well to consider how much less expensive it is to hire a thousand psychologists than to make even a minuscule change in the social and economic structure." (p. 6)

And so as we end our introduction to psychology, we hope you will see it as an introduction for you and not merely as an end to a course.

Every exit is an entry somewhere else.
Tom Stoppard, *Rosencrantz and Guildenstern Are Dead*, 1967

We hope that "somewhere else" will be a good place for you to be.

Basic Concepts in Statistics

Statistics provide us with a method of reporting and evaluating the results of psychological research. Just as the student of business administration must learn accounting in order to derive the full meaning from sales and profit figures, the psychologist must employ statistical methods and formulas in order to draw valid generalizations about human behavior and mental processes from observations. Complicated as these methods may seem at first glance, they are really ways of reducing a mass of data to terms that the mind can grasp.

Psychologists, like any other scientists, devote a great deal of time to making observations. These observations are the raw material with which they work. Having made a series of observations, they try to integrate them into a theoretical framework or use them to find the solution to a particular problem or the answer to a question. This involves various statistical procedures. The first step is to put the observations into numerical form so that they can be handled statistically. This is done by means of *psychological measuring devices* based on one of the scales of measurement described below.

Once the psychologist's observations are put into numerical form, they may be used for two major purposes: description and inference. *Descriptive statistics* enable us to describe, organize, and summarize sets of data from observations of groups in a convenient and efficient way. For example, descriptive statistics would enable us to tell how bright a particular group of freshmen are, as a group, and whether they are all at about the same level of ability or vary widely among themselves. Descriptive statistics would also enable us to compare their scores on two or more tests. *Inferential statistics* would enable us to *infer* how typical they are of freshmen in general and would tell us how much confidence we could have in particular inferences that we might make about them.

Psychological Measurement

Measurement in psychology, as in other fields, may be defined as assigning numbers to persons, objects, or events in accordance with certain rules. Psychologists make use of four different *scales of measurement: nominal, ordinal, interval,* and *ratio* scales. Each of these scales has certain distinguishing characteristics, as described below.

Nominal Scales

The lowest level of measurement—that is, the level of measurement that imparts the least information—is the nominal scale. Numbers are used only to distinguish one individual or group from another. Examples of the use of the nominal scale are the numbering of football players, of congressional districts, and of license plates. The numbers used do not represent an *amount* of anything, nor does a high number stand for more of something than a low number. The numbers merely differentiate one individual or class from another. Some argument might be made as to whether this is measurement at all, but it does fall under the definition, "assigning numbers to persons, objects, or events according to certain rules."

The essence of measurement on the nominal scale is *qualitative classification*. We might classify registered voters by assigning to them the number of the congressional district in which they live. Since there are many persons in the same congressional district, each number would be assigned to more than one individual. In some uses of nominal measurement, such as the numbering of license plates, there is only one person per class.

While a particular category may contain more than one individual, no individual may be assigned to more than one category. A person cannot be in two congressional districts, nor can a football player have two numbers. Thus in nominal measurement persons, objects, or events are put into *mutually exclusive* categories.

Ordinal Scales

Measurement on an ordinal scale not only distinguishes one individual from another, but also tells us whether a person has more or less of the trait being measured than other persons in the group. An example of the ordinal scale is the order in which runners cross the finish line in a race. The runner who finishes first is faster than the runner who finishes second, who in turn is faster than the runner who finishes third, and so on. By noting the order in which the runners cross the finish line, we have measured their speed on the ordinal scale.

Ordinal measurement, however, gives no information as to the amount of difference between two individuals in the trait being measured. Thus, although we know that the first-place runner is faster than the second-place runner, we do not know how much faster. Nor do we know whether the difference in speed between the first- and second-place runners is the same as between the third- and fourth-place runners. Ordinal measurement is used quite frequently by psychologists, because psychological traits are often difficult to measure on a quantitative scale.

Interval Scales

The interval scale has all the properties of the nominal and ordinal scales and in addition the property of equal units. This means that equal differences in scores represent equal differences in what is being measured. An example of the interval scale is the temperature scale, as found on a thermometer. The difference in temperature between 99 and 100 degrees centigrade is the same as the difference between 49 and 50 degrees centigrade, or any other difference of one degree centigrade. In other words, the *intervals* are equal throughout the scale. By measuring temperature on an *interval* scale, we know not only that one object is hotter or colder than another, but also *how much* hotter or colder.

Measurement on the interval scale does not, however, give us information as to the ratio of two objects with respect to the quantity being measured. Thus, it would be incorrect to say that an object whose temperature is 50 degrees centigrade is twice as warm as an object of 25 degrees. This statement would be correct if 0 degrees centigrade were an absolute zero—that is, if an object at 0 degrees had no warmth at all. In fact, however, absolute zero occurs at −273 degrees centigrade. Thus, an object at 25 degrees is really 298 degrees warmer than absolute zero, and an object at 50 degrees is 323 degrees warmer than absolute zero. The second object, then, is clearly not twice as warm as the first.

Ratio Scales

The ratio scale is the highest level of measurement. It has all the properties of the other previously mentioned scales, and the additional property of an absolute zero as its point of origin. This is the scale upon which the common physical measurements of length, time, and weight are made. Since the scale has an absolute zero, statements of ratios are meaningful. Thus, a six-inch line is twice as long as a three-inch line, a two-pound object is one fifth as heavy as a ten-pound object, and so on.

Psychologists usually have no knowledge of the absolute zero point of the measuring devices they use and therefore must be wary about comparing percentages or other proportions. For example, given that Mary has an IQ of 100 and Susan has an IQ of 110, we cannot say that Susan is 10 percent brighter than Mary. There are, however, rare instances in psychological measurement where such statements are possible.

The properties of these four common measurement scales can be summarized as follows:

Properties	Nominal Scale	Ordinal Scale	Interval Scale	Ratio Scale
Classification	X	X	X	X
Order		X	X	X
Equal Units			X	X
Absolute Zero				X

As can be seen in the table, each of these levels of measurement has all the properties of lower levels, plus an additional property. The higher the level of measurement, the more information is given about the attribute being measured. It is for this reason that psychologists, like other scientists, strive to use the highest level of measurement possible in a given situation.

The Use of Descriptive Statistics

Once data have been collected by means of psychological measurement, descriptive statistics are used to summarize them so that conclusions may be drawn. A descriptive statistic is a single number that stands for a series of measurements collected on a group. There are a great many different statistics used in psychological research. The choice of a statistic will depend on both the measurement scale used and the information wanted.

Since different statistics require different numerical operations, the level of measurement must be a consideration in determining which statistic to use. The higher the level of measurement, the more numerical operations are possible. We have seen that measurement on the nominal scale has only the property of classification. The numbers that represent the various classes are only labels; they do not express quantity. It would therefore be meaningless or even misleading to add them, subtract them, or perform any other numerical operation. Ratio-scale data, on the other hand, may be added, subtracted, multiplied, and divided.

The more basic consideration in choosing a statistic is, of course, what information we want. The three types of information most commonly needed in psychological research are: (a) what is the average or most representative score value (central value), (b) how much do the other scores differ from the average score (variability), and (c) what is the interrelationship between two or more variables, as represented by different sets of scores?

Measures of Central Value

Suppose some psychologists were studying the attributes of various religious groups. They would first have to classify their subjects by religion. Their measuring instrument might be a questionnaire asking each subject to state his or her religion. If they succeed in putting each subject into one and only one class from a list of several religions, they have measured the subjects' religion on the nominal scale. Suppose they now want to describe their sample by stating the religion of the "average" subject. There are several statistics that indicate a group's average measurement, but since they used only nominal measurement, they must use the central value statistic that is applicable to the nominal scale. This is the *mode*.

The mode. The mode of a group of nominal measurements is the class with the most members. For example, in the table below, the mode is Protestant since more subjects in the group are of the Protestant religion than any other religion.

Religion	Number of Subjects
1. Protestant	88 mode
2. Catholic	37
3. Jewish	17
4. Other	5

Since a table such as this shows how the individuals are distributed among the various classes, it is called a *distribution*. We often refer to a group of measurements as a distribution; when they are arranged in order from highest to lowest frequency, the array is called a *frequency distribution*.

The median. If we have at least ordinal measurement — that is, if the classifications can be put in order so that each class represents more of what we are measuring than those classes following it — another central value statistic may be used to describe the group.

Suppose we wanted to summarize the ranks of a group of army officers attending a military conference. By noting the insignia on their shoulders we could measure their ranks. Since these measurements can be put in order, we have measurement on the ordinal scale. In this table every rank is higher than the ranks below it and lower than the ranks above it.

Rank	Number of Cases
7. General	2
6. Colonel	3
5. Lieutenant Colonel	6
4. Major	9
3. Captain	10 median
2. First Lieutenant	8
1. Second Lieutenant	12 mode
	50 total cases

Higher numbers have been used to label higher ranks to preserve this order. These numbers are arbitrary in some respects; we might just as well have used 99 for General, 98 for Colonel, and so on down to Second Lieutenant. As long as the higher of two numbers always stands for the higher of the two ranks, the ordinal property is preserved.

A measure of central value that we can use for these data is the *median*. The median is the number that splits the distribution in half, so that half the cases are higher and half are lower. Since there are 50 cases altogether, the median is the rank that 25 cases are below and 25 are above. We see from the table that 20 officers are First Lieutenant or below and 20 are Major or higher. Since it is impossible to split the distribution exactly in half, we come as close to it as possible and say the median is somewhere in Rank 3 — Captain.

If we wished, we could also use the mode as a measure of central value. The mode of this distribution of measurements is 1, since there are more Second Lieutenants than any other rank. The choice between these two statistics will depend on what information is wanted. If we use the mode to represent all members of the group, we will be exactly right more times than if we use any other value. However, if we want the central value of rank that will have as many officers above it as below it, we will choose the median. To state this another way, suppose we wanted to guess the rank of an officer. If we used the mode, we would have the highest probability of being exactly right. If we used the median, the probability of guessing too low would be the same as the probability of guessing too high.

The mean. If measurement is on the interval scale or higher, still a third measure of central value may be used. This is the *mean*.[1] The mean is calculated by adding together all the measurements and dividing by the number of cases.

If we want to know the average verbal comprehension ability of a group of high-school students, we can begin by measuring their verbal comprehension with a test. If a test has been carefully constructed, we usually assume that it yields measurements on an interval scale. Here, we will assume that equal differences in test

[1]The exact term is *arithmetic mean*, as distinguished from other means, such as the geometric mean. Since these other statistics are seldom used in psychology, *arithmetic mean* is usually abbreviated to *mean;* or M or $\bar{X}$.

scores stand for equal differences in verbal comprehension. Suppose the scores on the test, arranged in order from highest to lowest, are as follows:

Student	Verbal Comprehension Score (X)
John	20
Mary	18
Shirley	18
Peter	17
Alice	16
Nancy	13 ⎫ mean
Henry	13 ⎭
Diane	12 median
Douglas	11
Sam	11
Harvey	10 ⎫
Jane	10 ⎬ mode
Barbara	10 ⎭
David	9
Roger	7
	Sum = ΣX = 195

The first step in calculating the mean is to add all the scores. The sum of all the scores is denoted by the symbol, ΣX, which is read, "sum of the X's." The capital Greek letter *sigma* (Σ) stands for "the sum of . . . ." The capital letter X stands for each of the scores in turn. By adding up all the scores, we find that $\Sigma X = 195$.

The second step in computing the mean is to divide ΣX by N, the total number of cases. The formula for the mean is:

$$\text{mean (or } \overline{X}) = \frac{\Sigma X}{N}$$

where $\overline{X}$ stands for the mean. This formula is read, "The *mean* is equal to the *sum* of the X's divided by the *number* of X's." Since there are 15 scores, we can calculate the mean as follows:

$$\overline{X} = \frac{\Sigma X}{N} = \frac{195}{15} = 13$$

Thus, the mean of the above scores is 13. That is, the average verbal comprehension score of this group of students is 13.

The verbal comprehension scores are interval data, so the mode, median, or mean *can* be used. Each of these central value statistics represents a different kind of "best guess."

If our purpose is to be exactly right most often, we would use the mode. More persons had a score of 10 than any other score, so 10 is the mode. In guessing the scores of individuals in the group, we would be exactly right 3 times if we guessed each student's score at 10. Of course, we would be wrong by some amount in guessing the scores of the other 12 students. In this case, too, we would usually be guessing too low, since 10 students have scores above the mode and only 2 have scores below it. If we wanted a guess that was too high as often as it was too low, we would use the median score, 12. This guess would be exactly right only once, but would be high 7 times and low 7 times.

Thus the median is in the "middle" of a distribution of scores in the sense that the same *number* of scores (though not the same *value* or *weight* of scores) are on both sides of it. But suppose that the three high scorers, John, Mary, and Shirley, had each gotten a score of 100. The median would still be 12, but this guess would be 88 points too low in three cases. The median would be too low the same *number* of times as it was too high, but the total *amount* by which it was too low would be much greater than the amount by which it was too high. If we want a guess that takes the amount of error into consideration, we will use the mean. The mean score of the fifteen students on verbal comprehension is 13. If we guess each student's verbal comprehension score at 13, the total amount by which this guess it too low will be equal to the total amount by which it is too high.

Central value statistics describing a group are the best guesses we can make about any member of that group. The mode is the guess most often right, the median has an equal chance of being too high or too low, and the mean may be too high by the same total amount as it may be too low.

Measures of Variability

Human beings differ, as we have seen throughout this text. They differ in the way they respond to stimuli. They differ in their ability to learn and to perceive.

The purpose of a variability statistic is to tell us how spread out a distribution is. Stated another way, it tells us how well or how poorly a single central value statistic represents all of the scores in a distribution. If all the scores are closely bunched together, each score is well represented by a central value statistic such as the mean. But if not, if the distribution is spread widely apart, then the central value statistic will be off target as the average estimate for many of the individual scores represented in the distribution. There are several measures that indicate the variability within a group.

The range. Perhaps the simplest way to get an idea of how spread out a distribution is, is to find the *range*. The range is the difference between the highest and lowest scores. In the table of verbal comprehension scores, the highest score is 20 and the lowest is 7. Therefore, the range is $20 - 7 = 13$.

Variability statistics, like central value statistics, must be appropriate to the level of measurement used. The range requires *interval* measurement, since subtraction is involved. On a scale without equal units, subtraction would be meaningless.

The range is a relatively uninformative measure of variability, since it depends on only two of the scores. Suppose one student had made a score of 3 on the verbal comprehension test. This single score would have increased the range by nearly one third. A variability measure, or any other statistic, that uses all of the scores in a distribution will give more information than one that uses just a few.

The standard deviation. With measurements on the interval scale, the most common measure of variability is the standard deviation. Every score in the distribution is used in its computation. More specifically, it is based on each score's deviation from the mean. A score's deviation from the mean is denoted by the small letter x. Mathematically it may be expressed by the formula:

$$x = X - \overline{X}$$

which means, "The *deviation* is equal to the *score* minus the *mean*."

At first thought, it might seem that a good way to measure variability, using all the scores, would be simply to average all these deviations. To do so, however, would prove disappointing. Remember, the deviation of a score is equal to that score minus the mean. If a score is above the mean it will have a positive deviation. If it is below the mean it will have a negative deviation. We have seen that the total amount by which the mean is too low (the positive deviation) is equal to the amount by which the mean is too high (the negative deviation). Thus if all the plus and minus deviations are added together, they cancel out, and the result is zero. Mathematically,

$$\Sigma x = 0$$

This will be true of any group of scores. To avoid this, each deviation can be squared (multiplied by itself) before adding.[2] Since a positive number multiplied by a positive number results in a positive number, and a negative number multiplied by a negative number also results in a positive number, all squared deviations must be positive, and the average of these *squared* deviations can easily be obtained:

$$s^2 = \frac{\Sigma x^2}{N}$$

The symbol s^2 is called the *variance*. The above formula is read, "The *variance* is equal to the *sum of the squared deviations* divided by the *number of cases*."

The reason that the variance is shown as the square of a quantity is to reflect the fact that all the deviations were squared before averaging. The variance is therefore expressed in terms of a different unit from the original measurements. If the original measurements were verbal comprehension scores, the variance would be in terms of squared verbal comprehension scores. To remove the squaring operation and provide a

[2]There are other, more mathematically sophisticated reasons for squaring the deviations, but a discussion of them is beyond the scope of this book.

VARIANCE AND STANDARD DEVIATION

Student	Verbal Comprehension Score X	Deviation from Mean x	Deviation Squared x^2
John	20	7	49
Mary	18	5	25
Shirley	18	5	25
Peter	17	4	16
Alice	16	3	9
Nancy	13 ⎫ mean	0	0
Henry	13 ⎭	0	0
Diane	12	−1	1
Douglas	11	−2	4
Sam	11	−2	4
Harvey	10	−3	9
Jane	10	−3	9
Barbara	10	−3	9
David	9	−4	16
Roger	7	−6	36
Sums	195	0	212

1. Add all the scores. This sum is called ΣX.

$$\Sigma X = 195$$

2. Divide this sum by the number of scores (N). This is the mean, $\bar{X}$.

$$\bar{X} = \frac{\Sigma X}{N} = \frac{195}{15} = 13$$

3. Subtract the mean from each score to find each deviation, x. (See "Deviation from Mean" column)

$$x = X - \bar{X}$$

4. Square each deviation. That is, multiply each deviation by itself. (See "Deviation Squared" column)

$$x^2 = (X - \bar{X})^2$$

5. Add all the squared deviations. The result is designated as Σx^2.

$$\Sigma x^2 = 212$$

6. Divide this sum by the number of scores to find the variance, s^2.

$$s^2 = \frac{\Sigma x^2}{N} = \frac{212}{15} = 14.13$$

7. Find the square root of the variance. This is the standard deviation, s.

$$s = \sqrt{\frac{\Sigma x^2}{N}} = \sqrt{14.13} = 3.8$$

measure of variability in terms of the same units as the measurements from which it was derived, the square root of the variance is often used as a measure of variability. This is called the *standard deviation,* and its symbol is the letter s. It is computed by the formula:

$$s = \sqrt{\frac{\Sigma x^2}{N}}$$

The steps used to compute the standard deviation are given in the figure. The verbal comprehension test scores are used for this example. ■

The mean score is 13, and the standard deviation is 3.8. These two statistics give us a summary of the fifteen scores. The mean gives us a representative figure for the level of the group as a whole and the standard deviation a representative figure for all the deviations, because it indicates how closely the scores cluster around the mean.

Standard scores. We have seen that measures of variability are useful ways of summarizing the individual differences in a group. They can also serve to establish a standard unit. Suppose that the high-school students who took the verbal comprehension test were also given a spelling test. We might then wonder if a student is as good in verbal comprehension as in spelling. Suppose the means on the tests and the scores of one student, John, are as follows:

Test	Mean Scores	John's Scores
Verbal Comprehension	13	20
Spelling	44	48

We know that John is above average on both tests. But we do not know *how much* above average. We cannot compare his two scores because we do not know whether one point on one test is equivalent to one point on the other test. Chances are that it is not. Suppose that one point on the spelling test is worth 2 points on the verbal comprehension test. This would mean that the 4 points that John is above the mean on spelling would be equivalent to 8 points above the mean on verbal comprehension. Since John was only 7 points above average on verbal comprehension, we would know that his spelling score was higher. On the other hand, if the units on the two tests are equivalent, he is better in verbal comprehension.

In order to relate the units on one test to the units on the other, we can make use of our measures of variability. We know that the standard deviation of the verbal comprehension scores is 3.8. John's score of 20 is 7 points above the mean, or almost 2 standard deviations above it (1.8 to be exact). Suppose we computed the standard deviation of the distribution of scores on the spelling test, and found it to be equal to 4. This would mean that John was one standard deviation above the mean in spelling, while he was almost two standard deviations above the mean in verbal comprehension. We could then say that John did better in verbal comprehension than in spelling.

The standard deviation, then, can be used as a unit for comparing a person's standing on two tests. Any individual's deviation from the mean can be expressed in terms of this unit. Scores expressed this way are called *standard scores* and are given the symbol z. John's score, at 1.8 standard deviations above the mean, gives him a standard score of 1.8. If John had made the mean score, 13, his z score would be 0. If he had scored below the mean, his z score would be a negative number.

Often two different tests will be of different length or difficulty or will use different units of measurement with the result that scores on the two tests are not comparable. If someone got 82 on one test and 450 on another, for example, you would have no idea just looking at the scores whether one was better than the other. On the other hand, the standard scores on the two tests would be expressed in comparable units—standard deviations—so that you could tell at once whether one was better than the other.

What a standard score gives us is a person's position in the group in which he or she took the test. Therefore, if we compared John's standard score in verbal comprehension with his standard score in spelling, we would be answering the question, "Is John's *relative* performance in spelling better or worse than his *relative* performance in verbal comprehension?"

The standard deviation can be computed only if there is a measurement scale of equal units. The standard deviation, like the arithmetic mean, may therefore be used only when measurement is at least at the interval scale.

Measures of Correlation

Up to this point we have been discussing statistics that describe a single set of measurements. Psychology is usually concerned with many different variables, hence with many different sets of measurements. A question frequently asked in psychological research is, "To what extent are two sets of scores related?" For example, if we gave a verbal comprehension test and a spelling test to the same group of individuals, we might wonder to what extent persons who scored high on one test also scored high on the other. One way to find out would be to write down the names of all the persons scoring above the mean on the verbal comprehension test and see how many of them scored above the mean on the spelling test. This would give us a rough idea of the *correlation* between the two tests. If most of the high scorers on one test scored high on the other test too, we would say there was a high *positive correlation*. If most of the high scorers on one scored low on the other, we would say there was a high *negative correlation*.

Correlation coefficients and what they mean. Let us now approach an understanding of correlation by building on our knowledge of standard scores (z scores). Suppose that all the scores on the spelling and verbal comprehension tests are converted to standard scores, and assume further that each individual's z score on the spelling test is the same as his or her z score on the verbal comprehension test. In such a case, the tests are said to have a perfect positive correlation. This result is shown in the graph below, in which each dot represents an individual, and the scores of any individual can be read from the horizontal and vertical axes. For example, John (the circled dot) made a z score of 1.8 on both tests. With a perfect correlation, individual scores on one test can be predicted exactly if we know their scores on the other test.

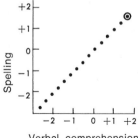

Verbal comprehension

Suppose now that every individual who scored high on verbal comprehension scored low, by an equal amount, on spelling. That is, everyone was as poor on one test as he or she was good on the other; the best speller was worst on verbal comprehension, and vice versa. A graph of this result follows:

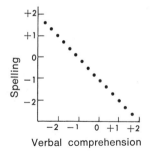

Verbal comprehension

In both of these examples, scores on one test were perfectly related to scores on the other. At the other extreme, suppose the scores are completely unrelated. In this case the best speller might be good, average, or poor on verbal comprehension. Knowledge of an individual's spelling ability would tell us nothing about that person's verbal comprehension. The graph of such a result might look like this:

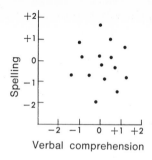

Verbal comprehension

Often two variables are correlated, but not perfectly correlated. In a graph of such a relationship, the dots are not in a straight line, nor do they form a circle; their pattern is oval. The flatter the oval—the nearer it is to a straight line—the higher the correlation.

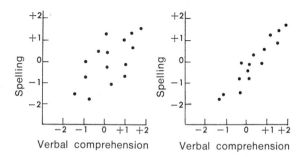

Verbal comprehension   Verbal comprehension

As you saw in Chapter 1 (p. 36), the amount by which two variables are correlated is expressed in the *coefficient of correlation (r)*. In computing a correlation, z scores are used according to the following formula:

$$r = \frac{\Sigma z_x z_y}{N}$$

According to this formula, "The correlation coefficient is equal to the sum of each person's z score on one test multiplied by his or her z score on the other test, divided by the number of people." The actual calculation looks complicated but is simple and straightforward. The steps in computing a correlation using the spelling and verbal comprehension test scores are shown in the figure. ● In this case, z_x is the standard score for the verbal comprehension test and z_y is the standard score for the spelling test.

Correlation coefficients, as you also saw in Chapter 1, can range from +1 (perfect positive correlation) through 0 (no correlation) to −1 (perfect negative correlation). In actual practice, perfect correlations, either positive or negative, are rare; they are only approached — a correlation of .90 being a very high one.

The correlation coefficient in prediction. Statisticians have determined what percentage of those who fall in the upper half of the distribution on one trait can be expected to fall in the upper half of the distribution on another when there is a given correlation between two normally distributed traits. Below are representative correlation coefficients and their corresponding percentages:

	Percent in Better Half on Test A Who Will Fall:	
Correlation Coefficient	in better half on Test B	in worse half on Test B
.00	50	50
.05	52	48
.10	53	47
.20	56	44
.30	60	40
.40	63	37
.50	67	33
.60	70	30
.70	75	25
.80	80	20
.90	86	14
.95	90	10
1.00	100	0

As you can see from the table, the accuracy of prediction varies with the degree of correlation between the two variables being considered. For example, if you know that the correlation between two tests is .90, you can predict that 86 percent of those who were in the upper half on the verbal comprehension test will also be in the upper half on the spelling test. But 14 percent will not be, and there is always the possibility that the particular individual you are concerned about is among this 14 percent. Thus in predicting a particular individual's score, the most you can do is indicate a probability. In this case, you can say the person's chances of being in the upper half on the second test are 86 out of 100.

● **CORRELATION**

Student	Verbal Comprehension		Spelling		
	X	$z_x = \dfrac{X - \bar{X}}{s_x}$	Y	$z_y = \dfrac{Y - \bar{Y}}{s_y}$	$z_x z_y$
John	20	1.8	48	0.8	1.44
Mary	18	1.3	45	0.2	0.26
Shirley	18	1.3	45	0.2	0.26
Peter	17	1.1	57	2.5	2.75
Alice	16	0.8	39	−0.9	−0.72
Nancy	13	0.0	42	−0.4	0.0
Henry	13	0.0	52	1.5	0.0
Diane	12	−0.3	43	−0.2	0.06
Douglas	11	−0.5	47	0.6	−0.30
Sam	11	−0.5	44	0.0	0.0
Harvey	10	−0.8	41	−0.6	0.48
Jane	10	−0.8	37	−1.3	1.04
Barbara	10	−0.8	43	−0.2	0.16
David	9	−1.1	40	−0.8	0.88
Roger	7	−1.6	37	−1.3	2.08

$$\Sigma z_x z_y = 8.39$$

1. Compute the means and the standard deviations for both of the variables being correlated.

$$\bar{X} = 13 \qquad s_x = 3.8$$

(See p. 688)

$$\bar{Y} = 44 \qquad s_y = 5.3$$

(Obtained in the same manner as $\bar{X}$)

2. Convert each score to a standard score by subtracting its mean and dividing by its standard deviation.

(See z_x and z_y columns)

3. Multiply the two standard scores together for each individual in the group.

(See $z_x z_y$ column)

4. Find the arithmetic mean of these products by adding them together and dividing by the number of individuals.

$$r = \frac{\Sigma z_x z_y}{N} = \frac{8.39}{15} = .56$$

Conclusion: There is a moderate positive correlation.

The Use of Statistical Inference

The greatest value of statistical methodology lies in the fact that it allows us to generalize. Psychologists do not usually wish to confine their conclusions to the specific groups that they select for observation or experimentation. Instead, they hope to find relationships that will apply to much larger groups or to human beings in general. This procedure of drawing general conclusions by studying samples is called *statistical inference*. In developing general theories of human behavior, it would be impossible to study all human beings under all conditions. Experimental psychologists will, therefore, deduce a specific hypothesis from a theory and design an experiment to test it on a sample. If the results come out as hypothesized, they have increased their confidence in the validity of the theory. If the results are contrary to the hypothesis, they have reason to suspect the validity of the theory.

Statistical inference is sometimes used in investigations that are not concerned with theory, but that attempt to find the answer to a specific practical question. This is the area of applied research. A common example of statistical inference in applied research is the public opinion poll. The accuracy of the pollsters in making predictions of group behavior after interviewing only a small sample of the group is an example of the power of statistical inference techniques.

The basic steps in statistical inference, whether theoretical or applied, are as follows:

1. Define a *population*. The population (sometimes called a *universe*) is the whole group in which the researcher is ultimately interested. It may be as general as all human beings, or even all living organisms. It may be as specific as all freshmen in a certain college or all registered voters in a certain congressional district.

2. Draw a *sample* from the population. The sample is the group of subjects upon which the research is conducted.

3. *Measure* the sample. This is the actual research or experimentation. Depending on the nature of the research, this measurement might be as simple as asking the subjects whom they intend to vote for in the next election. On the other hand, it might be extremely complex, perhaps including dividing the sample into several experimental groups, exposing each group to different experimental conditions, and measuring their responses to these conditions.

4. Compute one or more *descriptive statistics*. As we have seen, descriptive statistics summarize a series of measurements.

5. Use the descriptive statistics to make *inferences* about the population, with the aid of tests of statistical inference.

Sampling

Sampling, as you might surmise, is the process of drawing a sample from a population. Whatever sampling procedure is used, it must be one that assures that the sample is truly representative of the population. More specifically, the sample must represent, within known limits, all characteristics of the population that are related to the experimental problem. Otherwise, the sample is called a *biased* one.

There are many methods of sampling, the most common of which is *random sampling*. In random sampling there are two requirements: (a) each member of the population must have the same probability of appearing in the sample; (b) the probability of each member being selected must be independent of whether or not any other member is selected. An example of random sampling is the choosing of the winners in a well-run lottery. All the tickets (the population) are thoroughly mixed, and the winners (the sample) are selected blindly. Technically, random sampling requires the replacement of each winning ticket before drawing the next, so that it is possible for the same ticket to be drawn more than once. If the population is large, however, this refinement is insignificant. A less cumbersome method of random sampling is to assign consecutive numbers to each member of the population and then select numbers from a table in which all numbers appear in random order. These tables are so constructed that the probability of any number appearing in any position on the list is the same. One such table is published in book form (Rand, 1955).

Once a sample is drawn, measurements are taken and descriptive statistics computed. Such statistics may then serve as estimates of their counterparts in the population as a whole. These counterparts are called *parameters*.

Even the best estimate of a parameter contains a certain margin of error. It is important to know just how great this error is. Such knowledge is obtained by means of a mathematical model. A model is an abstraction that is used to describe real-world phenomena. The model most often used by psychologists in this case is called the *normal distribution*.

The Normal Distribution

As explained in Chapter 10, a very typical finding in psychological research is that most individuals cluster near the mean of a distribution of scores. The farther from the mean a given score is, the fewer individuals will have that score. On page 451 we showed how the scores of 1000 persons selected at random and administered a test of some psychological characteristic would probably be distributed.

We can identify three properties of this distribution of scores: (a) the number of persons with a given score diminishes as the distance of that score from the mean increases; (b) the distribution is symmetrical about the mean; (c) the mode, the median, and the mean are equal.

This frequency distribution can be approximated by a *bell-shaped curve* that encloses all the scores. Because frequency distributions of psychological measurements are so often closely approximated by the bell-shaped curve, it is convenient to take this curve as a model, or ideal case. This model, the *normal distribution,* is a generalization about frequency distributions, just as "50-50," for example, is a generalization about the odds in tossing coins. If a number of coins are tossed, the "model" expectation is that half will turn up heads. This is seldom exactly true, but as more coins are tossed, the

model is more closely approximated. The same thing is true also for the normal distribution: a perfect normal curve is never obtained from a sample of measurements, although the larger the sample, the more closely it will approximate the normal curve. An infinitely large population would be required to fit the mathematical definition of the curve perfectly. When obtained measurements closely approximate the normal curve, the assumption is often made that the sample has been drawn from a population that *does* fit the model exactly.

The normal distribution is an extremely useful model. If the distribution of a sample is approximately normal and we know its mean and standard deviation, we can construct a curve that supposedly will show what the distribution would be in the whole population from which the sample was drawn.

Approximately two thirds of the scores are within one standard deviation from the mean. Thus in the case of IQs, about two thirds of the area under the curve is between IQ values of 84 and 116, since the standard deviation is equal to 16.

Less than 3/10 of 1 percent of the scores are farther than three standard deviations from the mean. For this reason, the range of six standard deviations—three below the mean and three above it—is taken as representing the "practical" limits of a normal distribution. Unless a sample is extremely large, we will seldom find scores which exceed these limits.

Questions Answered by Inferential Statistics

Whenever you collect two groups of scores in randomly drawn samples, you are likely to find that their means differ to some extent, due to the operation of chance factors. If you flip a coin 1000 times, you should get heads approximately 500 times. But on only ten trials, you might not get exactly half heads. Thus when you observe only a small sample of data, you need some way of determining whether your observations are due to chance or can be attributed to some real, nonrandom event or process that is operating—a systematic source of bias.

The procedures of statistical inference introduce order into any attempt to draw conclusions that go beyond the observations made on particular samples. Some of the questions that can be answered by statistical inference are: (a) whether the sample of scores you have is really representative of some specified population, (b) whether an obtained difference between means of different samples is large enough that you can conclude they are probably drawn from different populations, and (c) whether the variance in scores *between* groups that have received different experimental treatments is greater than the scattering of the scores *within* each group. If two groups have different means but overlap a great deal, the difference between the two means may be due to chance rather than to the experimental treatments.

Every time you compare the scores of an experimental group with those of a control group at the end of an experiment, you are looking to see whether they are now representatives of two different populations as a result of the experimental treatment. The more different their new means and the less overlap there is, the more confidence you can have that there is a real difference. Thus you would expect to find it again if you were to replicate the experiment with two more samples from the original population. You can have more confidence that your statistical test is revealing a valid, meaningful effect, or a difference upon which you can rely: the more often and the more consistently you find the difference, the bigger it is, the larger your samples, and the greater your between-group differences as compared with your within-group differences.

Various statistical tests are available to use in answering the general questions posed above and the particular questions being raised by a given researcher. We can only name a few common ones here and indicate what they do. For example, the most common test for comparing the frequencies of various possible events that you actually find with the frequencies that would be predicted is called the *Chi-square* (χ^2) test. The test for comparing the differences between two sets of scores is called the *t-test*. The test for comparing between-group variability with within-group variability for two or more groups is called the *analysis of variance* or *F-test*.

This short appendix has been an extremely quick survey of concepts normally covered in a first course in statistics. Only the highlights have been covered, and these very briefly. Nonetheless, a general grasp of the material presented here will be of great help in interpreting the results of much published psychological research.

Psychology and Life · Ninth Edition

Glossary
References
Acknowledgments
Name Index
Subject Index

Glossary

Abnormal behavior. Behavior considered to be maladaptive or deviant by the individual or the social group of which the person is a member. (463)

Absolute rating scale. See *Rating scale.*

Absolute refractory period. Period of a few milliseconds after an axon has fired during which the membrane is temporarily unexcitable, and during which the axon cannot be fired again regardless of the stimulus energy level. (61)

Abstinence syndrome. Commonly called withdrawal; a range of symptoms evidenced when individuals physically dependent on a drug are deprived further administration of that drug. (474)

Accommodation. Process postulated by Piaget by which previously developed cognitive structures are modified on the basis of new experiences. (189)

Acetylcholine. Chemical transmitter substance that probably facilitates the passage of a nerve impulse from one neuron to another across the synapse. (63)

Acquiescence set. Tendency to agree frequently and thus to answer "yes" to test questions, even when "no" would be more appropriate. (441)

ACTH. A hormone secreted by the anterior pituitary, which interacts with the secretions of the adrenal cortex—an important factor in physiological reactions to prolonged stress. (381)

Activation. Arousal or energy mobilization, which enables an organism to pursue its goals. (334)

Addiction. Physical or psychological dependence on such substances as drugs, alcohol, tobacco, or food, which results in compulsive behavior over which an individual does not have adequate self-control. (467)

Adenine. One of the four nucleotide bases that make up the DNA molecule; found paired with thymine. (54)

Adipocytes. Specialized cells that store body fat in the form of fatty acids; obese individuals have a greater number of these cells than do normal individuals. (343)

Adolescence. In humans, a transitional stage between puberty and maturity; an arbitrary classification. (666)

Adrenal cortex. Outer part of the pituitary glands, which secretes cortin, a hormone important in physiological reactions to prolonged stress. (381)

Adrenal glands. A pair of endocrine glands located at the upper end of the kidneys; consist of inner adrenal medulla, which secretes the hormones adrenaline and noradrenaline during strong emotion, and outer adrenal cortex, which secretes hormones that influence maturation. (372)

Adrenaline. See *Epinephrine.*

Affective reactions. Category of psychotic disorders characterized by severe fluctuations of mood or feeling. (487)

Affective states. Emotional states or experiences whether the emotions involved are mild or intense, pleasant or unpleasant. (367)

Afferent nerve fiber. Carries messages toward the central nervous system from a sensory receptor cell, for instance in the eye or ear; also known as a *sensory nerve fiber.* (67)

Affiliation. Tendency or desire to be with other people; a basic social need or motive of gregariousness basic for common life. (573)

Age regression. A special case of memory distortion in which hypnotized subjects are induced to reexperience events that occurred at some earlier period of their lives. (312)

Aggression. A response that destroys objects, causes harm to others or to oneself (or the explicit intention to do so); assumes many forms. (378)

Agnosia. An "inability to know"; a disorder of perception in which sensations cannot be organized into normal perceptions. (84)

Agnosticism. From the Greek word for "unknowable." A stand which holds that from a scientific, empirical standpoint, no conclusions about religious faith and the existence of God can be made on the grounds of unknowability. (12)

Alarm reaction. See *General adaptation syndrome.*

Alcohol. A type of psychoactive drug that acts to depress the central nervous system; it has a high potential for psychological and physiological dependence and leads to irreversible tissue damage. (293)

Alcoholism. A dependence on or addiction to alcohol; perhaps best described as a disease process wherein physical damage becomes progressively greater with the increased consumption of alcohol over time. (468)

Algorithm. Diagrammatic representation of the sequence of steps, choices, and actions in a process or activity; also known as *flow chart.* (220)

All-or-none principle. Principle stating that if a nerve fiber responds at all, it responds at its full strength. That is, as long as the stimulus strength is above the stimulus threshold, the nerve impulse fired by a particular neuron is always the same magnitude. (61)

Alpha waves. The electrical rhythm or EEG frequency typical of the brain during a relaxed state. (307)

Altered states of consciousness. States of consciousness in which an individual feels that there has been a qualitative shift in his or her pattern of mental functioning away from the "normal" waking state of experiencing consciousness. (277)

Altruism. Any conduct that helps others in the absence of anticipated external rewards for the helping deed. (574)

Amnesia. Loss of memory, especially of past personal experiences; may be a type of dissociative state. (480)

Amplitude of response. A measure of conditioning strength based on the extent or amount of the response (e.g., the amount of saliva secreted by Pavlov's dogs). (102)

Amygdala. Structure in the limbic area of the brain associated with flight and defense responses, primitive emotion, and sexual behavior. (80)

Anal stage. In psychoanalytic theory, the second stage of psychosexual development during which bowel control is achieved and the focus of pleasure is the eliminative processes. (413)

Androgynous personality. Individual who exhibits both ''masculine'' and ''feminine'' characteristics. (227)

Anonymity. State of being unknown; not imparting a sense of clearly marked individuality. (The anonymity of urban living robs individuals of their sense of identity.) (632)

Anorexia nervosa. Self-induced hunger; it is a rare, chronic disease that is difficult to treat, which almost exclusively afflicts young girls. (340)

Anthropomorphism. Attributing human qualities, feelings, and thoughts to lower animals or things. (20)

Antianxiety drugs. Drugs used for relieving anxiety; used in chemotherapy. (511)

Antidepressant drugs. Drugs that elevate mood and relieve depression; used in chemotherapy. (511)

Antipsychotic drugs. Drugs that suppress psychotic reactions; used in chemotherapy. (511)

Antisocial aggression. Aggression expressed in socially unacceptable ways. For example, rape. (611)

Anxiety neurosis. Type of neurosis characterized by chronic anxiety and apprehension; the felt anxiety is ''free floating,'' that is, it is not something perceived as threatening others in the same situation or anchored to a specific source. (476)

Aphasia. Impairment of ability to use or understand language, even though hearing and speech mechanisms are unimpaired; due to disease or damage to certain association areas of the brain. (84)

Appetitive conditioning. A form of respondent conditioning in which the conditioned response is a kind of ''seeking,'' appetitive behavior, such as salivation. (98)

Appraisal. The evaluation and judgment of the significance of a stimulus; it may result in moving the organism to action. Primary appraisal establishes threat potential, secondary appraisal assesses coping strategies to use on perceived threat. (376)

Approach gradient. Strengthening of the tendency to approach a desired goal as the subject draws nearer to it. Important in the understanding of certain conflict situations. (428)

Archetypes. In Jung's personality theory, universal symbols and predispositions inherited in the ''collective unconscious''; may appear in dreams. (287)

Arousal. General energizing component of attention and motivation; involves organs controlled by both central and autonomic nervous systems. (327)

Assimilation. Process whereby new cognitive elements are altered to make them more similar to familiar, already experienced ones, and to fit more easily into existing cognitive structures. (189)

Association areas. Areas of the cerebral cortex that serve to correlate and integrate simpler functions of the sensory and motor areas. (83)

Atmospheric perspective. A cue in depth perception based on the learned difference in clarity between near and far objects. (264)

Attribution. Process of attributing to individuals or their behavior inferred underlying conditions and causes. (563)

Attribution error. Tendency, in explaining or understanding a given action, for an individual to overestimate the importance of the actor's disposition while underestimating the importance of situational factors. (565)

Attribution theory. Heider's theory that we give both meaning and predictability to the events of our lives by developing both a reality orientation and a control orientation to the world through finding causal attributions for actions and events we perceive. (566)

Attribution therapy. Therapy based on the principle that a patient's problem often lies not so much in symptoms and feelings as in the meaning attached to them and the causes attributed to them; it operates by providing new or different interpretations for what is being experienced, and what are the causal agents of the experience. (470)

Audience. Those to whom a message is directed; a variable in the study of attitude change. (587)

Auditory nerve. Nerve that carries impulses from the auditory receptors in the inner ear to the brain. (248)

Authoritarian personality. A personality type characterized by individuals high in rigidity, prejudice, political and economic conservatism, and fascistic traits. (440)

Autism. Extreme form of childhood mental disturbance in which the child does not communicate or relate well to others or to the environment, or form an adequate self-concept. (491)

Autistic thinking. Thinking as an end in itself and not a means to an end; determined primarily by the individual's needs or desires, as in daydreaming. (185)

Autoerotic. Sexual arousal or excitement arising through oneself, without the participation or stimulation of another individual. (358)

Autonomic nervous system (ANS). The part of the peripheral nervous system that regulates bodily activities not ordinarily subject to voluntary control, including the visceral changes that occur during emotion; composed of the *sympathetic* and *parasympathetic* divisions. (66)

Autoshaping. Learning process in which a response increases in frequency through self-generated reinforcers rather than being shaped by contingent extrinsic reinforcement. (133)

Autosuggestion. A process of influencing one's own attitudes, behavior, or physical condition by mental processes other than conscious thought. For example, through the use of self-hypnosis. (314)

Aversive conditioning. A form of respondent conditioning in which the conditioned response is an attempt to avoid or escape from an aversive stimulus. (98)

Aversive learning. Form of counterconditioning through punishment, sometimes used in treating such disorders as homosexuality, stuttering, and alcoholism. (526)

Avoidance conditioning. A form of operant conditioning in which an organism can prevent (avoid) an aversive stimulus by making an appropriate response. (116–17)

Avoidance gradient. Strengthening of the tendency to go away from a feared place or object as the subject draws nearer to it; it is steeper in slope than approach gradient; important in the understanding of certain types of conflict situations. (428)

Axon. Long fiber leading away from the cell body of the neuron; transmits nerve impulses to other neurons or to a muscle or gland. (59)

Axonal conduction. Nerve impulse transmission in which the depolarization of the nerve membrane triggers an all-or-none impulse which rapidly moves down the length of the axon. (61)

Bait shyness. Avoidance of contaminated bait. If an animal becomes ill after eating some food, it will avoid the food on future encounters; unusual because it is rapidly learned (often after one trial) and because the negative reinforcement is so far removed from the stimulus and response. (135)

Basilar membrane. Membrane of the ear within the cochlea; movements of this membrane stimulate the hair cells of the organ of corti, producing the neural effects of auditory stimulation. (248)

Battered children. Children who are seriously beaten, tortured, and injured by their parents, siblings, or other relatives. (621)

Behavioral variability. The observed phenomenon that different individuals respond differently to the same external situation; motivational analysis is an attempt to explain this occurrence. (324)

Behaviorism. Psychological school concerned with the objective study of stimulus-response relationships. (105)

Behavioristic therapy. Type of psychotherapy that focuses on observable behavior, using learning principles (such as the use of reinforcement) to discover the stimulus conditions that maintain behavior pathology and to change them so as to modify such behavior. (522)

Behaviorists. Psychologists whose work can be described as the scientific study of the overt behavior of organisms. They are concerned only with observable, objectively measurable behavior and the discovery of predictable and specific stimulus-response relationships. (15)

Behavior modification. Behavioristic therapy that involves the use of operant conditioning procedures, emphasizing observation of behavior, its controlling variables, and contingent reinforcement. (523)

Behavior sampling. Personality measurement technique in which the examiner observes the subject's behavior in a specified situation. (446)

Beliefs. A component of attitudes, they are propositions about the way things are or ought to be. (586)

Bell-shaped curve. See *Normal curve.*

Beta waves. The EEG frequency associated with problem solving and tension. (307)

Biofeedback. Technique by which organisms are taught to change and control internal body processes formerly thought to be involuntary (e.g., blood pressure and brain waves); it involves giving the subject immediate feedback or knowledge of the bodily changes as they occur. (307)

Bipolar cells. First neurons in the visual pathway; conduct messages from the rods and cones to ganglion cells. (242)

Blind obedience to authority. Compliance with the wishes or orders of another even in violation of one's self-image and moral values; may be fostered or enhanced by the presence of a legitimate authority, social norms, and when a superior-subordinate role relation is established. (642)

Blind spot. Region of the retina where the optic nerve leaves the eye; thus it contains no receptor cells. (242)

Body image distortion. A perceptual distortion that is often characteristic of altered states of consciousness; a condition in which awareness of the body or its parts may be considerably altered. For example, there may be a sense of being separated from one's body or a feeling that certain portions of the body are enlarged or weightless. (278)

Brain stem. A collection of structures lying between the new brain and the spinal cord; includes the thalamus, the hypothalamus, and the reticular formation, (78)

Brainstorming. Group technique used to bolster or encourage creativity; participants try to generate all possible solutions to a problem prior to evaluating and choosing one of them. (227)

Brainwashing. Intensive form of propaganda conducted under stressful conditions designed to induce major changes in thinking; a journalistic term derived from Korean war experiences. (582)

British empiricists (associationists). Seventeenth-century philosophers who stated that knowledge of reality could only come from information processed through the sensory apparatus; complex thoughts were seen as being built by association between simple sensory elements. (255)

Cannibis sativa. Group of psychoactive drugs consisting of marijuana and hashish; behavioral effects of these drugs depend to a great extent upon personal and social factors, but there is no potential for physical addiction. (294)

Cannula. A double tube (a tube within a tube) inserted into a body cavity, duct, or blood vessel and used for various purposes such as drainage of fluids or the administration of chemical substances into selected brain sites or other body parts. (76)

Catatonia. Type of schizophrenia characterized by motionless, unresponsive stupor; vegetative existence, but responds well to therapy. (491)

Causation. Relationship between behavior and stimulus condition whereby the occurrence of the stimulus invariably results in the simultaneous or subsequent occurrence of the behavior and is a necessary condition for it. (25, 26)

Cell body. Part of a cell that contains the nucleus and from which, in neurons, the axon and several dendrites project. (59)

Central nervous system (CNS). The brain and spinal cord, as distinct from the peripheral nervous system. (64)

Central tendency error. An error in perceptual judgment that occurs when raters ignore the variability among individuals or among the traits of one individual. For example, to rate or judge them all as "fair," or "good," or "average." (564)

Cerebellum. The part of the brain that controls the coordination of movements necessary to maintain balance, posture, and other regulatory mechanisms least involved in psychological functions. (80)

Cerebral dominance. Condition of asymmetry of brain function by which competition between the cerebral hemispheres is avoided by the dominance of one hemisphere over the other, usually of verbal controlling hemisphere over "silent" hemisphere (in most right-handed people the left hemisphere is dominant). (85)

Cerebral hemispheres. The two halves of the new brain. (77)

Cerebral specialization. The two cerebral hemispheres have a specialization of functions. The dominant hemisphere controls speech, writing, and mathematical calculations, while the nondominant hemisphere controls perceptive tasks; also referred to as *lateralization of function.* (85)

Chaining. Type of operant conditioning in which the subject learns to perform a *series* of responses in order to obtain reinforcement. (128)

Charisma. An extraordinary personal quality of leadership, actual or perceived, marked by a special emotional appeal and attraction on the part of the leader to a group of followers. (595)

Chemotherapy. A form of biological or somatic therapy using drugs in the treatment of mental and emotional disorders; heavily used in institutional settings for patient management as well as rehabilitation. (511)

Chi-square (χ^2) test. Test of statistical inference; a test for comparing the obtained frequencies of various possible events with the frequencies that would be predicted by chance alone. (694)

Chlorpromazine. Tranquilizing drug widely used in treatment of schizophrenia; it facilitates the production of serotonin. (286)

Chromosomes. Large molecules consisting of DNA and proteins, which contain the genes responsible for hereditary traits. Every human cell contains 46 chromosomes except the sex cells, or *gametes,* which have 23.

Chronological age (CA). An individual's age in years. (450)

Chunking. Organization of material to be learned or remembered into smaller units that are familiar; increases recall ability. (181)

Circadian rhythms. The rhythmic biological cycle of sleep and activity peculiar to each species. It reflects the energy requirements of the individual and the ecological character of its habitat. (284)

Clairvoyance. Form of extrasensory perception in which a person supposedly becomes aware of an external object without the use of the sense organs. (269)

Client-centered therapy. A nondirective technique of humanistic psychotherapy based on the theory that many individuals can work through their own problems by "talking them out" in a permissive and supportive atmosphere. (535)

Clinical psychologist. A psychologist with a Ph.D. whose training involves hospital and/or clinical experience; involved in the practice of psychotherapy using verbal-behavioral treatment; trained in diagnosis using methods of testing, interviewing, and research. (508)

"Cloak" theory of language. Theory that the structure of language reflects and is caused by the thought patterns of a cultural group. (212)

Cochlea. Part of the inner ear containing fluid that is set in motion by vibrations of the oval window and which in turn stimulates the basilar membrane. (248)

Cognitive control. Control of motivational, emotional, perceptual, and behavioral responses through engagement of cognitive processes, such as cognitive dissonance, choice, helplessness, beliefs in placebos or in taboos. (391)

Cognitive dissonance theory. Principle that dissonant (discrepant or incongruous) cognitions motivate the individual to reduce the perceived inconsistency, to achieve greater consonance. This can happen if one of the cognitions is changed, or if new ones are added; theory developed by Festinger. (575)

Cognitive maps. Learning of stimulus (S–S) relationships in the environment which help structure and give purpose to one's behavior; used by Tolman to account for expectancies and learning without responding. (110)

Cognitive processes. Those processes by which individuals think, know, and gain an awareness of objects and events; includes learning, reasoning, remembering, decision-making, creating, etc. (186)

Collective unconscious. In Jungian theory, that part of an individual's unconscious which is inherited, evolutionarily developed, and common to all members of the species; a sort of storehouse of racial memories deeper than the personal unconscious. (287)

Communication. Process by which individuals give and receive information. (144)

Community mental health. Approach to mental health that emphasizes the prevention of mental illness and the need for broader and more effective mental health services based within the community; stresses local needs and resources. (550)

Compartmentalization. A defense mechanism or technique of dehumanization by which a particular activity or situation can be separated from an individual's life, values, and feelings; also called *isolation.* (653)

Complementarity. Possession of traits that complement (go well with) those of another individual; a property that makes one person attractive to another. (578)

Compulsion. Bizarre, irrational, repetitive action which the individual does not understand but nevertheless feels impelled to perform; usually symbolic in nature. (478)

Concordance rate. Probability that one of a pair of twins in a population studied will show a particular characteristic, such as a schizophrenic reaction, given that the other twin has the characteristic. (493)

Concrete operations. Third of Piaget's stages of cognitive development (from 7–11 years); characterized by logical-mathematical thinking and conservation. (192)

Conditional regard. Approval of a certain behavior of an individual, rather than approval of the individual as a person; approval is contingent upon meeting specific criteria. (421)

Conditioned reinforcement. See *Secondary reinforcement.*

Conditioned response (CR). The learned or acquired response to a conditioned stimulus. (97)

Conditioned stimulus (CS). An originally neutral stimulus that, through repeated pairings with an unconditioned stimulus, acquires the ability to elicit the response originally elicited only by the unconditioned stimulus. (97)

Cones. Retinal receptor cells responsible for color vision and high visual acuity. (241)

Conflict. The simultaneous presence of opposing or mutually exclusive impulses, desires, or incompatible responses (i.e., to approach and to avoid). (428)

Conformity. Adherence of attitudes, values, and/or behavior to social norms. (465)

Confrontation. The culminating act in a sequence of violent interaction; a result of escalation. (623)

Conscience. Internal functioning of socially learned standards of right and wrong by which an individual judges his or her own behavior; corresponds to the superego. (414)

Conscious. In Freudian theory, the thoughts, ideas, feelings, and desires that an individual is aware of at any given moment. (413)

Consciousness. State of awareness of internal events (such as thought processes) and of the external environment; normal waking state. (275)

Conservation. The ability to recognize that an object or property (such as volume or surface area) remains the same despite transformations that may change its appearance. (192)

Consummatory response. Action that represents the completion of goal-seeking activity. For example, eating. (331)

Contact comfort. A significant aspect of the mother-child relationship; first studied and observed in a series of experiments with motherless monkeys reared with various kinds of terry-cloth "artificial mothers." (351)

Contiguity. Relationship between a conditioned stimulus and a response in the environment, which appear close together in space and time. According to current psychological theories it is a necessary, but not sufficient, condition to account for learning associations. (94)

Contingency, behavioral. A specified relationship between a given response and the timing or frequency of reinforcement. (115)

Continuity hypothesis. Theory that problem solving is essentially a gradual learning procedure based on trial-and-error behavior. (218)

Continuous reinforcement. Reinforcement given regularly after each correct response. (123)

Control group. Group of subjects that shares all of the characteristics and procedures of the experimental group except exposure to the independent variable the effect of which is being studied. A control group establishes a no-treatment baseline against which to compare the treatment effects on the experimental group. (34)

Control orientation. A view of the world that recognizes our need to be able to predict and influence events important in our lives; assumed by attribution theory. (566)

Convergence. Distributing process in the nervous system whereby impulses from many neurons or receptor cells reach the same neuron or effector. (242)

Conversion hysteria. Neurotic reaction to stress or anxiety in which psychological distress is converted into bodily symptoms. (479)

Coping strategies. The possible means of dealing with a situation that an organism perceives as threatening; various coping strategies possible in a given situation are assessed in the process of secondary appraisal. (376)

Corpus callosum. Heavy bundle of nerve fibers connecting the two cerebral hemispheres. When this is severed, separate functions of each hemisphere are not integrated, leading to "two minds in one brain." (77)

Correctional psychologists. Psychologist who works within the correctional system, the system which deals with and treats convicted criminals. (681)

Correlation. Measure of the degree to which two variables are related; generally a prediction relating one behavior to another rather than relating behavior to a stimulus condition. A precise quantitative measure of the degree of correlation is given by the coefficient of correlation. (24, 689)

Cortex. A thin, grayish rind of tissue covering the cerebrum and consisting of neurons and their connectors; active in conscious experience and higher mental processes; also called *gray matter.* (48)

Cortin. A hormone secreted by the adrenal cortex, which interacts with ACTH, a pituitary hormone, and is an important factor in the physiological reaction to prolonged stress. (381)

Counterconditioning. The replacement of a particular response to a stimulus by the establishment of another, often quite different, response; often used in behavior therapy to eliminate unwanted behavior and replace it with a more desirable response. (102, 526)

Counternorm. An alternative standard of behavioral appropriateness; an alternative to prevailing social norms. (466)

Countertransference. Process in which the analyst develops personal feelings about the patient because of perceived similarity of the patient to significant others in the therapist's life; reversal of the usual process of transference. (520)

Covert. Not directly observable; rather hidden or concealed from public scrutiny, as are one's thoughts.

Creative thinking. Uninhibited, imaginative thinking used in the service of reality. (184)

Cross-cultural psychology. The empirical study of members of various culture groups who have had different experiences that lead to predictable and significant differences in behavior. (195)

Cross-tolerance. A tolerance developed under one drug that generalizes to suppress the action of another chemically similar drug. (299)

Cueing. Specific function of motivation, it serves to trigger certain response patterns in an organism in selected directions. (327)

Cumulative record. Measure of response rate; a graph plotting the responses as they occur and recording a cumulative total for a given time interval. (122)

Curiosity. An organism's drive to explore and know its environment; also referred to as *exploratory drive* or *investigatory reflex.*

Cutaneous senses. Senses of pressure, pain, warmth, and cold, receptors for which are located primarily in the skin. (241)

Cytoplasm. Substance comprising a cell (excluding the nucleus), in which most of the biochemical reactions of the cell take place. (58)

Cytosine. One of the four nucleotide bases that make up the DNA molecule; found paired with guanine. (54)

Dark adaptation. Process by which the eyes become more sensitive so that they can see under low illumination. (243)

Data. Reports or measurements of observed events. (17)

Decay theory. Theory of forgetting that states that learned material leaves a trace in the brain, which fades away if unused. (173)

Decibel (db). Unit of measurement of the intensity of sound. (250)

Decortication. Surgical removal of the brain or its separation from the spinal cord. (68)

Deductive reasoning. The mode of reasoning that starts with propositions and derives inescapable conclusions from them. (217)

Deep structure. The basic, underlying meaning of a sentence; the same deep structure can be used to generate several different surface structures by the use of transformational rules. (155)

Defense mechanism. An unconscious mode of coping with situations that arouse anxiety or threaten self-esteem; examples include displacement, projection, rationalization, regression, and sublimation. (415, 586)

Deficiency cravings. Hungers for specific foods that are the result of biological needs and deficits. (337)

Deficiency motivation. Motivation in which the individual seeks to restore his or her physical or psychological equilibrium rather than move toward personal growth. (422)

Dehumanization. Psychological erasure or cancellation of human qualities and values of other people; leads to the treatment and perception of people as objects or subhuman animals. (647)

Deindividuation. Subjective state of the loss of one's identity as an accountable, responsible self. It results in weakening of the usual controls that restrain impulsive and antisocial behavior; may be fostered by anonymity or altered states of consciousness, among others. (643)

Delayed effect. An effect resulting from a given intervention, which does not appear immediately, but rather occurs after some time has elapsed. (663)

Delay of reinforcement. Principle which states that responses occurring close in time or space to the delivery of the reinforcement are learned more quickly than responses remote from reinforcement. (124)

Delusion. A strong belief opposed to reality and maintained in spite of logical persuasion and evidence to the contrary; symptom of paranoid states. Three main types: *delusion of grandeur* (belief that one is an exalted personage), *delusion of persecution* (belief that one is being plotted against), and *delusion of reference* (egocentric belief that chance happenings and conversations concern oneself). (486)

Dementia praecox. Former name for schizophrenia. (491)

Demonic possession. Archaic conception of mental illness, based on the belief that physical sickness and mental aberrations were caused by the ''possession'' of the patient's body by evil spirits. (457)

Dendrites. Highly branched fibers that extend from the cell body at the receiving end of a neuron; usually quite short. (59)

Denial. A defense mechanism by means of which an individual protects self from external threat by refusing to perceive or think about it; however, this unrealistic fear level may have negative results. (384)

Depolarization. A process that occurs in the neuron when the stimulation threshold is exceeded; the selective permeability of the axon membrane changes, allowing sodium ions to rush in and upset the polarized conditions of the neurons at rest, thus initiating a nerve impulse along the axon. (61)

Depression. Emotional state of dejection, feelings of worthlessness, and usually apprehension; it is the most prevalent psychiatric disorder in the United States and bears a marked similarity to the symptoms of learned helplessness. (400)

Depressive episodes or reactions. Psychotic reactions characterized by periods of extreme depression; may alternate with manic episodes. (487)

Depressive neurosis. A type of neurosis characterized by exaggerated sadness and depression in response to a loss or threatened loss; a reactive expression of helplessness and feelings of failure. (483)

Deprivation. Lack of, or withholding of, need-satisfying stimulation or of something necessary for biological or psychological functioning. (327)

Deprivation dwarfism. A condition of defective physical growth and maturation in children as a consequence of emotional deprivation. (6)

Deprogramming. Systematic attempt to force individuals to renounce their beliefs, usually newly acquired beliefs assumed to have been coercively programmed in. (582)

Descriptive statistic. A single number that represents or describes a series of measurements collected on a group, such as central tendency, variability, coefficient of correlation. (684)

Desensitization. Behavioral therapy process of reconditioning in which stimuli lose their power to elicit anxiety through the individual's graded exposure to them from mild forms to more severe ones. (524)

Determinism. The theory that all events are determined by preceding causes. The theory assumes that this relationship is invariant and, therefore, that an event is predictable when the relevant causes are known. (11)

Deviance. Behavior that is viewed by society as being markedly different from the group average or norm expected in a given situation under given conditions. (462)

Discontinuity hypothesis. Theory that problem solving is primarily a matter of insight and perceptual reorganization, and that solutions are discovered or realized all at once, rather than in a gradual fashion. (218)

Discrimination. The ability to detect differences between two stimuli; in conditioning, the ability to pick out and respond to relevant stimuli and to inhibit responses to irrelevant stimuli. (100) Prejudicial response or behavior, as in racial discrimination. (595)

Discriminative stimulus (S^D). In operant conditioning, a stimulus that signals that reinforcement is or is not available following the operant behavior. (113)

Dishabituation. The loss of habituation; the return of the orienting response after habituation when the stimulus input becomes distinguishably different from previous inputs. (71)

Disinhibition. Temporary reappearance of a conditioned response that has been extinguished, in response to an extraneous stimulus different from the conditioned stimulus; inhibition of an inhibition. (431)

Disobedience. Refusal or negligence to obey, to carry out a rule or command. (644)

Displaced aggression. Transfer of hostility from the object or person actually causing frustration to some other object or person or to the self. (615)

Displacement. A dream process by which material is disguised so that something important in real life is unimportant in a dream or vice versa. (286) A defense mechanism by which feelings of hostility, etc., are discharged against a substitute object. (415)

Displacement theory. Theory of forgetting which states that the capacity of an individual's memory store is limited, and that beyond a certain limit new information can only enter the store if it pushes out or displaces information previously in the store. (174)

Dispositional attribution. Attribution of causes of an action or event to relatively stable, internal, nonmodifiable characteristics within the individual; that is, his or her personality traits, character, and inner dispositions to act. It allows for the categorization of ''problem people'' rather than analysis of problem situations. (14, 564)

Dissent. Objection, a withholding of assent based on a difference of opinion; does not necessarily imply contrary action. (644)

Dissociated states. Neurotic reactions to extreme stress in which entire episodes of life are repressed from consciousness; mental processes may be split off from the main personality or lose their normal thought-affect relationships, as in *amnesia, fugue,* and *multiple personality.* (480)

Distal stimulus. The actual object providing stimulation of the retina. (239)

Divergence. Distributing process in the nervous system whereby impulses from a single neuron or receptor cell reach many neurons or muscles. (242)

Dizygotic twins. Fraternal twins; twins who develop from separate fertilized ova. (199)

DNA. Deoxyribonucleic acid; the principle component of genes, consisting of long chains of pairs of nucleotide bases arranged like a twisted ladder or spiral staircase. (53)

Dose-response function. An empirically determined relationship for an individual that shows how the size or amount of the dose is reflected in the effect of a drug. (298)

Double-bind. Situation that involves two or more inconsistent messages that require incompatible responses. (162)

Double-blind test. A methodological control used to conceal the treatment from the subject as well as from the person (researcher) who administers the treatment. A safeguard against expectation or set effects; especially used in drug evaluation research. (18)

Dream analysis. Psychoanalytic technique involving the interpretation of dreams in order to gain insight into the patient's unconscious motivation; based on the belief of Freud and others that dreams are symbolic representations of unconscious impulses, conflicts, and desires. (286, 518)

Dream work. The unconscious process by which the emotionally painful latent content of a dream is transformed into the less painful manifest content. (519)

Drive. Motive; internal conditions directing an organism towards a specific goal, usually involving biological processes. (323)

Drive reduction. Theory of learning stating that a motivated sequence of behavior is best explained as moving from an aversive state of tension (drive) to a goal state in which the drive is reduced. (110)

Drive state. Thorndike's term for strong *internal* stimuli that impel organisms to action. (107)

Drug abuse. Use of a drug to the point where it interferes with the individual's health or with economic or social adjustment; the third stage of drug use. (475)

Drug addiction. Dependence on any of a number of psychoactive drugs; both physical and psychological dependence are often involved. (471)

Dualism. Descartes' view of the human organism as comprising two independent elements: the mechanistic body and brain, and the spiritualistic soul and ephemeral mind. (50)

Duality of consciousness. The separateness of the functions of consciousness carried out by the two hemispheres of the brain. (318)

Dyad. A two-person group. (519)

Dynamism. In Sullivan's personality theory, a prolonged, recurrent behavior pattern; a habit. (419)

Dyscontrol syndrome. Pattern of senseless brutality or other repeated offenses assumed to be brought about by disease of the limbic system or the temporal lobe of the brain. (613)

Dyslexia. Impairment of reading ability, which involves reversal of series of letters or numbers. (259)

Eardrum. Thin membrane at the end of the auditory canal between the outer and middle ear. (248)

Eclectic approach. Approach to the study of psychology that stresses a wide variety of theories, assumptions, kinds of research, and levels of analysis rather than advocating any one as superior to others. (44)

Ecological psychology. A new approach to psychology concerned with understanding the psychosocial interdependence between the individuals in a community and their physical and biological environment. (657)

Ecology. The mutual relations between organisms and their physical environment. (657)

Ecosystem. A total ecological community considered together with the nonliving elements of its environment as a unit. (657)

Effectors. The organs (muscles or glands) that perform the actual response functions upon receiving nerve impulses from motor neurons. (64)

Efferent nerve fiber. Carries messages from the central nervous system to an organ of response such as a muscle or gland; also known as a *motor nerve fiber.* (67)

Efficacy. Sense of personal competence, effectiveness, mastery, or self-worth. (190)

Ego. In Freud's psychoanalytic theory, the rational aspect of the personality; regulates the impulses of the id in order to meet the demands of reality and maintain social approval and self-esteem. More generally, the individual's concept of self. (414)

Egocentrism. The failure to differentiate between one's own point of view and that of others. (191)

Ego-defense mechanism. See *Defense mechanism.*

Ego ideal. The individual's view of the kind of person he or she should try to become; part of the *superego.* (414)

Ego transcendence. Condition often characteristic of altered states of consciousness; an experience of separation from self and personal needs, enabling one to view reality more objectively from a detached vantage point. (278)

Eidetic imagery. Ability to retain an image (usually visual) with great clarity and accuracy for a fairly long period of time. (207)

Electroconvulsive shock treatment. A form of shock treatment used for purposes of psychotherapy in which electric current is passed briefly through the patient's head, producing temporary coma and convulsions with the intention of alleviating depression or other severe symptoms. (510)

Electroencephalogram (EEG). Recording of the minute electrical oscillations in the cerebral cortex known as brain waves; used to detect disturbances or pathology in brain functioning. (88)

Electromyogram (EMG). Recording of electrical activity associated with muscular responses. (213)

Elicited behavior. In conditioning, a response already in the organism's repertoire which is initiated or drawn out by some recognizable, external, physical stimulus. (97, 108)

Emergency reaction. See *General adaptation syndrome.*

Emitted behavior. Behavior caused by internal conditions, which appears without the use of an external stimulus to initiate it; basis of instrumental conditioning. (108)

Emotion. A complex subjective, psychological process, which may be induced by environmental stimuli and mediated by physiological variables; it may have the power to motivate an organism to action. It is a felt tendency toward stimuli appraised as good, and away from those appraised as bad. (365, 376)

Emotional inoculation. Preparatory process to enable individuals to moderate anxiety and plan future reactions to an impending threatening event. (383)

Empathy. Experiencing the thoughts, feelings, and motives of others vicariously; may serve to explain altruism. (574)

Empiricism. The scientific method of relying on verifiable, factual information such as observation, sensory experience, or experimentation rather than on untestable or unobservable concepts and speculations. (12)

Encounter groups. Small therapy or personal growth groups designed to provide an intensive interpersonal experience, focusing on the current interactions and feelings that emerge within the group in an atmosphere of honesty and emotional sensitivity. (543)

End feet. Structures at the end of an axon that synapse with another cell; also called *synaptic knobs.* (59)

Endocrine system. System composed of glands that secrete hormones which act to regulate metabolism, coordinate various body processes, and may influence emotion. (372)

Endogenous depression. Type of depressive behavior assumed to be caused by internal biochemical or genetic factors; symptoms may include retardation, insomnia, suicidal tendencies, and severe depression. (489)

Energizer. Drug with a stimulating effect, used in chemotherapy to enable a patient to feel more energetic; *imipramine* is an example of such a drug. (514)

Energizing. General nondirectional energy-arousal function of motivation. (327)

Energy arousal. A characteristic of motivation wherein an organism readies itself to act. (324)

Engram. Hypothetical memory trace; formed and temporarily stored during learning but lost unless transferred to long-term memory system. (178)

Environmentalists. Psychologists who stress environmental rather than hereditary factors in the development of human nature, placing an emphasis on ''nurture'' as the determining factor. They see human nature as modifiable. (200)

Epigenesis. Theory of human development put forth by Aristotle that organs were formed gradually out of simple unformed substances in the fertilized egg; now used to mean the emergence, in the course of development, of new phenomena and properties which are undifferentiated in the germ cells; in opposition to *orthogenesis.* (56)

Epinephrine. Hormone secreted by the adrenal medulla, the inner part of the adrenal glands, in strong emotion; associated with fear and anger reactions; also called *adrenaline.* (372)

Epiphenomenon. A secondary phenomenon accompanying another phenomenon and thought to be caused by it; blushing is an epiphenomenon of embarrassment.

Equity theory. Theory that applies to human relationships, stating that people will try to maximize their outcomes by achieving the greatest possible rewards at the minimum costs. (579)

Erogenous body zones. Local body areas which upon tactile stimulation trigger sexual arousal or excitement. (358)

Eros. According to Freudian theory, the ''sex instinct'' or ''life instinct,'' one of the two drives present at birth; encompasses all striving for creative synthesis, thus being much broader than sex drive alone. (414)

Erotic. Tending to arouse sexual excitement. (358)

Escalation (of aggression). Second step of a violent interaction in which the individuals involved react to previous responses, the initial provocation, and the inferred perception of the intention behind the act. (623)

Escape conditioning. A form of operant conditioning in which a negative, aversive stimulus can be terminated if the organism makes the appropriate response. (116–17)

Estrus. The sexually receptive state of female mammals; it is a cyclical state also known as ''heat,'' and may be accompanied by suggestive or aggressive sexual behavior. (349)

Ethics. A set of principles or values dealing with what is good and bad or right and wrong or with moral duty and obligation. (670)

Ethnocentrism. Tendency to hold prejudiced attitudes toward all groups different from one's own, which is assumed to be the best. (440)

Ethologist. Researcher who studies the behavior of animals in their natural habitat, often with the purpose of studying species-specific characteristics. (135)

Etiology. Causation; the systematic study of the causes of disorders.

Eugenics. The science that deals with the improvement of species through the control of hereditary factors in mating.

Euphoria. A feeling of extreme well-being or elation.

Evaluative reasoning. Critical thinking that involves judging the soundness, appropriateness, condition, or significance of an idea or product. (217)

Evil. A modern definition applies this term to situations in which force, violence, and other forms of coercion exceed institutional or morally justifiable limits. (640)

Evoked potential. A method of studying the brain's activity which entails a stimulus presentation to "evoke" or elicit neural impulses that travel to the brain. The occurrence of the impulse is recorded by electrodes on the surface or implanted in the brain. (74)

Existential-humanistic psychotherapy. Type of therapy which emphasizes the here-and-now of an individual who must be treated, understood, and attended to; sees individual experience rather than physical events as the basic reality; focuses on the whole organism as a complex system and not just its biology, behavior, or unconscious; also encourages a more concerned, caring orientation of therapist toward patient. (534)

Existentialism. An introspective philosophy which emphasizes that individuals are responsible for their own lives and realize their existence fully through the art of choice. (404)

Exorcism. Various techniques practiced since ancient and medieval times for casting the "evil spirits" out of those "possessed" or mentally ill; based on the concept that mental disturbances were caused by demonic possession. (457)

Expectancy. A condition of anticipating or predicting future events based on past experience and the present stimulus conditions; expectancy of achieving a goal was seen by Tolman as a necessary condition of all voluntary behavior. (394)

Experiential groups. Groups like encounter groups that provide intensive interpersonal experience. (543)

Experiential psychotherapy. Therapeutic process developed by Gendlin based on interpersonal encounter wherein the analyst takes an active, self-expressive, self-revealing stance in therapy while at the same time helping clients trust their own inner feelings. (537)

Experimental group. Group of subjects for whom the experimenter alters the independent variable or treatment variables, the influence of which is being investigated. See *Control group.* (34)

Experimental method. Highly formalized version of the scientific method which attempts to establish a causal relationship between the independent and dependent variable. A hypothesis is tested under precisely specified conditions controlled to eliminate the effects of all extraneous variables. (34)

Experimental neurosis. Neurosis produced in animals when a conditioning process involves prolonged stress and inescapable conflicts. (104–5)

Extinction. Gradual disappearance of a conditioned response when the conditioned stimulus repeatedly occurs without being followed either by reinforcement or by the unconditioned stimulus. (101, 116, 117) May be used as a form of behavior-modifying psychotherapy to reduce or eliminate undesirable responses. (523)

Extrasensory perception (ESP). Perception or experience not mediated by any known stimulation of, or activity in, the sense organs. (269)

Extrinsic reward. Externally provided reinforcement (money, praise, etc.), which can be awarded to an individual and which has the effect of initially increasing the behavior preceding it; however, shown to lower intrinsic motivation to perform task for its own value. (567)

Facial display. A form of nonverbal expression that concerns facial movements, positions, or expressions; e.g., a smile. (156)

Factor analysis. Statistical technique used in identifying and measuring the relative importance of the underlying variables, or factors, which contribute to a complex ability, trait, or form of behavior. (423)

Factor theories of personality. Theories of personality that involve the description and accounting of various clusters of human characteristics in terms of mathematically derived factors. (423)

Fear. A rational reaction to an objective, identifiable, external danger; distinguished from free-floating, neurotic anxiety; social consequences usually depend on its situational appropriateness. (477)

Feature analyzers. Neurons that respond selectively to trigger features. (244)

Feedback. Process by which information about the correctness of previous responses under one's control returns to the individual's "control center" so that corrections and regulations can be made where necessary to guide subsequent responding; knowledge of results. (26, 215)

Field. Natural environment or habitat; ecological psychologists believe that this is the proper sphere for psychological study. (659)

Field theory. The systematization of psychology by analogy with fields of force in physics, maintaining that all experience represents a balance and interaction of many forces. (420)

Figure-ground relations. The tendency to perceive things as objects or events (figures) against a background, even when the stimuli are ambiguous and the foreground-background relationships are reversible. (262)

First impression. Judgment of an individual at first sight or exposure, often based on minimal clues; may have a considerable influence on subsequent judgments. (562)

Fissures. Deep clefts or grooves separating the lobes of the cortex; major ones are named *Rolando,* vertical groove separating frontal and parietal lobes, and *Sylvius,* horizontal groove separating temporal from parietal and frontal lobes. (77)

Fixation. In Freudian theory, arrested development through failure to pass beyond one of the psychosexual stages as a result of an excess of frustration or gratification at this stage. (413)

Fixed interval schedule (FI). Intermittent schedule by which reinforcement is given regularly at the end of a certain period of time, such as every two minutes. (124)

Fixed ratio schedule (FR). Intermittent schedule by which reinforcement is given regularly after a certain number of correct responses. (124)

Flattened affect. Characteristic of some schizophrenic states in which emotions are blunted, subdued, or not expressed. (484)

Flow chart. See *Algorithm.*

Formal operations. The fourth of Piaget's stages of cognitive development (from 11 years on); characterized by abstract thinking and conceptualization. (193)

Form board. A board with recesses into which the subject must fit blocks of the proper size and shape as quickly as he or she can; used as a performance test to measure intelligence. (452)

Forward conduction, law of. Sequence of neural activity; information is transmitted in only one direction along neurons and synapses, from dendrites to cell body to axon to synaptic knobs across synapse to next dendrites. (64)

Free association. Principal psychoanalytic procedure used to probe the unconscious; patient lets his or her mind wander freely, giving a running account of every thought and feeling. (459)

Free-floating anxiety. Anxiety not referable to any specific cause or situation; type of anxiety that is experienced in anxiety neurosis. (476)

Frequency distribution. An array of individual scores arranged in order from highest to lowest; the frequency with which each score is represented in a given distribution. (685)

Frequency of response. A measure of the strength of response based on the rate of making a given response. (102)

Frequency theory. Theory of sound coding stating that the frequency of auditory nerve impulses is directly correlated with the frequency of sound waves. (239)

Frustration. Denial or thwarting of motives by obstacles that lie between organism and goal. Physiological changes, as in heart rate and systolic blood pressure, may occur and persist if no opportunity for aggression against the frustration presents itself. (378)

Frustration-aggression hypothesis. A theory which holds that aggression is a drive acquired as a direct response to frustration; the greater the amount of frustration, the stronger the resulting aggressive response. (614)

F-test. Test of statistical inference; also known as the analysis of variance test; a test for comparing between-group variability with within-group variability for two or more groups. (694)

Fugue. Neurotic dissociative state; entails loss of memory accompanied by actual physical flight from one's present life situation to a new environment or less threatening former one. (480)

Functional invariants. A concept in Piaget's theory of cognitive development; primary shapers of intellectual growth that are basic modes of interacting with the environment to make behavior appropriate to what has previously been experienced, as well as to modify behavior to fit new intellectual challenges. *Assimilation* and *accommodation* are the most important functional invariants. (189)

Functional psychosis. Severe mental disorder precipitated primarily by psychological stress, and not attributable to organic, physical causes. (486)

Gain-loss theory of attraction. Model of interpersonal attraction stating that changes in positive or negative evaluation have more impact on interpersonal attraction than does constant, unvarying evaluation; a theory developed by Aronson. (580)

Galvanic skin response (GSR). Minute changes in electrical conductivity of, or activity in, the skin, detected by a sensitive galvanometer. The reactions are commonly used as an indicator of emotional reactivity. (228)

Gamete. Germ cell; male and female gamete unite to form the zygote. (54)

Ganglion. A collection of nerve cell bodies located outside the central nervous system. (66)

Ganglion cells. Neurons that connect the bipolar cells to relay areas in the brain. (242)

Gate-control theory of pain. Melzack's theory of pain involving a control system that continuously interacts to modulate pain; involves the control of afferent input by efferent processes. (386)

General adaptation syndrome. Theoretical approach developed by Selye to explain the body's reaction under continued stress, consisting of the *alarm reaction*, during which the body makes a number of complicated physiological changes in response to a stressor; the *stage of resistance*, during which the organism, with the aid of increased secretions of the adrenal glands, is able to withstand the stressor for a time without showing symptoms; and the *stage of exhaustion*, in which the organism can no longer resist the stressor and may die if stress does not cease. (381)

Generalization decrement. Process whereby responses to stimuli not directly subject to extinction will also extinguish in proportion to the similarity of the stimuli to the conditioned stimulus; the reverse of stimulus generalization. (101–2)

Genes. Ultramicroscopic areas of DNA within the chromosomes; the basic unit of hereditary transmission. (53)

Genital stage. In Freudian theory, last stage of psychosexual development, starting at puberty with turning away from autoeroticism to interest in genitalia of others. (413)

Germ cells. Reproductive cells (male sperm and female ovum) that unite to produce a new individual; contain only half the number of chromosomes found in other body cells. (54)

Gestalt psychology. A school of psychology which teaches that psychology should study the whole pattern of behavior instead of analyzing it into elements, since the whole is more than the sum of its parts. (256)

Gibson's perception theory. Theory that perception is a process of reduction of sensory input, filtering out essential signal elements from the abundance of stimulus "noise." (257)

Give-up-itis. Syndrome afflicting some prisoners of war characterized by the loss of all hope of ever being freed and consequent loss of interest in the future; the result is emotionally caused death. (390)

Grammar. See *syntax.*

Group dynamics movement. Psychological movement started by Lewin, concerned with studying the dynamic properties of social interaction within groups at empirical, theoretical, and applied levels. (589)

Group therapy. Any form of psychotherapy practiced on a group basis; more than one person treated at same time in same setting; usually nondirective in form and under the guidance of a therapist. (542)

Groupthink. Mode of decision making engaged in by people in highly cohesive groups in which a preoccupation with unanimity limits critical thinking and realistic appraisal of options. (644)

Growth motivation. Motivation in which the individual seeks to go beyond level attained in the past; to develop potentials. (422)

Guanine. One of the four nucleotide bases that make up the DNA molecule; found paired with cytosine. (54)

Habit strength. In Hull's theory of learning, a learned connection between stimulus and response; the unit of learning and a mediating variable. (110)

Habituation. Diminished physiological and psychological responsiveness to stimulus input; cessation of the orienting reaction, when the stimulus has become familiar, is constantly repeated, or is expected, thus lowering its informational value to the individual. (70)

Hallucination. Sensory impression of external objects in the absence of appropriate stimulus energy in the environment; origin of the perception is internal and not external. (289)

Hallucinogenic. Able to produce sensory hallucinations. (291)

Hallucinogens. A group of hallucinogenic, psychoactive drugs, also called the psychedelics; they include LSD-25, psilocybin, and mescaline among others, and can cause profound perceptual alteration. (296)

Halo effect. An error of judgment to which rating scales are subject; it is the tendency, when interviewing or rating an individual on a particular trait, to be influenced by one's opinion of some other trait or by one's overall impression of the individual. (446)

Hebephrenic schizophrenia. Form of schizophrenia in which the most severe disorganization appears; characterized by inappropriate affect, and silly, childlike behavior, frequent hallucinations, and other grossly inappropriate thoughts, affect, and behavior. (491)

Hedonism. Doctrine that asserts that personal pleasure or happiness is the sole good and chief goal in life. (13)

Hermaphrodite. Individual in whom there is a contradiction between the predominant external genital appearance and the sex chromosome pattern, gonads, and internal reproductive structures; one in whom psychosexual differentiation is not complete. (357)

Heterosexuality. Primary sexual interest in members of the opposite sex. (361)

Heuristics. Methods designed to stimulate further thought in problem solving; "rules of thumb" used in trying to solve problems. (221)

Hierarchy of needs. According to Maslow's theory of personality, the arrangement of a person's inborn needs according to certain priorities; needs at a low level in the hierarchy must be satisfied before those on higher levels take precedence. (422)

Higher-order conditioning. Process by which, once a conditioned response has been established, the conditioned stimulus may in turn function as an unconditioned stimulus in setting up a conditioned response to a third (or higher-order) stimulus. (101)

Hippocampus. A subcortical structure of the brain that is crucial for recent memory and important in mating. (80)

Holistic approach. A psychological approach to the study of behavior stating that the proper perspective for the analysis of behavior must be in terms of the whole organism, not merely in terms of its functioning parts. (52)

Homeostasis. The complex process of maintaining stability between the internal and external environment so that the body's chemical balance can be maintained and social and biological needs can be satisfied; homeostasis on the physiological level is largely automatic. (329)

Homosexuality. Primary sexual interest in members of one's own sex. (361)

Homunculus. Miniature human figure, thought by some early scientists to exist in the sperm cells, needing only nourishment and time to unfold and develop into an adult. (56)

Hope. Cognitive concept concerning the expectation of the instrumental value of one's behavior for effecting a change in the environment. (394)

Hopelessness. A state of being without hope, which results in apathy, inaction, and passive resignation. (394)

Hormetic traits. Direct motivational aspects of the person, which depend upon both tissue needs and the kinds of experience the individual has had; include needs, attitudes, and interests. (424)

Hybridization. Mating of genetically dissimilar individuals. (55)

Hyperphagia. Excessive feeding in animals, due to brain lesions, resulting in obesity. (345)

Hypnosis. An altered state of awareness induced by a variety of techniques and characterized by deep relaxation, increased susceptibility to hypnotic suggestions, changes in sense of self-control and in level of motivation. (308)

Hypnotic amnesia. Memory alteration that occurs as a result of hypnosis; may be spontaneous amnesia for some parts of the hypnotic experience or due to some specific suggestion given during the session. (311)

Hypnotic analgesia. Upon suggestion, the insensitivity to pain of a hypnotized subject. (388)

Hypnotics. Group of psychoactive drugs mainly composed of the barbiturates, the tranquilizers that serve to depress the central nervous system; they have a high potential for psychological abuse. (295)

Hypnotizability. The level of susceptibility to hypnosis of an individual; the ease with which one comes to be hypnotized as measured by a hypnotic susceptibility scale. (315)

Hypochondria. Neurotic preoccupation with the body's activities and the state of one's health. (483)

Hypoglycemia. Lowered blood-sugar level, as following an injection of insulin. (332)

Hypothalamus. A key structure of the subcortex, important in the regulation of metabolism, temperature, hunger, thirst, and emotional behavior; control center for much of the endocrine system through connections with the pituitary gland. (78–79)

Hypothesis. A tentative explanation or statement of the relation between two events or variables, often based on the results of previous observations, that is tested in an experiment; essential in predicting, explaining, and testing behavior. Experimental results may reject or support it although it can never be conclusively proven. (23)

Hysterical neurosis. Type of neurosis characterized by involuntary psychogenic loss of motor or sensory function. For example, physical paralysis or loss of memory. (478)

Iconic representation. Representation of stimuli that are conceptually stored according to their perceptual, sensory image. (192)

Id. In Freud's tripartite division of the personality, the primitive part of the unconscious, composed of instinctive organic cravings and characterized by unrestrained pleasure-seeking impulses. (414)

Identity crisis. Period of transition marked by confusion, experimentation, and emotionality; it comes about when one's former view of himself or herself is no longer appropriate to a changing life setting, as in adolescence or in middle age. (434)

Idiographic approach. Psychological approach to understanding human nature which focuses on the special circumstances and unique aspects of each individual's personality in order to understand him or her. (13)

Illusion. A misinterpretation of the relationships among presented stimuli, so that the percept does not correspond to the physical reality that gives rise to it. (236)

Images. Mental pictures of actual sensory experience in the absence of any external stimulus. (207)

Imitation of models. May be a form of behavioral therapy in which an individual acquires new behaviors through the observation and imitation of a model. (528)

Implosive therapy. Form of behavior therapy developed by Stampfl; extinction occurs as frightening stimuli are imagined without harmful result; called *implosive* because the frightening stimuli produce an inner explosion—an *implosion*—of panic. (525)

Imprinting. A form of learning that occurs very early in life during a critical period of development and determines the form that behavior will take, as in the case of ducklings that follow the first moving object they see and remain closely attached to it. (136)

Inappropriate affect. A symptom of psychotic patients in which an emotion expressed is not proper or rationally suited to the situation. (484)

Incentive motivation. Strategy to prod an organism to respond through threat or the promise of future reward. (126)

Incentive stimuli. Stimulus objects or events in the environment that may trigger certain response sequences if they interact with the appropriate physiological condition. (327)

Independent variable. Factor whose effects (on the dependent variable) are being studied, and which is systematically manipulated while the other variables are held constant; in psychological experiments it is often a stimulus condition (S) whose effect on a response (R) is being studied. The independent variable is also the *predictor* variable used to predict outcomes or behaviors. (34)

Inductive reasoning. Method of reasoning by which, on the basis of specific observations and instances, an inference is drawn about a general state or abstract concept which organizes and makes meaningful those separate elements.

Ineffability. Often characteristic of an altered state of consciousness; individuals often profess an inability to put into words, to communicate, a description of their experiences. (279)

Inference. A conclusion or decision reached by reasoning from known facts or evidence. The inference often goes beyond observations, is broader, more general than the evidence on which it is based. (18)

Information processing. Approach to the study of cognitive processes that uses computer programs as a precise, rigorous model for thought. (220)

Inhibition. Suppression or restraint of behavior or an event; term has many specific meanings at all levels of analysis. (70)

Innate. Inborn or inherited; not learned. (369)

Inner-directed person. An individual who is controlled by early implanted values and goal orientations; such individuals perceive themselves as having a greater amount of control over their environment than do "externals." (437)

Insanity. A legal concept applied to any mental condition that renders the individual incapable of ethical and moral judgment and legally not responsible for his or her actions. (484)

Insight. A sudden realization, discovery, or recognition of the correct solution to a problem. (218)

Instinct. Innate behavior pattern that is unaffected by practice; invariant sequence of complex behaviors that is observed in all members of a species and released by specific stimuli in the apparent absence of learning. (412)

Instinctual drift. Tendency of an organism to drift away from learned behavior that is being reinforced toward responses that are counterproductive but resemble responses that would be made in its natural environment. (135)

Institutionalized racism. The social-political-economic support in a society for prejudiced beliefs and acts of discrimination against minority-group members because of their race. (601)

Instrumental behavior. Often used interchangeably with "operant behavior" to refer to voluntarily emitted responses that are instrumental in achieving a goal or reward. However, as used by Thorndike, this term refers to a learned response rather than one that the organism was already performing. (111–12)

Instrumental conditioning. A type of behavioral conditioning in which the subject learns to make a response that leads to a reward or prevents a punishment; in contrast to respondent conditioning, no eliciting stimulus is presented. (107)

Instrumental response. The reinforcement-seeking response; in a motivational state, an organism's behavior of searching or working to obtain a goal or reward. (331)

Insulin. Hormone secreted by the pancreas which helps the body to metabolize sugar and keep the blood sugar level steady. (332)

Integrated therapy. Psychotherapy based on an eclectic approach, stressing no particular theory or procedure but using whatever methods of therapy seem appropriate to the individual case. (546)

Intellectualization. Process or defense mechanism that reduces anxiety in a threatening situation by turning it into an abstract problem or by explaining it in such a way as to reduce the threat. (382)

Intelligence. The global capacity to profit from experience; it is a complex mental ability that includes such primary abilities as verbal comprehension, space visualization, reasoning ability, numerical ability; operationally defined, intelligence is what intelligence tests measure. (448)

Intelligence quotient (IQ). Measure of intelligence obtained by dividing the individual's mental age (MA), as determined by performance on standardized test items, by chronological age (CA) and then multiplying by 100. An IQ of 100 is considered to be average. (450)

Interference theory. Theory that forgetting is caused by new information interfering with what has already been learned. (174)

Interneurons. Nerve cells with many short dendrites and a short axon, the latter often giving off branches called collaterals; interconnect sensory input pathways and motor output pathways within the central nervous system; also called *associative neurons* or *internuncial neurons.* (67)

Interval scale. Scale of measurement possessing all of the properties of the nominal and ordinal scales in addition to the property of equal units; i.e., that equal differences in scores represent equal differences in what is being measured. (683)

Interventionists. Those who believe that psychological research should be conducted under controlled circumstances in which the relevant variables can be manipulated circumstances which may not occur or be observable and controllable in a naturally occurring situation. (659)

Intrapsychic conflicts. Psychoanalytic concept referring to conflicts between the id, superego, and ego. (413)

Intrinsic fatigue. A mechanism of habituation also known as *synaptic depression;* a condition of the nervous pathways that occurs at the synaptic junctions. (70)

Intrinsic rewards. Pleasurable consequences that transpire within an individual as a result of his or her behavior, making it more likely that this behavior will occur in the future without the necessity for external reinforcement. (567)

Introspective analysis. Careful self-observation of mental content; technique for retrieving original elements of psychological experience, without the distortion of meaning and interpretation. (256)

Inverted-U function. Relation between arousal and excellence of performance—increased arousal increases efficiency only up to a point and beyond that has negative effects. (328)

Involuntary response. An unlearned, automatic response of an organism to an eliciting stimulus. (97)

Involutional melancholia. Psychotic reaction characterized by abnormal anxiety, agitation, delusions, and depression; occurs in later years without previous history of psychosis; may be characterized chiefly by depression or can center around paranoid ideas, more frequently diagnosed in women. (488)

Invulnerability. Inability to be injured, wounded, or damaged either physically or psychologically; an illusion or false perception of one's own invulnerability may lead an individual to underestimate external influences and result in failure to cope adequately. (467)

Iodopsin. Photopigment found in the cones of the eye; three types of iodopsin correspond to the wave lengths of blue, green, and red light. (242)

Item analysis. Statistical method for determining the extent to which the responses to each test item in a series differentiate between the groups being tested. (448)

James-Lange theory. Theory that emotion consists of the bodily changes that occur in response to an exciting event, holding that we feel sad because we cry rather than vice versa; it was the first to challenge the idea that mental processes control bodily reactions. (371)

jnd (just noticeable difference). Minimum change in a physical stimulus required to yield the perception (at least 75 percent of the time) that the stimulus has changed. (240)

Kernel sentence. A simple, active, declarative sentence which is the basic element of language, according to Chomsky's theory of linguistic analysis. (145)

Kinesics. Study of nonverbal expression that involves body positions, posture, gestures, and other body movements. (157)

Kinesthetic sense. Somatic sense of active movement. (241)

Labyrinthine sense. Somatic sense of passive movement and body position. (241)

Laissez-faire style of leadership. Nondirective, nonparticipatory style of leadership in which the leader provides resources only when requested to do so. (596)

Latency of response. A measure of the strength of conditioning based on the length of time elapsing between the onset of the conditioned stimulus and the response. (102)

Latent. Condition of existing in a hidden, dormant, or repressed form, but capable of being evoked or elicited at a later time.

Latent content. In Freudian dream analysis, the hidden content of a dream, which indicates the individual's true wishes; changed to the symbolic but more acceptable manifest content. (286)

Latent fat. Condition in which individuals with an abundance of adipocytes have a potential to become obese because of their high base level of fat stores, even if they are skinny as a result of dieting. (344)

Latent stage. In Freudian theory, fourth stage of psychosexual development, during which less conscious sexual interest is thought to be present. (413)

Lateral geniculate nucleus. Relay point in the thalamus, through which impulses pass going from the eye to the occipital cortex. (242)

Lateral inhibition. A perceptual process in which every stimulated visual receptor inhibits the cells adjacent to it. (247)

Lateral specialization. "Two sidedness" of brain function unique to humans, such that the two hemispheres of the brain are specialized to carry out different functions. (317)

Law of effect. A theory formulated by Thorndike that S–R connections are strengthened by satisfying events and weakened by unsatisfying or unsuccessful ones. (109)

Leadership. Capacity possessed by individuals who exert more influence than other members of a group; the traits possessed by an effective leader include intelligence, achievement, responsibility, participation, and status. (595)

Learned helplessness. A sense of helplessness when an organism learns as a result of prior experience that its responses have no effect on a noxious, aversive, traumatic environment; has negative effects on motivation, learning, and performance; analogous to depression in humans. (396)

Legitimate authority. One seen as a valid representative of society, authorized to demand compliance, and who controls significant reinforcers; presence may foster blind obedience to authority. (642)

Leniency error. A common error in perceptual judgment, it is a tendency on the part of a judge to rate nearly all persons near the positive side of a rating scale. (564)

Lens. Transparent structure of the eye which focuses light rays onto the sensitive retina. (237)

Lesion. Destruction of a portion of the brain (or other tissue) by accident, by disease, or through an operation of either an experimental or medical nature. (73)

Libido. Broadly conceived sexual forces; the energy of Freud's creative drive, *Eros*. (413)

Life change rating. A scale developed to measure the degree of adjustment required by various kinds of life changes, both positive and negative. (380)

Limbic system. Region around the upper end of the brain stem that is active in functions of attention, emotion, motivation, and memory. (79)

Limen. The magnitude of a stimulus that is strong enough to be accurately detected by the sensory receptors 50 percent of the time; absolute threshold. (240)

Linear perspective. Perceptual phenomenon of objects appearing both smaller and closer together as they become more distant. (264)

Logical error. In perceptual judgment, the error of assuming that certain traits always go together. (563)

Logotherapy. School of existential analysis originated by Frankl which focuses on the individual's need to see meaning in his or her life; emphasizes spiritual and ethical values; concepts beyond the material ones in a given life environment. (535)

Long-term memory. Relatively permanent memory system with a theoretically unlimited capacity; however, information is not always readily accessible. (176)

Loss of access theory. Theory that forgetting is a process of losing accessibility to the information because of inadequate retrieval cues. (174)

Lysergic acid diethylamide (LSD). Hallucinogenic drug capable of producing vivid imagery, hallucinations, disorganization of thought processes, and symptoms of mental disorder; has also been used in psychotherapy and in cases of terminal illness. (514)

Machiavellians. Individuals who share in common with Machiavelli a set of beliefs about manipulative tactics and relative standards of morality; those who score high on the Christie Mach scale. (439)

Mach scale. A scale of measurement that differentiates the degree to which individuals endorse Machiavelli's rules of conduct; Low Machs are those with absolute standards of behavior, while High Machs are those who have relative standards of manipulative behavior. (439)

Manic reactions or episodes. Psychotic reactions characterized by periods of extreme elation, unbounded euphoria usually without sufficient reason; may alternate with depressive episodes. (487)

Manifest content. In Freudian dream analysis, the surface content of a dream that we remember; masks the unacceptable, emotionally painful latent content. (286)

Mantra. A sound pattern that can be meditated on; in transcendental meditation, syllables drawn from the Hindu holy books that are silently chanted by meditators, who exclude all other thoughts from their minds. (302)

Masochism. A deviant use of pain motivation, it is a desire to inflict pain on oneself, or to suffer pain at the hands of others; a form of pain as pleasure. (390)

Mean. Measure of central tendency, more familiarly known as the average; obtained by adding a group of measurements together and dividing the sum by the number of measurements; also called the *arithmetic mean.* (36)

Measure of variability. Statistic that indicates how dispersed a distribution of scores is; how deviant or scattered scores are from average, typical score. (686)

Mechanistic approach. An approach to the study of physiological processes put forth by Descartes which holds that perception and other bodily processes are mechanistically determined, that is, completely explainable according to the scientific laws of physics and chemistry. (50)

Median. A measure of central tendency of scores or measures in a distribution; the median is the middle measure when the scores have been ordered in order of magnitude, that is, the same number of scores will be higher or lower than the median. (36)

Mediating variable. Unseen, inner process inferred to be intervening between observed stimuli and observed response, also called *intervening variable* or *hypothetical construct.* (107)

Medical model. Model of psychopathology in which psychological and psychiatric behavior problems are viewed as symptoms of a disease state. (461)

Meditation. Conscious concentration of attention and awareness on a single unvarying source of stimulation for an extended period of time; often practiced in the hope that it will facilitate altered states of consciousness in which one can perceive the spontaneous flow of experience. (302)

Memory drum. Apparatus used in memory studies to present items sequentially, each for a fixed amount of time. (169)

Mental age (MA). Degree of mental development as measured by standardized intelligence tests; based on age at which average children make a given score; used in determining IQ. (450)

Mental illness. Term from medical model of psychological disturbance referring to a variety of abnormal behavior patterns severe enough to interfere with the ordinary conduct of life; includes motivational, emotional, and social maladjustments. (456)

Mental retardation. Below-normal intelligence (IQ below approximately 68), due to chronic defects in cognitive capacity such that mental age lags far behind chronological age. (453)

Mescaline. A hallucinogenic drug derived from the peyote cactus, the action of which is similar to that of epinephrine; investigation has found that it can induce a state comparable to schizophrenia; has been used for therapeutic purposes. (296, 511)

Mesmerism. Hypnotic induction by Mesmer's method; believed to involve animal magnetism, an alleged spirit-like force from the planets which could be contained and transmitted to others for therapeutic purposes. (308)

Message. The content and ideas that are communicated; a variable in the study of attitude change. (587)

Metabolism. Chemical processes that take place in all living tissue involving the breakdown of nutrients, by which energy is provided to carry on the life processes. (58)

Metaphor. Figure of speech in which a word denoting one kind of object or action is used in place of another to suggest a likeness between them; it is an implied comparison (e.g., "I am a machine" or "the clock-work mind"). (485)

Microscopic level. Level of psychological analysis wherein interest centers on the smallest discernible parts, events, and subunits of the organism (e.g., study of biochemical reactions within a brain cell). (39)

Mind. The capacity for thought, where thought is the integrative activity of the brain. (364)

Mnemonic strategies. Techniques for encoding material to be learned for more efficient remembering. (181)

Mode. A measure of central tendency; the most frequently occurring measure in a distribution. (36)

Model. Theoretical framework or structure developed in one field, but applied to another in order to lend a clearer, more familiar perspective for understanding, although the model itself is not the explanation. (21)

Molar level. Level of psychological analysis concerned with the functioning of the whole organism or of whole systems within the organism. For example, the study of emotional disorders or vandalism. (44)

"Mold" theory of language. Theory that the language patterns of a cultural group shape the thought patterns and the perceptions of the individuals in that culture; also known as the *Whorf hypothesis*. (212)

Molecular level. Intermediate level of psychological analysis; concerned with processes larger than those at a microscopic level, yet still small, quantifiable units. For example, study of a specific brain-wave pattern of arousal or reaction times to stimulus events. (44)

Monozygotic twins. Identical twins who developed from the same fertilized ovum (zygote), and thus share the identical genetic makeup. (199)

More-or-less principle. Graded activity characteristic of synaptic transmission whereby impulse inputs of various strengths are responded to differently, in contrast to the all-or-none activity found in the conduction of impulses along the axon. (63)

Morpheme. The smallest unit of speech that has a definable meaning; it is made up of some combination of phonemes, and may or may not be a word. (145)

Morphology. The study and description of word formation in language that is concerned with the units of meaning (morphemes). (145)

Motivational theory of forgetting. Theory that forgetting may be intentional; that individuals will forget or remember items of information according to their value and importance to the individual. (175)

Motive. A condition, usually social or psychological, which serves to direct the individual toward a certain goal. (323)

Motoric reproduction processes. Factor influencing observational learning whereby the performance of learned behavior depends upon an individual's ability or skill to carry out the modeled activity. (431)

Motor nerve fiber. See *efferent nerve fiber*.

Multiple personality. Extreme neurotic dissociative state in which the individual develops two or more distinct personalities that alternate in consciousness, each personality being based on sets of motives which are in conflict with those of the others; though dramatic, multiple personality is a rare occurrence. (480)

Mutations. Alterations in the bases of the DNA molecule which change the corresponding amino acid sequence in the proteins formed; may be beneficial, harmful, or even lethal for the individual or offspring. (54)

Mutt-and-Jeff approach. A tactic used in police interrogations in which an investigator who seems pleasant is switched with a cruel or relentless investigator in order to increase belief in and willingness to confess to the friendly investigator. (584)

Myelin sheath. Fatty white covering that surrounds axons and nerve branches of large diameter. Nerve impulses travel faster and with less energy expenditure along these myelinated paths. (61)

Naive personality theories. Informal, everyday judgments that serve as premature personality assessments; based largely on intuition, common sense, and uncontrolled observation of self and others. (409)

Naive realism. Stage of cognitive development in which perception is relied upon to the point that appearance is trusted and accepted as the only reality. (188)

Narcotic analgesics. Group of psychoactive drugs containing opium and its derivatives, such as heroin and certain synthetic drugs. These are the pain killers that also bring a sense of general euphoria; tolerance develops quickly and great physiological dependence occurs, making withdrawal difficult and traumatic. (294)

Nativists. Psychologists who hold that human nature is determined by innate, hereditary factors. They believe that the environment merely develops a nature that is already genetically determined. (196)

Need. Biological or psychological motive condition that serves to direct an individual toward a certain goal. (323)

Need for achievement. Felt need to perform successfully or at least to avoid failure; a general tendency to approach success, the strength of which depends upon one's expectation of success, the incentive value of the type of success involved, and perception of personal responsibility for success. (569)

Negative reinforcer. A reinforcer whose termination increases the probability that the response it follows will occur again under similar circumstances. (118)

Negative transference. Instance of transference in which the feelings attached to the analyst are those of hostility, envy, or some other negative emotion. (519)

Neocortex. Cortex of the brain, which has become more complex during the upward development of more complex species of animals; most highly developed in humans. (77)

Neo-Freudian theories. A group of personality theories held by modern psychologists who have modified Freud's basic theory in various ways; includes Jung's and Adler's theories. (418)

Nerve fibers. Axons. (64)

Nerve impulse. Electrochemical excitation propagated along a neuron or chain of neurons; the means of receiving and transmitting information in the nervous system. (59)

Nerve tract. Nerve pathway; bundle of nerve fibers that have a common place of origin and destination. (64–65)

Neuroglia. Network of cells in which the entire complex of neurons is embedded and that nourish and protect the neurons; (65) also called *glial cells*.

Neurology. Psychiatric, medical study of the brain and nervous system and the diseases thereof. (458)

Neuron. Individual nerve cell; the basic unit of the nervous system. (59)

Neurosis. Emotional disorder characterized by loss of joy in living and excessive anxiety, the true cause of which is not recognized, and overuse of defense mechanisms against anxiety. (476)

Nodes of Ranvier. Regularly occurring points of constriction along the myelin sheath; they serve to improve the reliability and velocity of nervous signal transmission by allowing the impulse to skip from node to node along the axons. (61)

Noise. In physiology, low level energy in the environment picked up by receptor cells, but of insufficient magnitude to cause the firing of sensory neurons. In signal detection, the irrelevant source of energy that interferes with or masks the relevant signal. (60)

Nominal scale. Scale of measurement in which numbers are used solely to differentiate one individual or class from another; the numbers involved do not represent an amount; a qualitative classification, naming. (682)

Nomothetic approach. Psychological approach to understanding human nature which tries to establish general relationships between behavior and causal conditions presumed to be shared by all individuals. (14)

Nondirective therapy. A type of humanistic psychotherapy in which the therapist refrains from advice or direction of the therapy, merely reflecting back the patient's ideas, concerns, and feelings. (536) See also *Client-centered therapy.*

Nonsense syllable. Syllable consisting of a vowel between two consonants, which is meaningless; invented by Ebbinghaus for use in the study of memory. (169)

Nonverbal expression. Any transmission of information or communication without words or word symbols. (156)

Noradrenaline. See *Norepinephrine.*

Norepinephrine. Hormone secreted by the inner part of the adrenal glands, the adrenal medulla, during strong emotion; associated with anger reactions; brings about a number of bodily changes, including constriction of the blood vessels near the body's surface; also called *noradrenaline.* (51, 372)

Norm. Standard based on measurement of a large group of people; used for comparing the standardized score of an individual with those of others within a defined group. (445) See also *Social norm.*

Normal. Conforming to the usual or the norm of expected reactions or values; also used to mean healthy, adequate adjustment. (463)

Normal curve. Graph of the normal distribution in the ideal case, where mean, median, and mode are identical and distribution is symmetrical around this central value. (451, 693)

Normal distribution. Tendency for most members of a large population to cluster around a central point or average with respect to a given trait, with the rest spreading out to the two extremes in a symmetrical bell-shaped curve. (451)

Nosology. Systematic naming and classification of diseases; allows for more reliable diagnosis and standardized treatment. (458)

Nucleotide bases. Paired units in the structure of the DNA molecule. Genes consist of long strings of the nucleotide bases; their order and sequence provide the "instructions" for hereditary traits. (53)

Nucleus. Specialized protoplasm in each cell that directs activities in the cytoplasm. It contains the chromosomes, and is necessary for cell reproduction; also, a group of nerve cell bodies located within the CNS. (57, 65)

Null hypothesis. Hypothesis that the variable being manipulated has *no* effect on the behavior being measured; that following experimental treatment, there will be no difference between the experimental and control groups. Statistical inference tests are designed so as to reject or fail to reject the null hypotheses ($H°$). (33, 35)

Obesity. Excessive body weight; food addiction; a social disease common in an affluent society like our own, it has serious psychological and physiological effects. (341)

Object constancy. The perception of continuous existence of an object as the same object despite changes in size, shape, and position of the retinal image. (238)

Objective anxiety. See *Fear.*

Objective reality. The independently measurable and verifiable physical world. (238)

Observational learning. Learning by observing and identifying with a model; important in childhood learning; influenced by attentional, retention, motoric reproduction, and reinforcement and motivational processes. Concept important in social learning theories. (429)

Obsession. Persistent and irrational idea, usually unpleasant, that comes into consciousness and cannot be banished voluntarily. (478)

Obsessive-compulsive neurosis. A neurotic pattern characterized by the presence of anxiety, with persisting unwanted thoughts and/or the compulsion to repeat ritualistic acts over and over. (478)

Occipital cortex. Lobe at the back of the brain that receives nerve impulses from the eye. (242)

Occipital lobe. Portion of the new brain located at the back of the brain; location of visual projection area. (82)

Operant behavior. Voluntarily emitted response already within an organism's behavioral repertoire that serves to operate on (i.e., have an effect on) its environment. (111–12)

Operant level. The rate at which a freely available response (operant behavior) occurs when its consequences are neither negative nor positive. (112)

Operationism. A means of defining an abstract concept like hunger, or an internal event such as a dream, by framing the definition in terms of the operations used to measure or observe it. Hunger might be defined operationally as ''x number of hours without food.'' Such definitions are important in reducing ambiguity from scientific concepts for experimental replication. (18–19)

Opponent cells. Cells in the lateral geniculate nucleus that make color vision possible by subtracting the output of one type of cone from the output of another. (244)

Oral stage. In Freudian theory, the first stage of psychosexual development, in which the mouth is the primary source of pleasure. (413)

Ordinal scale. An ordered scale of measurement that serves to distinguish one individual or score from another, and also to indicate whether one individual has more or less of the trait being measured. (683)

Organic psychosis. Mental disorder resulting from injury to the nervous system or from such conditions as glandular deficiency or poisons. (486)

Organismic theory. Personality theory that stresses the organization natural to an organism, and the orderly unfolding of the inherited potentialities of the organism and its unity; based on field theory. (421)

Organ of Corti. The receptor for hearing, which is located in the cochlea and contains the hair cells where the fibers of the auditory nerve originate. (248)

Orienting reaction. The mechanism for paying attention to novel environmental stimuli; includes increased sensitivity, visceral changes, and changes in muscles and in brain waves; all responses that serve to maximize sensitivity to information input and to prepare the organism for emergency action. (69)

Orthogenesis. Theory concerning human development which holds that evolution is the progressive manifestation of latent forms of preexisting life, all of which were once infolded in a primordial cell. (56)

Oscilloscope. Instrument used for the study of the brain's activity in which the sudden voltage change that occurs with the firing of neurons appears as a visible wave pattern upon a fluorescent screen. (74–75)

Osmoreceptors. In a hypothesized explanation of the homeostatic control of thirst, they are special receptor cells, believed to be located in the hypothalamus, which respond to signals of increased osmotic pressure by initiating drinking. (347)

Osmosis. Process by which the concentrations of solutions on either side of a semipermeable membrane are equalized; a flow or diffusion of water through the cell membrane, that is, from the cell to the extracellular fluids or vice versa; occurs in the direction that will serve to dilute the more concentrated solution and will thus render the concentration of the two solutions equal. (347)

Ossicles. The three small bones (the hammer, anvil, and stirrup) located in the middle ear. (248)

Other-directed individuals. Individuals who are more responsive to influence by their contemporaries for direction and social influence than are inner-directed people. (437)

Outer membrane. Cell structure that contains the cell contents and separates the cellular material from the external environment. (58)

Oval window. Membrane situated between the middle and inner ear. (248)

Overlearning. Technique for improving memory that involves additional practice after achieving mastery. (180)

Overt. Open to view; not concealed; public and directly observable.

Ovum. Female gamete or germ cell. (54)

Paired-associate learning. Learning in which the subject is first presented with paired items and must then respond with one word or syllable when given the other word or syllable with which it had been paired. (170)

Paradigm. An example or pattern; in research it is a basic procedure or design which represents the essential features of a process being investigated. (97)

Paradoxical intention. A technique of logotherapy useful in the short-term treatment of obsessive-compulsive and phobic patients, which deals with their anticipatory anxiety by encouraging them to do or think about the very thing they fear; similar to implosive therapy. (535)

Paralanguage. A form of nonverbal expression encompassing aspects of communication that are vocal but not verbal, such as vocal pitch and laughing. (157)

Paranoia. Psychosis characterized by systematized, intricate delusions. (486)

Paranoid reactions. A psychotic pattern of reaction marked by the pathological symptom of persistent delusions. (486)

Paranoid schizophrenia. Type of schizophrenia characterized by poorly systematized, often hostile, suspicious, aggressive delusions, and delusions of grandeur; also personality disorganization. (491)

Paraprofessionals. Individuals who have been trained in some aspect of mental health service, but not to an advanced professional level of the M.D. or Ph.D. certified therapist; nevertheless, may perform many services for people in need. (532)

Parapsychology. The scientific study of psychical phenomena. (269)

Parasympathetic division. Division of the autonomic nervous system that controls most of the vital functions of life, such as digestion; its action is opposite to that of the sympathetic division in most cases; its nerves originate from the lower segments of the spinal cord and from the brain stem. (66–67)

Partial reinforcement. Intermittent reinforcement of a response; responses acquired under these conditions are more resistant to extinction than those developed under schedules of continuous reinforcement. (123)

Pathology. Diseased or abnormal physical, mental, emotional, or social state.

Peak experiences. According to Maslow's theory of personality, moments of highest happiness and fulfillment; experienced by self-actualized individuals. (423)

Perceived reality. An individual's experience of objective reality. (238)

Percept. That which is perceived, a perceptual experience; also a *phenomenological experience.* (236)

Perceptual defense. Selective perception caused by emotional and motivational factors; the unconscious screening out or misperception of stimuli that are unpleasant, threatening, or socially taboo. (267–68)

Performance test. Test in which muscular responses rather than verbal ones are required; may be used for intelligence testing. (452)

Peripheral nervous system. A system of fibers connecting the receptors to the central nervous system or connecting the central nervous system to muscles and glands (effectors). (64)

Personality. What characterizes an individual; the sum total of the ways in which an individual characteristically reacts to and interacts with others. (409)

Personification. In Sullivan's theory, an image a person has of someone else; largely determines how he will react to that individual. (420)

Persuasion. Systematic attempts to influence another person's thoughts, feelings, and actions by means of communicated arguments. (584)

Phallic stage. In psychoanalytic theory, the third stage of psychosexual development (between third and fifth year) when genital manipulation and exploration occurs and there is a strong attraction for the parent of the opposite sex, with jealousy toward the same-sexed parent. (413)

Pharmacotherapy. (511) See *Chemotherapy.*

Phenomenal absolutism. Uncritical certainty of the naive observer that he or she is perceiving in a direct, unmediated way the attributes of various objects. (234)

Phenomenal field. In Carl Rogers' personality theory, private world of individual experience, that makes up a person's unique frame of reference. (421)

Phenomenalism. Belief that sequential events can be causally related even if they occur in different places, without direct contact. (190)

Phenomenologists. Psychologists who approach the study of human nature by seeking to understand consciousness. In contrast to the behaviorists they are interested in making use of subjective individual experience, introspective reports, and mental processes to derive their understanding of the world from the subject's point of view. (16)

Pheromone. Odor cues that arouse sexual desire in animals. (349)

Phi phenomenon. Perception of a moving light when, in reality, the stimulus is two stationary lights going on and off in succession. (235)

Phobic reaction. A neurotic defense pattern, it is a process of displacing free-floating anxiety onto some external environmental object which there is no objective reason to fear; leads to avoidance of that specific object or situation. (477)

Phonemes. Basic, distinctive units of sound that make up a particular language. (144)

Phonological level. Level of linguistic analysis concerned with the units of sound (phonemes) that make up speech. (144)

Phrenology. The false belief that the personality consists of various distinct "faculties," each located in a specific area of the brain and evidenced through "bumps" on the skull. (77)

Physiological dependence. Property of certain addictive drugs such that prolonged drug use makes the body physically dependent on the chemical for continued normal functioning. (294, 474)

Physiological psychologist. Psychologist whose professional concern is to relate the biological and physiological functioning of an organism to its experience and behavior. (49)

Pineal gland. Small endocrine gland at the base of the brain that acts as a biological time-measuring system sensitive to the light-dark cycle of night and day; also secretes melatonin, an enzyme that influences sex hormones. Believed by Descartes to be the only point of interaction between body and soul. (50, 51)

Pituitary gland. Endocrine gland associated directly with growth. It releases pituitary growth hormone when activated by the hypothalamus. It is in turn responsible for activating many of the other endocrine glands. (6)

Pivot words. A small group of words that can be attached to a large number of other words to form a meaningful two-word sentence; used by children between 18 and 24 months of age. (150)

Placebo. A chemically inactive substance administered in such a way that patients or research subjects believe they are receiving an active drug. In some cases reactions to the placebo are comparable to those of the active drug. (297)

Place theory. A theory of hearing developed by Helmholtz, who maintained that the basilar membrane consisted of a series of resonating fibers each tuned to a different frequency. (249)

Pleasure centers. Certain sites in the brain, electrical stimulation of which is positively reinforcing to the organism. (74)

Population. The total group from which samples are selected for study; also called *universe.* (39)

Positive regard. Approval of an individual obtained both from self and others; need for positive regard may conflict with an individual's drive toward self-actualization in terms of overreliance on acceptance of others. (421)

Positive reinforcer. A reinforcer whose presentation increases the probability that the response it follows will occur again under similar circumstances. (118)

Positive transference. Instance of transference in which the feelings attached to the analyst are those of love, admiration, or some other positive emotion. (519)

Posthypnotic suggestion. A suggestion given a hypnotized subject to carry out at a time after the termination of the hypnotic experience in response to a given cue. (313)

Preconscious. In Freudian theory, the ideas, thoughts, and images which a person is not aware of at a given moment, but which can be brought into awareness, made conscious, with little or no difficulty; includes anxiety and defense mechanisms. (413)

Predictability. Foreknowledge of the likelihood of events, it prevents against learned helplessness by reducing uncertainty; it serves to increase a subject's perceptual control of the environment. (398)

Predisposition. Likelihood that an individual will develop certain symptoms (for example, schizophrenic reactions) under certain stressful conditions because of prior factors, such as hereditary ones and early life experiences. (493)

Prefrontal lobotomy. Form of psychosurgery in which the nerve fibers connecting the hypothalamus with the prefrontal lobes of the brain are severed, the purpose being to cut intellectual processes off from the emotional processes which normally accompany them; not currently as widely used as in earlier years. (516)

Prejudice. A cluster of learned beliefs, attitudes, and values (usually negative) that bias an individual toward the members of a particular group and give rise to behavioral discrimination; usually based on incomplete information and relative immunity to contrary informational input. (598)

Prelinguistic period. Period of language development preceding the appearance of the beginnings of "true" speech; covers approximately the first year of life. (148)

Preloading. Experimental technique used in the study of thirst in which an animal subject's stomach is injected with a large quantity of water. (346)

Preoperational thought. Second of Piaget's stages of cognitive development (from 2–7 years); characterized by transductive reasoning, egocentrism, and development of the capacity to represent the external world symbolically. (190–91)

Primary mental abilities. The relatively independent abilities, identified through factor analysis, which make up "general intelligence." Among them are verbal, spatial, numerical, and reasoning abilities. (453)

Primary motor area. The portion of the neocortex concerned with motor functions; located immediately in front of the fissure of Rolando. (82)

Principle of uncertainty. Important for understanding psychological experimentation and measurement although it was developed in the field of physics, it states that the very act of measuring a process may change the process itself; also known as the Heisenberg principle of indeterminacy after the physicist who originated it. (41)

Proactive interference. Difficulty in remembering certain material because of the interference of material or associations learned prior to it. (171)

Problem solving. Mode of response that will achieve a goal through the elimination of obstacles. (218)

Productive memory. Theory of memory as a process of active reconstruction, rather than simple retrieval. (169)

Projective techniques. Methods of measuring personality traits in which the subject is presented with a standardized set of ambiguous or neutral stimuli and is encouraged to interpret freely what he sees in them. (446)

Promotive tension. Tension related to another's goal attainment; the arousal of promotive tension may be an explanation of altruism. (574)

Propaganda. Systematic, widespread promotion of particular ideas, doctrines, or practices to further one's cause or to discredit that of the opposition; often the real purpose or source of this form of persuasion is hidden from the intended target; usually directed toward changing political beliefs. (584)

Prosocial aggression. Aggression directed toward socially acceptable purposes, such as punishment for rule-breaking or defending a child against a bully. (611)

Protocol. A code prescribing correct procedure; also used to mean the standardized record of an interview, testing session, or series of experimental observations.

Provocation. Inciting to action, the first step of a violent interaction; interpersonal aggression is often initiated by mutual provocation, often intentional. (623)

Proxemics. A form of nonverbal expression involving spatial distance between people interacting with each other and their orientation toward each other as reflected in touch and eye contact. (157)

Proximal stimulus. The retinal pattern of an object (as opposed to the object itself). (239)

Pseudoconditioning. Phenomenon in which behavior similar to conditioned behavior is obtained without the typical pairing of stimuli, which is the essence of true conditioning. (102)

Psychedelic. Term meaning "mind manifesting," originally a neutral term used to connote any psychoactive drug; now refers to hallucinogens. (291)

Psychiatrist. Medical doctor specializing in the treatment of mental, emotional, and neurological illness; may utilize physical-medical forms of therapy such as psychosurgery, shock, drugs, etc., in addition to verbal-behavioral therapies. (507)

Psychiatry. Field of medicine concerned with understanding, assessing, treating, and preventing mental and neurological disorders. (458)

Psychic determinism. Theory of behavior, both normal and abnormal, postulated by Freud, which holds that mental events are never random, but can be meaningfully or causally related if explored deeply enough. (416)

Psychic trauma. Stressful experience of a severely traumatic or disturbing nature; psychic traumas occurring early in life may not show their effects until many years later. (379)

Psychoactive drug. A drug that affects mental processes. (291)

Psychoanalyst. A psychotherapist who has received advanced training in the Freudian approach to understanding and treating neuroses and other psychological problems. (508)

Psychoanalytic movement. School of psychology, originated by Freud, which emphasizes the study of unconscious mental processes; also a theory of personality and a method of psychotherapy that seeks to bring unconscious desires into consciousness and make it possible to resolve conflicts that usually date back to early childhood experiences. (459)

Psychoanalytic theory. Systematic personality theory put forth by Freud emphasizes childhood experiences, sexuality, and unconscious processes as they affect personality development and its distortions. (412)

Psychobiological therapy. Eclectic approach to therapy advanced by Meyer and aimed at an understanding of all factors—biological, psychological, and social—that may have contributed to the development of disorder. (546)

Psychodynamic psychotherapy. View of psychotherapy emphasizing causes within the individual, but stressing ongoing intense psychological processes rather than physical deficits, excesses, or imbalances as set forth in the biological or somatic view. (518)

Psychogenic. Caused by psychological-emotional factors rather than organic or physiological factors. (378)

Psychokinesis (PK). A form of extrasensory perception in which objects and events are supposedly controlled by an act of thought or will. (269)

Psycholinguistic approach. A theory of language acquisition advocated by Chomsky stating that children learn a system of rules by which they generate sentences, rather than learning strings of words. (153)

Psycholinguistics. The psychological study of language and how it is learned. (144)

Psychological dependence. A strong emotional need for pleasure or the relief of discomfort, stress, or anxiety; often develops in connection with an addiction substance such as a drug. (470)

Psychology. The scientific study of the behavior of organisms; the study of the interactions of biological organisms and their social and physical environments. (4)

Psychophysical scaling. Techniques for measuring psychological response to physical stimuli. (240)

Psychosocial stages. Stages of ego development as formulated by Erikson, incorporating both sexual and social aspects. (418)

Psychosomatic illness. Physical symptoms, often including actual tissue damage, that are attributable to emotional stress or other psychological causes. (131)

Psychosurgery. A form of biological or somatic psychotherapy that involves brain surgery used in the treatment of severe emotional disorders by severing nerve fibers connecting various brain areas, by removing cortical matter, and by lesioning specific brain sites. Recent use in control of violence is in dispute. (516)

Psychotherapy. The general term for all psychological treatment of mental disorders and abnormalities in thought, emotion, or behavior. (506)

Psychotomimetic. Capable of producing abnormal patterns of thought and arousal; term used of certain psychoactive drugs. (291)

Punishment. An aversive stimulus that follows an undesired response, thus producing a decrease in the rate of that response. (116–18)

Purposiveness. An important principle of Tolman's theory of behavior stating that learning is rationally directed and involves hypotheses, expectations, explicit goals, etc. (110)

Qualitative change. Change in character, essential nature, or in a particular distinguishing attribute; change in kind rather than in quantity or amount. (277)

Random sampling. Method of drawing a sample so that each member of the population has an equal chance of being selected, and so that the probability of each member being selected is independent of whether or not any other member is selected; also chance sampling. A necessary feature of assigning subjects to experimental groups. (692)

Range. Simplest measure of variability; the difference between the highest and lowest measurements. (36)

Rapid eye movement sleep (REM). A state of sleep during which rapid eye movements occur; it is characterized by a suppression of voluntary muscle action, major changes in the autonomic nervous system, phasic activity, and an aroused, alert brain-wave pattern; dreaming is more probable during this time. (282)

Rating scale. Device for recording the rater's judgment of himself or others on defined traits. On relative rating scales, the rater ranks the subjects in order from highest to lowest in the group on the trait in question. On absolute rating scales, the judge assigns an absolute value or score to the individual on each trait being rated. (445)

Ratio scale. Scale of measurement that possesses all of the properties of nominal, ordinal, and interval scales with the additional property of an absolute zero as its point of origin; common physical measurements of weight and length are examples of such scales. (683)

Reactance. Need for freedom of action; when freedom of action is threatened, individuals experience adverse emotions and react in a way designed to restore freedom; a theory developed by Brehm. (570)

Reaction formation. Defense mechanism in which the individual's conscious attitudes and overt behavior patterns are the opposite of his or her unconscious wishes, which have been repressed; prevents dangerous desires from being expressed by endorsing opposing attitudes and behavior as a barrier. (415)

Reactive depression. Type of depressive behavior induced by external, situational stressors, not inner ''disease'' causality. (489)

Realistic thinking. Thinking closely tied to reality; concerned with the features, requirements, and demands of the objective, external situation. (185)

Reality orientation. A way of viewing the world that recognizes our need to develop an understanding of predictable relations in order to lend stability and meaning to our lives; assumed by attribution theory. (566)

Reality testing. Process by which individuals evaluate themselves (opinions, abilities, and other attributes) according to objective means, standards, and comparisons, or according to some physical aspect of the environment. (572)

Reasoning. Realistic thinking directed toward problem solving. (185)

Recall. Method of measuring retention; with a bare minimum of cues, subject must reproduce a response learned earlier. (168)

Receptive field. That specific area of the retina from which a given neuron receives its impulses. (246)

Receptors. Structures in the nervous system that are sensitive to specific stimulus qualities (light, sound, pressure, etc.) and that set up nerve impulses in the sensory nerve fibers. (64)

Recidivism. A shift back to one's original attitude, behavior, or condition after a period of therapy or rehabilitation treatment; a measure of the failure of the intervention. (491)

Reciprocal inhibition. Technique of desensitization developed by Wolpe and used in behavior therapy in which responses antagonistic to anxiety, like relaxation, are paired with anxiety-eliciting stimuli. (524)

Reciprocity norm. Norm holding that an individual should treat another as that person has treated him or her. (575)

Recognition. Method of measuring retention that involves the ability to pick out or recognize previously learned items from among alternative responses. (169)

Reconstruction. A form of recall in which only part of an informational item is stored and recalled; the rest is reconstructed from the clues provided by the stored information. (168)

Reductionism. An approach for understanding complex processes and phenomena through the study of their simpler units and component terms. Often used by physiological psychologists in understanding human behavior and the functioning of the brain as they study the many discrete neurological and biochemical events and substances of the brain. (52)

Redundancy. The duplication or multiple duplications of cells that perform specialized functions, thus allowing vital functions to be continued even if some cells are damaged, destroyed, or removed. In information theory, the concept of redundancy refers to the noninformational parts of a signal or message. (58)

Reflex. Specific, automatic response involving only a part of the body, such as salivation or the grasping reflex of an infant; unlearned reactions elicited by stimuli and important for survival of the organism. (68)

Reinforcement. Stimulation that serves to strengthen a response. In classical conditioning, the process of following the conditioned stimulus with the unconditioned stimulus; in instrumental conditioning, the reward of the learner for appropriate responses. (110)

Reinforcement scheduling. The pattern of administration of reinforcement, whether regular or haphazard. (123)

Relative rating scale. See *Rating scale*.

Relative refractory period. Short period during which a stronger than normal stimulus is required to cause the firing of another nerve impulse. It follows the absolute refractory period, and immediately precedes the membrane's return of responsiveness to its usual stimulus level. (61)

Relearning. Method of measuring retention; the subject relearns the original task under the original conditions, the difference in amount of practice needed to reach the original point of mastery providing the measure of retention. (168)

Releaser stimuli. External signal stimuli or cues, such as disliked objects or objects already associated with aggression, which interact with internal conditions to elicit aggression and provide a target for its expression. (615)

Reliability. The degree to which individuals earn the same relative scores each time they are measured according to a certain measuring instrument. (445)

Remission. Term used in the medical model of psychopathology to refer to the improvement or disappearance of the *symptoms* of a mental illness, with implication that the core of disease is still present in latent form. (461)

Remote effects. Effects resulting from an intervention that appears in some part of the system apart from that being specifically studied. (663)

REM rebound. A marked increase in amount of dreaming following deprivation of REM sleep. (285)

Replication. Repetition of an experiment under the same conditions to see if the same results can be obtained a second time—usually by an independent investigator. (30)

Repression. Defense mechanism in which painful or guilt-producing thoughts, feelings, or memories are excluded from conscious awareness; such repressed material may remain active at an unconscious level, resulting in bizarre behavior. (175)

Reproductive memory. Theory of memory as a reproductive process consisting of the retrieval of previously learned material stored in the brain. (169)

Reserpine. Tranquilizing drug widely used in the treatment of mental patients. (511)

Resistances. In psychoanalysis, inability or unwillingness to discuss certain ideas, desires, or experiences, particularly during free association; conceived to be psychological barriers preventing the return to consciousness of painful, repressed material and conflicts. (519)

Resistance to extinction. A measure of the strength of conditioning based on the persistence of a conditioned response during extinction trials or the number of trials necessary to cause extinction. (102)

Respondent behavior. Behavior that is an unlearned, involuntary response to an eliciting stimulus. Essentially a reflex action, it acts to change the organism in order to better adapt it to the environment, rather than changing the environment itself. (97)

Response hierarchy. Ranking of the responses in an individual's repertoire according to the probability that they will occur in a given situation; those at the top of the hierarchy are more likely to occur. (108)

Retention processes. Factor influencing observational learning whereby a model's influence depends on the individual's ability to remember its actions. (431)

Reticular activating system (RAS). The fibers going from the reticular formation to the higher center, acting as a general arousal system and mobilizing the organism for action. (77)

Reticular formation. Mass of nuclei and fibers in the brain stem just above the spinal cord; important in arousing and alerting the organism and also in controlling attention and perceptual discrimination. (77)

Retina. Inner layer of the eye, containing the light-sensitive rods and cones. (237)

Retinal disparity. The slight difference in the retinal image which the two eyes get from the same object; helps make depth perception possible. (265)

Retinine. One of the products formed when rhodopsin absorbs light and is broken down into its component parts. (242)

Retroactive interference. Difficulty in remembering certain material because of the interference of material or associations learned after it. (171)

Retroactive therapy. Treatment to alleviate a condition (e.g., learned helplessness) after it has already occurred or been established. (400)

Retrograde amnesia. A memory defect suffered by patients with damage to the hippocampus in which old habits are remembered, but more recent events are less well remembered; may be caused by a blow on the head or an electroshock convulsion. (80)

Reward conditioning. A form of operant conditioning in which a positive reinforcing stimulus occurs if the organism makes the appropriate responses. (116–17)

Rhinencephalon. Primitive area in the brain containing both olfactory and emotional centers; the "nose brain." (79)

Rhodopsin. Photopigment found in the rods of the eye. (243)

Rods. Retinal receptor cells extremely sensitive to low intensities of light and capable of producing sensations of black, white, and gray (but not color). (241)

Role relation. Relationship between the patterns of behavior expected of individuals because of their place within social arrangements; an expected role relation of subordination may enhance blind obedience to authority. (642)

Rorschach test. A projective test making use of a series of symmetrical inkblots. (447)

Rote recall. Recall for material leaned verbatim, without regard for meaning. (168)

R→S relationship. Relationship that expresses the effect of a response on stimulus events (the physical and social environment); characterizes consequence learning. (95)

Rule modeling. Modeling process by which individuals learn to govern their behavior by the same underlying rules that they have watched a model follow, even when confronted with superficially different situations. (431)

Saccadic movements. Irregular flicking movements of the eye. (237)

Sadism. A deviant use of pain motivation, it is the motive that leads to inflicting pain on others; a form of pain as pleasure. (390)

Sample. A specific group upon which measurements are taken; should be representative of some population or universe about which an inference is to be made. (39)

Satiation. Condition wherein an organism is satisfied or has had enough of a particular goal or activity. (331)

Savings. In the relearning method of measuring retention, the difference between the amount of practice required for the original learning of a given task and the amount of practice required to relearn it. (168)

Scalloping. Typical response pattern of FI schedules; the organism ceases relevant responding after reinforcement, and then sharply increases its response in the period immediately before reinforcement is due to occur. (124)

Scapegoat. A target other than the original source of frustration onto which aggression is displaced; minorities and unpopular, powerless groups are favorite targets of displaced aggression as applied to prejudice. (615)

Schemata. In Piaget's theory, cognitive patterns or structures formed through accommodation, relating one's actions to goals sought. (189–90)

Schizokinesis. Dual reaction in which visceral and physiological components of a conditioned response persist after the behavioral response has extinguished. (104)

Schizophrenia. Psychosis characterized by the breakdown of integrated personality functioning, withdrawal from reality, emotional blunting and distortion, and disturbed thought processes. (286)

Secondary gain. Reinforcement an individual receives from others for manifesting certain abnormal symptoms; positive side effects of negative reactions, such as attention. (490)

Secondary reinforcement. Reinforcement provided by a stimulus that has gained reward value by being previously associated with a primary reinforcing stimulus, although it does not directly satisfy a need. (115)

Selective attention. A characteristic of motivation wherein an organism displays selective attention, that is, is attentive to stimuli relevant or central to its goal-directed behavior, but shows decreased sensitivity to stimuli irrelevant or peripheral to this purpose. (324)

Selective permeability. Property of the cell membrane of a neuron that allows certain ions to pass through it more easily than other ions, thereby changing the polarization of the neuron and permitting the transmission of nerve impulses. (60–61)

Self-actualization. Constant striving to realize one's full inherent potentials, regarded by Goldstein, Rogers, Maslow, and others as the most fundamental goal of the human personality. (421)

Self-concept. According to Roger's theory of self, the individual's awareness of his or her continuing identity as a person; develops gradually from an infant's discovery of the parts of his or her own body and comes to include all of the individual's thoughts, feelings, attitudes, values, and aspirations; a differentiated portion of one's phenomenal field. (421)

Self-inventory. Instrument for measuring personality traits by having the individual give information about himself or herself, validity limited by subject's lack of self-understanding and by desire to put best self forward. (448)

Self-regulatory process. Capacity allowing individuals to control their own actions whereby they evaluate their own behavior according to personal standards and provide their own reinforcements; concept stressed in social learning theories. (429)

Self-system. A dynamism, according to Sullivan, which develops as the individual learns to avoid threats to his security; tends to interfere with ability to deal effectively with others because it becomes isolated from the rest of the personality. (419)

Semantics. The study of meaning. (145)

Semistarvation neurosis. Psychological symptoms that appear as a result of prolonged periods on a markedly insufficient diet; characterized by apathy, depression, and irritability. (339)

Sensation. Awareness of the stimulation of a sensory receptor; first stage in perception. (233)

Sensitizing. Specific function of motivation in which an organism is sensitive to cues that trigger particular response patterns. (327)

Sensory adaptation. Reduced responsiveness to prolonged stimulus input as a result of adaptation of the receptors or fatigue of the muscles rather than as a result of habituation. (70)

Sensory deprivation. Sensory stimulation well below the normal level of sensory input, achieved by eliminating as much visual/auditory/factual stimulation as possible; may lead to hallucinations and delusions. Deprivation may also be in terms of lack of the *variety* of sensory input required by our complex brain. (289)

Sensory information store. A memory system that retains sensory information for a very brief period of time, usually less than a half of a second. (176)

Sensory-motor arc. Functional unit or basic pattern of the nervous system; a chain composed of sensory input at a receptor neuron, one or more interneurons in the spinal cord or brain, and an effector neuron that initiates behavioral output. (67)

Sensory-motor period. First of Piaget's stages of cognitive development (from about 0–2 years); characterized by development in self-identification, efficacy, and causality. (190)

Sensory nerve fiber. See *Afferent nerve fiber*.

Sensory overload. Increased sensory input caused by excessive motor activity and/or intense emotional arousal, which may precipitate altered states of consciousness. (290)

Septal area. A part of the limbic system; lesioning in this area can induce rage in a tame animal. (Lesions of the *cingulate gyrus* of the limbic system can tame a wild animal.) (80)

Serendipity. Chance discovery of something not sought for, often while looking for something else. (30)

Serial anticipation. Method of recall in which the subject first learns a series of words or syllables one at a time so that on successive showings he or she can anticipate the item that comes next. (169)

Serial position effect. In memory, the tendency for the early items in a series to be easier to recall than later items and for the last items to be easier to recall than the middle ones. (170)

Serotonin. A neurotransmitter substance produced in the brain; important in inducing nightly sleep and implicated in schizophrenic behavior. Research with cats has shown that when its production is blocked, brain-wave patterns similar to those characteristic of animals deprived of REM sleep are produced. (51, 286)

Servomechanism. A goal-directed, error-sensitive, self-correcting machine involving four basic processes: input, throughput, output, and feedback. (216)

Set. Readiness to respond in a particular way to some stimulus situation. (266)

Set point level. The base level or initial stable level used as a point of reference. (344)

Sex drive. The motive that leads to the satisfaction of the individual (through tension reduction) and the perpetuation of the species through successful reproduction—enhancing sexual receptivity and increasing approach to a variety of sex-related goals. (348)

Sexism. Prejudice and discrimination solely on the basis of sex of the individual. (604)

Sex-role socialization. Socially accepted stereotypes presented by society that prescribe what is right, proper, and appropriate behavior, values, and appearance for its male and female members. (604)

Sexual reproduction. The union of the gametes of two parents of opposite sex to form a new individual, combining genetic characteristics from both parents. (54–55)

Sham feeding. Experimental procedure used in the study of the metering of food intake; it involves a surgical operation so that food entering an animal subject's mouth is chewed and swallowed, but passes through an opening in the esophagus and never reaches the stomach. (336)

Shaping. Form of operant conditioning used in training in which all responses that come close to the desired one are rewarded at first, then only the closest approximations, until the desired response is attained. (128)

Shared participation. A major source of group influence in which each member of a group is an *active* participant in the decision-making and goal-setting process. (598)

Shock therapy. A form of biological or somatic psychotherapy, it is a method of treating severe mental disturbances by inducing convulsions, which are followed by a state of coma; usually induced by electricity or insulin. (510)

Short-term memory. A limited capacity memory system in which information is stored for only a short length of time and is easily accessible. (176)

Shyness. An awareness of one's inability to take social action when one both wants to and knows how to; a subjective state influenced by the label one attaches to a given set of reactions. (442)

Sigma (Σ). Greek letter used to stand for the phrase "the sum of . . ." (686)

Signal learning. An acquired, learned expectation that one stimulus (the signal) will be followed by a certain other stimulus. (96)

Significant difference. A research convention which sets in advance the formulation of a probability estimate that can be regarded as a statistically trustworthy measure of change, that is, real change, not merely that which might be due to chance; usually that difference is: $p < .05$, probability less than 5 times in 100 by chance. (35)

Simile. Figure of speech comparing two things. For example, saying "I feel like a machine." (485)

Simple schizophrenia. Type of schizophrenia characterized by reduction in interpersonal relationships, apathy, withdrawal, disintegration of thought processes, and inconspicuous delusions or hallucinations. (491)

Simulation. A means of explaining behavior by the artificial representation of the essential elements of a system; often involves a computer which processes information as specified by a model (its program designed by psychologists in an attempt to simulate actual human behavioral processes. (21)

Situational attribution. Attributing actions or events to causes and properties in the environment, situation, or personal interaction, rather than to the individual. (564)

Size constancy. Tendency to perceive the actual size of a familiar object, regardless of its distance from the observer. (239)

Skinner box. Simplified apparatus used in experiments on operant conditioning; a box that contains a bar or other device that the experimental organism must manipulate (operant response) in order to obtain food or some other reward. (122)

Sleep deprivation. A prolonged period of time without sleep, which can alter various physiological and psychological reactions, and may result in fatigue, disorientation, brain-wave abnormalities, paranoid ideas, perceptual distortions, and other behavioral abnormalities depending on a variety of factors. (281)

Social approval. Reinforcement of one's being or actions by others; it comes to be seen as reinforcing in itself and sought after. (573)

Social behavior. Social response; an individual behavior involving or taken with respect to others; response to social stimuli. (562)

Social comparison. Process by which people who feel a need to evaluate their opinions, emotions, and abilities do so by comparing their reactions to those of other people, a test of social reality; a theory developed by Festinger. (572)

Social-emotion leaders. Leaders who stress creating and maintaining good psychological conditions within the group rather than efficiency; concerned with process more than product. (596)

Socialization. The process of social learning by which an individual (usually a child) comes to recognize, practice, and identify with the values, attitudes, and basic belief structure of the dominant institutions and representatives of his or her society. (591)

Social learning theory. Theory stating that current psychological functioning is best understood in terms of a continuous reciprocal interaction between behavior and its controlling conditions, i.e., the environmental influences which include social stimuli, social and personal reinforcement, and past learning history. (428)

Social norms. Group-defined standards concerning what behaviors are acceptable or objectionable in given situations. (642)

Social pathology. Abnormal social conditions in institutions, environments, or systems that create, facilitate, or sustain reactions that are pathological in individuals living under those conditions. (609)

Social psychology. Field of psychology that studies the effect of social variables on individual behavior, attitudes, motives, and perceptions; the study of the effect of others and social environments on an individual's responses. (562)

Social responsibility norm. Norm holding that people should help those dependent on them and in need of their help. (575)

Social selection theory of pathology. Theory concerning the relation between social class and mental illness that the greater incidence of severe pathology among the lower classes is due to genetic theory. (495)

Social stimuli. Independent variables of social significance in influencing individual behavior; may be directly emitted by other people, or may be indirect stimuli previously associated with others, or social norms, etc. (562)

Social stress theories of pathology. Theories concerning the relation between social class and mental illness stating that the greater factors of environmental stress facing the poor lead to their incidence of social and personal pathology. (495)

Social support. A major source of group influence in which individual decisions to act are bolstered when others in the group concur. (590)

Social-systems analysis. A method of understanding patterns of individual response as they relate to and are interdependent with larger social systems, rather than searching for simple causal relations to isolated stimuli. (658)

Social trap. Situation that occurs within a social system in which individuals discover themselves behaving in a manner that they perceive will be harmful in the long run, but that they do not know how to stop or control at present. For example, the nuclear arms race. (668)

Somatosensory areas. Areas of cerebral cortex concerned with kinesthesis and the cutaneous senses; primary area lies just back of the fissure of Rolando and body surface is projected onto it. (81)

Somnambulism. Sleepwalking; may be a kind of dissociative state. (480)

Sound localization cues. Cues that enable organisms to locate the position of sound sources in terms of distance and direction, including the difference in phase, time, and intensity of sound waves as they stimulate the two ears. (265)

Sound spectrograms. Visual representations of spoken sounds, with time shown along the horizontal axis, frequency along the vertical axis, and intensity indicated by the varying shades of darkness of the pattern. (145)

Source. The communicator of the message; that from which the message comes; it is a variable in the persuasive impact of a communication. (587)

Spatial summation. Nerve impulse inputs from several different axons or axon endings arrive at a postsynaptic neuron at the same time, and their effects are added (summed) together. (63)

Specialization. Adaptation of a structure for the performance of some particular, specific function. In multi-celled organisms, cell structures have become highly specialized as to the functions they perform. (58)

Species-specific characteristics. Characteristics found only in a given species. (135)

Sperm. Male gamete or germ cell. (54)

Spinal cord. Part of the central nervous system, it is a longitudinal cord of nervous tissue connecting the brain and the peripheral nervous system. (64)

Spontaneous recovery. The return of a conditioned response following extinction, after an interval of no stimulation. (101)

S–R psychology. A psychological approach that is concerned with the stimulus-response connection as a unit for studying an organism's overt behavior. It is assumed that reinforced practice establishes and stresses the S–R connection. (16) See *Behaviorists*.

S→R relationship. Relationship between a stimulus condition and a response. (95)

S–S relationship. Relationship between two stimulus events in the environment. (94)

Stage of resistance. See *General adaptation syndrome*.

Standard deviation. A measure of the average variation of scores from the group mean; equal to the square root of the variance. (36)

Standardized interview schedule. Interview in which predetermined questions are asked in a set order; a method of making the interview a more objective behavior sampling technique. (446)

Standardized measuring device. Property of a useful measuring device by which it is administered to a large group of subjects representative of the group for which it is intended; then it is administered to all subjects in the same way under the same conditions in order that comparison can be made. (445)

Standard score. Score expressed in terms of standard deviations from the mean. (689)

Stanford-Binet test. A version of the Binet intelligence test, it is an individual test using age level subtests; most widely used children's intelligence test. (452)

Statistical inference. Procedure of drawing general conclusions of a probabilistic nature by studying samples of behavior. (692)

Statistical prediction. Prediction of the future behavior of a given individual on the bases of objective tests and the application of various statistical processes and rules rather than prediction based on clinical judgment. (432)

Stereotype. According to Sullivan, a personification held in common by a group of people. (420) A preconceived, often biased, notion as to how people of a given race, nationality, or occupation will appear or behave. (563)

Stevens' power function. Psychophysical law stating that equal stimulus ratios produce equal subjective ratios. (241)

Stigmatize. To mark or label as deviating from a norm; to single out for discrimination because individual or group is assumed to possess an undesirable trait or history, as ex-convicts or former mental patients, for example.

Stimulants. A group of psychoactive drugs that stimulate the central nervous system, these are the "uppers," and include amphetamines, methamphetamine (speed), cocaine, and caffeine (found in coffee, tea, and colas); tolerance develops quickly and there is a high degree of psychological dependence on these drugs. (295)

Stimulation threshold. The transitional point at which the energy level of an incoming stimulus is sufficient to activate a sensory neuron, causing it to fire. (60)

Stimulus control. Control of the occurrence of a response by means of a dependable signal (S^D) that a reinforcer is available; the responses will thus occur consistently in the presence of the stimulus, but not in its absence. (113)

Stimulus generalization. Tendency for a conditioned response to be evoked by a range of stimuli similar (but not identical) to the conditioned stimulus. (100)

Stimulus generalization gradient. Expression of the functional relationship between stimulus similarity and response strength; as the stimulus becomes less similar to the original conditioned stimulus, the response probability decreases proportionately. (100)

Stress. Nonspecific physiological and psychological response of an individual to any environmental demand or challenge to the integrity of the individual. (377)

Stressor. Anything potentially injurious to the organism, either physically or psychologically, that taxes the adaptive capacity of the organism. (381)

Structure of intellect. Systematic framework used by Guilford to classify the intellectual factors according to content, operation, and production. (426)

Sublimation. A defense mechanism by means of which socially acceptable forms of activity are substituted for unacceptable motives or instinctual drives. (523)

Subliminal stimulus. Term applied to stimulus values too weak to be detected by the sensory receptors; below threshold. (240)

Successive reproduction. Technique used in the study of productive memory in which meaningful material is recalled several times by subjects, and any transformation of the original material is noted. (172)

Suicide. The act of taking one's own life. (496)

Superego. According to Freudian psychoanalytic theory, that part of the personality controlling the internalized moral values learned by the individual as a child; consists of two components, the conscience and the ego ideal. (414)

Superstitious behavior. Behavior based on a coincidental relationship between a response and a reinforcing stimulus event; individual perceives causality when in fact there is none. (116)

Superstitious control. Belief that one has control of one's environment, although this belief is mere superstition and false, which serves to prevent the development of learned helplessness. (399)

Surface structure. The component parts of a sentence and their relations; the superficial structure. (154)

Syllogism. A deductive analysis of a formal problem that consists of two premises and a conclusion. (217)

Symbols. Most sophisticated means of mental representation, which involves the use of an image or word to represent something else. (210)

Sympathetic division. Division of the autonomic nervous system that is active in emergency conditions, as in extreme cold, violent effort or exercise, and states of fear or rage; fibers originate in spinal cord segments between brain stem and lower back. (66)

Symptom. Evidence or manifestation of a disease. (461)

Synapse. The functional space between the end feet of one neuron and the dendrites of one or more other neurons. (63)

Synaptic knobs. See *End feet*.

Synaptic transmission. Nerve impulse transmission between neurons in which a chemical transmitter substance crosses the synaptic gap between an active neuron and adjacent ones; excitation or inhibition of postsynaptic neurons is critical in processing information. (62–63)

Syntax. A branch of linguistic analysis concerned with the order of and relation between words and phrases used to form sentences; (145) also called *grammar*.

Tachistoscope. Apparatus used for the brief exposure of words, symbols, pictures, or other visually presented material in an experimental procedure. (268)

Task leaders. Leaders oriented to complete a task or job as efficiently as possible; concerned chiefly with product. (596)

Telepathy. Form of extrasensory perception in which perceptions are supposedly based on thought transference from one person to another. (269)

Telephone theory. A frequency theory of hearing, according to which the basilar membrane plays the role of a telephone transmitter, relaying impulses of various frequencies to the brain. (249)

Temperament factors. Traits of personality that describe the manner in which an individual characteristically operates, according to Guilford's factor theory. (424)

Temporal conditioning. A form of respondent conditioning in which the time interval between repeated presentations of the unconditioned stimulus becomes the conditioned stimulus. Thus the interval itself comes to elicit the conditioned response just before the UCS is due to appear. (100)

Temporal lobe. Portion of the new brain separated from the frontal and parietal lobes by the fissure of Sylvius; lies just beneath the temples; location of the auditory projection areas. (77)

Temporal summation. Nerve impulse inputs arrive at the postsynaptic neuron in quick succession, and their effects are added (summed) together. (63)

T-groups. Sensitivity training groups used less as therapeutic treatment than for personal growth and training in improving interpersonal skills. (543) See *Encounter groups*.

Thalamus. Brain structure that is a part of the brain stem and a relay station for incoming sensory messages from all parts of the body; important in sensations of pain. (78)

Thanatos. According to Freudian theory, the "aggressive instinct" or "death instinct," one of two drives present at birth; includes all striving toward self-destruction or breaking down of order. (414)

Thematic Apperception Test (TAT). A projective technique making use of pictures about each of which the subject is asked to make up a story, the themes of which are then analyzed for the existence of various sources of motivation. (439)

Theory. A systematic statement of the organization and relationships of assumptions, principles of behavior, and various observed facts and deductions. Theories account for what is known, integrate phenomena, and help predict the unknown. (21–22)

Therapeutic community. Hospital or institutional environment that attempts to promote a sense of staff-patient social community for therapeutic purposes. (547)

Theta waves. An EEG frequency; a possible sign of inhibitory activity. (307)

Thinking. Behavior carried on in terms of ideas, which involves symbolic, representational, and transformational processes. (185)

Thymine. One of the four nucleotide bases that make up the DNA molecule; found paired with adenine. (54)

Time distortion. A perceptual distortion, characteristic of some altered states of consciousness; distortion can make an hour seem like a second, or a second seem like an hour, or distortion may be changes in past, present, or future orientation. (278)

Token economy. Technique of positive reinforcement often employed by mental hospitals and other custodial institutions in which patients are rewarded for socially constructive behavior by tokens, which may later be exchanged for privileges. Major virtues are clear goals and explicit behavioral criteria. (529)

Tolerance. Physiological process by which the effect of a particular drug is reduced by virtue of its having been taken before; thus increased amounts of a drug must be taken in order to achieve the same effects previously produced by a smaller dose. (298)

Trait. A relatively stable characteristic of individuals that can be observed or measured. (423)

Tranquilizers. Drugs used in chemotherapy for antipsychotic purposes; they serve to reduce anxiety and tension. (511)

Transactional approach to perception. Theory stating that perception is the result of our learned transactions with objects and events in our environment; reality is thus constructed from our assumptions and hypotheses about how things, people, and actions are related on the basis of prior transactions with them. (256)

Transadulthood. A newly proposed psychosocial stage extending from late teens to late twenties or early thirties, which has been described as a period of experimenting with different life-styles, searching for career orientation, and testing educational goals; a time in which responsibilities are minimized and personal freedom is maximized. (666)

Transcendental meditation (TM). A form of meditation that involves repeated chanting of and the focusing of attention on a mantra, away from the external material world. (302)

Transduction. Process by which an organism obtains information about the intensity of a stimulus. (240)

Transductive reasoning. Type of reasoning in which a child uses simile by comparing particulars and concluding that particulars similar in one respect are similar in all respects. (191)

Transference. Process by which a patient in psychoanalytic therapy attaches to the therapist feelings formerly held toward some person who figured in a past emotional conflict, often a parent or a lover; may be negative, positive, or ambivalent feelings. (519)

Transformational rules. Rules applied to a kernel sentence to achieve different meanings and kinds of expression; used in converting the deep structure of meaning into the surface structure of spoken sentences, according to Chomsky's theory of language. (145)

Transmitter substances. Chemical substances that facilitate the passage of a nerve impulse from one neuron to another; released at neuronal terminals, they diffuse across the synaptic gap, interact with specific receptor sites on the membranes of adjacent neurons, and either excite or inhibit the postsynaptic neurons; *acetylcholine* is one such substance. (63)

Traumatic events. A physical or psychological event that is injurious, stressful or shocking; such occurrences early in life may be the source of adult fears or neurosis. (412)

Trial and error. Attempts to solve a problem by trying out alternative possibilities and discarding those that prove to be unsatisfactory. (218)

Trigger features. Patterns of sensory stimulation that initiate responding in particular sensory neurons. (244)

t-test. Test of statistical inference; used to determine whether the probability that the means of two sets of scores come from the same population or can be assumed to be different. (694)

Unconditioned response (UCR). Response made to an unconditioned stimulus; often an inborn reflex, as in the case of salivation in response to food. (97)

Unconditioned stimulus (UCS). Stimulus that elicits a response in the absence of conditioning. (97)

Unconscious. Lack of conscious, rational awareness; in Freudian theory, that portion of the psyche that is a repository for repressed conflicts and desires not directly accessible to consciousness. (413)

Unity and fusion. Often characteristic of an altered state of consciousness; the notion of the separateness of self seems to vanish and be replaced by the experience of a collective identity. (279)

Validity. The extent to which an instrument actually measures what it is intended to measure; the "goodness" of the concept, idea, measuring instrument. Validity may be assessed by external criteria or by internal consistency. (445)

Vandalism. Seemingly senseless acts of destruction of property; however, it may serve a specific purpose: acquisitive, tactical, ideological, vindictive, malicious, or playful. (635)

Variable. Any quantity or property subject to change. (11)

Variable interval schedule (VI). Intermittent schedule by which reinforcement is given after differing lengths of time, regardless of the number of correct responses made in between. (124)

Variable ratio schedule (VR). Intermittent schedule by which reinforcement is given after a variable number of responses. (124)

Variance. A measure of variability that is computed by adding the square of the difference between each measurement and the mean, and dividing by the number of measurements; square of the standard deviation. (687)

Veridical perception. Perception in which the person's subjective perceptual experience of an object agrees with its objective physical characteristics, as measurable and verifiable independently. (236)

Visual domination. Domination of vision over auditory perception when a conflict occurs between the two; also known as *visual capture*. (262)

Volley theory. Auditory theory that nerve fibers operate in groups and that various fibers discharge their volleys of impulses at different times, making it possible for a bundle of fibers to reproduce high frequencies. (239)

Voodoo deaths. Sudden deaths that occur when individuals who believe in witchcraft, voodoo, or the like discover that they have committed some transgression against or have been stricken down by supernatural powers. (392)

Weber-Fechner law. A psychophysical law stating that the stimulus increment that produces a jnd is a constant proportion for most values of the stimulus. (240)

Wechsler Adult Intelligence Scale (WAIS). Intelligence test battery for adults which includes both performance and verbal subtests; used also to diagnose cognitive defects through variability in a pattern of subtest scores. Children's version (WISC) also available. (452)

Whorf hypothesis. See *"Mold" theory of language.*

Yoga. A system of beliefs and practices the goal of which is to attain a union of self with Supreme Reality; popularly, it is meditation based on physical posturing and breathing. (304)

Zeigarnik effect. Tendency to have greater recall of tasks interrupted before completion than of completed ones. (175–76)

Zen. A Japanese school of Buddhism that teaches self-discipline, deep meditation, and the attainment of enlightenment. (304)

Zygote. Cell formed by the union of the male and female gametes which develops into a new organism. (54)

References

Abelson, R. P., Aronson, E., McGuire, W. J., Newcomb, T. M., Rosenberg, M. J., & Tannenbaum, P. H. (Eds.) *Theories of cognitive consistency: A sourcebook.* Chicago: Rand McNally, 1968.

Abelson, R. P., & Carroll, J. D. Computer simulation of individual belief systems. *American Behavioral Scientist,* 1965, **8,** 24–30.

Adamson, R. E. Functional fixedness as related to problem solving: A repetition of three experiments. *Journal of Experimental Psychology,* 1952, **44,** 288–91.

Adolph, E. Regulation of body water content through water ingestion. In M. Wayner (Ed.), *Thirst.* New York: Macmillan, 1964.

Adorno, T. W., Frenkel-Brunswick, E., Levinson, D. J., & Sanford, R. N. *The authoritarian personality.* New York: Harper & Row, 1950.

Akishige, Y. A historical survey of the psychological studies on Zen. In Y. Akishige (Ed.), *Psychological studies on Zen.* Fukuoka, Japan: Kyushu University, 1970.

Akiskal, H. S., & McKinney, W. T., Jr. Depressive disorders: Toward a unified hypothesis. *Science,* 1973, **182,** 20–29.

Allport, F. H. *Theories of perception and the concept of structure.* New York: Wiley, 1955.

Allport, G. W. *Personality and social encounter.* Berkeley, Calif.: Beacon Press, 1960.

Almond, R. The therapeutic community. *Scientific American,* 1971, **224,** 34–42.

Altman, D., Levine, M., & Nadien, J. Unpublished research cited in S. Milgram, The experience of living in cities. *Science,* 1970, **167,** 1461–68.

Amarel, S. On the mechanization of creative processes. *IEEE Spectrum,* 1966, **3**(4), 112–14.

American Psychological Association. Ethical Standards of psychologists. *American Psychologist,* Jan. 1963, **18**(1).

American Psychological Association. Ad Hoc Committee on Ethical Standards in Psychological Research. Proposed ethical principles submitted to the American Psychological Association membership for criticism and modification, 1971, p. 10.

American Psychological Association. A resolution concerning behavior and heredity. *American Psychologist,* July 1972, **27**(7), 660. Excerpt reprinted by permission of the American Psychological Association.

American Psychological Association. Ethical principles in the conduct of research with human participants. *American Psychologist,* Jan. 1973, **28**(1), 79–80.

American Psychological Association Task Force Report. On issues of sexual bias in graduate education (Jan Birk, Chairperson), 1974.

Ames, A. Visual perception and the rotating trapezoidal window. *Psychological Monographs,* 1951, **65**(7, Whole No. 234).

Ammons, R. B. Effects of knowledge of performance: A survey and tentative theoretical formulation. *Journal of Genetic Psychology,* 1956, **54,** 279–99.

Anand, B. K., Chhina, G. S., & Singh, B. Some aspects of electroencephalographic studies in Yogis. *EEG Clinical Neurophysiology,* 1961, **13,** 452–56.

Arendt, H. *Eichmann in Jerusalem: A report on the banality of evil.* New York: Viking, 1965.

Argyle, M., & Little, R. Do personality traits apply to social behavior? *Journal of the Theory of Social Behavior,* 1972, **2,** 1–35.

Arling, G. L. *Effects of social deprivation on maternal behavior of rhesus monkeys.* Unpublished master's thesis, University of Wisconsin, 1966.

Arnold, M. B. *Emotion and personality.* New York: Columbia University Press, 1960. 2 vols.

Aronfreed, J. The socialization of altruistic and sympathetic behavior: Some theoretical and experimental analyses. In J. Macauley & L. Berkowitz (Eds.), *Altruism and helping behavior: Social psychological studies of some antecedents and consequences.* New York: Academic Press, 1970.

Aronson, E. Some antecedents of interpersonal attraction. In W. J. Arnold & D. Levine (Eds.), *Nebraska symposium on motivation.* Lincoln: University of Nebraska Press, 1969.

Aronson, E., & Carlsmith, M. J. Experimentation in social psychology. In G. Lindzey & E. Aronson (Eds.), *Handbook of Social Psychology.* Vol. 2. Reading, Mass.: Addison-Wesley, 1969.

Aronson, E., & Linder, D. Gain and loss of esteem as determinants of interpersonal attractiveness. *Journal of Experimental and Social Psychology,* 1965, **1,** 156–71.

Asch, S. E. Opinions and social pressure. *Scientific American,* 1955, **193**(5), 31–35.

Aserinsky, E., & Kleitman, N. Regularly occurring periods of eye mobility and concomitant phenomena during sleep. *Science,* 1953, **118,** 273–74.

Ashley, W. R., Harper R. S., & Runyon, D. L. The perceived size of coins in normal and hypnotically induced economic states. *American Journal of Psychology,* 1951, **64,** 564–72.

Asimov, I. *The intelligent man's guide to science.* Vol. 2. New York: Basic Books, 1960.

Asimov, I. *Twentieth century discovery.* Garden City, N.Y.: Doubleday, 1969.

Associated Press. Excerpt from "Solution for a Burning Issue" from *The Associated Press,* Aug. 16, 1971. Reprinted by permission.

Atkinson, J. W. (Ed.) *Motives in fantasy, action, and society.* Princeton, N.J.: Van Nostrand, 1958.

Atkinson, J. W. *An introduction to motivation.* Princeton: Van Nostrand, 1964.

Atkinson, R. C. Teaching children to read using a computer. *American Psychologist,* 1974, **29,** 169–178.

Axelrod, J., & Wurtman, R. Biological rhythms and the pineal gland. *Mental Health Program Reports, No. 4.* Chevy Chase, Md.: National Institute of Mental Health, 1970.

Ayllon, T., & Azrin, N. H. The measurement and reinforcement of behavior of psychotics. *Journal of the Experimental Analysis of Behavior,* 1965, **8,** 357–83.

Ayllon, T., & Michael, J. The psychiatric nurse as a behavioral engineer. *Journal of the Experimental Analysis of Behavior,* 1959, **2,** 323–34.

Azrin, N. H., & Holz, W. C. Punishment. In W. K. Honig (Ed.), *Operant behavior.* New York: Appleton-Century-Crofts, 1966.

Bachrach, A. J., Erwin, W. J., & Mohr, J. P. The control of eating behavior in an anoretic by operant conditioning techniques. In L. P. Ullmann & L. Krasner (Eds.), *Case studies in behavior modification.* New York: Holt, Rinehart & Winston, 1965.

Back, K. Intervention techniques: Small groups. In P. H. Mussen & M. R. R. Rosenzweig (Eds.), *Annual review of psychology, 1974.* Vol. 25. Palo Alto, Calif.: Annual Reviews, 1974.

Badia, P., Culbertson, S., & Harch, J. Choice of longer or stronger signalled shock over shorter or weaker unsignalled shock. *Journal of the Experimental Analysis of Behavior,* Jan. 1973, **19**(1), 25–32.

Baer, D. M. A case for the selective reinforcement of punishment. In C. Neuringer & J. L. Michael (Eds.), *Behavior modification in clinical psychology.* New York: Appleton-Century-Crofts, 1970.

Balagura, S. Influence of osmotic and caloric loads upon lateral hypothalamic self-stimulation. *Journal of Comparative and Physiological Psychology,* 1968, **66,** 325–28. (a)

Balagura, S. Conditioned glyceric responses in the control of food intake. *Journal of Comparative and Physiological Psychology,* 1968, **65,** 30–32. (b)

Bandura, A. Influence of models' reinforcement contingencies on the acquisition of imitative responses. *Journal of Personality and Social Psychology,* 1965, **1,** 589–95.

Bandura, A. *Principles of behavior modification.* New York: Holt, Rinehart & Winston, 1969.

Bandura, A. Modeling therapy. In W. S. Sahakian (Ed.), *Psychopathology today: Experimentation, theory, and research.* Itaska, Ill.: F. E. Peacock, 1970.

Bandura, A. *Social learning theory.* (Module) Morristown, N.J.: General Learning Corp., 1971.

Bandura, A. *Aggression: A social learning analysis.* Englewood Cliffs, N.J.: Prentice-Hall, 1973.

Bandura, A., Ross, D., & Ross, S. A. Imitation of film-mediated aggressive models. *Journal of Abnormal and Social Psychology,* 1963, **66,** 3–11.

Bandura, A., & Walters, R. H. *Adolescent aggression.* New York: Ronald, 1959.

Banks, W. C. Determinants of interpersonal influence strategies. Unpublished dissertation, Stanford University, 1973.

Banks, W. C., Zimbardo, P. G., & Phillips, S. Variables related to the choice of positive versus negative means of interpersonal influence. Unpublished manuscript, Stanford University, 1974.

Barber, T. X. *LSD, marihuana, yoga and hypnosis.* Chicago: Aldine, 1970.

Barefoot, J. C., & Girodo, M. The misattribution of smoking cessation symptoms. *Canadian Journal of Behavioral Science,* Oct. 1972, **4**(4), 358–63.

Barfield, R., & Geyer, L. Sexual behavior: Ultrasonic postejaculatory song of the male rat. *Science,* June 23, 1972, **176,** 1349–90.

Barker, R. G. The stream of behavior as an empirical problem. In R. G. Barker (Ed.), *The stream of behavior.* New York: Appleton-Century-Crofts, 1963.

Barlow, H. B. Action potentials from the frog's retina *and* Summation and inhibition in the frog's retina. *Journal of Physiology,* 1953, **119**(1), 58–68, 69–88.

Barlow, H. B. Single units and sensation: A neuron doctrine for perceptual psychology? *Perception,* 1972, **1,** 371–94.

Barnett, S. A. Attack and defense in animal societies. In C. D. Clemente & D. B. Lindsley (Eds.), *Aggression and defense.* Los Angeles: University of California Press, 1967.

Barron, F. X. *Creativity and psychological health: Origins of personal vitality and creative freedom.* Princeton, N.J.: Van Nostrand, 1963.

Barta, R. The representation of Poles, Italians, Latins and blacks in the executive suites of Chicago's largest corporations. Report of The Institute for Urban Life, Chicago, 1974.

Bartlett, F. C. *Remembering: A study in experimental and social psychology.* New York: Macmillan, 1932.

Bash, K. W. Contribution to a theory of the hunger drive. *Journal of Comparative Psychology,* 1939, **28,** 137–60.

Bateson, G., Jackson, D. D., Haley, J., & Weakland, J., Toward a theory of schizophrenia. *Behavioral Sciences,* 1956, **1,** 251–64.

Bavelas, A., Hastorf, A. H., Gross, A. E., & Kite, W. R. Experiments on the alteration of group structure. *Journal of Experimental and Social Psychology,* 1965, **1,** 55–70.

Bayley, N. Behavioral correlates of mental growth: Birth to thirty-six years. *American Psychologist,* 1968, **23,** 1–17.

Bazelon, D. L. Untitled mimeograph from address to the American Association of Correctional Psychologists' Conferences on "Psychology's roles and contributions in problems of crime, delinquency and corrections." Lake Wales, Florida, Jan. 20, 1972. Cited in Caplan, N., & Nelson, S., On being useful. *American Psychologist,* 1973, **28**(3), 199–211.

Beadle, G. W. The new genetics: The threads of life. In *1964 Britannica book of the year.* Chicago: Britannica, 1964.

Beck, A. T. *Depression.* New York: Harper & Row, 1967.

Beck, A. T., Kovacs, M., & Weissman, A. Hopelessness and suicidal behavior. *Journal of the American Medical Association,* 1975. **234,** 1146–49.

Becker, H. S. *Outsiders: Studies in the sociology of deviance.* New York: The Free Press, 1963.

Becker, H. S. History, culture and subjective experience: An exploration on the social bases of drug-induced experiences. *Journal of Health and Social Behavior,* 1967, **8,** 163–76.

Beecher, H. K. Generalization from pain of various types and diverse origins. *Science,* 1959, **130,** 267–68.

Bellugi-Klima, U. Linguistic mechanisms underlying child speech. In E. M. Zale (Ed.), *Proceedings of the conference on language and language behavior.* New York: Appleton-Century-Crofts, 1968.

Bem, D. J. An experimental analysis of self-persuasion. *Journal of Experimental and Social Psychology,* 1965, **1,** 199–218.

Bem, D. J. Self-perception theory. In L. Berkowitz (Ed.), *Advances in experimental social psychology.* Vol. 6. New York: Academic Press, 1972.

Bem, D. J., & Allen, A. On predicting some of the people some of the time: The search for cross-situational consistencies in behavior. *Psychological Review,* 1974, in press.

Bem, S. L., & Bem, D. J. Homogenizing the American woman: The power of an unconscious ideology. In P. Zimbardo & C. Maslach (Eds.), *Psychology for our times: Readings.* Glenview, Ill.: Scott, Foresman, 1973.

Berger, E. *The psychology of gambling.* New York: Hill & Wang, 1957.

Bergin, A. E. Some implications of psychotherapy research for therapeutic practice. *Journal of Abnormal Psychology,* 1966, **71,** 235–46.

Berko, J. The child's learning of English morphology. *Word,* 1958, **14,** 150–77.

Berkowitz, L. The concept of aggressive drive: Some additional considerations. In L. Berkowitz (Ed.), *Advances in experimental social psychology.* Vol. 2. New York: Academic Press, 1965.

Berkowitz, L. Social norms, feelings, and other factors affecting helping and altruism. In L. Berkowitz (Ed.), *Advances in experimental social psychology.* Vol. 6. New York: Academic Press, 1972.

Berkowitz, L., & LePage, A. Weapons as aggression-eliciting stimuli. *Journal of Personality and Social Psychology,* 1967, **7,** 202–7.

Berkum, M. M., Bialek, H. M., Kern, R. P., & Yagi, K. Experimental studies of psychological stress in man. *Psychological Monographs,* 1962, **76** (15, Whole No. 534).

Berlyne, D. E. *Conflict, arousal, and curiosity.* New York: McGraw-Hill, 1960.

Bernard, L. L. *Instinct.* New York: Holt, Rinehart & Winston, 1924.

Bernstein, D. A. Modification of smoking behavior: An evaluative review. *Psychological Bulletin,* 1969, **71,** 418–20.

Bernstein, I. S. Alternatives to violence. *Mental Health Program Reports, No. 4.* Publication No. 5026. Chevy Chase, Md.: National Institute of Mental Health, 1970.

Bernstein, I. S. Personal communication, April, 22, 1974.

Berscheid, E., & Walster, E. Physical attractiveness. In L. Berkowitz (Ed.), *Advances in experimental social psychology.* Vol. 7. New York: Academic Press, 1974.

Bettelheim, B. Individual and mass behavior in extreme situations. *Journal of Abnormal and Social Psychology,* 1943, **38,** 417–52.

Bettelheim, B. Individual and mass behavior in extreme situations. In E. E. Maccoby, T. Newcomb, & E. Hartley (Eds.), *Readings in social psychology.* New York: Holt, Rinehart & Winston, 1958.

Bettelheim, B. *The informed heart.* New York: The Free Press, 1960.

Bichat, X. *Physiological researches upon life and death.* Philadelphia: Smith & Maxwell, 1809.

Bierbrauer, G. A. Attribution and perspective: Effects of time set and role on interpersonal inference. Unpublished doctoral dissertation, Stanford University, 1973.

Bindra, D. B. Interrelated mechanisms of reinforcement and motivation, and the nature of their influence on response. In W. J. Arnold & D. Levine (Eds.), *Nebraska symposium on motivation.* Lincoln: University of Nebraska Press, 1969.

Binet, A., & Simon, T. La mesure du développement de l'intelligence chez les jeunes enfants. *Bulletin de la Société Libre pour L'Étude Psychologique de L'Enfant,* 1911, **11,** 187–248.

Bingham, C. C. *A study of American intelligence.* Princeton, N.J.: Princeton University Press, 1923.

Birch, H. G. The relation of previous experience to insightful problem-solving. *Journal of Comparative Psychology,* 1945, **38,** 367–83.

Birch, H. G. Sources of order in the maternal behavior of animals. *American Journal of Orthopsychiatry,* 1956, **26,** 279–84.

Björntorp, P. Disturbances in the regulation of food intake. *Advances in Psychosomatic Medicine,* 1972, **7,** 116–27.

Blake, A. Coin collectors. *California Living Magazine,* Jan. 23, 1972. Reprinted with permission from *California Living,* the magazine of the *San Francisco Sunday Examiner & Chronicle.*

Blake, B. G. A follow-up of alcoholics treated by behavior therapy. *Behavior Research and Therapy,* 1967, **5,** 89–94.

Blakemore, C., & Cooper, G. F. Development of the brain depends on the visual environment. *Nature,* 1970, **228,** 477–78.

Blanchard, E. B., & Young, L. D. Self-control of cardiac functioning: A promise as yet unfulfilled. *Psychological Bulletin,* 1973, **79,** 145–63.

Bloom, B. L. *Community mental health: A historical and critical analysis.* (Module) Morristown, N.J.: General Learning Corp., 1973.

Blum, R. H. *I. Society and Drugs; II. Students and Drugs.* San Francisco: Jossey-Bass, 1969.

Blumenthal, M. Predicting attitudes toward violence. *Science,* 1972, **176,** 1296–1303.

Bolles, R. *Theory of motivation.* New York: Harper & Row, 1967.

Boring, E. G. *A history of experimental psychology.* New York: Appleton-Century-Crofts, 1950.

Boulding, K. E. The social system and the energy crisis. *Science,* April 19, 1974, **184,** 225–57. Copyright © 1974 by the American Association for the Advancement of Science. Excerpt reprinted by permission.

Bower, G. H., & Clark, M. C. Narrative stories as mediators for serial learning. *Psychonomic Science,* 1969, **14,** 181–82.

Bower, G. H., & Trabasso, T. Reversals prior to solution in concept identification. *Journal of Experimental Psychology,* 1963, **66,** 409–18.

Bower, T. G. R. Slant perception and shape constancy in infants. *Science,* 1966, **151,** 832–34. (a)

Bower, T. G. R. The visual world of infants. *Scientific American,* 1966, **215,** 85–92. (b)

Brady, J. P., & Levitt, E. E. Hypnotically induced visual hallucinating. *Psychosomatic Medicine,* 1966, **28,** 351–63.

Brady, J. V. Emotion and the sensitivity of psychoendocrine systems. In D. C. Glass (Ed.), *Neurophysiology and emotion.* New York: Rockefeller University Press, 1967.

Brady, J. V., Porter, R. W., Conrad, D. G., & Mason, J. W. Avoidance behavior and the development of gastroduodenal ulcers. *Journal of the Experimental Analysis of Behavior,* 1958, **1,** 69–73.

Braine, M. D. S. The ontogeny of English phrase structure: The first phase. *Language,* 1963, **39,** 1–13.

Bransford, J. D., & Franks, J. J. The abstraction of linguistic ideas. *Cognitive Psychology,* 1971, **2,** 331–50.

Breger, L. C., & McGaugh, J. L. Critique and reformulation of learning theory approaches to psychotherapy and neurosis. *Psychological Bulletin,* 1965, **63,** 338–58.

Brehm, J. W. *A theory of psychological reactance.* New York: Academic Press, 1966.

Brehm, J. W., & Cohen, A. R. *Explorations in cognitive dissonance.* New York: Wiley, 1962.

Breland, K. & Breland, M. *Animal behavior.* New York: Macmillan, 1966.

Brenner, M. Caring, love, and selective memory. Paper presented at the Annual Convention of American Psychological Association, Washington, D.C., 1971.

Brenner, M. The next-in-line effect. *Journal of Verbal Learning and Verbal Behavior,* 1973, **12,** 320–23.

Brenner, M. H. *Mental illness and the economy.* Cambridge. Mass.: Harvard University Press, 1973.

Bridgman, P. W. *The logic of modern physics.* New York: Macmillan, 1927.

Brislin, R. W., Lonner, W. J., & Thorndike, R. M. *Cross-cultural research methods.* New York: Wiley, 1973.

Broadbent, D. E. Cognitive psychology: Introduction. *British Medical Bulletin,* 1971, **27,** 191–94.

Brodeur, D. W. The effects of stimulant and tranquilizer placebos on healthy subjects in a real life situation. *Psychopharmacologia.* 1965, **7,** 444–52.

Brody, J. E. When illness follows a "giving up." *The New York Times,* April, 7, 1968, p. 11.

Brodsky, S. L. *Psychologists in the criminal justice system.* Urbana, Ill.: University of Illinois Press, 1973.

Brodzinsky, D. M., Jackson, J. P., & Overton, W. F. Effects of perceptual shielding in the development of spatial perspectives. *Child Development,* 1972, **43,** 1041–46.

Brower, L. P., & Cranston, P. Courtship of the Queen Butterfly, Danaus Gillippus Berenice. 16 mm. sound film, serial number PCR 2123K, Psychological Cinema Register, Pennsylvania State University, 1962.

Brown, C. *Manchild in the promised land.* New York: Macmillan, 1965. Copyright © Claude Brown 1965. Excerpt reprinted by permission of Macmillan Publishing Co., Inc., and Jonathan Cape Ltd.

Brown, J. S. A proposed program of research on psychological feedback (knowledge of results) in the performance of psychomotor tasks. *Conference Report 49–2*, USAF Air Training Command Human Resources Research Center, 1949, 81–87.

Brown, P. L., & Jenkins, H. M. Auto-shaping of the pigeon's key peck. *Journal of Experimental Analysis of Behavior*, 1968, **11**, 1–8.

Brown, R. W. Language and categories. In J. S. Bruner, J. J. Goodnow, & G. A. Austin (Eds.), *A study of thinking*. New York: Wiley, 1956.

Brown, R. W. The first sentences of child and chimpanzee. Unpublished mimeo report, Harvard University, 1970.

Brown, R. W., Cazden, C. B., & Bellugi-Klima, U. The child's grammar from I to III. In J. P. Hill (Ed.), *Minnesota symposia on child psychology*. Vol. 2. Minneapolis: University of Minnesota Press, 1969.

Brown, R. W., & McNeil, D. The "tip-of-the-tongue" phenomenon. *Journal of Verbal Learning and Verbal Behavior*, 1966, **5**, 325–37.

Brôzek, J. Experimental investigations on nutrition and human behavior: A postscript. *American Scientist*, June 1963, **51**, 139–63.

Bruch, H. Eating disorders in adolescence. In J. Zubin and A. M. Freedman (Eds.), *The psychopathology of adolescence*. New York: Grune & Stratton, 1971.

Bruch, H. *Eating disorders*. New York: Basic Books, 1973. Excerpt from Chapter 11, © 1973 Basic Books, Inc., Publishers, New York.

Bruner, J. S. The course of cognitive growth. *American Psychologist*, 1964, **19**, 1–15.

Bruner, J. S. *Beyond the information given*. New York: Norton, 1973.

Bruner, J. S., & Goodman, C. C. Value and need as organizing factors in perception. *Journal of Abnormal and Social Psychology*, 1947, **42**, 33–44.

Bruner, J. S., Olver, R. R., Greenfield, P. M., et al. *Studies in cognitive growth*. New York: Wiley, 1966.

Bryan, J. H., & Schwartz, T. The effects of film material upon children's behavior. *Psychological Bulletin*, 1971, **75**, 50–59.

Bryan, J. H., & Test, M. Models and helping: Naturalistic studies in aiding behavior. *Journal of Personality and Social Psychology*, 1967, **6**, 400–407.

Buber, M. *Pointing the way*. New York: Harper & Row, 1957.

Burger, R. E. Who cares for the aged? *Saturday Review*, 1969, **52**(4), 14–17.

Burks, B. S. The relative influence of nature and nurture upon mental development: A comparative study of foster parent-foster child resemblance and true parent-true child resemblance. In *National Society for the Study of Education*. 27th Yearbook, Part 1, 1928.

Burnham, J. *Beyond modern sculpture*. New York: George Braziller, 1968.

Burt, C. The evidence for the concept of intelligence. *British Journal of Educational Psychology*, 1955, **25**, 158–77.

Burt, C. The genetic determination of differences in intelligence: A study of monozygotic twins reared together and apart. *British Journal of Psychology*, 1966, **57**, 137–53.

Burt, C., & Howard, M. The relative influence of heredity and environment on assessments of intelligence. *British Journal of Statistical Psychology*, 1957, **10**, 99–104.

Bykov, K. M. *The cerebral cortex and the internal organs*. New York: Chemical Publishing Co., 1957.

Byrne, D. *The attraction paradigm*. New York: Academic Press, 1971.

Caldwell, D. K., & Caldwell, M. C. Dolphins communicate—but they don't talk. *Naval Reviews*, June–July 1972, 23–27.

Calhoun, J. B. A "behavioral sink." In E. L. Bliss (Ed.), *Roots of behavior*. New York: Harper & Row, 1962.

Calhoun, J. B. How the social organization of animal communities can lead to a population crisis which destroys them. Reported by M. Pines, *Mental Health Program Reports, No. 5*. (DHEW) Publication No. (HSM) 72-9042. Chevy Chase, Md.: National Institute of Mental Health, Dec. 1971.

Campbell, B. A., & Sheffield, F. D. Relation of random activity to food deprivation. *Journal of Comparative and Physiological Psychology*, 1953, **46**, 320–22.

Campbell, D. Ethnocentrism and other altruistic motives. In D. Levine (Ed.), *Nebraska symposium on motivation*. Lincoln: University of Nebraska Press, 1965.

Campbell, D., Sanderson, R. E., & Lavertz, S. G. Characteristics of a conditional response in human subjects during extinction trials following a single traumatic conditioning trial. *Journal of Abnormal and Social Psychology*, 1964, **68**, 627–39.

Campbell, L. S. Letter to the Editor. *The New York Times*, Feb. 4, 1972. © 1972 by The New York Times Company. Reprinted by permission of the author and The New York Times Company.

Cannon, W. B. *Bodily changes in pain, hunger, fear and rage*. (2nd ed.) New York: Appleton-Century-Crofts, 1929.

Cannon, W. B. Hunger and thirst. In C. Murchison (Ed.), *A handbook of general experimental psychology*. Worcester, Mass.: Clark University Press, 1934.

Cannon, W. B. "Voodoo" death. *American Anthropologist*, 1942, **44**, 169–81.

Cannon, W. B. "Voodoo" death. *Psychosomatic Medicine*, 1957, **19**, 182–90.

Caplan, N., & Nelson, S. D. On being useful: The nature and consequences of psychological research on social problems. *American Psychologist*, 1973, **28,** 199–211.

Caporael, L. R. Ergotism: the satan loosed in Salem? *Science,* 1976, **192,** 21–26.

Carlson, E. R. The affective tone of psychology. *Journal of General Psychology,* 1966, **75,** 65–78.

Carlson, J. G., & Wood, R. D. Need the final solution be justified? Unpublished manuscript, University of Hawaii, 1974.

Carmichael, L. Ontogenetic development. In S. S. Stevens (Ed.), *Handbook of experimental psychology.* New York: Wiley, 1951.

Carmichael, L., Hogan, H. P., & Walter, A. A. An experimental study of the effect of language on the reproduction of visually perceived form. *Journal of Experimental Psychology,* 1932, **15,** 73–86.

Cartwright, D., & Zander, A. (Eds.) *Group dynamics: Research and theory.* New York: Harper & Row, 1968.

Castaneda, C. *The teachings of Don Juan: A Yaqui way of knowledge.* New York: Ballantine Books, 1968. Copyright © 1968 by The Regents of The University of California. Excerpt reprinted by permission of The Regents of the University of California.

Castaneda, C. *A separate reality: Further conversations with Don Juan.* New York: Simon & Schuster, 1971.

Castaneda, C. *Journey to Ixtlan.* New York: Simon & Schuster, 1972.

Castiglione, B. *The book of the courtier.* Baltimore: Penguin Books, 1967. (Originally published, 1528.)

Cattell, R. B. *Personality and motivation: Structure and meaning.* New York: Harcourt Brace Jovanovich, 1957.

Cavalli-Sforza, L. L., & Bodmer, F. *Genetics of human populations.* San Francisco: Freeman, 1971.

Charatan, F. Personal communication to the author, Spring 1973.

Chase, M. H. The matriculating brain. *Psychology Today,* 1973, **7,** 82–87.

Chomsky, N. *Syntactic structures.* S'Gravenhage, Netherlands: Mouton, 1957.

Chomsky, N. *Language and mind.* New York: Harcourt Brace Jovanovich, 1968.

Chomsky, N. Language and the mind. *Readings in psychology today.* Del Mar, Calif.: CRM Books, 1969.

Christie, R., & Geis, F. L. (Eds.) *Studies in Machiavellianism.* New York: Academic Press, 1970.

Christie, R., & Jahoda, M. (Eds.) *Studies in the scope and method of the authoritarian personality.* New York: Free Press, 1954.

Christy, P. R., Gelfand, D. M., & Hartmann, D. P. Effects of competition-induced frustration on two classes of modeled behavior. *Developmental Psychology,* 1971, **5,** 104–11.

Cisler, L. Unfinished business: Birth control and women's liberation. In R. Morgan (Ed.), *Sisterhood is powerful.* New York: Random House, 1970.

Clark, K. B., & Clark, M. P. Racial identification and preference in Negro children. In E. E. Maccoby, T. M. Newcomb, & E. L. Hartley (Eds.), *Readings in social psychology.* New York: Holt, Rinehart & Winston, 1958.

Clausen, J. A. Drug use. In R. Merton & R. Nisbet (Eds.), *Comtemporary social problems.* New York: Harcourt Brace Jovanovich, 1971.

Clauser, G., & Klein, H. *Münchner Medizinische Wochenschrift,* 1957, **99,** 896. Cited in Haas et al., 1959.

Cline, V. B., Croft, R. G., & Courrier, S. The desensitization of children to television violence. Unpublished manuscript, University of Utah, 1972.

Coch, L., & French, J. R. P., Jr. Overcoming resistance to change. *Human Relations,* 1948, **11,** 512–32.

Cofer, C. N. Constructive processes in memory. *American Scientist,* 1973, **61,** 537–43.

Cofer, C. N., & Appley, M. H. *Motivation: Theory and research.* New York: Wiley, 1964.

Cohen, F. *Psychological factors in the etiology of somatic illness.* Unpublished report. Stanford University, 1975.

Cohen, H. L., & Filipczak, J. *A new learning environment.* San Francisco: Jossey-Bass, 1971.

Cohen, S. Property destruction: Motives and meanings. In C. Ward (Ed.), *Vandalism.* London: Architectural Press, 1973.

Colby, K. M. Computer simulation of neurotic processes. In R. W. Stacey & B. D. Waxman (Eds.), *Computers in biomedical research.* New York: Academic Press, 1965.

Colby, K. M., Watt, J., & Gilbert, J. P. A computer method of psychotherapy. *Journal of Nervous and Mental Diseases.* 1966, **142,** 148–52.

Coleman, J. C. *Abnormal psychology and modern life* (5th ed.). Glenview, Ill.: Scott, Foresman, 1976.

Collier, G. Consummatory and instrumental responding as functions of deprivation. *Journal of Experimental Psychology,* 1962, **64,** 410–14.

Collins, B. E., Martin, J. C., Ashmore, R. D., & Ross, L. Some dimensions of the internal-external metaphor in theories of personality. *Journal of Personality,* 1973, **41,** 471–92.

Congressional Hearings on Worker Alienation. Hearings before the Subcommittee on Employment, Manpower, and Poverty. Washington, D.C.: U.S. Government Printing Office, 1972.

Conklin, J. E. Dimensions of community response to the crime problem. *Social Problems,* 1971, **18,** 373–85.

Conrad, R. Acoustic confusions and immediate memory. *British Journal of Psychology,* 1964, **55,** 77–84.

Cooley, C. H. *Human nature and the social order.* New York: Scribner, 1902.

Cooper, L. A., & Shepard, R. N. The time required to prepare for a rotated stimulus. *Memory and Cognition*, 1973, **1**, 246–50.

Cooper, L. M. Hypnotic amnesia. In E. Fromm & R. E. Shor (Eds.), *Hypnosis: Research and developments.* Chicago: Aldine, 1972.

Cowen, E. L. Stress reduction and problem-solving rigidity. *Journal of Consulting Psychology*, 1952, **16**, 425–28.

Cowen, E. L., & Beier, E. S. Threat-expectancy, word frequencies, and perceptual prerecognition hypotheses. *Journal of Abnormal and Social Psychology*, 1954, **49**, 172–82.

Craddick, R. A. Size of witch drawings as a function of time before, on and after Halloween. *American Psychologist*, 1967, **17**, 307.

Craik, K. J. W. *The nature of explanation.* Cambridge, Mass.: Cambridge University Press, 1943.

Crandall, V. C. Sex differences in expectancy of intellectual and academic reinforcement. In C. P. Smith (Ed.), *Achievement related motives in children.* New York: Russell Sage Foundation, 1969.

Cranston, R. *The miracle of Lourdes.* New York: McGraw-Hill, 1955.

Crocket, R., Sandison, R., & Walk, A. (Eds.) *Hallucinogenic drugs and their psychotherapeutic use.* London: J. Q. Lewis, 1963.

Crombie, A. D. Early concepts of the senses and the mind. *Scientific American,* 1964, **215**, 108–16.

Cross, P. G., Cattell, R. B., & Butcher, H. J. The personality patterns of creative artists. *British Journal of Educational Psychology*, 1967, **37**, 292–99.

D'Andrade, R. G., Quinn, N. R., Nerlove, S. B., & Romney, A. I. *Categories of disease in American-English and Mexican-Spanish.* Unpublished paper, Stanford University, 1969.

Danziger, C., & Greenwald, M. *Alternatives: A look at unmarried couples and communes.* New York: Institute of Life Insurance, Research Services, 1974.

Darley, J. M., & Batson, C. O. From Jerusalem to Jericho: A study of situational variables in helping behavior. *Journal of Personality and Social Psychology*, 1973, **27**, 100–108.

Darley, J. M., & Latané, B. Bystander intervention in emergencies: Diffusion of responsibilities. *Journal of Personality and Social Psychology*, 1968, **8**(4), 377–83.

Darnton, R. *Mesmerism and the end of enlightenment in France.* Cambridge: Harvard University Press, 1968.

Darwin, C. *The expression of the emotions in man and animals.* London: Murray, 1872.

Davenport, W. Sexual patterns and their regulation in a society of the Southwest Pacific. In F. Beach (Ed.), *Sex and behavior.* New York: Wiley, 1965.

Davis, C. M. Self-selection of diet by newly weaned infants. *American Journal of Diseases of Children,* 1928, **36**, 651–79.

Davis, J. M. Efficacy of tranquilizing and antidepressant drugs. *Archives of General Psychiatry*, 1965, **13**, 552–72.

Davison, G. C., & Valins, S. Maintenance of self-attributed and drug-attributed behavior change. *Journal of Personality and Social Psychology*, 1969, **11**, 25–33.

Day, R. S., & Cutting, J. E. Perceptual competition between speech and nonspeech. Paper presented at the eighteenth annual meeting of the Acoustical Society of America, Houston, 1970.

Deci, E. L. Intrinsic motivation, extrinsic reinforcement, and inequity. *Journal of Personality and Social Psychology*, 1972, **22**, 113–20.

Dekker, E., & Groen, J. Reproducible psychogenic attacks of asthma. In C. F. Reed, I. E. Alexander, & S. S. Tomkins (Eds.), *Psychopathology: A source book.* Cambridge, Mass.: Harvard University Press, 1958.

Dellas, M., & Gaier, E. L. Identification of creativity: The individual. *Psychological Bulletin*, 1970, **73**, 55–73.

Dement, W. C. The effect of dream deprivation, *Science*, 1960, **131**, 1705–7.

Dement, W. C. A new look at the third state of existence. *Stanford M.D.,* 1969, **8**, 2–8.

Dement, W. C., & Kleitman, N. Cyclic variations in EEG during sleep and their relations to eye movement, body mobility and dreaming. *Electroencephalography and Clinical Neurophysiology*, 1957, **9**, 673–90.

Dement, W. C., & Mitler, M. M. An overview of sleep research: Past, present and future. In D. Hamburt & H. Brodie (Eds.), *American handbook of psychiatry.* Vol. 6. New York: Basic Books, 1975, in press.

Deutsch, J. A., & Deutsch, D. *Physiological psychology.* Homewood, Ill.: Dorsey Press, 1966.

Deutsch, M., & Gerard, H. B. A study of normative and informational social influence upon individual judgment. *Journal of Abnormal and Social Psychology*, 1955, **51**, 629–36.

De Vos, G., & Wagatsuma, H. *Japan's invisible race.* Berkeley: University of California Press, 1966.

Diamond, M. J. The use of observationally presented information to modify hypnotic susceptibility. *Journal of Abnormal Psychology*, 1972, **79**, 174–80.

Di Cara, L. V., & Miller, N. E. Instrumental learning of vasomotor responses by rats: Learning to respond differentially in the two ears. *Science,* 1968, **159**, 1485–86.

Dillard, J. L. Negro children's dialect in the inner city. *The Florida FL Reporter,* Fall 1967.

Dillard, J. L. Non-standard Negro dialects – convergence or divergence? *The Florida FL Reporter,* Fall 1968.

Dillard, J. L. *Black English.* New York: Random House, 1972.

Dobzhansky, T. On methods of evolutionary biology and anthropology. Part 1. Biology. *American Scientist,* 1957, **45**(5), 381 – 92.

Dohrenwend, B. P., & Dohrenwend, B. S. Social and cultural influences on psychopathology. In P. H. Mussen & M. R. R. Rosenzweig (Eds.), *Annual review of psychology, 1974.* Vol. 25. Palo Alto, Calif.: Annual Reviews, 1974.

Dolinar, L. Creationists issue a new challenge. *Learning,* April 1973, 52 – 55.

Dollard, J., Doob, L. W., Miller, N., Mowrer, O. H., & Sears, R. R. *Frustration and aggression.* New Haven: Yale University Press, 1939.

Dollard, J., & Miller, N. E. *Personality and psychotherapy.* New York: McGraw-Hill, 1950.

Dreyfus, E. A. Humanness: A therapeutic variable. *Personnel and Guidance Journal,* 1967, **45**, 573 – 78.

Duffy, E. *Activation and behavior.* New York: Wiley, 1962.

Dugdale, R. *The Jukes: A study in crime, pauperism, disease, and heredity.* New York: G. P. Putnam's Sons, 1877.

Duncan, S. When dieting goes berserk. *New York Magazine,* Jan. 29, 1973, 44 – 47.

Duncker, K. On problem-solving. *Psychological Monographs,* 1945, **58**(5).

Dunnette, M. D., Campbell, J., & Jaastad, K. The effects of group participation on brainstorming effectiveness for two industrial samples. *Journal of Applied Psychology,* 1963, **47**, 30 – 37.

DuPont, R. L., & Greene, M. H. The dynamics of a heroin addiction epidemic: Heroin abuse has declined in Washington, D.C. *Science,* Aug. 1973, **181**(4101), 716 – 22.

Dwornicka, B., Jasienska, A., Smolarz, W., & Wawryk, R. Attempt of determining the fetal reaction to acoustic stimulation. *Acta Oto-Laryngologica,* Stockholm, 1964, **57**, 571 – 74.

Ebbinghaus, H. *Memory.* New York: Teachers College, Columbia University, 1913. (Originally published: Leipzig: Altenberg, 1885.)

Edwards, A. E., & Acker, L. E. A demonstration of the long-term retention of a conditioned galvanic skin response. *Psychosomatic Medicine,* 1962, **24**, 459 – 63.

Edwards, D. A. Neonatal administration of androstenedione, testosterone, or testosterone propionate: Effects on ovulation, sexual receptivity, and aggressive behavior in female mice. *Physiological Behavior,* 1971, **6**, 223 – 28.

Egbert, L. Report of the American Society of Anesthesiologists, 1969.

Egbert, L., Battit, G., Welch, C., & Bartlett, M. Reduction of postoperative pain by encouragement and instruction of patients. *New England Journal of Medicine,* 1964, **270**, 825 – 27.

Eisner, B. G. Notes on the use of drugs to facilitate group psychotherapy. *Psychiatric Quarterly,* 1964, **38**, 310 – 28.

Ekman, P., & Friesen, W. V. Nonverbal behavior in psychotherapy research. *Research in Psychotherapy,* 1968, **3**, 179 – 216.

Ekman, P., & Friesen, W. V. The repertoire of nonverbal behavior categories, origins, usage, and coding. *Semiotica,* 1969, **1**, 49 – 98.

Ekman, P., Sorenson, E. R., & Friesen, W. V. Pancultural elements in facial displays of emotion. *Science,* 1969, **164**, 86 – 88.

Elliot, J. Personal communication to the authors, Oct. 1970.

Ellison, R. *The invisible man.* Random House: New York, 1952.

Ellsworth, P. C., & Carlsmith, J. M. Effects of eye contact and verbal contact on affective response to a dyadic interaction. *Journal of Personality and Social Psychology,* 1968, **10**, 15 – 20.

Ellsworth, P. C., Carlsmith, J., & Henson, A. The stare as a stimulus to flight in human subjects: A series of field experiments. *Journal of Personality and Social Psychology,* 1972, **21**(3), 302 – 11.

Elmer, E. *Children in jeopardy.* Pittsburgh: University of Pittsburgh Press, 1967.

Elmer, E. Studies of child abuse and infant accidents. *Mental Health Program Reports, No. 5.* (DHEW) Publication No. (HSM) 72-9042. Chevy Chase, Md.: National Institute of Mental Health, 1971.

Engel, G. Sudden and rapid death during psychological stress: Folklore or folk medicine? *Annals of Internal Medicine,* 1971, **74**, 771 – 82.

Engen, T., Lipsitt, L. P., & Kaye, H. Olfactory responses and adaptation in the human neonate. *Journal of Comparative and Physiological Psychology,* 1963, **56**, 73 – 77.

Erickson, M. Experimental demonstrations of the psychopathology of everyday life. *The Psychoanalytic Quarterly,* 1939, **8**, 338 – 53.

Erickson, M. H. A special inquiry with Aldous Huxley into the nature and character of various states of consciousness. *In American Journal of Clinical Hypnosis, 8,* 1965, 14 – 33.

Erikson, E. *Childhood and society.* New York: Norton, 1950.

Erikson, K. T. *Wayward puritans: A study in the sociology of deviance.* New York: Wiley, 1966.

Eron, L. D., Huesmann, L. R., Lefkowitz, M. M., & Walder, L. O. Does television violence cause aggression? *American Psychologist,* 1972, **27**, 253 – 63.

Evans, F. J., & Kihlstrom, J. F. Posthypnotic amnesia as disrupted retrieval. *Journal of Abnormal Psychology,* 1973, **82**, 317–23.

Evans, J. R., Rodnick, E. H., Goldstein, M. J., & Judd, L. L. Premorbid adjustment, phenothiazine treatment and remission in acute schizophrenics. *Archives of General Psychiatry,* 1972, **27**, 486–90.

Exline, R. V., & Winters, L. Affective relations and mutual glances in dyads. In S. Tomkins & C. Izard (Eds.), *Affect, cognition, and personality.* New York: Springer, 1965.

Eysenck, H. J. The effects of psychotherapy: An evaluation. *Journal of Consulting Psychology,* 1952, **16**, 319–24.

Eysenck, H. J., & Eysenck, S. *Eysenck personality.* San Diego: Educational and Industrial Testing Service, 1968.

Eysenck, H. J., & Rachman, S. *The causes and cures of neurosis.* San Diego, Calif.: Knapp, 1965.

Fairweather, G. W., et al. Relative effectiveness of psychotherapeutic programs: A multicriteria comparison of four programs for three different patient groups. *Psychological Monographs,* 1960, **74** (5, Whole No. 492).

Fairweather, G. W., Sanders, D. H., Maynard, R. F., & Cressler, D. L. *Community life for the mentally ill: Alternative to institutional care.* Chicago: Aldine, 1969.

Fantz, R. L. Pattern vision in newborn infants. *Science,* 1963, **140**, 296–97.

Farber, M. L. *Theory of suicide.* New York: Funk & Wagnalls, 1968.

Farberow, N. L., & Shneidman, E. F. *The cry for help.* New York: McGraw-Hill, 1965.

Farina, A., Gliha, D., Boudreau, L. A., Allen, J. G., & Sherman, M. Mental illness and the impact of believing others know about it. *Journal of Abnormal Psychology,* 1971, **77**, 1–5.

Farina, A., Holland, C. H., & Ring, K. The role of stigma and set in interpersonal interaction. *Journal of Abnormal Psychology,* 1966, **71**, 421–28.

Farina, A., & Ring, K. The influence of perceived mental illness on interpersonal relations. *Journal of Abnormal Psychology,* 1965, **70**, 47–51.

Faucheux, C., & Moscovici, S. Le style de compotement d'une minorite et son influence sur les reponses d'une majorite. *Bulletin du Centre d'Etudes et Recherches Psychologiques,* 1967, **16**, 337–60.

Feather, N. Valence of outcome and expectation of success in relation to task difficulty and perceived locus of control. *Journal of Personality and Social Psychology,* 1967, **7**, 372–86.

Fechner, G. T. *In sachen der psychophysik.* Leipzig: 1877.

Feldman, M. J., & Hersen, M. Attitudes toward death in nightmare subjects. *Journal of Abnormal Psychology,* 1967, **72**, 421–25.

Feldstein, A., Hoagland, H., Oktem, M. R., & Freeman, H. Mao inhibition and anti-depressant activities. *International Journal of Neuropsychiatry,* 1965, **1**, 384.

Fenichel, O. *The psychoanalytic theory of neurosis.* New York: Norton, 1945.

Fenz, W. D. Conflict and stress as related to physiological activation and sensory, perceptual, and cognitive functioning. *Psychological Monographs,* 1964, **78** (8, Whole No. 585).

Ferguson, L. R. *Personality development.* Belmont, Calif.: Brooks/Cole, 1970.

Ferguson, P. C., & Gowan, J. C. Psychological findings on transcendental meditation. *Journal of Humanistic Psychology,* 1976, **16**(3).

Ferrare, N. A. Institutionalization and attitude change in an aged population. Unpublished doctoral dissertation, Western Reserve University, 1962.

Ferriera, A. J., & Winter, W. W. Information exchange and silence in normal and abnormal families. In W. W. Winter & A. J. Ferriera (Eds.), *Research in family interaction.* Palo Alto, Calif.: Science & Behavior Books, 1964.

Feshbach, S., & Singer, R. D. *Television and aggression: An experimental field study.* San Francisco: Jossey-Bass, 1971.

Festinger, L. A theory of social comparison processes. *Human Relations,* 1954, **7**, 117–40.

Festinger, L. *A theory of cognitive dissonance.* Stanford: Stanford University Press, 1957.

Festinger, L., & Carlsmith, J. M. Cognitive consequences of forced compliance. *Journal of Abnormal and Social Psychology,* 1959, **58**, 203–11.

Fiedler, F. E. A contingency model of leadership effectiveness. In L. Berkowitz (Ed.), *Advances in experimental social psychology.* Vol. 1. New York: Academic Press, 1964.

Fiedler, F. E. *A theory of leadership effectiveness.* New York: McGraw-Hill, 1967.

Fine, R. The psychology of blindfold chess: An introspective account. *Acta Psychologia,* 1965, **24**, 352–70.

Firth, R. Suicide and risk-taking in Tikopia society. *Psychiatry,* 1961, **24**(1), 1–17.

Fisher, C., Byrne, J. V., Edwards, A., & Kahn, E. REM and NREM nightmares. In E. Hartman (Ed.), *Sleep and Dreaming.* Boston: Little, Brown, 1970.

Fiske, D. W., Luborsky, L., Parloff, M. B., Hunt, H. F., Orne, M. T., Reiser, M. F., & Tuma, A. H. Planning of research on effectiveness of psychotherapy. *American Psychologist,* 1970, **25**, 727–37.

Fitzsimmons, J., & Oatley, K. Additivity of stimuli for drinking in rats. *Journal of Comparative and Physiological Psychology,* 1968, **66**, 450–55.

Flavell, J. H. The development of inferences about others. In T. Misebel (Ed.), *Understanding other persons.* Oxford. Eng.: Blackwell Basil & Mott, 1973.

Fleming, J. D. Field report: The state of the apes. *Psychology Today,* 1974, **7**(8), 31–46.

Fletcher, C. R. Attributing responsibility to the deviant: A factor in psychiatric referrals by the general public. *Journal of Health and Social Behavior*, 1967, **8**, 185–96.

Fodor, J. A. *Psychological explanation: An introduction to the philosophy of psychology.* New York: Random House, 1968.

Folkins, C. H., Lawson, K. D., Opton, E. M., Jr., & Lazarus, R. S. Desensitization and the experimental reduction of threat. *Journal of Abnormal Psychology*, 1968, **73**, 100–13.

Fortune. A good man is hard to find. 1946, **33**(3), 92–95 ff.

Frank, J. D. *Persuasion and healing: A comparative study of psychotherapy.* Baltimore: Johns Hopkins Press, 1961.

Frank, J. D. *Persuasion and healing.* New York: Schocken Books, 1963.

Frankl, V. E. *Man's search for meaning.* Boston: Beacon Press, 1963. (Originally published, 1959.)

Frankl, V. E. Logotherapy. In W. S. Sahakian (Ed.), *Psychopathology today.* Itasca, Ill.: F. E. Peacock, 1970.

Fraser, S. C. Deindividuation: Effects of anonymity on aggression in children. Unpublished mimeograph report, University of Southern California, 1974.

Fraser, S. C., Kelem, R., Diener, E., & Beaman, A. The Halloween caper: The effects of deindividuation variables on stealing. *Journal of Personality and Social Psychology*, 1974, in press.

Freedman, J. L., & Fraser, S. C. Compliance without pressure: The foot-in-the-door technique. *Journal of Personality and Social Psychology*, 1966, **4**, 195–202.

Freedman, J., Levy, A., Buchanan, R., & Price, J. Crowding and human aggressiveness. *Journal of Experimental and Social Psychology*, 1972, **8**, 528–48.

Freeman, F. N., Holzinger, K. J., & Mitchell, B. C. The influence of environment on the intelligence, achievement, and conduct of foster children. In *National Society for the Study of Education.* 27th Yearbook, Part 1, 1928.

Freeman, W., & Watts, J. W. *Psychosurgery.* Springfield, Ill.: Charles C Thomas, 1942.

Freemon, F. R. *Sleep research: A critical review.* Springfield, Ill.: Charles C Thomas, 1972.

Freud, S. *The interpretation of dreams.* Vol. 5 *The standard edition of the complete psychological works of Sigmund Freud.* London: Hogarth Press, 1900.

Freud, S. Recommendations for physicians on the psycho-analytic method of treatment. In *Collected papers.* Vol. 2. London: Hogarth Press, 1956.

Freud, S. Psychopathology of everyday life. In J. Strachey (Ed.), *The standard edition of the complete psychological works of Sigmund Freud.* London: Hogarth Press, 1960. (First German edition, 1901.)

Freud, S. Introductory lectures on psycho-analysis. In J. Strachey (Ed.), *The standard edition of the complete psychological works of Sigmund Freud.* London: Hogarth Press, 1963. (First German edition, 1917.)

Friedman, M., & Rosenman, R. F. Overt behavior pattern in coronary disease. *Journal of the American Medical Association*, 1960, **173**, 1320–25.

Friedman, M., & Rosenman, R. F. *Type A behavior and your heart.* New York: Knopf, 1974.

Friedman, S. B., Ader, R., & Glasgow, L. A. Effects of psychological stress in adult mice inoculated with coxackie B viruses. *Psychosomatic Medicine*, 1965, **27**, 361–68.

Friedman, S. B., & Glasgow, L. A. Psychologic factors and resistance to infectious disease. *Pediatric Clinics of North America*, 1966, **13**, 315–35.

Frijda, N. H. Emotion and recognition of emotion. In M. Arnold (Ed.), *Feelings and emotions.* New York: Academic Press, 1970.

Funkenstein, D. H. The physiology of fear and anger. *Scientific American*, 1955, **192**(5), 74–80.

Funkenstein, D. H., King, S. H., & Drolette, M. E. *Mastery of stress.* Cambridge, Mass.: Harvard University Press, 1957.

Gage, N. L. I.Q., heritability, race differences, and educational research. *Phi Delta Kappan*, Jan. 1972, 308–12.

Galin, D., & Ornstein, R. Lateral specialization of cognitive mode: An EEG study. *Psychophysiology*, 1972, 412–18.

Galton, F. *Inquiries into human faculty and its development.* London: J. M. Dent & Sons, 1907. (Originally published: London: Macmillan, 1883.)

Gantt, W. H. Reflexology, schizokinesis, and autokinesis. *Conditional Reflex*, 1966, **1**, 57–68.

Garcia, J., McGowan, B. K., & Green, K. F. Sensory quality and integration: Constraints on conditioning. In A. H. Black & W. F. Prokasy (Eds.), *Classical conditions II: Current research and theory.* New York: Appleton-Century-Crofts, 1972.

Gardner, L. Deprivation dwarfism. *Scientific American*, 1972, **227**, 76–82.

Gardner, M. *Fads and fallacies in the name of science.* New York: Dover, 1957.

Gardner, R., & Gardner, B. T. Teaching sign language to a chimpanzee. *Science*, 1969, **165**, 664–72.

Gardner, R., & Heider, K. A. *Gardens of war: Life and death in the New Guinea stone age.* New York: Random House, 1968.

Gasset, J. O. *The dehumanization of art.* Princeton, N.J.: Princeton University Press, 1969. (Originally published, 1925.)

Gastaut, H., & Bert, J. Electroencephalographic detection of sleep by repetitive sensory stimuli. In G. E. W. Wolstenholme & M. O'Connor (Eds.), *The nature of sleep.* London: Churchill, 1961.

Gatland, K. Paranormal: Extrasensory perception: Party or tricks . . . Or hidden forces? *The Daily Telegraph Magazine,* Dec. 7, 1973, **475,** 62–63, 65.

Gazzaniga, M. S. *The bisected brain.* New York: Appleton-Century-Crofts, 1970.

Gebhard, P. H. Situational factors affecting human sexual behavior. In F. Beach (Ed.), *Sex and behavior.* New York: Wiley, 1965.

"Gee, Officer Krupke." Words by Stephen Sondheim and music by Leonard Bernstein. Copyright © 1957 by Leonard Bernstein and Stephen Sondheim. Excerpt used by permission of G. Shirmer, Inc.

Geen, R., & Berkowitz, L. Name-mediated aggressive cue properties. *Journal of Personality,* 1966, **34,** 456–65.

Gelernter, H. Realization of a geometry theorem proving machine. *Proceedings of the International Conference on Information Processing.* Paris: UNESCO, 1960.

Gendlin, E. Experiential psychotherapy. In R. Corsini (Ed.), *Current psychotherapies.* Itasca, Ill.: F. E. Peacock, 1973.

Gergen, K. J. *The concept of self.* New York: Holt, Rinehart & Winston, 1971.

Gershwin, G., & Gershwin, I. "They All Laughed." Copyright 1937 by Gershwin Publishing Corporation. Copyright renewed. Excerpt used by permission of Chappell & Co., Inc.

Gewirtz, J. L., & Baer, D. M. Deprivation and satiation of social reinforcers as drive conditions. *Journal of Abnormal and Social Psychology,* 1958, **57,** 165–72.

Gibbon, J. Discriminated punishment: Avoidable and unavoidable shock. *Journal of the Experimental Analysis of Behavior,* 1967, **10,** 451–60.

Gibson, E. J. *Principles of perceptual learning and development.* New York: Appleton-Century-Crofts, 1969.

Gibson, E. J. The development of perception as an adaptive process. *American Scientist,* 1970, **58,** 98–107.

Gibson, E. J., & Walk, R. D. The "visual cliff." *Scientific American,* 1960, **202**(4), 67–71.

Gilbert, G. M. Stereotype persistence and change among college students. *Journal of Abnormal and Social Psychology,* 1951, **46,** 245–54.

Glass, B. C., & Singer, J. E. *Urban stress: Experiments on noise and social stressors.* New York: Academic Press, 1972.

Gloor, P. Autonomic functions of the dienchephalon: A summary of the experimental work of Professor W. R. Hess. *Archives of Neurology and Psychiatry,* 1954, **71,** 773–90.

Glover, E. *The technique of psychoanalysis.* New York: International Universities Press, 1966.

Goddard, H. H. The Binet tests in relation to immigration. *Journal of Psycho-Asthenics,* 1913, **18,** 105–7.

Goddard, H. H. Mental tests and the immigrant. *Journal of Delinquency,* 1917, **2,** 243–77.

Goddard, H. H. *The Kallikak family.* New York: Arno Press, 1973. (Originally published: New York: Macmillan, 1912.)

Goffman, E. *Asylums: Essays on the social situation of mental patients and other inmates.* Garden City, N.Y.: Doubleday, 1961.

Goldberg, P. Are women prejudiced against women? *Transaction,* 1968, **5**(5), 28–30.

Goldfarb, W. The effects of early institutional care on adolescent personality. *Journal of Experimental Education,* 1943, **12,** 106–29.

Goldiamond, I. Fluent and nonfluent speech (stuttering): Analysis and operant techniques for control. In L. Krasner & L. P. Ullman (Eds.), *Research in behavior modification.* New York: Holt, Rinehart & Winston, 1965.

Goldstein, A. P., Heller, K., & Sechrest, L. B. *Psychotherapy and the psychology of behavior change.* New York: Wiley, 1966.

Goldstein, K. *The organism.* Boston: Beacon Press, 1963.

Gough, H. G. Techniques for identifying the creative research scientist. In *Conference on the creative person.* Berkeley: University of California, Institute of Personality Assessment and Research, 1961.

Gouldner, A. The norm of reciprocity: A preliminary statement. *American Sociological Review,* 1960, **25,** 161–78.

Graham, K. R. Eye movements during waking imagery and hypnotic hallucinations. Unpublished doctoral dissertation, Stanford University, 1969.

Granit, R. *The basis of motor control.* New York: Academic Press, 1970.

Gray, F., Graubard, P. S., & Rosenberg, H. Little brother is changing you. *Psychology Today,* March 1974, **7,** 42–46.

Green, E. E., Green, A., & Walter, E. D. A demonstration of voluntary control of bleeding and pain. Unpublished manuscript. The Menninger Foundation, 1972.

Greenblatt, G., Eastlake, D., & Crocker, S. The Greenblatt chess program. *Proceedings of the Fall Joint Computer Conference.* Washington, D.C.: Thompson, 1967.

Greenfield, P. M. On culture and conservation. In J. S. Bruner, R. R. Olver, & P. M. Greenfield, *Studies in cognitive growth.* New York: Wiley, 1966.

Greenfield, P. M., & Bruner, J. S. Culture and cognitive growth. In J. S. Bruner (Ed.), *Beyond the information given.* New York: Norton, 1973.

Greenwald, A. G., Brock, T. C., & Ostrom, T. M. *Psychological foundations of attitude.* New York: Academic Press, 1968.

Gregory, R. L. *Eye and brain: The psychology of seeing.* New York: McGraw-Hill, 1966.

Gresham, W. L. Fortune-tellers never starve by William Lindsay Gresham. *Esquire Magazine,* 1949, **32**(5). Copyright, 1949 by Fawcett Publications, Inc. Excerpt reprinted by permission of Brandt & Brandt.

Grimmett, H. Personal communication to the authors, Oct. 1970.

Grollman, E. A. *Suicide.* Boston: Beacon Press, 1971.

Gross, C. G. Visual functions of interotemporal cortex. In R. Jung (Ed.), *Handbook of sensory physiology.* Vol. 7, Part 3b. Berlin: Springer-Verlag, 1973.

Gross, C. G., Rocha-Miranda, C. E., & Bender, D. B. Visual properties of neurons in inferotemporal cortex of the macaque. *Journal of Neurophysiology,* 1972, **35,** 96–111.

Gross, L. Scarcity, unpredictability and eating behavior in rats. Unpublished doctoral dissertation, Columbia University, 1968.

Grossberg, J. M. Behavior therapy: A review. *Psychological Bulletin,* 1964, **109,** 73–88.

Grossman, S. P. Neuropharmacology of central mechanisms contributing to control of food and water intake. In C. Code (Ed.), *Handbook of physiology.* Baltimore: Williams & Wilkins, 1967.

Grossman, S. P. Physiological basis of specific and nonspecific motivational processes. In W. J. Arnold (Ed.), *Nebraska symposium on motivation.* Lincoln: University of Nebraska Press, 1968.

Gruber, R. P. Behavior therapy: Problems in generalization. *Behavior Therapy,* 1971, **2,** 361–68.

Gruen, W. Emotional encapsulation as a predictor of outcome in therapeutic discussion groups. *International Journal of Group Psychotherapy,* 1966, **16,** 93–97.

Grusec, J. Demand characteristics of the modeling experiment: Altruism as a function of age and aggression. *Journal of Personality and Social Psychology,* 1972, **22,** 139–48.

Gruver, G. G. College students as therapeutic agents. *Psychological Bulletin,* 1971, **76,** 111–27.

Guetzkow, H. S., & Bowman, P. H. *Men and hunger.* Elgin, Ill.: Brethren, 1946.

Guilford, J. P. Theories of intelligence. In B. B. Wolman (Ed.), *Handbook of general psychology.* Englewood Cliffs, N. J.: Prentice-Hall, 1973.

Gunter, R., Feigenson, L., & Blakeslee, P. Color vision in the cebus monkey. *Journal of Comparative and Physiological Psychology,* 1965, **60,** 107–13.

Gustavson, C. R., Garcia, J., Hankins, W. G., & Rusiniak, K. W. Coyote predation control by aversive conditioning. *Science,* 1974, **184,** 581–83.

Haas, H., Fink, H., & Hartfelder, G. Das placeboproblem. *Fortschoritte der Arzneimittleforschung,* 1959, **1,** 279–454. Translated in *Psychopharmacology Service Center Bulletin,* 1959, **2**(8), 1–65. U.S. Department of Health, Education and Welfare, Public Health Service.

Haber, R. N. (Ed.) *Contemporary theory and research in visual perception.* New York: Holt, Rinehart & Winston, 1968.

Haldeman-Julius, E. *First hundred million.* New York: Simon & Schuster, 1928.

Hall, C., & Van de Castle, R. *The content analysis of dreams.* New York: Appleton-Century-Crofts, 1966.

Hall, E. T. *The hidden dimension.* Garden City, N.Y.: Doubleday, 1966.

Hammer, E. F. Creativity and feminine ingredients in young male artists. *Perceptual and Motor Skills,* 1964, **19,** 414.

Hammond, A. L. Individual self-sufficiency in energy, *Science,* 1974, **184,** 278–82.

Hampson, S. L. Determinants of psychosexual orientation. In F. Beach (Ed.), *Sex and behavior.* New York: Wiley, 1965.

Hansel, C. E. M. *ESP: A scientific evaluation.* New York: Scribner's, 1966.

Harlow, H. F. Sexual behavior in the rhesus monkey. In F. Beach (Ed.), *Sex and behavior.* New York: Wiley, 1965.

Harlow, H. F. *Learning to love.* San Francisco: Albion, 1971.

Harlow, H. F., & Harlow, M. K. Learning to love. *American Scientist,* 1966, **54,** 244–72.

Harlow, H. F., & Zimmerman, R. R. The development of affectional responses in infant monkeys. *Proceedings of the American Philosophical Society,* 1958, **102,** 501–9.

Harriman, A. E. The effect of a preoperative preference for sugar over salt upon compensatory salt selection by adrenalectomized rats. *Journal of Nutrition,* 1955, **57,** 271–76.

Harris, S. J. Excerpt from "Strictly Personal" by Sydney J. Harris. *San Francisco Sunday Examiner/Chronicle,* Jan. 20, 1974, Sec. B, p. 3. Courtesy of Publishers-Hall Syndicate.

Hart, J. T. Memory and the memory-monitoring process. *Journal of Verbal Learning and Verbal Behavior,* 1967, **6,** 685–91.

Hartry, A. L., Keith-Lee, P., & Morton, W. D. Planaria: Memory transfer through cannibalism reexamined. *Science,* 1964, **146,** 274–75.

Hartshorne, H., & May, M. A. *Studies in the nature of character.* Vol. 1. *Studies in deceit.* New York: Macmillan, 1928.

Harvard Educational Review. The rights of children, Parts I & II, Nov. 1973, **43**(4) and Feb. 1974, 44(1).

Harvey, J. A. Behavioral tolerance. In J. A. Harvey (Ed.), *Behavioral analysis of drug action.* Glenview, Ill.: Scott, Foresman, 1971.

Hashim, S. A., & Van Itallie, T. B. Studies on normal and obese subjects with a monitored food dispensing device. *Annals of the New York Academy of Sciences,* 1965, **131,** 654–61.

Hatano, G. Personal communication, August 1975.

Hauserman, N., Walen, S. R., & Behling, M. Reinforced racial integration in the first grade: A study in generalization. *Journal of Applied Behavior Analysis,* Summer 1973, **6**(2), 193–200.

Hawkins, G. *Stonehenge decoded: An astronomer examines one of the great puzzles of the ancient world.* Garden City, N.Y.: Doubleday, 1965.

Hayes, K. J., & Hayes, C. Imitation in a home-raised chimpanzee. *Journal of Comparative and Physiological Psychology.* 1952, **45,** 450–59.

Heath, R. G., & Mickle, W. A. Evaluation of seven years' experience with depth electrode studies in human patients. In E. R. Ramey & D. S. O'Doherty, *Electrical studies of the unanesthetized brain.* New York: Holber, 1960.

Hebb, D. O. *A textbook of psychology.* Philadelphia: Saunders, 1958.

Hebb, D. O. What psychology is about. *American Psychologist,* 1974, **29,** 71–79.

Heider, F. *The psychology of interpersonal relations.* New York: Wiley, 1958.

Heider, F., & Simmel, M. An experimental study of apparent behavior. *American Journal of Psychology,* 1944, **57,** 243–59.

Held, R. Plasticity in sensory-motor systems. *Scientific American,* 1965, **213**(5), 84–94.

Helfer, R. E., & Kempe, C. H. *The battered child.* Chicago: University of Chicago Press, 1968.

Heller, C. S. *Mexican-American youth: Forgotten youth at the crossroads.* New York: Random House, 1966.

Helson, R. Sex differences in creative style. *Journal of Personality,* 1967, **35,** 214–33.

Heron, W. Perception as a function of retinal locus. *American Journal of Psychology,* 1957, **70,** 38–48.

Heron, W. Cognitive and physiological effects of perceptual isolation. In P. Solomon et al. (Eds.). *Sensory deprivation.* Cambridge: Harvard University Press, 1961.

Hersen, M. Nightmare behavior: A review. *Psychological Bulletin,* 1972, **78,** 37–48.

Hershenson, M., Munsinger, H., & Kessen, W. Preference for shapes of intermediate variability in the newborn human. *Science,* 1965, **147,** 630–31.

Hershkowitz, A. Personal communication to the authors, Nov. 1970.

Hess, E. H. Space perception in the chick. *Scientific American,* 1956, **195**(1), 71–80.

Hess, E. H. Imprinting. *Science,* 1959, **130,** 133–41.

Hess, E. H. Pupillometrics: A method of studying mental, emotional and sensory processes. In N. E. Greenfield & R. A. Steinbach (Eds.), *Handbook of psychophysiology.* New York: Holt, Rinehart & Winston, 1972.

Hicks, D. J. Effects of co-observer's sanctions and adult presence on imitative aggression. *Child Development,* 1968, **39,** 303–9.

Hilgard, E. R. *Hypnotic susceptibility.* New York: Harcourt Brace Jovanovich, 1965.

Hilgard, E. R. Pain as a puzzle for psychology and physiology. *American Psychologist,* 1969, **24,** 103–13.

Hilgard, E. R. *Personality and hypnosis: A study of imaginative involvement.* Chicago: University of Chicago Press, 1970.

Hilgard, E. R. The domain of hypnosis. With some comments on alternative paradigms. *American Psychologist,* 1973, **28,** 972–82.

Hilgard, E. R., & Nowlis, D. P. The contents of hypnotic dreams and night dreams: An exercise in method. In E. Fromm & R. E. Shor (Eds.), *Hypnosis: Research developments and perspectives.* Chicago: Aldine, 1972.

Hinkle, L. E., Jr., & Plummer, N. Life stress and industrial absenteeism. *Industrial Medicine and Surgery,* 1952, **21,** 363–75.

Hinkle, L. E., & Wolff, H. C. Communist interrogation and indoctrination of "Enemies of the state." *Archives of Neurology and Psychiatry,* 1956, **76,** 115–74.

Hiroto, D. S. Locus of control and learned helplessness. *Journal of Experimental Psychology,* 1974, **102**(2), 187–93.

Hirsch, H. V. B. Visual perception in cats after environmental surgery. *Experimental Brain Research,* 1972, **15,** 405–23.

Hirsch, H. V. B., & Jacobson, M. The perfectible brain: Principles of neuronal development. In M. S. Gazzaniga & C. Blakemore (Eds.), *Handbook of psychobiology.* New York: Academic Press, 1974, in press.

Hirsch, H. V. B., & Spinelli, D. N. Visual experience modifies distribution of horizontally and vertically oriented receptive fields of cats. *Science,* 1970, **168,** 869–71.

Hirsch, H. V. B., & Spinelli, D. N. Modification of the distribution of receptive field orientation in cats by selective visual exposure during development. *Experimental Brain Research,* 1971, **13,** 509–27.

Hirsch, J. Behavior–genetic analysis and its biosocial consequences. In *Seminars in psychiatry,* February 1970, **2**(1), 89–105.

Hirsch, J., & Han, D. W. Cellularity of rat adipose tissue: Effects of growth, starvation, and obesity. *Journal of Lipid Research,* 1969, **10,** 77–82.

Hitler, A. *My battle.* E. T. S. Dugdale (Trans.). New York: Houghton Mifflin, 1933.

Hitt, W. D. Two models of man. *American Psychologist,* 1969, **24**(7), 651–58.

Hoebel, B., & Teitelbaum, P. Hypothalamic control of feeding and self-stimulation. *Science,* 1962, **135,** 375–77.

Hogan, R. A., & Kirchner, J. H. Implosive, eclectic, verbal and bibliotherapy in the treatment of fears of snakes. *Behavior Research and Therapy,* 1968, **6,** 167–71.

Hogarty, G. E., Guy, W., Gross, M., & Gross, G. An evaluation of community based mental health programs. *Medical Care,* 1969, **7,** 271–80.

Hokanson, J. E., & Burgess, M. The effects of three types of aggression on vascular processes. *Journal of Abnormal and Social Psychology,* 1962, **64,** 446–49. (a)

Hokanson, J. E., DeGood, D. E., Forrest, M. S., & Brittain, T. M. Availability of avoidance behaviors in modulating vascular-stress responses. *Journal of Personality and Social Psychology,* July 1971, **19**(1), 60–68.

Hollander, E. P. Some future potentials in leadership research. Paper presented at the meeting of the American Psychological Association, Honolulu, Sept. 3, 1972.

Hollander, E. P., & Julian, J. W. Contemporary trends in the analysis of leadership processes. *Psychological Bulletin,* 1969, **71,** 387–97.

Hollingshead, A. B., & Redlich, F. C. *Social class and mental illness: A community study.* New York: Wiley, 1958.

Holmes, T. H., & Masuda, M. Life change and illness susceptibility. In B. S. Dohrenwend & B. P. Dohrenwend (Eds.), *Stressful life events; their nature and effects.* New York: Wiley, 1974.

Holmes, T. S., & Holmes, T. H. Short-term intrusions into the life-style routine. *Journal of Psychosomatic Research,* June 1970, **14,** 121–32.

Holt, H. Is psychoanalytic language obsolete? *Journal of Contemporary Psychotherapy,* 1970, **3,** 35–40.

Holt, R. R. *Assessing personality.* New York: Harcourt Brace Jovanovich, 1971.

Holzberg, J. D. The historical traditions of the state hospital as a force of resistance to the team. *American Journal of Orthopsychiatry,* 1960, **30,** 87–94.

Honzik, M. P. The development of intelligence. In B. B. Wolman (Ed.), *Handbook of general psychology.* Englewood Cliffs, N.J.: Prentice-Hall, 1973.

Hoover, J. E. *Crime in the United States: Uniform crime reports—1970.* Washington, D.C.: U.S. Government Printing Office, 1971.

Hoppe, A. Excerpt from Arthur Hoppe column from *San Francisco Chronicle,* June 11, 1973. © 1973, Chronicle Publishing Company. Reprinted by permission of the author.

Horner, M. S. Fail: Bright women. *Psychology Today,* November 1969, **3,** 36–38.

Hornstein, H. A. Promotive tension: The basis of prosocial behavior from a Lewinian perspective. *Journal of Social Issues,* 1972, **28,** 191–218.

Hovland, C. I., Janis, I. L., & Kelley, H. H. *Communication and persuasion.* New Haven: Yale University Press, 1953.

Howard, I. P. Perceptual learning and adaptation. *British Medical Bulletin,* 1971, **27,** 248–52.

Hraba, J., & Grant, G. Black is beautiful: A reexamination of racial preference and identification. *Journal of Personality and Social Psychology,* 1970, **16,** 398–402.

Hubel, D. H., & Wiesel, T. N. Receptive fields of single neurones in the cat's striate cortex. *Journal of Physiology.* London, 1959, **148,** 574–91.

Hull, C. L. *Principles of behavior: An introduction to behavior theory.* New York: Appleton-Century-Crofts, 1943.

Hull, C. L. *A behavior system: An introduction to behavior theory concerning the individual organism.* New Haven: Yale University Press, 1952.

"I'm Late." Words by Bob Hilliard and Music by Sammy Fain. Copyright 1949 by Walt Disney Music Company. Excerpt reprinted by permission.

Inbau, F., & Reid, J. E. *Criminal interrogations and confessions.* (2nd ed.) Baltimore: Williams & Wilkins, 1967.

Irwin, O. C. The effect on speech sound frequency of systematic reading of stories to infants. Unpublished Study by the Iowa Child Welfare Research Station, 1958. Reported in P. H. Mussen (Ed.), *Handbook of research methods in child development.* New York: Wiley, 1960.

Irwin, S. Drugs of abuse: An introduction to their actions and potential hazards. *Journal of Psychedelic Drugs,* 1971, **2,** 1–16.

Isaacs, W., Thomas, J., & Goldiamond, I. Application of operant conditioning to reinstate verbal behavior in psychotics. *Journal of Speech and Hearing Disorders,* 1960, **25,** 8–12.

Itard, J. M. G. *The wild boy of Aveyron.* New York: Appleton-Century-Crofts, 1962.

Ivey, A. E. *Microcounseling: Innovations in interview training.* Springfield, Ill.: Charles C Thomas, 1971.

Izard, C. E. *The face of emotion.* New York: Appleton-Century-Crofts, 1971.

Jackson, G. *Soledad brother: The prison letters of George Jackson.* New York: Bantam, 1971.

Jacobs, E., Winter, P. M., Alvis, H. J., & Small, S. M. Hyperbaric oxygen: Temporary aid for senile minds. *Journal of the American Medical Association,* 1969, **209,** 1435–38.

Jacobs, H. L., & Sharma, K. N. Taste versus calories: Sensory and metabolic signals in the control of food intake. *Annals of the New York Academy of Sciences,* 1968, **134.**

Jacobs, J. *Death and life of great American cities.* New York: Vintage Books, 1961. Copyright © 1961 by Jane Jacobs. Excerpt reprinted by permission of Random House, Inc.

James, W. What is an emotion? *Mind,* 1884, **9,** 188–205.

James, W. *The principles of psychology.* Vol. 1. New York: Holt, 1890.

James, W. *The varieties of religious experience.* New York: Longmans, Green, 1902.

James, W. An analysis of esophageal feeding as a form of operant reinforcement in the dog. *Psychological Reports,* 1963, **12,** 31–39.

Janis, I. L. *Psychological stress.* New York: Wiley, 1958.

Janis, I. L. *Victims of groupthink: A psychological study of foreign-policy decisions and fiascoes.* Boston: Houghton Mifflin, 1972.

Jellinck, E. M. *The disease-concept of alcoholism.* New Haven, Conn.: Hillhouse Press, 1960.

Jenkins, D. C., Rosenman, R. H., & Friedman, M. Development of an objective psychological test for the determination of the coronary-prone behavior pattern in employed men. *Journal of Chronic Diseases,* 1967, **20,** 371–79.

Jenkins, J. G., & Dallenbach, K. M. Oblivescence during sleep and waking. *The American Journal of Psychology,* 1924, **35,** 605–12.

Jensen, A. R. How much can we boost I.Q. and scholastic achievement? *Harvard Educational Review,* 1969, **39,** 1–123.

Jensen, A. R. I.Q.'s of identical twins reared apart. *Behavior Genetics,* 1970, **1,** 133–46.

Jensen, A. R. The heritability of intelligence. *Saturday Evening Post,* Summer 1972, 149.

Jensen, D. D. Paramecia, planaria and pseudo-learning. Learning and associated phenomena in invertebrates. *Animal Behavior Supplement,* 1965, **1,** 9–20.

Johnson, F. G. LSD in the treatment of alcoholism. Paper presented at the American Psychiatric Meeting, Boston, June 1968.

Johnson, J. M. Punishment of human behavior. *American Psychologist,* 1972, **27,** 1033–54.

Johnson, K. R. Black kinesics: Some non-verbal communication patterns in the black culture. *The Florida FL Reporter,* Spring/Fall 1971.

Joint Commission on Mental Illness and Health. *Action for mental health.* New York: Basic Books, 1961.

Jones, A., Bentler, P. M., & Petry, G. The reduction of uncertainty concerning future pain. *Journal of Abnormal Psychology,* 1966, **71,** 87–94.

Jones, D., & Davis, K. From acts to dispositions: The attribution process in person perception. In L. Berkowitz (Ed.), *Advances in experimental social psychology.* Vol. 2. New York: Academic Press 1965.

Jones, E. E., & Nisbett, R. E. The actor and the observer: Divergent perceptions on the causes of behavior. (Module) In E. E. Jones et al. (Eds.), *Attribution: Perceiving the causes of behavior.* Morristown, N.J.: General Learning Corp., 1972.

Julez, B. *Foundations of cyclopean perception.* Chicago: University of Chicago Press, 1971.

Kahn, M. The physiology of catharsis. *Journal of Personality and Social Psychology,* 1966, **3,** 278–86.

Kamin, L. *The Science and Politics of IQ.* Potomac, Md.: L. Erlbaum Associates, 1974.

Kandel, D. Adolescent marijuana use: Role of parents and peers. *Science,* 1973, **181,** 1067–70.

Kanellakos, D. P., & Ferguson, P. *The psychobiology of transcendental meditation.* Los Angeles: Maharishi International University, Spring 1973.

Kaplan, B. (Ed.) *The inner world of mental illness.* New York: Harper & Row, 1964, pp. 191–92. Excerpt reprinted by permission.

Kaplan, E. L., & Kaplan, G. A. Is there such a thing as a prelinguistic child? In J. Eliot (Ed.), *Human development and cognitive processes.* New York: Holt, Rinehart & Winston, 1970.

Karlins, M., Coffman, T. L., & Walters, G. On the fading of social stereotypes: Studies in three generations of college students. *Journal of Personality and Social Psychology,* 1969, **13,** 1–16.

Kasamatsu, A., & Hirai, T. An EEG study on the Zen meditation. *Folia Psyckiatria Neurologica Japonica,* 1966, **20,** 315–36

Katchadourian, H., & Lunde, D. I. *Fundamentals of human sexuality.* New York: Holt, Rinehart & Winston, 1972.

Katz, D., & Braly, K. W. Racial stereotypes of one hundred college students. *Journal of Abnormal and Social Psychology,* 1933, **28,** 280–90.

Katz, I. Experimental studies of negro-white relationships. In L. Berkowitz (Ed.), *Advances in experimental social psychology.* Vol. 5. New York: Academic Press, 1970.

Katz, M. P. The assessment and treatment of mental patients as a function of their attractiveness. Unpublished dissertation, Stanford University, 1974.

Kaufman, I., & Rock, I. The moon illusion. *Scientific American,* 1962, **204,** 120–30.

Kaufmann, W. *Existentialism from Dostoevsky to Sartre.* New York: Meridian, 1956.

Kelley, H. H. The warm-cold variable in first impressions of persons. *Journal of Personality,* 1950, **18,** 431–39.

Kelley, H. H. Attribution theory in social psychology. In D. Levine (Ed.), *Nebraska symposium on motivation.* Lincoln: University of Nebraska Press, 1967.

Kelley, H. H. Attribution in social psychology. (Module) In E. E. Jones et al. (Eds.), *Attribution: Perceiving the causes of behavior.* Morristown, N.J.: General Learning Corp., 1972.

Kellogg, J. H. *The ladies' guide in health and disease.* Chicago: Modern Medicine Publishing Co., 1902.

Kellogg, W. N., & Kellogg, L. A. *The ape and the child: A study of environmental influence on early behavior.* New York: Hafner, 1967. (Originally published: New York: McGraw-Hill, 1933.)

Kelly, G. A. Man's construction of his alternatives. In G. Lindzey (Ed.), *Assessment of human motives.* New York: Holt, Rinehart & Winston, 1958.

Kelman, H. C. Human use of human subjects: The problem of deception in psychological experiences. *Psychological Bulletin,* 1967, **67,** 1 – 11.

Kelman, H. C. *A time to speak on human values and social research.* (1st ed.) San Francisco: Jossey-Bass, 1968.

Kelman, H. C., & Lawrence, L. H. Assignment of responsibility in the case of Lt. Calley: Preliminary report on a national survey. *Journal of Social Issues,* 1972, **28,** 177 – 212.

Kendler, H. H., & Kendler, T. S. Mediation and conceptual behavior. In K. W. Spence & J. T. Spence (Eds.), *The psychology of learning and motivation: Advances in research and theory.* Vol. 2. New York: Academic Press, 1968.

Kerckhoff, A. C., & Davis, K. E. Value consensus and need complementarity in mate selection. *American Sociological Review,* 1962, **27,** 295 – 303.

Kessen, W. *The child.* New York: Wiley, 1965.

Kessler, J. W. *Psychopathology of childhood.* Englewood Cliffs, N.J.: Prentice-Hall, 1966.

Kety, S. S. Psychoendocrine systems and emotions: Biological aspects. In D. C. Glass (Ed.), *Neurophysiology and emotion.* New York: Rockefeller University Press, 1967. (a)

Kety, S. S. Relationship between energy metabolism of the brain and functional activity. In S. S. Kety, E. V. Evarts, & H. L. Williams (Eds.), *Sleep and altered states of consciousness.* Baltimore: Williams & Wilkins, 1967. (b)

Keys, A., Brôzek, J., Henschel, A., Mickelson, O., & Taylor, H. L. *The biology of human starvation.* Minneapolis: University of Minnesota Press, 1950.

Kiesler, C. *The psychology of commitment: Experiments linking behavior to belief.* New York: Academic Press, 1971.

King, J. H. Brief account of the sufferings of a detachment of United States Cavalry, from deprivation of water, during a period of eighty-six hours while scouting on the "Llano Estacado," or "Staked Plains," Texas. *American Journal of Medical Science,* 1878, **75,** 404 – 8.

Kinsey, A. C., Martin, C. E., & Pomeroy, W. B. *Sexual behavior in the human male.* Philadelphia: Saunders, 1948.

Kinsey, A. C., Pomeroy, W. B., Martin, C. E., & Gebhard, R. H. *Sexual behavior in the human female.* Philadelphia: Saunders, 1953.

Kirtner, W. L., & Cartwright, D. S. Success and failure in client-centered therapy as a function of client personality variables. *Journal of Consulting Psychology,* 1958, **22,** 259 – 64.

Kitsuse, J. I. Societal reactions to deviant behavior: Problems of theory and methods. In H. S. Becker (Ed.), *The other side: Perspectives on deviance.* New York: The Free Press, 1964.

Klee, G. D., Bertino, J., Weintraub, W., & Calloway, E. The influence of varying dosage on the effects of lysergic acid diethylamide (LSD-25) in humans. *Journal of Nervous and Mental Diseases,* 1961, **132,** 404 – 9.

Klerman, G. L., & Cole, J. O. *Pharmacological Review,* 1965, **17,** 101.

Klimova, V. I. The properties of the components of some orientation reactions. In *The orientation reaction and orienting-investigation of activity.* Moscow: Academy of Pedagogical Sciences, 1958.

Knapp, R., Kause, R., & Perkins, C. Immediate vs. delayed shock in t-maze performance. *Journal of Experimental Psychology,* 1959, **58,** 357 – 62.

Kohlberg, L. Moral and religious education and the public schools: A developmental view. In T. Sizer (Ed.), *Religion and Public Education.* Boston: Houghton Mifflin, 1967.

Kohlberg, L. Stage and sequence: The cognitive-developmental approach to socialization. In D. A. Goslin (Ed.), *Handbook of socialization theory and research.* Chicago: Rand McNally, 1969.

Kohlberg, L., & Kramer, R. Continuities and discontinuities in childhood and adult moral development. *Human Development,* 1969, **12,** 93 – 120.

Kohler, L. Experiments with goggles. *Scientific American,* 1962, **206,** 62 – 86.

Kohler, W. *The mentality of apes.* New York: Harcourt Brace Jovanovich, 1926.

Kollar, E. J., et al. Psychological, psychophysiological, and biochemical correlates of prolonged sleep deprivation. *American Journal of Psychiatry,* 1969, **126,** 488 – 97.

Kopp, S. The Zaddik. *Psychology Today,* May 1969, **2,** 26 – 31.

Koriat, A., Melkman, R., Averill, J. R., & Lazarus, R. S. The self-control of emotional reactions to a stressful film. *Journal of Personality,* 1972, **40,** 601 – 19.

Krafft-Ebing, R. V. *Psychopathia sexualis.* New York: Physicians & Surgeons Book Company, 1932.

Kringlen, E. Schizophrenia in twins. *Schizophrenia Bulletin,* Dec. 1969, **1,** 27 – 39.

Krippner, S. Psychedelic experience and the language process. *Journal of Psychedelic Drugs,* September 1970, **3**(1), 41 – 51.

Krueger, W. C. F. The effect of overlearning on retention. *Journal of Experimental Psychology,* 1929, **12,** 71–78.

Kuhn, M. H., & McPartland, T. S. An empirical investigation of self attitudes. *American Social Review,* 1954, **19,** 68–76.

Kupalov, P. S. Some normal and pathological properties of nervous processes in the brain. In N. S. Kline (Ed.), *Pavlovian conference on higher nervous activity. Annals of the New York Academy of Sciences,* 1961, **92,** 1046–53.

Kutschinsky, B. The effect of pornography: A pilot experiment on perception, behavior and attitudes. *Technical Report of the Commission on Obscenity and Pornography.* Vol. 8. Washington, D.C.: U.S. Government Printing Office, 1971.

Labov, W. The logic of non-standard English. *The Florida FL Reporter,* Spring/Summer 1969, 60–169.

Labov, W., Cohen, P., Robins, C., & Lewis, J. *A study of the non-standard English of Negro and Puerto Rican speakers in New York City.* Vols. 1 & 2. Columbia University, Cooperative Research Project No. 3288, U.S. Office of Education, 1968.

Lachman, S. J. A behavioristic rationale for the development of psychosomatic phenomenon. *Journal of Psychology,* 1963, **56,** 239–48.

Laing, R. D. *The politics of experience.* New York: Pantheon, 1967.

Lakin, M. *Experiential groups: The uses of interpersonal encounter, psychotherapy groups, and sensitivity training.* (Module) Morristown, N.J.: General Learning Corp., 1972.

Landis, C., & Cushman, J. F. The relation of national prohibition to the incidence of mental disease. *Quarterly Journal of Studies on Alcohol,* 1945, **5,** 527–34.

Landreth, C., & Johnson, B. C. Young children's responses to a picture inset test designed to reveal reactions to presence of different skin color. *Child Development Monographs,* 1953, **24,** 63–80.

Lane, R. C., & Singer, J. L. Familial attitudes in paranoid schizophrenia and normals from two socioeconomic classes. *Journal of Abnormal and Social Psychology,* 1959, **59,** 328–39.

Langner, T. S., et al. Reported in *The New York Times,* March 2, 1970, p. 28.

Larsen, K. S., Coleman, D., Forbes, J., & Johnson, R. Is the subject's personality or the experimental situation a better predictor of a subject's willingness to administer shock to a victim? *Journal of Personality and Social Psychology,* 1972, **22,** 287–95.

Lasagna, L., Mosteller, F., von Felsinger, J. M., & Beecher, H. K. A study of the placebo response. *American Journal of Medicine,* 1954, **16,** 770–79.

Lashley, K. S. *Brain mechanisms and intelligence.* Chicago: University of Chicago Press, 1929.

Lashley, K. S. In search of the engram. In *Physiological mechanisms in animal behavior: Symposium of the Society for Experimental Biology.* New York: Academic Press, 1950.

Latane, B. (Ed.) Studies in social comparison: Introduction and overview. *Journal of Experimental Social Psychology,* 1966, **2,** Supplement No. 1.

Lazarus, R. S. Emotions and adaptation: Conceptual and empirical relations. In W. J. Arnold (Ed.), *Nebraska symposium on motivation.* Lincoln: University of Nebraska Press, 1968.

Leahy, A. M. Nature-nurture and intelligence. *Genetic Psychology Monographs,* 1935, **17,** 23–308.

Lederberg, J. Genetic engineering, or the amelioration of genetic defect. *The Pharos of Alpha Omega Alpha,* 1971, **34,** 9–12.

Leeper, R. W. A study of a neglected portion of the field of learning: The development of sensory organization. *Pedagogical Seminary and Journal of Genetic Psychology,* 1935, **46,** 41–75.

Leeper, R. W. A motivational theory of emotion to replace "emotion as disorganized response." *Psychological Review,* 1948, **55,** 5–21.

Lefcourt, H. M. Internal versus external control of reinforcement: A review. *Psychological Bulletin,* 1966, **65,** 206–20.

Lefcourt, H. M. Recent development in the study of locus of control. In B. A. Maher (Ed.), *Progress in experimental personality research.* Vol. 6. New York: Academic Press, 1972.

Lefford, A. The influence of emotional subject matter on logical reasoning. *Journal of General Psychology,* 1946, **34,** 127–51.

Lenneberg, E. H. On explaining language. *Science,* 1969, **164,** 635–43.

Leo, J. Women are said to be infringing on another men's prerogative: The freedom to curse. *The New York Times,* Oct. 20, 1968, p. 49.

Lepper, M. R., & Greene, D. Turning play into work: Effects of adult surveillance and extrinsic rewards on children's intrinsic motivation. *Journal of Personality and Social Psychology,* 1975, **31,** 479–486.

Lepper, M. R., Greene, D., & Nisbett, R. E. Undermining children's intrinsic interest with extrinsic reward: A test of the overjustification hypothesis. *Journal of Personality and Social Psychology,* 1973, **28**(1), 129–37.

LeShan, L. An emotional life-history pattern associated with neoplactic disease. *Annals of the New York Academy of Sciences,* 1966, **125,** 780–93.

Leslie, J. Ethics and practice of placebo therapy. *American Journal of Medicine,* 1954, **16,** 854.

Leukel, F. A comparison of the effects of ECS and anesthesia on acquisition of the maze habit. *Journal of Comparative and Physiological Psychology,* 1957, **50,** 300–306.

Leventhal, H. Fear communications in the acceptance of preventive health practices. *Bulletin of the New York Academy of Sciences,* 1965, **41,** 1144–68.

Levi, L. Occupational stress: A psychophysiological overview. *Occupational Mental Health,* 1972, **2,** 6–9.

Levingood, R., Lowinger, P., & Schoof, K. Heroin addiction in the suburbs: An epidemiologic study. Paper presented at the meeting of the American Public Health Association, 1971.

Levy, S., & Kennard, M. A study of electroencephalogram as related to personality structure in a group of inmates in a state penitentiary. *American Journal of Psychiatry,* 1953, **109,** 382–89.

Lewin, K. Group decision and social change. In T. M. Newcomb & E. L. Hartley (Eds.), *Readings in social psychology.* New York: Holt, Rinehart & Winston, 1947.

Lewin, K., Lippitt, R., & White, R. K. Patterns of aggressive behavior in experimentally created social climates. *Journal of Social Psychology,* 1939, **10,** 271–99.

Lichtenstein, E. How to quit smoking. *Psychology Today,* 1971, **4**(8), 42–45.

Liddell, H. S. The conditioned reflex. In F. A. Moss (Ed.), *Comparative psychology.* New York: Prentice-Hall, 1934.

Liddell, H. S. *Emotional hazards in animals and man.* Springfield, Ill.: Charles C Thomas, 1956.

Lieberman, M. A., Yalom, I. D., & Miles, M. D. *Encounter groups: First facts.* New York: Basic Books, 1973.

Lief, H. I., & Fox, R. C. Training for "detached concern" in medical students. In H. I. Lief, V. F. Lief, & N. R. Lief (Eds.), *The psychological basis of medical practice.* New York: Harper & Row, 1963.

Lifton, R. J. Existential evil. In N. Sanford (Ed.), *Sanctions for evil.* San Francisco: Jossey-Bass, 1971.

Lindauer, M. S. Pleasant and unpleasant emotions in literature: A comparison with the affective tone of psychology. *Journal of Psychology,* 1968, **70,** 55–67.

Lindsay, P. H., & Norman, D. A. *Human information processing.* New York: Academic Press, 1972.

Linton, H. B., & Langs, R. J. Empirical dimensions of LSD-25 reactions. *Archives of General Psychiatry,* 1964, **10,** 469–85.

Lipsitt, L. P. Learning processes of human newborns. *Merrill-Palmer Quarterly of Behavior and Development,* 1966, **12,** 45–71.

Lipsitt, L. P., Engen, T., & Kaye, H. Developmental changes in the olfactory threshold of the neonate. *Child Development,* 1963, **34,** 371–76.

Lockard, J. S. Choice of a warning signal or no warning signal in an unavoidable shock situation. *Journal of Comparative and Physiological Psychology,* 1963, **56,** 526–30.

Logan, F. A. *Incentive.* New Haven: Yale University Press, 1960.

Logan, F. A. Experimental psychology of animal learning and now. *American Psychologist,* Nov. 1972, **27**(11), 1055–62.

Loo, C. M. The effects of spatial density on the social behavior of children. *Journal of Applied Social Psychology.* 1972, **2,** 372–81.

Loomis, A. L., Harvey, E. N., & Hobart, G. A. Cerebral status during sleep as studied by human brain potentials. *Journal of Experimental Psychology,* 1937, **21,** 127–44.

Lorenz, K. Der Kumpan in der Umvelt des Vogels. Der Artgenosse als auslösendes Moment sozialer Verhaltungsweisen. *Journal of Ornithology,* 1935, **83,** 137–213.

Lorenz, K. *On aggression.* New York: Harcourt Brace Jovanovich, 1966.

Lovaas, O. I. Learning theory approach to the treatment of childhood schizophrenia. In California Mental Health Research Symposium, No. 2. *Behavior theory and therapy.* Sacramento, California: Dept. of Mental Hygiene, 1968.

Lowen, A. *A practical guide to psychotherapy.* New York: Harper & Row, 1968.

Luce, G. G. *Current research on sleep and dreams.* Public Health Service Publication No. 1389. Bethesda, Md.: National Institutes of Health, 1965.

Luce, G. G. Biological rhythms in psychiatry and medicine. *Mental Health Program Reports, No. 4.* (PHS) Publication No. 2088. Chevy Chase, Md.: National Institute of Mental Health, 1970.

Luchins, A. S. Mechanization in problem solving—The effect of Einstellung. *Psychological Monographs,* 1942, **54**(6, Whole No. 248).

Luchins, A. S. An approach to evaluating the achievement of group psychotherapy. *Journal of Social Psychology,* 1960, **52,** 345–53.

Luchins, A. S., & Luchins, E. H. *Rigidity of behavior.* Portland: University of Oregon Press, 1959.

Luckhardt, A. B., & Carlson, A. J. Contributions to the physiology of the stomach. XVII. On the chemical control of the gastric hunger contractions. *American Journal of Physiology,* 1915, **36,** 37–46.

Ludwig, A. M. Altered states of consciousness. *Archives of General Psychiatry,* 1966, **15,** 225–34.

Lundin, R. W. *Personality: An experimental approach.* New York: Macmillan, 1961.

Luria, A. R. *The mind of a mnemonist.* New York: Basic Books, 1968.

Luria, A. R. The functional organization of the brain. *Scientific American,* 1970, **222**(3), 66–78.

Maccoby, E. E., & Jacklin, C. N. *The psychology of sex differences.* Palo Alto, Calif.: Stanford University Press, 1974.

MacKinnon, D. W. The study of creativity and creativity in architects. In *Conference on the creative person.* Berkeley: University of California, Institute of Personality Assessment and Research, 1961.

MacLean, P. D. Contrasting functions of limbic and neocortical systems of the brain and their relevance to psychophysiological aspects of medicine. *American Journal of Medicine,* 1958, **25,** 611–26.

Magoun, H. W. The ascending reticular system and wakefulness. In J. F. Delafresnaye (Ed.), *Brain mechanisms and consciousness.* Oxford: Blackwell, 1954.

Maher, B. A. *Principles of psychopathology: An experimental approach.* New York: McGraw-Hill, 1966.

Maller, O., Clark, J. M., & Kare, M. R. Short-term caloric regulation in the adult opossum. *Proceedings of the Society for Experimental Biology and Medicine,* 1965, **118,** 275–77.

Mallick, S. K., & McCandless, B. R. A study of catharsis of aggression. *Journal of Personality and Social Psychology,* 1966, **4,** 591–96.

Maltzman, I. On the training of originality. *Psychological Review,* 1960, **67,** 229–42.

Manes, A. L., & Melynk, P. Televised models of female achievement. *Journal of Applied Social Psychology,* 1974, 4, 365–374.

Manis, M. *An introduction to cognitive psychology.* Belmont, Calif.: Wadsworth, 1971.

Mann, J., Sidman, J., & Starr, S. Effects of erotic films on sexual behavior of married couples. *Technical report of the Commission on Obscenity and Pornography.* Vol. 8. Washington, D.C.: U.S. Government Printing Office, 1971.

Mann, T. Mario and the magician. In H. T. Lowe-Porter (Trans.), *Death in Venice and seven other stories by Thomas Mann.* New York: Vintage Books, 1957.

Mansson, H. H. Justifying the final solution. *Omega,* 3(2), 1972, 79–87.

Maranon, G. Contribution à l'étude de l'action émotive de l'adrénaline. *Revue Fr. Endocrinal,* 1924, **2,** 301–25.

Margotta, R. Nervous and mental diseases. In P. Lewis (Ed.), *The story of medicine.* New York: Golden Press, 1967.

Mark, V., & Ervin, F. R. *Violence and the brain.* New York: Harper & Row, 1970.

Marks, I. M., & Gelder, M. G. Transvetism and fetishism: Clinical and psychological changes during faradic aversion. *British Journal of Psychiatry,* 1967, **113,** 711–29.

Marks, L. E., & Miller, G. A. The role of semantic and syntactic constraints in the memorization of English sentences. *Journal of Verbal Learning and Verbal Behavior,* 1964, **3,** 1–5.

Marler, P. Acoustical influences in bird song development. *The Rockefeller University Review,* Sept./Oct. 1967, 8–13.

Marshall, G. *Affective consequences of "inadequately explained" physiological arousal.* Unpublished doctoral dissertation, Stanford University, 1976.

Martindale, D. Torment in the tower. *Chicago,* April 1976, 96–101.

Masangkay, Z. S., McCluskey, K. A., McIntyre, C. W., Sims-Knight, J., Vaughn, B. E., & Flavell, J. H. The early development of inferences about the visual perceptions of others. *Child Development.* 1974, in press.

Maslach, C. Social and personal bases of individuation. *Journal of Personality and Social Psychology,* March 1974, **29**(3), 411–25.

Maslach, C., Marshall, G., & Zimbardo, P. G. Hypnotic control of peripheral skin temperature: A case report. *Psychophysiology,* 1972, **2,** 600–605.

Maslach, C., & Zimbardo, P. G. Dehumanization in institutional settings. Paper presented at the American Psychological Association Convention, Montreal, Canada, 1973.

Maslow, A. H. *Motivation and personality.* New York: Harper & Row, 1954.

Maslow, A. H. Psychological data and value theory. In A. H. Maslow (Ed.), *New knowledge in human values.* New York: Harper & Row, 1959.

Masters, R. E., & Houston, J. *The varieties of psychedelic experience.* New York: Holt, Rinehart & Winston, 1966.

Masters, W. H., & Johnson, V. E. *Human sexual response.* Boston: Little, Brown, 1966.

Masters, W. H., & Johnson, V. E. *Human sexual inadequacy.* Boston: Little, Brown, 1970.

Masterton, R. B., & Berkley, M. A. Brain functions: Changing ideas on the role of sensory, motor, and association cortex in behavior. In P. H. Mussen & M. R. R. Rosenzweig (Eds.), *Annual review of psychology, 1974.* Vol. 25. Palo Alto, Calif.: Annual Reviews, 1974.

Matson, F. W. Humanistic theory: The third foul in psychology. *The Humanist,* March/April 1971, 7–11.

Mayer, J. *Overweight: Causes, cost and control.* Englewood Cliffs, N.J.: Prentice-Hall, 1968.

McClelland, D. C. *The achieving society.* Princeton: Van Nostrand, 1961.

McClelland, D. C. Do I.Q. tests measure intelligence? *Saturday Evening Post,* Summer 1972.

McConnell, J. V., Memory transfer through cannibalism in planaria. *Journal of Neuropsychiatry,* 1962, **3,** 45.

McConnell, J. V., Jacobson, A. L., & Kimble, D. P. The effects of regeneration upon retention of a conditioned response in the planarian. *Journal of Comparative and Physiological Psychology,* 1959, **52,** 1–5.

McConnell, R. A. *ESP curriculum guide.* New York: Simon & Schuster, 1971.

McGinnies, E. Emotionality and perceptual defense. *Psychological Review,* 1949, **56,** 244–51.

McGinnies, E., & Sherman, H. Generalization of perceptual defense. *Journal of Abnormal and Social Psychology,* 1952, **47,** 81–85.

McGlashin, T. H., Evans, F. J., & Orne, M. T. The nature of hypnotic analgesic and placebo response to experimental pain. *Psychosomatic Medicine,* 1969, **31,** 227–46.

McGlothlin, W., Cohen, S., & McGlothlin, M. S. Long lasting effects of LSD on normals. *Archives of General Psychiatry,* 1967, **17,** 521–32.

McGregor, D. *The human side of enterprise.* New York: McGraw-Hill, 1960.

McGuigan, F. J. Electrical measurement of covert processes as an explication of higher mental events. In F. J. McGuigan & R. A. Schoonover (Eds.), *The psychophysiology of thinking: Studies of covert processes.* New York: Academic Press, 1973.

McGuigan, F. J., Keller, B., & Stanton, E. Covert language responses during silent reading. *Journal of Educational Psychology,* 1964, 55, 339–43.

McGuigan, F. J., & Schoonover, R. A. *The psychophysiology of thinking.* New York: Academic Press, 1973.

McGuigan, F. J., & Tanner, R. G. Covert oral behavior during conversational and visual dreams. *Psychonomic Science,* 1971, **23,** 263–64.

McNeil, D. Developmental psycholinguistics. In F. Smith & G. A. Miller (Eds.), *The genesis of language: A psycholinguistic approach.* Cambridge, Mass.: M.I.T. Press, 1966.

McNemar, Q. *The revision of the Stanford-Binet Scale.* Boston: Houghton Mifflin, 1942.

Mead, M. *Coming of age in Samoa.* New York: Morrow, 1961. (Originally published, 1938.)

Meader, B. D., & Rogers, C. R. Client-centered therapy. In R. Corsini (Ed.), *Current psychotherapies.* Itasca, Ill.: F. E. Peacock, 1973.

Meehl, P. E. *Clinical versus statistical prediction.* Minneapolis: University of Minneapolis Press, 1954.

Meehl, P. E. Seer over sign: The first good example. *Journal of Experimental Research in Personality,* 1965, **1,** 27–32.

Megargee, E. I. Undercontrolled and overcontrolled personality types in extreme antisocial aggression. *Psychological Monographs,* 1966, **80**(Whole No. 611).

Mehrabian, A. Significance of posture and position in the communication of attitude and status relationships. *Psychological Bulletin,* 1969, **71,** 359–72.

Mehrabian, A. *Silent messages.* Belmont, Calif.: Wadsworth, 1971. (a)

Mehrabian, A. Verbal and nonverbal interaction of strangers in a waiting situation. *Journal of Experimental Research in Personality,* 1971, **5,** 127–38. (b)

Melzack, R. How acupuncture works: A sophisticated Western theory takes the mystery out. *Psychology Today,* June 1973, **7,** 28–37.

Melzack, R., & Scott, T. H. The effects of early experience on the response to pain. *Journal of Comparative and Physiological Psychology,* 1957, **50,** 155–61.

Melzack, R., & Wall, P. D. Pain mechanisms: A new theory. *Science,* 1965, **150,** 971–79.

Mendel, W. M. Effect of length of hospitalization on rate and quality of remission from acute psychotic episodes. *Journal of Nervous and Mental Diseases,* 1966, **143,** 226–33.

Mendels, J. *Concepts of depression.* New York: Wiley, 1970.

Metzler, J. & Shepard, R. N. Transformational studies of the internal representation of three-dimensional objects. In R. L. Solso (Ed.), *Theories of cognitive psychology: The Loyola symposium.* Potomac, Md.: Lawrence Erlbaum Associates, 1974.

Meyer, J. The case for a national commission on advertising. In S. Divita (Ed.), *Advertising in the Public Interest.* Chicago: American Marketing Association, 1974.

Meyer, M. M., & Ekstein, R. The psychotic pursuit of reality. *Journal of Contemporary Psychotherapy,* 1970, **3,** 3–12.

Meyer, P. M. Recovery from neocortical damage. In G. M. French (Ed.), *Cortical functioning in behavior.* Glenview, Ill.: Scott, Foresman, 1973.

Meyer, P. M., Horel, J. A., & Meyer, D. R. Effects of DL-Amphetamine upon placing responses in neodecorticate cats. *Journal of Comparative and Physiological Psychology,* 1963, **56,** 402–4.

Meyer, W. U. Reported in W. J. Arnold (Ed.), *Nebraska symposium on motivation.* Lincoln: University of Nebraska Press, 1968.

Michelet, J. *Satanism and witchcraft: A study in medieval superstition.* New York: Citadel, 1962.

Middlebrook, P. *Social psychology and modern life,* New York: Knopf, 1973.

Milgram, S. Issues in the study of obedience: A reply to Baumrind. *American Psychologist,* 1964, **19,** 848–52.

Milgram, S. Some conditions of obedience and disobedience to authority. *Human Relations,* 1965, **18**(1), 57–76.

Milgram, S. *Obedience to authority.* New York: Harper & Row, 1974.

Miller, G. A. The magical number seven plus or minus two: Some limits on our capacity for processing information. *Psychological Review*, 1956, **63**, 81–97.

Miller, G. A. *The psychology of communication: Seven essays*. New York: Basic Books, 1967.

Miller, G. A. Psychology as a means of promoting human welfare. *American Psychologist*, Dec. 1969, **24**(12), 1063–75.

Miller, G. A., Galanter, E., & Pribram, K. H. *Plans and the structure of behavior*. New York: Holt, Rinehart & Winston, 1960.

Miller, G. A., & Isard, S. Some perceptual consequences of linguistic rules. *Journal of Verbal Learning and Verbal Behavior*, 1963, **2**, 217–28.

Miller, J. M., Sutton, D., Pfingst, B., Ryan, A., Beaton, R., & Gourevitch, G. Single cell activity in the auditory cortex of Rhesus monkeys: Behavioral dependency. *Science*, 1972, **177**, 449–51.

Miller, N. E. The frustration-aggression hypothesis. *Psychological Review*, 1941, **48**, 337–42.

Miller, N. E. Experimental studies of conflict. In J. McV. Hunt (Ed.), *Personality and the behavior disorders*. Vol. 1. New York: Ronald Press, 1944.

Miller, N. E. Experiments on motivation. *Science*, 1957, **126**, 1271–78.

Miller, N. E. Learning of visceral and glandular responses. *Science*, 1969, **163**, 434–45.

Miller, N. E. Applications of learning and biofeedback to psychiatry and medicine. In A. M. Freedman, H. I. Kaplan, & B. J. Sadock (Eds.), *Comprehensive textbook of psychiatry*. (2nd ed.) Baltimore: Williams & Wilkins, 1974.

Miller, N. E., & Di Cara, L. V. Instrumental training of visceral functions. *Mental Health Program Reports, No. 6*. (DHEW) Publication No. (HSM) 73-9139. Chevy Chase, Md.: National Institute of Mental Health, 1973.

Miller, N. E., Di Cara, L. V., Solomon, H., Weiss, J., & Dworkin, B. Learned modifications of autonomic functions: A review and some new data. *Circulation Research*, 1970, **27**, 3–11. (Supplement 1)

Miller, W. Violent crime in city gangs. *The American Academy of Political and Social Science*, March 1966.

Miller, W. R., & Ervin, S. M. The development of grammar in child language. In U. Bellugi-Klima & R. Brown (Eds.), *The acquisition of language. Monographs of the Society for Research in Child Development*, 1964, **29**(1), 9–33.

Milner, B., & Penfield, W. The effect of hippocampal lesion on recent memory. *Transactions of the American Neurological Association*, 1955, **80**, 42–48.

Mischel, W. *Personality and assessment*. New York: Wiley, 1968.

Mishkin, M., & Forgays, D. G. Word recognition as a function of retinal locus. *Journal of Experimental Psychology*, 1952, **43**, 43–48.

Mogar, R. E. Current status and future trends in psychedelic (LSD) research. In C. Tart (Ed.), *Altered states of consciousness*. New York: Wiley, 1969.

Mohsin, S. M. Effect of frustration on problem-solving behavior. *Journal of Abnormal and Social Psychology*, 1954, **49**, 152–55.

Money, J., & Ehrhardt, A. A. *Man and woman, boy and girl*. Baltimore: Johns Hopkins University Press, 1972.

Moniz, E. Prefrontal leucotomy in the treatment of mental disorders. *American Journal of Psychiatry*, 1937, **93**, 1379–85.

Montgomery, J., & McBurney, R. D. *Operant conditioning token economy*. Camarillo, Calif.: Report of the Child Health and Human Development Center, 1970.

Montor, K. Brain-wave research. *Naval Research Reviews*, April 1973, 7–11.

Moore, B. R. The role of directed Pavlovian reactions in simple instrumental learning in the pigeon. In R. A. Hind & J. S. Hinde (Eds.), *Constraints on learning: Limitations and predispositions*. London: Academic Press, 1973.

Moore, S. C. Editorial. *Parachutist*, 1963, **4**, 5–7.

Moos, R. H. Conceptualizations of human environments. *American Psychologist*, 1973, **28**, 652–65.

Morgan, A. H. The heritability of hypnotic susceptibility in twins. *Journal of Abnormal Psychology*, 1973, **82**, 55–61.

Moritz, A. P., & Zamchech, N. Sudden and unexpected deaths of young soldiers. *American Medical Association Archives of Pathology*, 1946, **42**, 459–94.

Morland, J. K. A comparison race awareness in northern and southern children. *American Journal of Orthopsychiatry*, 1966, **36**, 22–31.

Mosak, H., & Dreikers, R. Adlerian psychotherapy. In R. Corsini (Ed.), *Current Psychotherapies*. Itasca, Ill.: F. E. Peacock, 1973.

Moscovici, S., Lage, E., & Naffrechoux, M. Influence of a consistent minority on the responses of a majority in a color perception task. *Sociometry*, 1969, **32**, 365–80.

Mosher, L. R., & Feinsilver, D. *Special report on schizophrenia*. Chevy Chase, Md.: National Institute of Mental Health, April 1970.

Mosher, L. R., & Feinsilver, D. *Special report: Schizophrenia*. Chevy Chase, Md.: National Institute of Mental Health, 1971.

Moskowitz, M. The big profits in tension relief. *San Francisco Chronicle*, Sept. 17, 1973.

Mowrer, O. H. *Learning theory and behavior*. New York: Wiley, 1960.

Mowrer, O. H., & Viek, P. An experimental analogue of fear from a sense of helplessness. *Journal of Abnormal and Social Psychology*, 1948, **43**, 193–200.

Moyer, K. E. Kinds of aggression and their physiological basis. *Communications in Behavioral Biology*, 1968, **2**, 65–87.

Munn, N. L. The effect of the knowledge of the situation upon judgment of emotion from facial expressions. *Journal of Abnormal and Social Psychology,* 1940, **35,** 324–38.

Münsterberg, H. *On the witness stand: Essays on psychology and crime.* New York: Clark Boardman, 1927. (Originally published: New York: Doubleday, 1908.)

Murray, J. R., Minor, M. J., Bradburn, N. M., Cotterman, R. F., Frandel, M., & Pisarski, A. E. Evolution of public response to the energy crisis. *Science,* 1974, **184,** 257–63.

Myerson, A. The attitude of neurologists, psychiatrists, and psychologists toward psychoanalysis. *American Journal of Psychiatry,* 1939, **96,** 623–41.

Nardini, J. E. Survival factors in American prisoners of war of the Japanese. *American Journal of Psychiatry,* 1952, **109,** 241–47.

National Clearinghouse for Mental Health Information. Publication No. 5027, March 1970.

Neisser, U. *Cognitive psychology.* New York: Appleton-Century-Crofts, 1967.

Nelson, K. Accommodation of visual-tracking patterns in human infants to object movement patterns. Unpublished doctoral dissertation, Yale University, 1970.

Newcomb, T. M. Attitude development as a function of reference groups. In E. E. Maccoby, T. M. Newcomb, & E. L. Hartley (Eds.), *Readings in social psychology.* New York: Holt, Rinehart & Winston, 1958.

Newcomb, T. M. Persistence and regression of changed attitudes: Long-range studies. *Journal of Social Issues,* 1963, **19,** 3–14.

Newell, A., Shaw, J. C., & Simon, H. A. Elements of a theory of human problem solving. *Psychological Review,* 1958, **65,** 151–66.

Newell, A., Shaw, J. C., & Simon, H. A. Report on a general problem-solving program. In *Proceedings of the International Conference on Information Processing.* Paris: UNESCO, 1960.

Newsweek. Quote from "Drinking Like a Pig," from *Newsweek,* July 30, 1973. Copyright Newsweek, Inc. 1973 reprinted by permission.

Newsweek. Quote from "The Power of Positive Non-Thinking," from *Newsweek* Magazine, Jan. 7, 1974, **83**(1), 74. Copyright Newsweek, Inc. 1974 reprinted by permission.

Nichols, R. C. The National Merit twin study. In S. G. Vandenberg (Ed.), *Methods and goals in human behavior genetics.* New York: Academic Press, 1965.

Niebuhr, R. In F. S. Mead (Ed.), *The encyclopedia of religious quotations.* Westwood, N.J.: Fleming H. Revell Co., 1965.

Nievergelt, J., & Farrar, J. C. What machines can and cannot do. *American Scientist,* 1973, **61,** 309–15.

Nisbett, R. E. Hunger, obesity, and the ventromedial hypothalamus. *Psychological Review,* 1972, **79,** 433–53.

Nisbett, R. E., & Schachter, S. The cognitive manipulation of pain. *Journal of Experimental Social Psychology,* 1966, **2,** 227–36.

Nissen, H. W., Chow, K. L., & Semmes, J. Effects of restricted opportunity for tactual, kinesthetic, and manipulative experience on the behavior of a chimpanzee. *American Journal of Psychology,* 1951, **64,** 485–507.

Nizer, L. *My life in court.* New York: Pyramid, 1961.

Nyswander, M. *The drug addict as a patient.* New York: Grune & Stratton, 1956.

O'Connell, D. N., Shore, R. E., & Orne, M. T. Hypnotic age regression: An empirical and methodological analysis. *Journal of Abnormal Psychology,* 1970, **76,** 32.

O'Connor, R. D. Modification of social withdrawal through symbolic modeling. *Journal of Applied Behavioral Analysis,* 1969, **2,** 15–22.

O'Hara. From "What Do You Think a Hangover Is?" *San Francisco Chronicle,* Jan. 1, 1972. © Chronicle Publishing Co., 1972.

Olcott, R. C. Personal correspondence to the author in letter dated Jan. 15, 1974, from speech delivered to Toastmasters Club, "Just a Spoonful." Excerpt reprinted by permission of the author.

Olds, J. Commentary on positive reinforcement produced by electrical stimulation of septal areas and other regions of rat brain. In E. S. Valenstein (Ed.), *Brain stimulation and motivation: Research and commentary.* Glenview, Ill.: Scott, Foresman, 1973.

Olds, J., & Milner, P. Positive reinforcement produced by electrical stimulation of septal area and other regions of the rat brain. *Journal of Comparative and Physiological Psychology,* 1954, **47,** 419–27.

O'Leary, K. D., Kaufman, K. F., Kass, R. E., & Drabran, R. S. The effects of loud and soft reprimands on the behavior of disruptive students. *Exceptional Children,* 1970, **37,** 145–55.

Oppenheimer, R. Analogy in science. *American Psychologist,* 1956, **11,** 127–35.

Opton, N. Lessons of My Lai. In R. Buckhout (Ed.), *Toward social change.* New York: Harper & Row, 1971.

Orlando, N. J. The mock ward: A study in simulation. In O. Milton & R. G. Wahler (Eds.), *Behavior disorders: Perspectives and trends.* Philadelphia: Lippincott, 1973.

Orne, M. T. Mechanisms of post-hypnotic amnesia. *International Journal of Clinical and Experimental Hypnosis,* 1966, **14,** 121–34.

Orne, M. T. Hypnosis, motivation and the ecological validity of the psychological experiment. In W. J. Arnold & M. M. Page (Eds.), *Nebraska symposium on motivation.* Lincoln: University of Nebraska Press, 1970.

Orne, M. T., & Hammer, A. G. Hypnosis. *Encyclopaedia Britannica.* Chicago: William Benton, 1974.

Ornstein, R. E. *The psychology of consciousness.* San Francisco: Freeman, 1972.

Osborn, A. F. *Applied imagination: Principles and procedures of creative thinking.* (2nd ed.) New York: Scribner's, 1957.

Osborn, D. K., & Endsley, R. C. Emotional reactions of young children to TV violence. *Child Development,* 1971, **42,** 321–31.

Osgood, C. *Method and theory in experimental psychology.* New York: Oxford University Press, 1953.

Osler, S. F., & Fivel, M. W. Concept attainment. I. The role of age and intelligence in concept attainment by induction. *Journal of Experimental Psychology,* 1961, **62,** 1–8.

Osmond, H., & Smythies, J. Schizophrenia: New approach. *Journal of Mental Science,* 1952, **98,** 300–315.

Ostwald, P. F., & Peltzman, P. The cry of the human infant. *Scientific American,* 1974, **230,** 84–90.

Overmier, J. B., & Seligman, M. E. Effects of inescapable shock upon subsequent escape and avoidance responding. *Journal of Comparative and Physiological Psychology,* 1967, **63**(1), 28–33.

Pahnke, W. N. Drugs and mysticism: An analysis of the relationship between psychedelic drugs and mystical consciousness. Unpublished doctoral dissertation, Harvard University, 1963.

Pahnke, W. N. LSD and religious experience. In R. C. DeBold & R. C. Leaf (Eds.), *LSD, man and society.* Middletown, Conn.: Wesleyan University Press, 1967.

Parke, R. D., Berkowitz, L., Leyens, J., West, S., & Sebastian, R. The effects of repeated exposure to movie violence on aggressive behavior in juvenile delinquent boys: A field experimental approach. Unpublished manuscript, University of Wisconsin, 1972.

Parke, R. D., & Walters, R. H. Some factors influencing the efficacy of punishment training for inducing response inhibition. *Monographs of the Society for Research in Child Development,* 1967, **32**(1, Whole No. 109).

Parkes, A. S., & Bruce, H. M. Olfactory stimuli in mammalian reproduction. Odor excites neurohumoral responses affecting olstrus, pseudopregnancy and pregnancy in the mouse. *Science,* 1961, **134,** 1049–54.

Paul, G. L. Outcome of systematic desensitization. II. Controlled investigations of individual treatment technique variations, and current status. In C. M. Franks (Ed.), *Behavior therapy: Appraisal and status.* New York: McGraw-Hill, 1969.

Pearson, K., & Moul, M. The problem of alien immigration into Great Britain, illustrated by an examination of Russian and Polish Jewish children. *Annals of Eugenics,* 1925, **1,** 5–127.

Pelletier, K. R. Neurological psychophysiological, and clinical differentiation of the alpha and theta altered states of consciousness. Unpublished doctoral dissertation, University of California, Berkeley, 1974.

Penfield, W. *The excitable cortex in conscious man.* Liverpool: Liverpool University Press, 1958.

Penfield, W., & Baldwin, M. Temporal lobe seizures and the technique of subtotal temporal lobectomy. *Annals of Surgery,* 1952, **136,** 625–34.

Penick, S., Smith, G., Wienske, K., & Hinkle, L. An experimental evaluation of the relationship between hunger and gastric motility. *American Journal of Physiology,* 1963, **205,** 421–26.

Peterson, G. B., Ackil, J. E., Frommer, G. P., & Hearst, E. S. Conditioned approach and contact behavior toward signals for food or brain-stimulation reinforcement. *Science,* 1972, **177,** 1009–11.

Pfungst, O. *Clever Hans (the horse of Mr. Von Osten).* R. Rosenthal (Trans.). New York: Holt, Rinehart & Winston, 1911. Copyright © 1965 by Holt, Rinehart & Winston, Inc. Excerpt reprinted by permission of Holt, Rinehart & Winston, Inc.

Phares, E. J. *Locus of control in personality.* Morristown, N.J.: General Learning Press, 1976.

Piaget, J. Genetic epistemology. New York: Columbia University Press, 1970.

Pick, H. L., Warren, D. H., & Hay, J. C. Sensory conflict in judgments of spatial direction. *Perception and Psychophysics,* 1969, **6**(4), 203–5.

Pierrel, R., & Sherman, J. G. Train your pet the Barnabus way. *Brown Alumni Monthly,* Feb. 1963, 8–14.

Piliavan, I. M., Rodin, J., & Piliavan, J. A. Good Samaritanism: An underground phenomenon? *Journal of Personality and Social Psychology,* 1969, **13,** 289–300.

Piliavan, J. A., & Piliavan, I. M. Effect of blood on reactions to a victim. *Journal of Personality and Social Psychology,* 1972, **23,** 353–61.

Pinkerton, J. (Ed.) *A general collection of the best and most interesting voyages and travels in all parts of the world.* London: Longman, Hurst, Rees, & Orne, 1808–14.

Pitts, F. N. The biochemistry of anxiety. *Scientific American,* 1969, **220,** 69–75.

Platt, J. Social traps. *American Psychologist,* 1973, **28,** 641–51.

Playboy, 1969, **16**(2), 46.

Posner, E. G. The effect of therapists' training on group therapeutic outcome. *Journal of Consulting Psychology,* 1966, **30,** 283–89.

Postman, L., & Rau, L. Retention as a function of the method of measurement. *University of California Publications in Psychology,* 1957, **8**(3).

Potter, V. R. *Bioethics: Bridge to the future.* Englewood Cliffs, N.J.: Prentice-Hall, 1971.

Powledge, T. M. The new ghetto hustle. *Saturday Review of the Sciences,* Jan. 27, 1973, **1**(1).

Premack, D. A functional analysis of language. Paper presented at the meeting of the American Psychological Association, Washington, D.C., 1969.

Premack, D. The education of Sarah. *Psychology Today,* 1970, **4**(4), 54–58.

Pribram, K. H. A review of theory in physiological psychology. *American Review of Psychology,* 1960, **11,** 1–40.

Pribram, K. H. Emotion: Steps toward a neurophysiological theory. In D. C. Glass (Ed.), *Neurophysiology and emotion.* New York: Rockefeller University Press, 1967.

Pribram, K. H. *Languages of the brain: Experimental paradoxes and principles in neuropsychology.* Englewood Cliffs, N.J.: Prentice-Hall, 1971.

Price, C. R. *New directions in the world of work.* Kalamazoo, Mich.: UpJohn Institute for Employment Research, March 1972.

Price-Williams, D. R. A study concerning concepts of conservation of quantities among primitive children. *Acta Psychological,* 1961, **18,** 297–305.

Price-Williams, D. R., Gordon, W., & Ramirez, M. Skill and conservation. *Developmental Psychology,* 1969, **1,** 769.

Prien, R. F., Caffey, E. M., & Klett, C. J. *Pharmacotherapy in chronic schizophrenia.* Washington, D.C.: Dept. of Medicine and Surgery, Veterans Administration, May 1973.

Prien, R. F., Levine, J., & Switalski, R. W. Discontinuation of chemotherapy for chronic schizophrenics. *Hospital and Community Pyschiatry,* 1971, **22,** 20.

Prytulak, L. S. Natural language mediation. *Cognitive Psychology,* 1971, **2,** 1–56.

Rahe, R. H. The pathway between subjects' recent life changes and their near-future illness reports: representative results and methodological issues. In B. S. Dohrenwend & B. P. Dohrenwend (Eds.), *Stressful life events: their nature and effects.* New York: Wiley, 1974.

Rahe, R. H., & Holmes, T. H. Life crisis and major health change. *Psychosomatic Medicine,* 1966, **28,** 774.

Rand, C., & Wapner, S. Postural status as a factor in memory. *Journal of Verbal Learning and Behavior,* 1967, **6,** 268–71.

Rand Corporation. *A million random digits with 100,000 normal deviates.* New York: The Free Press, 1955.

Rappaport, M., & Silverman, J. A sensor for schizophrenics. *Behavior Today,* 1970, **1**(21), 1.

Raush, H. L., & Raush, C. L. *The halfway house movement: A search for sanity.* New York: Appleton-Century-Crofts, 1968.

Rawlings, E. Reactive guilt and anticipatory guilt in altruistic behavior. In J. Macauley & L. Berkowitz (Eds.), *Altruism and helping behavior: Social psychological studies of some antecedents and consequences.* New York: Academic Press, 1970.

Razran, G. Introductory remarks. In N. S. Kline (Ed.), *Pavlovian conference on higher nervous activity. Annals of the New York Academy of Sciences,* 1961, **92,** 816–17.

Rechtschaffen, A., & Kales, A. (Eds.) *A manual of standardized terminology, techniques and scoring systems for sleep stages of human subjects.* Publication No. 204. Bethesda, Md.: National Institutes of Health, 1968.

Regan, D., Williams, M., & Sparling, S. Voluntary expiation of guilt: A field experiment. *Journal of Personality and Social Psychology,* 1972, **24,** 42–45.

Reisman, D., Glazer, N., & Denney, R. *The lonely crowd: A study of the changing American character.* New Haven: Yale University Press, 1950.

Reitman, J. S. Mechanisms of forgetting in short-term memory. *Cognitive Psychology,* 1971, **2,** 185–95.

Reitman, W. R. *Cognition and thought.* New York: Wiley, 1965.

Reuben, D. Letter to Dr. David Reuben. *San Francisco Examiner/Chronicle,* Dec. 16, 1973. Copyright 1973 Chicago Tribune-New York News Syndicate, Inc. Excerpt reprinted by permission.

Reynolds, G. S. The effect of stress upon problem solving. *Journal of General Psychology,* 1960, **62,** 83–88.

Rheingold, H. L., Gewirtz, J. L., & Ross, H. W. Social conditioning of vocalizations in the infant. *Journal of Comparative and Physiological Psychology,* 1959, **52,** 68–73.

Rhine, J. B. *New world of the mind.* London: Faber & Faber, 1954.

Ribble, M. A. Infantile experience in relation to personality development. In J. McV. Hunt (Ed.), *Personality and the behavior disorders.* New York: Ronald Press, 1944.

Richards, W., Grof, S., Goodman, L., & Kurland, A. LSD-assisted psychotherapy and the human encounter with death. *Journal of Transpersonal Psychology,* 1972, **4,** 121–50.

Richter, C. P. The self-selection of diets. In *Essays in biology.* Berkeley: University of California Press, 1943.

Richter, C. P. On the phenomenon of sudden death in animals and man. *Psychosomatic Medicine,* 1957, **19,** 191–98.

Rickles, K. Non-specific factors in drug therapy of neurotic patients. In K. Rickles (Ed.), *Non-specific factors in drug therapy.* Springfield, Ill.: Charles C Thomas, 1968.

Riesen, A. H. Arrested vision. *Scientific American,* 1950, **183**(1), 16–19.

Riesen, A. H. Stimulation as a requirement for growth and function in behavioral development. In D. W. Fiske & S. R. Maddi (Eds.), *Functions of varied experience.* Homewood, Ill.: Dorsey, 1961.

Rivlin, A. M. Social experiments: Promise and problems. *Science,* January 1974, **183**(4120), 35.

Robertson, J. Uncontainable joy. In R. Metzner (Ed.), *The ecstatic adventure.* New York: Macmillan, 1968.

Robinson, M. F., & Freeman, W. J. *Psychosurgery and the self.* New York: Grune & Stratton, 1955.

Rodgers, R. "Oklahoma." Copyright © 1943 by Williamson Music, Inc. Copyright renewed. Excerpt used by permission of Williamson Music, Inc.

Roffwarg, H. P., Muzio, J. N., & Dement, W. C. Ontogenetic development of the human sleep-dream cycle. *Science,* April 1966, **152**(29).

Rogers, C. R. Significant aspects of client-centered therapy. *American Psychologist,* 1946, **1,** 415–22.

Rogers, C. R. The case of Mary Jane Tilden. In W. U. Snyder (Ed.), *Casebook of non-directive counseling.* Boston: Houghton Mifflin, 1947. Copyright 1947 by Houghton Mifflin Company. Excerpt reprinted by permission.

Rogers, C. R. *On becoming a person: A therapist's view of psychotherapy.* Boston: Houghton Mifflin, 1961.

Rohrer, J. H., Baron, S. H., Hoffman, E. L., & Swander, D. V. The stability of autokinetic judgments. *Journal of Abnormal Psychology,* 1954, **49,** 595–97.

Rorvik, D. M. Jack Schwartz feels no pain. *Esquire,* December 1972, 209–64.

Rosenhan, D. Some origins of concern for others. In P. H. Mussen, J. Langer, & M. Covington (Eds.), *Trends and issues in developmental psychology.* New York: Holt, Rinehart & Winston, 1969.

Rosenhan, D. L. On being sane in insane places. *Science,* 1973, **179,** 250–58.

Rosenzweig, M. R., Bennett, E. L., Diamond, M. C., Wu, Su-Yu, Slagle, R. W., & Saffran, E. Influences of environmental complexity and visual stimulation on development of occipital cortex in rats. *Brain Research,* 1969, **14,** 427–45.

Ross, L., Bierbrauer, G., & Polly, S. Attribution of educational outcomes by professional and non-professional instructors. *Journal of Personality and Social Psychology,* 1974, **29,** 609–618.

Ross, L., Lepper, M. R., & Hubbard, M. Perseverance in self-perception and social perception: Biased attributional process in the debriefing paradigm. *Journal of Personality and Social Psychology,* 1975, **32,** 880–892.

Ross, L., Rodin, J., & Zimbardo, P. G. Toward an attribution therapy: The reduction of fear through induced cognitive-emotional misattribution. *Journal of Personality and Social Psychology,* 1969, **12,** 279–88.

Rothblat, L., & Pribram, K. H. Selective attention: Input filter or response selection? *Brain Research,* 1972, **39,** 427–36.

Rothman, D. J. *The discovery of the asylum: Social order and disorder in the new republic.* Boston: Little, Brown, 1971.

Rothman, M. A. Response to McConnell. *American Psychologist,* 1970, **25,** 280–81.

Rotter, J. B. *Social learning and clinical psychology.* New York: Prentice-Hall, 1954.

Rotter, J. B. Generalized expectancies for internal versus external controls of reinforcement. *Psychological Monographs,* 1966, **80**(1, Whole No. 609).

Rotter, J. B. External control and internal control. *Psychology Today,* 1971, **5**(1), 37–42, 58–59.

Rouse, L., & Reilly, S. Proposal for continued development of a treatment program for chronic patients. Unpublished mimeo report. Palo Alto, Calif.: Veterans Hospital, 1974.

Routh, D. K. Conditioning of vocal response differentiation in infants. *Journal of Developmental Psychology,* 1969, **1,** 219–26.

Rozin, P. Specific hunger for thiamine: Recovery from deficiency and thiamine preference, *Journal of Comparative and Physiological Psychology,* 1965, **59,** 98–101.

Rozin, P., & Kalat, J. Adaptive specialization in learning and memory. Salience: A factor which can override temporal contiguity in taste-aversion learning. *Journal of Comparative and Physiological Psychology,* 1970, **71**(2), 192–97.

Rubel, A. J. *Across the tracks: Mexican-Americans in a Texas city.* Austin: University of Texas, 1966.

Rubin, E. Figure and ground. In D. C. Beardslee & M. Wertheimer (Eds.), *Readings in perception.* Princeton: Van Nostrand, 1958. (Originally published, 1921.)

Rubin, J. *Do it: A revolutionary manifesto.* New York: Simon & Schuster, 1970. Copyright © 1970 by the Social Education Foundation. Excerpt reprinted by permission of Simon & Schuster, Inc., and Jonathan Cape Ltd.

Rubin, R. T., Miller, R. G., Arthur, R. J., & Clark, B. R. Differential adrenocortical stress responses in naval aviators during aircraft landing practice. *Navy Medical Neuropsychiatric Research Unit Report No. 12.* San Diego, Calif., 1969.

Rubin, Z. Measurement of romantic love. *Journal of Personality and Social Psychology,* 1970, **16,** 265–73.

Rubin, Z. *Liking and loving.* New York: Holt, Rinehart & Winston, 1973.

Ruma, S. J. Easier said than done . . . . Paper presented at the Conference on Applications of Social Psychology, Majorca, April 1973.

Rumbaugh, D. M., Gill, T. V., & von Glasersfeld, E. C. Reading and sentence completion by a chimpanzee. *Science*, 1973, **182**, 731–33.

Russell, B. *Human knowledge: Its scope and limits.* New York: Simon & Schuster, 1948.

Rustin, S. L. Therapist authenticity in group and individual psychotherapy with college students. *Journal of Contemporary Psychology*, 1970, **3**, 45–50.

Ryan, W. *Blaming the victim.* New York: Pantheon, 1971.

Saario, T. N., Jacklin, C. N., & Tittle, C. K. Sex role stereotyping in the public schools. *Harvard Educational Review*, 1973, **43**, 386–416.

Sacerdote, P. Hypnosis in cancer patients. *American Journal of Clinical Hypnosis*, 1966, **9**, 100–108.

Sachs, J. S. Recognition memory for syntactic and semantic aspects of connected discourse. *Perception and Psychophysics*, 1967, **2**(9), 441.

San Francisco Chronicle. Excerpt from "The Hangups of Bored Animals" by Michael Grieg from *San Francisco Chronicle*, Friday, Nov. 2, 1973. © 1973, Chronicle Publishing Co. Reprinted by permission.

Sarbin, T. R. On the futility of the proposition that some people be labeled "mentally ill." *Journal of Consulting Psychology*, 1967, **31**, 445–53.

Sarnoff, I. Psychoanalytic theory and social attitudes. *Public Opinion Quarterly*, 1960, **24**, 251–79.

Sarnoff, I. *Society with tears.* New York: Citadel, 1966.

Sartre, J. P. *Existentialism and human emotions.* New York: Philosophical Library, 1957.

Sawyer, J. Measurement and prediction, clinical and statistical. *Psychological Bulletin*, 1966, **66**, 178–200.

Schachter, S. *The psychology of affiliation.* Stanford: Stanford University Press, 1959.

Schachter, S. *Emotion, obesity and crime.* New York: Academic Press, 1971.

Schachter, S., & Freedman, J. Effects of work and cue prominence. In S. Schachter and J. Rodin (Eds.), *Obese humans and rats.* Potomac, Md.: Erlbaum Associates, 1974, in press.

Schachter, S., & Singer, J. Cognitive, social and physiological determinants of emotional state. *Psychological Review*, 1962, **69**, 379–99.

Schein, E. H. Reaction patterns to severe, chronic stress in American Army prisoners of war of the Chinese. *Journal of Social Issues*, 1957, **13**(3), 21–30.

Schein, E. H., with Schneier, I., & Barker, C. H. *Coercive persuasion: A socio-psychological analysis of the "brainwashing" of American civilian prisoners by the Chinese Communists.* New York: Norton, 1961.

Schein, M. W., & Hale, E. B. Stimuli eliciting sexual behavior. In F. Beach (Ed.), *Sex and behavior.* New York: Wiley, 1965.

Schildkrau, J. J., & Kety, S. S. Biogenic amines and emotion. *Science*, 1967, **156**, 21–30.

Schlosberg, H. The description of facial expressions in terms of two dimensions. *Journal of Experimental Psychology*, 1952, **44**, 229–37.

Schlosberg, H. Three dimensions of emotion. *Psychological Review*, 1954, **61**, 81–88.

Schoen, E. Lawrence Halprin: Humanizing the city environment. *The American Way*, Nov. 1972, 13–23.

Schutz, F. Differences between the imprinting of the following and sexual reactions in mallards. Paper presented at the meeting of the XIXth International Congress of Psychology, London, 1969.

Schwartz, C. G. Perspectives on deviance: Wives' definitions of their husbands' mental illness. *Psychiatry*, 1957, **20**, 275–91.

Schwartz, G. E. The facts on transcendental meditation: Part II. TM relaxes some people and makes them feel good. *Psychology Today*, April 1974, **7**, 39–44.

Scott, J. P. *Aggression.* Chicago: University of Chicago Press, 1958.

Scott, R. A. A proposed framework for analyzing deviance as a property of social order. In R. A. Scott & J. D. Douglas (Eds.), *Theoretical perspectives on deviance.* New York: Basic Books, 1972.

Scott, W. A. Research definitions of mental health and mental illness. *Psychological Bulletin*, 1958, **55**, 29–45.

Sears, R. R. Relation of early socialization experiences to aggression in middle childhood. *Journal of Abnormal and Social Psychology*, 1961, **63**, 466–92.

Sears, R. R., Maccoby, E. E., & Levin, H. *Patterns of child rearing.* New York: Harper & Row, 1957.

Seeman, M., & Evans, J. W. Alienation and learning in a hospital setting. *American Sociological Review*, 1962, **27**, 772–83.

Segall, M. H., Campbell, D. T., & Herskovits, M. J. *The influence of culture on perception.* New York: Bobbs-Merrill, 1966.

Seiden, L. S. Neurochemical basis of drug action: Introduction. In J. A. Harvey (Ed.), *Behavioral analysis of drug action.* Glenview, Ill.: Scott, Foresman, 1970.

Sekuler, R., Tynan, P., & Levinson, E. Visual temporal order: A new illusion. *Science*, 1973, **180**, 210–12.

Seligman, M. E. P. Chronic fear produced by unpredictable electric shock. *Journal of Comparative and Physiological Psychology*, 1968, **66**, 402–11.

Seligman, M. E. P. Fall into helplessness. *Psychology Today*, June 1973, **7**(1), 43–48.

Seligman, M. E. P. Depression and learned helplessness. In R. J. Friedman & M. M. Katz (Eds.), *The psychology of depression: Contemporary theory and research.* Washington, D.C.: V. H. Winston & Sons, 1974.

Seligman, M. E. P. *Helplessness: On depression, development and death.* San Francisco: W. H. Freeman, 1975.

Seligman, M. E. P., & Maier, S. F. Failure to escape traumatic shock. *Journal of Experimental Psychology,* 1967, **74**(1), 1–9.

Selye, H. *The stress of life.* New York: McGraw-Hill, 1956.

Selye, H. The evolution of the stress concept. *American Scientist,* 1973, **61**, 692–99.

Semmes, J. Protopathic and epicritic sensation: A reappraisal. In A. L. Benton (Ed.), *Contributions to clinical neuropsychology.* Chicago: Aldine, 1969.

Senden, M. *Raum-und Gestaltauffassung bei operierten Blindgeborenen vor und nach der Operation.* Leipzig: Barth, 1932. Cited in D. O. Hebb, *The organization of behavior.* New York: Wiley, 1949.

Shapiro, J. L., & Diamond, M. J. Increases in hypnotizability as a function of encounter group training. *Journal of Abnormal Psychology,* 1972, **79**(1), 112–15.

Sheffield, F. D., & Campbell, B. A. The role of experience in the "spontaneous" activity of hungry rats. *Journal of Comparative and Physiological Psychology,* 1954, **47**, 97–100.

Shepard, R. N., & Feng, C. A chronometric study of mental paper folding. *Cognitive Psychology,* 1972, **3**, 228–43.

Shepard, R. N., & Metzler, J. Mental rotation of three-dimensional objects. *Science,* 1971, **171**, 701–3.

Sheridan, C. L., & King, R. G. Obedience to authority with an authentic victim. *Proceedings of the 80th Annual Convention, American Psychological Association,* Part 1, 1972, **7**, 165–66.

Sherif, M. A study of some social factors in perception. *Archives of Psychology,* 1935, **27**(187).

Sherif, M., & Sherif, C. W. *An outline of social psychology.* (2nd ed.) New York: Harper & Row, 1956.

Sherman, J. A. Reinstatement of verbal behavior in a psychotic by reinforcement methods. *Journal of Speech and Hearing Disorders,* 1963, **28**, 398–401.

Shettlesworth, S. J. Constraints on learning. In D. S. Lehrman, R. A. Hinde, & E. Shaw (Eds.), *Advances in the study of behavior.* Vol. 4. New York: Academic Press, 1972.

Shields, J. *Monozygotic twins brought up apart or brought up together.* London: Oxford University Press, 1962.

Shockley, W. Dysgenics, geneticity, raceology: A challenge to the intellectual responsibility of educators. *Phi Delta Kappan,* Jan. 1972, 297–307.

Shockley, W. The nature of heritability of IQ and its social, economic, and political implications. Pre-debate hand-out for *Stanford Psychology Department Colloquium,* Jan. 23, 1973.

Shor, R. The fundamental problem in hypnoses research as viewed from historic perspectives. In E. Fromm & R. Shor (Eds.), *Hypnosis: Research developments and perspectives.* Chicago: Aldine, 1972.

Shulgin, A. Psychotomenetic agents related to the catecholamines. *Journal of Psychedelic Drugs,* Fall 1969, **2**, 17–29.

Sidman, M., & Stoddard, L. T. Programming perception and learning for retarded children. In N. R. Ellis (Ed.), *International review of research on mental retardation.* Vol. 2. New York: Academic Press, 1969.

Sigusch, V., Schmidt, G., Reinfeld, A., & Wiedemann-Sutor, I. Psychological stimulation: Sex differences. *Journal of Sex Research,* 1970, **6**, 10–24.

Silver, L. B., Dublin, C. C., & Lourie, R. S. Does violence breed violence? Contributions from a study of the child abuse syndrome. *American Journal of Psychiatry,* 1969, **126**, 404–7.

Simmel, E. C., Hoppe, R. A., & Milton, G. A. (Eds.) *Social facilitation and imitative behavior.* Boston: Allyn & Bacon, 1968.

Simon, H. A. Motivational and emotional controls of cognition. *Psychological Review,* 1967, **74**, 29–39.

Simpson, M. E., & Evans, H. M. Occurrence of faint bleeding on a definite intermenstrual day in man. *Science.* Vol. 68. New York: The Science Press, 1928.

Sims, J. H., & Baumann, D. D. The tornado threat: Coping styles of the north and south. *Science,* 1972, **176**, 1386–91.

Singh, D., & Sikes, S. Role of past experience on food-motivated behavior of obese humans. *Journal of Comparative and Physiological Psychology,* 1974, **83**, 503–508.

Skinner, B. F. *Walden II.* New York: Macmillan, 1948.

Skinner, B. F. *Verbal behavior.* New York: Appleton-Century-Crofts, 1957.

Skinner, B. F. Pigeons in a pelican. *American Psychologist.* 1960, **15**, 28–37.

Skinner, B. F. Teaching machines. *Scientific American,* 1961, **205**(5), 90–102.

Skinner, B. F. What is the experimental analysis of behavior? *Journal of the Experimental Analysis of Behavior,* 1966, **9**, 213–18.

Skinner, B. F. *Beyond freedom and dignity.* New York: Knopf, 1971.

Skinner, B. F., Solomon, H. C., & Lindsley, O. R. A new method for the experimental analysis of the behavior of psychotic patients. *Journal of Nervous and Mental Disease,* 1954, **120**, 403–6.

Slater, P. E., Morimoto, K., & Hyde, R. W. The effects of group administration upon symptom formation under LSD. *Journal of Nervous and Mental Diseases,* 1957, **125**, 312–15.

Slobin, D. I. *Psycholinguistics.* Glenview, Ill.: Scott, Foresman, 1971.

Smelser, N. J. Some determinants of destructive behavior. In N. Sanford (Eds.), *Sanctions for evil.* San Francisco: Jossey-Bass, 1971.

Smith, D. E. Drug use and abuse. In F. L. Ruch & P. G. Zimbardo, *Psychology and Life.* (8th Ed.) Glenview, Ill.: Scott, Foresman, 1971. Excerpt reprinted by permission of the author.

Smith, D. E., & Gay, G. R. Editor's note. *Journal of Psychedelic Drugs.* Fall 1971, **4**(2), 5–14.

Smith, D. E., King, M. B., & Hoebel, B. C. Lateral hypothalamic control of killing: Evidence for a cholinoceptive mechanism. *Science,* 1970, **167,** 900–901.

Smith, D. E., & Mehl, C. An analysis of marijuana toxicity. In D. E. Smith (Ed.), *The new social drug: Cultural, medical and legal perspectives on marijuana.* Englewood Cliffs, N.J.: Prentice-Hall, 1970. © 1970, p. 71. Excerpt reprinted by permission of Prentice-Hall, Inc., Englewood Cliffs, N.J.

Smith, K. V. *Delayed sensory feedback and behavior.* Philadelphia: Saunders, 1962.

Smith, M. B. Review of authoritarian personality. In T. W. Adorno, E. Frenkel-Brunswik, D. J. Levinson, & R. N. Sanford (Eds.), *Journal of Abnormal and Social Psychology,* 1950, **45,** 775–79.

Snow, C. P. Either-or. *Progressive,* 1961, **25**(2), 24–25.

Sobey, F. *The nonprofessional revolution in mental health.* New York: Columbia University, 1970.

Sokolov, E. N. Neuronal models and the orienting reflex. In M. A. Brazier (Ed.), *The central nervous system and behavior.* New York: Josiah Macy, 1960.

Solley, C. M., & Haigh, G. A. A note to Santa Claus. *Topical research papers, The Menninger Foundation,* 1957, **18,** 4–5.

Solomans, G. Drug therapy: Initiation and follow-up. *Annals: New York Academy of Sciences,* 1973, **205,** 335–44.

Solomon, R. L. Punishment. *American Psychologist,* 1964, **19,** 239–53.

Solomon, R. L., Kamin, L., & Wynne, L. C. Traumatic avoidance learning: The outcome of several extinction procedures with dogs. *Journal of Abnormal Social Psychology,* 1953, **48,** 291–302.

Solomon, R. W., & Wheeler, R. G. Peer reinforcement control of classroom problem behavior. *Journal of Applied Behavior Analysis,* 1973, **6,** 49–56.

Solzhenitsyn, A. I. Solzhenitsyn's Statement. *The New York Times,* June 17, 1970, 6. Excerpt © 1970 by The New York Times Company. Reprinted by permission.

Sontag, L. W., Baker, C. T., & Nelson, V. L. Mental growth and personality development: A longitudinal study. *Monographs of the Society for Research in Child Development,* 1958, **23**(2), 11–85.

Spaner, F. E. The psychotherapist as an activist in social change: A proponent. In F. F. Korten, S. W. Cook, & J. I. Lacey (Eds.), *Psychology and the problems of society.* Washington, D.C.: American Psychological Association, 1970.

Spears, W. C. Assessment of visual preference and discrimination in the four-month-old infant. *Journal of Comparative and Physiological Psychology,* 1964, **57,** 381–86.

Speisman, J. C., Lazarus, R. S., Mordkoff, A. M., & Davison, L. A. The experimental reduction of stress based on ego-defense theory. *Journal of Abnormal and Social Psychology,* 1964, **68,** 367–80.

Spence, K. W. *Behavior theory and conditioning.* New Haven: Yale University Press, 1956.

Sperry, R. W. Restoration of vision after crossing of optical nerves and after contralateral transposition of the eye. *Journal of Neurophysiology,* 1945, **8,** 15–28.

Sperry, R. W. Mental unity following surgical disconnection of the cerebral hemispheres. *The Harvey Lectures,* Series 62. New York: Academic Press, 1968.

Sperry, R. W., Gassaniga, M. S., & Bogen, J. E. Interhemispheric relationships: The neocortical commissures—syndromes of hemispheric disconnection. *Handbook of clinical neurology.* Vol. 4. New York: Wiley, 1969.

Spitz, R. A., & Wolf, K. Anaclitic depression. *Psychoanalytical Study of Children,* 1946, **2,** 313–42.

Stace, W. (Ed.) *The teachings of the mystics.* New York: New American Library, 1960.

Stampfl, T. G., & Levis, D. J. Essentials of implosive therapy: A learning theory-based psychodynamic behavioral therapy. *Journal of Abnormal Psychology,* 1967, **72,** 496–503.

Stayton, S. E., & Weiner, M. Value, magnitude, and accentuation. *Journal of Abnormal and Social Psychology,* 1961, **62,** 145–47.

Sterman, M. B. Learning to control brain functions through biological feedback techniques. Reported by G. Luce, *Mental Health Program Reports, No. 5.* (DHEW) Publication No. (HSM) 72-9042. Chevy Chase, Md.: National Institute of Mental Health, 1971.

Sternbach, R. A. *Pain: A psychophysiological analysis.* New York: Academic Press, 1968.

Sternbach, R. A., & Tursky, B. Ethnic differences among housewives in psychophysical and skin potential responses to electric shock. *Psychophysiology,* 1965, **1,** 241–46.

Stevens, S. S. *Psychophysics and social scaling.* Morristown, N.J.: General Learning Press, 1972.

Stevenson, H., & Stewart, E. A development study of racial awareness in young children. *Child Development,* 1966, **61,** 37–75.

Stogdill, R. M. Personality factors associated with leadership: A survey of the literature. *Journal of Psychology,* 1948, **25,** 35–71.

Stone, C. P., & Bakhtiari, A. B. Effects of electroconvulsive shock on maze relearning by albino rats. *Journal of Comparative and Physiological Psychology,* 1956, **49,** 318–20.

Stoppard, T. *Rosencrantz and Guildenstern are dead.* London: Faber, 1967.

Strayer, J., Bigelow, A., Ames, E. W. "I," "you," and point of view. Unpublished study, Simon Fraser University, 1973.

Strickland, L. Surveillance and trust. *Journal of Personality,* 1958, **26,** 200–215.

Stromeyer, C. F., & Psotka, J. The detailed texture of eidetic images. *Nature,* 1970, **225,** 346–49.

Stuart, R. B. *Trick or treatment: How and why psychotherapy fails.* Champaign, Ill.: Research Press, 1970.

Stunkard, A. New therapies for the eating disorders behavior modification of obesity and anorexia nervosa. *Archives of General Psychology,* May 1972, **26**(5), 391–98.

Stunkard, A., & Koch, C. The interpretation of gastric motility: Apparent bias in the report of hunger by obese persons. *Archives of General Psychology,* 1964, **11,** 74–82.

Suffolk, P. "The Eyewitness." From *A Big Bowl of Punch,* 1964 Simon & Schuster. © *Punch,* London. Poem reprinted by permission of Rothco Cartoons, Inc.

Sullivan, H. S. *The interpersonal theory of psychiatry.* New York: Norton, 1953.

Suppes, P. Mathematical concept formation in children. *American Psychologist,* 1966, **21,** 139–50.

Surgeon General's Report. *The health consequences of smoking.* Public Health Service Publication No. (HSM) 72–7516. Washington, D.C., U.S. Department of Health, Education and Welfare, 1972.

Surgeon General's Report by the Scientific Advisory Committee on Television and Social Behavior. Television and growing up: The impact of televised violence. Hearings before Subcommittee on Communications, 92nd Congress, 2nd session, March 21–24, 1972.

Sutherland, E. H. *White-collar crime.* New York: Holt, Rinehart & Winston, 1949.

Sutherland, E. H. Crime of corporations. In G. Geis (Ed.), *White-collar criminal.* New York: Atherton, 1968.

Sweet, W. H., Ervin, F., & Mark, V. H. The relationship of violent behavior to focal cerebral disease. In S. Garattini & E. Sigg (Eds.), *Aggressive behavior.* New York: Wiley, 1969.

Szasz, T. S. *The myth of mental illness.* New York: Harper & Row, 1961.

Szasz, T. S. *Psychiatric justice.* New York: Macmillan, 1965.

Szasz, T. S. *The age of madness.* Garden City, N.Y.: Anchor Press, 1973.

Tapp, J., Mathewson, D., D'Encarnacas, P., & Long, C. The effect of the onset of stimuli on reactivity in the rat. *Psychonomic Science,* 1970, **19,** 61–62.

Tart, C. *Altered states of consciousness.* New York: Wiley, 1969.

Tasaki, I. *Nervous transmission.* Springfield, Ill.: Charles C Thomas, 1953.

Taylor, D. W., Berry, P. C., & Block, C. H. Does group participation when using brainstorming facilitate or inhibit creative thinking? *Administrative Science Quarterly,* 1958, **3,** 23–47.

Teitelbaum, P. The use of operant methods in the assessment and control of motivational states. In W. K. Honig (Ed.), *Operant behavior.* New York: Appleton-Century-Crofts, 1966.

Teitelbaum, P., & Epstein, A. The lateral hypothalamic syndrome: Recovery of feeding and drinking after lateral hypothalamic lesions. *Psychological Review,* 1962, **69,** 74–90.

Terkel, S. *Working: People talk about what they do all day and how they feel about what they do.* New York: Pantheon Books, 1974.

Terman, L. M. *The measurement of intelligence.* Boston: Houghton Mifflin, 1916.

Terman, L. M. Feeble-minded children in the public schools of California. *School and Society,* 1917, **5,** 161–65.

Terman, L. M., & Merrill, M. A. *Measuring intelligence.* Boston: Houghton Mifflin, 1937.

Terman, L. M., & Merrill, M. A. *The Stanford-Binet intelligence scale.* Boston: Houghton Mifflin, 1960.

Terrace, H. S. Errorless transfer of a discrimination across two continua. *Journal of the Experimental Analysis of Behavior,* 1963, **6,** 224–32.

Thigpen, C. H. Personal communication to the authors, Aug. 1961.

Thigpen, C. H., & Cleckley, H. A. A case of multiple personality. *Journal of Abnormal and Social Psychology,* 1954, **49**(1), 135–44.

Thigpen, C. H., & Cleckley, H. A. *The three faces of Eve.* New York: McGraw-Hill, 1957.

Thompson, R., & McConnell, J. V. Classical conditioning in the Planarian, Dugesia Dorotocephala. *Journal of Comparative and Physiological Psychology,* 1955, **48,** 65–68.

Thompson, R. F., Robertson, R. T., & Mayers, K. S. Commentary on cortical association response areas. In G. M. French (Ed.), *Cortical functioning in behavior.* Glenview, Ill.: Scott, Foresman, 1973.

Thorndike, E. L. Animal intelligence. *Psychological Review Monograph Supplement*, 1898, **2** (4, Whole No. 8).

Thorndike, E. L. *The elements of psychology.* New York: Seiler, 1905.

Tillich, P. *The courage to be.* New Haven, Conn.: Yale University Press, 1952.

Tilly, C. Collective violence in European perspective. In H. D. Graham & T. R. Gurr (Eds.), *Violence in America: Historical and comparative perspectives.* New York: New American Library, 1969.

Tinklepaugh, O. L. An experimental study of representational factors in monkeys. *Journal of Comparative Psychology*, 1928, **8**, 197–236.

Toch, H. *Violent men.* Chicago: Aldine, 1969.

Tolman, E. C. *Purposive behavior in animals and men.* Berkeley: University of California Press, 1949. (Originally published, 1932.)

Tolman, E. C. Operational behaviorism and current trends in psychology. *Collected papers in psychology.* Berkeley: University of California Press, 1950. (Originally published, 1936.)

Trauax, C. B. Effective ingredients in psychotherapy. *Journal of Counseling Psychology*, 1963, **16**, 256–63.

Triandis, H. C. *Attitude and attitude change.* New York: Wiley, 1971.

Triplett, N. The dynamogenic factors in pacemaking and competition. *American Journal of Psychology*, 1897, **9**, 507–33.

Trotter, R. J. Psychosurgery, the courts and Congress. *Science News*, May 1973, **103**, 310–11.

Trotter, W. *Instincts of the herd in peace and war.* London: T. Fisher Unwin, 1916.

Tschukitschew. *Contributions of the Timiriazer Institute*, 1929, 36. Cited in R. D. Templeton & J. P. Quigley, The action of insulin on the motility of the gastrointestinal tract. *American Journal of Physiology*, 1930, **91**, 467–74.

Turing, A. M. Computing machinery and intelligence. *Mind*, 1950, **59**, 433–60.

Turnbull, C. M. Some observations regarding the experiences and behavior of BaMbuti Pygmies. *American Journal of Psychology*, 1961, **74**, 304–08.

Unger, S. M. Mescaline, LDS, psilocybin, and personality change. *Psychiatry*, 1963, **26**, 111–25.

Valenstein, E., Cox, V., & Kakolewski, J. Modification of motivated behavior elicited by electrical stimulation of the hypothalamus. *Science*, 1968, **159**, 1119–21. (a)

Valenstein, E., Cox, V., & Kakolewski, J. The motivation underlying eating elicited by lateral hypothalamic stimulation. *Physiology and Behavior*, 1968, **3**, 969–71. (b)

Valenstein, E., Cox, V., & Kakolewski, J. Re-examination of the role of the hypothalamus in motivation. *Psychological Review*, 1970, **77**, 16–31.

Van de Castle, R. L. *The psychology of dreaming.* (Module) Morristown, N.J.: General Learning Corp., 1971.

Verhave, T. The pigeon as a quality-control inspector. In R. Ulrich, T. Stachnik, & J. Mabry (Eds.), *Control of human behavior.* Glenview, Ill.: Scott, Foresman, 1966.

Verville, E. *Behavior problems of children.* Philadelphia: Saunders, 1967.

Vidmar, N., & Rokeach, M. Archie Bunker's bigotry: A study in selective perception and exposure. *Journal of Communication*, Winter 1974, **24**(1), 36–47.

Von Békésy, G. The ear. *Scientific American*, 1957, **197**(2), 66–78.

Wallace, B., & Garrett, J. B. Reduced felt arm sensation effects on visual adaptation. *Perception and Psychophysics*, 1973, **14**(3), 597–600.

Wallace, R. K., & Benson, H. The physiology of meditation. *Scientific American*, 1972, **226**, 84–90.

Wallach, M. A., & Kogan, N. *Modes of thinking in young children: A study of the creativity-intelligence distinction.* New York: Holt, Rinehart & Winston, 1965.

Walster, E., Berscheid, E., & Walster, G. W. New directions in equity research. *Journal of Personality and Social Psychology*, 1973, **25**, 151–76.

Ward, W. C., & Kogan, N. Motivation and ability in children's creativity. Unpublished report, 1970.

Warden, C. J. *Animal motivation: Experimental studies on the albino rat.* New York: Columbia University Press, 1931.

Warner, D. M. The bystander phenomenon: A critical review of the research. Unpublished manuscript, University of Nevada, Reno, 1972.

Wason, P. C. Problem solving and reasoning. *British Medical Bulletin*, 1971, **27**(3), 206–10. Excerpt reproduced by permission of the Medical Department, The British Council.

Watson, G., & Johnson, D. *Social psychology: Issues and insights*, New York: Lippincott, 1972.

Watson, J. B. Experimental studies on the growth of emotions. In C. Murchison (Ed.), *Psychologies of 1925.* Worcester, Mass.: Clark University Press, 1926.

Watson, J. B., & Rayner, R. Conditioned emotional reactions. *Journal of Experimental Psychology*, 1920, **3**, 1–14.

Watson, J. D. *The double helix.* New York: Atheneum, 1968.

Watson, R. I., Jr. Investigation into deindividuation using a cross-cultural survey technique. *Journal of Personality and Social Psychology*, 1973, **25,** 342–45.

Watts, A. W. *The way of Zen.* New York: Vintage Books, 1957.

Waugh, N. C., & Norman, D. A. Primary memory. *Psychological Review*, 1965, **72,** 89–104.

Webb, W. B. Sleep behavior as a biorhythm. In P. Coloquohon (Ed.), *Biological rhythms and human performance.* London: Academic Press, 1971.

Wechsler, D. *Wechsler intelligence scale for children.* New York: Psychological Corp., 1949.

Wechsler, D. *Wechsler adult intelligence scale.* New York: Psychological Corp., 1955.

Wechsler, H., Grosser, G. H., & Greenblatt, M. Research evaluating antidepressant medications on hospitalized mental patients: A survey of published reports during a 5-year period. *Journal of Nervous and Mental Disease,* 1965, **141,** 231–39.

Wegrocki, H. J. A critique of cultural and statistical concepts of abnormality. *Journal of Abnormal and Social Psychology*, 1939, **34,** 166–78.

Weiner, N. *The human use of human beings.* Boston: Houghton Mifflin, 1954.

Weiss, J. M. Effects of coping responses on stress. *Journal of Comparative and Physiological Psychology*, 1968, **65,** 251–60.

Weiss, J. M. Effects of coping behavior in different warning signal conditions on stress pathology in rats. *Journal of Comparative and Physiological Psychology*, 1971, **77,** 1–13.

Weiss, R. F., Buchanan, W., Altstatt, L., & Lombardo, J. P. Altruism is rewarding. *Science*, 1971, **171,** 1262–63.

Weiss, T., & Engel, B. Operant conditioning of heart rate in patients with premature ventricular contractions. *Psychosomatic Medicine*, 1971, **33,** 301–21.

Weisskopf-Joelson, E. Some comments on a Viennese school of psychiatry. *Journal of Abnormal and Social Psychology*, 1955, **51,** 701–3.

Weitzman, B. Behavior therapy and psychotherapy. *Psychological Review*, 1967, **74,** 300–17.

Welker, W. I. An analysis of exploratory and play behavior in animals. In D. W. Fiske & S. R. Maddi (Eds.), *Functions of varied experience.* Homewood, Ill.: Dorsey, 1961.

Wells, D. T. Large magnitude voluntary heart rate changes. *Psychophysiology*, 1973, **10,** 260–69.

Wells, W. D. Television and aggression: Replication of an experimental field study. Unpublished manuscript, University of Chicago, 1971.

Wertheimer, M. *Fundamental issues in psychology.* New York: Holt, Rinehart & Winston, 1972.

Wever, E. G. *Theory of hearing.* New York: Wiley, 1949.

Wever, E. G., & Bray, C. W. Present possibilities for auditory theory. *Psychological Review*, 1930, **37,** 365–80.

White, B. L., & Held, R. Plasticity of sensorimotor development in the human infant. In J. F. Rosenblith & W. Allinsmith (Eds.), *The causes of behavior.* Vol. 1. (2nd ed.) Boston: Allyn & Bacon, 1966.

White, R. W. Motivation reconsidered: The concept of competence. *Psychological Review*, 1959, **66,** 297–33.

Whiting, J. W. M., Kluckhohn, R., & Anthony, A. The function of male initiation ceremonies at puberty. In E. E. Maccoby, T. Newcomb, & E. D. Hartley (Eds.), *Readings in social psychology.* New York: Holt, Rinehart & Winston, 1958.

Whorf, B. L. *Language, thought, and reality.* J. B. Carroll (Ed.). New York: Wiley, 1956.

Willems, E. P. Go ye into all the world and modify behavior: An ecologist's view. *Representative Research in Social Psychology*, 1973, **4,** 93–105.

Williams, D. R., & Williams, H. Auto-maintenance in pigeons: Sustained pecking despite contingent non-reinforcement. *Journal of Experimental Analysis of Behavior*, 1969, **12,** 511–20.

Williams, H. L., Holloway, F., & Griffiths, W. J. Physiological psychology: Sleep. *Annual Review of Psychology, 1973.* Palo Alto, Calif.: Annual Reviews, 1973.

Williams, R. J. *Biochemical individuality.* New York: Wiley, 1956.

Williams, T. A., Friedman, R. J., & Secunda, S. K. *Special report: The depressive illnesses.* Chevy Chase, Md.: National Institute of Mental Health, 1970.

Wilson, M. *Rituals of kinship among the Nyakusa.* Oxford: Oxford University Press, 1970.

Wilson, M. Cortical function in somesthesis. In G. M. French (Ed.), *Cortical functioning in behavior.* Glenview, Ill.: Scott, Foresman, 1973.

Winick, M., Meyer, K. K., & Harris, R. C. Malnutrition and environmental enrichment by early adoption. *Science*, 1975, **190,** 1173–75.

Winokur, G. The types of affective disorders. *Journal of Nervous and Mental Diseases*, Feb. 1973, **156**(2), 82–96.

Winterbottom, M. R. The relation of childhood training in independence to achievement motivation. Unpublished doctoral dissertation, University of Michigan, 1953.

Witkin, H. A., et al. *Personality through perception.* New York: Harper & Row, 1954.

Wolf, A. V. *Thirst: Physiology of the urge to drink and problems of water lack.* Springfield, Ill.: Charles C Thomas, 1958.

Wolf, M., Risley, T., & Mees, H. Application of operant conditioning procedures to the behavior problems of an autistic child. *Behavior Research and Therapy,* 1964, **1,** 305–12.

Wolf, S., & Wolff, H. G. *Human gastric function.* (2nd ed.) New York: Oxford University Press, 1947.

Wolpe, J. *Psychotherapy by reciprocal inhibition.* Stanford: Stanford University Press, 1958.

Wolpe, J. Reciprocal inhibition as the main basis of psychotherapeutic effects. In H. J. Eysenck (Ed.), *Behavior therapy and the neuroses.* New York: Pergamon Press, 1960.

Wolpe, J. *The practice of behavior therapy.* New York: Pergamon Press, 1969.

Woods, J. *The yoga-system of pantanjali.* Cambridge, Mass.: Harvard University Press, 1914.

Worchel, S., & Brehm, J. W. Direct and implied social restoration of freedom. *Journal of Personality and Social Psychology,* 1971, **18,** 294–304.

Wurtman, R. J., Axelrod, J., & Kelly, D. E. *The pineal.* New York: Academic Press, 1968.

Yablonsky, L. The violent gang. In S. Endleman (Ed.), *Violence in the streets.* Chicago: Quadrangle Books, 1968.

Yamaoka, T. Psychological study of mental self-control. In Y. Akishige (Ed.), *Psychological studies in Zen.* Fukuoka, Japan: Kyushu University, 1968.

Yarrow, M. R., Schwartz, C. G., Murphy, G. S., & Deasy, L. C. The psychological meaning of mental illness in the family. *Journal of Social Issues,* 1955, **11,** 12–24.

Yates, A. J. Delayed auditory feedback. *Psychological Bulletin,* 1963, **60,** 213–32.

Young, P. T. *Motivation and emotion.* New York: Wiley, 1961.

Young, P. T. Evolution and preference in behavioral development. *Psychological Review,* 1968, **75,** 222–41.

Zajonc, R. B. Social facilitation. *Science,* 1965, **149,** 269–74.

Zajonc, R. B. Social facilitation in cockroaches. In E. C. Simmel, R. A. Hoppe, & G. A. Milton (Eds.), *Social facilitation and imitative behavior.* Boston: Allyn & Bacon, 1968.

Zarcone, V., Gulevick, G., Pivik, T., & Dement, W. Partial REM phase deprivation and schizophrenia. *Archives of General Psychiatry,* 1968, **18,** 194–202.

Zborowski, M. *People in pain.* San Francisco: Jossey-Bass, 1969.

Zeaman, D., & Smith, R. W. Review and analysis of some recent findings in human cardiac conditioning. In W. F. Prokasky (Ed.), *Classical conditioning.* New York: Appleton-Century-Crofts, 1965.

Zeigarnik, B. Uber das Behalten von erledigten und unerledigten Handlungen. *Psychologische Forschung,* 1927, **9,** 1–85.

Zimbardo, P. G. The effects of early avoidance training and rearing conditions upon the sexual behavior of the male rat. *Journal of Comparative and Physiological Psychology,* 1958, **51,** 764–69.

Zimbardo, P. G. *The cognitive control of motivation.* Glenview, Ill.: Scott, Foresman, 1969. (a)

Zimbardo, P. G. The human choice: Individuation, reason, and order versus deindividuation, impulse, and chaos. In W. J. Arnold & D. Levine (Eds.), *Nebraska symposium on motivation.* Lincoln: University of Nebraska Press, 1969. (b)

Zimbardo, P. G. A field experiment in auto-shaping. In C. Ward (Ed.), *Vandalism.* London: Architectural Press, 1973.

Zimbardo, P. G., & Formica, R. Emotional comparison and self-esteem as determinants of affiliation. *Journal of Personality,* 1963, **31,** 141–62.

Zimbardo, P. G., Haney, C., Banks, W. C., & Jaffe, D. The mind is a formidable jailer: A Pirandellian prison. *The New York Times,* April 8, 1973, 38–60.

Zimbardo, P. G., Marshall, G., & Maslach, C. Liberating behavior from time-bound control: Expanding the present through hypnosis. *Journal of Applied Social Psychology,* 1971, **4,** 305–23.

Zimbardo, P. G., & Meadow, W. Sexism in the *Readers Digest,* or Laugh and the world laughs at you. Paper presented at the meeting of the Western Psychological Association, San Francisco, April 1974.

Zimbardo, P. G., & Miller, N. E. Facilitation of exploration by hunger in rats. *Journal of Comparative and Physiological Psychology,* 1958. **51,** 43–46.

Zimbardo, P. G., Pilkonis, P. A., & Norwood, R. M. The social disease called shyness. *Psychology Today,* May 1975, **8**(12), 69–72.

Zimbardo, P. G., Rapaport, C., & Baron, J. Pain control by hypnotic induction of motivational states. In P. Zimbardo (Ed.), *The cognitive control of motivation.* Glenview, Ill.: Scott, Foresman, 1969.

Zimbardo, P. G., Weisenberg, M., Firestone, I., & Levy, B. Communicator effectiveness in producing public conformity and private attitude change. *Journal of Personality,* 1965, **33,** 233–55.

Zobrist, A. L., & Carlson, F. R. An advice-taking chess computer. *Scientific American,* 1973, **228**(6), 92–105.

Zubeck, J. P., Pushkar, D., Sansom, W., & Gowing, J. Perceptual changes after prolonged sensory isolation (darkness and silence). *Canadian Journal of Psychology,* 1961, **15,** 83–100.

Zurcher, L. A. The mutable self. *The Futurist,* Oct. 1972, 181–85.

Acknowledgments

Credits for illustrations and photographs not given on the page where they appear are listed below. Complete citations of these sources appear in the References, as do credits for quoted material. To all, the authors and publisher wish to express their appreciation.

3 "Identity"/© by Alfred Gescheidt.
6 From "Deprivation Dwarfism" by Lytt I. Gardner. Copyright © 1972 by Scientific American, Inc. All rights reserved.
8 Courtesy of Dr. Philip G. Zimbardo.
13 Woodcut by M. C. Escher, *Heaven and Hell*. From the collection of C. V. S. Roosevelt, Washington, D.C.
22 Aerofilms, Ltd.
25 Photo courtesy of Dr. Irwin Bernstein, Department of Psychology, University of Georgia.
28 Photo by Dr. Philip G. Zimbardo (top); Wide World Photos (lower left); Jester, Columbia University (lower right).
29 © 1971 by Saturday Review, Inc.
33 Scott, Foresman staff photographer.
38 From "Psychological Clues Detected in Elderly," New York *Times,* Nov. 12, 1968, p. 22 L, © 1968 by The New York Times Company, reprinted by permission (left); from "Theories Abound on Birth Increase" by Martin Tolchin, New York *Times,* Aug. 11, 1966, p. 35, © 1966 by The New York Times Company, reprinted by permission (center); from "Smoking Linked to Poor Grades" by Jane E. Brody, New York *Times,* Jan. 3, 1967, p. 13 L, © 1967 by The New York Times Company, reprinted by permission (right).
41 © Punch 1972.
43 By permission of L. M. Boyd.
49 Photo by Jean Martin, Montreal Neurological Institute. Courtesy of Dr. W. Penfield, from Penfield, W., *The Excitable Cortex in Conscious Man.* Liverpool: Liverpool University Press, 1958.
51 The Bettmann Archive, Inc.
52 From "The New Genetics: The Threads of Life" by G. W. Beadle in *Britannica Book of the Year,* 1964, by permission.
56 Drawing by Niklaas Hartsoeker, courtesy of Clarendon Press, Oxford (left); photo by A. G. Schering, Berlin, as published in *Nature,* courtesy of *Science News* (right).
57 Photos by Arnold Ryan Chalfant.
62 Courtesy of Dr. Edwin R. Lewis (left); courtesy of Dr. Sanford L. Palay (right).

71 Photo courtesy of Dr. Lewis P. Lipsitt, Hunter Laboratory, Brown University (top); from the *Journal of Comparative and Physiological Psychology,* Vol. 56, 1963, pp. 73–77. Copyright 1963 by the American Psychological Association. Reprinted by permission (center); from the *Journal of Comparative and Physiological Psychology,* 1965, Vol. 59, pp. 312–16. Copyright 1965 by the American Psychological Association. Reprinted by permission (bottom).
72 From *The Central Nervous System and Behavior,* edited by M. A. Brazier, 1960. Reprinted by permission of the Josiah Macy Jr. Foundation.
75 Tektronix, Inc.
76 From *A Handbook of Physiology, Phrenology, and Physiognomy,* by Fowler and Wells.
79 University College, London.
80 Courtesy of Dr. José M. Delgado.
83 Courtesy of Dr. C. G. Gross, *Journal of Neurophysiology,* 1972, *35,* 96–111.
87 From *The Harvey Lectures,* Series 62, 1968, by permission of Academic Press, Inc., and the author.
97 The Bettmann Archive, Inc.
99 Scott, Foresman staff photographer.
101 Scott, Foresman staff photographer.
109 Charles Biasiny.
110 Ken Heyman.
114 Courtesy of Professor Thom Verhave, Arizona State University (left); courtesy of Professor B. F. Skinner (right).
119 "Miss Peach," courtesy of Mell Lazarus and Publishers-Hall Syndicate, © Field Enterprises, Inc., 1973.
120 From *Exceptional Children,* 1970, Vol. 37, pp. 145–55, reprinted by permission of the Council for Exceptional Children.
122 Courtesy of Charles Pfizer & Co., Inc., photo by Art Green (left); photo by Will Rapport, courtesy of Professor B. F. Skinner (right).
124 Warren Street, Central Washington State College/ Reprinted by permission of *APA Monitor.*
129 The New York *Times* (both).
132 Courtesy of Dr. Neal E. Miller.

134 From *Science,* 1972, Vol. 177, 1009–11. Copyright 1972 by the American Association for the Advancement of Science.

136 Thomas McAvoy/Time-Life Picture Agency, © 1973.

137 From "Imprinting" by E. H. Hess, *Science,* Vol. 130, July 17, 1959, pp. 133–41, Figs. 1 & 2. Copyright 1959 by the American Association for the Advancement of Science.

146 From *Word,* Vol. 14, 1958, p. 154. Reprinted by permission of Johnson Reprint Corporation (right).

149 Copyright, 1973, G. B. Trudeau/Distributed by Universal Press Syndicate.

150 Courtesy of Children's Television Workshop.

151 Reprinted from *The Genesis of Language* by Frank Smith & George A. Miller by permission of The MIT Press, Cambridge, Massachusetts. Copyright © 1966 by The Massachusetts Institute of Technology.

154 From *Science,* Vol. 164, May 9, 1969, pp. 635–43, Table 1. Copyright 1969 by the American Association for the Advancement of Science.

157 Chris Reeberg/DPI.

159 Courtesy of Dr. Philip G. Zimbardo.

160 Harvey Stein.

161 © 1963 United Feature Syndicate, Inc.

163 Photo by David K. Caldwell, by permission of Biological Systems, Inc.

165 Courtesy of Dr. R. Allen Gardner and Dr. Beatrice T. Gardner, Research Association, University of Nevada, Reno, Nevada (top); courtesy of Dr. David Premack (middle); courtesy of the Department of Psychology, Georgia State University (bottom).

170 From "Retention as a Function of the Method of Measurement" by L. Postman and L. Rau, University of California Publications in Psychology, 1957, Vol. 8:3, p. 236. Originally published by the University of California Press; reprinted by permission of The Regents of the University of California.

172 From *Remembering: A Study in Experimental and Social Psychology* by F. C. Bartlett, 1932, by permission of Cambridge University Press.

173 From *Perception and Psychophysics,* Vol. 2, No. 9, 1967, p. 441, by permission of Psychonomic Journals, Inc.

174 After the *American Journal of Psychology,* Vol. 35, 1924, pp. 605–12, by permission of the University of Illinois Press.

180 From the *Journal of Experimental Psychology,* Vol. 12, 1929, pp. 71–78. Copyright 1929 by the American Psychological Association. Reprinted by permission.

182 From *Psychonomic Science,* Vol. 14, 1969, pp. 181–82, by permission of Psychonomic Journals, Inc.

188 Wide World Photos.

191 Courtesy of Dr. Keith Nelson.

207 Scott, Foresman staff photographer.

209 Courtesy of Bela Julesz, Bell Telephone Laboratories.

210 From *Science,* Vol. 171, Feb. 19, 1971, pp. 701–3, Figs. 1, 2. Copyright 1971 by the American Association for the Advancement of Science.

212 Reprinted from the *Journal of Experimental Psychology,* Vol. 15, 1932, pp. 73–86. Copyright 1932 by the American Psychological Association. Reprinted by permission.

214 From the *Journal of Educational Psychology,* Vol. 55, 1964, pp. 339–43. Copyright 1964 by the American Psychological Association. Reprinted by permission (left); courtesy of Dr. F. J. McGuigan (right).

215 From *Perception and Motion: An Analysis of Space-Structured Behavior* by Karl U. Smith & W. M. Smith, 1962 W. B. Saunders Company, Fig. 4-1, p. 59, and Fig. 5-16, p. 83, by permission of W. B. Saunders Company and the author.

217 Fred J. Picker/DPI.

224 Courtesy of Dr. Frank Barron.

227 The Welsh Figure Preference Test by George S. Welsh, Ph.D. Copyright 1959, published by Consulting Psychologists Press, Inc.

234 Courtesy of Dr. Herman A. Witkin.

236 Photos by Alan Ross.

237 Paul Sequeira.

239 Courtesy of the Institute for International Social Research.

246 From *Frontiers in Physiological Psychology* by R. W. Russell, Editor, by permission of Academic Press and the author. Copyright © 1966 Academic Press, Inc.

253 Reprinted by permission from *Scientific American,* photos by William Vandivert.

254 From the *Journal of Comparative and Physiological Psychology,* Vol. 56, No. 5, Oct. 1963, p. 873. Copyright 1963 by the American Psychological Association. Reprinted by permission.

259 From *American Journal of Psychology,* Vol. 70, 1957, pp. 38–48, by permission of the University of Illinois Press.

260 From *Eye and Brain: The Psychology of Seeing* by R. L. Gregory. Reprinted by permission of George Weidenfeld & Nicolson Ltd., London.

263 From *Patterns of Discovery* by Dr. Norwood R. Hanson, 1958, by permission of Cambridge University Press.

264 Courtesy of Dr. L. D. Harmon and Dr. K. C. Knowlton, Bell Telephone Laboratories.

266, 268, 271 From "A Study of a Neglected Portion of the Field of Learning—The Development of Sensory Organization" by Robert Leeper, the *Journal of Genetic Psychology,* 1935, Vol. 46, pp. 41–75, by permission of The Journal Press and the author.

267 From the *American Journal of Psychology,* Vol. 64, 1951, pp. 564–72, by permission of the University of Illinois Press.

270 The Daily Telegraph Magazine/Woodfin Camp and Associates.

277 Les Klug.

283 Adapted from Robert L. Van de Castle, *The Psychology of Dreaming* (Morristown, N.J.: General Learning Corporation, 1971), p. 26.

284 From *Sleep Research: A Critical Review* by F. R. Freemon, 1972, by permission.

285 Courtesy of Dr. William Dement.

288 The Bettmann Archive, Inc.

292 ©1911 by The New York Times Company. Reprinted by permission.

293 From *Science,* Vol. 181, Sept. 14, 1973, pp. 1067–70, Fig. 2. Copyright 1973 by the American Association for the Advancement of Science.

302 Dennis Stock/Magnum Photos.

303 From *Journal of Humanistic Psychology,* Vol. 16, No. 3. Reprinted by permission.

305 Courtesy of Kenneth Pelletier.

306 Photo by René Burri/Magnum Photos.

308 The Bettmann Archive, Inc.

309 The Bettmann Archive, Inc.

310 Courtesy of Dr. Philip G. Zimbardo.

313 Courtesy of Dr. Philip G. Zimbardo.

314 Courtesy of Dr. Philip G. Zimbardo.

315 From *Hypnotic Susceptibility* by E. R. Hilgard, 1965, published by Harcourt Brace Jovanovich.

316 From *Psychosomatic Medicine,* 1969, Vol. 31, pp. 227–46, Figure 1, by permission of Harper & Row, Inc., Medical Department (left); after "Liberating Behavior from Time-Bound Control: Expanding the Present Through Hypnosis" by P. G. Zimbardo, G. Marshall, & C. Maslach, in *Journal of Applied Social Psychology,* Vol. 1, No. 4, 1971, pp. 305–23. Reprinted by permission of V. H. Winston & Sons, Inc.

317 From *The Psychology of Consciousness* by Robert E. Ornstein. W. H. Freeman and Company. Copyright © 1972.

323 © 1974 Chicago-Tribune-New York News Syndicate.

327 From *Brain Mechanisms and Consciousness* edited by J. F. Delafresnaye, 1954, by permission of Blackwell Scientific Publications, Ltd.

328 From *A Textbook of Psychology* by D. O. Hebb, 2nd ed., 1966, p. 235, Fig. 75, by permission of W. B. Saunders Company and the author.

330 From *Animal Motivation: Experimental Studies on the Albino Rat* by C. J. Warden, 1931 Columbia University Press, by permission of the publisher.

331 John Sanderson.

334 From *Psychonomic Science,* Vol. 19, 1970, pp. 61–62, Fig. 2, by permission of Psychonomic Journals, Inc.

335 From the *Journal of Comparative and Physiological Psychology,* Vol. 51, 1958, pp. 43–46. Copyright 1958 by the American Psychological Association. Reprinted by permission.

339 R. Dourdin/Rapho Guillumette Pictures.

340 Wallace Kirkland/Time-Life Picture Agency, © 1973.

342 From "The Control of Eating Behavior in an Anorexia by Operant Conditioning Techniques" by Arthur J. Bachrach, William J. Erwin, & Jay P. Mohr, from *Case Studies in Behavior Modification,* ed. by Leonard P. Ullmann & Leonard Krasner. Copyright © 1965 by Holt, Rinehart and Winston, Inc. Reproduced by permission of Holt, Rinehart and Winston, Inc.

343 Harvey Stein.

346 Reprinted with permission from Matthew Wayner, *Thirst.* Copyright 1964, Pergamon Press.

350 By permission of Dr. L. P. Brower.

351 Courtesy of Dr. Harry F. Harlow, University of Wisconsin Primate Laboratory.

352 From the *American Psychologist,* Vol. 13, 1958, pp. 673–85. Copyright 1958 by the American Psychological Association. Reprinted by permission.

353 Courtesy of Dr. Harry F. Harlow, University of Wisconsin Primate Laboratory.

356 Courtesy of Dr. Philip G. Zimbardo.

361 Charles Gatewood/Magnum Photos.

365 Charles Gatewood.

369 Wide World Photos.

370 From the *Journal of Experimental Psychology,* Vol. 44, 1952, pp. 229–37. Copyright 1952 by the American Psychological Association. Reprinted by permission.

373 From *Human Gastric Functions* by Wolf and Wolff, Oxford University Press 1947, by permission.

375 From *Psychological Review,* Vol. 69, 1962, pp. 379–99. Copyright 1962 by the American Psychological Association. Reprinted by permission.

377 Nacio Jan Brown/BBM Associates.

380 From "Short Term Intrusions into the Life Style Routine" by T. S. Holmes and T. H. Holmes. *Journal of Psychosomatic Research,* Vol. 14, pp 121–132, June 1970. Reprinted by permission of Pergamon Press, Ltd. and T. H. Holmes.

383 From the *Journal of Abnormal Psychology,* Vol. 73, 1968, pp. 100–113. Copyright 1968 by the American Psychological Association. Reprinted by permission.

384 Adapted from *Psychological Stress* by I. Janis, 1958 John Wiley & Sons, Inc. Reprinted by permission of the publisher.

385 From *Psychological Monographs,* Vol. 78, No. 585, 1964, p. 13, Fig. 11. Copyright 1964 by the American Psychological Association. Reprinted by permission.

387 The Bettmann Archive, Inc.

389 From *The Cognitive Control of Motivation,* ed. by Philip G. Zimbardo. Copyright © 1969 by Scott, Foresman and Company.

390 Alinari/Art Reference Bureau.
395 Danny Lyon/Magnum Photos.
398 From the *Journal of Comparative and Physiological Psychology,* Vol. 66, No. 2, 1968, p. 405. Copyright 1968 by the American Psychological Association. Reprinted by permission.
399 From the *Journal of Personality and Social Psychology,* Vol. 19, No. 1, 1971. Copyright © 1971 by the American Psychological Association. Reprinted by permission.
409 Harvey Stein.
414 Pictorial Parade, Inc.
417 © Punch, London.
420 Courtesy of Carl Rogers, photo by John T. Wood.
421 Laurence Fink.
422 Data from "Hierarchy of Needs" in *Motivation and Personality,* 2nd ed., by Abraham H. Maslow (Harper & Row, 1970).
426 From *Psychological Review,* Vol. 68, 1961, pp. 1–20. Copyright 1961 by the American Psychological Association. Reprinted by permission.
429 From Neal E. Miller—"Experimental Studies of Conflict" in *Personality and the Behavior Disorders,* ed. by J. McVicker Hunt. Copyright 1944, Renewed © 1972 The Ronald Press Company, New York.
433 Copyright, 1973, Universal Press Syndicate.
435 From *Religion and Public Education* by Theodore R. Sizer, 1967. Copyright © 1967, Houghton Mifflin Company. Reprinted by permission of the publishers.
447 Prepared by John Mayahara.
457 The Bettmann Archive, Inc. (top, middle, bottom).
463 From *Understanding Ourselves and Others* by K. Haas, © 1965 by Prentice-Hall, Inc. Reprinted by permission.
464 "Miss Peach," courtesy of Mell Lazarus and Publishers-Hall Syndicate, © Field Enterprises, Inc., 1974.
468 Charles Gatewood.
471 C. Wolinsky/Stock, Boston (left); from *Psychological Bulletin,* Vol. 71, 1969, pp. 418–20. Copyright 1969 by the American Psychological Association. Reprinted by permission.
472 Photo by DAK/BBM Associates.
474 From *Science,* Vol. 181, pp. 716–22, Aug. 24, 1973. Copyright 1973 by the American Association for the Advancement of Science.
495 From *Social Class and Mental Illness* by E. P. Hollingshead & F. C. Redlich, 1958, John Wiley & Sons, Inc., by permission.
496 Gordon Lameyer (top); Ken Regan/Camera 5 (middle); Ralph Jakia/Camera 5 (bottom).
497 From *Theory of Suicide* by Maurice L. Farber. Copyright © 1968 by Maurice L. Farber, with permission of Funk & Wagnalls Publishing Company, Inc.
500 Courtesy of Dr. Daryl Bem.
501 National Gallery, Oslo, Norway.
509 Bob Towers (top); Marc J. Pokempner (middle); Ken Regan/Camera 5 (bottom).
513 Copyright 1968, Chelsea House Publishers, a division of Chelsea House Educational Communications, Inc., reprinted by permission.
525 From *The Causes and Cures of Neurosis* by H. J. Eysenck & S. Rachman (San Diego: R. Knapp, 1965), by permission of the publishers, Routledge & Kegan Paul, Ltd., and the authors.
529 Courtesy of Dr. Philip G. Zimbardo.
530 Reproduced by permission of the publisher, F. E. Peacock Publishers, Inc., Itasca, Illinois. From A. Bandura, "Modeling Therapy," *Psychopathology Today: Experimentation,* in W. S. Sahakian's *Theory and Research,* 1970, p. 553.
531 From "Proposal for Continued Development of a Treatment Program for Chronic Patients" by L. Rouse & S. Reilly. Unpublished Mimeo Report, Aug. 26, 1973, by permission.
547 From "The Therapeutic Community" by Richard Almond. Copyright © 1971 by Scientific American, Inc. All rights reserved.
550 Table adapted from B. L. Bloom, *Community Mental Health: A Historical and Critical Analysis.* © 1973 General Learning Corporation. Adapted by permission.
560–61 Courtesy of Dr. Philip G. Zimbardo.
563 Reprinted by permission of Newspaper Enterprise Association.
564 From the *Journal of Personality and Social Psychology,* Vol. 13, 1969, pp. 1–16. Copyright 1969 by the American Psychological Association. Reprinted by permission.
565 From the *American Journal of Psychology,* Vol. 57, 1944, pp. 243–59, by permission of the University of Illinois Press.
570 From the *Nebraska Symposium on Motivation,* edited by W. J. Arnold, © 1968 University of Nebraska Press. Reprinted by permission.
572 Mitchell Payne/Jeroboam, Inc.
574 Adapted from *The Psychology of Affiliation* by S. Schachter, 1959, Stanford University Press, by permission of the publisher.
575 Adapted from *Social Psychology and Modern Life* by Patricia Niles Middlebrook. Copyright © 1973 by Alfred A. Knopf, Inc. Reprinted by permission of the publisher.
577 From *The Cognitive Control of Motivation: The Consequences of Choice and Dissonance* by Philip G. Zimbardo. Copyright © 1969 Scott, Foresman and Company.
581 From *Liking and Loving* by Zick Rubin. Copyright © 1973 by Holt, Rinehart and Winston, Inc. Reprinted by permission of Holt, Rinehart and Winston, Inc.
582 Adapted from "Informational Loss in a Social Setting" by Malcolm Brenner, from Mimeographed Technical Report, University of Michigan, 1970. Used by permission of the author.
583 U.P.I.
590 Dennis Stock/Magnum Photos.

592 From "Opinions and Social Pressure" by Solomon E. Asch. Copyright 1955 by Scientific American, Inc. All rights reserved (both).

595 Courtesy of Dr. Muzafer Sherif, from Sherif, M. & Sherif, C., *An Outline of Social Psychology.* (Rev. ed.) New York: Harper & Row, 1956.

599 Courtesy of Mrs. Jane Elliott and ABC Television, photo by Charlotte Button.

600 From *Children of Crisis: A Study of Courage and Fear,* by permission of Atlantic-Little, Brown and Co. Copyright © 1964, 1965, 1966, 1967 by Robert Coles.

601 Hugues Vassal/Gamma.

605 Alice Kandell/Rapho Guillumette Pictures.

612 Reprinted from the *Journal of Abnormal and Social Psychology,* Vol. 63, 1961, pp. 466–92. Copyright 1961 by the American Psychological Association. Reprinted by permission.

615 Photo by Bob Bryant/*San Francisco Examiner.*

617 Courtesy of Dr. Albert Bandura.

619 Gilles Peress/Magnum Photos.

620 From *Aggression: A Social Learning Analysis* by Albert Bandura, 1973. Reprinted by permission of the publishers, Prentice-Hall, Inc.

621 U.P.I. (top, bottom).

626 Charles Gatewood.

629 Reprinted from the *Journal of Personality and Social Psychology,* Vol. 8, No. 4, 1968, pp. 377–83. Copyright 1968 by the American Psychological Association. Reprinted by permission.

630 Geoffrey Gove.

632 Wide World Photos.

633 Courtesy of Dr. Philip G. Zimbardo.

635 Reprinted from the *Journal of Personality and Social Psychology,* Vol. 25, 1973, pp. 342–45. Copyright 1973 by the American Psychological Association. Reprinted by permission.

636 Wide World Photos (top); Ken Heyman (bottom).

637 Courtesy of Dr. Philip G. Zimbardo.

638 Courtesy of Dr. Scott C. Fraser.

647 Joel Meyerwitz.

648 Martha Cooper Guthrie.

649 Courtesy of Dr. Philip G. Zimbardo.

653 From "Justifying the Final Solution" by H. H. Mansson from a paper presented at the International Congress of Psychology, London, 1969. Reprinted by permission.

660 From *The Stream of Behavior* by Roger G. Barker, p. 15. Copyright © 1963 by Appleton-Century-Crofts, reprinted by permission.

678 Photo by Paul Ryan (left); photo by Maude Dorr (right).

679 From *A New Learning Environment* by Harold L. Cohen & James Filipczak, 1971. Reprinted by permission of the publishers Jossey-Bass, Inc., San Francisco.

Color Section (beginning opposite page 22)

1 Charles Harbutt/Magnum Photos.

2 Bill Stanton/Magnum Photos (top left, center left, bottom left); Burk Uzzle/Magnum Photos (top right, bottom right).

3 Richard Howard/Camera 5 (top); Geoffrey Gove/Photos Trends (bottom).

4 Allan B. Richardson courtesy R. Gordon Wasson (top); Michael Alexander (bottom left); Owen Franken/Stock. Boston (bottom right).

5 Guttman-Maclay Collection, Institute of Psychiatry, London (all).

6 Steve McCarroll © 1975 by CRM Books, a division of Ziff-Davis Publishing Company (top left, top center, top right); Geoffrey Gove/Rapho Guillumette Pictures (bottom).

7 Michael Mattei/Camera 5 (top); Michael Alexander (bottom left); C. R. Tony Fletcher (bottom right).

8 By courtesy of the Metropolitan Museum of Art, George A. Hearn Fund, 1956 (top); Harry Crosby/Photophile (bottom left); Elliott Erwitt/Magnum Photos (bottom right).

9 John Oldenkamp (top); Will Kirkland/Photophile (bottom).

10 Burk Uzzle/Magnum Photos (top left); Russ Kinne/Photo Researchers (top right); Tony Linck/Shostal (bottom).

11 Bob Fitch/Black Star (top); Dave Bellak/Jeroboam, Inc. (bottom left); Tom McHugh/Photo Researchers (bottom right).

12 R. Herzog/FPG.

Charts and graphs by Paul Hazelrigg and James Minnick. Physiological drawings by Arnold Ryan Chalfant, John Pfiffner, and Joanna Adamska-Koperska. Artwork for Illusions Transparency Insert by James Minnick. Original cartoons by John Everds.

Name Index

Carlson, E. R., 368
Carlson, F. R., 222
Carlson, J. G., 652
Carmichael, L., 212, 251
Carnegie, D., 27, 586
Carroll, J. D., 223
Cartwright, D. S., 541, 589
Castaneda, C., 291
Castiglione, B., 276
Cattell, R. B., 227, 423, 424
Cavalli-Sforza, L. L., 202
Cazden, C. B., 153
Charatan, F., 626
Charcot, J., 309
Chase, M. H., 89
Chhina, G. S., 304
Chomsky, N., 145, 153, 154–55
Chow, K. L., 254
Christie, R., 439–40, 441
Christy, P. R., 617
Cisler, L., 60
Clark, B. R., 381–82
Clark, J. M., 336
Clark, K. B., 600, 677
Clark, M. C., 181–82
Clark, M. P., 600
Clausen, J. A., 475
Cleckley, H. A., 482–83
Cline, V. B., 620
Cobbs, P. M., 118
Coch, L., 590
Cofer, C. N., 173, 332
Coffman, T. L., 563, 564
Cohen, A. R., 576
Cohen, F., 381
Cohen, H. L., 679
Cohen, P., 149
Cohen, S., 300, 639
Colby, K. M., 222, 223, 487
Cole, J. O., 514
Coleman, D., 565
Coleman, J. C., 499
Coles, R., 600
Collier, G., 347
Collins, B. E., 437
Conklin, J. E., 627
Conrad, D. G., 397
Conrad, R., 177
Cooley, D. H., 433
Cooper, G. F., 255
Cooper, L. A., 210
Cooper, L. M., 311
Copernicus, 22, 31, 50
Cotterman, R. F., 661
Courrier, S., 620
Cowen, E. L., 268
Cox, V., 333
Craddick, R. A., 267
Craik, K. J. W., 220
Crandall, V. C., 605

Cranston, P., 350
Cranston, R., 400
Cressler, D. L., 552–53
Crick, F., 53
Crocker, S., 222
Crocket, R., 514
Croft, R. G., 620
Crombie, A. D., 50
Cross, P. G., 227
Culbertson, S., 398
Cushman, J. F., 469

Dallenbach, K. M., 174
D'Andrade, R. G., 392
Danziger, C., 665
Darley, J. M., 629–30, 631
Darnton, R., 308
Darwin, C., 57, 197, 369, 404, 412
Davenport, W., 360–61
Davis, C. M., 337
Davis, J. M., 511
Davis, K. E., 566, 579
Davison, G. C., 516
Davison, L. A., 382
Day, R., 145–46
Deasy, L. C., 463
Deci, E. L., 567
DeGood, D. E., 398–99
Dekker, E., 378
Delgado, J., 80
Dellas, M., 226
Dement, W. C., 283, 284, 285, 286
D'Encarnacus, P., 334
Denney, R., 437
Descartes, R., 50, 51, 90, 178, 184, 191, 226, 276
Deutsch, D., 178
Deutsch, J. A., 178
Deutsch, M., 572
DeValois, R. L., 246
De Vos, G., 602
Diamond, M. C., 200
Diamond, M. J., 315
Di Cora, L. V., 131–32
Diener, E., 634
Dillard, J. L., 148
Divorkin, B., 131–32
Dobzhansky, T., 53
Dohrenwend, B. P., 495
Dohrenwend, B. S., 495
Dolinar, L., 57
Dollard, J., 427–28, 454, 459, 614
Donders, F. C., 211
Doob, L. W., 614
Doyle, A. C., 269
Drabran, R. S., 120–21
Dreikurs, R., 521
Dreyfus, E. A., 539
Drolette, M. E., 373

Dublin, C. C., 622
Duffy, E., 373
Dugdale, R., 197
Duncan, S., 341
Dunnette, M. D., 228
DuPont, R. L., 473, 474
Dwornicka, B., 251

Eagleton, T., 465
Eastlake, D., 222
Ebbinghaus, H., 169–70, 172, 183
Edwards, A., 288
Edwards, A. E., 104
Edwards, D. B., 613
Egbert, L., 384, 400
Ehrhardt, A. A., 357
Eisner, B. G., 514
Ekman, P., 160, 370, 371
Ekstein, R., 485
Elliott, J., 598–99
Ellison, R., 433
Ellsworth, P. C., 157–58
Elmer, E., 121, 662
Endsley, R. C., 620
Engel, B., 133
Engel, G., 393
Engen, T., 71, 251
Epstein, A., 336, 347
Erickson, M., 310
Erikson, E., 418–19, 454
Erikson, K. T., 462
Ervin, F. R., 613, 614
Ervin, S. M., 151
Erwin, W. J., 342
Esdaile, J., 309
Evans, F. J., 311, 315–16
Evans, H. M., 605
Evans, J. R., 516
Evans, J. W., 438
Exline, R. V., 157
Eysenck, H. J., 424, 437, 525, 539
Eysenck, S., 437

Fairweather, G. W., 542, 552–53
Fantz, R. L., 252
Farber, M. L., 497
Farberow, N. L., 497
Farina, A., 463, 464
Farrar, J. C., 221
Faucheux, C., 593
Feather, N., 569
Fechner, G. T., 170, 240–41
Feinsilver, D., 490, 492, 494
Feldman, M. J., 288
Feldstein, A., 514
Feng, C., 210
Fenichel, O., 475
Fenz, W. D., 385

Ferguson, L. R., 409
Ferguson, P., 303
Ferrare, N. A., 403–4
Ferriera, A. J., 494
Feshbach, S., 620
Festinger, L., 572, 575, 576, 673
Fiedler, F. E., 596
Filipczak, J., 679
Fine, R., 208
Fink, L., 402
Firestone, I., 577
Firth, R., 497
Fisher, C., 288
Fitzsimmons, J., 347
Flavell, J., 191, 192
Fleming, A., 30
Fleming, J. D., 164
Fletcher, C. R., 463
Fodor, J. A., 21
Folkins, C. H., 382, 383
Forbes, J., 565
Ford, G., 465
Forgays, D. G., 259
Formica, R., 574
Forrest, M. S., 398–99
Fouts. R., 164
Fox, R. C., 654
Frandel, M., 661
Frank, J., 392–93, 538
Frank, J. D., 315
Frankl, V. E., 535, 537
Franks, J. J., 173
Fraser, S. C., 588, 634
Freedman, J. L., 345, 588, 632
Freeman, F. N., 203
Freeman, H., 514
Freeman, W., 516
Freemon, F. R., 281, 284
French, J. R. P., Jr., 590
Frenkel-Brunswick, E., 440
Freud, A., 414, 601
Freud, S., 16, 17, 21, 111, 175, 286–87, 309, 318, 409, 412–18, 419, 422, 427, 453–54, 518–20, 521, 535, 539, 542, 554, 611, 612, 614, 654
Friedman, M., 378
Friedman, R. J., 489
Friedman, S. B., 379
Fries, J., 343
Friesen, W. V., 160, 370, 371
Frijda, N. H., 371
Fromm, E., 318
Frommer, G. P., 134
Funkenstein, D. H., 372–73

McConnell, J. V., 103
McConnell, R. A., 269
McDougall, W., 269
McGaugh, J. L., 532
McGinnies, E., 268
McGlashlin, T. H., 315–16
McGlothlin, M. S., 300
McGlothlin, W., 300
McGowan, B. K., 135, 661
McGregor, D., 569
McGuigan, F. J., 213–14
McGuire, W. J., 575
McKinney, W. T., 489, 490
McNeil, D., 151, 179
McNemar, Q., 199
McPartland, T. S., 432
Mead, G. H., 433
Mead, M., 195, 360
Meader, B. D., 537
Meadow, W., 605
Medvedev, Z. A., 675
Meehl, P. E., 432
Mees, H., 527–28
Megaree, E. I., 611–12
Mehl, C., 299
Mehrabian, A., 156, 158, 159, 161
Melkman, R., 652
Melynk, P., 605
Melzack, R., 254, 386, 387
Mendel, W. M., 549
Mendels, J., 489
Merrill, M. A., 452
Mesmer, A., 308–9
Metzler, J., 210
Metzner, R., 279
Meyer, A., 546
Meyer, D. R., 82–83
Meyer, J., 675
Meyer, M. M., 485
Meyer, P. M., 73, 82–83
Meyer, W. U., 570
Michael, J., 523
Michelet, J., 389
Mickelson, O., 338–39
Mickle, W. A., 74
Middlebrook, P., 575
Miles, M. D., 545
Milgram, S., 8, 10, 15, 565, 641, 642, 643, 666, 673
Miller, G. A., 30, 87, 147, 180–81, 657
Miller, J. M., 72
Miller, N. E., 104, 131–32, 307, 334, 335, 347, 348, 379, 427–28, 429, 454, 459, 614
Miller, R. G., 381–82
Miller, W., 637
Miller, W. R., 151

Milner, B., 177
Milner, P., 74
Milton, G. A., 586
Minor, M. J., 661
Mischel, W., 15, 427, 454
Mishkin, M., 259
Mitchell, B. C., 203
Mitchell, E., 269
Mitler, M. M., 283
Mogar, R. E., 515
Mohr, J. P., 342
Money, J., 357
Moniz, E., 516
Montessori, M., 449
Montgomery, J., 531
Montor, K., 88–89
Moore, B., 133
Moore, S. C., 385
Moos, R. H., 678
Mordkoff, A. M., 382
Morgan, A. H., 315
Morinoto, K., 300
Moritz, A. P., 393
Morland, J. K., 600
Morton, W. D., 103
Mosak, H., 521
Moscovici, S., 593
Mosher, L. R., 490, 492, 494
Moskowitz, M., 512
Mosteller, F., 402
Mowrer, O. H., 395–96, 614
Moyer, K. E., 613
Munch, E., 501
Munn, N. L., 371
Munsinger, H., 252
Murphy, G., 269
Murphy, G. S., 463
Murray, J. R., 661
Müsterberg, H., 18
Muzio, 284
Myerson, A., 538

Nadien, J., 632
Naffrechoux, M., 593
Nardini, J. E., 391
Neisser, U., 172, 187
Nelson, K., 191
Nelson, S. D., 674
Nelson, V. L., 204–5
Nerlove, S. B., 392
Newcomb, T. M., 575, 593
Newell, A., 21, 221, 222
Nichols, R. C., 199
Nievergelt, J., 221
Nisbett, R. E., 343, 344, 470, 566, 567
Nissen, H. W., 254
Nizer, L., 584
Norman, D. A., 174, 177
Norwood, R., 442, 443
Nowlis, D. P., 312–13
Nyswander, M., 475

Oatley, K., 347
O'Connell, D. N., 312
O'Connor, R. D., 529
O'Hara, C. E., 21
Oktem, M. R., 514
Olcott, R. C., 434
Olds, J., 74
O'Leary, K. D., 120–21
Olver, R. R., 196
Oppenheimer, R., 29
Opton, E. M., Jr., 382, 383
Opton, N., 640
Orlando, N. J., 549
Orne, M. T., 310, 311, 312, 315–16
Ornstein, R., 85–86, 302, 317, 318
Osborn, A. F., 227
Osborn, D. K., 620
Osmond, H., 291, 511
Ostwald, P. F., 149
Overmier, J. B., 137, 396
Overton, W. F., 258

Pahnke, W. N., 297
Pantanjali, 276
Parke, R. D., 119, 620
Pastore, J. O., 621
Patrick, T., 582
Paul, G. L., 525
Pavlov, I. P., 30, 92–93, 97–98, 101, 102, 105, 107, 111, 130, 133, 134, 137
Pearson, K., 197, 202
Pelletier, K., 305
Peltzman, P., 149
Penfield, W., 49, 74, 177
Penick, S., 332
Perkins, C., 398
Peterson, G. B., 134
Petry, G., 398
Pfingst, B., 72
Pfungst, O., 32
Phares, E. J., 438
Phillips, S., 121
Piaget, J., 16, 188–93, 194, 228, 258, 435, 566
Pick, H. L., 262
Pierrel, R., 128
Piliavan, J. A., 631
Piliavan, I. M., 631
Pilkonis, P., 442, 443
Pinkerton, J., 392
Pisarski, A. E., 661
Pitts, F. N., 476, 477
Pivik, T., 286
Platt, J., 668
Plummer, N., 378
Plunkett, J., 261
Poincaré, J. H., 207

Polly, S., 565
Pomeroy, W. B., 356
Porter, R. W., 397
Posner, E. G., 542, 552
Postman, L., 170
Potter, V. R., 670
Powledge, T. M., 54
Premack, D., 164–65
Pribram, K. H., 85, 86, 87, 372
Price, C. R., 649
Price, J., 632
Price-Williams, D. R., 195, 196
Prien, R. F., 511, 512
Prytulak, L. S., 170
Psotka, J., 209
Pushkar, D., 289–90

Quinn, N. R., 392

Rachman, S., 525
Rahe, R. H., 380
Ramirez, M., 195
Rand, C., 175
Rapaport, C., 310, 389
Rapaport, R., 418
Rappaport, M., 517
Rau, L., 170
Raush, C. L., 553
Raush, H. L., 553
Rawlings, E., 575
Rayner, R., 106
Razran, G. H. S., 105
Rechtschaffen, A., 282
Redlich, F. C., 495
Regan, D., 575
Reich, C., 196
Reid, J. E., 585
Reilly, S., 531
Reinfeld, A., 358
Reisman, D., 437
Reitman, W. R., 177, 223
Reynolds, G., 325
Rheingold, H. L., 152
Rhine, J. B., 269, 271
Ribble, M., 6
Richards, W., 514
Richter, C. P., 337, 380, 393
Rickles, K., 512
Riesen, A. H., 254
Ring, K., 463
Risley, T., 527–28
Rivlin, A. M., 676
Robertson, J., 279

Trotter, W., 573, 595
Truax, C. B., 539
Tschukitschew, 332
Tumbleson, M., 19–20
Turing, A. M., 220
Turnbull, C., 235–36
Tursky, B., 388
Tynan, P., 259

Udrey, J. R., 40
Unger, S. M., 300

Valenstein, E., 333
Valins, S., 516
Van de Castle, R., 283, 287
Van Itallie, T. B., 344
Verhave, T., 114
Verville, E., 341
Vidmar, N., 603
Viek, P., 395–96
von Békésy, G., 249
von Felsinger, J. M., 402
von Glasersfeld, E. C., 165
Von Senden, M., 259

Wagatsuma, H., 602
Walen, S. R., 677
Walk, A., 514
Walk, R. D., 252–53
Wall, P. D., 386

Wallace, B., 262
Wallace, J., 267
Wallace, R., 303
Wallach, M. A., 226
Walster, E., 578, 579
Walster, G. W., 579
Walter, A. A., 212
Walter, E. D., 305
Walters, G., 563, 564
Walters, R. H., 119, 618
Wapner, S., 175
Ward, W. C., 224–25
Warden, C. J., 330
Warner, D. M., 631
Warren, D. H., 262
Washburn, A. L., 331
Wason, P. A., 219–20
Watson, G., 436
Watson, J., 214
Watson, J. B., 105–6
Watson, J. D., 53
Watson, R. I., Jr., 195, 635
Watt, J., 223
Watts, A. W., 279
Watts, J. W., 516
Waugh, N. C., 174
Wawryk, R., 251
Weakland, J., 162
Webb, W. B., 284
Weber, E. H., 240
Wechsler, D., 452
Wechsler, H., 514
Wegrocki, H. J., 460
Weiner, M., 267
Weiner, N., 26
Weintraub, W., 298
Weisenberg, M., 577
Weiss, J., 131–32
Weiss, J. M., 397

Weiss, R. F., 574
Weiss, T., 133
Weisskopf-Joelson, E., 535
Weissman, A., 501
Weitzman, B., 532
Welch, C., 384
Welker, W. I., 307
Wells, D. T., 307
Wells, W. D., 620
Wertheimer, M., 12, 256
West, S., 620
Wever, E. G., 249–50
Wheeler, R. G., 679–80
White, B. L., 255
White, R. K., 597
White, R. W., 394
Whiting, J. W. M., 601
Whorf, B., 212–13, 229
Wiedemann-Sutor, I., 358
Wienske, K., 332
Wiesel, T. N., 247
Willems, E. P., 665
Williams, D. R., 133
Williams, H., 133
Williams, H. L., 284
Williams, M., 575
Williams, R. J., 410
Williams, T. A., 489
Wilson, M., 14, 73
Winick, M., 205
Winokur, G., 488
Winter, P. M., 80
Winter, W. W., 494
Winterbottom, M. R., 569
Winters, L., 157
Witkin, H. A., 234
Wolf, A. V., 347
Wolf, K., 6
Wolf, M., 527–28
Wolf, S., 373
Wolff, H. C., 586
Wolff, H. G., 373
Wolpe, J., 524, 532
Wood, R. D., 652
Woods, J., 276
Worchel, S., 571

Wu, Su-Yu, 200
Wundt, W., 29, 256, 681
Wurtman, R. J., 51
Wynne, L. C., 102

Yablonsky, L., 637
Yagi, K., 672–73
Yalom, I. D., 545
Yamaoka, T., 306
Yarrow, M. R., 463
Yates, A. J., 216
Yezhov, N., 281, 282
Young, L. D., 307
Young, P. T., 337

Zajonc, R. B., 586
Zamchech, N., 393
Zander, A., 589
Zarcone, V., 286
Zborowski, M., 386, 388
Zeaman, D., 102
Zeigarnik, B., 175–76
Zimbardo, P. G., 42–43, 121, 201–3, 279–80, 296, 313–14, 316, 334, 335, 350, 389, 403, 442, 443, 470, 559–61, 605, 633–34, 635, 638–39, 643, 652, 680, 681
Zimmerman, R. R., 351–52
Zobrist, A. L., 222
Zubeck, J. P., 289–90
Zurcher, L. A., 433

Subject Index

Conflict: and experimental neurosis, 105; intergroup, 594–95; and personality theories, 413, 414, 415, 418, 454; therapy to eliminate, 509, 518, 519, 520, 521, 554

Conformity, 300, 365, 434, 435, 436, 437, 533; and anonymity, 633, 634; and attribution, 566, 606; and groupthink, 644; and social pressure, 592–93, 605, 607, 673

Confrontation, and violence, 623, 655

Conscience, 286, 413, 414, 435, 459, 646

Consciousness, 21, 208, 263, 415, 421, 453, 519; altered states of, 274–319; and deprivation, 289; and drugs, 291–301, 471; and hypnosis, 308–16; and meditation, yoga, and Zen, 302–7; and neurosis, 476, 482; sleeping and dreaming, 280–88

Consensual validation, 289

Consensus, 644, 646

Consequence learning, 96. See also Instrumental conditioning and Operant conditioning

Conservation, 192, 193, 194, 195, 258

Consistency: and attribution, 563–64, 606; of behavior, 94–95; need for, 575–77, 578; and personality, 410–12, 419, 421, 423, 426, 427, 428, 431, 442, 444, 453, 480

Consonance, 576

Constitutional factors and stress, 378–79

Consummatory behavior, and motivation, 330, 331, 333, 335, 348, 362

Contact comfort, 351–52, 363

Contiguity, 94

Contingencies. See Response-Reinforcer contingencies

Continuity position, of learning, 218

Continuous reinforcement, 123

Contradictory perception, and adaptation, 261–62

Control: need for, 394, 399–400, 401, 473; as a psychological goal, 17, 26–29, 46–47; social, 591; source of, 399, 437–38

Control groups, 34, 35, 47, 271, 541, 542, 545, 674, 694

Control orientation, 566, 606

Convergence: of eyes, 265, 273; and stimulation, 68, 69, 91

Conversion hysteria, 479–80, 504

Coordination, 87, 215–16; and drugs, 293, 294, 295; and perception, 254–55, 260

Coping strategies, 376, 381–85, 386, 390, 405

Coronary-prone men, 378

Corpus callosum, 77, 78, 85, 91

Correlation, 24–26, 36, 38–39, 40, 46; and authoritarianism, 441; in factor analysis, 424, 427; in IQ testing, 201, 202, 203, 205, 206; measures of, 689–91; positive and negative, 36, 689, 690–91

Correlation coefficient, 199, 201, 689–91

Cortex, 48, 49, 72, 73, 77–80, 81–84, 86, 88, 91, 327, 372; and enrichment, 200; and pain, 386, 387; and perception, 244, 246, 247, 249; and memory, 178; and sleep, 282, 283

Cortin, 381, 382

Counseling, 444, 452, 469, 532

Counterconditioning, 102, 105, 526–27

Counterculture, 295–96

Countertransference, 520

Covert oral behavior, and thinking, 213–15, 229

Creativity, 86, 184, 185–86, 208, 217, 224–28, 229, 436; and drugs, 294; and self-actualization, 423, 437

Crime, 41–42, 301, 325, 460, 467, 623–24, 625, 627, 655

Crisis intervention, 501, 505, 550

Critical periods, 136–37, 255, 357

Cross-cultural psychology and studies, 195, 371, 392, 444, 601, 635

Cross-tolerance, 299

Cry for help, 497, 501, 502

Crying, 95, 367, 404, 434, 489

Cues: for aggression, 615–16; in communications, 158, 183; and conditioning, 107, 108, 110, 133, 139; and drives, 327, 328, 335, 336, 343, 344, 346, 362, 363; to emotion, 369, 371, 372, 374, 404–5; internal and external, 334–36, 343, 362; and memory, 143, 174–75, 177; and perception, 235, 239, 253, 261, 264–66, 270, 273; and personality theories, 428, 454

Culture: and cognitive growth, 194–96, 228, 229; and drug usage, 472; and emotions, 369, 370, 404; and language, 212–13; and pain reactions, 386, 405; and perception, 235–36, 262, 265–66, 273; and personality, 422, 423, 504, 505; and sexual behavior, 356, 360–61, 363; and social norms, 591, 674; and views of disease, 391–93, 401

Cumulative recorder, 122, 123, 139

Cumulative response curve, 122, 139

Curiosity, 328, 395, 473, 569

Cutaneous senses, 241, 251, 253, 254, 272, 273

Cybernetic control, 26

Dark adaptation, 243–44

Data and data collection, 17–18, 22, 33–34, 37, 44, 375, 459, 473

Daydreams, 88, 184, 185, 217, 228, 275, 340, 415

Death: cognitive control of, 403–4; and drugs, 294, 295, 296; and hopelessness, 143, 365, 391–93, 394, 396, 405, 496; and neurosis, 477, 478; and stress, 105, 379, 380, 382; and suicide, 496–502; Voodoo, 365, 391–93, 394, 405

Death instinct, 414, 454, 611–12, 654

Decay theory, 173–74, 175, 177, 183

Deception, and research, 672–74

Decibel, 240, 250, 251

Decision making, 383, 438, 484; by group, 589, 644–45, 655

Decision steps for computer, 220

Decortication, 68

Deductive reasoning, 191, 217, 229

Deep structure, 155, 183

Defense mechanisms, 413, 415, 454, 459, 476, 525, 586, 607, 652, 653–54

Deficiency cravings, 337, 362

Deficiency motivation, 422

Dehumanization, 620, 646, 647–54, 655

Dehydration, 347

Deindividuation, 632–35, 655

Dejection, 339

Delinquency, 460, 679

Delusions, 278, 486, 491, 505, 553

Democratic personality, 423, 440

Dendrite, 62, 64, 65, 77, 90

Denial: of fear, 385, 386; of reality, 415

Density, and violence, 630–32

Deoxyrebonucleic acid (DNA), 52, 53, 54, 90

Dependency: on alcohol, 467–69, 504; on cigarettes, 469–71, 504; on drugs, 291, 293, 294, 295, 296, 319, 472–75, 504; and helplessness, 390; on parents, 341

Dependent variable, 34, 36, 47

Depolarization, 60, 90

Heart rate, 66, 69, 71, 78, 102, 104, 131, 132, 138, 410; during altered consciousness, 283, 284, 301, 304, 307; during sleep, 283, 284; and drugs, 301; stress and emotion and, 374, 378, 379, 382, 393

Hebephrenic schizophrenia, 486, 491, 505

Hedonism, 13, 109, 356, 413

Helplessness, 384, 391–400, 401, 404, 405, 416, 469, 483, 505; control of, 397–400, 401; learned, 137–38, 139, 394–97, 437, 455, 489, 500, 662; and suicide, 500; and violence, 627

Hemispheres, of brain, 85–86, 87, 91, 317–18

"Herd instinct," 573

Heredity: and adaptation, 53–55; and development, 12–13, 46, 187, 189, 196–203, 228–29, 255, 369; and hypnotizability, 315, 319; and intelligence, 196, 197–203, 204, 206, 229, 449; and learning, 130, 134–37; and personality, 413, 418, 421, 423

Hermaphrodite, 357, 363

Heroin, 292, 294, 296, 299, 301, 319, 328, 466, 471, 473–74

Heterosexuality, 136, 137, 200, 358, 361, 363

Heuristics, 221, 222

Hierarchical processing, and perception, 247, 272, 273

Hierarchy of needs, 422, 454

Higher-order conditioning, 101, 138

Hippocampus, 72, 91, 177

Holistic approach, 52, 90

Holograms, 85

Homeostasis, 329, 330, 347, 349, 362

Homosexuality, 361, 363, 366, 464, 487, 492, 526

Homunculus, 56

Hope, 365, 390, 394, 395, 396

Hopelessness: feelings of, 365, 390–93, 395, 404, 405; and suicide, 496, 498, 499, 500

Horizontal-vertical illusion, 265–66

Hormetic personality factors, 424, 454

Hostility, 206, 300, 303, 369, 373, 441, 616; and defense mechanisms, 415, 430; and groups, 594, 597; in psychosis, 491, 497. See also Aggression

Hull's learning theory, 109–10, 139

Humanism, 17, 276, 520

Humanistic therapy, 534–35, 535–38, 555

Human nature: and aggression, 608–9, 611–14, 654; assumptions about, 12–15, 46, 326, 508–9

Human sexuality, 354–61, 363, 417, 465

Humor: and dehumanization, 654, 655; sense of, 339, 423, 489; and sexism, 605

Hunger, 78, 79, 285, 294, 299, 318, 470; control of, 402, 403; as a drive, 322, 323, 325, 327, 328, 330–45, 348, 362, 422; and food addiction, 341, 343–45

Hybridization, 55

Hyperactivity, 295, 373, 393, 405

Hypersensitivity, after deprivation, 290

Hypertension, 104, 131, 307, 378

Hypnosis, 143, 214, 275, 279, 289, 308–16, 318, 319, 479; and control of pain, 311, 365, 388–89, 405; and perception, 262, 267, 310–11, 319; in therapy, 470, 471, 524, 546

Hypnotics, 292, 295, 319

Hypochondria, 483, 484, 505

Hypochondriasis, 491

Hypoglycemia, 332

Hypothalamus, 6, 78–79, 80, 91, 516; and aggression, 613; and drives, 333, 347, 362; and emotions, 372

Hypothesis: in predictions, 23–24, 30, 33, 34, 35, 36, 37, 46, 459, 691; in reasoning, 217, 218–19, 220, 229

Hysterical anesthesia, 479

Hysterical neurosis, 309, 355, 478–83, 484, 504

Id, 21, 414, 418, 454, 518, 521

Identification, 442, 654–55; with aggressor, 601; as a defense mechanism, 415; and gender role, 357–58; with group, 590–91, 595, 596, 601, 606

Identification graffiti, 637

Identity crises, 419, 432–35, 455, 472

Idiographic approach, 13, 14, 46, 432, 455

I-E Scale, 437, 438

"I-It" relationships, 647, 655

Illness: and faith, 400–402; and stress, 378–82, 391, 405

Illusions, 235, 236–37, 239, 265–66, 272, 278, 289

Images: in altered consciousness, 284, 297, 318; in perception, 237, 243, 258, 262, 290; in thinking, 187, 192, 207–12, 229

Imitation, 494, 575; and aggression, 616–18; and language, 152–53, 183; of response, 126, 127; in therapy, 523, 528–29, 555

Immaturity, and maladjustment, 475, 480

Immigrants, and intelligence, 198, 199, 202

Immunization, against helplessness, 397, 405

Implicit personality theory, 411

Implosive therapy, 525–26, 535, 555

Imprinting, 136–37, 139, 200, 662

Improving quality of life, 17, 29–30, 46, 659–60, 677–81

Impulses, repression of, 286, 414, 416, 459, 476, 478, 518

Impulsivity, 226, 366, 436, 516

Inadequacy, feelings of, 379, 464

Incentive motivation, 126

Incentive stimuli, 327

Inconsistency, 439, 441

Independence, 226–27, 436, 437

Independent variables, 34, 35, 36, 47, 660–63

Indirect learning, 533

Individual: and behavior, 432, 455, 464, 466; vs. group, 15, 46, 561, 646; and humanistic-existential therapy, 534–37; and phenomenology, 16, 17, 46; vs. universal laws, 13, 46

Individual differences, 410, 431–36; and effect of drugs, 298–301; and perception, 210, 211, 262, 265–68

Inductive reasoning, 191, 217, 229

Ineffability, and altered consciousness, 279, 318

Infancy: and cognitive development, 189, 190, 191, 200, 205, 206; and deprivation, 5–7, 351–53, 363; and dishabituation, 71; and eating behavior, 335, 337, 344; and language development, 5, 148, 149, 150, 152, 154, 182, 183; and learning, 105–6; and perceptual development, 250, 251, 273; and personality, 410, 418, 420; and stages of sleep, 283–84

Inferences, 18, 46, 193, 210, 229, 256

Inferential statistics, 682, 692–94

Inferiority feelings, 126, 148, 149, 409, 418, 487

Information, and attitudes, 586, 607

Information processing approach, 44, 220–23, 229

In-group vs. out-group, 440, 594–95, 607, 615

Psychotherapy, 13, 464, 484, 502, 503, 506–55; assessment prior to, 444–45; computerized, 222, 223; and ethics, 553–54, 658, 674–75; facilities for, 546–53; group, 539, 541–45; for helplessness, 397–400; individual, 510–37, 541–42; judging success of, 522, 538–41, 545, 555; to reduce addiction, 469, 470, 527; and suicide prevention, 501–2

Psychotic depression, 486, 487–90

Psychotomimetic drugs, 291, 319

Puberty. See *Adolescence*

Punishment, 421, 431; in conditioning, 116, 117, 118–21, 131, 139; counterproductive, 119; effect of, on aggression, 616–18; in therapy, 510, 511

Puzzle boxes and conditioning, 107–9, 112, 126, 138–39, 218

Qualitative classification, 683

Race: and intelligence, 198, 201–2; and personality variables, 438; and suicide rates, 499–500, 505

Racism, 472, 562, 598–604, 607

Raja Yoga, 304

Random sampling, 34, 47, 692–93

Range, of scores, 687

Rapid eye movement (REM) sleep, 282–86, 288, 318; REM rebound, 285, 286, 318, 328

Rate of responding, 116, 117, 122, 139

Rating scales, 445–46, 455

Rationalization, 402, 415, 640, 644

Reactance, 570–71, 606

Reaction formation, 415

Reaction time, 50, 210–12, 216, 229

Realistic thinking. See *Reasoning*

Reality: and altered consciousness, 278, 279, 301, 310, 314; and cognitive control, 365; and cognitive development, 188, 193; denial of, 415; in neurosis, 478, 482, 483; and perception, 232, 238, 255–56, 272, 273; and psychosis, 484, 485, 489, 495, 505, 510; and social and physical, 572–73, 590, 591–92; testing of, 485, 572, 598; and thinking, 184–85, 187, 217

Reality orientation, 566, 606

Reasoning, 184, 185, 191, 192–93, 217–20, 228, 229, 367, 450

Rebellion, 118, 361

Recall, 168, 174, 175–76, 179, 180, 181, 183, 212, 312, 581–82

Recall for uncompleted tasks, 175–76, 183

Recency effect, 588

Receptive field, and perception, 246, 255

Receptors: and nervous system, 64, 65, 67, 68, 69, 70, 88; and perception, 240, 241, 242, 243, 244, 247, 248, 249, 250, 259, 262, 272; and thirst, 347

Reciprocal inhibition, 524, 555

Reciprocity, norm of, 575

Recitation, and memory, 180, 183

Recognition, 168, 183

Reconstruction, and recall, 168

Reducing redundancy, 247, 273

Reductionism, 45, 52, 90

Reduction theory of perception, 257, 273

Redundancy of cells, 58, 84, 91

Reflex arc, 67–68, 69, 87

Reflexes, 67–68, 91, 200, 324, 386, 405

Refractory period, 60, 61

Regression, 142–43, 312, 319, 415, 481, 491, 514

Reinforcement and reinforcers, 110, 111, 112, 113, 114, 115, 116, 117, 119, 122, 123, 124–28, 130, 132, 133, 134, 139, 226, 490; delay of, 124–25; intermittent, 123–25, 139; and language development, 152, 153, 183; and motivation, 325, 330, 342, 347, 431; in personality theories, 424, 428, 431, 437, 454; positive and negative, 117, 118, 119, 121, 130, 139, 215; social, 567, 573, 606; in therapy, 508, 523, 524, 527–28; tokens in, 115, 529–32, 607

Rejection, 352–53, 361, 408, 430, 498, 570, 571, 573, 637

Relabeling, 653, 655

Relaxation, 314, 316, 319, 424

Relearning, 168–69, 183, 522–33

Releasers, for aggression, 615–16, 654

Reliability, of tests, 445, 455

Religious feeling, and drugs, 277, 278, 297, 299, 301, 319

Remission, 461

REM sleep and REM rebound, 282–86, 288, 318, 328

Reorganization, 167

Repetitiveness, 94

Repression, 175, 176, 183, 354, 415, 459, 487, 518, 520, 521, 525, 554, 586

Reproductive memory, 169

Reserpine, 511

Resignation, feelings of, 390–91, 394

Resistances, analysis of, 519, 521, 554

Resistance to extinction, 102, 138

Respiratory rate, 69, 71, 102, 104, 214; and altered consciousness, 284, 304; during sleep, 284; and stimulation, 251

Respondent conditioning, 97–106, 109, 130, 133–34, 138, 139, 526

Response: conditioned, 97–99, 101, 102, 103, 104, 130, 138; and consequences (R→S relationships), 95–96, 130, 139; correlations (R-R relationships), 94–95, 130, 139; learning new, 125–28, 139; in personality theory, 428, 454; rate of, 116, 117, 122, 139; unconditioned, 97–99, 102, 130, 138

Response hierarchy, 107, 108, 139

Response plasticity, 84

Response-reinforcer contingencies, 115–16, 117, 130, 133, 139

Responsibility, 569–70, 596, 607, 642, 654, 655, 666; motives and, 325–27, 362, 610; as stress, 381–82, 383, 397; in therapy, 534, 535, 547

Retention, of learned material, 169, 170, 180, 183, 431. See also *Memory*

Reticular activating system (RAS), 79, 327, 362

Reticular formation, 72, 78, 79, 91, 386

Retina, 232, 237, 239, 242, 243, 244, 246, 247, 254, 259, 262, 272, 374

Retinal disparity, 265, 273

Retinal image, 237, 238, 239, 252, 256, 262, 272

Retrieval cues, 174–75, 183

Retroactive interference, 171, 174, 183

Retroactive therapy, for helplessness, 400, 405

Retrograde amnesia, 80

Review, and learning, 180, 183

Rewards, 37, 431, 437, 567, 568, 569, 586, 607; in conditioning, 108, 110, 117, 124, 125, 126 (see also *Reinforcement*); in therapy, 527–32, 533

Rhinencephalon, 79, 82, 91

Rigidity, and personality, 300, 440–41, 442

Rods, of eye, 241–42, 243, 272

Role learning, 326, 357–58, 435; models for, 198; and obedience, 642, 655; and personality, 413, 418–19; sex (see *Sex role*)

Role playing, 463, 471, 503, 549, 558–61, 565, 645

Stimulus intensity, and perception, 240–41, 272
Stimulus-response mechanism in nervous system, 67–68, 91
Stimulus-response (S→R) relationships, 34, 94–95, 130, 139, 187
Stomach activity, and hunger, 331–32, 344, 362
Stress, 105, 277, 289, 348, 373, 377–85, 398–99, 405, 413, 444, 489, 551, 672; and change, 379–80; coping with, 390–404, 550; and overcrowding, 630–32; and psychosomatic reactions, 378–81, 391, 393
Stressors, 381–82, 489
Strong Vocational Interest Blank, 448
Structure of intellect model, 426, 454
Structures: cognitive, 189; of perception, 262–65
Stuttering, 523, 526
Subcortex, 78–80, 91, 177
Sublimation, 415
Subliminal values, 240
Success: fear of, 570, 571, 572, 606; need for (see *Achievement*); predicting, 444
Successive approximation, 128, 139
Successive reproduction, 172, 183
"Sudden-death" phenomenon, 391–94, 403–4, 405
Suggestibility, in altered consciousness, 280, 314, 319
Suicide, 206, 294, 466, 496–502, 505; and depression, 400, 460, 487; prevention of, 501–2, 505, 551; and violence, 650, 658
Superego, 44, 286, 414, 418, 454, 459, 518
Superstition, 116, 391–94, 399–400, 401, 405, 440
Superstitious relationships, 116, 130, 139
Support, 388, 393, 622; social, 589, 590, 607, 654, 655; in therapy, 469, 551
Surface structure, 154–55, 183
Surface traits, 423–24
Surveillance: and punishment, 120; and trust, 567
Syllogisms, 217
Symbionese Liberation Army (SLA), 583
Symbolized experiences, 421
Symbols, 99, 138, 418, 428, 477; in dreams, 286–87, 318, 519; language and, 144, 145, 147–48, 165, 183; in thinking, 184, 185, 186, 190–91, 208, 210, 212, 229, 258, 273, 449
Sympathetic nervous system, 66, 91, 97, 132, 301, 303

Sympathy, desire for, 119, 480, 483, 505
Synaptic depression, 70
Synaptic transmission, 61–64, 65, 66, 88, 90, 178, 183, 242, 386
Syntax, 145, 147, 154, 155, 164, 182
Systems vs. collections of entities, 665–69

Taboos, 392–93, 649–50
Tachistoscope, 268
Task leaders, 596, 607
Taste, sense of, 251, 272, 273, 337
Telepathy, 269, 270, 271, 273
Telephone theory of hearing, 249
Television: and social engineering, 675; and violence, 619–20, 621, 655
Temperament factors, 424, 454
Temperature: brain's control of, 78, 79, 328, 329, 346; individual's control of, 305, 307; sensitivity to external, 241, 251, 273; and stress, 393
Temporal conditioning, 100, 130
Temporal lobe, 82, 91, 613
Temporal patterning (CS-UCS interval), 93, 100
Temporal summation, 63, 90
Tension, 285, 286, 310, 340, 381, 385, 549; in Freudian psychology, 412–20, 427, 428
Testes, 349, 357
Tests: intelligence, 198, 199–200, 201–6, 255, 449–53, 455, 684, 693; projective, 385, 446–48, 455, 573; psychological, 425, 444–46, 508, 682–94
T-groups, 144, 543, 544, 589
Thalamus, 78, 91, 242, 372, 386
Thanatos, 414, 454, 611–12
Thematic Apperception Test (TAT), 447–48, 455
Theoretical explanation, 21–22, 46
Theory X and Theory Y, 569
Therapeutic community, 547, 555
Therapist's role, 507–8, 538, 539, 551; in behavior therapies, 532–33; and ethics, 553–54, 674–75; in group therapy, 541, 542–43, 545; in humanistic-existential therapies, 535–37, 541; in judging success, 432, 455, 538–41, 555; in psychoanalysis, 508, 518–20, 521, 522, 538, 539
Therapy. See *Psychotherapy*

Thinking, 184–85, 207–29, 300, 365; computers and, 220–23; and creativity, 224–28; disturbances in, 486, 491, 492; images in, 207–12; and problem solving, 212, 217, 218–20; reasoning, 192–93, 217–20, 228; words and, 212–13
Thirst, 78, 79, 294, 299, 323, 327, 328, 330, 333, 346–48, 362, 402, 403, 422
Threat, 376, 382, 401, 419
Threshold: and drives, 334, 362; of pain, 304, 315, 388, 397; and perception, 69, 240, 250, 268, 272
Throughput, 216, 229
Time-out periods, 119, 124
Time sense, 610; distortion of, 278, 294, 297, 300, 301, 318; hypnosis and, 313–14, 319
"Tip of the tongue" reaction (TOT), 179
Tobacco, 292, 293, 319
Token economies, 115, 529–32, 555, 607
Tolerance, 423, 440; to drugs, 293, 294, 295, 298–99, 319, 468, 470; to pain, 388
Torture, 389, 405
Touch, 241, 251, 253, 273
Traces, in memory, 173–74, 178, 183
Traits, 411, 419, 432, 444, 475; assessment of, 445, 446, 451, 683, 691; attribution of, 562–64; and leadership, 595–97, 607; Machiavellian, 439–40; and personality theory, 411–12, 423–27, 430, 454
Tranquilizers: and drug abuse, 286, 292, 295, 319, 467, 471; in therapy, 511–12, 515, 516, 554
Transactional approach to perception, 256, 273
Transadults, 666
Transcendental experiences, 276, 278, 297, 299, 301, 319
Transcendental meditation (TM), 302–3, 304, 319
Transduction, 240, 250, 272
Transductive reasoning, 191
Transference, analysis of, 519–20, 521, 525, 554
Transformational rules, 145, 152, 153, 155, 183
Transformation of input, 167, 170, 187, 210, 222
Transmitter substances, 63, 90
Trauma: and illness, 379–80, 461, 514; and memory, 176, 177, 178; and personality, 412, 413, 417
Treatment. See *Psychotherapy*

BF
121
.R77
1977

44202

Zimbardo

Psychology and life

DATE DUE

FEB 1 0 1978			
OCT 8 1978			
OCT 8			
MAR 4 1981			
OCT 12			
OCT 03 1994			
OCT 1994			
MAR 15 1996			
APR 2 8 2002			
DISCARDED			
GAYLORD			PRINTED IN U.S.A